T0254242

Lecture Notes in Computer Science　　　10801

Commenced Publication in 1973
Founding and Former Series Editors:
Gerhard Goos, Juris Hartmanis, and Jan van Leeuwen

Advanced Research in Computing and Software Science
Subline of Lecture Notes in Computer Science

More information about this series at http://www.springer.com/series/7407

Amal Ahmed (Ed.)

Programming Languages and Systems

27th European Symposium on Programming, ESOP 2018
Held as Part of the European Joint Conferences
on Theory and Practice of Software, ETAPS 2018
Thessaloniki, Greece, April 14–20, 2018
Proceedings

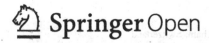

Editor
Amal Ahmed
Northeastern University
Boston, MA
USA

ISSN 0302-9743   ISSN 1611-3349   (electronic)
Lecture Notes in Computer Science
ISBN 978-3-319-89883-4   ISBN 978-3-319-89884-1   (eBook)
https://doi.org/10.1007/978-3-319-89884-1

Library of Congress Control Number: 2018940640

LNCS Sublibrary: SL1 – Theoretical Computer Science and General Issues

Printed on acid-free paper

This Springer imprint is published by the registered company Springer International Publishing AG
part of Springer Nature
The registered company address is: Gewerbestrasse 11, 6330 Cham, Switzerland

ETAPS Foreword

Welcome to the proceedings of ETAPS 2018! After a somewhat coldish ETAPS 2017 in Uppsala in the north, ETAPS this year took place in Thessaloniki, Greece. I am happy to announce that this is the first ETAPS with gold open access proceedings. This means that all papers are accessible by anyone for free.

ETAPS 2018 was the 21st instance of the European Joint Conferences on Theory and Practice of Software. ETAPS is an annual federated conference established in 1998, and consists of five conferences: ESOP, FASE, FoSSaCS, TACAS, and POST. Each conference has its own Program Committee (PC) and its own Steering Committee. The conferences cover various aspects of software systems, ranging from theoretical computer science to foundations to programming language developments, analysis tools, formal approaches to software engineering, and security. Organizing these conferences in a coherent, highly synchronized conference program facilitates participation in an exciting event, offering attendees the possibility to meet many researchers working in different directions in the field, and to easily attend talks of different conferences. Before and after the main conference, numerous satellite workshops take place and attract many researchers from all over the globe.

ETAPS 2018 received 479 submissions in total, 144 of which were accepted, yielding an overall acceptance rate of 30%. I thank all the authors for their interest in ETAPS, all the reviewers for their peer reviewing efforts, the PC members for their contributions, and in particular the PC (co-)chairs for their hard work in running this entire intensive process. Last but not least, my congratulations to all authors of the accepted papers!

ETAPS 2018 was enriched by the unifying invited speaker Martin Abadi (Google Brain, USA) and the conference-specific invited speakers (FASE) Pamela Zave (AT & T Labs, USA), (POST) Benjamin C. Pierce (University of Pennsylvania, USA), and (ESOP) Derek Dreyer (Max Planck Institute for Software Systems, Germany). Invited tutorials were provided by Armin Biere (Johannes Kepler University, Linz, Austria) on modern SAT solving and Fabio Somenzi (University of Colorado, Boulder, USA) on hardware verification. My sincere thanks to all these speakers for their inspiring and interesting talks!

ETAPS 2018 took place in Thessaloniki, Greece, and was organised by the Department of Informatics of the Aristotle University of Thessaloniki. The university was founded in 1925 and currently has around 75,000 students; it is the largest university in Greece. ETAPS 2018 was further supported by the following associations and societies: ETAPS e.V., EATCS (European Association for Theoretical Computer Science), EAPLS (European Association for Programming Languages and Systems), and EASST (European Association of Software Science and Technology). The local organization team consisted of Panagiotis Katsaros (general chair), Ioannis Stamelos,

Lefteris Angelis, George Rahonis, Nick Bassiliades, Alexander Chatzigeorgiou, Ezio Bartocci, Simon Bliudze, Emmanouela Stachtiari, Kyriakos Georgiadis, and Petros Stratis (EasyConferences).

The overall planning for ETAPS is the main responsibility of the Steering Committee, and in particular of its Executive Board. The ETAPS Steering Committee consists of an Executive Board and representatives of the individual ETAPS conferences, as well as representatives of EATCS, EAPLS, and EASST. The Executive Board consists of Gilles Barthe (Madrid), Holger Hermanns (Saarbrücken), Joost-Pieter Katoen (chair, Aachen and Twente), Gerald Lüttgen (Bamberg), Vladimiro Sassone (Southampton), Tarmo Uustalu (Tallinn), and Lenore Zuck (Chicago). Other members of the Steering Committee are: Wil van der Aalst (Aachen), Parosh Abdulla (Uppsala), Amal Ahmed (Boston), Christel Baier (Dresden), Lujo Bauer (Pittsburgh), Dirk Beyer (Munich), Mikolaj Bojanczyk (Warsaw), Luis Caires (Lisbon), Jurriaan Hage (Utrecht), Rainer Hähnle (Darmstadt), Reiko Heckel (Leicester), Marieke Huisman (Twente), Panagiotis Katsaros (Thessaloniki), Ralf Küsters (Stuttgart), Ugo Dal Lago (Bologna), Kim G. Larsen (Aalborg), Matteo Maffei (Vienna), Tiziana Margaria (Limerick), Flemming Nielson (Copenhagen), Catuscia Palamidessi (Palaiseau), Andrew M. Pitts (Cambridge), Alessandra Russo (London), Dave Sands (Göteborg), Don Sannella (Edinburgh), Andy Schürr (Darmstadt), Alex Simpson (Ljubljana), Gabriele Taentzer (Marburg), Peter Thiemann (Freiburg), Jan Vitek (Prague), Tomas Vojnar (Brno), and Lijun Zhang (Beijing).

I would like to take this opportunity to thank all speakers, attendees, organizers of the satellite workshops, and Springer for their support. I hope you all enjoy the proceedings of ETAPS 2018. Finally, a big thanks to Panagiotis and his local organization team for all their enormous efforts that led to a fantastic ETAPS in Thessaloniki!

February 2018   Joost-Pieter Katoen

Preface

This volume contains the papers presented at the 27th European Symposium on Programming (ESOP 2018) held April 16–19, 2018, in Thessaloniki, Greece. ESOP is one of the European Joint Conferences on Theory and Practice of Software (ETAPS). It is devoted to fundamental issues in the specification, design, analysis, and implementation of programming languages and systems.

The 36 papers in this volume were selected from 114 submissions based on originality and quality. Each submission was reviewed by three to six Program Committee (PC) members and external reviewers, with an average of 3.3 reviews per paper. Authors were given a chance to respond to these reviews during the rebuttal period from December 6 to 8, 2017. All submissions, reviews, and author responses were considered during the online discussion, which identified 74 submissions to be discussed further at the physical PC meeting held at Inria Paris, December 13–14, 2017. Each paper was assigned a guardian, who was responsible for making sure that external reviews were solicited if there was not enough non-conflicted expertise among the PC, and for presenting a summary of the reviews and author responses at the PC meeting. All non-conflicted PC members participated in the discussion of a paper's merits. PC members wrote reactions to author responses, including summaries of online discussions and discussions during the physical PC meeting, so as to help the authors understand decisions. Papers co-authored by members of the PC were held to a higher standard and discussed toward the end of the physical PC meeting. There were ten such submissions and five were accepted. Papers for which the program chair had a conflict of interest were kindly handled by Fritz Henglein.

My sincere thanks to all who contributed to the success of the conference. This includes the authors who submitted papers for consideration; the external reviewers, who provided timely expert reviews, sometimes on short notice; and the PC, who worked hard to provide extensive reviews, engaged in high-quality discussions about the submissions, and added detailed comments to help authors understand the PC discussion and decisions. I am grateful to the past ESOP PC chairs, particularly Jan Vitek and Hongseok Yang, and to the ESOP SC chairs, Giuseppe Castagna and Peter Thiemann, who helped with numerous procedural matters. I would like to thank the ETAPS SC chair, Joost-Pieter Katoen, for his amazing work and his responsiveness. HotCRP was used to handle submissions and online discussion, and helped smoothly run the physical PC meeting. Finally, I would like to thank Cătălin Hrițcu for sponsoring the physical PC meeting through ERC grant SECOMP, Mathieu Mourey and the Inria Paris staff for their help organizing the meeting, and William Bowman for assisting with the PC meeting.

February 2018   Amal Ahmed

Organization

Program Committee

Amal Ahmed	Northeastern University, USA and Inria, France
Nick Benton	Facebook, UK
Josh Berdine	Facebook, UK
Viviana Bono	Università di Torino, Italy
Dominique Devriese	KU Leuven, Belgium
Marco Gaboardi	University at Buffalo, SUNY, USA
Roberto Giacobazzi	Università di Verona, Italy and IMDEA Software Institute, Spain
Philipp Haller	KTH Royal Institute of Technology, Sweden
Matthew Hammer	University of Colorado Boulder, USA
Fritz Henglein	University of Copenhagen, Denmark
Jan Hoffmann	Carnegie Mellon University, USA
Cătălin Hrițcu	Inria Paris, France
Suresh Jagannathan	Purdue University, USA
Limin Jia	Carnegie Mellon University, USA
Naoki Kobayashi	University of Tokyo, Japan
Xavier Leroy	Inria Paris, France
Aleksandar Nanevski	IMDEA Software Institute, Spain
Michael Norrish	Data61 and CSIRO, Australia
Andreas Rossberg	Google, Germany
Davide Sangiorgi	Università di Bologna, Italy and Inria, France
Peter Sewell	University of Cambridge, UK
Éric Tanter	University of Chile, Chile
Niki Vazou	University of Maryland, USA
Steve Zdancewic	University of Pennsylvania, USA

Additional Reviewers

Danel Ahman	Mariangiola Dezani
S. Akshay	Derek Dreyer
Aws Albarghouthi	Ronald Garcia
Jade Alglave	Deepak Garg
Vincenzo Arceri	Samir Genaim
Samik Basu	Victor Gomes
Gavin Bierman	Peter Habermehl
Filippo Bonchi	Matthew Hague
Thierry Coquand	Justin Hsu

Zhenjiang Hu
Peter Jipsen
Shin-ya Katsumata
Andrew Kennedy
Heidy Khlaaf
Neelakantan Krishnaswami
César Kunz
Ugo Dal Lago
Paul Levy
Kenji Maillard
Roman Manevich
Paulo Mateus
Antoine Miné
Stefan Monnier
Andrzej Murawski
Anders Møller
Vivek Notani

Andreas Nuyts
Paulo Oliva
Dominic Orchard
Luca Padovani
Brigitte Pientka
Benjamin C. Pierce
Andreas Podelski
Chris Poskitt
Francesco Ranzato
Andrey Rybalchenko
Sriram Sankaranarayanan
Tetsuya Sato
Sandro Stucki
Zachary Tatlock
Bernardo Toninho
Viktor Vafeiadis

RustBelt: Logical Foundations for the Future of Safe Systems Programming

Derek Dreyer

Max Planck Institute for Software Systems (MPI-SWS), Germany
dreyer@mpi-sws.org

Abstract. Rust is a new systems programming language, developed at Mozilla, that promises to overcome the seemingly fundamental tradeoff in language design between high-level safety guarantees and low-level control over resource management. Unfortunately, none of Rust's safety claims have been formally proven, and there is good reason to question whether they actually hold. Specifically, Rust employs a strong, ownership-based type system, but then extends the expressive power of this core type system through libraries that internally use unsafe features.

In this talk, I will present RustBelt (http://plv.mpi-sws.org/rustbelt), the first formal (and machine-checked) safety proof for a language representing a realistic subset of Rust. Our proof is extensible in the sense that, for each new Rust library that uses unsafe features, we can say what verification condition it must satisfy in order for it to be deemed a safe extension to the language. We have carried out this verification for some of the most important libraries that are used throughout the Rust ecosystem.

After reviewing some essential features of the Rust language, I will describe the high-level structure of the RustBelt verification and then delve into detail about the secret weapon that makes RustBelt possible: the Iris framework for higher-order concurrent separation logic in Coq (http://iris-project.org). I will explain by example how Iris generalizes the expressive power of O'Hearn's original concurrent separation logic in ways that are essential for verifying the safety of Rust libraries. I will not assume any prior familiarity with concurrent separation logic or Rust.

This is joint work with Ralf Jung, Jacques-Henri Jourdan, Robbert Krebbers, and the rest of the Iris team.

Contents

Concurrency

Security

Program Verification

Program Analysis and Automated Verification

Session Types and Concurrency

Concurrency and Distribution

Compiler Verification

Language Design

Consistent Subtyping for All

Ningning Xie[✉], Xuan Bi, and Bruno C. d. S. Oliveira

The University of Hong Kong, Pokfulam, Hong Kong
{nnxie,xbi,bruno}@cs.hku.hk

Abstract. Consistent subtyping is employed in some gradual type systems to validate type conversions. The original definition by Siek and Taha serves as a guideline for designing gradual type systems with subtyping. Polymorphic types à la System F also induce a subtyping relation that relates polymorphic types to their instantiations. However Siek and Taha's definition is not adequate for polymorphic subtyping. The first goal of this paper is to propose a generalization of consistent subtyping that is adequate for polymorphic subtyping, and subsumes the original definition by Siek and Taha. The new definition of consistent subtyping provides novel insights with respect to previous polymorphic gradual type systems, which did not employ consistent subtyping. The second goal of this paper is to present a gradually typed calculus for implicit (higher-rank) polymorphism that uses our new notion of consistent subtyping. We develop both declarative and (bidirectional) algorithmic versions for the type system. We prove that the new calculus satisfies all static aspects of the refined criteria for gradual typing, which are mechanically formalized using the Coq proof assistant.

1 Introduction

Gradual typing [21] is an increasingly popular topic in both programming language practice and theory. On the practical side there is a growing number of programming languages adopting gradual typing. Those languages include Clojure [6], Python [27], TypeScript [5], Hack [26], and the addition of Dynamic to C# [4], to cite a few. On the theoretical side, recent years have seen a large body of research that defines the foundations of gradual typing [8,9,13], explores their use for both functional and object-oriented programming [21,22], as well as its applications to many other areas [3,24].

A key concept in gradual type systems is *consistency* [21]. Consistency weakens type equality to allow for the presence of *unknown* types. In some gradual type systems with subtyping, consistency is combined with subtyping to give rise to the notion of *consistent subtyping* [22]. Consistent subtyping is employed by gradual type systems to validate type conversions arising from conventional subtyping. One nice feature of consistent subtyping is that it is derivable from the more primitive notions of *consistency* and *subtyping*. As Siek and Taha [22] put it this shows that *"gradual typing and subtyping are orthogonal and can be combined in a principled fashion"*. Thus consistent subtyping is often used as a guideline for designing gradual type systems with subtyping.

© The Author(s) 2018
A. Ahmed (Ed.): ESOP 2018, LNCS 10801, pp. 3–30, 2018.
https://doi.org/10.1007/978-3-319-89884-1_1

Unfortunately, as noted by Garcia et al. [13], notions of consistency and/or consistent subtyping *"become more difficult to adapt as type systems get more complex"*. In particular, for the case of type systems with subtyping, certain kinds of subtyping do not fit well with the original definition of consistent subtyping by Siek and Taha [22]. One important case where such mismatch happens is in type systems supporting implicit (higher-rank) polymorphism [11,18]. It is well-known that polymorphic types à la System F induce a subtyping relation that relates polymorphic types to their instantiations [16,17]. However Siek and Taha's [22] definition is not adequate for this kind of subtyping. Moreover the current framework for *Abstracting Gradual Typing* (AGT) [13] also does not account for polymorphism, with the authors acknowledging that this is one of the interesting avenues for future work.

Existing work on gradual type systems with polymorphism does not use consistent subtyping. The Polymorphic Blame Calculus (λB) [1] is an *explicitly* polymorphic calculus with explicit casts, which is often used as a target language for gradual type systems with polymorphism. In λB a notion of *compatibility* is employed to validate conversions allowed by casts. Interestingly λB *allows conversions from polymorphic types to their instantiations*. For example, it is possible to cast a value with type $\forall a.a \to a$ into $\mathsf{Int} \to \mathsf{Int}$. Thus an important remark here is that while λB is explicitly polymorphic, casting and conversions are closer to *implicit* polymorphism. That is, in a conventional explicitly polymorphic calculus (such as System F), the primary notion is type equality, where instantiation is not taken into account. Thus the types $\forall a.a \to a$ and $\mathsf{Int} \to \mathsf{Int}$ are deemed *incompatible*. However in *implicitly* polymorphic calculi [11,18] $\forall a.a \to a$ and $\mathsf{Int} \to \mathsf{Int}$ are deemed *compatible*, since the latter type is an instantiation of the former. Therefore λB is in a sense a hybrid between implicit and explicit polymorphism, utilizing type equality (à la System F) for validating applications, and *compatibility* for validating casts.

An alternative approach to polymorphism has recently been proposed by Igarashi et al. [14]. Like λB their calculus is explicitly polymorphic. However, in that work they employ type consistency to validate cast conversions, and forbid conversions from $\forall a.a \to a$ to $\mathsf{Int} \to \mathsf{Int}$. This makes their casts closer to explicit polymorphism, in contrast to λB. Nonetheless, there is still same flavour of implicit polymorphism in their calculus when it comes to interactions between dynamically typed and polymorphically typed code. For example, in their calculus type consistency allows types such as $\forall a.a \to \mathsf{Int}$ to be related to $\star \to \mathsf{Int}$, where some sort of (implicit) polymorphic subtyping is involved.

The first goal of this paper is to study the gradually typed subtyping and consistent subtyping relations for *predicative implicit polymorphism*. To accomplish this, we first show how to reconcile consistent subtyping with polymorphism by generalizing the original consistent subtyping definition by Siek and Taha [22]. The new definition of consistent subtyping can deal with polymorphism, and preserves the orthogonality between consistency and subtyping. To slightly rephrase Siek and Taha [22], the motto of our paper is that:

Gradual typing and **polymorphism** *are orthogonal and can be combined in a principled fashion.*[1]

With the insights gained from our work, we argue that, for implicit polymorphism, Ahmed et al.'s [1] notion of compatibility is too permissive (i.e. too many programs are allowed to type-check), and that Igarashi et al.'s [14] notion of type consistency is too conservative. As a step towards an algorithmic version of consistent subtyping, we present a syntax-directed version of consistent subtyping that is sound and complete with respect to our formal definition of consistent subtyping. The syntax-directed version of consistent subtyping is remarkably simple and well-behaved, without the ad-hoc *restriction* operator [22]. Moreover, to further illustrate the generality of our consistent subtyping definition, we show that it can also account for *top types*, which cannot be dealt with by Siek and Taha's [22] definition either.

The second goal of this paper is to present a (source-level) gradually typed calculus for (predicative) implicit higher-rank polymorphism that uses our new notion of consistent subtyping. As far as we are aware, there is no work on bridging the gap between implicit higher-rank polymorphism and gradual typing, which is interesting for two reasons. On one hand, modern functional languages (such as Haskell) employ sophisticated type-inference algorithms that, aided by type annotations, can deal with implicit higher-rank polymorphism. So a natural question is how gradual typing can be integrated in such languages. On the other hand, there is several existing work on integrating *explicit* polymorphism into gradual typing [1,14]. Yet no work investigates how to move such expressive power into a source language with implicit polymorphism. Therefore as a step towards gradualizing such type systems, this paper develops both declarative and algorithmic versions for a gradual type system with implicit higher-rank polymorphism. The new calculus brings the expressive power of full implicit higher-rank polymorphic into a gradually typed source language. We prove that our calculus satisfies all of the *static* aspects of the refined criteria for gradual typing [25], while discussing some issues related with the *dynamic guarantee*.

In summary, the contributions of this paper are:

- We define a framework for consistent subtyping with:
  - a new definition of consistent subtyping that subsumes and generalizes that of Siek and Taha [22], and can deal with polymorphism and top types.
  - a syntax-directed version of consistent subtyping that is sound and complete with respect to our definition of consistent subtyping, but still guesses polymorphic instantiations.

---

[1] Note here that we borrow Siek and Taha's [22] motto mostly to talk about the static semantics. As Ahmed et al. [1] show there are several non-trivial interactions between polymorphism and casts at the level of the dynamic semantics.

$$\boxed{A <: B}$$

$$\text{Int} <: \text{Int} \qquad \text{Bool} <: \text{Bool} \qquad \text{Float} <: \text{Float} \qquad \text{Int} <: \text{Float}$$

$$\frac{B_1 <: A_1 \qquad A_2 <: B_2}{A_1 \to A_2 <: B_1 \to B_2} \qquad [l_i : A_i^{i \in 1 \ldots n+m}] <: [l_i : A_i^{i \in 1 \ldots n}] \qquad \star <: \star$$

$$\boxed{A \sim B}$$

$$A \sim A \qquad A \sim \star \qquad \star \sim A \qquad \frac{A_1 \sim B_1 \qquad A_2 \sim B_2}{A_1 \to A_2 \sim B_1 \to B_2} \qquad \frac{A_i \sim B_i}{[l_i : A_i] \sim [l_i : B_i]}$$

Fig. 1. Subtyping and type consistency in $\mathbf{FOb}^?_{<:}$.

- Based on consistent subtyping, we present a declarative gradual type system with predicative implicit higher-rank polymorphism. We prove that our calculus satisfies the static aspects of the refined criteria for gradual typing [25], and is type-safe by a type-directed translation to $\lambda\mathsf{B}$, and thus hereditarily preserves parametricity [2].
- We present a complete and sound bidirectional algorithm for implementing the declarative system based on the design principle of Garcia and Cimini [12] and the approach of Dunfield and Krishnaswami [11].
- All of the metatheory of this paper, except some manual proofs for the algorithmic type system, has been mechanically formalized in Coq[2].

2 Background and Motivation

In this section we review a simple gradually typed language with objects [22], to introduce the concept of consistency subtyping. We also briefly talk about the Odersky-Läufer type system for higher-rank types [17], which serves as the original language on which our gradually typed calculus with implicit higher-rank polymorphism is based.

2.1 Gradual Subtyping

Siek and Taha [22] developed a gradual typed system for object-oriented languages that they call $\mathbf{FOb}^?_{<:}$. Central to gradual typing is the concept of *consistency* (written $\sim$) between gradual types, which are types that may involve the unknown type $\star$. The intuition is that consistency relaxes the structure of a type system to tolerate unknown positions in a gradual type. They also defined the subtyping relation in a way that static type safety is preserved. Their key

---

[2] All supplementary materials are available at https://bitbucket.org/xieningning/consistent-subtyping.

insight is that the unknown type $\star$ is neutral to subtyping, with only $\star <: \star$. Both relations are found in Fig. 1.

A primary contribution of their work is to show that consistency and subtyping are orthogonal. To compose subtyping and consistency, Siek and Taha [22] defined *consistent subtyping* (written $\lesssim$) in two equivalent ways:

Definition 1 (Consistent Subtyping à la Siek and Taha [22])

- $A \lesssim B$ if and only if $A \sim C$ and $C <: B$ for some C.
- $A \lesssim B$ if and only if $A <: C$ and $C \sim B$ for some C.

Both definitions are non-deterministic because of the intermediate type C. To remove non-determinism, they proposed a so-called *restriction operator*, written $A|_B$ that masks off the parts of a type A that are unknown in a type B.

$A|_B = $ **case** A, B **of** $| (-, \star) \Rightarrow \star$
$\quad | A_1 \rightarrow A_2, B_1 \rightarrow B_2 = A_1|_{B_1} \rightarrow A_2|_{B_2}$
$\quad | [l_1 : A_1, ..., l_n : A_n], [l_1 : B_1, ..., l_m : B_m]$ **if** $n \leq m \Rightarrow [l_1 : A_1|_{B_1}, ..., l_n : A_n|_{B_n}]$
$\quad | [l_1 : A_1, ..., l_n : A_n], [l_1 : B_1, ..., l_m : B_m]$ **if** $n > m \Rightarrow$
$\qquad [l_1 : A_1|_{B_1}, ..., l_m : A_m|_{B_m}, ..., l_n : A_n]$
$\quad |$ **otherwise** $\Rightarrow A$

With the restriction operator, consistent subtyping is simply defined as $A \lesssim B \equiv A|_B <: B|_A$. Then they proved that this definition is equivalent to Definition 1.

2.2 The Odersky-Läufer Type System

The calculus we are combining gradual typing with is the well-established predicative type system for higher-rank types proposed by Odersky and Läufer [17]. One difference is that, for simplicity, we do not account for a let expression, as there is already existing work about gradual type systems with let expressions and let generalization (for example, see Garcia and Cimini [12]). Similar techniques can be applied to our calculus to enable let generalization.

The syntax of the type system, along with the typing and subtyping judgments is given in Fig. 2. An implicit assumption throughout the paper is that variables in contexts are distinct. We save the explanations for the static semantics to Sect. 4, where we present our gradually typed version of the calculus.

2.3 Motivation: Gradually Typed Higher-Rank Polymorphism

Our work combines implicit (higher-rank) polymorphism with gradual typing. As is well known, a gradually typed language supports both fully static and fully dynamic checking of program properties, as well as the continuum between these two extremes. It also offers programmers fine-grained control over the static-to-dynamic spectrum, i.e., a program can be evolved by introducing more or less precise types as needed [13].

$$
\begin{array}{ll}
\text{Expressions} & e ::= x \mid n \mid \lambda x : A.\ e \mid \lambda x.\ e \mid e\ e \\
\text{Types} & A, B ::= \text{Int} \mid a \mid A \to B \mid \forall a.A \\
\text{Monotypes} & \tau, \sigma ::= \text{Int} \mid a \mid \tau \to \sigma \\
\text{Contexts} & \Psi ::= \varnothing \mid \Psi, x : A \mid \Psi, a
\end{array}
$$

$$\boxed{\Psi \vdash^{OL} e : A}$$

$$
\dfrac{x : A \in \Psi}{\Psi \vdash^{OL} x : A}\ \text{Var}
\qquad
\dfrac{}{\Psi \vdash^{OL} n : \text{Int}}\ \text{Nat}
\qquad
\dfrac{\Psi, x : A \vdash^{OL} e : B}{\Psi \vdash^{OL} \lambda x : A.\ e : A \to B}\ \text{LamAnn}
$$

$$
\dfrac{\Psi \vdash^{OL} e_1 : A_1 \to A_2 \quad \Psi \vdash^{OL} e_2 : A_1}{\Psi \vdash^{OL} e_1\ e_2 : A_2}\ \text{App}
\qquad
\dfrac{\Psi \vdash^{OL} e : A_1 \quad \Psi \vdash A_1 <: A_2}{\Psi \vdash^{OL} e : A_2}\ \text{Sub}
$$

$$
\dfrac{\Psi, x : \tau \vdash^{OL} e : B}{\Psi \vdash^{OL} \lambda x.\ e : \tau \to B}\ \text{Lam}
\qquad
\dfrac{\Psi, a \vdash^{OL} e : A}{\Psi \vdash^{OL} e : \forall a.A}\ \text{Gen}
$$

$$\boxed{\Psi \vdash A <: B}$$

$$
\dfrac{a \in \Psi}{\Psi \vdash a <: a}\ \text{CS-TVar}
\qquad
\dfrac{}{\Psi \vdash \text{Int} <: \text{Int}}\ \text{CS-Int}
\qquad
\dfrac{\Psi \vdash \tau \quad \Psi \vdash A[a \mapsto \tau] <: B}{\Psi \vdash \forall a.A <: B}\ \text{ForallL}
$$

$$
\dfrac{\Psi, a \vdash A <: B}{\Psi \vdash A <: \forall a.B}\ \text{ForallR}
\qquad
\dfrac{\Psi \vdash B_1 <: A_1 \quad \Psi \vdash A_2 <: B_2}{\Psi \vdash A_1 \to A_2 <: B_1 \to B_2}\ \text{CS-Fun}
$$

Fig. 2. Syntax and static semantics of the Odersky-Läufer type system.

Haskell is a language that supports implicit higher-rank polymorphism, but no gradual typing. Therefore some programs that are safe at run-time may be rejected due to the conservativity of the type system. For example, consider the following Haskell program adapted from Jones et al. [18]:

foo :: (**[Int]**, **[Char]**)
foo = **let** $f\ x = (x\ [1, 2]\ ,\ x\ ['a', 'b'])$ **in** f **reverse**

This program is rejected by Haskell's type checker because Haskell implements the Damas-Milner rule that a lambda-bound argument (such as x) can only have a monotype, i.e., the type checker can only assign x the type **[Int]** → **[Int]**, or **[Char]** → **[Char]**, but not $\forall a.[a] \to [a]$. Finding such manual polymorphic annotations can be non-trivial. Instead of rejecting the program outright, due to missing type annotations, gradual typing provides a simple alternative by giving x the unknown type (denoted $\star$). With such typing the same program type-checks and produces $([2,1], ['b', 'a'])$. By running the program, programmers can gain some additional insight about the run-time behaviour. Then, with such insight, they can also give x a more precise type $(\forall a.[a] \to [a])$ a posteriori so that the program continues to type-check via implicit polymorphism and also grants

$$\begin{array}{ll} \text{Types} & A, B ::= \text{Int} \mid a \mid A \to B \mid \forall a.A \mid \star \\ \text{Monotypes} & \tau, \sigma ::= \text{Int} \mid a \mid \tau \to \sigma \\ \text{Contexts} & \Psi ::= \varnothing \mid \Psi, x : A \mid \Psi, a \end{array}$$

$$\boxed{A \sim B}$$

$$A \sim A \qquad A \sim \star \qquad \star \sim A \qquad \dfrac{A_1 \sim B_1 \quad A_2 \sim B_2}{A_1 \to A_2 \sim B_1 \to B_2} \qquad \dfrac{A \sim B}{\forall a.A \sim \forall a.B}$$

$$\boxed{\Psi \vdash A <: B}$$

$$\dfrac{\Psi, a \vdash A <: B}{\Psi \vdash A <: \forall a.B} \text{ S-ForallR} \qquad \dfrac{\Psi \vdash \tau \quad \Psi \vdash A[a \mapsto \tau] <: B}{\Psi \vdash \forall a.A <: B} \text{ S-ForallL} \qquad \dfrac{a \in \Psi}{\Psi \vdash a <: a} \text{ S-TVar}$$

$$\dfrac{}{\Psi \vdash \text{Int} <: \text{Int}} \text{ S-Int} \qquad \dfrac{\Psi \vdash B_1 <: A_1 \quad \Psi \vdash A_2 <: B_2}{\Psi \vdash A_1 \to A_2 <: B_1 \to B_2} \text{ S-Fun} \qquad \dfrac{}{\Psi \vdash \star <: \star} \text{ S-Unknown}$$

Fig. 3. Syntax of types, consistency, and subtyping in the declarative system.

more static safety. In this paper, we envision such a language that combines the benefits of both implicit higher-rank polymorphism and gradual typing.

3 Revisiting Consistent Subtyping

In this section we explore the design space of consistent subtyping. We start with the definitions of consistency and subtyping for polymorphic types, and compare with some relevant work. We then discuss the design decisions involved towards our new definition of consistent subtyping, and justify the new definition by demonstrating its equivalence with that of Siek and Taha [22] and the AGT approach [13] on simple types.

The syntax of types is given at the top of Fig. 3. We write A, B for types. Types are either the integer type Int, type variables a, functions types $A \to B$, universal quantification $\forall a.A$, or the unknown type $\star$. Though we only have one base type Int, we also use Bool for the purpose of illustration. Note that mono-types τ contain all types other than the universal quantifier and the unknown type $\star$. We will discuss this restriction when we present the subtyping rules. Contexts Ψ are *ordered* lists of type variable declarations and term variables.

3.1 Consistency and Subtyping

We start by giving the definitions of consistency and subtyping for polymorphic types, and comparing our definitions with the compatibility relation by Ahmed et al. [1] and type consistency by Igarashi et al. [14].

Consistency. The key observation here is that consistency is mostly a structural relation, except that the unknown type $\star$ can be regarded as any type. Following this observation, we naturally extend the definition from Fig. 1 with polymorphic types, as shown at the middle of Fig. 3. In particular a polymorphic type $\forall a.A$ is consistent with another polymorphic type $\forall a.B$ if A is consistent with B.

Subtyping. We express the fact that one type is a polymorphic generalization of another by means of the subtyping judgment $\Psi \vdash A <: B$. Compared with the subtyping rules of Odersky and Läufer [17] in Fig. 2, the only addition is the neutral subtyping of $\star$. Notice that, in the rule S-FORALLL, the universal quantifier is only allowed to be instantiated with a *monotype*. The judgment $\Psi \vdash \tau$ checks all the type variables in τ are bound in the context Ψ. For space reasons, we omit the definition. According to the syntax in Fig. 3, monotypes do not include the unknown type $\star$. This is because if we were to allow the unknown type to be used for instantiation, we could have $\forall a.a \to a <: \star \to \star$ by instantiating a with $\star$. Since $\star \to \star$ is consistent with any functions $A \to B$, for instance, Int $\to$ Bool, this means that we could provide an expression of type $\forall a.a \to a$ to a function where the input type is supposed to be Int $\to$ Bool. However, as we might expect, $\forall a.a \to a$ is definitely not compatible with Int $\to$ Bool. This does not hold in any polymorphic type systems without gradual typing. So the gradual type system should not accept it either. (This is the so-called *conservative extension* property that will be made precise in Sect. 4.3.)

Importantly there is a subtle but crucial distinction between a type variable and the unknown type, although they all represent a kind of "arbitrary" type. The unknown type stands for the absence of type information: it could be *any type* at *any instance*. Therefore, the unknown type is consistent with any type, and additional type-checks have to be performed at runtime. On the other hand, a type variable indicates *parametricity*. In other words, a type variable can only be instantiated to a single type. For example, in the type $\forall a.a \to a$, the two occurrences of a represent an arbitrary but single type (e.g., Int $\to$ Int, Bool $\to$ Bool), while $\star \to \star$ could be an arbitrary function (e.g., Int $\to$ Bool) at runtime.

Comparison with Other Relations. In other polymorphic gradual calculi, consistency and subtyping are often mixed up to some extent. In λB [1], the compatibility relation for polymorphic types is defined as follows:

$$\frac{A \prec B}{A \prec \forall X.B} \text{ COMP-ALLR} \qquad \frac{A[X \mapsto \star] \prec B}{\forall X.A \prec B} \text{ COMP-ALLL}$$

Notice that, in rule COMP-ALLL, the universal quantifier is *always* instantiated to $\star$. However, this way, λB allows $\forall a.a \to a \prec$ Int $\to$ Bool, which as we discussed before might not be what we expect. Indeed λB relies on sophisticated runtime checks to rule out such instances of the compatibility relation a posteriori.

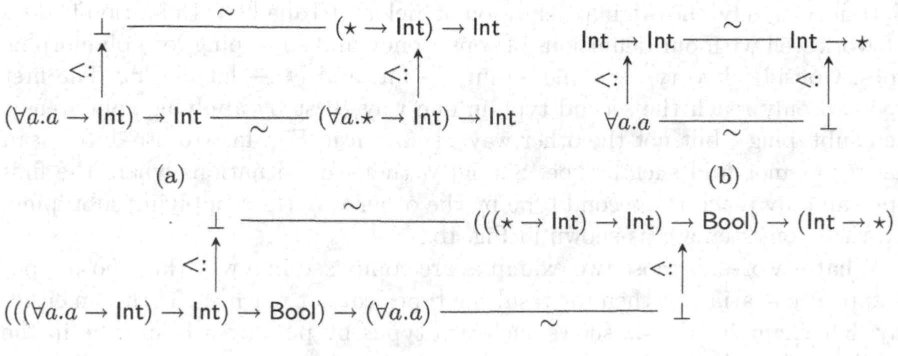

$$\bot \xrightarrow{\quad\sim\quad} (\star \to \mathsf{Int}) \to \mathsf{Int} \qquad\qquad \mathsf{Int} \to \mathsf{Int} \xrightarrow{\quad\sim\quad} \mathsf{Int} \to \star$$

(a)   (b)

(c)

Fig. 4. Examples that break the original definition of consistent subtyping.

Igarashi et al. [14] introduced the so-called *quasi-polymorphic* types for types that may be used where a ∀-type is expected, which is important for their purpose of conservativity over System F. Their type consistency relation, involving polymorphism, is defined as follows[3]:

$$\frac{A \sim B}{\forall a.A \sim \forall a.B} \qquad\qquad \frac{A \sim B \qquad B \neq \forall a.B' \qquad \star \in \mathsf{Types}(B)}{\forall a.A \sim B}$$

Compared with our consistency definition in Fig. 3, their first rule is the same as ours. The second rule says that a non ∀-type can be consistent with a ∀-type only if it contains ⋆. In this way, their type system is able to reject $\forall a.a \to a \sim$ $\mathsf{Int} \to \mathsf{Bool}$. However, in order to keep conservativity, they also reject $\forall a.a \to a \sim$ $\mathsf{Int} \to \mathsf{Int}$, which is perfectly sensible in their setting (i.e., explicit polymorphism). However with implicit polymorphism, we would expect $\forall a.a \to a$ to be related with $\mathsf{Int} \to \mathsf{Int}$, since a can be instantiated to Int.

Nonetheless, when it comes to interactions between dynamically typed and polymorphically typed terms, both relations allow $\forall a.a \to \mathsf{Int}$ to be related with $\star \to \mathsf{Int}$ for example, which in our view, is some sort of (implicit) polymorphic subtyping combined with type consistency, and that should be derivable by the more primitive notions in the type system (instead of inventing new relations). One of our design principles is that subtyping and consistency is *orthogonal*, and can be naturally superimposed, echoing the same opinion of Siek and Taha [22].

3.2 Towards Consistent Subtyping

With the definitions of consistency and subtyping, the question now is how to compose these two relations so that two types can be compared in a way that takes these two relations into account.

---

[3] This is a simplified version.

Unfortunately, the original definition of Siek and Taha [22] (Definition 1) does not work well with our definitions of consistency and subtyping for polymorphic types. Consider two types: $(\forall a.a \rightarrow \mathsf{Int}) \rightarrow \mathsf{Int}$, and $(\star \rightarrow \mathsf{Int}) \rightarrow \mathsf{Int}$. The first type can only reach the second type in one way (first by applying consistency, then subtyping), but not the other way, as shown in Fig. 4a. We use $\perp$ to mean that we cannot find such a type. Similarly, there are situations where the first type can only reach the second type by the other way (first applying subtyping, and then consistency), as shown in Fig. 4b.

What is worse, if those two examples are composed in a way that those types all appear co-variantly, then the resulting types cannot reach each other in either way. For example, Fig. 4c shows such two types by putting a Bool type in the middle, and neither definition of consistent subtyping works.

Observations on Consistent Subtyping Based on Information Propagation. In order to develop the correct definition of consistent subtyping for polymorphic types, we need to understand how consistent subtyping works. We first review two important properties of subtyping: (1) subtyping induces the subsumption rule: if $A <: B$, then an expression of type A can be used where B is expected; (2) subtyping is transitive: if $A <: B$, and $B <: C$, then $A <: C$. Though consistent subtyping takes the unknown type into consideration, the subsumption rule should also apply: if $A \lesssim B$, then an expression of type A can also be used where B is expected, given that there might be some information lost by consistency. A crucial difference from subtyping is that consistent subtyping is *not* transitive because information can only be lost once (otherwise, any two types are a consistent subtype of each other). Now consider a situation where we have both $A <: B$, and $B \lesssim C$, this means that A can be used where B is expected, and B can be used where C is expected, with possibly some loss of information. In other words, we should expect that A can be used where C is expected, since there is at most one-time loss of information.

Observation 1. *If $A <: B$, and $B \lesssim C$, then $A \lesssim C$.*

This is reflected in Fig. 5a. A symmetrical observation is given in Fig. 5b:

Observation 2. *If $C \lesssim B$, and $B <: A$, then $C \lesssim A$.*

From the above observations, we see what the problem is with the original definition. In Fig. 5a, if B can reach C by T_1, then by subtyping transitivity, A can reach C by T_1. However, if B can only reach C by T_2, then A cannot reach C through the original definition. A similar problem is shown in Fig. 5b.

However, it turns out that those two problems can be fixed using the same strategy: instead of taking one-step subtyping and one-step consistency, our definition of consistent subtyping allows types to take *one-step subtyping, one-step consistency, and one more step subtyping*. Specifically, $A <: B \sim T_2 <: C$ (in Fig. 5a) and $C <: T_1 \sim B <: A$ (in Fig. 5b) have the same relation chain: subtyping, consistency, and subtyping.

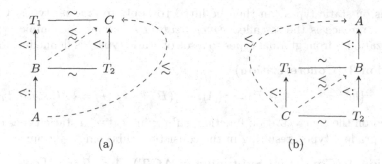

Fig. 5. Observations of consistent subtyping

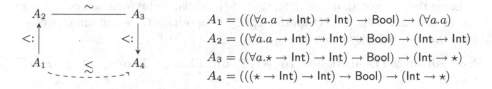

$$A_1 = (((\forall a.a \to \mathsf{Int}) \to \mathsf{Int}) \to \mathsf{Bool}) \to (\forall a.a)$$
$$A_2 = ((\forall a.a \to \mathsf{Int}) \to \mathsf{Int}) \to \mathsf{Bool}) \to (\mathsf{Int} \to \mathsf{Int})$$
$$A_3 = ((\forall a.\star \to \mathsf{Int}) \to \mathsf{Int}) \to \mathsf{Bool}) \to (\mathsf{Int} \to \star)$$
$$A_4 = (((\star \to \mathsf{Int}) \to \mathsf{Int}) \to \mathsf{Bool}) \to (\mathsf{Int} \to \star)$$

Fig. 6. Example that is fixed by the new definition of consistent subtyping.

Definition of Consistent Subtyping. From the above discussion, we are ready to modify Definition 1, and adapt it to our notation:

Definition 2 (Consistent Subtyping)

$$\frac{\Psi \vdash A <: C \qquad C \sim D \qquad \Psi \vdash D <: B}{\Psi \vdash A \lesssim B}$$

With Definition 2, Fig. 6 illustrates the correct relation chain for the broken example shown in Fig. 4c. At first sight, Definition 2 seems worse than the original; we need to guess *two* types! It turns out that Definition 2 is a generalization of Definition 1, and they are equivalent in the system of Siek and Taha [22]. However, more generally, Definition 2 is compatible with polymorphic types.

Proposition 1 (Generalization of Consistent Subtyping)

– *Definition 2 subsumes Definition 1.*
– *Definition 1 is equivalent to Definition 2 in the system of Siek and Taha [22].*

3.3   Abstracting Gradual Typing

Garcia et al. [13] presented a new foundation for gradual typing that they call the *Abstracting Gradual Typing* (AGT) approach. In the AGT approach, gradual types are interpreted as sets of static types, where static types refer to types containing no unknown types. In this interpretation, predicates and functions on static types can then be lifted to apply to gradual types. Central to their approach is the so-called *concretization* function. For simple types, a concretization γ from gradual types to a set of static types[4] is defined as follows:

Definition 3 (Concretization)

$$\gamma(\mathsf{Int}) = \{\mathsf{Int}\} \qquad \gamma(A \to B) = \gamma(A) \to \gamma(B) \qquad \gamma(\star) = \{\textit{All static types}\}$$

Based on the concretization function, subtyping between static types can be lifted to gradual types, resulting in the consistent subtyping relation:

Definition 4 (Consistent Subtyping in AGT). $A \mathrel{\widetilde{<:}} B$ *if and only if* $A_1 <: B_1$ *for some* $A_1 \in \gamma(A)$, $B_1 \in \gamma(B)$.

Later they proved that this definition of consistent subtyping coincides with that of Siek and Taha [22] (Definition 1). By Proposition 1, we can directly conclude that our definition coincides with AGT:

Proposition 2 (Equivalence to AGT on Simple Types). $A \lesssim B$ *iff* $A \mathrel{\widetilde{<:}} B$.

However, AGT does not show how to deal with polymorphism (e.g. the interpretation of type variables) yet. Still, as noted by Garcia et al. [13], it is a promising line of future work for AGT, and the question remains whether our definition would coincide with it.

Another note related to AGT is that the definition is later adopted by Castagna and Lanvin [7], where the static types A_1, B_1 in Definition 4 can be algorithmically computed by also accounting for top and bottom types.

3.4 Directed Consistency

Directed consistency [15] is defined in terms of precision and static subtyping:

$$\frac{A' \sqsubseteq A \qquad A <: B \qquad B' \sqsubseteq B}{A' \lesssim B'}$$

The judgment $A \sqsubseteq B$ is read "A is less precise than B". In their setting, precision is defined for type constructors and subtyping for static types. If we interpret this definition from AGT's point of view, finding a more precise static type[5] has the same effect as concretization. Namely, $A' \sqsubseteq A$ implies $A \in \gamma(A')$ and $B' \sqsubseteq B$ implies $B \in \gamma(B')$. Therefore we consider this definition as AGT-style. From this perspective, this definition naturally coincides with Definition 2.

The value of their definition is that consistent subtyping is derived compositionally from *static subtyping* and *precision*. These are two more atomic relations. At first sight, their definition looks very similar to Definition 2 (replacing $\sqsubseteq$ by $<:$ and $<:$ by $\sim$). Then a question arises as to *which one is more fundamental*. To answer this, we need to discuss the relation between consistency and precision.

---

[4] For simplification, we directly regard type constructor $\to$ as a set-level operator.

[5] The definition of precision of types is given in appendix.

Relating Consistency and Precision. Precision is a partial order (anti-symmetric and transitive), while consistency is symmetric but not transitive. Nonetheless, precision and consistency are related by the following proposition:

Proposition 3 (Consistency and Precision)

- If $A \sim B$, then there exists (static) C, such that $A \sqsubseteq C$, and $B \sqsubseteq C$.
- If for some (static) C, we have $A \sqsubseteq C$, and $B \sqsubseteq C$, then we have $A \sim B$.

It may seem that precision is a more atomic relation, since consistency can be derived from precision. However, recall that consistency is in fact an equivalence relation lifted from static types to gradual types. Therefore defining consistency independently is straightforward, and it is theoretically viable to validate the definition of consistency directly. On the other hand, precision is usually connected with the gradual criteria [25], and finding a correct partial order that adheres to the criteria is not always an easy task. For example, Igarashi et al. [14] argued that term precision for System F_G is actually nontrivial, leaving the gradual guarantee of the semantics as a conjecture. Thus precision can be difficult to extend to more sophisticated type systems, e.g. dependent types.

Still, it is interesting that those two definitions illustrate the correspondence of different foundations (on simple types): one is defined directly on gradual types, and the other stems from AGT, which is based on static subtyping.

3.5   Consistent Subtyping Without Existentials

Definition 2 serves as a fine specification of how consistent subtyping should behave in general. But it is inherently non-deterministic because of the two intermediate types C and D. As with Definition 1, we need a combined relation to directly compare two types. A natural attempt is to try to extend the restriction operator for polymorphic types. Unfortunately, as we show below, this does not work. However it is possible to devise an equivalent inductive definition instead.

Attempt to Extend the Restriction Operator. Suppose that we try to extend the restriction operator to account for polymorphic types. The original restriction operator is structural, meaning that it works for types of similar structures. But for polymorphic types, two input types could have different structures due to universal quantifiers, e.g., $\forall a.a \rightarrow$ Int and (Int $\rightarrow \star) \rightarrow$ Int. If we try to mask the first type using the second, it seems hard to maintain the information that a should be instantiated to a function while ensuring that the return type is masked. There seems to be no satisfactory way to extend the restriction operator in order to support this kind of non-structural masking.

Interpretation of the Restriction Operator and Consistent Subtyping. If the restriction operator cannot be extended naturally, it is useful to take a step back and revisit what the restriction operator actually does. For consistent subtyping, two input types could have unknown types in different positions, but we only care about the known parts. What the restriction operator does is (1) erase

$$\Psi \vdash A \lesssim B$$

$$\frac{\Psi, a \vdash A \lesssim B}{\Psi \vdash A \lesssim \forall a.B} \text{ CS-FORALLR} \qquad \frac{\Psi \vdash \tau \quad \Psi \vdash A[a \mapsto \tau] \lesssim B}{\Psi \vdash \forall a.A \lesssim B} \text{ CS-FORALLL}$$

$$\frac{\Psi \vdash B_1 \lesssim A_1 \quad \Psi \vdash A_2 \lesssim B_2}{\Psi \vdash A_1 \rightarrow A_2 \lesssim B_1 \rightarrow B_2} \text{ CS-FUN} \qquad \frac{a \in \Psi}{\Psi \vdash a \lesssim a} \text{ CS-TVAR} \qquad \frac{}{\Psi \vdash \text{Int} \lesssim \text{Int}} \text{ CS-INT}$$

$$\frac{}{\Psi \vdash \star \lesssim A} \text{ CS-UNKNOWNL} \qquad \frac{}{\Psi \vdash A \lesssim \star} \text{ CS-UNKNOWNR}$$

Fig. 7. Consistent Subtyping for implicit polymorphism.

the type information in one type if the corresponding position in the other type is the unknown type; and (2) compare the resulting types using the normal subtyping relation. The example below shows the masking-off procedure for the types $\text{Int} \rightarrow \star \rightarrow \text{Bool}$ and $\text{Int} \rightarrow \text{Int} \rightarrow \star$. Since the known parts have the relation that $\text{Int} \rightarrow \star \rightarrow \star <: \text{Int} \rightarrow \star \rightarrow \star$, we conclude that $\text{Int} \rightarrow \star \rightarrow \text{Bool} \lesssim \text{Int} \rightarrow \text{Int} \rightarrow \star$.

$$
\left.
\begin{array}{l}
\text{Int} \rightarrow \boxed{\star} \rightarrow \boxed{\text{Bool}} \quad _{|\ \text{Int} \rightarrow \text{Int} \rightarrow \star} \quad = \text{Int} \rightarrow \star \rightarrow \star \\
\text{Int} \rightarrow \boxed{\text{Int}} \rightarrow \boxed{\star} \quad _{|\ \text{Int} \rightarrow \star \rightarrow \text{Bool}} \quad = \text{Int} \rightarrow \star \rightarrow \star
\end{array}
\right) <:
$$

Here differences of the types in boxes are erased because of the restriction operator. Now if we compare the types in boxes directly instead of through the lens of the restriction operator, we can observe that the *consistent subtyping relation always holds between the unknown type and an arbitrary type*. We can interpret this observation directly from Definition 2: the unknown type is neutral to subtyping ($\star <: \star$), the unknown type is consistent with any type ($\star \sim A$), and subtyping is reflexive ($A <: A$). Therefore, *the unknown type is a consistent subtype of any type ($\star \lesssim A$), and vice versa ($A \lesssim \star$)*. Note that this interpretation provides a general recipe on how to lift a (static) subtyping relation to a (gradual) consistent subtyping relation, as discussed below.

Defining Consistent Subtyping Directly. From the above discussion, we can define the consistent subtyping relation directly, *without* resorting to subtyping or consistency at all. The key idea is that we replace $<:$ with $\lesssim$ in Fig. 3, get rid of rule S-UNKNOWN and add two extra rules concerning $\star$, resulting in the rules of consistent subtyping in Fig. 7. Of particular interest are the rules CS-UNKNOWNL and CS-UNKNOWNR, both of which correspond to what we just said: the unknown type is a consistent subtype of any type, and vice versa. From now on, we use the symbol $\lesssim$ to refer to the consistent subtyping relation in Fig. 7. What is more, we can prove that those two are equivalent[6]:

Theorem 1. $\Psi \vdash A \lesssim B \Leftrightarrow \Psi \vdash A <: C, C \sim D, \Psi \vdash D <: B$ *for some* C, D.

---

[6] Theorems with $\mathcal{T}$ are those proved in Coq. The same applies to $\mathcal{L}$emmas.

$$\boxed{\Psi \vdash e : A \rightsquigarrow s}$$

$$\frac{x : A \in \Psi}{\Psi \vdash x : A \rightsquigarrow x} \text{ VAR} \qquad \frac{}{\Psi \vdash n : \text{Int} \rightsquigarrow n} \text{ NAT} \qquad \frac{\Psi, a \vdash e : A \rightsquigarrow s}{\Psi \vdash e : \forall a.A \rightsquigarrow \Lambda a.s} \text{ GEN}$$

$$\frac{\Psi, x : A \vdash e : B \rightsquigarrow s}{\Psi \vdash \lambda x : A.\ e : A \rightarrow B \rightsquigarrow \lambda x : A.\ s} \text{ LAMANN} \qquad \frac{\Psi, x : \tau \vdash e : B \rightsquigarrow s}{\Psi \vdash \lambda x.\ e : \tau \rightarrow B \rightsquigarrow \lambda x : \tau.\ s} \text{ LAM}$$

$$\frac{\Psi \vdash e_1 : A \rightsquigarrow s_1 \qquad \Psi \vdash A \rhd A_1 \rightarrow A_2 \qquad \Psi \vdash e_2 : A_3 \rightsquigarrow s_2 \qquad \Psi \vdash A_3 \lesssim A_1}{\Psi \vdash e_1\ e_2 : A_2 \rightsquigarrow ((\langle A \hookrightarrow A_1 \rightarrow A_2 \rangle\ s_1)\ (\langle A_3 \hookrightarrow A_1 \rangle\ s_2))} \text{ APP}$$

$$\boxed{\Psi \vdash A \rhd A_1 \rightarrow A_2}$$

$$\frac{\Psi \vdash \tau \qquad \Psi \vdash A[a \mapsto \tau] \rhd A_1 \rightarrow A_2}{\Psi \vdash \forall a.A \rhd A_1 \rightarrow A_2} \text{ M-FORALL}$$

$$\frac{}{\Psi \vdash (A_1 \rightarrow A_2) \rhd (A_1 \rightarrow A_2)} \text{ M-ARR} \qquad \frac{}{\Psi \vdash \star \rhd \star \rightarrow \star} \text{ M-UNKNOWN}$$

Fig. 8. Declarative typing

4   Gradually Typed Implicit Polymorphism

In Sect. 3 we introduced the consistent subtyping relation that accommodates polymorphic types. In this section we continue with the development by giving a declarative type system for predicative implicit polymorphism that employs the consistent subtyping relation. The declarative system itself is already quite interesting as it is equipped with both higher-rank polymorphism and the unknown type. The syntax of expressions in the declarative system is given below:

$$\text{Expressions} \quad e ::= x \mid n \mid \lambda x : A.\ e \mid \lambda x.\ e \mid e\ e$$

4.1   Typing in Detail

Figure 8 gives the typing rules for our declarative system (the reader is advised to ignore the gray-shaded parts for now). Rule VAR extracts the type of the variable from the typing context. Rule NAT always infers integer types. Rule LAMANN puts x with type annotation A into the context, and continues type checking the body e. Rule LAM assigns a monotype τ to x, and continues type checking the body e. Gradual types and polymorphic types are introduced via annotations explicitly. Rule GEN puts a fresh type variable a into the type context and generalizes the typing result A to $\forall a.A$. Rule APP first infers the type of e_1, then the matching judgment $\Psi \vdash A \rhd A_1 \rightarrow A_2$ extracts the domain type A_1 and the codomain type A_2 from type A. The type A_3 of the argument e_2 is then compared with A_1 using the consistent subtyping judgment.

Matching. The matching judgment of Siek et al. [25] can be extended to polymorphic types naturally, resulting in $\Psi \vdash A \rhd A_1 \rightarrow A_2$. In M-FORALL, a monotype τ is guessed to instantiate the universal quantifier a. This rule is inspired by the *application judgment* $\Phi \vdash A \bullet e \Rightarrow C$ [11], which says that if we apply a term of type A to an argument e, we get something of type C. If A is a polymorphic type, the judgment works by guessing instantiations until it reaches an arrow type. Matching further simplifies the application judgment, since it is independent of typing. Rule M-ARR and M-UNKNOWN are the same as Siek et al. [25]. M-ARR returns the domain type A_1 and range type A_2 as expected. If the input is $\star$, then M-UNKNOWN returns $\star$ as both the type for the domain and the range.

Note that matching saves us from having a subsumption rule (SUB in Fig. 2). the subsumption rule is incompatible with consistent subtyping, since the latter is not transitive. A discussion of a subsumption rule based on normal subtyping can be found in the appendix.

4.2   Type-Directed Translation

We give the dynamic semantics of our language by translating it to λB. Below we show a subset of the terms in λB that are used in the translation:

$$\text{Terms} \quad s ::= x \mid n \mid \lambda x : A.\ s \mid \Lambda a.s \mid s_1\ s_2 \mid \langle A \hookrightarrow B \rangle\ s$$

A cast $\langle A \hookrightarrow B \rangle\ s$ converts the value of term s from type A to type B. A cast from A to B is permitted only if the types are *compatible*, written $A \prec B$, as briefly mentioned in Sect. 3.1. The syntax of types in λB is the same as ours.

The translation is given in the gray-shaded parts in Fig. 8. The only interesting case here is to insert explicit casts in the application rule. Note that there is no need to translate matching or consistent subtyping, instead we insert the source and target types of a cast directly in the translated expressions, thanks to the following two lemmas:

ℒemma 1 ($\rhd$ to $\prec$).   *If $\Psi \vdash A \rhd A_1 \rightarrow A_2$, then $A \prec A_1 \rightarrow A_2$.*

ℒemma 2 ($\lesssim$ to $\prec$).   *If $\Psi \vdash A \lesssim B$, then $A \prec B$.*

In order to show the correctness of the translation, we prove that our translation always produces well-typed expressions in λB. By ℒammas 1 and 2, we have the following theorem:

𝒯heorem 2 (Type Safety).   *If $\Psi \vdash e : A \rightsquigarrow s$, then $\Psi \vdash^B s : A$.*

Parametricity. An important semantic property of polymorphic types is *relational parametricity* [19]. The parametricity property says that all instances of a polymorphic function should behave *uniformly*. A classic example is a function with the type $\forall a.a \rightarrow a$. The parametricity property guarantees that a value of this type must be either the identity function (i.e., $\lambda x.x$) or the undefined function (one which never returns a value). However, with the addition of the unknown type $\star$, careful measures are to be taken to ensure parametricity. This is exactly the circumstance that λB was designed to address. Ahmed et al. [2] proved that λB satisfies relational parametricity. Based on their result, and by 𝒯heorem 2, parametricity is preserved in our system.

Ambiguity from Casts. The translation does not always produce a unique target expression. This is because when we guess a monotype τ in rule M-FORALL and CS-FORALLL, we could have different choices, which inevitably leads to different types. Unlike (non-gradual) polymorphic type systems [11,18], the choice of monotypes could affect runtime behaviour of the translated programs, since they could appear inside the explicit casts. For example, the following shows two possible translations for the same source expression $\lambda x : \star.\ f\ x$, where the type of f is instantiated to $\mathsf{Int} \to \mathsf{Int}$ and $\mathsf{Bool} \to \mathsf{Bool}$, respectively:

$$f : \forall a.a \to a \vdash (\lambda x : \star.\ f\ x) : \star \to \mathsf{Int}$$

$$\leadsto (\lambda x : \star.\ ((\forall a.a \to a \hookrightarrow \mathsf{Int} \to \mathsf{Int})\ f)\ (\ \langle \star \hookrightarrow \mathsf{Int}\rangle\ x))$$

$$f : \forall a.a \to a \vdash (\lambda x : \star.\ f\ x) : \star \to \mathsf{Bool}$$

$$\leadsto (\lambda x : \star.\ ((\forall a.a \to a \hookrightarrow \mathsf{Bool} \to \mathsf{Bool})\ f)\ (\ \langle \star \hookrightarrow \mathsf{Bool}\rangle\ x))$$

If we apply $\lambda x : \star.\ f\ x$ to 3, which is fine since the function can take any input, the first translation runs smoothly in λB, while the second one will raise a cast error (Int cannot be cast to Bool). Similarly, if we apply it to true, then the second succeeds while the first fails. The culprit lies in the highlighted parts where any instantiation of a would be put inside the explicit cast. More generally, any choice introduces an explicit cast to that type in the translation, which causes a runtime cast error if the function is applied to a value whose type does not match the guessed type. Note that this does not compromise the type safety of the translated expressions, since cast errors are part of the type safety guarantees.

Coherence. The ambiguity of translation seems to imply that the declarative system is *incoherent*. A semantics is coherent if distinct typing derivations of the same typing judgment possess the same meaning [20]. We argue that the declarative system is "coherent up to cast errors" in the sense that a well-typed program produces a unique value, or results in a cast error. In the above example, whatever the translation might be, applying $\lambda x : \star.\ f\ x$ to 3 either results in a cast error, or produces 3, nothing else.

This discrepancy is due to the guessing nature of the *declarative* system. As far as the declarative system is concerned, both $\mathsf{Int} \to \mathsf{Int}$ and $\mathsf{Bool} \to \mathsf{Bool}$ are equally acceptable. But this is not the case at runtime. The acute reader may have found that the *only* appropriate choice is to instantiate f to $\star \to \star$. However, as specified by rule M-FORALL in Fig. 8, we can only instantiate type variables to monotypes, but $\star$ is *not* a monotype! We will get back to this issue in Sect. 6.2 after we present the corresponding algorithmic system in Sect. 5.

4.3   Correctness Criteria

Siek et al. [25] present a set of properties that a well-designed gradual typing calculus must have, which they call the refined criteria. Among all the criteria, those related to the static aspects of gradual typing are well summarized by Cimini and Siek [8]. Here we review those criteria and adapt them to our notation. We have proved in Coq that our type system satisfies all these criteria.

Lemma 3 (Correctness Criteria)

- **Conservative extension:** for all static Ψ, e, and A,
  - if $\Psi \vdash^{OL} e : A$, then there exists B, such that $\Psi \vdash e : B$, and $\Psi \vdash B <: A$.
  - if $\Psi \vdash e : A$, then $\Psi \vdash^{OL} e : A$
- **Monotonicity w.r.t. precision:** for all Ψ, e, e', A, if $\Psi \vdash e : A$, and $e' \sqsubseteq e$, then $\Psi \vdash e' : B$, and $B \sqsubseteq A$ for some B.
- **Type Preservation of cast insertion:** for all Ψ, e, A, if $\Psi \vdash e : A$, then $\Psi \vdash e : A \rightsquigarrow s$, and $\Psi \vdash^B s : A$ for some s.
- **Monotonicity of cast insertion:** for all $\Psi, e_1, e_2, e'_1, e'_2, A$, if $\Psi \vdash e_1 : A \rightsquigarrow e'_1$, and $\Psi \vdash e_2 : A \rightsquigarrow e'_2$, and $e_1 \sqsubseteq e_2$, then $\Psi \upharpoonright \Psi \vdash e'_1 \sqsubseteq^B e'_2$.

The first criterion states that the gradual type system should be a conservative extension of the original system. In other words, a *static* program that is typeable in the Odersky-Läufer type system if and only if it is typeable in the gradual type system. A static program is one that does not contain any type $\star$[7]. However since our gradual type system does not have the subsumption rule, it produces more general types.

The second criterion states that if a typeable expression loses some type information, it remains typeable. This criterion depends on the definition of the precision relation, written $A \sqsubseteq B$, which is given in the appendix. The relation intuitively captures a notion of types containing more or less unknown types $(\star)$. The precision relation over types lifts to programs, i.e., $e_1 \sqsubseteq e_2$ means that e_1 and e_2 are the same program except that e_2 has more unknown types.

The first two criteria are fundamental to gradual typing. They explain for example why these two programs $(\lambda x : \mathsf{Int}.\ x + 1)$ and $(\lambda x : \star.\ x + 1)$ are typeable, as the former is typeable in the Odersky-Läufer type system and the latter is a less-precise version of it.

The last two criteria relate the compilation to the cast calculus. The third criterion is essentially the same as *Theorem 2*, given that a target expression should always exist, which can be easily seen from Fig. 8. The last criterion ensures that the translation must be monotonic over the precision relation $\sqsubseteq$.

As for the dynamic guarantee, things become a bit murky for two reasons: (1) as we discussed before, our declarative system is incoherent in that the runtime behaviour of the same source program can vary depending on the particular translation; (2) it is still unknown whether dynamic guarantee holds in λB. We will have more discussion on the dynamic guarantee in Sect. 6.3.

5   Algorithmic Type System

In this section we give a bidirectional account of the algorithmic type system that implements the declarative specification. The algorithm is largely inspired by the

---

[7] Note that the term *static* has appeared several times with different meanings.

Expressions	$e ::= x \mid n \mid \lambda x : A.\, e \mid \lambda x.\, e \mid e\, e \mid e : A$
Types	$A, B ::= \mathsf{Int} \mid a \mid \widehat{a} \mid A \to B \mid \forall a.A \mid \star$
Monotypes	$\tau, \sigma ::= \mathsf{Int} \mid a \mid \widehat{a} \mid \tau \to \sigma$
Contexts	$\Gamma, \Delta, \Theta ::= \varnothing \mid \Gamma, x : A \mid \Gamma, a \mid \Gamma, \widehat{a} \mid \Gamma, \widehat{a} = \tau$
Complete Contexts	$\Omega ::= \varnothing \mid \Omega, x : A \mid \Omega, a \mid \Omega, \widehat{a} = \tau$

Fig. 9. Syntax of the algorithmic system

$$\boxed{\Gamma \vdash A \lesssim B \dashv \Delta}$$

$$\frac{}{\Gamma[a] \vdash a \lesssim a \dashv \Gamma[a]}\ \text{ACS-TVar} \qquad \frac{}{\Gamma[\widehat{a}] \vdash \widehat{a} \lesssim \widehat{a} \dashv \Gamma[\widehat{a}]}\ \text{ACS-ExVar}$$

$$\frac{}{\Gamma \vdash \mathsf{Int} \lesssim \mathsf{Int} \dashv \Gamma}\ \text{ACS-Int} \qquad \frac{}{\Gamma \vdash \star \lesssim A \dashv \Gamma}\ \text{ACS-UnknownL} \qquad \frac{}{\Gamma \vdash A \lesssim \star \dashv \Gamma}\ \text{ACS-UnknownR}$$

$$\frac{\Gamma \vdash B_1 \lesssim A_1 \dashv \Theta \qquad \Theta \vdash [\Theta]A_2 \lesssim [\Theta]B_2 \dashv \Delta}{\Gamma \vdash A_1 \to A_2 \lesssim B_1 \to B_2 \dashv \Delta}\ \text{ACS-Fun}$$

$$\frac{\Gamma, a \vdash A \lesssim B \dashv \Delta, a, \Theta}{\Gamma \vdash A \lesssim \forall a.B \dashv \Delta}\ \text{ACS-ForallR} \qquad \frac{\Gamma, \widehat{a} \vdash A[a \mapsto \widehat{a}] \lesssim B \dashv \Delta}{\Gamma \vdash \forall a.A \lesssim B \dashv \Delta}\ \text{ACS-ForallL}$$

$$\frac{\widehat{a} \notin fv(A) \qquad \Gamma[\widehat{a}] \vdash \widehat{a} \lessgtr A \dashv \Delta}{\Gamma[\widehat{a}] \vdash \widehat{a} \lesssim A \dashv \Delta}\ \text{ACS-InstL} \qquad \frac{\widehat{a} \notin fv(A) \qquad \Gamma[\widehat{a}] \vdash A \lessgtr \widehat{a} \dashv \Delta}{\Gamma[\widehat{a}] \vdash A \lesssim \widehat{a} \dashv \Delta}\ \text{ACS-InstR}$$

Fig. 10. Algorithmic consistent subtyping

algorithmic bidirectional system of Dunfield and Krishnaswami [11] (henceforth DK system). However our algorithmic system differs from theirs in three aspects: (1) the addition of the unknown type $\star$; (2) the use of the matching judgment; and (3) the approach of *gradual inference only producing static types* [12]. We then prove that our algorithm is both sound and complete with respect to the declarative type system. Full proofs can be found in the appendix.

Algorithmic Contexts. The algorithmic context Γ is an *ordered* list containing declarations of type variables a and term variables $x : A$. Unlike declarative contexts, algorithmic contexts also contain declarations of existential type variables $\widehat{a}$, which can be either unsolved (written $\widehat{a}$) or solved to some monotype (written $\widehat{a} = \tau$). Complete contexts Ω are those that contain no unsolved existential type variables. Figure 9 shows the syntax of the algorithmic system. Apart from expressions in the declarative system, we have annotated expressions $e : A$.

5.1   Algorithmic Consistent Subtyping and Instantiation

Figure 10 shows the algorithmic consistent subtyping rules. The first five rules do not manipulate contexts. Rule ACS-Fun is a natural extension of its declarative counterpart. The output context of the first premise is used by the second

$$\boxed{\Gamma \vdash \widehat{a} \lesssim A \dashv \Delta}$$

$$\frac{\Gamma \vdash \tau}{\Gamma, \widehat{a}, \Gamma' \vdash \widehat{a} \lesssim \tau \dashv \Gamma, \widehat{a} = \tau, \Gamma'} \text{ InstLSolve} \qquad \frac{}{\Gamma[\widehat{a}][\widehat{b}] \vdash \widehat{a} \lesssim \widehat{b} \dashv \Gamma[\widehat{a}][\widehat{b} = \widehat{a}]} \text{ InstLReach}$$

$$\frac{}{\Gamma[\widehat{a}] \vdash \widehat{a} \lesssim \star \dashv \Gamma[\widehat{a}]} \text{ InstLSolveU} \qquad \frac{\Gamma[\widehat{a}], b \vdash \widehat{a} \lesssim B \dashv \Delta, b, \Delta'}{\Gamma[\widehat{a}] \vdash \widehat{a} \lesssim \forall b.B \dashv \Delta} \text{ InstLAllR}$$

$$\frac{\Gamma[\widehat{a}_2, \widehat{a}_1, \widehat{a} = \widehat{a}_1 \to \widehat{a}_2] \vdash A_1 \lesssim \widehat{a}_1 \dashv \Theta \qquad \Theta \vdash \widehat{a}_2 \lesssim [\Theta]A_2 \dashv \Delta}{\Gamma[\widehat{a}] \vdash \widehat{a} \lesssim A_1 \to A_2 \dashv \Delta} \text{ InstLArr}$$

Fig. 11. Algorithmic instantiation

premise, and the output context of the second premise is the output context of the conclusion. Note that we do not simply check $A_2 \lesssim B_2$, but apply Θ to both types (e.g., $[\Theta]A_2$). This is to maintain an important invariant that types are fully applied under input context Γ (they contain no existential variables already solved in Γ). The same invariant applies to every algorithmic judgment. Rule ACS-FORALLR looks similar to its declarative counterpart, except that we need to drop the trailing context a, Θ from the concluding output context since they become out of scope. Rule ACS-FORALLL generates a fresh existential variable $\widehat{a}$, and replaces a with $\widehat{a}$ in the body A. The new existential variable $\widehat{a}$ is then added to the premise's input context. As a side note, when both types are quantifiers, then either ACS-FORALLR or ACS-FORALLR could be tried. In practice, one can apply ACS-FORALLR eagerly. The last two rules together check consistent subtyping with an unsolved existential variable on one side and an arbitrary type on the other side by the help of the instantiation judgment.

The judgment $\Gamma \vdash \widehat{a} \lesssim A \dashv \Delta$ defined in Fig. 11 instantiates unsolved existential variables. Judgment $\widehat{a} \lesssim A$ reads "instantiate $\widehat{a}$ to a consistent subtype of A". For space reasons, we omit its symmetric judgement $\Gamma \vdash A \lesssim \widehat{a} \dashv \Delta$. Rule INSTLSOLVE and rule INSTLREACH set $\widehat{a}$ to τ and $\widehat{b}$ in the output context, respectively. Rule INSTLSOLVEU is similar to ACS-UNKNOWNR in that we put no constraint on $\widehat{a}$ when it meets the unknown type $\star$. This design decision reflects the point that type inference only produces static types [12]. We will get back to this point in Sect. 6.2. Rule INSTLALLR is the instantiation version of rule ACS-FORALLR. The last rule INSTLARR applies when $\widehat{a}$ meets a function type. It follows that the solution must also be a function type. That is why, in the first premise, we generate two fresh existential variables $\widehat{a}_1$ and $\widehat{a}_2$, and insert them just before $\widehat{a}$ in the input context, so that the solution of $\widehat{a}$ can mention them. Note that $A_1 \lesssim \widehat{a}_1$ switches to the other instantiation judgment.

5.2 Algorithmic Typing

We now turn to the algorithmic typing rules in Fig. 12. The algorithmic system uses bidirectional type checking to accommodate polymorphism. Most of

$$\boxed{\Gamma \vdash e \Rightarrow A \dashv \Delta}$$

$$\frac{(x : A) \in \Gamma}{\Gamma \vdash x \Rightarrow A \dashv \Gamma} \text{ AVar} \qquad\qquad \frac{}{\Gamma \vdash n \Rightarrow \text{Int} \dashv \Gamma} \text{ ANat}$$

$$\frac{\Gamma, \widehat{a}, \widehat{b}, x : \widehat{a} \vdash e \Leftarrow \widehat{b} \dashv \Delta, x : \widehat{a}, \Theta}{\Gamma \vdash \lambda x.\, e \Rightarrow \widehat{a} \rightarrow \widehat{b} \dashv \Delta} \text{ ALamU} \qquad \frac{\Gamma, x : A \vdash e \Rightarrow B \dashv \Delta, x : A, \Theta}{\Gamma \vdash \lambda x : A.\, e \Rightarrow A \rightarrow B \dashv \Delta} \text{ ALamAnnA}$$

$$\frac{\Gamma \vdash A \qquad \Gamma \vdash e \Leftarrow A \dashv \Delta}{\Gamma \vdash e : A \Rightarrow A \dashv \Delta} \text{ AAnno}$$

$$\frac{\Gamma \vdash e_1 \Rightarrow A \dashv \Theta_1 \qquad \Theta_1 \vdash [\Theta_1] A \rhd A_1 \rightarrow A_2 \dashv \Theta_2 \qquad \Theta_2 \vdash e_2 \Leftarrow [\Theta_2] A_1 \dashv \Delta}{\Gamma \vdash e_1\, e_2 \Rightarrow A_2 \dashv \Delta} \text{ AApp}$$

$$\boxed{\Gamma \vdash e \Leftarrow A \dashv \Delta}$$

$$\frac{\Gamma, x : A \vdash e \Leftarrow B \dashv \Delta, x : A, \Theta}{\Gamma \vdash \lambda x.\, e \Leftarrow A \rightarrow B \dashv \Delta} \text{ ALam} \qquad \frac{\Gamma, a \vdash e \Leftarrow A \dashv \Delta, a, \Theta}{\Gamma \vdash e \Leftarrow \forall a.A \dashv \Delta} \text{ AGen}$$

$$\frac{\Gamma \vdash e \Rightarrow A \dashv \Theta \qquad \Theta \vdash [\Theta] A \lesssim [\Theta] B \dashv \Delta}{\Gamma \vdash e \Leftarrow B \dashv \Delta} \text{ ASub}$$

$$\boxed{\Gamma \vdash A \rhd A_1 \rightarrow A_2 \dashv \Delta}$$

$$\frac{\Gamma, \widehat{a} \vdash A[a \mapsto \widehat{a}] \rhd A_1 \rightarrow A_2 \dashv \Delta}{\Gamma \vdash \forall a.A \rhd A_1 \rightarrow A_2 \dashv \Delta} \text{ AM-Forall} \qquad \frac{}{\Gamma \vdash (A_1 \rightarrow A_2) \rhd (A_1 \rightarrow A_2) \dashv \Gamma} \text{ AM-Arr}$$

$$\frac{}{\Gamma \vdash \star \rhd \star \rightarrow \star \dashv \Gamma} \text{ AM-Unknown} \qquad \frac{}{\Gamma[\widehat{c}] \vdash \widehat{c} \rhd \widehat{a} \rightarrow \widehat{b} \dashv \Gamma[\widehat{a}, \widehat{b}, \widehat{c} = \widehat{a} \rightarrow \widehat{b}]} \text{ AM-Var}$$

Fig. 12. Algorithmic typing

them are quite standard. Perhaps rule AApp (which differs significantly from that in the DK system) deserves attention. It relies on the algorithmic matching judgment $\Gamma \vdash A \rhd A_1 \rightarrow A_2 \dashv \Delta$. Rule AM-ForallL replaces a with a fresh existential variable $\widehat{a}$, thus eliminating guessing. Rule AM-Arr and AM-Unknown correspond directly to the declarative rules. Rule AM-Var, which has no corresponding declarative version, is similar to InstRArr/InstLArr: we create $\widehat{a}$ and $\widehat{b}$ and add $\widehat{c} = \widehat{a} \rightarrow \widehat{b}$ to the context.

5.3 Completeness and Soundness

We prove that the algorithmic rules are sound and complete with respect to the declarative specifications. We need an auxiliary judgment $\Gamma \longrightarrow \Delta$ that captures a notion of information increase from input contexts Γ to output contexts Δ [11].

Soundness. Roughly speaking, soundness of the algorithmic system says that given an expression e that type checks in the algorithmic system, there exists a corresponding expression e' that type checks in the declarative system. However there is one complication: e does not necessarily have more annotations than e'. For example, by ALAM we have $\lambda x.\ x \Leftarrow (\forall a.a) \rightarrow (\forall a.a)$, but $\lambda x.\ x$ itself cannot have type $(\forall a.a) \rightarrow (\forall a.a)$ in the declarative system. To circumvent that, we add an annotation to the lambda abstraction, resulting in $\lambda x : (\forall a.a).\ x$, which is typeable in the declarative system with the same type. To relate $\lambda x.\ x$ and $\lambda x : (\forall a.a).\ x$, we erase all annotations on both expressions. The definition of erasure $\lfloor \cdot \rfloor$ is standard and thus omitted.

Theorem 1 (Soundness of Algorithmic Typing). *Given* $\Delta \longrightarrow \Omega$,

1. *If* $\Gamma \vdash e \Rightarrow A \dashv \Delta$ *then* $\exists e'$ *such that* $[\Omega]\Delta \vdash e' : [\Omega]A$ *and* $\lfloor e \rfloor = \lfloor e' \rfloor$.
2. *If* $\Gamma \vdash e \Leftarrow A \dashv \Delta$ *then* $\exists e'$ *such that* $[\Omega]\Delta \vdash e' : [\Omega]A$ *and* $\lfloor e \rfloor = \lfloor e' \rfloor$.

Completeness. Completeness of the algorithmic system is the reverse of soundness: given a declarative judgment of the form $[\Omega]\Gamma \vdash [\Omega]\ldots$, we want to get an algorithmic derivation of $\Gamma \vdash \cdots \dashv \Delta$. It turns out that completeness is a bit trickier to state in that the algorithmic rules generate existential variables on the fly, so Δ could contain unsolved existential variables that are not found in Γ, nor in Ω. Therefore the completeness proof must produce another complete context Ω' that extends both the output context Δ, and the given complete context Ω. As with soundness, we need erasure to relate both expressions.

Theorem 2 (Completeness of Algorithmic Typing). *Given* $\Gamma \longrightarrow \Omega$ *and* $\Gamma \vdash A$, *if* $[\Omega]\Gamma \vdash e : A$ *then there exist* Δ, Ω', A' *and* e' *such that* $\Delta \longrightarrow \Omega'$ *and* $\Omega \longrightarrow \Omega'$ *and* $\Gamma \vdash e' \Rightarrow A' \dashv \Delta$ *and* $A = [\Omega']A'$ *and* $\lfloor e \rfloor = \lfloor e' \rfloor$.

6   Discussion

6.1   Top Types

To demonstrate that our definition of consistent subtyping (Definition 2) is applicable to other features, we show how to extend our approach to Top types with all the desired properties preserved.

In order to preserve the orthogonality between subtyping and consistency, we require $\top$ to be a common supertype of all static types, as shown in rule S-TOP. This rule might seem strange at first glance, since even if we remove the requirement A *static*, the rule seems reasonable. However, an important point is that because of the orthogonality between subtyping and consistency, subtyping itself should not contain a potential information loss! Therefore, subtyping instances such as $\star <: \top$ are not allowed. For consistency, we add the rule that $\top$ is consistent with $\top$, which is actually included in the original reflexive rule

$A \sim A$. For consistent subtyping, every type is a consistent subtype of $\top$, for example, $\mathsf{Int} \to \star \lesssim \top$.

$$\frac{A \; static}{\Psi \vdash A <: \top} \; \text{S-Top} \qquad\qquad \top \sim \top \qquad\qquad \frac{}{\Psi \vdash A \lesssim \top} \; \text{CS-Top}$$

It is easy to verify that Definition 2 is still equivalent to that in Fig. 7 extended with rule CS-Top. That is, *Theorem 1* holds:

Proposition 4 (Extension with $\top$). $\Psi \vdash A \lesssim B \Leftrightarrow \Psi \vdash A <: C, \; C \sim D,$ $\Psi \vdash D <: B$, for some C, D.

We extend the definition of concretization (Definition 3) with $\top$ by adding another equation $\gamma(\top) = \{\top\}$. Note that Castagna and Lanvin [7] also have this equation in their calculus. It is easy to verify that Proposition 2 still holds:

Proposition 5 (Equivalent to AGT on $\top$). $A \lesssim B$ if only if $A \; \widetilde{<:} \; B$.

Siek and Taha's [22] *Definition of Consistent Subtyping Does Not Work for $\top$.* As the analysis in Sect. 3.2, $\mathsf{Int} \to \star \lesssim \top$ only holds when we first apply consistency, then subtyping. However we cannot find a type A such that $\mathsf{Int} \to \star <: A$ and $A \sim \top$. Also we have a similar problem in extending the restriction operator: *non-structural* masking between $\mathsf{Int} \to \star$ and $\top$ cannot be easily achieved.

6.2 Interpretation of the Dynamic Semantics

In Sect. 4.2 we have seen an example where a source expression could produce two different target expressions with different runtime behaviour. As we explained, this is due to the guessing nature of the declarative system, and from the typing point of view, no type is particularly better than others. However, in practice, this is not desirable. Let us revisit the same example, now from the algorithmic point of view (we omit the translation for space reasons):

$$f : \forall a.a \to a \vdash (\lambda x : \star. \; f \; x) \Rightarrow \star \to \widehat{a} \dashv f : \forall a.a \to a, \widehat{a}$$

Compared with declarative typing, which produces many types ($\star \to \mathsf{Int}$, $\star \to \mathsf{Bool}$, and so on), the algorithm computes the type $\star \to \widehat{a}$ with $\widehat{a}$ unsolved in the output context. What can we know from the output context? The only thing we know is that $\widehat{a}$ is not constrained at all! However, it is possible to make a more refined distinction between different kinds of existential variables. The first kind of existential variables are those that indeed have no constraints at all, as they do not affect the dynamic semantics. The second kind of existential variables (as in this example) are those where the only constraint is that *the variable was once compared with an unknown type* [12].

To emphasize the difference and have better support for dynamic semantics, we could have *gradual variables* in addition to existential variables, with the difference that only unsolved gradual variables are allowed to be unified with the unknown type. An irreversible transition from existential variables to gradual variables occurs when an existential variable is compared with $\star$. After the algorithm terminates, we can set all unsolved existential variables to be any (static) type (or more precisely, as Garcia and Cimini [12], with *static type parameters*), and all unsolved gradual variables to be $\star$ (or *gradual type parameters*). However, this approach requires a more sophisticated declarative/algorithmic type system than the ones presented in this paper, where we only produce static monotypes in type inference. We believe this is a typical trade-off in existing gradual type systems with inference [12,23]. Here we suppress the complexity of dynamic semantics in favour of the conciseness of static typing.

6.3 The Dynamic Guarantee

In Sect. 4.3 we mentioned that the dynamic guarantee is closely related to the coherence issue. To aid discussion, we first give the definition of dynamic guarantee as follows:

Definition 5 (Dynamic guarantee). *Suppose* $e' \sqsubseteq e$, $\emptyset \vdash e : A \rightsquigarrow s$ *and* $\emptyset \vdash e' : A' \rightsquigarrow s'$, *if* $s \Downarrow v$, *then* $s' \Downarrow v'$ *and* $v' \sqsubseteq v$.

The dynamic guarantee says that if a gradually typed program evaluates to a value, then removing type annotations always produces a program that evaluates to an equivalent value (modulo type annotations). Now apparently the coherence issue of the declarative system breaks the dynamic guarantee. For instance:

$$(\lambda f : \forall a.a \to a. \ \lambda x : \mathsf{Int}. \ f \ x) \ (\lambda x.x) \ 3 \qquad (\lambda f : \forall a.a \to a. \ \lambda x : \star. \ f \ x) \ (\lambda x.x) \ 3$$

The left one evaluates to 3, whereas its less precise version (right) will give a cast error if a is instantiated to Bool for example.

As discussed in Sect. 6.2, we could design a more sophisticated declarative/algorithmic type system where coherence is retained. However, even with a coherent source language, the dynamic guarantee is still a question. Currently, the dynamic guarantee for our target language λB is still an open question. According to Igarashi et al. [14], the difficulty lies in the definition of term precision that preserves the semantics.

7   Related Work

Along the way we discussed some of the most relevant work to motivate, compare and promote our gradual typing design. In what follows, we briefly discuss related work on gradual typing and polymorphism.

Gradual Typing. The seminal paper by Siek and Taha [21] is the first to propose gradual typing. The original proposal extends the simply typed lambda calculus by introducing the unknown type $\star$ and replacing type equality with type consistency. Later Siek and Taha [22] incorporated gradual typing into a simple object oriented language, and showed that subtyping and consistency are orthogonal – an insight that partly inspired our work. We show that subtyping and consistency are orthogonal in a much richer type system with higher-rank polymorphism. Siek et al. [25] proposed a set of criteria that provides important guidelines for designers of gradually typed languages. Cimini and Siek [8] introduced the *Gradualizer*, a general methodology for generating gradual type systems from static type systems. Later they also develop an algorithm to generate dynamic semantics [9]. Garcia et al. [13] introduced the AGT approach based on abstract interpretation.

Gradual Type Systems with Explicit Polymorphism. Ahmed et al. [1] proposed λB that extends the blame calculus [29] to incorporate polymorphism. The key novelty of their work is to use dynamic sealing to enforce parametricity. Devriese et al. [10] proved that embedding of System F terms into λB is not fully abstract. Igarashi et al. [14] also studied integrating gradual typing with parametric polymorphism. They proposed System F_G, a gradually typed extension of System F, and System F_C, a new polymorphic blame calculus. As has been discussed extensively, their definition of type consistency does not apply to our setting (implicit polymorphism). All of these approaches mix consistency with subtyping to some extent, which we argue should be orthogonal.

Gradual Type Inference. Siek and Vachharajani [23] studied unification-based type inference for gradual typing, where they show why three straightforward approaches fail to meet their design goals. Their type system infers gradual types, which results in a complicated type system and inference algorithm. Garcia and Cimini [12] presented a new approach where gradual type inference only produces static types, which is adopted in our type system. They also deal with let-polymorphism (rank 1 types). However none of these works deals with higher-ranked implicit polymorphism.

Higher-Rank Implicit Polymorphism. Odersky and Läufer [17] introduced a type system for higher-rank types. Based on that, Peyton Jones et al. [18] developed an approach for type checking higher-rank predicative polymorphism. Dunfield and Krishnaswami [11] proposed a bidirectional account of higher-rank polymorphism, and an algorithm for implementing the declarative system, which serves as a sole inspiration for our algorithmic system. The key difference, however, is the integration of gradual typing. Vytiniotis et al. [28] defers static type errors to runtime, which is fundamentally different from gradual typing, where programmers can control over static or runtime checks by precision of the annotations.

8   Conclusion

In this paper, we present a generalized definition of consistent subtyping, which is proved to be applicable to both polymorphic and top types. Based on the new definition of consistent subtyping, we have developed a gradually typed calculus with predicative implicit higher-rank polymorphism, and an algorithm to implement it. As future work, we are interested to investigate if our results can scale to real world languages and other programming language features.

Acknowledgements. We thank Ronald Garcia and the anonymous reviewers for their helpful comments. This work has been sponsored by the Hong Kong Research Grant Council projects number 17210617 and 17258816.

References

1. Ahmed, A., Findler, R.B., Siek, J.G., Wadler, P.: Blame for all. In: Proceedings of the 38th Symposium on Principles of Programming Languages (2011)
2. Ahmed, A., Jamner, D., Siek, J.G., Wadler, P.: Theorems for free for free: parametricity, with and without types. In: Proceedings of the 22nd International Conference on Functional Programming (2017)
3. Schwerter, F.B., Garcia, R., Tanter, É.: A theory of gradual effect systems. In: Proceedings of the 19th International Conference on Functional Programming (2014)
4. Bierman, G., Meijer, E., Torgersen, M.: Adding dynamic types to C$^\sharp$. In: D'Hondt, T. (ed.) ECOOP 2010. LNCS, vol. 6183, pp. 76–100. Springer, Heidelberg (2010). https://doi.org/10.1007/978-3-642-14107-2_5
5. Bierman, G., Abadi, M., Torgersen, M.: Understanding TypeScript. In: Jones, R. (ed.) ECOOP 2014. LNCS, vol. 8586, pp. 257–281. Springer, Heidelberg (2014). https://doi.org/10.1007/978-3-662-44202-9_11
6. Bonnaire-Sergeant, A., Davies, R., Tobin-Hochstadt, S.: Practical optional types for clojure. In: Thiemann, P. (ed.) ESOP 2016. LNCS, vol. 9632, pp. 68–94. Springer, Heidelberg (2016). https://doi.org/10.1007/978-3-662-49498-1_4
7. Castagna, G., Lanvin, V.: Gradual typing with union and intersection types. Proc. ACM Program. Lang. 1(ICFP), 41:1–41:28 (2017)
8. Cimini, M., Siek, J.G.: The gradualizer: a methodology and algorithm for generating gradual type systems. In: Proceedings of the 43rd Symposium on Principles of Programming Languages (2016)
9. Cimini, M., Siek, J.G.: Automatically generating the dynamic semantics of gradually typed languages. In: Proceedings of the 44th Symposium on Principles of Programming Languages (2017)
10. Devriese, D., Patrignani, M., Piessens, F.: Parametricity versus the universal type. Proc. ACM Program. Lang. 2(POPL), 38 (2017)
11. Dunfield, J., Krishnaswami, N.R.: Complete and easy bidirectional typechecking for higher-rank polymorphism. In: International Conference on Functional Programming (2013)
12. Garcia, R., Cimini, M.: Principal type schemes for gradual programs. In: Proceedings of the 42nd Symposium on Principles of Programming Languages (2015)
13. Garcia, R., Clark, A.M., Tanter, É.: Abstracting gradual typing. In: Proceedings of the 43rd Symposium on Principles of Programming Languages (2016)

14. Igarashi, Y., Sekiyama, T., Igarashi, A.: On polymorphic gradual typing. In: Proceedings of the 22nd International Conference on Functional Programming (2017)
15. Jafery, K.A., Dunfield, J.: Sums of uncertainty: refinements go gradual. In: Proceedings of the 44th Symposium on Principles of Programming Languages (2017)
16. Mitchell, J.C.: Polymorphic type inference and containment. In: Logical Foundations of Functional Programming (1990)
17. Odersky, M., Läufer, K.: Putting type annotations to work. In: Proceedings of the 23rd Symposium on Principles of Programming Languages (1996)
18. Jones, S.P., Vytiniotis, D., Weirich, S., Shields, M.: Practical type inference for arbitrary-rank types. J. Funct. Program. **17**(1), 1–82 (2007)
19. Reynolds, J.C.: Types, abstraction and parametric polymorphism. In: Proceedings of the IFIP 9th World Computer Congress (1983)
20. Reynolds, J.C.: The coherence of languages with intersection types. In: Ito, T., Meyer, A.R. (eds.) TACS 1991. LNCS, vol. 526, pp. 675–700. Springer, Heidelberg (1991). https://doi.org/10.1007/3-540-54415-1_70
21. Siek, J.G., Taha, W.: Gradual typing for functional languages. In: Proceedings of the 2006 Scheme and Functional Programming Workshop (2006)
22. Siek, J., Taha, W.: Gradual typing for objects. In: Ernst, E. (ed.) ECOOP 2007. LNCS, vol. 4609, pp. 2–27. Springer, Heidelberg (2007). https://doi.org/10.1007/978-3-540-73589-2_2
23. Siek, J.G., Vachharajani, M.: Gradual typing with unification-based inference. In: Proceedings of the 2008 Symposium on Dynamic Languages (2008)
24. Siek, J.G., Wadler, P.: The key to blame: gradual typing meets cryptography (draft) (2016)
25. Siek, J.G., Vitousek, M.M., Cimini, M., Boyland, J.T.: Refined criteria for gradual typing. In: LIPIcs-Leibniz International Proceedings in Informatics (2015)
26. Verlaguet, J.: Facebook: analyzing PHP statically. In: Proceedings of Commercial Users of Functional Programming (2013)
27. Vitousek, M.M., Kent, A.M., Siek, J.G., Baker, J.: Design and evaluation of gradual typing for Python. In: Proceedings of the 10th Symposium on Dynamic Languages (2014)
28. Vytiniotis, D., Jones, S.P., Magalhães, J.P.: Equality proofs and deferred type errors: a compiler pearl. In: Proceedings of the 17th International Conference on Functional Programming, ICFP 2012, New York (2012)
29. Wadler, P., Findler, R.B.: Well-typed programs can't be blamed. In: Castagna, G. (ed.) ESOP 2009. LNCS, vol. 5502, pp. 1–16. Springer, Heidelberg (2009). https://doi.org/10.1007/978-3-642-00590-9_1

HOBiT: Programming Lenses Without Using Lens Combinators

Kazutaka Matsuda[1]([✉]) and Meng Wang[2]

[1] Tohoku University, Sendai 980-8579, Japan
kztk@ecei.tohoku.ac.jp
[2] University of Bristol, Bristol BS8 1TH, UK

Abstract. We propose HOBiT, a higher-order bidirectional programming language, in which users can write bidirectional programs in the familiar style of conventional functional programming, while enjoying the full expressiveness of lenses. A bidirectional transformation, or a lens, is a pair of mappings between source and view data objects, one in each direction. When the view is modified, the source is updated accordingly with respect to some laws—a pattern that is found in databases, model-driven development, compiler construction, and so on. The most common way of programming lenses is with lens combinators, which are lens-to-lens functions that compose simpler lenses to form more complex ones. Lens combinators preserve the bidirectionality of lenses and are expressive; but they compel programmers to a specialised point-free style—i.e., no naming of intermediate computation results—limiting the scalability of bidirectional programming. To address this issue, we propose a new bidirectional programming language HOBiT, in which lenses are represented as standard functions, and combinators are mapped to language constructs with binders. This design transforms bidirectional programming, enabling programmers to write bidirectional programs in a flexible functional style and at the same time access the full expressiveness of lenses. We formally define the syntax, type system, and the semantics of the language, and then show that programs in HOBiT satisfy bidirectionality. Additionally, we demonstrate HOBiT's programmability with examples.

1 Introduction

Transforming data from one format to another is a common task of programming: compilers transform program texts into syntax trees, manipulate the trees and then generate low-level code; database queries transform base relations into views; model transformations generate lower-level implementations from higher-level models; and so on. Very often, such transformations will benefit from being bidirectional, allowing changes to the targets to be mapped back to the sources too. For example, if one can run a compiler front-end (preprocessing, parsing, desugaring, etc.) backwards, then all sorts of program analysis tools will be able to focus on a much smaller core language, without sacrificing usability, as

© The Author(s) 2018
A. Ahmed (Ed.): ESOP 2018, LNCS 10801, pp. 31–59, 2018.
https://doi.org/10.1007/978-3-319-89884-1_2

their outputs in term of the core language will be transformed backwards to the source language. In the same way, such needs arise in databases (the *view-update problem* [1,6,12]) and model-driven engineering (bidirectional model transformation) [28,33,35].

As a response to this challenge, programming language researchers have started to design languages that execute deterministically in both directions, and the lens framework is the most prominent among all. In the lens framework, a *bidirectional transformation* (or a *lens*) $\ell \in Lens\ S\ V$, consists of $get\ \ell \in S \to V$, and $put\ \ell \in S \to V \to S$ [3,7,8]. (When clear from the context, or unimportant, we sometimes omit the lens name and write simply get/put.) Function get extracts a view from a source, and put takes both an updated view and the original source as inputs to produce an updated source. The additional parameter of put makes it possible to recover some of the source data that is not present in the view. In other words, get needs not to be injective to have a put. Not all pairs of get/put are considered correct lenses. The following round-triping laws of a lens ℓ are generally required to establish bidirectionality:

$$put\ \ell\ s\ v = s \quad \text{if} \quad get\ \ell\ s = v \qquad \qquad \textbf{(Acceptability)}$$

$$get\ \ell\ s' = v \quad \text{if} \quad put\ \ell\ s\ v = s' \qquad \qquad \textbf{(Consistency)}$$

for all s, s' and v. (In this paper we write $e = e'$ with the assumption that neither e nor e' is undefined. Stronger variants of the laws enforcing totality exist elsewhere, for example in [7].) Here *consistency* ensures that all updates on a view are captured by the updated source, and *acceptability* prohibits changes to the source if no update has been made on the view. Collectively, the two laws defines *well-behavedness* [1,7,12].

The most common way of programming lenses is with lens combinators [3,7,8], which are basically a selection of lens-to-lens functions that compose simpler lenses to form more complex ones. This combinator-based approach follows the long history of lightweight language development in functional programming. The distinctive advantage of this approach is that by restricting the lens language to a few selected combinators, well-behavedness can be more easily preserved in programming, and therefore given well-behaved lenses as inputs, the combinators are guaranteed to produce well-behaved lenses. This idea of lens combinators is very influential academically, and various designs and implementations have been proposed [2,3,7–9,16,17,27,32] over the years.

1.1 The Challenge of Programmability

The complexity of a piece of software can be classified as either intrinsic or accidental. Intrinsic complexity reflects the inherent difficulty of the problem at hand, whereas accidental complexity arises from the particular programming language, design or tools used to implement the solution. This work aims at reducing the accidental complexity of bidirectional programming by contributing to the design of bidirectional languages. In particularly, we identify a language restriction—i.e., no naming of intermediate computation results—which complicates lens programming, and propose a new design that removes it.

As a teaser to demonstrate the problem, let us consider the list append function. In standard unidirectional programming, it can be defined simply as *append x y* = **case** *x* **of** {[] → *y*; *a* : *x′* → *a* : *append x′ y*}. Astute readers may have already noticed that *append* is defined by structural recursion on *x*, which can be made explicit by using *foldr* as in *append x y* = *foldr* (:) *y x*.

But in a lens language based on combinators, things are more difficult. Specifically, *append* now requires a more complicated recursion pattern, as below.

$appendL :: Lens\ ([A], [A])\ [A]$
$appendL =$
    $cond\ idL\ (\lambda\_.\text{True})\ (\lambda\_.\lambda\_.[\,])\ (consL\ \hat{o}\ (idL \times appendL))\ (not \circ null)\ (\lambda\_.\lambda\_.\bot)$
    $\hat{o}\ rearr\ \hat{o}\ (outListL \times idL)$
  where $outListL :: Lens\ [A]\ (Either\ (\,)\ (A, [A]))$
     $rearr\ \ \ :: Lens\ (Either\ (\,)\ (a, b), c)\ (Either\ c\ (a, (b, c)))$
     $(\hat{o})\ \ \ \ \ :: Lens\ b\ c \to Lens\ a\ b \to Lens\ a\ c$
     $cond\ \ \ :: Lens\ a\ c \to \ldots \to Lens\ b\ c \to \ldots \to Lens\ (Either\ a\ b)\ c$
     $\ldots$

It is beyond the scope of this paper to explain how exactly the definition of *appendL* works, as its obscurity is what this work aims to remove. Instead, we informally describe its behaviour and the various components of the code. The above code defines a lens: forwards, it behaves as the standard *append*, and backwards, it splits the updated view list, and when the length of the list changes, this definition implements (with the grayed part) the bias of keeping the length of the first source list whenever possible (to disambiguate multiple candidate source changes). Here, *cond*, (ô), etc. are lens combinators and *outListL* and *rearr* are auxiliary lenses, as can be seen from their types. Unlike its unidirectional counterpart, *appendL* can no longer be defined as a structural recursion on list; instead it traverses a pair of lists with rather complex rearrangement *rearr*.

Intuitively, the additional grayed parts is intrinsic complexity, as they are needed for directing backwards execution. However, the complicated recursion scheme, which is a direct result of the underlying limitation of lens languages, is certainly accidental. Recall that in the definition of *append*, we were able to use the variable *y*, which is bound outside of the recursion pattern, inside the body of *foldr*. But the same is not possible with lens combinators which are strictly 'pointfree'. Moreover, even if one could name such variables (points), their usage with lens combinators will be very restricted in order to guarantee well-behavedness [21, 23]. This problem is specific to opaque non-function objects such as lenses, and goes well beyond the traditional issues associated with the pointfree programming style.

In this paper, we design a new bidirectional language HOBiT, which aims to remove much of the accidental difficulty found in combinator-based lens programming, and reduces the gap between bidirectional programming and standard functional programming. For example, the following definition in HOBiT implements the same lens as *appendL*.

$appendB :: \mathbf{B}[A] \to \mathbf{B}[A] \to \mathbf{B}[A]$

$appendB\ x\ y = \underline{\mathbf{case}}\ x\ \underline{\mathbf{of}}\ []\quad \to y$ with $\lambda\_.$True   by $(\lambda\_.\lambda\_.[])$

$\qquad\qquad\qquad\qquad a : x' \to a \underline{:} appendB\ x'\ y$ with $not \circ null$ by $(\lambda\_.\lambda\_.\bot)$

As expected, the above code shares the grayed part with the definition of *appendL* as the two implement the same backwards behaviour. The difference is that *appendB* uses structural recursion in the same way as the standard unidirectional *append*, greatly simplifying programming. This is made possible by the HOBiT's type system and semantics, allowing unrestricted use of free variables. This difference in approach is also reflected in the types: *appendB* is a proper function (instead of the abstract lens type of *appendL*), which readily lends itself to conventional functional programming. At the same time, *appendB* is also a proper lens, which when executed by the HOBiT interpreter behave exactly like *appendL*. A major technical challenge in the design of HOBiT is to guarantee this duality, so that functions like *appendB* are well-behaved by construction despite the flexibility in their construction.

1.2 Contributions

As we can already see from the very simple example above, the use of HOBiT simplifies bidirectional programming by removing much of the accidental complexity. Specifically, HOBiT stands out from existing bidirectional languages in two ways:

1. It supports the conventional programming style that is used in unidirectional programming. As a result, a program in HOBiT can be defined in a way similar to how one would define only its *get* component. For example, *appendB* is defined in the same way as the unidirectional *append*.
2. It supports incremental improvement. Given the very often close resemblance of a bidirectional-program definition and that of its *get* component, it becomes possible to write an initial version of a bidirectional program almost identical to its *get* component and then to adjust the backwards behaviour gradually, without having to significantly restructure the existing definition.

Thanks to these distinctive advantages, HOBiT for the first time allows us to construct realistically-sized bidirectional programs with relative ease. Of course, this does not mean free lunch: the ability to control backwards behaviours will not magically come without additional code (for example the grayed part above). What HOBiT achieves is that programming effort may now focus on the productive part of specifying backwards behaviours, instead of being consumed by circumventing language restrictions.

In summary, we make the following contributions in this paper.

- We design a higher-order bidirectional programming language HOBiT, which supports convenient bidirectional programming with control of backwards behaviours (Sect. 3). We also discuss several extensions to the language (Sect. 5).

– We present the semantics of HOBiT inspired by the idea of staging [5], and prove the well-behavedness property using Kripke logical relations [18] (Sect. 4).
– We demonstrate the programmability of HOBiT with examples such as desugaring/resugaring [26] (Sect. 6). Additional examples including a bidirectional evaluator for λ-calculus [21,23], a parser/printer for S-expressions, and bookmark extraction for Netscape [7] can be found at https://bitbucket.org/kztk/hibx together with a prototype implementation of HOBiT.

2   Overview: Bidirectional Programming Without Combinators

In this section, we informally introduce the essential constructs of HOBiT and demonstrate their use by a few small examples. Recall that, as seen in the *appendB* example, the strength of HOBiT lies in allowing programmers to access λ-abstractions without restrictions on the use of λ-bound variables.

2.1   The case Construct

The most important language construct in HOBiT is **case** (pronounced as *bidirectional case*), which provides pattern matching and easy access to bidirectional branching, and also importantly, allows unrestricted use of λ-bound variables.

In general, a **case** expression has the following form.

$$\underline{\textbf{case}}\ e\ \underline{\textbf{of}}\ \{p_1 \to e_1\ \underline{\textbf{with}}\ \phi_1\ \underline{\textbf{by}}\ \rho_1; \ldots ; p_n \to e_n\ \underline{\textbf{with}}\ \phi_n\ \underline{\textbf{by}}\ \rho_n\}$$

(Like Haskell, we shall omit "{", "}" and ";" if they are clear from the layout.) In the type system of HOBiT, a **case**-expression has type $\mathbf{B}B$, if e and e_i have types $\mathbf{B}A$ and $\mathbf{B}B$, and ϕ_i and ρ_i have types $B \to Bool$ and $A \to B \to A$, where A and B contains neither ($\to$) nor $\mathbf{B}$. The type $\mathbf{B}A$ can be understood intuitively as "updatable A". Typically, the source and view data are given such $\mathbf{B}$-types, and a function of type $\mathbf{B}A \to \mathbf{B}B$ is the HOBiT equivalent of *Lens A B*.

The pattern matching part of **case** performs two implicit operations: it first unwraps the $\mathbf{B}$-typed value, exposing its content for normal pattern matching, and then it wraps the variables bound by the pattern matching, turning them into 'updatable' $\mathbf{B}$-typed values to be used in the bodies. For example, in the second branch of *appendB*, a and x' can be seen as having types A and $[A]$ in the pattern, but $\mathbf{B}A$ and $\mathbf{B}[A]$ types in the body; and the bidirectional constructor $(\underline{:})::\mathbf{B}A \to \mathbf{B}[A] \to \mathbf{B}[A]$ combines them to produce a $\mathbf{B}$-typed list.

In addition to the standard conditional branches, **case**-expression has two unique components ϕ_i and ρ_i called *exit conditions* and *reconciliation functions* respectively, which are used in backwards executions. Exit condition ϕ_i is an over-approximation of the forwards-execution results of the expressions e_i. In other words, if branch i is choosen, then $\phi_i\ e_i$ must evaluate to True. This assertion is checked dynamically in HOBiT, though could be checked statically with a sophisticated type system [7]. In the backwards direction the exit condition is used for deciding branching: the branch with its exit condition satisfied by the updated view (when more than one match, the original branch used in the forwards direction has higher priority) will be picked for execution. The idea is that due to the update in the view, the branch taken in the backwards direction may be different from the one taken in the original forwards execution, a feature that is commonly supported by lens languages [7] which we call *branch switching*.

Branch switching is crucial to *put*'s *robustness*, i.e., the ability to handle a wide range of view updates (including those affect the branching decisions) without failing. We explain its working in details in the following.

Branch Switching. Being able to choose a different branch in the backwards direction only solves part of the problem. Let us consider the case where a forward execution chooses the nth branch, and the backwards execution, based on the updated view, chooses the mth $(m \neq n)$ branch. In this case, the original value of the pattern-matched expression e, which is the reason for the nth branch being chosen, is not compatible with the *put* of the mth branch.

As an example, let us consider a simple function that pattern-matches on an *Either* structure and returns an list. Note that we have purposely omitted the reconciliation functions.

$$f :: \mathbf{B}(Either\ [A]\ (A, [A])) \to \mathbf{B}[A]$$
$$f\ x = \underline{\text{case}}\ x\ \underline{\text{of}}\ \textsf{Left}\ ys \qquad \to ys \qquad \underline{\text{with}}\ \lambda\_.\textsf{True}\quad \{\text{- no }\underline{\text{by}}\text{ here -}\}$$
$$\qquad\qquad\qquad \textsf{Right}\ (y, ys) \to y : ys\ \underline{\text{with}}\ not \circ null$$

We have said that functions of type $\mathbf{B}A \to \mathbf{B}B$ are also fully functioning lenses of type *Lens A B*. In HOBiT, the above code runs as follows, where HOBiT> is the prompt of HOBiT's read-eval-print loop, and :get and :put are meta-language operations to perform *get* and *put* respectively.

```
HOBiT> :get f (Left [1, 2, 3])
[1, 2, 3]
HOBiT> :get f (Right (1, [2, 3]))
[1, 2, 3]
HOBiT> :put f (Left [1, 2, 3]) [4, 5]        -- The view [1, 2, 3] is updated to [4, 5].
Left [4, 5]                                   -- Both exit conditions are true with [4, 5],
                                              -- so the original branch (Left) is taken.
HOBiT> :put f (Right (1, [2, 3])) [4, 5]
Right (4, [5])                                -- Similar, but the original branch is Right.
HOBiT> :put f (Right (1, [2, 3])) []
⊥                                             -- Branch switches, but computation fails.
```

As we have explained above, exit conditions are used to decide which branch will be used in the backwards direction. For the first and second evaluations of *put*, the exit conditions corresponding to the original branches were true for the updated view. For the last evaluation of *put*, since the exit condition of

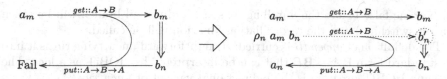

Fig. 1. Reconciliation function: assuming exit conditions ϕ_m and ϕ_n where $\phi_m\, b_n =$ False but $\phi_n\, b_n =$ True, and reconciliation functions ρ_m and ρ_n.

the original branch was false but that of the other branch was true, branch switching is required here. However, a direct *put*-execution of f with the inputs (Right $(1,[2,3])$) and $[]$ crashes (represented by $\bot$ above), for a good reason, as the two inputs are in an inconsistent state with respect to f.

This is where reconciliation functions come into the picture. For the Left branch above, a sensible reconciliation function will be $(\lambda\_.\lambda\_.\text{Left } [])$, which when applied turns the conflicting source (Right $(1,[2,3])$) into Left $[]$, and consequently the *put*-execution may succeed with the new inputs and returns Left $[]$. It is not difficult to verify that the "reconciled" *put*-execution still satisfies well-behavedness. Note that despite the similarity in types, reconciliation functions are not *put*; they merely provide a default source value to allow stuck *put*-executions to proceed. We visualise the effect of reconciliation functions in Fig. 1. The left-hand side is bidirectional execution without successful branch-switching, and since $\phi_m\, b_n$ is false (indicating that b_n is not in the range of the mth branch) the execution of *put* must (rightfully) fail in order to guarantee well-behavedness. On the right-hand side, reconciliation function ρ_n produces a suitable source from a_m and b_n (where $\phi_n\, (get\, (\rho_n\, a_m\, b_n))$ is True), and *put* executes with b_n and the new source $\rho_n\, a_m\, b_n$. It is worth mentioning that branch switching with reconciliation functions does not compromise correctness: though the quality of the user-defined reconciliation functions affects robustness as they may or may not be able to resolve conflicts, successful *put*-executions always guarantee well-behavedness, regardless the involvement of reconciliation functions.

Revisiting *appendB*. Recall *appendB* from Sect. 1.1 (reproduced below).

$$appendB :: \mathbf{B}[A] \rightarrow \mathbf{B}[A] \rightarrow \mathbf{B}[A]$$
$$appendB\; x\; y = \underline{\mathbf{case}}\; x\; \underline{\mathbf{of}}\; [\,] \qquad \rightarrow y \qquad\qquad \underline{\text{with}}\; \lambda\_.\text{True} \quad \underline{\mathbf{by}}\; (\lambda\_.\lambda\_.[\,])$$
$$a:x' \rightarrow a \mathrel{\underline{:}} appendB\; x'\; y\; \underline{\text{with}}\; not \circ null\; \underline{\mathbf{by}}\; (\lambda\_.\lambda\_.\bot)$$

The exit condition for the nil case always returns true as there is no restriction on the value of y, and for the cons case it requires the returned list to be non-empty. In the backwards direction, when the updated view is non-empty, both exit conditions will be true, and then the original branch will be taken. This means that since *appendB* is defined as a recursion on x, the backwards execution will try to unroll the original recursion step by step (i.e., the cons branch will be taken for a number of times that is the same as the length of x) as long as the view remains non-empty. If an updated view list is shorter than x, then $not \circ null$

will become false before the unrolling finishes, and the nil branch will be taken (branch-switching) and the reconciliation function will be called.

The definition of *appendB* is curried; straightforward uncurrying turns it into the standard form $\mathbf{B}A \to \mathbf{B}B$ that can be interpreted by HOBiT as a lens. The following HOBiT program is the bidirectional variant of *uncurry*.

$uncurryB :: (\mathbf{B}A \to \mathbf{B}B \to \mathbf{B}C) \to \mathbf{B}(A, B) \to \mathbf{B}C$
$uncurryB\ f\ z = \underline{\text{let}}\ (x, y) = z\ \underline{\text{in}}\ f\ x\ y$

Here, $\underline{\text{let}}\ p = e\ \underline{\text{in}}\ e'$ is syntactic sugar for $\underline{\text{case}}\ e\ \underline{\text{of}}\ \{p \to e'\ \underline{\text{with}}\ (\lambda\_.\text{True})\ \underline{\text{by}}$ $(\lambda s.\lambda\_.s)\}$, in which the reconciliation function is never called as there is only one branch. Let $appendB' = uncurryB\ appendB$, then we can run $appendB'$ as:

```
HOBiT> :get appendB' ([1, 2], [3, 4, 5])
[1, 2, 3, 4, 5]
HOBiT> :put appendB' ([1, 2], [3, 4, 5]) [6, 7, 8, 9, 10]
([6, 7], [8, 9, 10])     -- No structural change, no branch switching.
HOBiT> :put appendB' ([1, 2], [3, 4, 5]) [6, 7]
([6, 7], [])     -- No branch switching, still.
HOBiT> :put appendB' ([1, 2], [3, 4, 5]) [6]
([6], [])     -- Branch-switching happens and the recursion terminates early.
```

Difference from Lens Combinators. As mentioned above, the idea of branch switching can be traced back to lens languages. In particular, the design of **case** is inspired by the combinator *cond* [7]. Despite the similarities, it is important to recognise that **case** is not only a more convenient syntax for *cond*, but also crucially supports the unrestricted use of λ-bound variables. This more fundamental difference is the reason why we could define *appendB* in the conventional functional style as the variables x and y are used freely in the body of **case**. In other words, the novelty of HOBiT is its ability to combine the traditional (higher-order) functional programming and the bidirectional constructs as found in lens combinators, effectively establishing a new way of bidirectional programming.

2.2 A More Elaborate Example: *linesB*

In addition to supporting convenient programming and robustness in *put* execution, the **case** constructs can also be used to express intricate details of backwards behaviours. Let us consider the *lines* function in Haskell as an example, which splits a string into a list of strings by newlines, for example, *lines* "AA\nBB\n" = ["AA", "BB"], except that the last newline character in its input is optional. For example, *lines* returns ["AA", "BB"] for both "AA\nBB\n" and "AA\nBB". Suppose that we want the backwards transformation of *lines* to exhibit a behaviour that depends on the original source:

$linesB :: \mathbf{B}String \to \mathbf{B}[String]$
$linesB\ str =$
   $\underline{\mathbf{let}}\ (f, b) = breakNLB\ str$
   $\underline{\mathbf{in}}\ \underline{\mathbf{case}}\ b\ \underline{\mathbf{of}}\ \texttt{'\textbackslash n'} : x : r \to f \underset{\cdot}{:} linesB\ (x \underset{\cdot}{:} r)$

                                       $\underline{\mathbf{with}}\ (> 1) \circ length\ \underline{\mathbf{by}}\ (\lambda b.\lambda\_.\texttt{'\textbackslash n'} : \texttt{' '} : b)$
           $b'\ \ \ \ \ \ \ \ \ \ \ \to f \underset{\cdot}{:} [\,]\ \underline{\mathbf{with}}\ (== 1) \circ length\ \underline{\mathbf{by}}\ (\lambda b.\lambda\_.lastNL\ b)$
  $\underline{\mathbf{where}}\ \{lastNL\ [\,] = [\,];\ lastNL\ [\texttt{'\textbackslash n'}] = [\texttt{'\textbackslash n'}];\ lastNL\ (a : x) = lastNL\ x\}$
$breakNLB :: \mathbf{B}String \to \mathbf{B}(String, String)$
$breakNLB\ str = \underline{\mathbf{case}}\ str\ \underline{\mathbf{of}}$
  $[\,]\ \ \ \ \ \to ([\,], [\,])$ $\underline{\mathbf{with}}\ p_1\ \underline{\mathbf{by}}\ (\lambda\_.\lambda\_.[\,])$
  $\texttt{'\textbackslash n'} : s \to ([\,], \texttt{'\textbackslash n'} \underset{\cdot}{:} s)$ $\underline{\mathbf{with}}\ p_2\ \underline{\mathbf{by}}\ (\lambda\_.\lambda\_.\texttt{"\textbackslash n"})$
  $c : s\ \ \ \to \underline{\mathbf{let}}\ (f, r) = breakNLB\ s\ \underline{\mathbf{in}}\ (c \underset{\cdot}{:} f, r)\ \underline{\mathbf{with}}\ p_3\ \underline{\mathbf{by}}\ (\lambda\_.\lambda\_.\texttt{" "})$
  $\underline{\mathbf{where}}\ \{p_1(x, y) = null\ y;\ p_2(x, y) = null\ x\ \&\&\ not\ (null\ y);\ p_3(x, y) = not\ (null\ x)\}$

Fig. 2. $linesB$ and $breakNLB$

```
HOBiT> :put linesB "AA\nBB" ["a","b"]
"a\nb"
HOBiT> :put linesB "AA\nBB" ["a","b","c"]
"a\nb\nc"
HOBiT> :put linesB "AA\nBB" ["a"]
"a"
HOBiT> :put linesB "AA\nBB\n" ["a","b","c"]
"a\nb\nc\n"
HOBiT> :put linesB "AA\nBB\n" ["a"]
"a\n"
```

This behaviour is achieved by the definition in Fig. 2, which makes good use of reconciliation functions. Note that we do not consider the contrived corner case where the string ends with duplicated newlines such as in "A\n\n". The function $breakNLB$ splits a string at the first newline; since $breakNLB$ is injective, its exit conditions and reconciliation functions are of little interest. The interesting part is in the definition of $linesB$, particularly its use of reconciliation functions to track the existence of a last newline character. We firstly explain the branching structure of the program. On the top level, when the first line is removed from the input, the remaining string b may contain more lines, or be the end (represented by either the empty list or the singleton list [$\texttt{'\textbackslash n'}$]). If the first branch is taken, the returned result will be a list of more than one element. In the second branch when it is the end of the text, b could contain a newline or simply be empty. We do not explicitly give patterns for the two cases as they have the same body $f \underset{\cdot}{:} [\,]$, but the reconciliation function distinguishes the two in order to preserve the original source structure in the backwards execution. Note that we intentionally use the same variable name b in the case analysis and the reconciliation function, to signify that the two represent the same source data. The use of argument b in the reconciliation functions serves the purpose of remembering the (non)existence of the last newline in the original source, which is then preserved in the new source.

$$e ::= x \mid \lambda x.e \mid e_1\ e_2 \mid \text{True} \mid \text{False} \mid [] \mid e_1 : e_2 \mid \textbf{case } e \textbf{ of } \{p_i \rightarrow e_i\}_{i=1,2} \mid \textbf{fix } (\lambda f.e)$$
$$\mid \underline{\text{True}} \mid \underline{\text{False}} \mid \underline{[]} \mid e_1 \underline{:} e_2 \mid \underline{\textbf{case}}\ e\ \underline{\textbf{of}}\ \{p_i \rightarrow e_i \underline{\textbf{with}}\ e_i' \underline{\textbf{by}}\ e_i''\}_{i=1,2}$$
$$p ::= x \mid \text{True} \mid \text{False} \mid [] \mid p_1 : p_2$$

Fig. 3. Syntax of HOBiT Core

It is worth noting that just like the other examples we have seen, this definition in HOBiT shares a similar structure with a definition of *lines* in Haskell.[1] The notable difference is that a Haskell definition is likely to have a different grouping of the three cases of *lines* into two branches, as there is no need to keep track of the last newline for backwards execution. Recall that reconciliation functions are called *after* branches are chosen by exit conditions; in the case of *linesB*, the reconciliation function is used to decide the reconciled value of b' to be "\n" or "". This, however, means that we cannot separate the pattern b' into two "\n" and "" with copying its branch body and exit condition, because then we lose a chance to choose a reconciled value of b based on its original value.

3   Syntax and Type System of HOBiT Core

In this section, we describe the syntax and the type system of the core of HOBiT.

3.1   Syntax

The syntax of HOBiT Core is given in Fig. 3. For simplicity, we only consider booleans and lists. The syntax is almost the same as the standard λ-calculus with the fixed-point combinator (**fix**), lists and booleans. For data constructors and case expressions, there are in addition bidirectional versions that are underlined. We allow the body of **fix** to be non-λs to make our semantics simple (Sect. 4), though such a definition like **fix**($\lambda x.$True $: x$) can diverge.

Although in examples we used **case**/<u>**case**</u>-expressions with an arbitrary number of branches having overlapping patterns under the first-match principle, we assume for simplicity that in HOBiT Core **case**/<u>**case**</u>-expressions must have exactly two branches whose patterns do not overlap; extensions to support these features are straightforward. As in Haskell, we sometimes omit the braces and semicolons if they are clear from the layout.

---

[1] Haskell's *lines*'s behaviour is a bit more complicated as it returns [] if and only if the input is "". This behaviour can be achieved by calling *linesB* only when the input list is nonempty.

$$\boxed{\Gamma; \Delta \vdash e : A}$$

$$\frac{\Gamma(x) = A}{\Gamma; \Delta \vdash x : A} \quad \frac{\Delta(x) = \sigma}{\Gamma; \Delta \vdash x : \mathbf{B}\sigma} \quad \frac{\Gamma, x : A; \Delta \vdash e : B}{\Gamma; \Delta \vdash \lambda x.e : A \to B} \quad \frac{\Gamma; \Delta \vdash e_1 : A \to B \quad \Gamma; \Delta \vdash e_2 : A}{\Gamma; \Delta \vdash e_1 \, e_2 : B}$$

$$\frac{\Gamma, f : A; \Delta \vdash e : A}{\Gamma; \Delta \vdash \mathbf{fix}(\lambda f.e) : A} \quad \frac{}{\Gamma; \Delta \vdash \mathsf{True} : Bool} \quad \frac{}{\Gamma; \Delta \vdash \mathsf{False} : Bool} \quad \frac{}{\Gamma; \Delta \vdash [\,] : [A]}$$

$$\frac{\Gamma; \Delta \vdash e_1 : A \quad \Gamma; \Delta \vdash e_2 : [A]}{\Gamma; \Delta \vdash e_1 : e_2 : [A]} \quad \frac{}{\Gamma; \Delta \vdash \underline{\mathsf{True}} : \mathbf{B}Bool} \quad \frac{}{\Gamma; \Delta \vdash \underline{\mathsf{False}} : \mathbf{B}Bool} \quad \frac{}{\Gamma; \Delta \vdash \underline{[\,]} : \mathbf{B}[\sigma]}$$

$$\frac{\Gamma; \Delta \vdash e_1 : \mathbf{B}\sigma \quad \Gamma; \Delta \vdash e_2 : \mathbf{B}[\sigma]}{\Gamma; \Delta \vdash e_1 \underline{:} e_2 : \mathbf{B}[\sigma]} \quad \frac{\Gamma; \Delta \vdash e : A \quad \Gamma_i \vdash p_i : A \quad \Gamma, \Gamma_i; \Delta \vdash e_i : B \quad (i = 1, 2)}{\Gamma; \Delta \vdash \mathbf{case}\ e\ \mathbf{of}\ \{p_i \to e_i\}_{i=1,2} : B}$$

$$\frac{\Gamma; \Delta \vdash e : \mathbf{B}\sigma \quad \Delta_i \vdash p_i : \sigma \quad \Gamma; \Delta, \Delta_i \vdash e_i : \mathbf{B}\tau}{\Gamma; \Delta \vdash e_i' : \tau \to Bool \quad \Gamma; \Delta \vdash e_i'' : \sigma \to \tau \to \sigma \quad (i = 1, 2)}$$
$$\frac{}{\Gamma; \Delta \vdash \underline{\mathbf{case}}\ e\ \underline{\mathbf{of}}\ \{p_i \to e_i\ \underline{\mathbf{with}}\ e_i'\ \underline{\mathbf{by}}\ e_i''\}_{i=1,2} : \mathbf{B}\tau}$$

$$\boxed{\Gamma \vdash p : A}$$

$$\frac{}{x : A \vdash x : A} \quad \frac{}{\emptyset \vdash \mathsf{True} : Bool} \quad \frac{}{\emptyset \vdash \mathsf{False} : Bool} \quad \frac{}{\emptyset \vdash [\,] : [A]} \quad \frac{\Gamma_1 \vdash e_1 : A \quad \Gamma_2 \vdash e_2 : [A]}{\Gamma_1, \Gamma_2 \vdash e_1 : e_2 : [A]}$$

Fig. 4. Typing rules: $\Delta \vdash p : \sigma$ is similar to $\Gamma \vdash p : A$ but asserts that the resulting environment is actually a bidirectional environment.

3.2   Type System

The types in HOBiT Core are defined as follows.

$$A, B ::= \mathbf{B}\sigma \mid A \to B \mid [A] \mid Bool$$

We use the metavariable $\sigma, \tau, \ldots$ for types that do not contain $\to$ nor $\mathbf{B}$, We call σ-types *pure datatypes*, which are used for sources and views of lenses. Intuitively, $\mathbf{B}\sigma$ represents "updatable σ"—data subject to update in bidirectional transformation. We keep the type system of HOBiT Core simple, though it is possible to include polymorphic types or intersection types to unify unidirectional and bidirectional constructors.

The typing judgment $\Gamma; \Delta \vdash e : A$, which reads that under environments Γ and Δ, expression e has type A, is defined by the typing rules in Fig. 4. We use two environments: Δ (the *bidirectional type environment*) is for variables introduced by pattern-matching through **case**, and Γ for everything else. It is interesting to observe that Δ only holds pure datatypes, as the pattern variables of **case** have pure datatypes, while Γ holds any types. We assume that the variables in Γ and those in Δ are disjoint, and appropriate α-renaming has been done to ensure this. This separation of Δ from Γ does not affect typeability, but is key to our semantics and correctness proof (Sect. 4). Most of the rules are standard except **case**; recall that we only use unidirectional constructors in patterns which have pure types, while the variables bound in the patterns are used as $\mathbf{B}$-typed values in branch bodies.

4   Semantics of HOBiT Core

Recall that the unique strength of HOBiT is its ability to mix higher-order uni-directional programming with bidirectional programming. A consequence of this mixture is that we can no longer specify its semantics in the same way as other *first-order* bidirectional languages such as [13], where two semantics—one for *get* and the other for *put*—suffice. This is because the category of lenses is believed to have no exponential objects [27] (and thus does not permit λs).

4.1   Basic Idea: Staging

Our solution to this problem is staging [5], which separates evaluation into two stages: the unidirectional parts is evaluated first to make way for a bidi-rectional semantics, which only has to deal with the residual first-order pro-grams. As a simple example, consider the expression $(\lambda z.z)\ (x : ((\lambda w.w)\ y) : [])$. The first-stage evaluation, $e \Downarrow_{\mathsf{U}} E$, eliminates λs from the expression as in $(\lambda z.z)\ (x : ((\lambda w.w)\ y) : []) \Downarrow_{\mathsf{U}} x : y : []$. Then, our bidirectional semantics will be able to treat the residual expression as a lens between value environments and values, following [13,20]. Specifically, we have the *get* evaluation relation $\mu \vdash_{\mathsf{G}} E \Rightarrow v$, which computes the value v of E under environment μ as usual, and the *put* evaluation relation $\mu \vdash_{\mathsf{P}} v \Leftarrow E \dashv \mu'$, which computes an updated environment μ' for E from the updated view v and the original environment μ. In pseudo syntax, it can be understood as *put* $E\ \mu\ v = \mu'$, where μ represents the original source and μ' the new source.

It is worth mentioning that a complete separation of the stages is not possible due to the combination of **fix** and **case**, as an attempt to fully evaluate them in the first stage will result in divergence. Thus, we delay the unidirectional eval-uation inside **case** to allow **fix**, and consequently the three evaluation relations (uni-directional, *get*, and *put*) are mutually dependent.

4.2   Three Evaluation Relations: Unidirectional, *get* and *put*

First, we formally define the set of residual expressions:

$$E ::= \mathsf{True} \mid \mathsf{False} \mid [] \mid E_1 : E_2 \mid \lambda x.e$$
$$\mid\ x \mid \underline{\mathsf{True}} \mid \underline{\mathsf{False}} \mid \underline{[]} \mid E_1 \mathbin{\underline{:}} E_2 \mid \mathbf{case}\ E_0\ \mathbf{of}\ \{p_i \to e_i\ \mathbf{with}\ E_i\ \mathbf{by}\ E'_i\}_{i=1,2}$$

They are treated as values in the unidirectional evaluation, and as expressions in the *get* and *put* evaluations. Notice that e or e_i appear under λ or **case**, meaning that their evaluations are delayed.

The set of *(first-order) values* is defined as below.

$$v ::= \mathsf{True} \mid \mathsf{False} \mid [] \mid v_1 : v_2$$

Accordingly, we define a *(first-order) value environment* μ as a finite mapping from variables to first-order values.

$$\frac{}{x \Downarrow_U x} \qquad \frac{e_1 \Downarrow_U \lambda x.e \quad e_2 \Downarrow_U E_2 \quad e[E_2/x] \Downarrow_U E}{e_1\, e_2 \Downarrow_U E} \qquad \frac{}{\lambda x.e \Downarrow_U \lambda x.e} \qquad \frac{e[\mathbf{fix}(\lambda f.e)/f] \Downarrow_U E}{\mathbf{fix}(\lambda f.e) \Downarrow_U E}$$

$$\frac{e_0 \Downarrow_U E_0 \quad e_i' \Downarrow_U E_i' \quad e_i'' \Downarrow_U E_i'' \quad (i=1,2)}{\underline{\mathbf{case}}\ e_0\ \underline{\mathbf{of}}\ \{p_i \to e_i\ \underline{\mathbf{with}}\ e_i'\ \underline{\mathbf{by}}\ e_i''\}_{i=1,2} \Downarrow_U \underline{\mathbf{case}}\ E_0\ \underline{\mathbf{of}}\ \{p_i \to e_i\ \underline{\mathbf{with}}\ E_i'\ \underline{\mathbf{by}}\ E_i''\}_{i=1,2}}$$

Fig. 5. Evaluation rules for unidirectional parts (excerpt)

Unidirectional Evaluation Relation. The rules for the unidirectional evaluation relation is rather standard, as excerpted in Fig. 5. The bidirectional constructs (i.e., bidirectional constructors and $\underline{\mathbf{case}}$) are frozen, i.e., behave just like ordinary constructors in this evaluation. Notice that we can evaluate an expression containing free variables; then the resulting residual expression may contain the free variables.

Bidirectional (*get* and *put*) Evaluation Relations. The *get* and *put* evaluation relations, $\mu \vdash_G E \Rightarrow v$ and $\mu \vdash_P v \Leftarrow E \dashv \mu'$, are defined so that they together form a lens.

Weakening of Environment. Before we lay out the semantics, it is worth explaining a subtlety in environment handling. In conventional evaluation semantics, a larger than necessary environment does no harm, as long as there is no name clashes. For example, whether the expression x is evaluated under the environment $\{x = 1\}$ or $\{x = 1, y = 2\}$ does not matter. However, the same is not true for bidirectional evaluation. Let us consider a residual expression $E = x \, \underline{:} \, y \, \underline{:} \, [\,]$, and a value environment $\mu = \{x = 1, y = 2\}$ as the original source. We expect to have $\mu \vdash_G E \Rightarrow 1 : 2 : [\,]$, which may be derived as:

$$\frac{\mu \vdash_G x \Rightarrow 1 \quad \dfrac{\vdots}{\mu \vdash_G y \, \underline{:} \, [\,] \Rightarrow 2 : [\,]}}{\mu \vdash_G x \, \underline{:} \, y \, \underline{:} \, [\,] \Rightarrow 1 : 2 : [\,]}$$

In the *put* direction, for an updated view say $3 : 4 : [\,]$, we expect to have $\mu \vdash_P 3 : 4 : [\,] \Leftarrow E \dashv \{x = 3, y = 4\}$ with the corresponding derivation:

$$\frac{\mu \vdash_P 3 \Leftarrow x \dashv ?_1 \quad \dfrac{\vdots}{\mu \vdash_P 4 : [\,] \Leftarrow y \, \underline{:} \, [\,] \dashv ?_2}}{\mu \vdash_P 3 : 4 : [\,] \Leftarrow x \, \underline{:} \, y \, \underline{:} \, [\,] \dashv \{x = 3, y = 4\}}$$

What shall the environments $?_1$ and $?_2$ be? One way is to have $\mu \vdash_P 3 \Leftarrow x \dashv \{x = 3, y = 2\}$, and $\mu \vdash_P 4 : [\,] \Leftarrow y \, \underline{:} \, [\,] \dashv \{x = 1, y = 4\}$, where the variables do not appear free in the residual expression takes their values from the original source environment μ. However, the evaluation will get stuck here, as there is no reasonable way to produce the expected result $\{x = 3, y = 4\}$ from $?_1 = \{x = 3, y = 2\}$ and $?_2 = \{x = 1, y = 4\}$. In other words, the redundancy in environment is harmful as it may cause conflicts downstream.

Our solution to this problem, which follows from [21–23, 29], is to allow *put* to return value environments containing only bindings that are relevant for the residual expressions under evaluation. For example, we have $\mu \vdash_P 3 \Leftarrow x \dashv \{x = 3\}$, and $\mu \vdash_P 4 : [] \Leftarrow y : [] \dashv \{y = 4\}$. Then, we can merge the two value environments $?_1 = \{x = 3\}$ and $?_2 = \{y = 4\}$ to obtain the expected result $\{x = 3, y = 4\}$. As a remark, this seemingly simple solution actually has a non-trivial effect on the reasoning of well-behavedness. We defer a detailed discussion on this to Sect. 4.3.

Now we are ready to define *get* and *put* evaluation rules for each bidirectional constructs. For variables, we just lookup or update environments. Recall that μ is a mapping (i.e., function) from variables to (first-order) values, while we use a record-like notation such as $\{x = v\}$.

$$\overline{\mu \vdash_G x \Rightarrow \mu(x)} \qquad \overline{\mu \vdash_P v \Leftarrow x \dashv \{x = v\}}$$

For constants $\underline{c}$ where $c = $ False, True, $[]$, the evaluation rules are straightforward.

$$\overline{\mu \vdash_G \underline{c} \Rightarrow c} \qquad \overline{\mu \vdash_P c \Leftarrow \underline{c} \dashv \emptyset}$$

The above-mentioned behaviour of the bidirectional cons expression $E_1 : E_2$ is formally given as:

$$\frac{\mu \vdash_G E_1 \Rightarrow v_1 \quad \mu \vdash_G E_2 \Rightarrow v_2}{\mu \vdash_G E_1 : E_2 \Rightarrow v_1 : v_2} \qquad \frac{\mu \vdash_P v_1 \Leftarrow E_1 \dashv \mu'_1 \quad \mu \vdash_P v_2 \Leftarrow E_2 \dashv \mu'_2}{\mu \vdash_P v_1 : v_2 \Leftarrow E_1 : E_2 \dashv \mu'_1 \curlyvee \mu'_2}$$

(Note that the variable rules guarantee that only free variables in the residual expressions end up in the resulting environments.) Here, $\curlyvee$ is the merging operator defined as: $\mu \curlyvee \mu' = \mu \cup \mu'$ if there is no x such that $\mu(x) \neq \mu'(x)$. For example, $\{x = 3\} \curlyvee \{y = 4\} = \{x = 3, y = 4\}$, and $\{x = 3, y = 4\} \curlyvee \{y = 4\} = \{x = 3, y = 4\}$, but $\{x = 3, y = 2\} \curlyvee \{y = 4\}$ is undefined.

The most interesting rules are for **case**. In the *get* direction, it is not different from the ordinary **case** except that exit conditions are asserted, as shown in Fig. 6. We use the following predicate for pattern matching.

$$match(p_k, v_0, \mu_k) = (p_k \mu_k = v_0) \wedge (\mathsf{dom}(\mu_k) = \mathsf{fv}(p_k))$$

Here, we abuse the notation to write $p_k \mu_k$ for the value obtained from p_k by replacing the free variables x in p_k with $\mu_k(x)$. One might notice that we have the disjoint union $\mu \uplus \mu_i$ in Fig. 6 where μ_i holds the values of the variables in p_i, as we assume α-renaming of bound variables that is consistent in *get* and *put*. Recall that p_1 and p_2 are assumed not to overlap, and hence the evaluation is deterministic. Note that the reconciliation functions E''_i are untouched by the rule.

The *put* evaluation rule of **case** shown in Fig. 6 is more involved. In addition to checking which branch should be chosen by using exit conditions, we need two rules to handle the cases with and without branch switching. Basically,

$$\cfrac{\mu \vdash_G E_0 \Rightarrow v_0 \quad match(p_i, v_0, \mu_i) \quad e_i \Downarrow_U E_i \quad \mu \uplus \mu_i \vdash_G E_i \Rightarrow v \quad E_i' \, v \Downarrow_U \mathsf{True}}{\mu \vdash_G \underline{\mathbf{case}} \ E_0 \ \underline{\mathbf{of}} \ \{p_i \to e_i \ \underline{\mathbf{with}} \ E_i' \ \underline{\mathbf{by}} \ E_i''\}_{i=1,2} \Rightarrow v}$$

$$\cfrac{\mu \vdash_G E_0 \Rightarrow v_0 \quad match(p_i, v_0, \mu_i) \quad E_i' \, v \Downarrow_U \mathsf{True} \quad e_i \Downarrow_U E_i}{\mu \uplus \mu_i \vdash_P v \Leftarrow E_i \dashv \mu' \uplus_{\mathsf{dom}(\mu), \mathsf{dom}(\mu_i)} \mu_i' \quad v_0' = p_i(\mu_i' \lhd \mu_i) \quad \mu \vdash_P v_0' \Leftarrow E_0 \dashv \mu_0'}{\mu \vdash_P v \Leftarrow \underline{\mathbf{case}} \ E_0 \ \underline{\mathbf{of}} \ \{p_i \to e_i \ \underline{\mathbf{with}} \ E_i' \ \underline{\mathbf{by}} \ E_i''\}_{i=1,2} \dashv \mu_0' \curlyvee \mu'}$$

$$\cfrac{\mu \vdash_G E_0 \Rightarrow v_0 \quad match(p_i, v_0, \mu_i) \quad E_i' \, v \Downarrow_U \mathsf{False} \quad j = 3 - i \quad E_j' \, v \Downarrow_U \mathsf{True} \quad e_j \Downarrow_U E_j}{E_j'' \, v_0 \, v \Downarrow_U u_0 \quad match(p_j, u_0, \mu_j)}{\mu \uplus \mu_j \vdash_P v \Leftarrow E_j \dashv \mu' \uplus_{\mathsf{dom}(\mu), \mathsf{dom}(\mu_j)} \mu_j' \quad v_0' = p_j(\mu_j' \lhd \mu_j) \quad \mu \vdash_P v_0' \Leftarrow E_0 \dashv \mu_0'}{\mu \vdash_P v \Leftarrow \underline{\mathbf{case}} \ E_0 \ \underline{\mathbf{of}} \ \{p_i \to e_i \ \underline{\mathbf{with}} \ E_i' \ \underline{\mathbf{by}} \ E_i''\}_{i=1,2} \dashv \mu_0' \curlyvee \mu'}$$

Fig. 6. *get-* and *put-*Evaluation of **case**: we write $\mu \uplus_{X,Y} \mu'$ to ensure that $\mathsf{dom}(\mu) \subseteq X$ and $\mathsf{dom}(\mu') \subseteq Y$.

the branch to be taken in the backwards direction is decided first, by the *get-*evaluation of the case condition E_0 and the checking of the exit condition E_i' against the updated view v. After that, the body of the chosen branch e_i is firstly uni-directionally evaluated, and then its residual expression E_i is *put-*evaluated. The last step is *put-*evaluation of the case-condition E_0. When branch switching happens, there is the additional step of applying the reconciliation function E_j''.

Note the use of operator $\lhd$ in computing the updated case condition v_0'.

$$(\mu' \lhd \mu)(x) = \begin{cases} \mu'(x) & \text{if } x \in \mathsf{dom}(\mu') \\ \mu(x) & \text{otherwise} \end{cases}$$

Recall that in the beginning of this subsection, we discussed our approach of avoiding conflicts by producing environments with only relevant variables. This means the μ_i' above contains only variables that appear free in E_i, which may or may not be all the variables in p_i. Since this is the point where these variables are introduced, we need to supplement μ_i' with μ_i from the original pattern matching so that p_i can be properly instantiated.

Construction of Lens. Let us write $\mathcal{L}_0[\![E]\!]$ for a lens between value environments and values, defined as:

$$get \ \mathcal{L}_0[\![E]\!] \ \mu = v \qquad \text{if } \mu \vdash_G E \Rightarrow v$$
$$put \ \mathcal{L}_0[\![E]\!] \ \mu \, v = \mu' \qquad \text{if } \mu \vdash_P v \Leftarrow E \dashv \mu'$$

Then, we can define the lens $\mathcal{L}[\![e]\!]$ induced from e (a closed function expression), where $e \, x \Downarrow_U E$ for some fresh variable x.

$$get \ \mathcal{L}[\![e]\!] \ s = get \ \mathcal{L}_0[\![E]\!] \ \{x = s\}$$
$$put \ \mathcal{L}[\![e]\!] \ s \, v = (\mu' \lhd \{x = s\})(x) \qquad \text{where } \mu' = put \ \mathcal{L}_0[\![E]\!] \ \{x = s\} \ v$$

Actually, :get and :put in Sect. 2 are realised by $get \ \mathcal{L}[\![e]\!]$ and $put \ \mathcal{L}[\![e]\!]$.

4.3   Correctness

We establish the correctness of HOBiT Core: $\mathcal{L}[\![e]\!] \in Lens\ [\![\sigma]\!]\ [\![\tau]\!]$ is well-behaved for closed e of type $\mathbf{B}\sigma \to \mathbf{B}\tau$. Recall that $Lens\ S\ V$ is a set of lenses ℓ, where $get\ \ell \in S \to V$ and $put\ \ell \in S \to V \to S$. We only provide proof sketches in this subsection due to space limitation.

$\preceq$-**well-behavedness.** Recall that in the previous subsection, we allow environments to be weakened during put-evaluation. Since not all variables in a source may appear in the view, during some intermediate evaluation steps (for example within **case**-branches) the weakened environment may not be sufficient to fully construct a new source. Recall that, in $\mu \vdash_P v \Leftarrow e \dashv \mu'$, $\mathsf{dom}(\mu')$ can be smaller than $\mathsf{dom}(\mu)$, a gap that is fixed at a later stage of evaluation by merging ($\curlyvee$) and defaulting ($\lhd$) with other environments. This technique reduces conflicts, but at the same time complicates the compositional reasoning of correctness. Specifically, due to the potentially missing information in the intermediate environments, well-behavedness may be temporally broken during evaluation. Instead, we use a variant of well-behavedness that is weakening aware, which will then be used to establish the standard well-behavedness for the final result.

Definition 1 ($\preceq$-well-behavedness). Let $(S, \preceq)$ and $(V, \preceq)$ be partially-ordered sets. A lens $\ell \in Lens\ S\ V$ is called $\preceq$-*well-behaved* if it satisfies

$$get\ \ell\ s = v \implies v \text{ is maximal} \wedge (\forall v'.\ v' \preceq v \implies put\ \ell\ s\ v' \preceq s)$$
$$(\preceq\text{-}\mathbf{Acceptability})$$
$$put\ \ell\ s\ v = s' \implies (\forall s''.\ s' \preceq s'' \implies v \preceq get\ \ell\ s'')\quad (\preceq\text{-}\mathbf{Consistency})$$

for any $s, s' \in S$ and $v \in V$, where s is maximal.   □

We write $Lens^{\preceq \mathrm{wb}}\ S\ V$ for the set of lenses in $Lens\ S\ V$ that are $\preceq$-well-behaved. In this section, we only consider the case where S and V are value environments and first-order values, where value environments are ordered by weakening ($\mu \preceq \mu'$ if $\mu(x) = \mu'(x)$ for all $x \in \mathsf{dom}(\mu)$), and $(\preceq) = (=)$ for first-order values. In Sect. 5.2 we consider a slightly more general situation.

The $\preceq$-well-behavedness is a generalisation of the ordinary well-behavedness, as it coincides with the ordinary well-behavedness when $(\preceq) = (=)$.

Theorem 1. *For S and V with $(\preceq) = (=)$, a lens $\ell \in Lens\ S\ V$ is $\preceq$-well-behaved iff it is well-behaved.*   □

Kripke Logical Relation. The key step to prove the correctness of HOBiT Core is to prove that $\mathcal{L}_0[\![E]\!]$ is always $\preceq$-well-behaved if E is an evaluation result of a well-typed expression e. The basic idea is to prove this by logical relation that expression e of type $\mathbf{B}\sigma$ under the context Δ is evaluated to E, assuming termination, such that $\mathcal{L}_0[\![E]\!]$ is a $\preceq$-well-behaved lens between $[\![\Delta]\!]$ and $[\![\sigma]\!]$.

Usually a logical relation is defined only by induction on the type. In our case, as we need to consider Δ in the interpretation of $\mathbf{B}\sigma$, the relation should be indexed by Δ too. However, naive indexing does not work due to substitutions.

For example, we could define a (unary) relation $\mathcal{E}_\Delta(\mathbf{B}\sigma)$ as a set of expressions that evaluate to "good" (i.e., $\preceq$-well-behaved) lenses between (the semantics of) Δ and σ, and $\mathcal{E}_\Delta(\mathbf{B}\sigma \to \mathbf{B}\tau)$ as a set of expressions that evaluate to "good" functions that map good lenses between Δ and σ to those between Δ and τ. This naive relation, however, does not respect substitution, which can substitute a value obtained from an expression typed under Δ to a variable typed under Δ' such that $\Delta \subseteq \Delta'$, where Δ and Δ' need not be the same. With the naive definition, good functions at Δ need not be good functions at Δ', as a good lens between Δ' and σ is not always a good lens between Δ and σ.

To remedy the situation, inspired by the denotation semantics in [24], we use Kripke logical relations [18] where worlds are Δs.

Definition 2. We define the set $\mathcal{E}_\Delta[\![A]\!]$ of expressions, the set $\mathcal{R}_\Delta[\![A]\!]$ of residual expressions, the set $[\![\sigma]\!]$ of values and the set $[\![\Delta]\!]$ of value environments as below.

$$\mathcal{E}_\Delta[\![A]\!] = \{e \mid \forall E.\ e \Downarrow_U E \text{ implies } E \in \mathcal{R}_\Delta[\![A]\!]\}$$

$$\mathcal{R}_\Delta[\![Bool]\!] = \{\mathsf{True}, \mathsf{False}\}$$

$$\mathcal{R}_\Delta[\![[A]]\!] = List\ \mathcal{R}_\Delta[\![A]\!]$$

$$\mathcal{R}_\Delta[\![\mathbf{B}\sigma]\!] = \{E \mid \forall \Delta'.\ \Delta \subseteq \Delta' \text{ implies } \mathcal{L}_0[\![E]\!] \in Lens^{\preceq \mathrm{wb}}\ [\![\Delta']\!]\ [\![\sigma]\!]\}$$

$$\mathcal{R}_\Delta[\![A \to B]\!] = \{F \mid \forall \Delta'.\ \Delta \subseteq \Delta' \text{ implies } (\forall E \in \mathcal{R}_{\Delta'}[\![A]\!].\ F\ E \in \mathcal{E}_{\Delta'}[\![B]\!])\}$$

$$[\![Bool]\!] = \{\mathsf{True}, \mathsf{False}\}$$

$$[\![[\sigma]]\!] = List\ [\![\sigma]\!]$$

$$[\![\Delta]\!] = \{\mu \mid \mathsf{dom}(\mu) \subseteq \mathsf{dom}(\Delta) \text{ and } \forall x \in \mathsf{dom}(\mu).\mu(x) \in [\![\Delta(x)]\!]\}$$

Here, for a set S, $List\ S$ is inductively defined as: $[\ ] \in List\ S$, and $s : t \in List\ S$ for all $s \in S$ and $t \in List\ S$. $\qquad\square$

The notable difference from ordinary logical relations is the definition of $\mathcal{R}_\Delta[\![A \to B]\!]$ where we consider an arbitrary Δ' such that $\Delta \subseteq \Delta'$. This is the key to state $\mathcal{R}_\Delta[\![A]\!] \subseteq \mathcal{R}_{\Delta'}[\![A]\!]$ if $\Delta \subseteq \Delta'$. Notice that $[\![\sigma]\!] = \mathcal{R}_\Delta[\![\sigma]\!]$ for any Δ.

We have the following lemmas.

Lemma 1. *If $\Delta \subseteq \Delta'$, $v \in \mathcal{R}_\Delta[\![A]\!]$ implies $v \in \mathcal{R}_{\Delta'}[\![A]\!]$.* $\qquad\square$

Lemma 2. *$x \in \mathcal{R}_\Delta[\![\mathbf{B}\sigma]\!]$ for any Δ such that $\Delta(x) = \sigma$.* $\qquad\square$

Lemma 3. *For any σ and Δ, $\mathsf{True}, \mathsf{False} \in \mathcal{R}_\Delta[\![\mathbf{B}Bool]\!]$ and $[\ ] \in \mathcal{R}_\Delta[\![\mathbf{B}[\sigma]]\!]$.* $\qquad\square$

Lemma 4. *If $E_1 \in \mathcal{R}_\Delta[\![\mathbf{B}\sigma]\!]$ and $E_2 \in \mathcal{R}_\Delta[\![\mathbf{B}[\sigma]]\!]$, then $E_1 : E_2 \in \mathcal{R}_\Delta[\![\mathbf{B}[\sigma]]\!]$.* $\qquad\square$

Lemma 5. *Let σ and τ be pure types and Δ a pure type environment. Suppose that $e_i \in \mathcal{E}_{\Delta \uplus \Delta_i}[\![\tau]\!]$ for $\Delta_i \vdash p_i : \sigma$ $(i = 1, 2)$, and that $E_0 \in \mathcal{R}_\Delta[\![\mathbf{B}\sigma]\!]$, $E_1', E_2' \in \mathcal{R}_\Delta[\![\tau \to Bool]\!]$ and $E_1'', E_2'' \in \mathcal{R}_\Delta[\![\sigma \to \tau \to \sigma]\!]$. Then, $\underline{\mathbf{case}}\ E_0\ \underline{\mathbf{of}}\ \{p_i \to e_i\ \underline{\mathbf{with}}\ E_i'\ \underline{\mathbf{by}}\ E_i''\}_{i=1,2} \in \mathcal{R}_\Delta[\![\mathbf{B}\tau]\!]$.*

Proof (Sketch). The proof itself is straightforward by case analysis. The key property is that *get* and *put* use the same branches in both proofs of $\preceq$-**Acceptability** and $\preceq$-**Consistency**. Slight care is required for unidirectional evaluations of e_1 and e_2, and applications of E'_1, E'_2, E''_1 and E''_2. However, the semantics is carefully designed so that in the proof of $\preceq$-**Acceptability**, unidirectional evaluations that happen in *put* have already happened in the evaluation of *get*, and a similar discussion applies to $\preceq$-**Consistency**.   □

As a remark, recall that we assumed α-renaming of p_i so that the disjoint unions ($\uplus$) in Fig. 6 succeed. This renaming depends on the μs received in *get* and *put* evaluations, and can be realised by using de Bruijn levels.

Lemma 6 (Fundamental Lemma). *For* $\Gamma; \Delta \vdash e : A$, *for any* Δ' *with* $\Delta \subseteq \Delta'$ *and* $E_x \in \mathcal{R}_{\Delta'}[\![\Gamma(x)]\!]$, *we have* $e[E_x/x]_x \in \mathcal{E}_{\Delta'}[\![A]\!]$.

Proof (Sketch). We prove the lemma by induction on typing derivation. For bidirectional constructs, we just apply the above lemmas appropriately. The other parts are rather routine.   □

Now we are ready to state the correctness of our construction of lenses.

Corollary 1. *If* $\varepsilon; \varepsilon \vdash e : \mathbf{B}\sigma \rightarrow \mathbf{B}\tau$, *then* $e\ x \in \mathcal{E}_{\{x:\sigma\}}[\![\mathbf{B}\tau]\!]$.   □

Lemma 7. *If* $e \in \mathcal{E}_{\{x:\sigma\}}[\![\mathbf{B}\tau]\!]$, $\mathcal{L}[\![e]\!]$ *(if defined) is in* $Lens^{\preceq\mathrm{wb}}\ [\![\sigma]\!]\ [\![\tau]\!]$ *(and thus well-behaved by Theorem 1).*   □

Theorem 2. *If* $\varepsilon; \varepsilon \vdash e : \mathbf{B}\sigma \rightarrow \mathbf{B}\tau$, *then* $\mathcal{L}[\![e]\!] \in Lens\ [\![\sigma]\!]\ [\![\tau]\!]$ *(if defined) is well-behaved.*   □

5   Extensions

Before presenting a larger example, we discuss a few extensions of HOBiT Core which facilitate programming.

5.1   In-Language Lens Definition

In HOBiT programming, it is still sometimes useful to allow manually defined primitive lenses (i.e., lenses constructed from independently specified *get/put* functions), for backwards compatibility and also for programs with relatively simple computation logic but complicated backwards behaviours. This feature is supported by the construct **appLens** $e_1\ e_2\ e_3$ in HOBiT. For example, we can write $incB\ x = \mathbf{appLens}\ (\lambda s.s + 1)\ (\lambda\_.\lambda v.v - 1)\ x$ to define a bidirectional increment function $incB :: \mathbf{B}Int \rightarrow \mathbf{B}Int$. Note that for simplicity we require the additional expression x (represented by e_3 in the general case) to convert between normal functions and lenses. The typing rule for **appLens** e_1 e_2 e_3 is as below.

$$\frac{\Gamma; \Delta \vdash e_1 : \sigma \to \tau \quad \Gamma; \Delta \vdash e_2 : \sigma \to \tau \to \sigma \quad \Gamma; \Delta \vdash e_3 : \mathbf{B}\sigma}{\Gamma; \Delta \vdash \mathbf{appLens}\ e_1\ e_2\ e_3 : \mathbf{B}\tau}$$

Accordingly, we add the following unidirectional evaluation rule.

$$\frac{e_i \Downarrow_\mathsf{U} E_i \quad (i = 1, 2, 3)}{\mathbf{appLens}\ e_1\ e_2\ e_3 \Downarrow_\mathsf{U} \mathbf{appLens}\ E_1\ E_2\ E_3}$$

Also, we add the following *get/put* evaluation rules for **appLens**.

$$\frac{\mu \vdash_\mathsf{G} E_3 \Rightarrow v \quad E_1\ v \Downarrow_\mathsf{U} u}{\mu \vdash_\mathsf{G} \mathbf{appLens}\ E_1\ E_2\ E_3 \Rightarrow u} \qquad \frac{\mu \vdash_\mathsf{G} E_3 \Rightarrow v \quad E_2\ v\ u' \Downarrow_\mathsf{U} v' \quad \mu \vdash_\mathsf{P} v' \Leftarrow E_3 \dashv \mu'}{\mu \vdash_\mathsf{P} u' \Leftarrow \mathbf{appLens}\ E_1\ E_2\ E_3 \dashv \mu'}$$

Notice that **appLens** e_1 e_2 e_3 is "good" if e_3 is so, i.e., **appLens** e_1 e_2 $e_3 \in \overline{\mathcal{E}_\Delta[\![\mathbf{B}\tau]\!]}$ if $e_3 \in \overline{\mathcal{E}_\Delta[\![\mathbf{B}\sigma]\!]}$, provided that the *get/put* pair (e_1, e_2) is well-behaved.

5.2   Lens Combinators as Language Constructs

In this paper, we have focused on the **case** construct, which is inspired by the *cond* combinator [7]. Although *cond* is certainly an important lens combinator, it is not the only one worth considering. Actually, we can obtain language constructs from a number of lens combinators including those that take care of alignment [2]. For the sake of demonstration, we outline the derivation of a simpler example $comb \in Lens\ [\![\sigma]\!]\ [\![\tau]\!] \to Lens\ [\![\sigma']\!]\ [\![\tau']\!]$. As the construction depends solely on types, we purposely leave the combinator abstract.

A naive way of lifting combinators can already be found in [21,23]. For example, for *comb*, we might prepare the construct $\underline{\mathbf{comb}}_\mathrm{bad}$ with the following typing rule (where ε is the empty environment):

$$\frac{\varepsilon; \varepsilon \vdash e : \mathbf{B}\sigma \to \mathbf{B}\tau \quad \Gamma; \Delta \vdash e' : \mathbf{B}\tau'}{\Gamma; \Delta \vdash \underline{\mathbf{comb}}_\mathrm{bad}\ e\ e' : \mathbf{B}\tau'}$$

Notice that in this version e is required to be closed so that we can turn the function directly into a lens by $\mathcal{L}[\![-]\!]$, and the evaluation of $\underline{\mathbf{comb}}_\mathrm{bad}$ can then be based on standard lens composition: $\mathcal{L}_0[\![\underline{\mathbf{comb}}_\mathrm{bad}\ E\ E']\!] = comb\ \mathcal{L}[\![E]\!] \mathbin{\hat{\circ}} \mathcal{L}_0[\![E']\!]$ (we omit the straightforward concrete evaluation rules), where E and E' is the unidirectional evaluation results of e and e' (notice that a residual expression is also an expression), and $\hat{\circ}$ is the lens composition combinator [7] defined by:

$(\hat{\circ}) \in Lens\ B\ C \to Lens\ A\ B \to Lens\ A\ C$
$get\ (\ell_2 \mathbin{\hat{\circ}} \ell_1)\ a \quad = get\ \ell_2\ (get\ \ell_1\ a)$
$put\ (\ell_2 \mathbin{\hat{\circ}} \ell_1)\ a\ c' = put\ \ell_1\ a\ (put\ \ell_2\ (get\ \ell_1\ a)\ c')$

The combinator preserves $\preceq$-well-behavedness, and thus $\underline{\mathbf{comb}}_\mathrm{bad}$ guarantees correctness. However, as discussed extensively in the case of **case**, this "closedness" requirements prevents flexible use of variables and creates a major obstacle in programming.

So instead of the plain *comb*, we shall assume a parameterised version $pcomb \in Lens\ (T \times [\![\sigma]\!])\ [\![\tau]\!] \to Lens\ (T \times [\![\sigma']\!])\ [\![\tau']\!]$ that allows each source to have an extra component T, which is expected to be kept track of by the combinator without modification. Here T is assumed to have a partial merging operator $(\Upsilon) \in T \to T \to T$ and a minimum element, and *pcomb* may use these facts in its definition. By using *pcomb*, we can give a corresponding language construct **comb** with a binder, typed as follows.

$$\frac{\Gamma; \Delta, x : \sigma \vdash e : \mathbf{B}\tau \quad \Gamma; \Delta \vdash e' : \mathbf{B}\sigma'}{\Gamma; \Delta \vdash \mathbf{comb}\ (x.e)\ e' : \mathbf{B}\tau'}$$

We give its unidirectional evaluation rule as

$$\frac{e \Downarrow_U E \quad e' \Downarrow_U E'}{\mathbf{comb}\ (x.e)\ e' \Downarrow_U \mathbf{comb}\ E\ E'}$$

We omit the *get/put* evaluation rules, which are straightforwardly obtained from the following equation.

$$\mathcal{L}_0[\![\mathbf{comb}\ E\ E']\!] = pcomb\ (unEnv_x\ \mathcal{L}_0[\![E]\!])\ \hat{\circ}\ \langle idL, \mathcal{L}_0[\![E']\!] \rangle$$

where $unEnv_x \in Lens\ ([\![\Delta \uplus \{x : \sigma\}]\!])\ [\![\tau]\!] \to Lens\ ([\![\Delta]\!] \times [\![\sigma]\!])\ [\![\tau]\!]$ and $\langle -, - \rangle \in Lens\ [\![\Delta]\!]\ A \to Lens\ [\![\Delta]\!]\ B \to Lens\ [\![\Delta]\!]\ (A \times B)$ are lens combinators defined for any Δ as:

$$get\ (unEnv_x\ \ell)\ (\mu, v)\ = get\ \ell\ (\mu \uplus \{x = v\})$$
$$put\ (unEnv_x\ \ell)\ (\mu, v)\ u = (\mu', v')$$
$$\mathbf{where}\ \mu' \uplus \{x = v'\} = (put\ \ell\ (\mu \uplus \{x = v\})\ v) \triangleleft \{x = v\}$$

$$get\ \langle \ell_1, \ell_2 \rangle\ \mu\ = (get\ \ell_1\ \mu, get\ \ell_2\ \mu)$$
$$put\ \langle \ell_1, \ell_2 \rangle\ \mu\ (a, b) = put\ \ell_1\ \mu\ a \Upsilon\ put\ \ell_2\ \mu\ b$$

Both combinators preserve $\preceq$-well-behavedness, where we assume the component-wise ordering on pairs. No "closedness" requirement is imposed on e in this version. From the construct, we can construct a higher-order function $\lambda f.\lambda z.\mathbf{comb}\ (x.f\ x)\ z : (\mathbf{B}\sigma \to \mathbf{B}\tau) \to \mathbf{B}\sigma' \to \mathbf{B}\tau'$. That is, in HOBiT, lens combinators are just higher-order functions, as long as they permit the above-mentioned parameterisation. This observation means that we are able to systematically derive language constructs from lens combinators; as a matter of fact, the semantics of **case** is derived from a variant of the *cond* combinator [7].

Even better, the parametrised *pcomb* can be systematically constructed from the definition of *comb*. For *comb*, it is typical that $get\ (comb\ \ell)$ only uses $get\ \ell$, and $put\ (comb\ \ell)$ uses $put\ \ell$; that is, *comb* essentially consists of two functions of types $([\![\sigma]\!] \to [\![\tau]\!]) \to ([\![\sigma']\!] \to [\![\tau']\!])$ and $([\![\sigma]\!] \to [\![\tau]\!] \to [\![\sigma]\!]) \to ([\![\sigma']\!] \to [\![\tau']\!] \to [\![\sigma']\!])$. Then, we can obtain *pcomb* of the above type merely by "monad"ifying the two functions: using the reader monad $T \to -$ for the former and the composition of the reader and writer monads $T \to (-, T)$ backwards for the latter suffice to construct *pcomb*.

A remaining issue is to ensure that *pcomb* preserves $\preceq$-well-behavedness, which ensures **comb** $(x.e)\ e' \in \mathcal{E}_\Delta[\![\mathbf{B}\tau']\!]$ under the assumptions $e \in \mathcal{E}_{\Delta \uplus \{x:\sigma\}}[\![\mathbf{B}\tau]\!]$ and $e' \in \mathcal{E}_\Delta[\![\mathbf{B}\sigma']\!]$. Currently, such a proof has to be done manually, even though *comb* preserves well-behavedness and *pcomb* is systematically constructed. Whether we can lift the correctness proof for *comb* to *pcomb* in a systematic way will be an interesting future exploration.

5.3 Guards

Guards used for branching are merely syntactic sugar in ordinary unidirectional languages such as Haskell. But interestingly, they actually increase the expressive power of HOBiT, by enabling inspection of updatable values without making the inspection functions bidirectional.

For example, Glück and Kawabe's reversible equivalence check [10] can be implemented in HOBiT as follows.

$eqCheck :: \mathbf{B}\sigma \to \mathbf{B}\sigma \to \mathbf{B}(Either\ (\sigma, \sigma)\ \sigma)$
$eqCheck\ x\ y = \underline{\mathbf{case}}\ (x, y)\ \underline{\mathbf{of}}$
$\quad (x', y')\ |\ x' == y'\ \to \underline{\mathsf{Right}}\ x'\quad \underline{\mathbf{with}}\ isRight\ \underline{\mathbf{by}}\ (\lambda\_.\lambda(\mathsf{Right}\ x).(x, x))$
$\quad (x', y')\ |\ otherwise\ \to \underline{\mathsf{Left}}\ (x', y')\ \underline{\mathbf{with}}\ isLeft\ \ \underline{\mathbf{by}}\ (\lambda\_.\lambda(\mathsf{Left}\ (x, y)).(x, y))$

Here, $(-, -)$ is the bidirectional version of the pair constructor. The exit condition *isRight* checks whether a value is headed by the constructor Right, and *isLeft* by Left. Notice that the backwards transformation of *eqCheck* fails when the updated view is Left (v, v) for some v.

5.4 Syntax Sugar for Reconciliation Functions

In the general form, reconciliation functions take in two arguments for the computation of the new source. But as we have seen, very often the arguments are not used in the definition and therefore redundant. This observation motivates the following syntax sugar.

$$p \to e\ \underline{\mathbf{with}}\ e'\ \underline{\mathbf{default}}\ \{x_1 = e_1''; \ldots; x_n = e_n''\}$$

Here, $x_1, \ldots, x_n$ are the free variables in p. This syntax sugar is translated as:

$$p \to e\ \underline{\mathbf{with}}\ e'\ \underline{\mathbf{by}}\ \lambda\_.\lambda\_.p[e_1''/x_1, \ldots, e_n''/x_n]$$

Furthermore, it is also possible to automatically derive some default values from their types. This idea can be effectively implemented if we extend HOBiT with type classes.

5.5   Inference of Exit Conditions

It is possible to infer exit conditions from their surrounding contexts; an idea that has been studied in the literature of invertible programming [11,20], and may benefit from range analysis.

Our prototype implementation adopts a very simple inference that constructs an exit condition $\lambda x.\mathbf{case}\ x\ \mathbf{of}\ \{p_e \to \mathsf{True};\ \_ \to \mathsf{False}\}$ for each branch, where p_e is the skeleton of the branch body e, constructed by replacing bidirectional constructors with the unidirectional counterparts, and non-constructor expressions with $\_$. For example, from $a : appendB\ x'\ y$, we obtain the pattern $\_ : \_$. This embarrassingly simple inference has proven to be handy for developing larger HOBiT programs as we will see in Sect. 6.

6   An Involved Example: Desugaring

In this section, we demonstrate the programmability of HOBiT using the example of bidirectional desugaring [26]. Desugaring is a standard process for most programming languages, and making it bidirectional allows information in desugared form to be propagated back to the surface programs. It is argued convincingly in [26] that such bidirectional propagation (coined *resugaring*) is effective in mapping reduction sequences of desugared programs into those of the surface programs.

Let us consider a small programming language that consists of **let**, **if**, Boolean constants, and predefined operators.

> **data** $E = \mathsf{ELet}\ E\ E\ |\ \mathsf{EVar}\ Int\ |\ \mathsf{EIf}\ E\ E\ E\ |\ \mathsf{ETrue}\ |\ \mathsf{EFalse}\ |\ \mathsf{EOp}\ Name\ [E]$
> **type** $Name = String$

Variables are represented as de Bruijn indices.

Some operators in this language are syntactic sugar. For example, we may want to desugar

> $\mathsf{EOp}\ \texttt{"not"}\ [e]$ as $\mathsf{EIf}\ e\ \mathsf{EFalse}\ \mathsf{ETrue}.$

Also, $e_1\ |\ |\ e_2$ can be transformed to **let** $x = e_1$ **in if** x **then** x **else** e_2, which in our mini-language is the following.

> $\mathsf{EOp}\ \texttt{"or"}\ [e_1, e_2]$ as $\mathsf{ELet}\ e_1\ (\mathsf{EIf}\ (\mathsf{EVar}\ 0)\ (\mathsf{EVar}\ 0)\ (shift\ 0\ e_2))$

Here, $shift\ n$ is the standard shifting operator for de Bruijn indexed-term that increments the variables that have indices greater than n (these variables are "free" in the given expression). We will program a bidirectional version of the above desugaring process in Figs. 7 and 8, with the particular goal of keeping the result of a backward execution as close as possible to the original sugared form (so that it is not merely a "decompilation" in the sense that the original source has to be consulted).

$composB :: (BE \to BE) \to BE \to BE$

$composB\ f\ x = \underline{\text{case}}\ x\ \underline{\text{of}}$

Elf $e_1\ e_2\ e_3$	$\to \underline{\text{Elf}}\ (f\ e_1)\ (f\ e_2)\ (f\ e_3)$	$\underline{\text{by}}\ recE$
ELet $e_1\ e_2$	$\to \underline{\text{ELet}}\ (f\ e_1)\ (f\ e_2)$	$\underline{\text{by}}\ recE$
EVar n	$\to \underline{\text{EVar}}\ n$	$\underline{\text{by}}\ recE$
ETrue	$\to \underline{\text{ETrue}}$	
EFalse	$\to \underline{\text{EFalse}}$	
EOp $n\ es$	$\to \underline{\text{EOp}}\ n\ (mapB\ \text{ETrue}\ f\ es')$	$\underline{\text{by}}\ recE$

$mapB :: a \to (Ba \to Bb) \to B[a] \to B[b]$

$mapB\ def\ z = \underline{\text{case}}\ z\ \underline{\text{of}}$

$[] \quad \to \underline{[]}$

$a : x \to f\ a \underline{:}\ mapB\ def\ x\ \underline{\text{default}}\ \{a = def; x = []\}$

$recE :: E \to E \to E$

$recE\ e\ (\text{Elf}\ \_\ \_\ \_) = \text{Elf ETrue}\ e\ e$

$recE\ e\ (\text{ELet}\ \_\ \_) = \text{ELet}\ e\ (shift\ 0\ e)$

$recE\ e\ (\text{EOp}\ n\ \_) = toOp\ n\ e$

$recE\ e\ e' \qquad = e'$

$toOp :: Name \to E \to E$

$toOp\ n\ e =$

$\quad \text{let}\ k = fromJust\ (lookup\ n\ arities)$

$\quad \text{in EOp}\ (replicate\ k\ e)$

Fig. 7. $composB$: a useful building block

$shiftB :: Int \to BE \to BE$

$shiftB\ n\ e = \underline{\text{case}}\ e\ \underline{\text{of}}$

ELet $e_1\ e_2$	$\to \underline{\text{ELet}}\ (shiftB\ n\ e_1)\ (shiftB\ (n+1)\ e_2)$		$\underline{\text{default}}\ \{e_1 = \text{ETrue}; e_2 = \text{EFalse}\}$
EVar $m \mid m < n$	$\to \underline{\text{EVar}}\ m$	$\underline{\text{with}}\ varLT\ n$	$\underline{\text{default}}\ m = 0$
EVar $m \mid m \geq n$	$\to \underline{\text{EVar}}\ (incB\ m)$	$\underline{\text{with}}\ varGT\ n$	$\underline{\text{default}}\ m = n+1$
e'	$\to composB\ (shiftB\ n)\ e'$	$\underline{\text{with}}\ nonLetVar$	$\underline{\text{by}}\ recE$

$desugarB :: BE \to BE$

$desugarB\ e = \underline{\text{case}}\ e\ \underline{\text{of}}$

EOp "or" $[e_1, e_2]$	$\to \underline{\text{ELet}}\ (desugarB\ e_1)\ (\underline{\text{Elf}}\ (\underline{\text{EVar}}\ 0)\ (\underline{\text{EVar}}\ 0)\ (desugarB\ (shiftB\ 0\ e_2)))$
	$\qquad\qquad\qquad\qquad\qquad \underline{\text{by}}\ (\lambda s.\lambda\_.toOp\ \text{"or"}\ s)$
EOp "not" $[e]$	$\to \underline{\text{Elf}}\ e\ \underline{\text{EFalse}}\ \underline{\text{ETrue}}\quad \underline{\text{by}}\ (\lambda s.\lambda\_.toOp\ \text{"not"}\ s)$
e'	$\to composB\ desugarB\ e'\ \underline{\text{by}}\ recE$

$varLT\ n\ (\text{EVar}\ m)$	$= m < n$	$nonLetVar\ (\text{ELet}\ \_\ \_)$	$= \text{False}$
$varLT\ n\ \_$	$= \text{False}$	$nonLetVar\ (\text{EVar}\ \_)$	$= \text{False}$
$varGT\ n\ (\text{EVar}\ m)$	$= m > n$	$nonLetVar\ e$	$= \text{True}$
$varGT\ n\ \_$	$= \text{False}$		

Fig. 8. $desugarB$: bidirectional desugring

We start with an auxiliary function $compos$ [4] in Fig. 7, which is a useful building block for defining shifting and desugaring. We have omitted the straightforward exit conditions; they will be inferred as explained in Sect. 5.5. The function $mapB$ is the bidirectional map. The reconciliation function $recE$ tries to preserves as much source structure as possible by reusing the original source e. Here, $arities :: [(Name, Int)]$ maps operator names to their arities (i.e. $arities = [(\text{"or"}, 2), (\text{"not"}, 1)]$). The function $shift$ is the standard uni-directional shifting function. We omit its definition as it is similar to the bidirectional version in Fig. 8. Note that **default** is syntactic sugar for reconciliation function introduced in Sect. 5.4. Here, $incB$ is the bidirectional increment function defined in Sect. 5.1. Thanks to $composB$, we only need to define the interesting parts in the definitions of $shiftB$ and $desugarB$. The reconciliation functions *recE* and *toOp* try to keep as much source information as possible, which enables the behaviour that the backwards execution produces "not" and "or" in the sugared form only if the original expression has the sugar.

Consider a sugared expression EOp "or" [EOp "not" [ETrue], EOp "not" [EFalse]] as a source *source*.

```
HOBiT> :get desugarB source
ELet (EIf ETrue EFalse ETrue) (EIf (EVar 0) (EVar 0) (EIf EFalse EFalse ETrue)
{- let x = (if True then False else True)
   in if x then x else (if False then False else True) -}
```

The following updated views may be obtained by reductions from the view.

{- *view*₁ ≡ let x = False in if x then x else (if False then False else True) -}
*view*₁ = ELet EFalse (EIf (EVar 0) (EVar 0) (EIf EFalse EFalse ETrue))

{- *view*₂ ≡ if False then False else (if False then False else True) -}
*view*₂ = EIf EFalse EFalse (EIf EFalse EFalse ETrue)

{- *view*₃ ≡ if False then False else True -}
*view*₃ = EIf EFalse EFalse ETrue

The following are the corresponding backward transformation results.

```
HOBiT> :put desugarB source view₁
EOp "or" [EFalse, EOp "not" [EFalse]]
HOBiT> :put desugarB source view₂
EIf EFalse EFalse (EOp "not" [EFalse]
HOBiT> :put desugarB source view₃
EOp "not" [False]
```

As the AST structure of the view is changed, all of the three cases require branch-switching in the backwards executions; our program handles it with ease. For *view*₂, the top-level expression EIf EFalse EFalse ... does not have a corresponding sugared form. Our program keeps the top level unchanged, and proceeds to the subexpression with correct resugaring, a behaviour enabled by the appropriate use of reconciliation function (the first line of *recE* for this particular case) in *composB*.

If we were to present the above results as the evaluation steps in the surface language, one may argue that the second result above does not correspond to a valid evaluation step in the surface language. In [26], AST nodes introduced in desugaring are marked with the information of the original sugared syntax, and resugaring results containing the marked nodes will be skipped, as they do not correspond to any reduction step in the surface language. The marking also makes the backwards behaviour more predictable and stable for drastic changes on the view, as the desugaring becomes injective with this change. This technique is orthogonal to our exploration here, and may be combined with our approach.

7 Related Work

Controlling Backwards Behaviour. In addition to $put \in S \rightarrow V \rightarrow S$, many lens languages [3] supply a *create* $\in V \rightarrow S$ (which is in essence a right-inverse of *get*) to be used when the original source data is unavailable. This happens when new data is inserted in the view, which does not have any corresponding source for *put* to execute, or when branch-switching happens but with no reconciliation function available. Being a right-inverse, *create* does not fail (assuming it terminates), but since it is not guided by the original source, the results are more arbitrary. We do not include *create* in HOBiT, as it complicates the system without offering obvious benefits. Our branch-switching facilities are perfectly capable of handling missing source data via reconciliation functions.

Using exit conditions in branching constructs for backwards evaluation can be found in a number of related fields: bidirectional transformation [7], reversible computation [34] and program inversion [11,20]. Our design of **case** is inspired by the *cond* combinator in the lens framework [7] and the if-statement in Janus [34]. A similar combinator is *Case* in BiGUL [16], where a branch has a function performing a similar role as an exit condition, but taking the original source in addition. This difference makes *Case* more expressive than *cond*; for example, *Case* can implement matching lenses [2]. Our design of **case** follows *cond* for its relative simplicity, but the same underlying technique can be applied to *Case* as mentioned in Sect. 5.2. In the context of *bidirectionalization* [19,29,30] there is the idea of "Plug-ins" [31] that are similar to reconciliation functions in the sense that source values can be adapted to direct backwards execution.

Applicative Lenses. The applicative lens framework [21,23] provides a way to use λ-abstraction and function application as in normal functional programming to compose lenses. Note that this use of "applicative" refers to the classical applicative (functional) programming style, and is not directly related to Applicative functor in Haskell. In this sense, it shares a similar goal to us. But crucially, applicative lens lacks HOBiT's ability to allow λ-bound variables to be used freely, and as a result suffers from the same limitation of lens languages. There are also a couple of technical differences between applicative lens and our work: applicative lens is based on Yoneda embedding while ours is based on separating Γ and Δ and having three semantics (Sect. 4); and applicative lens is implemented as an embedded DSL, while HOBiT is given as a standalone language. Embedded implementation of HOBiT is possible, but a type-correct embedding would expose the handling of environment Δ to programmers, which is undesirable.

Lenses and Their Extensions. As mentioned in Sect. 1, the most common way to construct lenses is by using combinators [3,7,8], in which lenses are treated as opaque objects and composed by using lens combinators. Our goal in this paper is to enhance the programmability of lens programming, while keeping its expressive power as possible. In HOBiT, primitive lenses can be represented as functions on **B**-typed values (Sect. 5.1), and lens combinators satisfying certain conditions can be represented as language construct with binders (Sect. 5.2), which is at least enough to express the original lenses in [7].

Among extensions of the lens language [2,3,7–9,16,17,27,32], there exists a few that extend the classical lens model [7], namely quotient lenses [8], symmetric lenses [14], and edit-based lenses [15]. A natural question to ask is whether our development, which is based on the classical lenses, can be extended to them. The answer depends on treatment of value environments μ in *get* and *put*. In our semantics, we assume a non-linear system as we can use the same variable in μ any number of times. This requires us to extend the classical lens to allow merging (Υ) and defaulting ($\lhd$) operations in *put* with $\preceq$-well-behavedness, but makes the syntax and type system of HOBiT simple, and HOBiT free from the design issues of linear programming languages [25]. Such extension of lenses would be applicable to some kinds of lens models, including quotient lenses and symmetric lenses, but its applicability is not clear in general. Also, we want to mention that allowing duplications in bidirectional transformation is still open, as it essentially entails multiple views and the synchronization among them.

8   Conclusion

We have designed HOBiT, a higher-order bidirectional programming language in which lenses are represented as functions and lens combinators are represented as language constructs with binders. The main advantage of HOBiT is that users can program in a style similar to conventional functional programming, while still enjoying the benefits of lenses (i.e., the expressive power and well-behavedness guarantee). This has allowed us to program realistic examples with relative ease.

HOBiT for the first time introduces a truly "functional" way of constructing bidirectional programs, which opens up a new area of future explorations. Particularly, we have just started to look at programming techniques in HOBiT. Moreover, given the resemblance of HOBiT code to that in conventional languages, the application of existing programming tools becomes plausible.

Acknowledgements. We thank Shin-ya Katsumata, Makoto Hamana and Kazuyuki Asada for their helpful comments on the category theory and denotational semantics, from which our formal discussions originate. The work was partially supported by JSPS KAKENHI Grant Numbers 24700020, 15K15966, and 15H02681.

References

1. Bancilhon, F., Spyratos, N.: Update semantics of relational views. ACM Trans. Database Syst. **6**(4), 557–575 (1981). https://doi.org/10.1145/319628.319634
2. Barbosa, D.M.J., Cretin, J., Foster, N., Greenberg, M., Pierce, B.C.: Matching lenses: alignment and view update. In: Hudak, P., Weirich, S. (eds.) ICFP, pp. 193–204. ACM (2010). https://doi.org/10.1145/1863543.1863572
3. Bohannon, A., Foster, J.N., Pierce, B.C., Pilkiewicz, A., Schmitt, A.: Boomerang: resourceful lenses for string data. In: Necula, G.C., Wadler, P. (eds.) POPL, pp. 407–419. ACM (2008). https://doi.org/10.1145/1328438.1328487
4. Bringert, B., Ranta, A.: A pattern for almost compositional functions. J. Funct. Program. **18**(5–6), 567–598 (2008). https://doi.org/10.1017/S0956796808006898

5. Davies, R., Pfenning, F.: A modal analysis of staged computation. J. ACM **48**(3), 555–604 (2001). https://doi.org/10.1145/382780.382785
6. Fegaras, L.: Propagating updates through XML views using lineage tracing. In: Li, F., Moro, M.M., Ghandeharizadeh, S., Haritsa, J.R., Weikum, G., Carey, M.J., Casati, F., Chang, E.Y., Manolescu, I., Mehrotra, S., Dayal, U., Tsotras, V.J. (eds.) ICDE, pp. 309–320. IEEE (2010). https://doi.org/10.1109/ICDE.2010.5447896
7. Foster, J.N., Greenwald, M.B., Moore, J.T., Pierce, B.C., Schmitt, A.: Combinators for bidirectional tree transformations: a linguistic approach to the view-update problem. ACM Trans. Program. Lang. Syst. **29**(3) (2007). https://doi.org/10.1145/1232420.1232424
8. Foster, J.N., Pilkiewicz, A., Pierce, B.C.: Quotient lenses. In: Hook, J., Thiemann, P. (eds.) ICFP, pp. 383–396. ACM (2008). https://doi.org/10.1145/1411204.1411257
9. Foster, N., Matsuda, K., Voigtländer, J.: Three complementary approaches to bidirectional programming. In: Gibbons, J. (ed.) Generic and Indexed Programming. LNCS, vol. 7470, pp. 1–46. Springer, Heidelberg (2012). https://doi.org/10.1007/978-3-642-32202-0_1
10. Glück, R., Kawabe, M.: A program inverter for a functional language with equality and constructors. In: Ohori, A. (ed.) APLAS 2003. LNCS, vol. 2895, pp. 246–264. Springer, Heidelberg (2003). https://doi.org/10.1007/978-3-540-40018-9_17
11. Glück, R., Kawabe, M.: Revisiting an automatic program inverter for lisp. SIGPLAN Not. **40**(5), 8–17 (2005). https://doi.org/10.1145/1071221.1071222
12. Hegner, S.J.: Foundations of canonical update support for closed database views. In: Abiteboul, S., Kanellakis, P.C. (eds.) ICDT 1990. LNCS, vol. 470, pp. 422–436. Springer, Heidelberg (1990). https://doi.org/10.1007/3-540-53507-1_93
13. Hidaka, S., Hu, Z., Inaba, K., Kato, H., Matsuda, K., Nakano, K.: Bidirectionalizing graph transformations. In: Hudak, P., Weirich, S. (eds.) ICFP, pp. 205–216. ACM (2010). https://doi.org/10.1145/1863543.1863573
14. Hofmann, M., Pierce, B.C., Wagner, D.: Symmetric lenses. In: Ball, T., Sagiv, M. (eds.) POPL, pp. 371–384. ACM (2011). https://doi.org/10.1145/1926385.1926428
15. Hofmann, M., Pierce, B.C., Wagner, D.: Edit lenses. In: Field, J., Hicks, M. (eds.) POPL, pp. 495–508. ACM (2012). https://doi.org/10.1145/2103656.2103715
16. Hu, Z., Ko, H.S.: Principles and practice of bidirectional programming in BiGUL. Oxford Summer School on Bidirectional Transformations (2017). https://bitbucket.org/prl_tokyo/bigul/raw/master/SSBX16/tutorial.pdf. Accessed 18 Oct 2017
17. Hu, Z., Mu, S.-C., Takeichi, M.: A programmable editor for developing structured documents based on bidirectional transformations. In: Heintze, N., Sestoft, P. (eds.) PEPM, pp. 178–189. ACM (2004). https://doi.org/10.1145/1014007.1014025
18. Jung, A., Tiuryn, J.: A new characterization of lambda definability. In: Bezem, M., Groote, J.F. (eds.) TLCA 1993. LNCS, vol. 664, pp. 245–257. Springer, Heidelberg (1993). https://doi.org/10.1007/BFb0037110
19. Matsuda, K., Hu, Z., Nakano, K., Hamana, M., Takeichi, M.: Bidirectionalization transformation based on automatic derivation of view complement functions. In: Hinze, R., Ramsey, N. (eds.) ICFP, pp. 47–58. ACM (2007). https://doi.org/10.1145/1291151.1291162
20. Matsuda, K., Mu, S.-C., Hu, Z., Takeichi, M.: A grammar-based approach to invertible programs. In: Gordon, A.D. (ed.) ESOP 2010. LNCS, vol. 6012, pp. 448–467. Springer, Heidelberg (2010). https://doi.org/10.1007/978-3-642-11957-6_24
21. Matsuda, K., Wang, M.: Applicative bidirectional programming: mixing lenses and semantic bidirectionalization. J. Funct. Program. Accepted 14 Feb 2018

22. Matsuda, K., Wang, M.: "Bidirectionalization for free" for monomorphic transformations. Sci. Comput. Program. **111**(1), 79–109 (2014). https://doi.org/10.1016/j.scico.2014.07.008

23. Matsuda, K., Wang, M.: Applicative bidirectional programming with lenses. In: Fisher, K., Reppy, J.H. (eds.) ICFP, pp. 62–74. ACM (2015). https://doi.org/10.1145/2784731.2784750

24. Moggi, E.: Functor categories and two-level languages. In: Nivat, M. (ed.) FoSSaCS 1998. LNCS, vol. 1378, pp. 211–225. Springer, Heidelberg (1998). https://doi.org/10.1007/BFb0053552

25. Morris, J.G.: The best of both worlds: linear functional programming without compromise. In: Garrigue, J., Keller, G., Sumii, E. (eds.) ICFP, pp. 448–461. ACM (2016). https://doi.org/10.1145/2951913.2951925

26. Pombrio, J., Krishnamurthi, S.: Resugaring: lifting evaluation sequences through syntactic sugar. In: O'Boyle, M.F.P., Pingali, K. (eds.) PLDI, pp. 361–371. ACM (2014). https://doi.org/10.1145/2594291.2594319

27. Rajkumar, R., Foster, N., Lindley, S., Cheney, J.: Lenses for web data. ECEASST **57** (2013). https://doi.org/10.14279/tuj.eceasst.57.879

28. Stevens, P.: A landscape of bidirectional model transformations. In: Lämmel, R., Visser, J., Saraiva, J. (eds.) GTTSE 2007. LNCS, vol. 5235, pp. 408–424. Springer, Heidelberg (2008). https://doi.org/10.1007/978-3-540-88643-3_10

29. Voigtländer, J.: Bidirectionalization for free! (pearl). In: Shao, Z., Pierce, B.C. (eds.) POPL, pp. 165–176. ACM (2009). https://doi.org/10.1145/1480881.1480904

30. Voigtländer, J., Hu, Z., Matsuda, K., Wang, M.: Combining syntactic and semantic bidirectionalization. In: Hudak, P., Weirich, S. (eds.) ICFP, pp. 181–192. ACM (2010). https://doi.org/10.1145/1863543.1863571

31. Voigtländer, J., Hu, Z., Matsuda, K., Wang, M.: Enhancing semantic bidirectionalization via shape bidirectionalizer plug-ins. J. Funct. Program. **23**(5), 515–551 (2013). https://doi.org/10.1017/S0956796813000130

32. Wang, M., Gibbons, J., Matsuda, K., Hu, Z.: Refactoring pattern matching. Sci. Comput. Program. **78**(11), 2216–2242 (2013). https://doi.org/10.1016/j.scico.2012.07.014

33. Xiong, Y., Liu, D., Hu, Z., Zhao, H., Takeichi, M., Mei, H.: Towards automatic model synchronization from model transformations. In: Stirewalt, R.E.K., Egyed, A., Fischer, B. (eds.) ASE, pp. 164–173. ACM (2007). https://doi.org/10.1145/1321631.1321657

34. Yokoyama, T., Axelsen, H.B., Glück, R.: Principles of a reversible programming language. In: Ramírez, A., Bilardi, G., Gschwind, M. (eds.) CF, pp. 43–54. ACM (2008). https://doi.org/10.1145/1366230.1366239

35. Yu, Y., Lin, Y., Hu, Z., Hidaka, S., Kato, H., Montrieux, L.: Maintaining invariant traceability through bidirectional transformations. In: Glinz, M., Murphy, G.C., Pezzè, M. (eds.) ICSE, pp. 540–550. IEEE (2012). https://doi.org/10.1109/ICSE.2012.6227162

Dualizing Generalized Algebraic Data Types by Matrix Transposition

Klaus Ostermann$^{(\boxtimes)}$ and Julian Jabs

University of Tübingen, Tübingen, Germany
{klaus.ostermann,julian.jabs}@uni-tuebingen.de

Abstract. We characterize the relation between generalized algebraic datatypes (GADTs) with pattern matching on their constructors one hand, and generalized algebraic co-datatypes (GAcoDTs) with copattern matching on their destructors on the other hand: GADTs can be converted mechanically to GAcoDTs by refunctionalization, GAcoDTs can be converted mechanically to GADTs by defunctionalization, and both defunctionalization and refunctionalization correspond to a transposition of the matrix in which the equations for each constructor/destructor pair of the (co-)datatype are organized. We have defined a calculus, $GADT^T$, which unifies GADTs and GAcoDTs in such a way that GADTs and GAcoDTs are merely different ways to partition the program.

We have formalized the type system and operational semantics of $GADT^T$ in the Coq proof assistant and have mechanically verified the following results: (1) The type system of $GADT^T$ is sound, (2) defunctionalization and refunctionalization can translate GADTs to GAcoDTs and back, (3) both transformations are type- and semantics-preserving and are inverses of each other, (4) (co-)datatypes can be represented by matrices in such a way the aforementioned transformations correspond to matrix transposition, (5) GADTs are extensible in an exactly dual way to GAcoDTs; we thereby clarify folklore knowledge about the "expression problem".

We believe that the identification of this relationship can guide future language design of "dual features" for data and codata.

1 Introduction

The duality between data and codata, between construction and destruction, between smallest and largest fixed points, is a long-standing topic in the PL community. While some languages, such as Haskell, do not distinguish explicitly between data and codata, there has been a "growing consensus" [1] that the two should not be mixed up. Many ideas that are well-known from the data world have counterparts in the codata world. One work that is particularly relevant for this paper are copatterns, also proposed by Abel et al. [1]. Using copatterns,

Electronic supplementary material The online version of this chapter (https://doi.org/10.1007/978-3-319-89884-1_3) contains supplementary material, which is available to authorized users.

© The Author(s) 2018
A. Ahmed (Ed.): ESOP 2018, LNCS 10801, pp. 60–85, 2018.
https://doi.org/10.1007/978-3-319-89884-1_3

the language support for codata is very symmetrical to that for data: Data types are defined in terms of constructors, functions consuming data are defined using pattern matching on constructors; codata types are defined in terms of destructors, functions producing codata are defined using copattern matching on destructors.

Another example of designing dual features for codata is the recently proposed codata version of inductive data types [36]. However, coming up with these counterparts requires ingenuity. The overarching goal of this work is to replace the required ingenuity by a mechanical derivation. A key idea towards this goal has been proposed by Rendel et al. [31], namely to relate the data and codata worlds by refunctionalization [16] and defunctionalization [17,32].

Defunctionalization is a global program transformation to transform higher-order programs into first-order programs. By defunctionalizing a program, higher-order function types are replaced by sum types with one variant per function that exists in the program. For instance, if a program contains two functions of type $Nat \rightarrow Nat$, then these functions are represented by a sum type with two variants, one for each function, whereby the type components of each variant store the content of the free variables that show up in the function definition. Defunctionalized function calls become calls to a special first-order $apply$ function which pattern-matches on the aforementioned sum type to dispatch the call to the right function body.

Refunctionalization is the inverse transformation, but traditionally it only works (easily) on programs that are in the image of defunctionalization [16]. In particular, it is not clear how to refunctionalize programs when there is more than one function (like $apply$) that pattern-matches on the same data type. Rendel et al. [31] have shown that this problem goes away when functions are generalized to arbitrary codata (with functions being the special codata type with only one $apply$ destructor), because then every pattern-matching function in a program to be refunctionalized can be expressed as another destructor.

The main goal of this work is to extend the de- and refunctionalization correspondence between data and codata to generalized algebraic datatypes (GADTs) [8,40] and their codata counterpart, which we call Generalized Algebraic Codata types (GAcoDTs). More concretely, this paper makes the following contributions.

- We present the syntax, operational semantics, and type system of a language, $GADT^T$, that can express both GADTs and GAcoDTs. In this language, GADTs and GAcoDTs are unified in such a way that they are merely two different representations of an abstract "matrix" interface.
- We show that the type system is sound by proving progress and preservation [39].
- We formally define defunctionalization and refunctionalization, observe that they correspond to matrix transposition, and prove that GADTs and GAcoDTs are indistinguishable after hiding them behind the aforementioned matrix interface. We conclude that defunctionalization and refunctionalization preserve both operational semantics and typing.

- We prove that both GADTs and GAcoDTs can be extended in a modular way (with separate type checking) by "adding rows" to the corresponding matrix. Due to their matrix transposition relation, this means that the extensibility is exactly dual, which clarifies earlier informal results on the "expression problem" [11,33,37].
- The language and all results have been formalized and mechanically verified in the Coq proof assistant. The Coq sources are available in the supplemental material that accompanies this submission.
- As a small side contribution, if one considers only the GADT part of the language, this is to the best of our knowledge the first mechanically verified formalization of GADTs. It is also simpler than previous formalizations of GADTs because it is explicitly typed and hence avoids the complications of type inference.

The remainder of this paper is structured as follows. In Sect. 2 we give an informal overview of our main contributions by means of an example and using conventional concrete syntax. In Sect. 3 we present the syntax, operational semantics, and type system of $GADT^T$. Section 4 presents the aforementioned mechanically verified properties of $GADT^T$. In Sect. 5, we discuss applications and limitations of $GADT^T$, talk about termination/productivity and directions for future work, and describe how we formalized $GADT^T$ in Coq. Finally, Sect. 6 discusses related work and Sect. 7 concludes.

2   Informal Overview

Figure 1 illustrates the language design of $GADT^T$ in terms of an example. The left-hand side shows an example using GADTs and functions that pattern-match on GADT constructors. The right-hand side shows the same example using GAcoDTs and functions that copattern-match on GAcoDT destructors. The right-hand side is the refunctionalization of the left hand side; the left-hand side is the defunctionalization of the right-hand side.

Simply-Typed (Co)Datatypes. Let us first look at the Nat (co)datatype. Every data or codata type has an *arity*: The number of type arguments it receives. Since $GADT^T$ does only feature types of kind *, we simply state the number of type arguments in the (co)data type declaration. Nat receives zero type arguments, hence Nat illustrates the simply-typed setting with no type parameters. Functions in $GADT^T$, like add on the left-hand side, are first-order only; higher-order functions can be encoded as codata instead. Functions always (co)pattern-match on their first argument. (Co)pattern matching on multiple argument as well as nested and deep (co)pattern matching are not supported directly and must be encoded via auxiliary functions. We see that the refunctionalized version of Nat on the right-hand side turns constructors into functions, functions into destructors, and pattern matching into copattern matching. Abel et al. [1] use "dot notation" for copattern matching and destructor application; for instance, they

```
data Nat[0] where
  zero(): Nat
  succ(Nat): Nat

function add(Nat,Nat): Nat where
  add(zero(), x) = x
  add(succ(y),x) = succ(add(y,x))

data List[1] where
  nil[A](): List[A]
  cons[A](A, List[A]): List[A]

function length[A](List[A]): Nat w..
  length[_](nil[_]) = 0
  length[B](cons[_](x,xs)) =
    succ(length[B](xs))

function sum(List[Nat]): Nat
  sum(nil[_]) = 0
  sum(cons[_](x,xs)) = x + sum(xs)

data Tree[1] where
  node(Nat): Tree[Nat]
  branch[A](List[Tree[A]])
              : Tree[List[A]]

function unwrap(Tree[Nat]): Nat w..
  unwrap(node(n)) = n
  unwrap(branch[_](xs)) = impossible

function width[A](Tree[A]): Nat w..
  width[_](node(n)) = 0
  width[_](branch[C](xs)) =
    length[C](xs)
```

```
codata Nat[0] where
  add(Nat,Nat) : Nat

function zero(): Nat where
  add(zero(),x) = x

function succ(Nat): Nat where
  add(succ(y),x) = succ(add(y,x))

codata List[1] where
  length[A](List[A]): Nat
  sum(List[Nat]): Nat

function nil[A](): List[A] where
  length[_](nil[_]) = 0
  sum(nil[_]) = 0

function cons[A](A, List[A]): List[A] w..
  length[B](cons[_](x,xs)) =
    succ(length[B](xs))
  sum(cons[_](x,xs)) = x + sum(xs)

codata Tree[1] where
  unwrap(Tree[Nat]) : Nat
  width[A](Tree[A]): Nat

function node(Nat): Tree[Nat] where
  unwrap(node(n)) = n
  width[_](node(n)) = 0

function branch[A](List[Tree[A]])
              : Tree[List[A]] where
  unwrap(branch[_](xs)) = impossible
  width[_](branch[C](xs)) =
    length[C](xs)
```

Fig. 1. The same example in the data fragment (left) and codata fragment (right)

List[1]	nil[A](): List[A]	cons[A](A, List[A]): List[A]
length[A](List[A]): Nat	length[_](nil[_]) = 0	length[B](cons[_](x,xs)) = succ(length[B](xs))
sum(List[Nat]): Nat	sum(nil[_]) = 0	sum(cons[_](x,xs)) = x + sum(xs)

Fig. 2. Matrix representation of List GADT from Fig. 1 (left)

List[1]	length[A](List[A]): Nat	sum(List[Nat]): Nat
nil[A](): List[A]	length[_](nil[_]) = 0	sum(nil[_]) = 0
cons[A](A, List[A]): List[A]	length[B](cons[_](x,xs)) = succ(length[B](xs))	sum(cons[_](x,xs)) = x + sum(xs)

Fig. 3. Matrix representation of List GAcoDT from Fig. 1 (right). This matrix is the transposition of Fig. 2.

would write `succ(y).add(x)` = `succ(y.add(x))` instead of `add(succ(y),x)` = `succ(add(y,x))` on the right-hand side of Fig. 1. We use the same syntax for constructor calls, function calls, and destructor calls because then the equations are not affected by de- and refunctionalization.

Parametric (Co)Datatypes. The `List` datatype illustrates the classical special case of GADTs with no indexing. Type arguments of constructors, functions, and destructors are both declared and passed via rectangular brackets `[...]` (loosely like in Scala). Like System F, $GADT^T$ has no type inference; all type annotations and type applications must be given explicitly. $GADT^T$ has a redundant way of binding type parameters. When defining an equation of a polymorphic function with a polymorphic first argument, we use square brackets to bind both the type parameters of the function and of the constructor/destructor on which we (co)pattern-match. For instance, in the equation `length[B](cons[_](x,xs))` = ... on the left hand side, `B` is the type parameter of the `length` function, whereas the underscore (which we use if the type argument is not relevant, we could replace it by a proper type variable name) binds the type argument of the constructor with which the list was created. In this example, we could have also written the equation as `length[_](cons[B](x,xs))` = ... because both type parameters must necessarily be the same, but in the general case we need access to both sets of type variables (as the next example will illustrate). It is important that we do not (co)pattern-match on type arguments, since this would destroy parametricity; rather, the `[...]` notation on the left hand side of an equation is only a binding construct for type variables.

Codatatypes also serve as a generalization of first-class functions. The code below shows how a definition of a general function type together with a specific family of first-class function `addn` (that can be passed as an argument and returned as a result), defined by a codata generator function with return type `Function[Nat,Nat]`.

```
codata Function[2] where
  apply[A,B](Function[A,B], A): B

function addn(Nat): Function[Nat,Nat] where
  apply(addn(n),m) = add(n,m)
```

Type Parameter Binding. Of those two sets of type parameter bindings, the one for functions is in a way always redundant because we could use the type variable declaration inside the function declaration instead. For instance, in the equation `length[B](cons[_](x,xs))` = `succ(length[B](xs))` on the left hand side we could use the type parameter `A` of the enclosing function declaration instead. However, in $GADT^T$ the scope of the type variables in the function declaration does not extend to the equations and the type arguments must be bound anew in every equation. The reason for that is that we want to design the equations in such a way that they do not need to be touched when de/refunctionalizing a (co)datatype. For instance, when refunctionalizing a datatype, a function declaration is turned into a destructor declaration and what used to be a type argument that was bound in the enclosing function declaration becomes a type argument that is bound in a remote destructor declaration; to make type-checking modular we hence need a local binding construct. Our main goal in designing $GADT^T$ was not to make it convenient for programmers but to make the relation between GADTs and GAcoDTs as simple as possible; furthermore, a less verbose surface syntax could easily be added on top.

If we look at the corresponding List codatatype on the right-hand side, we see that the sum function from the left-hand side, which accepts only a list of numbers, turns into a destructor that is only applicable to those instances of List whose type parameter is Nat. This is similar to methods in object-oriented programming whose availability depends on type parameters [28], but here we see that this feature arises "mechanically" by the de/refunctionalization correspondence.

GA(co)DTs. The Tree (co)datatype illustrates a usage of GA(co)DTs that cannot be expressed with traditional parametric data types. We can see that by looking at the return type of the constructors of the Tree datatype; they are Tree[Nat] and Tree[List[A]] instead of Tree[A]. The Tree codatatype is also using the power of GAcoDTs in the unwrap destructor[1] because its first argument is different from Tree[A]. The GADT constructor node(Nat): Tree[Nat] turns into a function that returns a Tree[Nat] on the right hand side. The Tree example illustrates two additional issues that did not show up in the earlier examples.

First, it illustrates that type unification may make some pattern matches impossible, as illustrated by the unwrap(branch[_](xs)) = impossible equation on the left hand side. The equation is impossible, because the function argument type Tree[Nat] cannot be unified with the constructor return type Tree[List[A]].[2] In $GADT^T$, we require that pattern matching is always complete, but impossible equations are not type-checked; the right-hand side can hence be filled with any dummy term. Second, the equation width[_](branch[C] (xs)) = length[C](xs) illustrates the case where it is essential that we can bind constructor type arguments; otherwise we would have no name for the type argument we need to pass to length. Such type arguments are sometimes called *existential* or *phantom* [8] because if we have a branch of type Tree[A], we only know that there exists some type that was used in the invocation of the branch constructor, but that type does not show up in the structure of Tree[A].

We see again how both impossible equations and the need to access constructor type arguments translate naturally into corresponding features in the codata world. For impossible equations, we need to check whether the first destructor argument type can be unified with the function return type. Access to existential

---

[1] The unwrap destructor is meant to be used to extract the number from a tree that directly contains a number, i.e., a tree constructed with constructor node.

[2] This fits with our intention that unwrap should only work on a node (which directly contains a number).

constructor type arguments turns into access to local function types; conversely, access to existential destructor type arguments in the codata world turns into access to local function type arguments.

$GADT = GAcoDT^T$. We can see that the relation between GADTs and GAcoDTs is as promised when looking at Figs. 2 and 3. These two figures show a slightly different representation of the List (co)datatype and associated functions from Fig. 1. In this presentation, we have dropped all keywords from the language, such as function, data and codata. The reason for dropping these keywords is that now function signatures in the data fragment look the same as destructor signatures in the codata fragment, and constructor signatures in the data fragment look the same as function signatures in the codata fragment. Figure 2 organizes the datatype in the form of a matrix: the first row lists the datatype and its constructor signatures, the first column lists the signatures of the functions that pattern-match on the datatype, the inner cells represent the equations for each combination of constructor and function. Figure 3 does the same for the List codatatype: The first row lists the codatatype and its destructor signatures, the first column lists the signatures of functions that copattern-match on the codatatype, the inner cells represent the equations for each combination of function and destructor. We can now see that the relation between GADTs and GAcoDTs is now indeed rather simple: It is just matrix transposition.

An essential property of this transformation is that other (co)datatypes and functions are completely unaffected by the transformation. For instance, the Tree datatype (or codatatype, regardless of which version we use) looks the same, regardless of whether we encode List in data or in codata style. Defunctionalization and refunctionalization are still global transformations in that we need to find all functions that pattern-match on a datatype (for refunctionalization) or find all functions that copattern-match on a codatatype (for defunctionalization), but the rest of the program, including all clients of those (co)datatypes and functions, remain the same.

Infinite Codata, Termination, Productivity. The semantics of codata is usually defined via greatest fixed point constructions that include the possibility to represent "infinite" structures, such as streams. This is not the focus of this work, but since our examples so far did not feature such "infinite" structures but we do not want to give the impression that our codata types do somehow lack the expressiveness to express streams and the like, hence we show here an example of how to encode a stream of zeros, both in the codata representation (left) and, defunctionalized, in the data representation (right).

```
codata Stream where                 data Stream where
  head(Stream) : Nat                  zeros() : Stream
  tail(Stream) : Stream
                                    function head(Stream) : Nat
function zeros() : Stream             head(zeros()) = zero()
  head(zeros()) = zero()
  tail(zeros()) = zeros()           function tail(Stream) : Stream
                                      tail(zeros()) = zeros()
```

Codata is also often associated with guarded corecursion to ensure productivity. In the copattern formulation of codata, productivity and termination coincide [2]. Due to our unified treatment of data and codata, a single check is sufficient for both termination/productivity of programs. In Sect. 5.3, we discuss a simple syntactic check that corresponds to both structural recursion and guarded corecursion.

Properties of $GADT^T$. In the remainder of this paper, we formalize $GADT^T$ in a style similar to the matrix representation of (co)datatypes we have just seen. We define typing rules and a small-step operational semantics and prove formal versions of the following informal theorems: (1) The type system of $GADT^T$ is sound (progress and preservation), (2) Defunctionalization and refunctionalization (that is, matrix transposition) of (co)datatypes preserves well-typedness and operational semantics, (3) Both types of matrices are modularly extensible in one dimension, namely by adding more rows to the matrix. This means that we can modularly add constructors or destructors and their respective equations without breaking type soundness as long as the new equations are sound themselves.

3   Formal Semantics

We have formalized $GADT^T$ and all associated theorems and proofs in Coq[3]. Here we present a traditional representation of the formal syntax using context-free grammars, a small-step operational semantics, and a type system.

We have formalized the language in such a way that we abstract over the physical representation of matrices as described in the previous section, hence we do not need to distinguish between GADTs and GAcoDTs. In the following, we say *constructor* to denote either a constructor of a datatype, or a function that copattern-matches on a codatatype. We say *destructor* to denote either a function that pattern-matches on a datatype, or a destructor of a codatatype. The language is defined in terms of constructors and destructors; we will later see that GADTs and GAcoDTs are merely different organizations of destructors and constructors.

3.1   Language Design Rationale

Our main goal in the formalization is to clarify the relation between GADTs and GAcoDTs, and not to design a calculus that is convenient to use as a

---

[3] Full Coq sources are available in the supplemental material.

programming language. Hence we have left out many standard features of programming calculi that would have made the description of that relation more complicated. In particular:

- Like System F, $GADT^T$ requires explicit type annotations and explicit type application. Type inference could be added on top of the calculus, but this is not in the scope of this work.
- (Co)pattern matching is restricted in that every function must necessarily (co)pattern-match on its first argument, hence (co)pattern-matching on multiple arguments or "deep" (co)pattern matching must be encoded by auxiliary functions. Pattern matching is only supported for top-level function definitions; there is no "case" or "match" construct. Functions that are not supposed to (co)pattern-match (like the polymorphic identity function) must be encoded by a function that (co)pattern-matches on a dummy argument of type Unit.
- First-class functions are supported in the form of codata, but anonymous local first-class functions must be encoded via lambda lifting [3,25], that is, they must be encoded as top-level functions where the bindings for the free variables are passed as an extra parameter.
- Due to the abstraction over the physical representation of matrices we have not fixed the physical modular structure (a linearization of the matrix as text) of programs. Type checking of matrices simply iterates over all cells in an unspecified order. However, later on we will characterize GADTs and GAcoDTs as two physical renderings of matrices and formally prove the way in which those program organizations are extensible.

3.2 Notational Conventions

As usual, we use the same letters for both non-terminal symbols and meta-variables, e.g., t stands both for the non-terminal in the grammar for terms but inside inference rules it is a meta-variable that stands for any term. We use the notation $\bar{t}$ to denote a list $t_1, t_2, \ldots, t_{|\bar{t}|}$, where $|\bar{t}|$ is the length of the list. We also use list notation to denote iteration, e.g., $P, \Gamma \vdash \bar{t} : \overline{T}$ means $P, \Gamma \vdash t_1 : T_1, \ldots, P, \Gamma \vdash t_{|\bar{t}|} : T_{|\bar{t}|}$. To keep the notation readable, we write $\bar{x} : \overline{T}$ instead of $\overline{x : T}$ to denote $x_1 : T_1, \ldots, x_n : T_n$.

We use the notation $t[x := t']$ to denote the substitution of all free occurrences of x in t by t', and similarly $T[X := T']$ and $t[X := T']$ for the substitution of type variables in types and terms, respectively.

3.3 Syntax

The syntax of $GADT^T$ is defined in Fig. 4. Types have the form $m[\overline{T}]$, where m is the name of a GADT or GAcoDT (in the following referred to as *matrix name*), and square brackets to denote type application. Types can contain type variables X. In the syntax of terms t, x denotes parameters that are bound by (co)pattern matching and y denotes other parameters. A constructor call $c[\overline{T}](\bar{t})$ takes zero or

$\boxed{\text{Syntax}}$

$$
\begin{array}{llr}
S, T & ::= m[\overline{T}] \mid X & \textit{Types} \\
t & ::= x \mid y \mid c[\overline{T}](\overline{t}) \mid d[\overline{T}](t, \overline{t}) & \textit{Terms} \\
C & ::= c[\overline{X}](\overline{T}) : m[\overline{T}] & \textit{Constructor Signature} \\
D & ::= d[\overline{X}](m[\overline{T}], \overline{T}) : T & \textit{Destructor Signature} \\
e & ::= d[\overline{Y}](c[\overline{X}](\overline{x}), \overline{y}) = t & \textit{Equations} \\
M & = (a, \gamma \in \overline{C}, \delta \in \overline{D}, \gamma \to \delta \to e) & \textit{Matrices} \\
P & = m \mapsto_{fin} M & \textit{Programs} \\
m & \in \textbf{Matrix names} \\
d & \in \textbf{Destructor names} \\
c & \in \textbf{Constructor names} \\
x & \in \textbf{Pattern Variable Names} \\
y & \in \textbf{Variable Names} \\
X, Y & \in \textbf{Type Variables} \\
a & \in \mathbb{N} & \textit{Arities}
\end{array}
$$

$\boxed{\text{Operational Semantics} : P \vdash t \to t'}$

$$
\begin{array}{llr}
u, v & ::= c[\overline{T}](\overline{v}) & \textit{Values} \\
E & ::= c[\overline{T}](\overline{v}, [], \overline{t}) \mid d[\overline{T}](\overline{v}, [], \overline{t}) & \textit{Evaluation Context}
\end{array}
$$

$$
\frac{P \vdash t \to t'}{P \vdash E[t] \to E[t']} \qquad \text{(E-CTX)}
$$

$$
\frac{
\begin{array}{c}
m \mapsto (a, \overline{C}, \overline{D}, lookup) \in P \\
D \in \overline{D} \qquad D = d[\ldots](m[\ldots], \ldots) \\
C \in \overline{C} \qquad C = c[\ldots](\ldots) \\
lookup(C, D) = d[\overline{Y}](c[\overline{X}](\overline{x}), \overline{y}) = t
\end{array}
}{
P \vdash d[\overline{S}](c[\overline{T}](\overline{v}), \overline{u}) \to t[\overline{X} := \overline{S}, \overline{Y} := \overline{T}][\overline{x} := \overline{v}, \overline{y} := \overline{u}]
} \qquad \text{(E-FIRE)}
$$

Fig. 4. Syntax and operational semantics of $GADT^T$

more arguments, whereas a destructor call $d[\overline{T}](t, \overline{t})$ takes at least one argument (namely the one to be destructed). Both destructors and constructors can have type parameters, which must be passed via square brackets.

A constructor signature $c[\overline{X}](\overline{T}) : m[\overline{T}]$ defines the number and types of parameters and the type parameters to the constructed type. Its output type cannot be a type variable but must be some concrete matrix type $m[\overline{T}]$. A destructor signature, on the other hand, must have a concrete matrix type as its first argument and can have an arbitrary return type. Equations $d[\overline{Y}](c[\overline{X}](\overline{x}), \overline{y}) = t$ define what happens when a constructor c meets a destructor d. The $\overline{x}$ bind the components of the constructor, whereas the $\overline{y}$ bind the remaining parameters of the destructor call. We also bind both the type arguments to the constructor $\overline{X}$

and the destructor $\overline{Y}$, such that they can be used inside t. In many cases, the $\overline{X}$ will provide access to the same types as $\overline{Y}$, but in the general case we need both because both constructors and destructors may contain phantom types [8].

Matrices M are an abstract representation of both GADTs and GAcoDTs, together with the functions that pattern-match (for GADTs) or copattern-match (for GAcoDTs) on the GA(co)DTs. A matrix has an arity a (the number of type parameters it receives), a list of constructors γ, and a list of destructors δ. It also has a lookup function that returns an equation for every constructor/destructor pair on which the matrix is defined (hence the type of matrices is a dependent type). There must be an equation for each constructor/destructor pair, but in the case of impossible combinations, the equations are not type-checked and some dummy term can be inserted. A program P is just a finite mapping from matrix names to matrices.

3.4 Operational Semantics

We define the operational semantics, also in Fig. 4, via an evaluation context E, which, together with E-CTX, defines a standard call-by-value left-to-right evaluation order. Not surprisingly, the only interesting rule is E-FIRE, which defines the reduction behavior when a destructor meets a constructor. We look up the corresponding matrix in the program and look up the equation for that constructor/destructor pair. In the body of the equation, t, we perform two substitutions: (1) We substitute the formal type arguments $\overline{X}$ and $\overline{Y}$ by the current type arguments $\overline{S}$ and $\overline{T}$, and (2) we substitute the pattern variables $\overline{x}$ by the components $\overline{v}$ of the constructor and the variables $\overline{y}$ by the current arguments $\overline{u}$.

3.5 Typing

The typing and well-formedness rules are defined in Fig. 5. Let us first look at the typing of terms. The rules for variable lookup are standard. The constructor rule T-CONST checks that the number of type- and term arguments matches the declaration and checks the type of all arguments, whereby the type variables are substituted by the type arguments of the actual constructor call. Constructor names must be globally unique, hence the matrix to which the constructor belongs is not relevant.

This is different for typing destructor calls (T-DEST). A destructor is resolved by first determining the matrix m of the first destructor argument, and then the destructor is looked up in that matrix. It is hence OK if the same destructor name shows up in multiple matrices. When considering codata as "objects" like in object-oriented programming [24], this corresponds to the familiar situation that different classes can define methods with the same name. In the GADT case, this corresponds to allowing multiple pattern-matching functions of the same name that are disambiguated by the type of their first argument.

In WF-EQ, we construct the appropriate typing context to type-check the right hand side of equations. We allow implicit α-renaming of type variables

$$\boxed{\text{Term Typing}: P, \Gamma \vdash t : T}$$

$$\Gamma ::= \epsilon \mid x : T, \Gamma \mid y : T, \Gamma \quad \textit{Typing Contexts}$$

$$\frac{x : T \in \Gamma}{P, \Gamma \vdash x : T} \text{(T-Pvar)}$$

$$\frac{y : T \in \Gamma}{P, \Gamma \vdash y : T} \text{(T-Var)}$$

$$\frac{\begin{array}{c} P, \Gamma \vdash t : m[\overline{T}][\overline{X} := \overline{S}] \\ m \mapsto (\ldots, \ldots d[\overline{X}](m[\overline{T}], \overline{U}) : T \ldots, \ldots) \in P \\ \forall i. P, \Gamma \vdash t_i : U_i[\overline{X} := \overline{S}] \\ |\overline{X}| = |\overline{S}| \qquad |\overline{U}| = |\overline{t}| \end{array}}{P, \Gamma \vdash d[\overline{S}](t, \overline{t}) : T[\overline{X} := \overline{S}]} \text{(T-Dest)}$$

$$\frac{\begin{array}{c} \ldots \mapsto (\ldots c[\overline{X}](\overline{T}) : T \ldots, \ldots, \ldots) \in P \\ \forall i. P, \Gamma \vdash t_i : T_i[\overline{X} := \overline{S}] \\ |\overline{X}| = |\overline{S}| \qquad |\overline{T}| = |\overline{t}| \end{array}}{P, \Gamma \vdash c[\overline{S}](\overline{t}) : T[\overline{X} := \overline{S}]} \text{(T-Const)}$$

$$\boxed{\text{Well-Formedness}}$$

$$\frac{\begin{array}{c} C = c[\overline{X'}](\overline{T}) : m[\overline{S}] \qquad |\overline{X}| = |\overline{X'}| \\ D = d[\overline{Y'}](m[\overline{S'}], \overline{T'}) : T \qquad |\overline{Y}| = |\overline{Y'}| \\ \textit{all-distinct}(\overline{X}, \overline{Y}) \qquad \textit{all-distinct}(\overline{X'}, \overline{Y'}) \\ \textit{most-general-unifier}(m[\overline{S}], m[\overline{S'}]) = \sigma \\ P, \overline{x} : \sigma(\overline{T}), \overline{y} : \sigma(\overline{T'}) \vdash \sigma(t[\overline{X} := \overline{X'}, \overline{Y} := \overline{Y'}]) : \sigma(T) \end{array}}{P, m \vdash d[\overline{Y}](c[\overline{X}](\overline{x}), \overline{y}) = t \text{ OK in } C, D} \text{(Wf-Eq)}$$

$$\frac{\begin{array}{c} C = \ldots : m[\overline{S}] \qquad D = \ldots (m[\overline{S'}], \ldots) : \ldots \\ \textit{most-general-unifier}(m[\overline{S}], m[\overline{S'}]) = \text{error} \end{array}}{P, m \vdash d[\overline{Y}](c[\overline{X}](\overline{x}), \overline{y}) = t \text{ OK in } C, D} \text{(Wf-Infsble)}$$

$$\frac{|\overline{S}| = a \qquad FV(\overline{T}) \subseteq \overline{X} \qquad FV(\overline{S}) \subseteq \overline{X}}{c[\overline{X}](\overline{T}) : m[\overline{S}] \text{ OK in } m, a} \text{(Wf-Constr)}$$

$$\frac{|\overline{S}| = a \qquad FV(\overline{S}) \subseteq \overline{Y} \qquad FV(\overline{T}) \subseteq \overline{Y}}{d[\overline{Y}](m[\overline{S}], \overline{T}) : T \text{ OK in } m, a} \text{(Wf-Destr)}$$

$$\frac{\begin{array}{c} \forall C \in \overline{C}, \forall D \in \overline{D}, \\ C \text{ OK in } m, a \\ D \text{ OK in } m, a \\ P, m \vdash \textit{lookup}(C, D) \text{ OK in } C, D \\ \textit{all-names-distinct}(\overline{D}) \end{array}}{m \mapsto (a, \overline{C}, \overline{D}, \textit{lookup}) \text{ OK in } P} \text{(Wf-Matr)}$$

$$\frac{\begin{array}{c} \forall m \in \textit{dom}(P), m \mapsto P(m) \text{ OK in } P \\ \textit{all-names-distinct}(\textit{ctors}(P)) \end{array}}{P \text{ OK}} \text{(Wf-Prog)}$$

Fig. 5. Typing and well-formedness

to prevent accidental name clashes (checked by *all-distinct*). We compute the most general unifier of the two matrix types in the constructor and destructor, respectively, to combine the type knowledge about the matrix type from the constructor and destructor type. If no such unifier exists, the equation is vacuously well-formed because the particular combination of constructor and destructor can never occur during execution of well-typed terms (WF-INFSBLE). Otherwise, we use the unifier σ and apply it to the given type annotations to type-check the term t. A unifier σ is a mapping from type variables to types, but we also use the notation $\sigma(t)$ and $\sigma(T)$ to apply σ to all occurrences of type variables inside a term t or a type T, respectively.

Constructor and destructor signatures are well-formed if they apply the correct number of type parameters to the matrix type and contain no free type variables (WF-CONSTR and WF-DESTR). A matrix is type-checked by making sure that all constructor and destructor signatures are well-formed, that all equations are well-formed for every constructor/destructor combination, and that destructor names are unique in the matrix (WF-MATR). To check uniqueness of names, we use *all-names-distinct*, which checks for a given list of signatures that all of their names are distinct. A program is well-formed if all of its matrices typecheck and the constructor signatures of the program (retrieved by *ctors*) are globally unique (WF-PROG).

3.6 GADTs and GAcoDTs

In the formalization so far, we have deliberately kept matrices abstract as a kind of abstract data type. Now we can bring in the harvest of our language design. GADTs and GAcoDTs are two different physical representations of matrices, see Fig. 6. They both contain nested vectors of equations and differ only in the order of the indices. With GADTs, the column labels are constructors and the row labels functions and a row corresponds to a function defined by pattern matching, with one equation for each case of the GADT. With GAcoDTs, the column labels are destructors, the row labels are functions, and a row corresponds to a function defined by copattern matching, with one equation for each case of

$$
\begin{aligned}
M_{GADT} &= (a, \gamma \in \overline{C}, \delta \in \overline{D}, \{e_{D,C} | D \in \delta, C \in \gamma\}) \\
M_{GAcoDT} &= (a, \gamma \in \overline{C}, \delta \in \overline{D}, \{e_{C,D} | C \in \gamma, D \in \delta\})
\end{aligned}
$$

$$
\begin{aligned}
mkmatrix \quad &: \; M_{GADT} + M_{GAcoDT} \rightarrow M \\
mkmatrix \quad &= \text{— obvious; omitted}
\end{aligned}
$$

$$
\begin{aligned}
refunctionalize \; &: \; M_{GADT} \rightarrow M_{GAcoDT} \\
refunctionalize \; &= transpose
\end{aligned}
$$

$$
\begin{aligned}
defunctionalize \; &: \; M_{GAcoDT} \rightarrow M_{GADT} \\
defunctionalize \; &= transpose
\end{aligned}
$$

Fig. 6. GADTs and GAcoDTs

the GAcoDT. Hence both *defunctionalize* and *refunctionalize*, which swap the respective organization of the matrix, are just matrix transposition.

4   Properties of $GADT^T$

In this section, we prove type soundness for $GADT^T$, the preservation of typing and operational semantics under de- and refunctionalization, and that our physical matrix representations of GADTs and GAcoDTs are accurate with respect to extension. All of these properties have been formalized and proven in Coq, based upon our Coq formalization of the previous section's formal syntax, semantics, and type system.

4.1   Type Soundness

We start with the usual progress and preservation theorems.

Theorem 1 (Progress). *If P is a well-formed program and t is a term with no free type variables and $P, \epsilon \vdash t : T$, then t is either a value v, or there exists a term t' such that $P \vdash t \rightarrow t'$.*

The proof of this theorem is a simple induction proof using a standard canonical forms lemma [30].

Preservation is much harder to prove. Often, preservation is proved using a substitution lemma which states that the substitution of a (term) variable by a term of the same type does not change the type of terms containing that term variable [30]. In $GADT^T$, this lemma looks as follows:

Lemma 1 (Term Substitution). *If $\bar{t}$ is a list of terms with $P, \epsilon \vdash \bar{t} : \overline{T}$ and $\overline{t'}$ is a list of terms with $P, \epsilon \vdash \overline{t'} : \overline{T'}$ and t is a term with $P, \overline{x} : \overline{T}, \overline{y} : \overline{T'} \vdash t : T$, then $P, \epsilon \vdash t[\overline{x} := \bar{t}, \overline{y} := \overline{t'}] : T$.*

However, in E-FIRE we perform both a substitution of terms and of types, hence the term substitution lemma is not enough to prove preservation; we also need a type substitution lemma.

Lemma 2 (Type Substitution). *If $P, \Gamma \vdash t : T$, then $P, \Gamma[\overline{X} := \overline{T}] \vdash t[\overline{X} := \overline{T}] : T[\overline{X} := \overline{T}]$*

The proof of this lemma requires various auxiliary lemmas about properties (such as associativity) of type substitution. Taken together, these two lemmas are the two main intermediate results to prove the desired preservation theorem.

Theorem 2 (Preservation). *If P is a well-formed program and t is a term with no free type variables and $P, \epsilon \vdash t : T$ and $P \vdash t \rightarrow t'$, then $P, \epsilon \vdash t' : T$.*

4.2 Defunctionalization and Refunctionalization

The preservation of typing and operational semantics by de/refunctionalization is a trivial consequence of the lemma below, which holds due to the fact that both de- and refunctionalization is merely matrix transposition, see Fig. 6, and that the embedding *mkmatrix* of the physical matrices into the abstract representation ignores the organization of the physical matrices.

Lemma 3 (Matrix Transposition)
$\forall m \in M_{GADT}$, $mkmatrix(m) = mkmatrix(refunctionalize(m))$.
$\forall m \in M_{GAcoDT}$, $mkmatrix(m) = mkmatrix(defunctionalize(m))$.

Corollary 1 (Preservation of typing and reduction). *De/refunctionalization of a matrix does not change the well-typedness of a program or the operational semantics of a term.*

4.3 Extensibility

So far, we have seen that our chosen physical matrix representations are amenable to easy proofs of the preservation of properties under de- and refunctionalization. However, are they also indeed accurate representations of GADTs and GAcoDTs? GADTs and GAcoDTs are utilized due to their *extensibility* along the destructor or constructor dimension, respectively, so we want this to be reflected by our representations.

We assume that matrices are represented as a traditional linear program by reading them row-by-row. Adding a new row is a non-invasive operation (adding to the program), whereas adding a column requires changes to the existing program.

We want to be able to extend our matrix representations with a new row, respectively representing the addition of a new destructor or constructor, without breaking well-typedness as long as the *newly added* equations typecheck with respect to the complete new program, and uniqueness of destructor/constructor names is preserved (globally, in the constructor case)[4].

In order to formally state that this is indeed the case, we first formally capture extension of GADT and GAcoDT matrices with the following definitions. These already include the preservation of local uniqueness as a condition, i.e., the name of the newly added destructor or constructor must be fresh within the matrix.

Definition 1 (GADT extension). *Consider an $m \in M_{GADT}$ with $m = (a, \gamma, \delta, \{e_{D,C}|D \in \delta, C \in \gamma\})$. For any $D' \in \overline{D}, D' \notin \delta$, and equations $e_{D',C}$, for each $C \in \gamma$, we call $(a, \gamma, \delta \cup \{D'\}, \{e_{D,C}|D \in \delta \cup \{D'\}, C \in \gamma\})$ a GADT extension of m with D' and $\{e_{D',C}|C \in \gamma\}$.*

---

[4] The counterpart to this property on the side of the operational semantics is that the reduction relation of the new program restricted to terms befitting the old program equals the reduction relation of the old program; this however we omitted as it holds trivially when uniqueness is preserved.

Definition 2 (GAcoDT extension). *Consider an* $m \in M_{GAcoDT}$ *with* $m = (a, \gamma, \delta, \{e_{C,D} | C \in \gamma, D \in \delta\})$. *For any* $C' \in \overline{C}, C' \notin \gamma$, *and equations* $e_{C',D}$, *for each* $D \in \delta$, *we call* $(a, \gamma \cup \{C'\}, \delta, \{e_{C,D} | C \in \gamma \cup \{C'\}, D \in \delta\})$ *a GAcoDT extension of* m *with* C' *and* $\{e_{C',D} | D \in \delta\}$.

We now straightforwardly lift these definitions to programs: A program P' is *a GA(co)DT extension (with some signature and equations) of another program P* if their matrices are identical except for one matrix name, and the underlying physical matrix (packed with *mkmatrix*) assigned to this name under P' is GA(co)DT extension (with this signature and equations) of the underlying physical matrix assigned under P.

Using this terminology we can now formally state and prove the extensibility of GADTs and GAcoDTs:

Theorem 3 (Datatype Extensibility). *If P is a well-formed program, and P' is a GADT extension of P with D' and equations $\{e_{D',C} | C \in \gamma\}$, for the constructor signatures γ of the matrix to be extended, such that $P', m \vdash e_{D',C}$ OK in C, D' for each $C \in \gamma$, then P' is well-formed.*

Theorem 4 (Codatatype Extensibility). *If P is a well-formed program, and P' is a GAcoDT extension of P with C', where the name of C' is different from all constructor names in P, and equations $\{e_{C',D} | D \in \delta\}$, for the destructor signatures δ of the matrix to be extended, such that $P', m \vdash e_{C',D}$ OK in C', D for each $D \in \delta$, then P' is well-formed.*

In other words, in both cases we can type-check each row of a matrix in isolation, and if we put those rows together the resulting matrix and program containing that matrix will be well-formed. The results justify the familiar physical representation of programs where the variants of a GADT are fixed but we can freely add new functions that pattern-match on that GADT (and correspondingly for GAcoDTs).

5   Discussion

In this section we discuss applications and limitations of our work, talk about directions for future work, and describe the Coq formalization of the definitions and proofs.

5.1   Applications

Language Design. The most obvious application of our approach is to guide programming language design, namely by designing its features in such a way that the correspondence by de/refunctionalization is preserved. We believe that we can find "gaps" in existing languages by checking whether the corresponding dual feature exists, or massaging the language feature in such a way that a clear dual exists. For instance, on the datatype and pattern matching side, many features exist that have no clear counterpart on the codata side yet, such as pattern matching on multiple arguments, non-linear pattern matching, or pattern guards [22]. Some vaguely dual features exist on the codata side understood as "objects", e.g. in the form of multi dispatch (such as [10]) or predicate dispatch [21]. We believe that the relation between pattern matching on multiple arguments and multi dispatch is a particularly interesting direction for future work, since it would entail generalizing our two-dimensional matrices to matrices of arbitrary dimension.

Arguably, codata is the essence of object-oriented programming [12]. In any case, we believe that our design can also help to design object-oriented language features. For instance, there has been previous works on "object-oriented" GADTs [20,26] using extensions of generic types with certain classes of constraints. For instance, in Kennedy and Russo's [26] work, a list interface could be defined like this:

```
interface List<A> {
  Integer size();
  Integer sum() where A=Integer; // Kennedy & Russo's syntax
}
```

If we compare this interface with the List codata type in Fig. 1 (right hand side), then we can see that such constraints are readily supported by GAcoDTs; not because this feature was explicitly added but because it arises mechanically from dualizing GADTs.

As another potential influence on language design, we believe that "closedness" under defunctionalization and refunctionalization can be a desirable language design quality that prevents oddities that things can be expressed better using codata than using data (or vice versa). For instance, Carette et al. [5] propose a program representation (basically again a form of Church encoding, hence a codata encoding) that works in a simple Haskell'98 language but whose datatype representation would require GADTs. This suggests a language design flaw in that the codata fragment of functions supports a more powerful type system than the data fragment of (non-generalized) algebraic data types. That is, the type arguments of a codata generator function's result type may be arbitrarily specialized, e.g., the result type might be List[Nat], while the type of a constructor must be fully generic, e.g., List[A]. Our approach gives a criterion on when the type systems for both sides are "in sync".

De/Refunctionalization as a Programmer Tool. Semantics-preserving program transformations are not only interesting on the meta-level of programming language design but also because they define an equivalence relation on programs. For instance, consider the program on the left-hand side of Fig. 7, written in our GAcoDT language. Nat is a representation of Church-encoded[5] natural numbers as a GAcoDT with arity zero and a singular destructor fold with a type

---

[5] This form of typed Church encoding is sometimes called Böhm-Berarducci encoding [4].

```
codata Func[2] where
  apply[A,B](Func[A,B], A) : B

codata Nat[0] where
  fold[A](Nat,A,Func[A,A]) : A

fun zero(): Nat where
  fold[A](zero(),z,s) = z

fun succ(Nat): Nat where
  fold[A](succ(n),z,s) =
    apply[A,A](s,fold[A](n,z,s))
```

```
data Nat[0] where
  zero() : Nat
  succ(Nat) : Nat

fun fold[A](Nat,A,Func[A,A]) : A where
  fold[A](zero(),z,s) = z
  fold[A](succ(n),z,s) =
    apply[A,A](s, fold[A](n,z,s))
```

Fig. 7. Defunctionalizing Church-encoded numbers (left) yields Peano numbers with a fold function (right)

parameter A. Defunctionalizing Nat yields the familiar Peano numbers with the standard fold function (right-hand side).

Such equivalences have been identified as being useful to identify different forms of programs that are "the same elephant". For instance, Olivier Danvy and associates [16,17] have used defunctionalization, refunctionalization, and some other transformations such as CPS-transformation to inter-derive "semantic artifacts" such as big-step semantics, small-step semantics, and abstract machines ("The inter-derivations illustrated here witness a striking unity of computation, be this for reduction semantics, abstract machines, and normalization function: they all truly define the same elephant." – Danvy et al. [15]).

The applicability of these transformations is widened by our approach since we support arbitrary codata and not just functions. Exploring these new possibilities is an interesting area of future work.

Furthermore, programmers can employ our transformation as a tool for a more practical purpose. Consider that at some point during the development of a large software, it might have been determined that the extensibility dimension for a particular aspect should be switched. That is, it is now thought that instead of allowing to add new variants (constructors), the software would be better poised by fixing the variants and allowing the addition of new operations (destructors), or vice versa. In the case that at this point it is further possible to make a closed-world assumption with regards to the particular type (represented as a matrix), since clients of the code are known and can be dealt with, it might seem reasonable to transpose the matrix representing that type. With $GADT^T$, it is possible to do this independently of the other matrices in the program. (As already discussed, $GADT^T$ in its present form doesn't aim to be particularly developer-friendly, but we expect further language layers to be placed on top of $GADT^T$ to remedy this eventually.)

Compiler Optimizations. To be able to use our automatizable transformation as a programmer tool, it was important to be able to make a closed-world assumption, where we have the entire program, or more precisely, the part which involves the matrix under consideration, at our disposal. A more automated process where such a kind of assumption can often be readily made is compilation. There, our matrix transposition transformation can be employed for a whole program optimization (such as [6]), as follows. An opportunity for optimization presents itself to the compiler when it is basically able to recognize an abstract machine in the code; optimizing this abstract machine is then an intermediate step, more generally applicable, that precedes hardware-specific optimizations [18]. As outlined above, defunctionalization can turn higher-order programs into first-order programs where this machine might be apparent. With our pair of languages, using our readily automatizable defunctionalization (matrix transposition), it is possible to turn GAcoDT code into GADT code during the compilation phase. Then the compiler can leverage the potentially recognizable abstract machine form of the GADT code for its optimizations.

5.2   Limitations

As we said, our design rationale for $GADT^T$ was to clarify the relation between GADTs and GAcoDTs, not to provide a convenient language for developers. Here we discuss some ways to address the limitations resulting from that decision.

Local (Co)Pattern Matching, Including λ. A significant limitation of $GADT^T$ is that (co)pattern matching is only allowed on the top-level; we don't have "case" (or "match") constructs on the term level. Any local (co)pattern matching, however, can be converted to the top-level form by extracting it to a new top-level function definition. Variables free within the (co)pattern matching term must be passed to this function as arguments. In particular, anonymous local first-class functions, i.e., λ expressions, are a form of local copattern matching which can be encoded in this way; this particular conversion is traditionally called lambda lifting.

(Co)Pattern Matching on Zero or More Arguments. (Co)pattern matching in $GADT^T$ is only possible on a single, distinguished argument (in our presentation, the first, but this is not important). Nested and multiple-argument matching can be encoded by *unnesting* à la Setzer et al. [35], producing auxiliary functions.

In $GADT^T$, it is further not possible to define a function without any (co) pattern matching entirely. The workaround of (co)pattern matching on a dummy argument of type Unit is simple, but it is not obvious how to reconcile this encoding with the symmetry of de/refunctionalization.

Type Inference. We have deliberately avoided the question of type inference in this work. In general, we expect that the ample existing works on type inference for GADTs (such as Peyton Jones et al. [29], Schrijvers et al. [34], Chen and Erwig [7]) can be adapted to our setting and will also work for GAcoDTs. We see one complication, though: Due to the fact that destructors are only locally unique in $GADT^T$, the (co)datatype the destructor belongs to must first be found via the type inferred for its distinguished, destructed argument. In other words, we do not know which destructor signature to consider before we know the destructed argument's type. This means that a type inference system which works inwards only, i.e., it discovers the types of the destructor arguments by looking at the signature, possibly leaving unification variables, and then checks that the recursively discovered types for the arguments conform, will not work.

5.3   Termination and Productivity

While termination and productivity are not in the focus of this paper, we want to mention that our unified treatment of data and codata can also lead to a unified treatment of termination and productivity.

Here we want to illustrate informally that a simple syntactic criterion is sufficient to allow structural recursion and guarded corecursion. Syntactic termination checks are not expressive enough for many situations, hence we leave a proper treatment of termination/productivity checking (such as with sized types [2]) for future work; the purpose of this discussion is merely to illustrate that termination checking could also benefit from unified data and codata and not to propose a practically useful termination checker.

The basic idea is to restrict destructor calls in the right-hand sides of equations to have the form $d[\overline{T}](x, \overline{t})$ instead of $d[\overline{T}](t, \overline{t})$. That is to say, in destructor calls, we only allow variables from *within* the constructor pattern of the left-hand side. This criterion already guarantees termination (and hence also productivity [2]) in our system, i.e. the finiteness of all reduction sequences, which can be shown with the usual argument of a property that strictly decreases under reduction. A reduction step in $GADT^T$ with right-hand sides restricted like that strictly decreases, under lexicographic order, the pair of

1. the maximum of all the first (destructed) arguments depths in destructor calls of the term, and
2. the sequence which counts how often each destructed argument depth appears in the term, starting with the maximum depth and going downward; those sequences are themselves lexicographically ordered.

This strict decrease can be proved by induction on the derivation of the reduction step. Since there are no infinitely decreasing sequences of these pairs, any reduction sequence must be finite. Note that our criterion in itself excludes far too many programs to be anywhere near practical, but it is readily conceivable how to relax it to only *recursive* calls together with a check that excludes mutual recursion.[6]

Let's look at Fig. 7 once more to illustrate that this criterion corresponds to both structural recursion and guarded corecursion. In the right-hand side of Fig. 7 we see that the first argument to the recursive call in the last line is n, which is allowed by our restriction because it is a syntactic part of the original input,

---

[6] For instance one might request the programmer to order the destructor names such that in equations for a certain destructor only destructors of lower order may be called.

succ(n) (structural recursion). The call to apply is not a problem because it is not a recursive call.[7] At the same time, if we look at the last line in the left-hand side of Fig. 7, we see that the criterion also corresponds to guarded corecursion. With copatterns, guarded corecursion means that we do not destruct the result of a recursive call (the "guard" itself is implicit in the pattern on the left-hand side of the equation). However, destructing that result would mean that we would have to call a destructor with the recursive call as its first argument, which is again forbidden by the syntactic criterion.

5.4 Going Beyond System F-like Polymorphism

A particularly interesting direction for future work is to extend $GADT^T$ and go beyond the System F-like polymorphism. For instance, F_ω contains a copy of the simply-typed lambda calculus on the type level. Could one also generalize type-level functions to arbitrary codata and maybe use a variant of $GADT^T$ on the type level? Can dependent products like in the calculus of constructions [13] be generalized in a similar way? Can inductive types like in the calculus of inductive constructions be formulated such that there is a dual that is also related by de/refunctionalization? Thibodeau et al. [36] have formulated such a dual, but whether it can be massaged to fit into the setting described here is not obvious.

5.5 Coq Formalization

Our Coq formalization is quite close to the traditional presentation chosen for this paper, but there are some technical differences. Both term and type variables are encoded via de Bruijn indices, which is rather standard for programming language mechanization. More interestingly, the syntax of the language in the Coq formalization expresses some of the constraints we express here via typing rules instead via dependent types. Specifically, terms and types are indexed by the type variables that can appear inside. To represent matrices, we have developed a small library of dependently typed tables (where the cell types can depend on the row and column labels), such that the matrix type already guarantees that all type variables that show up in terms and types are bound. An earlier version of the formalization and the soundness proof used explicit well-formedness constraints to guarantee that all type variables are bound; the type soundness proof for this version was about twice as long as the one using dependent types. On the flip side, we had to "pay" for using the dependent types in the form of many annoying "type casts" in definitions and theorems owing to the fact that Coq's equality is intensional and not extensional [9, Sect. 10.3]. Finally, instead of using an evaluation context to define evaluation order like we did in Fig. 4, we have used traditional congruence rules. In the reduction relation as formalized in Coq, a single step can actually correspond to multiple steps in the formalization presented in the paper; however, this is just a minor technicality to slightly simplify the proofs.

---

[7] As long as we avoid mutual recursion, for instance by ensuring fold > apply.

6   Related Work

"Theoreticians appreciate duality because it reveals deep symmetries. Practitioners appreciate duality because it offers two-for-the-price-of-one economy." This quote from Wadler [38] describes the spirit behind the design of $GADT^T$, but of course this is not the first paper to talk about duality in programming languages. We have already discussed the most closely related works in previous sections; here, we compare $GADT^T$ with theoretical calculi with related duality properties and point out an aspect of practical programming for which the duality of $GADT^T$ is relevant.

Codata. Hagino [23] pioneered the idea of dualizing data types: Whereas data types are used to define a type by the ways to *construct* it, codatatypes are dual to them in the sense that they are specified by their *deconstructions*. Abel et al. [1] introduce copatterns which allow functions producing codata to be defined by matching on the destructors of the result codatatype, dually to matching on the constructors of the argument datatype. All these developments occur in a world where function types are a given. The symmetric codata and data language fragments proposed by Rendel et al. [31] deviate from this: By enhancing destructor signatures with argument types, they provide a form of codata that is a generalization of first-class functions. Both the works by Rendel et al. [31] and Abel et al. [1] are simply-typed.

The (co)datatypes in the calculus of ownen and Ariola [19] also allow for user-defined function types. Their focus is different from ours, though, as they are mostly interested in evaluation strategies and their duality, and with regards to their calculus itself they work in an untyped setting. What is interesting in comparison with $GADT^T$ is how their (co)datatype declarations and signatures are inherently more symmetric as they essentially describe a type system for the parametric sequent calculus. As such, the position of additional arguments in the destructor signatures has a mirror counterparts in constructor signatures (to highlight this, Downen and Ariola [19] refer to destructors as "co-constructors").

Duality of Computations and Values. Staying on with the idea of avoiding function types as primitives for a moment, Wadler [38] presents a "dual calculus" in which the previously astonishing result that call-by-name is De Morgan-dual to call-by-value [14] is clarified by defining implication (corresponding to function types via the Curry-Howard isomorphism) in two different ways dependent on the intended corresponding evaluation regime. A somewhat similar approach, but perhaps more directly related to the data/codata duality, that also deals with the "troubling" coexistence of call-by-value and call-by-name, was proposed by Levy [27]. Levy [27] presents a calculus with a new evaluation regime, *call-by-push value* (CBPV), which subsumes call-by-value and call-by-name by encoding the local choice for either in the terms of the calculus. More specifically, there are two kinds of terms in the CBPV calculus: computations and values, which can be inter-converted by "thunking" and "forcing". The terms for computations and values are said to be of *positive* type and of *negative* type, respectively. Thibodeau et al. [36] have built their calculus, which extends codatatypes to indexed codatatypes, on top of CBPV, with datatypes being positive and codatatypes being negative. We think that, when extending $GADT^T$ with local (co)pattern matching on the term level, perhaps with pattern and copattern matching terms mixed, it might be helpful to similarly recast the resulting language as a modification of the CBPV calculus of Levy [27].

7 Conclusions

We have presented a formal calculus, $GADT^T$, which uniformly describes both GADTs and their dual, GAcoDTs. GADTs and GAcoDTs can be converted back and forth by defunctionalization and refunctionalization, both of which correspond to a transposition of the matrix of the equations for each pair of constructor/destructor. We have formalized the calculus in Coq and mechanically verified its type soundness, its extensibility properties, and the preservation of typing and operational semantics by defunctionalization and refunctionalization.

We believe that our work can be of help for future language design since it describes a methodology to get a kind of "sweet spot" where data and codata constructs (including functions) are "in sync". We think that it can also be useful as a general program transformation tool, both on the program level as a kind of refactoring tool, but also as part of compilers and runtime systems. Finally, since codata is quite related to objects in object-oriented programming, we hope that our approach can help to clarify their relation and design languages which subsume both traditional functional and object-oriented languages.

Acknowledgments. We would like to thank Tillmann Rendel and Julia Trieflinger for providing some early ideas for the design of what eventually became $GADT^T$. This work was supported by DFG project OS 293/3-1.

References

1. Abel, A., Pientka, B., Thibodeau, D., Setzer, A.: Copatterns: programming infinite structures by observations. In: Proceedings of the Symposium on Principles of Programming Languages, pp. 27–38. ACM (2013)
2. Abel, A.M., Pientka, B.: Wellfounded recursion with copatterns: a unified approach to termination and productivity. In: Proceedings of the 18th ACM SIGPLAN International Conference on Functional Programming, ICFP 2013, pp. 185–196. ACM, New York (2013)
3. Augustsson, L.: A compiler for lazy ML. In: Proceedings of the 1984 ACM Symposium on LISP and Functional Programming, LFP 1984, pp. 218–227. ACM, New York (1984)
4. Böhm, C., Berarducci, A.: Automatic synthesis of typed lambda-programs on term algebras. Theor. Comput. Sci. **39**, 135–154 (1985)
5. Carette, J., Kiselyov, O., Shan, C.: Finally tagless, partially evaluated: tagless staged interpreters for simpler typed languages. J. Funct. Program. **19**(5), 509–543 (2009)

6. Chambers, C., Dean, J., Grove, D.: Whole-program optimization of object-oriented languages. University of Washington Seattle, Technical report 96-06 2 (1996)
7. Chen, S., Erwig, M.: Principal type inference for GADTs. In: Proceedings of the 43rd Annual ACM SIGPLAN-SIGACT Symposium on Principles of Programming Languages, POPL 2016, pp. 416–428. ACM, New York (2016)
8. Cheney, J., Hinze, R.: First-class phantom types. Technical report. Cornell University (2003)
9. Chlipala, A.: Certified Programming with Dependent Types. MIT Press, Cambridge (2017). http://adam.chlipala.net/cpdt/
10. Clifton, C., Leavens, G.T., Chambers, C., Millstein, T.: MultiJava: modular open classes and symmetric multiple dispatch for Java. In: Proceedings of the Conference on Object-Oriented Programming, Systems, Languages and Applications, pp. 130–145. ACM (2000)
11. Cook, W.R.: Object-oriented programming versus abstract data types. In: de Bakker, J.W., de Roever, W.P., Rozenberg, G. (eds.) REX 1990. LNCS, vol. 489, pp. 151–178. Springer, Heidelberg (1991). https://doi.org/10.1007/BFb0019443
12. Cook, W.R.: On understanding data abstraction, revisited. In: Proceedings of the Conference on Object-Oriented Programming, Systems, Languages and Applications, pp. 557–572. ACM (2009)
13. Coquand, T., Huet, G.: The calculus of constructions. Inf. Comput. **76**(2–3), 95–120 (1988)
14. Curien, P.L., Herbelin, H.: The duality of computation. In: Proceedings of the Fifth ACM SIGPLAN International Conference on Functional Programming, ICFP 2000, pp. 233–243. ACM, New York (2000)
15. Danvy, O., Johannsen, J., Zerny, I.: A walk in the semantic park. In: Proceedings of the 20th ACM SIGPLAN Workshop on Partial Evaluation and Program Manipulation, PEPM 2011, pp. 1–12. ACM, New York (2011)
16. Danvy, O., Millikin, K.: Refunctionalization at work. Sci. Comput. Program. **74**(8), 534–549 (2009)
17. Danvy, O., Nielsen, L.R.: Defunctionalization at work. In: Proceedings of the Conference on Principles and Practice of Declarative Programming, pp. 162–174 (2001)
18. Diehl, S., Hartel, P., Sestoft, P.: Abstract machines for programming language implementation. Future Gener. Comput. Syst. **16**(7), 739–751 (2000)
19. Downen, P., Ariola, Z.M.: The duality of construction. In: Shao, Z. (ed.) ESOP 2014. LNCS, vol. 8410, pp. 249–269. Springer, Heidelberg (2014). https://doi.org/10.1007/978-3-642-54833-8_14
20. Emir, B., Kennedy, A., Russo, C., Yu, D.: Variance and generalized constraints for C♯ generics. In: Thomas, D. (ed.) ECOOP 2006. LNCS, vol. 4067, pp. 279–303. Springer, Heidelberg (2006). https://doi.org/10.1007/11785477_18
21. Ernst, M.D., Kaplan, C., Chambers, C.: Predicate dispatching: a unified theory of dispatch. In: Jul, E. (ed.) ECOOP 1998. LNCS, vol. 1445, pp. 186–211. Springer, Heidelberg (1998). https://doi.org/10.1007/BFb0054092
22. Erwig, M., Jones, S.P.: Pattern guards and transformational patterns. Electron. Notes Theor. Comput. Sci. **41**(1), 3 (2001)
23. Hagino, T.: Codatatypes in ML. J. Symb. Comput. **8**(6), 629–650 (1989)
24. Jacobs, B.: Objects and classes, coalgebraically. In: Freitag, B., Jones, C.B., Lengauer, C., Schek, H.J. (eds.) Object Orientation with Parallelism and Persistence, vol. 370, pp. 83–103. Springer, Boston (1995). https://doi.org/10.1007/978-1-4613-1437-0_5

25. Johnsson, T.: Lambda lifting: transforming programs to recursive equations. In: Jouannaud, J.-P. (ed.) FPCA 1985. LNCS, vol. 201, pp. 190–203. Springer, Heidelberg (1985). https://doi.org/10.1007/3-540-15975-4_37

26. Kennedy, A., Russo, C.V.: Generalized algebraic data types and object-oriented programming. In: Proceedings of the Conference on Object-Oriented Programming, Systems, Languages and Applications, pp. 21–40. ACM (2005)

27. Levy, P.B.: Call-by-push-value: a subsuming paradigm. In: Girard, J.-Y. (ed.) TLCA 1999. LNCS, vol. 1581, pp. 228–243. Springer, Heidelberg (1999). https://doi.org/10.1007/3-540-48959-2_17

28. Oliveira, B.C., Moors, A., Odersky, M.: Type classes as objects and implicits. In: Proceedings of the ACM International Conference on Object Oriented Programming Systems Languages and Applications, OOPSLA 2010, pp. 341–360. ACM, New York (2010)

29. Peyton Jones, S., Vytiniotis, D., Weirich, S., Washburn, G.: Simple unification-based type inference for GADTs. In: Proceedings of the Eleventh ACM SIGPLAN International Conference on Functional Programming, ICFP 2006, pp. 50–61. ACM, New York (2006)

30. Pierce, B.C.: Types and Programming Languages. Massachusetts Institute of Technology, Cambridge (2002)

31. Rendel, T., Trieflinger, J., Ostermann, K.: Automatic refunctionalization to a language with copattern matching: with applications to the expression problem. In: Proceedings of the 20th ACM SIGPLAN International Conference on Functional Programming, ICFP 2015, pp. 269–279. ACM, New York (2015)

32. Reynolds, J.C.: Definitional interpreters for higher-order programming languages. In: Proceedings of the ACM Annual Conference, pp. 717–740. ACM (1972)

33. Reynolds, J.C.: User-defined types and procedural data structures as complementary approaches to data abstraction. In: Schuman, S. (ed.) New Directions in Algorithmic Languages 1975, pp. 157–168. IFIP Working Group 2.1 on Algol, INRIA, Rocquencourt, France (1975)

34. Schrijvers, T., Peyton Jones, S., Sulzmann, M., Vytiniotis, D.: Complete and decidable type inference for GADTs. In: Proceedings of the 14th ACM SIGPLAN International Conference on Functional Programming, ICFP 2009, pp. 341–352. ACM, New York (2009)

35. Setzer, A., Abel, A., Pientka, B., Thibodeau, D.: Unnesting of copatterns. In: Dowek, G. (ed.) RTA 2014. LNCS, vol. 8560, pp. 31–45. Springer, Cham (2014). https://doi.org/10.1007/978-3-319-08918-8_3

36. Thibodeau, D., Cave, A., Pientka, B.: Indexed codata types. In: Proceedings of the 21st ACM SIGPLAN International Conference on Functional Programming, ICFP 2016, pp. 351–363. ACM, New York (2016)

37. Wadler, P.: The expression problem. Note to Java Genericity mailing list, November 1998

38. Wadler, P.: Call-by-value is dual to call-by-name. In: Proceedings of the Eighth ACM SIGPLAN International Conference on Functional Programming, ICFP 2003, pp. 189–201. ACM, New York (2003)

39. Wright, A., Felleisen, M.: A syntactic approach to type soundness. Inf. Comput. **115**(1), 38–94 (1994)

40. Xi, H.X., Chiyan, C., Chen, G.: Guarded recursive datatype constructors. In: Proceedings of the Symposium on Principles of Programming Languages, pp. 224–235. ACM (2003)

Deterministic Concurrency:
A Clock-Synchronised Shared Memory
Approach

Joaquín Aguado[1]([✉]), Michael Mendler[1], Marc Pouzet[2], Partha Roop[3],
and Reinhard von Hanxleden[4]

[1] Otto-Friedrich-Universität Bamberg, Bamberg, Germany
`joaquin.aguado@uni-bamberg.de`
[2] École Normale Supérieure, Paris, France
[3] University of Auckland, Auckland, New Zealand
[4] Christian-Albrechts-Universität zu Kiel, Kiel, Germany

Abstract. Synchronous Programming (SP) is a universal computational principle that provides deterministic concurrency. The same input sequence with the same timing always results in the same externally observable output sequence, even if the internal behaviour generates uncertainty in the scheduling of concurrent memory accesses. Consequently, SP languages have always been strongly founded on mathematical semantics that support formal program analysis. So far, however, communication has been constrained to a set of primitive clock-synchronised shared memory (CSM) data types, such as data-flow registers, streams and signals with restricted read and write accesses that limit modularity and behavioural abstractions.

This paper proposes an extension to the SP theory which retains the advantages of deterministic concurrency, but allows communication to occur at higher levels of abstraction than currently supported by SP data types. Our approach is as follows. To avoid data races, each CSM type publishes a *policy interface* for specifying the admissibility and precedence of its access methods. Each instance of the CSM type has to be policy-coherent, meaning it must behave deterministically under its own policy—a natural requirement if the goal is to build deterministic systems that use these types. In a policy-constructive system, all access methods can be scheduled in a policy-conformant way for all the types without deadlocking. In this paper, we show that a policy-constructive program exhibits deterministic concurrency in the sense that all policy-conformant interleavings produce the same input-output behaviour. Policies are conservative and support the CSM types existing in current SP languages. Technically, we introduce a kernel SP language that uses arbitrary policy-driven CSM types. A big-step fixed-point semantics for this language is developed for which we prove determinism and termination of constructive programs.

© The Author(s) 2018
A. Ahmed (Ed.): ESOP 2018, LNCS 10801, pp. 86–113, 2018.
https://doi.org/10.1007/978-3-319-89884-1_4

Keywords: Synchronous programming · Data abstraction
Clock-synchronised shared memory · Determinacy · Concurrency
Constructive semantics

1   Introduction

Concurrent programming is challenging. Arbitrary interleavings of concurrent threads lead to non-determinism with data races imposing significant integrity and consistency issues [1]. Moreover, in many application domains such as safety-critical systems, *determinism* is indeed a matter of life and death. In a medical-device software, for instance, the same input sequence from the sensors (with the same timing) must always result in the same output sequence for the actuators, even if the run-time software architecture regime is unpredictable.

Synchronous programming (SP) delivers *deterministic concurrency* out of the box[1] which explains its success in the design, implementation and validation of embedded, reactive and safety-critical systems for avionics, automotive, energy and nuclear industries. Right now SP-generated code is flying on the Airbus 380 in systems like flight control, cockpit display, flight warning, and anti-icing just to mention a few. The SP mathematical theory has been fundamental for implementing correct-by-construction program-derivation algorithms and establishing formal analysis, verification and testing techniques [2]. For SCADE[2], the SP industrial modelling language and software development toolkit, the formal SP background has been a key aspect for its certification at the highest level A of the aerospace standard DO-178B/C. This SP rigour has also been important for obtaining certifications in railway and transportation (EN 50128), industry and energy (IEC 61508), automotive (TÜV and ISO 26262) as well as for ensuring full compliance with the safety standards of nuclear instrumentation and control (IEC 60880) and medical systems (IEC 62304) [3].

Synchronous Programming in a Nutshell. At the top level, we can imagine an SP system as a black-box with inputs and outputs for interacting with its environment. There is a special input, called the *clock*, that determines when the communication between system and environment can occur. The clock gets an input stimulus from the environment at discrete times. At those moments we say that the clock *ticks*. When there is no tick, there is no possible communication, as if system and environment were disconnected. At every tick, the system *reacts* by reading the current inputs and executing a *step function* that delivers outputs and changes the internal memory. For its part, the environment must synchronise with this reaction and do not go ahead with more ticks. Thus,

---

[1] Milner's distinction between *determinacy* and *determinism* is that a computation is *determinate* if the same input sequence produces the same output sequence, as opposed to *deterministic* computations which in addition have identical internal behaviour/scheduling. In this paper we use both terms synonymously to mean determinacy in Milner's sense, i.e., observable determinism.

[2] SCADE is a product of ANSYS Inc. (http://www.esterel-technologies.com/).

in SP, we assume (*Synchrony Hypothesis*) that the time interval of a system reaction, also called *macro-step* or (*synchronous*) *instant*, appears instantaneous (has zero-delay) to the environment. Since each system reaction takes exactly one clock tick, we describe the evolution of the system-environment interaction as a synchronous (lock-step) sequence of macro-steps. The SP theory guarantees that all externally observable interaction sequences derived from the macro-step reactions define a functional input-output relation.

The fact that the sequences of macro-steps take place in time and space (memory) has motivated two orthogonal developments of SP. The *data-flow* view regards input-output sequences as synchronous streams of data changing over time and studies the functional relationships between streams. Dually, the *control-flow* approach projects the information of the input-output sequences at each point in time and studies the changes of this global state as time progresses, i.e., from one tick to the next. The SP paradigm includes languages such as Esterel [4], Quartz [5] and SC [6] in the imperative control-flow style and languages like Signal [7], Lustre [8] and Lucid Synchrone [9] that support the declarative data-flow view. There are even mixed control-data flow language such as Esterel V7 [10] or SCADE [3]. Independently of the execution model, the common strength to all of these SP languages is a precise formal semantics—an indispensable feature when dealing with the complexities of concurrency.

At a more concrete level, we can visualise an SP system as a white-box where inside we find (graphical or textual) code. In the SP domain, the program must be divided into fragments corresponding to the macro-step reactions that will be executed instantaneously at each tick. Declarative languages usually organise these macro-steps by means of (internally generated) activation clocks that prescribe the blocks (nodes) that are performed at each tick. Instead, imperative textual languages provide a `pause` statement for explicitly delimiting code execution within a synchronous instant. In either case, the Synchrony Hypothesis conveniently abstracts away all the, typically concurrent, low-level *micro-steps* needed to produce a system reaction. The SP theory explains how the micro-step accesses to shared memory must be controlled so as to ensure that all internal (white-box) behaviour eventually stabilises, completing a deterministic macro-step (black-box) response. For more details on SP, the reader is referred to [2].

State of the Art. Traditional imperative SP languages provide constructs to model control-dominated systems. Typically, these include a concurrent composition of *threads* (sequential processes) that guarantees determinism and offers *signals* as the main means for data communication between threads. Signals behave like shared variables for which the concurrent accesses occurring within a macro-step are scheduled according to the following principles: A *pure signal* has a *status* that can be *present* (1) or *absent* (0). At the beginning of each macro-step, pure signals have status 0 by default. In any instant, a signal s can be explicitly *emitted* with the statement `s.emit()` which atomically sets its status to 1. We can read the status of s with the statement `s.pres()`, so the control-flow can branch depending on run-time signal statuses. Specifically, inside programs, if-then-else constructions await for the appropriate combination of present and absent signal statuses to emit (or not) more signals. The main issue is to avoid inconsistencies due to circular causality resulting from decisions based on absent statuses. Thus, the order in which the access methods emit, pres are scheduled matters for the final result. The usual SP rule for ensuring determinism is that the pres test must wait until the final signal status is decided. If all signal accesses can be scheduled in this *decide-then-read* way then the program is *constructive*. All schedules that keep the decide-then-read order will produce the same input-output result. This is how SP reconciles concurrency and observable determinism and generates much of its algebraic appeal. Constructiveness of programs is what static techniques like the *must-can* analysis [4,11–13] verify although in a more abstract manner. Pure signals are a simple form of *clock-synchronised shared memory* (CSM) data types with access methods (operations) specific to this CSM type. Existing SP control-flow languages also support other restricted CSM types such valued signals and arrays [10] or sequentially constructive variables [6].

Contribution. This paper proposes an extension to the SP model which retains the advantages of deterministic concurrency while widening the notion of constructiveness to cover more general CSM types. This allows shared-memory communication to occur at higher levels of abstraction than currently supported. In particular, our approach subsumes both the notions of *Berry-constructiveness* [4] for Esterel and *sequential constructiveness* for SCL [14]. This is the first time that these SP communication principles are combined side-by-side in a single language. Moreover, our theory permits other predefined communication structures to coexist safely under the same uniform framework, such as data-flow variables [8], registers [15], Kahn channels [16], priority queues, arrays as well as other CSM types currently unsupported in SP.

Synopsis and Overview. The core of our approach is presented in Sect. 2 where *policies* are introduced as a (constructive) synchronisation mechanism for arbitrary *abstract data types* (ADT). For instance, the policy of a pure signal is depicted in Fig. 1. It has two control *states* 0 and 1 corresponding to the two possible signal statuses. Transitions are decorated with method names pres, emit or with σ to indicate a clock tick.

The policy tells us whether a given method or tick is *admissible*, i.e., if it can be scheduled from a particular state[3]. In addition, transitions include a *blocking* set of method names as part of their *action* labels. This set determines a *precedence* between methods from a given state. A label $m : L$ specifies that all methods in L take precedence over m.

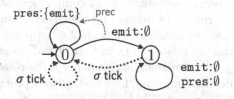

Fig. 1. Pure signal policy.

An empty blocking set $\emptyset$ indicates no precedences. To improve visualisation, we

---

[3] The signal policy in Fig. 1 does not impose any admissibility restriction since methods pres and emit can be scheduled from every policy state.

highlight precedences by dotted (red) arrows tagged $\texttt{prec}$[4]. The *policy interface* in Fig. 1 specifies the decide-then-read protocol of pure signals as follows. At any instant, if the signal status is 0 then the $\texttt{pres}$ test can only be scheduled if there are no more potential $\texttt{emit}$ statements that can still update the status to 1. This explains the precedence of the $\texttt{emit}$ transition over the self loop with action label $\texttt{pres}$: $\{\texttt{emit}\}$ from state 0. Conversely, transitions $\texttt{pres}$ and $\texttt{emit}$ from state 1 have no precedences, meaning that the $\texttt{pres}$ and $\texttt{emit}$ methods are *confluent* so they can be freely scheduled (interleaved). The reason is that a signal status 1 is already decided and can no longer be changed by either method in the same instant. In general, any two admissible methods that do not block each other must be confluent in the sense that the same policy state is reached independently of their order of execution. Note that all the σ transition go to the *initial* state 0 since at each tick the SP system enters a new macro-step where all pure signals get initialised to the 0 status.

Section 2 describes in detail the idea of a scheduling policy on general CSM types. This leads to a type-level *coherence* property, which is a local form of determinism. Specifically, a CSM type is *policy-coherent* if it satisfies the (policy) specification of admissibility and precedence of its access methods. The point is that a policy-coherent CSM type per se behaves deterministically under its own policy—a very natural requirement if the goal is to build deterministic systems that use this type. For instance, the fact that Esterel signals are deterministic (policy-coherent) in the first place permits techniques such as the must-can analysis to get constructive information about deterministic programs. We show how policy-coherence implies a global determinacy property called *commutation*. Now, in a *policy-constructive* program all access methods can be scheduled in a *policy-conforming* way for all the CSM types without deadlocking. We also show that, for policy-coherent types, a policy-constructive program exhibits deterministic concurrency in the sense that all policy-conforming interleavings produce the same input-output behaviour.

To implement a constructive scheduling mechanism parameterised in arbitrary CSM type policies, we present the synchronous kernel language, called *Deterministic Concurrent Language* (DCoL), in Sect. 2.1. DCoL is both a minimal language to study the new mathematical concepts but can also act as an intermediate language for compiling existing SP Sect. 3 presents its policy-driven operational semantics for which determinacy and termination is proven. Section 3 also explains how this model generalises existing notions of constructiveness. We discuss related work in Sect. 4 and present our conclusions in Sect. 5.

A companion of this paper is the research report (https://www.uni-bamberg. de/fileadmin/uni/fakultaeten/wiai_professuren/grundlagen_informatik/papers MM/report-WIAI-102-Feb-2018.pdf) [17] which contains detailed proofs and additional examples of CSM types.

---

[4] We tacitly assume that the tick transitions σ have the lowest *priority* since only when the reaction is over, the clock may tick. We could be more explicit and write σ : $\{\texttt{pres}, \texttt{emit}\}$ as action labels for these transitions.

2 Synchronous Policies

This section introduces a kernel synchronous *Deterministic Concurrent Language* (DCoL) for policy-conformant constructive scheduling which integrates policy-controlled CSM types within a simple syntax. DCoL is used to discuss the behavioural (clock) abstraction limitations of current SP. Then policies are introduced as a mechanism for specifying the scheduling discipline for CSM types which, in this form, can encapsulate arbitrary ADTs.

2.1 Syntax

The syntax of DCoL is given by the following operators:

$$
\begin{array}{lll}
P ::= & \texttt{skip} & \text{instantaneous termination} \\
| & \texttt{pause} & \text{wait for next instant (clock tick)} \\
| & P \parallel P & \text{parallel composition} \\
| & P\,;P & \text{sequential composition} \\
| & \texttt{let } x = c.m(e)\texttt{ in } P & \text{access method call, } x \text{ value variable} \\
| & \texttt{if } e \texttt{ then } P \texttt{ else } P & \text{conditional branching, } e \text{ value expression} \\
| & \texttt{rec}\,p.\,P & \text{recursive closure} \\
| & p & \text{process variable}
\end{array}
$$

The first two statements correspond to the two forms of immediate *completion*: skip terminates instantaneously and pause waits for the logical clock to terminate. The operators $P \parallel Q$ and $P\,;Q$ are *parallel interleaving* and *imperative sequential* composition of threads with the standard operational interpretation. Reading and destructive updating is performed through the execution of method calls $c.m(e)$ on a CSM *variable* $c \in O$ with a method $m \in M_c$. The sets O and M_c define the granularity of the available memory accesses. The construct $\texttt{let } x = c.m(e)\texttt{ in } P$ calls m on c with an input parameter determined by *value expression* e. It binds the return value to variable x and then executes program P, which may depend on x, sequentially afterwards. The execution of $c.m(e)$ in general has the side-effect of changing the internal memory of c. In contrast, the evaluation of expression e is side-effect free. For convenience we write $x = c.m(e)\,;P$ for $\texttt{let } x = c.m(e)\texttt{ in } P$. When P does not depend on x then we write $c.m(e)\,;P$ and $c.m(e)$; for $c.m(e)\,;\texttt{skip}$. The exact syntax of value expressions e is irrelevant for this work and left open. It could be as simple as permitting only constant value literals or a full-fledged functional language. The *conditional* $\texttt{if } e \texttt{ then } P \texttt{ else } P$ has the usual interpretation. For simplicity, we may write $\texttt{if } c.m(e) \texttt{ then } P \texttt{ else } Q$ to mean $x = c.m(e)\,;\,\texttt{if } x \texttt{ then } P \texttt{ else } Q$. The *recursive closure* $\texttt{rec}\,p.\,P$ binds the behaviour P to the program label p so it can be called from within P. Using this construct we can build iterative behaviours. For instance, $\texttt{loop}\,P\,\texttt{end} =_{df} \texttt{rec}\,p.\,P\,;\,\texttt{pause}\,;p$ indefinitely repeats P in each tick. We assume that in a closure $\texttt{rec}\,p.\,P$ the label p is (i) *clock guarded*, i.e., it occurs in the scope of at least one pause (meaning no instantaneous loops) and (ii) all occurrences of p are in the same thread. Thus, $\texttt{rec}\,p.\,p$ is illegal because of (i) and $\texttt{rec}\,p.\,(\texttt{pause}\,;\,p \parallel \texttt{pause}\,;\,p)$ is not permitted because of (ii).

This syntax seems minimalistic compared to existing SP languages. For instance, it does not provide primitives for pre-emption, suspension or traps as in Quartz or Esterel. Recent work [18] has shown how these control primitives can be translated into the constructs of the SCL language, exploiting destructive update of sequentially constructive (SC) variables. Since SC variables are a special case of policy-controlled CSM variables, DCoL is at least as expressive as SCL.

2.2 Limited Abstraction in SP

The pertinent feature of standard SP languages is that they do not permit the programmer to express sequential execution order inside a tick, for destructive updates of signals. All such updates are considered concurrent and thus must either be combined or concern distinct signals. For instance, in languages such as Esterel V7 or Quartz, a parallel composition

$$(v = \text{xs.read}() \,;\, \text{ys.emit}(v + 1)) \;\|\; (\text{xs.emit}(1) \,;\, \text{xs.emit}(5)) \tag{1}$$

of signal emissions is only constructive if a commutative and associative function is defined on the shared signal xs to combine the values assigned to it. But then, by the properties of this *combination function*, we get the same behaviour if we swap the assignments of values 1 and 5, or execute all in parallel as in

$$v = \text{xs.read}() \;\|\; \text{ys.emit}(v + 1) \;\|\; \text{xs.emit}(1) \;\|\; \text{xs.emit}(5).$$

If what we intended with the second emission xs.emit(5) in (1) was to override the first xs.emit(1) like in normal imperative programming so that the concurrent thread $v = \text{xs.read}() \,;\, \text{ys.emit}(v + 1)$ will read the updated value as $v = 5$? Then we need to introduce a **pause** statement to separate the emissions by a clock tick and delay the assignment to ys as in

$$(\textbf{pause} \,;\, v = \text{xs.read}() \,;\, \text{ys.emit}(v + 1)) \;\|\; (\text{xs.emit}(1) \,;\, \textbf{pause} \,;\, \text{xs.emit}(5)).$$

This makes behavioural abstraction difficult. For instance, suppose **nats** is a synchronous reaction module, possibly composite and with its own internal clocking, which returns the stream of natural numbers. Every time its step function **nats.step**() is called it returns the next number and increments its internal state. If we want to pair up two successive numbers within one tick of an outer clock and emit them in a single signal ys we would write something like $x_1 = \text{nats.step}() \,;\, x_2 = \text{nats.step}() \,;\, \text{y.emit}(x_1, x_2)$ where x_1, x_2 are thread-local value variables. This over-clocking is impossible in traditional SP because there is no imperative sequential composition by virtue of which we can call the step function of the same module instance twice within a tick. Instead, the two calls **nats.step**() are considered concurrent and thus create non-determinacy in the value of y.[5] To avoid a compiler error we must separate the calls by a clock as

---

[5] In Esterel V7 it is possible to use a module twice in a "sequential" composition $x_1 = \text{nats.step}(); x_2 = \text{nats.step}()$. However, the two occurrences of **nats** are distinct instances with their own internal state. Both calls will thus return the same value.

in $x_1 = $ nats.step() ; pause ; $x_2 = $ nats.step() ; y. emit(x_1, x_2) which breaks the intended clock abstraction.

The data abstraction limitation of traditional SP is that it is not directly possible to encapsulate a composite behaviour on synchronised signals as a shared synchronised object. For this, the simple decide-then-read signal protocol must be generalised, in particular, to distinguish between concurrent and sequential accesses to the shared data structure. A concurrent access $x_1 = $ nats.step() $\parallel$ $x_2 = $ nats.step() must give the same value for x_1 and x_2, while a sequential access $x_1 = $ nats.step() ; $x_2 = $ nats.step() must yield successive values of the stream. In a sequence $x = $ xs.read() ; xs. emit(v) the x does not see the value v but in a parallel $x = $ xs.read() $\parallel$ xs. emit(v) we may want the read to wait for the emission. The rest of this section covers our theory on policies in which this is possible. The modularity issue is reconsidered in Sect. 2.6.

2.3   Concurrent Access Policies

In the white-box view of SP, an imperative program consists of a set of threads (sequential processes) and some CSM variables for communication. Due to concurrency, a given *thread under control* (TUC) has the chance to access the shared variables only from time to time. For a given CSM variable, a *concurrent access policy* (CAP) is the locking mechanism used to control the accesses of the current TUC and its environment. The locking is to ensure that determinacy of the CSM type is not broken by the concurrent accesses. A CAP is like a policy which has extra transitions to model potential environment accesses outside the TUC. Concretely, a CAP is given by a state machine where each transition label $a : L$ codifies an *action* a taking place on the shared variable with *blocking set* L, where L is a set of methods that take precedence over a. The action is either a *method* $m : L$, a *silent action* $\tau : L$ or a *clock tick* $\sigma : L$. A transition $m : L$ expresses that in the current CAP control state, the method m can be called by the TUC, provided that no method in L is called concurrently. There is a *Determinacy Requirement* that guarantees that each method call by the TUC has a blocking set and successor state. Additionally, the execution of methods by the CAP must be *confluent* in the sense that if two methods are admissible and do not block each other, then the CAP reaches the same policy state no matter the order in which they are executed. This is to preserve determinism for concurrent variable accesses. A transition $\tau : L$ internalises method calls by the TUC's concurrent environment which are uncontrollable for the TUC. In the sequel, the actions in $\mathsf{M_c} \cup \{\sigma\}$ will be called *observable*. A transition $\sigma : L$ models a clock synchronisation step of the TUC. Like method calls, such clock ticks must be determinate as stated by the Determinacy Requirement. Additionally, the clock must always wait for any predicted concurrent τ-activity to complete. This is the *Maximal Progress Requirement*. Note that we do not need confluence for clock transitions since they are not concurrent.

Definition 1. *A concurrent access policy* (CAP) $\Vdash_c$ *of a* CSM *variable* c *with* (*access*) *methods* $\mathsf{M_c}$ *is a state machine consisting of a set of control states* $\mathbb{P}_c$, *an* initial state $\varepsilon \in \mathbb{P}_c$ *and a labelled* transition relation $\rightarrow \subseteq \mathbb{P}_c \times A_c \times \mathbb{P}_c$ *with* action *labels* $A_c = (M_c \cup \{\tau, \sigma\}) \times 2^{M_c}$. *Instead of* $(\mu_1, (a, L), \mu_2) \in \rightarrow$ *we write* $\mu_1 -a{:}L\rightarrow \mu_2$. *We then say action a is* admissible *in state* μ_1 *and* blocked *by all methods* $m \in L \subseteq M_c$. *When the* blocking set *L is irrelevant we drop it and write* $\mu_1 -a\rightarrow \mu_2$. *A* CAP *must satisfy the following conditions:*

- Determinacy. *If* $\mu -a{:}L_1\rightarrow \mu_1$ *and* $\mu -a{:}L_2\rightarrow \mu_2$ *then* $L_1 = L_2$ *and* $\mu_1 = \mu_2$ *provided a is* observable, *i.e.,* $a \neq \tau$.
- Confluence. *If* $\mu -m_1{:}L_1\rightarrow \mu_1$ *and* $\mu -m_2{:}L_2\rightarrow \mu_2$ *do not block each other, i.e.,* $m_1 \in M_c \setminus L_2$ *and* $m_2 \in M_c \setminus L_1$, *then for some* μ' *both* $\mu_1 -m_2\rightarrow \mu'$ *and* $\mu_2 -m_1\rightarrow \mu'$.
- Maximal Progress. $\mu -a{:}L_1\rightarrow \mu_1$ *and* $\mu -\sigma{:}L_2\rightarrow \mu_2$ *imply a is* observable.

A policy *is a* CAP *without any (concurrent) τ activity, i.e., every* $\mu -a\rightarrow \mu'$ *implies that a is* observable. □

The use of a CAP as a concurrent policy arises from the notion of enabling. Informally, an observable action $a \in M_c \cup \{\sigma\}$ is enabled in a state μ of a CAP if it is admissible in μ *and* in all subsequent states reachable under arbitrary silent steps. To formalise this we define *weak transitions* $\mu_1 \Rightarrow \mu_2$ inductively to express that either $\mu_1 = \mu_2$ or $\mu_1 \Rightarrow \mu'$ and $\mu' -\tau\rightarrow \mu_2$. We exploit the determinacy for observable actions $a \in M_c \cup \{\sigma\}$ and write $\mu \odot a$ for the unique μ' such that $\mu -a\rightarrow \mu'$, if it exists.

Definition 2. *Given a* CAP $\Vdash_c = (\mathbb{P}_c, \varepsilon, \longrightarrow)$; *an observable action* $a \in M_c \cup \{\sigma\}$ *is* enabled *in state* $\mu \in \mathbb{P}_c$, *written* $\mu \Vdash_c \downarrow a$, *if* $\mu' \odot a$ *exists for all* μ' *such that* $\mu \Rightarrow \mu'$. *A sequence* $\boldsymbol{a} \in (M_c \cup \{\sigma\})^*$ *of observable actions is* enabled *in* $\mu \in \mathbb{P}_c$, *written* $\mu \Vdash_c \downarrow \boldsymbol{a}$, *if (i)* $\boldsymbol{a} = \varepsilon$ *or (ii)* $\boldsymbol{a} = a\,\boldsymbol{b}$, $\mu \Vdash_c \downarrow a$ *and* $\mu \odot a \Vdash_c \downarrow \boldsymbol{b}$. □

Example 1. Consider the policy $\Vdash_s$ in Fig. 1 of an Esterel pure signal s. An edge labelled $a{:}L$ from state μ_1 to μ_2 corresponds to a transition $\mu_1 -a{:}L\rightarrow \mu_2$ in $\Vdash_s$. The start state is $\varepsilon = 0$ and the methods $M_s = \{\mathtt{pres}, \mathtt{emit}\}$ are always admissible, i.e., $\mu \odot m$ is defined in each state μ for all methods m. The presence test does not change the state and any emission sets it to 1, i.e., $\mu \odot \mathtt{pres} = \mu$ and $\mu \odot \mathtt{emit} = 1$ for

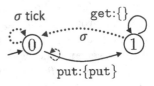

Fig. 2. Synchronous IVar.

all $\mu \in \mathbb{P}_s$. Each signal status is reset to 0 with the clock tick, i.e., $\mu \odot \sigma = 0$. Clearly, $\Vdash_s$ satisfies Determinacy. A presence test on a signal that is not emitted yet has to wait for all pending concurrent emissions, that is $\mathtt{emit}$ blocks $\mathtt{pres}$ in state 0, i.e., $0 -\mathtt{pres}{:}\{\mathtt{emit}\}\rightarrow 0$. Otherwise, no transition is blocked. Also, all competing transitions $\mu -m_1{:}L_1\rightarrow \mu_1$ and $\mu -m_2{:}L_2\rightarrow \mu_2$ that do not block each other, are of the form $\mu_1 = \mu_2$, from which Confluence follows. Note that since there are no silent transitions, Maximal Progress is always fulfilled too. Moreover, an action sequence is enabled in a state μ (Definition 2) iff it corresponds to a path in the automaton starting from μ. Hence, for $\boldsymbol{m} \in M_s^*$ we have

$0 \Vdash_s \downarrow m$ iff m is in the regular language[6] $\mathtt{pres}^* + \mathtt{pres}^* \, \mathtt{emit}(\mathtt{pres} + \mathtt{emit})^*$ and $1 \Vdash_s \downarrow m$ for all $m \in M_s^*$.

Contrast $\Vdash_s$ with the policy $\Vdash_c$ of a synchronous *immutable variable* (IVar) c shown in Fig. 2 with methods $M_c = \{\mathtt{get}, \mathtt{put}\}$. During each instant an IVar can be written (put) at most once and cannot be read (get) until it has been written. No value is stored between ticks, which means the memory is only temporary and can be reused, e.g., IVars can be implemented by wires. Formally, $\mu \Vdash_c \downarrow \mathtt{put}$ iff $\mu = 0$, where 0 is the initial empty state and $\mu \Vdash_c \downarrow \mathtt{get}$ iff $\mu = 1$, where 1 is the filled state. The transition $0 -\mathtt{put}:\{\mathtt{put}\} \rightarrow 1$ switches to filled state where get is admissible but put is not, anymore. The blocking $\{\mathtt{put}\}$ means there cannot be other concurrent threads writing c at the same time.   □

2.4   Enabling and Policy Conformance

A policy describes what a single thread can do to a CSM variable c when it operates alone. In a CAP all potential activities of the environment are added as τ-transitions to block the TUC's accesses. To implement this τ-locking we define an operation that generates a CAP $[\mu, \gamma]$ out of a policy. In this construction, $\mu \in \mathbb{P}_c$ is a policy state recording the history of methods that have been performed on c so far (*must* information). The second component $\gamma \subseteq M_c^*$ is a prediction for the sequences of methods that can still potentially be executed by the concurrent environment (*can* information).

Definition 3. *Let $(\mathbb{P}_c, \varepsilon, \rightarrow)$ be a policy. We define a CAP $\Vdash_c$ where states are pairs $[\mu, \gamma]$ such that $\mu \in \mathbb{P}_c$ is a policy state and $\gamma \subseteq M_c^*$ is a prediction. The initial state is $[\varepsilon, M_c^*]$ and the transitions are as follows:*

1. *The observable transitions $[\mu_1, \gamma_1] -m:L \rightarrow [\mu_2, \gamma_2]$ are such that $\gamma_1 = \gamma_2$ and $\mu_1 -m:L \rightarrow \mu_2$ provided that for all sequences $n\,\boldsymbol{n} \in \gamma_1$ with $\mu_1 -n \rightarrow \mu'$ we have $n \notin L$.*
2. *The silent transitions are $[\mu_1, \gamma_1] -\tau:L \rightarrow [\mu_2, \gamma_2]$ such that $\emptyset \neq m\,\gamma_2 \subseteq \gamma_1$ and $\mu_1 -m:L \rightarrow \mu_2$.*
3. *The clock transitions are $[\mu_1, \gamma_1] -\sigma:L \rightarrow [\mu_2, \gamma_2]$ such that $\gamma_1 = \emptyset$ and $\mu_1 -\sigma:L \rightarrow \mu_2$.*   □

Silent steps arise from the concurrent environment: A step $[\mu_1, \gamma_1] -\tau:L \rightarrow [\mu_2, \gamma_2]$ removes some prefix method m from the environment prediction γ_1, which contracts to an updated suffix prediction γ_2 with $m\,\gamma_2 \subseteq \gamma_1$. This method m is executed on the CSM variable, changing the policy state to $\mu_2 = \mu_1 \odot m$. A method m is enabled, $[\mu, \gamma] \Vdash_c \downarrow m$, if for all $[\mu_1, \gamma_1]$ which are τ-reachable from $[\mu, \gamma]$, method m is admissible, i.e., $[\mu_1, \gamma_1] -m \rightarrow [\mu_2, \gamma_1]$ for some μ_2.

Example 2. Consider concurrent threads $P_1 \parallel P_2$, where $P_2 = \mathtt{zs.put}(5)\,;\, u = \mathtt{ys.get}()$ and $P_1 = v = \mathtt{zs.get}()\,;\, \mathtt{ys.put}(v+1)$ with IVars zs, ys according to

---

[6] We are more liberal than Esterel where emit cannot be called sequentially after pres.

Example 1. Under the IVar policy the execution is deterministic, so that first P_2 writes on zs, then P_1 reads from zs and writes to ys, whereupon finally P_1 reads ys. Suppose the variables have reached policy states μ_{zs} and μ_{ys} and the threads are ready to execute the residual programs P_i' waiting at some method call $c_i.m_i(v_i)$, respectively. Since thread P_i' is concurrent with the other P_{3-i}', it can only proceed if m_i is not blocked by P_{3-i}', i.e., if $[\mu_{c_i}, can_{c_i}(P_{3-i}')] \Vdash_{c_i} \downarrow m_i$, where $can_c(P) \subseteq M_c^*$ is the set of method sequences predicted for P on c.

Initially we have $\mu_{zs} = 0 = \mu_{ys}$. Since method get is not admissible in state 0, we get $[0, can_{zs}(P_2)] \nVdash_{zs} \downarrow$ get by Definitions 3 and 2. So, P_1 is blocked. The zs.put of P_2, however, can proceed. First, since no predicted method sequence $can_{zs}(P_1) = \{$get$\}$ of P_1 starts with put, the transition 0 $-$put:$\{$put$\}\rightarrow$ 1 implies that $[0, can_{zs}(P_1)]$ $-$put:$\{$put$\}\rightarrow$ $[1, can_{zs}(P_1)]$ by Definition 3(1). Moreover, since get of P_1 is not admissible in 0, there are no silent transitions out of $[0, can_{zs}(P_1)]$ according to Definition 3(2). Thus, $[0, can_{zs}(P_1)] \Vdash_{zs} \downarrow$ put, as claimed.

When the zs.put is executed by P_2 it turns into $P_2' = u =$ys.get() and the policy state for zs advances to $\mu_{zs}' = 1$, while ys is still at $\mu_{ys} = 0$. Now ys.get of P_2' blocks for the same reason as zs was blocked in P_1 before. But since P_2 has advanced, its prediction on zs reduces to $can_{zs}(P_2') = \emptyset$. Therefore, the transition 1 $-$get:$\emptyset\rightarrow$ 1 implies $[1, can_{zs}(P_2')]$ $-$get:$\emptyset\rightarrow$ $[1, can_{zs}(P_2')]$ by Definition 3(1). Also, there are no silent transitions out of $[1, can_{zs}(P_2')]$ by Definition 3(2) and so $[\mu_{zs}', can_{zs}(P_2')] \Vdash_{zs} \downarrow$ get by Definition 2. This permits P_1 to execute zs.get() and proceed to $P_1' =$ ys.put$(5 + 1)$. The policy state of zs is not changed by this, neither is the state of ys, whence P_2' is still blocked. Yet, we have $[\mu_{ys}, can_{zs}(P_2')] \Vdash_{ys} \downarrow$ put which lets P_1' complete ys.put. It reaches P_1'' with $can_{ys}(P_1'') = \emptyset$ and changes the policy state of ys to $\mu_{ys}' = 1$. At this point, $[\mu_{ys}', can_{zs}(P_1'')] \Vdash_{ys} \downarrow$ get which means P_2' unblocks to execute ys.get. □

Definition 4. *Let $\Vdash_c$ be a policy for c. A method sequence m_1 blocks another m_2 in state μ, written $\mu \Vdash_c m_1 \rightarrow m_2$, if $\mu \Vdash_c \downarrow m_2$ but $[\mu, \{m_1\}] \nVdash_c \downarrow m_2$. Two method sequences m_1 and m_2 are concurrently enabled, denoted $\mu \Vdash_c m_1 \diamond m_2$ if $\mu \Vdash_c \downarrow m_1$, $\mu \Vdash_c \downarrow m_2$ and both $\mu \nVdash_c m_1 \rightarrow m_2$ and $\mu \nVdash_c m_2 \rightarrow m_1$.* □

Our operational semantics will only let a TUC execute a sequence m provided $[\mu, \gamma] \Vdash_c \downarrow m$, where μ is the current policy state of c and γ the predicted activity in the TUC's concurrent environment. Symmetrically, the environment will execute any $n \in \gamma$ only if it is enabled with respect to m, i.e., if $[\mu, \{m\}] \Vdash \downarrow n$. This means $\mu \Vdash_c m \diamond n$. Policy coherence (Definition 5 below) then implies that every interleaving of the sequences m and any $n \in \gamma$ leads to the same return values and final variable state (Proposition 1).

2.5   Coherence and Determinacy

A *method call* $m(v)$ combines a method $m \in M_c$ with a method parameter[7] $v \in \mathbb{D}$, where $\mathbb{D}$ is a universal domain for method arguments and return values,

---

[7] This is without loss of generality since $\mathbb{D}$ may contain value tuples.

including the special don't care value $_- \in \mathbb{D}$. We denote by $A_c = \{m(v) \mid m \in M_c, v \in \mathbb{D}\}$ the set of all method calls on object c. Sequences of method calls $\alpha \in A_c^*$ can be abstracted back into sequences of methods $\alpha^{\#} \in M_c^*$ by dropping the method parameters: $\varepsilon^{\#} = \varepsilon$ and $(m(v)\,\alpha)^{\#} = m\,\alpha^{\#}$.

Coherence concerns the semantics of method calls as state transformations. Let $\mathbb{S}_c$ be the domain of memory states of the object c with initial state $init_c \in \mathbb{S}_c$. Each method call $m(v) \in A_c$ corresponds to a semantical action $[\![m(v)]\!]_c \in \mathbb{S}_c \to (\mathbb{D} \times \mathbb{S}_c)$. If $s \in \mathbb{S}_c$ is the current state of the object then executing a call $m(v)$ on c returns a pair $(u, s') = [\![m(v)]\!]_c(s)$ where the first projection $u \in \mathbb{D}$ is the return value from the call and the second projection $s' \in \mathbb{S}_c$ is the new updated state of the variable. For convenience, we will denote $u = \pi_1[\![m(v)]\!]_c(s)$ by $u = s.m(v)$ and $s' = \pi_2[\![m(v)]\!]_c(s)$ by $s' = s \odot m(v)$. The action notation is extended to sequences of calls $\alpha \in A_c^*$ in the natural way: $s \odot \varepsilon = s$ and $s \odot (m(v)\,\alpha) = (s \odot m(v)) \odot \alpha$.

For policy-based scheduling we assume an abstraction function mapping a memory state $s \in \mathbb{S}_c$ into a policy state $s^{\#} \in \mathbb{P}_c$. Specifically, $init_c^{\#} = \varepsilon$. Further, we assume the abstraction commutes with method execution in the sense that if we execute a sequence of calls and then abstract the final state, we get the same as if we executed the policy automaton on the abstracted state in the first place. Formally, $(s \odot \alpha)^{\#} = s^{\#} \odot \alpha^{\#}$ for all $s \in \mathbb{S}_c$ and $\alpha \in A_c^*$.

Definition 5 (Coherence). *A* CSM *variable* c *is* policy-coherent *if for all method calls* $a, b \in A_c$ *whenever* $s^{\#} \Vdash_c a^{\#} \diamond b^{\#}$ *for a state* $s \in \mathbb{S}_c$, *then a and b are* confluent *in the sense that* $s.a = (s \odot b).a$, $s.b = (s \odot a).b$ *and* $s \odot a \odot b = s \odot b \odot a$. □

Example 3. Esterel pure signals do not carry any data value, so their memory state coincides with the policy state, $\mathbb{S}_s = \mathbb{P}_s = \{0, 1\}$ and $s^{\#} = s$. An emission emit does not return any value but sets the state of s to 1, i.e., $s.\mathtt{emit}(_-) = _- \in \mathbb{D}$ and $s \odot \mathtt{emit}(_-) = 1 \in \mathbb{S}_s$. A present test returns the state, $s.\mathtt{pres}(_-) = s$, but does not modify it, $s \odot \mathtt{pres}(_-) = s$. From the policy Fig. 1 we find that the concurrent enablings $s^{\#} \Vdash_s a^{\#} \diamond b^{\#}$ according to Definition 4 are (i) $a = b \in \{\mathtt{pres}(_-), \mathtt{emit}(_-)\}$ for arbitrary s, or (ii) $s = 1$, $a = \mathtt{emit}(_-)$ and $b = \mathtt{pres}(_-)$. In each of these cases we verify $s.a = (s \odot b).a$, $s.b = (s \odot a).b$ and $s \odot a \odot b = s \odot b \odot a$ without difficulty. Note that $1 \Vdash_s \mathtt{emit} \diamond \mathtt{pres}$ since the order of execution is irrelevant if $s = 1$. On the other hand, $0 \nVdash_s \mathtt{emit} \diamond \mathtt{pres}$ because in state 0 both methods are not confluent. Specifically, $0.\mathtt{pres}(_-) = 0 \neq 1 = (0 \odot \mathtt{emit}(_-)).\mathtt{pres}(_-)$. □

A special case are *linear precedence policies* where $\mu \Vdash_c \downarrow m$ for all $m \in M_c$ and $\mu \Vdash_c m \to n$ is a linear ordering on M_c, for all policy states μ. Then, for no state we have $\mu \Vdash_c m_1 \diamond m_2$, so there is no concurrency and thus no confluence requirement to satisfy at all. Coherence of c is trivially satisfied whatever the semantics of method calls. For any two admissible methods one takes precedence over the other and thus the enabling relation becomes deterministic. There is however a risk of deadlock which can be excluded if we assume that threads always call methods in order of decreasing precedence.

The other extreme case is where the policy makes all methods concurrently enabled, i.e., $\mu \Vdash_c m_1 \diamond m_2$ for all policy states μ and methods m_1, m_2. This avoids deadlock completely and gives maximal concurrency but imposes the strongest confluence condition, viz. independently of the scheduling order of any two methods, the resulting variable state must be the same. This requires complete isolation of the effects of any two methods. Such an extreme is used, e. g., in the CR library [19]. The typical CSM variable, however, will strike a trade-off between these two extremes. It will impose a sensible set of precedences that are strong enough to ensure coherent implementations and thus determinacy for policy-conformant scheduling, while at the same time being sufficiently relaxed to permit concurrent implementations and avoiding unnecessary deadlocks risking that programs are rejected by the compiler as un-scheduleable.

Whatever the policies, if the variables are coherent, then all policy-conformant interleavings are indistinguishable for each CSM variable. To state schedule invariance in its general form we lift method actions and independence to multi-variable sequences of methods calls $A = \{c.m(v) \mid c \in O, m(v) \in A_c\}$. For a given sequence $\alpha \in A^*$ let $\pi_c(\alpha) \in A_c^*$ be the projection of α on c, formally $\pi_c(\varepsilon) = \varepsilon$, $\pi_c(c.m(v)\,\alpha) = m(v)\,\pi_c(\alpha)$ and $\pi_c(c'.m(v)\,\alpha) = \pi_c(\alpha)$ for $c' \neq c$. A global memory $\Sigma \in \mathbb{S} = \prod_{c \in O} \mathbb{S}_c$ assigns a local memory $\Sigma.c \in \mathbb{S}_c$ to each variable c. We write $init$ for the initial memory that has $init.c = init_c$ and $(init.c)^\# = \varepsilon \in \mathbb{P}_c$.

Given a global memory $\Sigma \in \mathbb{S}$ and sequences $\alpha, \beta \in A^*$ of method calls, we extend the independence relation of Definition 4 variable-wise, defining $\Sigma \Vdash \alpha \diamond \beta$ iff $(\Sigma.c)^\# \Vdash_c (\pi_c(\alpha))^\# \diamond (\pi_c(\beta))^\#$. The application of a method call $a \in A$ to a memory $\Sigma \in \mathbb{S}$ is written $\Sigma.a \in \mathbb{S}$ and defined $(\Sigma.(c.m(v))).c = (\Sigma.c).m(v)$ and $(\Sigma.(c.m(v))).c' = \Sigma.c'$ for $c' \neq c$. Analogously, method actions are lifted to global memories, i.e., $(\Sigma \odot c.m(v)).c' = \Sigma.c'$ if $c' \neq c$ and $(\Sigma \odot c.m(v)).c = \Sigma.c \odot m(v)$.

Proposition 1 (Commutation). *Let all CSM variables be policy-coherent and $\Sigma \Vdash a \diamond \alpha$ for a memory $\Sigma \in \mathbb{S}$, method call $a \in V$ and sequences of method calls $\alpha \in V^*$. Then, $\Sigma \odot a \odot \alpha = \Sigma \odot \alpha \odot a$ and $\Sigma.a = (\Sigma \odot \alpha).a$.*

2.6   Policies and Modularity

Consider the synchronous data-flow network cnt in Fig. 3b with three process nodes, a multiplexer mux, a register reg and an incrementor inc. Their DCoL code is given in Fig. 3a. The network implements a settable counter, which produces at its output ys a stream of consecutive integers, incremented with each clock tick. The wires ys, zs and ws are IVars (see Example 2) carrying a single integer value per tick. The input xs is a pure Esterel signal (see Example 1). The counter state is stored by reg in a local variable xv with read and write methods that can be called by a single thread only. The register is initialised to value 0 and in each subsequent tick the value at ys is stored. The inc takes the value at zs and increments it. When the signal xs is absent, mux passes the incremented value on ws to ys for the next tick. Otherwise, if xs is present then mux resets ys.

The evaluation order is implemented by the policies of the IVars ys, zs and ws. In each case the put method takes precedence over get which makes sure that the latter is blocked until the former has been executed. The causality cycle of the feedback loop is broken by the fact that the reg node first sends the current counter value to zs before it waits for the new value at ys. The other nodes mux and inc, in contrast, first read their inputs and then send to their output.

(b) Block diagram of the feedback network.

```
module cnt
[ % mux node
  loop
    v = xs.pres();
    if v then ys.put(0);
          else u = ws.get();
               ys.put(u);
  end
] ||
[ % reg node
  xv.write(0);
  loop
    v = xv.read(); zs.send(v);
    u = ys.get(); xv.write(u);
  end
] ||
[ % inc node
  loop
    v = zs.get(); ws.put(v+1);
  end
]
```

(a) Network with mux, reg, inc threads.

```
module cnt-cmp
reg.init(0);
[ % mux-cmp node
  loop
    v = xs.pres();
    if v then reg.set(0);
          else u = ws.get();
               reg.set(u);
  end
] ||
[ % inc-cmp node
  loop
    v = reg.get(); ws.put(v+1);
  end
]
```

(c) Network with reg as a precompiled DCoL object.

Fig. 3. Synchronous data-flow network cnt built from control-flow processes.

Now suppose, for modularity, the reg node is pre-compiled into a synchronous IO automaton to be used by mux and inc as a black box component. Then, reg must be split into three *modes* [20] reg.init, reg.get and reg.set that can be called independently in each instant. The init mode initialises the register memory with 0. The get mode extracts the buffered value and set stores a new value into the register. Since there may be data races if get and set are called concurrently on reg, a policy must be imposed. In the scheduling of Fig. 3b, first reg.get is executed to place the output on zs. Then, reg waits for mux to produce the next value of ys from xs or ws. Finally, reg.set is executed to store the current value of ys for the next tick. Thus, the natural policy for the register is to require that in each tick set is called by at most one thread and if so no concurrent call to get by another thread happens afterwards. In addition, the policy requires init to take place at least once before any set or get. Hence, the policy has two states $\mathbb{P}_{reg} = \{0, 1\}$ with initial $\varepsilon = 0$ and admissibility such that $0 \Vdash_{reg} \downarrow m$ iff $m = $ init and $1 \Vdash_{reg} \downarrow m$ for all m. The transitions are $0 \odot$ init $= 1$ and $1 \odot m = 1$ for all $m \in \mathsf{M}_{reg}$. Further, for coherence, in state 1 no set may be concurrent and every get must take place before any concurrent set. This means, we have $1 \Vdash_{reg} m \to$ set for all $m \in \{$get, set$\}$. Figure 3c shows the partially compiled code in which reg is treated as a compiled object. The policy on reg makes sure the accesses by mux and inc are scheduled in the right way (see Example 4). Note that reg is not an IVar because it has memory.

The cnt example exhibits a general pattern found in the modular compilation of SP: Modules (here reg) may be exercised *several times* in a synchronous tick through *modes* which are executed in a specific *prescribed order*. Mode calls (here reg.set, reg.get) in the same module are coupled via common *shared memory* (here the local variable xs) while mode calls in distinct modules are isolated from each other [15, 20].

3   Constructive Semantics of DCoL

To formalise our semantics it is technically expedient to keep track of the *completion status* of each active thread inside the program expression. This results in a syntax for *processes* distinguished from programs in that each parallel composition $P_1 \,_{k_1} \| \,_{k_2} P_2$ is labelled by *completion codes* $k_i \in \{\bot, 0, 1\}$ which indicate whether each thread is *waiting* $k_i = \bot$, *terminated* 0 or *pausing* $k_i = 1$. Since we remove a process from the parallel as soon as it terminates then the code $k_i = 0$ cannot occur. An expression $P_1 \| P_2$ is considered a special case of a process with $k_i = \bot$. The formal semantics is given by a reduction relation on processes

$$\Sigma; \Pi \vdash P \overset{m}{\Rightarrow} \Sigma' \vdash_{k'} P' \tag{2}$$

specified by the inductive rules in Figs. 4 and 5. The relation (2) determines an instantaneous *sequential reduction step* of process P, called an *sstep*, that follows a sequence of enabled method calls $m \in \mathsf{M}^*$ in sequential program order in P. This does not include any context switches between concurrent threads inside P. For thread communication, several ssteps must be chained up, as described later. The sstep (2) results in an updated memory Σ' and residual process P'. The subscript k' is a completion code, described below. The reduction (2) is performed in a context consisting of a global memory $\Sigma \in \mathbb{S}$ (*must* context) containing the current state of all CSM variables and an environment prediction $\Pi \subseteq \mathsf{M}^*$ (*can* context). The prediction records all potentially outstanding methods sequences from threads running *concurrently* with P.

We write $\pi_c(m) \in \mathsf{M}_c^*$ for the projection of a method sequence $m \in \mathsf{M}^*$ to variable c and write $\pi_c(\Pi)$ for its lifting to sets of sequences. Prefixing is lifted, too, i.e., $c.m \odot \Pi = \{c.m\, m \mid m \in \Pi\}$ for any $c.m \in \mathsf{M}$.

Performing a method call $\mathsf{c}.m(v)$ in $\Sigma; \Pi$ advances the *must* context to $\Sigma \odot \mathsf{c}.m(v)$ but leaves Π unchanged. The sequence of methods $\boldsymbol{m} \in \mathsf{M}^*$ in (2) is *enabled* in $\Sigma; \Pi$, written $[\Sigma, \Pi] \Vdash \downarrow \boldsymbol{m}$ meaning that $[(\Sigma.\mathsf{c})^\#, \pi_\mathsf{c}(\Pi)] \Vdash_\mathsf{c} \downarrow \pi_\mathsf{c}(\boldsymbol{m})$ for all $\mathsf{c} \in \mathsf{O}$. In this way, the context $[\Sigma, \Pi]$ forms a joint policy state for all variables for the TUC P, in the sense of Sect. 2 (Definition 3).

Sequence

$$\frac{\Sigma; \Pi \vdash P \overset{m}{\Rightarrow} \Sigma' \vdash_{k'} P' \qquad k' \neq 0}{\Sigma; \Pi \vdash P \mathbin{;} Q \overset{m}{\Rightarrow} \Sigma' \vdash_{k'} P' \mathbin{;} Q} \; \mathsf{Seq}_1$$

$$\frac{\Sigma; \Pi \vdash P \overset{m_1}{\Rightarrow} \Sigma' \vdash_0 P' \qquad \Sigma'; \Pi \vdash Q \overset{m_2}{\Rightarrow} \Sigma'' \vdash_{k'} Q'}{\Sigma; \Pi \vdash P \mathbin{;} Q \overset{m_1 m_2}{\Rightarrow} \Sigma'' \vdash_{k'} Q'} \; \mathsf{Seq}_2$$

Completion

$$\frac{}{\Sigma; \Pi \vdash \mathsf{skip} \overset{\epsilon}{\Rightarrow} \Sigma \vdash_0 \mathsf{skip}} \; \mathsf{Cmp}_1 \qquad\qquad \frac{}{\Sigma; \Pi \vdash \mathsf{pause} \overset{\epsilon}{\Rightarrow} \Sigma \vdash_1 \mathsf{pause}} \; \mathsf{Cmp}_2$$

Recursion

$$\frac{\Sigma; \Pi \vdash P\{\mathsf{rec}\,p.\,P/p\} \overset{m}{\Rightarrow} \Sigma' \vdash_{k'} P'}{\Sigma; \Pi \vdash \mathsf{rec}\,p.\,P \overset{m}{\Rightarrow} \Sigma' \vdash_{k'} P'} \; \mathsf{Rec}$$

Fig. 4. SStep reductions for sequence, completion and recursion.

Most of the rules in Figs. 4 and 5 should be straightforward for the reader familiar with structural operational semantics. Seq_1 is the case of a sequential $P; Q$ where P pauses or waits ($k' \neq 0$) and Seq_2 is where P terminates and control passes into Q. The statements skip and pause are handled by rules Cmp_1 and Cmp_2. The rule Rec explains recursion $\mathsf{rec}\,p.P$ by syntactic unfolding of the recursion body P. All interaction with the memory takes place in the method calls $\mathsf{let}\,x = \mathsf{c}.m(e)$ in P. Rule Let_1 is applicable when the method call is enabled, i.e., $[\Sigma, \Pi] \Vdash \downarrow \mathsf{c}.m$. Since processes are closed, the argument expression e must evaluate, $eval(e) = v$, and we obtain the new memory $\Sigma \odot \mathsf{c}.m(v)$ and return value $\Sigma.\mathsf{c}.m(v)$. The return value is substituted for the local (stack allocated) identifier x, giving the continuation process $P\{\Sigma.\mathsf{c}.m(v)/x\}$ which is run in the updated context $\Sigma \odot \mathsf{c}.m(v); \Pi$. The prediction Π remains the same. The second rule Let_2 is used when the method call is blocked or the thread wants to wait and yield to the scheduler. The rules for conditionals Cnd_1, Cnd_2 are canonical. More interesting are the rules Par_1–Par_4 for parallel composition, which implement non-deterministic thread switching. It is here where we need to generate predictions and pass them between the threads to exercise the policy control.

The key operation is the computation of the *can*-prediction of a process P to obtain an over-approximation of the set of possible method sequences potentially executed by P. For compositionality we work with sequences $can^s(P) \subseteq \mathsf{M}^* \times \{0, 1\}$ *stoppered* with a completion code 0 if the sequence ends in termination or

Method Call

$$\frac{[\Sigma, \Pi] \Vdash \downarrow c.m \quad eval(e) = v \quad \Sigma \odot c.m(v); \Pi \vdash P\{\Sigma.c.m(v)/x\} \overset{m}{\Rightarrow} \Sigma' \vdash_{k'} P'}{\Sigma; \Pi \vdash \mathtt{let}\ x = c.m(e)\ \mathtt{in}\ P \xRightarrow{c.m\ m} \Sigma' \vdash_{k'} P'} \ \text{Let}_1$$

$$\frac{}{\Sigma; \Pi \vdash \mathtt{let}\ x = c.m(e)\ \mathtt{in}\ P \overset{\varepsilon}{\Rightarrow} \Sigma \vdash_{\perp} \mathtt{let}\ x = c.m(e)\ \mathtt{in}\ P} \ \text{Let}_2$$

Conditional

$$\frac{eval(e) = \mathsf{true} \quad \Sigma; \Pi \vdash P \overset{m}{\Rightarrow} \Sigma' \vdash_{k'} P'}{\Sigma; \Pi \vdash \mathtt{if}\ e\ \mathtt{then}\ P\ \mathtt{else}\ Q \overset{m}{\Rightarrow} \Sigma' \vdash_{k'} P'} \ \text{Cnd}_1$$

$$\frac{eval(e) = \mathsf{false} \quad \Sigma; \Pi \vdash Q \overset{m}{\Rightarrow} \Sigma' \vdash_{k'} Q'}{\Sigma; \Pi \vdash \mathtt{if}\ e\ \mathtt{then}\ P\ \mathtt{else}\ Q \overset{m}{\Rightarrow} \Sigma' \vdash_{k'} Q'} \ \text{Cnd}_2$$

Parallel

$$\frac{\Sigma; \Pi \otimes can(Q) \vdash P \overset{m}{\Rightarrow} \Sigma' \vdash_{k'} P' \quad k' \neq 0}{\Sigma; \Pi \vdash P\ _k\|\ _{k_Q} Q \overset{m}{\Rightarrow} \Sigma' \vdash_{k' \sqcap k_Q} P'\ _{k'}\|\ _{k_Q} Q} \ \text{Par}_1$$

$$\frac{\Sigma; \Pi \otimes can(Q) \vdash P \overset{m}{\Rightarrow} \Sigma' \vdash_0 P'}{\Sigma; \Pi \vdash P\ _k\|\ _{k_Q} Q \overset{m}{\Rightarrow} \Sigma' \vdash_{k_Q} Q} \ \text{Par}_2$$

$$\frac{\Sigma; \Pi \otimes can(P) \vdash Q \overset{m}{\Rightarrow} \Sigma' \vdash_{k'} Q' \quad k' \neq 0}{\Sigma; \Pi \vdash P\ _{k_P}\|\ _k Q \overset{m}{\Rightarrow} \Sigma' \vdash_{k_P \sqcap k'} P\ _{k_P}\|\ _{k'} Q'} \ \text{Par}_3$$

$$\frac{\Sigma; \Pi \otimes can(P) \vdash Q \overset{m}{\Rightarrow} \Sigma' \vdash_0 Q'}{\Sigma; \Pi \vdash P\ _{k_P}\|\ _k Q \overset{m}{\Rightarrow} \Sigma' \vdash_{k_P} P} \ \text{Par}_4$$

Fig. 5. SStep reductions for method calls, conditional and parallel.

1 if it ends in pausing. The symbols $\perp_0$, $\perp_1$ and $\top$ are the *terminated, paused* and *fully unconstrained can* contexts, respectively, with $\perp_0 = \{(\varepsilon, 0)\}$, $\perp_1 = \{(\varepsilon, 1)\}$ and $\top = M^* \times \{0, 1\}$. The set $can^s(P)$, defined in Fig. 6, is extracted from the structure of P using prefixing $c.m \odot \Pi'$, choice $\Pi'_1 \oplus \Pi'_2 = \Pi'_1 \cup \Pi'_2$, parallel $\Pi'_1 \otimes \Pi'_2$ and sequential composition $\Pi'_1 \cdot \Pi'_2$. Sequential composition is obtained pairwise on stoppered sequences such that $(m, 0) \cdot (n, c) = (m\,n, c)$ and $(m, 1) \cdot (n, c) = (m, 1)$. As a consequence, $\perp_0 \cdot \Pi' = \Pi'$ and $\perp_1 \cdot \Pi' = \perp_1$. Parallel composition is pairwise free interleaving with synchronisation on completion codes. Specifically, a product $(m, c) \otimes (n, d)$ generates all interleavings of m and n with a completion that models a parallel composition that terminates iff both threads terminate and pauses if one pauses. Formally, $(m, c) \otimes (n, d) = \{(c, max(c, d)) \mid c \in m \otimes n\}$. Thus, $\Pi'_P \otimes \Pi'_Q = \perp_0$ iff $\Pi'_P = \perp_0 = \Pi'_Q$ and $\Pi'_P \otimes \Pi'_Q = \perp_1$ if $\Pi'_P = \perp_1 = \Pi'_Q$, or $\Pi'_P = \perp_0$ and $\Pi'_Q = \perp_1$, or $\Pi'_P = \perp_1$ and $\Pi'_Q = \perp_0$. From $can^s(P)$ we obtain $can(P) \subseteq M^*$ by dropping all stopper codes, i.e., $can(P) = \{m \mid \exists d. \ (m, d) \in can^s(P)\}$.

The rule Par_1 exercises a parallel $P\ _k\|\ _{k_Q} Q$ by performing an sstep in P. This sstep is taken in the extended context $\Sigma; \Pi \otimes can(Q)$ in which the prediction of the sibling Q is added to the method prediction Π for the outer environment

$$can^s(\text{skip}) = can^s(p) = \perp_0 \qquad can^s(\text{pause}) = \perp_1$$

$$can^s(\text{rec}\,p.\,P) = can^s(P) \qquad can^s(P \parallel Q) = can^s(P) \otimes can^s(Q)$$

$$can^s(P\,;\,Q) = \begin{cases} can^s(P) & \text{if } can^s(P) \subseteq \mathsf{M}^* \times \{1\} \\ can^s(P) \cdot can^s(Q) & \text{otherwise} \end{cases}$$

$$can^s(\text{let}\,x = c.m(e)\,\text{in}\,P) = c.m \odot can^s(P)$$

$$can^s(\text{if}\,e\,\text{then}\,P\,\text{else}\,Q) = \begin{cases} can^s(P) & \text{if } eval(e) = \text{true} \\ can^s(Q) & \text{if } eval(e) = \text{false} \\ can^s(P) \oplus can^s(Q) & \text{otherwise.} \end{cases}$$

Fig. 6. Computing the *can* prediction.

in which the parent $P \parallel Q$ is running. In this way, Q can block method calls of P. When P finally yields as P' with a non-terminating completion code, $0 \neq k' \in \{\perp, 1\}$, the parallel completes as $P'\,_{k'}\!\parallel_{k_Q} Q$ with code $k' \sqcap k_Q$. This operation is defined $k_1 \sqcap k_2 = 1$ if $k_1 = 1 = k_2$ and $k_1 \sqcap k_2 = \perp$, otherwise. When P terminates its sstep with code $k' = 0$ then we need rule Par_2 which removes child P' from the parallel composition. The rules $\mathsf{Par}_3, \mathsf{Par}_4$ are symmetrical to $\mathsf{Par}_1, \mathsf{Par}_2$. They run the right child Q of a parallel $P\,_{k_P}\!\parallel_k Q$.

Completion and Stability. A process P' is *0-stable* if $P' = \text{skip}$ and *1-stable* if $P' = \text{pause}$ or $P' = P_1'\,;\,P_2'$ and P_1' is *1-stable*, or $P' = P_1'\,_1\!\parallel_1 P_2'$, and P_i' are 1-stable. A process is *stable* if it is 0-stable or 1-stable. A process expression is *well-formed* if in each sub-expression $P_1\,_{k_1}\!\parallel_{k_2} P_2$ of P the completion annotations are matching with the processes, i.e., if $k_i \neq \perp$ then P_i is k_i-stable. Stable processes are well-formed by definition. For stable processes we define a *(syntactic) tick function* which steps a stable process to the next tick. It is defined such that $\sigma(\text{skip}) = \text{skip}$, $\sigma(\text{pause}) = \text{skip}$, $\sigma(P_1'\,;\,P_2') = \sigma(P_1')\,;\,P_2'$ and $\sigma(P_1'\,_{k_1}\!\parallel_{k_2} P_2') = \sigma(P_1') \parallel \sigma(P_2')$.

Example 4. The data-flow `cnt-cmp` from Fig. 3c can be represented as a DCoL process in the form $C = \text{reg.init}(0)\,;\,(M\,_{\perp}\!\parallel_{\perp} I)$ with

$$M =_{df} \text{rec}\,p.\,\text{v} = \text{xs.pres}()\,;\,P(v)\,;\,\text{pause}\,;\,p$$

$$P(v) =_{df} \text{if}\,v\,\text{then}\,\text{reg.set}(0)\,;\,\text{else}\,Q$$

$$Q =_{df} u = \text{ws.get}()\,;\,\text{reg.set}(u)\,;$$

$$I =_{df} \text{rec}\,q.\,\text{v} = \text{reg.get}()\,;\,\text{ws.put}(v+1)\,;\,\text{pause}\,;\,q.$$

Let us evaluate process C from an initialised memory Σ_0 such that $\Sigma_0.\text{xs} = 0 = \Sigma_0.\text{ws}$, and empty environment prediction $\{\epsilon\}$.

The first sstep is executed from the context $\Sigma_0;\{\epsilon\}$ with empty *can* prediction. Note that $\text{reg.init}(0)\,;\,(M\,_{\perp}\!\parallel_{\perp} I)$ abbreviates $\text{let}\,\_ = \text{reg.init}(0)$ in $(M\,_{\perp}\!\parallel_{\perp} I)$. In context $\Sigma_0;\{\epsilon\}$ the method call $\text{reg.init}(0)$ is enabled, i.e., $[\Sigma_0, \{\epsilon\}] \Vdash\,\downarrow \text{reg.init}$. Since $eval(0) = 0$, we can execute the first method call of C using rule Let_1. This advances the memory to $\Sigma_1 = \Sigma_0 \odot \text{reg.init}(0)$.

The continuation process $M \perp \| \perp I$ is now executed in context $\Sigma_1; \perp_0$. The left child M starts with method call $\mathtt{xs.pres}()$ and the right child I with $\mathtt{reg.get}()$. The latter is admissible, since $(\Sigma_1.\mathtt{reg})^\# = 1$. Moreover, $\mathtt{get}$ does not need to honour any precedences, whence it is enabled, $[\Sigma_1, \Pi] \Vdash \downarrow \mathtt{reg.get}$ for any Π. On the other hand, $\mathtt{xs.pres}$ in M is enabled only if $(\Sigma_1.\mathtt{xs})^\# = 1$ or if there is no concurrent $\mathtt{emit}$ predicted for $\mathtt{xs}$. Indeed, this is the case: The concurrent context of M is $\Pi_I = \{\epsilon\} \otimes can(I) = can(I) = \{\mathtt{reg.get} \cdot \mathtt{ws.put}\}$. We project $\pi_{\mathtt{xs}}(\Pi_I) = \{\epsilon\}$ and find $[\Sigma_1, \Pi_I] \Vdash \downarrow \mathtt{xs.pres}$. Hence, we have a non-deterministic choice to take an sstep in M or in I. Let us use rule $\mathsf{Par}_1/\mathsf{Par}_2$ to run M in context $\Sigma; \Pi_I$. By loop unfolding Rec and rule Let_1 we execute the present test of M which returns the value $\Sigma_1.\mathtt{xs.pres}() = \mathtt{false}$. This leads to an updated memory $\Sigma_2 = \Sigma_1 \odot \mathtt{xs.pres}() = \Sigma_1$ and continuation process $P(\mathtt{false}); \mathtt{pause}; M$. In this (right associated) sequential composition we first execute $P(\mathtt{false})$ where the conditional rule Cnd_2 switches to the $\mathtt{else}$ branch Q which is $u = \mathtt{ws.get}(); \mathtt{reg.set}(u);$, still in the context Σ_2, Π_I. The reading of the data-flow variable $\mathtt{ws}$, however, is not enabled, $[\Sigma_2, \Pi_I] \not\Vdash \downarrow \mathtt{ws.get}$, because $(\Sigma_2.\mathtt{ws})^\# = 0$ and thus $\mathtt{get}$ not admissible. The sstep blocks with rule Let_2:

$$\dfrac{\dfrac{\dfrac{\dfrac{\dfrac{\dfrac{\Sigma_2; \Pi_I \vdash Q \overset{\epsilon}{\Rightarrow} \Sigma_2 \vdash_\perp Q}{\Sigma_2; \Pi_I \vdash P(\mathtt{false}) \overset{\epsilon}{\Rightarrow} \Sigma_2 \vdash_\perp Q} \mathsf{Cnd}_2}{\Sigma_2; \Pi_I \vdash P(\mathtt{false}); \mathtt{pause}; M \overset{\epsilon}{\Rightarrow} \Sigma_2 \vdash_\perp Q; \mathtt{pause}; M} \mathsf{Seq}_1}{\Sigma_1; \Pi_I \vdash \mathtt{v} = \mathtt{xs.pres}(); P(v); \mathtt{pause}; M \overset{\epsilon}{\Rightarrow} \Sigma_2 \vdash_\perp Q; \mathtt{pause}; M} \mathsf{Let}_1(\Sigma_1; \Pi_I \vdash \downarrow \mathtt{xs.pres})}{\Sigma_1; \Pi_I \vdash M \overset{m_2}{\Longrightarrow} \Sigma_2 \vdash_\perp Q; \mathtt{pause}; M} \mathsf{Rec}}{\Sigma_1; \{\epsilon\} \vdash M \perp \| \perp I \overset{m_2}{\Longrightarrow} \Sigma_2 \vdash_\perp (Q; \mathtt{pause}; M) \perp \| \perp I} \mathsf{Par}_1}{\Sigma; \{\epsilon\} \vdash C \overset{m_1 m_2}{\Longrightarrow} \Sigma_2 \vdash_\perp (Q; \mathtt{pause}; M) \perp \| \perp I} \mathsf{Let}_1(\Sigma; \perp_0 \Vdash \downarrow \mathtt{reg.init})$$

where $m_1 = \mathtt{reg.init}$ and $m_2 = \mathtt{xs.pres}$. In the next sstep, from $\Sigma_2; \Pi_Q$ with $\Pi_Q = \{\epsilon\} \otimes can(Q; \mathtt{pause}; M) = can(Q; \mathtt{pause}; M) = \{\mathtt{ws.get} \cdot \mathtt{reg.set}\}$ we let the process I execute its $\mathtt{reg.get}()$ with rules Rec and Let_1. The return value is $v = \Sigma_2.\mathtt{reg.get}() = 0$. Then, from the updated memory $\Sigma_3 = \Sigma_2 \odot \mathtt{reg.get}()$ we run the continuation process $\mathtt{ws.put}(0 + 1); \mathtt{pause}; I$. The $\mathtt{ws.put}$ is enabled if the IVar is empty and there is no concurrent $\mathtt{put}$ on $\mathtt{ws}$ predicted from M. Both conditions hold since $(\Sigma_3.\mathtt{ws})^\# = (\Sigma.\mathtt{ws})^\# = 0$ and $\pi_{\mathtt{ws}}(\Pi_Q) = \{\mathtt{get}\}$. Therefore, $[\Sigma_3, \Pi_Q] \Vdash \downarrow \mathtt{ws.put}$. With the evaluation $eval(0 + 1) = 1$ the rule Let_1 permits us to update the memory as $\Sigma_4 = \Sigma_3 \odot \mathtt{ws.put}(1)$ and continue with process $\mathtt{pause}; I$ which completes by pausing. Formally, this sstep is:

$$\dfrac{\dfrac{\dfrac{\dfrac{\dfrac{\Sigma_4; \Pi_Q \vdash \mathtt{pause} \overset{\epsilon}{\Rightarrow} \Sigma_4 \vdash_1 \mathtt{pause}}{\Sigma_4; \Pi_Q \vdash \mathtt{pause}; I \overset{\epsilon}{\Rightarrow} \Sigma_4 \vdash_1 \mathtt{pause}; I} \mathsf{Cmp}_2 \quad \mathsf{Seq}_1}{\Sigma_3; \Pi_Q \vdash \mathtt{ws.put}(0+1); \mathtt{pause}; I \overset{m_4}{\Longrightarrow} \Sigma_4 \vdash_1 \mathtt{pause}; I} \mathsf{Let}_2}{\Sigma_2; \Pi_Q \vdash v = \mathtt{reg.get}(); \mathtt{ws.put}(v+1); \mathtt{pause}; I \overset{m_3 m_4}{\Longrightarrow} \Sigma_4 \vdash_1 \mathtt{pause}; I} \mathsf{Let}_1}{\Sigma_2; \Pi_Q \vdash I \overset{m_3 m_4}{\Longrightarrow} \Sigma_4 \vdash_1 \mathtt{pause}; I} \mathsf{Rec}}{\Sigma_2; \{\epsilon\} \vdash (Q; \mathtt{pause}; M) \perp \| \perp I \overset{m_3 m_4}{\Longrightarrow} \Sigma_4 \vdash_\perp (Q; \mathtt{pause}; M) \perp \|_1 (\mathtt{pause}; I)} \mathsf{Par}_3$$

where $m_3 = $ reg.get and $m_4 = $ ws.put. In the next sstep the waiting method $u = $ ws.get in Q is now admissible and can proceed, $(\Sigma_4.\text{ws})^\# = ((\Sigma_3 \odot \text{ws.put}(1)).\text{ws})^\# = 1$ and thus $[\Sigma_4, \Pi] \Vdash \downarrow \text{ws.get}$ for all Π. The return value is $u = \Sigma_4.\text{ws.get}() = 1$, the updated memory $\Sigma_5 = \Sigma_4 \odot \text{ws.put}(1)$ and the continuation process reg.set(1); pause; M. The register set method is admissible since $(\Sigma_4.\text{reg})^\# = 1$ and also enabled because there is no get predicted in the concurrent environment $\perp_0$. Thus, $[\Sigma_5, \perp_0] \Vdash \downarrow \text{reg.set}$. The execution of the method yields the memory $\Sigma_6 = \Sigma_5 \odot \text{reg.set}(1)$ with continuation process pause ; M which completes by pausing. This yields the derivation tree:

$$\cfrac{\cfrac{\cfrac{\Sigma_6; \{\epsilon\} \vdash \text{pause}; M \xRightarrow{\varsigma} \Sigma_6 \vdash_1 \text{pause}; M}{\Sigma_5; \{\epsilon\} \vdash \text{reg.set}(1); \text{pause}; M \xRightarrow{m_6} \Sigma_6 \vdash_1 \text{pause}; M} \text{Cmp}_2}{\Sigma_4; \{\epsilon\} \vdash Q; \text{pause}; M \xRightarrow{m_5 m_6} \Sigma_6 \vdash_1 \text{pause}; M} \text{Let}_1}{\Sigma_4; \{\epsilon\} \vdash (Q; \text{pause}; M) {}_\perp\|{}_1 (\text{pause}; I) \xRightarrow{m_5 m_6} \Sigma_6 \vdash_1 (\text{pause}; M) {}_1\|{}_1 (\text{pause}; I)} \text{Par}_2$$

where $m_5 = $ ws.get and $m_6 = $ reg.set. To justify the rule Par_2 consider that $\{\epsilon\} \otimes can(\text{pause}; I) = \{\epsilon\} \otimes \{\epsilon\} = \{\epsilon\}$. At this point we have reached a 1-stable process. With the tick function we advance to the next tick, $\sigma((\text{pause}; M) {}_1\|{}_1 (\text{pause}; I)) = (\text{skip}; M) {}_\perp\|{}_\perp (\text{skip}; I)$ which behaves like $M {}_\perp\|{}_\perp I$.   □

3.1   Determinacy, Termination and Constructiveness

Determinacy of DCoL is a result of two components, monotonicity of policy-conformant scheduling and CSM coherence. Monotonicity ensures that whenever a method is executable and policy-enabled, then it remains policy-enabled under arbitrary ssteps of the environment. Symmetrically, the environment cannot be blocked by a thread taking policy-enabled computation steps.

The second building block for determinacy is CSM variable coherence. Consider a context $\Sigma; \Pi_Q$ in which we run an sstep of P with prediction Π_Q for concurrent process Q, resulting in a final memory Σ'_P arising from executing a sequence m_P of method calls from P. Because of the policy constraint, the sequence m_P must be enabled under all predictions $n \in \Pi_Q$, i.e., $[\Sigma, n] \Vdash \downarrow m_P$. Suppose, on the other side, we sstep the process Q in the same memory Σ with prediction Π_P for P, resulting in an action sequence m_Q and final memory Σ'_Q. Then, by the same reasoning, $[\Sigma, n] \Vdash \downarrow m_Q$ for all $n \in \Pi_P$. But since m_P is an actual execution of P it must be in the prediction for P, i.e., $m_P \in \Pi_P$ and symmetrically, $m_Q \in \Pi_Q$. But then we have $[\Sigma, m_Q] \Vdash \downarrow m_P$ and $[\Sigma, m_P] \Vdash \downarrow m_P$ which means $\Sigma \Vdash m_P \diamond m_Q$. Now if the semantics of method calls is policy-coherent then the Monotonicity can be exploited to derive a confluence property for processes which guarantees that m_P can still be executed by P in state Σ'_Q and m_Q by Q in state Σ'_P, and both lead to the same final memory.

Theorem 1 (Diamond Property). *If all* CSM *variables are policy-coherent then the sstep semantics is confluent. Formally, given two derivations* $\Sigma; \Pi \vdash P \overset{m_1}{\Rightarrow} \Sigma_1 \vdash_{k_1} P_1$ *and* $\Sigma; \Pi \vdash P \overset{m_2}{\Rightarrow} \Sigma_2 \vdash_{k_2} P_2$, *Then, there exist* Σ', k' *and* P' *such that* $\Sigma_1; \Pi \vdash P_1 \overset{n_1}{\Rightarrow} \Sigma' \vdash_{k'} P'$ *and* $\Sigma_1; \Pi \vdash P_2 \overset{n_2}{\Rightarrow} \Sigma' \vdash_{k'} P'$.

Theorem 1 shows that no matter how we schedule the ssteps of local threads to create an sstep of a parallel composition, the final result will not diverge. This does not guarantee completion of a process. However, it implies that the question of whether P blocks or makes progress does not depend on the order in which concurrent threads are scheduled. Either a process completes or it does not. All ssteps in a process can be scheduled with maximal parallelism without interference.

A main program P is run at the top level in an "environmentally closed" form of ssteps (2) where the prediction is empty $\Pi = \{\epsilon\}$ and thus acts neutrally. We iterate such ssteps to construct a macro-step reaction. Let us write

$$\Sigma \vdash P \Rightarrow \Sigma' \vdash P' \tag{3}$$

if there exists k', m such that $\Sigma; \bot_0 \vdash P \overset{m}{\Rightarrow} \Sigma' \vdash_{k'} P'$. The relation $\Rightarrow$ is well-founded for clock-guarded processes in the sense that it has no infinite chains.

Theorem 2 (Termination). *Let* $P_0, P_1, P_2, \ldots$ *and* $\Sigma_0, \Sigma_1, \Sigma_2, \ldots$ *be infinite sequences of processes and memories, respectively, with* $\Sigma_i \vdash P_i \Rightarrow \Sigma_{i+1} \vdash P_{i+1}$. *If* P_0 *is clock-guarded then there is* $n \geq 0$ *with* $\Sigma_n = \Sigma_i$, $P_n = P_i$ *for all* $i \geq n$.

The fixed point semantics will iterate (3) until it reaches a P^* such that $\Sigma^* \vdash P^* \Rightarrow \Sigma^* \vdash P^*$. By Termination Theorem 2 this must exist for clock-guarded processes. If $can^s(P^*) = \bot_0$ then P^* is 0-stable and the program P has terminated. If $can^s(P^*) = \bot_1$, the residual P^* is pausing.

Definition 6 (Macro Step). *A run* $\Sigma \vdash P \Rightarrow \Sigma' \vdash P'$ *is a sequence of ssteps with processes* $P_0, P_1, P_2, \ldots, P_n$ *and sequences of method calls* $m_1, m_2, \ldots m_n$ *such that for all* $1 \leq i \leq n$,

$$\Sigma_{i-1}; \bot_0 \vdash P_{i-1} \Rightarrow \Sigma_i \vdash_{k_i} P_i,$$

where $P_0 = P$, $\Sigma_0 = \Sigma$, $\Sigma_n = \Sigma'$ *and* $P_n = P'$. *A run is called a* macro-step *if it is maximal, i.e., if* $\Sigma' \vdash P' \Rightarrow \Sigma'' \vdash P''$ *implies* $\Sigma' = \Sigma''$ *and* $P' = P''$. *The macro-step is called* stabilising *if the final* P' *is stable, i.e.,* $k_n \neq \bot$ *and the clock is admissible, i.e., if* $(\Sigma'.c)^{\#} \odot \sigma$ *is defined for all* $c \in O$. *The macro-step is* pausing *if* $k_n = 1$ *and* terminating *if* $k_n = 0$. □

Given a pausing macro-step $\Sigma \vdash P \Rightarrow \Sigma' \vdash P'$, then the next tick starts with process $\sigma(P')$ in memory Σ'' such that $(\pi_c(\Sigma'))^{\#} -\sigma\rightarrow (\pi_c(\Sigma''))^{\#}$ for all $c \in O$. This only constrains the abstract policy state of each variable in Σ'' not their memory content. In this way, CSM variables can introduce an arbitrary new memory Σ'' with every clock tick.

Theorem 3 (Macro-step Determinism). *If all* CSM *variables are policy-coherent then for two macro steps* $\Sigma \vdash P \Rightarrow \Sigma_1 \vdash P_1$ *and* $\Sigma \vdash P \Rightarrow \Sigma_2 \vdash P_2$ *we have* $\Sigma_1 = \Sigma_2$ *and* $P_1 = P_2$.

Definition 7 (Constructiveness). *A program P is* policy-constructive, *for a set of policy coherent* CSM *variables, if for arbitrary initial memory Σ all reachable macro-steps of P are stabilising.* □

A non-constructive program will, after some tick, end up in a fixed point P^* with $can^s(P^*) \notin \{\perp_0, \perp_1\}$. Then P^* is stuck involving a set of active child threads waiting for each other in a policy-induced cycle.

Finally, we present two important results for DCoL showing that we are conservatively extending existing SP semantics. A DCoL program using only sequentially constructive variables [14] (see [17] Sec. 5.7]) is called a *DCoL-SC* program. DCoL programs using only pure signals subject to the policy of Example 1 (Fig. 1) are expressive complete for the pure instantaneous fragment of Esterel [4]. Esterel signal emissions `emit s` are syntactic sugar for `s.emit();`. A presence test `pres s then P else Q` abbreviates `if s.pres() then P else Q`. Sequential composition P ; Q in Esterel behaves like a parallel composition in which the schedule is forced to run P to termination before it can pass control to Q. In DCoL this is $(P; \text{s}'.\text{emit}();) \parallel (\text{s}'.\text{pres}() \text{ then } Q \text{ else skip})$ with fresh signal s' not occurring in either P or Q. This suggests the following definition: A program P is a *(pure instantaneous) DCoL-Esterel* program if (i) P only uses pure signals and (ii) P does not use `pause` or `rec` and (iii) P does not contain sequentially nested occurrences of signal accesses.

Theorem 4 (Esterel and Sequential Constructiveness)

1. *If an DCoL-Esterel program P is policy-constructive according to Definition 7 iff it is Berry-constructive in the sense of [4].*
2. *If a DCoL-SC program P is policy-constructive according to Definition 7 then it is sequentially constructive in the sense of [14].*

It is interesting to note that the second statement in Theorem 4 is not invertible (for a counter example see [17]). Hence, policy-constructiveness for SC-variables induced by our semantics is more restrictive than that given in [14].

4   Related Work

Many languages have been proposed to offer determinism as a fundamental design principle. We consider these attempts under several categories.

Fixed Protocol for Shared Data. These approaches introduce an unique protocol for data exchange between concurrent processes. SHIM [21] provides a model for combined hardware software systems typically of embedded systems. Here, the concurrent processes communicate using point-to-point (restricted) Kahn channels with blocking reads and writes. SHIM programs are shown to be deterministic-by-construction as the states of each process are finite and deterministic and the data produced-consumed over any channel is also deterministic.

Concurrent revisions [19] introduce a generic and deterministic programming model for parallel programming. This model supports fork-join parallelism and processes are allowed to make concurrent modifications to shared data by creating local copies that are eventually merged using suitable (programmer specified) merge functions at join boundaries.

However, like the deterministic SP model [2], both SHIM and concurrent revisions lack support for more expressive shared ADTs essential for programming complex systems. Caromel et al. [22], on the other hand, offer determinism with asynchronously communicating active objects (ADTs) equipped with a process calculus semantics. Here, an active object is a sequential thread. Active objects communicate using *futures* and synchronise via Kahn-MacQueen co-routines [23] for deterministic data exchange. Our approach subsumes Kahn buffers of SHIM and the *local-copy-merge protocol* of concurrent revisions by an appropriate choice of method interface and policy. None of these approaches [19,21,22] uses a clock as a central barrier mechanism like our approach does.

In the Java-derived language X10, clocks are a form of synchronisation barrier for supporting deterministic and deadlock-free patterns of common parallel computations [24]. This allows multiple-clocks in contrast to our approach. These, however, are not abstracted in the objects in contrast to our clocks that are encapsulated inside the CSM types. Hence X10 clocks are invoked directly by the *activities* (i.e., concurrent threads) of programs and this manual synchronisation is as error-prone as other unsafe low-level primitives such as locks.

Coherent Memory Models for Shared Data. Whether clocked or not, our approach depends on the availability of CSM types that are provably coherent for their policy. Besides the standard types of SP (data-flow, sequentially constructive variables, Kahn channels, signals) such CSM types can be obtained from existing research on *coherent memory models* [25,26]. Unlike the protocol-oriented approaches above, some approaches have been developed based on coherency of the underlying memory models [26] especially for shared objects.

Bocchino et al. [25] propose deterministic parallel Java (DPJ) which has a type and effect system to ensure that parallel heap accesses remain safe. Data structures such as arrays, trees, and sets can be accessed in parallel as long as accesses can be shown to use non-overlapping regions.

Grace [27] promises a deterministic run-time through the adoption of *fork-join* parallelism combined with memory protection and a sequential commit protocol. However, there is no guarantee on the determinism of such custom synchronisation protocols. These must be verified using expensive proof systems.

A powerful technique to generate coherent shared memory structure for functional programs has recently been proposed by Kuper et al. [28]. They introduce lattice-based data structures, called LVars, in which all write accesses produce a monotonic value increase in the lattice and all read accesses are blocked until the memory value has passed a read-specific threshold. Each variable's domain is organised as a lattice of states with $\perp$ and $\top$ representing an empty new location and an error, respectively. Because of monotonicity all writes are confluent with each other. Since reads are blocked each LVar data type can thus be used in DCoL as a coherent CSM type of variables with a threshold-determined policy. Note that [25–28] do not consider CSM types and [28] also do not treat destructive sequential updates as we do.

Recently Haller et al. [29] have developed Reactive Async, a new event-based asynchronous concurrent programming model that improves on LVars. This approach extends futures and promises[8] with lattice-based operations in order to support destructive updates (refinement of results) in a deterministic concurrent setting. The basic abstractions are: *cells* which define interfaces for reading a value that is asynchronously computed and (ii) *cell completers* that allow multiple monotonic updates of values taken from a lattice type class. The model supports concurrent programming with cyclic data dependencies in contrast to LVars. The mechanism for resolving cycles combines the lattices with quiescence detection on a handler pool (execution context). The quiescence concept refers to a state where the cell values are not going to be changed anymore. The thread pool is able to detect this quiescent (synchronisation) phase and when this is the case the resolution of cyclic dependencies and reading of cells can take place. This is similar to our policies, where enabling of methods (e. g., read) is a state and prediction-dependent notion. Our developments may offer a theoretical background for the cell interfaces of this model. In Reactive Async the concurrent code is guaranteed to be deterministic provided that the API is used appropriately but this is not checked statically. It would be interesting to investigate whether our theory can contribute on this front. In the other direction, Reactive Async manages inter-cell dependencies which might support global policies between different CSM variables in our setting.

Clock-Driven Encapsulation. Encapsulation is not entirely unknown in reactive programming. The idea of *reactive object model (ROM)* [30] was first introduced by Boussinot et al. and subsequently refined [31] and combined with standards such as UML [32]. Here a program is a collection of reactive objects that operate synchronously relative to a global clock, similar to SP. Each object encapsulates a set of methods and data, where the methods share this data. ROM relied on a simplified assumption, where each method invocation is separated into instants.

André et al. [33] generalised the ROM idea to that of *synchronous objects*, which behave like synchronous modules (in Esterel or Lustre). The program is divided into a collection of synchronous and standard objects. While the latter interact using messages, the former use *signals* like in SP. Communication between standard and synchronous objects has to be managed using special *interface objects*. The framework supports features such as aggregation, encapsulation and inheritance yet communication is restricted to standard Esterel-style signals. However, the issue of determinism for the composition of synchronous objects with standard objects is not considered.

---

[8] A future can asynchronously be completed with a value of the appropriate type or it can fail with an exception. A promise allows completing a future at most once.

A concrete implementation of synchronous objects in Java is proposed in [34]. Here, a run-time system is used to provide a cyclic schedule of the objects during an instant. This approach assumes that outputs from the objects can be read only in the next instant (similar to the SL programming language [35]) and so does not support instantaneous communication like we do.

Synchronous objects arise naturally in modular compilation [15,36,37]. The first time these have been exposed at the language level is in [20]. That work has inspired our use of policies. While [20] offers a mechanism for deterministic management of shared variables through ADT-like interfaces it has three serious limitations: (1) Modes express data-flow equations rather than imperative method procedures and so are not directly suitable for control-flow programming; (2) Policies do not distinguish between two modes being called *sequentially* by the *same* thread, which can be permitted, and two methods being called by *different* threads in *parallel*, which may have to be prohibited. This makes policies too restrictive in the light of the recent more liberal notion of sequential constructiveness [14] and, most importantly, (3) the notion of policy-soundness does not use policies *prescriptively* as a contract to be fulfilled by the scheduler but instead only *descriptively* as an invariant of the program code. Hence, policies in [20] cannot be used to generalise the semantics of SP signals to shared ADTs.

The sequentially constructive model of synchronous computation [14] has shown how the constructive semantics of Esterel can be reconstructed from a scheduling view as standard destructive variables plus synchronisation protocol. SCL acts as an intermediate language for the graphical language SCCharts [38] and the textual language SCEst [18] which are proposed as sequentially constructive extensions of the well-known control-flow languages SyncCharts [39] and Esterel [4]. By presenting our new analysis of sequential constructiveness for SCL our results become applicable both for SCCharts and SCEst.

The term 'constructive' semantics has been coined by Berry [4]. In [40] it was shown how it can be recoded as a fixed-point in an interval domain which we generalise here to policy states $[\mu, \gamma]$. Talpin et al. [13] recently gave a constructive semantics of multi-clock synchronous programs. It is an open problem how our approach could be generalised to multiple clocks.

5   Conclusion

This work extends the SP theoretical foundations to allow communication at higher levels of abstraction. The paper explains deterministic concurrency of SP as a derived property from CSM types. Our results extend the SP-notion of constructiveness to general shared CSM types. We have made some simplifying assumptions that render the theory somewhat less general than it could be. A first limitation is our assumption that all method calls are atomic. We believe the theory can be generalised for non-atomic methods albeit at the price of a significant increase in the complexity of calculating *can* predictions. Second, method parameters are passed "by value" rather than "by reference". This is necessary for having types as black boxes ready to use. Method parameters passing variables "by reference" would also introduce aliasing issues which we do not address. Third, in our present setting the policy update $\mu \odot m$ does not observe method parameters. This is an abstraction to facilitate static analyses. In principle, to increase expressiveness, the method parameters could be included, too, but again complicate over-approximation for *can* information.

Acknowledgement. We thank Philipp Haller, Adrien Guatto and the three anonymous reviewers for their insightful comments and suggestions helping us improving the paper. This work has been supported by the German Research Council (DFG) under grant number ME-1427/6-2.

References

1. Lee, E.: The problem with threads. Computer **39**(5), 33–42 (2006)
2. Benveniste, A., Caspi, P., Edwards, S., Halbwachs, N., Guernic, P.L., de Simone, R.: The synchronous languages twelve years later. Proc. IEEE **91**(1), 64–83 (2003)
3. Colaço, J., Pagano, B., Pouzet, M.: SCADE 6: a formal language for embedded critical software development. In: TASE 2017, Sophia Antipolis, France, September 2017
4. Berry, G.: The Constructive Semantics of Pure Esterel. Draft Book (1999)
5. Schneider, K.: The synchronous programming language quartz. Internal report 375, Department of Computer Science, University of Kaiserslautern, Germany, December 2009
6. von Hanxleden, R.: SyncCharts in C – a proposal for light-weight, deterministic concurrency. In: EMSOFT 2009, Grenoble, France, pp. 225–234, October 2009
7. Guernic, P.L., Goutier, T., Borgne, M.L., Maire, C.L.: Programming real time applications with SIGNAL. Proc. IEEE **79**, 1321–1336 (1991)
8. Halbwachs, N., Caspi, P., Raymond, P., Pilaud, D.: The synchronous data-flow programming language LUSTRE. Proc. IEEE **79**(9), 1305–1320 (1991)
9. Pouzet, M.: Lucid Synchrone, un langage synchrone d'ordre supérieur. Mémoire d'habilitation, Université Paris 6, November 2002
10. The Esterel v7 Reference Manual Version v7_30, November 2005
11. Aguado, J., Mendler, M.: Constructive semantics for instantaneous reactions. Theor. Comput. Sci. **412**, 931–961 (2011)
12. Aguado, J., Mendler, M., von Hanxleden, R., Fuhrmann, I.: Grounding synchronous deterministic concurrency in sequential programming. In: Shao, Z. (ed.) ESOP 2014. LNCS, vol. 8410, pp. 229–248. Springer, Heidelberg (2014). https://doi.org/10.1007/978-3-642-54833-8_13
13. Talpin, J., Brandt, J., Gemünde, M., Schneider, K., Shukla, S.: Constructive polychronous systems. Sci. Comput. Prog. **96**(3), 377–394 (2014)
14. von Hanxleden, R., Mendler, M., Aguado, J., Duderstadt, B., Fuhrmann, I., Motika, C., Mercer, S., O'Brien, O., Roop, P.: Sequentially constructive concurrency—a conservative extension of the synchronous model of computation. ACM TECS **13**(4s), 144:1–144:26 (2014)
15. Pouzet, M., Raymond, P.: Modular static scheduling of synchronous data-flow networks - an efficient symbolic representation. Des. Autom. Embed. Syst. **14**(3), 165–192 (2010)

16. Kahn, G.: The semantics of simple language for parallel programming. In: IFIP Congress 1974, Stockholm, Sweden, pp. 471–475, August 1974
17. Aguado, J., Mendler, M., Pouzet, M., Roop, P., von Hanxleden, R.: Clock-synchronised shared objects for deterministic concurrency. Research report 102, University of Bamberg, Germany, July 2017. https://www.uni-bamberg.de/fileadmin/uni/fakultaeten/wiai_professuren/grundlagen_informatik/papersMM/report-WIAI-102-Feb-2018.pdf
18. Rathlev, K., Smyth, S., Motika, C., von Hanxleden, R., Mendler, M.: SCEst: sequentially constructive esterel. ACM TECS **17**(2), 33:1–33:26 (2018)
19. Burckhardt, S., Leijen, D., Fähndrich, M., Sagiv, M.: Eventually consistent transactions. In: Seidl, H. (ed.) ESOP 2012. LNCS, vol. 7211, pp. 67–86. Springer, Heidelberg (2012). https://doi.org/10.1007/978-3-642-28869-2_4
20. Caspi, P., Colaço, J., Gérard, L., Pouzet, M., Raymond, P.: Synchronous objects with scheduling policies: introducing safe shared memory in lustre. In: LCTES 2009, Dublin, Ireland, pp. 11–20, June 2009
21. Vasudevan, N.: Efficient, deterministic and deadlock-free concurrency. Ph.D. thesis, Department of Computer Science, Columbia University, March 2011
22. Caromel, D., Henrio, L., Serpette, B.: Asynchronous and deterministic objects. In: POPL 2004, Venice, Italy, pp. 123–134, January 2004
23. Kahn, G., MacQueen, D.: Coroutines and networks of parallel processes. In: IFIP Congress 1977, Toronto, Canada, pp. 993–998, August 1977
24. Charles, P., Grothoff, C., Saraswat, V., Donawa, C., Kielstra, A., Ebcioglu, K., von Praun, C., Sarkar, V.: X10: an object-oriented approach to non-uniform cluster computing. In: OOPSLA 2005, San Diego, USA, pp. 519–538, October 2005
25. Bocchino, R., Adve, V., Dig, D., Adve, S., Heumann, S., Komuravelli, R., Overbey, J., Simmons, P., Sung, H., Vakilian, M.: A type and effect system for deterministic parallel Java. In: OOPSLA 2009, Orlando, USA, pp. 97–116, October 2009
26. Flanagan, C., Qadeer, S.: A type and effect system for atomicity. In: PLDI 2003, San Diego, USA, pp. 338–349, June 2003
27. Berger, E., Yang, T., Liu, T., Novark, G.: Grace: safe multithreaded programming for C/C++. In: OOPSLA 2009, Orlando, USA, pp. 81–96, October 2009
28. Kuper, L., Turon, A., Krishnaswami, N., Newton, R.: Freeze after writing: quasi-deterministic parallel programming with LVars. In: POPL 2014, San Diego, USA, pp. 257–270, January 2014
29. Haller, P., Geries, S., Eichberg, M., Salvaneschi, G.: Reactive Async: expressive deterministic concurrency. In: SCALA 2016, Amsterdam, Netherlands, pp. 11–20, October 2016
30. Boussinot, F., Doumenc, G., Stefani, J.: Reactive objects. Annales des télécommunications **51**(9–10), 459–473 (1996)
31. Talpin, J., Benveniste, A., Caillaud, B., Jard, C., Bouziane, Z., Canon, H.: BDL, a language of distributed reactive objects. In: IEEE ISORC 1998, Kyoto, Japan, pp. 196–205, April 1998
32. André, C., Peraldi-Frati, M.-A., Rigault, J.-P.: Integrating the synchronous paradigm into UML: application to control-dominated systems. In: Jézéquel, J.-M., Hussmann, H., Cook, S. (eds.) UML 2002. LNCS, vol. 2460, pp. 163–178. Springer, Heidelberg (2002). https://doi.org/10.1007/3-540-45800-X_15
33. André, C., Boulanger, F., Péraldi, M., Rigault, J., Vidal-Naquet, G.: Objects and synchronous programming. RAIRO-APII-JESA-J. Eur. Syst. Autom. **31**(3), 417–432 (1997)

34. Passerone, C., Sansoe, C., Lavagno, L., McGeer, R., Martin, J., Passerone, R., Sangiovanni-Vincentelli, A.: Modeling reactive systems in Java. ACM TODAES **3**(4), 515–523 (1998)
35. Boussinot, F., Simone, R.D.: The SL synchronous language. IEEE TSE **22**(4), 256–266 (1996)
36. Biernacki, D., Colaço, J., Hamon, G., Pouzet, M.: Clock-directed modular code generation of synchronous data-flow languages. In: LCTES 2008, Tucson, USA, pp. 121–130, June 2008
37. Hainque, O., Pautet, L., Le Biannic, Y., Nassor, É.: Cronos: a separate compilation tool set for modular Esterel applications. In: Wing, J.M., Woodcock, J., Davies, J. (eds.) FM 1999. LNCS, vol. 1709, pp. 1836–1853. Springer, Heidelberg (1999). https://doi.org/10.1007/3-540-48118-4_47
38. von Hanxleden, R., Duderstadt, B., Motika, C., Smyth, S., Mendler, M., Aguado, J., Mercer, S., O'Brien, O.: SCCharts: sequentially constructive statecharts for safety-critical applications. SIGPLAN Not. **49**(6), 372–383 (2014)
39. André, C.: Semantics of SyncCharts. Technical report ISRN I3S/RR-2003-24-FR, I3S Laboratory, Sophia-Antipolis, France, April 2003
40. Aguado, J., Mendler, M., von Hanxleden, R., Fuhrmann, I.: Denotational fixed-point semantics for constructive scheduling of synchronous concurrency. Acta Informatica **52**(4), 393–442 (2015)

Probabilistic Programming

An Assertion-Based Program Logic
for Probabilistic Programs

Gilles Barthe[1], Thomas Espitau[2], Marco Gaboardi[3], Benjamin Grégoire[4],
Justin Hsu[5(✉)], and Pierre-Yves Strub[6]

[1] IMDEA Software Institute, Madrid, Spain
[2] Université Paris 6, Paris, France
[3] University at Buffalo, SUNY, Buffalo, USA
[4] Inria Sophia Antipolis–Méditerranée, Nice, France
[5] University College London, London, UK
[6] École Polytechnique, Palaiseau, France

Abstract. We present ELLORA, a sound and relatively complete assertion-based program logic, and demonstrate its expressivity by verifying several classical examples of randomized algorithms using an implementation in the EASYCRYPT proof assistant. ELLORA features new proof rules for loops and adversarial code, and supports richer assertions than existing program logics. We also show that ELLORA allows convenient reasoning about complex probabilistic concepts by developing a new program logic for probabilistic independence and distribution law, and then smoothly embedding it into ELLORA.

1 Introduction

The most mature systems for deductive verification of randomized algorithms are *expectation-based* techniques; seminal examples include PPDL [28] and PGCL [34]. These approaches reason about *expectations*, functions E from states to real numbers,[1] propagating them backwards through a program until they are transformed into a mathematical function of the input. Expectation-based systems are both theoretically elegant [16,23,24,35] and practically useful; implementations have verified numerous randomized algorithms [19,21]. However, properties involving multiple probabilities or expected values can be cumbersome to verify—each expectation must be analyzed separately.

An alternative approach envisioned by Ramshaw [37] is to work with predicates over distributions. A direct comparison with expectation-based techniques

---

This is the conference version of the paper.

[1] Treating a program as a function from input states s to output distributions $\mu(s)$, the expected value of E on $\mu(s)$ is an expectation.

Electronic supplementary material The online version of this chapter (https://doi.org/10.1007/978-3-319-89884-1_5) contains supplementary material, which is available to authorized users.

© The Author(s) 2018
A. Ahmed (Ed.): ESOP 2018, LNCS 10801, pp. 117–144, 2018.
https://doi.org/10.1007/978-3-319-89884-1_5

is difficult, as the approaches are quite different. In broad strokes, assertion-based systems can verify richer properties in one shot and have specifications that are arguably more intuitive, especially for reasoning about loops, while expectation-based approaches can transform expectations mechanically and can reason about non-determinism. However, the comparison is not very meaningful for an even simpler reason: existing assertion-based systems such as [8,18,38] are not as well developed as their expectation-based counterparts.

Restrictive Assertions. Existing probabilistic program logics do not support reasoning about expected values, only probabilities. As a result, many properties about average-case behavior are not even expressible.

Inconvenient Reasoning for Loops. The Hoare logic rule for deterministic loops does not directly generalize to probabilistic programs. Existing assertion-based systems either forbid loops, or impose complex semantic side conditions to control which assertions can be used as loop invariants. Such side conditions are restrictive and difficult to establish.

No Support for External or Adversarial Code. A strength of expectation-based techniques is reasoning about programs combining probabilities and *non-determinism*. In contrast, Morgan and McIver [30] argue that assertion-based techniques cannot support compositional reasoning for such a combination. For many applications, including cryptography, we would still like to reason about a commonly-encountered special case: programs using external or adversarial code. Many security properties in cryptography boil down to analyzing such programs, but existing program logics do not support adversarial code.

Few Concrete Implementations. There are by now several independent implementations of expectation-based techniques, capable of verifying interesting probabilistic programs. In contrast, there are only scattered implementations of probabilistic program logics.

These limitations raise two points. Compared to expectation-based approaches:

1. Can assertion-based approaches achieve similar expressivity?
2. Are there situations where assertion-based approaches are more suitable?

In this paper, we give positive evidence for both of these points.[2] Towards the first point, we give a new assertion-based logic ELLORA for probabilistic programs, overcoming limitations in existing probabilistic program logics. ELLORA supports a rich set of assertions that can express concepts like expected values and probabilistic independence, and novel proof rules for verifying loops and adversarial code. We prove that ELLORA is sound and relatively complete.

Towards the second point, we evaluate ELLORA in two ways. First, we define a new logic for proving probabilistic independence and distribution law

---

[2] Note that we do not give mathematically precise formulations of these points; as we are interested in the practical verification of probabilistic programs, a purely theoretical answer would not address our concerns.

properties—which are difficult to capture with expectation-based approaches—and then embed it into ELLORA. This sub-logic is more narrowly focused than ELLORA, but supports more concise reasoning for the target assertions. Our embedding demonstrates that the assertion-based approach can be flexibly integrated with intuitive, special-purpose reasoning principles. To further support this claim, we also provide an embedding of the Union Bound logic, a program logic for reasoning about accuracy bounds [4]. Then, we develop a full-featured implementation of ELLORA in the EASYCRYPT theorem prover and exercise the logic by mechanically verifying a series of complex randomized algorithms. Our results suggest that the assertion-based approach can indeed be practically viable.

Abstract Logic. To ease the presentation, we present ELLORA in two stages. First, we consider an abstract version of the logic where assertions are general predicates over distributions, with no compact syntax. Our abstract logic makes two contributions: reasoning for loops, and for adversarial code.

Reasoning About Loops. Proving a property of a probabilistic loop typically requires establishing a loop invariant, but the class of loop invariants that can be soundly used depends on the termination behavior—stronger termination assumptions allows richer loop invariants. We identify three classes of assertions that can be used for reasoning about probabilistic loops, and provide a proof rule for each one:

- arbitrary assertions for *certainly terminating* loops, i.e. loops that terminate in a finite amount of iterations;
- *topologically closed* assertions for *almost surely* terminating loops, i.e. loops terminating with probability 1;
- *downwards closed* assertions for arbitrary loops.

The definition of topologically closed assertion is reminiscent of Ramshaw [37]; the stronger notion of downwards closed assertion appears to be new.

Besides broadening the class of loops that can be analyzed, our rules often enable simpler proofs. For instance, if the loop is certainly terminating, then there is no need to prove semantic side-conditions. Likewise, there is no need to consider the termination behavior of the loop when the invariant is downwards and topologically closed. For example, in many applications in cryptography, the target property is that a "bad" event has low probability: $\Pr[E] \leq k$. In our framework this assertion is downwards and topologically closed, so it can be a loop invariant regardless of the termination behavior.

Reasoning About Adversaries. Existing assertion-based logics cannot reason about probabilistic programs with *adversarial* code. *Adversaries* are special probabilistic procedures consisting of an interface listing the concrete procedures that an adversary can call (*oracles*), along with restrictions like how many calls an adversary may make. Adversaries are useful in cryptography, where security notions are described using experiments in which adversaries interact with a challenger, and in game theory and mechanism design, where adversaries can represent strategic agents. Adversaries can also model inputs to *online* algorithms.

We provide proof rules for reasoning about adversary calls. Our rules are significantly more general than previously considered rules for reasoning about adversaries. For instance, the rule for adversary used by [4] is restricted to adversaries that cannot make oracle calls.

Metatheory. We show soundness and relative completeness of the core abstract logic, with mechanized proofs in the COQ proof assistant.

Concrete Logic. While the abstract logic is conceptually clean, it is inconvenient for practical formal verification—the assertions are too general and the rules involve semantic side-conditions. To address these issues, we flesh out a concrete version of ELLORA. Assertions are described by a grammar modeling a two-level assertion language. The first level contains state predicates—deterministic assertions about a single memory—while the second layer contains probabilistic predicates constructed from probabilities and expected values over discrete distributions. While the concrete assertions are theoretically less expressive than their counterparts in the abstract logic, they can already encode common properties and notions from existing proofs, like probabilities, expected values, distribution laws and probabilistic independence. Our assertions can express theorems from probability theory, enabling sophisticated reasoning about probabilistic concepts.

Furthermore, we leverage the concrete syntax to simplify verification.

- We develop an automated procedure for generating pre-conditions of non-looping commands, inspired by expectation-based systems.
- We give syntactic conditions for the closedness and termination properties required for soundness of the loop rules.

Implementation and Case Studies. We implement ELLORA on top of EASY-CRYPT, a general-purpose proof assistant for reasoning about probabilistic programs, and we mechanically verify a diverse collection of examples including textbook algorithms and a randomized routing procedure. We develop an EASY-CRYPT formalization of probability theory from the ground up, including tools like concentration bounds (e.g., the Chernoff bound), Markov's inequality, and theorems about probabilistic independence.

Embeddings. We propose a simple program logic for proving *probabilistic independence*. This logic is designed to reason about independence in a lightweight way, as is common in paper proofs. We prove that the logic can be embedded into ELLORA, and is therefore sound. Furthermore, we prove an embedding of the Union Bound logic [4].

2   Mathematical Preliminaries

As is standard, we will model randomized computations using *sub-distributions*.

Definition 1. *A sub-distribution over a set A is defined by a mass function $\mu : A \to [0,1]$ that gives the probability of the unitary events $a \in A$. This mass function must be s.t. $\sum_{a \in A} \mu(a)$ is well-defined and $|\mu| \triangleq \sum_{a \in A} \mu(a) \leq 1$. In particular, the support $\text{supp}(\mu) \triangleq \{a \in A \mid \mu(a) \neq 0\}$ is discrete.[3] The name "sub-distribution" emphasizes that the total probability may be strictly less than 1. When the weight $|\mu|$ is equal to 1, we call μ a distribution. We let $\textbf{SDist}(A)$ denote the set of sub-distributions over A. The probability of an event $E(x)$ w.r.t. a sub-distribution μ, written $\text{Pr}_{x \sim \mu}[E(x)]$, is defined as $\sum_{x \in A \mid E(x)} \mu(x)$.*

Simple examples of sub-distributions include the *null sub-distribution* $\textbf{0}$, which maps each element of the underlying space to 0; and the *Dirac distribution centered on x*, written δ_x, which maps x to 1 and all other elements to 0. The following standard construction gives a monadic structure to sub-distributions.

Definition 2. *Let $\mu \in \textbf{SDist}(A)$ and $f : A \to \textbf{SDist}(B)$. Then $\mathbb{E}_{a \sim \mu}[f] \in \textbf{SDist}(B)$ is defined by*

$$\mathbb{E}_{a \sim \mu}[f](b) \triangleq \sum_{a \in A} \mu(a) \cdot f(a)(b).$$

We use notation reminiscent of expected values, as the definition is quite similar.

We will need two constructions to model branching statements.

Definition 3. *Let $\mu_1, \mu_2 \in \textbf{SDist}(A)$ such that $|\mu_1| + |\mu_2| \leq 1$. Then $\mu_1 + \mu_2$ is the sub-distribution μ such that $\mu(a) = \mu_1(a) + \mu_2(a)$ for every $a \in A$.*

Definition 4. *Let $E \subseteq A$ and $\mu \in \textbf{SDist}(A)$. Then the restriction $\mu_{|E}$ of μ to E is the sub-distribution such that $\mu_{|E}(a) = \mu(a)$ if $a \in E$ and 0 otherwise.*

Sub-distributions are partially ordered under the pointwise order.

Definition 5. *Let $\mu_1, \mu_2 \in \textbf{SDist}(A)$. We say $\mu_1 \leq \mu_2$ if $\mu_1(a) \leq \mu_2(a)$ for every $a \in A$, and we say $\mu_1 = \mu_2$ if $\mu_1(a) = \mu_2(a)$ for every $a \in A$.*

We use the following lemma when reasoning about the semantics of loops.

Lemma 1. *If $\mu_1 \leq \mu_2$ and $|\mu_1| = 1$, then $\mu_1 = \mu_2$ and $|\mu_2| = 1$.*

Sub-distributions are stable under pointwise-limits.

---

[3] We work with discrete distributions to keep measure-theoretic technicalities to a minimum, though we do not see obstacles to generalizing to the continuous setting.

Definition 6. *A sequence* $(\mu_n)_{n\in\mathbb{N}} \in \mathbf{SDist}(A)$ *sub-distributions converges if for every* $a \in A$, *the sequence* $(\mu_n(a))_{n\in\mathbb{N}}$ *of real numbers converges. The* limit *sub-distribution is defined as*

$$\mu_\infty(a) \triangleq \lim_{n\to\infty} \mu_n(a)$$

for every $a \in A$. *We write* $\lim_{n\to\infty} \mu_n$ *for* μ_∞.

Lemma 2. *Let* $(\mu_n)_{n\in\mathbb{N}}$ *be a convergent sequence of sub-distributions. Then for any event* $E(x)$, *we have:*

$$\forall n \in \mathbb{N}. \Pr_{x\sim\mu_\infty}[E(x)] = \lim_{n\to\infty} \Pr_{x\sim\mu_n}[E(x)].$$

Any bounded increasing real sequence has a limit; the same is true of sub-distributions.

Lemma 3. *Let* $(\mu_n)_{n\in\mathbb{N}} \in \mathbf{SDist}(A)$ *be an increasing sequence of sub-distributions. Then, this sequence converges to* μ_∞ *and* $\mu_n \leq \mu_\infty$ *for every* $n \in \mathbb{N}$. *In particular, for any event* E, *we have* $\Pr_{x\sim\mu_n}[E] \leq \Pr_{x\sim\mu_\infty}[E]$ *for every* $n \in \mathbb{N}$.

3   Programs and Assertions

Now, we introduce our core programming language and its denotational semantics.

Programs. We base our development on PWHILE, a strongly-typed imperative language with deterministic assignments, probabilistic assignments, conditionals, loops, and an **abort** statement which halts the computation with no result. Probabilistic assignments $x \xleftarrow{\$} g$ assign a value sampled from a distribution g to a program variable x. The syntax of statements is defined by the grammar:

$$s ::= \mathbf{skip} \mid \mathbf{abort} \mid x \leftarrow e \mid x \xleftarrow{\$} g \mid s; s$$
$$\mid \mathbf{if}\ e\ \mathbf{then}\ s\ \mathbf{else}\ s \mid \mathbf{while}\ e\ \mathbf{do}\ s \mid x \leftarrow \mathcal{I}(e) \mid x \leftarrow \mathcal{A}(e)$$

where x, e, and g range over typed variables in $\mathcal{X}$, expressions in $\mathcal{E}$ and distribution expressions in $\mathcal{D}$ respectively. The set $\mathcal{E}$ of well-typed expressions is defined inductively from $\mathcal{X}$ and a set $\mathcal{F}$ of function symbols, while the set $\mathcal{D}$ of well-typed distribution expressions is defined by combining a set of distribution symbols $\mathcal{S}$ with expressions in $\mathcal{E}$. Programs may call a set $\mathcal{I}$ of internal procedures as well as a set $\mathcal{A}$ of external procedures. We assume that we have code for internal procedures but not for external procedures—we only know indirect information, like which internal procedures they may call. Borrowing a convention from cryptography, we call internal procedures *oracles* and external procedures *adversaries*.

Semantics. The denotational semantics of programs is adapted from the seminal work of [27] and interprets programs as sub-distribution transformers. We view

$$[\![\mathbf{skip}]\!]_m = \delta_m$$

$$[\![\mathbf{abort}]\!]_m = \mathbf{0}$$

$$[\![x \leftarrow e]\!]_m = \delta_{m[x:=[\![e]\!]_m]}$$

$$[\![x \xleftarrow{\$} g]\!]_m = \mathbb{E}_{v \sim [\![g]\!]_m}[\delta_{m[x:=v]}]$$

$$[\![s_1; s_2]\!]_m = \mathbb{E}_{m' \sim [\![s_1]\!]_m}[[\![s_2]\!]_{m'}]$$

$$[\![\mathbf{if}\ e\ \mathbf{then}\ s_1\ \mathbf{else}\ s_2]\!]_m = \mathbf{if}\ [\![e]\!]_m\ \mathbf{then}\ [\![s_1]\!]_m\ \mathbf{else}\ [\![s_2]\!]_m$$

$$[\![\mathbf{while}\ e\ \mathbf{do}\ s]\!]_m = \lim_{n \to \infty}[\![(\mathbf{if}\ e\ \mathbf{then}\ s)^n; \mathbf{if}\ e\ \mathbf{then}\ \mathbf{abort}]\!]_m$$

$$[\![x \leftarrow \mathcal{I}(e)]\!]_m = [\![f_{\mathbf{arg}} \leftarrow e; f_{\mathbf{body}}; x \leftarrow f_{\mathbf{res}}]\!]_m$$

$$[\![x \leftarrow \mathcal{A}(e)]\!]_m = [\![a_{\mathbf{arg}} \leftarrow e; a_{\mathbf{body}}; x \leftarrow a_{\mathbf{res}}]\!]_m$$

$$[\![s]\!]_\mu = \mathbb{E}_{m \sim \mu}[[\![s]\!]_m]$$

Fig. 1. Denotational semantics of programs

states as type-preserving mappings from variables to values; we write **State** for the set of states and **SDist(State)** for the set of probabilistic states. For each procedure name $f \in \mathcal{I} \cup \mathcal{A}$, we assume a set $\mathcal{X}_f^{\mathcal{L}} \subseteq \mathcal{X}$ of *local variables* s.t. $\mathcal{X}_f^{\mathcal{L}}$ are pairwise disjoint. The other variables $\mathcal{X} \setminus \bigcup_f \mathcal{X}_f^{\mathcal{L}}$ are *global variables*.

To define the interpretation of expressions and distribution expressions, we let $[\![e]\!]_m$ denote the interpretation of expression e with respect to state m, and $[\![e]\!]_\mu$ denote the interpretation of expression e with respect to an initial sub-distribution μ over states defined by the clause $[\![e]\!]_\mu \triangleq \mathbb{E}_{m \sim \mu}[[\![e]\!]_m]$. Likewise, we define the semantics of commands in two stages: first interpreted in a single input memory, then interpreted in an input sub-distribution over memories.

Definition 7. *The semantics of commands are given in Fig. 1.*

- *The semantics $[\![s]\!]_m$ of a statement s in initial state m is a sub-distribution over states.*
- *The (lifted) semantics $[\![s]\!]_\mu$ of a statement s in initial sub-distribution μ over states is a sub-distribution over states.*

We briefly comment on loops. The semantics of a loop **while** e **do** c is defined as the limit of its lower approximations, where the n-th *lower approximation* of $[\![\mathbf{while}\ e\ \mathbf{do}\ c]\!]_\mu$ is $[\![(\mathbf{if}\ e\ \mathbf{then}\ s)^n; \mathbf{if}\ e\ \mathbf{then}\ \mathbf{abort}]\!]_\mu$, where **if** e **then** s is shorthand for **if** e **then** s **else skip** and c^n is the n-fold composition $c; \cdots ; c$. Since the sequence is increasing, the limit is well-defined by Lemma 3. In contrast, the n-th *approximation* of $[\![\mathbf{while}\ e\ \mathbf{do}\ c]\!]_\mu$ defined by $[\![(\mathbf{if}\ e\ \mathbf{then}\ s)^n]\!]_\mu$ may not converge, since they are not necessarily increasing. However, in the special case where the output distribution has weight 1, the n-th lower approximations and the n-th approximations have the same limit.

Lemma 4. *If the sub-distribution* $[\![\textbf{while } e \textbf{ do } c]\!]_\mu$ *has weight* 1, *then the limit of* $[\![(\textbf{if } e \textbf{ then } s)^n]\!]_\mu$ *is defined and*

$$\lim_{n\to\infty} [\![(\textbf{if } e \textbf{ then } s)^n; \textbf{if } e \textbf{ then abort}]\!]_\mu = \lim_{n\to\infty} [\![(\textbf{if } e \textbf{ then } s)^n]\!]_\mu.$$

This follows by Lemma 1, since lower approximations are below approximations so the limit of their weights (and the weight of their limit) is 1. It will be useful to identify programs that terminate with probability 1.

Definition 8 (Lossless). *A statement* s *is* lossless *if for every sub-distribution* μ, $|[\![s]\!]_\mu| = |\mu|$, *where* $|\mu|$ *is the total probability of* μ. *Programs that are not lossless are called* lossy.

Informally, a program is lossless if all probabilistic assignments sample from full distributions rather than sub-distributions, there are no **abort** instructions, and the program is almost surely terminating, i.e. infinite traces have probability zero. Note that if we restrict the language to sample from full distributions, then losslessness coincides with almost sure termination.

Another important class of loops are loops with a uniform upper bound on the number of iterations. Formally, we say that a loop **while** e **do** s is *certainly terminating* if there exists k such that for every sub-distribution μ, we have $|[\![\textbf{while } e \textbf{ do } s]\!]_\mu| = |[\![(\textbf{if } e \textbf{ then } s)^k]\!]_\mu|$. Note that certain termination of a loop does not entail losslessness—the output distribution of the loop may not have weight 1, for instance, if the loop samples from a sub-distribution or if the loop aborts with positive probability.

Semantics of Procedure Calls and Adversaries. The semantics of internal procedure calls is straightforward. Associated to each procedure name $f \in \mathcal{I}$, we assume a designated input variable $f_{\textbf{arg}} \in \mathcal{X}_f^\mathcal{L}$, a piece of code $f_{\textbf{body}}$ that executes the function call, and a result expression $f_{\textbf{res}}$. A function call $x \leftarrow \mathcal{I}(e)$ is then equivalent to $f_{\textbf{arg}} \leftarrow e; f_{\textbf{body}}; x \leftarrow f_{\textbf{res}}$. Procedures are subject to well-formedness criteria: procedures should only use local variables in their scope and after initializing them, and should not perform recursive calls.

External procedure calls, also known as adversary calls, are a bit more involved. Each name $a \in \mathcal{A}$ is parametrized by a set $a_{\textbf{ocl}} \subseteq \mathcal{I}$ of internal procedures which the adversary may call, a designated input variable $a_{\textbf{arg}} \in \mathcal{X}_a^\mathcal{L}$, a (unspecified) piece of code $a_{\textbf{body}}$ that executes the function call, and a result expression $a_{\textbf{res}}$. We assume that adversarial code can only access its local variables in $\mathcal{X}_a^\mathcal{L}$ and can only make calls to procedures in $a_{\textbf{ocl}}$. It is possible to impose more restrictions on adversaries—say, that they are lossless—but for simplicity we do not impose additional assumptions on adversaries here.

4   Proof System

In this section we introduce a program logic for proving properties of probabilistic programs. The logic is abstract—assertions are arbitrary predicates on sub-distributions—but the meta-theoretic properties are clearest in this setting. In the following section, we will give a concrete version suitable for practical use.

Assertions and Closedness Conditions. We use predicates on state distribution.

Definition 9 (Assertions). *The set* Assn *of assertions is defined as* $\mathcal{P}(\mathbf{SDist}(\mathbf{State}))$. *We write* $\eta(\mu)$ *for* $\mu \in \eta$.

Usual set operations are lifted to assertions using their logical counterparts, e.g., $\eta \wedge \eta' \triangleq \eta \cap \eta'$ and $\neg\eta \triangleq \overline{\eta}$. Our program logic uses a few additional constructions. Given a predicate ϕ over states, we define

$$\Box\phi(\mu) \triangleq \forall m.\, m \in \mathrm{supp}(\mu) \implies \phi(m)$$

where $\mathrm{supp}(\mu)$ is the set of all states with non-zero probability under μ. Intuitively, ϕ holds deterministically on all states that we may sample from the distribution. To reason about branching commands, given two assertions η_1 and η_2, we let

$$(\eta_1 \oplus \eta_2)(\mu) \triangleq \exists\mu_1, \mu_2 .\ \mu = \mu_1 + \mu_2 \wedge \eta_1(\mu_1) \wedge \eta_2(\mu_2).$$

This assertion means that the sub-distribution is the sum of two sub-distributions such that η_1 holds on the first piece and η_2 holds on the second piece.

Given an assertion η and an event $E \subseteq \mathbf{State}$, we let $\eta_{|E}(\mu) \triangleq \eta(\mu_{|E})$. This assertion holds exactly when η is true on the portion of the sub-distribution satisfying E. Finally, given an assertion η and a function F from $\mathbf{SDist}(\mathbf{State})$ to $\mathbf{SDist}(\mathbf{State})$, we define $\eta[F] \triangleq \lambda\mu.\,\eta(F(\mu))$. Intuitively, $\eta[F]$ is true in a sub-distribution μ exactly when η holds on $F(\mu)$.

Now, we can define the closedness properties of assertions. These properties will be critical to our rules for **while** loops.

Definition 10 (Closedness properties). *A family of assertions* $(\eta_n)_{n \in \mathbb{N}^\infty}$ *is:*

- *u-closed if for every increasing sequence of sub-distributions* $(\mu_n)_{n \in \mathbb{N}}$ *such that* $\eta_n(\mu_n)$ *for all* $n \in \mathbb{N}$ *then* $\eta_\infty(\lim_{n \to \infty} \mu_n)$;
- *t-closed if for every converging sequence of sub-distributions* $(\mu_n)_{n \in \mathbb{N}}$ *such that* $\eta_n(\mu_n)$ *for all* $n \in \mathbb{N}$ *then* $\eta_\infty(\lim_{n \to \infty} \mu_n)$;
- *d-closed if it is t-closed and downward closed, that is for every sub-distributions* $\mu \leq \mu'$, $\eta_\infty(\mu')$ *implies* $\eta_\infty(\mu)$.

When $(\eta_n)_n$ *is constant and equal to* η, *we say that* η *is* u-/t-/d-closed.

Note that t-closedness implies u-closedness, but the converse does not hold. Moreover, u-closed, t-closed and d-closed assertions are closed under arbitrary intersections and finite unions, or in logical terms under finite boolean combinations, universal quantification over arbitrary sets and existential quantification over finite sets.

Finally, we introduce the necessary machinery for the frame rule. The set $\mathrm{mod}(s)$ of *modified* variables of a statement s consists of all the variables on the left of a deterministic or probabilistic assignment. In this setting, we say that an assertion η is *separated* from a set of variables X, written $\mathsf{separated}(\eta, X)$, if $\eta(\mu_1) \iff \eta(\mu_2)$ for any distributions μ_1, μ_2 s.t. $|\mu_1| = |\mu_2|$ and $\mu_{1|\overline{X}} = \mu_{2|\overline{X}}$ where for a set of variables X, the restricted sub-distribution $\mu_{|X}$ is

$$\mu_{|X} : m \in \mathbf{State}_{|X} \mapsto \Pr_{m' \sim \mu}[m = m'_{|X}]$$

where $\mathbf{State}_{|X}$ and $m_{|X}$ restrict $\mathbf{State}$ and m to the variables in X.

Intuitively, an assertion is separated from a set of variables X if every two sub-distributions that agree on the variables outside X either both satisfy the assertion, or both refute the assertion.

Judgments and Proof Rules. Judgments are of the form $\{\eta\}\, s\, \{\eta'\}$, where the assertions η and η' are drawn from Assn.

Definition 11. *A judgment $\{\eta\}\, s\, \{\eta'\}$ is valid, written $\models \{\eta\}\, s\, \{\eta'\}$, if $\eta'(\llbracket s \rrbracket_\mu)$ for every interpretation of adversarial procedures and every probabilistic state μ such that $\eta(\mu)$.*

Figure 2 describes the structural and basic rules of the proof system. Validity of judgments is preserved under standard structural rules, like the rule of consequence [CONSEQ]. As usual, the rule of consequence allows to weaken the post-condition and to strengthen the post-condition; in our system, this rule serves as the interface between the program logic and mathematical theorems from probability theory. The [EXISTS] rule is helpful to deal with existentially quantified pre-conditions.

$$\frac{\eta_0 \Rightarrow \eta_1 \quad \{\eta_1\}\, s\, \{\eta_2\} \quad \eta_2 \Rightarrow \eta_3}{\{\eta_0\}\, s\, \{\eta_3\}} \text{ [CONSEQ]} \qquad \frac{\forall x : T.\, \{\eta\}\, s\, \{\eta'\}}{\{\exists x : T.\, \eta\}\, s\, \{\eta'\}} \text{ [EXISTS]}$$

$$\frac{}{\{\eta\}\, \mathbf{abort}\, \{\Box\bot\}} \text{ [ABORT]} \qquad \frac{\eta' \triangleq \eta[\![x \leftarrow e]\!]}{\{\eta'\}\, x \leftarrow e\, \{\eta\}} \text{ [ASSGN]} \qquad \frac{}{\{\eta\}\, \mathbf{skip}\, \{\eta\}} \text{ [SKIP]}$$

$$\frac{\eta' \triangleq \eta[\![x \xleftarrow{\$} g]\!]}{\{\eta'\}\, x \xleftarrow{\$} g\, \{\eta\}} \text{ [SAMPLE]} \qquad \frac{\{\eta_0\}\, s_1\, \{\eta_1\} \quad \{\eta_1\}\, s_2\, \{\eta_2\}}{\{\eta_0\}\, s_1; s_2\, \{\eta_2\}} \text{ [SEQ]}$$

$$\frac{\{\eta_1 \wedge \Box e\}\, s_1\, \{\eta_1'\} \quad \{\eta_2 \wedge \Box\neg e\}\, s_2\, \{\eta_2'\}}{\{(\eta_1 \wedge \Box e) \oplus (\eta_2 \wedge \Box\neg e)\}\, \mathbf{if}\ e\ \mathbf{then}\ s_1\ \mathbf{else}\ s_2\, \{\eta_1' \oplus \eta_2'\}} \text{ [COND]}$$

$$\frac{\{\eta_1\}\, s\, \{\eta_1'\} \quad \{\eta_2\}\, s\, \{\eta_2'\}}{\{\eta_1 \oplus \eta_2\}\, s\, \{\eta_1' \oplus \eta_2'\}} \text{ [SPLIT]}$$

$$\frac{\mathsf{separated}(\eta, \mathsf{mod}(s)) \quad s \text{ is lossless}}{\{\eta\}\, s\, \{\eta\}} \text{ [FRAME]}$$

$$\frac{\{\eta\}\, f_{\mathbf{arg}} \leftarrow e; f_{\mathbf{body}}\, \{\eta'[\![x \leftarrow f_{\mathbf{res}}]\!]\}}{\{\eta\}\, x \leftarrow f(e)\, \{\eta'\}} \text{ [CALL]}$$

Fig. 2. Structural and basic rules

The rules for **skip**, assignments, random samplings and sequences are all straightforward. The rule for **abort** requires $\Box\bot$ to hold after execution; this assertion uniquely characterizes the resulting null sub-distribution. The rules for assignments and random samplings are semantical.

The rule [COND] for conditionals requires that the post-condition must be of the form $\eta_1 \oplus \eta_2$; this reflects the semantics of conditionals, which splits the initial probabilistic state depending on the guard, runs both branches, and recombines the resulting two probabilistic states.

The next two rules ([SPLIT] and [FRAME]) are useful for local reasoning. The [SPLIT] rule reflects the additivity of the semantics and combines the pre- and post-conditions using the $\oplus$ operator. The [FRAME] rule asserts that lossless statements preserve assertions that are not influenced by modified variables.

The rule [CALL] for internal procedures is as expected, replacing the procedure call f with its definition.

Figure 3 presents the rules for loops. We consider four rules specialized to the termination behavior. The [WHILE] rule is the most general rule, as it deals with arbitrary loops. For simplicity, we explain the rule in the special case where the family of assertions is constant, i.e. we have $\eta_n = \eta$ and $\eta'_n = \eta'$. Informally, the η is the loop invariant and η' is an auxiliary assertion used to prove the invariant. We require that η is u-closed, since the semantics of a loop is defined as the limit of its lower approximations. Moreover, the first premise ensures that starting from η, one guarded iteration of the loop establishes η'; the second premise ensures that restricting to $\neg e$ a probabilistic state μ' satisfying η' yields a probabilistic state μ satisfying η. It is possible to give an alternative formulation where the second premise is substituted by the logical constraint $\eta'_{|\neg e} \implies \eta$. As usual, the post-condition of the loop is the conjunction of the invariant with the negation of the guard (more precisely in our setting, that the guard has probability 0).

The [WHILE-AST] rule deals with lossless loops. For simplicity, we explain the rule in the special case where the family of assertions is constant, i.e. we have $\eta_n = \eta$. In this case, we know that lower approximations and approximations have the same limit, so we can directly prove an invariant that holds after one guarded iteration of the loop. On the other hand, we must now require that the η satisfies the stronger property of t-closedness.

The [WHILE-D] rule handles arbitrary loops with a d-closed invariant; intuitively, restricting a sub-distribution that satisfies a downwards closed assertion η yields a sub-distribution which also satisfies η.

The [WHILE-CT] rule deals with certainly terminating loops. In this case, there is no requirement on the assertions.

We briefly compare the rules from a verification perspective. If the assertion is d-closed, then the rule [WHILE-D] is easier to use, since there is no need to prove any termination requirement. Alternatively, if we can prove certain termination of the loop, then the rule [WHILE-CT] is the best to use since it does not impose any condition on assertions. When the loop is lossless, there is no need to introduce an auxiliary assertion η', which simplifies the proof goal.

$$\frac{\text{uclosed}((\eta_n')_{n\in\mathbb{N}^\infty})}{\forall n.\ \{\eta_n\}\ \textbf{if }e\textbf{ then }s\ \{\eta_{n+1}\} \qquad \forall n.\ \{\eta_n\}\ \textbf{if }e\textbf{ then abort}\ \{\eta_n'\}}{\{\eta_0\}\ \textbf{while }e\textbf{ do }s\ \{\eta_\infty'\wedge\square\neg e\}}\ [\text{While}]$$

$$\frac{\text{tclosed}((\eta_n)_{n\in\mathbb{N}^\infty}) \qquad \forall n.\ \{\eta_n\}\ \textbf{if }e\textbf{ then }s\ \{\eta_{n+1}\}}{\forall\mu.\ \eta_0(\mu)\implies |[\![(\textbf{while }e\textbf{ do }s)]\!]_\mu|=1}{\{\eta_0\}\ \textbf{while }e\textbf{ do }s\ \{\eta_\infty\wedge\square\neg e\}}\ [\text{While-AST}]$$

$$\frac{\text{dclosed}((\eta_n)_{n\in\mathbb{N}^\infty}) \qquad \forall n.\ \{\eta_n\}\ \textbf{if }e\textbf{ then }s\ \{\eta_{n+1}\}}{\{\eta_0\}\ \textbf{while }e\textbf{ do }s\ \{\eta_\infty\wedge\square\neg e\}}\ [\text{While-D}]$$

$$\frac{\forall n.\ \{\eta_n\}\ \textbf{if }e\textbf{ then }s\ \{\eta_{n+1}\}}{\forall\mu.\ \eta_0(\mu)\implies [\![(\textbf{if }e\textbf{ then }s)^k]\!]_\mu = [\![(\textbf{while }e\textbf{ do }s)]\!]_\mu}{\{\eta_0\}\ \textbf{while }e\textbf{ do }s\ \{\eta_k\wedge\square\neg e\}}\ [\text{While-CT}]$$

Fig. 3. Rules for loops

$$\frac{\forall n\in\mathbb{N}^\infty.\ \text{separated}(\eta_n,\{x,\mathfrak{s}\}) \qquad \text{dclosed}((\eta_n)_{n\in\mathbb{N}^\infty})}{\forall f\in a_{\textbf{ocl}}, x\in\mathcal{X}_a^\mathcal{L}, e\in\mathcal{E}, n\in\mathbb{N}.\ \{\eta_n\}\ x\leftarrow f(e)\ \{\eta_{n+1}\}}{\{\eta_0\}\ x\leftarrow a(e)\ \{\eta_\infty\}}\ [\text{Adv}]$$

Fig. 4. Rules for adversaries

Note however that it might still be beneficial to use the [While] rule, even for lossless loops, because of the weaker requirement that the invariant is u-closed rather than t-closed.

Finally, Fig. 4 gives the adversary rule for general adversaries. It is highly similar to the general rule [While-D] for loops since the adversary may make an arbitrary sequence of calls to the oracles in $a_{\textbf{ocl}}$ and may not be lossless. Intuitively, η plays the role of the invariant: it must be d-closed and it must be preserved by every oracle call with arbitrary arguments. If this holds, then η is also preserved by the adversary call. Some framing conditions are required, similar to the ones of the [Frame] rule: the invariant must not be influenced by the state writable by the external procedures.

It is possible to give other variants of the adversary rule with more general invariants by restricting the adversary, e.g., requiring losslessness or bounding the number of calls the external procedure can make to oracles, leading to rules akin to the almost surely terminating and certainly terminating loop rules, respectively.

Soundness and Relative Completeness. Our proof system is sound with respect to the semantics.

Theorem 1 (Soundness). *Every judgment $\{\eta\}\, s\, \{\eta'\}$ provable using the rules of our logic is valid.*

Completeness of the logic follows from the next lemma, whose proof makes an essential use of the [WHILE] rule. In the sequel, we use $\mathbf{1}_\mu$ to denote the characteristic function of a probabilistic state μ, an assertion stating that the current state is equal to μ.

Lemma 5. *For every probabilistic state μ, the following judgment is provable using the rule of the logic:*

$$\{\mathbf{1}_\mu\}\, s\, \{\mathbf{1}_{[\![s]\!]_\mu}\}.$$

Proof. By induction on the structure of s.

- $s = \mathbf{abort}$, $s = \mathbf{skip}$, $x \leftarrow e$ and $s = x \stackrel{\$}{\leftarrow} g$ are trivial;
- $s = s_1; s_2$, we have to prove

$$\{\mathbf{1}_\mu\}\, s_1; s_2\, \{\mathbf{1}_{[\![s_2]\!]_{[\![s_1]\!]_\mu}}\}.$$

We apply the [SEQ] rule with $\eta_1 = \mathbf{1}_{[\![s_1]\!]_\mu}$ premises can be directly proved using the induction hypothesis;
- $s = \mathbf{if}\ e\ \mathbf{then}\ s_1\ \mathbf{else}\ s_2$, we have to prove

$$\{\mathbf{1}_\mu\}\, \mathbf{if}\ e\ \mathbf{then}\ s_1\ \mathbf{else}\ s_2\, \{(\mathbf{1}_{[\![s_1]\!]_{\mu_{|e}}} \oplus \mathbf{1}_{[\![s_2]\!]_{\mu_{|\neg e}}})\}.$$

We apply the [CONSEQ] rule to be able to apply the [COND] rule with $\eta_1 = \mathbf{1}_{[\![s_1]\!]_{\mu_{|e}}}$ and $\eta_2 = \mathbf{1}_{[\![s_2]\!]_{\mu_{|\neg e}}}$ Both premises can be proved by an application of the [CONSEQ] rule followed by the application of the induction hypothesis.
- $s = \mathbf{while}\ e\ \mathbf{do}\ s$, we have to prove

$$\{\mathbf{1}_\mu\}\, \mathbf{while}\ e\ \mathbf{do}\ s\, \{\mathbf{1}_{\lim_{n\to\infty}\ [\![(\mathbf{if}\ e\ \mathbf{then}\ s)^n;\mathbf{if}\ e\ \mathbf{then}\ \mathbf{abort}]\!]_\mu}\}.$$

We first apply the [WHILE] rule with $\eta'_n = \mathbf{1}_{[\![(\mathbf{if}\ e\ \mathbf{then}\ s)^n]\!]_\mu}$ and

$$\eta_n = \mathbf{1}_{[\![(\mathbf{if}\ e\ \mathbf{then}\ s)^n;\mathbf{if}\ e\ \mathbf{then}\ \mathbf{abort}]\!]_\mu}.$$

For the first premise we apply the same process as for the conditional case: we apply the [CONSEQ] and [COND] rules and we conclude using the induction hypothesis (and the [SKIP] rule). For the second premise we follow the same process but we conclude using the [ABORT] rule instead of the induction hypothesis. Finally we conclude since $\mathsf{uclosed}((\eta_n)_{n\in\mathbb{N}^\infty})$. □

The abstract logic is also relatively complete. This property will be less important for our purposes, but it serves as a basic sanity check.

Theorem 2 (Relative completeness). *Every valid judgment is derivable.*

Proof. Consider a valid judgment $\{\eta\}s\{\eta'\}$. Let μ be a probabilistic state such that $\eta(\mu)$. By the above proposition, $\{\mathbf{1}_\mu\}s\{\mathbf{1}_{[\![s]\!]_\mu}\}$. Using the validity of the judgment and [CONSEQ], we have $\{\mathbf{1}_\mu \wedge \eta(\mu)\}s\{\eta'\}$. Using the [EXISTS] and [CONSEQ] rules, we conclude $\{\eta\}s\{\eta'\}$ as required. □

The side-conditions in the loop rules (e.g., $\mathsf{uclosed}/\mathsf{tclosed}/\mathsf{dclosed}$ and the weight conditions) are difficult to prove, since they are semantic properties. Next, we present a concrete version of the logic with give easy-to-check, syntactic sufficient conditions.

5   A Concrete Program Logic

To give a more practical version of the logic, we begin by setting a concrete syntax for assertions

Assertions. We use a two-level assertion language, presented in Fig. 5. A *probabilistic assertion* η is a formula built from comparison of probabilistic expressions, using first-order quantifiers and connectives, and the special connective $\oplus$. A *probabilistic expression* p can be a logical variable v, an operator applied to probabilistic expressions $o(\boldsymbol{p})$ (constants are 0-ary operators), or the expectation $\mathbb{E}[\tilde{e}]$ of a state expression $\tilde{e}$. A *state expression* $\tilde{e}$ is either a program variable x, the characteristic function $\mathbf{1}_\phi$ of a state assertion ϕ, an operator applied to state expressions $o(\tilde{e})$, or the expectation $\mathbb{E}_{v \sim g}[\tilde{e}]$ of state expression $\tilde{e}$ in a given distribution g. Finally, a *state assertion* ϕ is a first-order formula over program variables. Note that the set of operators is left unspecified but we assume that all the expressions in $\mathcal{E}$ and $\mathcal{D}$ can be encoded by operators.

$$\tilde{e} ::= x \mid v \mid \mathbf{1}_\phi \mid \mathbb{E}_{v \sim g}[\tilde{e}] \mid o(\tilde{\boldsymbol{e}}) \quad \text{(S-expr.)}$$
$$\phi ::= \tilde{e} \bowtie \tilde{e} \mid FO(\phi) \quad \text{(S-assn.)}$$
$$p ::= v \mid o(\boldsymbol{p}) \mid \mathbb{E}[\tilde{e}] \quad \text{(P-expr.)}$$
$$\eta ::= p \bowtie p \mid \eta \oplus \eta \mid FO(\eta) \quad \text{(P-assn.)}$$
$$\bowtie \in \{=, <, \leq\} \quad o \in Ops \quad \text{(Ops.)}$$

Fig. 5. Assertion syntax

The interpretation of the concrete syntax is as expected. The interpretation of probabilistic assertions is relative to a valuation ρ which maps logical variables to values, and is an element of Assn. The definition of the interpretation is straightforward; the only interesting case is $[\![\mathbb{E}[\tilde{e}]]\!]^\rho_\mu$ which is defined by $\mathbb{E}_{m \sim \mu}[[\![\tilde{e}]\!]^\rho_m]$, where $[\![\tilde{e}]\!]^\rho_m$ is the interpretation of the state expression $\tilde{e}$ in the memory m and valuation ρ. The interpretation of state expressions is a mapping from memories to values, which can be lifted to a mapping from distributions over memories to distributions over values. The definition of the interpretation is straightforward; the most interesting case is for expectation $[\![\mathbb{E}_{v \sim g}[\tilde{e}]]\!]^\rho_m \triangleq \mathbb{E}_{w \sim [\![g]\!]^\rho_m}[[\![\tilde{e}]\!]^{\rho[v:=w]}_m]$. We present the full interpretations in the supplementary materials.

Many standard concepts from probability theory have a natural representation in our syntax. For example:

- the probability that ϕ holds in some probabilistic state is represented by the probabilistic expression $\Pr[\phi] \triangleq \mathbb{E}[\mathbf{1}_\phi]$;
- probabilistic independence of state expressions $\tilde{e}_1, \ldots, \tilde{e}_n$ is modeled by the probabilistic assertion $\#\{\tilde{e}_1, \ldots, \tilde{e}_n\}$, defined by the clause[4]

$$\forall v_1 \ldots v_n, \ \Pr[\top]^{n-1} \Pr[\bigwedge_{i=1\ldots n} \tilde{e}_i = v_i] = \prod_{i=1\ldots n} \Pr[\tilde{e}_i = v_i];$$

- the fact that a distribution is proper is modeled by the probabilistic assertion $\mathcal{L} \triangleq \Pr[\top] = 1$;

---

[4] The term $\Pr[\top]^{n-1}$ is necessary since we work with sub-distributions.

– a state expression $\tilde{e}$ distributed according to a law g is modeled by the probabilistic assertion

$$\tilde{e} \sim g \triangleq \forall w, \quad \Pr[\tilde{e} = w] = \mathbb{E}[\mathbb{E}_{v \sim g}[\mathbf{1}_{v=w}]].$$

The inner expectation computes the probability that v drawn from g is equal to a fixed w; the outer expectation weights the inner probability by the probability of each value of w.

We can easily define $\square$ operator from the previous section in our new syntax: $\square \phi \triangleq \Pr[\neg \phi] = 0$.

Syntactic Proof Rules. Now that we have a concrete syntax for assertions, we can give syntactic versions of many of the existing proof rules. Such proof rules are often easier to use since they avoid reasoning about the semantics of commands and assertions. We tackle the non-looping rules first, beginning with the following syntactic rules for assignment and sampling:

$$\frac{}{\{\eta[x := e]\}x \leftarrow e\{\eta\}} \text{ [Assgn]} \qquad \frac{}{\{\mathcal{P}_x^g(\eta)\}x \xleftarrow{\$} g\{\eta\}} \text{ [Sample]}$$

The rule for assignment is the usual rule from Hoare logic, replacing the program variable x by its corresponding expression e in the pre-condition. The replacement $\eta[x := e]$ is done recursively on the probabilistic assertion η; for instance for expectations, it is defined by $\mathbb{E}[\tilde{e}][x := e] \triangleq \mathbb{E}[\tilde{e}[x := e]]$, where $\tilde{e}[x := e]$ is the syntactic substitution.

The rule for sampling uses probabilistic substitution operator $\mathcal{P}_x^g(\eta)$, which replaces all occurrences of x in η by a new integration variable t and records that t is drawn from g; the operator is defined in Fig. 6.

$$
\begin{aligned}
\mathcal{P}_x^g(v) &\triangleq v \\
\mathcal{P}_x^g(\mathbb{E}[\tilde{e}]) &\triangleq \mathbb{E}[\mathbb{E}_{t \sim g}[\tilde{e}[x := t]]] \\
\mathcal{P}_x^g(o(\boldsymbol{\eta})) &\triangleq o(\mathcal{P}_x^g(\eta_1), \dots, \mathcal{P}_x^g(\eta_n)) \\
\mathcal{P}_x^g(\eta_1 \bowtie \eta_2) &\triangleq \mathcal{P}_x^g(\eta_1) \bowtie \mathcal{P}_x^g(\eta_2)
\end{aligned}
$$

for $o \in \mathbf{Ops}, \bowtie \in \{\wedge, \vee, \Rightarrow\}$.

Fig. 6. Syntactic op. $\mathcal{P}$ (main cases)

Next, we turn to the loop rule. The side-conditions from Fig. 3 are purely semantic, while in practice it is more convenient to use a sufficient condition in the Hoare logic. We give sufficient conditions for ensuring certain and almost-sure termination in Fig. 7; $\tilde{e}$ is an integer-valued expression. The first side-condition $\mathcal{C}_{\text{CTerm}}$ shows certain termination given a strictly decreasing *variant* $\tilde{e}$ that is bounded below, similar to how a decreasing variant shows termination for deterministic programs. The second side-condition $\mathcal{C}_{\text{ASTerm}}$ shows almost-sure termination given a probabilistic variant $\tilde{e}$, which must be bounded both above and below. While $\tilde{e}$ may increase with some probability, it must decrease with strictly positive probability. This condition was previously considered by [17] for probabilistic transition systems and also used in expectation-based approaches [20,33]. Our framework can also support more refined conditions (e.g., based on super-martingales [9,31]), but the condition $\mathcal{C}_{\text{ASTerm}}$ already suffices for most randomized algorithms.

$$\mathcal{C}_{\text{CTerm}} \triangleq \{\mathcal{L} \wedge \square(\tilde{e} = k \wedge 0 < k \wedge b)\}\, s \,\{\mathcal{L} \wedge \square(\tilde{e} < k)\}$$
$$\models \eta \Rightarrow (\exists \dot{y}.\ \square \tilde{e} \leq \dot{y}) \wedge \square(\tilde{e} = 0 \Rightarrow \neg b)$$

$$\mathcal{C}_{\text{ASTerm}} \triangleq \{\mathcal{L} \wedge \square(\tilde{e} = k \wedge 0 < k \leq K \wedge b)\}\, s \,\{\mathcal{L} \wedge \square(0 \leq \tilde{e} \leq K) \wedge \Pr[\tilde{e} < k] \geq \epsilon\}$$
$$\models \eta \Rightarrow \square(0 \leq \tilde{e} \leq K \wedge \tilde{e} = 0 \Rightarrow \neg b)$$
$$\models \text{tclosed}(\eta)$$

Fig. 7. Side-conditions for loop rules

While t-closedness is a semantic condition (cf. Definition 10), there are simple syntactic conditions to guarantee it. For instance, assertions that carry a non-strict comparison $\bowtie\, \in \{\leq, \geq, =\}$ between two bounded probabilistic expressions are t-closed; the assertion stating probabilistic independence of a set of expressions is t-closed.

Precondition Calculus. With a concrete syntax for assertions, we are also able to incorporate syntactic reasoning principles. One classic tool is Morgan and McIver's *greatest pre-expectation*, which we take as inspiration for a pre-condition calculus for the loop-free fragment of ELLORA. Given an assertion η and a loop-free statement s, we mechanically construct an assertion η^* that is the pre-condition of s that implies η as a post-condition. The basic idea is to replace each expectation expression p inside η by an expression p^* that has the same denotation before running s as p after running s. This process yields an assertion η^* that, interpreted before running s, is logically equivalent to η interpreted after running s.

The computation rules for pre-conditions are defined in Fig. 8. For a probability assertion η, its pre-condition $\text{pc}(s, \eta)$ corresponds to η where the expectation expressions of the form $\mathbb{E}[\tilde{e}]$ are replaced by their corresponding *pre-term*, $\text{pe}(s, \mathbb{E}[\tilde{e}])$. Pre-terms correspond loosely to Morgan and McIver's *pre-expectations*—we will make this correspondence more precise in the next section. The main interesting cases for computing pre-terms are for random sampling and conditionals. For random sampling the result is $\mathcal{P}_x^g(\mathbb{E}[\tilde{e}])$, which corresponds to the [SAMPLE] rule. For conditionals, the expectation expression is split into a part where e is true and a part where e is not true. We restrict the expectation to a part satisfying e with the operator $\mathbb{E}[\tilde{e}]_{|e} \triangleq \mathbb{E}[\tilde{e} \cdot \mathbf{1}_e]$. This corresponds to the expected value of $\tilde{e}$ on the portion of the distribution where e is true. Then, we can build the pre-condition calculus into ELLORA.

Theorem 1. *Let s be a non-looping command. Then, the following rule is derivable in the concrete version of* ELLORA:

$$\frac{}{\{pc(s, \eta)\}\, s\, \{\eta\}}\ [\text{PC}]$$

6   Case Studies: Embedding Lightweight Logics

While ELLORA is suitable for general-purpose reasoning about probabilistic programs, in practice humans typically use more special-purpose proof

$$\mathrm{pe}(s_1; s_2, \mathbb{E}[\tilde{e}]) \triangleq \mathrm{pe}(s_1, \mathrm{pe}(s_2, \mathbb{E}[\tilde{e}]))$$

$$\mathrm{pe}(x \leftarrow e, \mathbb{E}[\tilde{e}]) \triangleq \mathbb{E}[\tilde{e}][x := e]$$

$$\mathrm{pe}(x \xleftarrow{\$} g, \mathbb{E}[\tilde{e}]) \triangleq \mathcal{P}_x^g(\mathbb{E}[\tilde{e}])$$

$$\mathrm{pe}(\textbf{if } e \textbf{ then } s_1 \textbf{ else } s_2, \mathbb{E}[\tilde{e}]) \triangleq \mathrm{pe}(s_1, \mathbb{E}[\tilde{e}])_{|e} + \mathrm{pe}(s_2, \mathbb{E}[\tilde{e}])_{|\neg e}$$

$$\mathrm{pc}(s, p_1 \bowtie p_2) \triangleq \mathrm{pe}(s, p_1) \bowtie \mathrm{pe}(s, p_2)$$

Fig. 8. Precondition calculus (selected)

techniques—often targeting just a single, specific kind of property, like prob- abilistic independence—when proving probabilistic assertions. When these tech- niques apply, they can be a convenient and powerful tool.

To capture this intuitive style of reasoning, researchers have considered lightweight program logics where the assertions and proof rules are tailored to a specific proof technique. We demonstrate how to integrate these tools in an assertion-based logic by introducing and embedding a new logic for reason- ing about independence and distribution laws, useful properties when analyzing randomized algorithms. We crucially rely on the rich assertions in ELLORA— it is not clear how to extend expectation-based approaches to support similar, lightweight reasoning. Then, we show to embed the union bound logic [4] for proving accuracy bounds.

6.1   Law and Independence Logic

We begin by describing the law and independence logic IL, a proof system with intuitive rules that are easy to apply and amenable to automation. For simplicity, we only consider programs which sample from the binomial distribution, and have deterministic control flow—for lack of space, we also omit procedure calls.

Definition 12 (Assertions). IL *assertions have the grammar:*

$$\xi := \mathsf{det}(e) \mid \#E \mid e \sim \mathrm{B}(e, p) \mid \top \mid \bot \mid \xi \wedge \xi$$

where $e \in \mathcal{E}$, $E \subseteq \mathcal{E}$, *and* $p \in [0, 1]$.

The assertion $\mathsf{det}(e)$ states that e is deterministic in the current distribution, i.e., there is at most one element in the support of its interpretation. The asser- tion $\#E$ states that the expressions in E are independent, as formalized in the previous section. The assertion $e \sim \mathrm{B}(m, p)$ states that e is distributed according to a binomial distribution with parameter m (where m can be an expression) and constant probability p, i.e. the probability that $e = k$ is equal to the proba- bility that exactly k independent coin flips return heads using a biased coin that returns heads with probability p.

Assertions can be seen as an instance of a logical abstract domain, where the order between assertions is given by implication based on a small number of axioms. Examples of such axioms include independence of singletons, irreflexivity of independence, anti-monotonicity of independence, an axiom for the sum of binomial distributions, and rules for deterministic expressions:

$$\#\{x\} \qquad \#\{x,x\} \iff \mathsf{det}(x) \qquad \#(E \cup E') \implies \#E$$

$$e \sim \mathrm{B}(m,p) \wedge e' \sim \mathrm{B}(m',p) \wedge \# \{e,e'\} \implies e+e' \sim \mathrm{B}(m+m',p)$$

$$\bigwedge_{1 \leq i \leq n} \mathsf{det}(e_i) \implies \mathsf{det}(f(e_1,\dots,e_n))$$

Definition 13. *Judgments of the logic are of the form* $\{\xi\}$ s $\{\xi'\}$, *where* ξ *and* ξ' *are IL-assertions. A judgment is* valid *if it is derivable from the rules of Fig. 9; structural rules and rule for sequential composition are similar to those from Sect. 4 and omitted.*

The rule [IL-ASSGN] for deterministic assignments is as in Sect. 4. The rule [IL-SAMPLE] for random assignments yields as post-condition that the variable x and a set of expressions E are independent assuming that E is independent before the sampling, and moreover that x follows the law of the distribution that it is sampled from. The rule [IL-COND] for conditionals requires that the guard is deterministic, and that each of the branches satisfies the specification; if the guard is not deterministic, there are simple examples where the rule is not sound. The rule [IL-WHILE] for loops requires that the loop is certainly terminating with a deterministic guard. Note that the requirement of certain termination could be avoided by restricting the structural rules such that a statement s has deterministic control flow whenever $\{\xi\}$ s $\{\xi'\}$ is derivable.

We now turn to the embedding. The embedding of IL assertions into general assertions is immediate, except for $\mathsf{det}(e)$ which is translated as $\square e \vee \square \neg e$. We let $\bar{\xi}$ denote the translation of ξ.

Theorem 2 (Embedding and soundness of IL logic). *If* $\{\xi\}$ s $\{\xi'\}$ *is derivable in the IL logic, then* $\{\bar{\xi}\} s \{\bar{\xi'}\}$ *is derivable in (the syntactic variant of)* ELLORA. *As a consequence, every derivable judgment* $\{\xi\}$ s $\{\xi'\}$ *is valid.*

Proof sketch. By induction on the derivation. The interesting cases are conditionals and loops. For conditionals, the soundness follows from the soundness of the rule:

$$\frac{\{\eta\}\, s_1\, \{\eta'\} \qquad \{\eta\}\, s_2\, \{\eta'\} \qquad \square e \vee \square \neg e}{\{\eta\}\, \mathbf{if}\ e\ \mathbf{then}\ s_1\ \mathbf{else}\ s_2\, \{\eta'\}}$$

To prove the soundness of this rule, we proceed by case analysis on $\square e \vee \square \neg e$. We treat the case $\square e$; the other case is similar. In this case, η is equivalent to $\eta_1 \wedge \square e \oplus \eta_2 \wedge \square \neg e$, where $\eta_1 = \eta$ and $\eta_2 = \bot$. Let $\eta'_1 = \eta'$ and $\eta_2 = \square \bot$; again, $\eta'_1 \oplus \eta'_2$ is logically equivalent to η'. The soundness of the rule thus follows from

$$\frac{}{\{\xi[x := e]\}\ x \leftarrow e\ \{\xi\}}\ \text{[IL-Assgn]}$$

$$\frac{\{x\} \cap \mathrm{FV}(E) \cap \mathrm{FV}(e) = \emptyset}{\{\# E\}\ x \xleftarrow{\$} B(e, p)\ \{\#(E \cup \{x\}) \wedge x \sim B(e, p)\}}\ \text{[IL-Sample]}$$

$$\frac{\{\xi\}\ s_1\ \{\xi'\} \qquad \{\xi'\}\ s_2\ \{\xi''\}}{\{\xi\}\ s_1; s_2\ \{\xi''\}}\ \text{[IL-Seq]}$$

$$\frac{\{\xi\}\ s_1\ \{\xi'\} \qquad \{\xi\}\ s_2\ \{\xi'\} \\ \xi \implies \mathsf{det}(b)}{\{\xi\}\ \textbf{if}\ b\ \textbf{then}\ s_1\ \textbf{else}\ s_2\ \{\xi'\}}\ \text{[IL-Cond]}$$

$$\frac{\{\xi\}\ s\ \{\xi\} \qquad \xi \implies \mathsf{det}(b) \qquad \mathcal{C}_{\mathrm{CTerm}}}{\{\xi\}\ \textbf{while}\ b\ \textbf{do}\ s\ \{\xi\}}\ \text{[IL-While]}$$

Fig. 9. IL proof rules (selected)

the soundness of the [Cond] and [Conseq] rules. For loops, there exists a natural number n such that **while** b **do** s is semantically equivalent to (**if** b **then** s)^n. By assumption $\{\xi\}\ s\ \{\xi\}$ holds, and thus by induction hypothesis $\{\overline{\xi}\}\ s\ \{\overline{\xi}\}$. We also have $\xi \implies \mathsf{det}(b)$, and hence $\{\overline{\xi}\}$ **if** b **then** $s\ \{\overline{\xi}\}$. We conclude by [Seq]. $\square$

To illustrate our system IL, consider the statement s in Fig. 10 which flips a fair coin N times and counts the number of heads. Using the logic, we prove that $c \sim B(N \cdot (N+1)/2, 1/2)$ is a post-condition for s. We take the invariant:

$$c \sim B\left(\mathfrak{j}(\mathfrak{j}+1)/2, 1/2\right)$$

The invariant holds initially, as $0 \sim B(0, 1/2)$. For the inductive case, we show:

$$\{c \sim B(0, 1/2)\}\ s_0\ \{c \sim B\left((\mathfrak{j}+1)(\mathfrak{j}+2)/2, 1/2\right)\}$$

where s_0 represents the loop body, i.e. $x \xleftarrow{\$} B(\mathfrak{j}, 1/2)\,; c \leftarrow c + x$. First, we apply the rule for sequence taking as intermediate assertion

$$c \sim B\left(\mathfrak{j}(\mathfrak{j}+1)/2, 1/2\right) \wedge x \sim B(\mathfrak{j}, 1/2) \wedge \#\{x, c\}$$

```
proc sum () =
  var c:int, x:int;
  c ← 0;
  for j ← 1 to N do
    x ← B(j,1/2);
    c ← c + x;
  return c
```

Fig. 10. Sum of bin.

The first premise follows from the rule for random assignment and structural rules. The second premise follows from the rule for deterministic assignment and the rule of consequence, applying axioms about sums of binomial distributions.

We briefly comment on several limitations of IL. First, IL is restricted to programs with deterministic control flow, but this restriction could be partially relaxed by enriching IL with assertions for conditional independence. Such assertions are already expressible in the logic of ELLORA; adding conditional independence would significantly broaden the scope of the IL proof system and open the possibility to rely on axiomatizations of conditional independence (e.g., based on graphoids [36]). Second, the logic only supports sampling from binomial distributions. It is possible to enrich the language of assertions with clauses $c \sim g$ where g can model other distributions, like the uniform distribution or the Laplace distribution. The main design challenge is finding a core set of useful facts about these distributions. Enriching the logic and automating the analysis are interesting avenues for further work.

6.2   Embedding the Union Bound Logic

The program logic AHL [4] was recently introduced for estimating accuracy of randomized computations. One main application of AHL is proving accuracy of randomized algorithms, both in the offline and online settings—i.e. with adversary calls. AHL is based on the union bound, a basic tool from probability theory, and has judgments of the form $\models_\beta \{\Phi\} \ s \ \{\Psi\}$, where s is a statement, Φ and Ψ are first-order formulae over program variables, and β is a probability, i.e. $\beta \in [0,1]$. A judgment $\models_\beta \{\Phi\} \ s \ \{\Psi\}$ is valid if for every memory m such that $\Phi(m)$, the probability of $\neg\Psi$ in $[\![s]\!]_m$ is upper bounded by β, i.e. $\Pr_{[\![s]\!]_m}[\neg\Psi] \leq \beta$.

Figure 11 presents some key rules of AHL, including a rule for sampling from the Laplace distribution $\mathcal{L}_\epsilon$ centered around e. The predicate $\mathcal{C}_{\mathrm{CTerm}}(k)$ indicates that the loop terminates in at most k steps on any memory that satisfies the pre-condition. Moreover, β is a function of ϵ.

$$\frac{}{\models_\beta \{\top\} \ x \xleftarrow{\$} \mathcal{L}_\epsilon(e) \ \{|x - e| \leq \frac{1}{\epsilon}\log\frac{1}{\beta}\}} \ \text{[AHL-SAMPLE]}$$

$$\frac{\models_{\beta_1} \{\Phi\} \ s_1 \ \{\Theta\} \qquad \models_{\beta_2} \{\Theta\} \ s_2 \ \{\Psi\}}{\models_{\beta_1+\beta_2} \{\Phi\} \ s_1; s_2 \ \{\Psi\}} \ \text{[AHL-SEQ]}$$

$$\frac{\models_\beta \{\Phi\} \ c \ \{\Phi\} \qquad \mathcal{C}_{\mathrm{CTerm}}(k)}{\models_{k \cdot \beta} \{\Phi\} \ \mathbf{while} \ e \ \mathbf{do} \ c \ \{\Phi \wedge \neg e\}} \ \text{[AHL-WHILE]}$$

Fig. 11. AHL proof rules (selected)

AHL has a simple embedding into ELLORA.

Theorem 3 (Embedding of AHL). *If* $\models_\beta \{\Phi\} \ s \ \{\Psi\}$ *is derivable in* AHL, *then* $\{\Box\Phi\} \ s \ \{\mathbb{E}[\mathbf{1}_{\neg\Psi}] \leq \beta\}$ *is derivable in* ELLORA.

7   Case Studies: Verifying Randomized Algorithms

In this section, we will demonstrate ELLORA on a selection of examples; we present further examples in the supplemental material. Together, they exhibit a wide variety of different proof techniques and reasoning principles which are available in the ELLORA's implementation.

Hypercube Routing. will begin with the *hypercube routing* algorithm [41, 42]. Consider a network topology (the *hypercube*) where each node is labeled by a bit-string of length D and two nodes are connected by an edge if and only if the two corresponding labels differ in exactly one bit position.

In the network, there is initially one packet at each node, and each packet has a unique destination. The algorithm implements a routing strategy based on *bit fixing*: if the current position has bitstring i, and the target node has bitstring j, we compare the bits in i and j from left to right, moving along the edge that corrects the first differing bit. Valiant's algorithm uses randomization to guarantee that the total number of steps grows *logarithmically* in the number of packets. In the first phase, each packet i select an intermediate destination $\rho(i)$ uniformly at random, and use bit fixing to reach $\rho(i)$. In the second phase, each packet use bit fixing to go from $\rho(i)$ to the destination j. We will focus on the first phase since the reasoning for the second phase is nearly identical. We can model the strategy with the code in Fig. 12, using some syntactic sugar for the **for** loops.[5]

```
proc route (D T : int) :
  var ρ, pos, usedBy : node map;
  var nextE : edge;
  pos ← Map.init id 2^D; ρ ←Map.empty;
  for i ← 1 to 2^D do
    ρ[i] ←$ [1, 2^D]
    for t ← 1 to T do
      usedBy ← Map.empty;
      for i ← 1 to 2^D do
        if pos[i] ≠ ρ[i] then
          nextE ← getEdge pos[i] ρ[i];
          if usedBy[nextE] = ⊥ then
            // Mark edge used
            usedBy[nextE] ← i;
            // Move packet
            pos[i] ← dest nextE
  return (pos, ρ)
```

Fig. 12. Hypercube Routing

We assume that initially, the position of the packet i is at node i (see Map.init). Then, we initialize the random intermediate destinations ρ. The remaining loop encodes the evaluation of the routing strategy iterated T time. The variable usedBy is a map that logs if an edge is already used by a packet, it is empty at the beginning of each iteration. For each packet, we try to move it across one edge along the path to its intermediate destination. The function getEdge returns the next edge to follow, following the bit-fixing scheme. If the packet can progress (its edge is not used), then its current position is updated and the edge is marked as used.

We show that if the number of timesteps T is $4D + 1$, then all packets reach their intermediate destination in at most T steps, except with a small probability 2^{-2D} of failure. That is, the number of timesteps grows linearly in D, logarithmic in the number of packets. This is formalized in our system as:

$$\{T = 4D + 1\}\texttt{route}\{\Pr[\exists i.\ \texttt{pos}[i] \neq \rho[i]] \leq 2^{-2D}]\}$$

---

[5] Recall that the number of node in a hypercube of dimension D is 2^D so each node can be identified by a number in $[1, 2^D]$.

```
proc coupon (N : int) :
    var int cp[N], t[N];
    var int X ←0;
    for p ← 1 to N do
        ct ← 0;
        cur ←$ [1, N];
        while cp[cur] = 1 do
            ct ← ct + 1;
            cur ←$ [1, N];
        t[p]    ← ct;
        cp[cur] ← 1;
        X ←X + t[p];
    return X
```

Fig. 13. Coupon collector

Modeling Infinite Processes. Our second example is the *coupon collector* process. The algorithm draws a uniformly random coupon (we have N coupon) on each day, terminating when it has drawn at least one of each kind of coupon. The code of the algorithm is displayed in Fig. 13; the array cp records of the coupons seen so far, t holds the number of steps taken before seeing a new coupon, and X tracks of the total number of steps. Our goal is to bound the average number of iterations. This is formalized in our logic as:

$$\{\mathcal{L}\}\ \text{coupon}\ \left\{ \mathbb{E}[X] = \sum_{i \in [1,N]} \left(\frac{N}{N-i+1} \right) \right\}.$$

Limited Randomness. Pairwise independence says that if we see the result of X_i, we do not gain information about all other variables X_k. However, if we see the result of *two* variables X_i, X_j, we may gain information about X_k. There are many constructions in the algorithms literature that grow a small number of independent bits into more pairwise independent bits. Figure 14 gives one procedure, where $\oplus$ is exclusive-or, and bits(j) is the set of positions set to 1 in the binary expansion of j. The proof uses the following fact, which we fully verify: for a uniformly distributed Boolean random variable Y, and a random variable Z of any type,

```
proc pwInd (N : int) :
    var bool X[2^N], B[N];
    for i ← 1 to N do
        B[i] ←$ Ber(1/2);
    for j ← 1 to 2^N do
        X[j] ← 0;
        for k ← 1 to N do
            if k ∈ bits(j) then
                X[j] ← X[j] ⊕ B[k]
    return X
```

Fig. 14. Pairwise Independence

$$Y \mathbin{\#} Z \Rightarrow Y \oplus f(Z) \mathbin{\#} g(Z) \tag{1}$$

for any two Boolean functions f, g. Then, note that $\mathrm{x}[i] = \bigoplus_{\{j \in \text{bits}(i)\}} \mathrm{B}[j]$ where the big XOR operator ranges over the indices j where the bit representation of i has bit j set. For any two $i, k \in [1, \dots, 2^N]$ distinct, there is a bit position in $[1, \dots, \mathrm{N}]$ where i and k differ; call this position r and suppose it is set in i but not in k. By rewriting,

$$\mathrm{x}[i] = \mathrm{B}[r] \oplus \bigoplus_{\{j \in \text{bits}(i) \backslash r\}} \mathrm{B}[j] \quad \text{and} \quad \mathrm{x}[k] = \bigoplus_{\{j \in \text{bits}(k) \backslash r\}} \mathrm{B}[j].$$

Since $\mathrm{B}[j]$ are all independent, $\mathrm{x}[i] \mathbin{\#} \mathrm{x}[k]$ follows from Eq. (1) taking Z to be the distribution on tuples $\langle \mathrm{B}[1], \dots, \mathrm{B}[N] \rangle$ excluding $\mathrm{B}[r]$. This verifies pairwise independence:

$$\{\mathcal{L}\}\ \text{pwInd(N)}\ \{\mathcal{L} \wedge \forall i, k \in [2^N].\ i \neq k \Rightarrow \mathrm{x}[i] \mathbin{\#} \mathrm{x}[k]\}.$$

Adversarial Programs. Pseudorandom functions (PRF) and pseudorandom permutations (PRP) are two idealized primitives that play a central role in the design of symmetric-key systems. Although the most natural assumption to make about a blockcipher is that it behaves as a pseudorandom permutation, most commonly the security of such a system is analyzed by replacing the blockcipher with a perfectly random function. The PRP/PRF Switching Lemma [6, 22] fills the gap: given a bound for the security of a blockcipher as a pseudorandom function, it gives a bound for its security as a pseudorandom permutation.

Lemma 4 (PRP/PRF switching lemma). *Let A be an adversary with blackbox access to an oracle O implementing either a random permutation on $\{0,1\}^l$ or a random function from $\{0,1\}^l$ to $\{0,1\}^l$. Then the probability that the adversary A distinguishes between the two oracles in at most q calls is bounded by*

$$\left| \Pr_{PRP}[b \wedge |H| \leq q] - \Pr_{PRF}[b \wedge |H| \leq q] \right| \leq \frac{q(q-1)}{2^{l+1}},$$

where H is a map storing each adversary call and $|H|$ is its size.

Proving this lemma can be done using the Fundamental Lemma of Game-Playing, and bounding the probability of *bad* in the program from Fig. 15. We focus on the latter. Here we apply the [Adv] rule of ELLORA with the invariant $\forall k, \Pr[\text{bad} \wedge |H| \leq k] \leq \frac{k(k-1)}{2^{l+1}}$ where $|H|$ is the size of the map H, i.e. the number of adversary call. Intuitively, the invariant says that at each call to the oracle the probability that bad has been set before and that the number of adversary call is less than k is bounded by a polynomial in k.

The invariant is d-closed and true before the adversary call, since at that point $\Pr[\text{bad}] = 0$. Then we need to prove that the oracle preserves the invariant, which can be done easily using the precondition calculus ([PC] rule).

```
var H: ({0,1}^l, {0,1}^l) map;            proc main():
proc orcl (q:{0,1}^l):                      var b: bool;
  var a : {0,1}^l;                          bad ← false;
  if q ∉ H then                            H ← [];
    a ←$ {0,1}^l;                          b ← A();
    bad ← bad || a ∈ codom(H);             return b;
    H[q] ←a;
  return H[q];
```

Fig. 15. PRP/PRF game

8   Implementation and Mechanization

We have built a prototype implementation of ELLORA within EASYCRYPT [2,5], a theorem prover originally designed for verifying cryptographic protocols. EASY-CRYPT provides a convenient environment for constructing proofs in various Hoare logics, supporting interactive, tactic-based proofs for manipulating assertions and allowing users to invoke external tools, like SMT-solvers, to discharge proof obligations. EASYCRYPT provides a mature set of libraries for both data structures (sets, maps, lists, arrays, etc.) and mathematical theorems (algebra, real analysis, etc.), which we extended with theorems from probability theory.

Table 1. Benchmarks

Example	LC	FPLC
hypercube	100	1140
coupon	27	184
vertex-cover	30	61
pairwise-indep	30	231
private-sums	22	80
poly-id-test	22	32
random-walk	16	42
dice-sampling	10	64
matrix-prod-test	20	75

We used the implementation for verifying many examples from the literature, including all the programs presented in Sect. 7 as well as some additional examples in Table 1 (such as polynomial identity test, private running sums, properties about random walks, etc.). The verified proofs bear a strong resemblance to the existing, paper proofs. Independently of this work, ELLORA has been used to formalize the main theorem about a randomized gossip-based protocol for distributed systems [26, Theorem 2.1]. Some libraries developed in the scope of ELLORA have been incorporated into the main branch of EASYCRYPT, including a general library on probabilistic independence.

A New Library for Probabilistic Independence. In order to support assertions of the concrete program logic, we enhanced the standard libraries of EASYCRYPT, notably the ones dealing with big operators and sub-distributions. Like all EASY-CRYPT libraries, they are written in a foundational style, i.e. they are defined instead of axiomatized. A large part of our libraries are proved formally from first principles. However, some results, such as concentration bounds, are currently declared as axioms.

Our formalization of probabilistic independence deserves special mention. We formalized two different (but logically equivalent) notions of independence. The first is in terms of products of probabilities, and is based on heterogenous lists. Since ELLORA (like EASYCRYPT) has no support for heterogeneous lists, we use a smart encoding based on second-order predicates. The second definition is more abstract, in terms of product and marginal distributions. While the first definition is easier to use when reasoning about randomized algorithms, the second definition is more suited for proving mathematical facts. We prove the two definitions equivalent, and formalize a collection of related theorems.

Mechanized Meta-Theory. The proofs of soundness and relative completeness of the abstract logic, without adversary calls, and the syntactical termination arguments have been mechanized in the Coq proof assistant. The development is available in supplemental material.

9   Related Work

More on Assertion-Based Techniques. The earliest assertion-based system is due to Ramshaw [37], who proposes a program logic where assertions can be formulas involving *frequencies*, essentially probabilities on sub-distributions. Ramshaw's logic allows assertions to be combined with operators like $\oplus$, similar to our approach. [18] presents a Hoare-style logic with general assertions on the distribution, allowing expected values and probabilities. However, his **while** rule is based on a semantic condition on the guarded loop body, which is less desirable for verification because it requires reasoning about the semantics of programs. [8] give decidability results for a probabilistic Hoare logic without **while** loops. We are not aware of any existing system that supports assertions about general expected values; existing works also restrict to Boolean distributions. [38] formalize a Hoare logic for probabilistic programs but unlike our work, their assertions are interpreted on *distributions* rather than sub-distributions. For conditionals, their semantics rescales the distribution of states that enter each branch. However, their assertion language is limited and they impose strong restrictions on loops.

Other Approaches. Researchers have proposed many other approaches to verify probabilistic program. For instance, verification of Markov transition systems goes back to at least [17,40]; our condition for ensuring almost-sure termination in loops is directly inspired by their work. Automated methods include model checking (see e.g., [1,25,29]) and abstract interpretation (see e.g., [12,32]). Techniques for reasoning about higher-order (functional) probabilistic languages are an active subject of research (see e.g., [7,13,14]). For analyzing probabilistic loops, in particular, there are tools for reasoning about running time. There are also automated systems for synthesizing invariants [3,11]. [9,10] use a martingale method to compute the expected time of the coupon collector process for $N = 5$—fixing N lets them focus on a program where the outer **while** loop is fully unrolled. Martingales are also used by [15] for analyzing probabilistic termination. Finally, there are approaches involving symbolic execution; [39] use a mix of static and dynamic analysis to check probabilistic programs from the approximate computing literature.

10 Conclusion and Perspectives

We introduced an expressive program logic for probabilistic programs, and showed that assertion-based systems are suited for practical verification of probabilistic programs. Owing to their richer assertions, program logics are a more suitable foundation for specialized reasoning principles than expectation-based systems. As evidence, our program logic can be smoothly extended with custom reasoning for probabilistic independence and union bounds. Future work includes proving better accuracy bounds for differentially private algorithms, and exploring further integration of ELLORA into EASYCRYPT.

Acknowledgments. We thank the reviewers for their helpful comments. This work benefited from discussions with Dexter Kozen, Annabelle McIver, and Carroll Morgan. This work was partially supported by ERC Grant #679127, and NSF grant 1718220.

References

1. Baier, C.: Probabilistic model checking. In: Dependable Software Systems Engineering, NATO Science for Peace and Security Series - D: Information and Communication Security, vol. 45, pp. 1–23. IOS Press (2016), https://doi.org/10.3233/978-1-61499-627-9-1
2. Barthe, G., Dupressoir, F., Grégoire, B., Kunz, C., Schmidt, B., Strub, P.-Y.: EasyCrypt: A tutorial. In: Aldini, A., Lopez, J., Martinelli, F. (eds.) FOSAD 2012-2013. LNCS, vol. 8604, pp. 146–166. Springer, Cham (2014). https://doi.org/10.1007/978-3-319-10082-1_6
3. Barthe, G., Espitau, T., Ferrer Fioriti, L.M., Hsu, J.: Synthesizing probabilistic invariants via Doob's decomposition. In: International Conference on Computer Aided Verification (CAV), Toronto, Ontario (2016). https://arxiv.org/abs/1605.02765
4. Barthe, G., Gaboardi, M., Grégoire, B., Hsu, J., Strub, P.Y.: A program logic for union bounds. In: International Colloquium on Automata, Languages and Programming (ICALP), Rome, Italy (2016). http://arxiv.org/abs/1602.05681
5. Barthe, G., Grégoire, B., Heraud, S., Béguelin, S.Z.: Computer-aided security proofs for the working cryptographer. In: Rogaway, P. (ed.) CRYPTO 2011. LNCS, vol. 6841, pp. 71–90. Springer, Heidelberg (2011). https://doi.org/10.1007/978-3-642-22792-9_5
6. Bellare, M., Rogaway, P.: The security of triple encryption and a framework for code-based game-playing proofs. In: IACR International Conference on the Theory and Applications of Cryptographic Techniques (EUROCRYPT), Saint Petersburg, Russia, pp. 409–426 (2006). https://doi.org/10.1007/11761679_25
7. Bizjak, A., Birkedal, L.: Step-indexed logical relations for probability. In: Pitts, A. (ed.) FoSSaCS 2015. LNCS, vol. 9034, pp. 279–294. Springer, Heidelberg (2015). https://doi.org/10.1007/978-3-662-46678-0_18
8. Chadha, R., Cruz-Filipe, L., Mateus, P., Sernadas, A.: Reasoning about probabilistic sequential programs. Theoretical Computer Science **379**(1–2), 142–165 (2007)
9. Chakarov, A., Sankaranarayanan, S.: Probabilistic program analysis with martingales. In: Sharygina, N., Veith, H. (eds.) CAV 2013. LNCS, vol. 8044, pp. 511–526. Springer, Heidelberg (2013). https://doi.org/10.1007/978-3-642-39799-8_34
10. Chakarov, A., Sankaranarayanan, S.: Expectation invariants for probabilistic program loops as fixed points. In: Müller-Olm, M., Seidl, H. (eds.) SAS 2014. LNCS, vol. 8723, pp. 85–100. Springer, Cham (2014). https://doi.org/10.1007/978-3-319-10936-7_6
11. Chatterjee, K., Fu, H., Novotný, P., Hasheminezhad, R.: Algorithmic analysis of qualitative and quantitative termination problems for affine probabilistic programs. In: ACM SIGPLAN-SIGACT Symposium on Principles of Programming Languages (POPL), Saint Petersburg, Florida, pp. 327–342 (2016). https://doi.org/10.1145/2837614.2837639
12. Cousot, P., Monerau, M.: Probabilistic abstract interpretation. In: Seidl, H. (ed.) ESOP 2012. LNCS, vol. 7211, pp. 169–193. Springer, Heidelberg (2012). https://doi.org/10.1007/978-3-642-28869-2_9
13. Crubillé, R., Dal Lago, U.: On probabilistic applicative bisimulation and call-by-value λ-calculi. In: Shao, Z. (ed.) ESOP 2014. LNCS, vol. 8410, pp. 209–228. Springer, Heidelberg (2014). https://doi.org/10.1007/978-3-642-54833-8_12

14. Dal Lago, U., Sangiorgi, D., Alberti, M.: On coinductive equivalences for higher-order probabilistic functional programs. In: ACM SIGPLAN-SIGACT Symposium on Principles of Programming Languages (POPL), San Diego, California, pp. 297–308 (2014). https://arxiv.org/abs/1311.1722
15. Fioriti, L.M.F., Hermanns, H.: Probabilistic termination: Soundness, completeness, and compositionality. In: ACM SIGPLAN-SIGACT Symposium on Principles of Programming Languages (POPL), Mumbai, India, pp. 489–501 (2015)
16. Gretz, F., Katoen, J.P., McIver, A.: Operational versus weakest pre-expectation semantics for the probabilistic guarded command language. Perform. Eval. **73**, 110–132 (2014)
17. Hart, S., Sharir, M., Pnueli, A.: Termination of probabilistic concurrent programs. ACM Trans. Program. Lang. Syst. **5**(3), 356–380 (1983)
18. den Hartog, J.: Probabilistic extensions of semantical models. Ph.D. thesis, Vrije Universiteit Amsterdam (2002)
19. Hurd, J.: Formal verification of probabilistic algorithms. Technical report, UCAM-CL-TR-566, University of Cambridge, Computer Laboratory (2003)
20. Hurd, J.: Verification of the Miller-Rabin probabilistic primality test. J. Log. Algebr. Program. **56**(1–2), 3–21 (2003). https://doi.org/10.1016/S1567-8326(02)00065-6
21. Hurd, J., McIver, A., Morgan, C.: Probabilistic guarded commands mechanized in HOL. Theor. Comput. Sci. **346**(1), 96–112 (2005)
22. Impagliazzo, R., Rudich, S.: Limits on the provable consequences of one-way permutations. In: ACM SIGACT Symposium on Theory of Computing (STOC), Seattle, Washington, pp. 44–61 (1989). https://doi.org/10.1145/73007.73012
23. Kaminski, B.L., Katoen, J.-P., Matheja, C.: Inferring covariances for probabilistic programs. In: Agha, G., Van Houdt, B. (eds.) QEST 2016. LNCS, vol. 9826, pp. 191–206. Springer, Cham (2016). https://doi.org/10.1007/978-3-319-43425-4_14
24. Kaminski, B., Katoen, J.P., Matheja, C., Olmedo, F.: Weakest precondition reasoning for expected run-times of probabilistic programs. In: European Symposium on Programming (ESOP), Eindhoven, The Netherlands, January 2016
25. Katoen, J.P.: The probabilistic model-checking landscape. In: IEEE Symposium on Logic in Computer Science (LICS), New York (2016)
26. Kempe, D., Dobra, A., Gehrke, J.: Gossip-based computation of aggregate information. In: Proceedings of the 44th Annual IEEE Symposium on Foundations of Computer Science, pp. 482–491 (2003). https://doi.org/10.1109/SFCS.2003.1238221
27. Kozen, D.: Semantics of probabilistic programs. J. Comput. Syst. Sci. **22**, 328–350 (1981). https://www.sciencedirect.com/science/article/pii/0022000081900362
28. Kozen, D.: A probabilistic PDL. J. Comput. Syst. Sci. **30**(2), 162–178 (1985)
29. Kwiatkowska, M., Norman, G., Parker, D.: PRISM 4.0: Verification of probabilistic real-time systems. In: Gopalakrishnan, G., Qadeer, S. (eds.) CAV 2011. LNCS, vol. 6806, pp. 585–591. Springer, Heidelberg (2011). https://doi.org/10.1007/978-3-642-22110-1_47
30. McIver, A., Morgan, C.: Abstraction, refinement, and proof for probabilistic systems. Monographs in Computer Science. Springer, New York (2005)
31. McIver, A., Morgan, C., Kaminski, B.L., Katoen, J.P.: A new rule for almost-certain termination. In: Proceedings of the ACM on Programming Languages 1(POPL) (2018). https://arxiv.org/abs/1612.01091, appeared at ACM SIGPLAN-SIGACT Symposium on Principles of Programming Languages (POPL), Los Angeles, California

32. Monniaux, D.: Abstract interpretation of probabilistic semantics. In: Palsberg, J. (ed.) SAS 2000. LNCS, vol. 1824, pp. 322–339. Springer, Heidelberg (2000). https://doi.org/10.1007/978-3-540-45099-3_17
33. Morgan, C.: Proof rules for probabilistic loops. In: BCS-FACS Conference on Refinement, Bath, England (1996)
34. Morgan, C., McIver, A., Seidel, K.: Probabilistic predicate transformers. ACM Trans. Program. Lang. Syst. **18**(3), 325–353 (1996)
35. Olmedo, F., Kaminski, B.L., Katoen, J.P., Matheja, C.: Reasoning about recursive probabilistic programs. In: IEEE Symposium on Logic in Computer Science (LICS), New York, pp. 672–681 (2016)
36. Pearl, J., Paz, A.: Graphoids: graph-based logic for reasoning about relevance relations. In: ECAI, pp. 357–363 (1986)
37. Ramshaw, L.H.: Formalizing the Analysis of Algorithms. Ph.D. thesis, Computer Science (1979)
38. Rand, R., Zdancewic, S.: VPHL: a verified partial-correctness logic for probabilistic programs. In: Conference on the Mathematical Foundations of Programming Semantics (MFPS), Nijmegen, The Netherlands (2015)
39. Sampson, A., Panchekha, P., Mytkowicz, T., McKinley, K.S., Grossman, D., Ceze, L.: Expressing and verifying probabilistic assertions. In: ACM SIGPLAN Conference on Programming Language Design and Implementation (PLDI), Edinburgh, Scotland, p. 14 (2014)
40. Sharir, M., Pnueli, A., Hart, S.: Verification of probabilistic programs. SIAM J. Comput. **13**(2), 292–314 (1984)
41. Valiant, L.G.: A scheme for fast parallel communication. SIAM J. Comput. **11**(2), 350–361 (1982)
42. Valiant, L.G., Brebner, G.J.: Universal schemes for parallel communication. In: ACM SIGACT Symposium on Theory of Computing (STOC), Milwaukee, Wisconsin, pp. 263–277 (1981). https://doi.org/10.1145/800076.802479

Fine-Grained Semantics
for Probabilistic Programs

Benjamin Bichsel$^{(\boxtimes)}$, Timon Gehr, and Martin Vechev

ETH Zürich, Zürich, Switzerland
{benjamin.bichsel,timon.gehr,martin.vechev}@inf.ethz.ch

Abstract. Probabilistic programming is an emerging technique for modeling processes involving uncertainty. Thus, it is important to ensure these programs are assigned precise formal semantics that also cleanly handle typical exceptions such as non-termination or division by zero. However, existing semantics of probabilistic programs do not fully accommodate different exceptions and their interaction, often ignoring some or conflating multiple ones into a single exception state, making it impossible to distinguish exceptions or to study their interaction.

In this paper, we provide an expressive probabilistic programming language together with a fine-grained measure-theoretic denotational semantics that handles and distinguishes non-termination, observation failures and error states. We then investigate the properties of this semantics, focusing on the interaction of different kinds of exceptions. Our work helps to better understand the intricacies of probabilistic programs and ensures their behavior matches the intended semantics.

1 Introduction

A probabilistic programming language allows probabilistic models to be specified independently of the particular inference algorithms that make predictions using the model. Probabilistic programs are formed using standard language primitives as well as constructs for drawing random values and conditioning. The overall approach is general and applicable to many different settings (e.g., building cognitive models). In recent years, the interest in probabilistic programming systems has grown rapidly with various languages and probabilistic inference algorithms (ranging from approximate to exact). Examples include [10,11,13,14,25–27,29,36]; for a recent survey, please see [15]. An important branch of recent probabilistic programming research is concerned with providing a suitable semantics for these programs enabling one to formally reason about the program's behaviors [2–4,33–35].

Often, probabilistic programs require access to primitives that may result in unwanted behavior. For example, the standard deviation σ of a Gaussian distribution must be positive (sampling from a Gaussian distribution with negative standard deviation should result in an error). If a program samples from a Gaussian distribution with a non-constant standard deviation, it is in general

© The Author(s) 2018
A. Ahmed (Ed.): ESOP 2018, LNCS 10801, pp. 145–185, 2018.
https://doi.org/10.1007/978-3-319-89884-1_6

undecidable if that standard deviation is guaranteed to be positive. A similar situation occurs for while loops: except in some trivial cases, it is hard to decide if a program terminates with probability one (even harder than checking termination of deterministic programs [20]). However, general while loops are important for many probabilistic programs. As an example, a Markov Chain Monte Carlo sampler is essentially a special probabilistic program, which in practice requires a non-trivial stopping criterion (see e.g. [6] for such a stopping criterion). In addition to offering primitives that may result in such unwanted behavior, many probabilistic programming languages also provide an **observe** primitive that intuitively allows to filter out executions violating some constraint.

Motivation. Measure-theoretic denotational semantics for probabilistic programs is desirable as it enables reasoning about probabilistic programs within the rigorous and general framework of measure theory. While existing research has made substantial progress towards a rigorous semantic foundation of probabilistic programming, existing denotational semantics based on measure theory usually conflate failing **observe** statements (i.e., conditioning), error states and non-termination, often modeling at least some of these as missing weight in a sub-probability measure (we show why this is practically problematic in later examples). This means that even semantically, it is impossible to distinguish these types of exceptions[1]. However, distinguishing exceptions is essential for a solid understanding of probabilistic programs: it is insufficient if the semantics of a probabilistic programming language can only express that *something* went wrong during the execution of the program, lacking the capability to distinguish for example non-termination and errors. Concretely, programmers often want to avoid non-termination and assertion failure, while observation failure is acceptable (or even desirable). When a program runs into an exception, the programmer should be able determine the type of exception, from the semantics.

This Work. This paper presents a clean denotational semantics for a Turing complete first-order probabilistic programming language that supports mixing continuous and discrete distributions, arrays, observations, partial functions and loops. This semantics distinguishes observation failures, error states and non-termination by tracking them as explicit program states. Our semantics allows for fine-grained reasoning, such as determining the termination probability of a probabilistic program making observations from a sequence of concrete values.

In addition, we explain the consequences of our treatment of exceptions by providing interesting examples and properties of our semantics, such as commutativity in the absence of exceptions, or associativity regardless of the presence of exceptions. We also investigate the interaction between exceptions and the **score** primitive, concluding in particular that the probability of non-termination cannot be defined in this case. **score** intuitively allows to increase or decrease the probability of specific runs of a program (for more details, see Sect. 5.3).

---

[1] In this paper, we refer to errors, non-termination and observation failures collectively as *exceptions*. For example, a division by zero is an error (and hence and exception), while non-termination is an exception but not an error.

2   Overview

In this section we demonstrate several important features of our probabilistic programming language (PPL) using examples, followed by a discussion involving different kinds of exception interactions.

2.1   Features of Probabilistic Programs

In the following, we informally discuss the most important features of our PPL.

Discrete and Continuous Primitive Distributions. Listing 1 illustrates a simple Gaussian mixture model (the figure only shows the function body). Depending on the outcome of a fair coin flip x (resulting in 0 or 1), y is sampled from a Gaussian distribution with mean 0 or mean 2 (and standard deviation 1). Note that in our PPL, we represent **gauss**$(\cdot, \cdot)$ by the more general construct **sampleFrom**$_f(\cdot, \cdot)$, with $f : \mathbb{R} \times [0, \infty) \to \mathbb{R} \to \mathbb{R}$ being the probability density function of the Gaussian distribution

$$f(\mu, \sigma)(x) = \frac{1}{\sqrt{2\pi\sigma^2}} e^{-\frac{(x-\mu)^2}{2\sigma^2}}.$$

```
y:=0;
if flip(½) {
   y=gauss(0,1);
}else{
   y=gauss(2,1);
}
return y;
```

Listing 1. Simple Gaussian mixture

Conditioning. Listing 2 samples two independent values from the uniform distribution on the interval $[0, 1]$ and conditions the possible values of x and y on the observation $x + y > 1$ before returning x. Intuitively, the first two lines express a-priori knowledge about the uncertain values of x and y. Then, a measurement determines that $x + y$ is greater than 1. We combine this new information with the existing knowledge. Because $x + y > 1$ is more likely for larger values of

```
x:=uniform(0,1);
y:=uniform(0,1);
observe(x+y>1);
return x;
```

Listing 2. Conditioning on a continuous distribution

x, the return value has larger weight on larger values. Formally, our semantics handles **observe** by introducing an extra program state for observation failure $\frac{1}{2}$. Hence, the probability distribution after the third line of Listing 2 will put weight $\frac{1}{2}$ on $\frac{1}{2}$ and weight $\frac{1}{2}$ on those x and y satisfying $x + y > 1$.

In practice, one will usually condition the output distribution on there being no observation failure ($\frac{1}{2}$). For discrete distributions, this amounts to computing:

$$Pr[X = x \mid X \neq \frac{1}{2}] = \frac{Pr[X = x \land X \neq \frac{1}{2}]}{Pr[X \neq \frac{1}{2}]} = \frac{Pr[X = x]}{1 - Pr[X = \frac{1}{2}]}$$

where x is the outcome of the program (a value, non-termination or an error) and $Pr[X = x]$ is the probability that the program results in x. Of course, this conditioning only works when the probability of $\frac{1}{2}$ is not 1. Note that tracking the probability of $\frac{1}{2}$ has the practical benefit of rendering the (often expensive) marginalization $Pr[X \neq \frac{1}{2}] = \sum_{x \neq \frac{1}{2}} Pr[X = x]$ unnecessary.

Other semantics often use sub-probability measures to express failed observations [4, 34, 35]. These semantics would say that Listing 2 results in a return value between 0 and 1 with probability $\frac{1}{2}$ (and infer that the missing weight of $\frac{1}{2}$ is due to failed observations). We believe one should improve upon this approach as the semantics only implicitly states that the program sometimes fails an observation. Further, this strategy only allows tracking a single kind of exception (in this case, failed observations). This has led some works to conflate observation failure and non-termination [18,34]. We believe there is an important distinction between the two: observation failure means that the program behavior is inconsistent with observed facts, non-termination means that the program did not return a result.

Listing 3 illustrates that it is not possible to condition parts of the program on there being no observation failure. In Listing 3, conditioning the first branch $x := 0; \mathbf{observe}(\mathbf{flip}(\frac{1}{2}))$ on there being no observation failure yields $Pr[x = 0] = 1$, rendering the observation irrelevant. The same situation arises for the second branch. Hence, conditioning the two branches in isolation yields $Pr[x = 0] = \frac{1}{2}$ instead of $Pr[x = 0] = \frac{2}{3}$.

```
if flip(½) {
  x:=0;
  observe(flip(½));
}else{
  x:=1;
  observe(flip(¼));
}
```

Listing 3. The need for tracking ⨑

Loops. Listing 4 shows a probabilistic program with a while loop. It samples from the **geometric**($\frac{1}{2}$) distribution, which counts the number of failures (**flip** returns 0) until the first success occurs (**flip** returns 1). This program terminates with probability 1, but it is of course possible that a probabilistic program fails to terminate with positive probability. Listing 5 demonstrates this possibility.

```
n:=0;
while !flip(½) {
  n=n+1;
}
return n;
```

Listing 4. Geometric distribution

Listing 5 modifies x until either $x = 0$ or $x = 10$. In each iteration, x is either increased or decreased, each with probability $\frac{1}{2}$. If x reaches 0, the loop terminates. If x reaches 10, the loop never terminates. By symmetry, both termination and non-termination are equally likely. Hence, the program either returns 0 or does not terminate, each with probability $\frac{1}{2}$.

```
x := 5;
while x>0 {
  if x<10 {
    x+=2*flip(½)-1;
  }
}
return x;
```

Listing 5. Program that may not terminate

Other semantics often use sub-probability measures to express non-termination [4,23]. Thus, these semantics would say that Listing 5 results in 0 with probability $\frac{1}{2}$ (and nothing else). We propose to track the probability of non-termination explicitly by an additional state ↻, just as we track the probability of observation failure (⨑).

Partial Functions. Many functions that are practically useful are only partial (meaning they are not defined for some inputs). Examples include **uniform**(a, b) (undefined for $b < a$) and $\sqrt{x}$ (undefined for $x < 0$). Listing 6 shows an example program using $\sqrt{x}$. Usually, semantics do not explicitly address partial functions [23,24,28,33] or use

```
x:=uniform(-1,1);
x=√x;
return x;
```

Listing 6. Using partial functions

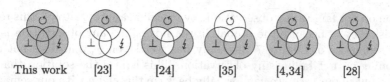

This work   [23]   [24]   [35]   [4,34]   [28]

Fig. 1. Visual comparison of the exception handling capabilities of different semantics. For example, ↻ is filled in [34] because its semantics can handle non-termination. However, the intersection between ↻ and ⚡ is not filled because [34] cannot distinguish non-termination from observation failure.

partial functions without dealing with failure (e.g. [19] use **Bernoulli**(p) without stating what happens if $p \notin [0,1]$). Most of these languages could use a sub-probability distribution that misses weight in the presence of errors (in these languages, this results in conflating errors with non-termination and observation failures).

We introduce a third exception state $\perp$ that can be produced when partial functions are evaluated outside of their domain. Thus, Listing 6 results in $\perp$ with probability $\frac{1}{2}$ and returns a value from $[0,1]$ with probability $\frac{1}{2}$ (larger values are more likely). Some previous work uses an error state to capture failing computations, but does not propagate this failure implicitly [34,35]. In particular, if an early expression in a long program may fail evaluating $\sqrt{-4}$, every expression in the program that depends on this failing computation has to check whether an exception has occurred. While it may seem possible to skip the rest of the function in case of a failing computation (by applying the pattern **if** $(x = \perp)$ {**return** $\perp$} **else** {rest of function}), this is non-modular and does not address the result of the function being used in other parts of a program.

Although our semantics treat $\perp$ and ⚡ similarly, there is an important distinction between the two: $\perp$ means the program terminated due to an error, while ⚡ means that according to observed evidence, the program did not actually run.

2.2   Interaction of Exception States

Next, we illustrate the interaction of different exception states. We explain how our semantics handles these interactions when compared to existing semantics. Fig. 1 gives an overview of which existing semantics can handle which (interactions of) exceptions. We note that our semantics could easily distinguish more kinds of exceptions, such as division by zero or out of bounds accesses to arrays.

Non-termination and Observation Failure. Listing 7 shows a program that has been investigated in [22]. Based on the observations, it only admits a single behavior, namely always sampling $x = 0$ in the third line. This behavior results in non-termination, but it occurs with probability 0. Hence, the program fails an observation (ending up in state ⚡) with probability 1. If we try to

```
x:=0;
while x=0 {
  x=flip(½);
  observe(x=0);
}
```

Listing 7. Mixing loops and observations

condition on not failing any observation (by rescaling appropriately), this results in a division by 0, because the probability of not failing any observation is 0.

The semantics of Listing 7 thus only has weight on $\frac{1}{2}$, and does not allow conditioning on not failing any observation. This is also the solution that [22] proposes, but in our case, we can formally back up this claim with our semantics.

Other languages handle both non-termination and observation failure by sub-probability distributions, which makes it impossible to conclude that the missing weight is due to observation failure (and not due to non-termination) [4,24,34]. The semantics in [28] cannot directly express that the missing weight is due to observation failure (rather, the semantics are undefined due to a division by zero). However, the semantics enables a careful reader to determine that the missing weight is due to observation failure (by investigating the conditional weakest precondition and the conditional weakest liberal precondition). Some other languages can express neither while loops nor observations [23,33,35].

Assertions and Non-termination. For some programs, it is useful to check assumptions explicitly. For example, the implementation of the factorial function in Listing 8 explicitly checks whether x is a valid argument to the factorial function. If $x \notin \mathbb{N}$, the program should run into an error (i.e. only have weight on $\bot$). If $x \in \mathbb{N}$, the program should return $x!$ (i.e. only have weight on $x!$). This example illustrates that earlier exceptions (like failing an assertion) should *bypass* later exceptions (like non-termination, which occurs for $x \notin \mathbb{N}$ if the programmer

```
assert(x≥0);
assert(x=⌊x⌋);
fac:=1;
while x≠0 {
  fac=fac*x;
  x=x-1;
}
return fac;
```

Listing 8. Explicitly checking assumptions

forgets the first two assertions). This is not surprising, given that this is also the semantics of exceptions in most deterministic languages. Most existing semantics either cannot express Listing 8 ([23,34] have no assertions, [35] has no iteration) or cannot distinguish failing an assertion from non-termination [24,28,33]. The consequence of the latter is that removing the first two assertions from Listing 8 does not affect the semantics. Handling assertion failure by sum types (as e.g. in [34]) could be a solution, but would force the programmer to deal with assertion failure explicitly. Only the semantics in [4] has the expressiveness to implicitly handle assertion errors in Listing 8 without conflating those errors with non-termination.

Listing 9 shows a different interaction between non-termination and failing assertions. Here, even though the loop condition is always true, the first iteration of the loop will run into an exception. Thus, Listing 9 results in $\bot$ with probability 1. Again, this behavior should not be surprising given the behavior of deterministic languages. For

```
x:=0;
while 1 {
  x=x/x;
}
```

Listing 9. Guaranteed failure

Listing 9, conflating errors with non-termination means the program semantics cannot express that the missing weight is due to an error and not due to non-termination.

Observation Failure and Assertion Failure. In our PPL, earlier exceptions bypass later exceptions, as illustrated in Listing 8. However, because we are operating in a probabilistic language, exceptions can occur probabilis-tically. Listing 10 shows a program that may run into

```
observe(flip(½));
assert(flip(½));
```
Listing 10. Observation or assertion failure

an observation failure, or into an assertion failure, or neither. If it runs into an observation failure (with probability $\frac{1}{2}$), it bypasses the rest of the program, resulting in $\frac{1}{2}$ with probability $\frac{1}{2}$ and in $\bot$ with probability $\frac{1}{4}$. Conditioning on the absence of observation failures, the probability of $\bot$ is $\frac{1}{2}$.

An important observation is that reordering the two statements of Listing 10 will result in a different behavior. This is the case, even though there is no obvious data-flow between the two statements. This is in sharp contrast to the semantics in [34], which guarantee (in the absence of exceptions) that only data flow is relevant and that expressions can be reordered. Our semantics illustrate that even if there is no explicit data-dependency, some seemingly obvious properties (like commutativity) may not hold in the presence of exceptions. Some languages either cannot express Listing 10 ([23,33] lack observations), cannot distinguish observation failure from assertion failure [24] or cannot handle exceptions implic-itly [34,35].

Summary. In this section, we showed examples of probabilistic programs that exhibit non-termination, observation failures and errors. Then, we provided examples that show how these exceptions can interact, and explained how exist-ing semantics handle these interactions.

3   Preliminaries

In this section, we provide the necessary theory. Most of the material is stan-dard, however, our treatment of exception states is interesting and important for providing semantics to probabilistic programs in the presence of exceptions. All key lemmas (together with additional definitions and examples) are proven in Appendix A.

Natural Numbers, $[n]$, Iverson Brackets, Restriction of Functions. We include 0 in the natural numbers, so that $\mathbb{N} := \{0, 1, \dots\}$. For $n \in \mathbb{N}$, $[n] := \{1, \dots, n\}$. The *Iverson brackets* $[\cdot]$ are defined by $[b] = 1$ if b is true and $[b] = 0$ if b is false. A particular application of the Iverson brackets is to characterize the indicator function of a specific set S by $[x \in S]$. For a function $f \colon X \to Y$ and a subset of the domain $S \subseteq X$, f restricted to S is denoted by $f_{|S} \colon S \to Y$.

Set of Variables, Generating Tuples, Preservation of Properties, Singleton Set. Let Vars be a set of admissible variable names. We refer to the elements of Vars by x, y, z and x_i, y_i, z_i, v_i, w_i, for $i \in \mathbb{N}$. For $v \in A$ and $n \in \mathbb{N}$, $v!n := (v, \dots, v) \in A^n$ denotes the tuple containing n copies of v. A function $f \colon A^n \to A$ *preserves a property* if whenever $a_1, \dots, a_n \in A$ have that property, $f(a_1, \dots, a_n) \in A$ has that property. Let $\mathbb{1}$ denote the set which only contains the empty tuple (), i.e. $\mathbb{1} := \{()\}$. For sets of tuples $S \subseteq \prod_{i=1}^n A_i$, there is an isomorphism $S \times \mathbb{1} \simeq \mathbb{1} \times S \simeq S$. This isomorphism is intuitive and we sometimes silently apply it.

Exception States, Lifting Functions to Exception States. We allow the extension of sets with some symbols that stand for the occurrence of special events in a program. This is important because it allows us to capture the event that a given program runs into specific exceptions. Let $\mathcal{X} := \{\bot, \frac{\iota}{\iota}, \circlearrowright\}$ be a (countable) set of exception states. We denote by $\overline{A} := A \cup \mathcal{X}$ the set A extended with $\mathcal{X}$ (we require that $A \cap \mathcal{X} = \emptyset$). Intuitively, $\bot$ corresponds to assertion failures, $\frac{\iota}{\iota}$ corresponds to observation failures and $\circlearrowright$ corresponds to non-termination. For a function $f \colon A \to B$, f *lifted to exception states*, denoted by $\overline{f} \colon \overline{A} \to \overline{B}$ is defined by $\overline{f}(a) = a$ if $a \in \mathcal{X}$ and $\overline{f}(a) = f(a)$ if $a \notin \mathcal{X}$. For a function $f \colon \prod_{i=1}^n A_i \to B$, f *lifted to exception states*, denoted by $\overline{f} \colon \prod_{i=1}^n \overline{A_i} \to \overline{B}$, propagates the first exception in its arguments, or evaluates f if none of its arguments are exceptions. Formally, it is defined by $\overline{f}(a_1, \ldots, a_n) = a_1$ if $a_1 \in \mathcal{X}$, $\overline{f}(a_1, \ldots, a_n) = a_2$ if $a_1 \notin \mathcal{X}$ and $a_2 \in \mathcal{X}$, and so on. Only if $a_1, \ldots, a_n \notin \mathcal{X}$, we have $\overline{f}(a_1, \ldots, a_n) = f(a_1, \ldots, a_n)$. Thus, $\overline{f}(\circlearrowright, a, \bot) = \circlearrowright$. In particular, we write $\overline{(a, b)}$ for lifting the tupling function, resulting in for example $\overline{(\frac{\iota}{\iota}, \circlearrowright)} = \frac{\iota}{\iota}$. To remove notation clutter, we do not distinguish the two different liftings $\overline{f} \colon \overline{A} \to \overline{B}$ and $\overline{f} \colon \prod_{i=1}^n \overline{A_i} \to \overline{B}$ notationally. Whenever we write $\overline{f}$, it will be clear from the context which lifting we mean. We write $S \overline{\times} T$ for $\{\overline{(s, t)} \mid s \in S, t \in T\}$.

Records. A *record* is a special type of tuple indexed by variable names. For sets $(S_i)_{i \in [n]}$, a record $r \in \prod_{i=1}^n (x_i \colon S_i)$ has the form $r = \{x_1 \mapsto v_1, \ldots, x_n \mapsto v_n\}$, where $v_i \in S_i$, with the convenient shorthand $r = \{x_i \mapsto v_i\}_{i \in [n]}$. We can access the elements of a record by their name: $r[x_i] = v_i$.

In what follows, we provide the measure theoretic background necessary to express our semantics.

σ-algebra, Measurable Set, σ-algebra Generated by a Set, Measurable Space, Measurable Functions. Let A be some set. A set $\Sigma_A \subseteq \mathcal{P}(A)$ is called a *σ-algebra on A* if it satisfies three conditions: $A \in \Sigma_A$, Σ_A is closed under complements ($S \in \Sigma_A$ implies $A \backslash S \in \Sigma_A$) and Σ_A is closed under countable unions (for any collection $\{S_i\}_{i \in \mathbb{N}}$ with $S_i \in \Sigma_A$, we have $\bigcup_{i \in \mathbb{N}} S_i \in \Sigma_A$). The elements of Σ_A are called *measurable sets*. For any set A, a trivial σ-algebra on A is its power set $\mathcal{P}(A)$. Unfortunately, the power set often contains sets that do not behave well. To come up with a σ-algebra on A whose sets do behave well, we often start with a set $S \subseteq \mathcal{P}(A)$ that is not a σ-algebra and extend it until we get a σ-algebra. For this purpose, let A be some set and $S \subseteq \mathcal{P}(A)$ a collection of subsets of A. The *σ-algebra generated by S* denoted by $\sigma(S)$ is the smallest σ-algebra that contains S. Formally, $\sigma(S)$ is the intersection of all σ-algebras on A containing S. For a set A and a σ-algebra Σ_A on A, (A, Σ_A) is called a *measurable space*. We often leave Σ_A implicit; whenever it is not mentioned explicitly, it is clear from the context. Table 1 provides the implicit σ-algebras for some common sets. As an example, some elements of $\Sigma_{\overline{\mathbb{R}}}$ include $[0, 1] \cup \{\bot\}$ and $\{1, 3, \pi\}$. For measurable spaces (A, Σ_A) and (B, Σ_B), a function $f \colon A \to B$ is called *measurable*,

Table 1. Implicit σ-algebras on common sets, for measurable spaces (A, Σ_A), (A_i, Σ_{A_i})

Set	σ-algebra on this set
$\mathbb{R}$	$\Sigma_{\mathbb{R}} = \mathcal{B} := \sigma(\{[a, b] \subseteq \mathbb{R} \mid a \leq b, a \in \mathbb{R}, b \in \mathbb{R}\})$, the Borel σ-algebra on $\mathbb{R}$ generated by all intervals
S for $S \in \mathcal{B}$	$\Sigma_S = \{T \in \mathcal{B} \mid T \subseteq S\}$
$\prod_{i=1}^{n} A_i$	$\Sigma_{\prod_{i=1}^{n} A_i} = \sigma(\{\prod_{i=1}^{n} S_i \mid S_i \in \Sigma_{A_i}\})$
$\prod_{i=1}^{n}(x_i : A_i)$	$\Sigma_{\prod_{i=1}^{n}(x_i : A_i)} = \sigma(\{\prod_{i=1}^{n}(x_i : S_i) \mid S_i \in \Sigma_{A_i}\})$
$\overline{A}$	$\Sigma_{\overline{A}} = \{S \cup S' \mid S \in \Sigma_A, S' \in \mathcal{P}(\mathcal{X})\}$

if $\forall S \in \Sigma_B \colon f^{-1}(S) \in \Sigma_A$. Here, $f^{-1}(S) := \{a \in A \colon f(a) \in S\}$. If one is familiar with the notion of Lebesgue measurable functions, note that our definition does not include all Lebesgue measurable functions. As a motivation to why we need measurable functions, consider the following scenario. We know the distribution of some variable x, and want to know the distribution of $y = f(x)$. To figure out how likely it is that $y \in S$ for a measurable set S, we can determine how likely it is that $x \in f^{-1}(S)$, because $f^{-1}(S)$ is guaranteed to be a measurable set.

Measures, Examples of Measures. For a measurable space (A, Σ_A), a function $\mu \colon \Sigma_A \to [0, \infty]$ is called a *measure on A* if it satisfies two properties: null empty set ($\mu(\emptyset) = 0$) and countable additivity (for any countable collection $\{S_i\}_{i \in \mathcal{I}}$ of pairwise disjoint sets $S_i \in \Sigma_A$, we have $\mu\left(\bigcup_{i \in \mathcal{I}} S_i\right) = \sum_{i \in \mathcal{I}} \mu(S_i)$). Measures allow us to quantify the probability that a certain result lies in a measurable set. For example, $\mu([1, 2])$ can be interpreted as the probability that the outcome of a process is between 1 and 2.

The *Lebesgue measure* $\lambda \colon \mathcal{B} \to [0, \infty]$ is the (unique) measure that satisfies $\lambda([a, b]) = b - a$ for all $a, b \in \mathbb{R}$ with $a \leq b$. The *zero measure* $\mathbf{0} \colon \Sigma_A \to [0, \infty]$ is defined by $\mathbf{0}(S) = 0$ for all $S \in \Sigma_A$. For a measurable space (A, Σ_A) and some $a \in A$, the *Dirac measure* $\delta_a \colon \Sigma_A \to [0, \infty]$ is defined by $\delta_a(S) = [a \in S]$.

Unfortunately, there are measures that do not satisfy some important properties (for example, they may not satisfy Fubini's theorem, which we discuss later on). The usual way to deal with this is to restrict our attention to σ-finite measures, which are well-known and were studied in great detail. However, σ-finite measures are too restrictive for our purposes. In particular, the s-finite kernels that we introduce later on can induce measures that are not σ-finite. This is why in the following, we work with s-finite measures. Table 2 gives an overview of the different kinds of measures that are important for understanding our work. The expression $1/2 \cdot \delta_1$ stands for the pointwise multiplication of the measure δ_1 by $1/2 \colon 1/2 \cdot \delta_1 = \lambda S. 1/2 \cdot \delta_1(S)$. Here, the λ refers to λ-abstraction and not to the Lebesgue measure. To distinguish the two λs, we always write "λx." (with a dot) when we refer to λ-abstraction. For more details on the definitions and for proofs about the provided examples, see Appendix A.1.

Table 2. Definition and comparison of different measures $\mu\colon \Sigma_A \to [0,\infty]$ on measurable spaces (A, Σ_A). Reading the table top-down, we get from the most restrictive definition to the most permissive definition. For example, any sub-probability measure is also a σ-finite measure. We also provide an example for each type of measure that is not an example of the more restrictive type of measure. For example, the Lebesgue measure λ is σ-finite but not s-finite.

Type of measure	Characterization	Examples
Probability measure	μ is a measure and $\mu(A) = 1$	$\mu = \delta_1$
Sub-probability measure	μ is a measure and $\mu(A) \leq 1$	$\mu = \mathbf{0}$ or $\mu = 1/2 \cdot \delta_1$
σ-finite measure	μ is a measure and $A = \bigcup_{i\in\mathbb{N}} A_i$ for $A_i \in \Sigma_A$ with $\mu(A_i) < \infty$	$\mu = \lambda$
s-finite measure	$\mu = \sum_{i\in\mathbb{N}} \mu_i$ for sub-probability measures μ_i	$\mu(S) = \begin{cases} 0 & \lambda(S) = 0 \\ \infty & \lambda(S) > 0 \end{cases}$
Measure	$\mu(\emptyset) = 0$, countable additivity	$\mu(S) = \begin{cases} \lvert S \rvert & S \text{ finite} \\ \infty & \text{otherwise} \end{cases}$

Product of Measures, Product of Measures in the Presence of Exception States. For s-finite measures $\mu\colon \Sigma_A \to [0,\infty]$ and $\mu'\colon \Sigma_B \to [0,\infty]$, we denote the *product of measures* by $\mu \times \mu'\colon \Sigma_{A\times B} \to [0,\infty]$, and define it by

$$(\mu \times \mu')(S) = \int_{a\in A} \int_{b\in B} [(a,b) \in S]\mu'(db)\mu(da)$$

For s-finite measures $\mu\colon \Sigma_{\overline{A}} \to [0,\infty]$ and $\mu'\colon \Sigma_{\overline{B}} \to [0,\infty]$, we denote the *lifted product of measures* by $\mu\overline{\times}\mu'\colon \Sigma_{\overline{A\times B}} \to [0,\infty]$ and define it using the lifted tupling function: $(\mu\overline{\times}\mu')(S) = \int_{a\in\overline{A}} \int_{b\in\overline{B}} \overline{[(a,b)} \in S]\mu'(db)\mu(da)$. While the product of measures $\mu \times \mu'$ is well known for combining two measures to a joint measure, the concept of a lifted product of measures $\mu\overline{\times}\mu'$ is required to do the same for combining measures that have weight on exception states. Because the formal semantics of our probabilistic programming language makes use of exception states, we always use $\overline{\times}$ to combine measures, appropriately handling exception states implicitly.

Lemma 1. *For measures* $\mu\colon \Sigma_A \to [0,\infty]$, $\mu'\colon \Sigma_B \to [0,\infty]$, *let* $S \in \Sigma_A$ *and* $T \in \Sigma_B$. *Then,* $(\mu \times \mu')(S \times T) = \mu(S) \cdot \mu'(T)$.

For $\mu\colon \Sigma_{\overline{A}} \to [0,\infty]$, $\mu'\colon \Sigma_{\overline{B}} \to [0,\infty]$ and $S \in \Sigma_{\overline{A}}$, $T \in \Sigma_{\overline{B}}$, in general we have $(\mu\overline{\times}\mu')(S \times T) \neq \mu(S) \cdot \mu'(T)$, due to interactions of exception states.

Lemma 2. $\times$ *and* $\overline{\times}$ *for s-finite measures are associative, left- and right-distributive and preserve (sub-)probability and s-finite measures.*

Lebesgue Integrals, Fubini's Theorem for s-finite Measures. Our definition of the Lebesgue integral is based on [31]. It allows integrating functions that sometimes evaluate to ∞, and Lebesgue integrals evaluating to ∞.

Here, (A, Σ_A) and (B, Σ_B) are measurable spaces and $\mu \colon \Sigma_A \to [0, \infty]$ and $\mu' \colon \Sigma_B \to [0, \infty]$ are measures on A and B, respectively. Also, $E \in \Sigma_A$ and $F \in \Sigma_B$. Let $s \colon A \to [0, \infty)$ be a measurable function. s is a *simple function* if $s(x) = \sum_{i=1}^{n} \alpha_i [x \in A_i]$ for $A_i \in \Sigma_A$ and $\alpha_i \in \mathbb{R}$. For any simple function s, the Lebesgue integral of s over E with respect to μ, denoted by $\int_{a \in E} s(a) \mu(da)$, is defined by $\sum_{i=1}^{n} \alpha_i \cdot \mu(A_i \cap E)$, making use of the convention $0 \cdot \infty = 0$. Let $f \colon A \to [0, \infty]$ be measurable but not necessarily simple. Then, the *Lebesgue integral* of f over E with respect to μ is defined by

$$\int_{a \in E} f(a) \mu(da) := \sup \left\{ \int_{a \in E} s(a) \mu(da) \;\middle|\; s \colon A \to [0, \infty) \text{ is simple}, 0 \leq s \leq f \right\}$$

Here, the inequalities on functions are pointwise. Appendix A.2 lists some useful properties of the Lebesgue integral. Here, we only mention Fubini's theorem, which is important because it entails a commutativity-like property of the product of measures: $(\mu \times \mu')(S) = (\mu' \times \mu)(\text{swap}(S))$, where swap switches the dimensions of S: $\text{swap}(S) = \{(b, a) \mid (a, b) \in S\}$. The proof of this property is straightforward, by expanding the definition of the product of measures and applying Fubini's theorem. As we show in Sect. 5, this property is crucial for the commutativity of expressions. In the presence of exceptions, it does not hold: $(\mu \overline{\times} \mu')(S) \neq (\mu' \overline{\times} \mu)(\text{swap}(S))$ in general.

Theorem 1 (Fubini's theorem). *For s-finite measures $\mu \colon \Sigma_A \to [0, \infty]$ and $\mu' \colon \Sigma_B \to [0, \infty]$ and any measurable function $f \colon A \times B \to [0, \infty]$,*

$$\int_{a \in A} \int_{b \in B} f(a, b) \mu'(db) \mu(da) = \int_{b \in B} \int_{a \in A} f(a, b) \mu(da) \mu'(db)$$

For s-finite measures $\mu \colon \Sigma_{\overline{A}} \to [0, \infty]$ and $\mu' \colon \Sigma_{\overline{B}} \to [0, \infty]$ and any measurable function $f \colon A \times B \to [0, \infty]$,

$$\int_{a \in \overline{A}} \int_{b \in \overline{B}} \overline{f}(a, b) \mu'(db) \mu(da) = \int_{b \in \overline{B}} \int_{a \in \overline{A}} \overline{f}(a, b) \mu(da) \mu'(db)$$

(Sub-)probability Kernels, s-finite Kernels, Dirac Delta, Lebesgue Kernel, Motivation for s-finite Kernels. In the following, let (A, Σ_A) and (B, Σ_B) be measurable spaces. A *(sub-)probability kernel with source A and target B* is a function $\kappa \colon A \times \Sigma_B \to [0, \infty)$ such that for all $a \in A \colon \kappa(a, \cdot) \colon \Sigma_B \to [0, \infty)$ is a (sub-)probability measure, and $\forall S \in \Sigma_B \colon \kappa(\cdot, S) \colon A \to [0, \infty)$ is measurable. $\kappa \colon A \times \Sigma_B \to [0, \infty]$ is an *s-finite kernel with source A and target B* if κ is a pointwise sum of sub-probability kernels $\kappa_i \colon A \times \Sigma_B \to [0, \infty)$, meaning $\kappa = \sum_{i \in \mathbb{N}} \kappa_i$. We denote the set of s-finite kernels with source A and target B by $A \mapsto B \subseteq A \times \Sigma_B \to [0, \infty]$. Because we only ever deal with s-finite kernels, we often refer to them simply as kernels.

We can understand the Dirac measure as a probability kernel. For a measurable space (A, Σ_A), the *Dirac delta* $\delta \colon A \mapsto A$ is defined by $\delta(a, S) = [a \in S]$. Note that for any a, $\delta(a, \cdot) \colon \Sigma_A \to [0, \infty]$ is the Dirac measure. We often write

$\delta(a)(S)$ or $\delta_a(S)$ for $\delta(a, S)$. Note that we can also interpret $\delta \colon A \mapsto A$ as an s-finite kernel from $A \mapsto B$ for $A \subseteq B$. The *Lebesgue kernel* $\lambda^* \colon A \mapsto \mathbb{R}$ is defined by $\lambda^*(a)(S) = \lambda(S)$, where λ is the Lebesgue measure. The definition of s-finite kernels is a lifting of the notion of s-finite measures. Note that for an s-finite kernel κ, $\kappa(a, \cdot)$ is an s-finite measure for all $a \in A$. In the context of probabilistic programming, s-finite kernels have been used before [34].

Working in the space of sub-probability kernels is inconvenient, because, for example, $\lambda^* \colon \mathbb{R} \mapsto \mathbb{R}$ is not a sub-probability kernel. Even though $\lambda^*(x)$ is σ-finite measure for all $x \in \mathbb{R}$, not all s-finite kernels induce σ-finite measures in this sense. As an example, $(\lambda^*; \lambda^*)(x)$ is not a σ-finite measure for any $x \in \mathbb{R}$ (see Lemma 15 in Appendix A.1). We introduce (;) shortly in Definition 1.

Working in the space of s-finite kernels is convenient because s-finite kernels have many nice properties. In particular, the set of s-finite kernels $A \mapsto B$ is the smallest set that contains all sub-probability kernels with source A and target B and is closed under countable sums.

Lifting Kernels to Exception States, Removing Weight from Exception States. For kernels $\kappa \colon A \mapsto B$ or kernels $\kappa \colon A \mapsto \overline{B}$, κ lifted to exception states $\overline{\kappa} \colon \overline{A} \mapsto \overline{B}$ is defined by $\overline{\kappa}(a) = \kappa(a)$ if $a \in A$ and $\overline{\kappa}(a) = \delta(a)$ if $a \notin A$. When transforming κ into $\overline{\kappa}$, we preserve (sub-)probability and s-finite kernels.

Composing kernels, composing kernels in the presence of exception states.

Definition 1. *Let* $(;) \colon (A \mapsto B) \to (B \mapsto C) \to (A \mapsto C)$ *be defined by* $(f;g)(a)(S) = \int_{b \in B} g(b)(S) \, f(a)(db)$.

Note that $f;g$ intuitively corresponds to first applying f and then g. Throughout this paper, we mostly use $\ggg$ instead of (;), but we introduce (;) because it is well-known and it is instructive to show how our definition of $\ggg$ relates to (;).

Lemma 3. (;) *is associative, left- and right-distributive, has neutral element*[2] δ *and preserves (sub-)probability and s-finite kernels.*

Definition 2. *Let* $(\ggg) \colon (A \mapsto \overline{B}) \to (B \mapsto \overline{C}) \to (A \mapsto \overline{C})$ *be defined by* $(f \ggg g)(a)(S) = \int_{b \in \overline{B}} \overline{g}(b)(S) \, f(a)(db)$.

We sometimes write $f(a) \ggg g$ for $(f \ggg g)(a)$.

Lemma 4. *For* $f \colon A \mapsto \overline{B}$ *and* $g \colon B \mapsto \overline{C}$, $a \in A$ *and* $S \in \Sigma_{\overline{C}}$,

$$(f \ggg g)(a)(S) = (f;g)(a)(S) + \sum_{x \in \mathcal{X}} \delta(x)(S) f(a)(\{x\})$$

Lemma 4 shows how $\ggg$ relates to (;), by splitting $f \ggg g$ into non-exceptional behavior of f (handled by (;)) and exceptional behavior of f (handled by a sum). Intuitively, if f produces an exception state $\star \in \mathcal{X}$, then g is not even evaluated. Instead, this exception is directly passed on, as indicated by $\delta(x)(S)$.

---

[2] δ is a neutral element of (;) if $(\delta; \kappa) = (\kappa; \delta) = \kappa$ for all kernels κ.

If $f(a)(\mathcal{X}) = 0$ for all $a \in A$, or if $S \cap \mathcal{X} = \emptyset$, then the definitions are equivalent in the sense that $(f;g)(a)(S) = (f \ggg g)(a)(S)$. The difference between $\ggg$ and $(;)$ is the treatment of exception states produced by f. Note that technically, the target $\overline{B}$ of $f \colon A \mapsto \overline{B}$ does not match the source B of $g \colon B \mapsto \overline{C}$. Therefore, to formally interpret $f;g$, we silently restrict the domain of f to $A \times \Sigma_B$.

Lemma 5. $\ggg$ *is associative, left-distributive (but not right-distributive), has neutral element δ and preserves (sub-)probability and s-finite kernels.*

Product of Kernels, Product of Kernels in the Presence of Exception States. For s-finite kernels $\kappa \colon A \mapsto B$, $\kappa' \colon A \mapsto C$, we define the *product of kernels*, denoted by $\kappa \times \kappa' \colon A \mapsto B \times C$, as $(\kappa \times \kappa')(a)(S) = (\kappa(a) \times \kappa'(a))(S)$. For s-finite kernels $\kappa \colon A \mapsto \overline{B}$ and $\kappa' \colon A \mapsto \overline{C}$, we define the *lifted product of kernels*, denoted by $\kappa \overline{\times} \kappa' \colon A \mapsto \overline{B \times C}$, as $(\kappa \overline{\times} \kappa')(a)(S) = (\kappa(a) \overline{\times} \kappa'(a))(S)$. $\times$ and $\overline{\times}$ allow us to combine kernels to a joint kernel. Essentially, this definition reduces the product of kernels to the product of measures.

Lemma 6. $\times$ *and $\overline{\times}$ for kernels preserve (sub-)probability and s-finite kernels, are associative, left- and right-distributive.*

Binding Conventions. To avoid too many parentheses, we make use of some binding conventions, ordering (in decreasing binding strength) $\overline{\times}, \times, ;, \ggg, +$.

Summary. The most important concepts introduced in this section are exception states, records, Lebesgue integration, Fubini's theorem and (s-finite) kernels.

4   A Probabilistic Language and Its Semantics

We now describe our probabilistic programming language, the typing rules and the denotational semantics of our language.

4.1   Syntax

Let $\mathbb{V} := \mathbb{Q} \cup \{\pi, e\} \subseteq \mathbb{R}$ be a (countable) set of constants expressible in our programs. Let $i, n \in \mathbb{N}$, $r \in \mathbb{V}$, $x \in \text{Vars}$, $\ominus$ a generic unary operator (e.g., $-$ inverts the sign of a value, $!$ is logical negation mapping 0 to 1 and all other numbers to 0, $\lfloor \cdot \rfloor$ and $\lceil \cdot \rceil$ round down and up respectively), $\oplus$ a generic binary operator (e.g., $+, -, *, /, {}^{\wedge}$ for addition, subtraction, multiplication, division and exponentiation, $\&\&, \|$ for logical conjunction and disjunction, $=, \neq, <, \leq, >, \geq$ to compare values). Let $f \colon A \rightarrow \mathbb{R} \rightarrow [0, \infty)$ be a measurable function that maps $a \in A$ to a probability density function. We check if f is measurable by uncurrying f to $f \colon A \times \mathbb{R} \rightarrow [0, \infty)$. Fig. 2 shows the syntax of our language.

Our expressions capture $()$ (the only element of $\mathbb{1}$), r (real numbers), x (variables), $(e_1, \ldots, e_n)$ (tuples), $e[i]$ (accessing elements of tuples for $i \in \mathbb{N}$), $\ominus e$ (unary operators), $e_1 \oplus e_2$ (binary operators), $e_1[e_2]$ (accessing array elements), $e_1[e_2 \mapsto e_3]$ (updating array elements), **array**(e_1, e_2) (creating array of length e_1

$$e ::= () \mid r \mid x \mid (e_1, \ldots, e_n) \mid e[i] \mid \ominus e \mid e_1 \oplus e_2 \mid e_1[e_2] \mid \qquad \text{(Expressions)}$$
$$\quad \text{array}(e_1, e_2) \mid e_1[e_2 \mapsto e_3] \mid F(e)$$
$$F ::= \lambda x.\{P; \text{return } e; \} \mid \text{flip} \mid \text{uniform} \mid \text{sampleFrom}_f \qquad \text{(Functions)}$$
$$P ::= \text{skip} \mid x := e \mid x = e \mid P_1; P_2 \mid \text{if } e \ \{P_1\} \ \text{else } \{P_2\} \mid \{P\} \mid \qquad \text{(Statements)}$$
$$\quad \text{assert}(e) \mid \text{observe}(e) \mid \text{while } e \ \{P\}$$

Fig. 2. The syntax of our probabilistic language.

containing e_2 at every index) and $F(e)$ (evaluating function F on argument e). To handle functions $F(e_1, \ldots, e_n)$ with multiple arguments, we interpret $(e_1, \ldots, e_n)$ as a tuple and apply F to that tuple.

Our functions express $\lambda x.\{P; \text{return } e; \}$ (function taking argument x running P on x and returning e), $\text{flip}(e)$ (random choice from $\{0, 1\}$, 1 with probability e), $\text{uniform}(e_1, e_2)$ (continuous uniform distribution between e_1 and e_2) and $\text{sampleFrom}_f(e)$ (sample value distributed according to probability density function $f(e)$). An example for f is the density of the exponential distribution, indexed with rate λ. Formally, $f: (0, \infty) \to \mathbb{R} \to [0, \infty)$ is defined by $f(\lambda)(x) = \lambda e^{-\lambda x}$ if $x \geq 0$ and $f(\lambda)(x) = 0$ otherwise. Often, f is partial (e.g., $\lambda \leq 0$ is not allowed). Intuitively, arguments outside the allowed range of f produce the error state $\bot$.

Our statements express skip (no operation), $x := e$ (assigning to a fresh variable), $x = e$ (assigning to an existing variable), $P_1; P_2$ (sequential composition of programs), $\text{if } e \ \{P_1\} \ \text{else } \{P_2\}$ (if-then-else), $\{P\}$ (static scoping), $\text{assert}(e)$ (asserting that an expression evaluates to true, assertion failure results in $\bot$), $\text{observe}(e)$ (observing that an expression evaluates to true, observation failure results in $\lightning$) and $\text{while } e \ \{P\}$ (while loops, non-termination results in $\circlearrowleft$). We additionally introduce syntactic sugar $e_1[e_2] = e_3$ for $e_1 = e_1[e_2 \mapsto e_3]$, $\text{if } (e) \ \{P\}$ for $\text{if } e \ \{P\} \ \text{else } \{\text{skip}\}$ and $\text{func}(e_2)$ for $\lambda x.\{P; \text{return } e_1; \}(e_2)$ (using the name func for the function with argument x and body $\{P; \text{return } e_1\}$).

4.2   Typing Judgments

Let $n \in \mathbb{N}$. We define types by the following grammar in BNF, where $\tau[]$ denotes arrays over type τ. We sometimes write $\prod_{i=1}^{n} \tau_i$ for the product type $\tau_1 \times \cdots \times \tau_n$.

$$\tau :: = \mathbb{1} \mid \mathbb{R} \mid \tau[] \mid \tau_1 \times \cdots \times \tau_n$$

Note that we also use the type $\tau_1 \mapsto \tau_2$ of kernels with source τ_1 and target τ_2, but we do not list it here to avoid higher-order functions (discussed in Sect. 4.5).

Formally, a *context* Γ is a set $\{x_i : \tau_i\}_{i \in [n]}$ that assigns a type τ_i to each variable $x_i \in \text{Vars}$. In slight abuse of notation, we sometimes write $x \in \Gamma$ if there is a type τ with $x : \tau \in \Gamma$. We also write $\Gamma, x : \tau$ for $\Gamma \cup \{x : \tau\}$ (where $x \notin \Gamma$) and Γ, Γ' for $\Gamma \cup \Gamma'$ (where Γ and Γ' have no common variables).

$$\frac{}{\Gamma \vdash ():1} \quad \frac{}{\Gamma \vdash r:\mathbb{R}} \, r \in \mathbb{V} \quad \frac{}{\Gamma \vdash x:\tau} \, x:\tau \in \Gamma \quad \frac{\Gamma \vdash e_1:\tau_1 \quad \cdots \quad \Gamma \vdash e_n:\tau_n}{\Gamma \vdash (e_1,\ldots,e_n):\tau_1 \times \cdots \times \tau_n}$$

$$\frac{\Gamma \vdash e:\tau_0 \times \cdots \times \tau_{n-1}}{\Gamma \vdash e[i]:\tau_i} \, i \in \{0,\ldots,n-1\} \quad \frac{\Gamma \vdash e:\mathbb{R}}{\Gamma \vdash \ominus e:\mathbb{R}} \quad \frac{\Gamma \vdash e_1:\mathbb{R} \quad \Gamma \vdash e_2:\mathbb{R}}{\Gamma \vdash e_1 \oplus e_2:\mathbb{R}}$$

$$\frac{\Gamma \vdash e_1:\tau[] \quad \Gamma \vdash e_2:\mathbb{R}}{\Gamma \vdash e_1[e_2]:\tau} \quad \frac{\Gamma \vdash e_1:\mathbb{R} \quad \Gamma \vdash e_2:\tau}{\Gamma \vdash \mathbf{array}(e_1,e_2):\tau[]}$$

$$\frac{\Gamma \vdash e_1:\tau[] \quad \Gamma \vdash e_2:\mathbb{R} \quad \Gamma \vdash e_3:\tau}{\Gamma \vdash e_1[e_2 \mapsto e_3]:\tau[]} \quad \frac{\Gamma \vdash e:\tau_1 \quad \vdash F:\tau_1 \mapsto \tau_2}{\Gamma \vdash F(e):\tau_2}$$

$$\frac{x:\tau_1 \xrightarrow{P} \Gamma \quad \Gamma \vdash e:\tau_2}{\vdash \lambda x.\{P; \mathbf{return}\ e;\}:\tau_1 \mapsto \tau_2} \quad \frac{}{\vdash \mathbf{flip}:\mathbb{R} \mapsto \mathbb{R}} \quad \frac{}{\vdash \mathbf{uniform}:\mathbb{R} \times \mathbb{R} \mapsto \mathbb{R}}$$

$$\frac{}{\vdash \mathbf{sampleFrom}_f:\tau \mapsto \mathbb{R}} \, f:A \to \mathbb{R} \to [0,\infty), A \in \Sigma_\tau$$

Fig. 3. The typing rules for expressions and functions in our language

$$\frac{}{\Gamma \xrightarrow{\mathbf{skip}} \Gamma} \quad \frac{\Gamma \vdash e:\tau}{\Gamma \xrightarrow{x:=e} \Gamma,x:\tau} \, x \notin \Gamma \quad \frac{\Gamma \vdash e:\tau}{\Gamma \xrightarrow{x:=e} \Gamma} \, x:\tau \in \Gamma \quad \frac{\Gamma \xrightarrow{P} \Gamma' \quad \Gamma' \xrightarrow{Q} \Gamma''}{\Gamma \xrightarrow{P;Q} \Gamma''}$$

$$\frac{\Gamma \xrightarrow{P} \Gamma'}{\Gamma \xrightarrow{\{P\}} \Gamma} \quad \frac{\Gamma \vdash e:\mathbb{R} \quad \Gamma \xrightarrow{P_1} \Gamma' \quad \Gamma \xrightarrow{P_2} \Gamma'}{\Gamma \xrightarrow{\mathbf{if}\ e\ \{P_1\}\ \mathbf{else}\ \{P_2\}} \Gamma'} \quad \frac{\Gamma \vdash e:\mathbb{R}}{\Gamma \xrightarrow{\mathbf{assert}(e)} \Gamma} \quad \frac{\Gamma \vdash e:\mathbb{R}}{\Gamma \xrightarrow{\mathbf{observe}(e)} \Gamma}$$

$$\frac{\Gamma \vdash e:\mathbb{R} \quad \Gamma \xrightarrow{P} \Gamma}{\Gamma \xrightarrow{\mathbf{while}\ e\ \{P\}} \Gamma}$$

Fig. 4. The typing rules for statements

The rules in Figs. 3 and 4 allow deriving the type of expressions, functions and statements. To state that an expression e is of type τ under a context Γ, we write $\Gamma \vdash e:\tau$. Likewise, $\vdash F:\tau \mapsto \tau'$ indicates that F is a kernel from τ to τ'. Finally, $\Gamma \xrightarrow{P} \Gamma'$ states that a context Γ is transformed to Γ' by a statement P. For $\mathbf{sampleFrom}_f$, we intuitively want f to map values from τ to probability density functions. To allow f to be partial, i.e., to be undefined for some values from τ, we use $A \in \Sigma_\tau$ (and hence $A \subseteq [\![\tau]\!]$) as the domain of f (see Sect. 4.3).

4.3 Semantics

Semantic Domains. We assign to each type τ a set $[\![\tau]\!]$ together with an implicit σ-algebra Σ_τ on that set. Additionally, we assign a set $[\![\Gamma]\!]$ to each context $\Gamma = \{x_i:\tau_i\}_{i \in [n]}$. Concretely, we have $[\![1]\!] = 1 := \{()\}$ with $\Sigma_1 = \{\emptyset,()\}$, $[\![\mathbb{R}]\!] = \mathbb{R}$ and $\Sigma_\mathbb{R} = \mathcal{B}$. The remaining semantic domains are outlined in Fig. 5.

$$[\![\tau[]]\!] = \bigcup_{i \in \mathbb{N}} [\![\tau]\!]^i \qquad \Sigma_{\tau[]} \text{ is generated by } \bigcup_{i \in \mathbb{N}} \left\{ \prod_{j=1}^{i} S_j \,\middle|\, S_j \in \Sigma_\tau \right\}$$

$$[\![\tau_1 \times \cdots \times \tau_n]\!] = \prod_{i=1}^{n} [\![\tau_i]\!] \qquad \Sigma_{\tau_1 \times \cdots \times \tau_n} \text{ is generated by } \left\{ \prod_{i=1}^{n} S_i \,\middle|\, S_i \in \Sigma_{\tau_i} \right\}$$

$$[\![\Gamma]\!] = \prod_{i=1}^{n} (x_i : [\![\tau_i]\!]) \qquad \Sigma_\Gamma \text{ is generated by } \left\{ \prod_{i=1}^{n} (x_i : S_i) \,\middle|\, S_i \in \Sigma_{\tau_i} \right\}$$

Fig. 5. Semantic domains for types

$$[\![()]\!]_{\mathbf{1}}(\sigma)(S) = [() \in S] \qquad [\![r]\!]_{\mathbb{R}}(\sigma)(S) = [r \in S] \qquad [\![x]\!]_\tau(\sigma)(S) = [\sigma[x] \in S]$$

$$[\![(e_1, \ldots, e_n)]\!]_{\tau_1 \times \cdots \times \tau_n} = [\![e_1]\!]_{\tau_1} \overline{\times} \cdots \overline{\times} [\![e_n]\!]_{\tau_n} \qquad [\![e[i]]\!]_{\tau_i} = [\![e]\!]_{\tau_1 \times \cdots \times \tau_n} \ggg \lambda t.\delta(t[i])$$

$$[\![e_1/e_2]\!]_{\mathbb{R}} = \quad [\![e_1]\!]_{\mathbb{R}} \overline{\times} [\![e_2]\!]_{\mathbb{R}} \quad \ggg \lambda(x,y). \begin{cases} \delta(x/y) & y \neq 0 \\ \delta(\bot) & y = 0 \end{cases}$$

$$[\![e_1[e_2]]\!]_\tau = \quad [\![e_1]\!]_{\tau[]} \overline{\times} [\![e_2]\!]_{\mathbb{R}} \quad \ggg \lambda(t,i). \begin{cases} \delta(t[i]) & i \in \mathbb{N}, i < |t| \\ \delta(\bot) & \text{otherwise} \end{cases}$$

$$[\![e_1[e_2 \mapsto e_3]]\!]_{\tau[]} = [\![e_1]\!]_{\tau[]} \overline{\times} [\![e_2]\!]_{\mathbb{R}} \overline{\times} [\![e_3]\!]_\tau \ggg \lambda(t,i,v). \begin{cases} \delta(t[i \mapsto v]) & i \in \mathbb{N}, i < |t| \\ \delta(\bot) & \text{otherwise} \end{cases}$$

$$[\![\mathbf{array}(e_1, e_2)]\!]_{\tau[]} = \quad [\![e_1]\!]_{\mathbb{R}} \overline{\times} [\![e_2]\!]_\tau \quad \ggg \lambda(n,v). \begin{cases} \delta(v!n) & n \in \mathbb{N} \\ \delta(\bot) & \text{otherwise} \end{cases}$$

Fig. 6. The semantics of expressions. $v!n$ stands for the n-tuple $(v, \ldots, v)$. $t[i]$ stands for the i-th element (0-indexed) of the tuple t and $t[i \mapsto v]$ is the tuple t, where the i-th element is replaced by v. $|t|$ is the length of a tuple t. σ stands for a program state over all variables in some Γ, with $\sigma \in [\![\Gamma]\!]$.

Expressions. Fig. 6 assigns to each expression e typed by $\Gamma \vdash e : \tau$ a probability kernel $[\![e]\!]_\tau : [\![\Gamma]\!] \mapsto \overline{[\![\tau]\!]}$. When τ is irrelevant or clear from the context, we may drop it and write $[\![e]\!]$. The formal interpretation of $[\![\Gamma]\!] \mapsto \overline{[\![\tau]\!]}$ is explained in Sect. 3.[3] Note that Fig. 6 is incomplete, but extending it is straightforward. When we need to evaluate multiple terms (as in $(e_1, \ldots, e_n)$), we combine the results using $\overline{\times}$. This makes sure that in the presence of exceptions, the first exception that occurs will have priority over later exceptions. In addition, deterministic functions (like $x + y$) are lifted to probabilistic functions by the Dirac delta (e.g. $\delta(x + y)$) and incomplete functions (like x/y) are lifted to complete functions via the explicit error state $\bot$.

---

[3] As a quick and intuitive reminder, $\kappa : A \mapsto \overline{B}$ means that for every $a \in A$, $\kappa(a)$ will be a distribution over $\overline{B}$, where $\overline{B}$ is B enriched with exception states. Hence, $\kappa(a)$ may have weight on elements of B, on exception states, or on both.

Fig. 7 assigns to each function F typed by $\vdash F \colon \tau_1 \mapsto \tau_2$ a probability kernel $[\![F]\!]_{\tau_1 \mapsto \tau_2} \colon [\![\tau_1]\!] \mapsto \overline{[\![\tau_2]\!]}$. In the semantics of $\mathtt{flip}$, $\delta(1) \colon \Sigma_{\overline{\mathbb{R}}} \to [0, \infty]$ is a measure on $\overline{\mathbb{R}}$, and $p \cdot \delta(1)$ rescales this measure pointwise. Similarly, the sum $p \cdot \delta(1) + (1 - p) \cdot \delta(0)$ is also meant pointwise, resulting in a measure on $\overline{\mathbb{R}}$. Finally, $\lambda p.\, p \cdot \delta(1) + (1 - p) \cdot \delta(0)$ is a kernel with source $[0, 1]$ and target $\overline{\mathbb{R}}$. For $\mathtt{sampleFrom}_f(e)$, remember that $f(p)(\cdot)$ is a probability density function.

$$[\![\mathtt{flip}]\!]_{\mathbb{R} \to \mathbb{R}} = \lambda p. \begin{cases} p \cdot \delta(1) + (1 - p) \cdot \delta(0) & p \in [0, 1] \\ \delta(\bot) & \text{otherwise} \end{cases}$$

$$[\![\mathtt{uniform}]\!]_{\mathbb{R} \to \mathbb{R}} = \lambda(l, r). \begin{cases} \lambda S. \frac{1}{r - l} \lambda([l, r] \cap S) & l < r \\ \delta(\bot) & \text{otherwise} \end{cases}$$

$$[\![\mathtt{sampleFrom}_f]\!]_{\tau \to \mathbb{R}} = \lambda p. \begin{cases} \lambda S. \int_{x \in \mathbb{R} \cap S} f(p)(x)\lambda(dx) & p \in A \\ \delta(\bot) & p \notin A \end{cases}$$

$$[\![\lambda x.\{P; \mathtt{return}\ e;\}]\!]_{\tau_1 \mapsto \tau_2} = \lambda v. \delta(\{x \mapsto v\}) \ggg [\![P]\!] \ggg [\![e_2]\!]_{\tau_2}$$

Fig. 7. The semantics of functions.

$$[\![\mathtt{skip}]\!] = \delta \qquad [\![x := e]\!] = [\![x = e]\!] = \delta \overline{\times} [\![e]\!] \ggg \lambda(\sigma, v).\delta(\sigma[x \mapsto v])$$

$$[\![P_1; P_2]\!] = [\![P_1]\!] \ggg [\![P_2]\!] \qquad [\![\{P\}]\!] = [\![P]\!] \ggg \lambda \sigma'.\delta(\sigma'(\Gamma))$$

$$[\![\mathtt{if}\ e\ \{P_1\}\ \mathtt{else}\ \{P_2\}]\!] = \delta \overline{\times} [\![e]\!]_{\mathbb{R}} \ggg \lambda(\sigma, b). \begin{cases} [\![P_1]\!](\sigma) & b \neq 0 \\ [\![P_2]\!](\sigma) & b = 0 \end{cases}$$

$$[\![\mathtt{assert}(e)]\!] = \delta \overline{\times} [\![e]\!]_{\mathbb{R}} \ggg \lambda(\sigma, b). \begin{cases} \delta(\sigma) & b \neq 0 \\ \delta(\bot) & b = 0 \end{cases}$$

$$[\![\mathtt{observe}(e)]\!] = \delta \overline{\times} [\![e]\!]_{\mathbb{R}} \ggg \lambda(\sigma, b). \begin{cases} \delta(\sigma) & b \neq 0 \\ \delta(\xi) & b = 0 \end{cases}$$

Fig. 8. The semantics of programs in our probabilistic language. Here, $\sigma[x \mapsto v]$ results in σ with the value stored under x updated to v. $\sigma'(\Gamma)$ selects only those variables from σ' that occur in Γ, meaning $\{x_i \mapsto v_i\}_{i \in \mathcal{I}}(\{x_i \colon \tau_i\}_{i \in \mathcal{I}'}) = \{x_i \mapsto v_i\}_{i \in \mathcal{I} \cap \mathcal{I}'}$.

Statements. Fig. 8 assigns to each statement P with $\Gamma \overset{P}{\rightsquigarrow} \Gamma'$ a probability kernel $[\![P]\!] \colon [\![\Gamma]\!] \mapsto \overline{[\![\Gamma']\!]}$. Note the use of $\overline{\times}$ in $\delta \overline{\times} [\![e]\!]$, which allows evaluating e while keeping the state σ in which e is being evaluated. Intuitively, if evaluating e results in an exception from $\mathcal{X}$, the previous state σ is irrelevant, and the result of $\delta \overline{\times} [\![e]\!]$ will be that exception from $\mathcal{X}$.

While Loop. To define the semantics of the while loop `while` $e\ \{P\}$, we introduce a *kernel transformer* $[\![\texttt{while}\ e\ \{P\}]\!]^{\text{trans}} \colon (\![\varGamma]\!] \mapsto \overline{[\![\varGamma]\!]}) \to ([\![\varGamma]\!] \mapsto \overline{[\![\varGamma]\!]})$ that transforms the semantics for n runs of the loop to the semantics for $n+1$ runs of the loop. Concretely,

$$[\![\texttt{while}\ e\ \{P\}]\!]^{\text{trans}}(\kappa) = \delta \overline{\times} [\![e]\!] \ggg \lambda(\sigma, b). \begin{cases} [\![P]\!](\sigma) \ggg \kappa & b \neq 0 \\ \delta(\sigma) & b = 0 \end{cases}$$

This semantics first evaluates e, while keeping the program state around using δ. If e evaluates to 0, the while loop terminates and we return the current program state σ. If e does not evaluate to 0, we run the loop body P and feed the result to the next iteration of the loop, using κ.

We can then define the semantics of `while` $e\ \{P\}$ using a special fixed point operator $\text{fix} \colon ((A \mapsto \overline{A}) \to (A \mapsto \overline{A})) \to (A \mapsto \overline{A})$, defined by the pointwise limit $\text{fix}(\varDelta) = \lim_{n \to \infty} \varDelta^n(\circlearrowright)$, where $\circlearrowright := \lambda\sigma.\,\delta(\circlearrowright)$ and $\varDelta^n$ denotes the n-fold composition of $\varDelta$. $\varDelta^n(\circlearrowright)$ puts all runs of the while loop that do not terminate within n steps into the state $\circlearrowright$. In the limit, $\circlearrowright$ only has weight on those runs of the loop that never terminate. $\text{fix}(\varDelta)$ is only defined if its pointwise limit exists. Making use of fix, we can define the semantics of the while loop as follows:

$$[\![\texttt{while}\ e\ \{P\}]\!] = \text{fix}\Big([\![\texttt{while}\ e\ \{P\}]\!]^{\text{trans}}\Big)$$

Lemma 7. *For $\varDelta$ as in the semantics of the while loop, and for each σ and each S, the limit $\lim_{n \to \infty} \varDelta^n(\circlearrowright)(\sigma)(S)$ exists.*

Lemma 7 holds because increasing n may only shift probability mass from $\circlearrowright$ to other states (we provide a formal proof in Appendix B). Kozen shows a different way of defining the semantics of the while loop [23], using least fixed points. Lemma 8 describes the relation of the semantics of our while loop to the semantics of the while loop of [23]. For more details on the formal interpretation of Lemma 8 and for its proof, see Appendix B.

Lemma 8. *In the absence of exception states, and using sub-probability kernels instead of distribution transformers, the definition of the semantics of the while loop from [23] is equivalent to ours.*

Theorem 2. *The semantics of each expression $[\![e]\!]$ and statement $[\![P]\!]$ is indeed a probability kernel.*

Proof. The proof proceeds by induction. Some lemmas that are crucial for the proof are listed in Appendix C. Conveniently, most functions that come up in our definition are continuous (like $a+b$) or continuous except on some countable subset (like $\frac{a}{b}$) and thus measurable.

4.4   Recursion

To extend our language with recursion, we apply the same ideas as for the while loop. Given the source code of a function F that uses recursion, we define its

$$\delta\bar{\times}\left[\!\!\left[\texttt{!flip}\left(\frac{1}{2}\right)\right]\!\!\right] \ggg \lambda(\sigma,b).\begin{cases}\left(\kappa\bar{\times}[\![1]\!] \ggg \lambda(x,y).\,\delta(x+y)\right)(\sigma) & b\neq 0 \\ [\![0]\!](\sigma) & b=0\end{cases}$$

Fig. 9. Kernel transformer $[\![\texttt{geom}]\!]^{\text{trans}}(\kappa)$ for geom given in Listing 11.

semantics in terms of a kernel transformer $[\![F]\!]^{\text{trans}}$. This kernel transformer takes semantics for F up to a recursion depth of n and returns semantics for F up to recursion depth $n+1$. Formally, $[\![F]\!]^{\text{trans}}(\kappa)$ follows the usual semantics, but uses κ as the semantics for recursive calls to F (we will provide an example shortly). Finally, we define the semantics of F by $[\![F]\!] := \text{fix}\left([\![F]\!]^{\text{trans}}\right)$. Just as for the while loop, $\text{fix}\left([\![F]\!]^{\text{trans}}\right)$ is well-defined because stepping from recursion depth n to $n+1$ can only shift probability mass from $\circlearrowleft$ to other states. We note that we could generalize our approach to mutual recursion.

To demonstrate how we define the kernel transformer, consider the recursive implementation of the geometric distribution in Listing 11 (to simplify presentation, Listing 11 uses early return). Given semantics κ for geom : $1 \mapsto \mathbb{R}$ up to recursion depth n, we can define the semantics of geom up to recursion depth $n+1$, as illustrated in Fig. 9.

```
geom(){
    if !flip(½){
        return geom()+1;
    }else{
        return 0;
    }
}
```

Listing 11. Geometric distribution

4.5 Higher-Order Functions

Our language cannot express higher-order functions. When trying to give semantics to higher-order probabilistic programs, an important step is to define a σ-algebra on the set of functions from real numbers to real numbers. Unfortunately, no matter which σ-algebra is picked, function evaluation (i.e. the function that takes f and x as arguments and returns $f(x)$) is not measurable [1]. This is a known limitation that previous work has looked into (e.g. [35] address it by restricting the set of functions to those expressible by their source code).

A promising recent approach is replacing measurable spaces by quasi-Borel spaces [16]. This allows expressing higher-order functions, at the price of replacing the well-known and well-understood measurable spaces by a new concept.

4.6 Non-determinism

To extend our language with non-determinism, we may define the semantics of expressions, functions and statements in terms of sets of kernels. For an expression e typed by $\Gamma \vdash e : \tau$, this means that $[\![e]\!]_\tau \in \mathcal{P}([\![\Gamma]\!] \mapsto [\![\tau]\!])$, where $\mathcal{P}(S)$ denotes the power set of S. Lifting our semantics to non-determinism is mostly straightforward, except for loops. There, $[\![\texttt{while } e \ \{P\}]\!]$ contains all kernels of the form $\lim_{n\to\infty}(\Delta_1 \circ \cdots \circ \Delta_n)(\circlearrowleft)$, where $\Delta_i \in [\![\texttt{while } e \ \{P\}]\!]^{\text{trans}}$. Previous work has studied non-determinism in more detail, see e.g. [21,22].

5   Properties of Semantics

We now investigate two properties of our semantics: commutativity and associativity. These are useful in practice, e.g. because they enable rewriting programs to a form that allows for more efficient inference [5].

In this section, we write $e_1 \simeq e_2$ when expressions e_1 and e_2 are equivalent (i.e. when $[\![e_1]\!] = [\![e_2]\!]$). Analogously, we write $P_1 \simeq P_2$ for $[\![P_1]\!] = [\![P_2]\!]$.

5.1   Commutativity

In the presence of exception states, our language cannot guarantee commutativity of expressions such as $e_1 + e_2$. This is not surprising, as in our semantics the first exception bypasses all later exceptions.

Lemma 9. *For function* $F()\{$`while` 1 $\{$`skip`$\}$; `return` $0\}$,

$$\frac{1}{0} + F() \not\simeq F() + \frac{1}{0}$$

Formally, this is because if we evaluate $\frac{1}{0}$ first, we only have weight on $\bot$. If instead, we evaluate $F()$ first, we only have weight on $\circlearrowright$, by an analogous calculation. A more detailed proof is included in Appendix D.

However, the only reason for non-commutativity is the presence of exceptions. Assuming that e_1 and e_2 cannot produce exceptions, we obtain commutativity:

Lemma 10. *If* $[\![e_1]\!](\sigma)(\mathcal{X}) = [\![e_2]\!](\sigma)(\mathcal{X}) = 0$ *for all* σ, *then* $e_1 \oplus e_2 \simeq e_2 \oplus e_1$, *for any commutative operator* $\oplus$.

The proof of Lemma 10 (provided in Appendix D) relies on the absence of exceptions and Fubini's Theorem. This commutativity result is in line with the results from [34], which proves commutativity in the absence of exceptions.

In the analogous situation for statements, we cannot assume commutativity $P_1; P_2 \simeq P_2; P_1$, even if there is no dataflow from P_1 to P_2. We already illustrated this in Listing 10, where swapping two lines changes the program semantics. However, in the absence of exceptions and dataflow from P_1 to P_2, we can guarantee $P_1; P_2 \simeq P_2; P_1$.

5.2   Associativity

A careful reader might suspect that since commutativity does not always hold in the presence of exceptions, a similar situation might arise for associativity of some expressions. As an example, can we guarantee $e_1 + (e_2 + e_3) \simeq (e_1 + e_2) + e_3$, even in the presence of exceptions? The answer is yes, intuitively because exceptions can only change the behavior of a program if the order of their occurrence is changed. This is not the case for associativity. Formally, we derive the following:

Lemma 11. $e_1 \oplus (e_2 \oplus e_3) \simeq (e_1 \oplus e_2) \oplus e_3$, *for any associative operator* $\oplus$.

We include notes on the proof of Lemma 11 in Appendix D, mainly relying on the associativity of $\overline{\times}$ (Lemma 6). Likewise, sequential composition is associative: $(P_1; P_2); P_3 \simeq P_1; (P_2; P_3)$. This is due to the associativity of $>\!\!=\!\!>$ (Lemma 5).

5.3   Adding the score Primitive

Some languages include the primitive **score**, which allows to increase or decrease the probability of a certain event (or trace) [34,35].

Listing 12 shows an example program using **score**.
Without normalization, it returns 0 with probability $\frac{1}{2}$ and 1 with "probability" $\frac{1}{2} \cdot 2 = 1$. After normalization, it returns 0 with probability $\frac{1}{3}$ and 1 with probability $\frac{2}{3}$. Because **score** allows decreasing the probability of a specific event, it renders **observe** unnecessary. In general, we can replace **observe**(e) by **score**$(e \neq 0)$. However, performing this replacement means losing the explicit knowledge of the weight on $\frac{1}{2}$.

```
x:=flip(½);
if x=1 {
    score(2);
}
return x;
```

Listing 12. Using score

score can be useful to modify the shape of a given distribution. For example, Listing 13 turns the distribution of x, which is a Gaussian distribution, into the Lebesgue measure λ, by multiplying the density of x by its inverse. Hence, the density of x at any location is 1. Note that the distribution over x cannot be described by a probability measure, because e.g. the "probability" that x lies in the interval $[0, 2]$ is 2.

```
x:=gauss(0,1);
score(√(2π)e^(x²/2));
return x;
```

Listing 13. Reshaping a distribution.

Unfortunately, termination in the presence of **score** is not well-defined, as illustrated in Listing 14. In this program, the only non-terminating trace keeps changing its weight, switching between 1 and 2. In the limit, it is impossible to determine the weight of non-termination.

Hence, allowing the use of the **score** primitive only makes sense after abolishing the tracking of non-termination ($\circlearrowleft$), which can be achieved by only measuring sets that do not contain non-termination. Formally, this means restricting the semantics of expressions e typed by $\Gamma \vdash e : \tau$ to $[\![e]\!]_\tau : \Gamma \mapsto \left(\overline{[\![\tau]\!]} - \{\circlearrowleft\} \right)$.

```
i:=0;
while 1 {
    if i=0 {
        score(2);
    }else{
        score(½);
    }
    i=1-i;
}
```

Listing 14. score vs non-termination

Intuitively, abolishing non-termination means that we ignore non-terminating runs (these result in weight on non-termination). After doing this, we can give well-defined semantics to the **score** primitive.

The typing rule and semantics of **score** are:

$$\frac{\Gamma \vdash e : \mathbb{R}}{\Gamma \overset{\text{score}(e)}{\rightsquigarrow} \Gamma} \qquad \text{and} \qquad [\![\textbf{score}(e)]\!] = \delta \overline{\times} [\![e]\!]_\mathbb{R} \ggg \lambda(\sigma, c).c * \delta(\sigma)$$

After including **score** into our language, the semantics of the language can no longer be expressed in terms of probability kernels as stated in Theorem 2, because the probability of any event can be inflated beyond 1. Instead, the semantics must be expressed in terms of s-finite kernels.

Theorem 3. *After adding the* **score** *primitive and abolishing non-termination, the semantics of each expression $[\![e]\!]$ and statement $[\![P]\!]$ is an s-finite kernel.*

Table 3. Comparison of existing semantics to ours. When adding **score** to our language (Sect. 5.3), our semantics use s-finite kernels (not probability kernels).

Work	Language	Semantics	Typed	Higher-order	Loops	Constraints
We	Imperative	Probability kernels	Typed	First-order	Loops (FP)	Yes
[4]	Functional	Sub-probability kernels	Untyped	Higher-order	Recursion (FP)	Yes
[23]	Imperative	Distribution transformers	Limited	First-order	Loops (LFP)	No
[24]	Imperative	Sub-probability kernels	Limited	First-order	Loops (LFP)	Yes
[28]	Imperative	Weakest precondition	Untyped	First-order	Loops (LFP)	Yes
[33]	Declarative	Probability kernels	Limited	First-order	Loops (LFP)	No
[34]	Functional	s-finite kernels	Typed	First-order	Counting measure	$\mathbf{score}(x)$
[35]	Functional	Measurable functions	Typed	Higher-order	No	$\mathbf{score}(x)$

Proof. As for Theorem 2, the proof proceeds by induction. Most parts of the proof are analogous (e.g. $\ggg$ preserves s-finite kernels instead of probability kernels). For while loops, the limit still exists (Lemma 7 still holds), but it is not bounded from above anymore. The limit indeed corresponds to an s-finite kernel because the limit of strictly increasing s-finite kernels is an s-finite kernel.

In the presence of **score**, we can still talk about the interaction of different exceptions, assuming that we do track different types of exceptions (e.g. division by zero and out of bounds access of arrays). Then, we keep the commutativity and associativity properties studied in the previous sections, because these still hold for s-finite kernels.

```
score(2);
assert(false);
```

Listing 15. Interaction of **score** and **assert**

Listing 15 shows an interaction of **score** with **assert**. As one would expect, our semantics will assign weight 2 to $\bot$ in this case. If the two statements are switched, our semantics will ignore **score**(2) and assign weight 1 to $\bot$. Hence again, commutativity does not hold.

```
while 1 {
    score(2);
    assert(flip(½));
}
```

Listing 16. Interaction of **score**, **assert** and loops

Listing 16 shows a program that keeps increasing the probability of an error. In every loop iteration, there is a "probability" of 1 of running into an error. Overall, Listing 16 results in weight ∞ on state $\bot$.

6   Related Work

Kozen provides classic semantics to probabilistic programs [23]. We follow his main ideas, but deviate in some aspects in order to introduce additional features or to make our presentation cleaner. The semantics by Hur et al. [19] is heavily based on [23], so we do not go into more detail here. Table 3 summarizes the comparison of our approach to that of others.

Kernels. Like our work, most modern approaches use kernels (i.e., functions from values to distributions) to provide semantics to probabilistic programs [4, 24, 33, 34]. Borgström et al. [4] use sub-probability kernels on (symbolic) expressions.

Staton [34] uses s-finite kernels to capture the semantics of the **score** primitive (when we discuss **score** in Sect. 5.3, we do the same).

In the classic semantics of [23], Kozen uses distribution transformers (i.e., functions from distributions to distributions). For later work [24], Kozen also switches to sub-probability kernels, which has the advantage of avoiding redundancies. A different approach uses weakest precondition to define the semantics, as in [28]. Staton et al. [35] use a different concept of measurable functions $A \to P(\mathbb{R}_{\geq 0} \times B)$ (where $P(S)$ denotes the set of all probability measures on S).

Typing. Some probabilistic languages are untyped [4, 28], while others are limited to just a single type: $\mathbb{R}^n$ [23, 24] or $\bigcup_{i=1}^{\infty} \mathbb{N}^i \cup \mathbb{N}^{\infty}$ [33]. Some languages provide more interesting types including sum types, distribution types and tuples [34, 35]. We allow tuples and array types, and we could easily account for sum types.

Loops. Because the semantics of while loops is not always straightforward, some languages avoid while loops and recursion altogether [35]. Borgström et al. handle recursion instead of while loops, defining the semantics in terms of a fixed point [4]. Many languages handle while loops by least fixed points [23, 24, 28, 33]. Staton defines while loops in terms of the counting measure [34], which is similar to defining them by a fixed point. We define the semantics of while loops in terms of a fixed point, which avoids the need to prove the least fixed point exists (still, the classic while loop semantics of [23] and our formulation are equivalent).

Most languages do not explicitly track non-termination, but lose probability weight by non-termination [4, 23, 24, 34]. This missing weight can be used to identify the probability of non-termination, but only if other exceptions (such as **fail** in [24] or observation failure in [4]) do not also result in missing weight. The semantics of [33] are tailored to applications in networks and lose *non-terminating packet histories* instead of weight (due to a particular least fixed point construction of Scott-continuous maps on algebraic and continuous directed complete partial orders). Some works define non-termination as missing weight in the weakest precondition [28]. Specifically, the semantics in [28] can also explicitly express probability of non-termination *or* ending up in some state (using the separate construct of a weakest liberal precondition). We model non-termination by an explicit state $\circlearrowleft$, which has the advantage that in the context of lost weight, we know what part of that lost weight is due to non-termination.

Kaminski et al. [21] investigate the run-time of probabilistic program with loops and **fail** (interpreted as early termination), but without observations. In [21], non-termination corresponds to an infinite run-time.

Error States. Many languages do not consider partial functions (like fractions $\frac{a}{b}$) and thus never run into an exception state [23, 24, 33]. Olmedo et al. [28] do not consider partial functions, but support the related concept of an explicit **abort**. The semantics of **abort** relies on missing weight in the final distribution. Some languages handle expressions whose evaluation may fail using sum types [34, 35], forcing the programmer to deal with errors explicitly (we discuss the disadvantages of this approach at Listing 6). Formally, a sum type $A + B$ is a disjoint union of the two sets A and B. Defining the semantics of an expression in terms of the sum type $A+\{\perp\}$ allows that expression to evaluate to *either* a value $a \in A$ *or* to $\perp$. Borgström et al. [4] have a single state **fail** expressing exceptions such as dynamically detected type errors (without forcing the programmer to deal with exceptions explicitly). Our semantics also uses sum types to handle exceptions, but the handling is implicit, by defining semantics in terms of ($\ggeq$) (which defines how exceptions propagate in a program) instead of (;).

Constraints. To enforce hard constraints, we use the **observe**(e) statement, which puts the program into a special failure state $\frac{1}{2}$ if it does not satisfy e. We can encode soft constraints by **observe**(e), where e is probabilistic (this is a general technique). Borgström et al. [4] allow both soft constraints that reduce the probability of some program traces and hard constraints whose failure leads to the error state **fail**. Some languages can handle generalized soft constraints: they can not only decrease the probability of certain traces using soft constraints, but also increase them, using **score**(x) [34,35]. We investigate the consequences of adding **score** to our language in Sect. 5.3. Kozen [24] handles hard (and hence soft) constraints using **fail** (which results in a sub-probability distribution). Some languages can handle neither hard nor soft constraints [23,33]. Note though that the semantics of ProbNetKAT in [33] can drop certain packages, which is a similar behavior. Olmedo et al. [28] handle hard (and hence soft) constraints by a conditional weakest precondition that tracks both the probability of not failing any observation and the probability of ending in specific states. Unfortunately, this work is restricted to discrete distributions and is specifically designed to handle observation failures and non-termination. Thus, it is not obvious how to adapt the semantics if a different kind of exception is to be added.

Interaction of Different Exceptions. Most existing work handles at least some exceptions by sub-probability distributions [4,23,24,33,34]. Then, any missing weight in the final distribution must be due to exceptions. However, this leads to a conflation of all exceptions handled by sub-probability distributions (for the consequences of this, see, e.g., our discussion of Listing 8). Note that semantics based on sub-probability kernels can add more exceptions, but they will simply be conflated with all other exceptions.

Some previous work does not (exclusively) rely on sub-probability distributions. Borgström et al. [4] handle errors implicitly, but still use sub-probability kernels to handle non-termination and **score**. Olmedo et al. can distinguish non-termination (which is conflated with exception failure) from failing observations by introducing two separate semantic primitives (conditional weakest precondition and conditional liberal weakest precondition) [28]. Because their solution specifically addresses non-termination, it is non-trivial to generalize this treatment to more than two exception states. By using sum types, some semantics avoid interactions of errors with non-termination or constraint failures, but still cannot distinguish the latter [34,35]. Note that semantics based on sum types can easily add more exceptions (although it is impossible to add non-termination).

However, the interaction of different exceptions cannot be observed, because the programmer has to handle exceptions explicitly.

To the best of our knowledge, we are the first to give formal semantics to programs that may produce exceptions in this generality. One work investigates assertions in probabilistic programs, but explicitly disallows non-terminating loops [32]. Moreover, the semantics in [32] are operational, leaving the distribution (in terms of measure theory) of program outputs unclear. Cho et al. [8] investigate the interaction of partial programs and observe, but are restricted to discrete distributions and to only two exception states. In addition, this investigation treats these two exception states differently, making it non-trivial to extend the results to three or more exception states. Katoen et al. [22] investigate the intuitive problems when combining non-termination and observations, but restrict their discussions to discrete distributions and do not provide formal semantics. Huang [17] treats partial functions, but not different kinds of exceptions. In general, we know of no probabilistic programming language that distinguishes more than two different kinds of exceptions. Distinguishing two kinds of exceptions is simpler than three, because it is possible to handle one exception as an explicit exception state and the other one by missing weight (as e.g. in [4]).

Cousot and Monerau [9] provide a trace semantics that captures probabilistic behavior by an explicit randomness source given to the program as an argument. This allows handling non-termination by non-terminating traces. While the work does not discuss errors or observation failure, it is possible to add both. However, using an explicit randomness source has other disadvantages, already discussed by Kozen [23]. Most notably, this approach requires a distribution over the randomness source and a translation from the randomness source to random choices in the program, even though we only care about the distribution of the latter.

7   Conclusion

In this work we presented an expressive probabilistic programming language that supports important features such as mixing continuous and discrete distributions, arrays, observations, partial functions and while-loops. Unlike prior work, our semantics distinguishes non-termination, observation failures and error states. This allows us to investigate the subtle interaction of different exceptions, which is not possible for semantics that conflate different kinds of exceptions. Our investigation confirms the intuitive understanding of the interaction of exceptions presented in Sect. 2. However, it also shows that some desirable properties, like commutativity, only hold in the absence of exceptions. This situation is unavoidable, and largely analogous to the situation in deterministic languages.

Even though our semantics only distinguish three exception states, it can be trivially extended to handle any countable set of exception states. This allows for an even finer-grained distinction of e.g. division by zero, out of bounds array accesses or casting failures (in a language that allows type casting). Our semantics also allows enriching exceptions with the line number that the exception originated from (of course, this is not possible for non-termination). For an uncountable set of exception states, an extension is possible but not trivial.

A   Proofs for Preliminaries

In this section, we provide lemmas, proofs and some definitions that were left out or cut short in Sect. 3. For a more detailed introduction into measure theory, we recommend the book *A crash course on the Lebesgue integral and measure theory* [7].

A.1   Measures

Definition 3. *Let* (A, Σ_A) *be a measurable space and* $\mu \colon \Sigma_A \to [0, \infty]$ *a measure on* A.

- *We call* μ *s-finite if* μ *can be written as a countable sum* $\sum_{i \in \mathbb{N}} \mu_i$ *of sub-probability measures* μ_i.
- *We call* μ *σ-finite if* $A = \bigcup_{i \in \mathbb{N}} A_i$ *for* $A_i \in \Sigma_A$, *with* $\mu(A_i) < \infty$.
- *We call* μ *finite if* $\mu(A) < \infty$.
- *We call* μ *a sub-probability measure if* $\mu(A) \leq 1$.
- *We call* μ *a probability measure if* $\mu(A) = 1$.

Note that for a σ-finite measure μ, $\mu(A) = \infty$ is possible, even though $\mu(A_i) < \infty$ for all i. As an example, the Lebesgue measure is σ-finite because $\mathbb{R} = \bigcup_{i \in \mathbb{N}} [-i, i]$ with $\lambda([-i, i]) = 2 * i$, but $\lambda(\mathbb{R}) = \infty$.

Lemma 12. *The following definition of s-finite measures is equivalent to our definition of s-finite measures (the difference is that the μ_is are only required to be finite):*

We call $\mu \colon \Sigma_A \to [0, \infty]$ *an s-finite measure if it can be written as* $\mu = \sum_{i \in \mathbb{N}} \mu_i$ *for finite measures* $\mu_i \colon \Sigma_A \to [0, \infty]$.

Proof. Since any sub-probability measure is finite, one direction is trivial. For the other direction, let $\mu = \sum_{i \in \mathbb{N}} \mu_i'$ for finite measures μ_i'. Obviously, $\mu \geq 0$, $\mu(\emptyset) = 0$ and $\mu(\bigcup_{i \in \mathbb{N}} A_i) = \sum_{i \in \mathbb{N}} A_i$ for mutually disjoint $A_i \in \Sigma_A$, so μ is a measure. To show that μ can be written as a sum of sub-probability measures, let $n_i := \lceil \mu_i'(A) \rceil$. Then, $\mu = \sum_{i \in \mathbb{N}} \mu_i' = \sum_{i \in \mathbb{N}} \frac{n_i}{n_i} \mu_i' = \sum_{i \in \mathbb{N}} \sum_{j \in [n_i]} \frac{1}{n_i} \mu_i'$. We let $\mu_i := \frac{1}{n_i} \mu_i' \leq 1$.

Lemma 13. *Any σ-finite measure* $\mu \colon \Sigma_A \to [0, \infty]$ *is s-finite.*

Proof. Since μ is σ-finite, $A = \bigcup_{i \in \mathbb{N}} A_i$ with $A_i \in \Sigma_A$ and $\mu(A_i) < \infty$. Without loss of generality, assume that the A_i form a partition of A. Then, $\mu(S) = \sum_{i \in \mathbb{N}} \mu(S \cap A_i)$, with $\mu(\cdot \cap A_i) < \infty$. Thus, μ is a countable sum of finite measures.

Definition 4. *The counting measure $c \colon \mathcal{B} \to [0, \infty]$ is defined by*

$$c(S) = \begin{cases} |S| & S \text{ finite} \\ \infty & \text{otherwise} \end{cases}$$

Definition 5. *The infinity measure $\mu \colon \mathcal{B} \to [0, \infty]$ is defined by*

$$\mu(S) = \begin{cases} 0 & S = \emptyset \\ \infty & \text{otherwise} \end{cases}$$

Lemma 14. *Neither the counting measure nor the infinity measure are s-finite.*

Proof. For the counting measure c, assume (toward a contradiction) $c = \sum_{i \in \mathbb{N}} c_i$. We have $\mathbb{R} = \{r \in \mathbb{R} \mid c(\{r\}) > 0\} = \bigcup_{i \in \mathbb{N}} \{r \in \mathbb{R} \mid c_i(\{r\}) > 0\} = \bigcup_{i \in \mathbb{N}} \bigcup_{n \in \mathbb{N}} \{r \in \mathbb{R} \mid c_i(\{r\}) > \frac{1}{n}\}$. Because $\mathbb{R}$ is uncountable, there must be $i, n \in \mathbb{N}$ for which $S := \{r \in \mathbb{R} \mid c_i(\{r\}) > \frac{1}{n}\}$ is uncountable. Thus for any measurable, countably infinite $S' \subseteq S$, $c_i(S') = \infty$, which means that c_i is not finite. Proceed analogously for the infinity measure.

Lemma 15. *The measure $\mu \colon \mathcal{B} \to [0, \infty]$ with $\mu(S) = \left\{ \begin{matrix} 0 & \lambda(S) = 0 \\ \infty & \lambda(S) > 0 \end{matrix} \right\}$ is s-finite but not σ-finite.*

Proof. $\mu = \sum_{i \in \mathbb{N}} \lambda$, and λ is s-finite, so μ is s-finite. Assume (toward a contradiction) that μ is σ-finite. Then $\mathbb{R} = \bigcup_{i \in \mathbb{N}} A_i$ with $A_i \in \mathcal{B}$ and $\mu(A_i) < \infty$. Thus, $\mu(A_i) = 0$ and hence $\mu(\mathbb{R}) = \mu(\bigcup_{i \in \mathbb{N}} A_i) \leq \sum_{i \in \mathbb{N}} \mu(A_i) = 0$, a contradiction.

Lemma 16

$$\forall S \in \Sigma_{A \times B} \colon (\mu \times \mu')(S) = \int_{a \in A} \mu'(\{b \in B \mid (a, b) \in S\}) \mu(da)$$

$$= \int_{b \in B} \mu(\{a \in A \mid (a, b) \in S\}) \mu'(db)$$

$$\forall S \in \Sigma_{\overline{A \times B}} \colon (\mu \overline{\times} \mu')(S) = \int_{a \in \overline{A}} \mu'(\{b \in \overline{B} \mid \overline{(a, b)} \in S\}) \mu(da)$$

$$= \int_{b \in \overline{B}} \mu(\{a \in \overline{A} \mid \overline{(a, b)} \in S\}) \mu'(db)$$

Proof

$$(\mu \times \mu')(S) = \int_{a \in A} \int_{b \in B} [(a, b) \in S] \mu'(db) \mu(da)$$

$$= \int_{a \in A} \int_{b \in B} [b \in \{b' \in B \mid (a, b') \in S\}] \mu'(db) \mu(da)$$

$$= \int_{a \in A} \mu'(\{b' \in B \mid (a, b') \in S\}) \mu(da)$$

$$(\mu \times \mu')(S) = \int\limits_{a \in A} \int\limits_{b \in B} [(a, b) \in S]\mu'(db)\mu(da)$$

$$= \int\limits_{b \in B} \int\limits_{a \in A} [(a, b) \in S]\mu(da)\mu'(db) \qquad \text{Fubini}$$

$$= \ldots$$

$$= \int\limits_{b \in B} \mu(\{a' \in A \mid (a', b) \in S\})\mu'(db)$$

In the second line, we have used that $(a, b) \in S \iff b \in \{b' \in B \mid (a, b') \in S\}$. The proof works analogously for $\overline{\times}$.

Lemma 17. *Let* $\delta \colon A \mapsto A$, $\kappa \colon A \mapsto B$. *Then,*

$$(\delta \overline{\times} \kappa)(a)(S) = \kappa(a)(\{b \in \overline{B} \mid \overline{(a, b)} \in S\})$$

Proof

$$(\delta \overline{\times} \kappa)(a)(S) = \int_{b \in \overline{B}} \delta(a)(\{a' \in A \mid \overline{(a', b)} \in S\})\kappa(a)(db) \qquad \text{Lemma 16}$$

$$= \int_{b \in \overline{B}} \overline{[(a, b)} \in S]\kappa(a)(db)$$

$$= \kappa(a)(\{b \in \overline{B} \mid \overline{(a, b)} \in S\})$$

Lemma 1. *For measures* $\mu \colon \Sigma_A \to [0, \infty]$, $\mu' \colon \Sigma_B \to [0, \infty]$, *let* $S \in \Sigma_A$ *and* $T \in \Sigma_B$. *Then,* $(\mu \times \mu')(S \times T) = \mu(S) \cdot \mu'(T)$.

Proof

$$(\mu \times \mu')(S \times T) = \int_{a \in A} \mu'(\{b \in B \mid (a, b) \in S \times T\})\mu(da) \qquad \text{Lemma 16}$$

$$= \int_{a \in A} \mu'\left(\left\{ \begin{matrix} T & a \in S \\ \emptyset & \text{otherwise} \end{matrix} \right\}\right)\mu(da)$$

$$= \int_{a \in S} \mu'(T)\mu(da)$$

$$= \mu(S) * \mu'(T)$$

Lemma 2. $\times$ *and* $\overline{\times}$ *for s-finite measures are associative, left- and right-distributive and preserve (sub-)probability and s-finite measures.*

Proof. Remember that $(\mu \times \mu')(S) = \int_{a \in A} \int_{b \in B} [(a, b) \in S]\mu'(db)\mu(da)$ and that $(\mu \overline{\times} \mu')(S) = \int_{a \in \overline{A}} \int_{b \in \overline{B}} \overline{[(a, b)} \in S]\mu'(db)\mu(da)$. Preservation of (sub-)probability measures is trivial. Distributivity and preservation of s-finite measures are easily established by properties of the Lebesgue integral in Lemma 19.

For associativity, let $\mu \colon \Sigma_A \to [0, \infty]$, $\mu \colon \Sigma_B \to [0, \infty]$ and $\mu \colon \Sigma_C \to [0, \infty]$.

$$((\mu \times \mu') \times \mu'')(S)$$

$$= \int_{c \in C} (\mu \times \mu')(\{t \in A \times B \mid (t,c) \in S\})\mu''(dc) \qquad \text{Lemma 16}$$

$$= \int_{c \in C} \int_{a \in A} \int_{b \in B} [(a,b) \in \{t \in A \times B \mid (t,c) \in S\}]\mu'(db)\mu(da)\mu''(dc)$$

$$= \int_{c \in C} \int_{a \in A} \int_{b \in B} [(a,b,c) \in S]\mu'(db)\mu(da)\mu''(dc)$$

$$= \int_{a \in A} \int_{b \in B} \int_{c \in C} [(a,b,c) \in S]\mu''(dc)\mu'(db)\mu(da) \qquad \text{Fubini}$$

$$= \int_{a \in A} \int_{b \in B} \int_{c \in C} [(b,c) \in \{t \in B \times C \mid (a,t) \in S\}]\mu''(dc)\mu'(db)\mu(da)$$

$$= \int_{a \in A} (\mu' \times \mu'')(\{t \in B \times C \mid (a,t) \in S\})\mu(da)$$

$$= (\mu \times (\mu' \times \mu''))(S)\mu(da) \qquad \text{Lemma 16}$$

The proof proceeds analogously for $\overline{\times}$.

Lemma 18. *Let (A, Σ_A) and (B, Σ_B) be measurable spaces. Consider measures $\mu, \mu_1, \mu_2 \colon \Sigma_A \to [0, \infty]$ and $\nu, \nu_1, \nu_2 \colon \Sigma_B \to [0, \infty]$. We assume that $\nu_1 \leq \nu_2$ and $\mu_1 \leq \mu_2$ hold pointwise. Then,*

$$\mu \overline{\times} \nu_1 \leq \mu \overline{\times} \nu_2$$
$$\mu_1 \overline{\times} \nu \leq \mu_2 \overline{\times} \nu$$

Proof. Let $S \in \Sigma_{A \times B}$ and $\nu_1 \leq \nu_2$. Then, we have

$$\nu_1 \leq \nu_2$$

$$\implies \underbrace{\int_{b \in \overline{B}} [\overline{(a,b)} \in S]\nu_1(db)}_{=:f(a)} \leq \underbrace{\int_{b \in \overline{B}} [\overline{(a,b)} \in S]\nu_2(db)}_{=:g(a)} \qquad \text{Lemma 19}$$

$$\implies \int_{a \in \overline{A}} f(a)\mu(da) \leq \int_{a \in \overline{A}} g(a)\mu(da) \qquad \text{Lemma 19}$$

$$\implies (\mu \overline{\times} \nu_1)(S) \leq (\mu \overline{\times} \nu_2)(S)$$

The proof for $\mu_1 \overline{\times} \nu \leq \mu_2 \overline{\times} \nu$ is similar.

A.2   Lebesgue Integral

Lemma 19. *Let (A, Σ_A) and (B, Σ_B) be measurable spaces, $E \in \Sigma_A$ and $E' \in \Sigma_B$ measurable sets, $f, f_i, g \colon A \to \mathbb{R}$ and $h \colon A \times B \to \mathbb{R}$ measurable functions,*

$\mu, \mu_i, \nu \colon \Sigma_A \to [0, \infty]$ and $\mu' \colon \Sigma_B \to [0, \infty]$ measures.

$$\int_{a \in E} f(a)\mu(da) \in [0, \infty]$$

$$0 \le f \le g \le \infty \implies \int_{a \in E} f(a)\mu(da) \le \int_{a \in E} g(a)\mu(da)$$

$$\mu \le \nu \implies \int_{a \in E} f(a)\mu(da) \le \int_{a \in E} f(a)\nu(da)$$

$$\sum_{n=1}^{\infty} \int_{a \in E} f_n(a)\mu(da) = \int_{a \in E} \sum_{n=1}^{\infty} f_n(a)\mu(da)$$

$$\int_{a \in E} \int_{b \in E'} f(a,b)\mu'(db)\mu(da) = \int_{b \in E'} \int_{a \in E} f(a,b)\mu'(da)\mu(db) \qquad \mu, \mu'\,\sigma\text{-finite}$$

$$\int_{a \in E} f(a)\left(\sum_{n=1}^{\infty} \mu_i\right)(da) = \sum_{n=1}^{\infty} \int_{a \in E} f(a)\mu_i(da)$$

$$\int_{a \in E} f(a)\delta(x)(da) = f(x) \qquad\qquad x \in E$$

Finally, if $f_1 \le f_2 \le \cdots \le \infty$, we have

$$\lim_{n \to \infty} \int_{a \in E} f_n(a)\mu(da) = \int_{a \in E} \lim_{n \to \infty} f_n(a)\mu(da)$$

Proof. The following properties can be proven for simple functions and limits of simple functions (this suffices):

$$\int_{a \in E} f(a)\left(\sum_{n=1}^{\infty} \mu_i\right)(da) = \sum_{n=1}^{\infty} \int_{a \in E} f(a)\mu_i(da)$$

$$\mu \le \nu \implies \int_{a \in E} f(a)\mu(da) \le \int_{a \in E} f(a)\nu(da)$$

$\int_{a \in E} f(a)\delta(x)(da) = f(x)$ is straightforward. For the other properties, see [31].

Theorem 1 (Fubini's theorem). For s-finite measures $\mu \colon \Sigma_A \to [0, \infty]$ and $\mu' \colon \Sigma_B \to [0, \infty]$ and any measurable function $f \colon A \times B \to [0, \infty]$,

$$\int_{a \in A} \int_{b \in B} f(a,b)\mu'(db)\mu(da) = \int_{b \in B} \int_{a \in A} f(a,b)\mu(da)\mu'(db)$$

For s-finite measures $\mu \colon \Sigma_{\overline{A}} \to [0, \infty]$ and $\mu' \colon \Sigma_{\overline{B}} \to [0, \infty]$ and any measurable function $f \colon A \times B \to [0, \infty]$,

$$\int_{a \in \overline{A}} \int_{b \in \overline{B}} \overline{f}(a,b)\mu'(db)\mu(da) = \int_{b \in \overline{B}} \int_{a \in \overline{A}} \overline{f}(a,b)\mu(da)\mu'(db)$$

Proof. Let $\mu = \sum_{i\in\mathbb{N}} \mu_i$ and $\mu' = \sum_{i\in\mathbb{N}} \mu'_i$ for bounded measures μ_i and μ'_i.

$$\int_{a\in A} \int_{b\in B} f(a,b)\mu'(db)\mu(da)$$

$$= \sum_{i,j\in\mathbb{N}} \int_{a\in A} \int_{b\in B} f(a,b)\mu'_j(db)\mu_i(da) \qquad \text{Lemma 19}$$

$$= \sum_{i,j\in\mathbb{N}} \int_{b\in B} \int_{a\in A} f(a,b)\mu_i(da)\mu'_j(db) \qquad \text{Fubini for } \sigma\text{-finite measures } \mu_i, \mu'_j$$

$$= \int_{b\in B} \int_{a\in A} f(a,b)\mu(da)\mu'(db)$$

The proof in the presence of exception state is analogous.

Lemma 20. *Fubini does not hold for the counting measure* $c\colon \mathcal{B} \to [0,\infty]$ *and the Lebesgue measure* $\lambda\colon \mathcal{B} \to [0,\infty]$ *(because c is not s-finite).*

Proof

$$\int_{x\in[0,1]} \int_{y\in[0,1]} [x=y]c(dy)\lambda(dx) = \int_{x\in[0,1]} 1\lambda(dx) = 1$$

$$\int_{y\in[0,1]} \int_{x\in[0,1]} [x=y]\lambda(dx)c(dy) = \int_{y\in[0,1]} 0c(dy) = 0$$

A.3   Kernels

Lemma 21. *Let* $\kappa_1, \kappa'_1\colon A \mapsto \overline{B}$ *and* $\kappa_2, \kappa'_2\colon B \mapsto \overline{C}$ *be s-finite kernels. If* $\kappa_1 \leq \kappa'_1$ *holds pointwise, then*

$$\kappa_1 \ggg \kappa_2 \leq \kappa'_1 \ggg \kappa_2$$

If $\kappa_2 \leq \kappa'_2$ *holds pointwise, then*

$$\kappa_1 \ggg \kappa_2 \leq \kappa_1 \ggg \kappa'_2$$

Proof. Assume $\kappa_2 \leq \kappa'_2$. Thus, $\overline{\kappa_2} \leq \overline{\kappa'_2}$. Now, let $a \in A$, $S \in \Sigma_{\overline{C}}$.

$$(\kappa_1 \ggg \kappa_2)(a)(S) = \int_{b\in\overline{B}} \overline{\kappa_2}(b)(S)\,\kappa_1(a)(db)$$

$$\leq \int_{b\in\overline{B}} \overline{\kappa'_2}(b)(S)\,\kappa_1(a)(db) \qquad \overline{\kappa_2} \leq \overline{\kappa'_2}, \text{Lemma 19}$$

$$= (\kappa_1 \ggg \kappa'_2)(a)(S)$$

The proof for $\kappa_1 \ggg \kappa_2 \leq \kappa'_1 \ggg \kappa_2$ works analogously.

Lemma 3. *(;) is associative, left- and right-distributive, has neutral element[4] δ and preserves (sub-)probability and s-finite kernels.*

---

[4] δ is a neutral element of (;) if $(\delta;\kappa) = (\kappa;\delta) = \kappa$ for all kernels κ.

Proof. Remember that $(f;g)(a)(S) = \int_{b \in B} g(b)(S) f(a)(db)$. Left- and right-distributivity and the neutral element δ follow from properties of the Lebesgue integral in Lemma 19.

Associativity and preservation of (sub-)probability kernels is well known (see for example [12]). For s-finite kernels $f = \sum_{i \in \mathbb{N}} f_i$ and $g = \sum_{i \in \mathbb{N}} g_i$ and $h = \sum_{i \in \mathbb{N}} h_i$, we have (for sub-probability kernels f_i, g_i, h_i)

$$
(f;g);h = \left(\left(\sum_{i \in \mathbb{N}} f_i \right) ; \left(\sum_{j \in \mathbb{N}} g_j \right) \right) ; \sum_{k \in \mathbb{N}} h_k = \sum_{i,j,k \in \mathbb{N}} (f_i;g_j);h_k
$$

$$
= \sum_{i,j,k \in \mathbb{N}} f_i;(g_j;h_k) = f;(g;h)
$$

(;) preserves s-finite kernels because for s-finite kernels f and g, we have (for sub-probability kernels f_i, g_i) $f;g = \sum_{i,j \in \mathbb{N}} f_i;g_i$, a sum of kernels.

Lemma 4. *For $f \colon A \mapsto \overline{B}$ and $g \colon B \mapsto \overline{C}$, $a \in A$ and $S \in \Sigma_{\overline{C}}$,*

$$
(f \Longrightarrow g)(a)(S) = (f;g)(a)(S) + \sum_{x \in \mathcal{X}} \delta(x)(S) f(a)(\{x\})
$$

Proof

$$
(f \Longrightarrow g)(a)(S) = \int_{b \in \overline{B}} \overline{g}(b)(S) \, f(a)(db)
$$

$$
= \int_{b \in B} \overline{g}(b)(S) \, f(a)(db) + \int_{b \in \mathcal{X}} \overline{g}(b)(S) \, f(a)(db)
$$

$$
= \int_{b \in B} g(b)(S) \, f(a)(db) + \sum_{b \in \mathcal{X}} \overline{g}(b)(S) \, f(a)(\{x\})
$$

$$
= (f;g)(a)(S) + \sum_{x \in \mathcal{X}} \delta(x)(S) f(a)(\{x\})
$$

Lemma 5. $\Longrightarrow$ *is associative, left-distributive (but not right-distributive), has neutral element δ and preserves (sub-)probability and s-finite kernels.*

Proof. Remember that $(f \Longrightarrow g)(a)(S) = \int_{b \in \overline{B}} \overline{g}(b)(S) \, f(a)(db)$. Left-distributivity follows from the properties of the Lebesgue integral in Lemma 19. Right-distributivity does not necessarily hold because $\overline{g_1 + g_2}(\bot) \neq \overline{g_1}(\bot) + \overline{g_2}(\bot)$. Associativity for $f \colon A \mapsto \overline{B}$, $g \colon B \mapsto \overline{C}$ and $h \colon C \mapsto \overline{D}$ can be derived by

$$((f \ggg g) \ggg h)(a)(S)$$

$$= \Big(\big(f \ggg g\big);h\Big)(a)(S) + \sum_{x \in \mathcal{X}} \delta(x)(S)(f \ggg g)(a)(\{x\})$$

$$= \Big(\big(f;g + \lambda a'.\lambda S'.\sum_{x \in \mathcal{X}} \delta(x)(S')f(a')(\{x\})\big);h\Big)(a)(S)$$

$$+ \sum_{x \in \mathcal{X}} \delta(x)(S)(f \ggg g)(a)(\{x\})$$

$$= (f;g;h)(a)(S) + \underbrace{\Big(\big(\lambda a'.\lambda S'.\sum_{x \in \mathcal{X}} \delta(x)(S')f(a')(\{x\})\big);h\Big)(a)(S)}_{=0(\;\text{(integrates over non-exception states)}}$$

$$+ \sum_{x \in \mathcal{X}} \delta(x)(S)(f \ggg g)(a)(\{x\})$$

$$= (f;g;h)(a)(S) + \sum_{x \in \mathcal{X}} \delta(x)(S)\Big((f;g)(a)(\{x\}) + \sum_{x' \in \mathcal{X}} \delta(x')(\{x\})f(a)(\{x'\})\Big)$$

$$= (f;g;h)(a)(S) + \sum_{x \in \mathcal{X}} \delta(x)(S)\Big((f;g)(a)(\{x\}) + f(a)(\{x\})\Big)$$

$$= (f;g;h)(a)(S) + \sum_{x \in \mathcal{X}} \delta(x)(S)(f;\lambda a'.\lambda S'.g(a')(S'))(a)(\{x\})$$

$$+ \sum_{x \in \mathcal{X}} \delta(x)(S)f(a)(\{x\})$$

$$= (f;g;h)(a)(S) + \Big(f;\big(\lambda a'.\lambda S'.\sum_{x \in \mathcal{X}} \delta(x)(S')g(a')(\{x\})\big)\Big)(a)(S)$$

$$+ \sum_{x \in \mathcal{X}} \delta(x)(S)f(a)(\{x\})$$

$$= \Big(f;\big(g;h + \lambda a'.\lambda S'.\sum_{x \in \mathcal{X}} \delta(x)(S')g(a')(\{x\})\big)\Big)(a)(S) + \sum_{x \in \mathcal{X}} \delta(x)(S)f(a)(\{x\})$$

$$= \Big(f;\big(g \ggg h\big)\Big)(a)(S) + \sum_{x \in \mathcal{X}} \delta(x)(S)f(a)(\{x\})$$

$$= (f \ggg (g \ggg h))(a)(S)$$

Here, we have used Lemma 4, left- and right-distributivity of $(;)$.

To show that $f \ggg g$ preserves s-finite kernels, let $f \colon A \mapsto \overline{B}$ and $g \colon B \mapsto \overline{C}$ be s-finite kernels. Then, for sub-probability kernels f_i,

$$(f \ggg g)(a)(S) = (f;g)(a)(S) + \sum_{x \in \mathcal{X}} \delta(x)(S)f(a)(\{x\})$$

$$= (f;g)(a)(S) + \sum_{x \in \mathcal{X}} \sum_{i \in \mathbb{N}} \delta(x)(S)f_i(a)(\{x\})$$

Note that for each $x \in \mathcal{X}$ and $i \in \mathbb{N}$, $\lambda a.\lambda S.\delta(x)(S)f_i(a)(\{x\})$ is a sub-probability kernel. Thus, $f \ggg g$ is a sum of s-finite kernels and hence s-finite.

Proving that for sub-probability kernels f and g, $f \ggg g$ is also a (sub-) probability kernel is trivial, since we only need to show that $(f \ggg g)(a)(\overline{C}) = 1$ (or ≤ 1).

Lemma 22. *Let (A, Σ_A) and (B, Σ_B) be measurable spaces. Let $f: A \times B \to [0, \infty]$ be measurable and $\kappa: A \mapsto B$ be a sub-probability kernel. Then, $f': A \to [0, \infty]$ defined by*

$$f'(a) := \int_{b \in B} f(a, b) \kappa(a)(db)$$

is measurable.

Proof. See Theorem 20 of [30].

Lemma 23. $\times$ *and* $\overline{\times}$ *preserve (sub-)probability kernels.*

Proof. Let $\kappa: A \mapsto B$ and $\kappa': A \mapsto C$ be (sub-)probability kernels. The fact that $(\kappa \times \kappa')(a)(\cdot)$ for all $a \in A$ is a (sub-)probability measure is inherited from Lemma 2. It remains to show that $(\kappa \times \kappa')(\cdot)(S)$ is measurable for all $S \in \Sigma_{B \times C}$, with

$$(\kappa \times \kappa')(a)(S) = \int_{b \in B} \int_{c \in C} [(b, c) \in S] \kappa'(a)(dc) \kappa(a)(db)$$

By Lemma 22, $f': A \times B \to [0, \infty]$ defined by $f'(a, b) = \int_{c \in C} [(b, c) \in S] \kappa'(a)(dc)$ is measurable, using the measurable function $f: (A \times B) \times C \to [0, \infty]$ defined by $f((a, b), c) = [(b, c) \in S]$. Again by Lemma 22, $\int_{b \in B} \int_{c \in C} [(b, c) \in S] \kappa'(a)(dc) \kappa(a)(db)$ is measurable.

Proving that for (sub-)probability kernels $\kappa: A \mapsto \overline{B}$ and $\kappa': A \mapsto \overline{C}$, $\kappa \overline{\times} \kappa'$ is a (sub-)probability kernel proceeds analogously.

Lemma 6. $\times$ *and* $\overline{\times}$ *for kernels preserve (sub-)probability and s-finite kernels, are associative, left- and right-distributive.*

Proof. Associativity, left- and right-distributivity are inherited from respective properties of the product of measures established by Lemma 2. Sub-probability kernels are preserved by Lemma 23.

S-finite kernels are preserved because $\kappa \times \kappa' = (\sum_{i \in \mathbb{N}} \kappa_i) \times (\sum_{i \in \mathbb{N}} \kappa'_i) = \sum_{i,j \in \mathbb{N}} \kappa_i \times \kappa'_j$ (analogously for $\overline{\times}$).

B   Proofs for Semantics

Lemma 7. *For Δ as in the semantics of the while loop, and for each σ and each S, the limit $\lim_{n \to \infty} \Delta^n(\circlearrowleft)(\sigma)(S)$ exists.*

Proof. In general, $0 \leq \Delta^n(\circlearrowleft)(\sigma)(S) \leq 1$. First, we restrict the allowed arguments for $\lim_{n \to \infty} \Delta^n(\circlearrowleft)(\sigma)(S)$ to only those S with $\circlearrowleft \in S$. We prove by induction that $\Delta^{n+1}(\circlearrowleft) \leq \Delta^n(\circlearrowleft)$, meaning $\forall \sigma: \forall S: \circlearrowleft \in S \implies \Delta^{n+1}(\circlearrowleft)(\sigma)(S) \leq \Delta^n(\circlearrowleft)(\sigma)(S)$. Hence, $\Delta^n(\circlearrowleft)$ is monotone decreasing in n and lower bounded by 0, which means that the limit must exist.

As a base case, we have $\Delta^1(\circlearrowright)(\sigma)(S) \leq 1 = \delta_{\circlearrowright}(S) = \Delta^0(\circlearrowright)(\sigma)(S)$, because $\circlearrowright \in S$. We proceed by induction with

$$
\Delta^{n+1}(\circlearrowright)(\sigma)(S) = \left(\delta\overline{\times}[\![e]\!] \ggg \lambda(\sigma,b). \left\{ \begin{array}{ll} [\![P]\!](\sigma) \ggg \Delta^n(\circlearrowright) & b \neq 0 \\ \delta(\sigma) & b = 0 \end{array} \right\} \right)(\sigma)(S)
$$

$$
\leq \left(\delta\overline{\times}[\![e]\!] \ggg \lambda(\sigma,b). \left\{ \begin{array}{ll} [\![P]\!](\sigma) \ggg \Delta^{n-1}(\circlearrowright) & b \neq 0 \\ \delta(\sigma) & b = 0 \end{array} \right\} \right)(\sigma)(S)
$$

$$
= \Delta^n(\circlearrowright)(\sigma)(S)
$$

In the second line, we have used the induction hypothesis. This application is valid because $\kappa_2 \leq \kappa_2'$ implies $\kappa_1 \ggg \kappa_2 \leq \kappa_1 \ggg \kappa_2'$ (Lemma 21).

We proceed analogously when we restrict the allowed arguments for the kernel $\lim_{n\to\infty} \Delta^n(\circlearrowright)(\sigma)(S)$ to only those S with $\circlearrowright \notin S$, proving $\Delta^{n+1}(\circlearrowright) \geq \Delta^n(\circlearrowright)$ for that case.

Lemma 8. *In the absence of exception states, and using sub-probability kernels instead of distribution transformers, the definition of the semantics of the while loop from [23] is equivalent to ours.*

Definition 6. *In [23], Kozen shows a different way of defining the semantics of the while loop. In our notation, and in terms of probability kernels instead of distribution transformers, that definition becomes*

$$
[\![\textbf{while } e \, \{P\}]\!] = \sup_{n\in\mathbb{N}} \sum_{k=0}^{n} \left([\![\textbf{filter}(e)]\!] \ggg [\![P]\!] \right)^k \ggg [\![\textbf{filter}(\neg e)]\!]
$$

Here, exponentiation is in terms of Kleisli composition, i.e. $\kappa^0 = \delta$ and $\kappa^{n+1} = \kappa \ggg \kappa^n$. The sum and limit are meant pointwise. Furthermore, we define filter by the following expression (note that $[\![\textbf{filter}(e)]\!]$ and $[\![\textbf{filter}(\neg e)]\!]$ are only sub-probability kernels, not probability kernels).

$$
[\![\textbf{filter}(e)]\!] = \delta\overline{\times}[\![e]\!] \ggg \lambda(\sigma,b). \left\{ \begin{array}{ll} \delta(\sigma) & b \neq 0 \\ 0 & b = 0 \end{array} \right\}
$$

$$
[\![\textbf{filter}(\neg e)]\!] = \delta\overline{\times}[\![e]\!] \ggg \lambda(\sigma,b). \left\{ \begin{array}{ll} \delta(\sigma) & b = 0 \\ 0 & b \neq 0 \end{array} \right\}
$$

To justify Lemma 8, we prove the more formal Lemma 24. Note that in the presence of exceptions (e.g. P is just $\textbf{assert}(0)$), Definition 6 does not make sense, because if

Lemma 24. *For all S with $S \cap \mathcal{X} = \emptyset$*

$$
\left(\sum_{k=0}^{n} \left([\![\textbf{filter}(e)]\!] \ggg [\![P]\!] \right)^k \ggg [\![\textbf{filter}(\neg e)]\!] \right)(\sigma)(S) = \Delta^{n+1}(\circlearrowright)(\sigma)(S)
$$

Proof. For $n = 0$, we have

$$\left(\sum_{k=0}^{0} \left([\![\texttt{filter}(e)]\!] \ggg [\![P]\!] \right)^{k} \ggg [\![\texttt{filter}(\neg e)]\!] \right)(\sigma)(S)$$

$$= \left(\left([\![\texttt{filter}(e)]\!] \ggg [\![P]\!] \right)^{0} \ggg [\![\texttt{filter}(\neg e)]\!] \right)(\sigma)(S)$$

$$= \left(\delta \ggg [\![\texttt{filter}(\neg e)]\!] \right)(\sigma)(S)$$

$$= [\![\texttt{filter}(\neg e)]\!](\sigma)(S)$$

$$= \left(\delta \overline{\times} [\![e]\!] \ggg \lambda(\sigma', b). \left\{ \begin{matrix} \delta(\sigma') & b = 0 \\ \mathbf{0} & b \neq 0 \end{matrix} \right\} \right)(\sigma)(S)$$

$$= \left(\delta \overline{\times} [\![e]\!] \ggg \lambda(\sigma', b). \left\{ \begin{matrix} \delta(\sigma') & b = 0 \\ \circlearrowleft(\sigma') & b \neq 0 \end{matrix} \right\} \right)(\sigma)(S) \qquad \circlearrowleft \notin S$$

$$= \left(\delta \overline{\times} [\![e]\!] \ggg \lambda(\sigma', b). \left\{ \begin{matrix} \delta(\sigma') & b = 0 \\ ([\![P]\!] \ggg \circlearrowleft)(\sigma') & b \neq 0 \end{matrix} \right\} \right)(\sigma)(S) \qquad S \cap \mathcal{X} = \emptyset$$

$$= \Delta^1(\circlearrowleft)$$

For $n \geq 0$, we have

$$\left(\sum_{k=0}^{n+1} \left([\![\texttt{filter}(e)]\!] \ggg [\![P]\!] \right)^{k} \ggg [\![\texttt{filter}(\neg e)]\!] \right)(\sigma)(S)$$

$$= \left(\left(\sum_{k=0}^{n} \left([\![\texttt{filter}(e)]\!] \ggg [\![P]\!] \right)^{k+1} + ([\![\texttt{filter}(e)]\!] \ggg P)^{0} \right) \ggg [\![\texttt{filter}(\neg e)]\!] \right)(\sigma)(S)$$

$$= \left(\left(\sum_{k=0}^{n} \left([\![\texttt{filter}(e)]\!] \ggg [\![P]\!] \right)^{k+1} + \delta \right) \ggg [\![\texttt{filter}(\neg e)]\!] \right)(\sigma)(S)$$

$$= \left(\left(\sum_{k=0}^{n} \left([\![\texttt{filter}(e)]\!] \ggg [\![P]\!] \right)^{k+1} \right) \ggg [\![\texttt{filter}(\neg e)]\!] \right)(\sigma)(S) \qquad \text{since } S \cap \mathcal{X} = \emptyset$$

$$+ \left(\delta \ggg [\![\texttt{filter}(\neg e)]\!] \right)(\sigma)(S)$$

$$= \left(\left(\sum_{k=0}^{n} \left([\![\texttt{filter}(e)]\!] \ggg [\![P]\!] \right)^{k+1} \right) \ggg [\![\texttt{filter}(\neg e)]\!] \right)(\sigma)(S) + [\![\texttt{filter}(\neg e)]\!](\sigma)(S)$$

$$= \left(\left([\![\texttt{filter}(e)]\!] \ggg [\![P]\!] \ggg \sum_{k=0}^{n}([\![\texttt{filter}(e)]\!] \ggg [\![P]\!])^{k} \right) \ggg [\![\texttt{filter}(\neg e)]\!] \right)(\sigma)(S)$$

$$+ [\![\texttt{filter}(\neg e)]\!](\sigma)(S)$$

$$= \left([\![\texttt{filter}(e)]\!] \ggg [\![P]\!] \ggg \left(\sum_{k=0}^{n}([\![\texttt{filter}(e)]\!] \ggg [\![P]\!])^{k} \ggg [\![\texttt{filter}(\neg e)]\!] \right) \right)(\sigma)(S)$$

$$+ [\![\texttt{filter}(\neg e)]\!](\sigma)(S)$$

$$= \left([\![\texttt{filter}(e)]\!] \ggg [\![P]\!] \ggg \Delta^{n+1}(\circlearrowleft) \right)(\sigma)(S) + [\![\texttt{filter}(\neg e)]\!](\sigma)(S)$$

$$= \left(\delta \overline{\times} [\![e]\!] \ggg \lambda(\sigma', b). \left\{ \begin{matrix} [\![P]\!](\sigma') \ggg \Delta^{n+1}(\circlearrowleft) & b \neq 0 \\ \delta(\sigma') & b = 0 \end{matrix} \right\} \right)(\sigma)(S)$$

$$= \Delta^{n+2}(\circlearrowleft)(\sigma)(S)$$

In particular, have have used that left-distributivity does hold in this case since $S \cap \mathcal{X} = \emptyset$.

C   Probability Kernel

In the following, we list lemmas that are crucial to prove Theorem 2 (restated for convenience).

Theorem 2. *The semantics of each expression $[\![e]\!]$ and statement $[\![P]\!]$ is indeed a probability kernel.*

Lemma 25. *Any measurable function $f\colon A \to [0,\infty]$ can be viewed as an s-finite kernel $f\colon A \mapsto \mathbb{1}$, defined by $f(x)(\emptyset) = 0$ and $f(x)(\mathbb{1}) = f(x)$.*

Proof. We prove that f is an s-finite kernel. Let $A_\infty := \{x \in A \mid f(x) = \infty\}$. Since f is measurable, the set A_∞ must be measurable. $f(x)(S) = \sum_{i\in\mathbb{N}}[x \in A_\infty][() \in S] + \sum_{i\in\mathbb{N}} f(x)[i \le f(x) < i + 1][() \in S]$, which is a sum of finite kernels because the sets A_∞ and $\{x \mid i \le f(x) < i + 1\} = f^{-1}([i, i + 1))$ are measurable. Note that any sum of finite kernels can be rewritten as a sum of sub-probability kernels.

Lemma 26. *Let $\kappa'\colon X \mapsto Y$ and $\kappa''\colon X \mapsto Y$ be kernels, and $f\colon X \to \mathbb{R}$ measurable. Then,*

$$\kappa(x)(S) = \begin{cases} \kappa'(x)(S) & \text{if } f(x) = 0 \\ \kappa''(x)(S) & \text{otherwise} \end{cases}$$

is a kernel.

Proof. Let $f_{=0}(x) := [f(x) = 0]$, $f_{\neq 0}(x) := [f(x) \neq 0]$. Then, $\kappa = f_{=0} \times \kappa' + f_{\neq 0} \times \kappa''$. Viewing $f_{=0}$ and $f_{\neq 0}$ as kernels $X \mapsto \mathbb{1}$ immediately gives the desired result.

Lemma 27. *Let (A, Σ_A) and (B, Σ_B) be measurable spaces. Let $\{A_i\}_{i\in\mathcal{I}}$ be a partition of A into measurable sets, for a countable set of indices $\mathcal{I}$. Consider a function $f\colon A \to B$. If $f_{|A_i}\colon A_i \to B$ is measurable for each $i \in \mathcal{I}$, then f is measurable.*

Lemma 28. *Let $f\colon A \to B$ be measurable. Then $\kappa\colon A \mapsto B$ with $\kappa(a) = \delta(f(a))$ is a kernel.*

The following lemma is important to show that the semantics of the while loop is a probability kernel.

Lemma 29. *Suppose $\{\kappa_n\}_{n\in\mathbb{N}}$ is a sequence of (sub-)probability kernels $A \mapsto B$. Then, if the limit $\kappa = \lim_{n\to\infty} \kappa_n$ exists, it is also a (sub-)probability kernel. Here, the limit is pointwise in the sense $\forall a \in A\colon \forall S \in \Sigma_B\colon \kappa(a, S) = \lim_{n\to\infty} \kappa_n(a)(S)$.*

Proof. For every $a \in A$, $\kappa(a, \cdot)$ is a measure, because the pointwise limit of finite measures is a measure. For every $S \in \Sigma_B$, $\kappa(\cdot, S)$ is measurable, because the pointwise limit of measurable functions $f_n\colon A \to \mathbb{R}$ (with $\mathcal{B}$ as the σ-algebra on $\mathbb{R}$) is measurable.

D   Proofs for Consequences

In this section, we provide some proofs of consequences of our semantics, explained in Sect. 5.

Lemma 9. *For function* $F()\{\texttt{while}\ 1\ \{\texttt{skip}\};\ \texttt{return}\ 0\}$,

$$\frac{1}{0} + F() \not\simeq F() + \frac{1}{0}$$

Proof. If we evaluate $\frac{1}{0}$ first, we will only have weight on $\bot$.

$$\left[\!\!\left[\frac{1}{0} + F()\right]\!\!\right]$$
$$= \left[\!\!\left[\frac{1}{0}\right]\!\!\right]\overline{\times}[\![F()]\!] \ggg \lambda(x,y).\delta(x+y)$$
$$= \delta(\bot)\overline{\times}[\![F()]\!] \ggg \lambda(x,y).\delta(x+y)$$
$$= \delta(\bot) \ggg \lambda(x,y).\delta(x+y)$$
$$= \delta(\bot)$$

If instead, we first evaluate $F()$, we only have weight on $\circlearrowleft$, by an analogous calculation.

Lemma 10. *If* $[\![e_1]\!](\sigma)(\mathcal{X}) = [\![e_2]\!](\sigma)(\mathcal{X}) = 0$ *for all* σ, *then* $e_1 \oplus e_2 \simeq e_2 \oplus e_1$, *for any commutative operator* $\oplus$.

Proof

$$[\![e_1 \oplus e_2]\!](\sigma)(S) = [\![e_1]\!]\overline{\times}[\![e_2]\!] \ggg \lambda(x,y).\delta(x \oplus y)$$
$$= \int_{z \in \overline{\mathbb{R} \times \mathbb{R}}} \overline{\lambda(x,y).\delta(x \oplus y)}(z)(S)([\![e_1]\!]\overline{\times}[\![e_2]\!])(\sigma)(dz)$$
$$= \int_{(x,y) \in \mathbb{R} \times \mathbb{R}} \delta(x \oplus y)(S)([\![e_1]\!] \times [\![e_2]\!])(\sigma)(d(x,y))$$
$$= \int_{(y,x) \in \mathbb{R} \times \mathbb{R}} \delta(y \oplus x)(S)([\![e_2]\!] \times [\![e_1]\!])(\sigma)(d(y,x))$$
$$= [\![e_2 \oplus e_1]\!](\sigma)(S)$$

Here, we crucially rely on the absence of exceptions (for the third equality) and Fubini's Theorem (for the fourth equality).

Lemma 11. $e_1 \oplus (e_2 \oplus e_3) \simeq (e_1 \oplus e_2) \oplus e_3$, *for any associative operator* $\oplus$.

Proof. The important steps of the proof are the following.

$$
\begin{aligned}
\llbracket e_1 \oplus (e_2 \oplus e_3) \rrbracket &= \llbracket e_1 \rrbracket \overline{\times} \llbracket e_2 \oplus e_3 \rrbracket \ggg \lambda(x,s).\delta(x \oplus s) \\
&= \llbracket e_1 \rrbracket \overline{\times} \Big(\llbracket e_2 \rrbracket \overline{\times} \llbracket e_3 \rrbracket \ggg \lambda(y,z).\delta(y \oplus z) \Big) \ggg \lambda(x,s).\delta(x \oplus s) \\
&= \llbracket e_1 \rrbracket \overline{\times} \Big(\llbracket e_2 \rrbracket \overline{\times} \llbracket e_3 \rrbracket \Big) \ggg \lambda(x,(y,z)).\delta(x \oplus y \oplus z) \\
&= \Big(\llbracket e_1 \rrbracket \overline{\times} \llbracket e_2 \rrbracket \Big) \overline{\times} \llbracket e_3 \rrbracket \ggg \lambda((x,y),z).\delta(x \oplus y \oplus z) \\
&= \llbracket (e_1 \oplus e_2) \oplus e_3 \rrbracket
\end{aligned}
$$

Here, we make crucial use of associativity for the lifted product of measures in Lemma 6.

References

1. Aumann, R.J.: Borel structures for function spaces. Ill. J. Math. **5**(4), 614–630 (1961)
2. Barthe, G., Grégoire, B., Hsu, J., Strub, P.-Y.: Coupling proofs are probabilistic product programs. In: Proceedings of the 44th ACM SIGPLAN Symposium on Principles of Programming Languages, POPL 2017, pp. 161–174. ACM, New York (2017)
3. Barthe, G., Köpf, B., Olmedo, F., Zanella Béguelin, S.: Probabilistic relational reasoning for differential privacy. In: Proceedings of the 39th Annual ACM SIGPLAN-SIGACT Symposium on Principles of Programming Languages, POPL 2012, pp. 97–110. ACM, New York (2012)
4. Borgström, J., Dal Lago, U., Gordon, A.D., Szymczak, M.: A lambda-calculus foundation for universal probabilistic programming. In: Proceedings of the 21st ACM SIGPLAN International Conference on Functional Programming, ICFP 2016, pp. 33–46. ACM, New York (2016)
5. Chaganty, A., Nori, A., Rajamani, S.: Efficiently sampling probabilistic programs via program analysis. In: Artificial Intelligence and Statistics, pp. 153–160 (2013)
6. Chauveau, D., Diebolt, J.: An automated stopping rule for mcmc convergence assessment. Comput. Stat. **3**(14), 419–442 (1999)
7. Cheng, S.: A crash course on the lebesgue integral and measure theory (2008)
8. Cho, K., Jacobs, B.: Kleisli semantics for conditioning in probabilistic programming (2017)
9. Cousot, P., Monerau, M.: Probabilistic abstract interpretation. In: Seidl, H. (ed.) ESOP 2012. LNCS, vol. 7211, pp. 169–193. Springer, Heidelberg (2012). https://doi.org/10.1007/978-3-642-28869-2_9
10. Gehr, T., Misailovic, S., Vechev, M.: PSI: exact symbolic inference for probabilistic programs. In: Chaudhuri, S., Farzan, A. (eds.) CAV 2016. LNCS, vol. 9779, pp. 62–83. Springer, Cham (2016). https://doi.org/10.1007/978-3-319-41528-4_4
11. Gelman, A., Lee, D., Guo, J.: Stan a probabilistic programming language for bayesian inference and optimization. J. Educ. Behav. Stat. **40**, 530–543 (2015)
12. Giry, M.: A categorical approach to probability theory. In: Banaschewski, B. (ed.) Categorical Aspects of Topology and Analysis. LNM, vol. 915, pp. 68–85. Springer, Heidelberg (1982). https://doi.org/10.1007/BFb0092872

13. Goodman, N.D., Mansinghka, V.K., Roy, D.M., Bonawitz, K., Tenenbaum, J.B.: Church: a language for generative models. In: UAI, pp. 220–229 (2008)

14. Goodman, N.D., Stuhlmüller, A.: The design and implementation of probabilistic programming languages (2014). http://dippl.org. Accessed 15 May 2017

15. Gordon, A.D., Henzinger, T.A., Nori, A.V., Rajamani, S.K.: Probabilistic programming. In: Proceedings of the on Future of Software Engineering (2014)

16. Heunen, C., Kammar, O., Staton, S., Yang, H.: A convenient category for higher-order probability theory. CoRR, abs/1701.02547 (2017)

17. Huang, D.E.: On programming languages for probabilistic modeling (2017). https://danehuang.github.io/papers/dissertation.pdf. Accessed 28 June 2017

18. Hur, C.-K., Nori, A.V., Rajamani, S.K., Samuel, S.: Slicing probabilistic programs. In: Proceedings of the 35th ACM SIGPLAN Conference on Programming Language Design and Implementation, PLDI 2014, pp. 133–144. ACM, New York (2014)

19. Hur, C.-K., Nori, A.V., Rajamani, S.K., Samuel, S.: A provably correct sampler for probabilistic programs. In: LIPIcs-Leibniz International Proceedings in Informatics, vol. 45. Schloss Dagstuhl-Leibniz-Zentrum fuer Informatik (2015)

20. Kaminski, B.L., Katoen, J.-P.: On the hardness of almost–sure termination. In: Italiano, G.F., Pighizzini, G., Sannella, D.T. (eds.) MFCS 2015. LNCS, vol. 9234, pp. 307–318. Springer, Heidelberg (2015). https://doi.org/10.1007/978-3-662-48057-1_24

21. Kaminski, B.L., Katoen, J.-P., Matheja, C., Olmedo, F.: Weakest precondition reasoning for expected run–times of probabilistic programs. In: Thiemann, P. (ed.) ESOP 2016. LNCS, vol. 9632, pp. 364–389. Springer, Heidelberg (2016). https://doi.org/10.1007/978-3-662-49498-1_15

22. Katoen, J.-P., Gretz, F., Jansen, N., Kaminski, B.L., Olmedo, F.: Understanding probabilistic programs. In: Meyer, R., Platzer, A., Wehrheim, H. (eds.) Correct System Design. LNCS, vol. 9360, pp. 15–32. Springer, Cham (2015). https://doi.org/10.1007/978-3-319-23506-6_4

23. Kozen, D.: Semantics of probabilistic programs. In: Proceedings of the 20th Annual Symposium on Foundations of Computer Science, SFCS 1979, pp. 101–114. IEEE Computer Society, Washington, DC (1979)

24. Kozen, D.: A probabilistic pdl. In: Proceedings of the Fifteenth Annual ACM Symposium on Theory of Computing, STOC 1983, pp. 291–297. ACM, New York (1983)

25. Mansinghka, V., Selsam, D., Perov, Y.: Venture: a higher-order probabilistic programming platform with programmable inference. ArXiv e-prints, March 2014

26. Minka, T., Winn, J., Guiver, J., Webster, S., Zaykov, Y., Yangel, B., Spengler, A., Bronskill, J.: Infer.NET 2.5. Microsoft Research Cambridge (2013). http://research.microsoft.com/infernet

27. Narayanan, P., Carette, J., Romano, W., Shan, C., Zinkov, R.: Probabilistic inference by program transformation in Hakaru (system description). In: Kiselyov, O., King, A. (eds.) FLOPS 2016. LNCS, vol. 9613, pp. 62–79. Springer, Cham (2016). https://doi.org/10.1007/978-3-319-29604-3_5

28. Olmedo, F., Gretz, F., Jansen, N., Kaminski, B.L., Katoen, J.-P., McIver, A.: Conditioning in probabilistic programming. ACM Trans. Program. Lang. Syst. (2018, to appear)

29. Paige, B., Wood, F.: A compilation target for probabilistic programming languages. In: International Conference on Machine Learning, pp. 1935–1943 (2014)

30. Pollard, D.: A User's Guide to Measure Theoretic Probability, vol. 8. Cambridge University Press, Cambridge (2002)

31. Rudin, W.: Real and Complex Analysis. Tata McGraw-Hill Education, London (1987)
32. Sampson, A., Panchekha, P., Mytkowicz, T., McKinley, K.S., Grossman, D., Ceze, L.: Expressing and verifying probabilistic assertions. ACM SIGPLAN Not. **49**(6), 112–122 (2014)
33. Smolka, S., Kumar, P., Foster, N., Kozen, D., Silva, A.: Cantor meets scott: Semantic foundations for probabilistic networks. In: Proceedings of the 44th ACM SIGPLAN Symposium on Principles of Programming Languages, POPL 2017, pp. 557–571. ACM, New York (2017)
34. Staton, S.: Commutative semantics for probabilistic programming. In: Yang, H. (ed.) ESOP 2017. LNCS, vol. 10201, pp. 855–879. Springer, Heidelberg (2017). https://doi.org/10.1007/978-3-662-54434-1_32
35. Staton, S., Yang, H., Wood, F., Heunen, C., Kammar, O.: Semantics for probabilistic programming: higher-order functions, continuous distributions, and soft constraints. In: Proceedings of the 31st Annual ACM/IEEE Symposium on Logic in Computer Science, LICS 2016, pp. 525–534. ACM, New York (2016)
36. Wood, F., van de Meent, J., Mansinghka, V.: A new approach to probabilistic programming inference. CoRR, abs/1507.00996 (2015)

How long, O Bayesian network, will I sample thee?
A program analysis perspective on expected sampling times

Kevin Batz[✉], Benjamin Lucien Kaminski[✉], Joost-Pieter Katoen[✉], and Christoph Matheja[✉]

RWTH Aachen University, Aachen, Germany
kevin.batz@rwth-aachen.de,
{benjamin.kaminski,katoen,matheja}@cs.rwth-aachen.de

Abstract. Bayesian networks (BNs) are probabilistic graphical models for describing complex joint probability distributions. The main problem for BNs is inference: Determine the probability of an event given observed evidence. Since exact inference is often infeasible for large BNs, popular approximate inference methods rely on sampling.

We study the problem of determining the expected time to obtain a single valid sample from a BN. To this end, we translate the BN together with observations into a probabilistic program. We provide proof rules that yield the exact expected runtime of this program in a fully automated fashion. We implemented our approach and successfully analyzed various real–world BNs taken from the Bayesian network repository.

Keywords: Probabilistic programs · Expected runtimes
Weakest preconditions · Program verification

1 Introduction

Bayesian networks (BNs) are *probabilistic graphical models* representing joint probability distributions of sets of random variables with conditional dependencies. Graphical models are a popular and appealing modeling formalism, as they allow to succinctly represent complex distributions in a human–readable way. BNs have been intensively studied at least since 1985 [43] and have a wide range of applications including machine learning [24], speech recognition [50], sports betting [11], gene regulatory networks [18], diagnosis of diseases [27], and finance [39].

Probabilistic programs are programs with the key ability to draw values at random. Seminal papers by Kozen from the 1980s consider formal semantics [32] as well as initial work on verification [33,47]. McIver and Morgan [35] build on this work to further weakest–precondition style verification for imperative probabilistic programs.

A. Ahmed (Ed.): ESOP 2018, LNCS 10801, pp. 186–213, 2018.
https://doi.org/10.1007/978-3-319-89884-1_7

The interest in probabilistic programs has been rapidly growing in recent years [20,23]. Part of the reason for this déjà vu is their use for representing probabilistic graphical models [31] such as BNs. The full potential of modern probabilistic programming languages like Anglican [48], Church [21], Figaro [44], R2 [40], or Tabular [22] is that they enable rapid prototyping and obviate the need to manually provide inference methods tailored to an individual model.

Probabilistic inference is the problem of determining the probability of an event given observed evidence. It is a major problem for both BNs and probabilistic programs, and has been subject to intense investigations by both theoreticians and practitioners for more than three decades; see [31] for a survey. In particular, it has been shown that for probabilistic programs exact inference is highly unde-cidable [28], while for BNs both *exact inference* as well as *approximate inference* to an arbitrary precision are NP–hard [12,13]. In light of these complexity-theoretical hurdles, a popular way to analyze probabilistic graphical models as well as probabilistic programs is to gather a large number of independent and identically distributed (i.i.d. for short) samples and then do statistical reasoning on these samples. In fact, all of the aforementioned probabilistic programming languages support sampling based inference methods.

Rejection sampling is a fundamental approach to obtain valid samples from BNs with observed evidence. In a nutshell, this method first samples from the joint (unconditional) distribution of the BN. If the sample complies with all evidence, it is valid and accepted; otherwise it is rejected and one has to resample.

Apart from rejection sampling, there are more sophisticated sampling techniques, which mainly fall in two categories: Markov Chain Monte Carlo (MCMC) and importance sampling. But while MCMC requires heavy hand–tuning and suffers from slow convergence rates on real–world instances [31, Chapter 12.3], virtually all variants of importance sampling rely again on rejection sampling [31,49].

A major problem with rejection sampling is that for poorly conditioned data, this approach might have to reject and resample very often in order to obtain just a single accepting sample. Even worse, being poorly conditioned need not be immediately evident for a given BN, let alone a probabilistic program. In fact, Gordon et al. [23, p. 177] point out that

> "the main challenge in this setting [i.e. sampling based approaches] is that many samples that are generated during execution are ultimately rejected for not satisfying the observations."

If too many samples are rejected, the expected sampling time grows so large that sampling becomes infeasible. The expected sampling time of a BN is therefore a key figure for deciding whether sampling based inference is the method of choice.

How Long, O Bayesian Network, will I Sample Thee? More precisely, we use techniques from program verification to give an answer to the following question:

> Given a Bayesian network with observed evidence, how long does it take in expectation to obtain a *single* sample that satisfies the observations?

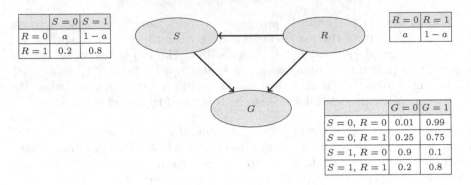

Fig. 1. A simple Bayesian network.

As an example, consider the BN in Fig. 1 which consists of just three nodes (random variables) that can each assume values 0 or 1. Each node X comes with a conditional probability table determining the probability of X assuming some value given the values of all nodes Y that X depends on (i.e. X has an incoming edge from Y), see [3, Appendix A.1] for detailed calculations. For instance, the probability that G assumes value 0, given that S and R are both assume 1, is 0.2. Note that this BN is paramterized by $a \in [0, 1]$.

Now, assume that our observed evidence is the event $G = 0$ and we apply rejection sampling to obtain *one* accepting sample from this BN. Then our approach will yield that a rejection sampling algorithm will, on average, require

$$\frac{200a^2 - 40a - 460}{89a^2 - 69a - 21}$$

guard evaluations, random assignments, etc. until it obtains a single sample that complies with the observation $G = 0$ (the underlying runtime model is discussed in detail in Sect. 3.3). By examination of this function, we see that for large ranges of values of a the BN is rather well–behaved: For $a \in [0.08,\ 0.78]$ the expected sampling time stays below 18. Above $a = 0.95$ the expected sampling time starts to grow rapidly up to 300.

While 300 is still moderate, we will see later that expected sampling times of real–world BNs can be much larger. For some BNs, the expected sampling time even exceeded 10^{18}, rendering sampling based methods infeasible. In this case, exact inference (despite NP–hardness) was a viable alternative (see Sect. 6).

Our Approach. We apply weakest precondition style reasoning a lá McIver and Morgan [35] and Kaminski et al. [30] to analyze both expected outcomes and *expected runtimes* (ERT) of a *syntactic fragment of* pGCL, which we call the *Bayesian Network Language* (BNL). Note that since BNL is a syntactic fragment of pGCL, every BNL program is a pGCL program but *not vice versa*. The main restriction of BNL is that (in contrast to pGCL) loops are of a special form that prohibits undesired data flow across multiple loop iterations. While this restriction renders BNL incapable of, for instance, counting the number of loop iterations[1], BNL is expressive enough to encode Bayesian networks with observed evidence.

For BNL, we develop dedicated proof rules to determine *exact* expected values and the *exact* ERT of any BNL program, including loops, without any user–supplied data, such as invariants [30,35], ranking or metering functions [19], (super)martingales [8–10], etc.

As a central notion behind these rules, we introduce *f–i.i.d.–ness* of probabilistic loops, a concept closely related to stochastic independence, that allows us to *rule out undesired parts of the data flow across loop iterations*. Furthermore, we show how every BN with observations is translated into a BNLprogram, such that

(a) executing the BNL program corresponds to sampling from the *conditional* joint distribution given by the BN and observed data, and
(b) the ERT of the BNL program corresponds to the expected time until a sample that satisfies the observations is obtained from the BN.

As a consequence, exact expected sampling times of BNs can be inferred by means of weakest precondition reasoning in a fully automated fashion. This can be seen as a first step towards formally evaluating the quality of a plethora of different sampling methods (cf. [31,49]) on source code level.

Contributions. To summarize, our main contributions are as follows:

- We develop easy–to–apply proof rules to reason about expected outcomes and expected runtimes of probabilistic programs with f–i.i.d. loops.
- We study a syntactic fragment of probabilistic programs, the Bayesian network language (BNL), and show that our proof rules are applicable to every BNL program; expected runtimes of BNL programs can thus be inferred.
- We give a formal translation from Bayesian networks with observations to BNL programs; expected sampling times of BNs can thus be inferred.
- We implemented a prototype tool that automatically analyzes the expected sampling time of BNs with observations. An experimental evaluation on real–world BNs demonstrates that very large expected sampling times (in the magnitude of millions of years) can be inferred within less than a second; This provides practitioners the means to decide whether sampling based methods are appropriate for their models.

Outline. We discuss related work in Sect. 2. Syntax and semantics of the probabilistic programming language pGCL are presented in Sect. 3. Our proof rules are introduced in Sect. 4 and applied to BNs in Sect. 5. Section 6 reports on experimental results and Sect. 7 concludes.

---

[1] An example of a program that is *not* expressible in BNL is given in Example 1.

2 Related Work

While various techniques for formal reasoning about runtimes and expected outcomes of probabilistic programs have been developed, e.g. [6,7,17,25,38], none of them explicitly apply formal methods to reason about Bayesian networks on source code level. In the following, we focus on approaches close to our work.

Weakest Preexpectation Calculus. Our approach builds upon the expected runtime calculus [30], which is itself based on work by Kozen [32,33] and McIver and Morgan [35]. In contrast to [30], we develop specialized proof rules for a clearly specified program fragment *without* requiring user–supplied invariants. Since finding invariants often requires heavy calculations, our proof rules contribute towards simplifying and automating verification of probabilistic programs.

Ranking Supermartingales. Reasoning about almost–sure termination is often based on ranking (super)martingales (cf. [8,10]). In particular, Chatterjee et al. [9] consider the class of affine probabilistic programs for which linear ranking supermartingales exist (LRAPP); thus proving (positive[2]) almost–sure termination for all programs within this class. They also present a doubly–exponential algorithm to approximate ERTs of LRAPP programs. While all BNL programs lie within LRAPP, our proof rules yield *exact* ERTs as *expectations* (thus allowing for compositional proofs), in contrast to a single number for a fixed initial state.

Bayesian Networks and Probabilistic Programs. Bayesian networks are a—if not the most—popular probabilistic graphical model (cf. [4,31] for details) for reasoning about conditional probabilities. They are closely tied to (a fragment of) probabilistic programs. For example, INFER.NET [36] performs inference by compiling a probabilistic program into a Bayesian network. While correspondences between probabilistic graphical models, such as BNs, have been considered in the literature [21,23,37], we are not aware of a formal soudness proof for a translation from classical BNs into probabilistic programs including conditioning.

Conversely, some probabilistic programming languages such as CHURCH [21], STAN [26], and R2 [40] directly perform inference on the program level using sampling techniques similar to those developed for Bayesian networks. Our approach is a step towards understanding sampling based approaches formally: We obtain the exact expected runtime required to generate a sample that satisfies all observations. This may ultimately be used to evaluate the quality of a plethora of proposed sampling methods for Bayesian inference (cf. [31,49]).

3 Probabilistic Programs

We briefly present the probabilistic programming language that is used throughout this paper. Since our approach is embedded into weakest-precondition style approaches, we also recap calculi for reasoning about both expected outcomes and expected runtimes of probabilistic programs.

---

[2] Positive almost–sure termination means termination in finite expected time [5].

3.1 The Probabilistic Guarded Command Language

We enhance Dijkstra's Guarded Command Language [14,15] by a probabilistic construct, namely a random assignment. We thereby obtain a *probabilistic Guarded Command Language* (for a closely related language, see [35]).

Let Vars be a finite set of *program variables*. Moreover, let $\mathbb{Q}$ be the set of rational numbers, and let $\mathcal{D}(\mathbb{Q})$ be the set of discrete probability distributions over $\mathbb{Q}$. The set of *program states* is given by $\Sigma = \{\, \sigma \mid \sigma \colon \text{Vars} \to \mathbb{Q} \,\}$.

A *distribution expression* μ is a function of type $\mu \colon \Sigma \to \mathcal{D}(\mathbb{Q})$ that takes a program state and maps it to a probability distribution on values from $\mathbb{Q}$. We denote by μ_σ the distribution obtained from applying σ to μ.

The probabilistic guarded command language (pGCL) is given by the grammar

$$
\begin{array}{lll}
C & \longrightarrow & \texttt{skip} & \text{(effectless program)} \\
& \mid & \texttt{diverge} & \text{(endless loop)} \\
& \mid & x \mathrel{:\approx} \mu & \text{(random assignment)} \\
& \mid & C;\, C & \text{(sequential composition)} \\
& \mid & \texttt{if}\,(\varphi)\,\{C\}\,\texttt{else}\,\{C\} & \text{(conditional choice)} \\
& \mid & \texttt{while}\,(\varphi)\,\{C\} & \text{(while loop)} \\
& \mid & \texttt{repeat}\,\{C\}\,\texttt{until}\,(\varphi)\ , & \text{(repeat–until loop)}
\end{array}
$$

where $x \in \text{Vars}$ is a program variable, μ is a distribution expression, and φ is a Boolean expression guarding a choice or a loop. A pGCL program that contains neither `diverge`, nor `while`, nor `repeat` − `until` loops is called loop–free.

For $\sigma \in \Sigma$ and an arithmetical expression E over Vars, we denote by $\sigma(E)$ the evaluation of E in σ, i.e. the value that is obtained by evaluating E after replacing any occurrence of any program variable x in E by the value $\sigma(x)$. Analogously, we denote by $\sigma(\varphi)$ the evaluation of a guard φ in state σ to either true or false. Furthermore, for a value $v \in \mathbb{Q}$ we write $\sigma\,[x \mapsto v]$ to indicate that we set program variable x to value v in program state σ, i.e.[3]

$$
\sigma\,[x \mapsto v] \;=\; \lambda y \bullet \begin{cases} v, & \text{if } y = x \\ \sigma(y), & \text{if } y \neq x\ . \end{cases}
$$

We use the Iverson bracket notation to associate with each guard its according indicator function. Formally, the Iverson bracket $[\varphi]$ of φ is thus defined as the function $[\varphi] = \lambda\sigma \bullet \sigma(\varphi)$.

Let us briefly go over the pGCL constructs and their effects: `skip` does not alter the current program state. The program `diverge` is an infinite busy loop, thus takes infinite time to execute. It returns no final state whatsoever.

The random assignment $x \mathrel{:\approx} \mu$ is (a) the only construct that can actually alter the program state and (b) the only construct that may introduce random

---

[3] We use λ–expressions to construct functions: Function $\lambda X \bullet \epsilon$ applied to an argument α evaluates to ϵ in which every occurrence of X is replaced by α.

behavior into the computation. It takes the current program state σ, then *samples* a value v from probability distribution μ_σ, and then assigns v to program variable x. An example of a random assignment is

$$x :\approx 1/2 \cdot \langle 5 \rangle + 1/6 \cdot \langle y + 1 \rangle + 1/3 \cdot \langle y - 1 \rangle .$$

If the current program state is σ, then the program state is altered to either $\sigma [x \mapsto 5]$ with probability $1/2$, or to $\sigma [x \mapsto \sigma(y) + 1]$ with probability $1/6$, or to $\sigma [x \mapsto \sigma(y) - 1]$ with probability $1/3$. The remainder of the pGCL constructs are standard programming language constructs.

In general, a pGCL program C is executed on an input state and yields a *probability distribution* over final states due to possibly occurring random assignments inside of C. We denote that resulting distribution by $[\![C]\!]_\sigma$. Strictly speaking, programs can yield *subdistributions*, i.e. probability distributions whose total mass may be below 1. The "missing" probability mass represents the probability of nontermination. Let us conclude our presentation of pGCL with an example:

Example 1 (Geometric Loop). Consider the program C_{geo} given by

$$x :\approx 0; \quad c :\approx 1/2 \cdot \langle 0 \rangle + 1/2 \cdot \langle 1 \rangle;$$
$$\text{while} (c = 1) \{ x :\approx x + 1; \ c :\approx 1/2 \cdot \langle 0 \rangle + 1/2 \cdot \langle 1 \rangle \}$$

This program basically keeps flipping coins until it flips, say, heads ($c = 0$). In x it counts the number of unsuccessful trials.[4] In effect, it almost surely sets c to 0 and moreover it establishes a geometric distribution on x. The resulting distribution is given by

$$[\![C_{geo}]\!]_\sigma (\tau) \ = \ \sum_{n=0}^{\omega} [\tau = \sigma [c, x \mapsto 0, n]] \cdot \frac{1}{2^{n+1}} . \qquad \triangle$$

3.2   The Weakest Preexpectation Transformer

We now present the weakest preexpectation transformer wp for reasoning about expected outcomes of executing probabilistic programs in the style of McIver and Morgan [35]. Given a random variable f mapping program states to reals, it allows us to reason about the expected value of f after executing a probabilistic program on a given state.

Expectations. The random variables the wp transformer acts upon are taken from a set of so-called expectations, a term coined by McIver and Morgan [35]:

---

[4] This counting is also the reason that C_{geo} is an example of a program that is not expressible in our BNL language that we present later.

Definition 1 (Expectations). *The set of expectations $\mathbb{E}$ is defined as*

$$\mathbb{E} = \{f \mid f \colon \Sigma \to \mathbb{R}_{\geq 0}^{\infty}\} \ .$$

We will use the notation $f[x/E]$ to indicate the replacement *of every occurrence of x in f by E. Since x, however, does not actually occur in f, we more formally define $f[x/E] = \lambda\sigma \bullet f(\sigma\,[x \mapsto \sigma(E)])$.*

A complete partial order $\leq$ on $\mathbb{E}$ is obtained by point–wise lifting the canonical total order on $\mathbb{R}_{\geq 0}^{\infty}$, i.e.

$$f_1 \preceq f_2 \quad \textit{iff} \quad \forall \sigma \in \Sigma \colon \ f_1(\sigma) \leq f_2(\sigma) \ .$$

Its least element is given by $\lambda\sigma \bullet 0$ which we (by slight abuse of notation) also denote by 0. Suprema are constructed pointwise, i.e. for $S \subseteq \mathbb{E}$ the supremum $\sup S$ is given by $\sup S = \lambda\sigma \bullet \sup_{f \in S} f(\sigma)$.

We allow expectations to map only to positive reals, so that we have a complete partial order readily available, which would not be the case for expectations of type $\Sigma \to \mathbb{R} \cup \{-\infty, +\infty\}$. A wp calculus that *can* handle expectations of such type needs more technical machinery and cannot make use of this underlying natural partial order [29]. Since we want to reason about ERTs which are by nature non–negative, we will not need such complicated calculi.

Notice that we use a slightly different definition of expectations than McIver and Morgan [35], as we allow for *unbounded* expectations, whereas [35] requires that expectations are *bounded*. This however would prevent us from capturing ERTs, which are potentially unbounded.

Expectation Transformers. For reasoning about the expected value of $f \in \mathbb{E}$ after execution of C, we employ a backward–moving weakest preexpectation transformer $\mathsf{wp}[\![C]\!]\colon \mathbb{E} \to \mathbb{E}$, that maps a *postexpectation* $f \in \mathbb{E}$ to a *preexpectation* $\mathsf{wp}\,[\![C]\!]\,(f) \in \mathbb{E}$, such that $\mathsf{wp}\,[\![C]\!]\,(f)\,(\sigma)$ is the expected value of f after executing C on initial state σ. Formally, if C executed on input σ yields final distribution $[\![C]\!]_\sigma$, then the *weakest preexpectation* $\mathsf{wp}\,[\![C]\!]\,(f)$ of C with respect to postexpectation f is given by

$$\mathsf{wp}\,[\![C]\!]\,(f)\,(\sigma) = \int_\Sigma f\,d[\![C]\!]_\sigma \ , \tag{1}$$

where we denote by $\int_A h\,d\nu$ the expected value of a random variable $h\colon A \to \mathbb{R}_{\geq 0}^{\infty}$ with respect to a probability distribution $\nu\colon A \to [0, 1]$. Weakest preexpectations can be defined in a very systematic way:

Definition 2 (The wp Transformer [35]). *The weakest preexpectation transformer $\mathsf{wp}\colon \mathsf{pGCL} \to \mathbb{E} \to \mathbb{E}$ is defined by induction on all pGCL programs according to the rules in Table 1. We call $F_f(X) = [\neg\varphi] \cdot f + [\varphi] \cdot \mathsf{wp}\,[\![C]\!]\,(X)$ the wp–characteristic functional of the loop $\mathtt{while}\,(\varphi)\,\{C\}$ with respect to postexpectation f. For a given wp–characteristic function F_f, we call the sequence $\{F_f^n(0)\}_{n \in \mathbb{N}}$ the orbit of F_f.*

Table 1. Rules for the wp–transformer.

C	$\text{wp}\,[\![C]\!]\,(f)$
$\texttt{skip}$	f
$\texttt{diverge}$	0
$x :\approx \mu$	$\lambda\sigma\bullet\ \int_{\mathbb{Q}}\ (\lambda v\bullet\ f[x/v])\ d\mu_\sigma$
$\texttt{if}\,(\varphi)\,\{C_1\}\,\texttt{else}\,\{C_2\}$	$[\varphi]\cdot\text{wp}\,[\![C_1]\!]\,(f) + [\neg\varphi]\cdot\text{wp}\,[\![C_2]\!]\,(f)$
$C_1;\ C_2$	$\text{wp}\,[\![C_1]\!]\,(\text{wp}\,[\![C_2]\!]\,(f))$
$\texttt{while}\,(\varphi)\,\{C'\}$	$\text{lfp}\,X\bullet\ [\neg\varphi]\cdot f + [\varphi]\cdot\text{wp}\,[\![C']\!]\,(X)$
$\texttt{repeat}\,\{C'\}\,\texttt{until}\,(\varphi)$	$\text{wp}\,[\![C';\ \texttt{while}\,(\neg\varphi)\,\{C'\}]\!]\,(f)$

Let us briefly go over the definitions in Table 1: For $\texttt{skip}$ the program state is not altered and thus the expected value of f is just f. The program $\texttt{diverge}$ will never yield any final state. The distribution over the final states yielded by $\texttt{diverge}$ is thus the null distribution $\nu_0(\tau) = 0$, that assigns probability 0 to *every* state. Consequently, the expected value of f after execution of $\texttt{diverge}$ is given by $\int_\Sigma f\ d\nu_0 = \sum_{\tau\in\Sigma} 0\cdot f(\tau) = 0$.

The rule for the random assignment $x :\approx \mu$ is a bit more technical: Let the current program state be σ. Then for every value $v \in \mathbb{Q}$, the random assignment assigns v to x with probability $\mu_\sigma(v)$, where σ is the current program state. The value of f after assigning v to x is $f(\sigma\,[x \mapsto v]) = f[x/v](\sigma)$ and therefore the expected value of f after executing the random assignment is given by

$$\sum_{v\in\mathbb{Q}} \mu_\sigma(v)\cdot f[x/v](\sigma)\ =\ \int_{\mathbb{Q}}\ (\lambda v\bullet\ f[x/v](\sigma))\ d\mu_\sigma\ .$$

Expressed as a function of σ, the latter yields precisely the definition in Table 1.

The definition for the conditional choice $\texttt{if}\,(\varphi)\,\{C_1\}\,\texttt{else}\,\{C_2\}$ is not surprising: if the current state satisfies φ, we have to opt for the weakest preexpectation of C_1, whereas if it does not satisfy φ, we have to choose the weakest preexpectation of C_2. This yields precisely the definition in Table 1.

The definition for the sequential composition $C_1;\ C_2$ is also straightforward: We first determine $\text{wp}\,[\![C_2]\!]\,(f)$ to obtain the expected value of f after executing C_2. Then we mentally prepend the program C_2 by C_1 and therefore determine the expected value of $\text{wp}\,[\![C_2]\!]\,(f)$ after executing C_1. This gives the weakest preexpectation of $C_1;\ C_2$ with respect to postexpectation f.

The definition for the while loop makes use of a least fixed point, which is a standard construction in program semantics. Intuitively, the fixed point iteration of the wp–characteristic functional, given by $0, F_f(0), F_f^2(0), F_f^3(0), \ldots$, corresponds to the portion the expected value of f after termination of the loop, that can be collected within at most $0, 1, 2, 3, \ldots$ loop guard evaluations.

The Kleene Fixed Point Theorem [34] ensures that this iteration converges to the least fixed point, i.e.

$$\sup_{n \in \mathbb{N}} F_f^n(0) = \mathsf{lfp}\ F_f = \mathsf{wp}\,[\![\mathtt{while}\,(\varphi)\,\{C\}]\!]\,(f).$$

By inspection of the above equality, we see that the least fixed point is exactly the construct that we want for while loops, since $\sup_{n \in \mathbb{N}} F_f^n(0)$ in principle allows the loop to run for any number of iterations, which captures precisely the semantics of a while loop, where the number of loop iterations is—in contrast to e.g. for loops—not determined upfront.

Finally, since $\mathtt{repeat}\,\{C\}\,\mathtt{until}\,(\varphi)$ is syntactic sugar for C; $\mathtt{while}\,(\varphi)\,\{C\}$, we simply define the weakest preexpectation of the former as the weakest preexpectation of the latter. Let us conclude our study of the effects of the wp transformer by means of an example:

Example 2. Consider the following program C:

$$c :\approx {}^1\!/\!_3 \cdot \langle 0 \rangle + {}^2\!/\!_3 \cdot \langle 1 \rangle;$$
$$\mathtt{if}\,(c = 0)\,\{x :\approx {}^1\!/\!_2 \cdot \langle 5 \rangle + {}^1\!/\!_6 \cdot \langle y + 1 \rangle + {}^1\!/\!_3 \cdot \langle y - 1 \rangle\}\,\mathtt{else}\,\{\mathtt{skip}\}$$

Say we wish to reason about the expected value of $x + c$ after execution of the above program. We can do so by calculating $\mathsf{wp}\,[\![C]\!]\,(x + c)$ using the rules in Table 1. This calculation in the end yields $\mathsf{wp}\,[\![C]\!]\,(x + c) = {}^{3y+26}\!/\!_{18}$ The expected valuation of the expression $x + c$ after executing C is thus ${}^{3y+26}\!/\!_{18}$. Note that $x + c$ can be thought of as an expression that is evaluated in the final states after execution, whereas ${}^{3y+26}\!/\!_{18}$ must be evaluated in the initial state before execution of C. $\triangle$

Healthiness Conditions of wp. The wp transformer enjoys some useful properties, sometimes called *healthiness conditions* [35]. Two of these healthiness conditions that we will heavily make use of are given below:

Theorem 1 (Healthiness Conditions for the wp Transformer [35]). *For all $C \in \mathsf{pGCL}$, $f_1, f_2 \in \mathbb{E}$, and $a \in \mathbb{R}_{\geq 0}$, the following holds:*

1. $\mathsf{wp}\,[\![C]\!]\,(a \cdot f_1 + f_2) = a \cdot \mathsf{wp}\,[\![C]\!]\,(f_1) + \mathsf{wp}\,[\![C]\!]\,(f_2)$ *(linearity)*

2. $\mathsf{wp}\,[\![C]\!]\,(0) = 0$ *(strictness).*

3.3   The Expected Runtime Transformer

While for deterministic programs we can speak of *the* runtime of a program on a given input, the situation is different for probabilistic programs: For those we instead have to speak of the *expected runtime* (ERT). Notice that the ERT can be finite (even constant) while the program may still admit infinite executions. An example of this is the geometric loop in Example 1.

A wp–like transformer designed specifically for reasoning about ERTs is the ert transformer [30]. Like wp, it is of type $\mathsf{ert}[\![C]\!]: \mathbb{E} \to \mathbb{E}$ and it can be shown that

Table 2. Rules for the ert–transformer.

C	ert $[\![C]\!]\,(f)$
skip	$1 + f$
diverge	∞
$x :\approx \mu$	$1 + \lambda\sigma \bullet\ \int_{\mathbb{Q}} \left(\lambda v \bullet\ f[x/v]\right)\, d\mu_\sigma$
if $(\varphi)\,\{C_1\}$ else $\{C_2\}$	$1 + [\varphi] \cdot \text{ert}\,[\![C_1]\!]\,(f) + [\neg\varphi] \cdot \text{ert}\,[\![C_2]\!]\,(f)$
$C_1;\ C_2$	$\text{ert}\,[\![C_1]\!]\,\big((\text{ert}\,[\![C_2]\!]\,(f))\big)$
while $(\varphi)\,\{C'\}$	$\text{lfp } X \bullet\ 1 + [\neg\varphi] \cdot f + [\varphi] \cdot \text{ert}\,[\![C']\!]\,(X)$
repeat $\{C'\}$ until (φ)	$\text{ert}\,[\![C';\ \text{while}\,(\neg\varphi)\,\{C'\}]\!]\,(f)$

ert $[\![C]\!]\,(0)\,(\sigma)$ is precisely the *expected runtime of executing C on input σ*. More generally, if $f \colon \Sigma \to \mathbb{R}_{\geq 0}^{\infty}$ measures the time that is needed after executing C (thus f is evaluated in the final states after termination of C), then ert $[\![C]\!]\,(f)\,(\sigma)$ is the expected time that is needed to run C on input σ and then let time f pass. For a more in–depth treatment of the ert transformer, see [30, Sect. 3]. The transformer is defined as follows:

Definition 3 (The ert Transformer [30]). *The expected runtime transformer* ert: pGCL $\to \mathbb{E} \to \mathbb{E}$ *is defined by induction on all* pGCL *programs according to the rules given in Table 2. We call* $F_f(X) = 1 + [\neg\varphi] \cdot f + [\varphi] \cdot \text{wp}\,[\![C]\!]\,(X)$ *the ert–characteristic functional of the loop* while $(\varphi)\,\{C\}$ *with respect to postexpectation* f. *As with* wp, *for a given ert–characteristic function* F_f, *we call the sequence* $\{F_f^n(0)\}_{n\in\mathbb{N}}$ *the orbit of* F_f. *Notice that*

$$\text{ert}\,[\![\text{while}\,(\varphi)\,\{C\}]\!]\,(f) \;=\; \text{lfp } F_f \;=\; \sup\ \{F_f^n(0)\}_{n\in\mathbb{N}}.$$

The rules for ert are very similar to the rules for wp. The runtime model we assume is that skip statements, random assignments, and guard evaluations for both conditional choice and while loops cost one unit of time. This runtime model can easily be adopted to count only the number of loop iterations or only the number of random assignments, etc. We conclude with a strong connection between the wp and the ert transformer, that is crucial in our proofs:

Theorem 2 (Decomposition of ert [41]). *For any* $C \in$ pGCL *and* $f \in \mathbb{E}$,

$$\text{ert}\,[\![C]\!]\,(f) \;=\; \text{ert}\,[\![C]\!]\,(0) + \text{wp}\,[\![C]\!]\,(f).$$

4   Expected Runtimes of i.i.d Loops

We derive a proof rule that allows to determine *exact ERTs of independent and identically distributed loops* (or *i.i.d. loops* for short). Intuitively, a loop

$$\texttt{while}\ \left((x-5)^2 + (y-5)^2 \geq 25\right)\ \{$$
$$x :\approx \texttt{Unif}[0 \dots 10];$$
$$y :\approx \texttt{Unif}[0 \dots 10]$$
$$\}$$

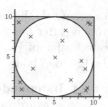

Fig. 2. An i.i.d. loop sampling a point within a circle uniformly at random using rejection sampling. The picture on the right–hand side visualizes the procedure: In each iteration a point (×) is sampled. If we obtain a point within the white area inside the square, we terminate. Otherwise, i.e. if we obtain a point within the gray area outside the circle, we resample.

is i.i.d. if the distributions of states that are reached at the end of different loop iterations are equal. This is the case whenever there is no data flow across different iterations. In the non–probabilistic case, such loops either terminate after exactly one iteration or never. This is different for probabilistic programs.

As a running example, consider the program C_{circle} in Fig. 2. C_{circle} samples a point within a circle with center $(5, 5)$ and radius $r = 5$ uniformly at random using rejection sampling. In each iteration, it samples a point $(x, y) \in [0, \dots, 10]^2$ within the square (with some fixed precision). The loop ensures that we resample if a sample is not located within the circle. Our proof rule will allow us to systematically determine the ERT of this loop, i.e. the average amount of time required until a single point within the circle is sampled.

Towards obtaining such a proof rule, we first present a syntactical notion of the i.i.d. property. It relies on expectations that are not affected by a pGCL program:

Definition 4. *Let $C \in$ pGCL and $f \in \mathbb{E}$. Moreover, let $\mathsf{Mod}(C)$ denote the set of all variables that occur on the left–hand side of an assignment in C, and let $\mathsf{Vars}(f)$ be the set of all variables that "occur in f", i.e. formally*

$$x \in \mathsf{Vars}(f) \qquad \textit{iff} \qquad \exists \sigma\, \exists v, v'\colon \quad f(\sigma\,[x \mapsto v]) \neq f(\sigma\,[x \mapsto v']).$$

Then f is unaffected *by C, denoted $f \not\Join C$, iff $\mathsf{Vars}(f) \cap \mathsf{Mod}(C) = \emptyset$.*

We are interested in expectations that are unaffected by pGCL programs because of a simple, yet useful observation: If $g \not\Join C$, then g *can be treated like a constant* w.r.t. the transformer wp (i.e. like the a in Theorem 1 (1)). For our running example C_{circle} (see Fig. 2), the expectation $f = \mathsf{wp}\,[\![C_{body}]\!]\,([x + y \leq 10])$ is unaffected by the loop body C_{body} of C_{circle}. Consequently, we have $\mathsf{wp}\,[\![C_{body}]\!]\,(f) = f \cdot \mathsf{wp}\,[\![C_{body}]\!]\,(1) = f$. In general, we obtain the following property:

Lemma 1 (Scaling by Unaffected Expectations). *Let $C \in$ pGCL and $f, g \in \mathbb{E}$. Then $g \not\Join C$ implies $\mathsf{wp}\,[\![C]\!]\,(g \cdot f) = g \cdot \mathsf{wp}\,[\![C]\!]\,(f)$.*

Proof. By induction on the structure of C. See [3, Appendix A.2]. $\qquad\qquad\square$

We develop a proof rule that only requires that both the probability of the guard evaluating to true after one iteration of the loop body (i.e. $\mathsf{wp}\,[\![C]\!]\,([\varphi])$) as well as the expected value of $[\neg\varphi]\cdot f$ after one iteration (i.e. $\mathsf{wp}\,[\![C]\!]\,([\neg\varphi]\cdot f)$) are unaffected by the loop body. We thus define the following:

Definition 5 (f-Independent and Identically Distributed Loops). *Let $C \in \mathsf{pGCL}$, φ be a guard, and $f \in \mathbb{E}$. Then we call the loop $\mathtt{while}\,(\varphi)\,\{C\}$ f-independent and identically distributed (or f-i.i.d. for short), if both*

$$\mathsf{wp}\,[\![C]\!]\,([\varphi])\ \text{\reflectbox{$\mathbb{A}$}}\ C \qquad and \qquad \mathsf{wp}\,[\![C]\!]\,([\neg\varphi]\cdot f)\ \text{\reflectbox{$\mathbb{A}$}}\ C.$$

Example 3. Our example program C_{circle} (see Fig. 2) is f-i.i.d. for all $f \in \mathbb{E}$. This is due to the fact that

$$\mathsf{wp}\,[\![C_{body}]\!]\,\left([(x-5)^2 + (y-5)^2 \geq 25]\right) \ =\ \frac{48}{121}\ \text{\reflectbox{$\mathbb{A}$}}\ C_{body} \qquad \text{(by Table 1)}$$

and (again for some fixed precision $p \in \mathbb{N}\setminus\{0\}$)

$$\mathsf{wp}\,[\![C_{body}]\!]\,\left([(x-5)^2 + (y-5)^2 > 25]\cdot f\right)$$

$$= \frac{1}{121}\cdot\sum_{i=0}^{10p}\sum_{j=0}^{10p}\left[(i/p-5)^2 + (j/p-5)^2 > 25\right]\cdot f[x/(i/p), y/(j/p)]\ \text{\reflectbox{$\mathbb{A}$}}\ C_{body}. \quad \triangle$$

Our main technical Lemma is that we can express the orbit of the wp–characteristic function as a partial geometric series:

Lemma 2 (Orbits of f-i.i.d. Loops). *Let $C \in \mathsf{pGCL}$, φ be a guard, $f \in \mathbb{E}$ such that the loop $\mathtt{while}\,(\varphi)\,\{C\}$ is f-i.i.d, and let F_f be the corresponding wp–characteristic function. Then for all $n \in \mathbb{N}\setminus\{0\}$, it holds that*

$$F_f^n(0)\ =\ [\varphi]\cdot\mathsf{wp}\,[\![C]\!]\,([\neg\varphi]\cdot f)\cdot\sum_{i=0}^{n-2}\left(\mathsf{wp}\,[\![C]\!]\,([\varphi])^i\right)\ +\ [\neg\varphi]\cdot f.$$

Proof. By use of Lemma 1, see [3, Appendix A.3]. ∎

Using this precise description of the wp orbits, we now establish proof rules for f-i.i.d. loops, first for wp and later for ert.

Theorem 3 (Weakest Preexpectations of f-i.i.d. Loops). *Let $C \in \mathsf{pGCL}$, φ be a guard, and $f \in \mathbb{E}$. If the loop $\mathtt{while}\,(\varphi)\,\{C\}$ is f-i.i.d., then*

$$\mathsf{wp}\,[\![\mathtt{while}\,(\varphi)\,\{C\}]\!]\,(f)\ =\ [\varphi]\cdot\frac{\mathsf{wp}\,[\![C]\!]\,([\neg\varphi]\cdot f)}{1 - \mathsf{wp}\,[\![C]\!]\,([\varphi])} + [\neg\varphi]\cdot f\,,$$

where we define $\frac{0}{0} := 0$.

Proof. We have

$$\text{wp}\,[\![\text{while}\,(\varphi)\,\{C\}]\!]\,(f)$$

$$= \sup_{n\in\mathbb{N}}\,F_f^n(0) \qquad\qquad\qquad\qquad\qquad\qquad\text{(by Definition 2)}$$

$$= \sup_{n\in\mathbb{N}}\,[\varphi]\cdot\text{wp}\,[\![C]\!]\,([\neg\varphi]\cdot f)\cdot\sum_{i=0}^{n-2}\left(\text{wp}\,[\![C]\!]\,([\varphi])^i\right)+[\neg\varphi]\cdot f \quad\text{(by Lemma 2)}$$

$$= [\varphi]\cdot\text{wp}\,[\![C]\!]\,([\neg\varphi]\cdot f)\cdot\sum_{i=0}^{\omega}\left(\text{wp}\,[\![C]\!]\,([\varphi])^i\right)+[\neg\varphi]\cdot f. \qquad\qquad(\dagger)$$

The preexpectation ($\dagger$) is to be evaluated in some state σ for which we have two cases: The first case is when $\text{wp}\,[\![C]\!]\,([\varphi])\,(\sigma) < 1$. Using the closed form of the geometric series, i.e. $\sum_{i=0}^{\omega}q = \frac{1}{1-q}$ if $|q| < 1$, we get

$$[\varphi]\,(\sigma)\cdot\text{wp}\,[\![C]\!]\,([\neg\varphi]\cdot f)\,(\sigma)\cdot\sum_{i=0}^{\omega}\left(\text{wp}\,[\![C]\!]\,([\varphi])\,(\sigma)^i\right)+[\neg\varphi]\,(\sigma)\cdot f(\sigma)$$

$$\text{($\dagger$ instantiated in σ)}$$

$$= [\varphi]\,(\sigma)\cdot\frac{\text{wp}\,[\![C]\!]\,([\neg\varphi]\cdot f)\,(\sigma)}{1-\text{wp}\,[\![C]\!]\,([\varphi])\,(\sigma)}+[\neg\varphi]\,(\sigma)\cdot f(\sigma).$$

$$\text{(closed form of geometric series)}$$

The second case is when $\text{wp}\,[\![C]\!]\,([\varphi])\,(\sigma) = 1$. This case is technically slightly more involved. The full proof can be found in [3, Appendix A.4]. $\qquad\qquad\square$

We now derive a similar proof rule for the ERT of an f–i.i.d. loop $\text{while}\,(\varphi)\,\{C\}$.

Theorem 4 (Proof Rule for ERTs of f–i.i.d. Loops). *Let $C \in$ pGCL, φ be a guard, and $f \in \mathbb{E}$ such that all of the following conditions hold:*

1. $\text{while}\,(\varphi)\,\{C\}$ *is f–i.i.d.*
2. $\text{wp}\,[\![C]\!]\,(1) = 1$ *(loop body terminates almost–surely).*
3. $\text{ert}\,[\![C]\!]\,(0)\,\text{⫫}\,C$ *(every iteration runs in the same expected time).*

Then for the ERT of the loop $\text{while}\,(\varphi)\,\{C\}$ w.r.t. postruntime f it holds that

$$\text{ert}\,[\![\text{while}\,(\varphi)\,\{C\}]\!]\,(f) = 1+\frac{[\varphi]\cdot(1+\text{ert}\,[\![C]\!]\,([\neg\varphi]\cdot f))}{1-\text{wp}\,[\![C]\!]\,([\varphi])}+[\neg\varphi]\cdot f,$$

where we define $\frac{0}{0}:=0$ and $\frac{a}{0}:=\infty$, for $a\neq 0$.

Proof. We first prove

$$\text{ert}\,[\![\text{while}\,(\varphi)\,\{C\}]\!]\,(0) = 1+[\varphi]\cdot\frac{1+\text{ert}\,[\![C]\!]\,(0)}{1-\text{wp}\,[\![C]\!]\,([\varphi])}. \qquad\qquad(\ddagger)$$

To this end, we propose the following expression as the orbit of the ert–characteristic function of the loop w.r.t. 0:

$$F_0^n(0) = 1 + [\varphi] \cdot \left(\text{ert} \, [\![C]\!] \, (0) \cdot \sum_{i=0}^{n} \text{wp} \, [\![C]\!] \, ([\varphi])^i \; + \; \sum_{i=0}^{n-1} \text{wp} \, [\![C]\!] \, ([\varphi])^i \right)$$

For a verification that the above expression is indeed the correct orbit, we refer to the rigorous proof of this theorem in [3, Appendix A.5]. Now, analogously to the reasoning in the proof of Theorem 3 (i.e. using the closed form of the geometric series and case distinction on whether $\text{wp} \, [\![C]\!] \, ([\varphi]) < 1$ or $\text{wp} \, [\![C]\!] \, ([\varphi]) = 1$), we get that the supremum of this orbit is indeed the right–hand side of ($\ddagger$). To complete the proof, consider the following:

$$\text{ert} \, [\![\text{while} \, (\varphi) \, \{C\}]\!] \, (f)$$
$$= \; \text{ert} \, [\![\text{while} \, (\varphi) \, \{C\}]\!] \, (0) + \text{wp} \, [\![\text{while} \, (\varphi) \, \{C\}]\!] \, (f) \qquad \text{(by Theorem 2)}$$
$$= \; 1 + [\varphi] \cdot \frac{1 + \text{ert} \, [\![C]\!] \, (0)}{1 - \text{wp} \, [\![C]\!] \, ([\varphi])} + [\varphi] \cdot \frac{\text{wp} \, [\![C]\!] \, ([\neg\varphi] \cdot f)}{1 - \text{wp} \, [\![C]\!] \, ([\varphi])} + [\neg\varphi] \cdot f$$
$$\qquad \qquad \qquad \qquad \qquad \qquad \qquad \qquad \qquad \text{(by ($\ddagger$) and Theorem 3)}$$
$$= \; 1 + [\varphi] \cdot \frac{1 + \text{ert} \, [\![C]\!] \, ([\neg\varphi] \cdot f)}{1 - \text{wp} \, [\![C]\!] \, ([\varphi])} + [\neg\varphi] \cdot f \qquad \qquad \text{(by Theorem 2)}$$

$$\square$$

5   A Programming Language for Bayesian Networks

So far we have derived proof rules for formal reasoning about expected outcomes and expected run-times of i.i.d. loops (Theorems 3 and 4). In this section, we apply these results to develop a syntactic pGCL fragment that allows exact computations of closed forms of ERTs. In particular, no invariants, (super)martingales or fixed point computations are required.

After that, we show how BNs with observations can be translated into pGCL programs within this fragment. Consequently, we call our pGCL fragment the *Bayesian Network Language*. As a result of the above translation, we obtain a systematic and automatable approach to compute the *expected sampling time* of a BN in the presence of observations. That is, the expected time it takes to obtain a single sample that satisfies all observations.

5.1   The Bayesian Network Language

Programs in the Bayesian Network Language are organized as sequences of blocks. Every block is associated with a single variable, say x, and satisfies two constraints: First, no variable other than x is modified inside the block, i.e. occurs on the left–hand side of a random assignment. Second, every variable accessed inside of a guard has been initialized before. These restrictions ensure that there is no data flow across multiple executions of the same block. Thus, intuitively, all loops whose body is composed from blocks (as described above) are f–i.i.d. loops.

Definition 6 (The Bayesian Network Language). *Let* $\mathsf{Vars} = \{x_1, x_2, \ldots\}$ *be a finite set of program variables as in Sect. 3. The set of programs in Bayesian Network Language, denoted* BNL, *is given by the grammar*

$$C \longrightarrow Seq \mid \texttt{repeat}\,\{Seq\}\,\texttt{until}\,(\psi) \mid C;\,C$$

$$Seq \longrightarrow Seq;\,Seq \mid B_{x_1} \mid B_{x_2} \mid \ldots$$

$$B_{x_i} \longrightarrow x_i :\approx \mu \mid \texttt{if}\,(\varphi)\,\{x_i :\approx \mu\}\,\texttt{else}\,\{B_{x_i}\}$$

$$\text{(rule exists for all } x_i \in \mathsf{Vars})$$

where $x_i \in \mathsf{Vars}$ *is a program variable, all variables in* φ *have been initialized before, and* B_{x_i} *is a non–terminal parameterized with program variable* $x_i \in \mathsf{Vars}$. *That is, for all* $x_i \in \mathsf{Vars}$ *there is a non–terminal* B_{x_i}. *Moreover,* ψ *is an arbitrary guard and* μ *is a distribution expression of the form* $\mu = \sum_{j=1}^{n} p_j \cdot \langle a_j \rangle$ *with* $a_j \in \mathbb{Q}$ *for* $1 \leq j \leq n$.

Example 4. Consider the BNL program C_{dice}:

$$x_1 :\approx \texttt{Unif}[1\ldots 6];\ \texttt{repeat}\,\{x_2 :\approx \texttt{Unif}[1\ldots 6]\}\,\texttt{until}\,(x_2 \geq x_1)$$

This program first throws a fair die. After that it keeps throwing a second die until its result is at least as large as the first die.   △

For any $C \in \mathsf{BNL}$, our goal is to compute the exact ERT of C, i.e. $\mathsf{ert}\,[\![C]\!]\,(0)$. In case of loop–free programs, this amounts to a straightforward application of the ert calculus presented in Sect. 3. To deal with loops, however, we have to perform fixed point computations or require user–supplied artifacts, e.g. invariants, supermartingales, etc. For BNL programs, on the other hand, it suffices to apply the proof rules developed in Sect. 4. As a result, we directly obtain an exact closed form solution for the ERT of a loop. This is a consequence of the fact that all loops in BNL are f–i.i.d., which we establish in the following.

By definition, every loop in BNL is of the form $\texttt{repeat}\,\{B_{x_i}\}\,\texttt{until}\,(\psi)$, which is equivalent to $B_{x_i};\,\texttt{while}\,(\neg\psi)\,\{B_{x_i}\}$. Hence, we want to apply Theorem 4 to that while loop. Our first step is to discharge the theorem's premises:

Lemma 3. *Let* Seq *be a sequence of* BNL*–blocks,* $g \in \mathbb{E}$, *and* ψ *be a guard. Then:*

1. *The expected value of* g *after executing* Seq *is unaffected by* Seq. *That is,* $\mathsf{wp}\,[\![Seq]\!]\,(g) \between Seq$.
2. *The ERT of* Seq *is unaffected by* Seq, *i.e.* $\mathsf{ert}\,[\![Seq]\!]\,(0) \between Seq$.
3. *For every* $f \in \mathbb{E}$, *the loop* $\texttt{while}\,(\neg\psi)\,\{Seq\}$ *is* f–*i.i.d.*

Proof. 1. is proven by induction on the length of the sequence of blocks Seq and 2. is a consequence of 1., see [3, Appendix A.6]. 3. follows immediately from 1. by instantiating g with $[\neg\psi]$ and $[\psi] \cdot f$, respectively.   □

We are now in a position to derive a closed form for the ERT of loops in BNL.

Theorem 5. *For every loop* $\mathtt{repeat}\,\{Seq\}\,\mathtt{until}\,(\psi) \in \mathrm{BNL}$ *and every* $f \in \mathbb{E}$,

$$\mathsf{ert}\,[\![\mathtt{repeat}\,\{Seq\}\,\mathtt{until}\,(\psi)]\!]\,(f) \;=\; \frac{1 + \mathsf{ert}\,[\![Seq]\!]\,([\psi]\cdot f)}{\mathsf{wp}\,[\![Seq]\!]\,([\psi])}.$$

Proof. Let $f \in \mathbb{E}$. Moreover, recall that $\mathtt{repeat}\,\{Seq\}\,\mathtt{until}\,(\psi)$ is equivalent to the program $Seq;\,\mathtt{while}\,(\neg\psi)\,\{Seq\} \in \mathrm{BNL}$. Applying the semantics of ert (Table 2), we proceed as follows:

$$\mathsf{ert}\,[\![\mathtt{repeat}\,\{Seq\}\,\mathtt{until}\,(\psi)]\!]\,(f) \;=\; \mathsf{ert}\,[\![Seq]\!]\,(\mathsf{ert}\,[\![\mathtt{while}\,(\neg\psi)\,\{Seq\}]\!]\,(f))$$

Since the loop body Seq is loop–free, it terminates certainly, i.e. $\mathsf{wp}\,[\![Seq]\!]\,(1) = 1$ (Premise 2. of Theorem 4). Together with Lemma 3.1. and 3., all premises of Theorem 4 are satisfied. Hence, we obtain a closed form for $\mathsf{ert}\,[\![\mathtt{while}\,(\neg\psi)\,\{Seq\}]\!]\,(f)$:

$$= \; \mathsf{ert}[\![Seq]\!]\Bigg(\underbrace{1 + \frac{[\neg\psi]\cdot(1+\mathsf{ert}\,[\![Seq]\!]\,([\psi]\cdot f))}{1 - \mathsf{wp}\,[\![Seq]\!]\,([\neg\psi])} + [\psi]\cdot f}_{=:g}\Bigg)$$

By Theorem 2, we know $\mathsf{ert}\,[\![Seq]\!]\,(g) = \mathsf{ert}\,[\![Seq]\!]\,(0) + \mathsf{wp}\,[\![C]\!]\,(g)$ for any g. Thus:

$$= \; \mathsf{ert}\,[\![Seq]\!]\,(0) + \mathsf{wp}[\![Seq]\!]\Bigg(\underbrace{1 + \frac{[\neg\psi]\cdot(1+\mathsf{ert}\,[\![Seq]\!]\,([\psi]\cdot f))}{1 - \mathsf{wp}\,[\![Seq]\!]\,([\neg\psi])} + [\psi]\cdot f}_{g}\Bigg)$$

Since wp is linear (Theorem 1 (2)), we obtain:

$$= \; \mathsf{ert}\,[\![Seq]\!]\,(0) + \underbrace{\mathsf{wp}\,[\![Seq]\!]\,(1)}_{=\,1} + \mathsf{wp}\,[\![Seq]\!]\,([\psi]\cdot f)$$
$$+ \mathsf{wp}\,[\![Seq]\!]\Bigg(\frac{[\neg\psi]\cdot(1+\mathsf{ert}\,[\![Seq]\!]\,([\psi]\cdot f))}{1 - \mathsf{wp}\,[\![Seq]\!]\,([\neg\psi])}\Bigg)$$

By a few simple algebraic transformations, this coincides with:

$$= \; 1 + \mathsf{ert}\,[\![Seq]\!]\,(0) + \mathsf{wp}\,[\![Seq]\!]\,([\psi]\cdot f) + \mathsf{wp}\,[\![Seq]\!]\Bigg([\neg\psi]\cdot\frac{1+\mathsf{ert}\,[\![Seq]\!]\,([\psi]\cdot f)}{1 - \mathsf{wp}\,[\![Seq]\!]\,([\neg\psi])}\Bigg)$$

Let R denote the fraction above. Then Lemma 3.1. and 2. implies $R \notin Seq$. We may thus apply Lemma 1 to derive $\mathsf{wp}\,[\![Seq]\!]\,([\neg\psi]\cdot R) = \mathsf{wp}\,[\![Seq]\!]\,([\neg\psi])\cdot R$. Hence:

$$= \; 1 + \mathsf{ert}\,[\![Seq]\!]\,(0) + \mathsf{wp}\,[\![Seq]\!]\,([\psi]\cdot f) + \mathsf{wp}\,[\![Seq]\!]\,([\neg\psi])\cdot\frac{1+\mathsf{ert}\,[\![Seq]\!]\,([\psi]\cdot f)}{1 - \mathsf{wp}\,[\![Seq]\!]\,([\neg\psi])}$$

Again, by Theorem 2, we know that $\mathsf{ert}\,[\![Seq]\!]\,(g) = \mathsf{ert}\,[\![Seq]\!]\,(0) + \mathsf{wp}\,[\![Seq]\!]\,(g)$ for any g. Thus, for $g = [\psi]\cdot f$, this yields:

$$= \; 1 + \mathsf{ert}\,[\![Seq]\!]\,([\psi]\cdot f) + \mathsf{wp}\,[\![Seq]\!]\,([\neg\psi])\cdot\frac{1+\mathsf{ert}\,[\![Seq]\!]\,([\psi]\cdot f)}{1 - \mathsf{wp}\,[\![Seq]\!]\,([\neg\psi])}$$

Then a few algebraic transformations lead us to the claimed ERT:

$$= \frac{1 + \text{ert} \llbracket Seq \rrbracket ([\psi] \cdot f)}{\text{wp} \llbracket Seq \rrbracket ([\psi])}. \qquad \square$$

Note that Theorem 5 holds for arbitrary postexpectations $f \in \mathbb{E}$. This enables *compositional reasoning* about ERTs of BNL programs. Since all other rules of the ert–calculus for loop–free programs amount to simple syntactical transformations (see Table 2), we conclude that

Corollary 1. *For any $C \in$ BNL, a closed form for* ert $\llbracket C \rrbracket (0)$ *can be computed compositionally.*

Example 5. Theorem 5 allows us to comfortably compute the ERT of the BNL program C_{dice} introduced in Example 4:

$$x_1 :\approx \text{Unif}[1 \dots 6]; \text{repeat} \{x_2 :\approx \text{Unif}[1 \dots 6]\} \text{until} (x_2 \geq x_1)$$

For the ERT, we have

$$\text{ert} \llbracket C_{dice} \rrbracket (0)$$
$$= \text{ert} \llbracket x_1 :\approx \text{Unif}[1 \dots 6] \rrbracket (\text{ert} \llbracket \text{repeat} \{\dots\} \text{until} ([x_2 \geq x_1]) \rrbracket (0)) \quad \text{(Table 2)}$$
$$= \text{ert} \llbracket x_1 :\approx \text{Unif}[1 \dots 6] \rrbracket \left(\frac{1 + \text{ert} \llbracket x_2 :\approx \text{Unif}[1 \dots 6] \rrbracket ([x_2 \geq x_1])}{\text{wp} \llbracket x_1 :\approx \text{Unif}[1 \dots 6] \rrbracket ([x_2 \geq x_1])} \right) \quad \text{(Thm. 5)}$$
$$= \sum_{1 \leq i \leq 6} {}^{1}/_{6} \cdot \frac{1 + \sum_{1 \leq j \leq 6} {}^{1}/_{6} \cdot [j \geq i]}{\sum_{1 \leq j \leq 6} {}^{1}/_{6} \cdot [j \geq i]} \quad \text{(Table 2)}$$
$$= 3.45. \qquad \triangle$$

5.2 Bayesian Networks

To reason about expected sampling times of BNs, it remains to develop a sound translation from BNs with observations into equivalent BNL programs. A BN is a probabilistic graphical model that is given by a directed acyclic graph. Every node is a random variable and a directed edge between two nodes expresses a probabilistic dependency between these nodes.

As a running example, consider the BN depicted in Fig. 3 (inspired by [31]) that models the mood of students after taking an exam. The network contains four random variables. They represent the difficulty of the exam (D), the level of preparation of a student (P), the achieved grade (G), and the resulting mood (M). For simplicity, let us assume that each random variable assumes either 0 or 1. The edges express that the student's mood depends on the achieved grade which, in turn, depends on the difficulty of the exam and the preparation of the student. Every node is accompanied by a table that provides the conditional probabilities of a node *given* the values of all the nodes it depends upon. We can then use the BN to answer queries such as "What is the probability that a

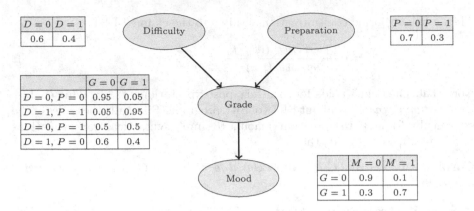

Fig. 3. A Bayesian network

student is well–prepared for an exam ($P = 1$), but ends up with a bad mood ($M = 0$)?"

In order to translate BNs into equivalent BNL programs, we need a formal representation first. Technically, we consider *extended* BNs in which nodes may additionally depend on inputs that are not represented by nodes in the network. This allows us to define a compositional translation without modifying conditional probability tables.

Towards a formal definition of extended BNs, we use the following notation. A tuple $(s_1, \ldots, s_k) \in S^k$ of length k over some set S is denoted by **s**. The empty tuple is ε. Moreover, for $1 \leq i \leq k$, the i-th element of tuple **s** is given by $\mathbf{s}(i)$. To simplify the presentation, we assume that all nodes and all inputs are represented by natural numbers.

Definition 7. *An* extended Bayesian network, *EBN for short, is a tuple* $\mathcal{B} = (V, I, E, \mathsf{Vals}, \mathsf{dep}, \mathsf{cpt})$, *where*

- $V \subseteq \mathbb{N}$ *and* $I \subseteq \mathbb{N}$ *are finite disjoint sets of* nodes *and* inputs.
- $E \subseteq V \times V$ *is a set of* edges *such that* (V, E) *is a directed acyclic graph.*
- Vals *is a finite set of possible* values *that can be assigned to each node.*
- $\mathsf{dep}: V \to (V \cup I)^*$ *is a function assigning each node v to an ordered sequence of dependencies. That is,* $\mathsf{dep}(v) = (u_1, \ldots, u_m)$ *such that $u_i < u_{i+1}$ ($1 \leq i < m$). Moreover, every dependency u_j ($1 \leq j \leq m$) is either an input, i.e. $u_j \in I$, or a node with an edge to v, i.e. $u_j \in V$ and $(u_j, v) \in E$.*
- cpt *is a function mapping each node v to its* conditional probability table $\mathsf{cpt}[v]$. *That is, for $k = |\mathsf{dep}(v)|$, $\mathsf{cpt}[v]$ is given by a function of the form*

$$\mathsf{cpt}[v] : \mathsf{Vals}^k \to \mathsf{Vals} \to [0, 1] \quad \text{such that} \quad \sum_{\mathbf{z} \in \mathsf{Vals}^k, a \in \mathsf{Vals}} \mathsf{cpt}[v](\mathbf{z})(a) = 1.$$

Here, the i-th entry in a tuple $\mathbf{z} \in \mathsf{Vals}^k$ corresponds to the value assigned to the i-th entry in the sequence of dependencies $\mathsf{dep}(v)$.

A Bayesian network *(BN) is an extended BN without inputs, i.e.* $I = \emptyset$. *In particular, the dependency function is of the form* $\mathsf{dep} \colon V \to V^*$.

Example 6. The formalization of our example BN (Fig. 3) is straightforward. For instance, the dependencies of variable G are given by $\mathsf{dep}(G) = (D, P)$ (assuming D is encoded by an integer less than P). Furthermore, every entry in the conditional probability table of node G corresponds to an evaluation of the function $\mathsf{cpt}[G]$. For example, if $D = 1$, $P = 0$, and $G = 1$, we have $\mathsf{cpt}[G](1,0)(1) = 0.4$. $\triangle$

In general, the conditional probability table cpt determines the conditional probability distribution of each node $v \in V$ given the nodes and inputs it depends on. Formally, we interpret an entry in a conditional probability table as follows:

$$\mathsf{Pr}\,(v = a \,|\, \mathsf{dep}(v) = \mathbf{z}) \;=\; \mathsf{cpt}[v](\mathbf{z})(a),$$

where $v \in V$ is a node, $a \in \mathsf{Vals}$ is a value, and $\mathbf{z}$ is a tuple of values of length $|\mathsf{dep}(v)|$. Then, by the chain rule, the joint probability of a BN is given by the product of its conditional probability tables (cf. [4]).

Definition 8. *Let* $\mathcal{B} = (V, I, E, \mathsf{Vals}, \mathsf{dep}, \mathsf{cpt})$ *be an extended Bayesian network. Moreover, let* $W \subseteq V$ *be a downward closed[5] set of nodes. With each* $w \in W \cup I$, *we associate a fixed value* $\underline{w} \in \mathsf{Vals}$. *This notation is lifted pointwise to tuples of nodes and inputs. Then the* joint probability *in which nodes in* W *assume values* $\underline{W}$ *is given by*

$$\mathsf{Pr}\,(W = \underline{W}) \;=\; \prod_{v \in W} \mathsf{Pr}\left(v = \underline{v} \,|\, \mathsf{dep}(v) = \underline{\mathsf{dep}(v)}\right) \;=\; \prod_{v \in W} \mathsf{cpt}[v](\underline{\mathsf{dep}(v)})(\underline{v}).$$

The conditional joint probability distribution of a set of nodes W, *given observations on a set of nodes* O, *is then given by the quotient* $\mathsf{Pr}(W=\underline{W})/\mathsf{Pr}(O=\underline{O})$.

For example, the probability of a student having a bad mood, i.e. $M = 0$, after getting a bad grade ($G = 0$) for an easy exam ($D = 0$) given that she was well–prepared, i.e. $P = 1$, is

$$\mathsf{Pr}\,(D = 0, G = 0, M = 0 \mid P = 1) \;=\; \frac{\mathsf{Pr}\,(D = 0, G = 0, M = 0, P = 1)}{\mathsf{Pr}\,(P = 1)}$$

$$= \frac{0.9 \cdot 0.5 \cdot 0.6 \cdot 0.3}{0.3} = 0.27.$$

5.3   From Bayesian Networks to BNL

We now develop a compositional translation from EBNs into BNL programs. Throughout this section, let $\mathcal{B} = (V, I, E, \mathsf{Vals}, \mathsf{dep}, \mathsf{cpt})$ be a fixed EBN. Moreover, with every node or input $v \in V \cup I$ we associate a program variable x_v.

We proceed in three steps: First, *every node together with its dependencies* is translated into a *block* of a BNL program. These blocks are then composed into a single BNL program that captures the whole BN. Finally, we implement conditioning by means of rejection sampling.

---

[5] W is downward closed if $v \in W$ and $(u, v) \in E$ implies $u \in E$.

Step 1: We first present the atomic building blocks of our translation. Let $v \in V$ be a node. Moreover, let $\mathbf{z} \in \mathsf{Vals}^{|\mathsf{dep}(v)|}$ be an evaluation of the dependencies of v. That is, $\mathbf{z}$ is a tuple that associates a value with every node and input that v depends on (in the same order as $\mathsf{dep}(v)$). For every node v and evaluation of its dependencies $\mathbf{z}$, we define a corresponding guard and a random assignment:

$$guard_B(v, \mathbf{z}) = \bigwedge_{1 \leq i \leq |\mathsf{dep}(v)|} x_{\mathsf{dep}(v)(i)} = \mathbf{z}(i)$$

$$assign_B(v, \mathbf{z}) = x_v :\approx \sum_{a \in \mathsf{Vals}} \mathsf{cpt}[v](\mathbf{z})(a) \cdot \langle a \rangle$$

Note that $\mathsf{dep}(v)(i)$ is the i-th element from the sequence of nodes $\mathsf{dep}(v)$.

Example 7. Continuing our previous example (see Fig. 1), assume we fixed the node $v = G$. Moreover, let $\mathbf{z} = (1,0)$ be an evaluation of $\mathsf{dep}(v) = (S, R)$. Then the guard and assignment corresponding to v and $\mathbf{z}$ are given by:

$$guard_B(G, (1,0)) = x_D = 1 \land x_P = 0, \text{ and}$$
$$assign_B(G, (1,0)) = x_G :\approx 0.6 \cdot \langle 0 \rangle + 0.4 \cdot \langle 1 \rangle. \qquad \triangle$$

We then translate every node $v \in V$ into a program block that uses guards to determine the rows in the conditional probability table under consideration. After that, the program samples from the resulting probability distribution using the previously constructed assignments. In case a node does neither depend on other nodes nor input variables we omit the guards. Formally,

$$block_B(v) = \begin{cases} assign_B(v, \varepsilon) & \text{if } |\mathsf{dep}(v)| = 0 \\ \texttt{if } (guard_B(v, \mathbf{z_1})) \, \{ \\ \quad assign_B(v, \mathbf{z_1}) \} \\ \texttt{else } \{ \texttt{if } (guard_B(v, \mathbf{z_2})) \, \{ & \text{if } |\mathsf{dep}(v)| = k > 0 \\ \quad assign_B(v, \mathbf{z_2}) \} & \text{and } \mathsf{Vals}^k = \{\mathbf{z_1}, \dots, \mathbf{z_m}\}. \\ \quad \dots \} \texttt{ else } \{ \\ \quad assign_B(v, \mathbf{z_m}) \} \dots \} \end{cases}$$

Remark 1. The guards under consideration are conjunctions of equalities between variables and literals. We could thus use a more efficient translation of conditional probability tables by adding a `switch-case` statement to our probabilistic programming language. Such a statement is of the form

$$\texttt{switch(x) \{ case } a_1 : C_1 \texttt{ case } a_2 : C_2 \ \dots \ \texttt{default} : C_m \},$$

where $\mathbf{x}$ is a tuple of variables, and $\mathbf{a}_1, \dots \mathbf{a}_{m-1}$ are tuples of rational numbers of the same length as $\mathbf{x}$. With respect to the wp semantics, a `switch-case` statement is syntactic sugar for nested `if-then-else` blocks as used in the above translation. However, the runtime model of a `switch-case` statement requires just a single guard evaluation (φ) instead of potentially multiple guard evaluations when evaluating nested `if-then-else` blocks. Since the above adaption is straightforward, we opted to use nested `if-then-else` blocks to keep our programming language simple and allow, in principle, more general guards. $\triangle$

Step 2: The next step is to translate a complete EBN into a BNL program. To this end, we compose the blocks obtained from each node starting at the roots of the network. That is, all nodes that contain no incoming edges. Formally,

$$roots(\mathcal{B}) = \{v \in V_{\mathcal{B}} \mid \neg \exists u \in V_{\mathcal{B}} \colon (u,v) \in E_{\mathcal{B}}\}.$$

After translating every node in the network, we remove them from the graph, i.e. every root becomes an input, and proceed with the translation until all nodes have been removed. More precisely, given a set of nodes $S \subseteq V$, the extended BN $\mathcal{B} \setminus S$ obtained by removing S from $\mathcal{B}$ is defined as

$$\mathcal{B} \setminus S \;=\; (V \setminus S,\, I \cup S,\, E \setminus (V \times S \cup S \times V),\, \mathsf{dep},\, \mathsf{cpt}).$$

With these auxiliary definitions readily available, an extended BN $\mathcal{B}$ is translated into a BNL program as follows:

$$BNL(\mathcal{B}) \;=\; \begin{cases} block_{\mathcal{B}}(r_1); \dots; block_{\mathcal{B}}(r_m) & \text{if } roots(\mathcal{B}) = \{r_1, \dots, r_m\} = V \\ block_{\mathcal{B}}(r_1); \dots; block_{\mathcal{B}}(r_m); & \text{if } roots(\mathcal{B}) = \{r_1, \dots, r_m\} \subsetneq V \\ BNL(\mathcal{B} \setminus roots(\mathcal{B})) \end{cases}$$

Step 3: To complete the translation, it remains to account for observations. Let $cond \colon V \to \mathsf{Vals} \cup \{\bot\}$ be a function mapping every node either to an observed value in Vals or to $\bot$. The former case is interpreted as an observation that node v has value $cond(v)$. Otherwise, i.e. if $cond(v) = \bot$, the value of node v is *not observed*. We collect all observed nodes in the set $O = \{v \in V \mid cond(v) \neq \bot\}$. It is then natural to incorporate conditioning into our translation by applying rejection sampling: We repeatedly execute a BNL program until every observed node has the desired value $cond(v)$. In the presence of observations, we translate the extended BN $\mathcal{B}$ into a BNL program as follows:

$$BNL(\mathcal{B}, cond) \;=\; \mathtt{repeat}\,\{BNL(\mathcal{B})\}\,\mathtt{until}\left(\bigwedge_{v \in O} x_v = cond(v)\right)$$

Example 8. Consider, again, the BN $\mathcal{B}$ depicted in Fig. 3. Moreover, assume we observe $P = 1$. Hence, the conditioning function $cond$ is given by $cond(P) = 1$ and $cond(v) = \bot$ for $v \in \{D, G, M\}$. Then the translation of $\mathcal{B}$ and $cond$, i.e. $BNL(\mathcal{B}, cond)$, is the BNL program C_{mood} depicted in Fig. 4.   △

Since our translation yields a BNL program for any given BN, we can compositionally compute a closed form for the expected simulation time of a BN. This is an immediate consequence of Corollary 1.

We still have to prove, however, that our translation is sound, i.e. the conditional joint probabilities inferred from a BN coincide with the (conditional) joint probabilities from the corresponding BNL program. Formally, we obtain the following soundness result.

```
1   repeat {                                  10        } else {
2       x_D :≈ 0.6 · ⟨0⟩ + 0.4 · ⟨1⟩;        11            x_G :≈ 0.6 · ⟨0⟩ + 0.4 · ⟨1⟩
3       x_P :≈ 0.7 · ⟨0⟩ + 0.3 · ⟨1⟩         12        };
4       if (x_D = 0 ∧ x_P = 0) {              13        if (x_G = 0) {
5           x_G :≈ 0.95 · ⟨0⟩ + 0.05 · ⟨1⟩   14            x_M :≈ 0.9 · ⟨0⟩ + 0.1 · ⟨1⟩
6       } else if (x_D = 1 ∧ x_P = 1) {       15        } else {
7           x_G :≈ 0.05 · ⟨0⟩ + 0.95 · ⟨1⟩   16            x_M :≈ 0.3 · ⟨0⟩ + 0.7 · ⟨1⟩
8       } else if (x_D = 0 ∧ x_P = 1) {       17        }
9           x_G :≈ 0.5 · ⟨0⟩ + 0.5 · ⟨1⟩      18   } until (x_P = 1)
```

Fig. 4. The BNL program C_{mood} obtained from the BN in Fig. 3.

Theorem 6 (Soundness of Translation). *Let $\mathcal{B} = (V, I, E, \mathsf{Vals}, \mathsf{dep}, \mathsf{cpt})$ be a BN and $cond : V \to \mathsf{Vals} \cup \{\bot\}$ be a function determining the observed nodes. For each node and input v, let $\underline{v} \in \mathsf{Vals}$ be a fixed value associated with v. In particular, we set $\underline{v} = cond(v)$ for each observed node $v \in O$. Then*

$$
\mathsf{wp}\,[\![BNL(\mathcal{B}, cond)]\!] \left(\left[\bigwedge_{v \in V \setminus O} x_v = \underline{v} \right] \right) = \frac{\mathsf{Pr}\left(\bigwedge_{v \in V} v = \underline{v} \right)}{\mathsf{Pr}\left(\bigwedge_{o \in O} o = \underline{o} \right)}.
$$

Proof. Without conditioning, i.e. $O = \emptyset$, the proof proceeds by induction on the number of nodes of $\mathcal{B}$. With conditioning, we additionally apply Theorems 3 and 5 to deal with loops introduced by observed nodes. See [3, Appendix A.7].   □

Example 9 (Expected Sampling Time of a BN). Consider, again, the BN $\mathcal{B}$ in Fig. 3. Moreover, recall the corresponding program C_{mood} derived from $\mathcal{B}$ in Fig. 4, where we observed $P = 1$. By Theorem 6 we can also determine the probability that a student who got a bad grade in an easy exam was well-prepared by means of weakest precondition reasoning. This yields

$$
\mathsf{wp}\,[\![C_{mood}]\!]\,([x_D = 0 \wedge x_G = 0 \wedge x_M = 0])
$$
$$
= \frac{\mathsf{Pr}\,(D = 0, G = 0, M = 0, P = 1)}{\mathsf{Pr}\,(P = 1)} = 0.27.
$$

Furthermore, by Corollary 1, it is straightforward to determine the expected time to obtain a single sample of $\mathcal{B}$ that satisfies the observation $P = 1$:

$$
\mathsf{ert}\,[\![C_{mood}]\!]\,(0) = \frac{1 + \mathsf{ert}\,[\![C_{loop\text{-}body}]\!]\,(0)}{\mathsf{wp}\,[\![C_{loop\text{-}body}]\!]\,([P = 1])} = 23.4 + {}^{1}/_{15} = 23.4\bar{6}. \quad \triangle
$$

6   Implementation

We implemented a prototype in Java to analyze expected sampling times of Bayesian networks. More concretely, our tool takes as input a BN together with observations in the popular Bayesian Network Interchange Format.[6] The BN is then translated into a BNL program as shown in Sect. 5. Our tool applies the ert–calculus together with our proof rules developed in Sect. 4 to compute the exact expected runtime of the BNL program.

The size of the resulting BNL program is linear in the total number of rows of all conditional probability tables in the BN. The program size is thus *not* the bottleneck of our analysis. As we are dealing with an NP–hard problem [12,13], it is not surprising that our algorithm has a worst–case exponential time complexity. However, also the space complexity of our algorithm is exponential in the worst case: As an expectation is propagated backwards through an if–clause of the BNL program, the size of the expectation is potentially multiplied. This is also the reason that our analysis runs out of memory on some benchmarks.

We evaluated our implementation on the *largest* BNs in the Bayesian Network Repository [46] that consists—to a large extent—of real–world BNs including expert systems for, e.g., electromyography (munin) [2], hematopathology diagnosis (hepar2) [42], weather forecasting (hailfinder) [1], and printer troubleshooting in Windows 95 (win95pts) [45, Sect. 5.6.2]. For a evaluation of *all* BNs in the repository, we refer to the extended version of this paper [3, Sect. 6].

All experiments were performed on an HP BL685C G7. Although up to 48 cores with 2.0 GHz were available, only one core was used apart from Java's garbage collection. The Java virtual machine was limited to 8 GB of RAM.

Our experimental results are shown in Table 3. The number of nodes of the considered BNs ranges from 56 to 1041. For each Bayesian network, we computed the expected sampling time (EST) for different collections of observed nodes (#obs). Furthermore, Table 3 provides the *average Markov Blanket size*, i.e. the average number of parents, children and children's parents of nodes in the BN [43], as an indicator measuring how independent nodes in the BN are.

Observations were picked at random. Note that the time required by our prototype varies depending on both the number of observed nodes and the actual observations. Thus, there are cases in which we run out of memory although the total number of observations is small.

In order to obtain an understanding of what the EST corresponds to in actual execution times on a real machine, we also performed simulations for the win95pts network. More precisely, we generated Java programs from this network analogously to the translation in Sect. 5. This allowed us to approximate that our Java setup can execute $9.714 \cdot 10^6$ steps (in terms of EST) per second.

For the win95pts with 17 observations, an EST of $1.11 \cdot 10^{15}$ then corresponds to an expected time of approximately 3.6 *years* in order to obtain a *single* valid sample. We were additionally able to find a case with 13 observed nodes where our tool discovered within 0.32 s an EST that corresponds to approximately 4.3 *million years*. In contrast, exact inference using variable elimination was almost instantaneous. This demonstrates that knowing expected sampling times upfront can indeed be beneficial when selecting an inference method.

---

[6] http://www.cs.cmu.edu/~fgcozman/Research/InterchangeFormat/.

Table 3. Experimental results. Time is in seconds. MO denotes out of memory.

BN	#obs	Time	EST	#obs	Time	EST	#obs	Time	EST
hailfinder	*#nodes: 56, #edges: 66, avg. Markov Blanket: 3.54*								
	0	0.23	$9.500 \cdot 10^1$	5	0.63	$5.016 \cdot 10^5$	9	0.46	$9.048 \cdot 10^6$
hepar2	*#nodes: 70, #edges: 123, avg. Markov Blanket: 4.51*								
	0	0.22	$1.310 \cdot 10^2$	1	1.84	$1.579 \cdot 10^2$	2	MO	–
win95pts	*#nodes: 76, #edges: 112, avg. Markov Blanket: 5.92*								
	0	0.20	$1.180 \cdot 10^2$	1	0.36	$2.284 \cdot 10^3$	3	0.36	$4.296 \cdot 10^5$
	7	0.91	$1.876 \cdot 10^6$	12	0.42	$3.973 \cdot 10^7$	17	61.73	$1.110 \cdot 10^{15}$
pathfinder	*#nodes: 135, #edges: 200, avg. Markov Blanket: 3.04*								
	0	0.37	217	1	0.53	$1.050 \cdot 10^4$	3	31.31	$2.872 \cdot 10^4$
	5	MO	–	7	5.44	∞	7	480.83	∞
andes	*#nodes: 223, #edges: 338, avg. Markov Blanket: 5.61*								
	0	0.46	$3.570 \cdot 10^2$	1	MO	–	3	1.66	$5.251 \cdot 10^3$
	5	1.41	$9.862 \cdot 10^3$	7	0.99	$8.904 \cdot 10^4$	9	0.90	$6.637 \cdot 10^5$
pigs	*#nodes: 441, #edges: 592, avg. Markov Blanket: 3.66*								
	0	0.57	$7.370 \cdot 10^2$	1	0.74	$2.952 \cdot 10^3$	3	0.88	$2.362 \cdot 10^3$
	5	0.85	$1.260 \cdot 10^5$	7	1.02	$1.511 \cdot 10^6$	8	MO	–
munin	*#nodes: 1041, #edges: 1397, avg. Markov Blanket: 3.54*								
	0	1.29	$1.823 \cdot 10^3$	1	1.47	$3.648 \cdot 10^4$	3	1.37	$1.824 \cdot 10^7$
	5	1.43	∞	9	1.79	$1.824 \cdot 10^{16}$	10	65.64	$1.153 \cdot 10^{18}$

7 Conclusion

We presented a syntactic notion of independent and identically distributed probabilistic loops and derived dedicated proof rules to determine exact expected outcomes and runtimes of such loops. These rules do not require any user–supplied information, such as invariants, (super)martingales, etc.

Moreover, we isolated a syntactic fragment of probabilistic programs that allows to compute expected runtimes in a highly automatable fashion. This fragment is non–trivial: We show that all Bayesian networks can be translated into programs within this fragment. Hence, we obtain an automated formal method for computing expected simulation times of Bayesian networks. We implemented this method and successfully applied it to various real–world BNs that stem from, amongst others, medical applications. Remarkably, our tool was capable of proving extremely large expected sampling times within seconds.

There are several directions for future work: For example, there exist subclasses of BNs for which exact inference is in P, e.g. polytrees. Are there analogies for probabilistic programs? Moreover, it would be interesting to consider more complex graphical models, such as recursive BNs [16].

References

1. Abramson, B., Brown, J., Edwards, W., Murphy, A., Winkler, R.L.: Hailfinder: a Bayesian system for forecasting severe weather. Int. J. Forecast. **12**(1), 57–71 (1996)
2. Andreassen, S., Jensen, F.V., Andersen, S.K., Falck, B., Kjærulff, U., Woldbye, M., Sørensen, A., Rosenfalck, A., Jensen, F.: MUNIN: an expert EMG Assistant. In: Computer-Aided Electromyography and Expert Systems, pp. 255–277. Pergamon Press (1989)
3. Batz, K., Kaminski, B.L., Katoen, J., Matheja, C.: How long, O Bayesian network, will I sample thee? arXiv extended version (2018)
4. Bishop, C.: Pattern Recognition and Machine Learning. Springer, New York (2006)
5. Bournez, O., Garnier, F.: Proving positive almost-sure termination. In: Giesl, J. (ed.) RTA 2005. LNCS, vol. 3467, pp. 323–337. Springer, Heidelberg (2005). https://doi.org/10.1007/978-3-540-32033-3_24
6. Brázdil, T., Kiefer, S., Kucera, A., Vareková, I.H.: Runtime analysis of probabilistic programs with unbounded recursion. J. Comput. Syst. Sci. **81**(1), 288–310 (2015)
7. Celiku, O., McIver, A.: Compositional specification and analysis of cost-based properties in probabilistic programs. In: Fitzgerald, J., Hayes, I.J., Tarlecki, A. (eds.) FM 2005. LNCS, vol. 3582, pp. 107–122. Springer, Heidelberg (2005). https://doi.org/10.1007/11526841_9
8. Chakarov, A., Sankaranarayanan, S.: Probabilistic program analysis with martingales. In: Sharygina, N., Veith, H. (eds.) CAV 2013. LNCS, vol. 8044, pp. 511–526. Springer, Heidelberg (2013). https://doi.org/10.1007/978-3-642-39799-8_34
9. Chatterjee, K., Fu, H., Novotný, P., Hasheminezhad, R.: Algorithmic analysis of qualitative and quantitative termination problems for affine probabilistic programs. In: POPL, pp. 327–342. ACM (2016)
10. Chatterjee, K., Novotný, P., Zikelic, D.: Stochastic invariants for probabilistic termination. In: POPL, pp. 145–160. ACM (2017)
11. Constantinou, A.C., Fenton, N.E., Neil, M.: pi-football: a Bayesian network model for forecasting association football match outcomes. Knowl. Based Syst. **36**, 322–339 (2012)
12. Cooper, G.F.: The computational complexity of probabilistic inference using Bayesian belief networks. Artif. Intell. **42**(2 3), 393–405 (1990)
13. Dagum, P., Luby, M.: Approximating probabilistic inference in Bayesian belief networks is NP-hard. Artif. Intell. **60**(1), 141–153 (1993)
14. Dijkstra, E.W.: Guarded commands, nondeterminacy and formal derivation of programs. Commun. ACM **18**(8), 453–457 (1975)
15. Dijkstra, E.W.: A Discipline of Programming. Prentice-Hall, Upper Saddle River (1976)
16. Etessami, K., Yannakakis, M.: Recursive Markov chains, stochastic grammars, and monotone systems of nonlinear equations. JACM **56**(1), 1:1–1:66 (2009)
17. Fioriti, L.M.F., Hermanns, H.: Probabilistic termination: soundness, completeness, and compositionality. In: POPL, pp. 489–501. ACM (2015)
18. Friedman, N., Linial, M., Nachman, I., Pe'er, D.: Using Bayesian networks to analyze expression data. In: RECOMB, pp. 127–135. ACM (2000)
19. Frohn, F., Naaf, M., Hensel, J., Brockschmidt, M., Giesl, J.: Lower runtime bounds for integer programs. In: Olivetti, N., Tiwari, A. (eds.) IJCAR 2016. LNCS (LNAI), vol. 9706, pp. 550–567. Springer, Cham (2016). https://doi.org/10.1007/978-3-319-40229-1_37

20. Goodman, N.D.: The principles and practice of probabilistic programming. In: POPL, pp. 399–402. ACM (2013)
21. Goodman, N.D., Mansinghka, V.K., Roy, D.M., Bonawitz, K., Tenenbaum, J.B.: Church: A language for generative models. In: UAI, pp. 220–229. AUAI Press (2008)
22. Gordon, A.D., Graepel, T., Rolland, N., Russo, C.V., Borgström, J., Guiver, J.: Tabular: a schema-driven probabilistic programming language. In: POPL, pp. 321–334. ACM (2014)
23. Gordon, A.D., Henzinger, T.A., Nori, A.V., Rajamani, S.K.: Probabilistic programming. In: Future of Software Engineering, pp. 167–181. ACM (2014)
24. Heckerman, D.: A tutorial on learning with Bayesian networks. In: Holmes, D.E., Jain, L.C. (eds.) Innovations in Bayesian Networks. Studies in Computational Intelligence, vol. 156, pp. 33–82. Springer, Heidelberg (2008)
25. Hehner, E.C.R.: A probability perspective. Formal Aspects Comput. **23**(4), 391–419 (2011)
26. Hoffman, M.D., Gelman, A.: The No-U-turn sampler: adaptively setting path lengths in Hamiltonian Monte Carlo. J. Mach. Learn. Res. **15**(1), 1593–1623 (2014)
27. Jiang, X., Cooper, G.F.: A Bayesian spatio-temporal method for disease outbreak detection. JAMIA **17**(4), 462–471 (2010)
28. Kaminski, B.L., Katoen, J.-P.: On the hardness of almost–sure termination. In: Italiano, G.F., Pighizzini, G., Sannella, D.T. (eds.) MFCS 2015. LNCS, vol. 9234, pp. 307–318. Springer, Heidelberg (2015). https://doi.org/10.1007/978-3-662-48057-1_24
29. Kaminski, B.L., Katoen, J.: A weakest pre-expectation semantics for mixed-sign expectations. In: LICS (2017)
30. Kaminski, B.L., Katoen, J.-P., Matheja, C., Olmedo, F.: Weakest precondition reasoning for expected run–times of probabilistic programs. In: Thiemann, P. (ed.) ESOP 2016. LNCS, vol. 9632, pp. 364–389. Springer, Heidelberg (2016). https://doi.org/10.1007/978-3-662-49498-1_15
31. Koller, D., Friedman, N.: Probabilistic Graphical Models - Principles and Techniques. MIT Press, Cambridge (2009)
32. Kozen, D.: Semantics of probabilistic programs. J. Comput. Syst. Sci. **22**(3), 328–350 (1981)
33. Kozen, D.: A probabilistic PDL. J. Comput. Syst. Sci. **30**(2), 162–178 (1985)
34. Lassez, J.L., Nguyen, V.L., Sonenberg, L.: Fixed point theorems and semantics: a folk tale. Inf. Process. Lett. **14**(3), 112–116 (1982)
35. McIver, A., Morgan, C.: Abstraction, Refinement and Proof for Probabilistic Systems. Springer, New York (2004). http://doi.org/10.1007/b138392
36. Minka, T., Winn, J.: Infer.NET (2017). http://infernet.azurewebsites.net/. Accessed Oct 17
37. Minka, T., Winn, J.M.: Gates. In: NIPS, pp. 1073–1080. Curran Associates (2008)
38. Monniaux, D.: An abstract analysis of the probabilistic termination of programs. In: Cousot, P. (ed.) SAS 2001. LNCS, vol. 2126, pp. 111–126. Springer, Heidelberg (2001). https://doi.org/10.1007/3-540-47764-0_7
39. Neapolitan, R.E., Jiang, X.: Probabilistic Methods for Financial and Marketing Informatics. Morgan Kaufmann, Burlington (2010)
40. Nori, A.V., Hur, C., Rajamani, S.K., Samuel, S.: R2: an efficient MCMC sampler for probabilistic programs. In: AAAI, pp. 2476–2482. AAAI Press (2014)
41. Olmedo, F., Kaminski, B.L., Katoen, J., Matheja, C.: Reasoning about recursive probabilistic programs. In: LICS, pp. 672–681. ACM (2016)

42. Onisko, A., Druzdzel, M.J., Wasyluk, H.: A probabilistic causal model for diagnosis of liver disorders. In: Proceedings of the Seventh International Symposium on Intelligent Information Systems (IIS-98), pp. 379–387 (1998)
43. Pearl, J.: Bayesian networks: a model of self-activated memory for evidential reasoning. In: Proceedings of CogSci, pp. 329–334 (1985)
44. Pfeffer, A.: Figaro: an object-oriented probabilistic programming language. Charles River Analytics Technical Report 137, 96 (2009)
45. Ramanna, S., Jain, L.C., Howlett, R.J.: Emerging Paradigms in Machine Learning. Springer, Heidelberg (2013)
46. Scutari, M.: Bayesian Network Repository (2017). http://www.bnlearn.com
47. Sharir, M., Pnueli, A., Hart, S.: Verification of probabilistic programs. SIAM J. Comput. **13**(2), 292–314 (1984)
48. Wood, F., van de Meent, J., Mansinghka, V.: A new approach to probabilistic programming inference. In: JMLR Workshop and Conference Proceedings, AISTATS, vol. 33, pp. 1024–1032 (2014). JMLR.org
49. Yuan, C., Druzdzel, M.J.: Importance sampling algorithms for Bayesian networks: principles and performance. Math. Comput. Model. **43**(9–10), 1189–1207 (2006)
50. Zweig, G., Russell, S.J.: Speech recognition with dynamic Bayesian networks. In: AAAI/IAAI, pp. 173–180. AAAI Press/The MIT Press (1998)

Relational Reasoning for Markov Chains in a Probabilistic Guarded Lambda Calculus

Alejandro Aguirre[1]([⊠]), Gilles Barthe[1], Lars Birkedal[2], Aleš Bizjak[2],
Marco Gaboardi[3], and Deepak Garg[4]

[1] IMDEA Software Institute, Madrid, Spain
alejandro.aguirre@imdea.org
[2] Aarhus University, Aarhus, Denmark
[3] University at Buffalo, SUNY, Buffalo, USA
[4] MPI-SWS, Kaiserslautern and Saarbrücken, Germany

Abstract. We extend the simply-typed guarded λ-calculus with discrete probabilities and endow it with a program logic for reasoning about relational properties of guarded probabilistic computations. This provides a framework for programming and reasoning about infinite stochastic processes like Markov chains. We demonstrate the logic sound by interpreting its judgements in the topos of trees and by using probabilistic couplings for the semantics of relational assertions over distributions on discrete types.

The program logic is designed to support syntax-directed proofs in the style of relational refinement types, but retains the expressiveness of higher-order logic extended with discrete distributions, and the ability to reason relationally about expressions that have different types or syntactic structure. In addition, our proof system leverages a well-known theorem from the coupling literature to justify better proof rules for relational reasoning about probabilistic expressions. We illustrate these benefits with a broad range of examples that were beyond the scope of previous systems, including shift couplings and lump couplings between random walks.

1 Introduction

Stochastic processes are often used in mathematics, physics, biology or finance to model evolution of systems with uncertainty. In particular, Markov chains are "memoryless" stochastic processes, in the sense that the evolution of the system depends only on the current state and not on its history. Perhaps the most emblematic example of a (discrete time) Markov chain is the simple random walk over the integers, that starts at 0, and that on each step moves one position either left or right with uniform probability. Let p_i be the position at time i. Then, this Markov chain can be described as:

$$p_0 = 0 \qquad p_{i+1} = \begin{cases} p_i + 1 \text{ with probability } 1/2 \\ p_i - 1 \text{ with probability } 1/2 \end{cases}$$

© The Author(s) 2018
A. Ahmed (Ed.): ESOP 2018, LNCS 10801, pp. 214–241, 2018.
https://doi.org/10.1007/978-3-319-89884-1_8

The goal of this paper is to develop a programming and reasoning framework for probabilistic computations over infinite objects, such as Markov chains. Although programming and reasoning frameworks for infinite objects and probabilistic computations are well-understood in isolation, their combination is challenging. In particular, one must develop a proof system that is powerful enough for proving interesting properties of probabilistic computations over infinite objects, and practical enough to support effective verification of these properties.

Modelling Probabilistic Infinite Objects. A first challenge is to model probabilistic infinite objects. We focus on the case of Markov chains, due to its importance. A (discrete-time) Markov chain is a sequence of random variables $\{X_i\}$ over some fixed type T satisfying some independence property. Thus, the straightforward way of modelling a Markov chain is as a *stream of distributions* over T. Going back to the simple example outlined above, it is natural to think about this kind of *discrete-time* Markov chain as characterized by the sequence of positions $\{p_i\}_{i \in \mathbb{N}}$, which in turn can be described as an infinite set indexed by the natural numbers. This suggests that a natural way to model such a Markov chain is to use *streams* in which each element is produced *probabilistically* from the previous one. However, there are some downsides to this representation. First of all, it requires explicit reasoning about probabilistic dependency, since X_{i+1} depends on X_i. Also, we might be interested in global properties of the executions of the Markov chain, such as "The probability of passing through the initial state infinitely many times is 1". These properties are naturally expressed as properties of the whole stream. For these reasons, we want to represent Markov chains as *distributions over streams*. Seemingly, one downside of this representation is that the set of streams is not countable, which suggests the need for introducing heavy measure-theoretic machinery in the semantics of the programming language, even when the underlying type is discrete or finite.

Fortunately, measure-theoretic machinery can be avoided (for discrete distributions) by developing a probabilistic extension of the simply-typed guarded λ-calculus and giving a semantic interpretation in the topos of trees [1]. Informally, the simply-typed guarded λ-calculus [1] extends the simply-typed lambda calculus with a *later* modality, denoted by $\triangleright$. The type $\triangleright A$ ascribes expressions that are available one unit of logical time in the future. The $\triangleright$ modality allows one to model infinite types by using "finite" approximations. For example, a stream of natural numbers is represented by the sequence of its (increasing) prefixes in the topos of trees. The prefix containing the first i elements has the type $S_i \triangleq \mathbb{N} \times \triangleright \mathbb{N} \times \ldots \times \triangleright^{(i-1)} \mathbb{N}$, representing that the first element is available now, the second element a unit time in the future, and so on. This is the key to representing probability distributions over infinite objects without measure-theoretic semantics: We model probability distributions over non-discrete sets as discrete distributions over their (the sets') approximations. For example, a distribution over streams of natural numbers (which a priori would be non-discrete since the set of streams is uncountable) would be modelled by a *sequence of distributions* over the finite approximations $S_1, S_2, \ldots$ of streams. Importantly, since each S_i is countable, each of these distributions can be discrete.

Reasoning About Probabilistic Computations. Probabilistic computations exhibit a rich set of properties. One natural class of properties is related to probabilities of events, saying, for instance, that the probability of some event E (or of an indexed family of events) increases at every iteration. However, several interesting properties of probabilistic computation, such as stochastic dominance or convergence (defined below) are relational, in the sense that they refer to two runs of two processes. In principle, both classes of properties can be proved using a higher-order logic for probabilistic expressions, e.g. the internal logic of the topos of trees, suitably extended with an axiomatization of finite distributions. However, we contend that an alternative approach inspired from refinement types is desirable and provides better support for effective verification. More specifically, reasoning in a higher-order logic, e.g. in the internal logic of the topos of trees, does not exploit the *structure of programs* for non-relational reasoning, nor the *structural similarities* between programs for relational reasoning. As a consequence, reasoning is more involved. To address this issue, we define a relational proof system that exploits the structure of the expressions and supports syntax-directed proofs, with necessary provisions for escaping the syntax-directed discipline when the expressions do not have the same structure. The proof system manipulates judgements of the form:

$$\Delta \mid \Sigma \mid \Gamma \mid \Psi \vdash t_1 : A_1 \sim t_2 : A_2 \mid \phi$$

where Δ and Γ are two typing contexts, Σ and Ψ respectively denote sets of assertions over variables in these two contexts, t_1 and t_2 are well-typed expressions of type A_1 and A_2, and ϕ is an assertion that may contain the special variables $\mathbf{r}_1$ and $\mathbf{r}_2$ that respectively correspond to the values of t_1 and t_2. The context Δ and Γ, the terms t_1 and t_2 and the types A_1 and A_2 provide a specification, while Σ, Ψ, and ϕ are useful for reasoning about relational properties over t_1, t_2, their inputs and their outputs. This form of judgement is similar to that of Relational Higher-Order Logic [2], from which our system draws inspiration.

In more detail, our relational logic comes with typing rules that allow one to reason about relational properties by exploiting as much as possible the syntactic similarities between t_1 and t_2, and to fall back on pure logical reasoning when these are not available. In order to apply relational reasoning to guarded computations the logic provides relational rules for the later modality $\triangleright$ and for a related modality $\square$, called "constant". These rules allow the relational verification of general relational properties that go beyond the traditional notion of program equivalence and, moreover, they allow the verification of properties of guarded computations over different types. The ability to reason about computations of different types provides significant benefits over alternative formalisms for relational reasoning. For example, it enables reasoning about relations between programs working on different data structures, e.g. a relation between a program working on a stream of natural numbers, and a program working on a stream of pairs of natural numbers, or having different structures, e.g. a relation between an application and a case expression.

Importantly, our approach for reasoning formally about probabilistic computations is based on *probabilistic couplings*, a standard tool from the analysis of Markov chains [3,4]. From a verification perspective, probabilistic couplings go beyond equivalence properties of probabilistic programs, which have been studied extensively in the verification literature, and yet support compositional reasoning [5,6]. The main attractive feature of coupling-based reasoning is that it limits the need of explicitly reasoning about the probabilities—this avoids complex verification conditions. We provide sound proof rules for reasoning about probabilistic couplings. Our rules make several improvements over prior relational verification logics based on couplings. First, we support reasoning over probabilistic processes of different types. Second, we use Strassen's theorem [7] a remarkable result about probabilistic couplings, to achieve greater expressivity. Previous systems required to prove a bijection between the sampling spaces to show the existence of a coupling [5,6], Strassen's theorem gives a way to show their existence which is applicable in settings where the bijection-based approach cannot be applied. And third, we support reasoning with what are called shift couplings, coupling which permits to relate the states of two Markov chains at possibly different times (more explanations below).

Case Studies. We show the flexibility of our formalism by verifying several examples of relational properties of probabilistic computations, and Markov chains in particular. These examples cannot be verified with existing approaches.

First, we verify a classic example of probabilistic non-interference which requires the reasoning about computations at different types. Second, in the context of Markov chains, we verify an example about stochastic dominance which exercises our more general rule for proving the existence of couplings modelled by expressions of different types. Finally, we verify an example involving shift relations in an infinite computation. This style of reasoning is motivated by "shift" couplings in Markov chains. In contrast to a standard coupling, which relates the states of two Markov chains at the same time t, a shift coupling relates the states of two Markov chains at possibly different times. Our specific example relates a standard random walk (described earlier) to a variant called a lazy random walk; the verification requires relating the state of standard random walk at time t to the state of the lazy random walk at time $2t$. We note that this kind of reasoning is impossible with conventional relational proof rules even in a non-probabilistic setting. Therefore, we provide a novel family of proof rules for reasoning about shift relations. At a high level, the rules combine a careful treatment of the later and constant modalities with a refined treatment of fixpoint operators, allowing us to relate different iterates of function bodies.

Summary of Contributions

With the aim of providing a general framework for programming and reasoning about Markov chains, the three main contributions of this work are:

1. A probabilistic extension of the guarded λ-calculus, that enables the definition of Markov chains as discrete probability distributions over streams.
2. A relational logic based on coupling to reason in a syntax-directed manner about (relational) properties of Markov chains. This logic supports reasoning

about programs that have different types and structures. Additionally, this logic uses results from the coupling literature to achieve greater expressivity than previous systems.
3. An extension of the relational logic that allows to relate the states of two streams at possibly different times. This extension supports reasoning principles, such as shift couplings, that escape conventional relational logics.

Omitted technical details can be found in the full version of the paper with appendix at https://arxiv.org/abs/1802.09787.

2 Mathematical Preliminaries

This section reviews the definition of discrete probability sub-distributions and introduces mathematical couplings.

Definition 1 (Discrete probability distribution). *Let C be a discrete (i.e., finite or countable) set. A (total) distribution over C is a function $\mu : C \to [0,1]$ such that $\sum_{x \in C} \mu(x) = 1$. The support of a distribution μ is the set of points with non-zero probability, $\operatorname{supp} \mu \triangleq \{x \in C \mid \mu(x) > 0\}$. We denote the set of distributions over C as $\mathsf{D}(C)$. Given a subset $E \subseteq C$, the probability of sampling from μ a point in E is denoted $\Pr_{x \leftarrow \mu}[x \in E]$, and is equal to $\sum_{x \in E} \mu(x)$.*

Definition 2 (Marginals). *Let μ be a distribution over a product space $C_1 \times C_2$. The first (second) marginal of μ is another distribution $\mathsf{D}(\pi_1)(\mu)$ $(\mathsf{D}(\pi_2)(\mu))$ over C_1 (C_2) defined as:*

$$\mathsf{D}(\pi_1)(\mu)(x) = \sum_{y \in C_2} \mu(x,y) \qquad \left(\mathsf{D}(\pi_2)(\mu)(y) = \sum_{x \in C_1} \mu(x,y) \right)$$

Probabilistic Couplings. Probabilistic couplings are a fundamental tool in the analysis of Markov chains. When analyzing a relation between two probability distributions it is sometimes useful to consider instead a distribution over the product space that somehow "couples" the randomness in a convenient manner.

Consider for instance the case of the following Markov chain, which counts the total amount of tails observed when tossing repeatedly a biased coin with probability of tails p:

$$n_0 = 0 \qquad n_{i+1} = \begin{cases} n_i + 1 \text{ with probability } p \\ n_i \text{ with probability } (1-p) \end{cases}$$

If we have two biased coins with probabilities of tails p and q with $p \leq q$ and we respectively observe $\{n_i\}$ and $\{m_i\}$ we would expect that, in some sense, $n_i \leq m_i$ should hold for all i (this property is known as stochastic dominance). A formal proof of this fact using elementary tools from probability theory would require to compute the cumulative distribution functions for n_i and m_i and then to compare them. The coupling method reduces this proof to showing a way to pair the coin flips so that if the first coin shows tails, so does the second coin.

We now review the definition of couplings and state relevant properties.

Definition 3 (Couplings). *Let $\mu_1 \in D(C_1)$ and $\mu_2 \in D(C_2)$, and $R \subseteq C_1 \times C_2$.*

- *A distribution $\mu \in D(C_1 \times C_2)$ is a coupling for μ_1 and μ_2 iff its first and second marginals coincide with μ_1 and μ_2 respectively, i.e. $D(\pi_1)(\mu) = \mu_1$ and $D(\pi_2)(\mu) = \mu_2$.*
- *A distribution $\mu \in D(C_1 \times C_2)$ is a R-coupling for μ_1 and μ_2 if it is a coupling for μ_1 and μ_2 and, moreover, $\Pr_{(x_1,x_2) \leftarrow \mu}[R\ x_1\ x_2] = 1$, i.e., if the support of the distribution μ is included in R.*

Moreover, we write $\diamond_{\mu_1,\mu_2}.R$ iff there exists a R-coupling for μ_1 and μ_2.

Couplings always exist. For instance, the product distribution of two distributions is always a coupling. Going back to the example about the two coins, it can be proven by computation that the following is a coupling that lifts the less-or-equal relation (0 indicating heads and 1 indicating tails):

$$\begin{cases} (0,0) \text{ w/ prob } (1-q) & (0,1) \text{ w/ prob } (q-p) \\ (1,0) \text{ w/ prob } 0 & (1,1) \text{ w/ prob } p \end{cases}$$

The following theorem in [7] gives a necessary and sufficient condition for the existence of R-couplings between two distributions. The theorem is remarkable in the sense that it proves an equivalence between an existential property (namely the existence of a particular coupling) and a universal property (checking, for each event, an inequality between probabilities).

Theorem 1 (Strassen's theorem). *Consider $\mu_1 \in D(C_1)$ and $\mu_2 \in D(C_2)$, and $R \subseteq C_1 \times C_2$. Then $\diamond_{\mu_1,\mu_2}.R$ iff for every $X \subseteq C_1$, $\Pr_{x_1 \leftarrow \mu_1}[x_1 \in X] \leq \Pr_{x_2 \leftarrow \mu_2}[x_2 \in R(X)]$, where $R(X)$ is the image of X under R, i.e. $R(X) = \{y \in C_2 \mid \exists x \in X. R\ x\ y\}$.*

An important property of couplings is closure under sequential composition.

Lemma 1 (Sequential composition couplings). *Let $\mu_1 \in D(C_1)$, $\mu_2 \in D(C_2)$, $M_1 : C_1 \to D(D_1)$ and $M_2 : C_2 \to D(D_2)$. Moreover, let $R \subseteq C_1 \times C_2$ and $S \subseteq D_1 \times D_2$. Assume: (1) $\diamond_{\mu_1,\mu_2}.R$; and (2) for every $x_1 \in C_1$ and $x_2 \in C_2$ such that $R\ x_1\ x_2$, we have $\diamond_{M_1(x_1),M_2(x_2)}.S$. Then $\diamond_{(\text{bind } \mu_1\ M_1),(\text{bind } \mu_2\ M_2)}.S$, where* bind $\mu\ M$ *is defined as*

$$(\text{bind } \mu\ M)(y) = \sum_x \mu(x) \cdot M(x)(y)$$

We conclude this section with the following lemma, which follows from Strassen's theorem:

Lemma 2 (Fundamental lemma of couplings). *Let $R \subseteq C_1 \times C_2$, $E_1 \subseteq C_1$ and $E_2 \subseteq C_2$ such that for every $x_1 \in E_1$ and $x_2 \in C_2$, $R\ x_1\ x_2$ implies $x_2 \in E_2$, i.e. $R(E_1) \subseteq E_2$. Moreover, let $\mu_1 \in D(C_1)$ and $\mu_2 \in D(C_2)$ such that $\diamond_{\mu_1,\mu_2}.R$. Then*

$$\Pr_{x_1 \leftarrow \mu_1}[x_1 \in E_1] \leq \Pr_{x_2 \leftarrow \mu_2}[x_2 \in E_2]$$

This lemma can be used to prove probabilistic inequalities from the existence of suitable couplings:

Corollary 1. *Let* $\mu_1, \mu_2 \in D(C)$:

1. *If* $\diamond_{\mu_1,\mu_2}.(=)$, *then for all* $x \in C$, $\mu_1(x) = \mu_2(x)$.
2. *If* $C = \mathbb{N}$ *and* $\diamond_{\mu_1,\mu_2}.(\geq)$, *then for all* $n \in \mathbb{N}$, $\mathrm{Pr}_{x \leftarrow \mu_1}[x \geq n] \geq \mathrm{Pr}_{x \leftarrow \mu_2}[x \geq n]$

In the example at the beginning of the section, the property we want to prove is precisely that, for every k and i, the following holds:

$$\Pr_{x_1 \leftarrow n_i}[x_1 \geq k] \leq \Pr_{x_2 \leftarrow m_i}[x_2 \geq k]$$

Since we have a $\leq$-coupling, this proof is immediate. This example is formalized in Subsect. 3.3.

3 Overview of the System

In this section we give a high-level overview of our system, with the details on Sects. 4, 5 and 6. We start by presenting the base logic, and then we show how to extend it with probabilities and how to build a relational reasoning system on top of it.

3.1 Base Logic: Guarded Higher-Order Logic

Our starting point is the Guarded Higher-Order Logic [1] (Guarded HOL) inspired by the topos of trees. In addition to the usual constructs of HOL to reason about lambda terms, this logic features the $\triangleright$ and $\square$ modalities to reason about infinite terms, in particular streams. The $\triangleright$ modality is used to reason about objects that will be available in the future, such as tails of streams. For instance, suppose we want to define an $\mathrm{All}(s, \phi)$ predicate, expressing that all elements of a stream $s \equiv n::xs$ satisfy a property ϕ. This can be axiomatized as follows:

$$\forall(xs : \triangleright \mathrm{Str}_\mathbb{N})(n : \mathbb{N}).\phi \ n \Rightarrow \triangleright[s \leftarrow xs] \, . \, \mathrm{All}(s, x.\phi) \Rightarrow \mathrm{All}(n::xs, x.\phi)$$

We use $x.\phi$ to denote that the formula ϕ depends on a free variable x, which will get replaced by the first argument of All. We have two antecedents. The first one states that the head n satisfies ϕ. The second one, $\triangleright[s \leftarrow xs] \, . \, \mathrm{All}(s, x.\phi)$, states that all elements of xs satisfy ϕ. Formally, xs is the tail of the stream and will be available in the future, so it has type $\triangleright \mathrm{Str}_\mathbb{N}$. The *delayed substitution* $\triangleright[s \leftarrow xs]$ replaces s of type $\mathrm{Str}_\mathbb{N}$ with xs of type $\triangleright \mathrm{Str}_\mathbb{N}$ inside All and shifts the whole formula one step into the future. In other words, $\triangleright[s \leftarrow xs] \, . \, \mathrm{All}(s, x.\phi)$ states that $\mathrm{All}(-, x.\phi)$ will be satisfied by xs in the future, once it is available.

3.2 A System for Relational Reasoning

When proving relational properties it is often convenient to build proofs guided by the syntactic structure of the two expressions to be related. This style of reasoning is particularly appealing when the two expressions have the same structure and control-flow, and is appealingly close to the traditional style of reasoning supported by refinement types. At the same time, a strict adherence to the syntax-directed discipline is detrimental to the expressiveness of the system; for instance, it makes it difficult or even impossible to reason about structurally dissimilar terms. To achieve the best of both worlds, we present a relational proof system built on top of Guarded HOL, which we call Guarded RHOL. Judgements have the shape:

$$\Delta \mid \Sigma \mid \Gamma \mid \Psi \vdash t_1 : A_1 \sim t_2 : A_2 \mid \phi$$

where ϕ is a logical formula that may contain two distinguished variables $\mathbf{r}_1$ and $\mathbf{r}_2$ that respectively represent the expressions t_1 and t_2. This judgement subsumes two typing judgements on t_1 and t_2 and a relation ϕ on these two expressions. However, this form of judgement does not tie the logical property to the type of the expressions, and is key to achieving flexibility while supporting syntax-directed proofs whenever needed. The proof system combines rules of two different flavours: two-sided rules, which relate expressions with the same top-level constructs, and one-sided rules, which operate on a single expression.

We then extend Guarded HOL with a modality $\diamond$ that lifts assertions over discrete types C_1 and C_2 to assertions over $\mathsf{D}(C_1)$ and $\mathsf{D}(C_2)$. Concretely, we define for every assertion ϕ, variables x_1 and x_2 of type C_1 and C_2 respectively, and expressions t_1 and t_2 of type $\mathsf{D}(C_1)$ and $\mathsf{D}(C_2)$ respectively, the modal assertion $\diamond_{[x_1 \leftarrow t_1, x_2 \leftarrow t_2]}\phi$ which holds iff the interpretations of t_1 and t_2 are related by the probabilistic lifting of the interpretation of ϕ. We call this new logic Probabilistic Guarded HOL.

We accordingly extend the relational proof system to support reasoning about probabilistic expressions by adding judgements of the form:

$$\Delta \mid \Sigma \mid \Gamma \mid \Psi \vdash t_1 : \mathsf{D}(C_1) \sim t_2 : \mathsf{D}(C_2) \mid \diamond_{[x_1 \leftarrow \mathbf{r}_1, x_2 \leftarrow \mathbf{r}_2]}\phi$$

expressing that t_1 and t_2 are distributions related by a ϕ-coupling. We call this proof system Probabilistic Guarded RHOL. These judgements can be built by using the following rule, that lifts relational judgements over discrete types C_1 and C_2 to judgements over distribution types $\mathsf{D}(C_1)$ and $\mathsf{D}(C_2)$ when the premises of Strassen's theorem are satisfied.

$$\frac{\Delta \mid \Sigma \mid \Gamma \mid \Psi \vdash \forall X_1 \subseteq C_1. \Pr_{y_1 \leftarrow t_1}[y_1 \in X_1] \leq \Pr_{y_2 \leftarrow t_2}[\exists y_1 \in X_1.\phi]}{\Delta \mid \Sigma \mid \Gamma \mid \Psi \vdash t_1 : \mathsf{D}(C_1) \sim t_2 : \mathsf{D}(C_2) \mid \diamond_{[y_1 \leftarrow \mathbf{r}_1, y_2 \leftarrow \mathbf{r}_2]}\phi} \text{ COUPLING}$$

Recall that (discrete time) Markov chains are "memoryless" probabilistic processes, whose specification is given by a (discrete) set C of states, an initial state s_0 and a probabilistic transition function step : $C \rightarrow \mathsf{D}(C)$, where $\mathsf{D}(S)$ represents the set of discrete distributions over C. As explained in the introduction, a convenient modelling of Markov chains is by means of probabilistic streams, i.e. to model a Markov chain as an element of $D(Str_S)$, where S is its underlying state space. To model Markov chains, we introduce a markov operator with type $C \to (C \to D(C)) \to D(Str_C)$ that, given an initial state and a transition function, returns a Markov chain. We can reason about Markov chains by the [Markov] rule (the context, omitted, does not change):

$$\frac{\begin{array}{c} \vdash t_1 : C_1 \sim t_2 : C_2 \mid \phi \\ \vdash h_1 : C_1 \to D(C_1) \sim h_2 : C_2 \to D(C_2) \mid \psi_3 \\ \vdash \psi_4 \end{array}}{\vdash \mathsf{markov}(t_1, h_1) : D(Str_{D_1}) \sim \mathsf{markov}(t_2, h_2) : D(Str_{D_2}) \mid \Diamond_{\substack{[y_1 \leftarrow \mathbf{r}_1] \\ [y_2 \leftarrow \mathbf{r}_2]}} \phi'} \text{ Markov}$$

$$\text{where} \begin{cases} \psi_3 \equiv \forall x_1 x_2. \phi[x_1/\mathbf{r}_1][x_2/\mathbf{r}_2] \Rightarrow \Diamond_{[y_1 \leftarrow \mathbf{r}_1 \ x_1, y_2 \leftarrow \mathbf{r}_2 \ x_2]} \phi[y_1/\mathbf{r}_1][y_2/\mathbf{r}_2] \\ \psi_4 \equiv \forall x_1 \ x_2 \ xs_1 \ xs_2. \phi[x_1/\mathbf{r}_1][x_2/\mathbf{r}_2] \Rightarrow \triangleright [y_1 \leftarrow xs_1, y_2 \leftarrow xs_2] . \phi' \Rightarrow \\ \qquad \phi'[x_1::xs_1/y_1][x_2::xs_2/y_2] \end{cases}$$

Informally, the rule stipulates the existence of an invariant ϕ over states. The first premise insists that the invariant hold on the initial states, the condition ψ_3 states that the transition functions preserve the invariant, and ψ_4 states that the invariant ϕ over pairs of states can be lifted to a stream property ϕ'.

Other rules of the logic are given in Fig. 1. The language construct munit creates a point distribution whose entire mass is at its argument. Accordingly, the [UNIT] rule creates a straightforward coupling. The [MLET] rule internalizes sequential composition of couplings (Lemma 1) into the proof system. The construct let $x = t$ in t' composes a distribution t with a probabilistic computation t' with one free variable x by sampling x from t and running t'. The [MLET-L] rule supports one-sided reasoning about let $x = t$ in t' and relies on the fact that couplings are closed under convex combinations. Note that one premise of the rule uses a unary judgement, with a non-relational modality $\Diamond_{[x \leftarrow \mathbf{r}]} \phi$ whose informal meaning is that ϕ holds with probability 1 in the distribution $\mathbf{r}$.

The following table summarizes the different base logics we consider, the relational systems we build on top of them, including the ones presented in [2], and the equivalences between both sides:

Relational logic		Base logic
RHOL [2] $\Gamma \mid \Psi \vdash t_1 \sim t_2 \mid \phi$	$\overset{[2]}{\Longleftrightarrow}$	HOL [2] $\Gamma \mid \Psi \vdash \phi[t_1/\mathbf{r}_1][t_2/\mathbf{r}_2]$
Guarded RHOL §6 $\Delta \mid \Sigma \mid \Gamma \mid \Psi \vdash t_1 \sim t_2 \mid \phi$	$\overset{\text{Thm } 3}{\Longleftrightarrow}$	Guarded HOL [1] $\Delta \mid \Sigma \mid \Gamma \mid \Psi \vdash \phi[t_1/\mathbf{r}_1][t_2/\mathbf{r}_2]$
Probabilistic Guarded RHOL §6 $\Delta \mid \Sigma \mid \Gamma \mid \Psi \vdash t_1 \sim t_2 \mid \Diamond_{[y_1 \leftarrow \mathbf{r}_1, y_2 \leftarrow \mathbf{r}_2]} . \phi$	$\overset{\text{Thm } 3}{\Longleftrightarrow}$	Probabilistic Guarded HOL §5 $\Delta \mid \Sigma \mid \Gamma \mid \Psi \vdash \Diamond_{[y_1 \leftarrow t_1, y_2 \leftarrow t_2]} . \phi$

3.3 Examples

We formalize elementary examples from the literature on security and Markov chains. None of these examples can be verified in prior systems. Uniformity of

$$\frac{\Delta \mid \Sigma \mid \Gamma \mid \Psi \vdash t_1 : C_1 \sim t_2 : C_2 \mid \phi[\mathbf{r}_1/x_1, \mathbf{r}_2/x_2]}{\Delta \mid \Sigma \mid \Gamma \mid \Psi \vdash \mathsf{munit}(t_1) : \mathsf{D}(C_1) \sim \mathsf{munit}(t_2) : \mathsf{D}(C_2) \mid \diamond_{[x_1 \leftarrow \mathbf{r}_1, x_2 \leftarrow \mathbf{r}_2]}\phi} \ \text{UNIT}$$

$$\frac{\Delta \mid \Sigma \mid \Gamma \mid \Psi \vdash t_1 : \mathsf{D}(C_1) \sim t_2 : \mathsf{D}(C_2) \mid \diamond_{[x_1 \leftarrow \mathbf{r}_1, x_2 \leftarrow \mathbf{r}_2]}\phi \quad \Delta \mid \Sigma \mid \Gamma, x_1 : C_1, x_2 : C_2 \mid \Psi, \phi \vdash t_1' : \mathsf{D}(D_1) \sim t_2' : \mathsf{D}(D_2) \mid \diamond_{[y_1 \leftarrow \mathbf{r}_1, y_2 \leftarrow \mathbf{r}_2]}\psi}{\Delta \mid \Sigma \mid \Gamma \mid \Psi \vdash \mathsf{let}\ x_1 = t_1\ \mathsf{in}\ t_1' : \mathsf{D}(D_1) \sim \mathsf{let}\ x_2 = t_2\ \mathsf{in}\ t_2' : \mathsf{D}(D_2) \mid \diamond_{[\substack{y_1 \leftarrow \mathbf{r}_1 \\ y_2 \leftarrow \mathbf{r}_2}]}\psi} \ \text{MLET}$$

$$\frac{\Delta \mid \Sigma \mid \Gamma \mid \Psi \vdash t_1 : \mathsf{D}(C_1) \mid \diamond_{[x \leftarrow \mathbf{r}]}\phi \quad \Delta \mid \Sigma \mid \Gamma, x_1 : C_1 \mid \Psi, \phi \vdash t_1' : \mathsf{D}(D_1) \sim t_2' : \mathsf{D}(D_2) \mid \diamond_{[y_1 \leftarrow \mathbf{r}_1, y_2 \leftarrow \mathbf{r}_2]}\psi}{\Delta \mid \Sigma \mid \Gamma \mid \Psi \vdash \mathsf{let}\ x_1 = t_1\ \mathsf{in}\ t_1' : \mathsf{D}(D_1) \sim t_2' : \mathsf{D}(D_2) \mid \diamond_{[y_1 \leftarrow \mathbf{r}_1, y_2 \leftarrow \mathbf{r}_2]}\psi} \ \text{MLET} - \text{L}$$

Fig. 1. Proof rules for probabilistic constructs

one-time pad and lumping of *random walks* cannot even be stated in prior systems because the two related expressions in these examples have different types. The *random walk vs lazy random walk* (shift coupling) cannot be proved in prior systems because it requires either asynchronous reasoning or code rewriting. Finally, the *biased coin example* (stochastic dominance) cannot be proved in prior work because it requires Strassen's formulation of the existence of coupling (rather than a bijection-based formulation) or code rewriting. We give additional details below.

One-Time Pad/Probabilistic Non-interference. Non-interference [8] is a baseline information flow policy that is often used to model confidentiality of computations. In its simplest form, non-interference distinguishes between public (or low) and private (or high) variables and expressions, and requires that the result of a public expression not depend on the value of its private parameters. This definition naturally extends to probabilistic expressions, except that in this case the evaluation of an expression yields a distribution rather than a value. There are deep connections between probabilistic non-interference and several notions of (information-theoretic) security from cryptography. In this paragraph, we illustrate different flavours of security properties for one-time pad encryption. Similar reasoning can be carried out for proving (passive) security of secure multiparty computation algorithms in the 3-party or multi-party setting [9, 10].

One-time pad is a perfectly secure symmetric encryption scheme. Its space of plaintexts, ciphertexts and keys is the set $\{0,1\}^\ell$—fixed-length bitstrings of size ℓ. The encryption algorithm is parametrized by a key k—sampled uniformly over the set of bitstrings $\{0,1\}^\ell$—and maps every plaintext m to the ciphertext $c = k \oplus m$, where the operator $\oplus$ denotes bitwise exclusive-or on bitstrings. We let otp denote the expression $\lambda m.\mathsf{let}\ k = \mathcal{U}_{\{0,1\}^\ell}$ in $\mathsf{munit}(k \oplus m)$, where $\mathcal{U}_X$ is the uniform distribution over a finite set X.

One-time pad achieves perfect security, i.e. the distributions of ciphertexts is independent of the plaintext. Perfect security can be captured as a probabilistic non-interference property:

$$\vdash \mathsf{otp} : \{0,1\}^\ell \to \mathsf{D}(\{0,1\}^\ell) \sim \mathsf{otp} : \{0,1\}^\ell \to \mathsf{D}(\{0,1\}^\ell) \mid \forall m_1 m_2.\mathbf{r}_1\ m_1 \overset{\diamond}{=} \mathbf{r}_2\ m_2$$

where $e_1 \overset{\diamond}{=} e_2$ is used as a shorthand for $\diamond_{[y_1 \leftarrow e_1, y_2 \leftarrow e_2]} y_1 = y_2$. The crux of the proof is to establish

$$m_1, m_2 : \{0,1\}^\ell \vdash \mathcal{U}_{\{0,1\}^\ell} : D(\{0,1\}^\ell) \sim \mathcal{U}_{\{0,1\}^\ell} : D(\{0,1\}^\ell) \mid r_1 \oplus m_2 \overset{\diamond}{=} r_2 \oplus m_1$$

using the [COUPLING] rule. It suffices to observe that the assertion induces a bijection, so the image of an arbitrary set X under the relation has the same cardinality as X, and hence their probabilities w.r.t. the uniform distributions are equal. One can then conclude the proof by applying the rules for monadic sequenciation ([MLET]) and abstraction (rule [ABS] in appendix), using algebraic properties of $\oplus$.

Interestingly, one can prove a stronger property: rather than proving that the ciphertext is independent of the plaintext, one can prove that the distribution of ciphertexts is uniform. This is captured by the following judgement:

$$c_1, c_2 : \{0,1\}^\ell \vdash \mathsf{otp} : \{0,1\}^\ell \to D(\{0,1\}^\ell) \sim \mathsf{otp} : \{0,1\}^\ell \to D(\{0,1\}^\ell) \mid \psi$$

where $\psi \triangleq \forall m_1\, m_2. m_1 = m_2 \Rightarrow \diamond_{[y_1 \leftarrow r_1\, m_1, y_2 \leftarrow r_2\, m_2]} y_1 = c_1 \Leftrightarrow y_2 = c_2$. This style of modelling uniformity as a relational property is inspired from [11]. The proof is similar to the previous one and omitted. However, it is arguably more natural to model uniformity of the distribution of ciphertexts by the judgement:

$$\vdash \mathsf{otp} : \{0,1\}^\ell \to D(\{0,1\}^\ell) \sim \mathcal{U}_{\{0,1\}^\ell} : D(\{0,1\}^\ell) \mid \forall m.\, r_1\, m \overset{\diamond}{=} r_2$$

This judgement is closer to the simulation-based notion of security that is used pervasively in cryptography, and notably in Universal Composability [12]. Specifically, the statement captures the fact that the one-time pad algorithm can be simulated without access to the message. It is interesting to note that the judgement above (and more generally simulation-based security) could not be expressed in prior works, since the two expressions of the judgement have different types—note that in this specific case, the right expression is a distribution but in the general case the right expression will also be a function, and its domain will be a projection of the domain of the left expression.

The proof proceeds as follows. First, we prove

$$\vdash \mathcal{U}_{\{0,1\}^\ell} \sim \mathcal{U}_{\{0,1\}^\ell} \mid \forall m.\, \diamond_{[y_1 \leftarrow r_1, y_2 \leftarrow r_2]}\, y_1 \oplus m = y_2$$

using the [COUPLING] rule. Then, we apply the [MLET] rule to obtain

$$\vdash\; \begin{array}{l} \mathsf{let}\ k = \mathcal{U}_{\{0,1\}^\ell}\ \mathsf{in} \\ \mathsf{munit}(k \oplus m) \end{array} \sim \begin{array}{l} \mathsf{let}\ k = \mathcal{U}_{\{0,1\}^\ell}\ \mathsf{in} \\ \mathsf{munit}(k) \end{array} \;\Big|\; \diamond_{[y_1 \leftarrow r_1, y_2 \leftarrow r_2]} y_1 = y_2$$

We have $\mathsf{let}\ k = \mathcal{U}_{\{0,1\}^\ell}\ \mathsf{in}\ \mathsf{munit}(k) \equiv \mathcal{U}_{\{0,1\}^\ell}$; hence by equivalence (rule [Equiv] in appendix), this entails

$$\vdash \mathsf{let}\ k = \mathcal{U}_{\{0,1\}^\ell}\ \mathsf{in}\ \mathsf{munit}(k \oplus m) \sim \mathcal{U}_{\{0,1\}^\ell} \mid \diamond_{[y_1 \leftarrow r_1, y_2 \leftarrow r_2]} y_1 = y_2$$

We conclude by applying the one-sided rule for abstraction.

Stochastic Dominance. Stochastic dominance defines a partial order between random variables whose underlying set is itself a partial order; it has many different applications in statistical biology (e.g. in the analysis of the birth-and-death processes), statistical physics (e.g. in percolation theory), and economics. First-order stochastic dominance, which we define below, is also an important application of probabilistic couplings. We demonstrate how to use our proof system for proving (first-order) stochastic dominance for a simple Markov process which samples biased coins. While the example is elementary, the proof method extends to more complex examples of stochastic dominance, and illustrates the benefits of Strassen's formulation of the coupling rule over alternative formulations stipulating the existence of bijections (explained later).

We start by recalling the definition of (first-order) stochastic dominance for the $\mathbb{N}$-valued case. The definition extends to arbitrary partial orders.

Definition 4 (Stochastic dominance). *Let* $\mu_1, \mu_2 \in D(\mathbb{N})$. *We say that* μ_2 *stochastically dominates* μ_1, *written* $\mu_1 \leq_{\mathrm{SD}} \mu_2$, *iff for every* $n \in \mathbb{N}$,

$$\Pr_{x \leftarrow \mu_1} [x \geq n] \leq \Pr_{x \leftarrow \mu_2} [x \geq n]$$

The following result, equivalent to Corollary 1, characterizes stochastic dominance using probabilistic couplings.

Proposition 1. *Let* $\mu_1, \mu_2 \in D(\mathbb{N})$. *Then* $\mu_1 \leq_{\mathrm{SD}} \mu_2$ *iff* $\diamond_{\mu_1, \mu_2}.(\leq)$.

We now turn to the definition of the Markov chain. For $p \in [0, 1]$, we consider the parametric $\mathbb{N}$-valued Markov chain coins $\triangleq$ markov$(0, h)$, with initial state 0 and (parametric) step function:

$$h \triangleq \lambda x.\mathsf{let}\ b = \mathcal{B}(p)\ \mathsf{in}\ \mathsf{munit}(x + b)$$

where, for $p \in [0, 1]$, $\mathcal{B}(p)$ is the Bernoulli distribution on $\{0, 1\}$ with probability p for 1 and $1 - p$ for 0. Our goal is to establish that coins is monotonic, i.e. for every $p_1, p_2 \in [0, 1]$, $p_1 \leq p_2$ implies coins $p_1 \leq_{\mathrm{SD}}$ coins p_2. We formalize this statement as

$$\vdash \mathsf{coins} : [0, 1] \to D(\mathrm{Str}_{\mathbb{N}}) \sim \mathsf{coins} : [0, 1] \to D(\mathrm{Str}_{\mathbb{N}}) \mid \psi$$

where $\psi \triangleq \forall p_1, p_2.p_1 \leq p_2 \Rightarrow \diamond_{[y_1 \leftarrow \mathbf{r}_1, y_2 \leftarrow \mathbf{r}_2]} \mathrm{All}(y_1, y_2, z_1.z_2.z_1 \leq z_2)$. The crux of the proof is to establish stochastic dominance for the Bernoulli distribution:

$$p_1 : [0, 1], p_2 : [0, 1] \mid p_1 \leq p_2 \vdash \mathcal{B}(p_1) : D(\mathbb{N}) \sim \mathcal{B}(p_2) : D(\mathbb{N}) \mid \mathbf{r}_1 \overset{\diamond}{\leq} \mathbf{r}_2$$

where we use $e_1 \overset{\diamond}{\leq} e_2$ as shorthand for $\diamond_{[y_1 \leftarrow e_1, y_2 \leftarrow e_2]} y_1 \leq y_2$. This is proved directly by the [COUPLING] rule and checking by simple calculations that the premise of the rule is valid.

We briefly explain how to conclude the proof. Let h_1 and h_2 be the step functions for p_1 and p_2 respectively. It is clear from the above that (context omitted):

$$x_1 \leq x_2 \vdash h_1\ x_1 : D(\mathbb{B}) \sim h_2\ x_2 : D(\mathbb{B}) \mid \diamond_{[y_1 \leftarrow \mathbf{r}_1, y_2 \leftarrow \mathbf{r}_2]}.y_1 \leq y_2$$

and by the definition of All:

$$x_1 \leq x_2 \Rightarrow \text{All}(xs_1, xs_2, z_1.z_2.z_1 \leq z_2) \Rightarrow \text{All}(x_1 :: \triangleright xs_1, x_2 :: \triangleright xs_2, z_1.z_2.z_1 \leq z_2)$$

So, we can conclude by applying the [Markov] rule.

It is instructive to compare our proof with prior formalizations, and in particular with the proof in [5]. Their proof is carried out in the pRHL logic, whose [COUPLING] rule is based on the existence of a bijection that satisfies some property, rather than on our formalization based on Strassen's Theorem. Their rule is motivated by applications in cryptography, and works well for many examples, but is inconvenient for our example at hand, which involves non-uniform probabilities. Indeed, their proof is based on code rewriting, and is done in two steps. First, they prove equivalence between sampling and returning x_1 from $\mathcal{B}(p_1)$; and sampling z_1 from $\mathcal{B}(p_2)$, z_2 from $\mathcal{B}(p_1/p_2)$ and returning $z = z_1 \wedge z_2$. Then, they find a coupling between z and $\mathcal{B}(p_2)$.

Shift Coupling: Random Walk vs Lazy Random Walk. The previous example is an instance of a lockstep coupling, in that it relates the k-th element of the first chain with the k-th element of the second chain. Many examples from the literature follow this lockstep pattern; however, it is not always possible to establish lockstep couplings. Shift couplings are a relaxation of lockstep couplings where we relate elements of the first and second chains without the requirement that their positions coincide.

We consider a simple example that motivates the use of shift couplings. Consider the random walk and lazy random walk (which, at each time step, either chooses to move or stay put), both defined as Markov chains over $\mathbb{Z}$. For simplicity, assume that both walks start at position 0. It is not immediate to find a coupling between the two walks, since the two walks necessarily get desynchronized whenever the lazy walk stays put. Instead, the trick is to consider a lazy random walk that moves two steps instead of one. The random walk and the lazy random walk of step 2 are defined by the step functions:

$$\text{step} \triangleq \lambda x.\text{let } z = \mathcal{U}_{\{-1,1\}} \text{ in munit}(z + x)$$
$$\text{lstep2} \triangleq \lambda x.\text{let } z = \mathcal{U}_{\{-1,1\}} \text{ in let } b = \mathcal{U}_{\{0,1\}} \text{ in munit}(x + 2 * z * b)$$

After 2 iterations of step, the position has either changed two steps to the left or to the right, or has returned to the initial position, which is the same behaviour lstep2 has on every iteration. Therefore, the coupling we want to find should equate the elements at position $2i$ in step with the elements at position i in lstep2. The details on how to prove the existence of this coupling are in Sect. 6.

Lumped Coupling: Random Walks on 3 and 4 Dimensions. A Markov chain is *recurrent* if it has probability 1 of returning to its initial state, and *transient* otherwise. It is relatively easy to show that the random walk over $\mathbb{Z}$ is recurrent. One can also show that the random walk over $\mathbb{Z}^2$ is recurrent. However, the random walk over $\mathbb{Z}^3$ is transient.

For higher dimensions, we can use a coupling argument to prove transience. Specifically, we can define a coupling between a lazy random walk in n dimensions and a random walk in $n+m$ dimensions, and derive transience of the latter from transience of the former. We define the (lazy) random walks below, and sketch the coupling arguments.

Specifically, we show here the particular case of the transience of the 4-dimensional random walk from the transience of the 3-dimensional lazy random walk. We start by defining the stepping functions:

$$\text{step}_4 : \mathbb{Z}^4 \to D(\mathbb{Z}^4) \triangleq \lambda z_1.\text{let } x_1 = \mathcal{U}_{U_4} \text{ in munit}(z_1 +_4 x_1)$$
$$\text{lstep}_3 : \mathbb{Z}^3 \to D(\mathbb{Z}^3) \triangleq \lambda z_2.\text{let } x_2 = \mathcal{U}_{U_3} \text{ in let } b_2 = \mathcal{B}(^3/_4) \text{ in munit}(z_2 +_3 b_2 * x_2)$$

where $U_i = \{(\pm 1, 0, \ldots 0), \ldots, (0, \ldots, 0, \pm 1)\}$ are the vectors of the basis of $\mathbb{Z}^i$ and their opposites. Then, the random walk of dimension 4 is modelled by $\text{rwalk4} \triangleq \text{markov}(0, \text{step}_4)$, and the lazy walk of dimension 3 is modelled by $\text{lwalk3} \triangleq \text{markov}(0, \text{step}_3)$. We want to prove:

$$\vdash \text{rwalk4} : D(\text{Str}_{\mathbb{Z}^4}) \sim \text{lwalk3} : D(\text{Str}_{\mathbb{Z}^3}) \mid \Diamond_{\substack{[y_1 \leftarrow r_1] \\ [y_2 \leftarrow r_2]}} \text{All}(y_1, y_2, z_1.z_2. \text{pr}_3^4(z_1) = z_2)$$

where $\text{pr}_{n_1}^{n_2}$ denotes the standard projection from $\mathbb{Z}^{n_2}$ to $\mathbb{Z}^{n_1}$.

We apply the [Markov] rule. The only interesting premise requires proving that the transition function preserves the coupling:

$$p_2 = \text{pr}_3^4(p_1) \vdash \text{step}_4 \sim \text{lstep}_3 \mid \forall x_1 x_2.x_2 = \text{pr}_3^4(x_1) \Rightarrow \Diamond_{\substack{[y_1 \leftarrow r_1 \ x_1] \\ [y_2 \leftarrow r_2 \ x_2]}} \text{pr}_3^4(y_1) = y_2$$

To prove this, we need to find the appropriate coupling, i.e., one that preserves the equality. The idea is that the step in $\mathbb{Z}^3$ must be the projection of the step in $\mathbb{Z}^4$. This corresponds to the following judgement:

$$\begin{matrix} \lambda z_1.\text{ let } x_1 = \mathcal{U}_{U_4} \text{ in} \\ \text{munit}(z_1 +_4 x_1) \end{matrix} \sim \begin{matrix} \lambda z_2.\text{ let } x_2 = \mathcal{U}_{U_3} \text{ in} \\ \text{let } b_2 = \mathcal{B}(^3/_4) \text{ in} \\ \text{munit}(z_2 +_3 b_2 * x_2) \end{matrix} \left| \begin{matrix} \forall z_1 z_2. \text{pr}_3^4(z_1) = z_2 \Rightarrow \\ \text{pr}_3^4(r_1 \ z_1) \stackrel{\Diamond}{=} r_2 \ z_2 \end{matrix} \right.$$

which by simple equational reasoning is the same as

$$\begin{matrix} \lambda z_1.\text{ let } x_1 = \mathcal{U}_{U_4} \text{ in} \\ \text{munit}(z_1 +_4 x_1) \end{matrix} \sim \begin{matrix} \lambda z_2.\text{ let } p_2 = \mathcal{U}_{U_3} \times \mathcal{B}(^3/_4) \text{ in} \\ \text{munit}(z_2 +_3 \pi_1(p_2) * \pi_2(p_2)) \end{matrix} \left| \begin{matrix} \forall z_1 z_2. \text{pr}_3^4(z_1) = z_2 \Rightarrow \\ \text{pr}_3^4(r_1 \ z_1) \stackrel{\Diamond}{=} r_2 \ z_2 \end{matrix} \right.$$

We want to build a coupling such that if we sample $(0, 0, 0, 1)$ or $(0, 0, 0, -1)$ from $\mathcal{U}_{U_3}$, then we sample 0 from $\mathcal{B}(^3/_4)$, and otherwise if we sample $(x_1, x_2, x_3, 0)$ from $\mathcal{U}_{U_4}$, we sample (x_1, x_2, x_3) from U_3. Formally, we prove this with the [Coupling] rule. Given $X : U_4 \to \mathbb{B}$, by simple computation we show that:

$$\Pr_{z_1 \sim \mathcal{U}_{U_4}} [z_1 \in X] \leq \Pr_{z_2 \sim \mathcal{U}_{U_3} \times \mathcal{B}(^3/_4)} [z_2 \in \{y \mid \exists x \in X.\text{pr}_3^4(x) = \pi_1(y) * \pi_2(y)\}]$$

This concludes the proof. From the previous example, it follows that the lazy walk in 3 dimensions is transient, since the random walk in 3 dimensions is transient. By simple reasoning, we now conclude that the random walk in 4 dimensions is also transient.

4   Probabilistic Guarded Lambda Calculus

To ensure that a function on infinite datatypes is well-defined, one must check that it is *productive*. This means that any finite prefix of the output can be computed in finite time. For instance, consider the following function on streams:

$$\texttt{letrec bad } (\texttt{x} : \texttt{xs}) = \texttt{x} : \texttt{tail}(\texttt{bad xs})$$

This function is not productive since only the first element can be computed. We can argue this as follows: Suppose that the tail of a stream is available one unit of time after its head, and that x:xs is available at time 0. How much time does it take for bad to start outputting its tail? Assume it takes k units of time. This means that tail(bad xs) will be available at time $k + 1$, since xs is only available at time 1. But tail(bad xs) is exactly the tail of bad(x:xs), and this is a contradiction, since x:xs is available at time 0 and therefore the tail of bad(x:xs) should be available at time k. Therefore, the tail of bad will never be available.

The guarded lambda calculus solves the productivity problem by distinguishing at type level between data that is available now and data that will be available in the future, and restricting when fixpoints can be defined. Specifically, the guarded lambda calculus extends the usual simply typed lambda calculus with two modalities: ▷ (pronounced *later*) and □ (*constant*). The later modality represents data that will be available one step in the future, and is introduced and removed by the term formers ▷ and prev respectively. This modality is used to guard recursive occurrences, so for the calculus to remain productive, we must restrict when it can be eliminated. This is achieved via the constant modality, which expresses that all the data is available at all times. In the remainder of this section we present a probabilistic extension of this calculus.

Syntax. Types of the calculus are defined by the grammar

$$A, B ::= b \mid \mathbb{N} \mid A \times B \mid A + B \mid A \to B \mid \text{Str}_A \mid \square\, A \mid \triangleright A \mid \mathsf{D}(C)$$

where b ranges over a collection of base types. Str_A is the type of guarded streams of elements of type A. Formally, the type Str_A is isomorphic to $A \times \triangleright \text{Str}_A$. This isomorphism gives a way to introduce streams with the function $(::) : A \to \triangleright \text{Str}_A \to \text{Str}_A$ and to eliminate them with the functions $\text{hd} : \text{Str}_A \to A$ and $\text{tl} : \text{Str}_A \to \triangleright \text{Str}_A$. $\mathsf{D}(C)$ is the type of distributions over *discrete types* C. Discrete types are defined by the following grammar, where b_0 are discrete base types, e.g., $\mathbb{Z}$.

$$C, D ::= b_0 \mid \mathbb{N} \mid C \times D \mid C + D \mid \text{Str}_C \mid \triangleright C.$$

Note that, in particular, arrow types are not discrete but streams are. This is due to the semantics of streams as sets of finite approximations, which we describe in the next subsection. Also note that $\square\, \text{Str}_A$ is not discrete since it makes the full infinite streams available.

We also need to distinguish between arbitrary types A, B and constant types S, T, which are defined by the following grammar

$$S, T ::= b_C \mid \mathbb{N} \mid S \times T \mid S + T \mid S \rightarrow T \mid \square \, A$$

where b_C is a collection of constant base types. Note in particular that for any type A the type $\square \, A$ is constant.

The terms of the language t are defined by the following grammar

$$t ::= x \mid c \mid 0 \mid St \mid \text{case } t \text{ of } 0 \mapsto t; S \mapsto t \mid \mu \mid \text{munit}(t) \mid \text{let } x = t \text{ in } t$$
$$\mid \langle t, t \rangle \mid \pi_1 t \mid \pi_2 t \mid \text{inj}_1 t \mid \text{inj}_2 t \mid \text{case } t \text{ of inj}_1 x.t; \text{inj}_2 y.t \mid \lambda x.t \mid tt \mid \text{fix } x.\, t$$
$$\mid t::ts \mid \text{hd}\, t \mid \text{tl}\, t \mid \text{box } t \mid \text{letb } x \leftarrow t \text{ in } t \mid \text{letc } x \leftarrow t \text{ in } t \mid \triangleright \xi.t \mid \text{prev } t$$

where ξ is a delayed substitution, a sequence of bindings $[x_1 \leftarrow t_1, \ldots, x_n \leftarrow t_n]$. The terms c are constants corresponding to the base types used and $\text{munit}(t)$ and $\text{let } x = t \text{ in } t$ are the introduction and sequencing construct for probability distributions. The meta-variable μ stands for base distributions like $\mathcal{U}_C$ and $\mathcal{B}(p)$.

Delayed substitutions were introduced in [13] in a dependent type theory to be able to work with types dependent on terms of type $\triangleright A$. In the setting of a simple type theory, such as the one considered in this paper, delayed substitutions are equivalent to having the applicative structure [14] $\circledast$ for the $\triangleright$ modality. However, delayed substitutions extend uniformly to the level of propositions, and thus we choose to use them in this paper in place of the applicative structure.

Denotational Semantics. The meaning of terms is given by a denotational model in the category $\mathcal{S}$ of presheaves over ω, the first infinite ordinal. This category $\mathcal{S}$ is also known as the *topos of trees* [15]. In previous work [1], it was shown how to model most of the constructions of the guarded lambda calculus and its internal logic, with the notable exception of the probabilistic features. Below we give an elementary presentation of the semantics.

Informally, the idea behind the topos of trees is to represent (infinite) objects from their finite approximations, which we observe incrementally as time passes. Given an object x, we can consider a sequence $\{x_i\}$ of its finite approximations observable at time i. These are trivial for finite objects, such as a natural number, since for any number n, $n_i = n$ at every i. But for infinite objects such as streams, the ith approximation is the prefix of length $i + 1$.

Concretely, the category $\mathcal{S}$ consists of:

- Objects X: families of sets $\{X_i\}_{i \in \mathbb{N}}$ together with *restriction functions* $r_n^X : X_{n+1} \rightarrow X_n$. We will write simply r_n if X is clear from the context.
- Morphisms $X \rightarrow Y$: families of functions $\alpha_n : X_n \rightarrow Y_n$ commuting with restriction functions in the sense of $r_n^Y \circ \alpha_{n+1} = \alpha_n \circ r_n^X$.

The full interpretation of types of the calculus can be found in Fig. 8 in the appendix. The main points we want to highlight are:

- Streams over a type A are interpreted as sequences of finite prefixes of elements of A with the restriction functions of A:

$$[\![\text{Str}_A]\!] \triangleq [\![A]\!]_0 \times \{*\} \xleftarrow{r_0 \times !} [\![A]\!]_1 \times [\![\text{Str}_A]\!]_0 \xleftarrow{r_1 \times r_0 \times !} [\![A]\!]_2 \times [\![\text{Str}_A]\!]_1 \leftarrow \cdots$$

- Distributions over a discrete object C are defined as a sequence of distributions over each $[\![C]\!]_i$:

$$[\![\mathsf{D}(C)]\!] \triangleq \mathsf{D}([\![C]\!]_0) \xleftarrow{\mathsf{D}(r_0)} \mathsf{D}([\![C]\!]_1) \xleftarrow{\mathsf{D}(r_1)} \mathsf{D}([\![C]\!]_2) \xleftarrow{\mathsf{D}(r_2)} \ldots,$$

where $\mathsf{D}([\![C]\!]_i)$ is the set of (probability density) functions $\mu : [\![C]\!]_i \to [0,1]$ such that $\sum_{x \in X} \mu x = 1$, and $\mathsf{D}(r_i)$ adds the probability density of all the points in $[\![C]\!]_{i+1}$ that are sent by r_i to the same point in the $[\![C]\!]_i$. In other words, $\mathsf{D}(r_i)(\mu)(x) = \Pr_{y \leftarrow \mu}[r_i(y) = x]$

An important property of the interpretation is that discrete types are interpreted as objects X such that X_i is finite or countably infinite for every i. This allows us to define distributions on these objects without the need for measure theory. In particular, the type of guarded streams Str_A is discrete provided A is, which is clear from the interpretation of the type Str_A. Conceptually this holds because $[\![\mathrm{Str}_A]\!]_i$ is an approximation of real streams, consisting of only the first $i+1$ elements.

An object X of $\mathcal{S}$ is *constant* if all its restriction functions are bijections. Constant types are interpreted as constant objects of $\mathcal{S}$ and for a constant type A the objects $[\![\Box A]\!]$ and $[\![A]\!]$ are isomorphic in $\mathcal{S}$.

Typing Rules. Terms are typed under a dual context $\Delta \mid \Gamma$, where Γ is a usual context that binds variables to a type, and Δ is a constant context containing variables bound to types that are *constant*. The term letc $x \leftarrow u$ in t allows us to shift variables between constant and non-constant contexts. The typing rules can be found in Fig. 2.

The semantics of such a dual context $\Delta \mid \Gamma$ is given as the product of types in Δ and Γ, except that we implicitly add $\Box$ in front of every type in Δ. In the particular case when both contexts are empty, the semantics of the dual context correspond to the terminal object 1, which is the singleton set $\{*\}$ at each time.

The interpretation of the well-typed term $\Delta \mid \Gamma \vdash t : A$ is defined by induction on the typing derivation, and can be found in Fig. 9 in the appendix.

Applicative Structure of the Later Modality. As in previous work we can define the operator $\circledast$ satisfying the typing rule

$$\frac{\Delta \mid \Gamma \vdash t : \rhd(A \to B) \qquad \Delta \mid \Gamma \vdash u : \rhd A}{\Delta \mid \Gamma \vdash t \circledast u : \rhd B}$$

and the equation $(\rhd t) \circledast (\rhd u) \equiv \rhd(t\ u)$ as the term $t \circledast u \triangleq \rhd[f \leftarrow t, x \leftarrow u].f\ x$.

Example: Modelling Markov Chains. As an application of $\circledast$ and an example of how to use guardedness and probabilities together, we now give the precise definition of the markov construct that we used to model Markov chains earlier:

markov $: C \to (C \to \mathsf{D}(C)) \to \mathsf{D}(\mathrm{Str}_C)$
markov $\triangleq$ fix f. $\lambda x.\lambda h$.
        let $z = h\ x$ in let $t = \mathrm{swap}_{\rhd \mathsf{D}}^{\mathrm{Str}_C}(f \circledast \rhd z \circledast \rhd h)$ in munit$(x::t)$

$$\frac{x:A \in \Gamma}{\Delta \mid \Gamma \vdash x:A} \qquad \frac{x:A \in \Delta}{\Delta \mid \Gamma \vdash x:A} \qquad \frac{\Delta \mid \Gamma, x:A \vdash t:B}{\Delta \mid \Gamma \vdash \lambda x.t:A \to B}$$

$$\frac{\Delta \mid \Gamma \vdash t:A \to B \qquad \Delta \mid \Gamma \vdash u:A}{\Delta \mid \Gamma \vdash tu:B} \qquad \frac{\Delta \mid \Gamma, f:\triangleright A \vdash t:A}{\Delta \mid \Gamma \vdash \text{fix } f.\, t:A} \qquad \frac{\Delta \mid \cdot \vdash t:\triangleright A}{\Delta \mid \Gamma \vdash \text{prev } t:A}$$

$$\frac{\Delta \mid \cdot \vdash t:A}{\Delta \mid \Gamma \vdash \text{box } t:\square A} \qquad \frac{\Delta \mid \Gamma \vdash u:\square B \qquad \Delta, x:B \mid \Gamma \vdash t:A}{\Delta \mid \Gamma \vdash \text{letb } x \leftarrow u \text{ in } t:A}$$

$$\frac{\Delta \mid \Gamma \vdash u:B \qquad \Delta, x:B \mid \Gamma \vdash t:A \qquad B \text{ constant}}{\Delta \mid \Gamma \vdash \text{letc } x \leftarrow u \text{ in } t:A}$$

$$\frac{\Delta \mid \Gamma, x_1:A_1, \cdots x_n:A_n \vdash t:A \qquad \Delta \mid \Gamma \vdash t_i:\triangleright A_i}{\Delta \mid \Gamma \vdash \triangleright [x_1 \leftarrow t_1, \ldots, x_n \leftarrow t_n].t:\triangleright A} \qquad \frac{\Delta \mid \Gamma \vdash t:A \qquad A \text{ discrete}}{\Delta \mid \Gamma \vdash \text{munit}(t):D(A)}$$

$$\frac{\Delta \mid \Gamma \vdash t:D(A) \qquad \Delta \mid \Gamma, x:A \vdash u:D(B)}{\Delta \mid \Gamma \vdash \text{let } x = t \text{ in } u:D(B)} \qquad \frac{\mu \text{ primitive distribution on type } A}{\Delta \mid \Gamma \vdash \mu:D(A)}$$

Fig. 2. A selection of the typing rules of the guarded lambda calculus. The rules for products, sums, and natural numbers are standard.

The guardedness condition gives f the type $\triangleright(C \to (C \to D(C)) \to D(\text{Str}_C))$ in the body of the fixpoint. Therefore, it needs to be applied functorially (via $\circledast$) to $\triangleright z$ and $\triangleright h$, which gives us a term of type $\triangleright D(\text{Str}_C)$. To complete the definition we need to build a term of type $D(\triangleright \text{Str}_C)$ and then sequence it with :: to build a term of type $D(\text{Str}_C)$. To achieve this, we use the primitive operator $\text{swap}_{\triangleright D}^C : \triangleright D(C) \to D(\triangleright C)$, which witnesses the isomorphism between $\triangleright D(C)$ and $D(\triangleright C)$. For this isomorphism to exist, it is crucial that distributions be total (i.e., we cannot use subdistributions). Indeed, the denotation for $\triangleright D(C)$ is the sequence $\{*\} \leftarrow D(C_1) \leftarrow D(C_2) \leftarrow \ldots$, while the denotation for $D(\triangleright C)$ is the sequence $D(\{*\}) \leftarrow D(C_1) \leftarrow D(C_2) \leftarrow \ldots$, and $\{*\}$ is isomorphic to $D(\{*\})$ in Set only if D considers only total distributions.

5   Guarded Higher-Order Logic

We now introduce Guarded HOL (GHOL), which is a higher-order logic to reason about terms of the guarded lambda calculus. The logic is essentially that of [1], but presented with the dual context formulation analogous to the dual-context typing judgement of the guarded lambda calculus. Compared to standard intuitionistic higher-order logic, the logic GHOL has two additional constructs, corresponding to additional constructs in the guarded lambda calculus. These are the later modality $(\triangleright)$ *on propositions*, with delayed substitutions, which expresses that a proposition holds one time unit into the future, and the "always" modality $\square$, which expresses that a proposition holds at all times. Formulas are defined by the grammar:

$$\phi, \psi ::= \top \mid \phi \wedge \psi \mid \phi \vee \psi \mid \neg \psi \mid \forall x.\phi \mid \exists x.\phi \mid \triangleright [x_1 \leftarrow t_1 \ldots x_n \leftarrow t_n].\phi \mid \square \phi$$

The basic judgement of the logic is $\Delta \mid \Sigma \mid \Gamma \mid \Psi \vdash \phi$ where Σ is a logical context for Δ (that is, a list of formulas well-formed in Δ) and Ψ is another logical context for the dual context $\Delta \mid \Gamma$. The formulas in context Σ must be *constant* propositions. We say that a proposition ϕ is *constant* if it is well-typed in context $\Delta \mid \cdot$ and moreover if every occurrence of the later modality in ϕ is under the $\square$ modality. Selected rules are displayed in Fig. 3. We highlight [Loeb] induction, which is the key to reasoning about fixpoints: to prove that ϕ holds now, one can assume that it holds in the future. The interpretation of the formula $\Delta \mid \Gamma \vdash \phi$ is a subobject of the interpretation $[\![\Delta \mid \Gamma]\!]$. Concretely the interpretation A of $\Delta \mid \Gamma \vdash \phi$ is a family $\{A_i\}_{i=0}^{\infty}$ of sets such that $A_i \subseteq [\![\Delta \mid \Gamma]\!]_i$. This family must satisfy the property that if $x \in A_{i+1}$ then $r_i(x) \in A_i$ where r_i are the restriction functions of $[\![\Delta \mid \Gamma]\!]$. The interpretation of formulas is defined by induction on the typing derivation. In the interpretation of the context $\Delta \mid \Sigma \mid \Gamma \mid \Psi$ the formulas in Σ are interpreted with the added $\square$ modality. Moreover all formulas ϕ in Σ are typeable in the context $\Delta \mid \cdot \vdash \phi$ and thus their interpretations are subsets of $[\![\square\Delta]\!]$. We treat these subsets of $[\![\Delta \mid \Gamma]\!]$ in the obvious way.

The cases for the semantics of the judgement $\Delta \mid \Gamma \vdash \phi$ can be found in the appendix. It can be shown that this logic is sound with respect to its model in the topos of trees.

Theorem 2 (Soundness of the semantics). *The semantics of guarded higher-order logic is sound: if* $\Delta \mid \Sigma \mid \Gamma \mid \Psi \vdash \phi$ *is derivable then for all* $n \in \mathbb{N}$, $[\![\square\Sigma]\!]_n \cap [\![\Psi]\!]_n \subseteq [\![\phi]\!]$.

In addition, Guarded HOL is expressive enough to axiomatize standard probabilities over discrete sets. This axiomatization can be used to define the $\diamond$ modality directly in Guarded HOL (as opposed to our relational proof system, were we use it as a primitive). Furthermore, we can derive from this axiomatization additional rules to reason about couplings, which can be seen in Fig. 4. These rules will be the key to proving the soundness of the probabilistic fragment of the relational proof system, and can be shown to be sound themselves.

Proposition 2 (Soundness of derived rules). *The additional rules are sound.*

6   Relational Proof System

We complete the formal description of the system by describing the proof rules for the non-probabilistic fragment of the relational proof system (the rules of the probabilistic fragment were described in Sect. 3.2).

6.1   Proof Rules

The rules for core λ-calculus constructs are identical to those of [2]; for convenience, we present a selection of the main rules in Fig. 7 in the appendix.

$$\frac{\phi \in \Psi}{\Delta \mid \Sigma \mid \Gamma \mid \Psi \vdash \phi} \ \mathsf{AX_U} \qquad \frac{\phi \in \Sigma}{\Delta \mid \Sigma \mid \Gamma \mid \Psi \vdash \phi} \ \mathsf{AX_G} \qquad \frac{\Gamma \vdash t : \tau \quad \Gamma \vdash t' : \tau \quad t \equiv t'}{\Delta \mid \Sigma \mid \Gamma \mid \Psi \vdash t = t'} \ \mathsf{CONV}$$

$$\frac{\Delta \mid \Sigma \mid \Gamma \mid \Psi \vdash \phi[t/x] \quad \Delta \mid \Sigma \mid \Gamma \mid \Psi \vdash t = u}{\Delta \mid \Sigma \mid \Gamma \mid \Psi \vdash \phi[u/x]} \ \mathsf{SUBST} \qquad \frac{\Delta \mid \Sigma \mid \Gamma \mid \Psi, \triangleright\phi \vdash \phi}{\Delta \mid \Sigma \mid \Gamma \mid \Psi \vdash \phi} \ \mathsf{Loeb}$$

$$\frac{\Delta \mid \Sigma \mid \Gamma, x_1 : A_1, \ldots, x_n : A_n \mid \Psi \vdash \phi \quad \Delta \mid \Gamma \vdash t_1 : \triangleright A_1 \quad \ldots \quad \Delta \mid \Gamma \vdash t_n : \triangleright A_n}{\Delta \mid \Sigma \mid \Gamma \mid \Psi \vdash \triangleright[x_1 \leftarrow t_1, \ldots, x_n \leftarrow t_n].\phi} \ \triangleright\mathsf{I}$$

$$\frac{\Delta \mid \Sigma \mid \cdot \mid \cdot \vdash \triangleright[x_1 \leftarrow t_1 \ldots x_n \leftarrow t_n].\phi \quad \Delta \mid \bullet \vdash t_1 : \triangleright A_1 \quad \ldots \quad \Delta \mid \bullet \vdash t_n : \triangleright A_n}{\Delta \mid \Sigma \mid \Gamma \mid \Psi \vdash \phi[\mathsf{prev}\ t_1/x_1] \ldots [\mathsf{prev}\ t_n/x_n]} \ \triangleright\mathsf{E}$$

$$\frac{\Delta \mid \Sigma \mid \Gamma \mid \Psi \vdash \triangleright[x_1 \leftarrow t_1, \ldots, x_n \leftarrow t_n].\psi \quad \Delta \mid \Gamma \vdash t_1 : \triangleright A_1 \ldots \Delta \mid \Gamma \vdash t_n : \triangleright A_n \quad \Delta \mid \Sigma \mid \Gamma, x_1 : A_1, \ldots, x_n : A_n \mid \Psi, \psi \vdash \phi}{\Delta \mid \Sigma \mid \Gamma \mid \Psi \vdash \triangleright[x_1 \leftarrow t_1, \ldots, x_n \leftarrow t_n].\phi} \ \triangleright\mathsf{App}$$

$$\frac{\Delta \mid \Sigma \mid \cdot \mid \cdot \vdash \phi}{\Delta \mid \Sigma \mid \Gamma \mid \Psi \vdash \Box\phi} \ \Box\mathsf{I} \qquad \frac{\Delta \mid \Sigma \mid \Gamma \mid \Psi \vdash \Box\psi \quad \Delta \mid \Sigma, \psi \mid \Gamma \mid \Psi \vdash \phi}{\Delta \mid \Sigma \mid \Gamma \mid \Psi \vdash \phi} \ \Box\mathsf{E}$$

Fig. 3. Selected Guarded Higher-Order Logic rules

$$\frac{\Delta \mid \Sigma \mid \Gamma \mid \Psi \vdash \Diamond_{[x_1 \leftarrow t_1, x_2 \leftarrow t_2]}\phi \quad \Delta \mid \Sigma \mid \Gamma, x_1 : C_1, x_2 : C_2 \mid \Psi, \phi \vdash \psi}{\Delta \mid \Sigma \mid \Gamma \mid \Psi \vdash \Diamond_{[x_1 \leftarrow t_1, x_2 \leftarrow t_2]}\psi} \ \mathsf{MONO2}$$

$$\frac{\Delta \mid \Sigma \mid \Gamma \mid \Psi \vdash \phi[t_1/x_1][t_2/x_2]}{\Delta \mid \Sigma \mid \Gamma \mid \Psi \vdash \Diamond_{[x_1 \leftarrow \mathsf{munit}(t_1), x_2 \leftarrow \mathsf{munit}(t_2)]}\phi} \ \mathsf{UNIT2}$$

$$\frac{\Delta \mid \Sigma \mid \Gamma \mid \Psi \vdash \Diamond_{[x_1 \leftarrow t_1, x_2 \leftarrow t_2]}\phi \quad \Delta \mid \Sigma \mid \Gamma, x_1 : C_1, x_2 : C_2 \mid \Psi, \phi \vdash \Diamond_{[y_1 \leftarrow t'_1, y_2 \leftarrow t'_2]}\psi}{\Delta \mid \Sigma \mid \Gamma \mid \Psi \vdash \Diamond_{[y_1 \leftarrow \mathsf{let}\ x_1 = t_1\ \mathsf{in}\ t'_1, y_2 \leftarrow \mathsf{let}\ x_2 = t_2\ \mathsf{in}\ t'_2]}\psi} \ \mathsf{MLET2}$$

$$\frac{\Delta \mid \Sigma \mid \Gamma \mid \Psi \vdash \Diamond_{[x_1 \leftarrow t_1]}\phi \quad \Delta \mid \Sigma \mid \Gamma, x_1 : C_1 \mid \Psi, \phi \vdash \Diamond_{[y_1 \leftarrow t'_1, y_2 \leftarrow t'_2]}\psi}{\Delta \mid \Sigma \mid \Gamma \mid \Psi \vdash \Diamond_{[y_1 \leftarrow \mathsf{let}\ x_1 = t_1\ \mathsf{in}\ t'_1, y_2 \leftarrow t'_2]}\psi} \ \mathsf{MLET\text{-}L}$$

Fig. 4. Derived rules for probabilistic constructs

We briefly comment on the two-sided rules for the new constructs (Fig. 5). The notation Ω abbreviates a context $\Delta \mid \Sigma \mid \Gamma \mid \Psi$. The rule [Next] relates two terms that have a $\triangleright$ term constructor at the top level. We require that both have one term in the delayed substitutions and that they are related pairwise. Then this relation is used to prove another relation between the main terms. This rule can be generalized to terms with more than one term in the delayed substitution. The rule [Prev] proves a relation between terms from the same delayed relation by applying prev to both terms. The rule [Box] proves a relation between two boxed terms if the same relation can be proven in a constant context. Dually, [LetBox] uses a relation between two boxed terms to prove a relation between their unboxings. [LetConst] is similar to [LetBox], but it requires instead a relation between two constant terms, rather than explicitly $\Box$-ed terms. The rule [Fix] relates two fixpoints following the [Loeb] rule from Guarded HOL. Notice that in the premise, the fixpoints need to appear in the delayed substitution so that the inductive hypothesis is well-formed. The rule [Cons] proves relations on streams from relations between their heads and tails, while [Head] and [Tail] behave as converses of [Cons].

Figure 6 contains the one-sided versions of the rules. We only present the left-sided versions as the right-sided versions are completely symmetric. The rule [Next-L] relates at ϕ a term that has a $\triangleright$ with a term that does not have a $\triangleright$. First, a unary property ϕ' is proven on the term u in the delayed substitution, and it is then used as a premise to prove ϕ on the terms with delays removed. Rules for proving unary judgements can be found in the appendix. Similarly, [LetBox-L] proves a unary property on the term that gets unboxed and then uses it as a precondition. The rule [Fix-L] builds a fixpoint just on the left, and relates it with an arbitrary term t_2 at a property ϕ. Since ϕ may contain the variable $\mathbf{r}_2$ which is not in the context, it has to be replaced when adding $\triangleright\phi$ to the logical context in the premise of the rule. The remaining rules are similar to their two-sided counterparts.

6.2   Metatheory

We review some of the most interesting metatheoretical properties of our relational proof system, highlighting the equivalence with Guarded HOL.

Theorem 3 (Equivalence with Guarded HOL).   *For all contexts Δ, Γ; types σ_1, σ_2; terms t_1, t_2; sets of assertions Σ, Ψ; and assertions ϕ:*

$$\Delta \mid \Sigma \mid \Gamma \mid \Psi \vdash t_1 : \sigma_1 \sim t_2 : \sigma_2 \mid \phi \quad \Longleftrightarrow \quad \Delta \mid \Sigma \mid \Gamma \mid \Psi \vdash \phi[t_1/\mathbf{r}_1][t_2/\mathbf{r}_2]$$

The forward implication follows by induction on the given derivation. The reverse implication is immediate from the rule which allows to fall back on Guarded HOL in relational proofs. (Rule [SUB] in the appendix). The full proof is in the appendix. The consequence of this theorem is that the syntax-directed, relational proof system we have built on top of Guarded HOL does not lose expressiveness.

The intended semantics of a judgement $\Delta \mid \Sigma \mid \Gamma \mid \Psi \vdash t_1 : A_1 \sim t_2 : A_2 \mid \phi$ is that, for every valuation $\delta \models \Delta$, $\gamma \models \Gamma$, if $[\![\Sigma]\!](\delta)$ and $[\![\Psi]\!](\delta, \gamma)$, then

$$[\![\phi]\!](\delta, \gamma[\mathbf{r}_1 \leftarrow [\![t_1]\!](\delta, \gamma), \mathbf{r}_2 \leftarrow [\![t_2]\!](\delta, \gamma)])$$

Since Guarded HOL is sound with respect to its semantics in the topos of trees, and our relational proof system is equivalent to Guarded HOL, we obtain that our relational proof system is also sound in the topos of trees.

Corollary 2 (Soundness and consistency).   *If $\Delta \mid \Sigma \mid \Gamma \mid \Psi \vdash t_1 : \sigma_2 \sim t_2 : \sigma_2 \mid \phi$, then for every valuation $\delta \models \Delta$, $\gamma \models \Gamma$:*

$$[\![\Delta \vdash \Box\Sigma]\!](\delta) \wedge [\![\Delta \mid \Gamma \vdash \Psi]\!](\delta, \gamma) \Rightarrow$$
$$[\![\Delta \mid \Gamma, \mathbf{r}_1 : \sigma_1, \mathbf{r}_1 : \sigma_2 \vdash \phi]\!](\delta, \gamma[\mathbf{r}_1 \leftarrow [\![\Delta \mid \Gamma \vdash t_1]\!](\delta, \gamma)][\mathbf{r}_2 \leftarrow [\![\Delta \mid \Gamma \vdash t_2]\!](\delta, \gamma)])$$

In particular, there is no proof of $\Delta \mid \emptyset \mid \Gamma \mid \emptyset \vdash t_1 : \sigma_1 \sim t_2 : \sigma_2 \mid \bot$.

$$\frac{\begin{array}{c}\Delta \mid \Sigma \mid \Gamma, x_1 : A_1, x_2 : A_2 \mid \Psi, \phi'[x_1/\mathbf{r}_1][x_2/\mathbf{r}_2] \vdash t_1 : A_1 \sim t_2 : A_2 \mid \phi \\ \Omega \vdash u_1 : \triangleright A_1 \sim u_2 : \triangleright A_2 \mid \triangleright[\mathbf{r}_1, \mathbf{r}_2 \leftarrow \mathbf{r}_1, \mathbf{r}_2].\phi'\end{array}}{\Omega \vdash \triangleright[x_1 \leftarrow u_1].t_1 : \triangleright A_1 \sim \triangleright[x_2 \leftarrow u_2].t_2 : \triangleright A_2 \mid \triangleright[x_1 \leftarrow u_1, x_2 \leftarrow u_2, \mathbf{r}_1 \leftarrow \mathbf{r}_1, \mathbf{r}_2 \leftarrow \mathbf{r}_2].\phi} \; \text{Next}$$

$$\frac{\Delta \mid \Sigma \mid \cdot \mid \cdot \vdash t_1 : \triangleright A_1 \sim t_2 : \triangleright A_2 \mid \triangleright[\mathbf{r}_1, \mathbf{r}_2 \leftarrow \mathbf{r}_1, \mathbf{r}_2].\phi}{\Omega \vdash \text{prev } t_1 : A_1 \sim \text{prev } t_2 : A_2 \mid \phi} \; \text{Prev}$$

$$\frac{\Delta \mid \Sigma \mid \cdot \mid \cdot \vdash t_1 : A_1 \sim t_2 : A_2 \mid \phi}{\Omega \vdash \text{box } t_1 : \square A_1 \sim \text{box } t_2 : \square A_2 \mid \square \phi[\text{letb } x_1 \leftarrow \mathbf{r}_1 \text{ in } x_1/\mathbf{r}_1][\text{letb } x_2 \leftarrow \mathbf{r}_2 \text{ in } x_2/\mathbf{r}_2]} \; \text{Box}$$

$$\frac{\begin{array}{c}\Omega \vdash u_1 : \square B_1 \sim u_2 : \square B_2 \mid \square \phi[\text{letb } x_1 \leftarrow \mathbf{r}_1 \text{ in } x_1/\mathbf{r}_1][\text{letb } x_2 \leftarrow \mathbf{r}_2 \text{ in } x_2/\mathbf{r}_2] \\ \Delta, x_1 : B_1, x_2 : B_2 \mid \Sigma, \phi[x_1/\mathbf{r}_1][x_2/\mathbf{r}_2] \mid \Gamma \mid \Psi \vdash t_1 : A_1 \sim t_2 : A_2 \mid \phi'\end{array}}{\Omega \vdash \text{letb } x_1 \leftarrow u_1 \text{ in } t_1 : A_1 \sim \text{letb } x_2 \leftarrow u_2 \text{ in } t_2 : A_2 \mid \phi'} \; \text{LetBox}$$

$$\frac{\begin{array}{c}B_1, B_2, \phi \text{ constant} \quad FV(\phi) \cap FV(\Gamma) = \emptyset \quad \Omega \vdash u_1 : B_1 \sim u_2 : B_2 \mid \phi \\ \Delta, x_1 : B_1, x_2 : B_2 \mid \Sigma, \phi[x_1/\mathbf{r}_1][x_2/\mathbf{r}_2] \mid \Gamma \mid \Psi \vdash t_1 : A_1 \sim t_2 : A_2 \mid \phi'\end{array}}{\Omega \vdash \text{letc } x_1 \leftarrow u_1 \text{ in } t_1 : A_1 \sim \text{letc } x_2 \leftarrow u_2 \text{ in } t_2 : A_2 \mid \phi'} \; \text{LetConst}$$

$$\frac{\Delta \mid \Sigma \mid \Gamma, f_1 : \triangleright A_1, f_2 : \triangleright A_2 \mid \Psi, \triangleright[\mathbf{r}_1, \mathbf{r}_2 \leftarrow f_1, f_2].\phi \vdash t_1 : A_1 \sim t_2 : A_2 \mid \phi}{\Omega \vdash \text{fix } f_1. \, t_1 : A_1 \sim \text{fix } f_2. \, t_2 : A_2 \mid \phi} \; \text{Fix}$$

$$\frac{\begin{array}{c}\Omega \vdash x_1 : A_1 \sim x_2 : A_2 \mid \phi_h \quad \Omega \vdash xs_1 : \triangleright \text{Str}_{A_1} \sim xs_2 : \triangleright \text{Str}_{A_2} \mid \phi_t \\ \Omega \vdash \forall x_1, x_2, s_1, s_2. \phi_h[x_1/\mathbf{r}_1][x_2/\mathbf{r}_2] \Rightarrow \phi_t[s_1/\mathbf{r}_1][s_2/\mathbf{r}_2] \Rightarrow \phi[x_1 :: s_1/\mathbf{r}_1][x_2 :: s_2/\mathbf{r}_2]\end{array}}{\Omega \vdash x_1 :: s_1 : \text{Str}_{A_1} \sim x_2 :: s_2 : \text{Str}_{A_2} \mid \phi} \; \text{Cons}$$

$$\frac{\Omega \vdash t_1 : \text{Str}_{A_1} \sim t_1 : \text{Str}_{A_1} \mid \phi[hd \, \mathbf{r}_1/\mathbf{r}_1][hd \, \mathbf{r}_2/\mathbf{r}_2]}{\Omega \vdash hd \, t_1 : A_1 \sim hd \, t_2 : A_2 \mid \phi} \; \text{Head}$$

$$\frac{\Omega \vdash t_1 : \text{Str}_{A_1} \sim t_2 : \text{Str}_{A_2} \mid \phi[tl \, \mathbf{r}_1/\mathbf{r}_1][tl \, \mathbf{r}_2/\mathbf{r}_2]}{\Omega \vdash tl \, t_1 : \triangleright \text{Str}_{A_1} \sim tl \, t_2 : \triangleright \text{Str}_{A_2} \mid \phi} \; \text{Tail}$$

Fig. 5. Two-sided rules for Guarded RHOL

6.3 Shift Couplings Revisited

We give further details on how to prove the example with shift couplings from Sect. 3.3. (Additional examples of relational reasoning on non-probabilistic streams can be found in the appendix) Recall the step functions:

$$\text{step} \triangleq \lambda x.\text{let } z = \mathcal{U}_{\{-1,1\}} \text{ in munit}(z + x)$$
$$\text{lstep2} \triangleq \lambda x.\text{let } z = \mathcal{U}_{\{-1,1\}} \text{ in let } b = \mathcal{U}_{\{0,1\}} \text{ in munit}(x + 2 * z * b)$$

We axiomatize the predicate $\text{All}_{2,1}$, which relates the element at position $2i$ in one stream to the element at position i in another stream, as follows.

$$\forall x_1 x_2 xs_1 xs_2 y_1. \phi[z_1/x_1][z_2/x_2] \Rightarrow$$
$$\triangleright [ys_1 \leftarrow xs_1] . \triangleright [zs_1 \leftarrow ys_1, ys_2 \leftarrow xs_2] . \text{All}_{2,1}(zs_1, ys_2, z_1.z_2.\phi) \Rightarrow$$
$$\text{All}_{2,1}(x_1 :: y_1 :: xs_1, x_2 :: xs_2, z_1.z_2.\phi)$$

In fact, we can assume that, in general, we have a family of All_{m_1, m_2} predicates relating two streams at positions $m_1 \cdot i$ and $m_2 \cdot i$ for every i.

$$\frac{\begin{array}{c} \Delta \mid \Sigma \mid \Gamma, x_1 : B_1 \mid \Psi, \phi'[x_1/\mathbf{r}] \vdash t_1 : A_1 \sim t_2 : A_2 \mid \phi \\ \Omega \vdash u_1 : {\triangleright} B_1 \mid {\triangleright}[\mathbf{r} \leftarrow \mathbf{r}].\phi' \end{array}}{\Omega \vdash {\triangleright}[x_1 \leftarrow u_1].t_1 : {\triangleright} A_1 \sim t_2 : A_2 \mid {\triangleright}[x_1 \leftarrow u_1, \mathbf{r}_1 \leftarrow \mathbf{r}_1].\phi} \text{ Next-L}$$

$$\frac{\Delta \mid \Sigma \mid \cdot \mid \cdot \vdash t_1 : {\triangleright} A_1 \sim t_2 : A_2 \mid {\triangleright}[\mathbf{r}_1 \leftarrow \mathbf{r}_1].\phi}{\Delta \mid \Sigma \mid \Gamma_1; \Gamma_2 \mid \Psi_1; \Psi_2 \vdash \text{prev } t_1 : A_1 \sim t_2 : A_2 \mid \phi} \text{ Prev-L}$$

$$\frac{\begin{array}{c} \Delta \mid \Sigma \mid \Gamma_2 \mid \Psi_2 \vdash t_1 : A_1 \sim t_2 : A_2 \mid \phi \\ FV(t_1) \not\subseteq FV(\Gamma_2) \qquad FV(\Psi_2) \subseteq FV(\Gamma_2) \end{array}}{\Delta \mid \Sigma \mid \Gamma_1; \Gamma_2 \mid \Psi_1; \Psi_2 \vdash \text{box } t_1 : \Box A_1 \sim t_2 : A_2 \mid \Box\phi[\text{letb } x_1 \leftarrow \mathbf{r}_1 \text{ in } x_1/\mathbf{r}_1]} \text{ Box-L}$$

$$\frac{\begin{array}{c} \Omega \vdash u_1 : \Box B_1 \mid \Box\phi[\text{letb } x_1 \leftarrow \mathbf{r}_1 \text{ in } x_1/\mathbf{r}] \\ \Delta, x_1 : B_1 \mid \Sigma, \phi[x_1/\mathbf{r}] \mid \Gamma \mid \Psi \vdash t_1 : A_1 \sim t_2 : A_2 \mid \phi' \end{array}}{\Omega \vdash \text{letb } x_1 \leftarrow u_1 \text{ in } t_1 : A_1 \sim t_2 : A_2 \mid \phi'} \text{ LetBox-L}$$

$$\frac{\begin{array}{c} B_1, \phi \text{ constant} \qquad FV(\phi) \cap FV(\Gamma) = \emptyset \qquad \Omega \vdash u_1 : B_1 \mid \phi \\ \Delta, x_1 : B_1 \mid \Sigma, \phi[x_1/\mathbf{r}] \mid \Gamma \mid \Psi \vdash t_1 : A_1 \sim t_2 : A_2 \mid \phi' \end{array}}{\Omega \vdash \text{letc } x_1 \leftarrow u_1 \text{ in } t_1 : A_1 \sim t_2 : A_2 \mid \phi'} \text{ LetConst-L}$$

$$\frac{\Delta \mid \Sigma \mid \Gamma, f_1 : {\triangleright} A_1 \mid \Psi, {\triangleright}[\mathbf{r}_1 \leftarrow f_1].(\phi[t_2/\mathbf{r}_2]) \vdash t_1 : A_1 \sim t_2 : A_2 \mid \phi}{\Delta \mid \Sigma \mid \Gamma \mid \Psi \vdash \text{fix } f_1.\, t_1 : A_1 \sim t_2 : A_2 \mid \phi} \text{ Fix-L}$$

$$\frac{\begin{array}{c} \Omega \vdash x_1 : A_1 \sim t_2 : A_2 \mid \phi_h \qquad \Omega \vdash xs_1 : {\triangleright}\text{Str}_{A_1} \sim t_2 : A_2 \mid \phi_t \\ \Omega \vdash \forall x_1, x_2, xs_1.\phi_h[x_1/\mathbf{r}_1][x_2/\mathbf{r}_2] \Rightarrow \phi_t[xs_1/\mathbf{r}_1][x_2/\mathbf{r}_2] \Rightarrow \phi[x_1::xs_1/\mathbf{r}_1][x_2/\mathbf{r}_2] \end{array}}{\Omega \vdash x_1::xs_1 : \text{Str}_{A_1} \sim t_2 : A_2 \mid \phi} \text{ Cons-L}$$

$$\frac{\Omega \vdash t_1 : \text{Str}_{A_1} \sim t_1 : A_2 \mid \phi[\text{hd } \mathbf{r}_1/\mathbf{r}_1]}{\Omega \vdash \text{hd } t_1 : A_1 \sim t_2 : A_2 \mid \phi} \text{ Head-L}$$

$$\frac{\Omega \vdash t_1 : \text{Str}_{A_1} \sim t_2 : A_2 \mid \phi[\text{tl } \mathbf{r}_1/\mathbf{r}_1]}{\Omega \vdash \text{tl } t_1 : {\triangleright}\text{Str}_{A_1} \sim t_2 : A_2 \mid \phi} \text{ Tail-L}$$

Fig. 6. One-sided rules for Guarded RHOL

We can now express the existence of a shift coupling by the statement:

$$p_1 = p_2 \vdash \text{markov}(p_1, \text{step}) \sim \text{markov}(p_2, \text{lstep2}) \mid \Diamond_{\substack{[y_1 \leftarrow \mathbf{r}_1] \\ [y_2 \leftarrow \mathbf{r}_2]}} \text{All}_{2,1}(y_1, y_2, z_1.z_2.z_1 = z_2)$$

For the proof, we need to introduce an asynchronous rule for Markov chains:

$$\frac{\begin{array}{c} \Omega \vdash t_1 : C_1 \sim t_2 : C_2 \mid \phi \\ \Omega \vdash (\lambda x_1.\text{let } x_1' = h_1\, x_1 \text{ in } h_1\, x_1') : C_1 \rightarrow \text{D}(C_1) \sim h_2 : C_2 \rightarrow \text{D}(C_2) \mid \\ \forall x_1 x_2.\phi[x_1/z_1][x_2/z_2] \Rightarrow \Diamond_{[z_1 \leftarrow \mathbf{r}_1\ x_1, z_2 \leftarrow \mathbf{r}_2\ x_2]}\phi \end{array}}{\begin{array}{c} \Omega \vdash \text{markov}(t_1, h_1) : \text{D}(\text{Str}_{C_1}) \sim \text{markov}(t_2, h_2) : \text{D}(\text{Str}_{C_2}) \mid \\ \Diamond_{[y_1 \leftarrow \mathbf{r}_1, y_2 \leftarrow \mathbf{r}_2]} \text{All}_{2,1}(y_1, y_2, z_1.z_2.\phi) \end{array}} \text{ Markov-2-1}$$

This asynchronous rule for Markov chains shares the motivations of the rule for loops proposed in [6]. Note that one can define a rule [Markov-m-n] for arbitrary m and n to prove a judgement of the form $\text{All}_{m,n}$ on two Markov chains.

We show the proof of the shift coupling. By equational reasoning, we get:

$$\lambda x_1.\text{let } x_1' = h_1 \; x_1 \text{ in } h_1 \; x_1' \equiv \lambda x_1.\text{let } z_1 = \mathcal{U}_{\{-1,1\}} \text{ in } h_1 \; (z_1 + x_1)$$
$$\equiv \lambda x_1.\text{let } z_1 = \mathcal{U}_{\{-1,1\}} \text{ in let } z_1' = \mathcal{U}_{\{-1,1\}} \text{ in } \mathsf{munit}(z_1' + z_1 + x_1')$$

and the only interesting premise of [Markov-2-1] is:

$$
\begin{array}{ccc}
\lambda x_1. \text{ let } z_1 = \mathcal{U}_{\{-1,1\}} \text{ in} & \lambda x_2. \text{ let } z_2 = \mathcal{U}_{\{-1,1\}} \text{ in} & \\
\text{let } z_1' = \mathcal{U}_{\{-1,1\}} \text{ in} \quad \sim & \text{let } b_2 = \mathcal{U}_{\{1,0\}} \text{ in} & \forall x_1 x_2. x_1 = x_2 \Rightarrow \\
\mathsf{munit}(z_1' + z_1 + x_1') & \mathsf{munit}(x_2 + 2 * b_2 * z_2) & \mathbf{r}_1 \; x_1 \overset{\diamond}{=} \mathbf{r}_2 \; x_2
\end{array}
$$

Couplings between z_1 and z_2 and between z_1' and b_2 can be found by simple computations. This completes the proof.

7   Related Work

Our probabilistic guarded λ-calculus and the associated logic Guarded HOL build on top of the guarded λ-calculus and its internal logic [1]. The guarded λ-calculus has been extended to guarded dependent type theory [13], which can be understood as a theory of guarded refinement types and as a foundation for proof assistants based on guarded type theory. These systems do not reason about probabilities, and do not support syntax-directed (relational) reasoning, both of which we support.

Relational models for higher-order programming languages are often defined using logical relations. [16] showed how to use second-order logic to define and reason about logical relations for the second-order lambda calculus. Recent work has extended this approach to logical relations for higher-order programming languages with computational effects such as nontermination, general references, and concurrency [17–20]. The logics used in *loc. cit.* are related to our work in two ways: (1) the logics in *loc. cit.* make use of the later modality for reasoning about recursion, and (2) the models of the logics in *loc. cit.* can in fact be defined using guarded type theory. Our work is more closely related to Relational Higher Order Logic [2], which applies the idea of logic-enriched type theories [21,22] to a relational setting. There exist alternative approaches for reasoning about relational properties of higher-order programs; for instance, [23] have recently proposed to use monadic reification for reducing relational verification of F^* to proof obligations in higher-order logic.

A series of work develops reasoning methods for probabilistic higher-order programs for different variations of the lambda calculus. One line of work has focused on operationally-based techniques for reasoning about contextual equivalence of programs. The methods are based on probabilistic bisimulations [24,25] or on logical relations [26]. Most of these approaches have been developed for languages with discrete distributions, but recently there has also been work on languages with continuous distributions [27,28]. Another line of work has focused on denotational models, starting with the seminal work in [29]. Recent work includes support for relational reasoning about equivalence of programs with continuous distributions for a total programming language [30]. Our approach is most closely related to prior work based on relational refinement types for higher-order probabilistic programs. These were initially considered by [31] for a stateful fragment of F^*, and later by [32,33] for a pure language. Both systems are specialized to building probabilistic couplings; however, the latter support approximate probabilistic couplings, which yield a natural interpretation of differential privacy [34], both in its vanilla and approximate forms (i.e. ϵ- and (ϵ, δ)-privacy). Technically, approximate couplings are modelled as a graded monad, where the index of the monad tracks the privacy budget (ϵ or (ϵ, δ)). Both systems are strictly syntax-directed, and cannot reason about computations that have different types or syntactic structures, while our system can.

8   Conclusion

We have developed a probabilistic extension of the (simply typed) guarded λ-calculus, and proposed a syntax-directed proof system for relational verification. Moreover, we have verified a series of examples that are beyond the reach of prior work. Finally, we have proved the soundness of the proof system with respect to the topos of trees.

There are several natural directions for future work. One first direction is to enhance the expressiveness of the underlying simply typed language. For instance, it would be interesting to introduce clock variables and some type dependency as in [13], and extend the proof system accordingly. This would allow us, for example, to type the function taking the n-th element of a *guarded* stream, which cannot be done in the current system. Another exciting direction is to consider approximate couplings, as in [32,33], and to develop differential privacy for infinite streams—preliminary work in this direction, such as [35], considers very large lists, but not arbitrary streams. A final direction would be to extend our approach to continuous distributions to support other application domains.

Acknowledgments. We would like to thank the anonymous reviewers for their time and their helpful input. This research was supported in part by the ModuRes Sapere Aude Advanced Grant from The Danish Council for Independent Research for the Natural Sciences (FNU), by a research grant (12386, Guarded Homotopy Type Theory) from the VILLUM foundation, and by NSF under grant 1718220.

References

1. Clouston, R., Bizjak, A., Grathwohl, H.B., Birkedal, L.: The guarded lambda-calculus: programming and reasoning with guarded recursion for coinductive types. Log. Methods Comput. Sci. **12**(3) (2016)
2. Aguirre, A., Barthe, G., Gaboardi, M., Garg, D., Strub, P.: A relational logic for higher-order programs. PACMPL **1**(ICFP), 21:1–21:29 (2017)
3. Lindvall, T.: Lectures on the Coupling Method. Courier Corporation (2002)

4. Thorisson, H.: Coupling, Stationarity, and Regeneration. Springer, New York (2000)

5. Barthe, G., Espitau, T., Grégoire, B., Hsu, J., Stefanesco, L., Strub, P.-Y.: Relational reasoning via probabilistic coupling. In: Davis, M., Fehnker, A., McIver, A., Voronkov, A. (eds.) LPAR 2015. LNCS, vol. 9450, pp. 387–401. Springer, Heidelberg (2015). https://doi.org/10.1007/978-3-662-48899-7_27

6. Barthe, G., Grégoire, B., Hsu, J., Strub, P.: Coupling proofs are probabilistic product programs. In: POPL 2017, Paris, France, 18–20 January 2017 (2017)

7. Strassen, V.: The existence of probability measures with given marginals. Ann. Math. Stat. **36**, 423–439 (1965)

8. Goguen, J.A., Meseguer, J.: Security policies and security models. In: IEEE Symposium on Security and Privacy, pp. 11–20 (1982)

9. Bogdanov, D., Niitsoo, M., Toft, T., Willemson, J.: High-performance secure multi-party computation for data mining applications. Int. J. Inf. Sec. **11**(6), 403–418 (2012)

10. Cramer, R., Damgard, I.B., Nielsen, J.B.: Secure Multiparty Computation and Secret Sharing, 1st edn. Cambridge University Press, New York (2015)

11. Barthe, G., Espitau, T., Grégoire, B., Hsu, J., Strub, P.: Proving uniformity and independence by self-composition and coupling. CoRR abs/1701.06477 (2017)

12. Canetti, R.: Universally composable security: a new paradigm for cryptographic protocols. In: Proceedings of Foundations of Computer Science. IEEE (2001)

13. Bizjak, A., Grathwohl, H.B., Clouston, R., Møgelberg, R.E., Birkedal, L.: Guarded dependent type theory with coinductive types. In: Jacobs, B., Löding, C. (eds.) FoSSaCS 2016. LNCS, vol. 9634, pp. 20–35. Springer, Heidelberg (2016). https://doi.org/10.1007/978-3-662-49630-5_2

14. McBride, C., Paterson, R.: Applicative programming with effects. J. Funct. Program. **18**(1), 1–13 (2008)

15. Birkedal, L., Møgelberg, R.E., Schwinghammer, J., Støvring, K.: First steps in synthetic guarded domain theory: step-indexing in the topos of trees. Log. Methods Comput. Sci. **8**(4) (2012)

16. Plotkin, G., Abadi, M.: A logic for parametric polymorphism. In: Bezem, M., Groote, J.F. (eds.) TLCA 1993. LNCS, vol. 664, pp. 361–375. Springer, Heidelberg (1993). https://doi.org/10.1007/BFb0037118

17. Dreyer, D., Ahmed, A., Birkedal, L.: Logical step-indexed logical relations. Log. Methods Comput. Sci. **7**(2) (2011)

18. Turon, A., Dreyer, D., Birkedal, L.: Unifying refinement and Hoare-style reasoning in a logic for higher-order concurrency. In: Morrisett, G., Uustalu, T. (eds.) ICFP 2013, Boston, MA, USA, 25–27 September 2013. ACM (2013)

19. Krebbers, R., Timany, A., Birkedal, L.: Interactive proofs in higher-order concurrent separation logic. In: Castagna, G., Gordon, A.D. (eds.) POPL 2017, Paris, France, 18–20 January 2017. ACM (2017)

20. Krogh-Jespersen, M., Svendsen, K., Birkedal, L.: A relational model of types-and-effects in higher-order concurrent separation logic. In: POPL 2017, Paris, France, 18–20 January 2017, pp. 218–231 (2017)

21. Aczel, P., Gambino, N.: Collection principles in dependent type theory. In: Callaghan, P., Luo, Z., McKinna, J., Pollack, R., Pollack, R. (eds.) TYPES 2000. LNCS, vol. 2277, pp. 1–23. Springer, Heidelberg (2002). https://doi.org/10.1007/3-540-45842-5_1

22. Aczel, P., Gambino, N.: The generalised type-theoretic interpretation of constructive set theory. J. Symb. Log. **71**(1), 67–103 (2006)

23. Grimm, N., Maillard, K., Fournet, C., Hritcu, C., Maffei, M., Protzenko, J., Rastogi, A., Swamy, N., Béguelin, S.Z.: A monadic framework for relational verification (functional pearl). CoRR abs/1703.00055 (2017)
24. Crubillé, R., Dal Lago, U.: On probabilistic applicative bisimulation and call-by-value λ-calculi. In: Shao, Z. (ed.) ESOP 2014. LNCS, vol. 8410, pp. 209–228. Springer, Heidelberg (2014). https://doi.org/10.1007/978-3-642-54833-8_12
25. Sangiorgi, D., Vignudelli, V.: Environmental bisimulations for probabilistic higher-order languages. In: Bodík, R., Majumdar, R. (eds.) POPL 2016, St. Petersburg, FL, USA, 20–22 January 2016. ACM (2016)
26. Bizjak, A., Birkedal, L.: Step-indexed logical relations for probability. In: Pitts, A. (ed.) FoSSaCS 2015. LNCS, vol. 9034, pp. 279–294. Springer, Heidelberg (2015). https://doi.org/10.1007/978-3-662-46678-0_18
27. Borgström, J., Lago, U.D., Gordon, A.D., Szymczak, M.: A lambda-calculus foundation for universal probabilistic programming. In: Garrigue, J., Keller, G., Sumii, E. (eds.) ICFP 2016, Nara, Japan, 18–22 September 2016. ACM (2016)
28. Culpepper, R., Cobb, A.: Contextual equivalence for probabilistic programs with continuous random variables and scoring. In: Yang, H. (ed.) ESOP 2017. LNCS, vol. 10201, pp. 368–392. Springer, Heidelberg (2017). https://doi.org/10.1007/978-3-662-54434-1_14
29. Jones, C., Plotkin, G.D.: A probabilistic powerdomain of evaluations. In: LICS 1989, Pacific Grove, California, USA, 5–8 June 1989. IEEE Computer Society (1989)
30. Staton, S., Yang, H., Wood, F., Heunen, C., Kammar, O.: Semantics for probabilistic programming: higher-order functions, continuous distributions, and soft constraints. In: LICS 2016, New York, NY, USA, 5–8 July 2016. ACM (2016)
31. Barthe, G., Fournet, C., Grégoire, B., Strub, P., Swamy, N., Béguelin, S.Z.: Probabilistic relational verification for cryptographic implementations. In: Jagannathan, S., Sewell, P. (eds.) POPL 2014 (2014)
32. Barthe, G., Gaboardi, M., Gallego Arias, E.J., Hsu, J., Roth, A., Strub, P.Y.: Higher-order approximate relational refinement types for mechanism design and differential privacy. In: POPL 2015, Mumbai, India, 15–17 January 2015 (2015)
33. Barthe, G., Farina, G.P., Gaboardi, M., Arias, E.J.G., Gordon, A., Hsu, J., Strub, P.: Differentially private Bayesian programming. In: CCS 2016, Vienna, Austria, 24–28 October 2016. ACM (2016)
34. Dwork, C., Roth, A.: The algorithmic foundations of differential privacy. Found. Trends Theor. Comput. Sci. 9(3–4), 211–407 (2014)
35. Kellaris, G., Papadopoulos, S., Xiao, X., Papadias, D.: Differentially private event sequences over infinite streams. PVLDB 7(12), 1155–1166 (2014)

Types and Effects

Failure is Not an Option
An Exceptional Type Theory

Pierre-Marie Pédrot[1](✉) and Nicolas Tabareau[2]

[1] MPI-SWS, Saarbrücken, Germany
ppedrot@mpi-sws.org
[2] Inria, Nantes, France
nicolas.tabareau@inria.fr

Abstract. We define the *exceptional translation*, a syntactic translation of the Calculus of Inductive Constructions (CIC) into itself, that covers full dependent elimination. The new resulting type theory features call-by-name exceptions with decidable type-checking and canonicity, but at the price of inconsistency. Then, noticing parametricity amounts to Kreisel's realizability in this setting, we provide an additional layer on top of the exceptional translation in order to tame exceptions and ensure that all exceptions used locally are caught, leading to the *parametric exceptional translation* which fully preserves consistency. This way, we can consistently extend the logical expressivity of CIC with independence of premises, Markov's rule, and the negation of function extensionality while retaining η-expansion. As a byproduct, we also show that Markov's principle is not provable in CIC. Both translations have been implemented in a Coq plugin, which we use to formalize the examples.

1 Introduction

Monadic translations constitute a canonical way to add effects to pure functional languages [1]. Until recently, this technique was not available for type theories such as CIC because of complex interactions with dependency. In a recent paper [2], we have presented a generic way to extend the monadic translation to dependent types, using the *weaning translation*, as soon as the monad under consideration satisfies a crucial property: being self-algebraic. Indeed, in the same way that the universe of types $\square_i$ is itself a type (of a higher universe) in type theory, the type of algebras of a monad T

$$\Sigma A : \square_i.\, \mathrm{T}\, A \to A$$

needs to be itself an algebra of the monad to allow a correct translation of the universe. However, in general, the weaning translation does not interpret all of CIC because dependent elimination needs to be restricted to linear predicates, that is, those that are intuitively call-by-value [3]. In this paper, we study the particular case of the error monad, and show that its weaning translation can be simplified and tweaked so that full dependent elimination is valid.

A. Ahmed (Ed.): ESOP 2018, LNCS 10801, pp. 245–271, 2018.
https://doi.org/10.1007/978-3-319-89884-1_9

This *exceptional translation* gives rise to a novel extension of CIC with new computational behaviours, namely call-by-name exceptions.[1] That is, the type theory induced by the exceptional translation features new operations to raise and catch exceptions. This new logical expressivity comes at a cost, as the resulting theory is not consistent anymore, although still being computationally relevant. This means that it is possible to prove a contradiction, but, thanks to a weak form of canonicity, only because of an unhandled exception. Furthermore, the translation allows us to reason directly in CIC on terms of the exceptional theory, letting us prove, e.g., that assuming some properties on its input, an exceptional function actually never raises an exception. We thus have a sound logical framework to prove safety properties about impure dependently-typed programs.

We then push this technique further by noticing that parametricity provides a systematic way to describe that a term is not allowed to produce uncaught exceptions, bridging the gap between Kreisel's modified realizability [4] and parametricity inside type theory [5]. This *parametric exceptional translation* ensures that no exception reaches toplevel, thus ensuring consistency of the resulting theory. Pure terms are automatically handled, while it is necessary to show parametricity manually for terms internally using exceptions. We exploit this computational extension of CIC to show various logical results over CIC.

Contributions

- We describe the *exceptional translation*, the first monadic translation for the error monad for CIC, including strong elimination of inductive types, resulting in a sound logical framework to reason about impure dependently-typed programs.
- We use parametricity to extend the exceptional translation, getting a consistent variant dubbed the *parametric exceptional translation*.
- We show that Markov's rule is admissible in CIC.
- We show that definitional η-expansion together with the negation of function extensionality is admissible in CIC.
- We show that there exists a syntactical model of CIC that validates the independence of premises (which is known to be generally not valid in intuitionistic logic [6]) and use it to recover the recent result of Coquand and Mannaa [7], *i.e.*, that Markov's principle is not provable in CIC.
- We provide a CoQ plugin[2] that implements both translations and with which we have formalized all the examples.

Plan of the Paper. In Sect. 2, we describe the exceptional translation and the resulting new computational principles arising from it. In Sect. 3, we present the parametric variant of the exceptional translation. Section 4 is devoted to the

---

[1] The fact that the resulting exception are call-by-name is explained in detailed in [2] using a call-by-push-value decomposition. Intuitively, it comes from the fact that CIC is naturally call-by-name.

[2] The plugin is available at https://github.com/CoqHott/exceptional-tt.

$$A, B, M, N ::= \square_i \mid x \mid M\ N \mid \lambda x : A.\ M \mid \Pi x : A.\ B$$

$$\Gamma, \Delta ::= \cdot \mid \Gamma, x : A$$

$$\frac{\vdash \Gamma \qquad i < j}{\Gamma \vdash \square_i : \square_j} \qquad\qquad \frac{\Gamma \vdash M : B \qquad \Gamma \vdash A : \square_i}{\Gamma, x : A \vdash M : B}$$

$$\frac{\Gamma \vdash A : \square_i \qquad \Gamma, x : A \vdash B : \square_j}{\Gamma \vdash \Pi x : A.\ B : \square_{\max(i,j)}} \qquad\qquad \frac{\Gamma \vdash M : B \qquad \Gamma \vdash A : \square_i \qquad A \equiv B}{\Gamma \vdash M : A}$$

$$\frac{\Gamma, x : A \vdash M : B \qquad \Gamma \vdash \Pi x : A.\ B : \square_i}{\Gamma \vdash \lambda x : A.\ M : \Pi x : A.\ B} \qquad\qquad \frac{\Gamma \vdash M : \Pi x : A.\ B \qquad \Gamma \vdash N : A}{\Gamma \vdash M\ N : B\{x := N\}}$$

$$\frac{}{\vdash \cdot} \qquad \frac{\Gamma \vdash A : \square_i}{\vdash \Gamma, x : A} \qquad\qquad \frac{\Gamma \vdash A : \square_i}{\Gamma, x : A \vdash x : A}$$

$$(\lambda x : A.\ M)\ N \equiv M\{x := N\} \qquad\qquad \text{(congruence rules ommitted)}$$

Fig. 1. Typing rules of CC_ω

various logical results resulting from the parametric exceptional translations. In Sect. 5, we discuss possible extensions of the translation with negative records and an impredicative universe. Section 6 describes the Coq plugin and illustrates its use on a concrete example. We discuss related work in Sect. 7 and conclude in Sect. 8.

2   The Exceptional Translation

We define in this section the exceptional translation as a syntactic translation between type theories. We call the target theory $\mathcal{T}$, upon which we will make various assumptions depending on the objects we want to translate.

2.1   Adding Exceptions to CC_ω

In this section, we describe the exceptional translation over a purely negative theory, *i.e.*, featuring only universes and dependent functions, called CC_ω, which is presented in Fig. 1. This theory is a predicative version of the Calculus of Constructions [8], with an infinite hierarchy of universes $\square_i$ instead of one impredicative sort. We assume from now on that $\mathcal{T}$ contains at least CC_ω itself.

The exceptional translation is a simplification of the weaning translation [2] applied to the error monad. Owing to the fact that it is specifically tailored for exceptions, this allows to give a more compact presentation of it.

Let $\mathbb{E} : \square_0$ be a fixed type of exceptions in $\mathcal{T}$. The weaning translation for the error monad amounts to interpret types as algebras, *i.e.*, as inhabitants of the dependent sum $\Sigma A : \square_i.\,(A + \mathbb{E}) \to A$. In this paper, we take advantage of the fact that the algebra morphism restricted to A is always the identity. Thus every type just comes with a way to interpret failure on this type, i.e. types are intuitively interpreted as a pair of an $A : \square_i$ with a default (raise) function $A_\varnothing : \mathbb{E} \to A$. In practice, it is slightly more complicated as the universe of types itself is a type, so its interpretation must comes with a default function. We overcome this issue by assuming a term $\mathtt{type}_i$, representing types that can raise exceptions. This type comes with two constructors: $\mathtt{TypeVal}_i$ which allows to construct a $\mathtt{type}_i$ from a type and a default function on this type ; and another constructor $\mathtt{TypeErr}_i$ that represents the default function at the level of $\mathtt{type}_i$. Furthermore, $\mathtt{type}_i$ is equipped with an eliminator $\mathtt{type\_elim}_i$ and thus can be thought of as an inductive definition. For simplicity, we axiomatize it instead of requiring inductive types in the target of the translation.

Definition 1. *We assume that* $\mathcal{T}$ *features the data below, where* i, j *indices stand for universe polymorphism.*

- $\Omega_i : \mathbb{E} \to \square_i$
- $\omega_i : \Pi e : \mathbb{E}.\,\Omega_i\, e$
- $\mathtt{type}_i : \square_j$, *where* $i < j$
- $\mathtt{TypeVal}_i : \Pi A : \square_i.\,(\mathbb{E} \to A) \to \mathtt{type}_i$
- $\mathtt{TypeErr}_i : \mathbb{E} \to \mathtt{type}_i$
- $\mathtt{type\_elim}_{i,j} : \quad \Pi P : \mathtt{type}_i \to \square_j.$
$$(\Pi(A : \square_i)\,(A_\varnothing : \mathbb{E} \to A).\,P\,(\mathtt{TypeVal}_i\, A\, A_\varnothing)) \to$$
$$(\Pi e : \mathbb{E}.\,P\,(\mathtt{TypeErr}_i\, e)) \to \Pi T : \mathtt{type}_i.\,P\,T$$

subject to the following definitional equations:

$$\mathtt{type\_elim}_{i,j}\, P\, p_v\, p_\varnothing\,(\mathtt{TypeVal}_i\, A\, A_\varnothing) \equiv p_v\, A\, A_\varnothing$$

$$\mathtt{type\_elim}_{i,j}\, P\, p_v\, p_\varnothing\,(\mathtt{TypeErr}_i\, e) \equiv p_\varnothing\, e$$

The Ω term describes what it means for a type to fail, i.e. it ascribes a meaning to sequents of the form $\Gamma \vdash M : \mathtt{fail}\ e$. In practice, it is irrelevant and can be chosen to be degenerate, e.g. $\Omega := \lambda\_ : \mathbb{E}.\,\mathtt{unit}$.

In what follows, we often leave the universe indices implicit although they can be retrieved at the cost of more explicit annotations.

Before defining the exceptional translation we need to derive a term El[3] that recovers the underlying type from an inhabitant of $\mathtt{type}$ and $\mathtt{Err}$ that lifts the default function to this underlying type.

Definition 2. *From the data of Definition 1, we derive the following terms.*

$$\begin{aligned}
\mathtt{El}_i \ :\ \ & \mathtt{type}_i \to \square_i \\
& := \lambda A : \mathtt{type}_i.\,\mathtt{type\_elim}\,(\lambda T : \mathtt{type}_i.\,\square_i) \\
& \quad\ (\lambda(A_0 : \square_i)\,(A_\varnothing : \mathbb{E} \to A_0).\,A_0)\,\Omega\,A \\
\mathtt{Err}_i \ :\ \ & \Pi A : \mathtt{type}_i.\,\mathbb{E} \to \mathtt{El}_i\, A \\
& := \lambda(A : \mathtt{type}_i)\,(e : \mathbb{E}).\,\mathtt{type\_elim}\,\mathtt{El}_i \\
& \quad\ (\lambda(A_0 : \square_i)\,(A_\varnothing : \mathbb{E} \to A_0).\,A_\varnothing\, e)\,\omega\,A
\end{aligned}$$

---

[3] The notation El refers to universes à la Tarski in Martin-Löf type theory.

$$[\square_i] \quad\quad := \texttt{TypeVal type}_i\ \texttt{TypeErr}_i$$

$$[x] \quad\quad := x$$

$$[\lambda x : A.\, M] := \lambda x : [\![A]\!].\,[M]$$

$$[M\ N] \quad := [M]\,[N]$$

$$[\Pi x : A.\, B] := \texttt{TypeVal}\,(\Pi x : [\![A]\!].\,[\![B]\!])\,(\lambda(e : \mathbb{E})\,(x : [\![A]\!]).\,[B]_\varnothing\ e)$$

$$[A]_\varnothing \quad\quad := \texttt{Err}\,[A]$$

$$[\![A]\!] \quad\quad := \texttt{El}\,[A]$$

$$[\cdot] \quad\quad := \cdot$$

$$[\Gamma, x : A] \quad := [\![\Gamma]\!], x : [\![A]\!]$$

Fig. 2. Exceptional translation

The exceptional translation is defined in Fig. 2. As usual for syntactic translations [9], the term translation is given by $[\cdot]$ and the type translation, written $[\![\cdot]\!]$, is derived from it using the function El. There is an additional macro $[\cdot]_\varnothing$, defined using $\texttt{Err}_i$, which corresponds to the way to inhabit a given type from an exception.

Note that we will often slightly abuse the translation and use the $[\cdot]$ and $[\![\cdot]\!]$ notation as macros acting on the target theory. This is merely for readability purposes, and the corresponding uses are easily expanded to the actual term.

The following lemma makes explicit how $[\![\cdot]\!]$ and $[\cdot]_\varnothing$ behave on universes and on the dependent function space.

Lemma 3 (Unfoldings). *The following definitional equations hold:*

- $[\![\square_i]\!] \equiv \texttt{type}_i$
- $[\![\Pi x : A.\, B]\!] \equiv \Pi x : [\![A]\!].\,[\![B]\!]$
- $[\square_i]_\varnothing\ e \equiv \texttt{TypeErr}_i\ e$
- $[\Pi x : A.\, B]_\varnothing\ e \equiv \lambda x : [\![A]\!].\,[B]_\varnothing\ e$

Proof. By unfolding and straightforward reductions.

The soundness of the translation follows from the following properties, which are fundamental but straightforward to prove.

Theorem 4 (Soundness). *The following properties hold.*

- $[M\{x := N\}] \equiv [M]\{x := [N]\}$ *(substitution lemma).*
- *If* $M \equiv N$ *then* $[M] \equiv [N]$ *(conversion lemma).*
- *If* $\Gamma \vdash M : A$ *then* $[\![\Gamma]\!] \vdash [M] : [\![A]\!]$ *(typing soundness).*
- *If* $\Gamma \vdash A : \square$ *then* $[\![\Gamma]\!] \vdash [A]_\varnothing : \mathbb{E} \to [\![A]\!]$ *(exception soundness).*

Proof. The first property is by routine induction on M, the second is direct by induction on the conversion derivation. The third is by induction on the typing derivation, the most important rule being $\square_i : \square_j$, which holds because $[\square_i] \equiv$ TypeVal type$_i$ TypeErr$_i$ has type type$_j$ which is convertible to $[\![\square_j]\!]$ by Lemma 3. The last property is a direct application of typing soundness and unfolding of Lemma 3 for universes.

We call $\mathcal{T}_\mathbb{E}$ the theory arising from this interpretation, which is formally defined in a way similar to standard categorical constructions over dependent type theory. Terms and contexts of $\mathcal{T}_\mathbb{E}$ are simply terms and contexts of $\mathcal{T}$. A context Γ is valid is $\mathcal{T}_\mathbb{E}$ whenever its translation $[\![\Gamma]\!]$ is valid in $\mathcal{T}$. Two terms M and N are convertible in $\mathcal{T}_\mathbb{E}$ whenever their translations $[M]$ and $[N]$ are convertible in $\mathcal{T}$. Finally, $\Gamma \vdash_{\mathcal{T}_\mathbb{E}} M : A$ whenever $[\![\Gamma]\!] \vdash_{\mathcal{T}} [M] : [\![A]\!]$.

That is, it is possible to extend $\mathcal{T}_\mathbb{E}$ with a new constant c of a given type A by providing an inhabitant c$_\mathbb{E}$ of the translated type $[\![A]\!]$. Then the translation is extended with $[c] := $ c$_\mathbb{E}$. The potential computational rules satisfied by this new constant are directly given by the computational rules satisfied by its translation. In some sense, the new constant c is just syntactic sugar for c$_\mathbb{E}$. Using $\mathcal{T}_\mathbb{E}$, Theorem 4 can be rephrased in the following way.

Theorem 5. *If $\mathcal{T}$ interprets CC_ω then so does $\mathcal{T}_\mathbb{E}$, that is, the exceptional translation is a syntactic model of CC_ω.*

2.2   Exceptional Inductive Types

The fact that the only effect we consider is raising exceptions does not really affect the negative fragment when compared to our previous work [2], but it sure shines when it comes to interpreting inductive datatypes. Indeed, as explained in the introduction, the weaning translation only interprets a subset of CIC, restricting dependent elimination to linear predicates. Furthermore, it also requires a few syntactic properties of the underlying monad ensuring that positivity criteria are preserved through the translation, which can be sometimes hard to obtain.

The exceptional translation diverges from the weaning translation precisely on inductives types. It allows a more compact translation of the latter, while at the same time providing a complete interpretation of CIC, that is, including full dependent elimination.

From now on, we assume that the target theory is a predicative restriction of CIC, i.e. that we can construct in it new inductive datatypes as we do in e.g. CoQ [10], but without considering an impredicative universe. That is, all the inductive types we consider in this section live in $\square$. As a matter of fact, we slightly abuse the usual nomenclature and simply call CIC this predicative fragment in the remainder of the paper. We refrain from describing the generic typing rules that extend CC_ω into CIC, as they are fairly standard and would take up too much space. See for instance Werner's thesis for a comprehensive presentation [11].

$$[\mathcal{I}] := \lambda(p_1 : [\![P_1]\!]) \ldots (p_n : [\![P_n]\!]) (i_1 : [\![I_1]\!]) \ldots (i_m : [\![I_m]\!]).$$
$$\text{TypeVal} \; (\mathcal{I}^\bullet \; p_1 \; \ldots \; p_n \; i_1 \; \ldots \; i_m) \; (\mathcal{I}_\varnothing \; p_1 \; \ldots \; p_n \; i_1 \; \ldots \; i_m)$$
$$[c_1] := c_1^\bullet$$
$$\ldots$$
$$[c_k] := c_k^\bullet$$

Fig. 3. Inductive type translation

Type and Constructor Translation. As explained before, the intuitive interpretation of a type through the exceptional translation is a pair of a type and a default function from exceptions into that type. In particular, when translating some inductive type $\mathcal{I}$, we must come up with a type $[\![\mathcal{I}]\!]$ together with a default function $\mathbb{E} \to [\![\mathcal{I}]\!]$. As soon as $\mathbb{E}$ is inhabited, that means that we need $[\![\mathcal{I}]\!]$ to be inhabited, preferably in a canonical way. The solution is simple: just as for types where we freely added the exceptional case by means of the `TypeErr` constructor, we freely add exceptions to every inductive type.

In practice, there is an elegant and simple way to do this. It just consists in translating constructors pointwise, while adding a new dedicated constructor standing for the exceptional case. We now turn to the formal construction.

Definition 6. *Let $\mathcal{I}$ be an inductive datatype with*

- *parameters $p_1 : P_1, \ldots, p_n : P_n$;*
- *indices $i_1 : I_1, \ldots, i_m : I_m$;*
- *constructors*

$$c_1 : \Pi(a_{1,1} : A_{1,1}) \ldots (a_{1,l_1} : A_{1,l_1}).\mathcal{I} \; p_1 \; \ldots \; p_n \; V_{1,1} \; \ldots \; V_{1,m}$$
$$\ldots$$
$$c_k : \Pi(a_{k,1} : A_{k,1}) \ldots (a_{k,l_k} : A_{k,l_k}).\mathcal{I} \; p_1 \; \ldots \; p_n \; V_{k,1} \; \ldots \; V_{k,m}$$

We define the exceptional translation of $\mathcal{I}$ and its constructors in Fig. 3, where $\mathcal{I}^\bullet$ is the inductive type defined by

- *parameters $p_1 : [\![P_1]\!], \ldots, p_n : [\![P_n]\!]$;*
- *indices $i_1 : [\![I_1]\!], \ldots, i_m : [\![I_m]\!]$;*
- *constructors*

$$c_1^\bullet : \Pi(a_{1,1} : [\![A_{1,1}]\!]) \ldots (a_{1,l_1} : [\![A_{1,l_1}]\!]).\mathcal{I}^\bullet \; p_1 \; \ldots \; p_n \; [V_{1,1}] \; \ldots \; [V_{1,m}]$$
$$\ldots$$
$$c_k^\bullet : \Pi(a_{k,1} : [\![A_{k,1}]\!]) \ldots (a_{k,l_k} : [\![A_{k,l_k}]\!]).\mathcal{I}^\bullet \; p_1 \; \ldots \; p_n \; [V_{k,1}] \; \ldots \; [V_{k,m}]$$
$$\mathcal{I}_\varnothing : \Pi(i_1 : [\![I_1]\!]) \ldots (i_m : [\![I_m]\!]).\mathbb{E} \to \mathcal{I}^\bullet \; p_1 \; \ldots \; p_n \; i_1 \; \ldots \; i_m$$

where in the recursive calls in the various A, we locally set

$$[\![\mathcal{I} \; M_1 \; \ldots \; M_n \; N_1 \; \ldots \; N_m]\!] := \mathcal{I}^\bullet \; [M_1] \; \ldots \; [M_n] \; [N_1] \; \ldots \; [N_m].$$

Example 7. We give a few representative examples of the inductive translation in Fig. 4 in a COQ-like syntax. They were chosen because they are simple instances of inductive types featuring parameters, indices and recursion in an orthogonal way. For convenience, we write $\Sigma \; A \; (\lambda x : A. B)$ as $\Sigma x : A. B$.

$$\text{Ind bool} : \square :=$$
$$\mid \text{true} : \text{bool}$$
$$\mid \text{false} : \text{bool}$$

$$\text{Ind bool}^\bullet : \square :=$$
$$\mid \text{true}^\bullet : \text{bool}^\bullet$$
$$\mid \text{false}^\bullet : \text{bool}^\bullet$$
$$\mid \text{bool}_\varnothing : \mathbb{E} \to \text{bool}^\bullet$$

$$\text{Ind list } (A : \square) : \square :=$$
$$\mid \text{nil} : \text{list } A$$
$$\mid \text{cons} : A \to \text{list } A \to \text{list } A$$

$$\text{Ind list}^\bullet \, (A : [\![\square]\!]) : \square :=$$
$$\mid \text{nil}^\bullet : \text{list}^\bullet \, A$$
$$\mid \text{cons}^\bullet : [\![A]\!] \to \text{list}^\bullet \, A \to \text{list}^\bullet \, A$$
$$\mid \text{list}_\varnothing : \mathbb{E} \to \text{list}^\bullet \, A$$

$$\text{Ind } \Sigma \, (A : \square)(B : A \to \square) : \square :=$$
$$\mid \text{ex} : \Pi(x : A)(y : B \, x).\Sigma \, A \, B$$

$$\text{Ind } \Sigma^\bullet \, (A : [\![\square]\!])(B : [\![A]\!] \to \square) : \square :=$$
$$\mid \text{ex}^\bullet : \Pi(x : [\![A]\!])(y : [\![B \, x]\!]).\Sigma^\bullet \, A \, B$$
$$\mid \Sigma_\varnothing : \mathbb{E} \to \Sigma^\bullet \, A \, B$$

$$\text{Ind eq } (A : \square)(x : A) : A \to \square :=$$
$$\mid \text{refl} : \text{eq } A \, x \, x$$

$$\text{Ind eq}^\bullet \, (A : [\![\square]\!])(x : [\![A]\!]) : [\![A]\!] \to \square :=$$
$$\mid \text{refl}^\bullet : \text{eq}^\bullet \, A \, x \, x$$
$$\mid \text{eq}_\varnothing : \Pi y : [\![A]\!].\mathbb{E} \to \text{eq}^\bullet \, A \, x \, y$$

Fig. 4. Examples of translations of inductive types

Remark 8. The fact the we locally override the translation for recursive calls on the $[\![\cdot]\!]$ translation of the type being defined means that we cannot handle cases where the translation of the type of a constructor actually contains an instance of $[\mathcal{I}]$. Because of the syntactic positivity criterion, the only possibility for such a situation to occur in CIC is in the so-called nested inductive definitions. However, nested inductive types are essentially a programming convenience, as most nested types can be rewritten in an isomorphic way that is not nested.

Lemma 9. *If $\mathcal{I}$ is given as in Definition 6, we have for any terms $\vec{M}$, $\vec{N}$*

$$[\![\mathcal{I} \, M_1 \ldots M_n \, N_1 \ldots N_m]\!] \equiv \mathcal{I}^\bullet \, [M_1] \ldots [M_n] \, [N_1] \ldots [N_m].$$

This justifies a posteriori the simplified local definition we used in the recursive calls of the translation of the constructors.

Theorem 10. *For any inductive type $\mathcal{I}$ not using nested inductive types, the translation from Definition 6 is well-typed and satisfies the positivity criterion.*

Proof. Preservation of typing is a consequence of Theorem 4. The restriction on nested types, which is slightly stronger than the usual positivity criterion of CIC, is due to the fact that $\mathcal{I}_\varnothing$ is not available in the recursive calls and thus cannot be used to build a term of type **type** via the **TypeVal** constructor.

Preservation of the positivity criterion is straightforward, as the shape of every constructor c_k is preserved, and furthermore by Lemma 3 the structure of every argument type is preserved by $[\![\cdot]\!]$ as well. The only additional constructor $\mathcal{I}_\varnothing$ does not mention the recursive type and is thus automatically positive.

Corollary 11. *Type soundness holds for the translation of inductive types and their constructors.*

Pattern-Matching Translation. We now turn to the translation of the elimination of inductive terms, that is, pattern matching. Once again, its definition originates from the fact that we are working with call-by-name exceptions. It is well-known that in call-by-name, pattern matching implements a delimited form of call-by-value, by forcing its scrutinee before proceeding, at least up to the head constructor. Therefore, as soon as the matched term (re-)raises an exception, the whole pattern-matching reraises the same exception. A little care has to be taken in order to accomodate for the fact that the return type of the pattern-matching depends on the scrutinee, in particular when it is the default constructor of the inductive type.

In what follows, we use the $i_1 \ldots i_n$ notation for clarity, but compact it to $\vec{i}$ for space reasons, when appropriate.

Definition 12. *Assume an inductive $\mathcal{I}$ as given in Definition 6. Let Q be the well-typed pattern-matching defined as*

```
match M return λ(i₁ : I₁)... (iₘ : Iₘ) (x : I X₁ ... Xₙ i₁ ... iₘ). R with
| c₁ a₁,₁ ... a₁,ₗ₁  ⇒  N₁
...
| cₖ aₖ,₁ ... aₖ,ₗₖ  ⇒  Nₖ
end
```

where

$$\Gamma \vdash \vec{X} : \vec{P} \qquad \Gamma \vdash \vec{Y} : \vec{I}\{\vec{p} := \vec{X}\} \qquad \Gamma \vdash M : \mathcal{I} \, X_1 \ldots X_n \, Y_1 \ldots Y_m$$

$$\Gamma, \vec{i} : \vec{I}\{\vec{p} := \vec{X}\}, x : \mathcal{I} \, \vec{X} \, \vec{i} \vdash R : \square \qquad \Gamma \vdash Q : R\{\vec{i} := \vec{Y}, x := M\}$$

$$\Gamma, \vec{a}_1 : \vec{A}_1 \vdash N_1 : R\{\vec{i} := \vec{V}_1\{\vec{p} := \vec{X}\}, x := c_1 \, \vec{X} \, \vec{a}_1\}$$

$$\ldots$$

$$\Gamma, \vec{a}_k : \vec{A}_k \vdash N_k : R\{\vec{i} := \vec{V}_k\{\vec{p} := \vec{X}\}, x := c_k \, \vec{X} \, \vec{a}_k\}$$

then we pose $[Q]$ to be the following pattern-matching.

```
match [M] return λ(i₁ : [I₁])...(iₘ : [Iₘ]) (x : I• [X₁]... [Xₙ] i₁ ... iₘ). [R] with
| c•₁ a₁,₁ ... a₁,ₗ₁  ⇒  [N₁]
...
| c•ₖ aₖ,₁ ... aₖ,ₗₖ  ⇒  [Nₖ]
| I∅ i₁ ... iₘ e  ⇒  [R]∅{x := I∅ X₁ ... Xₙ i₁ ... iₘ e} e
end
```

Lemma 13. *With notations and typing assumptions from Definition 12, we have*

$$[\![\Gamma]\!] \vdash [Q] : [\![R]\!]\{\vec{i} := [\vec{Y}], x := [M]\}.$$

Proof. Mostly a consequence of Theorem 4 applied to all of the premises of the pattern-matching rule. The only thing we have to check specifically is that the branch for the default constructor $\mathcal{I}_\varnothing$ is well-typed as

$$[\![\Gamma]\!], \vec{i} : \vec{I}\{\vec{p} := \vec{X}\}, e : \mathbb{E} \vdash [R]_\varnothing\{x := \mathcal{I}_\varnothing \, \vec{X} \, \vec{i} \, e\} \, e : [\![R]\!]\{x := \mathcal{I}_\varnothing \, \vec{X} \, \vec{i} \, e\}$$

which is also due to Theorem 4 applied to R.

Lemma 14. *The translation preserves ι-rules.*

Proof. Immediate, as the translation preserves the structure of the patterns.

The translation is also applicable to fixpoints, but for the sake of readability we do not want to fully spell it out, although it is simply defined by congruence (commutation with the syntax). As such, it trivially preserves typing and reduction rules. Note that the Coq plugin presented in Sect. 6 features a complete translation of inductive types, pattern-matching and fixpoints. So the interested reader may experiment with the plugin to see how fixpoints are translated.

Therefore, by summarizing all of the previous properties, we have the following result.

Theorem 15. *If T interprets CIC, then so does $T_{\mathbb{E}}$, and thus the exceptional translation is a syntactic model of CIC.*

2.3   Flirting with Inconsistency

It is now time to point at the elephant in the room. The exceptional translation has a lot of nice properties, but it has one grave defect.

Theorem 16. *If $\mathbb{E}$ is inhabited, then $T_{\mathbb{E}}$ is logically inconsistent.*

Proof. The empty type is translated as

$$\text{Ind empty}^{\bullet} : \square := \text{empty}_{\varnothing} : \mathbb{E} \to \text{empty}^{\bullet}$$

which is inhabited as soon as $\mathbb{E}$ is.

Note that when $\mathbb{E}$ is empty, the situation is hardly better, as the translation is essentially the identity. However, when T satisfies canonicity, the situation is not totally desperate as $T_{\mathbb{E}}$ enjoys the following weaker canonicity lemma.

Lemma 17 (Exceptional Canonicity). *Let $\mathcal{I}$ be an inductive type with constructors $c_1, \ldots, c_n$ and assume that T satisfies canonicity. The translation of any closed term $\vdash_{T_{\mathbb{E}}} M : \mathcal{I}$ evaluates either to a constructor of the form $c_i^{\bullet} \, N_1 \ldots N_{l_i}$ or to the default constructor $\mathcal{I}_{\varnothing} \, e$ for some $e : \mathbb{E}$.*

Proof. Direct application of Theorem 4 and canonicity of T.

A direct consequence of Lemma 17 is that any proof of the empty type is an exception. As we will see in Sect. 4.1, for some types it is also possible to dynamically check whether a term of this type is a correct proof, in the sense that it does not raise an uncaught exception. This means that while $T_{\mathbb{E}}$ is logically unsound, it is computationally relevant and can still be used as a *dependently-typed programming language with exceptions*, a shift into a realm where we would have called the weaker canonicity Lemma 17 a *progress lemma*.

This is not the end of the story, though. Recall that $T_{\mathbb{E}}$ only exists through its embedding $[\cdot]$ into T. In particular, if T is consistent, this means that one can reason about terms of $T_{\mathbb{E}}$ directly in T. For instance, it is possible to prove in $\mathcal{T}$ that assuming some properties about its input, a function in $\mathcal{T}_\mathbb{E}$ never raises an exception. Hence not only do we have an effectul programming language, but we also have a *sound logical framework* allowing to transparently prove safety properties about impure programs.

It is actually even better than that. We will show in Sect. 3 that safety properties can be derived automatically for pure programs, allowing to recover a consistent type theory as long as $\mathcal{T}$ is consistent itself.

2.4   Living in an Exceptional World

We describe here what $\mathcal{T}_\mathbb{E}$ feels like in direct style. The exceptional theory feature a new type $\mathbf{E}$ which reifies the underlying type $\mathbb{E}$ of exceptions in $\mathcal{T}_\mathbb{E}$. It uses the fact that for $\mathbb{E}$, the default function (here of type $\mathbb{E} \to \mathbb{E}$) can simply be defined as the identity function. Its translation is given by

$$[\mathbf{E}] : [\![\Box]\!] := \mathtt{TypeVal}\ \mathbb{E}\ (\lambda e : \mathbb{E}.\,e).$$

Then, it is possible to define in $\mathcal{T}_\mathbb{E}$ a function $\mathtt{raise} : \Pi A : \Box.\,\mathbf{E} \to A$ that raises the provided exception at any type as

$$[\mathtt{raise}] := \lambda(A : \mathtt{type})\,(e : \mathbb{E}).\,\mathtt{Err}\ A\ e.$$

As we have already mentioned, the reader should be aware that the exceptions arising from this translation are call-by-name. This means that they do not behave like their usual call-by-value counterpart. In particular, we have in $\mathcal{T}_\mathbb{E}$

$$\mathtt{raise}\ (\Pi x : A.\,B)\ e \equiv \lambda x : A.\,\mathtt{raise}\ B\ e$$

which means that exceptions cannot be caught on Π-types. We can catch them on universes and inductive types though, because in those cases they are freely added through an extra constructor which one can pattern-match on. For instance, there exists in $\mathcal{T}_\mathbb{E}$ a term

$$\mathtt{catch}_{\mathtt{bool}} : \Pi P : \mathtt{bool} \to \Box.\,P\ \mathtt{true} \to P\ \mathtt{false} \to$$
$$(\Pi e : \mathbf{E}.\,P\ (\mathtt{raise}\ \mathtt{bool}\ e)) \to \Pi b : \mathtt{bool}.\,P\ b$$

defined by

$$[\mathtt{catch}_{\mathtt{bool}}] := \lambda P\,p_t\,p_f\,p_e\,b.\,\mathtt{match}\ b\ \mathtt{return}\ \lambda b.\mathtt{El}\ (P\ b)\ \mathtt{with}$$
$$| \ \mathtt{true}^\bullet \Rightarrow p_t$$
$$| \ \mathtt{false}^\bullet \Rightarrow p_f$$
$$| \ \mathtt{bool}_\varnothing\ e \Rightarrow p_e\ e$$
$$\mathtt{end}$$

satisfying the expected reduction rules on all three cases.

In Sect. 6, we illustrate the use of the exceptional theory using the CoQ plugin to define a simple cast framework as in [12].

$$[\Box_i]_\varepsilon \quad := \lambda A : [\![\Box_i]\!].\,[\![A]\!] \to \Box_i$$

$$[x]_\varepsilon \quad := x_\varepsilon$$

$$[\lambda x : A.\,M]_\varepsilon := \lambda(x : [\![A]\!])\,(x_\varepsilon : [\![A]\!]_\varepsilon\ x).\,[M]_\varepsilon$$

$$[M\ N]_\varepsilon \quad := [M]_\varepsilon\ [N]\ [N]_\varepsilon$$

$$[\Pi x : A.\,B]_\varepsilon := \lambda(f : \Pi x : [\![A]\!].\,[\![B]\!]).\,\Pi(x : [\![A]\!])\,(x_\varepsilon : [\![A]\!]_\varepsilon\ x).\,[\![B]\!]_\varepsilon\ (f\ x)$$

$$[\![A]\!]_\varepsilon \quad := [A]_\varepsilon$$

$$[\![\cdot]\!]_\varepsilon \quad := \cdot$$

$$[\![\Gamma, x : A]\!]_\varepsilon := [\![\Gamma]\!]_\varepsilon, x : [\![A]\!], x_\varepsilon : [\![A]\!]_\varepsilon\ x$$

Fig. 5. Parametricity over exceptional translation

3   Kreisel Meets Martin-Löf

It is well-known that Reynolds' parametricity [13] and Kreisel's modified realizability [4] are two instances of the broader logical relation techniques. Usually, parametricity is used to derive theorems for free, while realizability constrains programs. In a surprising turn of events, we use Bernardy's variant of parametricity on CIC [5] as a realizability trick to evict undesirable behaviours of $\mathcal{T}_\mathbb{E}$. This leads to the *parametric exceptional translation*, which can be seen as the embodiment of Kreisel's realizability in type theory. In this section, we first present this translation on the negative fragment, then extend it to CIC and finally discuss its meta-theoretical properties.

3.1   Exceptional Parametricity in a Negative World

The exceptional parametricity translation for terms of CC_ω is defined in Fig. 5. Intuitively, any type A in $\mathcal{T}_\mathbb{E}$ is turned into a validity predicate $A_\varepsilon : A \to \Box$ which encodes the fact that an inhabitant of A is not allowed to generate unhandled exceptions. For instance, a function is valid if its application to a valid term produces a valid answer. It does not say anything about the application to invalid terms though, which amounts to a *garbage in, garbage out* policy. The translation then states that every pure term is automatically valid.

This translation is exactly standard parametricity for type theory [5] but parametrized by the exceptional translation. This means that any occurrence of a term of the original theory used in the parametricity translation is replaced by its exceptional translation, using $[\cdot]$ or $[\![\cdot]\!]$ depending on whether it is used as a term or as a type. For instance, the translation of an application $[M\ N]_\varepsilon$ is given by $[M]_\varepsilon\ [N]\ [N]_\varepsilon$ instead of just $[M]_\varepsilon\ N\ [N]_\varepsilon$.

Lemma 18 (Substitution lemma). *The translation satisfies the following conversion:* $[M\{x := N\}]_\varepsilon \equiv [M]_\varepsilon\{x := [N], x_\varepsilon := [N]_\varepsilon\}.$

Theorem 19 (Soundness). *The two following properties hold.*

– If $M \equiv N$ then $[M]_\varepsilon \equiv [N]_\varepsilon$.
– If $\Gamma \vdash M : A$ then $[\![\Gamma]\!]_\varepsilon \vdash [M]_\varepsilon : [\![A]\!]_\varepsilon [M]$.

Proof. By induction on the derivation.

We can use this result to construct another syntactic model of CC_ω. Contrarily to usual syntactic models where sequents are straightforwardly translated to sequents, this model is slightly more subtle as sequents are translated to pairs of sequents instead. This is similar to the usual parametricity translation.

Definition 20. *The theory T_E^p is defined by the following data.*

– *Terms of T_E^p are pairs of terms of T.*
– *Contexts of T_E^p are pairs of contexts of T.*
– $\vdash_{T_E^p} \Gamma$ *whenever* $\vdash_T [\![\Gamma]\!]$ *and* $\vdash_T [\![\Gamma]\!]_\varepsilon$.
– $M \equiv_{T_E^p} N$ *whenever* $[M] \equiv_T [N]$ *and* $[M]_\varepsilon \equiv_T [N]_\varepsilon$.
– $\Gamma \vdash_{T_E^p} M : A$ *whenever* $[\![\Gamma]\!] \vdash_T [M] : [\![A]\!]$ *and* $[\![\Gamma]\!]_\varepsilon \vdash_T [M]_\varepsilon : [\![A]\!]_\varepsilon [M]$.

Once again, Theorem 19 can be rephrased in terms of preservation of theories and syntactic models.

Theorem 21. *If T interprets CC_ω then so does T_E^p. That is, the parametric exceptional translation is a syntactic model of CC_ω.*

This construction preserves definitional η-expansion, as functions are mapped to (slightly more complicated) functions.

Lemma 22. *If T satisfies definitional η-expansion, then so does T_E^p.*

Proof. The first component of the translation preserves definitional η-expansion because functions are mapped to functions. It remains to show that

$$[\lambda x : A. \, M \, x]_\varepsilon := \lambda(x : [\![A]\!]) \, (x_\varepsilon : [\![A]\!]_\varepsilon \, x). \, [M]_\varepsilon \, x \, x_\varepsilon \equiv [M]_\varepsilon$$

which holds by applying η-expansion twice.

It is interesting to remark that Bernardy-style unary parametricity also leads to a syntactic model T^p that interprets CC_ω (as well as CIC), using the same kind of glueing construction. Nonetheless, this model is somewhat degenerate from the logical point of view. Namely it is a conservative extension of the target theory. Indeed, if $\Gamma \vdash_{T^p} M : A$ for some Γ, M and A from T, then there we also have $\Gamma \vdash_T M : A$, because the first component of the model is the identity, and the original sequent can be retrieved by the first projection.

This is definitely *not* the case with the T_E^p theory, because the first projection is not the identity. In particular, because of Theorem 16, every sequent in the first projection is inhabited, although it is not the case in T itself if it is consistent. This means that parametricity can actually bring additional expressivity when it applies to a theory which is not pure, as it is the case here.

> Ind $bool_\varepsilon$: $bool^\bullet \to \square$:=
> | $true_\varepsilon$: $bool_\varepsilon$ $true^\bullet$
> | $false_\varepsilon$: $bool_\varepsilon$ $false^\bullet$
>
> Ind $list_\varepsilon$ $(A : type)\,(A_\varepsilon : [\![A]\!] \to \square)$: $list^\bullet\ A \to \square$:=
> | nil_ε : $list_\varepsilon$ A A_ε $(nil^\bullet\ A)$
> | $cons_\varepsilon$: $\Pi(x : [\![A]\!])\,(x_\varepsilon : A_\varepsilon\ x)\,(l : list^\bullet\ A)\,(l_\varepsilon : list_\varepsilon\ A\ A_\varepsilon\ l).$
> $\qquad list_\varepsilon\ A\ A_\varepsilon\ (cons^\bullet\ A\ x\ l)$
>
> Ind eq_ε $(A : type)\,(A_\varepsilon : [\![A]\!] \to \square)\,(x : [\![A]\!])\,(x_\varepsilon : A_\varepsilon\ x)$:
> $\qquad \Pi(y : [\![A]\!])\,(y_\varepsilon : A_\varepsilon\ y).\,eq^\bullet\ A\ x\ y \to \square$:=
> | $refl_\varepsilon$: $refl_\varepsilon$ A A_ε x x_ε x x_ε $(refl^\bullet\ A\ x)$

Fig. 6. Examples of parametric translation of inductive types

3.2 Exceptional Parametric Translation of CIC

We now describe the parametricity translation of the positive fragment. The intuition is that as it stands for an exception, the default constructor is always invalid, while all other constructors are valid, assuming their arguments are.

Type and Constructor Translation

Definition 23. *Let $\mathcal{I}$ be an inductive type as given in Definition 6. We define the exceptional parametricity translation $\mathcal{I}_\varepsilon$ of $\mathcal{I}$ as the inductive type defined by:*

- *parameters $[\![p_1 : P_1, \ldots, p_n : P_n]\!]_\varepsilon$;*
- *indices $[\![i_1 : I_1, \ldots, i_m : I_m]\!]_\varepsilon, x : \mathcal{I}\ p_1 \ldots p_n\ i_1 \ldots i_m$;*
- *constructors*
  $c_{1\varepsilon}$: $\Pi[\![\vec{a}_1 : \vec{A}_1]\!]_\varepsilon.$
  $\qquad \mathcal{I}_\varepsilon\ p_1\ p_{1\varepsilon} \ \cdots\ p_n\ p_{n\varepsilon}\ [V_{1,1}]\ [V_{1,1}]_\varepsilon\ \cdots\ [V_{1,m}]\ [V_{1,m}]_\varepsilon\ (c_1^\bullet\ \vec{p}\ \vec{a}_1)$
  $\cdots$
  $c_{k\varepsilon}$: $\Pi[\![\vec{a}_k : \vec{A}_k]\!]_\varepsilon.$
  $\qquad \mathcal{I}_\varepsilon\ p_1\ p_{1\varepsilon} \ \cdots\ p_n\ p_{n\varepsilon}\ [V_{k,1}]\ [V_{k,1}]_\varepsilon\ \cdots\ [V_{k,m}]\ [V_{k,m}]_\varepsilon\ (c_k^\bullet\ \vec{p}\ \vec{a}_k).$

and we extend the translation as

$$[\mathcal{I}]_\varepsilon := \mathcal{I}_\varepsilon \quad [c_1]_\varepsilon := c_{1\varepsilon} \quad \cdots \quad [c_k]_\varepsilon := c_{k\varepsilon}.$$

Example 24. We give the exceptional parametric inductive translation of our running examples in Fig. 6.

Note that contrarily to the negative case, the exceptional parametricity translation on inductive types is *not* the same thing as the composition of Bernardy's parametricity together with the exceptional translation. Indeed, the latter would also have produced a constructor for the default case from the exceptional inductive translation, whereas our goal is precisely to rule this case out via the additional realizability-like interpretation.

It is also very different from our previous parametric weaning translation [2], which relies on internal parametricity to recover dependent elimination, enforcing by construction that no effectful term exists. Here, effectful terms may be used in the first component, but they are required after the fact to have no inconsistent behaviour. Intuitively, parametric weaning produces one pure sequent, while exceptional parametricity produces two, with the first one being potentially impure and the second one assuring the first one is harmless.

Pattern-Matching Translation

Definition 25. *Let Q be the pattern-matching defined in Definition 12. We pose $[Q]_\varepsilon$ to be the pattern-matching*

$$\texttt{match } [M]_\varepsilon \texttt{ return } \lambda[\![\vec{i} : \vec{I}]\!]_\varepsilon\,(x : \mathcal{I}^\bullet\ [X_1]\ \dots\ [X_n]\ i_1\ \dots\ i_m).$$
$$(x_\varepsilon : \mathcal{I}_\varepsilon\ [X_1]\ [X_1]_\varepsilon\ \dots\ [X_n]\ [X_n]_\varepsilon\ i_1\ i_{1\varepsilon}\ \dots\ i_m\ i_{m\varepsilon}\ x)$$
$$[\![R]\!]_\varepsilon\ [Q_x]$$

$$\texttt{with}$$
$$\mid\ c_{1\varepsilon}\ a_{1,1}\ a_{1,1\varepsilon}\ \dots\ a_{1,l_1}\ a_{1,l_1\varepsilon}\ \Rightarrow\ [N_1]_\varepsilon$$
$$\dots$$
$$\mid\ c_{k\varepsilon}\ a_{k,1}\ a_{k,1\varepsilon}\ \dots\ a_{k,l_k}\ a_{1,l_k\varepsilon}\ \Rightarrow\ [N_k]_\varepsilon$$
$$\texttt{end}$$

where Q_x is the following pattern-matching

$$\texttt{match } x \texttt{ return } \lambda(i_1 : I_1)\dots(i_m : I_m)\,(x : \mathcal{I}\ X_1\ \dots\ X_n\ i_1\ \dots\ i_m).\,R \texttt{ with}$$
$$\mid\ c_1\ a_{1,1}\ \dots\ a_{1,l_1}\ \Rightarrow\ N_1$$
$$\dots$$
$$\mid\ c_k\ a_{k,1}\ \dots\ a_{k,l_k}\ \Rightarrow\ N_k$$
$$\texttt{end}$$

that is Q where the scrutinee has been turned into the index variable of the parametricity predicate.

Lemma 26. *With notations and typing assumptions from Definition 12, we have*

$$[\![\Gamma]\!]_\varepsilon \vdash [Q]_\varepsilon : [\![R\{\vec{i} := \vec{Y}, x := M\}]\!]_\varepsilon\ [Q].$$

The exceptional parametricity translation can be extended to handle fixpoints as well, with a few limitations. Translating generic fixpoints uniformly is indeed an open problem in standard parametricity, and our variant faces the same issue. In practice, standard recursors can be automatically translated, and fancy fixpoints may require hand-writing the parametricity proof. We do not describe the recursor translation here though, as it is essentially the same as standard parametricity. Again, the interested reader may test the CoQ plugin exposed in Sect. 6 to see how recursors are translated.

Packing everything together allows to state the following result.

Theorem 27. *If $\mathcal{T}$ interprets CIC, then so does $\mathcal{T}_\mathbb{E}^p$, and thus the exceptional parametricity translation is a syntactic model of CIC.*

3.3 Meta-Theoretical Properties of $\mathcal{T}_{\mathbb{E}}^{p}$

Being built as a syntactic model, $\mathcal{T}_{\mathbb{E}}^{p}$ inherits a lot of meta-theoretical properties of $\mathcal{T}$. We list a few of interest below.

Theorem 28. *If $\mathcal{T}$ is consistent, then so is $\mathcal{T}_{\mathbb{E}}^{p}$.*

Proof. Assume $\vdash_{\mathcal{T}_{\mathbb{E}}^{p}} M_0$: empty for some M_0. Then by definition, there exists two terms M and M_ε such that $\vdash_{\mathcal{T}} M$: empty$^\bullet$ and $\vdash_{\mathcal{T}} M_\varepsilon$: empty$_\varepsilon$ M. But empty$_\varepsilon$ has no constructor, and $\mathcal{T}$ is inconsistent.

More generally, the same argument holds for any inductive type.

Theorem 29. *If $\mathcal{T}$ enjoys canonicity, then so does $\mathcal{T}_{\mathbb{E}}^{p}$.*

Proof. The exceptional parametricity translation for inductive types has the same structure as the original type, so any normal form in $\mathcal{T}_{\mathbb{E}}^{p}$ can be mapped back to a normal form in $\mathcal{T}$.

4 Effectively Extending CIC

The parametric exceptional translation allows to extend the logical expressivity of CIC in the following ways, which we develop in the remainder of this section.

We show in Sect. 4.1 that Markov's rule is admissible in CIC. We already sketched this result in our previous paper [2], but we come back to it in more details. More generally, we show a form of conservativity of double-negation elimination over the type-theoretic version of Π_2^0 formulae.

In Sect. 4.2, we exhibit a syntactic model of CIC which satisfies definitional η-expansion for functions but which negates function extensionality. As far as we know, this was not known.

Finally, in Sect. 4.3, we show that there exists a model of CIC which validates the independence of premises. This is a new result, that shows that CIC can feature traces of classical reasoning while staying computational. We use this result in Sect. 4.4 to give an alternative proof of the recent result of Coquand and Mannaa [7] that Markov's principle is not provable in CIC.

4.1 Markov's Rule

We show in this section that CIC is closed under a generalized Markov's rule. The technique used here is no more than a dependently-typed variant of Friedman's trick [14]. Indeed, Friedman's A-translation amounts to add exceptions to intuitionistic logic, which is precisely what $\mathcal{T}_{\mathbb{E}}$ does for CIC.

Definition 30. *An inductive type in CIC is said to be first-order if all the types of the arguments of its constructors, in its parameters and in its indices are recursively first-order.*

Example 31. The empty, unit and $\mathbb{N}$ types are first-order. If P and Q are first-order then so is $\Sigma p : P.Q$, $P + Q$ and eq $P\ p_0\ p_1$. Consequently, the CIC equivalent of Σ_1^0 formulae are in particular first-order.

First-order types enjoy uncommon properties, like the fact that they can be injected into effectful terms and purified away. This is then used to prove the generalized Markov's Rule.

Lemma 32. *For every first-order type* $\vec{p} : \vec{P} \vdash Q : \square$ *where all* $\vec{P}$ *are first-order, there are retractions* $\iota_{\vec{P}}$, ι_Q *and* $\theta_{\vec{P}}$, θ_Q *s.t.:*

$$\vec{p} : \vec{P} \vdash \iota_Q : Q \to [\![Q]\!]\{\vec{p} := \iota_{\vec{P}}\ \vec{p}\}$$
$$\vec{p} : \vec{P} \vdash \theta_Q : [\![Q]\!]\{\vec{p} := \iota_{\vec{P}}\ \vec{p}\} \to Q + \mathbb{E}.$$

Proof. The ι terms exist because effectful inductive types are a semantical superset of their pure equivalent, and the θ terms are implemented by recursively forcing the corresponding impure inductive term. One relies on decidability of equality of first-order type to fix the indices.

Theorem 33 (Generalized Markov's Rule). *For any first-order type* P *and first-order predicate* Q *over* P, *if* $\vdash_{\mathrm{CIC}} \Pi p : P.\ \neg\neg\ (Q\ p)$ *then* $\vdash_{\mathrm{CIC}} \Pi p : P.Q\ p$.

Proof. Let $\vdash M : \Pi p : P.\ \neg\neg\ (Q\ p)$. By taking $\mathbb{E} := Q\ p$ and apply the soundness theorem, one gets a proof

$$p : P \vdash [M] : \Pi \hat{p} : [\![P]\!].\ ([\![Q\ \hat{p}]\!] \to \mathtt{empty}^\bullet) \to \mathtt{empty}^\bullet.$$

But $\mathtt{empty}^\bullet \cong \mathbb{E} \equiv Q\ p$, so we can derive from $[M]$ a term $M^\sharp$ s.t.

$$p : P \vdash M^\sharp : \Pi \hat{p} : [\![P]\!].\ ([\![Q\ \hat{p}]\!] \to Q\ p + Q\ p) \to Q\ p.$$

The proofterm we were looking for is thus no more than $\lambda p : P.\ M^\sharp\ (\iota_P\ p)\ \theta_Q$.

4.2 Function Intensionality with η-expansion

In a previous paper [9], we already showed that there existed a syntactic model of CIC that allowed to internally disprove function extensionality. Yet, this model was clearly not preserving definitional η-expansion on functions, as it was adding additional structure to abstraction and application (namely a boolean). Thanks to our new model, we can now demonstrate that counterintuitively, it is possible to have a consistent type theory that enjoys definitional η-expansion while negating internally function extensionality. In this section we suppose that $\mathbb{E} := \mathtt{unit}$, although any inhabited type of exceptions would work.

By Lemma 22, we know that the parametric exceptional translation preserves definitional η-expansion. It is thus sufficient to find two functions that are extensionally equal but intensionally distinct in the model. Let us consider to this end the unit $\to$ unit functions

$$\mathtt{id}_\perp := \lambda u : \mathtt{unit}.\ u \qquad\qquad \mathtt{id}_\top := \lambda u : \mathtt{unit}.\mathtt{tt}.$$

Theorem 34. *The following sequents are derivable:*

$$\vdash_{\mathcal{T}_{\mathbb{E}}^p} \Pi u : \texttt{unit}.\,\texttt{id}_\perp\, u = \texttt{id}_\top\, u \qquad \vdash_{\mathcal{T}_{\mathbb{E}}^p} \texttt{id}_\perp = \texttt{id}_\top \to \texttt{empty}.$$

Proof. The main difference between the two functions is that $\texttt{id}_\perp$ preserves exceptions while $\texttt{id}_\top$ does not, which we exploit.

The first sequent is provable in CIC by dependent elimination and thus is derivable in $\mathcal{T}_{\mathbb{E}}^p$ by applying the soundness theorem.

To prove the first component of the second sequent, we exhibit a property that discriminates $[\texttt{id}_\perp]$ and $[\texttt{id}_\top]$, which is, as explained, their evaluation on the term $\texttt{unit}_\varnothing$ tt. Showing then that this proof is parametric is equivalent to showing $\Pi(p : [\texttt{id}_\perp = \texttt{id}_\top]) (p_\varepsilon : [\texttt{id}_\perp = \texttt{id}_\top]_\varepsilon\, p).\,\texttt{empty}$. But p_ε actually implies $[\texttt{id}_\perp] = [\texttt{id}_\top]$, which we just showed was absurd.

4.3   Independence of Premise

Independence of premise (IP) is a semi-classical principle from first-order logic whose CIC equivalent can be stated as follows.

$$\Pi(A : \square) (B : \mathbb{N} \to \square).\,(\neg A \to \Sigma n : \mathbb{N}.\,B\, n) \to \Sigma n : \mathbb{N}.\,\neg A \to B\, n \qquad \text{(IP)}$$

Although not derivable in intuitionistic logic, it is an admissible rule of **HA**. The standard proof of this property is to go through Kreisel's modified realizability interpretation of **HA** [4]. In a nutshell, the interpretation goes as follows: by induction over a formula A, define a simple type $\tau(A)$ of realizers of A together with a realizability predicate $\cdot \Vdash A$ over $\tau(A)$. Then show that whenever $\vdash_{\textbf{HA}} A$, there exists some simply-typed term $t : \tau(A)$ s.t. $t \Vdash A$. As the interpretation also implies that there is no t s.t. $t \Vdash \perp$, this gives a sound model of **HA**, which contains more than the latter. Most notably, there is for instance a term $\texttt{ip}$ s.t.

$$\texttt{ip} \Vdash (\neg A \to \exists n.\, B) \to \exists n.\, \neg A \to B$$

for any A, B. Intriguingly, the computational content of $\texttt{ip}$ did not seem to receive a fair treatment in the literature. To the best of our knowledge, it has never been explicitly stated that IP was realizable because of the following "bug" of Kreisel's modified realizability.

Lemma 35 (Kreisel's bug). *For every formula A, $\tau(A)$ is inhabited. In particular, $\tau(\perp) := \texttt{unit}$.*

We show that this is actually not a bug, but a hidden feature of Kreisel's modified realizability, which secretly allows to encode exceptions in the realizers. To this end, we implement IP in $\mathcal{T}_{\mathbb{E}}^p$ by relying internally on *paraproofs*, i.e. terms raising exceptions, while ensuring these exceptions never escape outside of the locally unsafe boundary. The resulting $\mathcal{T}_{\mathbb{E}}^p$ term has essentially the same computational content as its Kreisel's realizability counterpart. In this section we suppose that $\mathbb{E} := \texttt{unit}$, although assuming $\mathbb{E}$ to be inhabited is sufficient.

To ease the understanding of the definition, we rely on effectful combinators that can be defined in $\mathcal{T}_{\mathbb{E}}$.

Definition 36. *We define in* $\mathcal{T}_{\mathbb{E}}$ *the following terms.*

$$\texttt{fail} \;:\; \Pi A : \Box.\, A$$
$$[\texttt{fail}] := \lambda A : [\![\Box]\!].\, [A]_\varnothing \;\texttt{tt}$$

$\texttt{is}_\Sigma \;:\; \Pi A\,B.\,(\Sigma x : A.\,B) \to \texttt{bool}$
$[\texttt{is}_\Sigma] := \lambda A\,B\,p.\,\texttt{match } p \texttt{ with}$
$\qquad\quad |\; \texttt{ex}^\bullet \, \_\,\_ \Rightarrow \texttt{true}^\bullet$
$\qquad\quad |\; \Sigma_\varnothing\, \_ \Rightarrow \texttt{false}^\bullet$
$\qquad\quad \texttt{end}$

$\texttt{is}_{\mathbb{N}} \;:\; \mathbb{N} \to \texttt{bool}$
$[\texttt{is}_{\mathbb{N}}] := \texttt{fix } \texttt{is}_{\mathbb{N}}\, n \;:=\; \texttt{match } n \texttt{ with}$
$\qquad\quad |\; 0^\bullet \Rightarrow \texttt{true}^\bullet$
$\qquad\quad |\; \texttt{S}^\bullet\, n \Rightarrow \texttt{is}_{\mathbb{N}}\, n$
$\qquad\quad |\; \mathbb{N}_\varnothing\, \_ \Rightarrow \texttt{false}^\bullet$
$\qquad\quad \texttt{end}$

It is worth insisting that these combinators are not necessarily parametric. While it can be shown that $\texttt{is}_\Sigma$ and $\texttt{is}_{\mathbb{N}}$ actually are, $\texttt{fail}$ is luckily not. The $\texttt{is}_\Sigma$ and $\texttt{is}_{\mathbb{N}}$ functions are used in order to check that a value is actually pure and does not contain exceptions.

Definition 37. *We define* $\texttt{ip}$ *in* $\mathcal{T}_{\mathbb{E}}$ *in direct style below, using the available combinators from Definition 36 and a bit of syntactic sugar.*

$\texttt{ip} :\; \texttt{IP}$
$\texttt{ip} := \lambda(A : \Box)\,(B : \mathbb{N} \to \Box)\,(f : \neg A \to \Sigma n : \mathbb{N}.\,B\,n).$
$\qquad\quad \texttt{let } p := f\;(\texttt{fail}\;(\neg A)) \texttt{ in}$
$\qquad\quad \texttt{if } \texttt{is}_\Sigma\,\mathbb{N}\,B\,p \texttt{ then match } p \texttt{ with}$
$\qquad\quad |\; \texttt{ex}\,n\,b \Rightarrow \texttt{if } \texttt{is}_{\mathbb{N}}\,n \texttt{ then ex } \_\,\_\,n\;(\lambda\_ : \neg A.\,b)$
$\qquad\qquad\qquad\qquad\qquad \texttt{else ex } \_\,\_\;0\;(\texttt{fail}\;(\neg A \to B\;0))$
$\qquad\quad \texttt{end else ex } \_\,\_\;0\;(\texttt{fail}\;(\neg A \to B\;0))$

The intuition behind this term is the following. Given $f : \neg A \to \Sigma n : \mathbb{N}.\,B\,n$, we apply it to a dummy function which fails whenever it is used. Owing to the semantics of negation, we know *in the parametricity layer* that the only way for this application to return an exception is that f actually contained a proof of A and applied $\texttt{fail}$ to it. Therefore, given a true proof of $\neg A$, we are in an inconsistent setting and thus we are able to do whatever pleases us. The issue is that we do not have access to such a proof yet, and we do have to provide a valid integer now. Therefore, we check whether f actually provided us with a valid pair containing a valid integer. If so, this is our answer, otherwise we stuff a dummy integer value and we postpone the contradiction.

This is essentially the same realizer as the one from Kreisel's modified realizability, except that we have a fancy type system for realizers. In particular, because we have dependent types, integers also exist in the logical layer, so that they need to be checked for exceptions as well. The only thing that remains to be proved is that $\texttt{ip}$ also lives in $\mathcal{T}_{\mathbb{E}}^p$.

Theorem 38. *There is a proof of* $\vdash_{\mathcal{T}} [\![\texttt{IP}]\!]_\varepsilon\, [\texttt{ip}]$.

Proof. The proof is straightforward but tedious, so we do not give the full details. The file $\texttt{IPc.v}$ of the companion CoQ plugin contains an explicit proof. The essential properties that make it go through are the following.

- $\vdash_{\mathcal{T}} \Pi(n : \mathbb{N}^{\bullet})\,(p_1\,p_2 : \mathbb{N}_{\varepsilon}\ n).\,p_1 = p_2$
- $\vdash_{\mathcal{T}} \Pi n : \mathbb{N}^{\bullet}.\,[\mathsf{is}_{\mathbb{N}}]\ n = \mathsf{true}^{\bullet} \leftrightarrow \mathbb{N}_{\varepsilon}\ n$
- $\vdash_{\mathcal{T}} \Pi(p\,q : [\![\neg A]\!]).\,[\![\neg A]\!]_{\varepsilon}\ p \to [\![\neg A]\!]_{\varepsilon}\ q$

Corollary 39. *We have* $\vdash_{\mathcal{T}_{\mathbb{E}}^{p}} \mathrm{IP}$.

4.4   Non-provability of Markov's Principle

From this result, one can get a very easy syntactic proof of the independence result of Markov's principle from CIC. Markov's principle is usually stated as

$$\Pi P : \mathbb{N} \to \mathsf{bool}.\,\neg\neg\,(\Sigma n : \mathbb{N}.\,P\ n = \mathsf{true}) \to \Sigma n : \mathbb{N}.\,P\ n = \mathsf{true} \quad (\mathrm{MP})$$

An independence result was recently proved by Coquand and Mannaa by a semantic argument [7]. We leverage instead a property from realizability [15] that has been applied to type theory the other way around by Herbelin [16].

Lemma 40. *If $\mathcal{S}$ is a computable theory containing* CIC *and enjoying canonicity, then one cannot have both* $\vdash_{\mathcal{S}} \mathrm{IP}$ *and* $\vdash_{\mathcal{S}} \mathrm{MP}$.

Proof. By applying IP to MP, one easily obtains that

$$\vdash_{\mathcal{S}} \Pi P : \mathbb{N} \to \mathsf{bool}.\,\Sigma n : \mathbb{N}.\,\Pi m : \mathbb{N}.\,P\ m = \mathsf{true} \to P\ n = \mathsf{true}.$$

Thus, for every closed $P : \mathbb{N} \to \mathsf{bool}$, by canonicity there exists a closed $n_P : \mathbb{N}$ s.t. $\vdash_{\mathcal{S}} \Pi m : \mathbb{N}.\,P\ m = \mathsf{true} \to P\ n_P = \mathsf{true}$. But then one can decide whether P holds for some n by just computing $P\ n_P$, so that we effectively obtained an oracle deciding the halting problem (which is expressible in CIC).

Corollary 41. *We have* $\nvdash_{\mathrm{CIC}_{\mathbb{E}}^{p}} \mathrm{MP}$ *and thus also* $\nvdash_{\mathrm{CIC}} \mathrm{MP}$.

5   Possible Extensions

5.1   Negative Records

Interestingly, the fact that the translation introduces effects has unintented consequences on a few properties of type theory that are often taken for granted. Namely, because type theory is pure, there is a widespread confusion amongst type theorists between positive tuples and negative records.

- Positive tuples are defined as a one-constructor inductive type, introduced by this constructor and eliminated by pattern-matching. They do not (and in general cannot, for typing reasons) satisfy definitional η-laws, also known as *surjective pairing*.
- Negative records are defined as a record type, introduced by primitive packing and eliminated by projections. They naturally obey definitional η-laws.

$$A, B, M, N ::= \dots \mid \&x : A. B \mid \langle M, N \rangle \mid M.\pi_1 \mid M.\pi_2$$

$$\frac{\Gamma \vdash A : \Box_i \quad \Gamma, x : A \vdash B : \Box_j}{\Gamma \vdash \&x : A. B : \Box_{\max(i,j)}} \qquad \frac{\Gamma \vdash M : \&x : A. B}{\Gamma \vdash M.\pi_1 : A} \qquad \frac{\Gamma \vdash M : \&x : A. B}{\Gamma \vdash M.\pi_2 : B\{x := M.\pi_1\}}$$

$$\frac{\Gamma \vdash M : A \quad \Gamma, x : A \vdash B : \Box \quad \Gamma \vdash N : B\{x := M\}}{\Gamma \vdash \langle M, N \rangle : \&x : A. B}$$

$$\langle M.\pi_1, M.\pi_2 \rangle \equiv M \qquad \langle M, N \rangle.\pi_1 \equiv M \qquad \langle M, N \rangle.\pi_2 \equiv N$$

Fig. 7. Negative pairs

$$[\&x : A. B] := \texttt{TypeVal}\ (\&x : [\![A]\!].\,[\![B]\!])\ (\lambda e : \mathbb{E}.\,\langle [A]_\varnothing\ e, [B]_\varnothing\{x := [A]_\varnothing\ e\}\ e \rangle)$$

$$[\langle M, N \rangle] := \langle [M], [N] \rangle$$

$$[M.\pi_i] := [M].\pi_i$$

Fig. 8. Exceptional translation of negative pairs

In the remainder of this section, we will focus on the specific case of pairs, but the same arguments are generalizable to arbitrary records. Positive pairs $\Sigma x : A. B$ are defined by the inductive type from Fig. 4. Negative pairs $\&x : A. B$ are defined as a primitive structure in Fig. 7. We use the ampersand notation as a reference to linear logic.

In CIC, it is possible to show that negative and positive pairs are propositionally isomorphic, because positive pairs enjoy dependent elimination. Nonetheless, it is a well-known fact in the programming folklore that in a call-by-name language with effects, the two are sharply distinct. For instance, in presence of exceptions, assuming $\vdash M : \Sigma x : A. B$, one does not have in general

$$M \equiv \texttt{ex}\ A\ B\ (\texttt{fst}\ A\ B\ M)\ (\texttt{snd}\ A\ B\ M)$$

where $\texttt{fst}$ and $\texttt{snd}$ are defined by pattern-matching. Indeed, if M is itself an exception, the two sides can be discriminated by a pattern-matching. Matching on the left-hand side results in immediate reraising of the exception, while matching on the right-hand side succeeds as long as the arguments of the constructor are not forced. Forcefully equating those two terms would then result in a trivial equational theory.

Such a phenomenon is at work in the exceptional translation. It is actually possible to interpret negative pairs through the translation, but in a way that significantly differs from the translation of positive pairs. In this section, we assume that $\mathcal{T}$ contains negative pairs.

Definition 42. *The translation of negative pairs is given in Fig. 8.*

It is straightforward to check that the definitions of Fig. 8 preserve the conversion and typing rules from Fig. 7. The same translation can be extended to any record. We thus have the following theorem.

Theorem 43. *If $\mathcal{T}$ has negative records, then so has $\mathcal{T}_{\mathbb{E}}$.*

It is enlightening to look at the difference between negative and positive pairs through the translation, because now we have effects that allow to separate them clearly. Indeed, compare

$$[\![\&x : A. B]\!] \equiv \&x : [\![A]\!].[\![B]\!] \quad \text{with} \quad [\![\Sigma x : A. B]\!] \cong \mathbb{E} + \Sigma x : [\![A]\!].[\![B]\!].$$

Clearly, if $\mathbb{E}$ is inhabited, then the two types do not even have the same cardinal, assuming A and B are finite. Furthermore, their default inhabitant is not the same at all. It is defined pointwise for negative pairs, while it is a special constructor for positive ones. Finally, there is obviously not any chance that $[\![\Sigma x : A. B]\!]$ satisfies definitional surjective pairing in vanilla CIC, as it has two constructors. The trick is that the two types are externally distinguishable, but are not internally so, because $\mathcal{T}_{\mathbb{E}}$ is a model of CIC+& and thus proves that they are propositionally isomorphic.

It is possible to equip negative pairs with a parametricity relation defined as a primitive record which is the pointwise parametricity relation of each field, which naturally preserve typing and conversion rules.

Theorem 44. *If $\mathcal{T}$ has negative records, then so has $\mathcal{T}_{\mathbb{E}}^{p}$.*

5.2   Impredicative Universe

All the systems we have considered so far are predicative. It is nonetheless possible to implement an impredicative universe $*$ in $\mathcal{T}_{\mathbb{E}}$ if $\mathcal{T}$ features one.

Intuitively, it is sufficient to ask for an inductive type `prop` living in $\square_i$ for all i, which is defined just as `type`, except that its constructor `PropVal` corresponding to `TypeVal` contains elements of $*$ rather than $\square$. Then one can similarly define El_* and Err_* acting on `prop` rather than `type`. One then slightly tweaks the $[\![\cdot]\!]$ macro from Fig. 2 by defining it instead as

$$[\![A]\!] := \begin{cases} \text{El}_* \, [\![A]\!] \text{ if } A : * \\ \text{El} \, [\![A]\!] \text{ otherwise} \end{cases}$$

and similarly for type constructors. With this modified translation, one obtains a soundness theorem for CC_ω.

Theorem 45. *The exceptional translation is a syntactic model of $\text{CC}_\omega + *$.*

Likewise, the inductive translation is amenable to interpret an impredicative universe, with one major restriction though.

Theorem 46. *The exceptional translation is a syntactic model of $\text{CIC} + *$ without the singleton elimination rule.*

Indeed, the addition of the default constructor disrupts the singleton elimination criterion for all inductive types. Actually, this criterion is very fragile, and even if $\mathcal{T}_{\mathbb{E}}$ satisfied it, Keller and Lasson showed that the parametricity translation could not interpret inductive types in * for similar reasons [17], and $\mathcal{T}_{\mathbb{E}}^{p}$ would face the same issue.

6   The Exceptional Translation in Practice

6.1   Implementation as a Coq Plugin

The (parametric) exceptional translation is a translation of CIC into itself, which means that we can directly implement it as a Coq plugin. This way, we can use the translation to extend safely Coq with new logical principles, so that typechecking remains decidable.

Such a Coq plugin is simply a program that, given a Coq proof term M, produces the translations $[M]$ and $[M]_{\varepsilon}$ as Coq terms. For instance, the translations of type list, given in Figs. 4 and 6, are obtained by typing the following commands, which define each one new inductive type in Coq.

```
Effect Translate list.
Parametricity Translate list.
```

The first command produces only [list], while the second produces $[list]_{\varepsilon}$. But the main interest of the translation is that we can exhibit new constructors. For instance, the raise operation described in Sect. 2.4 is defined as

```
Effect Definition Exception : Type := fun E ⇒ TypeVal E E id.
Effect Definition raise : ∀ A, Exception → A := fun E (A : type E) ⇒ Err A.
```

6.2   Usecase: A Cast Framework

We can use the ability to raise exception to define partial function in the exceptional layer. For instance, given a decidable property (described by the type class below), it is then possible to define a cast function from A to Σ (a : A). P a returning the converted value if the property is satisfied and raising an exception otherwise (using an inhabitant cast_failed of Exception).

```
Class Decidable (A : Type) := dec : A + (not A).
Definition cast A (P : A → Type) (a:A) {Hdec : Decidable (P a)} : Σ (a : A). P a
:= match dec (P a) with
 | inl p ⇒ (a ; p)
 | inr _ ⇒ raise cast_failed
 end.
```

Using this cast mechanism, it is easy to define a function list_to_pair from lists to pairs by first converting the list into a list size two, using the impure function cast (list A) (fun l ⇒ List.length l = 2) and then recovering a pair from a list of size two using a pure function.

In the exceptional layer, it is possible to prove the following property

Definition list_to_pair_prop A (x y : A) : list_to_pair [x ; y] = (x,y).

in at least two way. One can perfectly prove it by simply raising an exception at top level, or by reflexivity—using the fact that list_to_pair [x ; y] actually reduces to (x,y).

However, there is a way to distinguish between those two proofs in the target theory, here CoQ, by stating the following lemma which can only proven for the proof not raising an exception.

Definition list_to_pair_prop_soundness A x y :
    list_to_pair_prop• A x y = eq_refl• _ _ _ := eq_refl _.

where underscores represent arguments inferred by CoQ.

7   Related Work

Adding Dependency to an Effectful Language. There are numerous works on adding dependent types in mainstream effectful programming languages. They all mostly focused on how to appropriately restrict effectful terms from appearing in types. Indeed, if types only depend on pure terms, the problem of having two different evaluations of the effect of the term (at the level of types and at the level of terms) disappear. This is the case for instance for Dependent ML of Xi and Pfenning [18], or more recently for Casinghino *et al.* [19] on how to combine proofs and programs when programs can be non-terminating. The F^* programming language of Swamy *et al.* [20] uses a notion of primitive effects including state, exceptions, divergence and IO. Each effect is described through a monadic predicate transformer semantics which allows to have a pure core dependent language to reason on those effects. On a more foundational side, there are two recent and overlapping lines of work on the description of a dependent call-by-push-value (CBPV) by Ahman *et al.* [21] and Vákár [22]. Those works also use a purity restriction for dependency, but using the CBPV language, deals with any effect described in monadic style. On another line of work, Brady advocates for the use of algebraic effects as an elegant way to allow combing effects more smoothly than with a monadic approach and gives an implementation in Idris [23].

Adding Effects to a Dependently-Typed Language. Nanevski *et al.* [24] have developed Hoare type theory (HTT) to extend CoQ with monadic style effects. To this end, they provide an axiomatic extension of CoQ with a monad in which to encapsulate imperative code. Important tools have been developed on HTT, most notably the Ynot project [25]. Apart from being axiomatic, their monadic approach does not allow to mix effectful programs and dependency but is rather made for proving inside CoQ properties on simply typed imperative programs.

Internal Translation of Type Theory. A non-axiomatic way to extend type theory with new features is to use internal translation, that is translation of type theory into itself as advocated by Boulier *et al.* [9]. The presentation of parametricity for type theory given by Bernardy and Lasson [5] can be seen as one of the first internal translation of type theory. However, this one does not add any new power to type theory as it is a conservative extension. Barthe *et al.* [26] have described a CPS translation for CC_ω featuring `call-cc`, but without dealing with inductive types and relying on a form of type stratification. A variant of this translation has been extended recently by Bowman *et al.* [27] to dependent sums using answer-type polymorphism $\Pi\alpha : \Box.\,(A \to \alpha) \to \alpha$. A generic class of internal translations has been defined by Jaber *et al.* [28] using forcing, which can be seen as a type theoretic version of the presheaf construction used in categorical logic. This class of translation works on all CIC but for a restricted version of dependent elimination, identical to the Baclofen type theory [2]. Therefore, to the best of our knowledge, the exceptional translation is the first complete internal translation of CIC adding a particular notion of effect.

8   Conclusion and Future Work

In this paper, we have defined the exceptional translation, the first syntactic translation of the Calculus of Inductive Constructions into itself, adding effects and that covers full dependent elimination. This results in a new type theory, which features call-by-name exceptions with decidable type-checking and a weaker form of canonicity. We have shown that although the resulting theory is inconsistent, it is possible to reason on exceptional programs and show that some of them actually never raise an exception by relying on the target theory. This provides a sound logical framework allowing to transparently prove safety properties about impure dependently-typed programs. Then, using parametricity, we have given an additional layer at the top of the exceptional translation in order to tame exceptions and preserve consistency. This way, we have consistently extended the logical expressivity of CIC with independence of premises, Markov's rule, and the negation of function extensionality while retaining η-expansion. Both translations have been implemented in a COQ plugin, which we use to formalize the examples.

One of the main directions of future work is to investigate whether other kind of effects can give rise to an internal translation of CIC. To that end, it seems promising to look at algebraic presentation of effects. Indeed, the recent work on the non-necessity of the value restriction policy for algebraic effects and handlers of Kammar and Pretnar [29] suggests that we should be able to perform similar translations on CIC with full dependent elimination for other algebraic effects and handlers than exceptions.

Acknowledgements. This research was supported in part by an ERC Consolidator Grant for the project "RustBelt", funded under Horizon 2020 grant agreement № 683289 and an ERC Starting Grant for the project "CoqHoTT", funded under Horizon 2020 grant agreement № 637339.

References

1. Moggi, E.: Notions of computation and monads. Inf. Comput. **93**(1), 55–92 (1991)
2. Pédrot, P., Tabareau, N.: An effectful way to eliminate addiction to dependence. In: 32nd Annual Symposium on Logic in Computer Science, LICS 2017, Reykjavik, Iceland, 20–23 June 2017, pp. 1–12 (2017)
3. Munch-Maccagnoni, G.: Models of a non-associative composition. In: Muscholl, A. (ed.) FoSSaCS 2014. LNCS, vol. 8412, pp. 396–410. Springer, Heidelberg (2014). https://doi.org/10.1007/978-3-642-54830-7_26
4. Kreisel, G.: Interpretation of analysis by means of constructive functionals of finite types. In: Heyting, A. (ed.) Constructivity in Mathematics, pp. 101–128. North-Holland Pub. Co., Amsterdam (1959)
5. Bernardy, J.-P., Lasson, M.: Realizability and parametricity in pure type systems. In: Hofmann, M. (ed.) FoSSaCS 2011. LNCS, vol. 6604, pp. 108–122. Springer, Heidelberg (2011). https://doi.org/10.1007/978-3-642-19805-2_8
6. Avigad, J., Feferman, S.: Gödel's functional ("Dialectica") interpretation. In: The Handbook of Proof Theory, pp. 337–405. North-Holland (1999)
7. Coquand, T., Mannaa, B.: The independence of Markov's principle in type theory. In: 1st International Conference on Formal Structures for Computation and Deduction, FSCD 2016, Porto, Portugal, 22–26 June 2016, pp. 17:1–17:18 (2016)
8. Coquand, T., Huet, G.P.: The calculus of constructions. Inf. Comput. **76**(2/3), 95–120 (1988)
9. Boulier, S., Pédrot, P., Tabareau, N.: The next 700 syntactical models of type theory. In: Proceedings of the 6th ACM SIGPLAN Conference on Certified Programs and Proofs, CPP 2017, Paris, France, 16–17 January 2017, pp. 182–194 (2017)
10. The Coq Development Team: The Coq proof assistant reference manual (2017)
11. Werner, B.: Une Théorie des Constructions Inductives. Ph.D. thesis, Université Paris-Diderot - Paris VII, May 1994
12. Tanter, É., Tabareau, N.: Gradual certified programming in Coq. In: Proceedings of the 11th ACM Dynamic Languages Symposium (DLS 2015), Pittsburgh, PA, USA, pp. 26–40. ACM Press, October 2015
13. Reynolds, J.C.: Types, abstraction and parametric polymorphism. In: IFIP Congress, pp. 513–523 (1983)
14. Friedman, H.: Classically and intuitionistically provably recursive functions. In: Miiller, G.H., Scott, D.S. (eds.) Higher Set Theory. Lecture Notes in Mathematics, pp. 21–27. Springer, Heidelberg (1978)
15. Troelstra, A. (ed.): Metamathematical Investigation of Intuitionistic Arithmetic and Analysis. Lecture Notes in Mathematics, vol. 344. Springer, Heidelberg (1973). https://doi.org/10.1007/BFb0066739
16. Herbelin, H.: An intuitionistic logic that proves Markov's principle. In: Proceedings of the 25th Annual Symposium on Logic in Computer Science, LICS 2010, Edinburgh, United Kingdom, 11–14 July 2010, pp. 50–56 (2010)
17. Keller, C., Lasson, M.: Parametricity in an impredicative sort. In: Computer Science Logic (CSL'12) - 26th International Workshop/21st Annual Conference of the EACSL, CSL 2012, Fontainebleau, France, 3–6 September 2012, pp. 381–395 (2012)
18. Xi, H., Pfenning, F.: Dependent types in practical programming. In: Proceedings of the 26th ACM SIGPLAN-SIGACT Symposium on Principles of Programming Languages, POPL 1999, pp. 214–227. ACM, New York (1999)

19. Casinghino, C., Sjöberg, V., Weirich, S.: Combining proofs and programs in a dependently typed language. In: Proceedings of the 41st ACM SIGPLAN-SIGACT Symposium on Principles of Programming Languages, POPL 2014, pp. 33–45. ACM, New York (2014)
20. Swamy, N., Hriţcu, C., Keller, C., Rastogi, A., Delignat-Lavaud, A., Forest, S., Bhargavan, K., Fournet, C., Strub, P.Y., Kohlweiss, M., Zinzindohoue, J.K., Zanella-Béguelin, S.: Dependent types and multi-monadic effects in F*. In: 43rd ACM SIGPLAN-SIGACT Symposium on Principles of Programming Languages (POPL), pp. 256–270. ACM, January 2016
21. Ahman, D., Ghani, N., Plotkin, G.D.: Dependent types and fibred computational effects. In: Jacobs, B., Löding, C. (eds.) FoSSaCS 2016. LNCS, vol. 9634, pp. 36–54. Springer, Heidelberg (2016). https://doi.org/10.1007/978-3-662-49630-5_3
22. Vákár, M.: A framework for dependent types and effects (2015) draft
23. Brady, E.: Idris, a general-purpose dependently typed programming language: design and implementation. J. Funct. Program. **23**(05), 552–593 (2013)
24. Nanevski, A., Morrisett, G., Birkedal, L.: Hoare type theory, polymorphism and separation. J. Funct. Program. **18**(5–6), 865–911 (2008)
25. Chlipala, A., Malecha, G., Morrisett, G., Shinnar, A., Wisnesky, R.: Effective interactive proofs for higher-order imperative programs. In: Proceedings of the 14th ACM SIGPLAN International Conference on Functional Programming, ICFP 2009, pp. 79–90. ACM, New York (2009)
26. Barthe, G., Hatcliff, J., Sørensen, M.H.B.: CPS translations and applications: the cube and beyond. High. Order Symbol. Comput. **12**(2), 125–170 (1999)
27. Bowman, W., Cong, Y., Rioux, N., Ahmed, A.: Type-preserving CPS translation of σ and π types is not possible. In: Proceedings of the 45th ACM SIGPLAN-SIGACT Symposium on Principles of Programming Languages, POPL 2018. ACM, New York (2018)
28. Jaber, G., Lewertowski, G., Pédrot, P., Sozeau, M., Tabareau, N.: The definitional side of the forcing. In: Proceedings of the 31st Annual ACM/IEEE Symposium on Logic in Computer Science, LICS 2016, New York, NY, USA, 5–8 July 2016, pp. 367–376 (2016)
29. Kammar, O., Pretnar, M.: No value restriction is needed for algebraic effects and handlers. J. Funct. Program. **27**, 367–376 (2017)

Let Arguments Go First

Ningning Xie[✉] and Bruno C. d. S. Oliveira

The University of Hong Kong, Pokfulam, Hong Kong
{nnxie,bruno}@cs.hku.hk

Abstract. Bi-directional type checking has proved to be an extremely useful and versatile tool for type checking and type inference. The conventional presentation of bi-directional type checking consists of two modes: *inference* mode and *checked* mode. In traditional bi-directional type-checking, type annotations are used to guide (via the checked mode) the type inference/checking procedure to determine the type of an expression, and *type information flows from functions to arguments*.

This paper presents a variant of bi-directional type checking where the *type information flows from arguments to functions*. This variant retains the inference mode, but adds a so-called *application* mode. Such design can remove annotations that basic bi-directional type checking cannot, and is useful when type information from arguments is required to type-check the functions being applied. We present two applications and develop the meta-theory (mostly verified in Coq) of the application mode.

1 Introduction

Bi-directional type checking has been known in the folklore of type systems for a long time. It was popularized by Pierce and Turner's work on *local type inference* [29]. Local type inference was introduced as an alternative to Hindley-Milner (henceforth HM system) type systems [11,17], which could easily deal with polymorphic languages with subtyping. Bi-directional type checking is one component of local type inference that, aided by some type annotations, enables type inference in an expressive language with polymorphism and subtyping. Since Pierce and Turner's work, various other authors have proved the effectiveness of bi-directional type checking in several other settings, including many different systems with subtyping [12,14,15], systems with dependent types [2,3,10,21,37], and various other works [1,7,13,22,28]. Furthermore, bi-directional type checking has also been combined with HM-style techniques for providing type inference in the presence of higher-ranked types [14,27].

The key idea in bi-directional type checking is simple. In its basic form typing is split into *inference* and *checked* modes. The most salient feature of a bi-directional type-checker is when information deduced from inference mode is used to guide checking of an expression in checked mode. One of such interactions between modes happens in the typing rule for function applications:

$$\frac{\Gamma \vdash e_1 \Rightarrow A \to B \qquad \Gamma \vdash e_2 \Leftarrow A}{\Gamma \vdash e_1\ e_2 \Rightarrow B}\ \text{APP}$$

© The Author(s) 2018
A. Ahmed (Ed.): ESOP 2018, LNCS 10801, pp. 272–299, 2018.
https://doi.org/10.1007/978-3-319-89884-1_10

In the above rule, which is a standard bi-directional rule for checking applications, the two modes are used. First we synthesize ($\Rightarrow$) the type $A \to B$ from e_1, and then check ($\Leftarrow$) e_2 against A, returning B as the type for the application.

This paper presents a variant of bi-directional type checking that employs a so-called *application* mode. With the application mode the design of the application rule (for a simply typed calculus) is as follows:

$$\frac{\Gamma \vdash e_2 \;\Rightarrow\; A \qquad \Gamma \mid \Psi, A \vdash e_1 \;\Rightarrow\; A \to B}{\Gamma \mid \Psi \vdash e_1\ e_2 \;\Rightarrow\; B} \text{ APP}$$

In this rule, there are two kinds of judgments. The first judgment is just the usual inference mode, which is used to infer the type of the argument e_2. The second judgment, the application mode, is similar to the inference mode, but it has an additional context Ψ. The context Ψ is a stack that tracks the types of the arguments of outer applications. In the rule for application, the type of the argument e_2 is inferred first, and then pushed into Ψ for inferring the type of e_1. Applications are themselves in the application mode, since they can be in the context of an outer application. With the application mode it is possible to infer the type for expressions such as (λx. x) 1 without additional annotations.

Bi-directional type checking with an application mode may still require type annotations and it gives different trade-offs with respect to the checked mode in terms of type annotations. However the different trade-offs open paths to different designs of type checking/inference algorithms. To illustrate the utility of the application mode, we present two different calculi as applications. The first calculus is a higher ranked implicit polymorphic type system, which infers higher-ranked types, generalizes the HM type system, and has polymorphic **let** as syntactic sugar. As far as we are aware, no previous work enables an HM-style let construct to be expressed as syntactic sugar. For this calculus many results are proved using the Coq proof assistant [9], including type-safety. Moreover a sound and complete algorithmic system, inspired by Peyton Jones et al. [27], is also developed. A second calculus with *explicit polymorphism* illustrates how the application mode is compatible with type applications, and how it adds expressiveness by enabling an encoding of type declarations in a System-F-like calculus. For this calculus, all proofs (including type soundness), are mechanized in Coq.

We believe that, similarly to standard bi-directional type checking, bi-directional type checking with an application mode can be applied to a wide range of type systems. Our work shows two particular and non-trivial applications. Other potential areas of applications are other type systems with subtyping, static overloading, implicit parameters or dependent types.

In summary the contributions of this paper are[1]:

- **A variant of bi-directional type checking** where the inference mode is combined with a new, so-called, application mode. The application mode naturally propagates type information from arguments to the functions.
- **A new design for type inference of higher-ranked types** which generalizes the HM type system, supports a polymorphic **let** as syntactic sugar, and infers higher rank types. We present a syntax-directed specification, an elaboration semantics to System F, some meta-theory in Coq, and an algorithmic type system with completeness and soundness proofs.
- **A System-F-like calculus** as a theoretical response to the challenge noted by Pierce and Turner [29]. It shows that the application mode is compatible with type applications, which also enables encoding type declarations. We present a type system and meta-theory, including proofs of type safety and uniqueness of typing in Coq.

2 Overview

2.1 Background: Bi-directional Type Checking

Traditional type checking rules can be heavyweight on annotations, in the sense that lambda-bound variables always need explicit annotations. Bi-directional type checking [29] provides an alternative, which allows types to propagate downward the syntax tree. For example, in the expression $(\lambda f : \mathtt{Int} \to \mathtt{Int}. \ f) \ (\lambda y. \ y)$, the type of y is provided by the type annotation on f. This is supported by the bi-directional typing rule for applications:

$$\frac{\Gamma \vdash e_1 \Rightarrow A \to B \qquad \Gamma \vdash e_2 \Leftarrow A}{\Gamma \vdash e_1 \ e_2 \Rightarrow B} \text{ App}$$

Specifically, if we know that the type of e_1 is a function from $\mathtt{A} \to \mathtt{B}$, we can check that e_2 has type $\mathtt{A}$. Notice that here the type information flows from functions to arguments.

One guideline for designing bi-directional type checking rules [15] is to distinguish introduction rules from elimination rules. Constructs which correspond to introduction forms are *checked* against a given type, while constructs corresponding to elimination forms *infer* (or synthesize) their types. For instance, under this design principle, the introduction rule for pairs is supposed to be in checked mode, as in the rule PAIR-C.

$$\frac{\Gamma \vdash e_1 \Leftarrow A \qquad \Gamma \vdash e_2 \Leftarrow B}{\Gamma \vdash (e_1, e_2) \Leftarrow (A, B)} \text{ Pair-C} \qquad \frac{\Gamma \vdash e_1 \Rightarrow A \qquad \Gamma \vdash e_2 \Rightarrow B}{\Gamma \vdash (e_1, e_2) \Rightarrow (A, B)} \text{ Pair-I}$$

---

[1] All supplementary materials are available in https://bitbucket.org/ningningxie/let-arguments-go-first.

Unfortunately, this means that the trivial program (1, 2) cannot type-check, which in this case has to be rewritten to (1, 2) : (Int , Int).

In this particular case, bi-directional type checking goes against its original intention of removing burden from programmers, since a seemingly unnecessary annotation is needed. Therefore, in practice, bi-directional type systems do not strictly follow the guideline, and usually have additional inference rules for the introduction form of constructs. For pairs, the corresponding rule is PAIR-I.

Now we can type check (1, 2), but the price to pay is that two typing rules for pairs are needed. Worse still, the same criticism applies to other constructs. This shows one drawback of bi-directional type checking: often to minimize annotations, many rules are duplicated for having both inference and checked mode, which scales up with the typing rules in a type system.

2.2 Bi-directional Type Checking with the Application Mode

We propose a variant of bi-directional type checking with a new *application mode*. The application mode preserves the advantage of bi-directional type checking, namely many redundant annotations are removed, while certain programs can type check with even fewer annotations. Also, with our proposal, the inference mode is a special case of the application mode, so it does not produce duplications of rules in the type system. Additionally, the checked mode can still be *easily* combined into the system (see Sect. 5.1 for details). The essential idea of the application mode is to enable the type information flow in applications to propagate from arguments to functions (instead of from functions to arguments as in traditional bi-directional type checking).

To motivate the design of bi-directional type checking with an application mode, consider the simple expression

$(\lambda x.\ x)\ 1$

This expression cannot type check in traditional bi-directional type checking because unannotated abstractions only have a checked mode, so annotations are required. For example, $((\lambda x.\ x) : \text{Int} \to \text{Int})\ 1$.

In this example we can observe that if the type of the argument is accounted for in inferring the type of $\lambda x.\ x$, then it is actually possible to deduce that the lambda expression has type $\text{Int} \to \text{Int}$, from the argument 1.

The Application Mode. If types flow from the arguments to the function, an alternative idea is to push the type of the arguments into the typing of the function, as the rule that is briefly introduced in Sect. 1:

$$\frac{\Gamma \vdash e_2 \Rightarrow A \quad \Gamma \mid \Psi, A \vdash e_1 \Rightarrow A \to B}{\Gamma \mid \Psi \vdash e_1\ e_2 \Rightarrow B} \text{ APP}$$

Here the argument e_2 synthesizes its type A, which then is pushed into the application context Ψ. Lambda expressions can now make use of the application context, leading to the following rule:

$$\frac{\Gamma, x : A \mid \Psi \vdash e \;\Rightarrow\; B}{\Gamma \mid \Psi, A \vdash \lambda x.\, e \;\Rightarrow\; A \rightarrow B} \;\text{LAM}$$

The type A that appears last in the application context serves as the type for x, and type checking continues with a smaller application context and x:A in the typing context. Therefore, using the rule APP and LAM, the expression $(\lambda x.\ x)\ 1$ can type-check without annotations, since the type Int of the argument 1 is used as the type of the binding x.

Note that, since the examples so far are based on simple types, obviously they can be solved by integrating type inference and relying on techniques like unification or constraint solving. However, here the point is that the application mode helps to reduce the number of annotations *without requiring such sophisticated techniques*. Also, the application mode helps with situations where those techniques cannot be easily applied, such as type systems with subtyping.

Interpretation of the Application Mode. As we have seen, the guideline for designing bi-directional type checking [15], based on introduction and elimination rules, is often not enough in practice. This leads to extra introduction rules in the inference mode. The application mode does not distinguish between introduction rules and elimination rules. Instead, to decide whether a rule should be in inference or application mode, we need to think whether the expression can be applied or not. Variables, lambda expressions and applications are all examples of expressions that can be applied, and they should have application mode rules. However pairs or literals cannot be applied and should have inference rules. For example, type checking pairs would simply lead to the rule PAIR-I. Nevertheless elimination rules of pairs could have non-empty application contexts (see Sect. 5.2 for details). In the application mode, arguments are always inferred first in applications and propagated through application contexts. An empty application context means that an expression is not being applied to anything, which allows us to model the inference mode as a particular case[2].

Partial Type Checking. The inference mode synthesizes the type of an expression, and the checked mode checks an expression against some type. A natural question is how do these modes compare to application mode. An answer is that, in some sense: the application mode is stronger than inference mode, but weaker than checked mode. Specifically, the inference mode means that we know nothing about the type an expression before hand. The checked mode means that the whole type of the expression is already known before hand. With the application mode we know some partial type information about the type of an expression:

---

[2] Although the application mode generalizes the inference mode, we refer to them as two different modes. Thus the variant of bi-directional type checking in this paper is interpreted as a type system with both *inference* and *application* modes.

we know some of its argument types (since it must be a function type when the application context is non-empty), but not the return type.

Instead of nothing or all, this partialness gives us a finer grain notion on how much we know about the type of an expression. For example, assume $e : A \rightarrow B \rightarrow C$. In the inference mode, we only have e. In the checked mode, we have both e and $A \rightarrow B \rightarrow C$. In the application mode, we have e, and maybe an empty context (which degenerates into inference mode), or an application context A (we know the type of first argument), or an application context B, A (we know the types of both arguments).

Trade-offs. Note that the application mode is *not* conservative over traditional bidirectional type checking due to the different information flow. However, it provides a new design choice for type inference/checking algorithms, especially for those where the information about arguments is useful. Therefore we next discuss some benefits of the application mode for two interesting cases where functions are either variables; or lambda (or type) abstractions.

2.3   Benefits of Information Flowing from Arguments to Functions

Local Constraint Solver for Function Variables. Many type systems, including type systems with *implicit polymorphism* and/or *static overloading*, need information about the types of the arguments when type checking function variables. For example, in conventional functional languages with implicit polymorphism, function calls such as (id 3) where id: ∀a. (a → a), are *pervasive*. In such a function call the type system must instantiate a to Int. Dealing with such implicit instantiation gets trickier in systems with *higher-ranked types*. For example, Peyton Jones et al. [27] require additional syntactic forms and relations, whereas Dunfield and Krishnaswami [14] add a special purpose *application judgment*.

With the application mode, all the type information about the arguments being applied is available in application contexts and can be used to solve instantiation constraints. To exploit such information, the type system employs a special subtyping judgment called *application subtyping*, with the form $\Psi \vdash A \leq B$. Unlike conventional subtyping, computationally Ψ and A are interpreted as inputs and B as output. In above example, we have that $\mathsf{Int} \vdash \forall a.a \rightarrow a \leq B$ and we can determine that $a = \mathsf{Int}$ and $B = \mathsf{Int} \rightarrow \mathsf{Int}$. In this way, type system is able to solve the constraints *locally* according to the application contexts since we no longer need to propagate the instantiation constraints to the typing process.

Declaration Desugaring for Lambda Abstractions. An interesting consequence of the usage of an application mode is that it enables the following **let** sugar:

let x = e_1 **in** e_2 ⤳ (λx. e_2) e_1

Such syntactic sugar for **let** is, of course, standard. However, in the context of implementations of typed languages it normally requires extra type annotations or a more sophisticated type-directed translation. Type checking (λx. e_2) e_1

would normally require annotations (for example an annotation for x), or otherwise such annotation should be inferred first. Nevertheless, with the application mode no extra annotations/inference is required, since from the type of the argument e_1 it is possible to deduce the type of x. Generally speaking, with the application mode *annotations are never needed for applied lambdas*. Thus **let** can be the usual sugar from the untyped lambda calculus, including HM-style **let** expression and even type declarations.

2.4   Application 1: Type Inference of Higher-Ranked Types

As a first illustration of the utility of the application mode, we present a calculus with *implicit predicative higher-ranked polymorphism*.

Higher-Ranked Types. Type systems with higher-ranked types generalize the traditional HM type system, and are useful in practice in languages like Haskell or other ML-like languages. Essentially higher-ranked types enable much of the expressive power of System F, with the advantage of implicit polymorphism. Complete type inference for System F is known to be undecidable [36]. Therefore, several partial type inference algorithms, exploiting additional type annotations, have been proposed in the past instead [15,25,27,31].

Higher-Ranked Types and Bi-directional Type Checking. Bi-directional type checking is also used to help with the inference of higher-ranked types [14,27]. Consider the following program:

$(\lambda f.\ (f\ 1,\ f\ ^{\prime}c^{\prime}))\ (\lambda x.\ x)$

which is not typeable under those type systems because they fail to infer the type of f, since it is supposed to be polymorphic. Using bi-directional type checking, we can rewrite this program as

$((\lambda f.\ (f\ 1,\ f\ ^{\prime}c^{\prime}))\ :\ (\forall a.\ a\ \rightarrow\ a)\ \rightarrow\ (Int,\ Char))\ (\lambda x\ .\ x)$

Here the type of f can be easily derived from the type signature using checked mode in bi-directional type checking. However, although some redundant annotations are removed by bi-directional type checking, the burden of inferring higher-ranked types is still carried by programmers: they are forced to add polymorphic annotations to help with the type derivation of higher-ranked types. For the above example, the type annotation is still *provided by programmers*, even though the necessary type information can be derived intuitively without any annotations: f is applied to $\lambda x.\ x$, which is of type $\forall a.\ a\ \rightarrow\ a$.

Generalization. Generalization is famous for its application in let polymorphism in the HM system, where generalization is adopted at let bindings. Let polymorphism is a useful component to introduce top-level quantifiers (rank 1 types) into a polymorphic type system. The previous example becomes typeable in the HM system if we rewrite it to: **let** $f = \lambda x.\ x$ **in** $(f\ 1,\ f\ ^{\prime}c^{\prime})$.

Type Inference for Higher-Ranked Types with the Application Mode. Using our bi-directional type system with an application mode, the original expression can type check without annotations or rewrites: (λf. (f 1, f 'c')) (λx. x).

This result comes naturally if we allow type information flow from arguments to functions. For inferring polymorphic types for arguments, we use *generalization*. In the above example, we first infer the type $\forall$a. a $\rightarrow$ a for the argument, then pass the type to the function. A nice consequence of such an approach is that HM-style polymorphic **let** expressions are simply regarded as syntactic sugar to a combination of lambda/application:

let x = e_1 **in** e_2 $\leadsto$ (λx. e_2) e_1

With this approach, nested lets can lead to types which are *more general* than HM. For example, **let** s = λx. x **in let** t = λy. s **in** e. The type of s is $\forall$a. a $\rightarrow$ a after generalization. Because t returns s as a result, we might expect t: $\forall$b. b $\rightarrow$ ($\forall$a. a $\rightarrow$ a), which is what our system will return. However, HM will return type t: $\forall$b. $\forall$a. b $\rightarrow$ (a $\rightarrow$ a), as it can only return rank 1 types, which is less general than the previous one according to Odersky and Läufer's subtyping relation for polymorphic types [24].

Conservativity over the Hindley-Milner Type System. Our type system is a conservative extension over the Hindley-Milner type system, in the sense that every program that can type-check in HM is accepted in our type system, which is explained in detail in Sect. 3.2. This result is not surprising: after desugaring **let** into a lambda and an application, programs remain typeable.

Comparing Predicative Higher-Ranked Type Inference Systems. We will give a full discussion and comparison of related work in Sect. 6. Among those works, we believe the work by Dunfield and Krishnaswami [14], and the work by Peyton Jones et al. [27] are the most closely related work to our system. Both their systems and ours are based on a *predicative* type system: universal quantifiers can only be instantiated by monotypes. So we would like to emphasize our system's properties in relation to those works. In particular, here we discuss two interesting differences, and also briefly (and informally) discuss how the works compare in terms of expressiveness.

(1) Inference of higher-ranked types. In both works, every polymorphic type inferred by the system must correspond to one annotation provided by the programmer. However, in our system, some higher-ranked types can be inferred from the expression itself without any annotation. The motivating expression above provides an example of this.

(2) Where are annotations needed? Since type annotations are useful for inferring higher rank types, a clear answer to the question where annotations are needed is necessary so that programmers know when they are required to write annotations. To this question, previous systems give a concrete answer: only on the binding of polymorphic types. Our answer is slightly different: only on the bindings of polymorphic types in abstractions *that are not applied to arguments*. Roughly speaking this means that our system ends up with fewer or smaller annotations.

(3) Expressiveness. Based on these two answers, it may seem that our system should accept all expressions that are typeable in their system. However, this is not true because the application mode is *not* conservative over traditional bi-directional type checking. Consider the expression (λf : (∀a. a → a) → (Int, Char). f) (λg. (g 1, g 'a')), which is typeable in their system. In this case, even if g is a polymorphic binding without a type annotation the expression can still type-check. This is because the original application rule propagates the information from the outer binding into the inner expressions. Note that the fact that such expression type-checks does not contradict their guideline of providing type annotations for every polymorphic binder. Programmers that strictly follow their guideline can still add a polymorphic type annotation for g. However it does mean that it is a little harder to understand where annotations for polymorphic binders can be *omitted* in their system. This requires understanding how the applications in checked mode operate.

In our system the above expression is not typeable, as a consequence of the information flow in the application mode. However, following our guideline for annotations leads to a program that can be type-checked with a smaller annotation: (λf. f) (λg : (∀a. a → a). (g 1, g 'a')). This means that our work is not conservative over their work, which is due to the design choice of the application typing rule. Nevertheless, we can always rewrite programs using our guideline, which often leads to fewer/smaller annotations.

2.5   Application 2: More Expressive Type Applications

The design choice of propagating arguments to functions was subject to consideration in the original work on local type inference [29], but was rejected due to possible non-determinism introduced by explicit type applications:

> "It is possible, of course, to come up with examples where it would be beneficial to synthesize the argument types first and then use the resulting information to avoid type annotations in the function part of an application expression.... Unfortunately this refinement does not help infer the type of polymorphic functions. For example, we cannot uniquely determine the type of x in the expression $(fun[X](x)\ e)$ [Int] 3." [29]

Therefore, as a response to this challenge, our second application is a variant of System F. Our development of the calculus shows that the application mode can actually work well with calculi with explicit type applications. To explain the new design, consider the expression:

(Λa. λx : a. x + 1) Int

which is not typeable in the traditional type system for System F. In System F the lambda abstractions do not account for the context of possible function applications. Therefore when type checking the inner body of the lambda abstraction, the expression x + 1 is ill-typed, because all that is known is that x has the (abstract) type a.

If we are allowed to propagate type information from arguments to functions, then we can verify that a = Int and x + 1 is well-typed. The key insight in the new type system is to use application contexts to track type equalities induced by type applications. This enables us to type check expressions such as the body of the lambda above (x + 1). Therefore, back to the problematic expression $(fun[X](x)\ e)$ [Int] 3, the type of x can be inferred as either X or Int since they are actually equivalent.

Sugar for Type Synonyms. In the same way that we can regard **let** expressions as syntactic sugar, in the new type system we further *gain built-in type synonyms for free*. A *type synonym* is a new name for an existing type. Type synonyms are common in languages such as Haskell. In our calculus a simple form of type synonyms can be desugared as follows:

type a = A **in** e ↝ (Λa. e) A

One practical benefit of such syntactic sugar is that it enables a direct encoding of a System F-like language with declarations (including type-synonyms). Although declarations are often viewed as a routine extension to a calculus, and are not formally studied, they are highly relevant in practice. Therefore, a more realistic formalization of a programming language should directly account for declarations. By providing a way to encode declarations, our new calculus enables a simple way to formalize declarations.

Type Abstraction. The type equalities introduced by type applications may seem like we are breaking System F type abstraction. However, we argue that *type abstraction* is still supported by our System F variant. For example:

let inc = Λa. λx : a. x + 1 **in** inc Int e

(after desugaring) does *not* type-check, as in a System-F like language. In our type system lambda abstractions that are immediatelly applied to an argument, and unapplied lambda abstractions behave differently. Unapplied lambda abstractions are just like System F abstractions and retain type abstraction. The example above illustrates this. In contrast the typeable example (Λa. λx : a. x + 1) Int, which uses a lambda abstraction directly applied to an argument, can be regarded as the desugared expression for **type** a = Int **in** λx : a . x + 1.

3   A Polymorphic Language with Higher-Ranked Types

This section first presents a declarative, *syntax-directed* type system for a lambda calculus with implicit higher-ranked polymorphism. The interesting aspects about the new type system are: (1) the typing rules, which employ a combination of inference and application modes; (2) the novel subtyping relation under an application context. Later, we prove our type system is type-safe by a type directed translation to System F [16,27] in Sect. 3.4. Finally an algorithmic type system is discussed in Sect. 3.5.

3.1 Syntax

The syntax of the language is:

Expr	$e ::= x \mid n \mid \lambda x : A.\ e \mid \lambda x.\ e \mid e_1\ e_2$
Type	$A, B ::= a \mid A \to B \mid \forall a.A \mid \mathsf{Int}$
Monotype	$\tau ::= a \mid \tau_1 \to \tau_2 \mid \mathsf{Int}$
Typing Context	$\Gamma ::= \varnothing \mid \Gamma, x : A$
Application Context	$\Psi ::= \varnothing \mid \Psi, A$

Expressions. Expressions e include variables (x), integers (n), annotated lambda abstractions $(\lambda x : A.\ e)$, lambda abstractions $(\lambda x.\ e)$, and applications $(e_1\ e_2)$. Letters x, y, z are used to denote term variables. Notably, the syntax does not include a **let** expression $(\mathbf{let}\ x = e_1\ \mathbf{in}\ e_2)$. Let expressions can be regarded as the standard syntax sugar $(\lambda x.\ e_2)\ e_1$, as illustrated in more detail later.

Types. Types include type variables (a), functions $(A \to B)$, polymorphic types $(\forall a.A)$ and integers (Int). We use capital letters (A, B) for types, and small letters (a, b) for type variables. Monotypes are types without universal quantifiers.

Contexts. Typing contexts Γ are standard: they map a term variable x to its type A. We implicitly assume that all the variables in Γ are distinct. The main novelty lies in the *application contexts* Ψ, which are the main data structure needed to allow types to flow from arguments to functions. Application contexts are modeled as a stack. The stack collects the types of arguments in applications. The context is a stack because if a type is pushed last then it will be popped first. For example, inferring expression e under application context (a, Int), means e is now being applied to two arguments e_1, e_2, with $e_1 : \mathsf{Int}$, $e_2 : a$, so e should be of type $\mathsf{Int} \to a \to A$ for some A.

3.2 Type System

The top part of Fig. 1 gives the typing rules for our language. The judgment $\Gamma \mid \Psi \vdash e \Rightarrow B$ is read as: under typing context Γ, and application context Ψ, e has type B. The standard inference mode $\Gamma \vdash e \Rightarrow B$ can be regarded as a special case when the application context is empty. Note that the variable names are assumed to be fresh enough when new variables are added into the typing context, or when generating new type variables.

Rule T-VAR says that if $x : A$ is in the typing context, and A is a subtype of B under application context Ψ, then x has type B. It depends on the subtyping rules that are explained in Sect. 3.3. Rule T-INT shows that integer literals are only inferred to have type Int under an empty application context. This is obvious since an integer cannot accept any arguments.

T-LAM shows the strength of application contexts. It states that, without annotations, if the application context is non-empty, a type can be popped from the application context to serve as the type for x. Inference of the body then continues with the rest of the application context. This is possible, because the

$$\boxed{\Gamma \mid \Psi \vdash e \Rightarrow B}$$

$$\dfrac{x : A \in \Gamma \qquad \Psi \vdash A \mathrel{<:} B}{\Gamma \mid \Psi \vdash x \Rightarrow B}\ \text{T-Var} \qquad\qquad \dfrac{}{\Gamma \vdash n \Rightarrow \mathsf{Int}}\ \text{T-Int}$$

$$\dfrac{\Gamma, x : A \mid \Psi \vdash e \Rightarrow B}{\Gamma \mid \Psi, A \vdash \lambda x.\, e \Rightarrow A \rightarrow B}\ \text{T-Lam} \qquad\qquad \dfrac{\Gamma, x : \tau \vdash e \Rightarrow B}{\Gamma \vdash \lambda x.\, e \Rightarrow \tau \rightarrow B}\ \text{T-Lam2}$$

$$\dfrac{\Gamma, x : A \vdash e \Rightarrow B}{\Gamma \vdash \lambda x : A.\, e \Rightarrow A \rightarrow B}\ \text{T-LamAnn1}$$

$$\dfrac{C \mathrel{<:} A \qquad \Gamma, x : A \mid \Psi \vdash e \Rightarrow B}{\Gamma \mid \Psi, C \vdash \lambda x : A.\, e \Rightarrow C \rightarrow B}\ \text{T-LamAnn2} \qquad\qquad \dfrac{\bar{a} = ftv(A) - ftv(\Gamma)}{\Gamma_{gen}(A) = \forall \bar{a}.A}\ \text{T-Gen}$$

$$\dfrac{\Gamma \vdash e_2 \Rightarrow A \qquad \Gamma_{gen}(A) = B \qquad \Gamma \mid \Psi, B \vdash e_1 \Rightarrow B \rightarrow C}{\Gamma \mid \Psi \vdash e_1\, e_2 \Rightarrow C}\ \text{T-App}$$

$$\boxed{A \mathrel{<:} B}$$

$$\dfrac{}{\mathsf{Int} \mathrel{<:} \mathsf{Int}}\ \text{S-Int} \qquad \dfrac{}{a \mathrel{<:} a}\ \text{S-Var} \qquad \dfrac{A \mathrel{<:} B}{A \mathrel{<:} \forall a.B}\ \text{S-ForallR}$$

$$\dfrac{A[\![a \mapsto \tau]\!] \mathrel{<:} B}{\forall a.A \mathrel{<:} B}\ \text{S-ForallL} \qquad \dfrac{C \mathrel{<:} A \qquad B \mathrel{<:} D}{A \rightarrow B \mathrel{<:} C \rightarrow D}\ \text{S-Fun}$$

$$\boxed{\Psi \vdash A \mathrel{<:} B}$$

$$\dfrac{}{\varnothing \vdash A \mathrel{<:} A}\ \text{S-Empty} \qquad \dfrac{\Psi, C \vdash A[\![a \mapsto \tau]\!] \mathrel{<:} B}{\Psi, C \vdash \forall a.A \mathrel{<:} B}\ \text{S-ForallL2}$$

$$\dfrac{C \mathrel{<:} A \qquad \Psi \vdash B \mathrel{<:} D}{\Psi, C \vdash A \rightarrow B \mathrel{<:} C \rightarrow D}\ \text{S-Fun2}$$

Fig. 1. Syntax-directed typing and subtyping.

expression $\lambda x.\, e$ is being applied to an argument of type A, which is the type at the top of the application context stack. Rule T-Lam2 deals with the case when the application context is empty. In this situation, a monotype τ is *guessed* for the argument, just like the Hindley-Milner system.

Rule T-LamAnn1 works as expected with an empty application context: a new variable x is put with its type A into the typing context, and inference continues on the abstraction body. If the application context is non-empty, then the rule T-LamAnn2 applies. It checks that C is a subtype of A before putting $x : A$ in the typing context. However, note that it is always possible to remove annotations in an abstraction if it has been applied to some arguments.

Rule T-App pushes types into the application context. The application rule first infers the type of the argument e_2 with type A. Then the type A is generalized in the same way that types in **let** expressions are generalized in the HM type system. The resulting generalized type is B. The generalization is shown in rule T-GEN, where all free type variables are extracted to quantifiers. Thus the type of e_1 is now inferred under an application context extended with type B. The generalization step is important to infer higher ranked types: since B is a possibly polymorphic type, which is the argument type of e_1, then e_1 is of possibly a higher rank type.

Let Expressions. The language does not have built-in **let** expressions, but instead supports **let** as syntactic sugar. The typing rule for **let** expressions in the HM system is (without the gray-shaded part):

$$\frac{\Gamma \vdash e_1 \Rightarrow A_1 \quad \Gamma_{gen}(A_1) = A_2 \quad \Gamma, x : A_2 \mid \Psi \vdash e_2 \Rightarrow B}{\Gamma \mid \Psi \vdash \textbf{let } x = e_1 \textbf{ in } e_2 \Rightarrow B} \text{ T-Let}$$

where we do generalization on the type of e_1, which is then assigned as the type of x while inferring e_2. Adapting this rule to our system with application contexts would result in the gray-shaded part, where the application context is only used for e_2, because e_2 is the expression being applied. If we desugar the **let** expression (**let** $x = e_1$ **in** e_2) to (($\lambda x.\ e_2$) e_1), we have the following derivation:

$$\frac{\Gamma \vdash e_1 \Rightarrow A_1 \quad \Gamma_{gen}(A_1) = A_2 \quad \dfrac{\dfrac{\Gamma, x : A_2 \mid \Psi \vdash e_2 \Rightarrow B}{\Gamma \mid \Psi, A_2 \vdash \lambda x.\ e_2 \Rightarrow A_2 \rightarrow B} \text{ T-Lam}}{\Gamma \mid \Psi \vdash (\lambda x.\ e_2)\ e_1 \Rightarrow B} \text{ T-App}}{\ }$$

The type A_2 is now pushed into application context in rule T-APP, and then assigned to x in T-LAM. Comparing this with the typing derivations with rule T-LET, we now have same preconditions. Thus we can see that the rules in Fig. 1 are sufficient to express an HM-style polymorphic let construct.

Meta-Theory. The type system enjoys several interesting properties, especially lemmas about application contexts. Before we present those lemmas, we need a helper definition of what it means to use arrows on application contexts.

Definition 1 ($\Psi \rightarrow B$). If $\Psi = A_1, A_2, ..., A_n$, then $\Psi \rightarrow B$ means the function type $A_n \rightarrow ... \rightarrow A_2 \rightarrow A_1 \rightarrow B$.

Such definition is useful to reason about the typing result with application contexts. One specific property is that the application context determines the form of the typing result.

Lemma 1 (Ψ Coincides with Typing Results). *If $\Gamma \mid \Psi \vdash e \Rightarrow A$, then for some A', we have $A = \Psi \rightarrow A'$.*

Having this lemma, we can always use the judgment $\Gamma \mid \Psi \vdash e \Rightarrow \Psi \rightarrow A'$ instead of $\Gamma \mid \Psi \vdash e \Rightarrow A$.

In traditional bi-directional type checking, we often have one subsumption rule that transfers between inference and checked mode, which states that if an expression can be inferred to some type, then it can be checked with this type. In our system, we regard the normal inference mode $\Gamma \vdash e \Rightarrow A$ as a special case, when the application context is empty. We can also turn from normal inference mode into application mode with an application context.

Lemma 2 (Subsumption). *If $\Gamma \vdash e \Rightarrow \Psi \rightarrow A$, then $\Gamma \mid \Psi \vdash e \Rightarrow \Psi \rightarrow A$.*

The relationship between our system and standard Hindley Milner type system can be established through the desugaring of let expressions. Namely, if e is typeable in Hindley Milner system, then the desugared expression $|e|$ is typeable in our system, with a more general typing result.

Lemma 3 (Conservative over HM). *If $\Gamma \vdash^{HM} e \Rightarrow A$, then for some B, we have $\Gamma \vdash |e| \Rightarrow B$, and $B <: A$.*

3.3 Subtyping

We present our subtyping rules at the bottom of Fig. 1. Interestingly, our subtyping has two different forms.

Subtyping. The first judgment follows Odersky and Läufer [24]. $A <: B$ means that A is more polymorphic than B and, equivalently, A is a subtype of B. Rules S-INT and S-VAR are trivial. Rule S-FORALLR states A is subtype of $\forall a.B$ only if A is a subtype of B, with the assumption a is a fresh variable. Rule S-FORALLL says $\forall a.A$ is a subtype of B if we can instantiate it with some τ and show the result is a subtype of B. In rule S-FUN, we see that subtyping is contra-variant on the argument type, and covariant on the return type.

Application Subtyping. The typing rule T-VAR uses the second subtyping judgment $\Psi \vdash A <: B$. To motivate this new kind of judgment, consider the expression id 1 for example, whose derivation is stuck at T-VAR (here we assume id : $\forall a.a \rightarrow a \in \Gamma$):

$$\frac{\Gamma \vdash 1 \Rightarrow \mathsf{Int} \quad \Gamma_{gen}(\mathsf{Int}) = \mathsf{Int} \quad \dfrac{\mathsf{id} : \forall a.a \rightarrow a \in \Gamma \quad ???}{\Gamma \mid \mathsf{Int} \vdash \mathsf{id} \Rightarrow} \text{ T-Var}}{\Gamma \vdash \mathsf{id}\ 1 \Rightarrow} \text{ T-App}$$

Here we know that id : $\forall a.a \rightarrow a$ and also, from the application context, that id is applied to an argument of type Int. Thus we need a mechanism for solving the instantiation $a = \mathsf{Int}$ and return a supertype $\mathsf{Int} \rightarrow \mathsf{Int}$ as the type of id. This is precisely what the application subtyping achieves: resolve instantiation constraints according to the application context. Notice that unlike existing works [14,27], application subtyping provides a way to solve instantiation more *locally*, since it does not mutually depend on typing.

Back to the rules in Fig. 1, one way to understand the judgment $\Psi \vdash A <: B$ from a computational point-of-view is that the type B is a *computed* output, rather than an input. In other words B is determined from Ψ and A. This is unlike the judgment $A <: B$, where both A and B would be computationally interpreted as inputs. Therefore it is not possible to view $A <: B$ as a special case of $\Psi \vdash A <: B$ where Ψ is empty.

There are three rules dealing with application contexts. Rule S-EMPTY is for case when the application context is empty. Because it is empty, we have no constraints on the type, so we return it back unchanged. Note that this is where HM systems (also Peyton Jones et al. [27]) would normally use a rule INST to remove top-level quantifiers:

$$\overline{\forall \bar{a}.A <: A[\![\bar{a} \mapsto \bar{\tau}]\!]} \text{ INST}$$

Our system does not need INST, because in applications, type information flows from arguments to the function, instead of function to arguments. In the latter case, INST is needed because a function type is wanted instead of a polymorphic type. In our approach, instantiation of type variables is avoided unless necessary.

The two remaining rules apply when the application context is non-empty, for polymorphic and function types respectively. Note that we only need to deal with these two cases because Int or type variables a cannot have a non-empty application context. In rule S-FORALL2, we instantiate the polymorphic type with some τ, and continue. This instantiation is forced by the application context. In rule S-FUN2, one function of type $A \to B$ is now being applied to an argument of type C. So we check $C <: A$. Then we continue with B and the rest application context, and return $C \to D$ as the result type of the function.

Meta-Theory. Application subtyping is novel in our system, and it enjoys some interesting properties. For example, similarly to typing, the application context decides the form of the supertype.

Lemma 4 (Ψ Coincides with Subtyping Results). *If $\Psi \vdash A <: B$, then for some B', $B = \Psi \to B'$.*

Therefore we can always use the judgment $\Psi \vdash A <: \Psi \to B'$, instead of $\Psi \vdash A <: B$. Application subtyping is also reflexive and transitive. Interestingly, in those lemmas, if we remove all applications contexts, they are exactly the reflexivity and transitivity of traditional subtyping.

Lemma 5 (Reflexivity). $\Psi \vdash \Psi \to A <: \Psi \to A$.

Lemma 6 (Transitivity). *If $\Psi_1 \vdash A <: \Psi_1 \to B$, and $\Psi_2 \vdash B <: \Psi_2 \to C$, then $\Psi_2, \Psi_1 \vdash A <: \Psi_1 \to \Psi_2 \to C$.*

Finally, we can convert between subtyping and application subtyping. We can remove the application context and still get a subtyping relation:

Lemma 7 ($\Psi \vdash <:$ to $<:$). *If $\Psi \vdash A <: B$, then $A <: B$.*

Transferring from subtyping to application subtyping will result in a more general type.

Lemma 8 (<: to $\Psi \vdash$ <:). *If A <: $\Psi \to B_1$, then for some B_2, we have $\Psi \vdash A$ <: $\Psi \to B_2$, and B_2 <: B_1.*

This lemma may not seem intuitive at first glance. Consider a concrete example $\mathsf{Int} \to \forall a.a$ <: $\mathsf{Int} \to \mathsf{Int}$, and $\mathsf{Int} \vdash \mathsf{Int} \to \forall a.a$ <: $\mathsf{Int} \to \forall a.a$. The former one, holds because we have $\forall a.a$ <: Int in the return type. But in the latter one, after Int is consumed from application context, we eventually reach S-EMPTY, which always returns the original type back.

3.4 Translation to System F, Coherence and Type-Safety

We translate the source language into a variant of System F that is also used in Peyton Jones et al. [27]. The translation is shown to be coherent and type safe. Due to space limitations, we only summarize the key aspects of the translation. Full details can be found in the supplementary materials of the paper.

The syntax of our target language is as follows:

$$\text{Expressions } s, f ::= x \mid n \mid \lambda x : A.\ s \mid \varLambda a.s \mid s_1\ s_2 \mid s_1\ A$$

In the translation, we use f to refer to the coercion function produced by the subtyping translation, and s to refer to the translated term in System F. We write $\Gamma \vdash^F s : A$ to mean the term s has type A in System F.

The type-directed translation follows the rules in Fig. 1, with a translation output in the forms of judgments. We summarize all judgments as:

Judgment	Translation Output	Soundness
A <: $B \rightsquigarrow f$	coercion function f	$\varnothing \vdash^F f : A \to B$
$\Psi \vdash A$ <: $B \rightsquigarrow f$	coercion function f	$\varnothing \vdash^F f : A \to B$
$\Gamma \mid \Psi \vdash e \Rightarrow A \rightsquigarrow s$	target expression s	$\Gamma \vdash^F s : A$

For example, A <: $B \rightsquigarrow f$ means that if A <: B holds in the source language, we can translate it into a System F term f, which is a coercion function and has type $A \to B$. We prove that our system is type safe by proving that the translation produces well-typed terms.

Lemma 9 (Typing Soundness). *If $\Gamma \mid \Psi \vdash e \Rightarrow A \rightsquigarrow s$, then $\Gamma \vdash^F s : A$.*

However, there could be multiple targets corresponding to one expression due to the multiple choices for τ. To prove that the translation is coherent, we prove that all the translations for one expression have the same operational semantics. We write $|e|$ for the expressions after type erasure since types are useless after type checking. Because multiple targets could have different number of coercion functions, we use η-id equality [5] instead of syntactic equality, where two expressions are regarded as equivalent if they can turn into the same expression through η-reduction or removal of redundant identity functions. We then prove that our translation actually generates a *unique* target:

Lemma 10 (Coherence). *If $\Gamma_1 \mid \Psi_1 \vdash e \Rightarrow A \rightsquigarrow s_1$, and $\Gamma_2 \mid \Psi_2 \vdash e \Rightarrow B \rightsquigarrow s_2$, then $|s_1| \rightsquigarrow_{\eta id} |s_2|$.*

3.5   Algorithmic System

Even though our specification is syntax-directed, it does not directly lead to an algorithm, because there are still many guesses in the system, such as in rule T-LAM2. This subsection presents a brief introduction of the algorithm, which essentially follows the approach by Peyton Jones et al. [27]. Full details can be found in the supplementary materials.

Instead of guessing, the algorithm creates meta type variables $\widehat{\alpha}, \widehat{\beta}$ which are waiting to be solved. The judgment for the algorithmic type system is $(S_0, N_0) \mid \Gamma \mid \Psi \vdash e \Rightarrow A \hookrightarrow (S_1, N_1)$. Here we use N as name supply, from which we can always extract new names. We use S as a notation for the substitution that maps meta type variables to their solutions. For example, rule T-LAM2 becomes

$$\frac{(S_0, N_0) \mid \Gamma, x : \widehat{\beta} \vdash e \Rightarrow A \hookrightarrow (S_1, N_1)}{(S_0, N_0\widehat{\beta}) \mid \Gamma \vdash \lambda x.\ e \Rightarrow \widehat{\beta} \to A \hookrightarrow (S_1, N_1)} \quad \text{AT-LAM1}$$

Comparing it to rule T-LAM2, τ is replaced by a new meta type variable $\widehat{\beta}$ from name supply $N_0\widehat{\beta}$. But despite of the name supply and substitution, the rule retains the structure of T-LAM2.

Having the name supply and substitutions, the algorithmic system is a direct extension of the specification in Fig. 1, with a process to do unifications that solve meta type variables. Such unification process is quite standard and similar to the one used in the Hindley-Milner system. We proved our algorithm is sound and complete with respect to the specification.

Theorem 1 (Soundness). *If* $([], N_0) \mid \Gamma \vdash e \Rightarrow A \hookrightarrow (S_1, N_1)$, *then for any substitution* V *with* $dom(V) = fmv(S_1\Gamma, S_1A)$, *we have* $VS_1\Gamma \vdash e \Rightarrow VS_1A$.

Theorem 2 (Completeness). *If* $\Gamma \vdash e \Rightarrow A$, *then for a fresh* N_0, *we have* $([], N_0) \mid \Gamma \vdash e \Rightarrow B \hookrightarrow (S_1, N_1)$, *and for some* S_2, *we have* $\Gamma(S_2S_1B) <: \Gamma(A)$.

4   More Expressive Type Applications

This section presents a System-F-like calculus, which shows that the application mode not only does work well for calculi with explicit type applications, but it also adds interesting expressive power, while at the same time retaining uniqueness of types for *explicitly* polymorphic functions. One additional novelty in this section is to present another possible variant of typing and subtyping rules for the application mode, by exploiting the lemmas presented in Sects. 3.2 and 3.3.

$$\langle \emptyset \rangle A = A \qquad\qquad \langle \Gamma, x : B \rangle A = \langle \Gamma \rangle A$$
$$\langle \Gamma, a \rangle A = \langle \Gamma \rangle A \qquad\qquad \langle \Gamma, a = B \rangle A = \langle \Gamma \rangle (A[\![a \mapsto B]\!])$$

Fig. 2. Apply contexts as substitutions on types.

$$\frac{a \in \Gamma}{\Gamma \vdash a}\ \text{WF-TVar} \qquad \frac{}{\Gamma \vdash \mathsf{Int}}\ \text{WF-Int} \qquad \frac{\Gamma \vdash A \quad \Gamma \vdash B}{\Gamma \vdash A \to B}\ \text{WF-Arrow} \qquad \frac{\Gamma, a \vdash A}{\Gamma \vdash \forall a.A}\ \text{WF-All}$$

Fig. 3. Well-formedness.

4.1 Syntax

We focus on a new variant of the standard System F. The syntax is as follows:

Expr	$e ::= x \mid n \mid \lambda x : A.\ e \mid \lambda x.\ e \mid e_1\ e_2 \mid \Lambda a.e \mid e\ [A]$
Type	$A ::= a \mid \mathsf{Int} \mid A \to B \mid \forall a.A$
Typing Context	$\Gamma ::= \varnothing \mid \Gamma, x : A \mid \Gamma, a \mid \Gamma, a = A$
Application Context	$\Psi ::= \varnothing \mid \Psi, A \mid \Psi, [A]$

The syntax is mostly standard. Expressions include variables x, integers n, annotated abstractions $\lambda x : A.\ s$, unannotated abstractions $\lambda x.\ e$, applications $e_1\ e_2$, type abstractions $\Lambda a.s$, and type applications $e_1\ [A]$. Types includes type variable a, integers Int, function types $A \to B$, and polymorphic types $\forall a.A$.

The main novelties are in the typing and application contexts. Typing contexts contain the usual term variable typing $x : A$, type variables a, and type equations $a = A$, which track equalities and are not available in System F. Application contexts use A for the *argument type* for term-level applications, and use $[A]$ for the *type argument itself* for type applications.

Applying Contexts. The typing contexts contain type equations, which can be used as substitutions. For example, $a = \mathsf{Int}, x : \mathsf{Int}, b = Bool$ can be applied to $a \to b$ to get the function type $\mathsf{Int} \to Bool$. We write $\langle \Gamma \rangle A$ for Γ applied as a substitution to type A. The formal definition is given in Fig. 2.

Well-Formedness. The type well-formedness under typing contexts is given in Fig. 3, which is quite straightforward. Notice that there is no rule corresponding to type variables in type equations. For example, a is not a well-formed type under typing context $a = \mathsf{Int}$, instead, $\langle a = \mathsf{Int} \rangle a$ is. In other words, we keep the invariant: *types are always fully substituted under the typing context.*

The well-formedness of typing contexts $\Gamma\ ctx$, and the well-formedness of application contexts $\Gamma \vdash \Psi$ can be defined naturally based on the well-formedness of types. The specific definitions can be found in the supplementary materials.

$$\boxed{\Gamma \mid \Psi \vdash e \;\Rightarrow\; B}$$

$$\frac{\Gamma \; ctx \qquad \Gamma \vdash \Psi \qquad x : A \in \Gamma \qquad \Psi \vdash A \;<:\; B}{\Gamma \mid \Psi \vdash x \;\Rightarrow\; B}\;\text{SF-Var} \qquad\qquad \frac{\Gamma \; ctx}{\Gamma \vdash n \;\Rightarrow\; \mathsf{Int}}\;\text{SF-Int}$$

$$\frac{\Gamma, x : \langle\Gamma\rangle A \vdash e \;\Rightarrow\; B}{\Gamma \vdash \lambda x : A.\, e \;\Rightarrow\; \langle\Gamma\rangle A \to B}\;\text{SF-LamAnn1}$$

$$\frac{\Gamma, x : \langle\Gamma\rangle A \mid \Psi \vdash e \;\Rightarrow\; B}{\Gamma \mid \Psi, \langle\Gamma\rangle A \vdash \lambda x : A.\, e \;\Rightarrow\; B}\;\text{SF-LamAnn2} \qquad \frac{\Gamma, x : A \mid \Psi \vdash e \;\Rightarrow\; B}{\Gamma \mid \Psi, A \vdash \lambda x.\, e \;\Rightarrow\; B}\;\text{SF-Lam}$$

$$\frac{\Gamma \vdash e_2 \;\Rightarrow\; A \qquad \Gamma \mid \Psi, A \vdash e_1 \;\Rightarrow\; B}{\Gamma \mid \Psi \vdash e_1 \, e_2 \;\Rightarrow\; B}\;\text{SF-App} \qquad \frac{\Gamma, a \vdash e \;\Rightarrow\; B}{\Gamma \vdash \Lambda a.e \;\Rightarrow\; \forall a.B}\;\text{SF-TLam1}$$

$$\frac{\Gamma, a = A \mid \Psi \vdash e \;\Rightarrow\; B}{\Gamma \mid \Psi, [A] \vdash \Lambda a.e \;\Rightarrow\; B}\;\text{SF-TLam2} \qquad \frac{\Gamma \mid \Psi, [\langle\Gamma\rangle A] \vdash e \;\Rightarrow\; B}{\Gamma \mid \Psi \vdash e\,[A] \;\Rightarrow\; B}\;\text{SF-TApp}$$

$$\boxed{\Psi \vdash A \;<:\; B}$$

$$\frac{}{\varnothing \vdash A \;<:\; A}\;\text{SF-SEmpty}$$

$$\frac{\Psi \vdash B[\![a \mapsto A]\!] \;<:\; C}{\Psi, [A] \vdash \forall a.B \;<:\; C}\;\text{SF-STApp} \qquad \frac{\Psi \vdash B \;<:\; C}{\Psi, A \vdash A \to B \;<:\; C}\;\text{SF-SApp}$$

Fig. 4. Type system for the new System F variant.

4.2   Type System

Typing Judgments. From Lemmas 1 and 4, we know that the application context always coincides with typing/subtyping results. This means that the types of the arguments can be recovered from the application context. So instead of the whole type, we can use only the return type as the output type. For example, we review the rule T-Lam in Fig. 1:

$$\frac{\Gamma, x : A \mid \Psi \vdash e \;\Rightarrow\; B}{\Gamma \mid \Psi, A \vdash \lambda x.\, e \;\Rightarrow\; A \to B}\;\text{T-Lam} \qquad \frac{\Gamma, x : A \mid \Psi \vdash e \;\Rightarrow\; C}{\Gamma \mid \Psi, A \vdash \lambda x.\, e \;\Rightarrow\; C}\;\text{T-Lam-Alt}$$

We have $B = \Psi \to C$ for some C by Lemma 1. Instead of B, we can directly return C as the output type, since we can derive from the application context that e is of type $\Psi \to C$, and $\lambda x.\, e$ is of type $(\Psi, A) \to C$. Thus we obtain the T-Lam-Alt rule.

Note that the choice of the style of the rules is only a matter of taste in the language in Sect. 3. However, it turns out to be very useful for our variant of System F, since it helps avoiding introducing types like $\forall a = \mathsf{Int}.a$. Therefore, we adopt the new form of judgment. Now the judgment $\Gamma \mid \Psi \vdash e \;\Rightarrow\; A$ is interpreted as: *under the typing context Γ, and the application context Ψ, the return type of e applied to the arguments whose types are in Ψ is A.*

Typing Rules. Using the new interpretation of the typing judgment, we give the typing rules in the top of Fig. 4. SF-VAR depends on the subtyping rules. Rule SF-INT always infers integer types. Rule SF-LAMANN1 first applies current context on A, then puts $x : \langle \Gamma \rangle A$ into the typing context to infer e. The return type is a function type because the application context is empty. Rule SF-LAMANN2 has a non-empty application context, so it requests that the type at the top of the application context is equivalent to $\langle \Gamma \rangle A$. The output type is B instead of a function type. Notice how the invariant that types are fully substituted under the typing context is preserved in these two rules.

Rule SF-LAM pops the type A from the application context, puts $x : A$ into the typing context, and returns only the return type B. In rule SF-APP, the argument type A is pushed into the application context for inferring e_1, so the output type B is the type of e_1 under application context (Ψ, A), which is exactly the return type of $e_1\ e_2$ under Ψ.

Rule SF-TLAM1 is for type abstractions. The type variable a is pushed into the typing context, and the return type is a polymorphic type. In rule SF-TLAM2, the application context has the type argument A at its top, which means the type abstraction is applied to A. We then put the type equation $a = A$ into the typing context to infer e. Like term-level applications, here we only return the type B instead of a polymorphic type. In rule SF-TAPP, we first apply the typing context on the type argument A, then we put the applied type argument $\langle \Gamma \rangle A$ into the application context to infer e, and return B as the output type.

Subtyping. The definition of subtyping is given at the bottom of Fig. 4. As with the typing rules, the part of argument types corresponding to the application context is omitted in the output. We interpret the rule form $\Psi \vdash A <: B$ as, under the application context Ψ, A is a subtype of the type whose type arguments are Ψ and the return type is B.

Rule SF-SEMPTY returns the input type under the empty application context. Rule SF-STAPP instantiates a with the type argument A, and returns C. Note how application subtyping can be extended naturally to deal with type applications. Rule SF-SAPP requests that the argument type is the same as the top type in the application context, and returns C.

4.3   Meta Theory

Applying the idea of the application mode to System F results in a well-behaved type system. For example, subtyping transitivity becomes more concise:

Lemma 11 (Subtyping transitivity). *If $\Psi_1 \vdash A <: B$, and $\Psi_2 \vdash B <: C$, then $\Psi_2, \Psi_1 \vdash A <: C$.*

Also, we still have the interesting subsumption lemma that transfers from the inference mode to the application mode:

Lemma 12 (Subsumption). *If $\Gamma \vdash e \Rightarrow A$, and $\Gamma \vdash \Psi$, and $\Psi \vdash A <: B$, then $\Gamma \mid \Psi \vdash e \Rightarrow B$.*

Furthermore, we prove the type safety by proving the progress lemma and the preservation lemma. The detailed definitions of operational semantics and values can be found in the supplementary materials.

Lemma 13 (Progress). *If $\varnothing \vdash e \Rightarrow T$, then either e is a value, or there exists e', such that $e \longrightarrow e'$.*

Lemma 14 (Preservation). *If $\Gamma \mid \Psi \vdash e \Rightarrow A$, and $e \longrightarrow e'$, then $\Gamma \mid \Psi \vdash e' \Rightarrow A$.*

Moreover, introducing type equality preserves unique types:

Lemma 15 (Uniqueness of typing). *If $\Gamma \mid \Psi \vdash e \Rightarrow A$, and $\Gamma \mid \Psi \vdash e \Rightarrow B$, then $A = B$.*

5   Discussion

This section discusses possible design choices regarding bi-directional type checking with the application mode, and talks about possible future work.

5.1   Combining Application and Checked Modes

Although the application mode provides us with alternative design choices in a bi-directional type system, a checked mode can still be *easily* added. One motivation for the checked mode would be annotated expressions $e : A$, where the type of expressions is known and is therefore used to check expressions.

Consider adding $e : A$ for introducing the third checked mode for the language in Sect. 3. Notice that, since the checked mode is stronger than application mode, when entering checked mode the application context is no longer useful. Instead we use application subtyping to satisfy the application context requirements. A possible typing rule for annotation expressions is:

$$\frac{\Psi \vdash A <: B \qquad \Gamma \vdash e \Leftarrow A}{\Gamma \mid \Psi \vdash (e : A) \Rightarrow B} \text{ T-Ann}$$

Here, e is checked using its annotation A, and then we instantiate A to B using subtyping with application context Ψ.

Now we can have a rule set of the checked mode for all expressions. For example, one useful rule for abstractions in checked mode could be ABS-CHK, where the parameter type A serves as the type of x, and typing checks the body with B. Also, combined with the information flow, the checked rule for application checks the function with the full type.

$$\frac{\Gamma, x : A \vdash e \Leftarrow B}{\Gamma \vdash \lambda x.\, e \Leftarrow A \to B} \text{ Abs-Chk} \qquad \frac{\Gamma \vdash e_2 \Rightarrow A \qquad \Gamma \vdash e_1 \Leftarrow A \to B}{\Gamma \vdash e_1\, e_2 \Leftarrow B} \text{ App-Chk}$$

Note that adding expression annotations might bring convenience for programmers, since annotations can be more freely placed in a program. For example, $(\lambda f.\ f\ 1) : (\text{Int} \to \text{Int}) \to \text{Int}$ becomes valid. However this does not add expressive power, since programs that are typeable under expression annotations, would remain typeable after moving the annotations to bindings. For example the previous program is equivalent to $(\lambda f : (\text{Int} \to \text{Int}).\ f\ 1)$.

This discussion is a sketch. We have not defined the corresponding declarative system nor algorithm. However we believe that the addition of a checked mode will *not* bring surprises to the meta-theory.

5.2 Additional Constructs

In this section, we show that the application mode is compatible with other constructs, by discussing how to add support for pairs in the language given in Sect. 3. A similar methodology would apply to other constructs like sum types, data types, if-then-else expressions and so on.

The introduction rule for pairs must be in the inference mode with an empty application context. Also, the subtyping rule for pairs is as expected.

$$\frac{\Gamma \vdash e_1 \Rightarrow A \qquad \Gamma \vdash e_2 \Rightarrow B}{\Gamma \vdash (e_1, e_2) \Rightarrow (A, B)} \text{ T-Pair} \qquad \frac{A_1 <: B_1 \qquad A_2 <: B_2}{(A_1, A_2) <: (B_1, B_2)} \text{ S-Pair}$$

The application mode can apply to the elimination constructs of pairs. If one component of the pair is a function, for example, $(\mathbf{fst}\ (\lambda x.\ x, 3)\ 4)$, then it is possible to have a judgment with a non-empty application context. Therefore, we can use the application subtyping to account for the application contexts:

$$\frac{\Gamma \vdash e \Rightarrow (A, B) \qquad \Psi \vdash A <: C}{\Gamma \mid \Psi \vdash \mathbf{fst}\ e \Rightarrow C} \text{ T-Fst1} \qquad \frac{\Gamma \vdash e \Rightarrow (A, B) \qquad \Psi \vdash B <: C}{\Gamma \mid \Psi \vdash \mathbf{snd}\ e \Rightarrow C} \text{ T-Snd1}$$

However, in polymorphic type systems, we need to take the subsumption rule into consideration. For example, in the expression $(\lambda x : (\forall a.(a, b)).\ \mathbf{fst}\ x)$, $\mathbf{fst}$ is applied to a polymorphic type. Interestingly, instead of a non-deterministic subsumption rule, having polymorphic types actually leads to a simpler solution. According to the philosophy of the application mode, the types of the arguments always flow into the functions. Therefore, instead of regarding $(\mathbf{fst}\ e)$ as an expression form, where e is itself an argument, we could regard $\mathbf{fst}$ as a function on its own, whose type is $(\forall ab.(a, b) \to a)$. Then as in the variable case, we use the subtyping rule to deal with application contexts. Thus the typing rules for $\mathbf{fst}$ and $\mathbf{snd}$ can be modeled as:

$$\frac{\Psi \vdash (\forall ab.(a, b) \to a) <: A}{\Gamma \mid \Psi \vdash \mathbf{fst} \Rightarrow A} \text{ T-Fst2} \qquad \frac{\Psi \vdash (\forall ab.(a, b) \to b) <: A}{\Gamma \mid \Psi \vdash \mathbf{snd} \Rightarrow A} \text{ T-Snd2}$$

Note that another way to model those two rules would be to simply have an initial typing environment $\Gamma_{initial} \equiv \mathbf{fst} : (\forall ab.(a, b) \to a), \mathbf{snd} : (\forall ab.(a, b) \to b)$. In this case the elimination of pairs be dealt directly by the rule for variables.

An extended version of the calculus presented in Sect. 3, which includes the rules for pairs (T-PAIR, S-PAIR, T-FST2 and T-SND2), has been formally studied. All the theorems presented in Sect. 3 hold with the extension of pairs.

5.3   Dependent Type Systems

One remark about the application mode is that the same idea is possibly applicable to systems with advanced features, where type inference is sophisticated or even undecidable. One promising application is, for instance, dependent type systems [2,3,10,21,37]. Type systems with dependent types usually unify the syntax for terms and types, with a single lambda abstraction generalizing both type and lambda abstractions. Unfortunately, this means that the **let** desugar is not valid in those systems. As a concrete example, consider desugaring the expression **let** $a = $ Int **in** $\lambda x : a.\ x + 1$ into $(\lambda a.\ \lambda x\ :\ a.\ x\ +\ 1)$ Int, which is ill-typed because the type of x in the abstraction body is a and not Int.

Because **let** cannot be encoded, declarations cannot be encoded either. Modeling declarations in dependently typed languages is a subtle matter, and normally requires some additional complexity [34].

We believe that the same technique presented in Sect. 4 can be adapted into a dependently typed language to enable a **let** encoding. In a dependent type system with unified syntax for terms and types, we can combine the two forms in the typing context ($x : A$ and $a = A$) into a unified form $x = e : A$. Then we can combine two application rules SF-APP and SF-TAPP into DE-APP, and also two abstraction rules SF-LAM and SF-TLAM1 into DE-LAM.

$$\frac{\Gamma \vdash e_2 \Rightarrow A \quad \Gamma \mid \Psi, e_2 : A \vdash e_1 \Rightarrow B}{\Gamma \mid \Psi \vdash e_1\ e_2 \Rightarrow B}\ \text{DE-APP} \qquad \frac{\Gamma, x = e_1 : A \mid \Psi \vdash e \Rightarrow B}{\Gamma \mid \Psi, e_1 : A \vdash \lambda x.\ e \Rightarrow B}\ \text{DE-LAM}$$

With such rules it would be possible to handle declarations easily in dependent type systems. Note this is still a rough idea and we have not fully worked out the typing rules for this type system yet.

6   Related Work

6.1   Bi-directional Type Checking

Bi-directional type checking was popularized by the work of Pierce and Turner [29]. It has since been applied to many type systems with advanced features. The alternative application mode introduced by us enables a variant of bi-directional type checking. There are many other efforts to refine bi-directional type checking.

Colored local type inference [25] refines local type inference for *explicit* polymorphism by propagating partial type information. Their work is built on distinguishing inherited types (known from the context) and synthesized types (inferred from terms). A similar distinction is achieved in our algorithm by manipulating type variables [14]. Also, their information flow is from functions to arguments, which is fundamentally different from the application mode.

The system of *tridirectional* type checking [15] is based on bi-directional type checking and has a rich set of property types including intersections, unions and quantified dependent types, but without parametric polymorphism. Tridirectional type checking has a new direction for supporting type checking unions and existential quantification. Their third mode is basically unrelated to our application mode, which propagates information from outer applications.

Greedy bi-directional polymorphism [13] adopts a greedy idea from Cardelli [4] on bi-directional type checking with higher ranked types, where the type variables in instantiations are determined by the first constraint. In this way, they support some uses of impredicative polymorphism. However, the greediness also makes many obvious programs rejected.

6.2   Type Inference for Higher-Ranked Types

As a reference, Fig. 5 [14, 20] gives a high-level comparison between related works and our system.

Predicative Systems. Peyton Jones et al. [27] developed an approach for type inference for higher rank types using traditional bi-directional type checking based on Odersky and Läufer [24]. However in their system, in order to do instantiation on higher rank types, they are forced to have an additional type category (ρ types) as a special kind of higher rank type without top-level quantifiers. This complicates their system since they need to have additional rule sets for such types. They also combine a variant of the containment relation from Mitchell [23] for deep skolemisation in subsumption rules, which we believe is compatible with our subtyping definition.

Dunfield and Krishnaswami [14] build a simple and concise algorithm for higher ranked polymorphism based on traditional bidirectional type checking. They deal with the same language of Peyton Jones et al. [27], except they do not have *let* expressions nor generalization (though it is discussed in design variations). They have a special *application judgment* which delays instantiation until the expression is applied to some argument. As with application mode, this avoids the additional category of types. Unlike their work, our work supports generalization and HM-style *let* expressions. Moreover the use of an application mode in our work introduces several differences as to when and where annotations are needed (see Sect. 2.4 for related discussion).

Impredicative Systems. ML^F [18,19,32] generalizes ML with first-class polymorphism. ML^F introduces a new type of bounded quantification (either rigid or flexible) for polymorphic types so that instantiation of polymorphic bindings is delayed until a principal type is found. The HML system [20] is proposed as a simplification and restriction of ML^F. HML only uses flexible types, which simplifies the type inference algorithm, but retains many interesting properties and features.

The FPH system [35] introduces boxy monotypes into System F types. One critique of boxy type inference is that the impredicativity is deeply hidden in the algorithmic type inference rules, which makes it hard to understand the interaction between its predicative constraints and impredicative instantiations [31].

System	Types	Impred	Let	Annotations
ML^F	flexible and rigid	yes	yes	on polymorphically used parameters
HML	flexible F-types	yes	yes	on polymorphic parameters
FPH	boxy F-types	yes	yes	on polymorphic parameters and some let bindings with higher-ranked types
Peyton Jones et al. (2007)	F-types	no	yes	on polymorphic parameters
Dunfield et al. (2013)	F-types	no	no	on polymorphic parameters
this paper	F-types	no	sugar	on polymorphic parameters that are not applied

Fig. 5. Comparison of higher-ranked type inference systems.

6.3 Tracking Type Equalities

Tracking type equalities is useful in various situations. Here we discuss specifically two related cases where tracking equalities plays an important role.

Type Equalities in Type Checking. Tracking type equalities is one essential part for type checking algorithms involving Generalized Algebraic Data Types (GADTs) [6,26,33]. For example, Peyton Jones et al. [26] propose a type inference algorithm based on unification for GADTs, where type equalities only apply to user-specified types. However, reasoning about type equalities in GADTs is essentially different from the approach in Sect. 4: type equalities are introduced by pattern matches in GADTs, while they are introduced through type applications in our system. Also, type equalities in GADTs are local, in the sense different branches in pattern matches have different type equalities for the same type variable. In our system, a type equality is introduced globally and is never changed. However, we believe that they can be made compatible by distinguishing different kinds of equalities.

Equalities in Declarations. In systems supporting dependent types, type equalities can be introduced by declarations. In the variant of pure type systems proposed by Severi and Poll [34], expressions $x = a : A$ **in** b generate an equality $x = a : A$ in the typing context, which can be fetched later through δ-reduction. However, δ-reduction rules require careful design, and the conversion rule of δ-reduction makes the type system non-deterministic. One potential usage of the application mode is to help reduce the complexity for introducing declarations in those type systems, as briefly discussed in Sect. 5.3.

7 Conclusion

We proposed a variant of bi-directional type checking with a new *application mode*, where type information flows from arguments to functions in applications. The application mode is essentially a generalization of the inference mode, can therefore work naturally with inference mode, and avoid the rule duplication that is often needed in traditional bi-directional type checking. The application mode can also be combined with the checked mode, but this often does not add expressiveness. Compared to traditional bi-directional type checking, the application mode opens a new path to the design of type inference/checking.

We have adopted the application mode in two type systems. Those two systems enjoy many interesting properties and features. However as bi-directional type checking can be applied to many type systems, we believe application mode is applicable to various type systems. One obvious potential future work is to investigate more systems where the application mode brings benefits. This includes systems with subtyping, intersection types [8,30], static overloading, or dependent types.

Acknowledgements. We thank the anonymous reviewers for their helpful comments. This work has been sponsored by the Hong Kong Research Grant Council projects number 17210617 and 17258816.

References

1. Abel, A.: Termination checking with types. RAIRO-Theor. Inform. Appl. **38**(4), 277–319 (2004)
2. Abel, A., Coquand, T., Dybjer, P.: Verifying a semantic $\beta\eta$-conversion test for Martin-Löf type theory. In: Audebaud, P., Paulin-Mohring, C. (eds.) MPC 2008. LNCS, vol. 5133, pp. 29–56. Springer, Heidelberg (2008). https://doi.org/10.1007/978-3-540-70594-9_4
3. Asperti, A., Ricciotti, W., Sacerdoti Coen, C., Tassi, E.: A bi-directional refinement algorithm for the calculus of (co) inductive constructions. Log. Meth. Comput. Sci. **8**, 1–49 (2012)
4. Cardelli, L.: An implementation of FSub. Technical report, Research report 97. Digital Equipment Corporation Systems Research Center (1993)
5. Chen, G.: Coercive subtyping for the calculus of constructions. In: POPL 2003 (2003)
6. Cheney, J., Hinze, R.: First-class phantom types. Technical Report CUCIS TR2003-1901. Cornell University (2003)
7. Chlipala, A., Petersen, L., Harper, R.: Strict bidirectional type checking. In: International Workshop on Types in Languages Design and Implementation (2005)
8. Coppo, M., Dezani-Ciancaglini, M., Venneri, B.: Functional characters of solvable terms. Math. Log. Q. **27**(2–6), 45–58 (1981)
9. Coq Development Team: The Coq proof assistant, Documentation, system download (2015)
10. Coquand, T.: An algorithm for type-checking dependent types. Sci. Comput. Program. **26**(1–3), 167–177 (1996)
11. Damas, L., Milner, R.: Principal type-schemes for functional programs. In: POPL 1982 (1982)
12. Davies, R., Pfenning, F.: Intersection types and computational effects. In: ICFP 2000 (2000)
13. Dunfield, J.: Greedy bidirectional polymorphism. In: Workshop on ML (2000)
14. Dunfield, J., Krishnaswami, N.R.: Complete and easy bidirectional typechecking for higher-rank polymorphism. In: ICFP 2013 (2013)

15. Dunfield, J., Pfenning, F.: Tridirectional typechecking. In: POPL 2004 (2004)
16. Girard, J.-Y.: The system F of variable types, fifteen years later. Theor. Comput. Sci. **45**, 159–192 (1986)
17. Hindley, J.R.: The principal type-scheme of an object in combinatory logic. Trans. Am. Math. Soc. **146**, 29–60 (1969)
18. Le Botlan, D., Rémy, D.: MLF: Raising ML to the power of system F. In: ICFP 2003 (2003)
19. Le Botlan, D., Rémy, D.: Recasting MLF. Inform. Comput. **207**(6), 726–785 (2009)
20. Leijen, D.: Flexible types: robust type inference for first-class polymorphism. In: POPL 2009 (2009)
21. Löh, A., McBride, C., Swierstra, W.: A tutorial implementation of a dependently typed lambda calculus. Fundamenta informaticae **102**(2), 177–207 (2010)
22. Lovas, W.: Refinement types for logical frameworks. Ph.D. thesis, Carnegie Mellon University (2010). AAI3456011
23. Mitchell, J.C.: Polymorphic type inference and containment. Inform. Comput. **76**(2–3), 211–249 (1988)
24. Odersky, M., Läufer, K.: Putting type annotations to work. In: POPL 1996 (1996)
25. Odersky, M., Zenger, C., Zenger, M.: Colored local type inference. In: POPL 2001 (2001)
26. Peyton Jones, S., Vytiniotis, D., Weirich, S., Washburn, G.: Simple unification-based type inference for gadts. In: ICFP 2006 (2006)
27. Peyton Jones, S., Vytiniotis, D., Weirich, S., Shields, M.: Practical type inference for arbitrary-rank types. J. Funct. Program. **17**(01), 1–82 (2007)
28. Pientka, B.: A type-theoretic foundation for programming with higher-order abstract syntax and first-class substitutions. In: POPL 2008 (2008)
29. Pierce, B.C., Turner, D.N.: Local type inference. TOPLAS **22**(1), 1–44 (2000)
30. Pottinger, G.: A type assignment for the strongly normalizable λ-terms. In: To HB Curry: essays on combinatory logic, lambda calculus and formalism. pp. 561–577 (1980)
31. Rémy, D.: Simple, partial type-inference for system F based on type-containment. In: ICFP 2005 (2005)
32. Rémy, D., Yakobowski, B.: From ML to MLF: graphic type constraints with efficient type inference. In: ICFP 2008 (2008)
33. Schrijvers, T., Peyton Jones, S., Sulzmann, M., Vytiniotis, D.: Complete and decidable type inference for gadts. In: ICFP 2009 (2009)
34. Severi, P., Poll, E.: Pure type systems with definitions. In: Nerode, A., Matiyasevich, Y.V. (eds.) LFCS 1994. LNCS, vol. 813, pp. 316–328. Springer, Heidelberg (1994). https://doi.org/10.1007/3-540-58140-5_30
35. Vytiniotis, D., Weirich, S., Peyton Jones, S.: FPH: First-class polymorphism for haskell. In: ICFP 2008 (2008)
36. Wells, J.B.: Typability and type checking in system F are equivalent and undecidable. Ann. Pure Appl. Log. **98**(1–3), 111–156 (1999)
37. Xi, H., Pfenning, F.: Dependent types in practical programming. In: POPL 1999 (1999)

Behavioural Equivalence via Modalities for Algebraic Effects

Alex Simpson and Niels Voorneveld[(✉)]

Faculty of Mathematics and Physics, University of Ljubljana, Ljubljana, Slovenia
{Alex.Simpson,Niels.Voorneveld}@fmf.uni-lj.si

Abstract. The paper investigates behavioural equivalence between programs in a call-by-value functional language extended with a signature of (algebraic) effect-triggering operations. Two programs are considered as being behaviourally equivalent if they enjoy the same behavioural properties. To formulate this, we define a logic whose formulas specify behavioural properties. A crucial ingredient is a collection of *modalities* expressing effect-specific aspects of behaviour. We give a general theory of such modalities. If two conditions, *openness* and *decomposability*, are satisfied by the modalities then the logically specified behavioural equivalence coincides with a modality-defined notion of applicative bisimilarity, which can be proven to be a congruence by a generalisation of Howe's method. We show that the openness and decomposability conditions hold for several examples of algebraic effects: nondeterminism, probabilistic choice, global store and input/output.

1 Introduction

The notion of *behavioural equivalence* between programs is a fundamental concept in the theory of programming languages. A conceptually natural approach to defining behavioural equivalence is to consider two programs as being equivalent if they enjoy the same 'behavioural properties'. This can be made precise by specifying a *behavioural logic* whose formulas express behavioural properties. Two programs M, N are then defined to be equivalent if, for all formulas Φ, it holds that $M \models \Phi$ iff $N \models \Phi$ (where $M \models \Phi$ expresses the satisfaction relation: program M enjoys property Φ).

This logical approach to defining behavioural equivalence has been particularly prominent in concurrency theory, where the classic result is that the equivalence defined by Hennessy-Milner logic [4] coincides with bisimilarity [14,17]. The aim of the present paper is to adapt the logical approach to the very different computational paradigm of *applicative programming with effects*.

A. Simpson—Supported by the Slovenian Research Agency, research core funding No. P1–0294.

N. Voorneveld—Supported by the Air Force Office of Scientific Research under award number FA9550-17-1-0326, and by EU-MSCA-RISE project 731143 (CID).

A. Ahmed (Ed.): ESOP 2018, LNCS 10801, pp. 300–326, 2018.
https://doi.org/10.1007/978-3-319-89884-1_11

More precisely, we consider a call-by-value functional programming language with *algebraic effects* in the sense of Plotkin and Power [21]. Broadly speaking, effects are those aspects of computation that involve a program interacting with its 'environment'; for example: nondeterminism, probabilistic choice (in both cases, the choice is deferred to the environment); input/output; mutable store (the machine state is modified); control operations such as exceptions, jumps and handlers (which interact with the continuation in the evaluation process); etc. Such general effects collectively enjoy common properties identified in the work of Moggi on monads [15]. Among them, algebraic effects play a special role. They can be included in a programming language by adding effect-triggering operations, whose 'algebraic' nature means that effects act independently of the continuation. From the aforementioned examples of effects, only jumps and handlers are non-algebraic. Thus the notion of algebraic effect covers a broad range of effectful computational behaviour. Call-by-value functional languages provide a natural context for exploring effectful programming. From a theoretical viewpoint, other programming paradigms are subsumed; for example, imperative programs can be recast as effectful functional ones. From a practical viewpoint, the combination of effects with call-by-value leads to the natural programming style supported by impure functional languages such as OCaml.

In order to focus on the main contributions of the paper (the behavioural logic and its induced behavioural equivalence), we instantiate "call-by-value functional language with algebraic effects" using a very simple language. Our language is a simply-typed λ-calculus with a base type of natural numbers, general recursion, call-by-value function evaluation, and algebraic effects, similar to [21]; although, for technical convenience, we adopt the (equivalent) formulation of fine-grained call-by-value [13]. The language is defined precisely in Sect. 2. Following [8,21], an operational semantics is given that evaluates programs to *effect trees*.

Section 3 introduces the behavioural logic. In our impure functional setting, the evaluation of a program of type τ results in a computational process that may or may not invoke effects, and which may or may not terminate with a return *value* of type τ. The key ingredient in our logic is an effect-specific family $\mathcal{O}$ of *modalities*, where each modality $o \in \mathcal{O}$ converts a property ϕ of values of type τ to a property $o\phi$ of general programs (called *computations*) of type τ. The idea is that such modalities capture all relevant effect-specific behavioural properties of the effects under consideration.

A main contribution of the paper is to give a general framework for defining such effect modalities, applicable across a wide range of algebraic effects. The general setting is that we have a signature Σ of effect operations, which determines the programming language, and a collection $\mathcal{O}$ of modalities, which determines the behavioural logic. In order to specify the semantics of the logic, we require each modality to be assigned a set of unit-type effect trees, which determines the meaning of the modality. Several concrete examples and a detailed general explanation are given in Sect. 3.

In Sect. 4, we consider the relation of *behavioural equivalence* between programs determined by the logic. A fundamental well-behavedness property is that any reasonable program equivalence should be a congruence with respect to the syntactic constructs of the programming language. Our main theorem (Theorem 1) is that, under two conditions on the collection $\mathcal{O}$ of modalities, which hold for all the examples of effects we consider, the logically induced behavioural equivalence is indeed a congruence.

In order to prove Theorem 1, we develop an alternative perspective on behavioural equivalence, which is of interest in its own right. In Sect. 5 we show how the modalities $\mathcal{O}$ determine a relation of *applicative $\mathcal{O}$-bisimilarity*, which is an effect-sensitive version of Abramsky's notion of *applicative bisimilarity* [1]. Theorem 2 shows that applicative $\mathcal{O}$-bisimilarity coincides with the logically defined relation of behavioural equivalence.

The proof of Theorem 1 is then concluded in Sect. 6, where we use Howe's method [5,6] to show that applicative $\mathcal{O}$-bisimilarity is a congruence. Although the proof is technically involved, we give only a brief outline, as the details closely follow the recent paper [9], in which Howe's method is applied to an untyped language with general algebraic effects.

In Sect. 7, we present a variation on our behavioural logic, in which we make the syntax of logical formulas independent of the syntax of the programming language.

Finally, in Sect. 8 we discuss related and further work.

2   A Simple Programming Language

As motivated in the introduction, our chosen base language is a simply-typed call-by-value functional language with general recursion and a ground type of natural numbers, to which we add (algebraic) effect-triggering operations. This means that our language is a call-by-value variant of PCF [20], extended with algebraic effects, resulting in a language similar to the one considered in [21]. In order to simplify the technical treatment of the language, we present it in the style of *fine-grained call-by-value* [13]. This means that we make a syntactic distinction between *values* and *computations*, representing the static and dynamic aspects of the language respectively. Furthermore, all *sequencing* of computations is performed using a single language construct, the **let** construct. The resulting language is straightforwardly intertranslatable with the more traditional call-by-value formulation. But the encapsulation of all sequencing within a single construct has the benefit of avoiding redundancy in proofs.

Our types are just the simple types obtained by iterating the function type construction over two base types: $\mathbf{N}$ of natural numbers, and also a unit type $\mathbf{1}$.

Types: $\tau, \rho ::= \mathbf{1} \mid \mathbf{N} \mid \rho \rightarrow \tau$
Contexts: $\Gamma ::= \emptyset \mid \Gamma, x : \tau$

As usual, term variables x are taken from a countably-infinite stock of such variables, and the context $\Gamma, x : \tau$ can only be formed if the variable x does not already appear in Γ.

As discussed above, program terms are separated into two mutually defined but disjoint categories: *values* and *computations*.

Values: $V, W ::= * \mid Z \mid S(V) \mid \lambda x.M \mid x$
Computations: $M, N ::= VW \mid \textbf{return } V \mid \textbf{let } M \Rightarrow x \textbf{ in } N \mid \textbf{fix } (V) \mid$
$\qquad \textbf{case } V \textbf{ in } \{Z \Rightarrow M, S(x) \Rightarrow N\}$

Here, $*$ is the unique value of the unit type. The values of the type of natural numbers are the *numerals* represented using zero Z and successor S. The values of function type are the λ-abstractions. And a variable x can be considered a value, because, under the call-by-value evaluation strategy of the language, it can only be instantiated with a value.

The computations are: function application VW; the computation that does nothing but return a value V; a **let** construct for sequencing; a **fix** construct for recursive definition; and a **case** construct that branches according to whether its natural-number argument is zero or positive. The computation **let** $M \Rightarrow x$ **in** N implements sequencing in the following sense. First the computation M is evaluated. Only in the case that the evaluation of M terminates, with return value V, does the thread of execution continue to N. In this case, the computation $N[V/x]$ is evaluated, and its return value (if any) is the one returned by the **let** construct.

To the pure functional language described above, we add *effect operations*. The collection of effect operations is specified by a set Σ (the *signature*) of such operations, together with, for each $\sigma \in \Sigma$ an associated *arity* which takes one of the four forms below

$$\alpha^n \to \alpha \quad \mathbf{N} \times \alpha^n \to \alpha \quad \alpha^{\mathbf{N}} \to \alpha \quad \mathbf{N} \times \alpha^{\mathbf{N}} \to \alpha.$$

The notation here is chosen to be suggestive of the way in which such arities are used in the typing rules below, viewing α as a type variable. Each of the forms of arity has an associated term constructor, for building additional computation terms, with which we extend the above grammar for computation terms.

Effects: $\sigma(M_0, M_1, \ldots, M_{n-1}) \mid \sigma(V; M_0, M_1, \ldots, M_{n-1}) \mid \sigma(V) \mid \sigma(W; V)$

Motivating examples of effect operations and their computation terms can be found in Examples 0–5 below.

The typing rules for the language are given in Fig. 1 below. Note that the choice of typing rule for an effect operation $\sigma \in \Sigma$ depends on its declared arity.

The terms of type τ are the values and computations generated by the constructors above. Every term has a unique *aspect* as either a value or computation. We write $Val(\tau)$ and $Com(\tau)$ respectively for closed values and computations. So the closed terms of τ are $Term(\tau) = Val(\tau) \cup Com(\tau)$. For $n \in \mathbb{N}$ a natural number, we write $\overline{n}$ for the numeral $S^n(Z)$, hence $Val(\mathbf{N}) := \{\overline{n} \mid n \in \mathbb{N}\}$.

We now consider some standard signatures of computationally interesting effect operations, which will be used as running examples throughout the paper. (We use the same examples as in [8].)

Example 0 (Pure functional computation). This is the trivial case (from an effect point of view) in which the signature Σ of effect operations is empty. The resulting language is a call-by-value variant of PCF [20].

$$\Gamma, x:\tau \vdash x:\tau \qquad \Gamma \vdash *:\mathbf{1} \qquad \Gamma \vdash Z:\mathbf{N} \qquad \dfrac{\Gamma \vdash V:\mathbf{N}}{\Gamma \vdash S(V):\mathbf{N}}$$

$$\dfrac{\Gamma \vdash V:\tau}{\Gamma \vdash \mathbf{return}(V):\tau} \qquad \dfrac{\Gamma, x:\tau \vdash M:\rho}{\Gamma \vdash (\lambda x:\tau.M):\tau \to \rho}$$

$$\dfrac{\Gamma \vdash V:\tau \to \rho \quad \Gamma \vdash W:\tau}{\Gamma \vdash (VW):\rho} \qquad \dfrac{\Gamma \vdash V:(\tau \to \rho) \to (\tau \to \rho)}{\Gamma \vdash \mathbf{fix}(V):\tau \to \rho}$$

$$\dfrac{\Gamma \vdash V:\mathbf{N} \quad \Gamma \vdash M:\tau \quad \Gamma, x:\mathbf{N} \vdash N:\tau}{\Gamma \vdash \mathbf{case}\ V\ \mathbf{of}\ \{Z \Rightarrow M; S(x) \Rightarrow N\}:\tau} \qquad \dfrac{\Gamma \vdash M:\tau \quad \Gamma, x:\tau \vdash N:\rho}{\Gamma \vdash \mathbf{let}\ M \Rightarrow x\ \mathbf{in}\ N:\rho}$$

$$\dfrac{\sigma:\alpha^n \to \alpha \quad \Gamma \vdash M_i:\tau}{\Gamma \vdash \sigma(M_0, M_1, \ldots, M_{n-1}):\tau} \qquad \dfrac{\sigma:\alpha^{\mathbf{N}} \to \alpha \quad \Gamma \vdash V:\mathbf{N} \to \tau}{\Gamma \vdash \sigma(V):\tau}$$

$$\dfrac{\sigma:\mathbf{N} \times \alpha^n \to \alpha \quad \Gamma \vdash V:\mathbf{N} \quad \Gamma \vdash M_i:\tau}{\Gamma \vdash \sigma(V; M_0, M_1, \ldots, M_{n-1}):\tau}$$

$$\dfrac{\sigma:\mathbf{N} \times \alpha^{\mathbf{N}} \to \alpha \quad \Gamma \vdash V:\mathbf{N} \quad \Gamma \vdash W:\mathbf{N} \to \tau}{\Gamma \vdash \sigma(V; W):\tau}$$

Fig. 1. Typing rules

Example 1 (Error). We take a set of error labels E. For each $e \in E$ there is an effect operator $raise_e : \alpha^0 \to \alpha$ which, when invoked by the computation $raise_e()$, aborts evaluation and outputs e as an error message.

Example 2 (Nondeterminism). There is a binary choice operator $or : \alpha^2 \to \alpha$ which gives two options for continuing the computation. The choice of continuation is under the control of some external agent, which one may wish to model as being cooperative (*angelic*), antagonistic (*demonic*), or *neutral*.

Example 3 (Probabilistic choice). Again there is a single binary choice operator $p\text{-}or : \alpha^2 \to \alpha$ which gives two options for continuing the computation. In this case, the choice of continuation is probabilistic, with a $\frac{1}{2}$ probability of either option being chosen. Other weighted probabilistic choices can be programmed in terms of this fair choice operation.

Example 4 (Global store). We take a set of locations L for storing natural numbers. For each $l \in L$ we have $lookup_l : \alpha^{\mathbf{N}} \to \alpha$ and $update_l : \mathbf{N} \times \alpha \to \alpha$. The computation $lookup_l(V)$ looks up the number at location l and passes it as an argument to the function V, and $update_l(\overline{n}; M)$ stores n at l and then continues with the computation M.

Example 5 (Input/output). Here we have two operators, $read : \alpha^{\mathbf{N}} \to \alpha$ which reads a number from an input channel and passes it as the argument to a function, and $write : \mathbf{N} \times \alpha \to \alpha$ which outputs a number (the first argument) and then continues as the computation given as the second argument.

We next present an operational semantics for our language, under which a computation term evaluates to an *effect tree*: essentially, a coinductively generated term using operations from Σ, and with values and $\bot$ (nontermination) as the generators. This idea appears in [8,21], and our technical treatment follows approach of the latter, adapted to call-by-value.

We define a single-step reduction relation $\rightarrowtail$ between configurations (S, M) consisting of a stack S and a computation M. The computation M is the term under current evaluation. The stack S represents a continuation computation awaiting the termination of M. First, we define a stack-independent reduction relation on computation terms that do not involve **let** at the top level.

$(\lambda x : \tau.M)V \rightsquigarrow M[V/x]$

case Z **of** $\{Z \Rightarrow M_1; S(x) \Rightarrow M_2\} \rightsquigarrow M_1$

case $S(V)$ **of** $\{Z \Rightarrow M_1; S(x) \Rightarrow M_2\} \rightsquigarrow M_2[V/x]$

fix$(F) \rightsquigarrow$ **return** $\lambda x : \tau.$ **let** $F(\lambda y : \tau.$**let fix** $F \Rightarrow z$ **in** $zy) \Rightarrow w$ **in** wx

The behaviour of **let** is implemented using a system of stacks where:

Stacks $S ::= id \mid S \circ ($ **let** $(-) \Rightarrow x$ **in** $M)$

We write $S\{N\}$ for the computation term obtained by 'applying' the stack S to N, defined by:

$$id\{N\} = N$$
$$(S \circ (\text{let } (-) \Rightarrow x \text{ in } M))\{N\} = S\{ \text{let } N \Rightarrow x \text{ in } M\}$$

We write $Stack(\tau, \rho)$ for the set of stacks S such that for any $N \in Com(\tau)$, it holds that $S\{N\}$ is a well-typed expression of type ρ. We define a reduction relation on pairs $Stack(\tau, \rho) \times Com(\tau)$ (denoted $(S_1, M_1) \rightarrowtail (S_2, M_2)$) by:

$(S, \text{ let } N \Rightarrow x \text{ in } M) \rightarrowtail (S \circ (\text{ let } (-) \Rightarrow x \text{ in } M), N)$

$(S, R) \rightarrowtail (S, R')$ \hfill if $R \rightsquigarrow R'$

$(S \circ (\text{ let } (-) \Rightarrow x \text{ in } M), \text{return } V) \rightarrowtail (S, M[V/x])$

We define the notion of *effect tree* for an arbitrary set X, where X is thought of as a set of abstract 'values'.

Definition 1. An *effect tree* (henceforth *tree*), over a set X, determined by a signature Σ of effect operations, is a labelled and possibly infinite tree whose nodes have the possible forms.

1. A leaf node labelled with $\perp$ (the symbol for nontermination).
2. A leaf node labelled with x where $x \in X$.
3. A node labelled σ with children $t_0, \ldots, t_{n-1}$, when $\sigma \in \Sigma$ has arity $\alpha^n \to \alpha$.
4. A node labelled σ with children $t_0, t_1, \ldots$, when $\sigma \in \Sigma$ has arity $\alpha^\mathbf{N} \to \alpha$.
5. A node labelled σ_m where $m \in \mathbb{N}$ with children $t_0, \ldots, t_{n-1}$, when $\sigma \in \Sigma$ has arity $\mathbf{N} \times \alpha^n \to \alpha$.
6. A node labelled σ_m where $m \in \mathbb{N}$ with children $t_0, t_1, \ldots$, when $\sigma \in \Sigma$ has arity $\mathbf{N} \times \alpha^\mathbf{N} \to \alpha$.

We write TX for the set of trees over X. We define a partial ordering on TX where $t_1 \leq t_2$, if t_1 can be obtained by replacing subtrees of t_2 by $\bot$. This forms an ω-*complete* partial order, meaning that every ascending sequence $t_1 \leq t_2 \leq \ldots$ has a least upper bound $\bigsqcup_n t_n$. Let $Tree(\tau) := T\,Val(\tau)$, we will define a reduction relation from computations to trees of values.

Given $f : X \to Y$ and a tree $t \in TX$, we write $t[x \mapsto f(x)] \in TY$ for the tree whose leaves $x \in X$ are renamed to $f(x)$. We have a function $\mu : TTX \to TX$, which takes a tree r of trees and flattens it to a tree $\mu r \in TX$, by taking the labelling tree at each non-$\bot$ leaf of r as the subtree at the corresponding node in μr. The function μ is the multiplication associated with the monad structure of the T operation. The unit of the monad is the map $\eta : X \to TX$ which takes an element $x \in X$ and returns a leaf labelled x.

The operational mapping from a computation $M \in Com(\tau)$ to an effect tree is defined intuitively as follows. Start evaluating the M in the empty stack id, until the evaluation process (which is deterministic) terminates (if this never happens the tree is $\bot$). If the evaluation process terminates at a configuration of the form $(id, \mathbf{return}\ V)$ then the tree is the leaf V. Otherwise the evaluation process can only terminate at a configuration of the form $(S, \sigma(\ldots))$ for some effect operation $\sigma \in \Sigma$. In this case, create an internal node in the tree of the appropriate kind (depending on σ) and continue generating each child tree of this node by repeating the above process by evaluating an appropriate continuation computation, starting from a configuration with the current stack S.

The following (somewhat technical) definition formalises the idea outlined above in a mathematically concise way. We define a family of maps $|-, -|_{(-)} :$ $Stack(\tau, \rho) \times Com(\tau) \times \mathbb{N} \to Tree(\rho)$ indexed over τ, and ρ by:

$$|S, M|_0 = \bot$$

$$|S, M|_{n+1} = \begin{cases} V & \text{if } S = id \wedge M = \mathbf{return}\ V \\ |S', M'|_n & \text{if } (S, M) \rightarrowtail (S', M') \\ \sigma(|S, M_0|_n, \ldots, |S, M_{m-1}|_n) & \sigma : \alpha^m \to \alpha, M = \sigma(M_0, \ldots, M_{m-1}) \\ \sigma(|S, V\overline{0}|_n, |S, V\overline{1}|_n, \ldots) & \sigma : \alpha^{\mathbf{N}} \to \alpha, M = \sigma(V) \\ \sigma_k(|S, M_0|_n, \ldots, |S, M_{m-1}|_n) & \sigma : \mathbf{N} \times \alpha^m \to \alpha, M = \sigma(\overline{k}, M_0, \ldots, M_{m-1}) \\ \sigma_k(|S, V\overline{0}|_n, |S, V\overline{1}|_n, \ldots) & \sigma : \mathbf{N} \times \alpha^{\mathbf{N}} \to \alpha, M = \sigma(\overline{k}, V) \\ \bot & \text{otherwise} \end{cases}$$

It follows that $|S, M|_n \leq |S, M|_{n+1}$ in the given ordering on trees. We write $|-|_{(-)} : Com(\tau) \times \mathbb{N} \to Tree(\tau)$ for the function defined by $|M|_n = |id, M|_n$. Using this we can give the operational interpretation of computation terms as effect trees by defining $|-| : Com(\tau) \to Tree(\tau)$ by $|M| := \bigsqcup_n |M|_n$.

Example 3 (Nondeterminism). Nondeterministically generate a natural number:

$$?N := \mathbf{let}\ \mathbf{fix}(\lambda x : 1 \to \mathbf{N}.\ or(\lambda y : 1.\ Z, \lambda y : 1.\ \mathbf{let}\ xy \Rightarrow z\ \mathbf{in}\ S(z))) \Rightarrow w\ \mathbf{in}\ w*$$

$$|?N| = \begin{array}{c} or \\ \diagup \quad \diagdown \\ \overline{0} \qquad\qquad or \\ \qquad \diagup \quad \diagdown \\ \qquad \overline{1} \qquad\qquad or \\ \qquad\qquad \diagup \quad \diagdown \\ \qquad\qquad \overline{2} \end{array}$$

3 Behavioural Logic and Modalities

The goal of this section is to motivate and formulate a logic for expressing *behavioural properties* of programs. In our language, program means (well-typed) term, and we shall be interested both in properties of *computations* and in properties of *values*. Accordingly, we define a logic that contains both *value formulas* and *computation formulas*. We shall use lower case Greek letters $\phi, \psi, \dots$ for the former, and upper case Greek letters $\Phi, \Psi, \dots$ for the latter. Our logic will thus have two satisfaction relations

$$V \models \phi \qquad\qquad M \models \Phi$$

which respectively assert that "value V enjoys the value property expressed by ϕ" and "computation M enjoys the computation property expressed by Φ".

In order to motivate the detailed formulation of the logic, it is useful to identify criteria that will guide the design.

(C1) The logic should express only 'behaviourally meaningful' properties of programs. This guides us to build the logic upon primitive notions that have a direct behavioural interpretation according to a natural understanding of program behaviour.

(C2) The logic should be as expressive as possible within the constraints imposed by criterion (C1).

For every type τ, we define a collection $VF(\tau)$ of *value formulas*, and a collection $CF(\tau)$ of *computation formulas*, as motivated above.

Since boolean logical connectives say nothing themselves about computational behaviour, it is a reasonable general principle that 'behavioural properties' should be closed under such connectives. Thus, in keeping with criterion (C2), which asks for maximal expressivity, we close each set $CF(\tau)$ and $VF(\tau)$, of computation and value formulas, under infinitary propositional logic.

In addition to closure under infinitary propositional logic, each set $VF(\tau)$ contains a collection of *basic* value formulas, from which compound formulas are constructed using (infinitary) propositional connectives.[1] The choice of basic formulas depends on the type τ.

---

[1] We call such formulas *basic* rather than *atomic* because they include formulas such as $(V \mapsto \Phi)$, discussed below, which are built from other formulas.

In the case of the natural numbers type, we include a basic value formula $\{n\} \in VF(\mathbf{N})$, for every $n \in \mathbb{N}$. The semantics of this formula are given by:

$$V \models \{n\} \quad \Leftrightarrow \quad V = \bar{n}.$$

By the closure of $VF(\mathbf{N})$ under infinitary disjunctions, every subset of $\mathbb{N}$ can be represented by some value formula. Moreover, since a general value formula in $VF(\mathbf{N})$ is an infinitary boolean combination of basic formulas of the form $\{n\}$, the value formulas represent exactly the subsets on $\mathbb{N}$.

For the unit type, we do not require any basic value formulas. The unit type has only one value, $*$. The two subsets of this singleton set of values are defined by the formulas $\bot$ ('falsum', given as an empty disjunction), and $\top$ (the truth constant, given as an empty conjunction).

For a function type $\tau \to \rho$, we want each basic formula to express a fundamental behavioural constraint on values (i.e., λ-abstractions) W of type $\tau \to \rho$. In keeping with the applicative nature of functional programming, the only way in which a λ-abstraction can be used to generate behaviour is to apply it to an argument of type τ, which, because we are in a call-by-value setting, must be a value V. The application of W to V results in a computation WV of type ρ, whose properties can be probed using computation formulas in $CF(\rho)$. Based on this, for every value $V \in Val(\tau)$ and computation formula $\Phi \in CF(\rho)$, we include a basic value formula $(V \mapsto \Phi) \in VF(\tau \to \rho)$ with the semantics:

$$W \models (V \mapsto \Phi) \quad \Leftrightarrow \quad WV \models \Phi.$$

Using this simple construct, based on application to a single argument V, other natural mechanisms for expressing properties of λ-abstractions are definable, using infinitary propositional logic. For example, given $\phi \in VF(\tau)$ and $\Psi \in CF(\rho)$, the definition

$$(\phi \mapsto \Psi) := \bigwedge \{(V \mapsto \Psi) \mid V \in Val(\tau), V \models \phi\} \tag{1}$$

defines a formula whose derived semantics is

$$W \models (\phi \mapsto \Psi) \quad \Leftrightarrow \quad \forall V \in Val(\tau). \; V \models \phi \text{ implies } WV \models \Psi. \tag{2}$$

In Sect. 7, we shall consider the possibility of changing the basic value formulas in $VF(\tau \to \rho)$ to formulas $(\phi \mapsto \Psi)$.

It remains to explain how the basic computation formulas in $CF(\tau)$ are formed. For this we require a given set $\mathcal{O}$ of *modalities*, which depends on the algebraic effects contained in the language. The basic computation formulas in $CF(\tau)$ then have the form $o\phi$, where $o \in \mathcal{O}$ is one of the available modalities, and ϕ is a value formula in $VF(\tau)$. Thus a modality 'lifts' properties of values of type τ to properties of computations of type τ.

In order to give semantics to computation formulas $o\phi$, we need a general theory of the kind of modality under consideration. This is one of the main contributions of the paper. Before presenting the general theory, we first consider motivating examples, using our running examples of algebraic effects.

Example 0 (Pure functional computation). Define $\mathcal{O} = \{\downarrow\}$. Here the single modality $\downarrow$ is the *termination modality*: $\downarrow\phi$ asserts that a computation terminates with a return value V satisfying ϕ. This is formalised using effect trees:

$$M \models \downarrow\phi \quad\Leftrightarrow\quad |M| \text{ is a leaf } V \text{ and } V \models \phi.$$

Note that, in the case of pure functional computation, all trees are leaves: either value leaves V, or nontermination leaves $\bot$.

Example 1 (Error). Define $\mathcal{O} = \{\downarrow\} \cup \{E_e \mid e \in E\}$. The semantics of the termination modality $\downarrow$ is defined as above. The *error modality* E_e flags error e:

$$M \models E_e\phi \quad\Leftrightarrow\quad |M| \text{ is a node labelled with } raise_e.$$

(Because $raise_e$ is an operation of arity 0, a $raise_e$ node in a tree has 0 children.) Note that the semantics of $E_e\phi$ makes no reference to ϕ. Indeed it would be natural to consider E_e as a basic computation formula in its own right, which could be done by introducing a notion of 0-argument modality, and considering E_e as such. In this paper, however, we keep the treatment uniform by always considering modalities as unary operations, with natural 0-argument modalities subsumed as unary modalities with redundant argument.

Example 2 (Nondeterminism). Define $\mathcal{O} = \{\Diamond, \Box\}$ with:

$$M \models \Diamond\phi \quad\Leftrightarrow\quad |M| \text{ has some leaf } V \text{ such that } V \models \phi$$
$$M \models \Box\phi \quad\Leftrightarrow\quad |M| \text{ has finite height and every leaf is a value } V \text{ s.t. } V \models \phi.$$

Including both modalities amounts to a neutral view of nondeterminism. In the case of angelic nondeterminism, one would include just the $\Diamond$ modality; in that of demonic nondeterminism, just the $\Box$ modality. Because of the way the semantic definitions interact with termination, the modalities $\Box$ and $\Diamond$ are not De Morgan duals. Indeed, each of the three possibilities $\{\Diamond, \Box\}, \{\Diamond\}, \{\Box\}$ for $\mathcal{O}$ leads to a logic with a different expressivity.

Example 3 (Probabilistic choice). Define $\mathcal{O} = \{P_{>q} \mid q \in \mathbb{Q}, 0 \leq q < 1\}$ with:

$$M \models P_{>q}\phi \quad\Leftrightarrow\quad \mathbf{P}(|M| \text{ terminates with a value in } \{V \mid V \models \phi\}) > q,$$

where the probability on the right is the probability that a run through the tree $|M|$, starting at the root, and making an independent fair probabilistic choice at each branching node, terminates at a value node with a value V in the set $\{V \mid V \models \phi\}$. We observe that the restriction to rational thresholds q is immaterial, as, for any real r with $0 \leq r < 1$, we can define:

$$P_{>r}\phi := \bigvee\{P_{>q}\phi \mid q \in \mathbb{Q}, r < q < 1\}.$$

Similarly, we can define non-strict threshold modalities, for $0 < r \leq 1$, by:

$$P_{\geq r}\phi := \bigwedge\{P_{>q}\phi \mid q \in \mathbb{Q}, 0 \leq q < r\}.$$

Also, we can exploit negation to define modalities expressing strict and non-strict upper bounds on probabilities. Notwithstanding the definability of non-strict and upper-bound thresholds, we shall see later that it is important that we include only strict lower-bound modalities in our set $\mathcal{O}$ of primitive modalities.

Example 4 (Global store). For a set of locations L, define the set of states by $State = \mathbb{N}^L$. The modalities are $\mathcal{O} = \{(s \rightarrowtail r) \mid s, r \in State\}$, where informally:

$$M \models (s \rightarrowtail r)\,\phi \quad \Leftrightarrow \quad \begin{array}{l} \text{the execution of } M, \text{ starting in state } s, \text{ terminates in} \\ \text{final state } r \text{ with return value } V \text{ such that } V \models \phi. \end{array}$$

We make the above definition precise using the effect tree of M. Define

$$exec : TX \times State \rightarrow X \times State,$$

for any set X, to be the least partial function satisfying:

$$exec(t, s) = \begin{cases} (x, s) & \text{if } t \text{ is a leaf labelled with } x \in X \\ exec(t_{s(l)}, s) & \text{if } t = lookup_l(t_0, t_1, \cdots) \text{ and } exec(t_{s(l)}, s) \text{ is defined} \\ exec(t', s[l := n]) & \text{if } t = update_{l,n}(t') \text{ and } exec(t', s[l := n]) \text{ is defined,} \end{cases}$$

where $s[l := n]$ is the evident modification of state s. Intuitively, $exec(t, s)$ defines the result of "executing" the tree of commands in effect tree t starting in state s, whenever this execution terminates. In terms of operational semantics, it can be viewed as defining a 'big-step' semantics for effect trees (in the signature of global store). We can now define the semantics of the $(s \rightarrowtail r)$ modality formally:

$$M \models (s \rightarrowtail r)\,\phi \quad \Leftrightarrow \quad exec(|M|, s) = (V, r) \text{ where } V \models \phi.$$

Example 5 (Input/output). Define an *i/o-trace* to be a word w over the alphabet

$$\{?n \mid n \in \mathbb{N}\} \cup \{!n \mid n \in \mathbb{N}\}.$$

The idea is that such a word represents an input/output sequence, where $?n$ means the number n is given in response to an input prompt, and $!n$ means that the program outputs n. Define the set of modalities

$$\mathcal{O} = \{\langle w \rangle \downarrow, \langle w \rangle_{...} \mid w \text{ an i/o-trace}\}.$$

The intuitive semantics of these modalities is as follows.

$$M \models \langle w \rangle \downarrow \phi \quad \Leftrightarrow \quad \begin{array}{l} w \text{ is a complete i/o-trace for the execution of } M \\ \text{resulting in termination with } V \text{ s.t. } V \models \phi \end{array}$$

$$M \models \langle w \rangle_{...}\,\phi \quad \Leftrightarrow \quad w \text{ is an initial i/o-trace for the execution of } M.$$

In order to define the semantics of formulas precisely, we first define relations $t \models \langle w \rangle \downarrow P$ and $t \models \langle w \rangle_{...}$, between $t \in TX$ and $P \subseteq X$, by induction on words

$$\frac{n \in \mathbb{N}}{\{n\} \in VF(\mathbf{N})}(1) \qquad \frac{V : \tau \quad \Phi \in CF(\rho)}{(V \mapsto \Phi) \in VF(\tau \to \rho)}(2) \qquad \frac{\phi \in VF(\tau) \quad o \in \mathcal{O}}{o\phi \in CF(\tau)}(3)$$

$$\frac{\phi : I \to VF(\tau)}{\bigvee_I \phi \in VF(\tau)}(4) \qquad \frac{\phi : I \to VF(\tau)}{\bigwedge_I \phi \in VF(\tau)}(5) \qquad \frac{\phi \in VF(\tau)}{\neg \phi \in VF(\tau)}(6)$$

$$\frac{\Phi : I \to CF(\tau)}{\bigvee_I \Phi \in CF(\tau)}(7) \qquad \frac{\Phi : I \to CF(\tau)}{\bigwedge_I \Phi \in CF(\tau)}(8) \qquad \frac{\Phi \in CF(\tau)}{\neg \Phi \in CF(\tau)}(9)$$

Fig. 2. The logic $\mathcal{V}$

(Note that we are overloading the $\models$ symbol.) In the following, we write ε for the empty word, and we use textual juxtaposition for concatenation of words.

$$
\begin{aligned}
t &\models \langle \varepsilon \rangle {\downarrow} P &\Leftrightarrow&\quad t \text{ is a leaf } x \text{ and } x \in P \\
t &\models \langle (?n)\, w \rangle {\downarrow} P &\Leftrightarrow&\quad t = read(t_0, t_1, \dots) \text{ and } t_n \models \langle w \rangle {\downarrow} P \\
t &\models \langle (!n)\, w \rangle {\downarrow} P &\Leftrightarrow&\quad t = write_n(t') \text{ and } t' \models \langle w \rangle {\downarrow} P \\
t &\models \langle \varepsilon \rangle_{...} &\Leftrightarrow&\quad \text{true} \\
t &\models \langle (?n)\, w \rangle_{...} &\Leftrightarrow&\quad t = read(t_0, t_1, \dots) \text{ and } t_n \models \langle w \rangle_{...} \\
t &\models \langle (!n)\, w \rangle_{...} &\Leftrightarrow&\quad t = write_n(t') \text{ and } t' \models \langle w \rangle_{...}
\end{aligned}
$$

The formal semantics of modalities is now easily defined by:

$$
\begin{aligned}
M &\models \langle w \rangle {\downarrow} \phi &\Leftrightarrow&\quad |M| \models \langle w \rangle {\downarrow} \{V \mid V \models \phi\} \\
M &\models \langle w \rangle_{...} \phi &\Leftrightarrow&\quad |M| \models \langle w \rangle_{...}.
\end{aligned}
$$

Note that, as in Example 1, the formula argument of the $\langle w \rangle_{...}$ modality is redundant. Also, note that our modalities for input/output could naturally be formed by combining the termination modality ${\downarrow}$, which lifts value formulas to computation formulas, with sequences of atomic modalities $\langle ?n \rangle$ and $\langle !n \rangle$ acting directly on computation formulas. In this paper, we do not include such modalities, acting on computation formulas, in our general theory. But this is a natural avenue for future consideration.

We now give a formal treatment of the logic and its semantics, in full generality. We assume given a signature Σ of effect operations, as in Sect. 2. And we assume given a set $\mathcal{O}$, whose elements we call *modalities*.

We call our main behavioural logic $\mathcal{V}$, where the letter $\mathcal{V}$ is chosen as a reference to the fact that the basic formula at function type specifies function behaviour on individual value arguments V.

Definition 2 (The logic $\mathcal{V}$). The classes $VF(\tau)$ and $CF(\tau)$ of *value* and *computation formulas*, for each type τ, are mutually inductively defined by the rules in Fig. 2. In this, I can be instantiated to any set, allowing for arbitrary conjunctions and disjunctions. When I is $\emptyset$, we get the special formulas $\top = \bigwedge_\emptyset$ and $\bot = \bigvee_\emptyset$. The use of arbitrary index sets means that formulas, as defined, form a proper class. However, we shall see below that countable index sets suffice.

In order to specify the semantics of modal formulas, we require a connection between modalities and effect trees, which is given by an interpretation function

$$[\![\cdot]\!] : \mathcal{O} \to \mathcal{P}(T1).$$

That is, every modality $o \in \mathcal{O}$ is mapped to a subset $[\![o]\!] \subseteq T1$ of unit-type effect trees. Given a subset $P \subseteq X$ (e.g. given by a formula) and a tree $t \in TX$ we can define a unit-type tree $t[\in P] \in T1$ as the tree created by replacing the leaves of t that belong to P by $*$ and the others by $\bot$. In the case that P is the subset $\{V \mid V \models \phi\}$ specified by a formula $\phi \in VF(\tau)$, we also write $t[\models \phi]$ for $t[\in P]$.

We can now formally define the two satisfaction relations $\models \subseteq Val(\tau) \times VF(\tau)$ and $\models \subseteq Com(\tau) \times CF(\tau)$, mutually inductively, by:

$$
\begin{aligned}
\overline{m} &\models \{n\} &\Leftrightarrow&\quad m = n \\
W &\models (V \mapsto \Phi) &\Leftrightarrow&\quad WV \models \Phi \\
M &\models o\phi &\Leftrightarrow&\quad |M|[\models \phi] \in [\![o]\!] \\
W &\models \neg\phi &\Leftrightarrow&\quad \neg(W \models \phi).
\end{aligned}
$$

We omit the evident clauses for the other propositional connectives. We remark that all conjunctions and disjunctions are semantically equivalent to countable ones, because value and computation formulas are interpreted over sets of terms, $Val(\tau)$ and $Com(\tau)$, which are countable.

We end this section by revisiting our running examples, and showing, in each case, that the example modalities presented above are all specified by suitable interpretation functions $[\![\cdot]\!] : \mathcal{O} \to \mathcal{P}(T1)$.

Example 0 (Pure functional computation). We have $\mathcal{O} = \{\downarrow\}$. Define:

$$[\![\downarrow]\!] = \{*\} \quad \text{(where } * \text{ is the tree with single node } *\text{)}$$

Example 1 (Error). We have $\mathcal{O} = \{\downarrow\} \cup \{\mathsf{E}_e \mid e \in E\}$. Define:

$$[\![\mathsf{E}_e]\!] = \{\, raise_e \,\}.$$

Example 2 (Nondeterminism). We have $\mathcal{O} = \{\Diamond, \Box\}$. Define:

$$
\begin{aligned}
[\![\Diamond]\!] &= \{t \mid t \text{ has some } * \text{ leaf}\} \\
[\![\Box]\!] &= \{t \mid t \text{ has finite height and every leaf is a } *\}.
\end{aligned}
$$

Example 3 (Probabilistic choice). $\mathcal{O} = \{\mathsf{P}_{>q} \mid q \in \mathbb{Q}, 0 \leq q < 1\}$. Define:

$$[\![\mathsf{P}_{>q}]\!] = \{t \mid \mathbf{P}(t \text{ terminates with a } * \text{ leaf}) > q\}.$$

Example 4 (Global store). $\mathcal{O} = \{(s \rightarrowtail r) \mid s, r \in State\}$. Define:

$$[\![(s \rightarrowtail r)]\!] = \{t \mid exec(t, s) = (*, r)\}.$$

Example 5 (Input/output). $\mathcal{O} = \{\langle w\rangle\downarrow, \langle w\rangle_{...} \mid w \text{ an i/o-trace}\}$. Define:

$$
\begin{aligned}
[\![\langle w\rangle\downarrow]\!] &= \{t \mid t \models \langle w\rangle\downarrow\{*\}\} \\
[\![\langle w\rangle_{...}]\!] &= \{t \mid t \models \langle w\rangle_{...}\}.
\end{aligned}
$$

4   Behavioural Equivalence

The goal of this section is to precisely formulate our main theorem: under suitable conditions, the behavioural equivalence determined by the logic $\mathcal{V}$ of Sect. 3 is a congruence. In order to achieve this, it will be useful to consider the *positive fragment* $\mathcal{V}^+$ of $\mathcal{V}$.

Definition 3 (The logic $\mathcal{V}^+$). The logic $\mathcal{V}^+$ is the fragment of $\mathcal{V}$ consisting of those formulas in $VF(\tau)$ and $CF(\tau)$ that do not contain negation.

Whenever we have a logic $\mathcal{L}$ whose value and computation formulas are given as subcollections $VF_\mathcal{L}(\tau) \subseteq VF(\tau)$ and $CF_\mathcal{L}(\tau) \subseteq CF(\tau)$, then $\mathcal{L}$ determines a preorder (and hence also an equivalence relation) between terms of the same type and aspect.

Definition 4 (Logical preorder and equivalence). Given a fragment $\mathcal{L}$ of $\mathcal{V}$, we define the *logical preorder* $\sqsubseteq_\mathcal{L}$, between well-typed terms of the same type and aspect, by:

$$V \sqsubseteq_\mathcal{L} W \quad \Leftrightarrow \quad \forall \phi \in VF_\mathcal{L}(\tau),\, V \models \phi \Rightarrow W \models \phi$$
$$M \sqsubseteq_\mathcal{L} N \quad \Leftrightarrow \quad \forall \Phi \in CF_\mathcal{L}(\tau),\, M \models \Phi \Rightarrow N \models \Phi$$

The *logical equivalence* $\equiv_\mathcal{L}$ on terms is the equivalence relation induced by the preorder (the intersection of $\sqsubseteq_\mathcal{L}$ and its converse).

In the case that formulas in $\mathcal{L}$ are closed under negation, it is trivial that the preorder $\sqsubseteq_\mathcal{L}$ is already an equivalence relation, and hence coincides with $\equiv_\mathcal{L}$. Thus we shall only refer specifically to the preorder $\sqsubseteq_\mathcal{L}$, for fragments, such as $\mathcal{V}^+$, that are not closed under negation.

The two main relations of interest to us in this paper are the primary relations determined by $\mathcal{V}$ and $\mathcal{V}^+$: full *behavioural equivalence* $\equiv_\mathcal{V}$; and the *positive behavioural preorder* $\sqsubseteq_{\mathcal{V}^+}$ (which induces *positive behavioural equivalence* $\equiv_{\mathcal{V}^+}$).

We next formulate the appropriate notion of (pre)congruence to apply to the relations $\equiv_\mathcal{V}$ and $\sqsubseteq_{\mathcal{V}^+}$. These two preorders are examples of *well-typed relations* on closed terms. Any such relation can be extended to a relation on open terms in the following way. Given a well-typed relation $\mathcal{R}$ on closed terms, we define the *open extension* $\mathcal{R}^\circ$ where $\Gamma \vdash M \mathcal{R}^\circ N : \tau$ precisely when, for every well-typed vector of closed values $\vec{V} : \Gamma$, it holds that $M[\vec{V}] \mathcal{R} N[\vec{V}]$. The correct notion of precongruence for a well-typed preorder on closed terms, is to ask for its open extension to be *compatible* in the sense of the definition below; see, e.g., [10,19] for further explanation.

Definition 5 (Compatibility). A well-typed open relation $\mathcal{R}$ is said to be *compatible* if it is closed under the rules in Fig. 3.

We now state our main congruence result, although we have not yet defined the conditions it depends upon.

$$\overline{\Gamma, x : \tau \vdash x \, \mathcal{R} \, x : \tau} \qquad \overline{\Gamma \vdash Z \, \mathcal{R} \, Z : \mathbf{N}} \qquad \frac{\Gamma \vdash V \, \mathcal{R} \, V' : \mathbf{N}}{\Gamma \vdash S(V) \, \mathcal{R} \, S(V') : \mathbf{N}}$$

$$\frac{\Gamma \vdash V \, \mathcal{R} \, V' : \tau}{\Gamma \vdash \mathbf{return}(V) \, \mathcal{R} \, \mathbf{return}(V') : \tau} \qquad \frac{\Gamma, x : \tau \vdash M \, \mathcal{R} \, M' : \rho}{\Gamma \vdash (\lambda x : \tau.M) \, \mathcal{R} \, (\lambda x : \tau.M') : \tau \to \rho}$$

$$\frac{\Gamma \vdash V \, \mathcal{R} \, V' : \tau \to \rho \quad \Gamma \vdash W \, \mathcal{R} \, W' : \tau}{\Gamma \vdash (VW) \, \mathcal{R} \, (V'W') : \rho} \qquad \frac{\Gamma \vdash V \, \mathcal{R} \, V' : (\tau \to \rho) \to (\tau \to \rho)}{\Gamma \vdash \mathbf{fix}(V) \, \mathcal{R} \, \mathbf{fix}(V') : \tau \to \rho}$$

$$\frac{\Gamma \vdash V \, \mathcal{R} \, V' : \mathbf{N} \quad \Gamma \vdash M \, \mathcal{R} \, M' : \tau \quad \Gamma, x : \mathbf{N} \vdash N \, \mathcal{R} \, N' : \tau}{\Gamma \vdash \ \mathbf{case} \ V \ \mathbf{of} \ \{Z \Rightarrow M; S(x) \Rightarrow N\} \, \mathcal{R} \ \mathbf{case} \ V' \ \mathbf{of} \ \{Z \Rightarrow M'; S(x) \Rightarrow N'\} : \tau}$$

$$\frac{\Gamma \vdash M \, \mathcal{R} \, M' : \tau \quad \Gamma, x : \tau \vdash N \, \mathcal{R} \, N' : \rho}{\Gamma \vdash \mathbf{let} \ M \Rightarrow x \ \mathbf{in} \ N \, \mathcal{R} \ \mathbf{let} \ M' \Rightarrow x \ \mathbf{in} \ N' : \rho}$$

$$\frac{\Gamma \vdash M_i \, \mathcal{R} \, M_i' : \tau}{\Gamma \vdash \sigma(M_0, M_1, ...) \, \mathcal{R} \, \sigma(M_0', M_1', ...) : \tau} \qquad \frac{\Gamma \vdash V \, \mathcal{R} \, V' : \mathbf{N} \quad \Gamma \vdash M_i \, \mathcal{R} \, M_i' : \tau}{\Gamma \vdash \sigma(V; M_0, M_1, ...) \, \mathcal{R} \, \sigma(V'; M_0', M_1', ...) : \tau}$$

$$\frac{\Gamma \vdash V \, \mathcal{R} \, V' : \mathbf{N} \to \tau}{\Gamma \vdash \sigma(V) \, \mathcal{R} \, \sigma(V') : \tau} \qquad \frac{\Gamma \vdash V \, \mathcal{R} \, V' : \mathbf{N} \quad \Gamma \vdash W \, \mathcal{R} \, W' : \mathbf{N} \to \tau}{\Gamma \vdash \sigma(V; W) \, \mathcal{R} \, \sigma(V'; W') : \tau}$$

Fig. 3. Rules for compatibility

Theorem 1. *If $\mathcal{O}$ is a decomposable set of Scott-open modalities then the open extensions of $\equiv_V$ and $\sqsubseteq_{V+}$ are both compatible. (It is an immediate consequence that the open extension of $\equiv_{V+}$ is also compatible.)*

The Scott-openness condition refers to the *Scott topology* on $T1$.

Definition 6. We say that $o \in \mathcal{O}$ is *upwards closed* if $[\![o]\!]$ is an upper-closed subset of $T1$; i.e., if $t \in [\![o]\!]$ implies $t' \in [\![o]\!]$ whenever $t \le t'$.

Definition 7. We say that $o \in \mathcal{O}$ is *Scott-open* if $[\![o]\!]$ is an open subset in the Scott topology on $T1$; i.e., $[\![o]\!]$ is upper closed and, whenever $t_1 \le t_2 \le \dots$ is an ascending chain in $T1$ with supremum $\sqcup_i t_i \in [\![o]\!]$, we have $t_n \in [\![o]\!]$ for some n.

Before formulating the property of *decomposability*, we make some simple observations about the positive preorder $\sqsubseteq_{V+}$.

Lemma 8. *For any $V_0, V_1 \in Val(\rho \to \tau)$, we have $V_0 \sqsubseteq_{V+} V_1$ if and only if:*

$$\forall W \in Val(\rho), \forall \Psi \in CF_{V+}(\tau), \ V_0 \models (W \mapsto \Psi) \ implies \ V_1 \models (W \mapsto \Psi).$$

Lemma 9. *For any $M_0, M_1 \in Com(\tau)$, we have $M_0 \sqsubseteq_{V+} M_1$ if and only if:*

$$\forall o \in \mathcal{O}, \forall \phi \in VF_{V+}(\tau), \ M_0 \models o \, \phi \ implies \ M_1 \models o \, \phi.$$

Similar characterisations, with appropriate adjustments, hold for behavioural equivalence $\equiv_V$.

The decomposability property is formulated using an extension of the positive preorder $\sqsubseteq_{V+}$, at unit type, from a relation on computations to a relation on arbitrary effect trees. Accordingly, we define a preorder $\preceq$ on $T1$ by:

$$t \preceq t' \quad \Leftrightarrow \quad \forall o \in \mathcal{O}, \ (t \in [\![o]\!] \Rightarrow t' \in [\![o]\!]) \wedge (t[\in \emptyset] \in [\![o]\!] \Rightarrow t'[\in \emptyset] \in [\![o]\!]).$$

Proposition 10. *For computations $M, N \in Com(1)$, it holds that $|M| \preceq |N|$ if and only if $M \sqsubseteq_{\mathcal{V}+} N$.*

Proof. The defining condition for $|M| \preceq |N|$ unwinds to:

$$\forall o \in \mathcal{O}, \ (M \models o\top \text{ implies } N \models o\top) \wedge (M \models o\bot \text{ implies } N \models o\bot).$$

This coincides with $M \sqsubseteq_{\mathcal{V}+} N$ by Lemma 9.   □

We now formulate the required notion of decomposability. We first give the general definition, and then follow it with a related notion of *strong decomposability*, which can be more convenient to establish in examples. Both definitions are unavoidably technical in nature.

For any relation $\mathcal{R} \subseteq X \times Y$ and subset $A \subseteq X$, we write $\mathcal{R}^\uparrow A$ for the right set $\{y \in Y \mid \exists x \in A, x\mathcal{R}y\}$. This allows use to easily define our required notion.

Definition 11 (Decomposability). We say that $\mathcal{O}$ is *decomposable* if, for all $r, r' \in TT1$, we have:

$$(\forall A \subseteq T1, \ r[\in A] \preceq r'[\in \preceq^\uparrow A]) \quad \Rightarrow \quad \mu r \preceq \mu r'.$$

Corollary 22 in Sect. 5, may help to motivate the formulation of the above property, which might otherwise appear purely technical. The following stronger version of decomposability, which suffices for all examples considered in the paper, is perhaps easier to understand in its own right.

Definition 12 (Strong decomposability). We say that $\mathcal{O}$ is *strongly decomposable* if, for every $r \in TT1$ and $o \in \mathcal{O}$ for which $\mu r \in [\![o]\!]$, there exists a collection $\{(o_i, o_i')\}_{i \in I}$ of pairs of modalities such that:

1. $\forall i \in I, \ r[\in [\![o_i']\!]] \in [\![o_i]\!]$; and
2. for every $r' \in TT1$, $(\forall i \in I, \ r'[\in [\![o_i']\!]] \in [\![o_i]\!])$ implies $\mu r' \in [\![o]\!]$.

Proposition 13. *If $\mathcal{O}$ is a strongly decomposable then it is decomposable.*

Proof. Suppose that $r[\in A] \preceq r'[\in (\preceq^\uparrow A)]$ holds for every $A \subseteq T1$. Assume that $\mu r \in [\![o]\!] \in \mathcal{O}$. Then strong decomposability gives a collection $\{(o_i, o_i')\}_I$. By the definition of $\preceq$, for each o_i' we have $\preceq^\uparrow [\![o_i']\!] = [\![o_i']\!]$. By the initial assumption, $r[\in [\![o_i']\!]] \in [\![o_i]\!]$ implies $r'[\in (\preceq^\uparrow [\![o_i']\!])] \in [\![o_i]\!]$, and hence $r'[\in [\![o_i']\!]] \in [\![o_i]\!]$. This holds for every i, so by strong decomposability $\mu r' \in [\![o]\!]$. We have shown that $\mu r \in [\![o]\!]$ implies $\mu r' \in [\![o]\!]$. One can prove similarly that $\mu r[\in \emptyset] \in [\![o]\!]$ implies that $\mu r'[\in \emptyset] \in [\![o]\!]$ by observing that $\preceq^\uparrow \{x \mid x[\in \emptyset] \in [\![o_i']\!]\} = \{x \mid x[\in \emptyset] \in [\![o_i']\!]\}$. Thus it holds that $\mu r \preceq \mu r'$ and hence $\mathcal{O}$ is decomposable.   □

We end this section by again looking at our running examples, and showing, in each case, that the identified collection $\mathcal{O}$ of modalities is Scott-closed (hence upwards closed) and strongly decomposable (hence decomposable). For any of the examples, upwards closure is easily established, so we will not show it here.

Example 0 (Pure functional computation). We have $\mathcal{O} = \{\downarrow\}$ and $[\![\downarrow]\!] = \{*\}$. Scott openness holds since if $\sqcup_i t_i = *$ then for some i we must already have $t_i = *$. It is strongly decomposable since: $\mu r \in [\![\downarrow]\!] \Leftrightarrow r[\in [\![\downarrow]\!]] \in [\![\downarrow]\!]$, which means r returns a tree t which is a leaf $*$.

Example 1 (Error). We have $\mathcal{O} = \{\downarrow\} \cup \{E_e \mid e \in E\}$ and $[\![E_e]\!] = \{raise_e\}$. Scott-openness holds for both modalities for the same reason as in the previous example, and its strongly decomposable since:

$$\mu r \in [\![\downarrow]\!] \quad \Leftrightarrow \quad r[\in [\![\downarrow]\!]] \in [\![\downarrow]\!].$$

Which means r returns a tree t which returns $*$.

$$\mu r \in [\![E_e]\!] \quad \Leftrightarrow \quad r[\in [\![E_e]\!]] \in [\![E_e]\!] \vee r[\in [\![E_e]\!]] \in [\![\downarrow]\!].$$

Which means r raises an error, or returns a tree that raises an error.

Example 2 (Nondeterminism). We have $\mathcal{O} = \{\Diamond, \Box\}$. The Scott-openness of $[\![\Diamond]\!] = \{t \mid t \text{ has some } * \text{ leaf}\}$ is because if $\sqcup_i t_i$ has a $*$ leaf, then that leaf must already be contained in t_i for some i. Similarly, if $\sqcup_i t_i \in [\![\Box]\!]$ then, because $[\![\Box]\!] = \{t \mid t \text{ has finite height and every leaf is a} *\}$, the tree $\sqcup_i t_i$ has finitely many leaves and all must be contained in t_i for some i. Hence $t_i \in [\![\Box]\!]$. Strong decomposability holds because:

$$\mu r \in [\![\Diamond]\!] \Leftrightarrow r[\in [\![\Diamond]\!]] \in [\![\Diamond]\!] \quad \text{and} \quad \mu r \in [\![\Box]\!] \Leftrightarrow r[\in [\![\Box]\!]] \in [\![\Box]\!].$$

The right-hand-side of the former states that r has as a leaf a tree t, which itself has a leaf $*$. That of the latter states that r is finite and all leaves are finite trees t that have only $*$ leaves. The same arguments show that $\{\Diamond\}$ and $\{\Box\}$ are also decomposable sets of Scott open modalities.

Example 3 (Probabilistic choice). $\mathcal{O} = \{P_{>q} \mid q \in \mathbb{Q}, 0 \leq q < 1\}$. For the Scott-openness of $[\![P_{>q}]\!] = \{t \mid \mathbf{P}(t \text{ terminates with a } * \text{ leaf}) > q\}$, note that $\mathbf{P}(\sqcup_i t_i \text{ terminates with a} * \text{leaf})$ is determined by some countable sum over the leaves of t_i. If this sum is greater than a rational q, then some finite approximation of the sum must already be above q. The finite sum is over finitely many leaves from $\sqcup_i t_i$, all of which will be present in t_i for some i. Hence $t_i \in [\![P_{>q}]\!]$.

We have strong decomposability, since $\mathbf{P}(\mu r \text{ terminates with a} * \text{leaf})$ equals the integral of the function $f_r(x) = sup\{y \in [0,1] \mid r[[\![P_{>x}]\!]] \in [\![P_{>y}]\!]\}$ from $[0,1]$ to $[0,1]$. Indeed, $f_r(x)$ gives the probability that r return a tree $t \in [\![P_{>x}]\!]$. So we know that if $\forall x, y, r[[\![P_{>x}]\!]] \in [\![P_{>y}]\!] \Rightarrow r'[[\![P_{>x}]\!]] \in [\![P_{>y}]\!]$, then $f_{r'}(x) \geq f_r(x)$ for any x. Hence if $\mu r \in [\![P_{>q}]\!]$ then $\int f_r > q$, whence also $\int f_{r'} > q$, which means $\mu r' \in [\![P_{>q}]\!]$.

Example 4 (Global store). We have $\mathcal{O} = \{(s \rightarrowtail s') \mid s, s' \in State\}$. For the Scott-openness of $[\![(s \rightarrowtail s')]\!] = \{t \mid exec(t, s) = (*, r)\}$, note that if $exec(\sqcup_i t_i, s) = (*, s')$, there is a single finite branch of t that follows the path the recursive function $exec$ took. This branch must already be contained in t_i for some i. We also have strong decomposability since:

$$\mu r \in [\![s \rightarrowtail s']\!] \quad \Leftrightarrow \quad \exists s'' \in State, r[\in [\![s'' \rightarrowtail s']\!]] \in [\![s \rightarrowtail s'']\!].$$

Which just means that $exec(r, s) = (t, s'')$ and $exec(t, s'') = (*, s')$ for some s''.

Example 5 (Input/output). We have $\mathcal{O} = \{\langle w\rangle\downarrow, \langle w\rangle_{...} \mid w \text{ an i/o-trace}\}$. For the Scott-openness of $[\![\langle w\rangle\downarrow]\!] = \{t \mid t \models \langle w\rangle\downarrow\{*\}\}$, note that the i/o-trace $\langle w\rangle\downarrow$ is given by some finite branch, which if in $\sqcup_i t_i$ must be in t_i for some i. The Scott-openness of $[\![\langle w\rangle_{...}]\!] = \{t \mid t \models \langle w\rangle_{...}\}$ holds for similar reasons. We have strong decomposability because of the implications:

$$\mu r \in [\![\langle w\rangle\downarrow]\!] \quad \Leftrightarrow \quad \exists v, u \text{ i/o-traces}, vu = w \wedge r[\in [\![\langle u\rangle\downarrow]\!]] \in [\![\langle v\rangle\downarrow]\!].$$

Which means r follows trace v returning t, and t follows trace u returning $*$.

$$\mu r \in [\![\langle w\rangle_{...}]\!] \quad \Leftrightarrow \quad r[\in [\![\downarrow]\!]] \in [\![\langle w\rangle_{...}]\!] \vee \exists v, u, vu = w \wedge r[\in [\![\langle u\rangle_{...}]\!]] \in [\![\langle v\rangle\downarrow]\!].$$

Which means either r follows trace w immediately, or it follows v returning a tree that follows u.

5 Applicative $\mathcal{O}$-(bi)similarity

In this section we look at an alternative description of our logical pre-order. Central to such a definition lies the concept of a *relator* [12,25], which we use to lift a relation on value terms to a relation on computation terms. With our family of modalities $\mathcal{O}$ we can define a relator which takes a relation $\mathcal{R} \subseteq X \times Y$ and returns the relation $\mathcal{O}(\mathcal{R}) \subseteq TX \times TY$, defined by:

$$t\,\mathcal{O}(\mathcal{R})\,t' \quad \Leftrightarrow \quad \forall A \subseteq X, \forall o \in \mathcal{O}, t[\in A] \in [\![o]\!] \Rightarrow t'[\in (\mathcal{R}^\uparrow A)] \in [\![o]\!].$$

Note that $\mathcal{O}(id_1) = (\preceq)$. Following [9], we use this relation-lifting operation to define notions of applicative similarity and bisimilarity.

Definition 14. An *applicative $\mathcal{O}$-simulation* is given by a pair of relations $\mathcal{R}^v_\tau$ and $\mathcal{R}^c_\tau$ for each type τ, where $\mathcal{R}^v_\tau \subseteq Val(\tau)^2$ and $\mathcal{R}^c_\tau \subseteq Com(\tau)^2$, such that:

1. $V \mathcal{R}^v_{\mathbf{N}} W \Rightarrow (V = W)$
2. $M \mathcal{R}^c_\tau N \Rightarrow |M|\,\mathcal{O}(\mathcal{R}^v_\tau)\,|N|$
3. $V \mathcal{R}^v_{\rho\to\tau} W \Rightarrow \forall U \in Val(\rho),\, VU\,\mathcal{R}^c_\tau\,WU$

Applicative $\mathcal{O}$-similarity is the largest applicative $\mathcal{O}$-simulation, which is equal to the union of all applicative $\mathcal{O}$-simulations.

Definition 15. An *applicative $\mathcal{O}$-bisimulation* is a symmetric $\mathcal{O}$-simulation. The relation of $\mathcal{O}$-*bisimilarity* is the largest applicative $\mathcal{O}$-bisimulation.

Lemma 16. *Applicative $\mathcal{O}$-bisimilarity is identical to the relation of applicative $(\mathcal{O} \cap \mathcal{O}^{op})$-similarity, where $t(\mathcal{O} \cap \mathcal{O}^{op})(\mathcal{R})r \Leftrightarrow t\mathcal{O}(\mathcal{R})r \wedge r\mathcal{O}(\mathcal{R}^{op})t$.*

Proof. Let $\mathcal{R}$ be the $\mathcal{O}$-bisimilarity, then by symmetry we have $\mathcal{R}^{op} = \mathcal{R}$. So if $M\mathcal{R}N$ we have $N\mathcal{R}M$, and by the simulation rules we derive $|M|\mathcal{O}(\mathcal{R})|N|$ and $|N|\mathcal{O}(\mathcal{R})|M|$ which is what we needed.

Let $\mathcal{R}$ be the $\mathcal{O} \cap \mathcal{O}^{op}$-similarity. If $M\mathcal{R}^{op}N$ then $|N|(\mathcal{O} \cap \mathcal{O}^{op})(\mathcal{R})|M|$ so $|N|\mathcal{O}(\mathcal{R})|M| \wedge |M|\mathcal{O}(\mathcal{R}^{op})|N|$ which results in $|M|(\mathcal{O} \cap \mathcal{O}^{op})(\mathcal{R}^{op})|N|$. Verifying the other simulation conditions as well, we can conclude that the symmetric closure $\mathcal{R} \cup \mathcal{R}^{op}$ is also a $\mathcal{O} \cap \mathcal{O}^{op}$-simulation. So $\mathcal{R}$ must, as the largest such simulation, be symmetric. Hence $\mathcal{R}$ is a symmetric $\mathcal{O}$-simulation as well.

For brevity, we will leave out the word "applicative" from here on, and write o to mean its denotation $[\![o]\!]$. We also introduce brackets, writing $o[\phi]$ for $o\,\phi$. The key result now is that the maximal relation, the $\mathcal{O}$-similarity is in most cases the same object as our logical preorder. We first give a short Lemma.

Lemma 17. *For any fragment $\mathcal{L}$ of $\mathcal{V}$ closed under countable conjunction, it holds that for each value V there is a formula $\chi_V \in \mathcal{L}$ s.t. $W \models_{\mathcal{L}} \chi_V \Leftrightarrow V \sqsubseteq_{\mathcal{L}} W$.*

Proof. For each U such that $(V \not\sqsubseteq_{\mathcal{L}} U)$, choose a formula $\phi^U \in \mathcal{L}$ such that $V \models_{\mathcal{L}} \phi^U$ and $(U \not\models \phi^U)$. Then if we define $\chi_V := \bigwedge_{\{U | V \not\sqsubseteq_{\mathcal{L}} U\}} \phi^U$ it holds that $V \not\sqsubseteq_{\mathcal{L}} U \Leftrightarrow U \not\models \chi_V$, which is what we want.

Theorem 2 (a). *For any family of upwards closed modalities $\mathcal{O}$, we have that the logical preorder $\sqsubseteq_{\mathcal{V}+}$ is identical to $\mathcal{O}$-similarity.*

Proof. We write $\sqsubseteq$ instead of $\sqsubseteq_{\mathcal{V}+}$ to make room for other annotations. We first prove that our logical preorder $\sqsubseteq$ is an $\mathcal{O}$-simulation by induction on types.

1. Values of **N**. If $\overline{n} \sqsubseteq_{\mathbf{N}}^v \overline{m}$, then since $\overline{n} \models \{n\}$ we have that $\overline{m} \models \{n\}$, hence $m = n$.
2. Computations of τ. Assume $M \sqsubseteq_{\tau}^c N$, we prove that $|M|\mathcal{O}(\sqsubseteq_{\tau}^v)|N|$. Take $A \subseteq Val(\tau)$ and $o \in \mathcal{O}$ such that $|M|[\in A] \in o$. Taking the following formula $\phi := \bigvee_{a \in A} \chi_a$ (where χ_a as in Lemma 17), then $b \models \phi \Leftrightarrow \exists a \in A, a \sqsubseteq_{\tau}^v b$ and $a \in A \Rightarrow a \models \phi$. So $|M|[\models \phi] \geq |M|[\in A]$, hence since o is upwards closed, $|M|[\models \phi] \in o$. By $M \sqsubseteq_{\tau}^c N$ we have $|N|[\in \{b \in Val(\tau) \mid \exists a \in A, a \sqsubseteq_{\tau}^v b\}] = |N|[\models \phi] \in o$. Hence we can conclude that $|M|\mathcal{O}(\sqsubseteq_{\tau}^v)|N|$.
3. Function values of $\rho \rightarrow \tau$, this follows from Lemma 8 and the Induction Hypothesis.

We can conclude that $\sqsubseteq$ is an $\mathcal{O}$-simulation. Now take an arbitrary $\mathcal{O}$-simulation $\mathcal{R}$. We prove by induction on types that $\mathcal{R} \subseteq (\sqsubseteq)$.

1. Values of **N**. If $V\mathcal{R}_{\mathbf{N}}^v W$ then $V = W$, hence by reflexivity we get $V \sqsubseteq_{\mathbf{N}}^v W$.
2. Computations of τ. Assume $M\mathcal{R}_{\tau}^c N$, we prove that $M \sqsubseteq_{\tau}^c N$ using the characterisation from Lemma 9. Say for $o \in \mathcal{O}$ and $\phi \in VF(\tau)$ we have $M \models o[\phi]$. Let $A_\phi := \{a \in Val(\tau) \mid a \models \phi\} \subseteq Val(\tau)$, then $|M|[\in A_\phi] = |M|[\models \phi] \in o$ hence by $M\mathcal{R}_{\tau}^c N$ we derive $|N|[\in \{b \in Val(\tau) \mid \exists a \in A_\phi, a\mathcal{R}_{\tau}^v b\}] \in o$. By Induction Hypothesis on values of τ, we know that $\mathcal{R}_{\tau}^v \subseteq (\sqsubseteq_{\tau}^v)$, hence '$\exists a \in A_\phi, a\mathcal{R}_{\tau}^v b$' implies $b \models \phi$. We get that $|N|[\models \phi] \geq |N|[\in \{b \in Val(\tau) \mid \exists a \in A_\phi, a\mathcal{R}_{\tau}^v b\}]$, so by upwards closure of o we have $|N|[\models \phi] \in o$ meaning $N \models o[\phi]$. We conclude that $M \sqsubseteq_{\tau}^c N$.
3. Function values of $\rho \rightarrow \tau$, assume $V\mathcal{R}_{\rho \rightarrow \tau}^v W$. We prove $V \sqsubseteq_{\rho \rightarrow \tau}^v W$ using the characterisation from Lemma 8. Assume $V \models (U \mapsto \Phi)$ where $U \in Val(\rho)$ and $\Phi \in CF(\tau)$, so $VU \models \Phi$. By $V\mathcal{R}_{\rho \rightarrow \tau}^v W$ we have $VU\,\mathcal{R}_{\tau}^c WU$ and by Induction Hypothesis we have $\mathcal{R}_{\tau}^c \subseteq (\sqsubseteq_{\tau}^c)$, so $VU \sqsubseteq_{\tau}^c WU$. Hence $WU \models \Phi$ meaning $W \models (U \mapsto \Phi)$. We can conclude that $V \sqsubseteq_{\rho \rightarrow \tau}^v W$.

4. Values of 1. If $V \mathcal{R}_1^v W$ then $V = * = W$ hence $V \sqsubseteq_1^v W$.

In conclusion: any $\mathcal{O}$-simulation $\mathcal{R}$ is a subset of the $\mathcal{O}$-simulation $\sqsubseteq_{V^+}$. So $\sqsubseteq_{V^+}$ is $\mathcal{O}$-similarity.   □

Alternatively, we can look at the variation of our logic with negation. This is related to applicative bisimulations.

Theorem 2 (b). *For any family of upwards closed modalities $\mathcal{O}$, we have that the logical equivalence $\equiv_V$ is identical to $\mathcal{O}$-bisimilarity.*

Proof. Note first that $\equiv_V$ is symmetric.

Secondly, note that since $\equiv_V = \sqsubseteq_V$ we know by Lemma 17, that for any V, there is a formula χ_V such that $W \models \chi_V \Leftrightarrow V \equiv_V W$.

Using these special formulas χ_V, the rest of the proof is very similar to the proof in Theorem 2(a). Here follow the non-trivial parts of the proof, different from the previous lemma. For proving $\equiv_V$ is an $\mathcal{O}$-simulation:

1. Computations of τ. Assume $M \equiv_\tau^c N$ and $|M|[\in A] \in o \in \mathcal{O}$. Then $M \models o[\bigvee_{V \in A} \chi_V]$ hence $N \models o[\bigvee_{V \in A} \chi_V]$ meaning $|N|[\in \{W \mid \exists V \in A, V \equiv_\tau^c W\}]$. So $|M|\mathcal{O}(\equiv_\tau^v)|N|$.
2. Functions of $\rho \to \tau$, if $V \equiv_{\rho \to \tau}^v W$ and $U \in Val(\rho)$. If $VU \models \Phi$, then $V \models U \mapsto \Phi$ hence $W \models U \mapsto \Phi$ so $WU \models \Phi$. Same vice versa, so $VU \equiv_\tau^c WU$.

So $\equiv_V$ is an $\mathcal{O}$-bisimulation. Now take any $\mathcal{O}$-bisimulation $\mathcal{R}$.

1. Computations of τ, if $M \mathcal{R} N$ and $M \models o[\phi]$ then $|M|[\models \phi] \in o$ hence $|N|[\in \{W \mid \exists V \models \phi, V \mathcal{R}_\tau^v W\}] \in o$. By Induction Hypothesis, $(\mathcal{R}_\tau^v) \subseteq (\equiv_\tau^v)$ so $\{W \mid \exists V \models \phi, V \mathcal{R}_\tau^v W\} \subseteq \{W \mid \exists V \models \phi, V \equiv_\tau^v W\}$. So by upwards closure of o we get that $|N|[\in \{W \mid \exists V \models \phi, V \equiv_\tau^v W\}] \in o$ and further that $N \models o[\phi]$. We can conclude $M \equiv_V N$.
2. Values of $\rho \to \tau$, if $V \mathcal{R} W$ and $V \models U \mapsto \Phi$, then $VU \models \Phi$ and $VU \mathcal{R} WU$ hence by Induction Hypothesis, $VU \equiv WU$ meaning $WU \models \Phi$ so $W \models U \mapsto \Phi$. If $V \models \neg(U \mapsto \Phi)$ then $\neg(VU \models \Phi)$ hence by $VU \equiv WU$ we have $\neg(WU \models \Phi)$ so $W \models \neg(U \mapsto \Phi)$. For the $\bigvee$ and $\bigwedge$ constructors, a simple Induction Step would suffice, and for higher level negation note that $\neg \bigvee \phi \Leftrightarrow \bigwedge \neg \phi$ and $\neg \bigwedge \phi \Leftrightarrow \bigvee \neg \phi$.

We can conclude that $(\mathcal{R}) \subseteq (\equiv_V)$, so $\equiv_V$ is indeed $\mathcal{O}$-bisimilarity.   □

We end this section by stating the abstract properties of our relational lifting $\mathcal{O}(\mathcal{R})$ required for the proof by Howe's method in Sect. 6 to go through. The necessary properties were identified in [9]. The contribution of this paper is that all the required properties follow from our modality-based definition of $\mathcal{O}(\mathcal{R})$. The first set of properties tell us that $\mathcal{O}(-)$ is a relator in the sense of [12]:

Lemma 18. *If the modalities from $\mathcal{O}$ are upwards closed, then $\mathcal{O}(-)$ is a relator, meaning that:*

1. If $\mathcal{R} \subseteq X \times X$ is reflexive, then so is $\mathcal{O}(\mathcal{R})$.
2. $\forall \mathcal{R}, \forall \mathcal{S}, \quad \mathcal{O}(\mathcal{R})\mathcal{O}(\mathcal{S}) \subseteq \mathcal{O}(\mathcal{RS})$, where $\mathcal{RS}$ is relation composition.
3. $\forall \mathcal{R}, \forall \mathcal{S}, \quad \mathcal{R} \subseteq \mathcal{S} \Rightarrow \mathcal{O}(\mathcal{R}) \subseteq \mathcal{O}(\mathcal{S})$.
4. $\forall f : X \to Z, g : Y \to W, \mathcal{R} \subseteq Z \times W, \mathcal{O}((f \times g)^{-1}\mathcal{R}) = (Tf \times Tg)^{-1}\mathcal{O}(\mathcal{R})$
   where $(f \times g)^{-1}(\mathcal{R}) = \{(x, y) \in X \times Y \mid f(x)\mathcal{R}g(y)\}$.

The next property together with the previous lemma establishes that $\mathcal{O}(-)$ is a *monotone relator* in the sense of [25].

Lemma 19. *If the modalities from $\mathcal{O}$ are upwards closed, then $\mathcal{O}(-)$ is monotone, meaning for any $f : X \to Z$, $g : Y \to W$, $\mathcal{R} \subseteq X \times Y$ and $\mathcal{S} \subseteq Z \times W$:*

$$(\forall x, y, x\mathcal{R}y \Rightarrow f(x)\,\mathcal{S}\,g(y)) \wedge t\mathcal{O}(\mathcal{R})r \Rightarrow t[x \mapsto f(x)]\,\mathcal{O}(\mathcal{S})\,r[y \mapsto g(y)]$$

The relator also interacts well with the monad structure on T.

Lemma 20. *If $\mathcal{O}$ is a decomposable set of upwards closed modalities, then:*

1. $x\mathcal{R}y \Rightarrow \eta(x)\mathcal{O}(\mathcal{R})\eta(y)$;
2. $t\mathcal{O}(\mathcal{O}(\mathcal{R}))r \Rightarrow \mu t\mathcal{O}(\mathcal{R})\mu r$.

Finally, the following properties show that relator behaves well with respect to the order on trees.

Lemma 21. *If $\mathcal{O}$ only contains Scott open modalities, then:*

1. *If $\mathcal{R}$ is reflexive, then $t \leq r \Rightarrow t\mathcal{O}(\mathcal{R})r$.*
2. *For any two sequences $u_0 \leq u_1 \leq u_2 \leq \dots$ and $v_0 \leq v_1 \leq v_2 \leq \dots$:*
   $$\forall n, (u_n\mathcal{O}(\mathcal{R})v_n) \Rightarrow (\sqcup_n u_n)\mathcal{O}(\mathcal{R})(\sqcup_n v_n)$$

The lemmas above list the core properties of the relator, which are satisfied when our family $\mathcal{O}$ is decomposable and contains only Scott open modalities. The results below follow from those above.

Corollary 22. *If $\mathcal{O}$ contains only upwards closed modalities, then:*

$$\mathcal{O} \text{ is decomposable} \quad \Leftrightarrow \quad \forall \mathcal{R} \subseteq X \times Y, \forall t, r \in TT1, (t\mathcal{O}(\mathcal{O}(\mathcal{R}))r \Rightarrow \mu t\,\mathcal{O}(\mathcal{R})\,\mu r)$$

Corollary 23. *If $\mathcal{O}$ is a decomposable family of upwards closed modalities, then lifted relations are preserved by Kleisli lifting and effect operators:*

1. *Given $f : X \to Z$, $g : Y \to W$, $\mathcal{R} \subseteq X \times Y$ and $\mathcal{S} \subseteq Z \times W$, if for all $x \in X$ and $y \in Y$ we have $x\mathcal{R}y \Rightarrow f(x)\,\mathcal{O}(\mathcal{S})\,g(y))$ and if $t\mathcal{O}(\mathcal{R})r$ then $\mu(t[x \mapsto f(x)])\,\mathcal{O}(\mathcal{S})\,\mu(r[y \mapsto g(y)])$*
2. $(\forall k, u_k\mathcal{O}(\mathcal{S})v_k) \Rightarrow \sigma(u_0, u_1, \dots)\mathcal{O}(\mathcal{S})\sigma(v_0, v_1, \dots)$

Point 2 of Corollary 23 has been stated in such a way that it contains both the infinite arity case $\alpha^{\mathbf{N}} \to \alpha$ and the finite arity case $\alpha^n \to \alpha$. So it states that any lifted relation is preserved under any of the predefined algebraic effects.

6   Howe's Method

In this section, we apply Howe's method, first developed in [5,6], to establish the compatibility of applicative (bi)similarity, and hence of the behavioural preorders. Given a relation $\mathcal{R}$ on terms, one defines its *Howe closure* $\mathcal{R}^\bullet$, which is compatible and contains the open extension $\mathcal{R}^\circ$. Our proof makes fundamental use of the relator properties from Sect. 5, closely following the approach of [9].

Proposition 24. *If $\mathcal{O}$ is a decomposable set of Scott open modalities, then for any $\mathcal{O}$-simulation preorder $\sqsubseteq$, the restriction of its Howe closure $\sqsubseteq^\bullet$ to closed terms is an $\mathcal{O}$-simulation.*

In the proof of the proposition, the relator properties are mainly used to show that $\sqsubseteq^\bullet$ satisfies condition (2) in Definition 14.

We can now establish the compatibility of applicative $\mathcal{O}$-similarity.

Theorem 3 (a). *If $\mathcal{O}$ is a decomposable set of Scott open modalities, then the open extension of the relation of $\mathcal{O}$-similarity is compatible.*

Proof (sketch). We write $\sqsubseteq_s$ for the relation of $\mathcal{O}$-similarity. Since $\sqsubseteq_s$ is an $\mathcal{O}$-simulation, we know by Proposition 24 that $\sqsubseteq_s^\bullet$ limited to closed terms is one as well, and hence is contained in the largest $\mathcal{O}$-simulation $\sqsubseteq_s$. Since $\sqsubseteq_s^\bullet$ is compatible, it is contained in the open extension $\sqsubseteq_s^\circ$. We can conclude that $\sqsubseteq_s^\circ$ is equal to the Howe closure $\sqsubseteq_s^\bullet$, which is compatible.   □

To prove that $\mathcal{O}$-bisimilarity is compatible, we use the following result from [10] (where we write $\mathcal{S}^*$ for the transitive-reflexive closure of a relation $\mathcal{S}$).

Lemma 25. *If $\mathcal{R}^\circ$ is symmetric and reflexive, then $\mathcal{R}^{\bullet*}$ is symmetric.*

Theorem 3 (b). *If $\mathcal{O}$ is a decomposable set of Scott open modalities, then the open extension of the relation of $\mathcal{O}$-bisimilarity is compatible.*

Proof (sketch). We write $\mathcal{O}$-bisimilarity as $\sqsubseteq_b$. From Proposition 24 we know that $\sqsubseteq_b^\bullet$ on closed terms is an $\mathcal{O}$-simulation, and so we know $\sqsubseteq_b^{\bullet*}$ is an $\mathcal{O}$-simulation as well (using Lemma 18). Since $\sqsubseteq_b$ is reflexive and symmetric, we know by the previous lemma that $\sqsubseteq_b^{\bullet*}$ is symmetric. Hence $\sqsubseteq_b^{\bullet*}$ is an $\mathcal{O}$-bisimulation, implying $(\sqsubseteq_b^{\bullet*}) \subseteq (\sqsubseteq_b^\circ)$ by compatibility of $\sqsubseteq_b^{\bullet*}$. Since $(\sqsubseteq_b^\circ) \subseteq (\sqsubseteq_b^\bullet) \subseteq (\sqsubseteq_b^{\bullet*})$ we have that $(\sqsubseteq_b^{\bullet*}) = (\sqsubseteq_b^\circ)$, and we can conclude that $\sqsubseteq_b^\circ$ is compatible.   □

Theorem 1 is an immediate consequence of Theorems 2 and 3.

7   Pure Behavioural Logic

In this section, we briefly explore an alternative formulation of our logic. This has both conceptual and practical motivations. Our very approach to behavioural logic, fits into the category of *endogenous* logics in the sense of Pnueli [24]. Formulas (ϕ and Φ) express properties of individual programs, through satisfaction relations ($V \models \phi$ and $M \models \Phi$). Programs are thus considered as 'models' of the logic, with the satisfaction relation being defined via program behaviour.

It is conceptually appealing to push the separation between program and logic to its natural conclusion, and ask for the syntax of the logic to be independent of the syntax of the programming language. Indeed, it seems natural that it should be possible to express properties of program behaviour without knowledge of the syntax of the programming language. Under our formulation of the logic $\mathcal{V}$, this desideratum is violated by the value formula ($V \mapsto \Psi$) at function type, which mentions the programming language value V.

This issue can be addressed, by replacing the basic value formula ($V \mapsto \Psi$) with the alternative ($\phi \mapsto \Psi$), already mentioned in Sect. 3. Such a change also has a practical motivation. The formula ($\phi \mapsto \Psi$) declares a precondition and postcondition for function application, supporting a useful specification style.

Definition 26. The *pure behavioural logic* $\mathcal{F}$ is defined by replacing rule (2) in Fig. 2 with the alternative:

$$\frac{\phi \in VF(\rho) \qquad \Psi \in CF(\tau)}{(\phi \mapsto \Psi) \in VF(\rho \to \tau)}(2^*)$$

The semantics is modified by defining $V \models (\phi \mapsto \Psi)$ using formula (2) of Sect. 3.

Proposition 27. *If the open extension of $\equiv_\mathcal{V}$ is compatible then the logics $\mathcal{V}$ and $\mathcal{F}$ are equi-expressive. Similarly, if the open extension of $\sqsubseteq_{\mathcal{V}^+}$ is compatible then the positive fragments $\mathcal{V}^+$ and $\mathcal{F}^+$ are equi-expressive.*

Proof. The definition of ($\phi \mapsto \Psi$) within $\mathcal{V}$, given in (1) of Sect. 3, can be used as the basis of an inductive translation from $\mathcal{F}$ to $\mathcal{V}$ (and from $\mathcal{F}^+$ to $\mathcal{V}^+$).

For the reverse translation, whose correctness proof is more interesting, we give a little more detail. Every value/computation formula, ϕ/Φ, of $\mathcal{V}$ is inductively translated to a corresponding formula $\widehat{\phi}/\widehat{\Phi}$ of $\mathcal{F}$. The interesting case is:

$$\widehat{(V \mapsto \Phi)} := (\psi_V \mapsto \widehat{\Phi}),$$

where ψ_V is a formula such that: $V \models_\mathcal{F} \psi_V$; and, for any ψ, if $V \models_\mathcal{F} \psi$ then $\psi_V \to \psi$ (meaning that $V' \models_\mathcal{F} \psi_V$ implies $V' \models_\mathcal{F} \psi$, for all V'). Such a formula ψ_V is easily constructed as a countable conjunction (cf. Lemma 17). One then proves, by induction on types, that the $\mathcal{F}$-semantics of $\widehat{\phi}$ (resp. $\widehat{\Phi}$) coincides with the $\mathcal{V}$-semantics of ϕ (resp. Φ). In the case for $\widehat{(V \mapsto \Phi)}$, the induction hypothesis is used to establish that any V' satisfying $V' \models_\mathcal{F} \psi_V$ enjoys the property that $V' \equiv_\mathcal{V} V$. It then follows from the compatibility of $\equiv_\mathcal{V}$ that $WV' \equiv_\mathcal{V} WV$, for any W of appropriate type, whence $WV' \equiv_\mathcal{F} WV$. The rest of the proof can easily be erected around these observations. □

Combining the above proposition with Theorem 1 we obtain the following.

Corollary 28. *Suppose $\mathcal{O}$ is a decomposable family of Scott-open modalities. Then $\equiv_{\mathcal{F}}$ coincides with $\equiv_{\mathcal{V}}$, and $\sqsubseteq_{\mathcal{F}+}$ coincides with $\sqsubseteq_{\mathcal{V}+}$. Hence the open extensions of $\equiv_{\mathcal{F}}$ and $\sqsubseteq_{\mathcal{F}+}$ are compatible.*

We do not know any proof of the compatibility of the $\equiv_{\mathcal{F}}$ and $\sqsubseteq_{\mathcal{F}+}$ relations that does not go via the logic $\mathcal{V}$. In particular, the compatibility property of the **fix** operator seems difficult to establish directly for $\equiv_{\mathcal{F}}$ and $\sqsubseteq_{\mathcal{F}+}$.

8   Discussion and Related Work

The behavioural logics considered in this paper are designed for the purpose of clarifying the notion of 'behavioural property', and for defining behavioural equivalence. As infinitary propositional logics, they are not directly suited to practical applications such as specification and verification. Nevertheless, they serve as low-level logics into which more practical finitary logics can be translated. For this, the closure of the logics under infinitary propositional logic is important. For example, there are standard translations of quantifiers and least and greatest fixed points into infinitary propositional logic. Also, in the case of global store, Hoare triples translate into logical combinations of modal formulas.

Our approach, of basing logics for effects on behavioural modalities, may potentially inform the design of practical logics for specifying and reasoning about effects. For example, Pitts' *evaluation logic* was an early logic for general computational effects [18]. In the light of the general theory of modalities in the present paper, it seems natural to replace the built-in $\square$ and $\lozenge$ modalities of evaluation logic, with effect-specific modalities, as in Sect. 3.

The *logic for algebraic effects*, of Plotkin and Pretnar [23], axiomatises effectful behaviour by means of an equational theory over the signature of effect operations, following the algebraic approach to effects advocated by Plotkin and Power [22]. Such equational axiomatisations are typically sound with respect to more than one notion of program equivalence. The logic of [23] can thus be used to soundly reason about program equivalence, but does not in itself determine a notion of program equivalence. Instead, our logic is specifically designed as a vehicle for defining program equivalence. In doing so, our modalities can be viewed as a chosen family of 'observations' that are compatible with the effects present in the language. It is the choice of modalities that determines the equational properties that the effect operations satisfy.

The logic of [23] itself makes use of modalities, called *operation modalities*, each associated with a single effect operations in Σ. It would be natural to replace these modalities, which are syntactic in nature, with behavioural modalities of the form we consider. Similarly, our behavioural modalities appear to offer a promising basis for developing a modality-based refinement-type system for algebraic effects. In general, an important advantage we see in the use of behavioural modalities is that our notion of *strong decomposability* appears related to the availability of compositional proof principles for modal properties. This is a promising avenue for future exploration.

A rather different approach to logics for effects has been proposed by Goncharov, Mossakowski and Schröder [3,16]. They assume a semantic setting in which the programming language is rich enough to contain a *pure fragment* that itself acts as a program logic. This approach is very powerful for certain effects. For example, Hoare logic can be derived in the case of global store. However, it appears not as widely adaptable across the range of effects as our approach.

Our logics exhibit certain similarities in form with the endogenous logic developed in Abramsky's *domain theory in logical form* [2]. Our motivation and approach are, however, quite different. Whereas Abramsky shows the usefulness of an axiomatic approach to a finitary logic as a way of characterising denotational equality, the present paper shows that there is a similar utility in considering an infinitary logic from a semantic perspective (based on operational semantics) as a method of defining behavioural equivalence.

The work in this paper has been carried out for fine-grained call-by-value [13], which is equivalent to call-by-value. The definitions can, however, be adapted to work for call-by-name, and even call-by-push-value [11]. Adding type constructors such as sum and product is also straightforward. We have not checked the generalisation to arbitrary recursive types, but we do not foresee any problem.

An omission from the present paper is that we have not said anything about *contextual equivalence*, which is often taken to be the default equivalence for applicative languages. In addition to determining the logically defined preorders/equivalences, the choice of the set $\mathcal{O}$ of modalities gives rise to a natural definition of *contextual preorder*, namely the largest compatible preorder that, on computations of unit type $\mathbf{1}$, is contained in the $\preceq$ relation from Sect. 4. The compatibility of $\sqsubseteq_{\mathcal{V}+}$ established in the present paper means that we have the expected relation inclusions $\equiv_{\mathcal{V}} \subseteq \sqsubseteq_{\mathcal{V}+} \subseteq \sqsubseteq_{\text{ctxt}}$. It is an interesting question whether the logic can be restricted to characterise contextual equivalence/preorder. A more comprehensive investigation of contextual equivalence is being undertaken, in ongoing work, by Aliame Lopez and the first author.

The crucial notion of modality, in the present paper, was adapted from the notion of *observation* in [8]. The change from a set of trees of type $\mathbf{N}$ (an observation) to a set of unit-type trees (a modality) allows value formulas to be lifted to computation formulas, analogously to *predicate lifting* in coalgebra [7], which is a key characteristic of our modalities. Properties of *Scott-openness* and *decomposability* play a similar role the present paper to the role they play in [8]. However, the notion of decomposability for modalities (Definition 11) is more subtle than the corresponding notion for observations in [8].

There are certain limitations to the theory of modalities in the present paper. For example, for the combination of probability and nondeterminism, one might naturally consider modalities $\Diamond P_r$ and $\Box P_r$ asserting the possibility and necessity of the termination probability exceeding r. However, the decomposability property fails. It appears that this situation can be rescued by changing to a quantitative logic, with a corresponding notion of quantitative modality. This is a topic of ongoing research.

Acknowledgements. We thank Francesco Gavazzo, Aliaume Lopez and the anonymous referees for helpful discussions and comments.

References

1. Abramsky, S.: The lazy λ-calculus. In: Research Topics in Functional Programming, pp. 65–117 (1990)
2. Abramsky, S.: Domain theory in logical form. Ann. Pure Appl. Log. **51**(1–2), 1–77 (1991)
3. Goncharov, S., Schröder, L.: A relatively complete generic Hoare logic for order-enriched effects. In: Proceedings of the 28th Annual Symposium on Logic in Computer Science (LICS 2013), pp. 273–282. IEEE (2013)
4. Hennessy, M., Milner, R.: Algebraic laws for nondeterminism and concurrency. J. ACM (JACM) **32**(1), 137–161 (1985)
5. Howe, D.J.: Equality in lazy computation systems. In: Proceedings of the 4th IEEE Symposium on Logic in Computer Science, pp. 198–203 (1989)
6. Howe, D.J.: Proving congruence of bisimulation in functional programming languages. Inf. Comput. **124**(2), 103–112 (1996)
7. Jacobs, B.: Introduction to Coalgebra: Towards Mathematics of States and Observation. Cambridge University Press, Cambridge (2016)
8. Johann, P., Simpson, A., Voigtländer, J.: A generic operational metatheory for algebraic effects. In: Logic in Computer Science, pp. 209–218 (2010)
9. Ugo, D.L., Gavazzo, F., Levy, P.B.: Effectful applicative bisimilarity: Monads, relators, and the Howe's method. In: Logic in Computer Science, pp. 1–12 (2017)
10. Lassen, S.B.: Relational Reasoning about Functions and Nondeterminism. Ph.D. thesis, BRICS (1998)
11. Levy, P.B.: Call-by-push-value: decomposing call-by-value and call-by-name. Higher-Order Symbol. Comput. **19**(4), 377–414 (2006)
12. Levy, P.B.: Similarity quotients as final coalgebras. In: Hofmann, M. (ed.) FoSSaCS 2011. LNCS, vol. 6604, pp. 27–41. Springer, Heidelberg (2011). https://doi.org/10.1007/978-3-642-19805-2_3
13. Levy, P.B., Power, J., Thielecke, H.: Modelling environments in call-by-value programming languages. Inf. Comput. **185**(2), 182–210 (2003)
14. Milner, R.: A Calculus of Communicating Systems. Springer, Heidelberg (1982). https://doi.org/10.1007/3-540-10235-3
15. Moggi, E.: Notions of computation and monads. Inf. Comput. **93**(1), 55–92 (1991)
16. Mossakowski, T., Schröder, L., Goncharov, S.: A generic complete dynamic logic for reasoning about purity and effects. Formal Aspects Comput. **22**(3–4), 363–384 (2010)
17. Park, D.: Concurrency and automata on infinite sequences. In: Deussen, P. (ed.) GI-TCS 1981. LNCS, vol. 104, pp. 167–183. Springer, Heidelberg (1981). https://doi.org/10.1007/BFb0017309
18. Pitts, A.: Evaluation logic. In: Birtwistle, G. (ed.) 4th Higher Order Workshop. Workshops in Computing, pp. 162–189. Springer, London (1990). https://doi.org/10.1007/978-1-4471-3182-3_11
19. Pitts, A.: Parametric polymorphism and operational equivalence. Math. Struct. Comput. Sci. **10**, 321–359 (2000)
20. Plotkin, G.: LCF considered as a programming language. Theor. Comput. Sci. **5**(3), 223–255 (1977)

21. Plotkin, G., Power, J.: Adequacy for algebraic effects. In: Honsell, F., Miculan, M. (eds.) FoSSaCS 2001. LNCS, vol. 2030, pp. 1–24. Springer, Heidelberg (2001). https://doi.org/10.1007/3-540-45315-6_1

22. Plotkin, G., Power, J.: Notions of computation determine monads. In: Nielsen, M., Engberg, U. (eds.) FoSSaCS 2002. LNCS, vol. 2303, pp. 342–356. Springer, Heidelberg (2002). https://doi.org/10.1007/3-540-45931-6_24

23. Plotkin, G., Pretnar, M.: A logic for algebraic effects. In: Proceedings of the Logic in Computer Science, pp. 118–129 (2008)

24. Pnueli, A.: The temporal logic of programs. In: Proceedings of the 18th Annual Symposium on the Foundations of Computer Science, pp. 46–57 (1977)

25. Thijs, A.M.: Simulation and fixpoint semantics. Ph.D. thesis (1996)

Explicit Effect Subtyping

Amr Hany Saleh[1]($\boxtimes$), Georgios Karachalias[1], Matija Pretnar[2],
and Tom Schrijvers[1]

[1] Department of Computer Science, KU Leuven, Leuven, Belgium
ah.saleh@cs.kuleuven.be
[2] Faculty of Mathematics and Physics, University of Ljubljana, Ljubljana, Slovenia

Abstract. As popularity of algebraic effects and handlers increases, so
does a demand for their efficient execution. Eff, an ML-like language
with native support for handlers, has a subtyping-based effect system
on which an effect-aware optimizing compiler could be built. Unfortunately, in our experience, implementing optimizations for Eff is overly
error-prone because its core language is implicitly-typed, making code
transformations very fragile.

To remedy this, we present an explicitly-typed polymorphic core calculus for algebraic effect handlers with a subtyping-based type-and-effect
system. It reifies appeals to subtyping in explicit casts with coercions
that witness the subtyping proof, quickly exposing typing bugs in program transformations.

Our typing-directed elaboration comes with a constraint-based inference algorithm that turns an implicitly-typed Eff-like language into our
calculus. Moreover, all coercions and effect information can be erased in
a straightforward way, demonstrating that coercions have no computational content.

1 Introduction

Algebraic effect handlers [17,18] are quickly maturing from a theoretical model
to a practical language feature for user-defined computational effects. Yet, in
practice they still incur a significant performance overhead compared to native
effects.

Our earlier efforts [22] to narrow this gap with an optimising compiler from
Eff [2] to OCaml showed promising results, in some cases reaching even the
performance of hand-tuned code, but were very fragile and have been postponed
until a more robust solution is found. We believe the main reason behind this
fragility is the complexity of subtyping in combination with the implicit typing of
Eff's core language, further aggravated by the "garbage collection" of subtyping
constraints (see Sect. 7).[1]

---

[1] For other issues stemming from the same combination see issues #11 and #16 at
https://github.com/matijapretnar/eff/issues/.

© The Author(s) 2018
A. Ahmed (Ed.): ESOP 2018, LNCS 10801, pp. 327–354, 2018.
https://doi.org/10.1007/978-3-319-89884-1_12

For efficient compilation, one must avoid the poisoning problem [26], where unification forces a pure computation to take the less precise impure type of the context (e.g. a pure and an impure branch of a conditional both receive the same impure type). Since this rules out existing (and likely simpler) effect systems for handlers based on row-polymorphism [8,12,14], we propose a polymorphic explicitly-typed calculus based on subtyping. More specifically, our contributions are as follows:

- First, in Sect. 3 we present IMPEFF, a polymorphic implicitly-typed calculus for algebraic effects and handlers with a subtyping-based type-and-effect system. IMPEFF is essentially a (desugared) source language as it appears in the compiler frontend of a language like Eff.
- Next, Sect. 4 presents EXEFF, the core calculus, which combines explicit System F-style polymorphism with explicit coercions for subtyping in the style of Breazu-Tannen et al. [3]. This calculus comes with a type-and-effect system, a small-step operational semantics and a proof of type-safety.
- Section 5 specifies the typing-directed elaboration of IMPEFF into EXEFF and presents a type inference algorithm for IMPEFF that produces the elaborated EXEFF term as a by-product. It also establishes that the elaboration preserves typing, and that the algorithm is sound with respect to the specification and yields principal types.
- Finally, Sect. 6 defines SKELEFF, which is a variant of EXEFF without effect information or coercions. SKELEFF is also representative of Multicore Ocaml's support for algebraic effects and handlers [6], which is a possible compilation target of Eff. By showing that the erasure from EXEFF to SKELEFF preserves semantics, we establish that EXEFF's coercions are computationally irrelevant and that, despite the existence of multiple proofs for the same subtyping, there is no coherence problem. To enable erasure, EXEFF annotates its types with *(type) skeletons*, which capture the erased counterpart and are, to our knowledge, a novel contribution.
- Our paper comes with two software artefacts: an ongoing implementation[2] of a compiler from Eff to OCaml with EXEFF at its core, and an Abella mechanisation[3] of Theorems 1, 2, 6, and 7. Remaining theorems all concern the inference algorithm, and their proofs closely follow [20].

The full version of this paper includes an appendix with omitted figures and can be found at http://www.cs.kuleuven.be/publicaties/rapporten/cw/CW711.abs. html.

2   Overview

This section presents an informal overview of the EXEFF calculus, and the main issues with elaborating to and erasing from it.

---

[2] https://github.com/matijapretnar/eff/tree/explicit-effect-subtyping.
[3] https://github.com/matijapretnar/proofs/tree/master/explicit-effect-subtyping.

2.1 Algebraic Effect Handlers

The main premise of algebraic effects is that impure behaviour arises from a set of *operations* such as Get and Set for mutable store, Read and Print for interactive input and output, or Raise for exceptions [17]. This allows generalizing exception handlers to other effects, to express backtracking, co-operative multithreading and other examples in a natural way [2,18].

Assume operations Tick : Unit → Unit and Tock : Unit → Unit that take a unit value as a parameter and yield a unit value as a result. Unlike special built-in operations, these operations have no intrinsic effectful behaviour, though we can give one through handlers. For example, the handler {Tick $x\,k$ ↦ (Print "tick"; k unit), Tock $x\,k$ ↦ Print "tock"} replaces all calls of Tick by printing out "tick" and similarly for Tock. But there is one significant difference between the two cases. Unlike exceptions, which always abort the evaluation, operations have a continuation waiting for their result. It is this continuation that the handler captures in the variable k and potentially uses in the handling clause. In the clause for Tick, the continuation is resumed by passing it the expected unit value, whereas in the clause for Tock, the operation is discarded. Thus, if we handle a computation emitting the two operations, it will print out "tick" until a first "tock" is printed, after which the evaluation stops.

2.2 Elaborating Subtyping

Consider the computation do x ← Tick unit; $f\,x$ and assume that f has the function type Unit → Unit ! {Tock}, taking unit values to unit values and perhaps calling Tock operations in the process. The whole computation then has the type Unit ! {Tick, Tock} as it returns the unit value and may call Tick and Tock.

The above typing implicitly appeals to subtyping in several places. For instance, Tick unit has type Unit ! {Tick} and $f\,x$ type Unit ! {Tock}. Yet, because they are sequenced with do, the type system expects they have the same set of effects. The discrepancies are implicitly reconciled by the subtyping which admits both {Tick} ⩽ {Tick, Tock} and {Tock} ⩽ {Tick, Tock}.

We elaborate the IMPEFF term into the explicitly-typed core language EXEFF to make those appeals to subtyping explicit by means of casts with coercions:
$$\text{do } x \leftarrow ((\text{Tick unit}) \rhd \gamma_1); (f\,x) \rhd \gamma_2$$
A coercion γ is a witness for a subtyping $A \mathbin{!} \Delta \leqslant A' \mathbin{!} \Delta'$ and can be used to cast a term c of type $A \mathbin{!} \Delta$ to a term $c \rhd \gamma$ of type $A' \mathbin{!} \Delta'$. In the above term, γ_1 and γ_2 respectively witness Unit ! {Tick} ⩽ Unit ! {Tick, Tock} and Unit ! {Tock} ⩽ Unit ! {Tick, Tock}.

2.3 Polymorphic Subtyping for Types and Effects

The above basic example only features monomorphic types and effects. Yet, our calculus also supports polymorphism, which makes it considerably more expressive. For instance the type of f in let $f = (\text{fun } g \mapsto g \text{ unit})$ in ... is generalised to:

$$\forall \alpha, \alpha'. \forall \delta, \delta'. \alpha \leqslant \alpha' \Rightarrow \delta \leqslant \delta' \Rightarrow (\text{Unit} \to \alpha \ ! \ \delta) \to \alpha' \ ! \ \delta'$$

This polymorphic type scheme follows the qualified types convention [9] where the type $(\text{Unit} \to \alpha \ ! \ \delta) \to \alpha' \ ! \ \delta'$ is subjected to several qualifiers, in this case $\alpha \leqslant \alpha'$ and $\delta \leqslant \delta'$. The universal quantifiers on the outside bind the type variables α and α', and the effect set variables δ and δ'.

The elaboration of f into EXEFF introduces explicit binders for both the quantifiers and the qualifiers, as well as the explicit casts where subtyping is used.

$$\Lambda\alpha.\Lambda\alpha'.\Lambda\delta.\Lambda\delta'.\Lambda(\omega : \alpha \leqslant \alpha').\Lambda(\omega' : \delta \leqslant \delta').\text{fun } (g : \text{Unit} \to \alpha \, ! \, \delta) \mapsto (g \, \text{unit}) \triangleright (\omega \, ! \, \omega')$$

Here the binders for qualifiers introduce coercion variables ω between pure types and ω' between operation sets, which are then combined into a computation coercion $\omega \ ! \ \omega'$ and used for casting the function application $g \, \text{unit}$ to the expected type.

Suppose that h has type $\text{Unit} \to \text{Unit} \,! \, \{\text{Tick}\}$ and $f \, h$ type $\text{Unit} \,! \, \{\text{Tick}, \text{Tock}\}$. In the EXEFF calculus the corresponding instantiation of f is made explicit through type and coercion applications

$$f \, \text{Unit} \, \text{Unit} \, \{\text{Tick}\} \, \{\text{Tick}, \text{Tock}\} \, \gamma_1 \, \gamma_2 \, h$$

where γ_1 needs to be a witness for $\text{Unit} \leqslant \text{Unit}$ and γ_2 for $\{\text{Tick}\} \leqslant \{\text{Tick}, \text{Tock}\}$.

2.4   Guaranteed Erasure with Skeletons

One of our main requirements for EXEFF is that its effect information and subtyping can be easily erased. The reason is twofold. Firstly, we want to show that neither plays a role in the runtime behaviour of EXEFF programs. Secondly and more importantly, we want to use a conventionally typed (System F-like) functional language as a backend for the Eff compiler.

At first, erasure of both effect information and subtyping seems easy: simply drop that information from types and terms. But by dropping the effect variables and subtyping constraints from the type of f, we get $\forall \alpha, \alpha'.(\text{Unit} \to \alpha) \to \alpha'$ instead of the expected type $\forall \alpha.(\text{Unit} \to \alpha) \to \alpha$. In our naive erasure attempt we have carelessly discarded the connection between α and α'. A more appropriate approach to erasure would be to unify the types in dropped subtyping constraints. However, unifying types may reduce the number of type variables when they become instantiated, so corresponding binders need to be dropped, greatly complicating the erasure procedure and its meta-theory.

Fortunately, there is an easier way by tagging all bound type variables with *skeletons*, which are barebone types without effect information. For example, the skeleton of a function type $A \to B \ ! \ \Delta$ is $\tau_1 \to \tau_2$, where τ_1 is the skeleton of

A and τ_2 the skeleton of B. In ExEff every well-formed type has an associated skeleton, and any two types $A_1 \leqslant A_2$ share the same skeleton. In particular, binders for type variables are explicitly annotated with skeleton variables ς. For instance, the actual type of f is:

$$\forall\varsigma.\forall(\alpha : \varsigma), (\alpha' : \varsigma).\forall\delta, \delta'.\alpha \leqslant \alpha' \Rightarrow \delta \leqslant \delta' \Rightarrow (\text{Unit} \to \alpha \ ! \ \delta) \to \alpha' \ ! \ \delta'$$

The skeleton quantifications and annotations also appear at the term-level:

$$\Lambda\varsigma.\Lambda(\alpha : \varsigma).\Lambda(\alpha' : \varsigma).\Lambda\delta.\Lambda\delta'.\Lambda(\omega : \alpha \leqslant \alpha').\Lambda(\omega' : \delta \leqslant \delta')....$$

Now erasure is really easy: we drop not only effect and subtyping-related term formers, but also type binders and application. We do retain skeleton binders and applications, which take over the role of (plain) types in the backend language. In terms, we replace types by their skeletons. For instance, for f we get:

$$\Lambda\varsigma.\text{fun} \ (g : \text{Unit} \to \varsigma) \mapsto g\,\text{unit} \quad : \quad \forall\varsigma.(\text{Unit} \to \varsigma) \to \varsigma$$

Terms

$$\text{value } v ::= x \mid \text{unit} \mid \text{fun } x \mapsto c \mid h$$
$$\text{handler } h ::= \{\text{return } x \mapsto c_r, \text{Op}_1 \, x\, k \mapsto c_{\text{Op}_1}, \ldots, \text{Op}_n \, x\, k \mapsto c_{\text{Op}_n}\}$$
$$\text{computation } c ::= \text{return } v \mid \text{Op } v \ (y.c) \mid \text{do } x \leftarrow c_1; c_2$$
$$\mid \ \text{handle } c \text{ with } v \mid v_1 \ v_2 \mid \text{let } x = v \text{ in } c$$

Types & Constraints

$$\text{skeleton } \tau ::= \varsigma \mid \text{Unit} \mid \tau_1 \to \tau_2 \mid \tau_1 \Rrightarrow \tau_2$$

$$\text{value type } A, B ::= \alpha \mid \text{Unit} \mid A \to \underline{C} \mid \underline{C} \Rrightarrow \underline{D}$$
$$\text{qualified type } K ::= A \mid \pi \Rightarrow K$$
$$\text{polytype } S ::= K \mid \forall\varsigma.S \mid \forall\alpha{:}\tau.S \mid \forall\delta.S$$
$$\text{computation type } \underline{C}, \underline{D} ::= A \, ! \, \Delta$$
$$\text{dirt } \Delta ::= \delta \mid \emptyset \mid \{\text{Op}\} \cup \Delta$$

$$\text{simple constraint } \pi ::= A_1 \leqslant A_2 \mid \Delta_1 \leqslant \Delta_2$$
$$\text{constraint } \rho ::= \pi \mid \underline{C} \leqslant \underline{D}$$

Fig. 1. ImpEff Syntax

3   The ImpEff Language

This section presents ImpEff, a basic functional calculus with support for algebraic effect handlers, which forms the core language of our optimising compiler. We describe the relevant concepts, but refer the reader to Pretnar's tutorial [21], which explains essentially the same calculus in more detail.

3.1   Syntax

Figure 1 presents the syntax of the source language. There are two main kinds of terms: (pure) values v and (dirty) computations c, which may call effectful operations. Handlers h are a subsidiary sort of values. We assume a given set of *operations* Op, such as Get and Put. We abbreviate $\text{Op}_1\, x\, k \mapsto c_{\text{Op}_1}, \ldots, \text{Op}_n\, x\, k \mapsto c_{\text{Op}_n}$ as $[\text{Op}\, x\, k \mapsto c_{\text{Op}}]_{\text{Op} \in \mathcal{O}}$, and write $\mathcal{O}$ to denote the set $\{\text{Op}_1, \ldots, \text{Op}_n\}$.

Similarly, we distinguish between two basic sorts of types: the value types A, B and the computation types $\underline{C}, \underline{D}$. There are four forms of value types: type variables α, function types $A \to \underline{C}$, handler types $\underline{C} \Rightarrow \underline{D}$ and the Unit type. Skeletons τ capture the shape of types, so, by design, their forms are identical. The computation type $A\,!\,\Delta$ is assigned to a computation returning values of type A and potentially calling operations from the *dirt* set Δ. A dirt set contains zero or more operations Op and is terminated either by an empty set or a dirt variable δ. Though we use cons-list syntax, the intended semantics of dirt sets Δ is that the order of operations Op is irrelevant. Similarly to all HM-based systems, we discriminate between value types (or monotypes) A, qualified types K and polytypes (or type schemes) S. (Simple) subtyping constraints π denote inequalities between either value types or dirts. We also present the more general form of constraints ρ that includes inequalities between computation types (as we illustrate in Sect. 3.2 below, this allows for a single, uniform constraint entailment relation). Finally, polytypes consist of zero or more skeleton, type or dirt abstractions followed by a qualified type.

3.2   Typing

Figure 2 presents the typing rules for values and computations, along with a typing-directed elaboration into our target language ExEff. In order to simplify the presentation, in this section we focus exclusively on typing. The parts of the rules that concern elaboration are highlighted in gray and are discussed in Sect. 5.

Values. Typing for values takes the form $\Gamma \vdash_v v : A \rightsquigarrow v'$, and, given a typing environment Γ, checks a value v against a value type A.

Rule TMVAR handles term variables. Given that x has type $(\forall \bar{\varsigma}.\overline{\alpha : \tau}.\forall \bar{\delta}.\overline{\pi} \Rightarrow A)$, we *appropriately* instantiate the skeleton $(\bar{\varsigma})$, type $(\bar{\alpha})$, and dirt $(\bar{\delta})$ variables, and ensure that the instantiated wanted constraints $\sigma(\pi)$ are satisfied, via side condition $\overline{\Gamma \vdash_{co} \gamma : \sigma(\pi)}$. Rule TMCASTV allows casting the type of a value v from A to B, if A is a subtype of B (upcasting). As illustrated by Rule TMTMABS, we omit freshness conditions by adopting the Barendregt convention [1]. Finally, Rule TMHAND gives typing for handlers. It requires that the right-hand sides of the return clause and all operation clauses have the same computation type $(B\,!\,\Delta)$, and that all operations mentioned are part of the top-level signature Σ.[4] The result type takes the form $A\,!\,\Delta \cup \mathcal{O} \Rightarrow B\,!\,\Delta$, capturing the intended handler semantics: given a computation of type $A\,!\,\Delta \cup \mathcal{O}$, the handler (a) produces a result of type B, (b) handles operations $\mathcal{O}$, and (c) propagates unhandled operations Δ to the output.

---

[4] We capture all defined operations along with their types in a global signature Σ.

typing environment $\Gamma ::= \epsilon \mid \Gamma, \varsigma \mid \Gamma, \alpha : \tau \mid \Gamma, \delta \mid \Gamma, x : S \mid \Gamma, \omega : \pi$

$\boxed{\Gamma \vdash_v v : A \rightsquigarrow v'}$ **Values**

$$\frac{(x : \forall \varsigma. \forall \overline{\alpha : \tau}. \forall \overline{\delta}. \overline{\pi} \Rightarrow A) \in \Gamma \quad \sigma = [\overline{\tau'/\varsigma}, \overline{B/\alpha}, \overline{\Delta/\delta}] \quad \Gamma \vdash_{co} \overline{\gamma} : \sigma(\overline{\pi})}{\Gamma \vdash_v x : \sigma(A) \rightsquigarrow x \; \overline{\tau'} \; \overline{B} \; \overline{\Delta} \; \overline{\gamma}} \; \text{TmVar}$$

$$\frac{\begin{array}{c} \Gamma \vdash_v v : A \rightsquigarrow v' \\ \Gamma \vdash_{co} \gamma : A \leqslant B \end{array}}{\Gamma \vdash_v v : B \rightsquigarrow v' \rhd \gamma} \; \text{TmCastV} \qquad\qquad \frac{}{\Gamma \vdash_v \text{unit} : \text{Unit} \rightsquigarrow \text{unit}} \; \text{TmUnit}$$

$$\frac{\Gamma, x : A \vdash_c c : \underline{C} \rightsquigarrow c' \quad \Gamma \vdash_{vty} A : \tau \rightsquigarrow T}{\Gamma \vdash_v (\text{fun } x \mapsto c) : A \to \underline{C} \rightsquigarrow \text{fun } (x : T) \mapsto c'} \; \text{TmTmAbs}$$

$$\frac{\begin{array}{c} \Gamma, x : A \vdash_c c_r : B \mathbin{!} \Delta \rightsquigarrow c'_r \quad \Gamma \vdash_{vty} A : \tau \rightsquigarrow T \\ \left[(\text{Op} : A_{\text{Op}} \to B_{\text{Op}}) \in \Sigma \quad \Gamma, x : A_{\text{Op}}, k : B_{\text{Op}} \to B \mathbin{!} \Delta \vdash_c c_{\text{Op}} : B \mathbin{!} \Delta \rightsquigarrow c'_{\text{Op}} \right]_{\text{Op} \in \mathcal{O}} \\ c_{res} = \{ \text{return } (x : T) \mapsto c'_r, [\text{Op } x \, k \mapsto c'_{\text{Op}}]_{\text{Op} \in \mathcal{O}} \} \end{array}}{\Gamma \vdash_v \{ \text{return } x \mapsto c_r, [\text{Op } x \, k \mapsto c_{\text{Op}}]_{\text{Op} \in \mathcal{O}} \} : A \mathbin{!} \Delta \cup \mathcal{O} \Rightarrow B \mathbin{!} \Delta \rightsquigarrow c_{res}} \; \text{TmHand}$$

$\boxed{\Gamma \vdash_c c : \underline{C} \rightsquigarrow c'}$ **Computations**

$$\frac{\begin{array}{c} \Gamma \vdash_c c : \underline{C_1} \rightsquigarrow c' \\ \Gamma \vdash_{co} \gamma : \underline{C_1} \leqslant \underline{C_2} \end{array}}{\Gamma \vdash_c c : \underline{C_2} \rightsquigarrow c' \rhd \gamma} \; \text{TmCastC} \qquad \frac{\begin{array}{c} \Gamma \vdash_v v_1 : A \to \underline{C} \rightsquigarrow v'_1 \\ \Gamma \vdash_v v_2 : A \rightsquigarrow v'_2 \end{array}}{\Gamma \vdash_c v_1 \, v_2 : \underline{C} \rightsquigarrow v'_1 \, v'_2} \; \text{TmTmApp}$$

$$\frac{\begin{array}{c} S = \forall \varsigma. \overline{\alpha : \tau}. \forall \overline{\delta}. \overline{\pi} \Rightarrow A \\ \Gamma, \overline{\varsigma}, \overline{\alpha : \tau}, \overline{\delta}, \overline{\omega : \pi} \vdash_v v : A \rightsquigarrow v' \quad \Gamma, x : S \vdash_c c : \underline{C} \rightsquigarrow c' \end{array}}{\Gamma \vdash_c \text{let } x = v \text{ in } c : \underline{C} \rightsquigarrow \text{let } x = \Lambda\varsigma.\Lambda\overline{\alpha : \tau}.\Lambda\overline{\delta}.\Lambda(\overline{\omega : \pi}).v' \text{ in } c'} \; \text{TmLet}$$

$$\frac{\Gamma \vdash_v v : A \rightsquigarrow v'}{\Gamma \vdash_c \text{return } v : A \mathbin{!} \emptyset \rightsquigarrow \text{return } v'} \; \text{TmReturn}$$

$$\frac{\begin{array}{c} (\text{Op} : A_{\text{Op}} \to B_{\text{Op}}) \in \Sigma \quad \Gamma \vdash_v v : A_{\text{Op}} \rightsquigarrow v' \\ \Gamma, y : B_{\text{Op}} \vdash_c c : A \mathbin{!} \Delta \rightsquigarrow c' \quad \Gamma \vdash_{vty} B_{\text{Op}} : \tau \rightsquigarrow T_{\text{Op}} \quad \text{Op} \in \Delta \end{array}}{\Gamma \vdash_c \text{Op } v \, (y.c) : A \mathbin{!} \Delta \rightsquigarrow \text{Op } v' \, (y : T_{\text{Op}}.c')} \; \text{TmOp}$$

$$\frac{\Gamma \vdash_c c_1 : A \mathbin{!} \Delta \rightsquigarrow c'_1 \quad \Gamma, x : A \vdash_c c_2 : B \mathbin{!} \Delta \rightsquigarrow c'_2}{\Gamma \vdash_c \text{do } x \leftarrow c_1; c_2 : B \mathbin{!} \Delta \rightsquigarrow \text{do } x \leftarrow c'_1; c'_2} \; \text{TmDo}$$

$$\frac{\Gamma \vdash_v v : \underline{C} \Rightarrow \underline{D} \rightsquigarrow v' \quad \Gamma \vdash_c c : \underline{C} \rightsquigarrow c'}{\Gamma \vdash_c \text{handle } c \text{ with } v : \underline{D} \rightsquigarrow \text{handle } c' \text{ with } v'} \; \text{TmHandle}$$

Fig. 2. ImpEff Typing & Elaboration

Computations. Typing for computations takes the form $\Gamma \vdash_c c : \underline{C} \rightsquigarrow \underline{c}'$, and, given a typing environment Γ, checks a computation c against a type $\underline{C}$.

Rule TMCASTC behaves like Rule TMCASTV, but for computation types. Rule TMLET handles polymorphic, non-recursive let-bindings. Rule TMRETURN handles **return** v computations. Keyword **return** effectively lifts a value v of type A into a computation of type $A \ ! \ \emptyset$. Rule TMOP checks operation calls. First, we ensure that v has the appropriate type, as specified by the signature of Op. Then, the continuation $(y.c)$ is checked. The side condition $\text{Op} \in \Delta$ ensures that the called operation Op is captured in the result type. Rule TMDO handles sequencing. Given that c_1 has type $A \,!\, \Delta$, the pure part of the result of type A is bound to term variable x, which is brought in scope for checking c_2. As we mentioned in Sect. 2, all computations in a do-construct should have the same effect set, Δ. Rule TMHANDLE eliminates handler types, just as Rule TMTMAPP eliminates arrow types.

Constraint Entailment. The specification of constraint entailment takes the form $\Gamma \vdash_{co} \gamma : \rho$ and is presented in Fig. 3. Notice that we use ρ instead of π, which allows us to capture subtyping between two value types, computation types or dirts, within the same relation. Subtyping can be established in several ways:

Rule CoVAR handles given assumptions. Rules VCOREFL and DCOREFL express that subtyping is reflexive, for both value types and dirts. Notice that we do not have a rule for the reflexivity of computation types since, as we illustrate below, it can be established using the reflexivity of their subparts. Rules VCOTRANS, CCOTRANS and DCOTRANS express the transitivity of subtyping for value types, computation types and dirts, respectively. Rule VCOARR establishes inequality of arrow types. As usual, the arrow type constructor is contravariant in the argument type. Rules VCOARRL and CCOARRR are the inversions of Rule VCOARR, allowing us to establish the relation between the subparts of the arrow types. Rules VCOHAND, CCOHL, and CCOHR work similarly, for handler types. Rule CCOCOMP captures the covariance of type constructor (!), establishing subtyping between two computation types if subtyping is established for their respective subparts. Rules VCOPURE and DCOIM-PURE are its inversions. Finally, Rules DCONIL and DCOOP establish subtyping between dirts. Rule DCONIL captures that the empty dirty set $\emptyset$ is a subdirt of any dirt Δ and Rule DCOOP expresses that dirt subtyping preserved under extension with the same operation Op.

Well-Formedness of Types, Constraints, Dirts, and Skeletons. The relations $\Gamma \vdash_{vty} A : \tau \rightsquigarrow T$ and $\Gamma \vdash_{cty} \underline{C} : \tau \rightsquigarrow \underline{C}$ check the well-formedness of value and computation types respectively. Similarly, relations $\Gamma \vdash_{ct} \rho \rightsquigarrow \rho$ and $\Gamma \vdash_{\Delta} \Delta$ check the well-formedness of constraints and dirts, respectively.

$\boxed{\Gamma \vdash_{co} \gamma : \rho}$ **Constraint Entailment**

$$\frac{(\omega : \pi) \in \Gamma}{\Gamma \vdash_{co} \omega : \pi} \text{ CoVar} \qquad \frac{\Gamma \vdash_{vty} A : \tau \leadsto T}{\Gamma \vdash_{co} \langle T \rangle : A \leqslant A} \text{ VCoRefl}$$

$$\frac{\Gamma \vdash_{\overline{h}} \Delta}{\Gamma \vdash_{co} \langle \Delta \rangle : \Delta \leqslant \Delta} \text{ DCoRefl} \qquad \frac{\begin{array}{c} \Gamma \vdash_{co} \gamma_1 : A_1 \leqslant A_2 \\ \Gamma \vdash_{co} \gamma_2 : A_2 \leqslant A_3 \end{array}}{\Gamma \vdash_{co} \gamma_1 \gg \gamma_2 : A_1 \leqslant A_3} \text{ VCoTrans}$$

$$\frac{\begin{array}{c} \Gamma \vdash_{co} \gamma_1 : \underline{C_1} \leqslant \underline{C_2} \\ \Gamma \vdash_{co} \gamma_2 : \underline{C_2} \leqslant \underline{C_3} \end{array}}{\Gamma \vdash_{co} \gamma_1 \gg \gamma_2 : \underline{C_1} \leqslant \underline{C_3}} \text{ CCoTrans} \qquad \frac{\begin{array}{c} \Gamma \vdash_{co} \gamma_1 : \Delta_1 \leqslant \Delta_2 \\ \Gamma \vdash_{co} \gamma_2 : \Delta_2 \leqslant \Delta_3 \end{array}}{\Gamma \vdash_{co} \gamma_1 \gg \gamma_2 : \Delta_1 \leqslant \Delta_3} \text{ DCoTrans}$$

$$\frac{\Gamma \vdash_{co} \gamma_1 : B \leqslant A \qquad \Gamma \vdash_{co} \gamma_2 : \underline{C} \leqslant \underline{D}}{\Gamma \vdash_{co} \gamma_1 \to \gamma_2 : A \to \underline{C} \leqslant B \to \underline{D}} \text{ VCoArr}$$

$$\frac{\Gamma \vdash_{co} \gamma : A \to \underline{C} \leqslant B \to \underline{D}}{\Gamma \vdash_{co} \mathsf{left}(\gamma) : B \leqslant A} \text{ VCoArrL} \qquad \frac{\Gamma \vdash_{co} \gamma : A \to \underline{C} \leqslant B \to \underline{D}}{\Gamma \vdash_{co} \mathsf{right}(\gamma) : \underline{C} \leqslant \underline{D}} \text{ CCoArrR}$$

$$\frac{\Gamma \vdash_{co} \gamma_1 : \underline{C_2} \leqslant \underline{C_1} \qquad \Gamma \vdash_{co} \gamma_2 : \underline{D_1} \leqslant \underline{D_2}}{\Gamma \vdash_{co} \gamma_1 \Rightarrow \gamma_2 : \underline{C_1} \Rightarrow \underline{D_1} \leqslant \underline{C_2} \Rightarrow \underline{D_2}} \text{ VCoHand}$$

$$\frac{\Gamma \vdash_{co} \gamma : \underline{C_1} \Rightarrow \underline{D_1} \leqslant \underline{C_2} \Rightarrow \underline{D_2}}{\Gamma \vdash_{co} \mathsf{left}(\gamma) : \underline{C_2} \leqslant \underline{C_1}} \text{ CCoHL} \qquad \frac{\Gamma \vdash_{co} \gamma : \underline{C_1} \Rightarrow \underline{D_1} \leqslant \underline{C_2} \Rightarrow \underline{D_2}}{\Gamma \vdash_{co} \mathsf{right}(\gamma) : \underline{D_1} \leqslant \underline{D_2}} \text{ CCoHR}$$

$$\frac{\Gamma \vdash_{co} \gamma_1 : A_1 \leqslant A_2 \qquad \Gamma \vdash_{co} \gamma_2 : \Delta_1 \leqslant \Delta_2}{\Gamma \vdash_{co} \gamma_1 \mathbin{!} \gamma_2 : A_1 \mathbin{!} \Delta_1 \leqslant A_2 \mathbin{!} \Delta_2} \text{ CCoComp}$$

$$\frac{\Gamma \vdash_{co} \gamma : A_1 \mathbin{!} \Delta_1 \leqslant A_2 \mathbin{!} \Delta_2}{\Gamma \vdash_{co} \mathsf{pure}(\gamma) : A_1 \leqslant A_2} \text{ VCoPure} \qquad \frac{\Gamma \vdash_{co} \gamma : A_1 \mathbin{!} \Delta_1 \leqslant A_2 \mathbin{!} \Delta_2}{\Gamma \vdash_{co} \mathsf{impure}(\gamma) : \Delta_1 \leqslant \Delta_2} \text{ DCoImpure}$$

$$\frac{}{\Gamma \vdash_{co} \emptyset_\Delta : \emptyset \leqslant \Delta} \text{ DCoNil} \qquad \frac{\Gamma \vdash_{co} \gamma : \Delta_1 \leqslant \Delta_2 \qquad (\mathsf{Op} : A_{\mathsf{Op}} \to B_{\mathsf{Op}}) \in \Sigma}{\Gamma \vdash_{co} \{\mathsf{Op}\} \cup \gamma : \{\mathsf{Op}\} \cup \Delta_1 \leqslant \{\mathsf{Op}\} \cup \Delta_2} \text{ DCoOp}$$

Fig. 3. IMPEFF Constraint Entailment

4   The ExEff Language

4.1   Syntax

Figure 4 presents EXEFF's syntax. EXEFF is an intensional type theory akin to
System F [7], where every term encodes its own typing derivation. In essence, all
abstractions and applications that are implicit in IMPEFF, are made explicit in
EXEFF via new syntactic forms. Additionally, EXEFF is impredicative, which is
reflected in the lack of discrimination between value types, qualified types and

Terms

$$\text{value } v ::= x \mid \text{unit} \mid \text{fun } (x : T) \mapsto c \mid h$$
$$\mid \; \Lambda\varsigma.v \mid v\,\tau \mid \Lambda\alpha:\tau.v \mid v\,T \mid \Lambda\delta.v \mid v\,\Delta \mid \Lambda(\omega:\pi).v \mid v\,\gamma \mid v \triangleright \gamma$$
$$\text{handler } h ::= \{\text{return } (x : T) \mapsto c_r, \text{Op}_1\,x\,k \mapsto c_{\text{Op}_1}, \ldots, \text{Op}_n\,x\,k \mapsto c_{\text{Op}_n}\}$$
$$\text{computation } c ::= \text{return } v \mid \text{Op } v\,(y : T.c) \mid \text{do } x \leftarrow c_1; c_2$$
$$\mid \; \text{handle } c \text{ with } v \mid v_1\,v_2 \mid \text{let } x = v \text{ in } c \mid c \triangleright \gamma$$

Types

$$\text{skeleton } \tau ::= \varsigma \mid \text{Unit} \mid \tau_1 \to \tau_2 \mid \tau_1 \Rightarrow \tau_2 \mid \forall\varsigma.\tau$$

$$\text{value type } T ::= \alpha \mid \text{Unit} \mid T \to \underline{C} \mid \underline{C}_1 \Rightarrow \underline{C}_2 \mid \forall\varsigma.T \mid \forall\alpha:\tau.T \mid \forall\delta.T \mid \pi \Rightarrow T$$
$$\text{simple coercion type } \pi ::= T_1 \leqslant T_2 \mid \Delta_1 \leqslant \Delta_2$$
$$\text{coercion type } \rho ::= \pi \mid \underline{C}_1 \leqslant \underline{C}_2$$

$$\text{computation type } \underline{C} ::= T\,!\,\Delta$$
$$\text{dirt } \Delta ::= \delta \mid \emptyset \mid \{\text{Op}\} \cup \Delta$$

Coercions

$$\gamma ::= \omega \mid \gamma_1 \gg \gamma_2 \mid \langle T \rangle \mid \gamma_1 \to \gamma_2 \mid \gamma_1 \Rightarrow \gamma_2 \mid \text{left}(\gamma) \mid \text{right}(\gamma) \mid \langle \Delta \rangle \mid \emptyset_\Delta \mid \{\text{Op}\} \cup \gamma$$
$$\mid \; \forall\varsigma.\gamma \mid \gamma[\tau] \mid \forall\alpha.\gamma \mid \gamma[T] \mid \forall\delta.\gamma \mid \gamma[\Delta] \mid \pi \Rightarrow \gamma \mid \gamma_1@\gamma_2 \mid \gamma_1\,!\,\gamma_2 \mid \text{pure}(\gamma) \mid \text{impure}(\gamma)$$

Fig. 4. ExEff Syntax

type schemes; all non-computation types are denoted by T. While the impredicativity is not strictly required for the purpose at hand, it makes for a cleaner system.

Coercions. Of particular interest is the use of explicit *subtyping coercions*, denoted by γ. ExEff uses these to replace the implicit casts of ImpEff (Rules TmCastV and TmCastC in Fig. 2) with explicit casts $(v \triangleright \gamma)$ and $(c \triangleright \gamma)$.

Essentially, coercions γ are explicit witnesses of subtyping derivations: each coercion form corresponds to a subtyping rule. Subtyping forms a partial order, which is reflected in coercion forms $\gamma_1 \gg \gamma_2$, $\langle T \rangle$, and $\langle \Delta \rangle$. Coercion form $\gamma_1 \gg \gamma_2$ captures transitivity, while forms $\langle T \rangle$ and $\langle \Delta \rangle$ capture reflexivity for value types and dirts (reflexivity for computation types can be derived from these).

Subtyping for skeleton abstraction, type abstraction, dirt abstraction, and qualification is witnessed by forms $\forall\varsigma.\gamma$, $\forall\alpha.\gamma$, $\forall\delta.\gamma$, and $\pi \Rightarrow \gamma$, respectively. Similarly, forms $\gamma[\tau]$, $\gamma[T]$, $\gamma[\Delta]$, and $\gamma_1@\gamma_2$ witness subtyping of skeleton instantiation, type instantiation, dirt instantiation, and coercion application, respectively.

Syntactic forms $\gamma_1 \to \gamma_2$ and $\gamma_1 \Rightarrow \gamma_2$ capture injection for the arrow and the handler type constructor, respectively. Similarly, inversion forms $\text{left}(\gamma)$ and $\text{right}(\gamma)$ capture projection, following from the injectivity of both type constructors.

Coercion form $\gamma_1 ! \gamma_2$ witnesses subtyping for computation types, using proofs for their components. Inversely, syntactic forms $pure(\gamma)$ and $impure(\gamma)$ witness subtyping between the value- and dirt-components of a computation coercion.

Finally, coercion forms $\emptyset_\Delta$ and $\{Op\} \cup \gamma$ are concerned with dirt subtyping. Form $\emptyset_\Delta$ witnesses that the empty dirt $\emptyset$ is a subdirt of any dirt Δ. Lastly, coercion form $\{Op\} \cup \gamma$ witnesses that subtyping between dirts is preserved under extension with a new operation. Note that we do not have an inversion form to extract a witness for $\Delta_1 \leqslant \Delta_2$ from a coercion for $\{Op\} \cup \Delta_1 \leqslant \{Op\} \cup \Delta_2$. The reason is that dirt sets are sets and not inductive structures. For instance, for $\Delta_1 = \{Op\}$ and $\Delta_2 = \emptyset$ the latter subtyping holds, but the former does not.

4.2 Typing

Value and Computation Typing. Typing for EXEFF values and computations is presented in Figs. 5 and 6 and is given by two mutually recursive relations of the form $\Gamma \vdash_v v : T$ (values) and $\Gamma \vdash_c c : \underline{C}$ (computations). EXEFF typing environments Γ contain bindings for variables of all sorts:

$$\Gamma ::= \epsilon \mid \Gamma, \varsigma \mid \Gamma, \alpha : \tau \mid \Gamma, \delta \mid \Gamma, x : T \mid \Gamma, \omega : \pi$$

Typing is entirely syntax-directed. Apart from the typing rules for skeleton, type, dirt, and coercion abstraction (and, subsequently, skeleton, type, dirt, and coercion application), the main difference between typing for IMPEFF and EXEFF lies in the explicit cast forms, $(v \rhd \gamma)$ and $(c \rhd \gamma)$. Given that a value v has type T_1 and that γ is a proof that T_1 is a subtype of T_2, we can upcast v with an explicit cast operation $(v \rhd \gamma)$. Upcasting for computations works analogously.

$$\frac{(x : T) \in \Gamma}{\Gamma \vdash_v x : T} \qquad \frac{}{\Gamma \vdash_v \mathbf{unit} : \mathbf{Unit}} \qquad \frac{\Gamma, x : T \vdash_c c : \underline{C} \qquad \Gamma \vdash_T T : \tau}{\Gamma \vdash_v (\mathbf{fun}\ x : T \mapsto c) : T \to \underline{C}}$$

$$\frac{\Gamma \vdash_v v : T_1 \qquad \Gamma \vdash_{co} \gamma : T_1 \leqslant T_2}{\Gamma \vdash_v v \rhd \gamma : T_2} \qquad \frac{\Gamma, \varsigma \vdash_v v : T}{\Gamma \vdash_v \Lambda\varsigma.v : \forall\varsigma.T} \qquad \frac{\Gamma, \alpha : \tau \vdash_v v : T}{\Gamma \vdash_v \Lambda\alpha : \tau.v : \forall\alpha : \tau.T}$$

$$\frac{\Gamma, \delta \vdash_v v : T}{\Gamma \vdash_v \Lambda\delta.v : \forall\delta.T} \qquad \frac{\Gamma, \omega : \pi \vdash_v v : T \qquad \Gamma \vdash_\rho \pi}{\Gamma \vdash_v \Lambda(\omega : \pi).v : \pi \Rightarrow T} \qquad \frac{\Gamma \vdash_v v : \pi \Rightarrow T \qquad \Gamma \vdash_{co} \gamma : \pi}{\Gamma \vdash_v v\ \gamma : T}$$

$$\frac{[(Op : T_1 \to T_2) \in \Sigma \qquad \Gamma, x : T_1, k : T_2 \to T!\Delta \vdash_c c_{op} : T!\Delta]_{Op \in \mathcal{O}}}{\Gamma \vdash_v \{\mathbf{return}\ (x : T_x) \mapsto c_r, [Op\ x\ k \mapsto c_{op}]_{Op \in \mathcal{O}}\} : T_x ! \Delta \cup \mathcal{O} \Rightarrow T!\Delta}$$

$$\frac{\Gamma \vdash_v v : \forall\varsigma.T \qquad \Gamma \vdash_T \tau}{\Gamma \vdash_v v\ \tau : T[\tau/\varsigma]} \qquad \frac{\Gamma \vdash_v v : \forall\alpha : \tau.T_1 \qquad \Gamma \vdash_T T_2 : \tau}{\Gamma \vdash_v v\ T_2 : T_1[T_2/\alpha]} \qquad \frac{\Gamma \vdash_v v : \forall\delta.T \qquad \Gamma \vdash_\Delta \Delta}{\Gamma \vdash_v v\ \Delta : T[\Delta/\delta]}$$

Fig. 5. EXEFF Value Typing

Well-Formedness of Types, Constraints, Dirts and Skeletons. The definitions of the judgements that check the well-formedness of EXEFF value types $(\Gamma \vdash_T T : \tau)$, computation types $(\Gamma \vdash_{\underline{C}} \underline{C} : \tau)$, dirts $(\Gamma \vdash_{\Delta} \Delta)$, and skeletons $(\Gamma \vdash_\tau \tau)$ are equally straightforward as those for IMPEFF.

Coercion Typing. Coercion typing formalizes the intuitive interpretation of coercions we gave in Sect. 4.1 and takes the form $\Gamma \vdash_{co} \gamma : \rho$. It is essentially an extension of the constraint entailment relation of Fig. 3.

4.3   Operational Semantics

Figure 7 presents selected rules of EXEFF's small-step, call-by-value operational semantics. For lack of space, we omit β-rules and other common rules and focus only on cases of interest.

Firstly, one of the non-conventional features of our system lies in the stratification of results in plain results and cast results:

$$\frac{\Gamma \vdash_v v_1 : T \to \underline{C} \quad \Gamma \vdash_v v_2 : T}{\Gamma \vdash_c v_1\, v_2 : \underline{C}} \qquad \frac{\Gamma \vdash_v v : T \quad \Gamma, x : T \vdash_c c : \underline{C}}{\Gamma \vdash_c \mathbf{let}\ x = v\ \mathbf{in}\ c : \underline{C}}$$

$$\frac{\Gamma \vdash_v v : T}{\Gamma \vdash_c \mathbf{return}\ v : T\,!\,\emptyset} \qquad \frac{\Gamma \vdash_c c_1 : T_1\,!\,\Delta \quad \Gamma, x : T_1 \vdash_c c_2 : T_2\,!\,\Delta}{\Gamma \vdash_c \mathbf{do}\ x \leftarrow c_1; c_2 : T_2\,!\,\Delta}$$

$$\frac{(\mathtt{Op} : T_1 \to T_2) \in \Sigma \quad \Gamma \vdash_v v : T_1 \quad \Gamma, y : T_2 \vdash_c c : T\,!\,\Delta \quad \mathtt{Op} \in \Delta}{\Gamma \vdash_c \mathtt{Op}\ v\ (y : T_2.c) : T\,!\,\Delta}$$

$$\frac{\Gamma \vdash_v v : \underline{C}_1 \Rightarrow \underline{C}_2 \quad \Gamma \vdash_c c : \underline{C}_1}{\Gamma \vdash_c \mathbf{handle}\ c\ \mathbf{with}\ v : \underline{C}_2} \qquad \frac{\Gamma \vdash_c c : \underline{C}_1 \quad \Gamma \vdash_{co} \gamma : \underline{C}_1 \leqslant \underline{C}_2}{\Gamma \vdash_c c \triangleright \gamma : \underline{C}_2}$$

Fig. 6. EXEFF Computation Typing

$$\text{terminal value}\ v^T ::= \mathbf{unit} \mid h \mid \mathbf{fun}\ x : T \mapsto c \mid \Lambda\alpha : \tau.v \mid \Lambda\delta.v \mid \lambda\omega : \pi.v$$
$$\text{value result}\ v^R ::= v^T \mid v^T \triangleright \gamma$$
$$\text{computation result}\ c^R ::= \mathbf{return}\ v^T \mid (\mathbf{return}\ v^T) \triangleright \gamma \mid \mathtt{Op}\ v^R\ (y : T.c)$$

Terminal values v^T represent conventional values, and value results v^R can either be plain terminal values v^T or terminal values with a cast: $v^T \triangleright \gamma$. The same applies to computation results c^R.[5]

Although unusual, this stratification can also be found in Crary's coercion calculus for inclusive subtyping [4], and, more recently, in System F_C [25]. Stratification is crucial for ensuring type preservation. Consider for example the expression

---

[5] Observe that operation values do not feature an outermost cast operation, as the coercion can always be pushed into its continuation.

($\mathtt{return}\ 5 \rhd \langle \mathtt{int} \rangle\,!\,\emptyset_{\{\mathtt{Op}\}}$), of type $\mathtt{int}\,!\,\{\mathtt{Op}\}$. We can not reduce the expression further without losing effect information; removing the cast would result in computation ($\mathtt{return}\ 5$), of type $\mathtt{int}\,!\,\emptyset$. Even if we consider type preservation only up to subtyping, the redex may still occur as a subterm in a context that expects solely the larger type.

Secondly, we need to make sure that casts do not stand in the way of evaluation. This is captured in the so-called "push" rules, all of which appear in Fig. 7.

In relation $v \leadsto_v v'$, the first rule groups nested casts into a single cast, by means of transitivity. The next three rules capture the essence of push rules: whenever a redex is "blocked" due to a cast, we take the coercion apart and redistribute it (in a type-preserving manner) over the subterms, so that evaluation can progress.

The situation in relation $c \leadsto_c c'$ is quite similar. The first rule uses transitivity to group nested casts into a single cast. The second rule is a push rule for β-reduction. The third rule pushes a cast out of a $\mathtt{return}$-computation. The fourth rule pushes a coercion inside an operation-computation, illustrating why the syntax for c^R does not require casts on operation-computations. The fifth rule is a push rule for sequencing computations and performs two tasks at once. Since we know that the computation bound to x calls no operations, we (a) safely "drop" the impure part of γ, and (b) substitute x with v^T, cast with the pure part of γ (so that types are preserved). The sixth rule handles operation calls in sequencing computations. If an operation is called in a sequencing computation, evaluation is suspended and the rest of the computation is captured in the continuation.

The last four rules are concerned with effect handling. The first of them pushes a coercion on the handler "outwards", such that the handler can be exposed and evaluation is not stuck (similarly to the push rule for term application). The second rule behaves similarly to the push/beta rule for sequencing computations. Finally, the last two rules are concerned with handling of operations. The first of the two captures cases where the called operation is handled by the handler, in which case the respective clause of the handler is called. As illustrated by the rule, like Pretnar [20], ExEff features *deep handlers*: the continuation is also wrapped within a $\mathtt{with\text{-}handle}$ construct. The last rule captures cases where the operation is not covered by the handler and thus remains unhandled.

We have shown that ExEff is type safe:

Theorem 1 (Type Safety)

- If $\Gamma \vdash_v v : T$ then either v is a result value or $v \leadsto_v v'$ and $\Gamma \vdash_v v' : T$.
- If $\Gamma \vdash_c c : \underline{C}$ then either c is a result computation or $c \leadsto_c c'$ and $\Gamma \vdash_c c' : \underline{C}$.

$\boxed{v \leadsto_{\mathrm{v}} v'}$ **Values**

$$(v^T \rhd \gamma_1) \rhd \gamma_2 \leadsto_{\mathrm{v}} v^T \rhd (\gamma_1 \gg \gamma_2) \qquad\qquad (v^T \rhd \gamma) \; T \leadsto_{\mathrm{v}} (v^T \; T) \rhd \gamma[T]$$

$$(v^T \rhd \gamma) \; \Delta \leadsto_{\mathrm{v}} (v^T \; \Delta) \rhd \gamma[\Delta] \qquad\qquad (v^T \rhd \gamma_1) \; \gamma_2 \leadsto_{\mathrm{v}} (v^T \; \gamma_2) \rhd \gamma_1 @ \gamma_2$$

$\boxed{c \leadsto_{\mathrm{c}} c'}$ **Computations**

$$(c^R \rhd \gamma_1) \rhd \gamma_2 \leadsto_{\mathrm{c}} c^R \rhd (\gamma_1 \gg \gamma_2) \qquad (v_1^T \rhd \gamma) \; v_2 \leadsto_{\mathrm{c}} (v_1^T \; (v_2 \rhd \mathit{left}(\gamma))) \rhd \mathit{right}(\gamma)$$

$$\mathtt{return} \; (v^T \rhd \gamma) \leadsto_{\mathrm{c}} (\mathtt{return} \; v^T) \rhd (\gamma \, ! \, \emptyset_\emptyset)$$

$$(\mathtt{Op} \; v^R \; (y : T.c)) \rhd \gamma \leadsto_{\mathrm{c}} \mathtt{Op} \; v^R \; (y : T.(c \rhd \gamma))$$

$$\mathtt{do} \; x \leftarrow ((\mathtt{return} \; v^T) \rhd \gamma); c_2 \leadsto_{\mathrm{c}} c_2[(v^T \rhd \mathit{pure}(\gamma))/x]$$

$$\mathtt{do} \; x \leftarrow \mathtt{Op} \; v^R \; (y : T.c_1); c_2 \leadsto_{\mathrm{c}} \mathtt{Op} \; v^R \; (y : T.\mathtt{do} \; x \leftarrow c_1; c_2)$$

$$\mathtt{handle} \; c \; \mathtt{with} \; (v^T \rhd \gamma) \leadsto_{\mathrm{c}} (\mathtt{handle} \; (c \rhd \mathit{left}(\gamma)) \; \mathtt{with} \; v^T) \rhd \mathit{right}(\gamma)$$

$$\mathtt{handle} \; ((\mathtt{return} \; v^T) \rhd \gamma) \; \mathtt{with} \; h \leadsto_{\mathrm{c}} c_r[v^T \rhd \mathit{pure}(\gamma)/x]$$

$$\mathtt{handle} \; (\mathtt{Op} \; v^R \; (y : T.c)) \; \mathtt{with} \; h \leadsto_{\mathrm{c}} c_{\mathrm{Op}}[v^R/x, (\mathtt{fun} \; (y : T) \mapsto \mathtt{handle} \; c \; \mathtt{with} \; h)/k]$$

$$\mathtt{handle} \; (\mathtt{Op} \; v^R \; (y : T.c)) \; \mathtt{with} \; h \leadsto_{\mathrm{c}} \mathtt{Op} \; v^R \; (y : T.\mathtt{handle} \; c \; \mathtt{with} \; h)$$

Fig. 7. EXEFF Operational Semantics (Selected Rules)

5   Type Inference and Elaboration

This section presents the typing-directed elaboration of IMPEFF into EXEFF. This elaboration makes all the implicit type and effect information explicit, and introduces explicit term-level coercions to witness the use of subtyping.

After covering the declarative specification of this elaboration, we present a constraint-based algorithm to infer IMPEFF types and at the same time elaborate into EXEFF. This algorithm alternates between two phases: (1) the syntax-directed generation of constraints from the IMPEFF term, and (2) solving these constraints.

5.1   Elaboration of ImpEff into ExEff

The grayed parts of Fig. 2 augment the typing rules for IMPEFF value and computation terms with typing-directed elaboration to corresponding EXEFF terms. The elaboration is mostly straightforward, mapping every IMPEFF construct onto its corresponding EXEFF construct while adding explicit type annotations to binders in Rules TMTMABS, TMHANDLER and TMOP. Implicit appeals to

subtyping are turned into explicit casts with coercions in Rules TMCASTV and
TMCASTC. Rule TMLET introduces explicit binders for skeleton, type, and dirt
variables, as well as for constraints. These last also introduce coercion variables
ω that can be used in casts. The binders are eliminated in rule TMVAR by means
of explicit application with skeletons, types, dirts and coercions. The coercions
are produced by the auxiliary judgement $\Gamma \vdash_{co} \gamma : \pi$, defined in Fig. 3, which
provides a coercion witness for every subtyping proof.

As a sanity check, we have shown that elaboration preserves types.

Theorem 2 (Type Preservation)

– *If* $\Gamma \vdash_v v : A \rightsquigarrow v'$ *then* $elab_\Gamma(\Gamma) \vdash_v v' : elab_s(A)$.
– *If* $\Gamma \vdash_c c : \underline{C} \rightsquigarrow c'$ *then* $elab_\Gamma(\Gamma) \vdash_c c' : elab_{\underline{c}}(\underline{C})$.

Here $elab_\Gamma(\Gamma)$, $elab_s(A)$ and $elab_{\underline{c}}(\underline{C})$ convert IMPEFF environments and types
into EXEFF environments and types.

5.2 Constraint Generation and Elaboration

Constraint generation with elaboration into EXEFF is presented in Figs. 8 (values) and 9 (computations). Before going into the details of each, we first introduce the three auxiliary constructs they use.

$$
\begin{aligned}
\text{constraint set } \mathcal{P}, \mathcal{Q} &::= \bullet \mid \tau_1 = \tau_2, \mathcal{P} \mid \alpha : \tau, \mathcal{P} \mid \omega : \pi, \mathcal{P} \\
\text{typing environment } \Gamma &::= \epsilon \mid \Gamma, x : S \\
\text{substitution } \sigma &::= \bullet \mid \sigma \cdot [\tau/\varsigma] \mid \sigma \cdot [A/\alpha] \mid \sigma \cdot [\Delta/\delta] \mid \sigma \cdot [\gamma/\omega]
\end{aligned}
$$

At the heart of our algorithm are sets $\mathcal{P}$, containing three different kinds of constraints: (a) skeleton equalities of the form $\tau_1 = \tau_2$, (b) skeleton constraints of the
form $\alpha : \tau$, and (c) wanted subtyping constraints of the form $\omega : \pi$. The purpose
of the first two becomes clear when we discuss constraint solving, in Sect. 5.3.
Next, typing environments Γ only contain term variable bindings, while other
variables represent unknowns of their sort and may end up being instantiated
after constraint solving. Finally, during type inference we compute substitutions
σ, for refining as of yet unknown skeletons, types, dirts, and coercions. The last
one is essential, since our algorithm simultaneously performs type inference and
elaboration into EXEFF.

A substitution σ is a solution of the set $\mathcal{P}$, written as $\sigma \models \mathcal{P}$, if we get
derivable judgements after applying σ to all constraints in $\mathcal{P}$.

Values. Constraint generation for values takes the form $\mathcal{Q}; \Gamma \vdash_v v : A \mid
\mathcal{Q}'; \sigma \rightsquigarrow v'$. It takes as inputs a set of wanted constraints $\mathcal{Q}$, a typing envi-
ronment Γ, and a IMPEFF value v, and produces a value type A, a new set of
wanted constraints $\mathcal{Q}'$, a substitution σ, and a EXEFF value v'.

Unlike standard HM, our inference algorithm does not keep constraint generation and solving separate. Instead, the two are interleaved, as indicated by

$$\boxed{\mathcal{Q}; \Gamma \vdash_{\overline{v}} v : A \mid \mathcal{Q}'; \sigma \rightsquigarrow v'} \quad \textbf{Values}$$

$$\frac{(x : \forall \varsigma.\overline{\alpha : \tau}.\forall \overline{\delta}.\overline{\pi} \Rightarrow A) \in \Gamma \qquad \sigma = [\overline{\varsigma'/\varsigma}, \overline{\alpha'/\alpha}, \overline{\delta'/\delta}]}{\mathcal{Q}; \Gamma \vdash_{\overline{v}} x : \sigma(A) \mid \overline{\omega : \sigma(\pi)}, \overline{\alpha' : \sigma(\tau)}, \mathcal{Q}; \bullet \rightsquigarrow x\,\overline{\varsigma'}\,\overline{\alpha'}\,\overline{\delta'}\,\overline{\omega}}$$

$$\overline{\mathcal{Q}; \Gamma \vdash_{\overline{v}} \mathtt{unit} : \mathtt{Unit} \mid \mathcal{Q}; \bullet \rightsquigarrow \mathtt{unit}}$$

$$\frac{\alpha : \varsigma, \mathcal{Q}; \Gamma, x : \alpha \vdash_{\overline{c}} c : \underline{C} \mid \mathcal{Q}'; \sigma \rightsquigarrow c'}{\mathcal{Q}; \Gamma \vdash_{\overline{v}} (\mathtt{fun}\ x \mapsto c) : \sigma(\alpha) \rightarrow \underline{C} \mid \mathcal{Q}'; \sigma \rightsquigarrow \mathtt{fun}\ x : \sigma(\alpha) \mapsto c'}$$

$$\alpha_r : \varsigma_r, \mathcal{Q}; \Gamma, x : \alpha_r \vdash_{\overline{c}} c_r : B_r\ !\ \Delta_r \mid \mathcal{Q}_0; \sigma_r \rightsquigarrow c'_r \qquad \sigma^i = \sigma_i \cdot \sigma_{i-1} \cdots \cdot \sigma_1$$

$$\mathtt{Op}_i \in \mathcal{O}:$$
$$(\mathtt{Op}_i : A_i \to B_i) \in \Sigma$$
$$\alpha_i : \varsigma_i, \mathcal{Q}_{i-1}; \sigma^{i-1}(\sigma_r(\Gamma)), x : A_i, k : B_i \to \alpha_i\,!\,\delta_i \vdash_{\overline{c}} c_{\mathtt{Op}_i} : B_{\mathtt{Op}_i}\,!\,\Delta_{\mathtt{Op}_i} \mid \mathcal{Q}_i; \sigma_i \rightsquigarrow c'_{\mathtt{Op}_i}$$
$$\mathcal{Q}' = \alpha_{in} : \varsigma_{in}, \alpha_{out} : \varsigma_{out}, \omega_1 : \sigma^n(B_r) \leqslant \alpha_{out}, \omega_2 : \sigma^n(\Delta_r) \leqslant \delta_{out}, \overline{\omega_{3_i} : \sigma^n(B_{\mathtt{Op}_i}) \leqslant \alpha_{out}}^n,$$
$$\overline{\omega_{4_i} : \sigma^n(\Delta_{\mathtt{Op}_i}) \leqslant \delta_{out}}^n, \overline{\omega_{5_i} : B_i \to \alpha_{out}\,!\,\delta_{out} \leqslant B_i \to \sigma^n(\alpha_i\,!\,\delta_i)}^n,$$
$$\omega_6 : \alpha_{in} \leqslant \sigma^n(\sigma_r(\alpha_r)), \omega_7 : \delta_{in} \leqslant \delta_{out} \cup \mathcal{O}, \mathcal{Q}_n$$
$$c_{res} = \{\mathtt{return}\ y : \sigma^n(\sigma_r(\alpha_r)) \mapsto \sigma^n(c'_r)[y \triangleright \omega_6/x] \triangleright \omega_1\,!\,\omega_2$$
$$, [\mathtt{Op}_i\ x\ l \mapsto \sigma^n(c'_{\mathtt{Op}_i})[l \triangleright \omega_{5_i}/k] \triangleright \omega_{3_i}\,!\,\omega_{4_i}]_{\mathtt{Op}_i \in \mathcal{O}}\} \triangleright ((\alpha_{in})\,!\,\omega_7 \Rightarrow \langle \alpha_{out} \rangle\,!\,\langle \delta_{out} \rangle)$$

$$\overline{\mathcal{Q}; \Gamma \vdash_{\overline{v}} \{\mathtt{return}\ x \mapsto c_r, [\mathtt{Op}\ x\ k \mapsto c_{\mathtt{Op}}]_{\mathtt{Op} \in \mathcal{O}}\} : \alpha_{in}\,!\,\delta_{in} \Rightarrow \alpha_{out}\,!\,\delta_{out} \mid \mathcal{Q}'; (\sigma^n \cdot \sigma_r) \rightsquigarrow c_{res}}$$

Fig. 8. Constraint Generation with Elaboration (Values)

the additional arguments of our relation: (a) constraints $\mathcal{Q}$ are passed around in a stateful manner (i.e., they are input and output), and (b) substitutions σ generated from constraint solving constitute part of the relation output. We discuss the reason for this interleaved approach in Sect. 5.4; we now focus on the algorithm.

The rules are syntax-directed on the input IMPEFF value. The first rule handles term variables x: as usual for constraint-based type inference the rule instantiates the polymorphic type ($\forall \varsigma.\overline{\alpha : \tau}.\forall \overline{\delta}.\overline{\pi} \Rightarrow A$) of x with fresh variables; these are placeholders that are determined during constraint solving. Moreover, the rule extends the wanted constraints $\mathcal{P}$ with $\overline{\pi}$, appropriately instantiated. In EXEFF, this corresponds to explicit skeleton, type, dirt, and coercion applications.

More interesting is the third rule, for term abstractions. Like in standard Hindley-Damas-Milner [5], it generates a fresh type variable α for the type of the abstracted term variable x. In addition, it generates a fresh skeleton variable ς, to capture the (yet unknown) shape of α.

As explained in detail in Sect. 5.3, the constraint solver instantiates type variables only through their skeletons annotations. Because we want to allow local constraint solving for the body c of the term abstraction the opportunity to produce a substitution σ that instantiates α, we have to pass in the annotation constraint $\alpha : \varsigma$.[6] We apply the resulting substitution σ to the result type $\sigma(\alpha) \to \underline{C}$.[7]

Finally, the fourth rule is concerned with handlers. Since it is the most complex of the rules, we discuss each of its premises separately:

Firstly, we infer a type $B_r ! \Delta_r$ for the right hand side of the **return**-clause. Since α_r is a fresh unification variable, just like for term abstraction we require $\alpha_r : \varsigma_r$, for a fresh skeleton variable ς_r.

Secondly, we check every operation clause in $\mathcal{O}$ in order. For each clause, we generate fresh skeleton, type, and dirt variables (ς_i, α_i, and δ_i), to account for the (yet unknown) result type $\alpha_i ! \delta_i$ of the continuation k, while inferring type $B_{\mathrm{Op}_i} ! \Delta_{\mathrm{Op}_i}$ for the right-hand-side c_{Op_i}.

More interesting is the (final) set of wanted constraints $\mathcal{Q}'$. First, we assign to the handler the overall type

$$\alpha_{in} ! \delta_{in} \Rightarrow \alpha_{out} ! \delta_{out}$$

where $\varsigma_{in}, \alpha_{in}, \delta_{in}, \varsigma_{out}, \alpha_{out}, \delta_{out}$ are fresh variables of the respective sorts. In turn, we require that (a) the type of the return clause is a subtype of $\alpha_{out} ! \delta_{out}$ (given by the combination of ω_1 and ω_2), (b) the right-hand-side type of each operation clause is a subtype of the overall result type: $\sigma^n(B_{\mathrm{Op}_i} ! \Delta_{\mathrm{Op}_i}) \leqslant \alpha_{out} ! \delta_{out}$ (witnessed by $\omega_{3_i} ! \omega_{4_i}$), (c) the actual types of the continuations $B_i \to \alpha_{out} ! \delta_{out}$ in the operation clauses should be subtypes of their assumed types $B_i \to \sigma^n(\alpha_i ! \delta_i)$ (witnessed by ω_{5_i}). (d) the overall argument type α_{in} is a subtype of the assumed type of x: $\sigma^n(\sigma_r(\alpha_r))$ (witnessed by ω_6), and (e) the input dirt set δ_{in} is a subtype of the resulting dirt set δ_{out}, extended with the handled operations $\mathcal{O}$ (witnessed by ω_7).

All the aforementioned implicit subtyping relations become explicit in the elaborated term c_{res}, via explicit casts.

Computations. The judgement $\mathcal{Q}; \Gamma \vdash_{\mathsf{c}} c : \underline{C} \mid \mathcal{Q}'; \sigma \rightsquigarrow c'$ generates constraints for computations.

The first rule handles term applications of the form $v_1 v_2$. After inferring a type for each subterm (A_1 for v_1 and A_2 for v_2), we generate the wanted constraint $\sigma_2(A_1) \leqslant A_2 \to \alpha ! \delta$, with fresh type and dirt variables α and δ, respectively. Associated coercion variable ω is then used in the elaborated term to explicitly (up)cast v_1' to the expected type $A_2 \to \alpha ! \delta$.

The third rule handles polymorphic let-bindings. First, we infer a type A for v, as well as wanted constraints $\mathcal{Q}_v$. Then, we simplify wanted constraints $\mathcal{Q}_v$ by means of function **solve** (which we explain in detail in Sect. 5.3 below), obtaining a substitution σ_1' and a set of *residual constraints* $\mathcal{Q}_v'$.

---

[6] This hints at why we need to pass constraints in a stateful manner.

[7] Though σ refers to IMPEFF types, we abuse notation to save clutter and apply it directly to EXEFF entities too.

$$\boxed{\mathcal{Q}; \Gamma \vdash_{\mathsf{c}} c : \underline{C} \mid \mathcal{Q}'; \sigma \leadsto c'} \quad \textbf{Computations}$$

$$\cfrac{\mathcal{Q}; \Gamma \vdash_{\mathsf{v}} v_1 : A_1 \mid \mathcal{Q}_1; \sigma_1 \leadsto v_1' \qquad \mathcal{Q}_1; \sigma_1(\Gamma) \vdash_{\mathsf{v}} v_2 : A_2 \mid \mathcal{Q}_2; \sigma_2 \leadsto v_2'}{\mathcal{Q}; \Gamma \vdash_{\mathsf{c}} v_1\, v_2 : \alpha\, !\, \delta \mid \alpha : \varsigma,\, \omega : \sigma_2(A_1) \leqslant A_2 \rightarrow \alpha\, !\, \delta, \mathcal{Q}_2; (\sigma_2 \cdot \sigma_1) \leadsto (\sigma_2(v_1') \rhd \omega)\, v_2'}$$

$$\cfrac{\mathcal{Q}; \Gamma \vdash_{\mathsf{v}} v : A \mid \mathcal{Q}'; \sigma \leadsto v'}{\mathcal{Q}; \Gamma \vdash_{\mathsf{c}} \mathbf{return}\, v : A\, !\, \emptyset \mid \mathcal{Q}'; \sigma \leadsto \mathbf{return}\, v'}$$

$$\cfrac{\begin{array}{c} \mathcal{Q}; \Gamma \vdash_{\mathsf{v}} v : A \mid \mathcal{Q}_v; \sigma_1 \leadsto v' \\ \mathbf{solve}(\bullet;\, \bullet;\, \mathcal{Q}_v) = (\sigma_1', \mathcal{Q}_v') \qquad split(\sigma_1'(\sigma_1(\Gamma)), \mathcal{Q}_v', \sigma_1'(A)) = \langle \bar{\varsigma}, \overline{\alpha : \tau}, \bar{\delta}, \overline{\omega : \pi}, \mathcal{Q}_1 \rangle \\ \mathcal{Q}_1; \sigma_1'(\sigma_1(\Gamma)), x : \forall \bar{\varsigma}.\forall \overline{\alpha : \tau}.\forall \bar{\delta}.\bar{\pi} \Rightarrow \sigma_1'(A) \vdash_{\mathsf{c}} c : \underline{C} \mid \mathcal{Q}_2; \sigma_2 \leadsto c' \\ c_{res} = \mathbf{let}\, x = \sigma_2(\Lambda\bar{\varsigma}.\Lambda\overline{\alpha : \tau}.\Lambda\bar{\delta}.\Lambda(\omega : elab_\rho(\pi)).v')\, \mathbf{in}\, c' \end{array}}{\mathcal{Q}; \Gamma \vdash_{\mathsf{c}} \mathbf{let}\, x = v\, \mathbf{in}\, c : \underline{C} \mid \mathcal{Q}_2; (\sigma_2 \cdot \sigma_1' \cdot \sigma_1) \leadsto c_{res}}$$

$$\cfrac{\begin{array}{c} \mathcal{Q}; \Gamma \vdash_{\mathsf{v}} v : A_1 \mid \mathcal{Q}_1; \sigma_1 \leadsto v' \qquad \mathcal{Q}_1; \sigma_1(\Gamma), y : B_{\mathsf{op}} \vdash_{\mathsf{c}} c : A_2\, !\, \Delta_2 \mid \mathcal{Q}_2; \sigma_2 \leadsto c' \\ (\mathbf{Op} : A_{\mathsf{op}} \rightarrow B_{\mathsf{op}}) \in \Sigma \qquad c_{res} = \mathbf{Op}\, (\sigma_2(v') \rhd \omega)\, (y : elab_S(B_{\mathsf{op}}).c') \end{array}}{\mathcal{Q}; \Gamma \vdash_{\mathsf{c}} \mathbf{Op}\, v\, (y : B_{\mathsf{op}}.c) : A_2\, !\, \{\mathbf{Op}\} \cup \Delta_2 \mid \omega : \sigma_2(A_1) \leqslant A_{\mathsf{op}}, \mathcal{Q}_2; (\sigma_2 \cdot \sigma_1) \leadsto c_{res}}$$

$$\cfrac{\begin{array}{c} \mathcal{Q}; \Gamma \vdash_{\mathsf{c}} c_1 : A_1\, !\, \Delta_1 \mid \mathcal{Q}_1; \sigma_1 \leadsto c_1' \qquad \mathcal{Q}_1; \sigma_1(\Gamma), x : A_1 \vdash_{\mathsf{c}} c_2 : A_2\, !\, \Delta_2 \mid \mathcal{Q}_2; \sigma_2 \leadsto c_2' \\ c_{res} = \mathbf{do}\, x \leftarrow (\sigma_2(c_1') \rhd \langle \sigma_2(\Delta_1) \rangle\, !\, \omega_1); (c_2' \rhd \langle \Delta_2 \rangle\, !\, \omega_2) \end{array}}{\mathcal{Q}; \Gamma \vdash_{\mathsf{c}} \mathbf{do}\, x \leftarrow c_1; c_2 : A_2\, !\, \delta \mid \omega_1 : \sigma_2(\Delta_1) \leqslant \delta,\, \omega_2 : \Delta_2 \leqslant \delta, \mathcal{Q}_2; (\sigma_2 \cdot \sigma_1) \leadsto c_{res}}$$

$$\cfrac{\begin{array}{c} \mathcal{Q}; \Gamma \vdash_{\mathsf{v}} v : A_1 \mid \mathcal{Q}_1; \sigma_1 \leadsto v' \qquad \mathcal{Q}_1; \sigma_1(\Gamma) \vdash_{\mathsf{c}} c : A_2\, !\, \Delta_2 \mid \mathcal{Q}_2; \sigma_2 \leadsto c' \\ \mathcal{Q}' = \alpha_1 : \varsigma_1, \alpha_2 : \varsigma_2,\, \omega_1 : \sigma_2(A_1) \leqslant (\alpha_1\, !\, \delta_1 \Rightarrow \alpha_2\, !\, \delta_2),\, \omega_2 : A_2 \leqslant \alpha_1,\, \omega_3 : \Delta_2 \leqslant \delta_1, \mathcal{Q}_2 \\ c_{res} = \mathbf{handle}\, (c' \rhd (\omega_2\, !\, \omega_3))\, \mathbf{with}\, (\sigma_2(v') \rhd \omega_1) \end{array}}{\mathcal{Q}; \Gamma \vdash_{\mathsf{c}} \mathbf{handle}\, c\, \mathbf{with}\, v : \alpha_2\, !\, \Delta_2 \mid \mathcal{Q}'; (\sigma_2 \cdot \sigma_1) \leadsto c_{res}}$$

Fig. 9. Constraint Generation with Elaboration (Computations)

Generalization of x's type is performed by auxiliary function *split*, given by the following clause:

$$\cfrac{\begin{array}{c} \bar{\varsigma} = \{\varsigma \mid (\alpha : \varsigma) \in \mathcal{Q}, \nexists \alpha'.\alpha' \notin \bar{\alpha} \wedge (\alpha' : \varsigma) \in \mathcal{Q}\} \\ \bar{\alpha} = fv_\alpha(\mathcal{Q}) \cup fv_\alpha(A) \setminus fv_\alpha(\Gamma) \qquad \mathcal{Q}_1 = \{(\omega : \pi) \mid (\omega : \pi) \in \mathcal{Q}, fv(\pi) \not\subseteq fv(\Gamma)\} \\ \bar{\delta} = fv_\delta(\mathcal{Q}) \cup fv_\delta(A) \setminus fv_\delta(\Gamma) \qquad \mathcal{Q}_2 = \mathcal{Q} - \mathcal{Q}_1 \end{array}}{split(\Gamma, \mathcal{Q}, A) = \langle \bar{\varsigma}, \overline{\alpha : \tau}, \bar{\delta}, \mathcal{Q}_1, \mathcal{Q}_2 \rangle}$$

In essence, *split* generates the type (scheme) of x in parts. Additionally, it computes the subset $\mathcal{Q}_2$ of the input constraints $\mathcal{Q}$ that do not depend on locally-bound variables. Such constraints can be floated "upwards", and are passed as input when inferring a type for c. The remainder of the rule is self-explanatory.

The fourth rule handles operation calls. Observe that in the elaborated term, we upcast the inferred type to match the expected type in the signature.

The fifth rule handles sequences. The requirement that all computations in a do-construct have the same dirt set is expressed in the wanted constraints $\sigma_2(\Delta_1) \leqslant \delta$ and $\Delta_2 \leqslant \delta$ (where δ is a fresh dirt variable; the resulting dirt set), witnessed by coercion variables ω_1 and ω_2. Both coercion variables are used in the elaborated term to upcast c_1 and c_2, such that both draw effects from the same dirt set δ.

Finally, the sixth rule is concerned with effect handling. After inferring type A_1 for the handler v, we require that it takes the form of a handler type, witnessed by coercion variable $\omega_1 : \sigma_2(A_1) \leqslant (\alpha_1 ! \delta_1 \Rightarrow \alpha_2 ! \delta_2)$, for fresh $\alpha_1, \alpha_2, \delta_1, \delta_2$. To ensure that the type $A_2 ! \Delta_2$ of c matches the expected type, we require that $A_2 ! \Delta_2 \leqslant \alpha_1 ! \delta_1$. Our syntax does not include coercion variables for computation subtyping; we achieve the same effect by combining $\omega_2 : A_2 \leqslant \alpha_1$ and $\omega_3 : \Delta_2 \leqslant \delta_1$.

Theorem 3 (Soundness of Inference). *If $\bullet; \Gamma \vdash_{\mathsf{v}} v : A \mid \mathcal{Q}; \sigma \rightsquigarrow v'$ then for any $\sigma' \models \mathcal{Q}$, we have $(\sigma' \cdot \sigma)(\Gamma) \vdash_v v : \sigma'(A) \rightsquigarrow \sigma'(v')$, and analogously for computations.*

Theorem 4 (Completeness of Inference). *If $\Gamma \vdash_v v : A \rightsquigarrow v'$ then we have $\bullet; \Gamma \vdash_{\mathsf{v}} v : A' \mid \mathcal{Q}; \sigma \rightsquigarrow v''$ and there exists $\sigma' \models \mathcal{Q}$ and γ, such that $\sigma'(v'') = v'$ and $\sigma(\Gamma) \vdash_{\mathsf{co}} \gamma : \sigma'(A') \leqslant A$. An analogous statement holds for computations.*

5.3 Constraint Solving

The second phase of our inference-and-elaboration algorithm is the constraint solver. It is defined by the `solve` function signature:

$$\boxed{\mathsf{solve}(\sigma; \mathcal{P}; \mathcal{Q}) = (\sigma', \mathcal{P}')}$$

It takes three inputs: the substitution σ accumulated so far, a list of already processed constraints $\mathcal{P}$, and a queue of still to be processed constraints $\mathcal{Q}$. There are two outputs: the substitution σ' that solves the constraints and the residual constraints $\mathcal{P}'$. The substitutions σ and σ' contain four kinds of mappings: $\varsigma \mapsto \tau$, $\alpha \mapsto A$, $\delta \mapsto \Delta$ and $\omega \to \gamma$ which instantiate respectively skeleton variables, type variables, dirt variables and coercion variables.

Theorem 5 (Correctness of Solving). *For any set $\mathcal{Q}$, the call $\mathsf{solve}(\bullet; \bullet; \mathcal{Q})$ either results in a failure, in which case $\mathcal{Q}$ has no solutions, or returns $(\sigma, \mathcal{P})$ such that for any $\sigma' \models \mathcal{Q}$, there exists $\sigma'' \models \mathcal{P}$ such that $\sigma' = \sigma'' \cdot \sigma$.*

The solver is invoked with $\mathsf{solve}(\bullet; \bullet; \mathcal{Q})$, to process the constraints $\mathcal{Q}$ generated in the first phase of the algorithm, i.e., with an empty substitution and no processed constraints. The `solve` function is defined by case analysis on the queue.

Empty Queue. When the queue is empty, all constraints have been processed. What remains are the residual constraints and the solving substitution σ, which are both returned as the result of the solver.

$$\text{solve}(\sigma; \mathcal{P}; \bullet) = (\sigma, \mathcal{P})$$

Skeleton Equalities. The next set of cases we consider are those where the queue is non-empty and its first element is an equality between skeletons $\tau_1 = \tau_2$. We consider seven possible cases based on the structure of τ_1 and τ_2 that together essentially implement conventional unification as used in Hindley-Milner type inference [5].

$\text{solve}(\sigma; \mathcal{P}; \tau_1 = \tau_2, \mathcal{Q}) =$
  $\text{match } \tau_1 = \tau_2 \text{ with}$
   $\mid \varsigma = \varsigma \mapsto \text{solve}(\sigma; \mathcal{P}; \mathcal{Q})$
   $\mid \varsigma = \tau \mapsto \text{if } \varsigma \notin fv_\varsigma(\tau) \text{ then let } \sigma' = [\tau/\varsigma] \text{ in } \text{solve}(\sigma' \cdot \sigma; \bullet; \sigma'(\mathcal{Q}, \mathcal{P})) \text{ else fail}$
   $\mid \tau = \varsigma \mapsto \text{if } \varsigma \notin fv_\varsigma(\tau) \text{ then let } \sigma' = [\tau/\varsigma] \text{ in } \text{solve}(\sigma' \cdot \sigma; \bullet; \sigma'(\mathcal{Q}, \mathcal{P})) \text{ else fail}$
   $\mid \text{Unit} = \text{Unit} \mapsto \text{solve}(\sigma; \mathcal{P}; \mathcal{Q})$
   $\mid (\tau_1 \to \tau_2) = (\tau_3 \to \tau_4) \mapsto \text{solve}(\sigma; \mathcal{P}; \tau_1 = \tau_3, \tau_2 = \tau_4, \mathcal{Q})$
   $\mid (\tau_1 \Rightarrow \tau_2) = (\tau_3 \Rightarrow \tau_4) \mapsto \text{solve}(\sigma; \mathcal{P}; \tau_1 = \tau_3, \tau_2 = \tau_4, \mathcal{Q})$
   $\mid \text{otherwise} \mapsto \text{fail}$

The first case applies when both skeletons are the same type variable ς. Then the equality trivially holds. Hence we drop it and proceed with solving the remaining constraints. The next two cases apply when either τ_1 or τ_2 is a skeleton variable ς. If the occurs check fails, there is no finite solution and the algorithm signals failure. Otherwise, the constraint is solved by instantiating the ς. This additional substitution is accumulated and applied to all other constraints $\mathcal{P}, \mathcal{Q}$. Because the substitution might have modified some of the already processed constraints $\mathcal{P}$, we have to revisit them. Hence, they are all pushed back onto the queue, which is processed recursively.

The next three cases consider three different ways in which the two skeletons can have the same instantiated top-level structure. In those cases the equality is decomposed into equalities on the subterms, which are pushed onto the queue and processed recursively.

The last catch-all case deals with all ways in which the two skeletons can be instantiated to different structures. Then there is no solution.

Skeleton Annotations. The next four cases consider a skeleton annotation $\alpha : \tau$ at the head of the queue, and propagate the skeleton instantiation to the type variable. The first case, where the skeleton is a variable ς, has nothing to do, moves the annotation to the processed constraints and proceeds with the remainder of the queue. In the other three cases, the skeleton is instantiated and the solver instantiates the type variable with the corresponding structure, introducing fresh variables for any subterms. The instantiating substitution is accumulated and applied to the remaining constraints, which are processed recursively.

$\mathrm{solve}(\sigma;\ \mathcal{P};\ \alpha:\tau,\mathcal{Q}) =$

$\quad \mathtt{match}\ \tau\ \mathtt{with}$

$\quad |\ \varsigma \mapsto \mathrm{solve}(\sigma;\ \mathcal{P},\alpha:\tau;\ \mathcal{Q})$

$\quad |\ \mathtt{Unit} \mapsto \mathtt{let}\ \sigma' = [\mathtt{Unit}/\alpha]\ \mathtt{in}\ \mathrm{solve}(\sigma'\cdot\sigma;\ \bullet;\ \sigma'(\mathcal{Q},\mathcal{P}))$

$\quad |\ \tau_1 \to \tau_2 \mapsto \mathtt{let}\ \sigma' = [(\alpha_1^{\tau_1} \to \alpha_2^{\tau_2}\,!\,\delta)/\alpha]\ \mathtt{in}\ \mathrm{solve}(\sigma'\cdot\sigma;\ \bullet;\ \alpha_1:\tau_1,\alpha_2:\tau_2,\sigma'(\mathcal{Q},\mathcal{P}))$

$\quad |\ \tau_1 \Rrightarrow \tau_2 \mapsto \mathtt{let}\ \sigma' = [(\alpha_1^{\tau_1}\,!\,\delta_1 \Rrightarrow \alpha_2^{\tau_2}\,!\,\delta_2)/\alpha]\ \mathtt{in}\ \mathrm{solve}(\sigma'\cdot\sigma;\ \bullet;\ \alpha_1:\tau_1,\alpha_2:\tau_2,\sigma'(\mathcal{Q},\mathcal{P}))$

Value Type Subtyping. Next are the cases where a subtyping constraint between two value types $A_1 \leqslant A_2$, with as evidence the coercion variable ω, is at the head of the queue. We consider six different situations.

$\mathrm{solve}(\sigma;\ \mathcal{P};\ \omega:A_1 \leqslant A_2,\mathcal{Q}) =$

$\quad \mathtt{match}\ A_1 \leqslant A_2\ \mathtt{with}$

$\quad |\ A \leqslant A \mapsto \mathtt{let}\ T = elab_s(A)\ \mathtt{in}\ \mathrm{solve}([\langle T\rangle/\omega]\cdot\sigma;\ \mathcal{P};\ \mathcal{Q})$

$\quad |\ \alpha^{\tau_1} \leqslant A \mapsto \mathtt{let}\ \tau_2 = skeleton(A)\ \mathtt{in}\ \mathrm{solve}(\sigma;\ \mathcal{P},\omega:\alpha^{\tau_1} \leqslant A;\ \tau_1 = \tau_2,\mathcal{Q})$

$\quad |\ A \leqslant \alpha^{\tau_1} \mapsto \mathtt{let}\ \tau_2 = skeleton(A)\ \mathtt{in}\ \mathrm{solve}(\sigma;\ \mathcal{P},\omega:A \leqslant \alpha^{\tau_1};\ \tau_2 = \tau_1,\mathcal{Q})$

$\quad |\ (A_1 \to B_1\,!\,\Delta_1) \leqslant (A_2 \to B_2\,!\,\Delta_2) \mapsto \mathtt{let}\ \sigma' = [(\omega_1 \to \omega_2\,!\,\omega_3)/\omega]\ \mathtt{in}$

$\qquad \mathrm{solve}(\sigma'\cdot\sigma;\ \mathcal{P};\ \omega_1:A_2 \leqslant A_1,\omega_2:B_1 \leqslant B_2,\omega_3:\Delta_1 \leqslant \Delta_2,\mathcal{Q})$

$\quad |\ (A_1\,!\,\Delta_1 \Rrightarrow A_2\,!\,\Delta_2) \leqslant (A_3\,!\,\Delta_3 \Rrightarrow A_4\,!\,\Delta_4) \mapsto \mathtt{let}\ \sigma' = [(\omega_1\,!\,\omega_2 \Rrightarrow \omega_3\,!\,\omega_4)/\omega]\ \mathtt{in}$

$\qquad \mathrm{solve}(\sigma'\cdot\sigma;\ \mathcal{P};\ \omega_1:A_3 \leqslant A_1,\omega_2:\Delta_3 \leqslant \Delta_1,\omega_3:A_2 \leqslant A_4,\omega_4:\Delta_2 \leqslant \Delta_4,\mathcal{Q})$

$\quad |\ \mathtt{otherwise} \mapsto \mathtt{fail}$

If the two types are equal, the subtyping holds trivially through reflexivity. The solver thus drops the constraint and instantiates ω with the reflexivity coercion $\langle T\rangle$. Note that each coercion variable only appears in one constraint. So we only accumulate the substitution and do not have to apply it to the other constraints. In the next two cases, one of the two types is a type variable α. Then we move the constraint to the processed set. We also add an equality constraint between the skeletons[8] to the queue. This enforces the invariant that only types with the same skeleton are compared. Through the skeleton equality the type structure (if any) from the type is also transferred to the type variable. The next two cases concern two types with the same top-level instantiation. The solver then decomposes the constraint into constraints on the corresponding subterms and appropriately relates the evidence of the old constraint to the new ones. The final case catches all situations where the two types are instantiated with a different structure and thus there is no solution.

Auxiliary function $skeleton(A)$ computes the skeleton of A.

Dirt Subtyping. The final six cases deal with subtyping constraints between dirts.

---

[8] We implicitly annotate every type variable with its skeleton: α^τ.

$\text{solve}(\sigma; \ \mathcal{P}; \omega : \Delta \leqslant \Delta', \mathcal{Q}) =$

  $\text{match } \Delta \leqslant \Delta' \text{ with}$

  $| \ \mathcal{O} \cup \delta \leqslant \mathcal{O}' \cup \delta' \mapsto \text{if } \mathcal{O} \neq \emptyset \text{ then } \text{let } \sigma' = [((\mathcal{O} \backslash \mathcal{O}') \cup \delta'')/\delta', \mathcal{O} \cup \omega'/\omega] \text{ in}$
  $\qquad\qquad\qquad\qquad\qquad\qquad\quad \text{solve}(\sigma' \cdot \sigma; \ \bullet; (\omega' : \delta \leq \sigma'(\Delta')), \sigma'(\mathcal{Q}, \mathcal{P}))$
  $\qquad\qquad\qquad\qquad\qquad \text{else } \text{solve}(\sigma; \ \mathcal{P}, (\omega : \Delta \leqslant \Delta'); \ \mathcal{Q})$

  $| \ \emptyset \leqslant \Delta' \mapsto \text{solve}([\emptyset_{\Delta'}/\omega] \cdot \sigma; \ \mathcal{P}; \ \mathcal{Q})$

  $| \ \delta \leqslant \emptyset \mapsto \text{let } \sigma' = [\emptyset/\delta; \ \emptyset_\emptyset/\omega] \text{ in } \text{solve}(\sigma' \cdot \sigma; \ \bullet; \ \sigma'(\mathcal{Q}, \mathcal{P}))$

  $| \ \mathcal{O} \cup \delta \leqslant \mathcal{O}' \mapsto$

  $\qquad \text{if } \mathcal{O} \subseteq \mathcal{O}' \text{ then } \text{let } \sigma' = [\mathcal{O} \cup \omega'/\omega] \text{ in } \text{solve}(\sigma' \cdot \sigma; \ \mathcal{P}, (\omega' : \delta \leqslant \mathcal{O}'); \ \mathcal{Q}) \text{ else fail}$

  $| \ \mathcal{O} \leqslant \mathcal{O}' \mapsto \text{if } \mathcal{O} \subseteq \mathcal{O}' \text{ then } \text{let } \sigma' = [\mathcal{O} \cup \emptyset_{\mathcal{O}' \backslash \mathcal{O}}/\omega] \text{ in } \text{solve}(\sigma' \cdot \sigma; \ \mathcal{P}; \ \mathcal{Q}) \text{ else fail}$

  $| \ \mathcal{O} \leqslant \mathcal{O}' \cup \delta' \mapsto \text{let } \sigma' = [(\mathcal{O} \backslash \mathcal{O}') \cup \delta''/\delta'; \ \mathcal{O}' \cup \emptyset_{(\mathcal{O}' \backslash \mathcal{O}) \cup \delta''}/\omega] \text{ in}$
  $\qquad\qquad\qquad \text{solve}(\sigma' \cdot \sigma; \ \bullet; \ \sigma'(\mathcal{Q}, \mathcal{P}))$

If the two dirts are of the general form $\mathcal{O} \cup \delta$ and $\mathcal{O}' \cup \delta'$, we distinguish two subcases. Firstly, if $\mathcal{O}$ is empty, there is nothing to be done and we move the constraint to the processed set. Secondly, if $\mathcal{O}$ is non-empty, we partially instantiate δ' with any of the operations that appear in $\mathcal{O}$ but not in $\mathcal{O}'$. We then drop $\mathcal{O}$ from the constraint, and, after substitution, proceed with processing all constraints. For instance, for $\{\mathtt{Op}_1\} \cup \delta \leqslant \{\mathtt{Op}_2\} \cup \delta'$, we instantiate δ' to $\{\mathtt{Op}_1\} \cup \delta''$—where δ'' is a fresh dirt variable—and proceed with the simplified constraint $\delta \leqslant \{\mathtt{Op}_1, \mathtt{Op}_2\} \cup \delta''$. Note that due to the set semantics of dirts, it is not valid to simplify the above constraint to $\delta \leqslant \{\mathtt{Op}_2\} \cup \delta''$. After all the substitution $[\delta \mapsto \{\mathtt{Op}_1\}, \delta'' \mapsto \emptyset]$ solves the former and the original constraint, but not the latter.

The second case, $\emptyset \leqslant \Delta'$, always holds and is discharged by instantiating ω to $\emptyset_{\Delta'}$. The third case, $\delta \leqslant \emptyset$, has only one solution: $\delta \mapsto \emptyset$ with coercion $\emptyset_\emptyset$. The fourth case, $\mathcal{O} \cup \delta \leqslant \mathcal{O}'$, has as many solutions as there are subsets of $\mathcal{O}'$, provided that $\mathcal{O} \subseteq \mathcal{O}'$. We then simplify the constraint to $\delta \leqslant \mathcal{O}'$, which we move to the set of processed constraints. The fifth case, $\mathcal{O} \leqslant \mathcal{O}'$, holds iff $\mathcal{O} \subseteq \mathcal{O}'$. The last case, $\mathcal{O} \leqslant \mathcal{O}' \cup \delta'$, is like the first, but without a dirt variable in the left-hand side. We can satisfy it in a similar fashion, by partially instantiating δ' with $(\mathcal{O} \backslash \mathcal{O}') \cup \delta''$—where δ'' is a fresh dirt variable. Now the constraint is satisfied and can be discarded.

Terms

$\qquad\qquad \text{value } v ::= x \mid \text{unit} \mid h \mid \text{fun } (x : \tau) \mapsto c \mid \Lambda\varsigma.v \mid v \ \tau$
$\qquad\qquad \text{handler } h ::= \{\text{return } (x : \tau) \mapsto c_r, \mathtt{Op}_1 \ x \ k \mapsto c_{\mathtt{Op}_1}, \ldots, \mathtt{Op}_n \ x \ k \mapsto c_{\mathtt{Op}_n}\}$
$\qquad \text{computation } c ::= v_1 \ v_2 \mid \text{let } x = v \text{ in } c \mid \text{return } v \mid \mathtt{Op} \ v \ (y : \tau.c)$
$\qquad\qquad\qquad\qquad\quad | \ \text{do } x \leftarrow c_1; c_2 \mid \text{handle } c \text{ with } v$

Types

$\qquad\qquad \text{type } \tau ::= \varsigma \mid \tau_1 \to \tau_2 \mid \tau_1 \Rightarrow \tau_2 \mid \text{Unit} \mid \forall \varsigma.\tau$

Fig. 10. SKELEFF Syntax

5.4 Discussion

At first glance, the constraint generation algorithm of Sect. 5.2 might seem needlessly complex, due to eager constraint solving for let-generalization. Yet, we want to generalize at local `let`-bound values over both type and skeleton variables,[9] which means that we must solve all equations between skeletons before generalizing. In turn, since skeleton constraints are generated when solving subtyping constraints (Sect. 5.3), all skeleton annotations should be available during constraint solving. This can not be achieved unless the generated constraints are propagated statefully.

6 Erasure of Effect Information from ExEff

6.1 The SkelEff Language

The target of the erasure is SKELEFF, which is essentially a copy of EXEFF from which all effect information Δ, type information T and coercions γ have been removed. Instead, skeletons τ play the role of plain types. Thus, SKELEFF is essentially System F extended with term-level (but not type-level) support for algebraic effects. Figure 10 defines the syntax of SKELEFF. The type system and operational semantics of SKELEFF follow from those of EXEFF.

Discussion. The main point of SKELEFF is to show that we can erase the effects and subtyping from EXEFF to obtain types that are compatible with a System F-like language. At the term-level SKELEFF also resembles a subset of Multicore OCaml [6], which provides native support for algebraic effects and handlers but features no explicit polymorphism. Moreover, SKELEFF can also serve as a staging area for further elaboration into System F-like languages without support for algebraic effects and handlers (e.g., Haskell or regular OCaml). In those cases, computation terms can be compiled to one of the known encodings in the literature, such as a free monad representation [10,22], with delimited control [11], or using continuation-passing style [13], while values can typically be carried over as they are.

6.2 Erasure

Figure 11 defines erasure functions $\epsilon_v^\sigma(v)$, $\epsilon_c^\sigma(c)$, $\epsilon_V^\sigma(T)$, $\epsilon_C^\sigma(\underline{C})$ and $\epsilon_E^\sigma(\Gamma)$ for values, computations, value types, computation types, and type environments respectively. All five functions take a substitution σ from the free type variables α to their skeleton τ as an additional parameter.

Thanks to the skeleton-based design of EXEFF, erasure is straightforward. All types are erased to their skeletons, dropping quantifiers for type variables and all occurrences of dirt sets. Moreover, coercions are dropped from values

---

[9] As will become apparent in Sect. 6, if we only generalize at the top over skeleton variables, the erasure does not yield local polymorphism.

$$\epsilon_v^\sigma(x) = x$$
$$\epsilon_v^\sigma(\text{unit}) = \text{unit}$$
$$\epsilon_v^\sigma(v \rhd \gamma) = \epsilon_v^\sigma(v)$$
$$\epsilon_v^\sigma(\text{fun } (x : T) \mapsto c) = \text{fun } (x : \epsilon_V^\sigma(T)) \mapsto \epsilon_c^\sigma(c)$$
$$\epsilon_v^\sigma(\Lambda\varsigma.v) = \Lambda\varsigma.\epsilon_v^\sigma(v)$$
$$\epsilon_v^\sigma(\Lambda(\alpha : \tau).v) = \epsilon_v^{\sigma \cdot \{\alpha \mapsto \tau\}}(v)$$

$$\epsilon_v^\sigma(\Lambda\delta.v) = \epsilon_v^\sigma(v)$$
$$\epsilon_v^\sigma(\Lambda(\omega : \pi).v) = \epsilon_v^\sigma(v)$$
$$\epsilon_v^\sigma(v \ \tau) = \epsilon_v^\sigma(v) \ \tau$$
$$\epsilon_v^\sigma(v \ T) = \epsilon_v^\sigma(v)$$
$$\epsilon_v^\sigma(v \ \Delta) = \epsilon_v^\sigma(v)$$
$$\epsilon_v^\sigma(v \ \gamma) = \epsilon_v^\sigma(v)$$

$$\epsilon_v^\sigma(\{\text{return } (x : T) \mapsto c_r, [\text{Op } x \ k \mapsto c_{\text{Op}}]_{\text{Op} \in O}\}) =$$
$$\{\text{return } (x : \epsilon_V^\sigma(T)) \mapsto \epsilon_c^\sigma(c_r), [\text{Op } x \ k \mapsto \epsilon_c^\sigma(c_{\text{Op}})]_{\text{Op} \in O}\}$$

$$\epsilon_c^\sigma(v_1 \ v_2) = \epsilon_v^\sigma(v_1) \ \epsilon_v^\sigma(v_2)$$
$$\epsilon_c^\sigma(\text{let } x = v \text{ in } c) = \text{let } x = \epsilon_v^\sigma(v) \text{ in } \epsilon_c^\sigma(c)$$
$$\epsilon_c^\sigma(\text{return } v) = \text{return } (\epsilon_v^\sigma(v))$$
$$\epsilon_c^\sigma(\text{Op } v \ (y : T.c)) = \text{Op } (\epsilon_v^\sigma(v)) \ (y : \epsilon_V^\sigma(T).\epsilon_c^\sigma(c))$$
$$\epsilon_c^\sigma(\text{do } x \leftarrow c_1; c_2) = \text{do } x \leftarrow \epsilon_c^\sigma(c_1); \epsilon_c^\sigma(c_2)$$
$$\epsilon_c^\sigma(\text{handle } c \text{ with } v) = \text{handle } \epsilon_c^\sigma(c) \text{ with } \epsilon_v^\sigma(v)$$
$$\epsilon_c^\sigma(c \rhd \gamma) = \epsilon_c^\sigma(c)$$

$$\epsilon_V^\sigma(\alpha) = \sigma(\alpha)$$
$$\epsilon_V^\sigma(T \to \underline{C}) = \epsilon_V^\sigma(T) \to \epsilon_C^\sigma(\underline{C})$$
$$\epsilon_V^\sigma(\underline{C_1} \Rightarrow \underline{C_2}) = \epsilon_C^\sigma(\underline{C_1}) \Rightarrow \epsilon_C^\sigma(\underline{C_2})$$
$$\epsilon_V^\sigma(\text{Unit}) = \text{Unit}$$
$$\epsilon_V^\sigma(\pi \Rightarrow T) = \epsilon_V^\sigma(T)$$
$$\epsilon_V^\sigma(\forall\varsigma.T) = \forall\varsigma.\epsilon_V^\sigma(T)$$
$$\epsilon_V^\sigma(\forall(\alpha : \tau).T) = \epsilon_V^{\sigma \cdot \{\alpha \mapsto \tau\}}(T)$$
$$\epsilon_V^\sigma(\forall\delta.T) = \epsilon_V^\sigma(T)$$

$$\epsilon_C^\sigma(T \ ! \ \Delta) = \epsilon_V^\sigma(T)$$

$$\epsilon_E^\sigma(\epsilon) = \epsilon$$
$$\epsilon_E^\sigma(\Gamma, \varsigma) = \epsilon_E^\sigma(\Gamma), \varsigma$$
$$\epsilon_E^\sigma(\Gamma, \alpha : \tau) = \epsilon_E^{\sigma \cdot \{\alpha \mapsto \tau\}}(\Gamma)$$
$$\epsilon_E^\sigma(\Gamma, \delta) = \epsilon_E^\sigma(\Gamma)$$
$$\epsilon_E^\sigma(\Gamma, x : T) = \epsilon_E^\sigma(\Gamma), x : \epsilon_V^\sigma(T)$$
$$\epsilon_E^\sigma(\Gamma, \omega : \pi) = \epsilon_E^\sigma(\Gamma)$$

Fig. 11. Definition of type erasure.

and computations. Finally, all binders and elimination forms for type variables, dirt set variables and coercions are dropped from values and type environments.

The expected theorems hold. Firstly, types are preserved by erasure.[10]

Theorem 6 (Type Preservation). *If* $\Gamma \vdash_v v : T$ *then* $\epsilon_E^\emptyset(\Gamma) \vdash_{ev} \epsilon_v^\Gamma(v) : \epsilon_V^\Gamma(T)$. *If* $\Gamma \vdash_c c : \underline{C}$ *then* $\epsilon_E^\emptyset(\Gamma) \vdash_{ec} \epsilon_c^\Gamma(c) : \epsilon_C^\Gamma(\underline{C})$.

Here we abuse of notation and use Γ as a substitution from type variables to skeletons used by the erasure functions.

Finally, we have that erasure preserves the operational semantics.

Theorem 7 (Semantic Preservation). *If* $v \rightsquigarrow_v v'$ *then* $\epsilon_v^\sigma(v) \equiv_v^{\rightsquigarrow} \epsilon_v^\sigma(v')$. *If* $c \rightsquigarrow_c c'$ *then* $\epsilon_c^\sigma(c) \equiv_c^{\rightsquigarrow} \epsilon_c^\sigma(c')$.

In both cases, $\equiv^{\rightsquigarrow}$ denotes the congruence closure of the step relation in SKEL-EFF. The choice of substitution σ does not matter as types do not affect the behaviour.

---

[10] Typing for SKELEFF values and computations take the form $\Gamma \vdash_{ev} v : \tau$ and $\Gamma \vdash_{ec} c : \tau$.

Discussion. Typically, when type information is erased from call-by-value languages, type binders are erased by replacing them with other (dummy) binders. For instance, the expected definition of erasure would be:

$$\epsilon_v^\sigma(\Lambda(\alpha : \tau).v) = \lambda(x : \text{Unit}).\epsilon_v^\sigma(v)$$

This replacement is motivated by a desire to preserve the behaviour of the typed terms. By dropping binders, values might be turned into computations that trigger their side-effects immediately, rather than at the later point where the original binder was eliminated. However, there is no call for this circumspect approach in our setting, as our grammatical partition of terms in values (without side-effects) and computations (with side-effects) guarantees that this problem cannot happen when we erase values to values and computations to computations.

7   Related Work and Conclusion

Eff's Implicit Type System. The most closely related work is that of Pretnar [20] on inferring algebraic effects for Eff, which is the basis for our implicitly-typed IMPEFF calculus, its type system and the type inference algorithm. There are three major differences with Pretnar's inference algorithm.

Firstly, our work introduces an explicitly-typed calculus. For this reason we have extended the constraint generation phase with the elaboration into EXEFF and the constraint solving phase with the construction of coercions.

Secondly, we add skeletons to guarantee erasure. Skeletons also allow us to use standard occurs-check during unification. In contrast, unification in Pretnar's algorithm is inspired by Simonet [24] and performs the occurs-check up to the equivalence closure of the subtyping relation. In order to maintain invariants, all variables in an equivalence class (also called a skeleton) must be instantiated simultaneously, whereas we can process one constraint at a time. As these classes turn out to be surrogates for the underlying skeleton types, we have decided to keep the name.

Finally, Pretnar incorporates garbage collection of constraints [19]. The aim of this approach is to obtain unique and simple type schemes by eliminating redundant constraints. Garbage collection is not suitable for our use as type variables and coercions witnessing subtyping constraints cannot simply be dropped, but must be instantiated in a suitable manner, which cannot be done in general.

Consider for instance a situation with type variables α_1, α_2, α_3, α_4, and α_5 where $\alpha_1 \leqslant \alpha_3$, $\alpha_2 \leqslant \alpha_3$, $\alpha_3 \leqslant \alpha_4$, and $\alpha_3 \leqslant \alpha_5$. Suppose that α_3 does not appear in the type. Then garbage collection would eliminate it and replace the constraints by $\alpha_1 \leqslant \alpha_4$, $\alpha_2 \leqslant \alpha_4$, $\alpha_1 \leqslant \alpha_5$, and $\alpha_2 \leqslant \alpha_5$. While garbage collection guarantees that for any ground instantiation of the remaining type variables, there exists a valid ground instantiation for α_3, EXEFF would need to be extended with joins (or meets) to express a generically valid instantiation like $\alpha_1 \sqcup \alpha_2$. Moreover, we would need additional coercion formers to establish $\alpha_1 \leqslant (\alpha_1 \sqcup \alpha_2)$ or $(\alpha_1 \sqcup \alpha_2) \leqslant \alpha_4$.

As these additional constructs considerably complicate the calculus, we propose a simpler solution. We use EXEFF as it is for internal purposes, but display types to programmers in their garbage-collected form.

Calculi with Explicit Coercions. The notion of explicit coercions is not new; Mitchell [15] introduced the idea of inserting coercions during type inference for ML-based languages, as a means for explicit casting between different numeric types.

Breazu-Tannen et al. [3] also present a translation of languages with inheritance polymorphism into System F, extended with coercions. Although their coercion combinators are very similar to our coercion forms, they do not include inversion forms, which are crucial for the proof of type safety for our system. Moreover, Breazu-Tannen et al.'s coercions are terms, and thus can not be erased.

Much closer to EXEFF is Crary's coercion calculus for inclusive subtyping [4], from which we borrowed the stratification of value results. Crary's system supports neither coercion abstraction nor coercion inversion forms.

System F_C [25] uses explicit type-equality coercions to encode complex language features (e.g. GADTs [16] or type families [23]). Though EXEFF's coercions are proofs of subtyping rather than type equality, our system has a lot in common with it, including the inversion coercion forms and the "push" rules.

Future Work. Our plans focus on resuming the postponed work on efficient compilation of handlers. First, we intend to adjust program transformations to the explicit type information. We hope that this will not only make the optimizer more robust, but also expose new optimization opportunities. Next, we plan to write compilers to both Multicore OCaml and standard OCaml, though for the latter, we must first adapt the notion of erasure to a target calculus without algebraic effect handlers. Finally, once the compiler shows promising preliminary results, we plan to extend it to other Eff features such as user-defined types or recursion, allowing us to benchmark it on more realistic programs.

Acknowledgements. We would like to thank the anonymous reviewers for careful reading and insightful comments. Part of this work is funded by the Flemish Fund for Scientific Research (FWO). This material is based upon work supported by the Air Force Office of Scientific Research under award number FA9550-17-1-0326.

References

1. Barendregt, H.: The Lambda Calculus: Its Syntax and Semantics. Studies in Logic and the Foundations of Mathematics, vol. 3. North-Holland, Amsterdam (1981)
2. Bauer, A., Pretnar, M.: Programming with algebraic effects and handlers. J. Logic Algebraic Program. **84**(1), 108–123 (2015)
3. Breazu-Tannen, V., Coquand, T., Gunter, C.A., Scedrov, A.: Inheritance as implicit coercion. Inf. Comput. **93**, 172–221 (1991)
4. Crary, K.: Typed compilation of inclusive subtyping. In: Proceedings of the Fifth ACM SIGPLAN International Conference on Functional Programming, ICFP 2000, pp, 68–81. ACM, New York (2000)

5. Damas, L., Milner, R.: Principal type-schemes for functional programs. In: Proceedings of the 9th ACM SIGPLAN-SIGACT Symposium on Principles of Programming Languages, POPL 1982, pp. 207–212. ACM, New York (1982)

6. Dolan, S., White, L., Sivaramakrishnan, K., Yallop, J., Madhavapeddy, A.: Effective concurrency through algebraic effects. In: OCaml Workshop (2015)

7. Girard, J.-Y., Taylor, P., Lafont, Y.: Proofs and Types. Cambridge University Press, Cambridge (1989)

8. Hillerström, D., Lindley, S.: Liberating effects with rows and handlers. In: Chapman, J., Swierstra, W. (eds.) Proceedings of the 1st International Workshop on Type-Driven Development, TyDe@ICFP 2016, Nara, Japan, 18 September 2016, pp. 15–27. ACM (2016)

9. Jones, M.P.: A theory of qualified types. In: Krieg-Brückner, B. (ed.) ESOP 1992. LNCS, vol. 582, pp. 287–306. Springer, Heidelberg (1992). https://doi.org/10.1007/3-540-55253-7_17

10. Kammar, O., Lindley, S., Oury, N.: Handlers in action. In: Proceedings of the 18th ACM SIGPLAN International Conference on Functional programming, ICFP 2014, pp. 145–158. ACM (2013)

11. Kiselyov, O., Sivaramakrishnan, K.: Eff directly in OCaml. In: OCaml Workshop (2016)

12. Leijen, D.: Koka: programming with row polymorphic effect types. In: Levy, P., Krishnaswami, N. (eds.) Proceedings of 5th Workshop on Mathematically Structured Functional Programming, MSFP@ETAPS 2014, Grenoble, France, 12 April 2014. EPTCS, vol. 153, pp. 100–126 (2014)

13. Leijen, D.: Type directed compilation of row-typed algebraic effects. In: Castagna, G., Gordon, A.D. (eds.) Proceedings of the 44th ACM SIGPLAN Symposium on Principles of Programming Languages, POPL 2017, Paris, France, 18–20 January 2017, pp. 486–499. ACM (2017)

14. Lindley, S., McBride, C., McLaughlin, C.: Do be do be do. In: Castagna, G., Gordon, A.D. (eds.) Proceedings of the 44th ACM SIGPLAN Symposium on Principles of Programming Languages, POPL 2017, Paris, France, 18–20 January 2017, pp. 500–514. ACM (2017). http://dl.acm.org/citation.cfm?id=3009897

15. Mitchell, J.C.: Coercion and type inference. In: Proceedings of the 11th ACM SIGACT-SIGPLAN Symposium on Principles of Programming Languages, POPL 1984, pp. 175–185. ACM, New York (1984)

16. Peyton Jones, S., Vytiniotis, D., Weirich, S., Washburn, G.: Simple unification-based type inference for GADTs. In: ICFP 2006 (2006)

17. Plotkin, G.D., Power, J.: Algebraic operations and generic effects. Appl. Categ. Struct. 11(1), 69–94 (2003)

18. Plotkin, G.D., Pretnar, M.: Handling algebraic effects. Log. Methods Comput. Sci. 9(4) (2013)

19. Pottier, F.: Simplifying subtyping constraints: a theory. Inf. Comput. 170(2), 153–183 (2001). https://doi.org/10.1006/inco.2001.2963

20. Pretnar, M.: Inferring algebraic effects. Log. Methods Comput. Sci. 10(3) (2014)

21. Pretnar, M.: An introduction to algebraic effects and handlers, invited tutorial. Electron. Notes Theoret. Comput. Sci. 319, 19–35 (2015)

22. Pretnar, M., Saleh, A.H., Faes, A., Schrijvers, T.: Efficient compilation of algebraic effects and handlers. Technical report CW 708, KU Leuven Department of Computer Science (2017)

23. Schrijvers, T., Peyton Jones, S., Chakravarty, M., Sulzmann, M.: Type checking with open type functions. In: ICFP 2008, pp. 51–62. ACM (2008)

24. Simonet, V.: Type inference with structural subtyping: a faithful formalization of an efficient constraint solver. In: Ohori, A. (ed.) APLAS 2003. LNCS, vol. 2895, pp. 283–302. Springer, Heidelberg (2003). https://doi.org/10.1007/978-3-540-40018-9_19
25. Sulzmann, M., Chakravarty, M.M.T., Peyton Jones, S., Donnelly, K.: System F with type equality coercions. In: Proceedings of the 2007 ACM SIGPLAN International Workshop on Types in Languages Design and Implementation, TLDI 2007, pp. 53–66. ACM, New York (2007)
26. Wansbrough, K., Peyton Jones, S.L.: Once upon a polymorphic type. In: POPL, pp. 15–28. ACM (1999)

Concurrency

A Separation Logic for a Promising Semantics

Kasper Svendsen[1], Jean Pichon-Pharabod[1], Marko Doko[2]($^{(\boxtimes)}$), Ori Lahav[3],
and Viktor Vafeiadis[2]

[1] University of Cambridge, Cambridge, UK
[2] MPI-SWS, Kaiserslautern and Saarbrücken, Germany
mdoko@mpi-sws.org
[3] Tel Aviv University, Tel Aviv, Israel

Abstract. We present SLR, the first expressive program logic for reasoning about concurrent programs under a weak memory model addressing the out-of-thin-air problem. Our logic includes the standard features from existing logics, such as RSL and GPS, that were previously known to be sound only under stronger memory models: (1) separation, (2) per-location invariants, and (3) ownership transfer via release-acquire synchronisation—as well as novel features for reasoning about (4) the absence of out-of-thin-air behaviours and (5) coherence. The logic is proved sound over the recent "promising" memory model of Kang et al., using a substantially different argument to soundness proofs of logics for simpler memory models.

1 Introduction

Recent years have seen the emergence of several program logics [2,6,8,16,23,24, 26–28] for reasoning about programs under weak memory models. These program logics are valuable tools for structuring program correctness proofs, and enabling programmers to reason about the correctness of their programs without necessarily knowing the formal semantics of the programming language. So far, however, they have only been applied to relatively strong memory models (such as TSO [19] or release/acquire consistency [15] that can be expressed as a constraint on individual candidate program executions) and provide little to no reasoning principles to deal with C/C++ "relaxed" accesses.

The main reason for this gap is that the behaviour of relaxed accesses is notoriously hard to specify [3,5]. Up until recently, memory models have either been too strong (e.g., [5,14,17]), forbidding some behaviours observed with modern hardware and compilers, or they have been too weak (e.g., [4]), allowing so-called out-of-thin-air (OOTA) behaviour even though it does not occur in practice and is highly problematic.

One observable behaviour forbidden by the strong models is the load buffering behaviour illustrated by the example below, which, when started with both locations x and y containing 0, can end with both r_1 and r_2 containing 1.

© The Author(s) 2018
A. Ahmed (Ed.): ESOP 2018, LNCS 10801, pp. 357–384, 2018.
https://doi.org/10.1007/978-3-319-89884-1_13

This behaviour is observable on certain ARMv7 processors after the compiler optimises $r_2 + 1 - r_2$ to 1.

$$\begin{array}{ll} r_1 := [x]_{\mathtt{rlx}}; \; // \text{ reads } 1 \; \Big\| \; r_2 := [y]_{\mathtt{rlx}}; \; // \text{ reads } 1 \\ [y]_{\mathtt{rlx}} := r_1 \Big\| \; [x]_{\mathtt{rlx}} := r_2 + 1 - r_2 \end{array} \qquad \text{(LB+data+fakedep)}$$

However, one OOTA behaviour they should not allow is the following example by Boehm and Demsky [5]. When started with two completely disjoint lists a and b, by updating them separately in parallel, it should not be allowed to end with a and b pointing to each other, as that would violate physical separation (for simplicity, in these lists, a location just holds the address of the next element):

$$\begin{array}{ll} r_1 := [a]_{\mathtt{rlx}}; \; // \text{ reads } b \; \Big\| \; r_2 := [b]_{\mathtt{rlx}}; \; // \text{ reads } a \\ [r_1]_{\mathtt{rlx}} := a \Big\| \; [r_2]_{\mathtt{rlx}} := b \end{array} \qquad \text{(Disjoint-Lists)}$$

Because of this specification gap, program logics either do not reason about relaxed accesses, or they assume overly strengthened models that disallow some behaviours that occur in practice (as discussed in Sect. 5).

Recently, there have been several proposals of programming language memory models that allow load buffering behaviour, but forbid obvious out-of-thin-air behaviours [10,13,20]. This development has enabled us to develop a program logic that provides expressive reasoning principles for relaxed accesses, without relying on overly strong models.

In this paper, we present SLR, a separation logic based on RSL [27], extended with strong reasoning principles for relaxed accesses, which we prove sound over the recent "promising" semantics of Kang et al. [13]. SLR features per-location invariants [27] and physical separation [22], as well as novel assertions that we use to show the absence of *OOTA behaviours* and to reason about various *coherence* examples. (Coherence is a property of memory models that requires the existence of a per-location total order on writes that reads respect.)

There are two main contributions of this work.

First, SLR is the first logic which can prove absence of OOTA in all the standard litmus tests. As such, it provides more evidence to the claim that the promising semantics solves the out-of-thin-air problem in a satisfactory way. The paper that introduced the promising semantics [13] comes with three DRF theorems and a simplistic value logic. These reasoning principles are enough to show absence of some simple out-of-thin-air behaviours, but it is still very easy to end up beyond the reasoning power of these two techniques. For instance, they cannot be used to prove that $r_1 = 0$ in the following "random number generator" litmus test[1], where both the x and y locations initially hold 0.

$$\begin{array}{ll} r_1 := [x]_{\mathtt{rlx}}; \; \Big\| \; r_2 := [y]_{\mathtt{rlx}}; \\ [y]_{\mathtt{rlx}} := r_1 + 1 \; \Big\| \; [x]_{\mathtt{rlx}} := r_2 \end{array} \qquad \text{(RNG)}$$

The subtlety of this litmus test is the following: if the first thread reads a certain value v from x, then it writes $v + 1$ to y, which the second thread can read, and

---

[1] The litmus test is called this way because some early attempts to solve the OOTA problem allowed this example to return arbitrary values for x and y.

write to x; this, however, does not enable the first thread to read $v + 1$. SLR features novel assertions that allow it to handle those and other examples, as shown in the following section.

The second major contribution is the proof of soundness of SLR over the promising semantics [13][2]. The promising semantics is an operational model that represents memory as a collection of timestamped write messages. Besides the usual steps that execute the next command of a thread, the model has a non-standard step that allows a thread to promise to perform a write in the future, provided that it can guarantee to be able to fulfil its promise. After a write is promised, other threads may read from that write as if it had already happened. Promises allow the load-store reordering needed to exhibit the load buffering behaviour above, and yet seem, from a series of litmus tests, constrained enough so as to not introduce out-of-thin-air behaviour.

Since the promising model is rather different from all other (operational and axiomatic) memory models for which a program logic has been developed, none of the existing approaches for proving soundness of concurrent program logics are applicable to our setting. Two key difficulties in the soundness proof come from dealing with promise steps.

1. Promises are very non-modular, as they can occur at every execution point and can affect locations that may only be accessed much later in the program.
2. Since promised writes can be immediately read by other threads, the soundness proof has to impose the same invariants on promised writes as the ones it imposes on ordinary writes (e.g., that only values satisfying the location's protocol are written). In a logic supporting ownership transfer,[3] however, establishing those invariants is challenging, because a thread may promise to write to x even without having permission to write to x.

To deal with the first challenge, our proof decouples promising steps from ordinary execution steps. We define two semantics of Hoare triples—one "promising", with respect to the full promising semantics, and one "non-promising", with respect to the promising semantics without promising steps—and prove that every Hoare triple that is correct with respect to its non-promising interpretation is also correct with respect to its promising interpretation. This way, we modularise reasoning about promise steps. Even in the non-promising semantics, however, we do allow threads to have outstanding promises. The main difference in the non-promising semantics is that threads are not allowed to issue new promises.

To resolve the second challenge, we observe that in programs verified by SLR, a thread may promise to write to x only if it is able to acquire the necessary write permission before performing the actual write. This follows from promise

---

[2] As the promising semantics comes with formal proofs of correctness of all the expected local program transformations and of compilation schemes to the x86-TSO, Power, and ARMv8-POP architectures [21], SLR is sound for these architectures too.

[3] Supporting ownership transfer is necessary to provide useful rules for C11 release and acquire accesses.

$$e \in Expr ::= n \qquad \text{integer} \qquad s \in Stm ::= \textbf{skip} \mid s_1; s_2 \mid \textbf{if } e \textbf{ then } s_1 \textbf{ else } s_2$$
$$\mid r \qquad \text{register} \qquad \mid \textbf{while } e \textbf{ do } s \mid r := e \mid r := [e]_{\text{rlx}}$$
$$\mid e_1 \ op \ e_2 \ \text{arithmetic} \qquad \mid r := [e]_{\text{acq}} \mid [e_1]_{\text{rlx}} := e_2 \mid [e_1]_{\text{rel}} := e_2$$

Fig. 1. Syntax of the programming language.

certification: the promising semantics requires all promises to be certifiable; that is, for every state of the promising machine, there must exist a non-promising execution of the machine that fulfils all outstanding promises.

We present the SLR assertions and rules informally in Sect. 2. We then give an overview of the promising semantics of Kang et al. [13] in Sect. 3, and use it in Sect. 4 to explain the proof of soundness of SLR. We discuss related work in Sect. 5. *Details of the rules of SLR and its soundness proof can be found in our technical appendix* [1].

2 Our Logic

The novelty of our program logic is to allow non-trivial reasoning about relaxed accesses. Unlike release/acquire accesses, relaxed accesses do not induce synchronisation between threads, so the usual approach of program logics, which relies on ownership transfer, does not apply. Therefore, in addition to reasoning about ownership transfer like a standard separation logic, our logic supports reasoning about relaxed accesses by collecting information about what reads have been observed, and in which order. When combined with information about which writes have been performed, we can deduce that certain executions are impossible.

For concreteness, we consider a minimal "WHILE" programming language with expressions, $e \in Expr$, and statements, $s \in Stm$, whose syntax is given in Fig. 1. Besides local register assignments, statements also include memory reads with relaxed or acquire mode, and memory writes with relaxed or release mode.

2.1 The Assertions of the Logic

The SLR assertion language is generated by the following grammar, where N, l, v, t, π and X all range over a simply-typed term language which we assume includes booleans, locations, values and expressions of the programming language, fractional permissions, and timestamps, and is closed under pairing, finite sets, and sequences. By convention, we assume that l, v, t, π and X range over terms of type location, value, timestamp, permission and sets of pairs of values, and timestamps, respectively.

$$P, Q \in Assn ::= \bot \mid \top \mid P \lor Q \mid P \land Q \mid P \Rightarrow Q \mid \forall x.\, P \mid \exists x.\, P \mid N_1 = N_2 \mid \phi(N)$$
$$\mid P * Q \mid \mathsf{Rel}(l, \phi) \mid \mathsf{Acq}(l, \phi) \mid \mathsf{O}(l, v, t) \mid \mathsf{W}^\pi(l, X) \mid \nabla P$$

$$\phi \in Pred ::= \lambda x.\, P$$

The grammar contains the standard operators from first order logic and separation logic, the Rel and Acq assertions from RSL [27], and a few novel constructs.

Rel(l, ϕ) grants permission to perform a release write to location l and transfer away the invariant $\phi(v)$, where v is the value written to that location. Conversely, Acq(l, ϕ) grants permission to perform an acquire read from location l and gain access to the invariant $\phi(v)$, where v is the value returned by the read.

The first novel assertion form, O(l, v, t), records the fact that location l was observed to have value v at timestamp t. The timestamp is used to order it with other reads from the same location. The information this assertion provides is very weak: it merely says that the owner of the assertion has observed that value, it does not imply that any other thread has ever observed it.

The other novel assertion form, W$^\pi(l, X)$, asserts ownership of location l and records a set of writes X to that location. The fractional permission $\pi \in \mathbb{Q}$ indicates whether ownership is shared or exclusive. Full permission, $\pi = 1$, confers exclusive ownership of location l and ensures that X is the set of all writes to location l; any fraction, $0 < \pi < 1$, confers shared ownership and enforces that X is a lower-bound on the set of writes to location l. The order of writes to l is tracked through timestamps; the set X is thus a set of pairs consisting of the value and the timestamp of the write.

In examples where we only need to refer to the order of writes and not the exact timestamps, we write W$^\pi(x, \ell)$, where $\ell = [v_1, ..., v_n]$ is a list of values, as shorthand for $\exists t_1, ..., t_n. t_1 > t_2 > \cdots > t_n * W^\pi(x, \{(v_1, t_1), ..., (v_n, t_n)\})$. The W$^\pi(x, \ell)$ assertion thus expresses ownership of location x with permission π, and that the writes to x are given by the list ℓ in order, with the most recent write at the front of the list.

Relation Between Reads and Writes. Records of reads and writes can be confronted by the thread owning the exclusive write assertion: all reads must have read values that were written. This is captured formally by the following property:

$$\text{W}^1(x, X) * \text{O}(x, a, t) \Rightarrow \text{W}^1(x, X) * \text{O}(x, a, t) * (a, t) \in X \quad \text{(Reads-from-Write)}$$

Random Number Generator. These assertions allow us to reason about the "random number generator" litmus test from the Introduction, and to show that it cannot read arbitrarily large values. As discussed in the Introduction, capturing the set of values that are written to x, as made possible by the "invariant-based program logic" of Kang et al. [13, Sect. 5.5] and of Jeffrey and Riley [10, Sect. 6], is not enough, and we make use of our stronger reasoning principles. We use O(x, a, t) to record what values reads read from each location, and W$^1(x, \ell)$ to record what sequences of values were written to each location, and then confront these records at the end of the execution. The proof sketch is then as follows:

$$\{\text{W}^1(y, [0]) * \ldots\} \quad \| \quad \{\text{W}^1(x, [0]) * \ldots\}$$
$$r_1 := [x]_{\texttt{rlx}}; \quad \| \quad r_2 := [y]_{\texttt{rlx}};$$
$$\{\text{W}^1(y, [0]) * \text{O}(x, r_1, \_) * \ldots\} \quad \| \quad \{\text{W}^1(x, [0]) * \text{O}(y, r_2, \_) * \ldots\}$$
$$[y]_{\texttt{rlx}} := r_1 + 1 \quad \| \quad [x]_{\texttt{rlx}} := r_2$$
$$\{\text{W}^1(y, [r_1 + 1; 0]) * \text{O}(x, r_1, \_) * \ldots\} \quad \| \quad \{\text{W}^1(x, [r_2; 0]) * \text{O}(y, r_2, \_) * \ldots\}$$

At the end of the execution, we are able to draw conclusions about the values of the registers. From $W^1(x, [r_2; 0])$ and $O(x, r_1, \_)$, we know that $r_1 \in \{r_2, 0\}$ by rule Reads-from-Write. Similarly, we know that $r_2 \in \{r_1 + 1, 0\}$, and so we can conclude that $r_1 = 0$. We discuss the distribution of resources at the beginning of a program, and their collection at the end of a program, in Theorem 2. Note that we are unable to establish what values the reads read before the end of the litmus test. Indeed, before the end of the execution, nothing enforces that there are no further writes that reads could read from.

2.2 The Rules of the Logic for Relaxed Accesses

We now introduce the rules of our logic by focusing on the rules for *relaxed* accesses. In addition, we support the standard rules from separation logic and Hoare logic, rules for release/acquire accesses (Sect. 2.4), and the following consequence rule:

$$\frac{P \Rrightarrow P' \quad \{P'\}\, c\, \{Q'\} \quad Q' \Rrightarrow Q}{\vdash \{P\}\, c\, \{Q\}} \tag{CONSEQ}$$

which allows one to use "view shifting" implications to strengthen the precondition and weaken the postcondition.

The rules for relaxed accesses are adapted from the rules of RSL [27] for release/acquire accesses, but use our novel resources to track the more subtle behaviour of relaxed accesses. Since relaxed accesses do not introduce synchronisation, they cannot be used to transfer ownership; they can, however, be used to transfer information. For this reason, as in RSL [27], we associate a predicate ϕ on values to a location x using paired $\mathsf{Rel}(x, \phi)$ and $\mathsf{Acq}(x, \phi)$ resources, for writers and readers, respectively. To write v to x, a writer has to provide $\phi(v)$, and in exchange, when reading v from x, a reader obtains $\phi(v)$. However, here, relaxed writes can only send *pure* predicates (i.e., ones which do not assert ownership of any resources), and relaxed reads can only obtain the assertion from the predicate guarded by a modality ∇[4] that only pure assertions filter through: if P is pure, then $\nabla P \Longrightarrow P$. All assertions expressible in first-order logic are pure.

Relaxed Write Rule. To write value v (to which the value expression e_2 evaluates) to location x (to which the location expression e_1 evaluates), the thread needs to own a write permission $W^\pi(x, X)$. Moreover, it needs to provide $\phi(v)$, the assertion associated to the written value, v, to location x by the $\mathsf{Rel}(x, \phi)$ assertion. Because the write is a relaxed write, and therefore does not induce synchronisation, $\phi(v)$ has to be a pure predicate. The write rule updates the record of writes with the value written, timestamped with a timestamp newer than any timestamp for that location that the thread has observed so far; this is expressed by relating it to a previous timestamp that the thread has to provide through an $O(x, \_, t)$ assertion in the precondition.

---

[4] This ∇ modality is similar in spirit, but weaker than that of FSL [8].

$$\frac{\phi(v) \text{ is pure}}{\vdash \left\{ \begin{array}{l} e_1 = x * e_2 = v * W^\pi(x, X) \\ {} * \text{Rel}(x, \phi) * \phi(v) * O(x, \_, t) \end{array} \right\} [e_1]_{\text{rlx}} := e_2 \left\{ \begin{array}{l} \exists t' > t. \\ W^\pi(x, \{(v, t')\} \cup X) \end{array} \right\}} \quad \text{(W-RLX)}$$

The $\text{Rel}(x, \phi)$ assertion is duplicable, so there is no need for the rule to keep it.

In practice, $O(x, \_, t)$ is taken to be that of the last read from x if it was the last operation on x, and $O(x, \mathit{fst}(\max(X)), \mathit{snd}(\max(X)))$ if the last operation on x was a write, including the initial write. The latter can be obtained by

$$W^\pi(x, X) * (v, t) \in X \Rightarrow W^\pi(x, X) * O(x, v, t) \qquad \text{(Write-Observed)}$$

Relaxed Read Rule. To read from location x (to which the location expression e evaluates), the thread needs to own an $\text{Acq}(x, \phi)$ assertion, which gives it the right to (almost) obtain assertion $\phi(v)$ upon reading value v from location x. The thread then keeps its $\text{Acq}(x, \phi)$, and obtains an assertion $O(x, r, t')$ stating that it has read the value now in register r from location x, timestamped with t'. This timestamp is no older than any timestamp for that location that the thread has observed so far, expressed again by relating it to an $O(x, \_, t)$ assertion in the precondition. Moreover, it obtains the pure portion $\nabla\phi(r)$ of the assertion $\phi(r)$ corresponding to the value read in register r

$$\vdash \left\{ e = x * \text{Acq}(x, \phi) * O(x, \_, t) \right\}$$
$$r := [e]_{\text{rlx}} \qquad\qquad\qquad\qquad \text{(R-RLX)}$$
$$\left\{ \exists t' \geq t.\ \text{Acq}(x, \phi) * O(x, r, t') * \nabla\phi(r) \right\}$$

Again, we can obtain $O(x, v_0^x, 0)$, where v_0^x is the initial value of x, from the initial write permission for x, and distribute it to all the threads that will read from x, expressing the fact that the initial value is available to all threads, and use it as the required $O(x, \_, t)$ in the precondition of the read rule.

Moreover, if a thread owns the exclusive write permission for a location x, then it can take advantage of the fact that it is the only writer at that location to obtain more precise information about its reads from that location: they will read the last value it has written to that location.

$$\vdash \left\{ e = x * \text{Acq}(x, \phi) * W^1(x, X) \right\}$$
$$r := [e]_{\text{rlx}} \qquad\qquad\qquad\qquad\qquad\qquad \text{(R-RLX*)}$$
$$\left\{ \exists t.\ (r, t) = \max(X) * \text{Acq}(x, \phi) * W^1(x, X) * O(x, r, t) * \nabla\phi(r) \right\}$$

Separation. With these assertions, we can straightforwardly specify and verify the Disjoint-Lists example. Ownership of an element of a list is simply expressed using a full write permission, $W^1(x, X)$. This allows including the Disjoint-Lists as a snippet in a larger program where the lists can be shared before or after, and still enforce the separation property we want to establish. While this reasoning sounds underwhelming (and we elide the details), we remark that it is unsound in models that allow OOTA behaviours.

2.3 Reasoning About Coherence

An important feature of many memory models is coherence, that is, the existence of a per-location total order on writes that reads respect. Coherence becomes interesting where there are multiple simultaneous writers to the same location (write/write races). In our logic, write assertions can be split and combined as follows: if $\pi_1 + \pi_2 \leq 1$, $0 < \pi_1$ and $0 < \pi_2$ then

$$\mathsf{W}^{\pi_1+\pi_2}(x, X_1 \cup X_2) \Leftrightarrow \mathsf{W}^{\pi_1}(x, X_1) * \mathsf{W}^{\pi_2}(x, X_2) \qquad \text{(Combine-Writes)}$$

To reason about coherence, the following rules capture the fact that the timestamps of the writes at a given location are all distinct, and totally ordered:

$$\mathsf{W}^{\pi}(x, X) * (v, t) \in X * (v', t') \in X * v \neq v' \Rightarrow \mathsf{W}^{\pi}(x, X) * t \neq t'$$
$$\text{(Different-Writes)}$$

$$\mathsf{W}^{\pi}(x, X) * (\_, t) \in X * (\_, t') \in X \Rightarrow \mathsf{W}^{\pi}(x, X) * (t < t' \vee t = t' \vee t' < t)$$
$$\text{(Writes-Ordered)}$$

CoRR2. One of the basic tests of coherence is the CoRR2 litmus test, which tests whether two threads can disagree on the order of two writes to the same location. The following program, starting with location x holding 0, should not be allowed to finish with $r_1 = 1 * r_2 = 2 * r_3 = 2 * r_4 = 1$, as that would mean that the third thread sees the write of 1 to x before the write of 2 to x, but that the fourth thread sees the write of 2 before the write of 1:

$$[x]_{\mathtt{rlx}} := 1 \;\Big\|\; [x]_{\mathtt{rlx}} := 2 \;\Big\|\; \begin{array}{l} r_1 := [x]_{\mathtt{rlx}}; \\ r_2 := [x]_{\mathtt{rlx}} \end{array} \Big\|\; \begin{array}{l} r_3 := [x]_{\mathtt{rlx}}; \\ r_4 := [x]_{\mathtt{rlx}} \end{array} \qquad \text{(CoRR2)}$$

Coherence enforces a total order on the writes to x that is respected by the reads, so if the third thread reads 1 then 2, then the fourth cannot read 2 then 1.

We use the timestamps in the $\mathsf{O}(x, a, t)$ assertions to record the order in which reads read values, and then link the timestamps of the reads with those of the writes. Because we do not transfer anything, the predicate for x is $\lambda v.\, \top$ again, and we elide the associated clutter below.

The proof outline for the writers just records what values have been written:

$$
\begin{array}{l}
\{\mathsf{W}^{1/2}(x, \{(0,0)\}) * \ldots\} \\
{[x]_{\mathtt{rlx}} := 1} \\
\{\exists t_1.\, \mathsf{W}^{1/2}(x, \{(1, t_1), (0,0)\}) * \ldots\}
\end{array}
\;\Big\|\;
\begin{array}{l}
\{\mathsf{W}^{1/2}(x, \{(0,0)\}) * \ldots\} \\
{[x]_{\mathtt{rlx}} := 2} \\
\{\exists t_2.\, \mathsf{W}^{1/2}(x, \{(2, t_2), (0,0)\}) * \ldots\}
\end{array}
$$

The proof outline for the readers just records what values have been read, and—crucially—in which order.

$$
\Big\|\;
\begin{array}{l}
\{\mathsf{Acq}(x, \lambda v.\, \top) * \mathsf{O}(x, 0, 0)\} \\
r_1 := [x]_{\mathtt{rlx}}; \\
\{\exists t_a.\, \mathsf{Acq}(x, \lambda v.\, \top) * \mathsf{O}(x, r_1, t_a) * 0 \leq t_a * \ldots\} \\
r_2 := [x]_{\mathtt{rlx}} \\
\{\exists t_a, t_b.\, \mathsf{O}(x, r_1, t_a) * \mathsf{O}(x, r_2, t_b) * 0 \leq t_a * t_a \leq t_b\}
\end{array}
\;\Big\|\;
\begin{array}{l}
r_3 := [x]_{\mathtt{rlx}}; \\
r_4 := [x]_{\mathtt{rlx}}
\end{array}
\;\Big\|\;
$$

At the end of the program, by combining the two write permissions using rule Combine-Writes, we obtain $W^1(x, \{(1, t_1), (2, t_2), (0, 0)\})$. From this, we have $t_1 < t_2$ or $t_2 < t_1$ by rules Different-Writes and Writes-Ordered. Now, assuming $r_1 = 1$ and $r_2 = 2$, we have $t_a < t_b$, and so $t_1 < t_2$ by rule Reads-from-Write. Similarly, assuming $r_3 = 2$ and $r_4 = 1$, we have $t_2 < t_1$. Therefore, we cannot have $r_1 = 1 * r_2 = 2 * r_3 = 2 * r_4 = 1$, so coherence is respected, as desired.

2.4 Handling Release and Acquire Accesses

Next, consider release and acquire accesses, which, in addition to coherence, provide synchronisation and enable the message passing idiom.

$$[x]_{\text{rlx}} := 1; \; \left\| \; \begin{array}{l} r_1 := [y]_{\text{acq}}; \\ \text{if } r_1 = 1 \text{ then } r_2 := [x]_{\text{rlx}} \end{array} \right. \tag{MP}$$
$$[y]_{\text{rel}} := 1$$

The first thread writes data (here, 1) to a location x, and signals that the data is ready by writing 1 to a "flag" location y with a release write. The second thread reads the flag location y with an acquire read, and, if it sees that the first thread has signalled that the data has been written, reads the data. The release/acquire pair is sufficient to ensure that the data is then visible to the second thread.

Release/acquire can be understood abstractly in terms of views [15]: a release write contains the view of the writing thread at the time of the writing, and an acquire read updates the view of the reading thread with that of the release write it is reading from. This allows one-way synchronisation of views between threads.

To handle release/acquire accesses in SLR, we can adapt the rules for relaxed accesses by enabling ownership transfer according to predicate associated with the Rel and Acq permissions. The resulting rules are strictly more powerful than the corresponding RSL [27] rules, as they also allow us to reason about coherence.

Release Write Rule. The release write rule is the same as for relaxed writes, but does not require the predicate to be a pure predicate, thereby allowing sending of actual resources, rather than just information:

$$\vdash \; \begin{array}{l} \{e_1 = x * e_2 = v * W^\pi(x, X) * \text{Rel}(x, \phi) * \phi(v) * O(x, \_, t)\} \\[4pt] [e_1]_{\text{rel}} := e_2 \\[4pt] \{\exists t' \geq t. \; W^\pi(x, \{(v, t')\} \cup X)\} \end{array} \tag{W-REL}$$

Acquire Read Rule. Symmetrically, the acquire read rule is the same as for relaxed reads, but allows the actual resource to be obtained, not just its pure portion:

$$\vdash \; \begin{array}{l} \{e = x * \text{Acq}(x, \phi) * O(x, \_, t)\} \\[4pt] r := [e]_{\text{acq}} \\[4pt] \{\exists t' \geq t. \; \text{Acq}(x, \phi[r \mapsto \top]) * O(x, r, t') * \phi(r)\} \end{array} \tag{R-ACQ}$$

We have to update ϕ to record the fact that we have obtained the resource associated with reading that value, so that we do not erroneously obtain that resource twice; $\phi[v' \mapsto P]$ stands for $\lambda v.$ *if* $v = v'$ *then* P *else* $\phi(v)$.

As for relaxed accesses, we can strengthen the read rule when the reader is also the exclusive writer to that location:

$$\vdash \left\{ \mathsf{Acq}(x, \phi) * \mathsf{W}^1(x, X) \right\}$$
$$r := [x]_{\mathsf{acq}}$$
$$\left\{ \begin{array}{l} \exists t.\ (r, t) = \max(X) * \mathsf{Acq}(x, \phi[r \mapsto \top]) \\ \qquad * \mathsf{W}^1(x, X) * \mathsf{O}(x, r, t) * \phi(r) \end{array} \right\} \qquad (\text{R-ACQ*})$$

Additionally, we allow duplicating of release assertions and splitting of acquire assertions, as expressed by the following two rules.

$$\mathsf{Rel}(x, \phi) \Leftrightarrow \mathsf{Rel}(x, \phi) * \mathsf{Rel}(x, \phi) \qquad (\text{Release-Duplicate})$$
$$\mathsf{Acq}(x, \lambda v.\ \phi_1(v) * \phi_2(v)) \Rightarrow \mathsf{Acq}(x, \phi_1) * \mathsf{Acq}(x, \phi_2) \qquad (\text{Acquire-Split})$$

Message Passing. With these rules, we can easify verify the message passing example. Here, we want to transfer a resource from the writer to the reader, namely the state of the data, x. By transferring the write permission for the data to the reader over the "flag" location, y, we allow the reader to use it to read the data precisely. We do that by picking the predicate

$$\phi_y = \lambda v.\ v = 1 \wedge \mathsf{W}^1(x, [1; 0]) \vee v \neq 1$$

for y. Since we do not transfer any resource using x, the predicate for x is $\lambda v. \top$.

The writer transfers the write permissions for x away on y using ϕ_y:

$$\left\{ \mathsf{W}^1(x, [0]) * \mathsf{Rel}(x, \lambda v. \top) * \mathsf{W}^1(y, [0]) * \mathsf{Rel}(y, \phi_y) \right\}$$
$$[x]_{\mathtt{rlx}} := 1;$$
$$\left\{ \mathsf{W}^1(x, [1; 0]) * \mathsf{W}^1(y, [0]) * \mathsf{Rel}(y, \phi_y) \right\}$$
$$\qquad \left\{ \mathsf{W}^1(y, \{(0,0)\}) * \mathsf{Rel}(y, \phi_y) * \phi_y(1) * \mathsf{O}(x, 0, 0) \right\}$$
$$[y]_{\mathtt{rel}} := 1$$
$$\qquad \left\{ \exists t_1.\ \mathsf{W}^1(y, \{(1, t_1)\} \cup \{(0, 0)\}) * 0 < t_1 \right\}$$
$$\left\{ \mathsf{W}^1(y, [1; 0]) * \mathsf{Rel}(y, \phi_y) \right\}$$

The proof outline for the reader uses the acquire permission ϕ_y for y to obtain $\mathsf{W}^1(x, [1; 0])$, which it then uses to know that it reads 1 from x.

$$\left\{ \mathsf{Acq}(y, \phi_y)) * \mathsf{O}(y, 0, 0) * \mathsf{Acq}(x, \lambda v. \top) \right\}$$
$$r_1 := [y]_{\mathsf{acq}};$$
$$\left\{ \exists t_1^y \geq 0.\ \mathsf{Acq}(y, \phi_y[r_1 \mapsto \top]) * \mathsf{O}(y, r_1, t_1^y) * \phi_y(r_1) * \mathsf{Acq}(x, \lambda v. \top) \right\}$$
$$\left\{ \phi_y(r_1) * \mathsf{Acq}(x, \lambda v. \top) \right\}$$
if $r_1 = 1$ **then**
$$\qquad \left\{ \mathsf{W}^1(x, [1; 0]) * \mathsf{Acq}(x, \lambda v. \top) \right\}$$
$$\qquad r_2 := [x]_{\mathtt{rlx}}$$
$$\qquad \left\{ \mathsf{Acq}(x, \lambda v. \top) * \mathsf{W}^1(x, [1; 0]) * (r_2 = 1) \right\}$$
$$\left\{ r_1 = 1 \implies r_2 = 1 \right\}$$

2.5 Plain Accesses

Our formal development (in the technical appendix) also features the usual "partial ownership" $x \xrightarrow{\pi} v$ assertion for "plain" (non-atomic) locations, and the usual corresponding rules.

3 The Promising Semantics

In this section, we provide an overview of the promising semantics [13], the model for which we prove SLR sound. Formal details can be found in [1,13].

The promising semantics is an operational semantics that interleaves execution of the threads of a program. Relaxed behaviour is introduced in two ways:

- As in the "strong release/acquire" model [15], the memory is a pool of timestamped messages, and each thread maintains a "view" thereof. A thread may read any value that is not older than the latest value observed by the thread for the given location; in particular, this may well not be the latest value written to that particular location. Timestamps and views model non-multi-copy-atomicity: writes performed by one thread do not become simultaneously visible by all other threads.
- The operational semantics contains a non-standard step: at any point a thread can nondeterministically *promise* a write, provided that, at every point before the write is actually performed, the thread can *certify* the promise, that is, execute the write by running on its own from the current state. Promises are used to enable load-store reordering.

The behaviour of promising steps can be illustrated on the LB+data+fakedep litmus test from the Introduction. The second thread can, at the very start of the execution, promise a write of 1 to x, because it can, by running on its own from the current state, read from y (it will read 0), then write 1 to x (because $0 + 1 - 0 = 1$), thereby fulfilling its promise. On the other hand, the first thread cannot promise a write of 1 to y at the beginning of the execution, because, by running on its own, it can only read 0 from x, and therefore only write 0 to y.

3.1 Storage Subsystem

Formally, the semantics keeps track of writes and promises in a *global configuration*, $gconf = \langle M, P \rangle$, where M is a memory and $P \subseteq M$ is the *promise memory*. We denote by $gconf$.M and $gconf$.P the components of $gconf$. Both *memories* are finite sets of messages, where a *message* is a tuple $\langle x :_i^o v, R@t] \rangle$, where $x \in Loc$ is the location of the message, $v \in Val$ its value, $i \in Tid$ its originating thread, $t \in Time$ its timestamp, R its message *view*, and $o \in \{\texttt{rlx}, \texttt{rel}\}$ its message mode, where $Time$ is an infinite set of timestamps, densely totally ordered by $\leq$, with a minimum element, 0. (We return to views later.) We denote $m.\texttt{loc}$,

m.val, m.time, m.view and m.mod the components of a message m. We use the following notation to restrict memories:

$$M(i) \stackrel{def}{=} \{m \in M \mid m.\mathtt{tid} = i\} \qquad M(\mathtt{rel}) \stackrel{def}{=} \{m \in M \mid m.\mathtt{mod} = \mathtt{rel}\}$$

$$M(x) \stackrel{def}{=} \{m \in M \mid m.\mathtt{loc} = x\} \qquad M(\mathtt{rlx}) \stackrel{def}{=} \{m \in M \mid m.\mathtt{mod} = \mathtt{rlx}\}$$

$$M(i, x) \stackrel{def}{=} M(i) \cap M(x)$$

A global configuration $gconf$ evolves in two ways. First, a message can be "promised" and be added both to $gconf$.M and $gconf$.P. Second, a message can be written, in which case it is either added to $gconf$.M, or removed from $gconf$.P (if it was promised before).

3.2 Thread Subsystem

A *thread state* is a pair $TS = \langle \sigma, V \rangle$, where σ is the internal state of the thread and V is a *view*. We denote by $TS.\sigma$ and $TS.V$ the components of TS.

Thread Internal State. The internal state σ consists of a thread store (denoted $\sigma.\mu$) that assigns values to local registers and a statement to execute (denoted $\sigma.s$). The transitions of the thread internal state are labeled with *memory actions* and are given by an ordinary sequential semantics. As these are routine, we leave their description to the technical appendix.

Views. Thread views are used to enforce coherence, that is, the existence of a per-location total order on writes that reads respect. A view is a function $V : Loc \rightarrow Time$, which records how far the thread has seen in the history of each location. To ensure that a thread does not read stale messages, its view restricts the messages the thread may read, and is increased whenever a thread observes a new message. Messages themselves also carry a view (the thread's view when the message comes from a release write, and the bottom view otherwise) which is incorporated in the thread view when the message is read by an acquire read.

Additional Notations. The order on timestamps, $\leq$, is extended pointwise to views. $\bot$ and $\sqcup$ denote the natural bottom elements and join operations for views. $\{x@t\}$ denotes the view assigning t to x and 0 to other locations.

3.3 Interaction Between a Thread and the Storage Subsystem

The interaction between a thread and the storage subsystem is given in terms of transitions of *thread configurations*. Thread configurations are tuples $\langle TS, \langle M, P \rangle \rangle$, where TS is a thread state, and $\langle M, P \rangle$ is a global configuration. These transitions are labelled with $\beta \in \{\mathrm{NP}, \mathrm{prom}\}$ in order to distinguish whether they involve promises or not. A thread can:

– Make an internal transition with no effect on the storage subsystem.
– Read the value v from location x, when there is a matching message in memory that is not outdated according to the thread's view. It then updates its view accordingly: it updates the timestamp for location x and, in addition, incorporates the message view if the read is an acquire read.
– Write the value v to location x. Here, the thread picks a timestamp greater than the one of its current view for the message it adds to memory (or removes from the promise set). If the write is a release write, the message carries the view of the writing thread. Moreover, a release write to x can only be performed when the thread has already fulfilled all its promises to x.
– Non-deterministically promise a relaxed write by adding a message to both M and P.

3.4   Constraining Promises

Now that we have described how threads and promises interact with memory, we can present the certification condition for promises, which is essential to avoid out-of-thin-air behaviours. Accordingly, we define another transition system, $\Longrightarrow$, on top of the previous one, which enforces that the memory remains "consistent", that is, all the promises that have been made can be certified. A thread configuration $\langle TS, \langle M, P \rangle \rangle$ is called *consistent* w.r.t. $i \in Tid$ if thread i can fulfil its promises by executing on its own, or more formally if $\langle TS, \langle M, P \rangle \rangle \xrightarrow{\mathrm{NP}}{}^{*}_{i} \langle TS', \langle M', P' \rangle \rangle$ for some TS', M', P' such that $P'(i) = \emptyset$. Certification is *local*, that is, only thread i is executing during its certification; this is crucial to avoid out-of-thin-air. Further, the certification itself cannot make additional promises, as it is restricted to NP-steps. Here is a visual representation of a promise machine run, together with certifications.

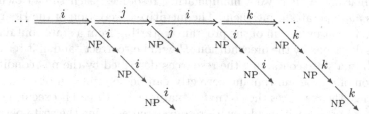

The thread configuration $\Longrightarrow$-transitions allow a thread to (1) take any number of non-promising steps, provided its thread configuration at the end of the sequence of step (intuitively speaking, when it gives control back to the scheduler) is consistent, or (2) take a promising step, again provided that its thread configuration after the step is consistent.

3.5   Full Machine

Finally, the full machine transitions simply lift the thread configuration $\Longrightarrow$-transitions to the machine level. A *machine state* is a tuple $\mathbf{MS} = \langle TS, \langle M, P \rangle \rangle$, where TS is a function assigning a thread state TS to every thread, and $\langle M, P \rangle$ is a global configuration. The initial state $\mathbf{MS}^0$ (for a given program) consists of the function $\mathcal{TS}^0$ mapping each thread i to its initial state $\langle \sigma_i^0, \bot \rangle$, where σ_i^0 is the thread's initial local state and $\bot$ is the zero view (all timestamps in views are 0); the initial memory M^0 consisting of one message $\langle x :_0^{rlx} 0, \bot@0] \rangle$ for each location x; and the empty set of promises.

4   Semantics and Soundness

In this section, we present the semantics of SLR, and give a short overview of the soundness proof. Our focus is not on the technical details of the proof, but on the two main challenges in defining the semantics and proving soundness:

1. *Reasoning about promises.* This difficulty arises because promise steps can be nondeterministically performed by the promise machine at any time.
2. *Reasoning about release-acquire ownership transfer in the presence of promises.* The problem is that writes may be promised before the thread has acquired enough resources to allow it to actually perform the write.

4.1   The Intuition

SLR assertions are interpreted by (sets of) *resources*, which represent permissions to write to a certain location and/or to obtain further resources by reading a certain message from memory. As is common in semantics of separation logics, the resources form a partial commutative monoid, and SLR's separating conjunction is interpreted as the composition operation of the monoid.

When defining the meaning of a Hoare triple $\{P\}\ s\ \{Q\}$, we think of the promise machine as if it were manipulating resources: each thread owns some resources and operates using them. The intuitive description of the Hoare triple semantics is that every run of the program s starting from a state containing the resources described by the precondition, P, will be "correct" and, if it terminates, will finish in a state containing the resources described by the postcondition, Q. The notion of a program running correctly can be described in terms of threads "respecting" the resources they own; for example, if a thread is executing a write or fulfilling a promise, it should own a resource representing the write permission.

4.2   A Closer Look at the Resources and the Assertion Semantics

We now take a closer look at the structure of resources and the semantics of assertions, whose formal definitions can be found in Figs. 2 and 3.

The idea is to interpret assertions as predicates over triples consisting of memory, a view, and a resource. We use the resource component to model assertions involving ownership (i.e., write assertions and acquire assertions), and model other assertions using the memory and view components. Once a resource is no longer needed, SLR allows us to drop these from assertions: $P * Q \Rightarrow P$.

To model this we interpret assertions as upwards-closed predicates, that may own more than explicitly asserted. The ordering on memories and views is given by the promising semantics, and the ordering on resources is induced by the composition operation in the resource monoid. For now, we leave the resource composition unspecified, and return to it later.

$$\iota \in PredId \stackrel{def}{=} \mathbb{N} \quad \text{(predicate identifiers)}$$
$$Perm \stackrel{def}{=} \{\pi \in \mathbb{Q} \mid 0 \leq \pi \leq 1\} \quad \text{(fractional permissions)}$$
$$Write \stackrel{def}{=} \mathcal{P}(Val \times Time)$$
$$WrPerm \stackrel{def}{=} Loc \rightarrow \{(\pi, X) \in Perm \times Write \mid \pi = 0 \Rightarrow X = \emptyset\}$$
$$AcqPerm \stackrel{def}{=} Loc \rightarrow \mathcal{P}(PredId)$$
$$r = (r.\mathbf{wr}, r.\mathbf{acq}) \in Res \stackrel{def}{=} WrPerm \times AcqPerm \quad \text{(resources)}$$
$$\mathcal{W} = (\mathcal{W}.\mathbf{rel}, \mathcal{W}.\mathbf{acq}) \in World \stackrel{def}{=} (Loc \rightarrow Pred) \times (PredId \rightarrow_{fin} Pred) \quad \text{(worlds)}$$
$$Prop \stackrel{def}{=} World \rightarrow_{mon} \mathcal{P}^{\uparrow}(Mem \times View \times Res)$$

Fig. 2. Semantic domains used in this section.

In addition, however, we have to deal with assertions that are parametrised by predicates (in our case, $\mathsf{Rel}(x, \phi)$ and $\mathsf{Acq}(x, \phi)$). Doing so is not straightforward because naïve attempts of giving semantics to such assertions result in circular definitions. A common technique for avoiding this circularity is to treat predicates stored in assertions syntactically, and to interpret assertions relative to a *world*, which is used to interpret those syntactic predicates. In our case, worlds consist of two components: the *WrPerm* component associates a syntactic SLR predicate with every location (this component is used to interpret release permissions), while the *AcqPerm* component associates a syntactic predicate with a finite number of currently allocated predicate identifiers (this component is used to interpret acquire permissions). The reason for the more complex structure for acquire permissions is that they can be split (see (Acquire-Split)). Therefore, we allow multiple predicate identifiers associated with a single location. When acquire permissions are divided and split between threads, new predicate identifiers are allocated and associated with predicates in the world. The world ordering, $\mathcal{W}_1 \leq \mathcal{W}_2$, expresses that world $\mathcal{W}_2$ is an extension of $\mathcal{W}_1$ in which new predicate identifiers may have been allocated, but all existing predicate identifiers are associated with the same predicates.

Let us now focus our attention on the assertion semantics. The semantics of assertions, $[\![P]\!]_\mu^\eta$, is relative to a thread store μ that assigns values to registers, and an environment η that assigns values to logical variables.

The standard logical connectives and quantifiers are interpreted following their usual intuitionistic semantics. The semantics of our novel assertions is given in Fig. 3 and can be explained as follows:

- The observed assertion $\mathsf{O}(x, v, t)$ says that the memory contains a message at location x with value v and timestamp t, and the current thread knows about it (i.e., the thread view contains it).

- The write assertion $W^\pi(x, X)$ asserts ownership of a (partial, with fraction π) write resource at location x, and requires that the largest timestamp recorded in X does not exceed the view of the current thread.
- The acquire assertion, $\mathsf{Acq}(x, \phi)$, asserts that location x has some predicate identifier ι associated with the ϕ predicate in the current world $\mathcal{W}$.
- The release assertion, $\mathsf{Rel}(x, \phi)$, asserts that location x is associated with some predicate ϕ' in the current world such that there exists a syntactic proof of the entailment, $\vdash \forall v.\, \phi(v) \Rightarrow \phi'(v)$. The implication allows us to strengthen the predicate in release assertions.
- Finally, ∇P states that P is satisfiable in the current world.

Note that $W^\pi(x, X)$, $\mathsf{Acq}(x, \phi)$, and $\mathsf{Rel}(x, \phi)$ only talk about owning certain resources, and do not constrain the memory itself at all. In the next subsection, we explain how we relate the abstract resources with the concrete machine state.

$$
\begin{aligned}
\llbracket O(x, v, t) \rrbracket_\mu^\eta(\mathcal{W}) &\stackrel{def}{=} \{(M, V, r) \mid \\
&\quad \exists j, R, o.\, \langle \llbracket x \rrbracket_\mu^\eta :_j^o \llbracket v \rrbracket_\mu^\eta, R@\llbracket t \rrbracket_\mu^\eta \rangle \in M \wedge \llbracket t \rrbracket_\mu^\eta \leq V(x)\} \\
\llbracket W^\pi(x, X) \rrbracket_\mu^\eta(\mathcal{W}) &\stackrel{def}{=} \{(M, V, r) \mid \exists \pi' \geq \llbracket \pi \rrbracket_\mu^\eta.\, r.\mathtt{wr}(\llbracket x \rrbracket_\mu^\eta) = (\pi', \llbracket X \rrbracket_\mu^\eta) \\
&\qquad\qquad\qquad\qquad\qquad \wedge\, snd(\max(\llbracket X \rrbracket_\mu^\eta)) \leq V(\llbracket x \rrbracket_\mu^\eta)\} \\
\llbracket \mathsf{Acq}(x, \phi) \rrbracket_\mu^\eta(\mathcal{W}) &\stackrel{def}{=} \{(M, V, r) \mid \exists \iota \in r.\mathtt{acq}(\llbracket x \rrbracket_\mu^\eta).\, \mathcal{W}.\mathtt{acq}(\iota) = \phi\} \\
\llbracket \mathsf{Rel}(x, \phi) \rrbracket_\mu^\eta(\mathcal{W}) &\stackrel{def}{=} \{(M, V, r) \mid \vdash \forall v.\, \phi(v) \Rightarrow \mathcal{W}.\mathtt{rel}(\llbracket x \rrbracket_\mu^\eta)(v)\} \\
\llbracket \nabla P \rrbracket_\mu^\eta(\mathcal{W}) &\stackrel{def}{=} \{(M, V, r) \mid \llbracket P \rrbracket_\mu^\eta(\mathcal{W}) \neq \emptyset\}
\end{aligned}
$$

Fig. 3. Interpretation of SLR assertions, $\llbracket \_ \rrbracket_\mu^\eta : Assn \to Prop$

4.3   Relating Concrete State and Resources

Before giving a formal description of the relationship between abstract resources and concrete machine states, we return to the intuition of threads manipulating resources presented in Sect. 4.1.

Consider what happens when a thread executes a release write to a location x. At that point, the thread has to own a release resource represented by $\mathsf{Rel}(x, \phi)$, and to store the value v, it has to own the resources represented by $\phi(v)$. As the write is executed, the thread gives up the ownership of the resources corresponding to $\phi(v)$. Conversely, when a thread that owns the resource represented by $\mathsf{Acq}(x, \phi)$ performs an acquire read of a value v from location x, it will gain ownership of resources satisfying $\phi(v)$. However, this picture does not account for *what happens to the resources that are "in flight"*, i.e., the resources that have been released, but not yet acquired.

Our approach is to associate in-flight resources to messages in the memory. When a thread does a release write, it attaches the resources it released to the message it just added to the memory. That way, a thread performing an acquire read from that message can easily take ownership of the resources that are associated to the message. Formally, as the execution progresses, we update the assignment of resources to messages,

$$u \colon M(\mathtt{rel}) \to (PredId \to Res).$$

For every release message in memory M, the message resource assignment u gives us a mapping from predicate identifiers to resources. Here, we again use predicate identifiers to be able to track which acquire predicate is being satisfied by which resource. The intended reading of $u(m)(\iota) = r$ is that the resource r attached to the message m satisfies the predicate with the identifier ι.

We also require that the resources attached to a message (i.e., the resources released by the thread that wrote the message) suffice to satisfy all the acquire predicates associated with that particular location. Together, these two properties of our message resource assignment, as formalised in Fig. 4, allow us to describe the release/acquire ownership transfer.

$$M \models r, u, \mathcal{W} \stackrel{def}{=}$$
$$\forall m \in M(\mathtt{rel}). \; r.\mathtt{acq}(m.\mathtt{loc}) = dom(u(m))$$
$$\wedge \; \forall \iota \in dom(u(m)). \left.\begin{array}{l} \\ \\ \\ \end{array}\right\} \begin{array}{l} \text{attached resources} \\ \text{satisfy predicates} \end{array}$$
$$(M, m.\mathtt{view}, u(m)(\iota)) \in [\![\mathcal{W}.\mathtt{acq}(\iota)(m.\mathtt{val})]\!]_{[]}^{[]}(\mathcal{W}) \left.\begin{array}{l} \\ \end{array}\right\} \text{they are supposed to}$$
$$\wedge \; \forall x, v. \vdash \mathcal{W}.\mathtt{rel}(x)(v) \Rightarrow \circledast_{\iota \in r.\mathtt{acq}(x)} \mathcal{W}.\mathtt{acq}(\iota)(v) \left.\begin{array}{l} \\ \end{array}\right\} \begin{array}{l} \text{released resources are} \end{array}$$
$$\wedge \; \forall m \in dom(u). \; dom(u(m)) \subseteq dom(\mathcal{W}.\mathtt{acq}) \left.\begin{array}{l} \\ \end{array}\right\} \text{enough to satisfy acquires}$$
$$\wedge \; \forall m \in M(\mathtt{rlx}). \left.\begin{array}{l} \\ \\ \end{array}\right\} \begin{array}{l} \text{no ownership transfer} \end{array}$$
$$(\langle \emptyset, \emptyset \rangle, \lambda x. \, 0, \varepsilon) \in [\![\mathcal{W}.\mathtt{rel}(m.\mathtt{loc})(m.\mathtt{val})]\!]_{[]}^{[]}(\mathcal{W}.\mathtt{rel}, [\,]) \left.\begin{array}{l} \\ \end{array}\right\} \text{via relaxed accesses}$$

Fig. 4. Message resource satisfaction.

The last condition in the message resource satisfaction relation has to do with relaxed accesses. Since relaxed accesses do not provide synchronisation, we disallow ownership transfer through them. Therefore, we require that the release predicates connected with the relaxed messages are satisfiable with the empty resource. This condition, together with the requirement that the released resources satisfy acquire predicates, forbids ownership transfer via relaxed accesses.

The resource missing from the discussion so far is the write resource (modelling the $\mathsf{W}^\pi(x, X)$ assertion). Intuitively, we would like to have the following property: whenever a thread adds a message to the memory, it has to own the corresponding write resource. Recall there are two ways a thread can produce a new message:

1. *A thread performs a write.* This is the straightforward case: we simply require the thread to own the write resource and to update the set of value-timestamp pairs recorded in the resource accordingly.
2. *A thread promises a write.* Here the situation is more subtle, because the thread might not own the write resource at the time it is issuing the promise,

but will acquire the appropriate resource by the time it fulfils the promise. So, in order to assert that the promise step respects the resources owned by the thread, we also need to be able to talk about the resources that the thread *can acquire* in the future.

When dealing with the promises, the saving grace comes from the fact that all promises have to be certifiable, i.e., when issuing a promise a thread has to be able to fulfil it without help from other threads.

Intuitively, the existence of a certification run tells us that even though at the moment a thread issues a promise, it might not have the resources necessary to actually perform the corresponding write, the thread should, by running uninterrupted, still be able to obtain the needed resources before it fulfils the promise. This, in turn, tells us that the needed resources have to be already released by the other threads by the time the promise is made: only resources attached to messages in the memory are available to be acquired, and only the thread that made the promise is allowed to run during the certification; therefore all the available resources have already been released.

The above reasoning shows what it means for the promise steps to "respect resources": when promises are issued, the resources currently owned by a thread, together with all the resources it is able to acquire according to the resources it owns and the current assignment of resources to messages, have to contain the appropriate write resource for the write being promised. The notion of "resources a thread is able to acquire" is expressed through the $\mathrm{canAcq}(r, u)$ predicate. $\mathrm{canAcq}(r, u)$ performs a fixpoint calculation: the resources we have (r) allow us to acquire some more resources from the messages in memory (assignment of resources to messages is given by u), which allows us to acquire some more, and so on. Its formal definition can be found in the technical appendix, and hinges on the fact that u precisely tracks which resources satisfy which predicates.

$$r_1 \bullet r_2 \overset{def}{=} (r_1.\mathbf{wr} \bullet_{\mathbf{wr}} r_2.\mathbf{wr}, r_1.\mathbf{acq} \bullet_{\mathbf{acq}} r_2.\mathbf{acq}) \qquad \varepsilon \overset{def}{=} ([], \lambda\_. \emptyset)$$

$$f_1 \bullet_{\mathbf{wr}} f_2 \overset{def}{=} \begin{cases} \lambda x. (f_1(x).\mathbf{perm} + f_2(x).\mathbf{perm}, f_1(x).\mathbf{msgs} \cup f_2(x).\mathbf{msgs}) \\ \quad \text{if } f_1(x).\mathbf{perm} + f_2(x).\mathbf{perm} \leq 1 \text{ for all locations } x \\ \text{undefined otherwise} \end{cases}$$

$$g_1 \bullet_{\mathbf{acq}} g_2 \overset{def}{=} \text{if } \forall x. \, g_1(x) \cap g_2(x) = \emptyset \text{ then } \lambda x. \, g_1(x) \cup g_2(x) \text{ else undefined}$$

Fig. 5. Resource composition.

An important element that was omitted from the discussion so far is the definition of the composition in the resource monoid *Res*. The resource composition, defined in Fig. 5, follows the expected notion of per-component composition. The most important feature is in the composition of write resources: a full permission write resource is only composable with the empty write resource.

At this point, we are equipped with all the necessary ingredients to relate abstract states represented by resources to concrete states $\langle M, P \rangle$ (where M is

$$\lfloor r_F, u, \mathcal{W} \rfloor_T \overset{\text{def}}{=} \{ \langle M, P \rangle \mid \textbf{let } r = \prod_{i \in TId} r_F(i) \bullet \prod_{m \in M} \prod_{\iota \in dom(u(m))} u(m)(\iota) \textbf{ in}$$

(1) $M \models r, u, \mathcal{W} \wedge$

(2) $\forall x. \{ (m.\texttt{val}, m.\texttt{time}) \mid m \in M(x) \setminus P \} = r.\texttt{wr}(x).\texttt{msgs} \wedge$

(3) $\forall m \in P. \; m.\texttt{tid} \notin T \Rightarrow$
$\qquad (r_F(m.\texttt{tid}) \bullet \texttt{canAcq}(r_F(m.\texttt{tid}), u)).\texttt{wr}(m.\texttt{loc}).\texttt{perm} > 0 \}$

r_F: *ThreadId* $\rightarrow$ *Res* maps threads to the resources they own.
r is the sum of all the resources distributed among the threads and messages.

Fig. 6. Erasure.

memory, and P is the set of promised messages). We define a function, called *erasure*, that given an assignment of resources to threads, r_F: *ThreadId* $\rightarrow$ *Res*, an assignment of resources to messages, u, and a world, $\mathcal{W}$, gives us a set of concrete states satisfying the following conditions:

1. Memory M is consistent with respect to the total resource r and the message resource assignment u at world $\mathcal{W}$.
2. The set of *fulfilled* writes to each location x in $\langle M, P \rangle$ must match the set of writes of all write permissions owned by any thread or associated with any messages, when combined.
3. For all unfulfilled promises to a location x by thread i, thread i must currently own or be able to acquire from u at least a shared write permission for x.

Our formal notion of erasure, defined in Fig. 6, has an additional parameter, a set of thread identifiers T. This set allows us to exclude promises of threads T from the requirement of respecting the resources. As we will see in the following subsection, this additional parameter plays a subtle, but key, role in the soundness proof. (The notion of erasure described above corresponds to the case when $T = \emptyset$.)

Note also that the arguments of erasure very precisely account for who owns which part of the total resource. This diverges from the usual approach in separation logic, where we just give the total resource as the argument to the erasure. Our approach is motivated by Lemma 1, which states that a reader that owns the full write resource for location x knows which value it is going to read from x. This is the key lemma in the soundness proof of the (R-RLX*) and (R-ACQ*) rules.

Lemma 1. If $(M, V, r_F(i)) \in [\![\mathsf{W}^1(x, X)]\!]_\mu^\eta(\mathcal{W})$, and $\langle M, P \rangle \in \lfloor r_F, u, \mathcal{W} \rfloor_{\{i\}}$ then for all messages $m \in M(x) \setminus P(i)$ such that $V(x) \leq m.\texttt{time}$, we have $m.\texttt{val} = fst(\max(X))$.

Lemma 1 is looking from the perspective of thread i that owns the full write resource for the location x. This is expressed by $(M, V, r_F(i)) \in [\![\mathsf{W}^1(x, X)]\!]_\mu^\eta(\mathcal{W})$ (recall that $r_F(i)$ are the resources owned by the thread i). Furthermore, the lemma assumes that the concrete state respects the abstract resources, expressed by $\langle M, P \rangle \in \lfloor r_F, u, \mathcal{W} \rfloor_{\{i\}}$. Under these assumptions, the lemma intuitively tells us that the current thread knows which value it will read from x. Formally, the lemma says that all the messages thread i is allowed to read (i.e., messages in the memory that are not outstanding promises of thread i and whose timestamp is greater or equal to the view of thread i) have the value that appears as the maximal element in the set X.

To see why this lemma holds, consider a message $m \in M(x) \setminus P(i)$. If m is an unfulfilled promise by a different thread j, then, by erasure, it follows that j currently owns or can acquire at least a shared write permission for x. However, this is a contradiction, since thread i currently owns the exclusive write permission, and, by erasure, $r_F(i)$ is disjoint from the resources of all other threads and all resources currently associated with messages by u. Hence, m must be a fulfilled write. By erasure, it follows that the set of fulfilled writes to x is given by the combination of all write permissions. Since $r_F(i)$ owns the exclusive write permission, this is just $r_F(i).\mathbf{wr}$. Hence, the set of fulfilled writes is X, and the value of the last fulfilled write is $fst(\max(X))$.

Note that in the reasoning above, it is crucial to know which thread and which message owns which resource. Without precisely tracking this information, we would be unable to prove Lemma 1.

4.4   Soundness

Now that we have our notion of erasure, we can proceed to formalise the meaning of triples, and present the key points of the soundness proof.

Recall our intuitive view of Hoare triples saying that the program only makes steps which respect the resources it owns. This notion is formalised using the *safety* predicate: safety (somewhat simplified; we give its formal definition in Fig. 7) states that it is always safe to perform zero steps, and performing $n + 1$ steps is safe if the following two conditions hold:

1. If no more steps can be taken, the current state and resources have to satisfy the postcondition B.
2. If we can take a step which takes us from the state $\langle M, P \rangle$ (which respects our current resources r, the assignment of resources to messages u, and world $\mathcal{W}$) to the state $\langle M', P' \rangle$, then

$$
\begin{aligned}
&\text{safe}_0(\sigma, B)(\mathcal{W}_1) \overset{def}{=} Mem \times View \times Res \\
&\text{safe}_{n+1}(\sigma, B)(\mathcal{W}_1) \overset{def}{=} \{(M_1, V_1, r_1) \mid \forall (M, V, r) \geq (M_1, V_1, r_1). \forall \mathcal{W} \geq \mathcal{W}_1. \\
&\qquad (\sigma.s = \mathbf{skip} \Rightarrow (M, V, r) \in vs(B(\sigma.\mu))(\mathcal{W})) \\
&\qquad \wedge\ (\forall P, r_F, \sigma', M', P', V', u, i.\ \langle M, P \rangle \in \lfloor r_F[i \mapsto r], u, \mathcal{W} \rfloor_\emptyset\ \wedge \\
&\qquad\qquad \langle \langle \sigma, V \rangle, \langle M, P \rangle \rangle \Longrightarrow_i \langle \langle \sigma', V' \rangle, \langle M', P' \rangle \rangle \\
&\qquad \Rightarrow \exists r', u', \mathcal{W}' \geq \mathcal{W}.\ \langle M', P' \rangle \in \lfloor r_F[i \mapsto r'], u', \mathcal{W}' \rfloor_\emptyset\ \wedge \\
&\qquad\qquad (\langle M', P' \rangle, V', r') \in \text{safe}_n(\sigma', B)(\mathcal{W}'))\}
\end{aligned}
$$

Fig. 7. Safety.

(a) there exist resources r', an assignment of resources to messages u', and a future world $\mathcal{W}'$, such that $\langle M', P' \rangle$ respects r', u', and $\mathcal{W}'$, and

(b) we are safe for n more steps starting in the state $\langle M', P' \rangle$ with resources given by r', u' and $\mathcal{W}'$.

Note the following:

- Upon termination, we are not required to satisfy exactly the postcondition B, but its *view shift*. A view shift is a standard notion in concurrent separation logics, which allows updates of the abstract resources which do not affect the concrete state. In our case, this means that resource r can be view-shifted into r' satisfying B as long as the erasure is unchanged. The formal definition of view shifts is given in the appendix.
- Again as is standard in separation logics, safety requires framed resources to be preserved. This is the role of r_F in the safety definition. Frame preservation allows us to compose safety of threads that own compatible resources. However, departing from the standard notion of frame preservation, we precisely track who owns which resource in the frame, because this is important for erasure.

The semantics of Hoare triples is simply defined in terms of the safety predicate. The triple $\{P\}\ s\ \{Q\}$ holds if every logical state satisfying the precondition is safe for any number of steps:

$$\llbracket \vdash \{P\}\ s\ \{Q\} \rrbracket \stackrel{def}{=} \forall n, \mu, \eta, \mathcal{W}.\ \llbracket P \rrbracket_\mu^\eta(\mathcal{W}) \subseteq \mathrm{safe}_n((\mu, s), \lambda\mu'.\ \llbracket Q \rrbracket_{\mu'}^\eta)(\mathcal{W})$$

To establish soundness of the SLR proof rules, we have to prove that the safety predicate holds for arbitrary number of steps, including promise steps. The trouble with reasoning about promise steps is that they can nondeterministically appear at any point of the execution. Therefore, we have to account for them in the soundness proof of every rule of our logic. To make this task manageable, we encapsulate reasoning about the promise steps in a theorem, thus enabling the proofs of soundness for proof rules to consider only the non-promise steps.

To do so, once again certification runs for promises play a pivotal role. Recall that whenever a thread makes a step, it has to be able to fulfil its promises without help from other threads (Sect. 3.4). Since there will be no interference by other threads, performing promise steps during certification is of no use (because promises can only be used by other threads). Therefore, we can assume that the certification runs are always promise-free.

Now that we have noted that certifications are promise-free, the key idea behind encapsulating the reasoning about promises is as follows. If we know that all executions of our program are safe for arbitrarily many non-promising steps, we can use this to conclude that they are safe for promising steps too. Here, we use the fact that certification runs are possible runs of the program, and the fact that certifications are promise-free.

Let us now formalise our key idea. First, we need a way to state that executions are safe for non-promising steps. This is expressed by the *non-promising safety* predicate defined in Fig. 8. What we want to conclude is that non-promising safety is enough to establish safety, as expressed by Theorem 1:

Theorem 1 (Non-promising safety implies safety)

$$\forall n, \sigma, B, \mathcal{W}. \ \text{npsafe}_{(n+1,0)}(\sigma, B)(\mathcal{W}) \subseteq \text{safe}_n(\sigma, B)(\mathcal{W})$$

We now discuss several important points in the definition of non-promising safety which enable us to prove this theorem.

Non-promising Safety is Indexed by Pairs of Natural Numbers. When proving Theorem 1, we use promise-free certification runs to establish the safety of the promise steps. A problem we face here is that the length of certification runs is unbounded. Somehow, we have to know that whenever the thread makes a step, it is npsafe for arbitrarily many steps. Our solution is to have npsafe transfinitely indexed over pairs of natural numbers ordered lexicographically. That way, if we are npsafe at index $(n + 1, 0)$ and we take a step, we know that we are npsafe at index (n, m) for every m. We are then free to choose a sufficiently large m depending on the length of the certification run we are considering.

Non-promising Safety Considers Configurations that May Contain Promises. It is important to note that the definition of non-promising safety does not require that there are no promises in the starting configuration. The only thing that is required is that no more promises are going to be issued. This is very important for Theorem 1, since safety considers all possible starting configurations (including the ones with existing promises), and if we want the lemma to hold, non-promising safety has to consider all possible starting configurations too.

Erasure Used in the Non-promising Safety does not Constrain Promises of the Current Thread. Non-promising safety does not require promises by the thread being reduced (i.e., thread i) to respect resources. Thus, when reasoning about non-promising safety of thread i, we cannot assume that existing promises by thread i respect resources, but crucially we also do not have to worry about recertifying thread i's promises. However, since the $\xrightarrow{\text{NP}}$ reduction does not recertify promises, we explicitly require that the promises are well formed (via wf_{prom} predicate) in order to ensure that we still only consider executions where threads do not read from their own promises.

Additional Constraints by the Non-promising Safety. Non-promising safety also imposes additional constraints on the reducing thread i. In particular, any write permissions owned or acquirable by i after the reduction were already owned or acquirable by i before the reduction step. Intuitively, this holds because thread i can only transfer away resources and take ownership of resources it was already allowed to acquire before reducing. Lastly, non-promising safety requires that if the reduction of i performs any new writes or fulfils any old promises, it must own the write permission for the location of the given message. Together, these two conditions ensure that if a promise is fulfilled during a thread-local certification

$$\text{npsafe}_{(0,m)}(\sigma, B)(\mathcal{W}) \overset{def}{=} \textit{Mem} \times \textit{View} \times \textit{Res}$$

$$\text{npsafe}_{(n+1,0)}(\sigma, B)(\mathcal{W}) \overset{def}{=} \bigcap_{m \in \mathbb{N}} \text{npsafe}_{(n,m)}(\sigma, B)(\mathcal{W})$$

$$\text{npsafe}_{(n+1,m+1)}(\sigma, B)(\mathcal{W}_1) \overset{def}{=} \{(M_1, V_1, r_1) \mid \forall (M, V, r) \ge (M_1, V_1, r_1). \, \forall \mathcal{W} \ge \mathcal{W}_1.$$

$$(\sigma.s = \text{skip} \Rightarrow (M, V, r) \in vs(B(\sigma.\mu))(\mathcal{W}))$$

$$\wedge \, (\forall P, r_F, f, \sigma', M', P', V', u, i.$$

$$\langle M, P \rangle \in \lfloor r_F[i \mapsto r \bullet f], u, \mathcal{W} \rfloor_{\{i\}} \quad \text{(weak erasure)}$$

$$\wedge \quad \langle\langle \sigma, V \rangle, \langle M, P \rangle\rangle \overset{\text{NP}}{\longrightarrow}_i \langle\langle \sigma', V' \rangle, \langle M', P' \rangle\rangle \quad \text{(only non-promising steps allowed)}$$

$$\wedge \, \text{wf}_{\text{prom}}(P(i), V) \wedge \text{wf}_{\text{prom}}(P'(i), V') \quad \text{(promises well formed)}$$

$$\Rightarrow \exists r', u', \mathcal{W}' \ge \mathcal{W}. \, M' \in \lfloor r_F[i \mapsto r' \bullet f], u', \mathcal{W}' \rfloor_{\{i\}} \quad \text{(weak erasure)}$$

$$\wedge \, (M', V', r') \in \text{npsafe}_{(n+1,m)}(\sigma', B)(\mathcal{W}')$$

$$\wedge \, r' \bullet \text{canAcq}(r', u') \le_o r \bullet \text{canAcq}(r, u) \quad \text{(no new res. acquirable after taking a step)}$$

$$\wedge \, \forall m \in (M' \setminus P') \setminus (M \setminus P). \, r.\text{wr}(m.\text{loc}).\text{perm} > 0\} \quad \text{(when performing a write}$$
or fulfiling a promise
the thread has to own
the appropriate write res.)

$$r_1 \le_o r_2 \overset{def}{=} \forall x. \, r_1.\text{wr}(x).\text{perm} \le r_2.\text{wr}(x).\text{perm}$$

$$\text{wf}_{\text{prom}}(P, V) \overset{def}{=} \forall m \in P. \, V(m.\text{loc}) < m.\text{time}$$

Fig. 8. Non-promising safety.

and the thread satisfies non-promising safety, then the thread already owned or could acquire the write permission for the location of the promise. This is expressed formally in Lemma 2.

Lemma 2. Assuming that $(\langle M, P \rangle, V, r) \in \text{npsafe}_{(n+1,k)}(\sigma, B)(\mathcal{W})$ and $\langle M, P \rangle \in \lfloor r_F[i \mapsto r \bullet f], u, \mathcal{W} \rfloor_{\{i\}}$ and $\langle\langle \sigma, V \rangle, \langle M, P \rangle\rangle \overset{\text{NP}\,k}{\longrightarrow}_i \langle\langle \sigma', V' \rangle, \langle M', P' \rangle\rangle$ and $m \in (M' \setminus P') \setminus (M \setminus P)$, we have $(r \bullet \text{canAcq}(r, u)).\text{wr}(m.\text{loc}).\text{perm} > 0$.

The intuition for why Lemma 2 holds is that since only thread i executes, we know by the definition of non-promising safety that any write permission owned or acquirable by i when the promise is fulfilled, it already owns or can acquire in the initial state. Furthermore, whenever a promise is fulfilled, the non-promising safety definition explicitly requires ownership of the corresponding write permission. It follows that the thread already owns or can acquire the write permission for the location of the given promise in the initial state.

Lemma 2 gives us exactly the property that we need to reestablish erasure after the operational semantics introduces a new promise. This makes Lemma 2 the key step in the proof of Theorem 1, which allows us to disentangle reasoning about promising steps and normal reduction steps. Theorem 1 tells us that, in order to prove a proof rule sound, it is enough to prove that the non-promising safety holds for arbitrary indices. This liberates us of the cumbersome reasoning about promise steps and allows us to focus on non-promising reduction steps when proving the proof rules sound.

We can now state our top-level correctness theorem, Theorem 2. Since our language only has top-level parallel composition, we need a way to distribute initial resources to the various threads, and to collect all the resources once all the threads have finished. The correctness theorem gives us precisely that:

Theorem 2 (Correctness). *If A is a finite set of locations and*

1. $\vdash \forall x \in A. \phi_x(0)$
2. $\vdash \circledast_{x \in A} \mathsf{Rel}(x, \phi_x) * \mathsf{Acq}(x, \phi_x) * \mathsf{W}^1(x, \{(0,0)\}) \Rrightarrow \circledast_{i \in Tid} P_i$
3. $\vdash \{P_i\}\, s_i\, \{Q_i\}$ *for all* i
4. $\langle \lambda i. \langle (\mu_i, s_i), \bot \rangle, \langle M^0, \emptyset \rangle \rangle \Longrightarrow^* \langle TS, gconf \rangle$ *and* $TS(i).\sigma = \mathsf{skip}$ *for all* i
5. $\vdash \circledast_{i \in Tid} Q_i \Rrightarrow Q$
6. $FRV(Q_i) \cap FRV(Q_j) = \emptyset$ *for all distinct* $i, j \in Tid$

then there exist $\mu, r,$ *and* $\mathcal{W}$ *such that* $(gconf.M, \sqcup_i TS(i).V, r) \in \llbracket Q \rrbracket_\mu^{\emptyset}(\mathcal{W})$ *and* $\forall i \in Tid. \forall a \in FRV(Q_i). \mu(a) = TS(i).\mu(a),$ *where* $FRV(P)$ *denotes the set of free register variables in* P.

5   Related Work

There are a number of techniques for reasoning under relaxed memory models, but besides the DRF theorems and some simple invariant logics [10,13], no other techniques have been proved sound for a model allowing the weak behaviour of LB+data+fakedep from the introduction. The "invariant-based program logics" are by design unable to reason about programs like the random number generator, where having a bound on the set of values written to a location is not enough, let alone reasoning about functional correctness of a program.

Relaxed Separation Logic (RSL). Among program logics for relaxed memory, the most closely related is RSL [27]. There are two versions of RSL: a weak one that is sound with respect to the C/C++11 memory model, which features out-of-thin-air reads, and a stronger one that is sound with respect to a variant of the C/C++11 memory that forbids load buffering.

The weak version of RSL forbids relaxed writes completely, and does not constrain the value returned by a relaxed read. The stronger version provides single-location invariants for relaxed accesses, but its soundness proof relies strongly on a strengthened version of C/C++11 without $po \cup rf$ cycles (where po is program order, and rf is the reads-from relation), which forbids load buffering.

When it comes to reasoning about coherence properties, even the strong version of RSL is surprisingly weak: it cannot be used to verify any of the coherence examples in this paper. In fact, RSL can be shown sound with respect to much weaker coherence axioms than what C/C++11 relaxed accesses provide.

One notable feature of RSL which we do not support is read-modify-write (RMW) instructions (such as compare-and-swap and fetch-and-add). However, the soundness proof of SLR makes no simplifying assumptions about the promising semantics which would affect the semantics of RMW instructions. Therefore, we are confident that enhancing SLR with rules for RMW instructions would not substantially affect the structure of the soundness proof, presented in Sect. 4.

Other Program Logics. FSL [8] extends (the strong version of) RSL with stronger rules for relaxed accesses in the presence of release/acquire fences. In FSL, a release fence can be used to package an assertion with a modality, which a relaxed write can then transfer. Conversely, the ownership obtained by a relaxed read is guarded by a symmetric modality than needs an acquire fence to be unpacked. The soundness proof of FSL also relies on $po \cup rf$ acyclicity. Moreover, it is known to be unsound in models where load buffering is allowed [9, Sect. 5.2].

A number of other logics—GPS [26], iGPS [12], OGRA [16], iCAP-TSO [24], the rely-guarantee proof system for TSO of Ridge [23], and the program logic for TSO of Wehrman and Berdine [28]—have been developed for even stronger memory models (release/acquire or TSO), and also rely quite strongly on—and try to expose—the stronger consistency guarantees provided by those models.

The framework of Alglave and Cousot [2] for reasoning about relaxed concurrent programs is parametric with respect to an axiomatic "per-execution" memory model. By construction, as argued by Batty et al. [3], such models cannot be used to define a language-level model allowing the weak behaviour of LB+data+fakedep and similar litmus tests while forbidding out-of-thin-air behaviours. Moreover, their framework does not provide the usual abstraction facilities of program logics.

The lace logic of Bornat et al. [6] targets hardware memory models, in particular Power. It relies on annotating the program with "per-execution" constraints, and on syntactic features of the program. For example, it distinguishes LB+data+fakedep from LB+data+po, its variant where the write of second thread is $[x]_{\text{rlx}} := 1$, and is thus unsuitable to address out-of-thin-air behaviours.

Other Approaches. Besides program logics, another way to reason about programs under weak memory models is to reduce the act of reasoning under a memory model M to reasoning under a stronger model M'—typically, but not necessarily, sequential consistency [7,18]. One can often establish DRF theorems stating that a program without any races when executed under M' has the same behaviours when executed under M as when executed under M'. For the promising semantics, Kang et al. [13, Sect. 5.4] have established such theorems for M' being release-acquire consistency, sequential consistency, and the promise-free promising semantics, for suitable notions of races. The last one, the "Promise-Free DRF" theorem, is applicable to the Disjoint-Lists program from the introduction, but none of these theorems can be applied to any of the other examples of this paper, as they are racy. Moreover, these theorems are not compositional, as they do not state anything about the Disjoint-Lists program when put inside a larger, racy program—for example, just an extra read of a from another thread.

6   Conclusion

In this paper, we have presented the first expressive logic that is sound under the promising semantics, and have demonstrated its expressiveness with a number of examples. Our logic can be seen both as a general proof technique for reasoning about concurrent programs, and also as tool for proving the absence of out-of-thin-air behaviour for challenging examples, and reasoning about coherence. In the future, we would like to extend the logic to cover more of relaxed memory, more advanced reasoning principles, such as those available in GPS [26], and mechanise its soundness proof.

Interesting aspects of relaxed memory we would like to also cover are read-modify-writes and fences. These would allow us to consider concurrent algorithms like circular buffers and the atomic reference counter verified in FSL++ [9]. This could be done by adapting the corresponding rules of RSL and GPS; moreover, we could adapt them with our new approach to reason about coherence.

To mechanise the soundness proof, we intend to use the Iris framework [11], which has already been used to prove the soundness of iGPS [12], a variant of the GPS program logic. To do this, however, we have to overcome one technical limitation of Iris. Namely, the current version of Iris is step-indexed over $\mathbb{N}$, while our semantics uses transfinite step-indexing over $\mathbb{N} \times \mathbb{N}$ to define non-promising safety and allow us to reason about certifications of arbitrary length for each reduction step. Progress has been made towards transfinitely step-indexed logical relations that may be applicable to a transfinitely step-indexed version of Iris [25].

Acknowledgments. We would like to thank the reviewers for their feedback. The research was supported in part by the Danish Council for Independent Research (project DFF – 4181-00273), by a European Research Council Consolidator Grant for the project "RustBelt" (grant agreement no. 683289), and by Len Blavatnik and the Blavatnik Family foundation.

References

1. Supplementary material for this paper. http://plv.mpi-sws.org/slr/appendix.pdf
2. Alglave, J., Cousot, P.: Ogre and Pythia: an invariance proof method for weak consistency models. In: POPL 2017, pp. 3–18. ACM, New York (2017). http://doi.acm.org/10.1145/2994593
3. Batty, M., Memarian, K., Nienhuis, K., Pichon-Pharabod, J., Sewell, P.: The problem of programming language concurrency semantics. In: Vitek, J. (ed.) ESOP 2015. LNCS, vol. 9032, pp. 283–307. Springer, Heidelberg (2015). https://doi.org/10.1007/978-3-662-46669-8_12
4. Batty, M., Owens, S., Sarkar, S., Sewell, P., Weber, T.: Mathematizing C++ concurrency. In: POPL 2011, pp. 55–66. ACM, New York (2011). http://doi.acm.org/10.1145/1926385.1926394

5. Boehm, H.J., Demsky, B.: Outlawing ghosts: avoiding out-of-thin-air results. In: Proceedings of the Workshop on Memory Systems Performance and Correctness, MSPC 2014, pp. 7:1–7:6. ACM, New York (2014). http://doi.acm.org/10.1145/2618128.2618134

6. Bornat, R., Alglave, J., Parkinson, M.: New lace and arsenic (2016). https://arxiv.org/abs/1512.01416

7. Bouajjani, A., Derevenetc, E., Meyer, R.: Robustness against relaxed memory models. In: Software Engineering 2014, Fachtagung des GI-Fachbereichs Softwaretechnik, 25–28 Februar 2014, Kiel, Deutschland, pp. 85–86 (2014)

8. Doko, M., Vafeiadis, V.: A program logic for C11 memory fences. In: Jobstmann, B., Leino, K.R.M. (eds.) VMCAI 2016. LNCS, vol. 9583, pp. 413–430. Springer, Heidelberg (2016). https://doi.org/10.1007/978-3-662-49122-5_20

9. Doko, M., Vafeiadis, V.: Tackling real-life relaxed concurrency with FSL++. In: Yang, H. (ed.) ESOP 2017. LNCS, vol. 10201, pp. 448–475. Springer, Heidelberg (2017). https://doi.org/10.1007/978-3-662-54434-1_17

10. Jeffrey, A., Riely, J.: On thin air reads towards an event structures model of relaxed memory. In: LICS 2016, pp. 759–767. ACM, New York (2016)

11. Jung, R., Krebbers, R., Jourdan, J.H., Bizjak, A., Birkedal, L., Dreyer, D.: Iris from the ground up (2017)

12. Kaiser, J.O., Dang, H.H., Dreyer, D., Lahav, O., Vafeiadis, V.: Strong logic for weak memory: reasoning about release-acquire consistency in Iris. In: ECOOP 2017 (2017)

13. Kang, J., Hur, C.K., Lahav, O., Vafeiadis, V., Dreyer, D.: A promising semantics for relaxed-memory concurrency. In: POPL 2017. ACM, New York (2017). http://doi.acm.org/10.1145/3009837.3009850

14. Lahav, O., Vafeiadis, V., Kang, J., Hur, C.K., Dreyer, D.: Repairing sequential consistency in C/C++11. In: PLDI (2017)

15. Lahav, O., Giannarakis, N., Vafeiadis, V.: Taming release-acquire consistency. In: POPL 2016, pp. 649–662. ACM, New York (2016). http://doi.acm.org/10.1145/2837614.2837643

16. Lahav, O., Vafeiadis, V.: Owicki-gries reasoning for weak memory models. In: Halldórsson, M.M., Iwama, K., Kobayashi, N., Speckmann, B. (eds.) ICALP 2015. LNCS, vol. 9135, pp. 311–323. Springer, Heidelberg (2015). https://doi.org/10.1007/978-3-662-47666-6_25

17. Manson, J., Pugh, W., Adve, S.V.: The Java memory model. In: POPL, pp. 378–391. ACM, New York (2005)

18. Owens, S.: Reasoning about the implementation of concurrency abstractions on x86-TSO. In: D'Hondt, T. (ed.) ECOOP 2010. LNCS, vol. 6183, pp. 478–503. Springer, Heidelberg (2010). https://doi.org/10.1007/978-3-642-14107-2_23

19. Owens, S., Sarkar, S., Sewell, P.: A better x86 memory model: x86-TSO. In: Berghofer, S., Nipkow, T., Urban, C., Wenzel, M. (eds.) TPHOLs 2009. LNCS, vol. 5674, pp. 391–407. Springer, Heidelberg (2009). https://doi.org/10.1007/978-3-642-03359-9_27

20. Pichon-Pharabod, J., Sewell, P.: A concurrency semantics for relaxed atomics that permits optimisation and avoids thin-air executions. In: POPL 2016, pp. 622–633. ACM, New York (2016)

21. Podkopaev, A., Lahav, O., Vafeiadis, V.: Promising compilation to ARMv8 POP. In: ECOOP 2017. LIPIcs, vol. 74, pp. 22:1–22:28. Schloss Dagstuhl - Leibniz-Zentrum fuer Informatik (2017)

22. Reynolds, J.C.: Separation logic: a logic for shared mutable data structures. In: Proceedings of the 17th IEEE Symposium on Logic in Computer Science (LICS 2002), 22–25 July 2002, Copenhagen, Denmark, pp. 55–74 (2002). https://doi.org/10.1109/LICS.2002.1029817
23. Ridge, T.: A rely-guarantee proof system for x86-TSO. In: Leavens, G.T., O'Hearn, P., Rajamani, S.K. (eds.) VSTTE 2010. LNCS, vol. 6217, pp. 55–70. Springer, Heidelberg (2010). https://doi.org/10.1007/978-3-642-15057-9_4
24. Sieczkowski, F., Svendsen, K., Birkedal, L., Pichon-Pharabod, J.: A separation logic for fictional sequential consistency. In: Vitek, J. (ed.) ESOP 2015. LNCS, vol. 9032, pp. 736–761. Springer, Heidelberg (2015). https://doi.org/10.1007/978-3-662-46669-8_30
25. Svendsen, K., Sieczkowski, F., Birkedal, L.: Transfinite step-indexing: decoupling concrete and logical steps. In: Thiemann, P. (ed.) ESOP 2016. LNCS, vol. 9632, pp. 727–751. Springer, Heidelberg (2016). https://doi.org/10.1007/978-3-662-49498-1_28
26. Turon, A., Vafeiadis, V., Dreyer, D.: GPS: navigating weak memory with ghosts, protocols, and separation. In: 2014 ACM International Conference on Object Oriented Programming Systems Languages and Applications, OOPSLA 2014, pp. 691–707. ACM, New York (2014)
27. Vafeiadis, V., Narayan, C.: Relaxed separation logic: a program logic for C11 concurrency. In: OOPSLA 2013, pp. 867–884. ACM, New York (2013)
28. Wehrman, I., Berdine, J.: A proposal for weak-memory local reasoning. In: LOLA (2011)

Logical Reasoning for Disjoint Permissions

Xuan-Bach Le[1](✉) and Aquinas Hobor[1,2]

[1] National University of Singapore, Singapore, Singapore
bachdylan@gmail.com
[2] Yale-NUS College, Singapore, Singapore

Abstract. Resource sharing is a fundamental phenomenon in concurrent programming where several threads have permissions to access a common resource. Logics for verification need to capture the notion of permission ownership and transfer. One typical practice is the use of rational numbers in $(0, 1]$ as permissions in which 1 is the full permission and the rest are fractional permissions. Rational permissions are not a good fit for separation logic because they remove the essential "disjointness" feature of the logic itself. We propose a general logic framework that supports permission reasoning in separation logic while preserving disjointness. Our framework is applicable to sophisticated verification tasks such as doing induction over the finiteness of the heap within the object logic or carrying out biabductive inference. We can also prove precision of recursive predicates within the object logic. We developed the ShareInfer tool to benchmark our techniques. We introduce "scaling separation algebras," a compositional extension of separation algebras, to model our logic, and use them to construct a concrete model.

1 Introduction

The last 15 years have witnessed great strides in program verification [7,27,39, 43,44,46]. One major area of focus has been concurrent programs following Concurrent Separation Logic (CSL) [40]. The key rule of CSL is PARALLEL:

$$\frac{\{P_1\}\ c_1\ \{Q_1\} \qquad \{P_2\}\ c_2\ \{Q_2\}}{\{P_1 \star P_2\}\ c_1 || c_2\ \{Q_1 \star Q_2\}}\ \text{PARALLEL}$$

In this rule, we write $c_1 || c_2$ to indicate the parallel execution of commands c_1 and c_2. The separating conjunction $\star$ indicates that the resources used by the threads is disjoint in some useful way, *i.e.* that there are no dangerous races. Many subsequent program logics [18,20,30,31,45] have introduced increasingly sophisticated notions of "resource disjointness" for the PARALLEL rule.

Fractional permissions (also called "shares") are a relatively simple enhancement to separation logic's original notion of disjointness [4]. Rather than owning a resource (e.g. a memory cell) entirely, a thread is permitted to own a part/fraction of that resource. The more of a resource a thread owns, the more

© The Author(s) 2018
A. Ahmed (Ed.): ESOP 2018, LNCS 10801, pp. 385–414, 2018.
https://doi.org/10.1007/978-3-319-89884-1_14

actions it is permitted to take, a mapping called a *policy*. In this paper we will use the original policy of Bornat [4] to keep the examples straightforward: non-zero ownership of a memory cell permits reading while full ownership also permits writing. More modern logics allow for a variety of more flexible share policies [13, 28, 42], but our techniques still apply. Fractional permissions are less expressive than the "protocol-based" notions of disjointness used in program logics such as FCSL [38, 44], Iris [30], and TaDa [16], but are well-suited for common concurrent programming patterns such as read sharing and so have been incorporated into many program logics and verification tools [19, 26, 28, 31, 36, 41].

Since fractionals are simpler and more uniform than protocol-based logics, they are amenable to automation [26, 33]. However, previous techniques had difficulty with the inductive predicates common in SL proofs. We introduce *predicate multiplication*, a concise method for specifying the fractional sharing of complex predicates, writing $\pi \cdot P$ to indicate that we own the π-share of the arbitrary predicate P, *e.g.* $0.5 \cdot \mathsf{tree}(x)$ indicates a tree rooted at x and we own half of each of the nodes in the tree. If set up properly, predicate multiplication handles inductive predicates smoothly and is well-suited for automation because:

Section 3 it distributes with bientailments—*e.g.* $\pi \cdot (P \wedge Q) \dashv\vdash (\pi \cdot P) \wedge (\pi \cdot Q)$—
enabling rewriting techniques and both forwards and backwards reasoning;
Section 4 it works smoothly with the inference process of biabduction [10]; and
Section 5 the side conditions required for bientailments and biabduction can be
verified directly in the object logic, leveraging existing entailment checkers.

There has been significant work in recent years on tool support for protocol-based approaches [15, 19, 29, 30, 48], but they require significant user input and provide essentially no inference. Fractional permissions and protocol-based approaches are thus complementary: fractionals can handle large amounts of relatively simple concurrent code with minimal user guidance, while protocol-based approaches are useful for reasoning about the implementations of fine-grained concurrent data structures whose correctness argument is more sophisticated.

In addition to Sects. 3, 4 and 5, the rest of this paper is organized as follows.

Section 2 We give the technical background necessary for our work.
Section 6 We document Shareinfer [1], a tool that uses the logical tools developed in Sects. 3, 4 and 5 to infer frames and antiframes and check the necessary side conditions. We benchmark Shareinfer with 27 selective examples.
Section 7 We introduce *scaling separation algebra* that allows us to construct predicate multiplication on an abstract structure in a compositional way. We show such model can be constructed from Dockins *et al.*'s tree shares [21]. The key technical proofs in Sects. 5 and 7 have been verified in Coq [1].
Section 8 We prove that there are no useful share models that simultaneously satisfy disjointness and two distributivity axioms. Consequently, at least one axioms has to be removed, which we choose to be the left distributivity. We also prove that the failure of two-sided distributivity forces a side condition on a key proof rule for predicate multiplication.
Section 9 We discuss related work before delivering our conclusion.

$$\text{root} \overset{0.3}{\mapsto} (3, \text{left}, \text{right}) \star$$
$$\text{left} \overset{0.3}{\mapsto} (1, \text{null}, \text{grand}) \star$$
$$\text{right} \overset{0.3}{\mapsto} (4, \text{grand}, \text{null}) \star$$
$$\text{grand} \overset{0.6}{\mapsto} (1, \text{null}, \text{null})$$

Fig. 1. This heap satisfies tree(root, 0.3) despite being a DAG

2 Technical Preliminaries

Share Models. An (additive) share model $(\mathcal{S}, \oplus)$ is a partial commutative monoid with a bottom/empty element $\mathcal{E}$ and top/full element $\mathcal{F}$. On the rationals in $[0, 1]$, $\oplus$ is partial addition, $\mathcal{E}$ is 0, and $\mathcal{F}$ is 1. We also require the existence of complements $\overline{\pi}$ satisfying $\pi \oplus \overline{\pi} = \mathcal{F}$; in $\mathbb{Q}$, $\overline{\pi} \overset{\text{def}}{=} 1 - \pi$.

Separation Logic. Our base separation logic has the following connectives:

$$P, Q, \text{ etc. } \overset{\text{def}}{=} \langle F \rangle \mid P \wedge Q \mid P \vee Q \mid \neg P \mid P \star Q \mid \forall x.P \mid \exists x.P \mid \mu X.P \mid e_1 \overset{\pi}{\mapsto} e_2$$

Pure facts F are put in angle brackets, *e.g.* $\langle even(12) \rangle$. Pure facts force the empty heap, *i.e.* the usual separation logic emp predicate is just a macro for $\langle \top \rangle$. Our propositional fragment has (classical) conjunction $\wedge$, disjunction $\vee$, negation $\neg$, and the separating conjunction $\star$. We have both universal $\forall$ and existential $\exists$ quantifiers, which can be impredicative if desired. To construct recursive predicates we have the usual Tarski least fixpoint μ. The fractional points-to $e_1 \overset{\pi}{\mapsto} e_2$ means we own the π-fraction of the memory cell pointed to by e_1, whose contents is e_2, and nothing more. To distinguish points-to from emp we require that π be non-$\mathcal{E}$. For notational convenience we sometimes elide the full share $\mathcal{F}$ over a fractional maps-to, writing just $e_1 \mapsto e_2$. The connection of $\oplus$ to the fractional maps-to predicate is given by the bi-entailment:

$$\frac{}{e \overset{\pi_1}{\mapsto} e_1 \star e \overset{\pi_2}{\mapsto} e_2 \;\; \dashv\vdash \;\; e \overset{\pi_1 \oplus \pi_2}{\mapsto} e_1 \wedge e_1 = e_2} \; \substack{\text{MapsTo} \\ \text{Split}}$$

Disjointness. Although intuitive, the rationals are not a good model for shares in SL. Consider this definition for π-fractional trees rooted at x:

$$\text{tree}(x, \pi) \overset{\text{def}}{=} \langle x = \text{null} \rangle \vee \exists d, l, r.\ x \overset{\pi}{\mapsto} (d, l, r) \star \text{tree}(l, \pi) \star \text{tree}(r, \pi) \quad (1)$$

This tree predicate is obtained directly from the standard recursive predicate for binary trees by asserting only π ownership of the root and recursively doing the same for the left and right substructures, and so at first glance looks straightforward[1]. The problem is that when $\pi \in (0, 0.5]$, then tree can describe some

---

[1] We write $x \overset{\pi}{\mapsto} (v_1, \ldots, v_n)$ for $x \overset{\pi}{\mapsto} v_1 \star (x+1) \overset{\pi}{\mapsto} v_2 \star \ldots \star (x+n-1) \overset{\pi}{\mapsto} v_n$.

non-tree directed acyclic graphs as in Fig. 1. Fractional trees are a little too easy to introduce and thus unexpectedly painful to eliminate.

To prevent the deformation of recursive structures shown in Fig. 1, we want to recover the "disjointness" property of basic SL: $e \mapsto e_1 \star e \mapsto e_2 \dashv\vdash \bot$. Disjointness can be specified either as an inference rule in separation logic [41] or as an algebraic rule on the share model [21] as follows:

$$\frac{}{e \overset{\pi}{\mapsto} e_1 \star e \overset{\pi}{\mapsto} e_2 \ \dashv\vdash\ \bot} \text{\scriptsize MapsTo Disjoint} \qquad\qquad \forall a, b.\ a \oplus a = b \ \Rightarrow\ a = \mathcal{E} \qquad (2)$$

In other words, **a nonempty share π cannot join with itself.** In Sect. 3 we will see how disjointness enables the distribution of predicate multiplication over $\star$ and in Sect. 4 we will see how disjointness enables antiframe inference during biabduction.

Tree Shares. Dockins *et al.* [21] proposed "tree shares" as a share model satisfying disjointness. For this paper the details of the model are not critical so we provide only a brief overview. A tree share $\tau \in \mathbb{T}$ is a binary tree with Boolean leaves, *i.e.* $\tau = \bullet \mid \circ \mid \widehat{\tau_1\, \tau_2}$, where $\circ$ is the empty share $\mathcal{E}$ and $\bullet$ is the full share $\mathcal{F}$. There are two "half" shares: $\widehat{\circ\, \bullet}$ and $\widehat{\bullet\, \circ}$, and four "quarter" shares, *e.g.* $\widehat{\bullet\, \circ\, \circ}$. Trees must be in *canonical form*, *i.e.*, the most compact representation under $\cong$:

$$\frac{}{\circ \cong \circ} \qquad \frac{}{\bullet \cong \bullet} \qquad \frac{}{\circ \cong \widehat{\circ\, \circ}} \qquad \frac{}{\bullet \cong \widehat{\bullet\, \bullet}} \qquad \frac{\tau_1 \cong \tau_1' \quad \tau_2 \cong \tau_2'}{\widehat{\tau_1\, \tau_2} \cong \widehat{\tau_1'\, \tau_2'}}$$

Union $\sqcup$, intersection $\sqcap$, and complement $\bar{\ }$ are the basic operations on tree shares; they operate leafwise after unfolding the operands under $\cong$ into the same shape:

$$\widehat{\bullet\, \widehat{\circ\, \circ}} \sqcup \widehat{\widehat{\circ\, \bullet}\, \bullet} \ \cong\ \widehat{\bullet\, \widehat{\circ\, \circ}} \sqcup \widehat{\widehat{\circ\, \bullet}\, \bullet} \ =\ \widehat{\widehat{\bullet\, \bullet}\, \circ} \ \cong\ \widehat{\bullet\, \circ}$$

The structure $\langle \mathbb{T}, \sqcup, \sqcap, \bar{\ }, \circ, \bullet \rangle$ forms a countable atomless Boolean algebra and thus enjoys decidable existential and first-order theories with precisely known complexity bounds [34]. The join operator $\oplus$ on trees is defined as $\tau_1 \oplus \tau_2 = \tau_3 \overset{\text{def}}{=} \tau_1 \sqcup \tau_2 = \tau_3 \wedge \tau_1 \sqcap \tau_2 = \circ$. Due to their good metatheoretic and computational properties, a variety of program logics [24,25] and verification tools [3,26,33,47] have used tree shares (or other isomorphic structures [19]).

3   Predicate Multiplication

The additive structure of share models is relatively well-understood [21,33,34]. The focus for this paper is exploring the benefits and consequences of incorporating a multiplicative operator $\otimes$ into a share model. The simplest motivation for multiplication is computationally dividing some share π of a resource "in half;"

```
1 struct tree {int d; struct tree* l; struct tree* r;};
2 void processTree(struct tree* x) {
3   if (x == 0) { return; }
4   print(x -> d);              7   print(x -> d);
5   processTree(x -> l);        8   processTree(x -> l);
6   processTree(x -> r);        9   processTree(x -> r);

10 }
```

Fig. 2. The parallel processTree function, written in a C-like language

the two halves of the resource are then given to separate threads for parallel processing. When shares themselves are rationals, $\otimes$ is just ordinary multiplication, e.g. we can divide $0.6 = (0.5 \otimes 0.6) \oplus (0.5 \otimes 0.6)$. Defining a notion of multiplication on a share model that satisfies disjointness is somewhat trickier, but we can do so with tree shares $\mathbb{T}$ as follows. Define $\tau_1 \otimes \tau_2$ to be the operation that replaces each • in τ_2 with a copy of τ_1, e.g.: $\widehat{\circ\bullet} \otimes \widehat{\bullet\circ\bullet} = \widehat{\swarrow\searrow}$. The structure

$(\mathbb{T}, \oplus, \otimes)$ is a kind of "near-semiring." The $\otimes$ operator is associative, has identity $\mathcal{F}$ and null point $\mathcal{E}$, and is right distributive, i.e. $(a \oplus b) \otimes c = (a \otimes c) \oplus (b \otimes c)$. It is not commutative, does not distribute on the left, or have inverses. It is hard to do better: adding axioms like multiplicative inverses forces any model satisfying disjointness $(\forall a, b. \ a \oplus a = b \ \Rightarrow \ a = \mathcal{E})$ to have no more than two elements (Sect. 8).

Now consider the toy program in Fig. 2. Starting from the tree rooted at x, the program itself is dead simple. First (line 3) we check if the x is null, i.e. if we have reached a leaf; if so, we **return**. If not, we split into parallel threads (lines 4–6 and 7–9) that do some processing on the root data in both branches. In the toy example, the processing just **print**s out the root data (lines 4 and 7); the **print** command is unimportant: what is important that we somehow access some of the data in the tree. After processing the root, both parallel branches call the **processTree** function recursively on the left x->l (lines 5 and 8) and right x->r (lines 6 and 9) branches, respectively. After both parallel processes have terminated, the function returns (line 10). The program is simple, so we would like its verification to be equally simple.

Predicate multiplication is the tool that leads to a simple proof. Specifically, we would like to verify that **processTree** has the specification:

$$\forall \pi, x. \ \left(\ \{\pi \cdot \mathsf{tree}(x)\} \ \mathsf{processTree}(x) \ \{\pi \cdot \mathsf{tree}(x)\} \ \right)$$

Here $\mathsf{tree}(x) \stackrel{\text{def}}{=} \langle x = \mathsf{null} \rangle \vee \exists d, l, r. \ x \mapsto (d, l, r) \star \mathsf{tree}(l) \star \mathsf{tree}(r)$ is exactly the usual definition of binary trees in separation logic. Predicate multiplication has allowed us to isolate the fractional ownership from the definition; compare with Eq. (1) above. Our precondition and postcondition both say that x is a pointer to a heap-represented π-owned tree. Critically, we want to ensure that our π-share at the end of the program is equal to the π-share at the beginning. This way if our initial caller had full $\mathcal{F}$ ownership before calling `processTree`, he will have full ownership afterwards (allowing him to *e.g.* deallocate the tree).

The intuition behind the proof is simple. First in line 3, we check if x is null; if so we are in the base case of the tree definition and can simply return. If not we can eliminate the left disjunct and can proceed to split the $\star$-separated bits into disjoint subtrees 1 and r, and then dividing the ownership of those bits into two "halves". Let $\mathcal{L} \overset{\text{def}}{=} \widehat{\bullet\,_\circ}$ and $\mathcal{R} \overset{\text{def}}{=} \overline{\mathcal{L}} = \widehat{_\circ\,\bullet}$. When we start the parallel computation on lines 4 and 7 we want to pass the left branch of the computation the $\mathcal{L} \otimes \pi$-share of the spatial resources, and the right branch of the computation the $\mathcal{R} \otimes \pi$. In both branches we then need to show that we can read from the data cell, which in the simple policy we use for this paper boils down to making sure that the product of two non-$\mathcal{E}$ shares cannot be $\mathcal{E}$. This is a basic property for reasonable share models with multiplication. In the remainder of the parallel code (lines 5–6 and 8–9) we need to make recursive calls, which is done by simply instantiating π with $\mathcal{L} \otimes \pi$ and $\mathcal{R} \otimes \pi$ in the recursive specification (as well as 1 and r for x). The later half proof after the parallel call is pleasantly symmetric to the first half in which we fold back the original tree predicate by merging the two halves $\mathcal{L} \otimes \pi$ and $\mathcal{R} \otimes \pi$ back into π. Consequently, we arrive at the postcondition $\pi \cdot \mathsf{tree}(x)$, which is identical to the precondition.

3.1   Proof Rules for Predicate Multiplication

In Fig. 4 we put the formal verification for `processTree`, which follows the informal argument very closely. However, before we go through it, let us consider the reason for this alignment: because the key rules for reasoning about predicate multiplication are bidirectional. These rules are given in Fig. 3. The non-spatial rules are all straightforward and follow the basic pattern that predicate multiplication both pushes into and pulls out of the operators of our logic without meaningful side conditions. The DOTPURE rule means that predicate multiplication ignores pure facts, too. Complicating the picture slightly, predicate multiplication pushes into implication $\Rightarrow$ but does not pull out of it. Combining DOTIMPL with DOTPURE we get a one-way rule for negation: $\pi \cdot (\neg P) \vdash \neg\pi\cdot$. We will explain why we cannot get both directions in Sects. 5.1 and 8.

Most of the spatial rules are also simple. Recall that emp $\overset{\text{def}}{=} \langle \top \rangle$, so DOT-PURE yields $\pi \cdot$emp $\dashv\vdash$ emp. The DOTFULL rule says that $\mathcal{F}$ is the scalar identity on predicates, just as it is the multiplicative identity on the share model itself. The DOTDOT rule allows us to "collapse" repeated predicate multiplication using share multiplication; we will shortly see how we use it to verify the recursive calls to `processTree`. Similarly, the DOTMAPSTO rule shows how predicate multiplication combines with basic maps-to by multiplying the associated shares together. All three rules are bidirectional and require no side conditions.

While the last two rules are both bidirectional, they both have side conditions. The DOTPLUS rule shows how predicate multiplication distributes over $\oplus$. The $\vdash$ direction does not require a side condition, but the $\dashv$ direction we require that P be *precise* in the usual separation logic sense. Precision will be discussed

$$\frac{P \vdash Q}{\pi \cdot P \vdash \pi \cdot Q} \; \text{Dot Pos} \qquad \frac{}{\pi \cdot \langle P \rangle \dashv\vdash \langle P \rangle} \; \text{Dot Pure} \qquad \frac{}{\pi \cdot (P \Rightarrow Q) \vdash (\pi \cdot P) \Rightarrow (\pi \cdot Q)} \; \text{Dot Impl}$$

$$\frac{}{\pi \cdot (P \wedge Q) \dashv\vdash (\pi \cdot P) \wedge (\pi \cdot Q)} \; \text{Dot Conj} \qquad \frac{}{\pi \cdot (P \vee Q) \dashv\vdash (\pi \cdot P) \vee (\pi \cdot Q)} \; \text{Dot Disj} \qquad \frac{}{\pi \cdot (\neg P) \vdash \neg \pi \cdot P} \; \text{Dot Neg}$$

$$\frac{\tau \neq \emptyset}{\pi \cdot (\forall x : \tau.\ P(x)) \dashv\vdash \forall x : \tau.\ \pi \cdot P(x)} \; \text{Dot Univ} \qquad \frac{}{\pi \cdot (\exists x : \tau.\ P(x)) \dashv\vdash \exists x : \tau.\ \pi \cdot P(x)} \; \text{Dot Exis}$$

$$\frac{}{\mathcal{F} \cdot P \dashv\vdash P} \; \text{Dot Full} \qquad \frac{}{\pi_1 \cdot (\pi_2 \cdot P) \dashv\vdash (\pi_1 \otimes \pi_2) \cdot P} \; \text{Dot Dot} \qquad \frac{}{\pi \cdot x \mapsto y \dashv\vdash x \overset{\pi}{\mapsto} y} \; \text{Dot MapsTo}$$

$$\frac{\text{precise}(P)}{(\pi_1 \oplus \pi_2) \cdot P \dashv\vdash (\pi_1 \cdot P) \star (\pi_2 \cdot P)} \; \text{Dot Plus} \qquad \frac{P \vdash \text{uniform}(\pi') \qquad Q \vdash \text{uniform}(\pi')}{\pi \cdot (P \star Q) \dashv\vdash (\pi \cdot P) \star (\pi \cdot Q)} \; \text{Dot Star}$$

Fig. 3. Distributivity of the scaling operator over pure and spatial connectives

in Sect. 5.2; for now a simple counterexample shows why it is necessary:

$$\mathcal{L} \cdot (x \mapsto a \vee (x + 1) \mapsto b) \star \mathcal{R} \cdot (x \mapsto a \vee (x + 1) \mapsto b) \;\; \not\vdash \;\; \mathcal{F} \cdot (x \mapsto a \vee (x + 1) \mapsto b)$$

The premise is also consistent with $x \overset{\mathcal{L}}{\mapsto} a \star (x + 1) \overset{\mathcal{R}}{\mapsto} b$.

The DotStar rule shows how predicate multiplication distributes into and out of the separating conjunction $\star$. It is also bidirectional. **Crucially, the $\dashv$ direction fails on non-disjoint share models like** $\mathbb{Q}$, which is the "deeper reason" for the deformation of recursive structures illustrated in Fig. 1. On disjoint share models like $\mathbb{T}$, we get equational reasoning $\dashv\vdash$ subject to the side condition of *uniformity*. Informally, $P \vdash \text{uniform}(\pi')$ asserts that any heap that satisfies P has the permission π' uniformly at each of its defined addresses. In Sect. 8 we explain why we cannot admit this rule without a side condition.

In the meantime, let us argue that most predicates used in practice in separation logic are uniform. First, every SL predicate defined in non-fractional settings, such as $\text{tree}(x)$, is $\mathcal{F}$-uniform. Second, P is a π-uniform predicate if and only if $\pi' \cdot P$ is $(\pi' \otimes \pi)$-uniform. Third, the $\star$-conjunction of two π-uniform predicates is also π-uniform. Since a significant motivation for predicate multiplication is to allow standard SL predicates to be used in fractional settings, these already cover many common cases in practice. It is useful to consider examples of non-uniform predicates for contrast. Here are three (we elide the base cases):

$$\text{slist}(x) \;\; \dashv\vdash \;\; \exists d, n. \big(((\langle d = 17 \rangle \star x \overset{\mathcal{L}}{\mapsto} (d, n)) \vee (\langle d \neq 17 \rangle \star x \overset{\mathcal{R}}{\mapsto} (d, n))) \big) \star \text{slist}(n)$$
$$\text{dlist}(x) \;\; \dashv\vdash \;\; \exists d, n. x \mapsto d, n \star \mathcal{L} \cdot \text{dlist}(n)$$
$$\text{dtree}(x) \;\; \dashv\vdash \;\; \exists d, l, r. x \mapsto d, l, r \star \mathcal{L} \cdot \text{dtree}(l) \star \mathcal{R} \cdot \text{dtree}(r)$$

The $\text{slist}(x)$ predicate owns different amounts of permissions at different memory cells depending on the value of those cells. The $\text{dlist}(x)$ predicate owns decreasing amounts of the list, *e.g.* the first cell is owned more than the second, which is owned more than the third. The $\text{dtree}(x)$ predicate is even stranger, owning different amounts of different branches of the tree, essentially depending on the

```
1  void processTree(struct tree* x) { // { π · tree(x) }
```
2 // $\left\{ \pi \cdot \Big(\langle x = \text{null} \rangle \ \vee \ \big(\exists d, l, r.\ x \mapsto (d, l, r)\ \star\ \text{tree}(l)\ \star\ \text{tree}(r) \big) \Big) \right\}$

3 // $\left\{ \langle x = \text{null} \rangle \ \vee \ \Big(\exists d, l, r.\ x \overset{\pi}{\mapsto} (d, l, r)\ \star\ \big(\pi \cdot \text{tree}(l) \big)\ \star\ \big(\pi \cdot \text{tree}(r) \big) \Big) \right\}$

```
4    if (x == null) { // {⟨x = null⟩}
5    return;} // { π · tree(x) }
```

6 // $\left\{ x \overset{\pi}{\mapsto} (d, l, r)\ \star\ \big(\pi \cdot \text{tree}(l) \big)\ \star\ \big(\pi \cdot \text{tree}(r) \big) \right\}$

7 // $\left\{ \mathcal{F} \cdot \Big(x \overset{\pi}{\mapsto} (d, l, r)\ \star\ \big(\pi \cdot \text{tree}(l) \big)\ \star\ \big(\pi \cdot \text{tree}(r) \big) \Big) \right\}$

8 // $\left\{ (\mathcal{L} \oplus \mathcal{R}) \cdot \Big(x \overset{\pi}{\mapsto} (d, l, r)\ \star\ \big(\pi \cdot \text{tree}(l) \big)\ \star\ \big(\pi \cdot \text{tree}(r) \big) \Big) \right\}$

9 // $\left\{ \begin{array}{l} \Big(\mathcal{L} \cdot \big(x \overset{\pi}{\mapsto} (d, l, r)\ \star\ \big(\pi \cdot \text{tree}(l) \big)\ \star\ \big(\pi \cdot \text{tree}(r) \big) \big) \Big)\ \star \\ \Big(\mathcal{R} \cdot \big(x \overset{\pi}{\mapsto} (d, l, r)\ \star\ \big(\pi \cdot \text{tree}(l) \big)\ \star\ \big(\pi \cdot \text{tree}(r) \big) \big) \Big) \end{array} \right\}$

10 // $\left\{ \mathcal{L} \cdot \Big(x \overset{\pi}{\mapsto} (d, l, r)\ \star\ \big(\pi \cdot \text{tree}(l) \big)\ \star\ \big(\pi \cdot \text{tree}(r) \big) \Big) \right\}$

11 // $\left\{ \mathcal{L} \cdot x \overset{\pi}{\mapsto} (d, l, r)\ \star\ \mathcal{L} \cdot \pi \cdot \text{tree}(l)\ \star\ \mathcal{L} \cdot \pi \cdot \text{tree}(r) \right\}$

12 // $\left\{ x \overset{\mathcal{L} \otimes \pi}{\mapsto} (d, l, r)\ \star\ \big((\mathcal{L} \otimes \pi) \cdot \text{tree}(l) \big)\ \star\ \big((\mathcal{L} \otimes \pi) \cdot \text{tree}(r) \big) \right\}$

```
13    print(x -> d);
14    processTree(x -> l);  processTree(x -> r);
```

15 // $\left\{ x \overset{\mathcal{L} \otimes \pi}{\mapsto} (d, l, r)\ \star\ \big((\mathcal{L} \otimes \pi) \cdot \text{tree}(l) \big)\ \star\ \big((\mathcal{L} \otimes \pi) \cdot \text{tree}(r) \big) \right\}$

16 // $\left\{ \mathcal{L} \cdot \pi \cdot x \mapsto (d, l, r)\ \star\ \mathcal{L} \cdot \pi \cdot \text{tree}(l)\ \star\ \mathcal{L} \cdot \pi \cdot \text{tree}(r) \right\}$

17 // $\left\{ \mathcal{L} \cdot \pi \cdot \big(x \mapsto (d, l, r)\ \star\ \text{tree}(l)\ \star\ \text{tree}(r) \big) \right\}$

18 // $\left\{ \begin{array}{l} \Big(\mathcal{L} \cdot \pi \cdot \big(x \mapsto (d, l, r)\ \star\ \text{tree}(l)\ \star\ \text{tree}(r) \big) \Big)\ \star \\ \Big(\mathcal{R} \cdot \pi \cdot \big(x \mapsto (d, l, r)\ \star\ \text{tree}(l)\ \star\ \text{tree}(r) \big) \Big) \end{array} \right\}$

19 // $\left\{ (\mathcal{L} \oplus \mathcal{R}) \cdot \pi \cdot \big(x \mapsto (d, l, r)\ \star\ \text{tree}(l)\ \star\ \text{tree}(r) \big) \right\}$

```
20  } // { π · tree(x) }
```

Fig. 4. Reasoning with the scaling operator $\pi \cdot P$.

path to the root. None of these predicates mix well with DOTSTAR, but perhaps they are not useful to verify many programs in practice, either. In Sects. 5.1 and 5.2 we will discuss how to prove predicates are precise and uniform. In Sect. 5.4 will demonstrate our techniques to do so by applying them to two examples.

3.2 Verification of processTree using predicate multiplication

We now explain how the proof of processTree is carried out in Fig. 4 using scaling rules in Fig. 3. In line 2, we unfold the definition of predicate $\text{tree}(x)$ which consists of one base case and one inductive case. We reach line 3 by pushing π inward using various rules DOTPURE, DOTDISJ, DOTEXIS, DOTMAPSTO and DOTSTAR. To use DOTSTAR we must prove that $\text{tree}(x)$ is $\mathcal{F}$-uniform, which we show how to do in Sect. 5.4. We prove this lemma once and use it many times.

The base base $\mathtt{x} = \mathtt{null}$ is handled in lines 4–5 by applying rule DOTPURE, *i.e.*, $\langle \mathtt{x} = \mathtt{null} \rangle \vdash \pi \cdot \langle \mathtt{x} = \mathtt{null} \rangle$ and then DOTPOS, $\pi \cdot \langle \mathtt{x} = \mathtt{null} \rangle \vdash \pi \cdot \mathsf{tree}(x)$. For the inductive case, we first apply DOTFULL in line 7 and then replace $\mathcal{F}$ with $\mathcal{L} \oplus \mathcal{R}$ (recall that $\mathcal{R}$ is $\mathcal{L}$'s compliment). On line 9 we use DOTPLUS to translate the split on shares with $\oplus$ into a split on heaps with $\star$.

We show only one parallel process; the other is a mirror image. Line 10 gives the precondition from the PARALLEL rule, and then in lines 11 and 12 we continue to "push in" the predicate multiplication. To verify the code in lines 13–14 just requires FRAME. Notice that we need the DOTDOT rule to "collapse" the two uses of predicate multiplication into one so that we can apply the recursive specification (with the new π' in the recursive precondition equal to $\mathcal{L} \otimes \pi$).

Having taken the predicate completely apart, it is now necessary to put Humpty Dumpty back together again. Here is why it is vital that all of our proof rules are bidirectional, without which we would not be able to reach the final postcondition $\pi \cdot \mathsf{tree}(x)$. The final wrinkle is that for line 19 we must prove the precision of the $\mathsf{tree}(x)$ predicate. We show how to do so with example in Sect. 5.4, but typically in a verification this is proved once per predicate as a lemma.

4   Bi-abductive Inference with Fractional Permissions

Biabduction is a separation logic inference process that helps to increase the scalability of verification for sizable programs [22,49]; in recent years it has been the focus of substantial research for (sequential) separation logic [8,10,11,32]. Biabduction aims to infer the missing information in an incomplete separation logic entailment. More precisely, given an incomplete entailment $A \star [??] \vdash B \star [??]$, we would like to find predicates for the two missing pieces [??] that complete the entailment in a nontrivial manner. The first piece is called the *antiframe* while the second is the *inference frame*. The standard approach consists of two sequential subroutines, namely the *abductive inference* and *frame inference* to construct the antiframe and frame respectively. Our task in this section is to show how to upgrade these routines to handle fractional permissions so that biabduction can extend to concurrent programs. As we will see, disjointness plays a crucial role in antiframe inference.

4.1   Fractional Residue Computation

Consider the fractional point-to bi-abduction problem with rationals:

$$a \xrightarrow{\pi_1} b \star [??] \vdash a \xrightarrow{\pi_2} b \star [??]$$

There are three cases to consider, namely $\pi_1 = \pi_2$, $\pi_1 < \pi_2$ or $\pi_1 > \pi_2$. In the first case, both the (minimal) antiframe F_a and frame F_f are emp; for the second case we have $F_a = \mathsf{emp}$, $F_f = a \xrightarrow{\pi_2 - \pi_1} b$ and the last case gives us $F_a = a \xrightarrow{\pi_1 - \pi_2} b$, $F_f = \mathsf{emp}$. Here we straightforwardly compute the residue permission using rational subtraction. In general, one can attempt to define subtraction $\ominus$ from a share model $\langle \mathcal{S}, \oplus \rangle$ as $a \ominus b = c \overset{\text{def}}{=} b \oplus c = a$. However, this definition is too coarse as we want subtraction to be a total function so that the residue is always computable efficiently. A solution to this issue is to relax the requirements for $\ominus$, asking only that it satisfies the following two properties:

$$C_1 : a \oplus (b \ominus a) = b \oplus (a \ominus b) \qquad C_2 : a \ll b \oplus c \Rightarrow a \ominus b \ll c$$

where $a \ll b \overset{\text{def}}{=} \exists c.\ a \oplus c = b$. The condition C_1 provides a convenient way to compute the fractional residue in both the frame and antiframe while C_2 asserts that $a \ominus b$ is effectively the minimal element that when joined with b becomes greater than a. In the rationals $\mathbb{Q}$, $a \ominus b \overset{\text{def}}{=} if (a > b)\ then\ a - b\ else\ 0$. On tree shares $\mathbb{T}$, $a \ominus b \overset{\text{def}}{=} a \sqcap \overline{b}$. Recalling that the case when $\pi_1 = \pi_2$ is simple (both the antiframe and frame are just emp), then if $\pi_1 \neq \pi_2$ we can compute the fractional antiframe and inference frames uniquely using $\ominus$:

$$\frac{}{a \overset{\pi_1}{\longmapsto} b \star a \overset{\pi_2 \ominus \pi_1}{\longmapsto} b \vdash a \overset{\pi_2}{\longmapsto} b \star a \overset{\pi_1 \ominus \pi_2}{\longmapsto} b} \text{ MSUB}$$

Generally, the following rule helps compute the residue of predicate P:

$$\frac{\text{precise}(P)}{\pi_1 \cdot P \star (\pi_2 \ominus \pi_1) \cdot P \vdash \pi_2 \cdot P \star (\pi_1 \ominus \pi_2) \cdot P} \text{ PSUB}$$

Using C_1 and C_2 it is easy to prove that the residue is minimal w.r.t. $\ll$, *i.e.*:

$$\pi_1 \oplus a = \pi_2 \oplus b \Rightarrow \pi_2 \ominus \pi_1 \ll a \wedge \pi_1 \ominus \pi_2 \ll b$$

4.2   Extension of Predicate Axioms

To support reasoning over recursive data structure such as lists or trees, the assertion language is enriched with the corresponding inductive predicates. To derive properties over inductive predicates, verification tools often contain a list of predicate axioms/facts and use them to aid the verification process [9,32]. These facts are represented as entailment rules $A \vdash B$ that can be classified into "folding" and "unfolding" rules to manipulate the representation of inductive predicates. For example, some axioms for the tree predicate are:

$$F_1 : x = 0 \wedge \text{emp} \vdash \text{tree}(x) \qquad F_2 : x \mapsto (v, x_1, x_2) \star \text{tree}(x_1) \star \text{tree}(x_2) \vdash \text{tree}(x)$$
$$U : \text{tree}(x) \wedge x \neq 0 \vdash \exists v, x_1, x_2.\ x \mapsto (v, x_1, x_2) \star \text{tree}(x_1) \star \text{tree}(x_2)$$

We want to transform these axioms into fractional forms. The key ingredient is the DOTPOS rule from Fig. 3, that lifts the fractional portion of an entailment, *i.e.* $(P \vdash Q) \Rightarrow (\pi \cdot P \vdash \pi \cdot Q)$. Using this and the other scaling rules from Fig. 3, we can upgrade the folding/unfolding rules into corresponding fractional forms:

$$F_1' : x = 0 \wedge \text{emp} \vdash \pi \cdot \text{tree}(x) \qquad F_2' : x \overset{\pi}{\mapsto} (v, x_1, x_2) \star \pi \cdot \text{tree}(x_1) \star \pi \cdot \text{tree}(x_2) \vdash \pi \cdot \text{tree}(x)$$
$$U : \text{tree}(x) \wedge x \neq 0 \vdash \exists v, x_1, x_2.\ x \mapsto (v, x_1, x_2) \star \text{tree}(x_1) \star \text{tree}(x_2)$$

As our scaling rules are bi-directional, they can be applied both in the antecedent and consequent to produce a smooth transformation to fractional axioms. Also, recall that our DOTSTAR rule $\pi \cdot (P \star Q) \dashv\vdash \pi \cdot P \star \pi \cdot Q$ has a side condition that both P and Q are π'-uniform. This condition is trivial in the transformation as standard predicates (*i.e.* those without permissions) are automatically $\mathcal{F}$-uniform. Furthermore, the precision and uniformity properties can be transferred directly to fractional forms by the following rules:

$$\text{precise}(\pi \cdot P) \Leftrightarrow \text{precise}(P) \qquad P \vdash \text{uniform}(\pi) \Leftrightarrow \pi' \cdot P \vdash \text{uniform}(\pi' \otimes \pi)$$

4.3   Abductive Inference and Frame Inference

To construct the antiframe, Calcagno *et al.* [10] presented a general framework for antiframe inference which contains rules of the form:

$$\frac{\Delta' \star [M'] \rhd H' \qquad \text{Cond}}{\Delta \star [M] \rhd H}$$

where Cond is the side condition, together with consequents (H, H'), heap formulas (Δ, Δ') and antiframes (M, M'). In principle, the abduction algorithm gradually matches fragments of consequent with antecedent, derives sound equalities among variables while applying various folding and unfolding rules for recursive predicates in both sides of the entailment. Ideally, the remaining unmatched fragments of the antecedent are returned to form the antiframe. During the process, certain conditions need to be maintained, *e.g.*, satisfiability of the antecedent or minimal choice for antiframe. After finding the antiframe, the inference process is invoked to construct the inference frame. In principle, the old antecedent is first combined with the antiframe to form a new antecedent whose fragments are matched with the consequent. Eventually, the remaining unmatched fragments of the antecedent are returned to construct the inference frame.

The discussion of fractional residue computation in Sect. 4.1 and extension of recursive predicate rules in Sect. 4.2 ensure a smooth upgrade of the biabduction algorithm to fractional form. We demonstrate this intuition using the example in Fig. 5. The partial consequent is a fractional $\text{tree}(x)$ predicate with permission π_3 while the partial antecedent is star conjunction of a fractional maps-to predicate of address x with permission π_1, a fractional $\text{tree}(x_1)$ predicate with permission π_2 and a null pointer x_2. Following the spirit of Calcagno *et al.* [10], the steps in both sub-routines include applying the folding and unfolding rules for predicate tree and then matching the corresponding pair of fragments from antecedent and consequent. On the other hand, the upgraded part is reflected through the use of the two new rules MSUB and PSUB to compute the fractional residues as well as a more general system of folding and unfolding rules for predicate tree. We are then able to compute the antiframe $a = x_1 \wedge (\pi_3 \ominus \pi_2) \cdot \text{tree}(x_1) \star x \xmapsto{\pi_3 \ominus \pi_2} (v, a, x_2)$ and the inference frame $x \xmapsto{\pi_1 \ominus \pi_3} (v, x_1, x_2) \star (\pi_2 \ominus \pi_3) \cdot \text{tree}(x_1)$ respectively.

$$x \xmapsto{\pi_1} (v, a, x_2) \star \pi_2 \cdot \mathsf{tree}(x_1) \star (x_2 = 0 \wedge \mathsf{emp}) \star [??] \vdash \pi_3 \cdot \mathsf{tree}(x) \star [??]$$

$$
\cfrac{
\cfrac{
\cfrac{
\cfrac{\overline{(x_2 = 0 \wedge \mathsf{emp}) \star [\mathsf{emp}] \rhd \mathsf{emp}} \; \text{BASE}}
{(x_2 = 0 \wedge \mathsf{emp}) \star [\mathsf{emp}] \rhd \pi_3 \cdot \mathsf{tree}(x_2)} \; \mathsf{F_1}'
}
{\pi_2 \cdot \mathsf{tree}(x_1) \star (x_2 = 0 \wedge \mathsf{emp}) \star [(\pi_3 \ominus \pi_2) \cdot \mathsf{tree}(x_1)] \rhd \pi_3 \cdot \mathsf{tree}(x_1) \star \pi_3 \cdot \mathsf{tree}(x_2)} \; \text{PSUB}
}
{
\begin{array}{c}
x \xmapsto{\pi_1} (v, a, x_2) \star \pi_2 \cdot \mathsf{tree}(x_1) \star (x_2 = 0 \wedge \mathsf{emp}) \star [(\pi_3 \ominus \pi_2) \cdot \mathsf{tree}(x_1) \\
\star x \xmapsto{\pi_3 \ominus \pi_1} (v, a, x_2)] \rhd x \xmapsto{\pi_3} (v, a, x_2) \star \pi_3 \cdot \mathsf{tree}(x_1) \star \pi_3 \cdot \mathsf{tree}(x_2)
\end{array}
} \; \substack{\text{MATCH} \\ +\mathsf{F_2}'}
}
{
\begin{array}{c}
x \xmapsto{\pi_1} (v, a, x_2) \star \pi_2 \cdot \mathsf{tree}(x_1) \star (x_2 = 0 \wedge \mathsf{emp}) \\
\star \; [a = x_1 \wedge (\pi_3 \ominus \pi_2) \cdot \mathsf{tree}(x_1) \star x \xmapsto{\pi_3 \ominus \pi_1} (v, a, x_2)] \rhd \pi_3 \cdot \mathsf{tree}(x)
\end{array}
} \; \substack{\text{PSUB} \\ \text{MSUB}}
$$

Abductive inference

$$
\cfrac{
\cfrac{
\cfrac{\overline{\mathsf{emp} \rhd \mathsf{emp} \star [\mathsf{emp}]} \; \text{BASE}}
{x \xmapsto{\pi_1 \oplus (\pi_3 \ominus \pi_1)} (v, x_1, x_2) \rhd x \xmapsto{\pi_3} (v, x_1, x_2) \star [x \xmapsto{(\pi_1 \ominus \pi_3)} (v, x_1, x_2)]} \; \text{MSUB}
}
{
\begin{array}{c}
x \xmapsto{\pi_1 \oplus (\pi_3 \ominus \pi_1)} (v, x_1, x_2) \star (\pi_2 \oplus (\pi_3 \ominus \pi_2)) \cdot \mathsf{tree}(x_1) \rhd \\
x \xmapsto{\pi_3} (v, x_1, x_2) \star \pi_3 \cdot \mathsf{tree}(x_1) \star [x \xmapsto{(\pi_1 \ominus \pi_3)} (v, x_1, x_2) \star (\pi_2 \ominus \pi_3) \cdot \mathsf{tree}(x_1)]
\end{array}
} \; \text{PSUB}
}
{
\begin{array}{c}
x \xmapsto{\pi_1 \oplus (\pi_3 \ominus \pi_1)} (v, x_1, x_2) \star (\pi_2 \oplus (\pi_3 \ominus \pi_2)) \cdot \mathsf{tree}(x_1) \star (x_2 = 0 \wedge \mathsf{emp}) \rhd \\
x \xmapsto{\pi_3} (v, x_1, x_2) \star \pi_3 \cdot \mathsf{tree}(x_1) \star \pi_3 \cdot \mathsf{tree}(x_2) \star [x \xmapsto{(\pi_1 \ominus \pi_3)} (v, x_1, x_2) \star (\pi_2 \ominus \pi_3) \cdot \mathsf{tree}(x_1)]
\end{array}
} \; \mathsf{F_1}'
$$

Frame inference

Fig. 5. An example of biabduction with fractional permissions

Antiframe Inference and Disjointness. Consider the following abduction problem:

$$x \mapsto (v, x_1, x_2) \star \mathsf{tree}(x_1) \star [??] \vdash \mathsf{tree}(x)$$

Using the folding rule F_2, we can identify the antiframe as $\mathsf{tree}(x_2)$. Now suppose we have a rational permission $\pi \in \mathbb{Q}$ distributed everywhere, *i.e.*:

$$x \xmapsto{\pi} (v, x_1, x_2) \star \pi \cdot \mathsf{tree}(x_1) \star [??] \vdash \pi \cdot \mathsf{tree}(x)$$

A naïve solution is to let the antiframe be $\pi \cdot \mathsf{tree}(x_2)$. However, in $\mathbb{Q}$ this choice is unsound due to the deformation of recursive structures issue illustrated in Fig. 1: if the antiframe is $\pi \cdot \mathsf{tree}(x_2)$, the left hand side can be a DAG, even though the right hand side must be a tree. However, in disjoint share models like $\mathbb{T}$, choosing $\pi \cdot \mathsf{tree}(x_2)$ for the antiframe is correct and the entailment holds. As is often the case, things are straightforward once the definitions are correct.

5   A Proof Theory for Fractional Permissions

Our main objective in this section is to show how to discharge the uniformity and precision side conditions required by the DOTSTAR and DOTPLUS rules.

To handle recursive predicates like tree(x) we develop set of novel modal-logic based proof rules to carry out induction in the heap. To allow tools to leverage existing entailment checkers, all of these techniques are done **in the object logic itself**, rather than in the metalogic. Thus, in Sect. 5, we do not assume a concrete model for our object logic (in Sect. 7 we will develop a model).

First we discuss new proof rules for predicate multiplication and fractional maps-to (Sect. 5.1), precision (Sect. 5.2), and induction over fractional heaps (Sect. 5.3). We then conclude (Sect. 5.4) with two examples of proving real properties using our proof theory: that tree(x) is $\mathcal{F}$-uniform and that list(x) is precise. Some of the theorems have delicate proofs, so all of them have been verified in Coq [1].

5.1 Proof Theory for Predicate Multiplication and Fractional Maps-To

In Sect. 3 we presented the key rules that someone who wants to verify programs using predicate multiplication is likely to find convenient. On page 13 we present a series of additional rules, mostly used to establish the "uniform" and "precise" side conditions necessary in our proofs.

Figure 6 is the simplest group, giving basic facts about the fractional points-to predicate. Only $\mapsto$ INVERSION is not immediate from the nonfractional case. It says that it is impossible to have two fractional maps-tos of the same address and with two different values. We need this fact to *e.g.* prove that predicates with existentials such as tree are precise.

$$\frac{}{(x \overset{\pi}{\mapsto} y_1 \star \top) \wedge (x \overset{\pi'}{\mapsto} y_2 \star \top) \vdash |y_1 = y_2|} \overset{\mapsto}{\text{INVERSION}} \qquad \frac{}{x \overset{\pi}{\mapsto} y \vdash \neg\mathsf{emp}} \overset{\mapsto}{\text{emp}} \qquad \frac{}{x \overset{\pi}{\mapsto} y \vdash |x \neq \mathtt{null}|} \overset{\mapsto}{\text{null}}$$

Fig. 6. Proof theory for fractional maps-to

$$\frac{}{\mathsf{emp} \vdash \mathsf{uniform}(\pi)} \text{uniform/emp} \qquad \frac{}{\mathsf{uniform}(\pi) \star \mathsf{uniform}(\pi) \dashv\vdash \mathsf{uniform}(\pi)} \text{uniform}\star$$

$$\frac{P \vdash \mathsf{uniform}(\pi)}{\pi' \cdot P \vdash \mathsf{uniform}(\pi' \otimes \pi)} \text{uniformDot} \qquad \frac{}{\mathsf{precise}(x \overset{\pi}{\mapsto} y)} \overset{\mapsto}{\text{PRECISE}}$$

$$\frac{}{x \overset{\pi}{\mapsto} y \vdash \mathsf{uniform}(\pi)} \overset{\mapsto}{\text{uniform}} \qquad \frac{\mathsf{precise}(P)}{\mathsf{precise}(\pi \cdot P)} \overset{\text{DOT}}{\text{PRECISE}}$$

Fig. 7. Uniformity and precision for predicate multiplication

$$\frac{G \vdash \mathsf{precisely}(P) \quad G \vdash \mathsf{precisely}(Q)}{G \vdash \mathsf{precisely}(P \star Q)} \; \text{precisely}\star$$

$$\frac{\top \vdash \mathsf{precisely}(P)}{\mathsf{precise}(P)} \; \begin{array}{l}\text{precisely}\\ \text{\scriptsize PRECISE}\end{array}$$

$$\frac{}{\mathsf{precisely}(P) \vdash \big((P{\star}Q) \wedge (P{\star}R)\big) \Rightarrow \big(P{\star}(Q{\wedge}R)\big)} \; \begin{array}{l}\text{precisely}\\ \text{\scriptsize LEFT}\end{array}$$

$$\frac{\exists x.\Big(G \vdash \mathsf{precisely}\big(P(x)\big)\Big)}{G \vdash \mathsf{precisely}\big(\forall x.P(x)\big)} \; \text{precisely}\forall$$

$$\frac{\forall Q,R.\Big(G \vdash \big((P{\star}Q) \wedge (P{\star}R)\big) \Rightarrow \big(P{\star}(Q{\wedge}R)\big)\Big)}{G \vdash \mathsf{precisely}(P)} \; \begin{array}{l}\text{precisely}\\ \text{\scriptsize RIGHT}\end{array}$$

$$\frac{G \vdash \mathsf{precisely}(P)}{G \vdash \mathsf{precisely}(P \wedge Q)} \; \text{precisely}\wedge$$

$$\frac{\forall x.\Big(G \vdash \mathsf{precisely}\big(P(x)\big)\Big) \qquad \forall x,y.\Big(G \wedge \big(P(x) \star \top\big) \wedge \big(P(y) \star \top\big) \vdash |x=y|\Big)}{G \vdash \mathsf{precisely}\big(\exists x.P(x)\big)} \; \text{precisely}\exists$$

$$\frac{G \vdash \mathsf{precisely}(P) \qquad G \vdash \mathsf{precisely}(Q) \qquad G \wedge (P \star \top) \wedge (Q \star \top) \vdash \bot}{G \vdash \mathsf{precisely}(P \vee Q)} \; \text{precisely}\vee$$

Fig. 8. Proof theory for precision

$$\frac{}{\odot P \vdash P} \; \text{T} \qquad \frac{}{\odot P \vdash \odot\odot P} \; \odot\odot \qquad \frac{}{\triangleright_\pi P \vdash \triangleright_\pi \triangleright_\pi P} \; \triangleright_\pi\triangleright_\pi$$

$$\frac{\triangleright_\pi P \vdash P}{\top \vdash P} \; \text{W} \qquad \frac{}{\triangleright_\pi P \dashv\vdash \triangleright_\pi \odot P} \; \triangleright_\pi\odot \qquad \frac{}{\triangleright_\pi P \dashv\vdash \odot \triangleright_\pi P} \; \odot\triangleright_\pi$$

$$\frac{}{(P \star Q) \wedge \odot R \vdash (P \wedge \odot R) \star (Q \wedge \odot R)} \; \odot\star \qquad \frac{P \vdash U(\pi) \wedge \neg\mathsf{emp}}{(P \star Q) \wedge \triangleright_\pi R \vdash (P \wedge \triangleright_\pi R) \star (Q \wedge R)} \; \triangleright_\pi\star$$

Fig. 9. Proof theory for substructural induction

Proving the side conditions for DOTPLUS *and* DOTSTAR. Figure 7 contains some rules for establishing that P is π-uniform (*i.e.* $P \vdash \mathsf{uniform}(\pi)$) and that P is precise. Since uniformity is a simple property, the rules are easy to state:

To use predicate multiplication we will need to prove two kinds of side conditions: uniform/emp tells us that emp is π-uniform for all π; the conclusion (all defined heap locations are held with share π) is vacuously true. The uniformDOT rule tells us that if P is π-uniform then when we multiply P by a fraction π' the result is $(\pi' \otimes \pi)$-uniform. The $\mapsto$ uniform rule tells us that points-to is uniform. The uniform$\star$ rule possesses interesting characteristics. The $\dashv$ direction follows from uniform/emp and the $\star$emp rule ($P \star \mathsf{emp} \dashv\vdash P$). The $\vdash$ direction is not automatic but very useful. One consequence is that from $P \vdash \mathsf{uniform}(\pi)$ and $Q \vdash \mathsf{uniform}(\pi)$ we can prove $P \star Q \vdash \mathsf{uniform}(\pi)$. The $\vdash$ direction follows from disjointness but fails over non-disjoint models such as rationals $\mathbb{Q}$.

The $\mapsto$ PRECISE rule tells us that points-tos are precise. The DOTPRECISE rule is a partial solution to proving precision. It states that $\pi \cdot P$ is precise if and only if P is precise. We will next show how to prove that P itself is precise.

5.2   Proof Theory for Proving that Predicates Are Precise

Proving that a predicate is π-uniform is relatively straightforward using the proof rules presented so far. However, proving that a predicate is precise is not as pleasant. Traditionally precision is defined (and checked for concrete predicates) in the metalogic [40] using the following definition:

$$\text{precise}(P) \overset{\text{def}}{=} \forall h, h_1, h_2.\ h_1 \subseteq h \Rightarrow h_2 \subseteq h \Rightarrow (h_1 \models P) \Rightarrow (h_2 \models P) \Rightarrow h_1 = h_2 \quad (3)$$

Here we write $h_1 \subseteq h_2$ to mean that h_1 is a subheap of h_2, i.e. $\exists h'.h_1 \oplus h' = h_2$, where $\oplus$ is the joining operation on the underlying separation algebra [21]. Essentially precision is a kind of uniqueness property: if a predicate P is precise then it can only be true on a single subheap.

Rather than checking precision in the metalogic, we wish to do so in the object logic. We give a proof theory that lets us do so in Fig. 8. Among other advantages, proving precision in the object logic lets tools build on existing separation logic entailment checkers to prove the precision of recursive predicates. The core idea is simple: we define a new object logic operator "precisely(P)" that captures the notion of precision relativized to the current heap; essentially it is a partially applied version of the definition of precise(P) in Eq. (3):

$$h \models \text{precisely}(P) \overset{\text{def}}{=} \forall h_1, h_2.h_1 \subseteq h \Rightarrow h_2 \subseteq h \Rightarrow (h_1 \models P) \Rightarrow (h_2 \models P) \Rightarrow h_1 = h_2 \quad (4)$$

Although we have given precisely's model to aid intuition, we emphasize that in Sect. 5 all of our proofs take place in the object logic; we never unfold precisely's definition. Note that precisely is also generally weaker than the typical notion of precision. For example, the predicate $x \mapsto 7 \vee y \mapsto 7$ is not precise; however the entailment $z \mapsto 8 \vdash \text{precisely}(x \mapsto 7 \vee y \mapsto 7)$ is provable from Fig. 8.

That said, two notions are closely connected as given in the preciselyPRECISE rule. We also give introduction preciselyRIGHT and elimination rules preciselyLEFT that make a connection between precision and an "antidistribution" of $\star$ over $\wedge$.

We also give a number of rules for showing how precisely combines with the connectives of our logic. The rules for propositional $\wedge$ and separating $\star$ conjunction follow well-understood patterns, with the addition of an arbitrary premise context G being the key feature. The rule for disjunction $\vee$ is a little trickier, with an additional premise that forces the disjunction to be exclusive rather than inclusive. An example of such an exclusive disjunction is in the standard definition of the tree predicate, where the first disjunct $\langle x = \texttt{null} \rangle$ is fundamentally incompatible with the second disjunct $\exists d, l, r.x \mapsto d, l, r \star \ldots$ since $\mapsto$ does not allow the address to be $\texttt{null}$ (by rule $\mapsto \texttt{null}$ from Fig. 6). The rules for universal quantification $\forall$ existential quantification $\exists$ are essentially generalizations of the rules for the traditional conjunction $\wedge$ and disjunction $\vee$.

It is now straightforward to prove the precision of simple predicates such as $\langle x = \texttt{null} \rangle \vee (\exists y.x \mapsto y \star y \mapsto 0)$. Finding and proving the key lemmas that enable the proof of the precision of recursive predicates remains a little subtle.

5.3   Proof Theory for Induction over the Finiteness of the Heap

Recursive predicates such as $\mathsf{list}(x)$ and $\mathsf{tree}(x)$ are common in SL. However, proving properties of such predicates, such as proving that $\mathsf{list}(x)$ is precise, is a little tricky since the μFOLDUNFOLD rule provided by the Tarski fixed point does not automatically provide an induction principle. Generally speaking such properties follow by some kind of induction argument, either over auxiliary parameters (*e.g.* if we augment trees to have the form $\mathsf{tree}(x, \tau)$, where τ is an inductively-defined type in the metalogic) or over the finiteness of the heap itself. Both arguments usually occur in the metalogic rather than the object logic.

We have two contributions to make for proving inductive properties. First, we show how to do induction over the heap in a fractional setting. Intuitively this is more complicated than in the non-fractional case because there are infinite sequences of strictly smaller subheaps. That is, for a given initial heap h_0, there are infinite sequences $h_1, h_2, \ldots$ such that $h_0 \supsetneq h_1 \supsetneq h_2 \supsetneq \ldots$. The disjointness property does not fundamentally change this issue, so we illustrate with an example with the shares in $\mathbb{Q}$. The heap h_0 satisfying $x \overset{1}{\mapsto} y$ is strictly larger than the heap h_1 satisfying $x \overset{\frac{1}{2}}{\mapsto} y$, which is strictly larger than the heap h_2 satisfying $x \overset{\frac{1}{4}}{\mapsto} y$; in general h_i satisfies $x \overset{\frac{1}{2^i}}{\mapsto} y$. Since our sequence is infinite, we cannot use it as the basis for an induction argument. The solution is that we require that the heaps decrease by at least some constant size c. If each heap subsequent heap must shrink by at least *e.g.* $c = 0.25$ of a memory cell then the sequence must be finite just as in the non-fractional case, *i.e.* $c = \mathcal{F}$. More sophisticated approaches are conceivable (*e.g.* limits) but they are not easy to automate and we did not find any practical examples that require such methods.

Our second contribution is the development of a proof theory in the object logic that can carry out these kinds of induction proofs in a relatively straightforward way. The proof rules that let us do so are given in Fig. 9. Once good lemmas are identified, we find doing induction proofs over the finite heap formally in the object logic simpler than doing the same proofs in the metalogic.

The key to our induction rules is two new operators: "within" $\odot$ and "shrinking" $\rhd_\pi$. Essentially $\rhd_\pi P$ is used as an induction guard, preventing us from applying our induction hypothesis P until we are on a π-smaller subheap. When $\pi = \mathcal{F}$ we sometimes write just $\rhd P$. Semantically, if h satisfies $\rhd_\pi P$ then P is true **on all strict subheaps of h that are smaller by at least a π-piece**. Accordingly, the key elimination rule $\rhd_\pi \star$ may seem natural: it verifies that the induction guard is satisfied and unlocks the underlying hypothesis. To start an induction proof to prove an arbitrary goal $\top \models P$, we use the rule W to introduce an induction hypothesis, resulting in the new entailment goal of $\rhd_\pi P \vdash P$.

Some definitions, such as $\mathsf{list}(x)$, have only one "recursive call"; others, such as $\mathsf{tree}(x)$ have more than one. Moreover, sometimes we wish to apply our inductive hypothesis immediately after satisfying the guard, whereas other times it is convenient to satisfy the guard somewhat before we need the inductive hypothesis. To handle both of these issues we use the "within" operator $\odot$ such that $h \models \odot P$ means P is true on all subheaps of h, which is the intuition behind the rule $\odot\star$. To apply our induction hypothesis somewhat after meeting its guard (or if we wish to apply it more than once) we use the $\triangleright_\pi\odot$ rule to add the $\odot$ modality before eliminating the guard. We will see an example of this shortly.

5.4 Using Our Proof Theory

We now turn to two examples of using our proof theory from page 13 to demonstrate that the rule set is strong and flexible enough to prove real properties.

Proving that $\mathsf{tree}(x)$ *is $\mathcal{F}$-uniform.* Our logical rules for induction and uniformity are able to establish the uniformity of predicates in a fairly simple way. Here we focus on the $\mathsf{tree}(x)$ predicate because it is a little harder due to the two recursive "calls" in its unfolding. For convenience, we will write $\mathsf{u}(\pi)$ instead of $\mathsf{uniform}(\pi)$.

Our initial proof goal is $\mathsf{tree}(x) \vdash \mathsf{u}(\mathcal{F})$. Standard natural deduction arguments then reach the goal $\top \vdash \forall x.\mathsf{tree}(x) \Rightarrow \mathsf{u}(\mathcal{F})$, after which we apply the W rule ($\pi = \mathcal{F}$ is convenient) to start the induction, adding the hypothesis $\triangleright\forall x.\mathsf{tree}(x) \Rightarrow \mathsf{u}(\mathcal{F})$, which we strengthen with the $\triangleright_\pi\odot$ rule to reach $\triangleright\odot\ \forall x.\mathsf{tree}(x) \Rightarrow \mathsf{u}(\mathcal{F})$. Natural deduction from there reaches

$$(\langle x = \mathtt{null}\rangle \vee \exists d,l,r.x \mapsto (d,l,r) \star \mathsf{tree}(l) \star \mathsf{tree}(r)) \wedge (\triangleright \odot\forall x.\mathsf{tree}(x) \Rightarrow \mathsf{u}(\mathcal{F})) \vdash \mathsf{u}(\mathcal{F})$$

The proof breaks into two cases. The first reduces to $\langle x = \mathtt{null}\rangle \wedge (\triangleright\cdots) \vdash \mathsf{u}(\mathcal{F})$, which follows from $\mathsf{uniform}/\mathsf{emp}$ rule. The second case reduces to $(x \mapsto (d,l,r) \star \mathsf{tree}(l)\star\mathsf{tree}(r)) \wedge (\triangleright \odot\forall x.\mathsf{tree}(x) \Rightarrow \mathsf{u}(\mathcal{F})) \vdash \mathsf{u}(\mathcal{F})$. Then the $\mathsf{uniform}\star$ rule gives

$$\left(x \mapsto (d,l,r) \star (\mathsf{tree}(l) \star \mathsf{tree}(r))\right) \wedge \left(\triangleright \odot\forall x.\mathsf{tree}(x) \Rightarrow \mathsf{u}(\mathcal{F})\right) \vdash \mathsf{u}(\mathcal{F}) \star \mathsf{u}(\mathcal{F})$$

We now can cut with the $\triangleright_\pi\star$ rule to meet the inductive guard since $x \mapsto (d,l,r) \vdash \mathsf{uniform}(\mathcal{F})\wedge\neg\mathsf{emp}$ due to the rules $\mapsto\mathsf{uniform}$ and $\mapsto\mathsf{emp}$. Our remaining goal is thus

$$\left(x \mapsto (d,l,r) \wedge \triangleright\cdots\right) \star \left((\mathsf{tree}(l) \star \mathsf{tree}(r)) \wedge \odot\forall x.\mathsf{tree}(x) \Rightarrow \mathsf{u}(\mathcal{F})\right) \vdash \mathsf{u}(\mathcal{F}) \star \mathsf{u}(\mathcal{F})$$

We split over $\star$. The first goal is $x \mapsto (d,l,r) \wedge \triangleright\cdots \vdash \mathsf{u}(\mathcal{F})$, which follows from $\mapsto\mathsf{u}$. The second goal is $(\mathsf{tree}(l) \star \mathsf{tree}(r)) \wedge \odot\forall x.\mathsf{tree}(x) \Rightarrow \mathsf{u}(\mathcal{F})) \vdash \mathsf{u}(\mathcal{F})$. We apply $\odot\star$ to distribute the inductive hypothesis into the $\star$, and $\mathsf{uniform}\star$ to split the right hand side, yielding

$$\left(\mathsf{tree}(l) \wedge \odot\forall x.\mathsf{tree}(x) \Rightarrow \mathsf{u}(\mathcal{F})\right) \star \left(\mathsf{tree}(r) \wedge \odot\forall x.\mathsf{tree}(x) \Rightarrow \mathsf{u}(\mathcal{F})\right) \vdash \mathsf{u}(\mathcal{F}) \star \mathsf{u}(\mathcal{F})$$

We again split over $\star$ to reach two essentially identical cases. We apply rule T to remove the $\odot$ and then reach *e.g.* $\forall x.\mathsf{tree}(x) \Rightarrow \mathsf{u}(\mathcal{F}) \vdash \mathsf{tree}(l) \Rightarrow \mathsf{u}(\mathcal{F})$, which is immediate. Further details on this proof can be found in the full paper [2].

Proving that $\mathsf{list}(x)$ *is precise.* Precision is more complex than π-uniformity, so it is harder to prove. We will use the simpler $\mathsf{list}(x)$ as an example; the additional trick we need to prove that $\mathsf{tree}(x)$ is precise are applications of the $\triangleright_\pi\odot$ and $\odot\star$ rules in the same manner as the proof that $\mathsf{tree}(x)$ is $\mathcal{F}$-uniform. We have proved that both $\mathsf{list}(x)$ and $\mathsf{tree}(x)$ are precise using our proof rules in Coq [1].

$$\frac{}{\mathsf{precisely}(P) \dashv\vdash (P \star \top) \Rightarrow \mathsf{precisely}(P)} \text{ (A)}$$

$$\frac{\mathsf{precise}(P)}{P \star \mathsf{precisely}(Q) \vdash \mathsf{precisely}(P \star Q)} \text{ (D)}$$

$$\frac{\begin{array}{c} Q \wedge (R \star \top) \vdash \mathsf{precisely}(R) \\ Q \wedge (S \star \top) \vdash \mathsf{precisely}(S) \\ (R \star \top) \wedge (S \star \top) \vdash \bot \end{array}}{Q \wedge ((R \vee S) \star \top) \vdash \mathsf{precisely}(R \vee S)} \text{ (B)}$$

$$\frac{\begin{array}{c} \forall x. \Big(Q \wedge (P(x) \star \top) \vdash \mathsf{precisely}\big(P(x)\big) \Big) \\ \forall x, y. \Big((P(x) \star \top) \wedge (P(y) \star \top) \vdash |x = y| \Big) \end{array}}{Q \wedge \Big((\exists x. P(x)) \star \top \Big) \vdash \mathsf{precisely}\big(\exists x. P(x)\big)} \text{ (C)}$$

Fig. 10. Key lemmas we use to prove recursive predicates precise

In Fig. 10 we give four key lemmas used in our proof[2]. All four are derived (with a little cleverness) from the proof rules given in Fig. 8. We sketch the proof as follows. To prove precise(list(x)) we first use the preciselyPRECISE rule to transform the goal into $\top \vdash$ precisely(list(x)). We cannot immediately apply rule W, however, since without a concrete $\star$-separated conjunct **outside** the precisely, we cannot dismiss the inductive guard with the $\rhd_\pi \star$ rule. Accordingly, we next use lemma (A) and standard natural deduction to reach the goal $\top \vdash \forall x.(\mathsf{list}(x) \star \top) \Rightarrow \mathsf{precisely}(\mathsf{list}(x))$, after which we apply rule W with $\pi = \mathcal{F}$.

Afterwards we do some standard natural deduction steps yielding the goal

$$\Big(\rhd \forall x. \big(\mathsf{list}(x) \star \top\big) \Rightarrow \mathsf{precisely}\big(\mathsf{list}(x)\big) \Big) \wedge \Big((\langle x = \mathtt{null} \rangle \vee \exists d, n. x \mapsto (d, n) \star \mathsf{list}(n)) \star \top \Big) \vdash$$
$$\mathsf{precisely}\big(\langle x = \mathtt{null} \rangle \vee \exists d, n. x \mapsto (d, n) \star \mathsf{list}(n)\big)$$

We are now in a position to apply lemma (B) to break up the conjunction. We now have three goals. The first goal is that $\langle x = \mathtt{null} \rangle$ is precise, which follows from the fact that emp is precise, which in turn can be proved using the rule preciselyRIGHT. The third goal is that the two branches of the disjunction are mutually incompatible, which follows from $\langle x = \mathtt{null} \rangle$ being incompatible with maps-to using rule $\mapsto \mathtt{null}$. The second (and last remaining) goal needs to use lemma (C) twice to break up the existentials. Two of the three new goals are to show that the two existentials are uniquely determined, which follow from $\mapsto$ INVERSION, leaving the goal

$$\Big(\rhd \forall x. (\mathsf{list}(x) \star \top) \Rightarrow \mathsf{precisely}\big(\mathsf{list}(x)\big) \Big) \wedge \Big(x \mapsto (d, n) \star (\mathsf{list}(n) \star \top) \Big) \vdash \mathsf{precisely}\big(x \mapsto (d, n) \star \mathsf{list}(n)\big)$$

We now cut with lemma (D), using rule $\mapsto$ PRECISE to prove its premise, yielding

$$\Big(\rhd \forall x. (\mathsf{list}(x) \star \top) \Rightarrow \mathsf{precisely}\big(\mathsf{list}(x)\big) \Big) \wedge \Big(x \mapsto (d, n) \star (\mathsf{list}(n) \star \top) \Big) \vdash x \mapsto (d, n) \star \mathsf{precisely}\big(\mathsf{list}(n)\big)$$

We now use $\rhd_\pi \star$ rule to defeat the inductive guard. The rest is straightforward. Further details on this proof can be found in the full paper [2].

6   The ShareInfer fractional biabduction engine

Having described our logical machinery in Sects. 3, 4 and 5, we now demonstrate that our techniques are well-suited to automation by documenting our ShareInfer

---

[2] We abuse notation by reusing the inference rule format to present derived lemmas.

Precision		Uniformity		Bi-abduction	
File name	Time (ms)	File name	Time (ms)	File name	Time (ms)
precise_map1	0.1	uni_map1	0.2	bi_map1	1.3
precise_map2	0.2	uni_map2	0.8	bi_map2	0.9
precise_map3	1.2	uni_map3	0.3	bi_map3	0.5
precise_list1	2.7	uni_list1	1.2	bi_list1	4.0
precise_list2	1.3	uni_list2	2.1	bi_list2	3.2
precise_list3	3.4	uni_list3	0.7	bi_list3	3.8
precise_tree1	1.4	uni_tree1	1.9	bi_tree1	5.1
precise_tree2	1.7	uni_tree2	1.0	bi_tree2	6.5
precise_tree3	12.2	uni_tree3	10.3	bi_tree3	7.9

Fig. 11. Evaluation of our proof systems using ShareInfer

prototype [1]. Our tool is capable of checking whether a user-defined recursive predicate such as list or tree is uniform and/or precise and then conducting biabductive inference over a separation logic entailment containing said predicates.

To check uniformity, the tool first uses heuristics to guess a potential tree share candidate π and then applies proof rules in Figs. 7 and 6 to derive the goal uniform(π). To support more flexibility, our tool also allows users to specify the candidate share π manually. To check precision, the tool maneuvers over the proof rules in Figs. 6 and 8 to achieve the desired goal. In both cases, recursive predicates are handled with the rules in Fig. 9. ShareInfer returns either Yes, No or Unknown together with a human-readable proof of its claim.

For bi-abduction, ShareInfer automatically checks precision and uniformity whenever it encounters a new recursive predicate. If the check returns Yes, the tool will unlock the corresponding rule, *i.e.*, DOTPLUS for precision and DOTSTAR for uniformity. ShareInfer then matches fragments between the consequent and antecedent while applying folding and unfolding rules for recursive predicates to construct the antiframe and inference frame respectively. For instance, here is the biabduction problem contained in file bi_tree2 (see Fig. 11):

$$a \xmapsto{\mathcal{F}} (b,c,d) \, \star \, \mathcal{L} \cdot \mathsf{tree}(c) \, \star \, \mathcal{R} \cdot \mathsf{tree}(d) \, \star \, [??] \; \vdash \; \mathcal{L} \cdot \mathsf{tree}(a) \, \star \, [??]$$

ShareInfer returns antiframe $\mathcal{L} \cdot \mathsf{tree}(d)$ and inference frame $a \xmapsto{\mathcal{R}} (b,c,d) \star \mathcal{R} \cdot \mathsf{tree}(d)$.

ShareInfer is around 2.5k LOC of Java. We benchmarked it with 27 selective examples from three categories: precision, uniformity and bi-abduction. The benchmark was conducted with a 3.4 GHz processor and 16 GB of memory. Our results are given in Fig. 11. Despite the complexity of our proof rules our performance is reasonable: ShareInfer only took 75.9 ms to run the entire example set, or around 2.8 ms per example. Our benchmark is small, but this performance indicates that more sophisticated separation logic verifiers such as HIP/SLEEK [14] or Infer [9] may be able to use our techniques at scale.

7   Building a Model for Our Logic

Our task now is to provide a model for our proof theories. We present our models in several parts. In Sect. 7.1 we begin with a brief review of Cancellative Separation Algebras (CSA). In Sect. 7.2 we explain what we need from our fractional share models. In Sect. 7.3 we develop an extension to CSAs called "Scaling Separation Algebras" (SSA). In Sect. 7.5 we develop the machinery necessary to support our rules for object-level induction over the heap. We have verified in Coq [1] that the models in Sect. 7.1 support the rules in Fig. 8, the models in Sect. 7.3 support the rules Figs. 3 and 7, and the models in Sect. 7.5 support the rules in Fig. 9.

7.1   Cancellative Separation Algebras

A Separation Algebra (SA) is a set H with an associative, commutative partial operation $\oplus$. Separation algebras can have a single unit or multiple units; we use $identity(x)$ to indicate that x is a unit. A Cancellative SA $\langle H, \oplus \rangle$ further requires that $a \oplus b_1 = c \Rightarrow a \oplus b_2 = c \Rightarrow b_1 = b_2$. We can define a partial order on H using $\oplus$ by $h_1 \subseteq h_2 \stackrel{\text{def}}{=} \exists h'.h_1 \oplus h' = h_2$. Calcagno *et al.* [12] showed that CSAs can model separation logic with the definitions

$$h \models P \star Q \stackrel{\text{def}}{=} \exists h_1, h_2.\ h_1 \oplus h_2 = h \wedge (h_1 \models P) \wedge (h_2 \models Q) \quad \text{and} \quad h \models \text{emp} \stackrel{\text{def}}{=} identity(h).$$

The standard definition of precise(P) was given as Eq. (3) in Sect. 5.2, together with the definition for our new precisely(P) operator in Eq. (4). What is difficult here is finding a set of axioms (Fig. 8) and derivable lemmas (*e.g.* Fig. 10) that are strong enough to be useful in the object-level inductive proofs. Once the axioms are found, proving them from the model given is straightforward. Cancellation is not necessary to model basic separation logic [18], but we need it to prove the introduction preciselyRIGHT and elimination rules preciselyLEFT for our new operator.

7.2   Fractional Share Algebras

A fractional share algebra $\langle S, \oplus, \otimes, \mathcal{E}, \mathcal{F} \rangle$ (FSA) is a set S with two operations: partial addition $\oplus$ and total multiplication $\otimes$. The substructure $\langle S, \oplus \rangle$ is a CSA with the single unit $\mathcal{E}$. For the reasons discussed in Sect. 2 we require that $\oplus$ satisfies the disjointness axiom $a \oplus a = b \Rightarrow a = \mathcal{E}$. Furthermore, we require that the existence of a top element $\mathcal{F}$, representing complete ownership, and assume that each element $s \in S$ has a complement $\overline{s}$ such that $s \oplus \overline{s} = \mathcal{F}$.

Often (*e.g.* in the fractional $\mapsto$ operator) we wish to restrict ourselves to the "positive shares" $S^+ \stackrel{\text{def}}{=} S \setminus \{\mathcal{E}\}$. To emphasize that a share is positive we often use the metavariable π rather than s. $\oplus$ is still associative, commutative, and cancellative; every element other than $\mathcal{F}$ still has a complement. To enjoy a partial order on S^+ and other SA- or CSA-like structures that lack identities (sometimes called "permission algebras") we define $\pi_1 \subseteq \pi_2 \stackrel{\text{def}}{=} (\exists \pi'. \pi_1 \oplus \pi' = \pi_2) \vee (\pi_1 = \pi_2)$.

For the multiplicative structure we require that $\langle S, \otimes, \mathcal{F} \rangle$ be a monoid, *i.e.* that $\otimes$ is associative and has identity $\mathcal{F}$. Since we restrict maps-tos and the permission scaling operator to be positive, we want $\langle S^+, \otimes, \mathcal{F} \rangle$ to be a submonoid. Accordingly, when $\{\pi_1, \pi_2\} \subset S^+$, we require that $\pi_1 \otimes \pi_2 \neq \mathcal{E}$. Finally, we require that $\otimes$ distributes over $\oplus$ on the right, that is $(s_1 \oplus s_2) \otimes s_3 = (s_1 \otimes s_3) \oplus (s_2 \otimes s_3)$; and that $\otimes$ is cancellative on the right given a positive left multiplicand, *i.e.* $\pi \otimes s_1 = \pi \otimes s_2 \Rightarrow s_1 = s_2$.

The tree share model we present in Sect. 2 satisfies all of the above axioms, so we have a nontrivial model. As we will see shortly, it would be very convenient if we could assume that $\otimes$ also distributed on the left, or if we had multiplicative inverses on the left rather than merely cancellation on the right. However, we will see in Sect. 8.2 that both assumptions are untenable.

7.3 Scaling Separation Algebra

A scaling separation algebra (SSA) is $\langle H, S, \oplus_H, \oplus_S, \otimes_S, \mathcal{E}, \mathcal{F}, mul, force \rangle$, where $\langle H, \oplus_H \rangle$ is a CSA for heaps and $\langle S, \oplus_S, \otimes_S, \mathcal{E}, \mathcal{F} \rangle$ is a FSA for shares. Intuitively, $mul(\pi, h_1)$ multiplies every share inside h_1 by π and returns the result h_2. The multiplication is on the left, so for each original share π' in h_1, the resulting share in h_2 is $\pi \otimes_S \pi'$. Recall that the informal meaning of $\pi \cdot P$ is that we have a π-fraction of predicate P. Formally this notion relies on a little trick:

$$h \models \pi \cdot P \stackrel{\text{def}}{=} \exists h'. \, mul(\pi, h') = \pi \wedge h' \models P \tag{5}$$

A heap h contains a π-fraction of P if there is a **bigger** heap h' satisfying P, and multiplying that bigger heap h' by the scalar π gets back to the smaller heap h.

The simpler $force(\pi, h_1)$ overwrites all shares in h_1 with the constant share π to reach the resulting heap h_2. We use $force$ to define the uniform predicate as $h \models \mathsf{uniform}(\pi) \stackrel{\text{def}}{=} force(\pi, h) = h$. A heap h is π-uniform when setting all the shares in h to π gets you back to h—*i.e.*, they must have been π to begin with.

$S_1.$ $force(\pi, force(\pi', a)) = force(\pi, a)$ $S_2.$ $force(\pi, mul(\pi', a)) = force(\pi, a)$

$S_3.$ $mul(\pi, force(\pi', a)) = force(\pi \otimes_S \pi', a)$ $S_4.$ $mul(\pi, mul(\pi', a)) = mul(\pi \otimes_S \pi', a)$

$S_5.$ $identity(a) \Rightarrow force(\pi, a) = a$ $S_6.$ $a \subseteq_H force(\mathcal{F}, a)$

$S_7.$ $\pi_1 \subseteq_S \pi_2 \Rightarrow force(\pi_1, a) \subseteq_H force(\pi_2, a)$ $S_8.$ $force(\pi, a) \oplus_H force(\pi, b) = c \Rightarrow force(\pi, c) = c$

$S_9.$ $identity(a) \Rightarrow mul(\pi, a) = a$ $S_{10}.$ $mul(\mathcal{F}, a) = a$

$S_{11}.$ $mul(\pi, a_1) = mul(\pi, a_2) \Rightarrow a_1 = a_2$ $S_{12}.$ $mul(\pi, a) \subseteq_H a$

$S_{13}.$ $\pi_1 \oplus_S \pi_2 = \pi_3 \Rightarrow \forall b, c. \left((mul(\pi_1, b) \oplus_H mul(\pi_2, b) = c) \Leftrightarrow (c = mul(\pi_3, b)) \right)$

$S_{14}.$ $force(\pi', a) \oplus_H force(\pi', b) = force(\pi', c) \Leftrightarrow$
       $mul(\pi, force(\pi', a)) \oplus_H mul(\pi, force(\pi', b)) = mul(\pi, force(\pi', c))$

Fig. 12. The 14 additional axioms for scaling separation algebras beyond those inherited from cancellative separation algebras

We need to understand how all of the ingredients in an SSA relate to each other to prove the core logical rules on page 13. We distill the various relationships we need to model our logic in Fig. 12. Although there are a goodly number of them, most are reasonably intuitive.

Axioms S_1 through S_4 describe how *force* and *mul* compose with each other. Axioms S_5, S_9, and S_{10} give conditions when *force* and *mul* are identity functions: when either is applied to empty heaps, and when *mul* is applied to the multiplicative identity on shares $\mathcal{F}$. Axioms S_6 and S_{12} relate heap order with forcing the full share $\mathcal{F}$ and multiplication by an arbitrary share π. Axiom S_7 says that *force* is order-preserving. Axiom S_8 is how the disjointness axiom on shares is expressed on heaps: when two π-uniform heaps are joined, the result is π-uniform. Axiom S_{11} says that *mul* is injective on heaps. Axiom S_{13} is delicate. In the $\Rightarrow$ direction, it states that *mul* preserves the share model's join structure on heaps. In the $\Leftarrow$ direction, S_{13} is similar to axiom S_8, saying that the share model's join structure **must** be preserved. Taking both directions together, S_{13} translates the **right** distribution property of $\oplus_S$ over $\otimes_S$ into heaps. The final axiom S_{14} is a bit of a compromise. We wish we could satisfy

$$S'_{14}. \qquad a \oplus_H b = c \iff mul(\pi, a) \oplus_H mul(\pi, b) = mul(\pi, c)$$

S'_{14} is a kind of dual for S_{13}, *i.e.* it would correspond to a **left** distributivity property of $\oplus_S$ over $\otimes_S$ in the share model into heaps. Unfortunately, as we will see in Sect. 8.2, the disjointness of $\oplus_S$ is incompatible with simultaneously supporting both left and right distributivity. Accordingly, S_{14} weakens S'_{14} so that it only holds when a and b are π'-uniform (which by S_8 forces c to be π'-uniform). We also wish we could satisfy S'_{15}: $\forall \pi, a. \exists b. mul(\pi, b) = a$, which corresponds to left multiplicative inverses, but again (Sect. 8.2) disjointness is incompatible.

7.4   Compositionality of Scaling Separation Algebras

Despite their complex axiomatization, we gain two advantages from developing SSAs rather than directly proving our logical axioms on a concrete model. First, they give us a precise understanding of exactly which operations and properties (S_1–S_{14}) are used to prove the logical axioms. Second, following Dockins *et al.* [21] we can build up large SSAs compositionally from smaller SSAs.

To do so cleanly it will be convenient to consider a slight variant of SSAs, "Weak SSAs" that allow, but do not require, the existence of identity elements in the underlying CSA model. A WSSA satisfies exactly the same axioms as an SSA, except that we use the weaker $\subseteq_H$ definition we defined for permission algebras, *i.e.* $a_1 \subseteq_H a_2 \stackrel{\text{def}}{=} (\exists a'. a_1 \oplus_H a' = a_2) \vee (a_1 = a_2)$. Note that S_5 and S_9 are vacuously true when the CSA does not have identity elements. We need identity elements to prove the logical axioms from the model; we only use WSSAs to gain compositionality as we construct a suitable final SSA. Keeping the share components $\langle S, \oplus_S, \otimes_S, \mathcal{E}, \mathcal{F} \rangle$ constant, we give three SSA constructors to get a flavor for what we can do with the remaining components $\langle H, \oplus_H, force, mul \rangle$.

Example 1 (Shares). The share model $\langle S, \oplus_S \rangle$ is an SSA, and the positive (non-$\mathcal{E}$) shares $\langle S^+, \oplus \rangle$ are a WSSA, with $force_S(\pi, \pi') \stackrel{\text{def}}{=} \pi$ and $mul_S(\pi, \pi') \stackrel{\text{def}}{=} \pi \otimes \pi'$.

Example 2 (Semiproduct). Let $\langle A, \oplus_A, force_A, mul_A \rangle$ be an SSA/WSSA, and B be a set. Define $(a_1, b_1) \oplus_{A \times B} (a_2, b_2) = (a_3, b_3) \stackrel{\text{def}}{=} a_1 \oplus_A a_2 = a_3 \wedge b_1 = b_2 = b_3$, $force_{A \times B}(\pi, (a, b)) \stackrel{\text{def}}{=} (force_A(\pi, a), b)$, and $mul_{A \times B}(\pi, (a, b)) \stackrel{\text{def}}{=} (mul_A(\pi, a), b)$. Then $\langle A \times B, \oplus_{A \times B}, force_{A \times B}, mul_{A \times B} \rangle$ is an SSA/WSSA.

Example 3 (Finite partial map). Let A be a set and $\langle B, \oplus_B, force_B, mul_B \rangle$ be an SSA/WSSA. Define $f \oplus_{A \stackrel{\text{fin}}{\rightharpoonup} B} g = h$ pointwise [21]. Define $force_{A \stackrel{\text{fin}}{\rightharpoonup} B}(\pi, f) \stackrel{\text{def}}{=} \lambda x.force_B(\pi, f(x))$ and likewise define $mul_{A \stackrel{\text{fin}}{\rightharpoonup} B}(\pi, f) \stackrel{\text{def}}{=} \lambda x.mul_B(\pi, f(x))$. The structure $\langle A \stackrel{\text{fin}}{\rightharpoonup} B, \oplus_{A \stackrel{\text{fin}}{\rightharpoonup} B}, force_{A \stackrel{\text{fin}}{\rightharpoonup} B}, mul_{A \stackrel{\text{fin}}{\rightharpoonup} B} \rangle$ is an SSA.

Using these constructors, $A \stackrel{\text{fin}}{\rightharpoonup} (S^+, V)$, *i.e.* finite partial maps from addresses to pairs of positive shares and values, is an SSA and thus can support a model for our logic. We also support other standard constructions *e.g.* sum types $+$.

7.5   Model for Inductive Logic

What remains is to give the model that yields the inductive logic in Fig. 9. The key induction guard modal $\triangleright_\pi$ operator is defined as follows:

$$h_1 \, S_\pi \, h_4 \stackrel{\text{def}}{=} \exists h_2, h_3. \ h_1 \sqsupseteq_H h_2 \wedge h_3 \oplus_H h_4 = h_2 \wedge (h_3 \models \mathsf{uniform}(\pi) \wedge \neg\mathsf{emp})$$
$$h \models \triangleright_\pi P \stackrel{\text{def}}{=} \forall h'. \ (h \, S_\pi \, h') \Rightarrow (h' \models P)$$

In other words, $\triangleright_\pi$ is a (boxy) modal operator over the relation S_π, which relates a heap h_1 with all heaps that are strict subheaps that are smaller by at least a π-piece. The model is a little subtle to enable the rules $\triangleright_\pi \circledcirc$ and $\circledcirc \triangleright_\pi$ that let us handle multiple recursive calls and simplify the engineering. The within operator $\circledcirc$ is much simpler to model:

$$h_1 \, W \, h_2 \stackrel{\text{def}}{=} h_1 \sqsupseteq_H h_2 \qquad\qquad h \models \circledcirc P \stackrel{\text{def}}{=} \forall h'. \ (h \, W \, h') \Rightarrow (h' \models P)$$

All of the rules in Fig. 9 follow from these definitions except for rule W. To prove this rule, we require that the heap model have an additional operator. The "π-quantum", written $|h|_\pi$, gives the number of times a non-empty π-sized piece can be taken out of h. For disjoint shares, the number of times is no more than the number of defined memory locations in h. We require two facts for $|h|_\pi$. First, that $h_1 \subseteq_H h_2 \Rightarrow |h_1|_\pi \leq |h_2|_\pi$, *i.e.* that subheaps do not have larger π-quanta than their parent. Second, that $h_1 \oplus_H h_2 = h_3 \Rightarrow (h_2 \models \mathsf{uniform}(\pi) \wedge \neg\mathsf{emp}) \Rightarrow |h_3|_\pi > |h_1|_\pi$, *i.e.* that taking out a π-piece strictly decreases the number of π-quanta. Given this setup, rule W follows immediately by induction on $|h|_\pi$. The rules that require the longest proofs in the model are $\triangleright_\pi \circledcirc$ and $\circledcirc \triangleright_\pi$.

8 Lower Bounds on Predicate Multiplication

In Sect. 7 we gave a model for the logical axioms we presented in Fig. 3 and on page 13. Our goal here is to show that it is difficult to do better, *e.g.* by having a premise-free DOTSTAR rules or a bidirectional DOTIMPL rule. In Sect. 8.1 we show that these logical rules force properties on the share model. In Sect. 8.2 we show that disjointness puts restrictions on the class of share models. There are no non-trivial models that have left inverses or satisfy both left and right distributivity.

8.1 Predicate Multiplication's Axioms Force Share Model Properties

The SSA structures we gave in Sect. 7.3 are good for building models that enable the rules for predicate multiplication from Fig. 3. However, since they impose intermediate algebraic and logical signatures between the concrete model and rules for predicate multiplication, they are not good for showing that we cannot do better. Accordingly here we disintermediate and focus on the concrete model $A \overset{\text{fin}}{\rightharpoonup} (S^+, V)$, that is finite partial maps from addresses to pairs of positive shares and values. The join operations on heaps operates pointwise [21], with $(\pi_1, v_1) \oplus (\pi_2, v_2) = (\pi_3, v_3) \overset{\text{def}}{=} \pi_1 \oplus_S \pi_2 = \pi_3 \wedge v_1 = v_2 = v_3$, from which we derive the usual SA model for $\star$ and emp (Sect. 7.1). We define $h \models x \overset{\pi}{\mapsto} y \overset{\text{def}}{=} dom(h) = \{x\} \wedge h(x) = (\pi, y)$. We define scalar multiplication over heaps $\otimes_H$ pointwise as well, with $\pi_1 \otimes (\pi_2, v) \overset{\text{def}}{=} (\pi_1 \otimes_S \pi_2, v)$, and then define predicate multiplication by $h \models \pi \cdot P \overset{\text{def}}{=} \exists h'. \ h' = \pi \otimes_H h' = h \wedge h' \models P$. All of the above definitions are standard except for $\otimes_H$, which strikes us as the only choice (up to commutativity), and predicate multiplication itself.

By Sect. 7 we already know that this model satisfies the rules for predicate multiplication, given the assumptions on the share model from Sect. 7.2. What is interesting is that we can prove the other direction: if we assume that the key logical rules from Fig. 3 hold, they force axioms on the share model. The key correspondences are: DOTFULL forces that $\mathcal{F}$ is the left identity of $\otimes_S$; DOTMAPSTO forces that $\mathcal{F}$ is the right identity of $\otimes_S$; DOTMAPSTO forces the associativity of $\otimes_S$; the $\dashv$ direction of DOTCONJ forces the right cancellativity of $\otimes_S$ (as does DOTIMPL and the $\dashv$ direction of DOTUNIV); and DOTPLUS, which forces right distributivity of $\otimes_S$ over $\oplus_S$.

The following rules force left distributivity of $\otimes_S$ over $\oplus_S$ and left $\otimes_S$ inverses:

$$\frac{}{\pi \cdot (P \star Q) \dashv\vdash (\pi \cdot P) \star (\pi \cdot Q)} \text{ DOT}_{\text{STAR}'} \qquad \frac{}{\pi \cdot (P \Rightarrow Q) \dashv (\pi \cdot P) \Rightarrow (\pi \cdot Q)} \text{ DOT}_{\text{IMPL}'}$$

The $\dashv$ direction of DOTSTAR$'$ also forces that $\oplus_S$ satisfies disjointness; this is the key reason that we cannot use rationals $\langle (0, 1], +, \times \rangle$. Clearly the side-condition-free DOTSTAR$'$ rule is preferable to the DOTSTAR in Fig. 3, and it would also be preferable to have bidirectionality for predicate multiplication over implication and negation. Unfortunately, as we will see shortly, the disjointness of $\oplus_S$ places strong multiplicative algebraic constraints on the share model. These constraints are the reason we cannot support the DotImpl$'$ rule and why we require the π'-uniformity side condition in our DotStar rule.

8.2 Disjointness in a Multiplicative Setting

Our goal now is to explore the algebraic consequences of the disjointness property in a multiplicative setting. Suppose $\langle S, \oplus \rangle$ is a CSA with a single unit $\mathcal{E}$, top element $\mathcal{F}$, and $\oplus$ complements $\overline{s}$. Suppose further that shares satisfy the disjointness property $a \oplus a = b \Rightarrow a = \mathcal{E}$. For the multiplicative structure, assume $\langle S, \otimes, \mathcal{F} \rangle$ is a monoid (i.e. the axioms forced by the DotDot, DotMapsTo, and DotFull rules). It is undesirable for a share model if multiplying two positive shares (e.g. the ability to read a memory cell) results in the empty permission, so we assume that when π_1 and π_2 are non-$\mathcal{E}$ then their product $\pi_1 \otimes \pi_2 \neq \mathcal{E}$.

Now add left or right distributivity. We choose right distributivity $(s_1 \oplus s_2) \otimes s_3 = (s_1 \otimes s_3) \oplus (s_2 \otimes s_3)$; the situation is mirrored with left. Let us show that we cannot have left inverses for $\pi \neq \mathcal{F}$. We prove by contradiction: suppose $\pi \neq \mathcal{F}$ and there exists π^{-1} such that $\pi^{-1} \otimes \pi = \mathcal{F}$. Then

$$\pi = \mathcal{F} \otimes \pi = (\pi^{-1} \oplus \overline{\pi^{-1}}) \otimes \pi = (\pi^{-1} \otimes \pi) \oplus (\overline{\pi^{-1}} \otimes \pi) = \mathcal{F} \oplus (\overline{\pi^{-1}} \otimes \pi)$$

Let $e = \overline{\pi^{-1}} \otimes \pi$. Now $\pi = \mathcal{F} \oplus e = (\overline{e} \oplus e) \oplus e$, which by associativity and disjointness forces $e = \mathcal{E}$, which in turn forces $\pi = \mathcal{F}$, a contradiction.

Now suppose that instead of adding multiplicative inverses we have both left and right distributivity. First we prove (Lemma 1) that for arbitrary $s \in S$, $s \otimes \overline{s} = \overline{s} \otimes s$. We calculate:

$$(s \otimes s) \oplus (s \otimes \overline{s}) = s \otimes (s \oplus \overline{s}) = s \otimes \mathcal{F} = s = \mathcal{F} \otimes s = (s \oplus \overline{s}) \otimes s = (s \otimes s) \oplus (\overline{s} \otimes s)$$

Lemma 1 follows by the cancellativity of $\oplus$ between the far left and the far right.

Now we show (Lemma 2) that $s \otimes \overline{s} = \mathcal{E}$. We calculate:

$$\mathcal{F} = \mathcal{F} \otimes \mathcal{F} = (s \oplus \overline{s}) \otimes (s \oplus \overline{s}) = (s \otimes s) \oplus (s \otimes \overline{s}) \oplus (\overline{s} \otimes s) \oplus (\overline{s} \otimes \overline{s})$$
$$= (s \otimes s) \oplus \underline{(s \otimes \overline{s}) \oplus (s \otimes \overline{s})} \oplus (\overline{s} \otimes \overline{s})$$

The final equality is by Lemma 1. The underlined portion implies $s \otimes \overline{s} = \mathcal{E}$ by disjointness. The upshot of Lemma 2, together with our requirement that the product of two positive shares be positive, is that we can have no more than the two elements $\mathcal{E}$ and $\mathcal{F}$ in our share model. Since the entire motivation for fractional share models is to allow ownership between $\mathcal{E}$ and $\mathcal{F}$, we must choose either left or right distributivity; we choose right since we are able to prove that the π'-uniformity side condition enables the bidirectional DotStar.

9 Related Work

Fractional permissions are essentially used to reason about resource ownership in concurrent programming. The well-known rational model $\langle [0, 1], + \rangle$ by Boyland *et al.* [5] is used to reason about join-fork programs. This structure has the disjointness problem mentioned in Sect. 2, first noticed by Bornat *et al.* [4], as well as other problems discussed in Sects. 3, 4, and [2]. Boyland [6] extended the framework to scale permissions uniformly over arbitrary predicates with multiplication, *e.g.*, he defined $\pi \cdot P$ as "multiply each permission π' in P with π". However, his framework cannot fit into SL and his scaling rules are not bidirectional. Jacobs and Piessens [28] also used rationals for scaling permissions $\pi \cdot P$ in SL but only obtained one direction for DOTSTAR and DOTPLUS. A different kind of scaling permission was used by Dinsdale-Young *et al.* [20] in which they used rationals to define permission assertions $[A]_\pi^r$ to indicate a thread with permission π can execute the action A over the shared region r.

There are other flavors of permission besides rationals. Bornat *et al.* [4] introduced integer counting permissions $\langle \mathbb{Z}, +, 0 \rangle$ to reason about semaphores and combined rationals and integers into a hybrid permission model. Heule *et al.* [23] flexibly allowed permissions to be either concretely rational or abstractly read-only to lower the nuisance of detailed accounting. A more general read-only permissions was proposed by Charguéraud and Pottier [13] that transforms a predicate P into read-only mode $RO(P)$ which can duplicated/merged with the bi-entailment $RO(P) \dashv\vdash RO(P) \star RO(P)$. Their permissions distribute pleasantly over disjunction and existential quantifier but only work one way for $\star$, *i.e.*, $RO(H_1 \star H_2) \vdash RO(H_1) \star RO(H_2)$. Parkinson [41] proposed subsets of the natural numbers for shares $\langle \mathcal{P}(\mathbb{N}), \uplus \rangle$ to fix the disjointness problem. Compared to tree shares, Parkinson's model is less practical computationally and does not have an obvious multiplicative structure.

Protocol-based logics like FCSL [38] and Iris [30] have been very successful in reasoning about fine-grained concurrent programs, but their high expressivity results in a heavyweight logic. Automation (*e.g.* inference such as we do in Sect. 4) has been hard to come by. We believe that fractional permissions and protocol-based logics are in a meaningful sense complementary rather than competitors.

Verification tools often implement rational permissions because of its simplicity. For example, VeriFast [29] uses rationals to verify programs with locks and semaphores. It also allows simple and restrictive forms of scaling permissions which can be applied uniformly over standard predicates. On the other hand, HIP/SLEEK [31] uses rationals to model "thread as resource" so that the ownership of a thread and its resources can be transferred. Chalice [36] has rational permissions to verify properties of multi-threaded, objected-based programs such as data races and dead-locks. Viper [37] has an expressive intermediate language that supports both rational and abstract permissions. However, a number of verification tools have chosen tree shares due to their better metatheoretical properties. VST [3] is equipped with tree share permissions and an extensive tree share library. HIP/SLEEK uses tree shares to verify the barrier structure [26] and has its own complete share solver [33,35] that reduces tree formulae to Boolean formulae handled by Z3 [17]. Lastly, tree share permissions are featured in Heap-Hop [47] to reason over asynchronous communications.

10   Conclusion

We presented a separation logic proof framework to reason about resource sharing using fractional permissions in concurrent verification. We support sophisticated verification tasks such as inductive predicates, proving predicates precise, and biabduction. We wrote ShareInfer to gauge how our theories could be automated. We developed scaling separation algebras as compositional models for our logic. We investigated why our logic cannot support certain desirable properties.

References

1. http://www.comp.nus.edu.sg/~lxbach/tools/share_infer/
2. http://www.comp.nus.edu.sg/~lxbach/publication/permission_full.pdf
3. Appel, A.W.: Verified software toolchain. In: Barthe, G. (ed.) ESOP 2011. LNCS, vol. 6602, pp. 1–17. Springer, Heidelberg (2011). https://doi.org/10.1007/978-3-642-19718-5_1
4. Bornat, R., Cristiano, C., O'Hearn, P., Parkinson, M.: Permission accounting in separation logic. In: POPL (2005)
5. Boyland, J.: Checking interference with fractional permissions. In: Cousot, R. (ed.) SAS 2003. LNCS, vol. 2694, pp. 55–72. Springer, Heidelberg (2003). https://doi.org/10.1007/3-540-44898-5_4
6. Boyland, J.T.: Semantics of fractional permissions with nesting. ACM Trans. Program. Lang. Syst. **32**(6), 22 (2010)
7. Brotherston, J., Bornat, R., Calcagno, C.: Cyclic proofs of program termination in separation logic. In: POPL (2008)
8. Brotherston, J., Gorogiannis, N., Kanovich, M.: Biabduction (and related problems) in array separation logic. In: de Moura, L. (ed.) CADE 2017. LNCS (LNAI), vol. 10395, pp. 472–490. Springer, Cham (2017). https://doi.org/10.1007/978-3-319-63046-5_29
9. Calcagno, C., Distefano, D., Dubreil, J., Gabi, D., Hooimeijer, P., Luca, M., O'Hearn, P., Papakonstantinou, I., Purbrick, J., Rodriguez, D.: Moving fast with software verification. In: Havelund, K., Holzmann, G., Joshi, R. (eds.) NFM 2015. LNCS, vol. 9058, pp. 3–11. Springer, Cham (2015). https://doi.org/10.1007/978-3-319-17524-9_1
10. Calcagno, C., Distefano, D., O'Hearn, P., Yang, H.: Compositional shape analysis by means of bi-abduction. In: POPL (2009)
11. Calcagno, C., Distefano, D., Vafeiadis, V.: Bi-abductive resource invariant synthesis. In: Hu, Z. (ed.) APLAS 2009. LNCS, vol. 5904, pp. 259–274. Springer, Heidelberg (2009). https://doi.org/10.1007/978-3-642-10672-9_19
12. Calcagno, C., O'Hearn, P.W., Yang, H.: Local action and abstract separation logic. In: LICS, pp. 366–378 (2007)
13. Charguéraud, A., Pottier, F.: Temporary read-only permissions for separation logic. In: Yang, H. (ed.) ESOP 2017. LNCS, vol. 10201, pp. 260–286. Springer, Heidelberg (2017). https://doi.org/10.1007/978-3-662-54434-1_10
14. Chin, W.-N., David, C., Nguyen, H.H., Qin, S.: Automated verification of shape, size and bag properties via user-defined predicates in separation logic. Sci. Comput. Program. **77**(9), 1006–1036 (2012)
15. Chin, W.N., Le, T.C., Qin, S.: Automated verification of countdownlatch (2017)

16. da Rocha Pinto, P., Dinsdale-Young, T., Gardner, P.: TaDA: a logic for time and data abstraction. In: Jones, R. (ed.) ECOOP 2014. LNCS, vol. 8586, pp. 207–231. Springer, Heidelberg (2014). https://doi.org/10.1007/978-3-662-44202-9_9

17. de Moura, L., Bjørner, N.: Z3: an efficient SMT solver. In: Ramakrishnan, C.R., Rehof, J. (eds.) TACAS 2008. LNCS, vol. 4963, pp. 337–340. Springer, Heidelberg (2008). https://doi.org/10.1007/978-3-540-78800-3_24

18. Dinsdale-Young, T., Birkedal, L., Gardner, P., Parkinson, M., Yang, H.: Views: compositional reasoning for concurrent programs. In: POPL (2013)

19. Dinsdale-Young, T., Pinto, P.D.R., Andersen, K.J., Birkedal, L.: Caper: automatic verification for fine-grained concurrency. In: ESOP (2017)

20. Dinsdale-Young, T., Dodds, M., Gardner, P., Parkinson, M.J., Vafeiadis, V.: Concurrent abstract predicates. In: D'Hondt, T. (ed.) ECOOP 2010. LNCS, vol. 6183, pp. 504–528. Springer, Heidelberg (2010). https://doi.org/10.1007/978-3-642-14107-2_24

21. Dockins, R., Hobor, A., Appel, A.W.: A fresh look at separation algebras and share accounting. In: Hu, Z. (ed.) APLAS 2009. LNCS, vol. 5904, pp. 161–177. Springer, Heidelberg (2009). https://doi.org/10.1007/978-3-642-10672-9_13

22. Guo, B., Vachharajani, N., August, D.I.: Shape analysis with inductive recursion synthesis. In: PLDI (2007)

23. Heule, S., Leino, K.R.M., Müller, P., Summers, A.J.: Fractional permissions without the fractions. In: FTfJP, pp. 1:1–1:6 (2011)

24. Hobor, A.: Oracle Semantics. Ph.D. thesis, Department of Computer Science, Princeton University, Princeton, October 2008

25. Hobor, A., Gherghina, C.: Barriers in concurrent separation logic. In: Barthe, G. (ed.) ESOP 2011. LNCS, vol. 6602, pp. 276–296. Springer, Heidelberg (2011). https://doi.org/10.1007/978-3-642-19718-5_15

26. Hobor, A., Gherghina, C.: Barriers in concurrent separation logic: now with tool support! Log. Methods Comput. Sci. 8(2) (2012)

27. Hoenicke, J., Majumdar, R., Podelski, A.: Thread modularity at many levels: a pearl in compositional verification. In: POPL (2017)

28. Jacobs, B., Piessens, F.: Expressive modular fine-grained concurrency specification. In: POPL (2011)

29. Jacobs, B., Smans, J., Piessens, F.: A quick tour of the verifast program verifier. In: Ueda, K. (ed.) APLAS 2010. LNCS, vol. 6461, pp. 304–311. Springer, Heidelberg (2010). https://doi.org/10.1007/978-3-642-17164-2_21

30. Jung, R., Swasey, D., Sieczkowski, F., Svendsen, K., Turon, A., Birkedal, L., Dreyer, D.: Iris: monoids and invariants as an orthogonal basis for concurrent reasoning. In: POPL (2015)

31. Le, D.-K., Chin, W.-N., Teo, Y.M.: Threads as resource for concurrency verification. In: PEPM (2015)

32. Le, Q.L., Gherghina, C., Qin, S., Chin, W.-N.: Shape analysis via second-order bi-abduction. In: Biere, A., Bloem, R. (eds.) CAV 2014. LNCS, vol. 8559, pp. 52–68. Springer, Cham (2014). https://doi.org/10.1007/978-3-319-08867-9_4

33. Le, X.B., Gherghina, C., Hobor, A.: Decision procedures over sophisticated fractional permissions. In: Jhala, R., Igarashi, A. (eds.) APLAS 2012. LNCS, vol. 7705, pp. 368–385. Springer, Heidelberg (2012). https://doi.org/10.1007/978-3-642-35182-2_26

34. Le, X.-B., Hobor, A., Lin, A.W.: Decidability and complexity of tree shares formulas. In: FSTTCS (2016)

35. Le, X.-B., Nguyen, T.-T., Chin, W.-N., Hobor, A.: A certified decision procedure for tree shares. In: Duan, Z., Ong, L. (eds.) ICFEM 2017. LNCS, vol. 10610, pp. 226–242. Springer, Cham (2017). https://doi.org/10.1007/978-3-319-68690-5_14
36. Leino, K.R.M., Müller, P.: A basis for verifying multi-threaded programs. In: Castagna, G. (ed.) ESOP 2009. LNCS, vol. 5502, pp. 378–393. Springer, Heidelberg (2009). https://doi.org/10.1007/978-3-642-00590-9_27
37. Müller, P., Schwerhoff, M., Summers, A.J.: Viper: a verification infrastructure for permission-based reasoning. In: Jobstmann, B., Leino, K.R.M. (eds.) VMCAI 2016. LNCS, vol. 9583, pp. 41–62. Springer, Heidelberg (2016). https://doi.org/10.1007/978-3-662-49122-5_2
38. Nanevski, A., Ley-Wild, R., Sergey, I., Delbianco, G.A.: Communicating state transition systems for fine-grained concurrent resources. In: Shao, Z. (ed.) ESOP 2014. LNCS, vol. 8410, pp. 290–310. Springer, Heidelberg (2014). https://doi.org/10.1007/978-3-642-54833-8_16
39. Nguyen, H.H., David, C., Qin, S., Chin, W.-N.: Automated verification of shape and size properties via separation logic. In: Cook, B., Podelski, A. (eds.) VMCAI 2007. LNCS, vol. 4349, pp. 251–266. Springer, Heidelberg (2007). https://doi.org/10.1007/978-3-540-69738-1_18
40. OHearn, P.W.: Resources, concurrency, and local reasoning. Theor. Comput. Sci. **375**(1–3), 271–307 (2007)
41. Parkinson, M.: Local Reasoning for Java. Ph.D. thesis, University of Cambridge (2005)
42. Parkinson, M.J., Bornat, R., O'Hearn, P.W.: Modular verification of a non-blocking stack. In: POPL (2007)
43. Reynolds, J.C.: Separation logic: a logic for shared mutable data structures. In: LICS (2002)
44. Sergey, I., Nanevski, A., Banerjee, A.: Mechanized verification of fine-grained concurrent programs. In: PLDI (2015)
45. Vafeiadis, V.: Modular fine-grained concurrency verification. Ph.D. thesis (2008)
46. Vafeiadis, V., Parkinson, M.: A marriage of rely/guarantee and separation logic. In: Caires, L., Vasconcelos, V.T. (eds.) CONCUR 2007. LNCS, vol. 4703, pp. 256–271. Springer, Heidelberg (2007). https://doi.org/10.1007/978-3-540-74407-8_18
47. Villard, J.: Heaps and Hops. Ph.D. thesis, Laboratoire Spécification et Vérification, École Normale Supérieure de Cachan, France, February 2011
48. Windsor, M., Dodds, M., Simner, B., Parkinson, M.J.: Starling: lightweight concurrency verification with views. In: Majumdar, R., Kunčak, V. (eds.) CAV 2017. LNCS, vol. 10426, pp. 544–569. Springer, Cham (2017). https://doi.org/10.1007/978-3-319-63387-9_27
49. Yang, H., Lee, O., Berdine, J., Calcagno, C., Cook, B., Distefano, D., O'Hearn, P.: Scalable shape analysis for systems code. In: Gupta, A., Malik, S. (eds.) CAV 2008. LNCS, vol. 5123, pp. 385–398. Springer, Heidelberg (2008). https://doi.org/10.1007/978-3-540-70545-1_36

Deadlock-Free Monitors

Jafar Hamin(✉) and Bart Jacobs

imec-DistriNet, Department of Computer Science, KU Leuven,
Celestijnenlaan 200A, 3001 Heverlee, Belgium
{jafar.hamin,bart.jacobs}@cs.kuleuven.be

Abstract. Monitors constitute one of the common techniques to synchronize threads in multithreaded programs, where calling a wait command on a condition variable suspends the caller thread and notifying a
condition variable causes the threads waiting for that condition variable
to resume their execution. One potential problem with these programs is
that a waiting thread might be suspended forever leading to deadlock, a
state where each thread of the program is waiting for a condition variable
or a lock. In this paper, a modular verification approach for deadlock-
freedom of such programs is presented, ensuring that in any state of the
execution of the program if there are some threads suspended then there
exists at least one thread running. The main idea behind this approach
is to make sure that for any condition variable v for which a thread is
waiting there exists a thread obliged to fulfil an obligation for v that
only waits for a waitable object whose wait level, an arbitrary number
associated with each waitable object, is less than the wait level of v. The
relaxed precedence relation introduced in this paper, aiming to avoid
cycles, can also benefit some other verification approaches, verifying
deadlock-freedom of other synchronization constructs such as channels
and semaphores, enabling them to accept a wider range of deadlock-free
programs. We encoded the proposed proof rules in the VeriFast program
verifier and by defining some appropriate invariants for the locks associated with some condition variables succeeded in verifying some popular use cases of monitors including unbounded/bounded buffer, sleeping
barber, barrier, and readers-writers locks. A soundness proof for the presented approach is provided; some of the trickiest lemmas in this proof
have been machine-checked with Coq.

1 Introduction

One of the popular mechanisms for synchronizing threads in multithreaded programs is using monitors, a synchronization construct allowing threads to have
mutual exclusion and also the ability to wait for a certain condition to become
true. These constructs, consisting of a mutex/lock and some condition variables,
provide some basic functions for their clients, namely wait(v, l), causing the calling thread to wait for the condition variable v and release lock l while doing
so, and notify(v)/notifyAll(v), causing one/all thread(s) waiting for v to resume
their execution. Each condition variable is associated with a lock; a thread must

A. Ahmed (Ed.): ESOP 2018, LNCS 10801, pp. 415–441, 2018.
https://doi.org/10.1007/978-3-319-89884-1_15

acquire the associated lock for waiting or notifying on a condition variable, and when a thread is notified it must reacquire the associated lock.

However, one potential problem with these synchronizers is deadlock, where all threads of the program are waiting for a condition variable or a lock. To clarify the problem consider the program in Fig. 1, where a channel consists of a queue q, a lock l and a condition variable v, protecting a thread from dequeuing q when it is empty. In this program the receiver thread first acquires lock l and while there is no item in q it releases l, suspends itself and waits for a notification on v. If this thread is notified while q is not empty it dequeues an item and finally releases l. The sender thread also acquires the same lock, enqueues an item into q, notifies one of the threads waiting for v, if any, and lastly releases l. After creating a channel ch, the main thread of the program first forks a thread to receive a message from ch and then sends a message on ch. Although this program is deadlock-free, it is easy to construct some variations of it that lead to deadlock: if the main thread itself, before sending any messages, tries to receive a message from ch, or if the number of receives is greater than the number of sends, or if the receiver thread waits for v even if q is not empty.

```
routine main()                routine send(channel ch, int d)    routine receive(channel ch)
{q := newqueue;               {acquire(ch.l);                     {acquire(ch.l);
 l := newlock;                 enqueue(ch.q, d);                   while(sizeof(ch.q) = 0)
 v := newcond;                 notify(ch.v);                        wait(ch.v, ch.l);
 ch := channel(q, l, v);       release(ch.l)}                      d := dequeue(ch.q);
 fork (receive(ch));                                               release(ch.l);
 send(ch, 12)}                                                     d}
```

Fig. 1. A message passing program synchronized using a monitor

Several approaches to verify termination, deadlock-freedom, liveness, and finite blocking of threads of programs have been presented. Some of these approaches only work with non-blocking algorithms [1–3], where the suspension of one thread cannot lead to the suspension of other threads. These approaches are not applicable for condition variables because suspension of a sender thread in Fig. 1, for example, might cause a receiver thread to be blocked forever. Some other approaches are also presented to verify termination of programs using some blocking constructs such as channels [4–6] and semaphores [7]. These approaches are not general enough to cover condition variables because unlike the channels and semaphores a notification of a condition variable is lost when there is no thread waiting for that condition variable. There are also some studies [8–10] to verify correctness of programs that support condition variables. However, these approaches either only cover a very specific application of condition variables, such as a buffer program with only one producer and one consumer, or are not modular and suffer from a long verification time when the size of the state space, such as the number of threads, is increased.

In this paper we present a modular approach to verify deadlock-freedom of programs in the presence of condition variables. More specifically, this approach makes sure that for any condition variable v for which a thread is waiting there exists a thread obliged to fulfil an obligation for v that only waits for a waitable object whose wait level, an arbitrary number associated with each waitable object, is less than the wait level of v. The presented approach is modular, meaning that different modules (functions) of a program can be verified individually. This approach is based on Leino *et al.* [4] approach for verification of deadlock-freedom in the presence of channels and locks, which in turn was based on Kobayashi's [6] type system for verifying deadlock-freedom of π-calculus processes, and extends the separation logic-based encoding [11] by covering condition variables. We implemented the proposed proof rules in the VeriFast verifier [12–14] and succeeded in verifying some common applications of condition variables such as bounded/unbounded buffer, sleeping barber [15], barrier, and readers-writers locks (see the full version of this paper [16] reporting the verification time of these programs).

This paper is structured as follows. Section 2 provides some background information on the existing approaches upon which we build our verification algorithm. Section 3 introduces a preliminary approach for verifying deadlock-freedom of some common applications of condition variables. In Sect. 4 the precedence relation, aiming to avoid cycles, is relaxed, making it possible to verify some trickier applications of condition variables. A soundness proof of the presented approach is lastly given in Sect. 5.

2   Background Information on the Underlying Approaches

In this section we provide some background information on the existing approaches that verify absence of data races and deadlock in the presence of locks and channels that we build on.

2.1   Verifying Absence of Data Races

Locks/mutexes are mostly used to avoid data races, an undesired situation where a heap location is being written and accessed concurrently by two different threads. One common approach to verify absence of these undesired conditions is ownership: ownership of heap locations is assigned to threads and it is verified that a thread accesses only the heap locations that it owns. Transferring ownership of heap locations between threads is supported through locks by allowing locks, too, to own heap locations. While a lock is not held by a thread, it owns the heap locations described by its *invariant*. More specifically, when a lock is created the resources specified by its invariant are transferred from the creating thread to the lock, when that lock is acquired these resources are transferred from the lock to the acquiring thread, and when that lock is released these resources, that must be again in possession of the thread, are again transferred from the thread to the lock [17]. Figure 2 illustrates how a program increasing a

$x:=$newint(0);   **routine** inc(counter ct){

$\{x\mapsto 0\}$ $\{\mathsf{lock}(ct.l) \wedge \mathsf{I}(l)=\mathsf{inv}(ct)\}$

$l :=$ newlock;   acquire$(ct.l)$;

$\{\mathsf{ulock}(l) * x\mapsto 0\}$ $\{\mathsf{locked}(ct.l) * \exists z.\ ct.x\mapsto z\}$

$ct :=$ counter$(x:=x, l:=l)$; $ct.x:=ct.x+1$;

$\{\mathsf{ulock}(ct.l) * ct.x\mapsto 0\}$ $\{\mathsf{locked}(ct.l) * \exists z.\ ct.x\mapsto z\}$

$\{\mathsf{ulock}(ct.l) * \mathsf{inv}(ct)\}$ release$(ct.l)$

$\{\mathsf{lock}(ct.l) \wedge \mathsf{I}(l)=\mathsf{inv}(ct)\}$ $\{\mathsf{lock}(ct.l)\}\}$

$\{\mathsf{lock}(ct.l) * \mathsf{lock}(ct.l)\}$

fork (inc(ct));

$\{\mathsf{lock}(ct.l)\}$

inc(ct)

Fig. 2. Verification of data-race-freedom of a program, where inv $= \lambda ct.\ \exists z.\ ct.x\mapsto z$

counter, which consists of an integer variable x and a lock l protecting this variable, can be verified, where two threads try to write on the variable x. We use separation logic [18] to reason about the ownership of permissions. As indicated below each command, creating the integer variable x initialized by zero provides a read/write access permission to x, denoted by $x\mapsto 0$. This ownership, that is going to be protected by lock l, is transferred to the lock because it is asserted by the lock invariant inv, which is associated with the lock, as denoted by function I, at the point where the lock is initialized. The resulting lock permission, that can be duplicated, is used in the routine inc, where x is increased under protection of lock l. Acquiring this lock in this routine provides a full access permission to x and transforms the lock permission to a locked permission, implying that the related lock has been acquired. Releasing that lock again consumes this access permission and transforms the locked permission to a lock one.

2.2   Verifying Absence of Deadlock

One potential problem with programs using locks and other synchronization mechanisms is deadlock, an undesired situation where all threads of the program are waiting for some waitable objects. For example, a program can deadlock if a thread acquires a lock and forgets to release it, because any other thread waiting for that lock never succeeds in acquiring that lock. As another example, if in a message passing program the number of threads trying to receive a message from a channel is greater than the number of messages sent on that channel there will be some threads waiting for that channel forever. One approach to verify deadlock-freedom of channels and locks is presented by Leino *et al.* [4] that guarantees deadlock-freedom of programs by ensuring that (1) for any *obligee* thread waiting for a waitable object, such as a channel or lock, there is an *obligation* for that object that must be fulfilled by an *obligor* thread, where a thread can fulfil an obligation for a channel/lock if it sends a message on that channel/releases that lock, and (2) each thread waits for an object only if the *wait level* of that object, an arbitrary number assigned to each waitable object, is lower than the wait levels of all obligations of that thread. The second rule is established by making sure that when a thread with some obligations O executes a command acquire(o)/receive(o) the precondition $o \prec O$ holds, i.e. the wait level of o is lower than the wait levels of obligations in O. To meet the first rule where the waitable object is a lock, as the example in the left side of Fig. 3 illustrates, after acquiring a lock, that lock is loaded onto the bag[1] (multiset) of obligations of the thread, denoted by obs(O). This ensures that if a thread tries to acquire a lock that has already been acquired then there is one thread obliged to fulfil an obligation for that lock.

$\{\mathsf{obs}(O) * \mathsf{lock}(l) \wedge l \prec O\}$
acquire(l);
$\{\mathsf{obs}(O \uplus \{l\}) * \mathsf{locked}(l) * \mathsf{l}(l)\}$
...
$\{\mathsf{obs}(O \uplus \{l\}) * \mathsf{locked}(l) * \mathsf{l}(l)\}$
release(l)
$\{\mathsf{obs}(O) * \mathsf{lock}(l)\}$

$\{\mathsf{obs}(O)\}$
$\{\mathsf{obs}(O \uplus \{ch\}) * \mathsf{credit}(ch)\}$
fork (
$\{\mathsf{obs}(\{\}) * \mathsf{credit}(ch) \wedge ch \prec \{\}\}$
receive(ch)
$\{\mathsf{obs}(\{\})\}$
);
$\{\mathsf{obs}(O \uplus \{ch\})\}$
send(ch, 12) $\{\mathsf{obs}(O)\}$

Fig. 3. Verification of deadlock-freedom of locks (left side) and channels (right side)

To establish the first rule where the waitable object is a channel any thread trying to receive a message from a channel ch must spend one *credit* for ch. This credit is normally obtained from the thread that has forked the receiver thread, where this credit is originally created by loading ch onto the bag of obligations of the forking thread. The forking thread can discharge the loaded obligation by either sending a message on the corresponding channel or delegating it to a child thread that can discharge it. The example on the right side of Fig. 3 shows the verification of deadlock-freedom a program in which the main routine, after forking a obligee thread trying to receive a message from channel ch, sends a message on this channel. Before forking the receiver thread, a credit and an obligation for the channel ch are created in the main thread. The former is given to the forked thread, where this credit is spent by the receive(ch) command, and the latter is fulfilled by the main thread when it executes the command send(ch, 12).

More formally, the mentioned verification approach satisfies the first rule by ensuring that for each channel ch in the program the number of obligations for ch is equal to/greater than the number of threads waiting for ch. This assurance is obtained by preserving the invariant $Wt(ch)+Ct(ch) \leqslant Ot(ch)+\mathsf{sizeof}(ch)$, while the programming language itself ensures that $\mathsf{sizeof}(ch) > 0 \Rightarrow Wt(ch) = 0$, where sizeof is a function mapping each channel to the size of its queue, $Wt(ch)$

---

[1] We treat bags of waitable objects as functions from waitable objects to natural numbers.

is the total number of threads currently waiting for channel ch, $Ot(ch)$ is the total number of obligations for channel ch held by all threads, and $Ct(ch)$ is the total number of credits for channel ch currently in the system.

2.3 Proof Rules

The separation logic-based proof rules, introduced by Jacobs et al. [11], avoiding data races and deadlock in the presence of locks and channels are shown in Fig. 4, where R and I are functions mapping a waitable object/lock to its wait level/invariant, respectively, and g_initl, and g_load are some *ghost commands* used to initialize an uninitialized lock permission and load a channel onto the bag of obligations and credits of a thread, respectively. When a lock is created, as shown in NEWLOCK, an uninitialized lock permission ulock(l) is provided for that thread. Additionally, an arbitrary integer number z can be decided as the wait level of that lock that is stored in R. Note that variable z in this rule is universally quantified over the rule, and different applications of the NEWLOCK rule can use different values for this variable. The uninitialized lock permission, as shown in INITLOCK, can be converted to a normal lock permission lock(l) provided that the resources described by the invariant of that lock, stored in I, that must be in possession of the thread, are transferred from the thread to the lock. By the rule ACQUIRE, having a lock permission, a thread can acquire that lock if the wait levels of obligations of that thread are all greater than the wait level of that lock. After acquiring the lock, the resources represented by the invariant of that lock are provided for the acquiring thread and the permission lock is converted to a locked permission. When a

NEWLOCK
$\{$true$\}$ newlock $\{\lambda l.\ \text{ulock}(l) \wedge R(l){=}z\}$

INITLOCK
$\{\text{ulock}(l) * i\}$ g_initl(l) $\{\lambda\_.\ \text{lock}(l) \wedge I(l){=}i\}$

ACQUIRE $\{\text{lock}(l) * \text{obs}(O) \wedge l{\prec}O\}$ acquire(l) $\{\lambda\_.\ \text{obs}(O{\uplus}\{l\}) * \text{locked}(l) * I(l)\}$

RELEASE $\{\text{obs}(O) * \text{locked}(l) * I(l)\}$ release(l) $\{\lambda\_.\ \text{obs}(O{-}\{l\}) * \text{lock}(l)\}$

NEWCHANNEL
$\{$true$\}$ newchannel $\{\lambda ch.\ R(ch){=}z\}$

SEND
$\{\text{obs}(O)\}$ send(ch, v) $\{\lambda\_.\ \text{obs}(O{-}\{ch\})\}$

RECEIVE
$\{\text{obs}(O) * \text{credit}(ch) \wedge ch{\prec}O\}$ receive(ch) $\{\lambda\_.\ \text{obs}(O)\}$

FORK
$$\frac{\{a * \text{obs}(O)\}\ c\ \{\lambda\_.\ \text{obs}(\{\})\}}{\{a * \text{obs}(O{\uplus}O')\}\ \text{fork}(c)\ \{\lambda\_.\ \text{obs}(O')\}}$$
DUPLOCK   lock(l) $\Leftrightarrow$ lock(l) * lock(l)

LOADOB $\{\text{obs}(O)\}$ g_load(ch) $\{\lambda\_.\ \text{obs}(O{\uplus}\{ch\}) * \text{credit}(ch)\}$

Fig. 4. Proof rules ensuring deadlock-freedom of channels and locks, where $o{\prec}O \Leftrightarrow \forall o' \in O.\ R(o) < R(o')$

thread releases a lock, as shown in the rule RELEASE, the resources indicated by the invariant of that lock, that must be in possession of the releasing thread, are transferred from the thread to the lock and the permission locked is again converted to a lock permission. By the rule RECEIVE a thread with obligations O can try to receive a message from a channel ch only if the wait level of ch is lower than the wait levels of all obligations in O. This thread must also spend one credit for ch, ensuring that there is another thread obliged to fulfil an obligation for ch. As shown in the rule SEND, an obligation for this channel can be discharged by sending a message on that channel. Alternatively, by the rule FORK, a thread can discharge an obligation for a channel if it delegates that obligation to a child thread, provided that the child thread discharges the delegated obligation. In this setting the verification of a program starts with an empty bag of obligations and must also end with such bag implying that there is no remaining obligation to fulfil.

However, this verification approach is not straightforwardly applicable to condition variables. A command notify cannot be treated like a command send because a notification on a condition variable is lost when there is no thread waiting for that variable. Accordingly, it does not make sense to discharge an obligation for a condition variable whenever it is notified. Similarly, a command wait cannot be treated like a command receive. A command wait is normally executed in a while loop, checking the *waiting condition* of the related condition variable. Accordingly, it is impossible to build a loop invariant for such a loop if we force the wait command to spend a credit for the related condition variable.

3 Deadlock-Free Monitors

3.1 High-Level Idea

In this section we introduce an approach to verify deadlock-freedom of programs in the presence of condition variables. This approach ensures that the verified program never deadlocks, i.e. there is always a running thread, that is not blocked, until the program terminates. The main idea behind this approach is to make sure that for any condition variable v for which a thread is waiting there exists a thread obliged to fulfil an obligation for v that only waits for a waitable object whose wait level is less than the wait level of v. As a consequence, if the program has some threads suspended, waiting for some obligations, there is always a thread obliged to fulfil the obligation o_{min} that is not suspended, where o_{min} has a minimal wait level among all waitable objects for which a thread is waiting. Accordingly, the proposed proof rules make sure that (1) when a command wait(v, l) is executed $Ot(v) > 0$, where Ot maps each condition variable v to the total number of obligations for v held by all threads (note that having a thread with permission obs(O) implies $O(v) \leqslant Ot(v)$), (2) a thread discharges an obligation for a condition variable only if after this discharge the invariant one_ob(v, Wt, Ot) defined as $Wt(v) > 0 \Rightarrow Ot(v) > 0$ still holds, where $Wt(v)$ denotes the number of threads waiting for condition variable v, and (3) a thread with obligations O executes a command wait(v, l) only if $v \prec O$.

3.2 Tracking Numbers of Waiting Threads and Obligations

For all condition variables associated with a lock l the value of functions Wt and Ot can only be changed by a thread that has locked l; $Wt(v)$ is changed only when one of the commands $\mathsf{wait}(v, l)/\mathsf{notify}(v)/\mathsf{notifyAll}(v)$ is executed, requiring holding lock l, and we allow $Ot(v)$ to be changed only when a permission locked for l is available. Accordingly, when a thread acquires a lock these two bags are stored in the related locked permission and are used to establish the rules number 1 and 2, when a thread executes a wait command or discharges one of its obligations. Note that the domain of these functions is the set of the condition variables associated with the related lock. The thread executing the critical section can change these two bags under some circumstances. If that thread loads/discharges a condition variable onto/from the list of its obligations this condition variable must also be loaded/discharged onto/from the bag Ot stored in the related locked permission. Note that unlike the approach presented by Leino *et al.* [4], an obligation for a condition variable can arbitrarily be loaded or discharged by a thread, provided that the rule number 2 is respected. At the start of the execution of a $\mathsf{wait}(v, l)$ command, $Wt(v)$ is incremented and after execution of commands $\mathsf{notify}(v)/\mathsf{notifyAll}(v)$ one/all instance(s) of v is/are removed from the bag Wt stored in the related locked permission, since these commands change the number of threads waiting for v.

A program can be successfully verified according to the mentioned rules, formally indicated in Fig. 5, if each lock associated with any condition variable v has an appropriate invariant such that it implies the desired invariant $\mathsf{one\_ob}(v, Wt, Ot)$. Accordingly, the proof rules allow locks to have invariants parametrized over the bags Wt and Ot. When a thread acquires a lock the result of applying the invariant of that lock to these two bags, stored in the related locked permission, is provided for the thread and when that lock is released it is expected that the result of applying the lock invariant to those bags, stored in the related locked permission, again holds. However, before execution of a command $\mathsf{wait}(v, l)$, when lock l with bags Wt and Ot stored in its locked permission is going to be released, it is expected that the invariant of l holds with bags $Wt \uplus \{v\}$ and Ot because the running thread is going to wait for v and this condition variable is going to be added to Wt. As this thread resumes its execution, when it has some bags Wt' and Ot' stored in the related locked permission, the result of applying the invariant of l to these bags is provided for that thread. Note that the total number of threads waiting for v, $Wt(v)$, is already decreased when a command $\mathsf{notify}(v)$ or $\mathsf{notifyAll}(v)$ is executed, causing the waiting thread(s) to wake up and try to acquire the lock associated with v.

3.3 Resource Transfer on Notification

In general, as we will see when looking at examples, it is sometimes necessary to transfer resources from a notifying thread to the threads being notified[2].

---

[2] This transfer is only sound in the absence of spurious wake-ups, where a thread is awoken from its waiting state even though no thread has signaled the related condition variable.

To this end, these resources, specified by a function M, are associated with each condition variable v when v is created, such that the commands notify(v)/notifyAll(v) consume one/ $Wt(v)$ instance(s) of these resources, respectively, and the command wait(v, l) produces one instance of such resources (see the rules WAIT, NOTIFY, and NOTIFYALL in Fig. 5).

NEWLOCK $\{$true$\}$ newlock $\{\lambda l. \text{ulock}(l, \{\}, \{\}) \wedge \mathsf{R}(l){=}z\}$

NEWCV $\{$true$\}$ newcond $\{\lambda v. \mathsf{R}(v){=}z \wedge \mathsf{L}(v){=}l \wedge \mathsf{M}(v){=}m\}$

ACQUIRE $\dfrac{\{\text{lock}(l) * \text{obs}(O) \wedge l{\prec}O\} \text{ acquire}(l)}{\{\lambda\_. \exists Wt, Ot. \text{locked}(l, Wt, Ot) * \mathsf{I}(l)(Wt, Ot) * \text{obs}(O{\uplus}\{l\})\}}$

RELEASE
$\{\text{locked}(l, Wt, Ot) * \mathsf{I}(l)(Wt, Ot) * \text{obs}(O{\uplus}\{l\})\}$ release(l) $\{\lambda\_. \text{lock}(l) * \text{obs}(O)\}$

WAIT $\dfrac{\{\text{locked}(l, Wt, Ot) * \mathsf{I}(l)(Wt{\uplus}\{v\}, Ot) * \text{obs}(O{\uplus}\{l\})}{\wedge\, l{=}\mathsf{L}(v) \wedge v{\prec}O \wedge l{\prec}O \wedge \text{safe\_obs}(v, Wt{\uplus}\{v\}, Ot)\} \text{ wait}(v, l)}{\{\lambda\_. \text{obs}(O{\uplus}\{l\}) * \exists Wt', Ot'. \text{locked}(l, Wt', Ot') * \mathsf{I}(l)(Wt', Ot') * \mathsf{M}(v)\}}$

NOTIFY $\dfrac{\{\text{locked}(\mathsf{L}(v), Wt, Ot) * (Wt(v) = 0 \vee \mathsf{M}(v))\} \text{ notify}(v)}{\{\lambda\_. \text{locked}(\mathsf{L}(v), Wt{-}\{v\}, Ot)\}}$

NOTIFYALL
$\{\text{locked}(\mathsf{L}(v), Wt, Ot) * (\overset{Wt(v)}{\underset{i:=0}{*}} \mathsf{M}(v))\}$ notifyAll(v) $\{\lambda\_. \text{locked}(\mathsf{L}(v), Wt[v{:=}0], Ot)\}$

INITLOCK
$\{\text{ulock}(l, Wt, Ot) * inv(Wt, Ot) * \text{obs}(O)\}$ g_initl(l) $\{\lambda\_. \text{lock}(l) * \text{obs}(O) \wedge \mathsf{I}(l){=}inv\}$

CHARGEOB $\dfrac{\{\text{obs}(O) * \text{ulock/locked}(\mathsf{L}(v), Wt, Ot)\} \text{ g\_chrg}(v)}{\{\lambda\_. \text{obs}(O{\uplus}\{v\}) * \text{ulock/locked}(\mathsf{L}(v), Wt, Ot{\uplus}\{v\})\}}$

DISOB $\dfrac{\{\text{obs}(O) * \text{ulock/locked}(\mathsf{L}(v), Wt, Ot) \wedge \text{safe\_obs}(v, Wt(v), Ot{-}\{v\})\}}{\text{g\_disch}(v) \ \{\lambda\_. \text{obs}(O{-}\{v\}) * \text{ulock/locked}(\mathsf{L}(v), Wt, Ot{-}\{v\})\}}$

Fig. 5. Proof rules to verify deadlock-freedom of condition variables, where $Wt(v)$ and $Ot(v)$ denote the total number of threads waiting for v and the total number of obligations for v, respectively, and $\text{safe\_obs}(v, Wt, Ot) \Leftrightarrow \text{one\_ob}(v, Wt, Ot)$ and $\text{one\_ob}(v, Wt, Ot) \Leftrightarrow (Wt(v) > 0 \Rightarrow Ot(v) > 0)$

3.4 Proof Rules

Figure 5 shows the proposed proof rules used to verify deadlock-freedom of condition variables, where L and M are functions mapping each condition variable to its associated lock and to the resources that are moved from the notifying thread to the notified one when that condition variable is notified, respectively.

Creating a lock, as shown in the rule NEWLOCK, produces a permission ulock storing the bags Wt and Ot, where these bags are initially empty. The bag Ot in this permission, similar to a locked one, can be changed provided that the obligations of the running thread are also updated by one of the ghost commands g_chrg(v) or g_disch(v) (see rules CHARGEOB and DISOB). The lock related to this permission can be initialized by transferring the resources described by the invariant of this lock, that is now parametrized over the bags Wt and Ot, applied to the bags stored in this permission from the thread to the lock (see rule INITLOCK). When this lock is acquired, as shown in the rule ACQUIRE, the resources indicated by its invariant are provided for the thread, and when it is released, as shown in the rule RELEASE, the resources described by its invariant that must hold with appropriate bags, are again transferred from the thread to the lock. The rules WAIT and DISOB ensure that for any condition variable v when the number of waiting threads is increased, by executing a command wait(v, l), or the number of the obligations is decreased, by (logically) executing a command g_disch(v), the desired invariant one_ob still holds. Additionally, the rules ACQUIRE and WAIT make sure that a thread only waits for a waitable object whose wait level is lower that the wait levels of obligations of that thread. Note that in the rule WAIT in the precondition of the command wait(v, l) it is not necessary that the wait level of v is lower that the wait level of l, since lock l is going to be released by this command. However, in this precondition the wait level of l must be lower that the wait levels of the obligations of the thread because when this thread is notified it tries to reacquire l, at which point $l \prec O$ must hold. The commands notify(v)/notifyAll(v), as shown in the rules NOTIFY and NOTIFYALL, remove one/all instance(s) of v, if any, from the bag Wt stored in the related locked permission. Additionally, notify(v) consumes the moving resources, indicated by M(v), that appear in the postcondition of the notified thread. Note that notifyAll(v) consumes $Wt(v)$ instances of these resources, since they are transferred to $Wt(v)$ threads waiting for v.

3.5   Verifying Channels

Ghost Counters. We will now use our proof system to prove deadlock-freedom of the program in Fig. 1. To do so, however, we will introduce a *ghost resource* that plays the role of *credits*, in such a way that we can prove the invariant $Wt(ch) + Ct(ch) \leqslant Ot(ch) + \text{sizeof}(ch)$. In particular, we want this property to follow from the lock invariant. This means we need to be able to talk, in the lock invariant, about the total number of credits in the system. To achieve this, we introduce a notion of *ghost counters* and corresponding *ghost counter tickets*, both of which are a particular kind of ghost resources. Specifically, we introduce three ghost commands: g_newctr, g_inc, and g_dec. g_newctr allocates a new ghost counter whose *value* is zero and returns a *ghost counter identifier* c for it. g_inc(c) increments the value of the ghost counter with identifier c and produces a *ticket* for the counter. g_dec(c), finally, consumes a ticket for ghost

$$\text{NEWCOUNTER } \{\text{true}\} \text{ g\_newctr } \{\lambda c.\ \text{ctr}(c, 0)\}$$

$$\text{INCCOUNTER } \{\text{ctr}(c, n)\} \text{ g\_inc}(c) \{\lambda\_.\ \text{ctr}(c, n{+}1) * \text{tic}(c)\}$$

$$\text{DECCOUNTER } \{\text{ctr}(c, n) * \text{tic}(c)\} \text{ g\_dec}(c) \{\lambda\_.\ \text{ctr}(c, n{-}1) \wedge 0{<}n\}$$

Fig. 6. Ghost counters

counter c and decrements the ghost counter's value. Since these are the only operations that manipulate ghost counters or ghost counter tickets, it follows that the value of a ghost counter c is always equal to the number of tickets for c in the system. Proof rules for these ghost commands are shown in Fig. 6[3].

The Channels Proof. Figure 7 illustrates how the program in Fig. 1 can be verified using our proof system. The invariant of lock $ch.l$ in this program, denoted by $\text{inv}(ch)$, is parametrized over bags Wt, Ot and implies the desired invariant $\text{one\_ob}(ch.v, Wt, Ot)$. The permission $\text{ctr}(ch.c, Ctv)$ in this invariant indicates that the total number of credits (tickets) for $ch.v$ is Ctv, where $ch.c$ is a *ghost field* added to the channel data structure, aiming to store a ghost counter identifier for the ghost counter of $ch.v$. Generally, a lock invariant can imply the invariant $\text{one\_ob}(v, Wt, Ot)$ if it asserts $Wt(v) + Ct(v) \leqslant Ot(v) + S(v)$ and $Wt(v) \leqslant Ot(v)$, where $Ct(v)$ is the total number of credits for v and $S(v)$ is an integer value such that the command $\text{wait}(v, l)$ is executed only if $S(v) \leqslant 0$. After initializing l in the main routine, there exists a credit for $ch.v$ (denoted by $\text{tic}(ch.c)$) that is consumed by the thread executing the receive routine, and also an obligation for $ch.v$ that is fulfilled by this thread after executing the send routine. The credit $\text{tic}(ch.c)$ in the precondition of the routine receive ensures that before execution of the command $\text{wait}(ch.v, ch.l)$, $Ot(ch.v) > 0$. This inequality follows from the invariant of lock l, which holds for $Wt \uplus \{ch.v\}$ and Ot when Ctv is decreased by $\text{g\_dec}(ch.c)$. This credit (or the one specified by $M(ch.v)$ that is moved from a notifier thread when the receiver thread wakes up) must be consumed after execution of the command $\text{dequeue}(ch.q)$ and before releasing $ch.l$ to make sure that the invariant still holds after decreasing the number of items in $ch.q$. The obligation for $ch.v$ in the precondition of the routine send is discharged by this routine, which is safe, since after the execution of the commands enqueue and notify the invariant $\text{one\_ob}(ch.v, Wt, Ot - \{ch.v\})$, which follows from the lock invariant, holds.

---

[3] Some logics for program verification, such as Iris [19], include general support for defining ghost resources such as our ghost counters. In particular, our ghost counters can be obtained in Iris as an instance of the *authoritative monoid* [19, p. 5].

inv(channel ch) ::= $\lambda Wt.\ \lambda Ot.\ \exists Ctv.\ \text{ctr}(ch.c, Ctv) * \exists s.\ \text{queue}(ch.q, s)\ \wedge$
$\quad L(ch.v)=ch.l \wedge M(ch.v)=\text{tic}(ch.c)\ \wedge$
$\quad Wt(ch.v) + Ctv \leqslant Ot(ch.v) + s\ \wedge$
$\quad Wt(ch.v) \leqslant Ot(ch.v)$

routine main(){{obs({})}
q:=newqueue; l:=newlock; v:=newcond; c:=g_newctr; g_inc(c);
{obs({}) $*$ ulock($l, \{\}, \{\}$) $*$ queue($q, 0$) $*$ ctr($c, 1$) $*$ tic(c)
$\wedge$ L(v)=l $\wedge$ M(v)=tic(c) $\wedge$ R(l)=0 $\wedge$ R(v)=1}
ch:=channel(q, l, v); $ch.c$:=c;
{obs({}) $*$ ulock($l, \{\}, \{\}$) $*$ inv(ch)({}, {v}) $*$ tic(c)} g_chrg(v);
{obs({v}) $*$ ulock($l, \{\}, \{v\}$) $*$ inv(ch)({}, {v}) $*$ tic(c)} g_initl(l);
{obs({v}) $*$ lock(l) $*$ tic(c) $\wedge$ l(l)=inv(ch)}
fork (receive(ch));
{obs({v}) $*$ lock(l)}
send($ch, 12$) {obs({})}}}

routine receive(channel ch){
{obs(O) $*$ tic($ch.c$) $*$ lock($ch.l$) $\wedge$ $ch.l{\prec}O$ $\wedge$ $ch.v{\prec}O$ $\wedge$ l($ch.l$)=inv(ch)}
acquire($ch.l$);
{obs($O{\uplus}\{ch.l\}$) $*$ tic($ch.c$) $*$ $\exists Wt, Ot.$ locked($ch.l, Wt, Ot$) $*$ inv(ch)(Wt, Ot)}
while(sizeof($ch.q$) = 0){ g_dec($ch.c$);
{obs($O{\uplus}\{ch.l\}$) $*$ $\exists Wt, Ot.$ locked($ch.l, Wt, Ot$) $*$ inv(ch)($Wt{\uplus}\{ch.v\}, Ot$)}}
wait($ch.v, ch.l$)
{obs($O{\uplus}\{ch.l\}$) $*$ M($ch.v$) $*$ $\exists Wt, Ot.$ locked($ch.l, Wt, Ot$) $*$ inv(ch)(Wt, Ot)}};
dequeue($ch.q$); g_dec($ch.c$);
{obs($O{\uplus}\{ch.l\}$) $*$ $\exists Wt, Ot.$ locked($ch.l, Wt, Ot$) $*$ inv(ch)(Wt, Ot)}
release($ch.l$) {obs(O) $*$ lock($ch.l$)}}

routine send(channel ch, int d){
{obs($O{\uplus}\{ch.v\}$) $*$ lock($ch.l$) $\wedge$ $ch.l{\prec}O{\uplus}\{ch.v\}$ $\wedge$ l($ch.l$)=inv(ch)}
acquire($ch.l$);
{obs($O{\uplus}\{ch.v, ch.l\}$) $*$ $\exists Wt, Ot.$ locked($ch.l, Wt, Ot$) $*$ inv(ch)(Wt, Ot)}
enqueue($ch.q, d$);
if ($Wt(ch.v){>}0$) g_inc($ch.c$);
notify($ch.v$);
{obs($O{\uplus}\{ch.v, ch.l\}$) $*$ $\exists Wt, Ot.$ locked($ch.l, Wt, Ot$) $*$ inv(ch)($Wt, Ot-\{ch.v\}$)}
g_disch($ch.v$);
{obs($O{\uplus}\{ch.l\}$) $*$ $\exists Wt, Ot.$ locked($ch.l, Wt, Ot$) $*$ inv(ch)(Wt, Ot)}
release($ch.l$) {obs(O) $*$ lock($ch.l$)}}}

Fig. 7. Verification of the program in Fig. 1

3.6   Other Examples

Using the proof system of this section we prove two other deadlock-free programs, namely *sleeping barber* [16], and *barrier*. In the barrier program shown in Fig. 8, a barrier b consists of an integer variable r indicating the number of the remaining

```
routine main(){                          routine wait_for_rest(barrier b){
r:=newint(3);                            acquire(b.l);
l:=newlock;                              b.r:=b.r−1;
v:=newcond;                              if(b.r=0)
b:=barrier(r, l, v);                        notifyAll();
fork (task₁(); wait_for_rest(b); task₂());  else
fork (task₁(); wait_for_rest(b); task₂());     while(b.r>0)
task₁(); wait_for_rest(b); task₂()}               wait(b.v, b.l);
                                            release(b.l)}
```

$$inv(\text{barrier } b) ::= \lambda Wt.\ \lambda Ot.\ \exists r \geqslant 0.\ b.r \mapsto r \wedge L(b.v) = b.l \wedge M(b.v) = \text{true} \wedge$$
$$(Wt(b.v) = 0 \vee 0 < r) \wedge (r \leqslant Ot(b.v))$$

```
routine main(){{obs({})}
r:=newint(3); l:=newlock; v:=newcond;
{obs({}) * r↦3 * ulock(l, {}, {}) ∧ L(v)=l ∧ M(v)=true ∧ R(l)=0 ∧ R(v)=1}
b:=barrier(r, l, v);
{obs({}) * inv(b)({}, {3·v}) * ulock(l, {}, {})}
g_chrg(v); g_chrg(v); g_chrg(v); g_initl(l);
{obs({3·v}) * lock(l) ∧ l(l)=inv(b)}
fork (wait_for_rest(b));
{obs({2·v}) * lock(l)}
fork (wait_for_rest(b));
{obs({v}) * lock(l)}
wait_for_rest(b) {obs({})}}

routine wait_for_rest(barrier b){
{obs(O⊎{b.v}) * lock(b.l) ∧ b.l≺O⊎{b.v} ∧ b.v≺O ∧ l(b.l)=inv(b)}
acquire(b.l);
{obs(O⊎{b.v, b.l}) * ∃Wt, Ot. locked(b.l, Wt, Ot) * inv(b)(Wt, Ot)}
b.r:=b.r−1;
if(b.r=0){
  notifyAll(b.v);
  {obs(O⊎{b.v, b.l}) * ∃Wt, Ot. locked(b.l, Wt[b.v:=0], Ot)
  *inv(b)(Wt[b.v:=0], Ot−{b.v})} g_disch(b.v)
  {obs(O⊎{b.l}) * ∃Wt, Ot. locked(b.l, Wt, Ot) * inv(b)(Wt, Ot)}}
else{
  {obs(O⊎{b.v, b.l}) * ∃Wt, Ot. locked(b.l, Wt, Ot)
  *inv(b)(Wt, Ot−{b.v})} g_disch(b.v);
  {obs(O⊎{b.l}) * ∃Wt, Ot. locked(b.l, Wt, Ot) * inv(b)(Wt, Ot)}
  while(b.r>0)
    {obs(O⊎{b.l}) * ∃Wt, Ot. locked(b.l, Wt, Ot) * inv(b)(Wt⊎{b.v}, Ot)}
  wait(b.v, b.l)
    {obs(O⊎{b.l}) * ∃Wt, Ot. locked(b.l, Wt, Ot) * inv(b)(Wt, Ot)}};
release(b.l) {obs(O) * lock(b.l)}}
```

Fig. 8. Verification of a barrier synchronized using a monitor

threads that must call the routine wait_for_rest, a lock l protecting r against data races, and a condition variable v. Each thread executing the routine wait_for_rest first decreases the variable r, and if the resulting value is still positive waits for v, otherwise it notifies all threads waiting for v. In this program the barrier is initialized to 3, implying that no thread must start $task_2$ unless all the three threads in this program finish $task_1$. This program is deadlock-free because the routine wait_for_rest is executed by three different threads. Figure 8 illustrates how this program can be verified by the presented proof rules. Note that before executing g_disch in the else branch, safe_obs holds because at this point we have $0 < b.r$, which implies $1 < b.r$ before the execution of $b.r := b.r - 1$, and by the invariant we have $1 < Ot(b.v)$, implying $0 < (Ot - \{b.v\})(b.v)$. The interesting point about the verification of this program is that since all the threads waiting for condition variable v in this program are notified by the command notifyAll, the invariant of the related lock, implying one_ob$(b.v, Wt, Ot)$, is significantly different from the ones defined in the channel and sleeping barber examples. Generally, for a condition variable v on which only notifyAll is executed (and not notify) a lock invariant can imply the invariant one_ob(v, Wt, Ot) if it asserts $Wt(v) = 0 \vee S(v) \leqslant Ct(v)$ and $Ct(v) < Ot(v) + S(v)$, where $Ct(v)$ is the total number of credits for v and $S(v)$ is an integer value such that the command wait(v, l) is executed only if $S(v) \leqslant 0$. For this particular example $S(b.v) = 1 - b.r$ and $Ct(b.v) = 0$, since this program can be verified without incorporating the notion of credits.

4   Relaxing the Precedence Relation

The precedence relation, in this paper denoted by $\prec$, introduced in [4] makes sure that all threads wait for the waitable objects in strict ascending order (with respect to the wait level associated with each waitable object), or here in this paper in descending order, ensuring that in any state of the execution there is no cycle in the corresponding wait-for graph. However, this relation is too restrictive and prevents verifying some programs that are actually deadlock-free, such as the one shown in the left side of Fig. 9. In this program a value is increased by two threads communicating through a channel. Each thread receives a value from the channel, increases that value, and then sends it back on the channel. Since an initial value is sent on the related channel this program is deadlock-free. The first attempt to verify this program is illustrated in the middle part of Fig. 9, where the required credit to verify the receive command in the routine inc is going to be provided by the send command, executed immediately after this command, and not by the precondition of this routine. In other words, the idea is to load a credit and an obligation for ch in the routine inc itself, and then spend the loaded credit to verify the receive(ch) command and fulfil the loaded obligation by the send(ch) command. However, this idea fails because the receive command in the routine inc cannot be verified since one of its preconditions, $ch \prec \{ch\}$, never holds. Kobayashi [6, 20] has addressed this problem in his type system by using the notion of *usages* and assigning levels to each *obligation/capability*, instead of

```
routine main(){                routine main(){                routine main(){
  ch:=channel;                   {obs({})}                      {obs({})}
  send(ch, 12);                  ch:=newchannel;                ch:=newchannel;
  fork (inc(ch));                send(ch, 12);                  {obs({ch}) ∧ P(ch)=true}
  fork (inc(ch))}                fork (inc(ch));                send(ch, 12);
                                 fork (inc(ch)) {obs({})}}      {obs({})}
routine inc(channel ch){                                        fork (inc(ch));
  d:=receive(ch);              routine inc(channel ch){         fork (inc(ch)) {obs({})}}
  send(ch, d+1)}                 {obs({})}
                                 {obs({ch}) * credit(ch)       routine inc(channel ch){
                                 ∧ ch⊀{ch}}                      {obs({}) ∧ ch≼{ch}}
                                 d:=receive(ch);                ⟨obs({ch}) * credit(ch)
                                 {obs({ch})}                     ∧ ch≼{ch}⟩
                                 send(ch, d+1) {obs({})}}        d:=receive(ch);
                                                                 {obs({ch})}
                                                                 send(ch, d+1) {obs({})}}
```

Fig. 9. A deadlock-free program verified by exploiting the relaxed precedence relation

waitable objects. However, in the next section we provide a novel idea to address this problem by just relaxing the precedence relation used in the presented proof rules.

4.1 A Relaxed Precedence Relation

To tackle the problem mentioned in the previous section we relax the precedence relation, enforced by $\prec$, by replacing $\prec$ by $\preccurlyeq$ satisfying the following property: $o\preccurlyeq O$ holds if either $o\prec O$ or (1) $o\prec O - \{o\}$, and (2) o satisfies the property that in any execution state, if a thread waits for o then there exists a thread that can discharge an obligation for o and is not waiting for any object whose wait level is equal to/greater than the wait level of o. This property still guarantees that in any state of the execution if the program has some threads suspended, waiting for some obligations, there is always a thread obliged to fulfil the obligation o_{min} that is not blocked, where o_{min} has a minimal wait level among all waitable objects for which a thread is waiting.

The condition number 2 is met if it is an invariant that for a condition variable o for which a thread is waiting the total number of obligations is greater than the total number of waiting threads. Since each thread waiting for o has at most one instance of o in the bag of its obligations, according to the *pigeonhole principle*, if the number obligations for o is higher than the number of threads waiting for o then there exists a thread that holds an obligation for o that is not waiting for o, implying the rule number 2 because this thread only waits for objects whose wait levels are lower than the wait level of o. Accordingly, we first introduce a new function P in the proof rules mapping each waitable object to a boolean value, and then make sure that for any object o for which a thread is waiting if

$P(o) = $ true then $Wt(o) < Ot(o)$. With the help of this function we define the relaxed precedence relation as shown in Definition 1.

Definition 1 (Relaxed precedence relation). *The relaxed precedence relation indexed over functions* R *and* P *holds for a waitable object* v *and a bag of obligations* O, *denoted by* $v \preccurlyeq O$, *if and only if:*

$$v \prec O \ \lor \ (v \prec O - \{v\} \land P(v) = \text{true}) \ , \ where \ v \prec O \Leftrightarrow \forall o \in O. \ R(v) < R(o)$$

Using this relaxed precedence relation the approach presented by Leino *et al.* [4] can also support more complex programs, such as the one in the left side of Fig. 9. This approach can exploit this relation by (1) replacing the original precedence relation $\prec$ by the relaxed one $\preccurlyeq$, and (2) replacing the rule associated with creating a channel by the one shown below. According to this proof rule for each channel ch the function P, in the definition of the relaxed precedence relation, is initialized when ch is created such that if $P(ch)$ is decided to be true then one obligation for ch is loaded onto the bag of obligations of the creating thread. The approach is still sound because for any channel ch for which P is true the invariant $Wt(ch) + Ct(ch) < Ot(ch) + \text{sizeof}(ch)$ holds. Combined with the fact that in this language, where channels are primitive constructs, $Wt(ch) > 0 \Rightarrow \text{sizeof}(ch) = 0$, we have $Wt(ch) > 0 \Rightarrow Wt(ch) < Ot(ch)$. Now consider a deadlocked state, where each thread is waiting for a waitable object. Among all of these waitable objects take the one having a minimal wait level, namely o_m. If o_m is a lock or a channel, where $P(o_m) = $ false, then at least one thread has an obligation for o_m and is waiting for an object o whose wait level is lower that the wait level of o_m, which contradicts minimality of the wait level of o_m. Otherwise, since $Wt(o_m) > 0$ we have $Wt(o_m) < Ot(o_m)$. Additionally, we know that each thread waiting for o_m has at most one obligation for o_m. Accordingly, there must be a thread holding an obligation for o_m that is not waiting for o_m. Consequently, this thread must be waiting for an object o whose wait level is lower than the wait level of o_m, which contradicts minimality of the wait level of o_m.

$$\{\text{obs}(O)\} \ \text{newchannel} \ \{\lambda ch. \ \text{obs}(O') \land \text{R}(ch) = z \land \text{P}(ch) = b$$
$$\land ((b = \text{false} \land O' = O) \lor (b = \text{true} \land O' = O \uplus \{ch\}))\}$$

To exploit the relaxed definition in the approach presented in this paper we only need to make sure that for any condition variable v for which a thread is waiting if $P(v)$ is true then $Ot(v)$ is greater than $Wt(v)$. To achieve this goal we include this invariant in the definition of the invariant safe_obs, shown in Definition 2, an invariant that must hold when a command wait or a ghost command g_disch is executed.

Definition 2 (Safe Obligations). *The relation* safe_obs(v, Wt, Ot), *indexed over function* P, *holds if and only if:*

one_ob$(v, Wt, Ot) \ \land \ (\text{P}(v) = \text{true} \Rightarrow \text{spare\_ob}(v, Wt, Ot))$, *where*
one_ob$(v, Wt, Ot) \Leftrightarrow (Wt(v) > 0 \Rightarrow Ot(v) > 0)$
spare_ob$(v, Wt, Ot) \Leftrightarrow (Wt(v) > 0 \Rightarrow Wt(v) < Ot(v))$

one_ob(v, Wt, Ot) $\wedge$ $(P(v)=$true $\Rightarrow$ spare_ob$(v, Wt, Ot))$, *where*
one_ob(v, Wt, Ot) $\Leftrightarrow$ $(Wt(v)>0 \Rightarrow Ot(v)>0)$
spare_ob(v, Wt, Ot) $\Leftrightarrow$ $(Wt(v)>0 \Rightarrow Wt(v)<Ot(v))$

```
routine main(){              routine reader(rdwr b){       routine writer(rdwr b){
 aw:=newint(0);               acquire(b.l);                 acquire(b.l);
 ww:=newint(0);               while(b.aw+b.ww>0)            while(b.aw+b.ar>0){
 ar:=newint(0);                wait(b.vr, b.l);              b.ww:=b.ww+1;
 l:=newlock;                  b.ar:=b.ar+1;                 wait(b.vw, b.l);
 vw:=newcond;                 release(b.l);                 if(b.ww<1)
 vr:=newcond;                 // Perform reading ...          abort();
 b := rdwr(aw, ww             acquire(b.l);                 b.ww:=b.ww−1
  , ar, l, vw, vr);           if(b.ar<1)                   };
 fork(                         abort;                       b.aw:=b.aw+1;
  while (true)                b.ar:=b.ar−1;                 release(b.l);
   fork(reader(b))            notify(b.vw);                 // Perform writing ...
 );                           release(b.l)}                 acquire(b.l);
 while (true)                                               if(b.aw≠1)
  fork(writer(b))                                            abort;
}                                                           b.aw:=b.aw−1;
                                                            notify(b.vw);
                                                            if(b.ww=0)
                                                             notifyAll(b.vr);
                                                            release(b.l)}
```

Fig. 10. A readers-writers program with variables aw, holding the number of threads writing, ww, holding the number of thread waiting to write, and ar, holding the number of threads reading, that is synchronized using a monitor consisting of condition variables v_w, preventing writers from writing while other threads are reading or writing, and v_r, preventing readers from reading while there is another thread writing or waiting to write.

Readers-Writes Locks. As another application of this relaxed definition consider a readers-writers program, shown in Fig. 10[4], where the condition variable v_w prevents writers from writing on a shared memory when that memory is being accessed by other threads. After reading the shared memory, a reader thread notifies this condition variable if there is no other thread reading that memory. This condition variable is also notified by a writer thread when it finishes its writing. Consequently, a writer thread first might wait for v_w and then fulfil an obligation for this condition variable. This program is verified if the writer thread itself produces a credit and an obligation for v_w and then uses the former for the command wait(v_w, l) and fulfils the latter at the end of its execution. Accordingly, since when the command wait(v_w, l) is executed v_w is in the bag of obligations of the

---

[4] The abort commands in this program can be eliminated using the ghost counters from Fig. 6. However, we leave them in for simplicity.

$inv(rdwr\ b) ::= \lambda Wt.\ \lambda Ot.\ \exists Ctw.\ ctr(b.c_w, Ctw)\ *$
$\exists aw{\geqslant}0,\ ww{\geqslant}0,\ ar{\geqslant}0.\ b.aw{\mapsto}aw * b.ww{\mapsto}ww * b.ar{\mapsto}ar\ \wedge$
$L(b.v_w){=}L(b.v_r){=}b.l \wedge M(b.v_w){=}tic(b.c_w) \wedge M(b.v_r){=}true \wedge P(v_w){=}true \wedge P(v_r){=}false \wedge$
$(Wt(b.v_r) = 0 \vee 0 < aw + ww)\ \wedge$
$aw + ww \leqslant Ot(b.v_r)\ \wedge$
$Wt(b.v_w) + Ctw + aw + ar \leqslant Ot(b.v_w)\ \wedge$
$(Wt(b.v_w) = 0 \vee Wt(b.v_w) < Ot(b.v_w))$

routine main(){
$\quad aw{:=}newint(0);\ \ ww{:=}newint(0);$
$\quad ar{:=}newint(0);\ \ l{:=}newlock;$
$\quad v_w{:=}newcond;\ \ v_r{:=}newcond;$
$\quad b := rdwr(aw, ww, ar, l, v_w, v_r);$
$\quad b.c_w{:=}g\_newctr;$
$\quad \{obs(\{\}) * inv(b)(\{\}, \{\}) * ulock(l, \{\}, \{\})\ *$
$\quad L(v_w){=}L(v_r){=}l \wedge M(v_w){=}tic(b.c_w)\ \wedge$
$\quad M(v_r){=}true \wedge R(l){=}0 \wedge R(v_w){=}1\ \wedge$
$\quad R(v_r){=}2 \wedge L(v_w){=}l \wedge L(v_r){=}l$
$\quad \wedge P(v_w){=}true \wedge P(v_r){=}false\}\ g\_initl(l);$
$\quad \{obs(\{\}) * lock(l) \wedge I(l){=}inv(b)\}$
fork($\{obs(\{\}) * lock(l)\}$
   while (true) fork(reader(b)));
$\quad \{obs(\{\}) * lock(l)\}$
   while (true) fork(writer(b))
$\quad \{obs(\{\}) * lock(l)\}\}$

routine reader(rdwr b){
$\quad \{obs(O) * lock(b.l) \wedge b.l{\preccurlyeq}O{\uplus}\{b.v_w\}$
$\quad \wedge\ b.v_r{\preccurlyeq}O \wedge I(b.l){=}inv(b)\}$
acquire($b.l$);
while($b.aw{+}b.ww{>}0$)
$\quad$**wait($b.v_r, b.l$);**
$b.ar{:=}b.ar{+}1;$
$g\_chrg(b.v_w);$
release($b.l$);
// Perform reading ...
acquire($b.l$);
if($b.ar{<}1$)
$\quad$**abort;**
$b.ar{:=}b.ar{-}1;$
if $(Wt(b.v_w) > 0)$ $g\_inc(b.c_w);$
notify($b.v_w$);
$g\_disch(b.v_w);$
release($b.l$) $\{obs(\{\}) * lock(b.l)\}\}$

routine writer(rdwr b){
$\quad \{obs(O) * lock(b.l) \wedge b.l{\preccurlyeq}O{\uplus}\{b.v_w, b.v_r\}$
$\quad \wedge\ b.v_w{\preccurlyeq}O{\uplus}\{b.v_w, b.v_r\} \wedge I(b.l){=}inv(b)\}$
acquire($b.l$);
$g\_chrg(b.v_w);\ g\_inc(b.c_w);$
$g\_chrg(b.v_r);$
while($b.aw{+}b.ar{>}0$){
$\quad g\_dec(b.c_w);$
$\quad b.ww{:=}b.ww{+}1;$
$\quad$**wait($b.v_w, b.l$);**
$\quad$**if($b.ww{<}1$)**
$\quad\quad$**abort();**
$\quad b.ww{:=}b.ww{-}1$
};
$b.aw{:=}b.aw{+}1;$
$g\_dec(b.c_w);$
release($b.l$);
// Perform writing ...
acquire($b.l$);
if($b.aw{\neq}1$)
$\quad$**abort;**
$b.aw{:=}b.aw{-}1;$
if $(Wt(b.v_w) > 0)$ $g\_inc(b.c_w);$
notify($b.v_w$);
if($b.ww{=}0$)
$\quad$**notifyAll($b.v_r$);**
$g\_disch(b.v_w);\ g\_disch(b.v_r);$
release($b.l$) $\{obs(\{\}) * lock(b.l)\}\}$

Fig. 11. Verification of the program in Fig. 10

writer thread, this command can be verified if $v_w \preccurlyeq \{v_w\}$, where $\mathsf{P}(v_w)$ must be true. The verification of this program is illustrated in Fig. 11. Generally, for a condition variable v for which $P(v) = \mathsf{true}$ a lock invariant can imply the invariant one_ob(v, Wt, Ot) if it asserts $Wt(v) + Ct(v) < Ot(v) + S(v)$ and $Wt(v) = 0 \vee Wt(v) < Ot(v)$, where $Ct(v)$ is the total number of credits for v and $S(v)$ is an integer value such that wait(v, l) is executed only if $S(v) \leqslant 0$.

4.2 A Further Relaxation

The relation $\preccurlyeq$ allows one to verify some deadlock-free programs where a thread waits for a condition variable while that thread is also obliged to fulfil an obligation for that variable. However, it is still possible to have a more general, more relaxed definition for this relation. Under this definition a thread with obligations O is allowed to wait for a condition variable v if either $v \prec O$, or there exists an obligation o such that (1) $v \prec O - \{o\}$, and (2) o satisfies the property that in any execution state, if a thread is waiting for o then there exists a thread that is not waiting for any waitable object whose wait level is equal to/greater than the wait levels of v and o. This new definition still guarantees that in any state of the execution if the program has some threads suspended, waiting for some obligations, there is always a thread obliged to fulfil the obligation o_{min} that is not suspended, where o_{min} has a minimal wait level among all waitable objects for which a thread is waiting. To satisfy the condition number 2 we introduce a new definition for $\preccurlyeq$, shown in Definition 3, that uses a new function X mapping each lock to a set of wait levels. This definition will be sound only if the proof rules ensure that for any condition variable v whose wait level is in $\mathsf{X}(\mathsf{L}(v))$ the number of obligations is equal to or greater than the number of the waiting threads.

This definition is still sound because of Lemma 1, that has been machine-checked in Coq[5], where G is a bag of waitable object-bag of obligations pairs such that each element t of G is associated with a thread in a state of the execution, where the first element of t is the object for which t is waiting and the second element is the bag of obligations of t. This lemma implies that if all the mentioned rules, denoted by H_1 to H_4, are respected in any state of the execution then it is impossible that all threads in that state are waiting for a waitable object. This lemma can be proved by induction on the number of elements of G and considering the element waiting for object whose wait level is minimal (see [16] representing its proof in details).

Definition 3 (Relaxed precedence relation). *The new precedence relation indexed over functions* $\mathsf{R}, \mathsf{L}, \mathsf{P}, \mathsf{X}$ *holds for a waitable object v and a bag of obligations O, denoted by $v \preccurlyeq O$, if and only if:*

---

[5] The machine-checked proof can be found at https://github.com/jafarhamin/deadlock-free-monitors-soundness.

$(v \prec O \lor v \preceq O) \land (\neg \mathsf{exc}(v) \lor v \bot O)$, *where*

$v \prec O \Leftrightarrow \forall o \in O.\ \mathsf{R}(v) < \mathsf{R}(o)$

$v \preceq O \Leftrightarrow \mathsf{P}(v) = \mathsf{true} \land \mathsf{exc}(v) \land$
$\qquad\qquad \exists o.\ v \prec O - \{o\} \land \mathsf{R}(v) \leqslant \mathsf{R}(o) + 1 \land \mathsf{L}(v) = \mathsf{L}(o) \land \mathsf{exc}(o)$

$\mathsf{exc}(v) = \mathsf{R}(v) \in \mathsf{X}(\mathsf{L}(v))$

$v \bot O \Leftrightarrow \mathsf{let}\ Ox = \lambda v'.\ \begin{cases} O(v') & \textit{if } \mathsf{R}(v') \in \mathsf{X}(\mathsf{L}(v)) \\ 0 & \textit{otherwise} \end{cases}$ in

$\qquad\qquad |Ox| \leqslant 1 \land$
$\qquad\qquad \forall v'.\ Ox(v') > 0 \Rightarrow \mathsf{L}(v') = \mathsf{L}(v)$

Lemma 1 (A Valid Graph Is Not Deadlocked)

$\forall\ G{:}Bags(WaitObjs \times Bags(WaitObjs)),\ R{:}WaitObjs {\rightarrow} WaitLevels,$
$L{:}WaitObjs {\rightarrow} Locks,\ P{:}WaitObjs {\rightarrow} Bools,\ X{:}Locks {\rightarrow} Sets(WaitLevels).$
$H_1 \land H_2 \land H_3 \land H_4 \Rightarrow G = \{\}$, *where*

$\quad H_1 : \forall (o, O) \in G.\ 0 < \mathsf{Ot}(o)$
$\quad H_2 : \forall (o, O) \in G.\ \mathsf{P}(o) = \mathsf{true} \Rightarrow \mathsf{Wt}(o) < \mathsf{Ot}(o)$
$\quad H_3 : \forall (o, O) \in G.\ R(o) \in X(L(o)) \Rightarrow \mathsf{Wt}(o) \leqslant \mathsf{Ot}(o)$
$\quad H_4 : \forall (o, O) \in G.\ o \preccurlyeq_{R,L,P,X} O$

where $\mathsf{Wt} = \biguplus_{(o,O) \in G} \{o\}$ *and* $\mathsf{Ot} = \biguplus_{(o,O) \in G} O$

NewLock $\{\mathsf{true}\}$ newlock $\{\lambda l.\ \mathsf{ulock}(l, \{\}, \{\}) \land \mathsf{R}(l){=}z \land \mathsf{X}(l){=}X\}$

NewCv $\{\mathsf{true}\}$ newcond $\{\lambda v.\ \mathsf{R}(v){=}z \land \mathsf{L}(v){=}l \land \mathsf{M}(v){=}m \land \mathsf{P}(v){=}b\}$

Fig. 12. New proof rules initializing functions X and P used in safe_obs and $\preccurlyeq$

To extend the proof rules with the new precedence relation it suffices to include a new invariant own_ob in the definition of safe_obs, as shown in Definition 4, an invariant that must hold when a command wait or a ghost command g_disch is executed, to make sure that for any condition variable for which exc holds, the number of obligations is equal to/greater than the number of the waiting threads. Additionally, the functions X and P, as indicated in Fig. 12, are initialized when a lock and a condition variable is created, respectively. The rest of the proof rules are the same as those defined in Fig. 5 except that the old precedence relation ($\prec$) is replaced by the new one ($\preccurlyeq$).

Definition 4 (Safe Obligations). *The relation* safe_obs(v, Wt, Ot), *indexed over functions* R, L, P, X, *holds if and only if:*

one_ob$(v, Wt, Ot) \land (\mathsf{P}(v) = \mathsf{true} \Rightarrow$ spare_ob$(v, Wt, Ot)) \land$
$(\mathsf{exc}(v) = \mathsf{true} \Rightarrow$ own_ob$(v, Wt, Ot))$, *where*
one_ob$(v, Wt, Ot) \Leftrightarrow (Wt(v) > 0 \Rightarrow Ot(v) > 0)$
spare_ob$(v, Wt, Ot) \Leftrightarrow (Wt(v) > 0 \Rightarrow Wt(v) < Ot(v))$
own_ob$(v, Wt, Ot) \Leftrightarrow (Wt(v) \leqslant Ot(v))$

Bounded Channels. One application of the new definition is a bounded channel program, shown in Fig. 13, where a sender thread waits for a receiver thread if the channel is full, synchronized by v_f, and a receiver thread waits for a sender thread if the channel is empty, synchronized by v_e. More precisely, the sender thread with an obligation for v_e might execute the command wait(v_f, l), and the receiver thread with an obligation for v_f might execute a command wait(v_e, l).

```
routine main(){              routine send(channel ch, int d)   routine receive(channel ch)
  q := newqueue;             {                                 {
  l := newlock;                acquire(ch.l);                    acquire(ch.l);
  v_f := newcvar;              while(sizeof(ch.q) = max)         while(sizeof(ch.q) = 0)
  v_e := newcvar;                wait(ch.v_f, ch.l);              wait(ch.v_e, ch.l);
  ch:=channel(q, l, v_f, v_e); enqueue(ch.q, d);                 dequeue(ch.q);
  fork (receive(ch));          notify(ch.v_e);                   notify(ch.v_f);
  send(ch, 12)}               release(ch.l)}                    release(ch.l)}
```

$inv(\text{channel } ch) ::= \lambda Wt. \lambda Ot. \exists Cte, Ctf. \; ctr(ch.c_e, Cte) * ctr(ch.c_f, Ctf) *$
$\exists s. \; queue(ch.q, s) \land P(v_e) = \text{false} \land M(v_e) = tic(ch.c_e) \land M(v_f) = tic(ch.c_f) \; land$
$L(ch.v_e) = L(ch.v_f) = ch.l \land$
$Wt(ch.v_e) + Cte \leqslant Ot(ch.v_e) + s \land Wt(ch.v_e) \leqslant Ot(ch.v_e) \land$
$Wt(ch.v_f) + Ctf + s < Ot(ch.v_f) + \text{max} \land (Wt(v_f) = 0 \lor Wt(ch.v_f) < Ot(ch.v_f))$

```
routine main(){              routine send(channel ch, int d)       routine receive(channel ch){
  q := newqueue;             {{obs(O⊎{ch.v_e}) * tic(ch.c_f) *    {obs(O⊎{ch.v_f}) * tic(ch.c_e) *
  l := newlock;                lock(ch.l) ∧ ch.l≼O⊎{ch.v_e} ∧       lock(ch.l) ∧ ch.l≼O⊎{ch.v_f} ∧
  v_f := newcvar;              ch.v_f≼O⊎{ch.v_e}∧I(ch.l)=inv}       ch.v_e≼O⊎{ch.v_f}∧I(ch.l)=inv}
  v_e := newcvar;            acquire(ch.l);                         acquire(ch.l);
  ch:=channel(q, l, v_f, v_e); while(sizeof(ch.q) = max){           while(sizeof(ch.q) = 0){
  ch.c_e:=g_newctr;            g_dec(ch.c_f);                         g_dec(ch.c_e);
  ch.c_f:=g_newctr;           wait(ch.v_f, ch.l)};                   wait(ch.v_e, ch.l)};
  g_inc(ch.c_e);              enqueue(ch.q, d);                      dequeue(ch.q);
  g_inc(ch.c_f);              if (Wt(b.v_e) > 0)                     if (Wt(b.v_f) > 0)
  g_chrg(v_e); g_chrg(v_f);     g_inc(b.c_e);                          g_inc(b.c_f);
  g_initl(l);                 notify(ch.v_e);                        notify(ch.v_f);
  {obs({v_e, v_f}) * lock(l) * g_disch(ch.v_e);                     g_disch(ch.v_f);
  tic(ch.c_e) * tic(ch.c_f) * g_dec(ch.c_f);                         g_dec(ch.c_e);
  L(v_f)=l ∧ L(v_e)=l ∧      release(ch.l)                          release(ch.l)
  M(v_e)=tic(ch.c_e) ∧       {obs(O) * lock(ch.l)}}}                {obs(O) * lock(ch.l)}}}
  M(v_f)=tic(ch.c_f) ∧
  P(v_f)=true ∧
  P(v_e)=false ∧
  R(l)=0 ∧
  R(v_e)=1 ∧ R(v_f)=2 ∧
  X(l)={1, 2} ∧ I(l)=inv}
  fork (receive(ch));
  send(ch, 12) {obs({})}}
```

Fig. 13. Verification of a bounded channel synchronized using a monitor consisting of condition variables v_f, preventing sending on a full channel, and v_e, preventing taking messages from an empty channel

Since v_e and v_f are not equal, it is impossible to verify this program by the old definition of $\preccurlyeq$ because the waiting levels of v_e and v_f cannot be lower than each other. Thanks to the new definition of $\preccurlyeq$, this program can be verified, as shown in Fig. 13, by initializing $\mathsf{P}(v_f)$ with true and $\mathsf{X}(l)$ with $\{1,2\}$, where two consecutive numbers 1 and 2 are the wait levels of v_e and v_f, respectively.

5 Soundness Proof

In this section we provide a soundness proof for the present approach[6], i.e. if a program is verified by the proposed proof rules, where the verification starts from an empty bag of obligations and also ends with such bag, this program is deadlock-free. To this end, we first define the syntax of programs and a small-step semantics for programs ($\leadsto$) relating two *configurations* (see [16] for formal definitions). A configuration is a thread table-heap pair (t, h), where heaps and thread tables are some partial functions from locations and thread identifiers to integers and command-*context* pairs $(c; \xi)$, respectively, where a context, denoted by ξ, is either done or let $x:=[]$ in $c; \xi$. Then we define *validity of configurations*, shown in Definition 5, and prove that (1) if a program c is verified by the proposed proof rules, where it starts from the precondition $\mathsf{obs}(\{\!\!\{\}\!\!\})$ and satisfies the post condition $\lambda_-.\mathsf{obs}(\{\!\!\{\}\!\!\})$, then the initial configuration, where the heap is empty, denoted by $\mathbf{0} = \lambda_-.\varnothing$, and there is only one thread with command c and context done, is a valid configuration (Theorem 4), (2) a valid configuration is not deadlocked (Theorem 5), and (3) starting from a valid configuration, all the subsequent configurations of the execution are also valid (Theorem 6).

In a valid configuration (t, h), h contains all the heap ownerships that are in possession of all threads in t and also those that are in possession of the locks that are not held, specified by a list A. Additionally, each thread must have all the required permissions to be successfully verified with no remaining obligation, enforced by wpcx. $\mathsf{wpcx}(c, \xi)$ in this definition is a function returning the weakest precondition of the command c with the context ξ w.r.t. the postcondition $\lambda_-.\mathsf{obs}(\{\!\!\{\}\!\!\})$ (see [16] for formal definitions). This function is defined with the help of a function $\mathsf{wp}(c, a)$ returning the weakest precondition the command c w.r.t. the postcondition a.

Definition 5 (Validity of Configurations). *A configuration is valid, denoted by* $\mathsf{valid}(t, h)$, *if there exist a list of augmented threads* T, *consisting of an identifier* (id), *a program* (c), *a context* (ξ), *a permission heap* (p), *a ghost resource heap* (C) *and a bag of obligations* (O) *associated with each thread; a list of assertions* A, *and some functions* R, I, L, M, P, X *such that:*

- $\forall id, c, \xi.\ t(id) = (c; \xi) \Leftrightarrow \exists p, O, C.\ (id, c, \xi, p, O, C) \in T$
- $h = \mathsf{pheap2heap}(\underset{a \in A}{*} a * \underset{(id,c,\xi,p,O,C) \in T}{*} p)$

---

[6] The machine-checked version of some lemmas and theorems in this proof, such as Theorems 4 and 5, can be found at https://github.com/jafarhamin/deadlock-free-monitors-soundness.

$-\ \forall (id, c, \xi, p, O, C) \in T.$

- $p, O, C \models \mathsf{wpcx}_{R,I,L,M,P,X}(c, \xi)$
- $\forall l, Wt, Ot.\ p(l) = \mathsf{Ulock/Locked}(Wt, Ot) \Rightarrow Wt = \mathsf{Wt}_l \wedge Ot = \mathsf{Ot}_l$
- $\forall l.\ p(l) = \mathsf{Lock} \wedge h(l) = 1 \Rightarrow \mathsf{I}(l)(\mathsf{Wt}_l, \mathsf{Ot}_l) \in A$
- $\forall l.\ p(l) = \mathsf{Lock} \vee p(l) = \mathsf{Locked}(\mathsf{Wt}_l, \mathsf{Ot}_l) \Rightarrow \neg P(l) \wedge \neg \mathsf{exc}(l) \wedge (h(l) = 0 \Rightarrow l \in \mathsf{Ot})$
- $\forall o.\ \mathsf{waiting\_for}(c, h) = o \Rightarrow \mathsf{safe\_obs}_{R,L,P,X}(o, \mathsf{Wt}, \mathsf{Ot})$

where

- $\mathsf{Ot} = \underset{(id,c,\xi,p,O,C)\in T}{\biguplus} O,\ \mathsf{Wt} = \underset{(id,c,\xi,p,O,C)\in T \wedge \mathsf{waiting\_for}(c,h)=o}{\biguplus} \{o\}$
- O_l *is a bag that given an object o returns $O(o)$ if $L(o) = l$ and 0 if $L(o) \neq l$*
- $\mathsf{waiting\_for}(c, h)$ *returns the object for which c is waiting, if any*
- $\mathsf{pheap2heap}(p)$ *returns the heap corresponding with permission heap p*

We finally prove that for each proof rule $\{a\}\ c\ \{a'\}$ we have $a \Rightarrow \mathsf{wp}(c, a')$. To this end, we first define *correctness of commands*, shown in Definition 6, and then for each proof rule $\{a\}\ c\ \{a'\}$ we prove $\mathsf{correct}(a, c, a')$. In addition to the proof rules presented in this paper, other useful rules such as the rules *consequence*, *frame* and *sequential*, shown in Theorems 1, 2, and 3 can also be proved with the help of some auxiliary lemmas in [16]. Note that the indexes R, I, L, M, P, X are omitted when they are unimportant.

Definition 6 (Correctness of Commands)

$$\mathsf{correct}_{R,I,L,M,P,X}(a, c, a') \Leftrightarrow (a \Rightarrow \mathsf{wp}_{R,I,L,M,P,X}(c, a'))$$

Theorem 1 (Rule Consequence)

$$\mathsf{correct}(a_1, c, a_2) \wedge (a_1' \Rightarrow a_1) \wedge (\forall z.\ a_2(z) \Rightarrow a_2'(z)) \Rightarrow \mathsf{correct}(a_1', c, a_2')$$

Theorem 2 (Rule Frame)

$$\mathsf{correct}(a, c, a') \Rightarrow \mathsf{correct}(a * f, c, \lambda z.\ a'(z) * f)$$

Theorem 3 (Rule Sequential Composition)

$$\mathsf{correct}(a, c_1, a') \wedge (\forall z.\ \mathsf{correct}(a'(z), c_2[z/x], a'')) \Rightarrow$$
$$\mathsf{correct}(a, \mathsf{let}\ x{:=}c_1\ \mathsf{in}\ c_2, a'')$$

Theorem 4 (The Initial Configuration is Valid)

$$\mathsf{correct}_{R,I,L,M,P,X}(\mathsf{obs}(\{\}), c, \lambda\_.\mathsf{obs}(\{\})) \Rightarrow \mathsf{valid}(0[id{:=}c; \mathsf{done}], 0)$$

Proof. The goal is achieved because there are an augmented thread list $T = [(id, c, \mathsf{done}, 0, \{\}, 0)]$, a list of assertions $A = []$, and functions R, I, L, M, P, X by which all the conditions in the definition of validity of configurations are satisfied.

Theorem 5 (A Valid Configuration is Not Deadlocked)

$$(\exists id, c, \xi, o.\ t(id) = (c; \xi) \wedge \mathsf{waiting\_for}(c, h) = o) \wedge \mathsf{valid}(t, h)$$
$$\Rightarrow \exists id', c', \xi',\ t(id') = (c'; \xi') \wedge \mathsf{waiting\_for}(c', h) = \varnothing$$

Proof. We assume that all threads in t are waiting for an object. Since (t, h) is a valid configuration there exists a valid augmented thread table T with a corresponding valid graph $G = g(T)$, where g maps any element such as (id, c, ξ, p, O, C) to a new one such as $(\mathsf{waiting\_for}(c), O)$. By Lemma 1, we have $G = \{\}$, implying $T = \{\}$, implying $t = \mathbf{0}$ which contradicts the assumption of the theorem.

Theorem 6 (Steps Preserve Validity of Configurations).[7]

$$\mathsf{valid}(\kappa) \wedge \kappa \rightsquigarrow \kappa' \Rightarrow \mathsf{valid}(\kappa')$$

Proof. By case analysis of the small step relation $\rightsquigarrow$ (see [16] explaining the proof of some non-trivial cases).

6   Related Work

Several approaches to verify termination [1,21], total correctness [3], and lock freedom [2] of concurrent programs have been proposed. These approaches are only applicable to non-blocking algorithms, where the suspension of one thread cannot lead to the suspension of other threads. Consequently, they cannot be used to verify deadlock-freedom of programs using condition variables, where the suspension of a notifying thread might lead a waiting thread to be infinitely blocked. In [22] a compositional approach to verify termination of multi-threaded programs is introduced, where *rely-guarantee reasoning* is used to reason about each thread individually while there are some assertions about other threads. In this approach a program is considered to be terminating if it does not have any infinite computations. As a consequence, it is not applicable to programs using condition variables because a waiting thread that is never notified cannot be considered as a terminating thread.

There are also some other approaches addressing some common synchronization bugs of programs in the presence of condition variables. In [8], for example, an approach to identify some potential problems of concurrent programs consisting waits and notifies commands is presented. However, it does not take the order of execution of theses commands into account. In other words, it might accept an undesired execution trace where the waiting thread is scheduled before the notifying thread, that might lead the waiting thread to be infinitely suspended. [9] uses Petri nets to identify some common problems in multithreaded programs such as data races, lost signals, and deadlocks. However the model introduced for condition variables in this approach only covers the communication of two threads and it is not clear how it deals with programs having

---

[7] The proof of this theorem has not been machine-checked with Coq yet.

more than two threads communicating through condition variables. Recently, [10] has introduced an approach ensuring that every thread synchronizing under a set of condition variables eventually exits the synchronization block if that thread eventually reaches that block. This approach succeeds in verifying one of the applications of condition variables, namely the buffer. However, since this approach is not modular and relies on a Petri net analysis tool to solve the termination problem, it suffers from a long verification time when the size of the state space is increased, such that the verification of a buffer application having 20 producer and 18 consumer threads, for example, takes more than two minutes.

Kobayashi [6, 20] proposed a type system for deadlock-free processes, ensuring that a well-typed process that is annotated with a finite *capability level* is deadlock free. He extended channel types with the notion of *usages*, describing how often and in which order a channel is used for input and output. For example, usage of x in the process $x?y|x!1|x!2$, where $?, !, |$ represent an input action, an output action, and parallel composition receptively, is expressed by $?|!|!$, which means that x is used once for input and twice for output possibly in parallel. Additionally, to avoid circular dependency each action α is associated with the levels of obligation o and capabilities c, denoted by α_c^o, such that (1) an obligation of level n must be fulfilled by using only capabilities of level less than n, and (2) for an action of capability level n, there must exist a co-action of obligation level less than or equal to n. Leino *et al.* [4] also proposed an approach to verify deadlock-freedom of channels and locks. In this approach each thread trying to receive a message from a channel must spend one credit for that channel, where a credit for a channel is obtained if a thread is obliged to fulfil an obligation for that channel. A thread can fulfil an obligation for a channel if either it sends a message on that channel or delegate that obligation to other thread. The same idea is also used to verify deadlock-freedom of semaphores [7], where acquiring (i.e. decreasing) a semaphore consumes one credit and releasing (i.e. increasing) that semaphore produces one credit for that semaphore. However, as it is acknowledged in [4], it is impossible to treat channels (and also semaphores) like condition variables; a wait cannot be treated like a receive and a notify cannot be treated like a send because a notification for a condition variable will be lost if no thread is waiting for that variable. We borrow many ideas, including the notion of obligations/credits(capabilities) and levels, from these works and also the one introduced in [11], where a corresponding separation logic based approach is presented to verify total correctness of programs in the presence of channels.

7   Conclusion

It this article we introduced a modular approach to verify deadlock-freedom of monitors. We also introduced a relax, more general precedence relation to avoid cycles in the wait-for graph of programs, allowing a verification approach to verify a wider range of deadlock-free programs in the presence of monitors, channels and other synchronization mechanisms.

Acknowledgements. This work was funded through Flemish Research Fund grant G.0058.13 and KU Leuven Research Fund grant OT/13/065. We thank three anonymous reviewers and Prof. Aleksandar Nanevski for their careful reading of our manuscript and their many insightful comments and suggestions.

References

1. Liang, H., Feng, X., Shao, Z.: Compositional verification of termination-preserving refinement of concurrent programs. In: Proceedings of the Joint Meeting of the Twenty-Third EACSL Annual Conference on Computer Science Logic (CSL) and the Twenty-Ninth Annual ACM/IEEE Symposium on Logic in Computer Science (LICS), ACM (2014), Article No. 65
2. Hoffmann, J., Marmar, M., Shao, Z.: Quantitative reasoning for proving lock-freedom. In: 28th Annual IEEE/ACM Symposium on Logic in Computer Science (LICS). IEEE, pp. 124–133 (2013)
3. da Rocha Pinto, P., Dinsdale-Young, T., Gardner, P., Sutherland, J.: Modular termination verification for non-blocking concurrency. In: Thiemann, P. (ed.) ESOP 2016. LNCS, vol. 9632, pp. 176–201. Springer, Heidelberg (2016). https://doi.org/10.1007/978-3-662-49498-1_8
4. Leino, K.R.M., Müller, P., Smans, J.: Deadlock-free channels and locks. In: Gordon, A.D. (ed.) ESOP 2010. LNCS, vol. 6012, pp. 407–426. Springer, Heidelberg (2010). https://doi.org/10.1007/978-3-642-11957-6_22
5. Boström, P., Müller, P.: Modular Verification of Finite Blocking in Non-terminating Programs, vol. 37. Schloss Dagstuhl-Leibniz-Zentrum fuer Informatik, Germany (2015)
6. Kobayashi, N.: A new type system for deadlock-free processes. In: Baier, C., Hermanns, H. (eds.) CONCUR 2006. LNCS, vol. 4137, pp. 233–247. Springer, Heidelberg (2006). https://doi.org/10.1007/11817949_16
7. Jacobs, B.: Provably live exception handling. In: Proceedings of the 17th Workshop on Formal Techniques for Java-like Programs. ACM (2015) Article No. 7
8. Wang, C., Hoang, K.: Precisely deciding control state reachability in concurrent traces with limited observability. In: McMillan, K.L., Rival, X. (eds.) VMCAI 2014. LNCS, vol. 8318, pp. 376–394. Springer, Heidelberg (2014). https://doi.org/10.1007/978-3-642-54013-4_21
9. Kavi, K.M., Moshtaghi, A., Chen, D.J.: Modeling multithreaded applications using petri nets. Int. J. Parallel Prog. **30**(5), 353–371 (2002)
10. de Carvalho Gomes, P., Gurov, D., Huisman, M.: Specification and verification of synchronization with condition variables. In: Artho, C., Ölveczky, P.C. (eds.) FTSCS 2016. CCIS, vol. 694, pp. 3–19. Springer, Cham (2017). https://doi.org/10.1007/978-3-319-53946-1_1
11. Jacobs, B., Bosnacki, D., Kuiper, R.: Modular termination verification. In: LIPIcs-Leibniz International Proceedings in Informatics, vol. 37. Schloss Dagstuhl-Leibniz-Zentrum fuer Informatik, Germany (2015)
12. Jacobs, B., Smans, J., Philippaerts, P., Vogels, F., Penninckx, W., Piessens, F.: VeriFast: a powerful, sound, predictable, fast verifier for C and Java. NASA Form. Methods **6617**, 41–55 (2011)
13. Jacobs, B., Smans, J., Piessens, F.: A quick tour of the VeriFast program verifier. In: Ueda, K. (ed.) APLAS 2010. LNCS, vol. 6461, pp. 304–311. Springer, Heidelberg (2010). https://doi.org/10.1007/978-3-642-17164-2_21

14. Jacobs, B., (ed.): VeriFast 18.02. Zenodo (2018). https://doi.org/10.5281/zenodo.1182724
15. Dijkstra, E.W.: Cooperating sequential processes. The origin of concurrent programming, pp. 65–138. Springer, New York (1968)
16. Hamin, J., Jacobs, B.: Deadlock-free monitors: extended version. Technical report CW712, Department of Computer Science, KU Leuven, Belgium (2018)
17. Jacobs, B., Piessens, F.: Expressive modular fine-grained concurrency specification. ACM SIGPLAN Not. **46**(1), 271–282 (2011)
18. Reynolds, J.C.: Separation logic: a logic for shared mutable data structures. In: Proceedings on 17th Annual IEEE Symposium on Logic in Computer Science, IEEE, pp. 55–74 (2002)
19. Jung, R., Swasey, D., Sieczkowski, F., Svendsen, K., Turon, A., Birkedal, L., Dreyer, D.: Iris: monoids and invariants as an orthogonal basis for concurrent reasoning. ACM SIGPLAN Not. **50**(1), 637–650 (2015)
20. Kobayashi, N.: Type systems for concurrent programs. In: Aichernig, B.K., Maibaum, T. (eds.) Formal Methods at the Crossroads. From Panacea to Foundational Support. LNCS, vol. 2757, pp. 439–453. Springer, Heidelberg (2003). https://doi.org/10.1007/978-3-540-40007-3_26
21. Hamin, J., Jacobs, B.: Modular verification of termination and execution time bounds using separation logic. In: 17th International Conference on Information Reuse and Integration (IRI), IEEE, pp. 110–117 (2016)
22. Popeea, C., Rybalchenko, A.: Compositional termination proofs for multi-threaded programs. In: Flanagan, C., König, B. (eds.) TACAS 2012. LNCS, vol. 7214, pp. 237–251. Springer, Heidelberg (2012). https://doi.org/10.1007/978-3-642-28756-5_17
23. Vafeiadis, V.: Concurrent separation logic and operational semantics. Electron. Notes Theor. Comput. Sci. **276**, 335–351 (2011)

Fragment Abstraction for Concurrent Shape Analysis

Parosh Aziz Abdulla, Bengt Jonsson, and Cong Quy Trinh[✉]

Uppsala University, Uppsala, Sweden
cong-quy.trinh@it.uu.se

Abstract. A major challenge in automated verification is to develop techniques that are able to reason about fine-grained concurrent algorithms that consist of an unbounded number of concurrent threads, which operate on an unbounded domain of data values, and use unbounded dynamically allocated memory. Existing automated techniques consider the case where shared data is organized into singly-linked lists. We present a novel shape analysis for automated verification of fine-grained concurrent algorithms that can handle heap structures which are more complex than just singly-linked lists, in particular skip lists and arrays of singly linked lists, while at the same time handling an unbounded number of concurrent threads, an unbounded domain of data values (including timestamps), and an unbounded shared heap. Our technique is based on a novel shape abstraction, which represents a set of heaps by a set of *fragments*. A fragment is an abstraction of a pair of heap cells that are connected by a pointer field. We have implemented our approach and applied it to automatically verify correctness, in the sense of linearizability, of most linearizable concurrent implementations of sets, stacks, and queues, which employ singly-linked lists, skip lists, or arrays of singly-linked lists with timestamps, which are known to us in the literature.

1 Introduction

Concurrent algorithms with an unbounded number of threads that concurrently access a dynamically allocated shared state are of central importance in a large number of software systems. They provide efficient concurrent realizations of common interface abstractions, and are widely used in libraries, such as the Intel Threading Building Blocks or the `java.util.concurrent` package. They are notoriously difficult to get correct and verify, since they often employ fine-grained synchronization and avoid locking when possible. A number of bugs in published algorithms have been reported [13,30]. Consequently, significant research efforts have been directed towards developing techniques to verify correctness of such algorithms. One widely-used correctness criterion is that of *linearizability*, meaning that each method invocation can be considered to occur atomically at some point between its call and return. Many of the developed verification techniques require significant *manual* effort for constructing correctness

© The Author(s) 2018
A. Ahmed (Ed.): ESOP 2018, LNCS 10801, pp. 442–471, 2018.
https://doi.org/10.1007/978-3-319-89884-1_16

proofs (e.g., [25,41]), in some cases with the support of an interactive theorem prover (e.g., [11,35,40]). Development of automated verification techniques remains a difficult challenge.

A major challenge for the development of automated verification techniques is that such techniques must be able to reason about fine-grained concurrent algorithms that are infinite-state in many dimensions: they consist of an unbounded number of concurrent threads, which operate on an unbounded domain of data values, and use unbounded dynamically allocated memory. Perhaps the hardest of these challenges is that of handling dynamically allocated memory. Consequently, existing techniques that can automatically prove correctness of such fine-grained concurrent algorithms restrict attention to the case where heap structures represent shared data by singly-linked lists [1,3,18,36,42]. Furthermore, many of these techniques impose additional restrictions on the considered verification problem, such as bounding the number of accessing threads [4,43,45]. However, in many concurrent data structure implementations the heap represents more sophisticated structures, such as skiplists [16,22,38] and arrays of singly-linked lists [12]. There are no techniques that have been applied to automatically verify concurrent algorithms that operate on such data structures.

Contributions. In this paper, we present a technique for automatic verification of concurrent data structure implementations that operate on dynamically allocated heap structures which are more complex than just singly-linked lists. Our framework is the first that can automatically verify concurrent data structure implementations that employ singly linked lists, skiplists [16,22,38], as well as arrays of singly linked lists [12], at the same time as handling an unbounded number of concurrent threads, an unbounded domain of data values (including timestamps), and an unbounded shared heap.

Our technique is based on a novel shape abstraction, called *fragment abstraction*, which in a simple and uniform way is able to represent several different classes of unbounded heap structures. Its main idea is to represent a set of heap states by a set of *fragments*. A fragment represents two heap cells that are connected by a pointer field. For each of its cells, the fragment represents the contents of its non-pointer fields, together with information about how the cell can be reached from the program's global pointer variables. The latter information consists of both: (i) *local* information, saying which pointer variables point directly to them, and (ii) *global* information, saying how the cell can reach to and be reached from (by following chains of pointers) heap cells that are globally significant, typically since some global variable points to them. A set of fragments represents the set of heap states in which any two pointer-connected nodes is represented by some fragment in the set. Thus, a set of fragments describes the set of heaps that can be formed by "piecing together" fragments in the set. The combination of local and global information in fragments supports reasoning about the sequence of cells that can be accessed by threads that traverse the heap by following pointer fields in cells and pointer variables: the local information captures properties of the cell fields that can be accessed as a thread dereferences a pointer variable or a pointer field; the global information also captures whether certain significant accesses will at all be possible by following a sequence of pointer fields. This support for reasoning about patterns of cell accesses enables automated verification of reachability and other functional properties.

Fragment abstraction can (and should) be combined, in a natural way, with data abstractions for handling unbounded data domains and with thread abstractions for handling an unbounded number of threads. For the latter we adapt the successful thread-modular approach [5], which represents the local state of a single, but arbitrary thread, together with the part of the global state and heap that is accessible to that thread. Our combination of fragment abstraction, thread abstraction, and data abstraction results in a finite abstract domain, thereby guaranteeing termination of our analysis.

We have implemented our approach and applied it to automatically verify correctness, in the sense of linearizability, of a large number of concurrent data structure algorithms, described in a C-like language. More specifically, we have automatically verified linearizability of most linearizable concurrent implementations of sets, stacks, and queues, and priority queues, which employ singly-linked lists, skiplists, or arrays of timestamped singly-linked lists, which are known to us in the literature on concurrent data structures. For this verification, we specify linearizability using the simple and powerful technique of *observers* [1,7,9], which reduces the criterion of linearizability to a simple reachability property. To verify implementations of stacks and queues, the application of observers can be done completely automatically without any manual steps, whereas for implementations of sets, the verification relies on light-weight user annotation of how linearization points are placed in each method [3].

The fact that our fragment abstraction has been able to automatically verify all supplied concurrent algorithms, also those that employ skiplists or arrays of SLLs, indicates that the fragment abstraction is a simple mechanism for capturing both the local and global information about heap cells that is necessary for verifying correctness, in particular for concurrent algorithms where an unbounded number of threads interact via a shared heap.

Outline. In the next section, we illustrate our fragment abstraction on the verification of a skiplist-based concurrent set implementation. In Sect. 3 we introduce our model for programs, and of observers for specifying linearizability. In Sect. 4 we describe in more detail our fragment abstraction for skiplists; note that singly-linked lists can be handled as a simple special case of skiplists. In Sect. 5 we describe how fragment abstraction applies to arrays of singly-linked lists with timestamp fields. Our implementation and experiments are reported in Sect. 6, followed by conclusions in Sect. 7.

Related Work. A large number of techniques have been developed for representing heap structures in automated analysis, including, e.g., separation logic and various related graph formalisms [10,15,47], other logics [33], automata [23], or graph grammars [19]. Most works apply these to sequential programs.

Approaches for automated verification of concurrent algorithms are limited to the case of singly-linked lists [1,3,18,36,42]. Furthermore, many of these techniques impose additional restrictions on the considered verification problem, such as bounding the number of accessing threads [4,43,45].

In [1], concurrent programs operating on SLLs are analyzed using an adaptation of a transitive closure logic [6], combined with tracking of simple sortedness properties between data elements; the approach does not allow to represent patterns observed by threads when following sequences of pointers inside the heap, and so has not been applied to concurrent set implementations. In our recent work [3], we extended this approach to handle SLL implementations of concurrent sets by adapting a well-known abstraction of singly-linked lists [28] for concurrent programs. The resulting technique is specifically tailored for singly-links. Our fragment abstraction is significantly simpler conceptually, and can therefore be adapted also for other classes of heap structures. The approach of [3] is the only one with a shape representation strong enough to verify concurrent set implementations based on sorted and non-sorted singly-linked lists having non-optimistic contains (or lookup) operations we consider, such as the lock-free sets of *HM* [22], *Harris* [17], or *Michael* [29], or unordered set of [48]. As shown in Sect. 6, our fragment abstraction can handle them as well as also algorithms employing skiplists and arrays of singly-linked lists.

There is no previous work on automated verification of skiplist-based concurrent algorithms. Verification of *sequential* algorithms have been addressed under restrictions, such as limiting the number of levels to two or three [2,23]. The work [34] generates verification conditions for statements in sequential skiplist implementations. All these works assume that skiplists have the well-formedness property that any higher-level lists is a sublist of any lower-level list, which is true for sequential skiplist algorithms, but false for several concurrent ones, such as [22,26].

Concurrent algorithms based on arrays of SLLs, and including timestamps, e.g., for verifying the algorithms in [12] have shown to be rather challenging. Only recently has the TS stack been verified by non-automated techniques [8] using a non-trivial extension of forward simulation, and the TS queue been verified manually by a new technique based on partial orders [24,37]. We have verified both these algorithms automatically using fragment abstraction.

Our fragment abstraction is related in spirit to other formalisms that abstract dynamic graph structures by defining some form of equivalence on its nodes (e.g., [23,33,46]). These have been applied to verify functional correctness fine-grained concurrent algorithms for a limited number of SLL-based algorithms. Fragment abstraction's representation of both local and global information allows to extend the applicability of this class of techniques.

2   Overview

In this section, we illustrate our technique on the verification of correctness, in the sense of linearizability, of a concurrent set data structure based on skiplists, namely the Lock-Free Concurrent Skiplist from [22, Sect. 14.4]. Skiplists provide expected logarithmic time search while avoiding some of the complications of tree structures. Informally, a skiplist consists of a collection of sorted linked lists, each of which is located at a *level*, ranging from 1 up to a maximum value. Each skiplist node has a key value and participates in the lists at levels 1 up to its *height*. The skiplist has sentinel head and tail nodes with maximum heights and key values $-\infty$ and $+\infty$, respectively. The lowest-level list (at level 1) constitutes an ordered list of all nodes in the skiplist. Higher-level lists are increasingly sparse sublists of the lowest-level list, and serve as shortcuts into lower-level lists. Figure 1 shows an example of a skiplist of height 3. It has head and tail nodes of height 3, two nodes of height 2, and one node of height 1.

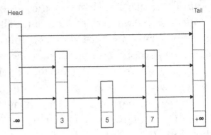

Fig. 1. An example of skiplist

The algorithm has three main methods, namely **add**, **contains** and **remove**. The method **add(x)** adds **x** to the set and returns true iff **x** was not already in the set; **remove(x)** removes **x** from the set and returns true iff **x** was in the set; and **contains(x)** returns true iff **x** is in the set. All methods rely on a method **find** to search for a given key. In this section, we shortly describe the **find** and **add** methods. Figure 2 shows code for these two methods.

In the algorithm, each heap node has a **key** field, a **height**, an array of **next** pointers indexed from 1 up to its **height**, and an array of **marked** fields which are true if the node has been logically removed at the corresponding level. Removal of a node (at a certain level k) occurs in two steps: first the node is logically removed by setting its **marked** flag at level k to **true**, thereafter the node is physically removed by unlinking it from the level-k list. The algorithm must be able to update the **next**[k] pointer and **marked**[k] field together as one atomic operation; this is standardly implemented by encoding them in a single word. The head and tail nodes of the skiplist are pointed to by global pointer variables H and T, respectively. The **find** method traverses the list at decreasing levels using two local variables **pred** and **curr**, starting at the head and at the maximum level (lines 5–6). At each level k it sets **curr** to **pred.next**[k] (line 7). During the traversal, the pointer variable **succ** and boolean variable **marked** are atomically assigned the values of **curr.next**[k] and **curr.marked**[k], respectively (line 9, 14). After that, the method repeatedly removes marked nodes at the current level (lines 10 to 14). This is done by using a **CompareAndSwap** (CAS) command (line 11), which tests whether **pred.next**[k] and **pred.marked**[k] are equal to **curr** and **false** respectively. If this test succeeds, it replaces them with **succ** and **false** and returns **true**; otherwise, the CAS returns **false**. During the traversal at level k, **pred** and **curr** are advanced until **pred** points to a node with the largest key at level k which is smaller than **x** (lines 15–18). Thereafter, the resulting values of **pred** and **curr** are recorded into **preds**[k] and **succs**[k] (lines 19, 20), whereafter traversal continues one level below until it reaches the bottom level. Finally, the method returns **true** if the **key** value of **curr** is equal to **x**; otherwise, it returns **false** meaning that a node with key **x** is not found.

```
struct Node { int key; int height; Node next[]; boolean marked[];}
```

```
boolean find(int x,Node preds[],Node succs[])
1  boolean marked = false;
2  boolean s;
3  retry:
4  while (true)
5    pred = H;
6    for (int k = MAXLEVEL; k >= 1; k--)
7      curr = pred.next[k];
8      while (true)
9        <succ, marked> =
                  <curr.next[k], curr.marked[k]>;
10       while (marked)
11         s=CAS(<pred.next[k],pred.marked[k]>
                  ,<curr,false>,<succ,false>);
12         if (!s) goto retry;
13         curr = pred.next[k]; •
14         <succ, marked =
                  <curr.next[k], curr.marked[k]>;
15       if (curr.key < x)
16         pred = curr;
17         curr = succ;
18       else break;
19     preds[k] = pred;
20     succs[k] = curr;
21     return (curr.key == x);
```

```
boolean add (int x):
1  int h = randomLevel;
2  Node* preds[1..h]; succs[1..h]
3  while (true);
4    if find(x,preds,succs)
5      return false;
6    else
7      Node* n = new Node(x, h);
8      for (int k = 1;k <= h; k++)
9        <n.next[k],n.marked[k]> =
                  <succ[k],false>;
10     Node* pred = preds[1];
11     Node* succ = succs[1];
12     <n.next[1],n.marked[1]>=<succ,false>
13     if !CAS(<pred.next[1],pred.marked[1]>
                  ,<succ,false>,<n,false>);
14       goto 3;
15     else •
16       for (int k = 2; k <= h; k++)
17         while (true);
18           pred = preds[k];
19           succ = succs[k];
20           if CAS(<pred.next[k],pred.marked
                  [k]>,<succ,false>,<n,false>)
21             break;
22       find(x,preds,succs);
23     return true;
```

Fig. 2. Code for the find and add methods of the skiplist algorithm. (Color figure online)

The add method uses find to check whether a node with key x is already in the list. If so it returns false; otherwise, a new node is created with randomly chosen height h (line 7), and with next pointers at levels from 1 to h initialised to corresponding elements of succ (line 8 to 9). Thereafter, the new node is added into the list by linking it into the bottom-level list between the preds[1] and succs[1] pointers returned by find. This is achieved by using a CAS to make preds[1].next[1] point to the new node (line 13). If the CAS fails, the add method will restart from the beginning (line 3) by calling find again, etc. Otherwise, add proceeds with linking the new node into the list at increasingly higher levels (lines 16 to 22). For each higher level k, it makes preds[k].next[k] point to the new node if it is still valid (line 20); otherwise find is called again to recompute preds[k] and succs[k] on the remaining unlinked levels (line 22). Once all levels are linked, the method returns true.

To prepare for verification, we add a specification which expresses that the skiplist algorithm of Fig. 2 is a linearizable implementation of a set data structure, using the technique of *observers* [1,3,7,9]. For our skiplist algorithm, the user first instruments statements in each method that correspond to linearization points (LPs), so that their execution announces the corresponding atomic set operation. In Fig. 2, the LP of a successful add operation is at line 15 of the add method (denoted by a blue dot) when the CAS succeeds, whereas the LP of an unsuccessful add operation is at line 13 of find method (denoted by a red dot). We must now verify that in any concurrent execution of a collection of method calls, the sequence of announced operations satisfies the semantics of the set data structure. This check is performed by an *observer*, which monitors the sequence of announced operations. The observer for the set data structure utilizes a register, which is initialized with a single, arbitrary key value. It checks that operations on this particular value follow set semantics, i.e., that successful add and remove operations on an element alternate and that contains are consistent with them. We form the cross-product of the program and the observer, synchronizing on operation announcements. This reduces the problem of checking linearizability to the problem of checking that in this cross-product, regardless of the initial observer register value, the observer cannot reach a state where the semantics of the set data structure has been violated.

To verify that the observer cannot reach a state where a violation is reported, we compute a symbolic representation of an invariant that is satisfied by all reachable configurations of the cross-product of a program and an observer. This symbolic representation combines thread abstraction, data abstraction and our novel *fragment abstraction* to represent the heap state. Our *thread abstraction* adapts the thread-modular approach by representing only the view of single, but arbitrary, thread th. Such a view consists of the local state of thread th, including the value of the program counter, the state of the observer, and the part of the heap that is accessible to thread th via pointer variables (local to th or global). Our *data abstraction* represents variables and cell fields that range over small finite domains by their concrete values, whereas variables and fields that range over the same domain as key fields are abstracted to constraints over their relative ordering (wrp. to $<$).

In our *fragment abstraction*, we represent the part of the heap that is accessible to thread th by a set of *fragments*. A fragment represents a pair of heap cells (accessible to th) that are connected by a pointer field, under the applied data abstraction. A fragment is a triple of form $\langle \mathtt{i}, \mathtt{o}, \phi \rangle$, where $\mathtt{i}$ and $\mathtt{o}$ are *tags* that represent the two cells, and ϕ is a subset of $\{<, =, >\}$ which constrains the order between the key fields of the cells. Each tag is a tuple $\mathtt{tag} = \langle \mathtt{dabs}, \mathtt{pvars}, \mathtt{reachfrom}, \mathtt{reachto}, \mathtt{private} \rangle$, where

- dabs represents the non-pointer fields of the cell under the applied data abstraction,
- pvars is the set of (local to th or global) pointer variables that point to the cell,
- reachfrom is the set of (i) global pointer variables from which the cell represented by the tag is reachable via a (possibly empty) sequence of next[1] pointers, and (ii) observer registers $\mathtt{x}_i$ such that the cell is reachable from some cell whose data value equals that of $\mathtt{x}_i$,

- **reachto** is the corresponding information, but now considering cells that are reachable from the cell represented by the tag.
- **private** is **true** only if c is private to **th**.

Thus, the fragment contains both (i) *local* information about the cell's fields and variables that point to it, as well as (ii) *global* information, representing how each cell in the pair can reach to and be reached from (by following a chain of pointers) a small set of globally significant heap cells.

A set of fragments represents the set of heap structures in which each pair of pointer-connected nodes is represented by some fragment in the set. Put differently, a set of fragments describes the set of heaps that can be formed by "piecing together" pairs of pointer-connected nodes that are represented by some fragment in the set. This "piecing together" must be both locally consistent (appending only fragments that agree on their common node), and globally consistent (respecting the global reachabil-

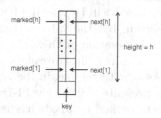

Fig. 3. A structure of a cell

ity information). When applying fragment abstraction to skiplists, we use two types of fragments: *level 1-fragments* for nodes connected by a **next**[1]-pointer, and *higher level-fragments* for nodes connected by a higher level pointer. In other words, we abstract all levels higher than 2 by the abstract element **higher**. Thus, a pointer or non-pointer variable of form v[k], indexed by a level $k \geq 2$, is abstracted to v[**higher**].

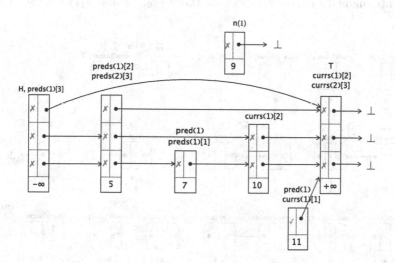

Fig. 4. A heap shape of a 3-level skiplist with two threads active

Let us illustrate how fragment abstraction applies to the skiplist algorithm. Figure 4 shows an example heap state of the skiplist algorithm with three levels.

Each heap cell is shown with the values of its fields as described in Fig. 3. In addition, each cell is labeled by the pointer variables that point to it; we use `preds(i)[k]` to denote the local variable `preds[k]` of thread th_i, and the same for other local variables. In the heap state of Fig. 4, thread th_1 is trying to add a new node of height 1 with key 9, and has reached line 8 of the add method. Thread th_2 is trying to add a new node with key 20 and it has done its first iteration of the `for` loop in the `find` method. The variables `preds(2)[3]` and `currs(2)[3]` have been assigned so that the new node (which has not yet been created) will be inserted between node 5 and the tail node. The observer is not shown, but the value of the observer register is 9; thus it currently tracks the add operation of th_1.

Figure 5 illustrates how pairs of heap nodes can be represented by fragments. As a first example, in the view of thread th_1, the two left-most cells in Fig. 4 are represented by the level 1-fragment v_1 in Fig. 5. Here, the variable `preds(1)[3]` is represented by `preds[higher]`. The mapping π_1 represents the data abstraction of the `key` field, here saying that it is smaller than the value 9 of the observer register. The two left-most cells are also represented by a higher-level fragment, viz. v_8. The pair consisting of the two sentinel cells (with keys $-\infty$ and $+\infty$) is represented by the higher-level fragment v_9. In each fragment, the abstraction `dabs` of non-pointer fields are shown represented inside each tag of the fragment. The ϕ is shown as a label on the arrow between two tags. Above each tag is `pvars`. The first row under each tag is `reachfrom`, whereas the second row is `reachto`.

Figure 5 shows a set of fragments that is sufficient to represent the part of the heap that is accessible to th_1 in the configuration in Fig. 4. There are 11 fragments, named $v_1, \ldots, v_{11}$. Two of these (v_6, v_7 and v_{11}) consist of a tag

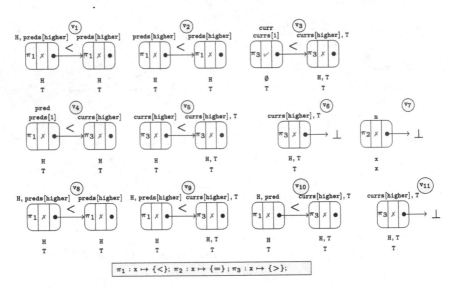

Fig. 5. Fragment abstraction of skiplist algorithm

that points to $\perp$. All other fragments consist of a pair of pointer-connected tags. The fragments $v_1, \ldots, v_6$ are level-1-fragments, whereas $v_7, \ldots, v_{11}$ are higher level-fragments. The private field of the input tag of v_7 is true, whereas the private field of tags of other fragments are false.

To verify linearizability of the algorithm in Fig. 2, we must represent several key invariants of the heap. These include (among others):

1. the bottom-level list is strictly sorted in key order,
2. a higher-level pointer from a globally reachable node is a shortcut into the level-1 list, i.e., it points to a node that is reachable by a sequence of next[1] pointers,
3. all nodes which are unreachable from the head of the list are marked, and
4. the variable pred points to a cell whose key field is never larger than the input parameter of its add method.

Let us illustrate how such invariants are captured by our fragment abstraction. (1) All level-1 fragments are strictly sorted, implying that the bottom-level list is strictly sorted. (2) For each higher-level fragment v, if $H \in$ v.i.reachfrom then also $H \in$ v.o.reachfrom, implying (together with v.$\phi = \{<\}$) that the cell represented by v.o it is reachable from that represented by v.i by a sequence of next[1]-pointers. (3) This is verified by inspecting each tag: v_3 contains the only unreachable tag, and it is also marked. (4) The fragments express this property in the case where the value of key is the same as the value of the observer register x. Since the invariant holds for any value of x, this property is sufficiently represented for purposes of verification.

3 Concurrent Data Structure Implementations

In this section, we introduce our representation of concurrent data structure implementations, we define the correctness criterion of linearizability, we introduce observers and how to use them for specifying linearizability.

3.1 Concurrent Data Structure Implementations

We first introduce (sequential) data structures. A *data structure* DS is a pair $\langle \mathbb{D}, \mathbb{M} \rangle$, where $\mathbb{D}$ is a (possibly infinite) *data domain* and $\mathbb{M}$ is an alphabet of *method names*. An *operation op* is of the form $\mathbf{m}(d^{in}, d^{out})$, where $\mathbf{m} \in \mathbb{M}$ is a method name, and d^{in}, d^{out} are the *input* resp. *output* values, each of which is either in $\mathbb{D}$ or in some small finite domain $\mathbb{F}$, which includes the booleans. For some method names, the input or output value is absent from the operation. A *trace* of DS is a sequence of operations. The (sequential) semantics of a data structure DS is given by a set $[\![DS]\!]$ of allowed traces. For example, a Set data structure has method names add, remove, and contains. An example of an allowed trace is add(3, true) contains(4, false) contains(3, true) remove(3, true).

A *concurrent data structure implementation* operates on a shared state consisting of shared global variables and a shared heap. It assigns, to each method name, a method which performs operations on the shared state. It also comes with a method named init, which initializes its shared state.

A *heap (state)* $\mathcal{H}$ consists of a finite set $\mathbb{C}$ of cells, including the two special cells null and $\bot$ (dangling). Heap cells have a fixed set $\mathcal{F}$ of fields, namely non-pointer fields that assume values in $\mathbb{D}$ or $\mathbb{F}$, and possibly lock fields. We use the term $\mathbb{D}$-*field* for a non-pointer field that assumes values in $\mathbb{D}$, and the terms $\mathbb{F}$-*field* and *lock field* with analogous meaning. Furthermore, each cell has one or several named pointer fields. For instance, in data structure implementations based on singly-linked lists, each heap cell has a pointer field named next; in implementations based on skiplists there is an array of pointer fields named next[k] where k ranges from 1 to a maximum level.

Each method declares local variables and a method body. The set of local variables includes the input parameter of the method and the program counter pc. A *local state* loc of a thread th defines the values of its local variables. The global variables can be accessed by all threads, whereas local variables can be accessed only by the thread which is invoking the corresponding method. Variables are either pointer variables (to heap cells), locks, or data variables assuming values in $\mathbb{D}$ or $\mathbb{F}$. We assume that all global variables are pointer variables. The body is built in the standard way from atomic commands, using standard control flow constructs (sequential composition, selection, and loop constructs). Atomic commands include assignments between variables, or fields of cells pointed to by a pointer variable. Method execution is terminated by executing a return command, which may return a value. The command new Node() allocates a new structure of type Node on the heap, and returns a reference to it. The compare-and-swap command CAS(a, b, c) atomically compares the values of a and b. If equal, it assigns the value of c to a and returns true, otherwise, it leaves a unchanged and returns false. We assume a memory management mechanism, which automatically collects garbage, and ensures that a new cell is fresh, i.e., has not been used before; this avoids the so-called ABA problem (e.g., [31]).

We define a *program* $\mathcal{P}$ (over a concurrent data structure) to consist of an arbitrary number of concurrently executing threads, each of which executes a method that performs an operation on the data structure. The shared state is initialized by the init method prior to the start of program execution. A *configuration* of a program $\mathcal{P}$ is a tuple $c_\mathcal{P} = \langle T, \text{LOC}, \mathcal{H} \rangle$ where T is a set of threads, $\mathcal{H}$ is a heap, and LOC maps each thread th $\in$ T to its local state LOC(th). We assume concurrent execution according to sequentially consistent memory model. The behavior of a thread th executing a method can be formalized as a transition relation $\rightarrow_{th}$ on pairs $\langle \text{loc}, \mathcal{H} \rangle$ consisting of a local state loc and a heap state $\mathcal{H}$. The behavior of a program $\mathcal{P}$ can be formalized by a transition relation $\rightarrow_\mathcal{P}$ on program configurations; each step corresponds to a move of a single thread. I.e., there is a transition of form $\langle T, \text{LOC}, \mathcal{H} \rangle \rightarrow_\mathcal{P} \langle T, \text{LOC}[\text{th} \leftarrow \text{loc}'], \mathcal{H}' \rangle$ whenever some thread th $\in$ T has a transition $\langle \text{loc}, \mathcal{H} \rangle \rightarrow_{th} \langle \text{loc}', \mathcal{H}' \rangle$ with LOC(th) = loc.

3.2   Linearizability

In a concurrent data structure implementation, we represent the calling of a method by a *call action* $\mathtt{call_o}\ \mathtt{m}\left(d^{in}\right)$, and the return of a method by a *return action* $\mathtt{ret_o}\ \mathtt{m}(d^{out})$, where $\mathtt{o} \in \mathbb{N}$ is an *action identifier*, which links the call and return of each method invocation. A *history* h is a sequence of actions such that (i) different occurrences of return actions have different action identifiers, and (ii) for each return action a_2 in h there is a unique *matching* call action a_1 with the same action identifier and method name, which occurs before a_2 in h. A call action which does not match any return action in h is said to be *pending*. A history without pending call actions is said to be *complete*. A *completed extension* of h is a complete history h' obtained from h by appending (at the end) zero or more return actions that are matched by pending call actions in h, and thereafter removing the call actions that are still pending. For action identifiers $\mathtt{o_1, o_2}$, we write $\mathtt{o_1} \preceq_h \mathtt{o_2}$ to denote that the return action with identifier $\mathtt{o_1}$ occurs before the call action with identifier $\mathtt{o_2}$ in h. A complete history is *sequential* if it is of the form $a_1 a_1' a_2 a_2' \cdots a_n a_n'$ where a_i' is the matching action of a_i for all $i : 1 \leq i \leq n$, i.e., each call action is immediately followed by its matching return action. We identify a sequential history of the above form with the corresponding trace $op_1 op_2 \cdots op_n$ where $op_i = \mathtt{m}(d_i^{in}, d_i^{out})$, $a_i = \mathtt{call_{o_i}}\ \mathtt{m}\left(d_i^{in}\right)$, and $a_i = \mathtt{ret_{o_i}}\ \mathtt{m}(d_i^{out})$, i.e., we merge each call action together with the matching return action into one operation. A complete history h' is a *linearization* of h if (i) h' is a permutation of h, (ii) h' is sequential, and (iii) $\mathtt{o_1} \preceq_{h'} \mathtt{o_2}$ if $\mathtt{o_1} \preceq_h \mathtt{o_2}$ for each pair of action identifiers $\mathtt{o_1}$ and $\mathtt{o_2}$. A sequential history h' is *valid* wrt. DS if the corresponding trace is in $[\![\mathtt{DS}]\!]$. We say that h is *linearizable* wrt. DS if there is a completed extension of h, which has a linearization that is valid wrt. DS. We say that a program $\mathcal{P}$ is linearizable wrt. DS if, in each possible execution, the sequence of call and return actions is *linearizable* wrt. DS.

We specify linearizability using the technique of *observers* [1,3,7,9]. Depending on the data structure, we apply it in two different ways.

- For implementations of sets and priority queues, the user instruments each method so that it announces a corresponding operation precisely when the method executes its LP, either directly or with lightweight instrumentation using the technique of linearization policies [3]. We represent such announcements by labels on the program transition relation $\rightarrow_{\mathcal{P}}$, resulting in transitions of form $c_{\mathcal{P}} \xrightarrow{\mathtt{m}(d^{in}, d^{out})}_{\mathcal{P}} c_{\mathcal{P}}'$. Thereafter, an *observer* is constructed, which monitors the sequence of operations that is announced by the instrumentation; it reports (by moving to an accepting error location) whenever this sequence violates the (sequential) semantics of the data structure.
- For stacks and queues, we use a recent result [7,9] that the set of linearizable histories, i.e., sequences of call and return actions, can be exactly specified by an observer. Thus, linearizability can be specified without any user-supplied instrumentation, by using an observer which monitors the sequences of call and return actions and reports violations of linearizability.

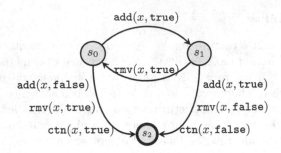

Fig. 6. Set observer.

Formally, an observer $\mathcal{O}$ is a tuple $\langle S^{\mathcal{O}}, s_{\text{init}}^{\mathcal{O}}, X^{\mathcal{O}}, \Delta^{\mathcal{O}}, s_{\text{acc}}^{\mathcal{O}} \rangle$ where $S^{\mathcal{O}}$ is a finite set of *observer locations* including the *initial location* $s_{\text{init}}^{\mathcal{O}}$ and the *accepting location* $s_{\text{acc}}^{\mathcal{O}}$, a finite set $X^{\mathcal{O}}$ of *registers*, and $\Delta^{\mathcal{O}}$ is a finite set of *transitions*. For observers that monitor sequences of operations, transitions are of the form $\langle s_1, \text{m}(x^{in}, x^{out}), s_2 \rangle$, where $\text{m} \in \mathbb{M}$ is a method name and x^{in} and x^{out} are either registers or constants, i.e., transitions are labeled by operations whose input or output data may be parameterized on registers. The observer processes a sequence of operations one operation at a time. If there is a transition, whose label (after replacing registers by their values) matches the operation, such a transition is performed. If there is no such transition, the observer remains in its current location. The observer accepts a sequence if it can be processed in such a way that an accepting location is reached. The observer is defined in such a way that it accepts precisely those sequences that are *not* in $[\![\text{DS}]\!]$. Figure 6 depicts an observer for the set data structure.

To check that no execution of the program announces a sequence of labels that can drive the observer to an accepting location, we form the cross-product $\mathcal{S} = \mathcal{P} \otimes \mathcal{O}$ of the program $\mathcal{P}$ and the observer $\mathcal{O}$, synchronizing on common transition labels. Thus, configurations of $\mathcal{S}$ are of the form $\langle c_{\mathcal{P}}, \langle s, \rho \rangle \rangle$, consisting of a program configuration $c_{\mathcal{P}}$, an observer location s, and an assignment ρ of values in $\mathbb{D}$ to the observer registers. Transitions of $\mathcal{S}$ are of the form $\langle c_{\mathcal{P}}, \langle s, \rho \rangle \rangle, \rightarrow_{\mathcal{S}}, \langle c_{\mathcal{P}}', \langle s', \rho \rangle \rangle$, obtained from a transition $c_{\mathcal{P}} \xrightarrow{\lambda}_{\mathcal{P}} c_{\mathcal{P}}'$ of the program with some (possibly empty) label λ, where the observer makes a transition $s \xrightarrow{\lambda} s'$ if it can perform such a matching transition, otherwise $s' = s$. Note that the observer registers are not changed. We also add straightforward instrumentation to check that each method invocation announces exactly one operation, whose input and output values agree with the method's parameters and return value. This reduces the problem of checking linearizability to the problem of checking that in this cross-product, the observer cannot reach an accepting error location.

4   Verification Using Fragment Abstraction for Skiplists

In the previous section, we reduced the problem of verifying linearizability to the problem of verifying that, in any execution of the cross-product of a program and an observer, the observer cannot reach an accepting location. We perform this verification by computing a symbolic representation of an invariant that is satisfied by all reachable configurations of the cross-product, using an abstract interpretation-based fixpoint procedure, starting from a symbolic representation of the set of initial configurations, thereafter repeatedly performing symbolic postcondition computations that extend the symbolic representation by the effect of any execution step of the program, until convergence.

In Sect. 4.1, we define in more detail our symbolic representation for skiplists, focusing in particular on the use of fragment abstraction, and thereafter (in Sect. 4.2) describe the symbolic postcondition computation. Since singly-linked lists is a trivial special case of skiplists, we can use the relevant part of this technique also for programs based on singly-linked lists.

4.1 Symbolic Representation

This subsection contains a more detailed description of our symbolic representation for programs that operate on skiplists, which was introduced in Sect. 2. We first describe the data abstraction, thereafter the fragment abstraction, and finally their combination into a symbolic representation.

Data Abstraction. Our data abstraction is defined by assigning a abstract domain to each concrete domain of data values, as follows.

- For small concrete domains (including that of the program counter, and of the observer location), the abstract domain is the same as the concrete one.
- For locks, the abstract domain is $\{me, other, free\}$, meaning that the lock is held by the concerned thread, held by some other thread, or is free, respectively.
- For the concrete domain $\mathbb{D}$ of data values, the abstract domain is the set of mappings from observer registers and local variables ranging over $\mathbb{D}$ to subsets of $\{<, =, >\}$. An mapping in this abstract domain represents the set of data values d such that it maps each local variable and observer register with a value $d' \in \mathbb{D}$ to a set which includes a relation $\sim$ such that $d \sim d'$.

Fragment Abstraction. Let us now define our fragment abstraction for skiplists. For presentation purposes, we assume that each heap cell has at most one $\mathbb{D}$-field, named **data**. For an observer register x_i, let a x_i-*cell* be a heap cell whose **data** field has the same value as x_i.

Since the number of levels is unbounded, we define an abstraction for levels. Let k be a level. Define the abstraction of a pointer variable of form $p[k]$, denoted $\widehat{p[k]}$, to be $p[1]$ if $k = 1$, and to be $p[\text{higher}]$ if $k \geq 2$. That is, this abstraction does not distinguish different higher levels.

A *tag* is a tuple $\text{tag} = \langle \text{dabs}, \text{pvars}, \text{reachfrom}, \text{reachto}, \text{private} \rangle$, where (i) **dabs** is a mapping from non-pointer fields to their corresponding abstract domains; if a non-pointer field is an array indexed by levels, then the abstract domain is that for single elements: e.g., the abstract domain for the array **marked** in Fig. 2 is simply the set of booleans, (ii) pvars is a set of abstracted pointer variables, (iii) reachfrom and reachto are sets of global pointer variables and observer registers, and (iv) private is a boolean value.

For a heap cell c that is accessible to thread th in a configuration c_S, and a tag tag $= \langle$dabs, pvars, reachfrom, reachto, private$\rangle$, we let $c \lhd_{\text{th},k}^{cs}$ tag denote that c satisfies the tag tag "at level k". More precisely, this means that

- dabs is an abstraction of the concrete values of the non-pointer fields of c; for array fields f we use the concrete value f[k],
- pvars is the set of abstractions of pointer variables (global or local to th) that point to c,
- reachfrom is the set of (i) abstractions of global pointer variables from which c is reachable via a (possibly empty) sequence of next[1] pointers, and (ii) observer registers x_i such that c is reachable from some x_i-cell (via a sequence of next[1] pointers),
- reachto is the set of (i) abstractions of global pointer variables pointing to a cell that is reachable (via a sequence of next[1] pointers) from c, and (ii) observer registers x_i such that some x_i-cell is reachable from c.
- private is true only if c is not accessible to any other thread than th.

Note that the global information represented by the fields reachfrom and reachto concerns *only* reachability via level-1 pointers.

A *skiplist fragment* v (or just fragment) is a triple of form $\langle i, o, \phi \rangle$, of form $\langle i, \text{null} \rangle$, or of form $\langle i, \bot \rangle$, where i and o are tags and ϕ is a subset of $\{<, =, >\}$. Each skiplist fragment additionally has a *type*, which is either *level-1* or *higher-level* (note that a level-1 fragment can otherwise be identical to a higher-level fragment). For a cell c which is accessible to thread th, and a fragment v of form $\langle i, o, \phi \rangle$, let $c \lhd_{\text{th},k}^{cs}$ v denote that the next[k] field of c points to a cell c' such that $c \lhd_{\text{th},k}^{cs} i$, and $c' \lhd_{\text{th},k}^{cs} o$, and $c.\text{data} \sim c'.\text{data}$ for some $\sim \in \phi$. The definition of $c \lhd_{\text{th},k}^{cs}$ v is adapted to fragments of form $\langle i, \text{null} \rangle$ and $\langle i, \bot \rangle$ in the obvious way. For a fragment $v = \langle i, o, \phi \rangle$, we often use v.i for i and v.o for o, etc.

Let V be a set of fragments. A global configuration c_S satisfies V wrp. to th, denoted $c_S \models_{\text{th}}^{heap} V$, if

- for any cell c that is accessible to th (different from null and $\bot$), there is a level-1 fragment v $\in V$ such that $c \lhd_{\text{th},1}^{cs}$ v, and
- for all levels k from 2 up to the height of c, there is a higher-level fragment v $\in V$ such that $c \lhd_{\text{th},k}^{cs}$ v.

Intuitively, a set of fragment represents the set of heap states, in which each pair of cells connected by a next[1] pointer is represented by a level-1 fragment, and each pair of cells connected by a next[k] pointer for $k \geq 2$ is represented by a higher-level fragment which represents array fields of cells at index k.

Symbolic Representation. We can now define our abstract symbolic representation.

Define a *local symbolic configuration* σ to be a mapping from local non-pointer variables (including the program counter) to their corresponding abstract domains. We let $c_S \models_{\text{th}}^{loc} \sigma$ denote that in the global configuration c_S, the local configuration of thread th satisfies the local symbolic configuration σ, defined in the natural way. For a local symbolic configuration σ, an observer location s, a pair V of fragments and a thread th, we write $c_S \models_{\text{th}} \langle \sigma, s, V \rangle$ to denote that (i) $c_S \models_{\text{th}}^{loc} \sigma$, (ii) the observer is in location s, and (iii) $c_S \models_{\text{th}}^{heap} V$.

Definition 1. *A symbolic representation Ψ is a partial mapping from pairs of local symbolic configurations and observer locations to sets of fragments. A system configuration c_S satisfies a symbolic representation Ψ, denoted c_S sat Ψ, if for each thread th, the domain of Ψ contains a pair $\langle \sigma, s \rangle$ such that $c_S \models_{\text{th}} \langle \sigma, s, \Psi(\langle \sigma, s \rangle) \rangle$.*

4.2 Symbolic Postcondition Computation

The symbolic postcondition computation must ensure that the symbolic representation of the reachable configurations of a program is closed under execution of a statement by some thread. That is, given a symbolic representation Ψ, the symbolic postcondition operation must produce an extension Ψ' of Ψ, such that whenever c_S sat Ψ and $c_S \rightarrow_{S} c_S'$ then c_S' sat Ψ'. Let th be an arbitrary thread. Then c_S sat Ψ means that $Dom(\Psi)$ contains some pair $\langle \sigma, s \rangle$ with $c_S \models_{\text{th}} \langle \sigma, s, \Psi(\langle \sigma, s \rangle) \rangle$. The symbolic postcondition computation must ensure that $Dom(\Psi')$ contains a pair $\langle \sigma', s' \rangle$ such that $c_S' \models_{\text{th}} \langle \sigma', s', \Psi'(\langle \sigma', s' \rangle) \rangle$. In the thread-modular approach, there are two cases to consider, depending on which thread causes the step from c_S to c_S'.

- *Local Steps:* The step is caused by th itself executing a statement which may change its local state, the location of the observer, and the state of the heap. In this case, we first compute a local symbolic configuration σ', an observer location s', and a set V' of fragments such that $c_S' \models_{\text{th}} \langle \sigma', s', V' \rangle$, and then (if necessary) extend Ψ so that $\langle \sigma', s' \rangle \in Dom(\Psi)$ and $V' \subseteq \Psi(\langle \sigma', s' \rangle)$.
- *Interference Steps:* The step is caused by another thread th_2, executing a statement which may change the location of the observer (to s') and the heap. By c_S sat Ψ there is a local symbolic configuration σ_2 with $\langle \sigma_2, s \rangle \in Dom(\Psi)$ such that $c_S \models_{\text{th}_2} \langle \sigma_2, s, \Psi(\langle \sigma_2, s \rangle) \rangle$. For any such σ_2 and statement of th_2, we must compute a set V' of fragments such that the resulting configuration c_S' satisfies $c_S' \models_{\text{th}}^{heap} V'$ and ensure that $\langle \sigma, s' \rangle \in Dom(\Psi)$ and $V' \subseteq \Psi(\langle \sigma, s' \rangle)$. To do this, we first combine the local symbolic configurations σ and σ_2 and the sets of fragments $\Psi(\langle \sigma, s \rangle)$ and $\Psi(\langle \sigma_2, s \rangle)$, using an operation called *intersection*, into a joint local symbolic configuration of th and th_2 and a set $V_{1,2}$ of fragments that represents the cells accessible to either th or th_2. We thereafter symbolically compute the postcondition of the statement executed by th_2, in the same was as for local steps, and finally project the set of resulting fragments back onto th to obtain V'.

In the following, we first describe the symbolic postcondition computation for local steps, and thereafter the intersection operation.

Symbolic Postcondition Computation for Local Steps. Let th be an arbitrary thread, assume that $\langle \sigma, s \rangle \in Dom(\Psi)$, and let $V = \Psi(\langle \sigma, s \rangle)$ For each statement that th can execute in a configuration c_S with $c_S \models_{\text{th}} \langle \sigma, s, V \rangle$, we must compute a local symbolic configuration σ', a new observer location s' and a set V' of fragments such that the resulting configuration c_{S}' satisfies $c_S' \models_{\text{th}} \langle \sigma', s', V' \rangle$. This computation is done differently for each statement. For statements that do not affect the heap or pointer variables, this computation is standard, and affects only the local symbolic configuration, the observer location, and the **dabs** component of tags. We therefore here describe how to compute the effect of statements that update pointer variables or pointer fields of heap cells, since these are the most interesting cases. In this computation, the set V' is constructed in two steps: (1) First, the level-1 fragments of V' are computed, based on the level-1 fragments in V. (2) Thereafter, the higher-level fragments of V' are computed, based on the higher-level fragments in V and how fragments in V are transformed when entered in to V'. We first describe the construction of level-1 fragments, and thereafter the construction of higher-level fragments.

Construction of Level-1 Fragments. Let us first intuitively introduce techniques used for constructing the level-1 fragments of V'. Consider a statement of form g := p, which assigns the value of a local pointer variable p to a global pointer variable g. The set V' of fragments is obtained by modifying fragments in V to reflect the effect of the assignment. For any tag in a fragment, the **dabs** field is not affected. The **pvars** field is updated to contain the variable g if and only if it contained the variable p before the statement. The difficulty is to update the reachability information represented by the fields **reachfrom** and **reachto**, and in particular to determine whether g should be in such a set after the statement (note that if p were a global variable, then the corresponding reachability information for p would be in the fields **reachfrom** and **reachto**, and the update would be simple, reflecting that g and p become aliases). In order to construct V' with sufficient precision, we therefore investigate whether the set of fragments V allows to form a heap in which a p-cell can reach or be reached from (by a sequence of **next**[1] pointers) a particular tag of a fragment. We also investigate whether a heap can be formed in which a p-cell can *not* reach or be reached from a particular tag. For each such successful investigation, the set V' will contain a level-1 fragment with corresponding contents of its **reachto** and **reachfrom** fields.

The postcondition computation performs this investigation by computing a set of transitive closure-like relations between level-1 fragments, which represent reachability via sequences of **next**[1] pointers (since only these are relevant for the **reachfrom** and **reachto** fields). First, say that two tags **tag** and **tag′** are *consistent* (wrp. to a set of fragments V) if the concretizations of their **dabs**-fields overlap, and if the other fields **pvars**, **reachfrom**, **reachto**, and **private**) agree. Thus, **tag** and **tag′** are consistent if there can exist a cell c accessible to th in some heap, with $c \lhd_{th}^{cs}$ tag and $c \lhd_{th}^{cs}$ tag'. Next, for two level-1 fragments v_1 and v_2 in a set V of fragments,

- let $v_1 \hookrightarrow_V v_2$ denote that $v_1.o$ and $v_2.i$ are consistent, and
- let $v_1 \leftrightarrow_V v_2$ denote that $v_1.o = v_2.o$ are consistent, and that either $v_1.i.pvars \cap v_2.i.pvars = \emptyset$ or the global variables in $v_1.i.reachfrom$ are disjoint from those in $v_2.i.reachfrom$.

Intuitively, $v_1 \hookrightarrow_V v_2$ denotes that it is possible that $c_1.next[1] = c_2$ for some cells with $c_1 \lhd_{th,1}^{cs} v_1$ and $c_2 \lhd_{th,1}^{cs} v_2$. Intuitively, $v_1 \leftrightarrow_V v_2$ denotes that it is possible that $c_1.next[1] = c_2.next[1]$ for different cells c_1 and c_2 with $c_1 \lhd_{th,1}^{cs} v_1$ and $c_2 \lhd_{th,1}^{cs} v_2$ (Note that these definitions also work for fragments containing null or $\bot$). We use these relations to define the following derived relations on level-1 fragments:

- $\overset{+}{\hookrightarrow}_V$ denotes the transitive closure, and $\overset{*}{\hookrightarrow}_V$ the reflexive transitive closure, of $\hookrightarrow_V$,
- $v_1 \overset{**}{\leftrightarrow}_V v_2$ denotes that $\exists v_1', v_2' \in V$ with $v_1' \leftrightarrow_V v_2'$ where $v_1 \overset{*}{\hookrightarrow}_V v_1'$ and $v_2 \overset{*}{\hookrightarrow}_V v_2'$,
- $v_1 \overset{*+}{\leftrightarrow}_V v_2$ denotes that $\exists v_1', v_2' \in V$ with $v_1' \leftrightarrow_V v_2'$ where $v_1 \overset{*}{\hookrightarrow}_V v_1'$ and $v_2 \overset{+}{\hookrightarrow}_V v_2'$,
- $v_1 \overset{*o}{\leftrightarrow}_V v_2$ denotes that $\exists v_1' \in V$ with $v_1' \leftrightarrow_V v_2$ where $v_1 \overset{*}{\hookrightarrow}_V v_1'$,
- $v_1 \overset{++}{\leftrightarrow}_V v_2$ denotes that $\exists v_1', v_2' \in V$ with $v_1' \leftrightarrow_V v_2'$ where $v_1 \overset{+}{\hookrightarrow}_V v_1'$ and $v_2 \overset{+}{\hookrightarrow}_V v_2'$,
- $v_1 \overset{+o}{\leftrightarrow}_V v_2$ denotes that $\exists v_1' \in V$ with $v_1' \leftrightarrow_V v_2$ where $v_1 \overset{+}{\hookrightarrow}_V v_1'$.

We sometimes use, e.g., $v_2 \overset{+*}{\leftrightarrow}_V v_1$ for $v_1 \overset{*+}{\leftrightarrow}_V v_2$. We say that v_1 and v_2 are *compatible* if $v_x \overset{*}{\hookrightarrow} v_y$, or $v_y \overset{*}{\hookrightarrow} v_x$, or $v_x \overset{**}{\leftrightarrow} v_y$. Intuitively, if v_1 and v_2 are satisfied by two cells in the same heap state, then they must be compatible.

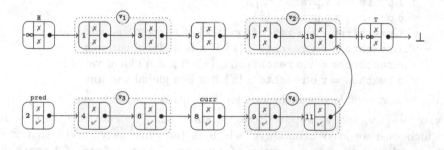

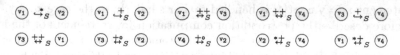

Fig. 7. Illustration of some transitive closure-like relations between fragments

Figure 7 illustrates the above relations for a heap state with 13 heap cells. The figure depicts, in green, four pairs of heap cells connected by a $\texttt{next}[1]$ pointer, which satisfy the four fragments v_1, v_2, v_3, and v_4, respectively. At the bottom are depicted the transitive-closure like relations that hold between these fragments.

We can now describe the symbolic postcondition computation for statements that affect pointer variables or fields. This is a case analysis, and for space reasons we only include some representative cases.

First, consider a statement of form $x := y$, where x and y are local (to thread th) or global pointer variables. We must compute a set V' of fragments which are satisfied by the configuration after the statement. We first compute the level-1-fragments in V' as follows (higher-level fragments will be computed later). We observe that for any cell c which is accessible to th after the statement, there must be some level-1 fragment v' in V' with $c \lhd_{th,1}^{cs} v'$. By assumption, c satisfies some fragment v in V before the statement, and is in the same heap state as the cell pointed to by y. This implies that v must be compatible with some fragment $v_y \in V$ such that $\widehat{y} \in v_y.i.\texttt{pvars}$ (recall that $\widehat{y}$ is the abstraction of y, which in the case that y is an array element maps higher level indices to that abstract index $\textbf{higher}$). This means that we can make a case analysis on the possible relationships between v and any such v_y. Thus, for each fragment $v_y \in V$ such that $\widehat{y} \in v_y.i.\texttt{pvars}$ we let V' contain the fragments obtained by any of the following transformations on any fragment in V.

1. First, for the fragment v_y itself, we let V' contain v'_y, which is the same as v_y, except that
   - $v'_y.i.\texttt{pvars} = v_y.i.\texttt{pvars} \cup \{\widehat{x}\}$ and $v'_y.o.\texttt{pvars} = v.o.\texttt{pvars} \setminus \{\widehat{x}\}$
   and furthermore, if x is a global variable, then
   - $v'_y.i.\texttt{reachto} = v_y.i.\texttt{reachto} \cup \{\widehat{x}\}$ and $v'_y.i.\texttt{reachfrom} = v_y.i.\texttt{reachfrom} \cup \{\widehat{x}\}$,
   - $v'_y.o.\texttt{reachfrom} = v_y.o.\texttt{reachfrom} \cup \{\widehat{x}\}$ and $v'_y.o.\texttt{reachto} = v_y.o.\texttt{reachto} \setminus \{\widehat{x}\}$.
2. for each v with $v \hookrightarrow_V v_y$, let V' contain v' which is the same as v except that
   - $v'.i.\texttt{pvars} = v.i.\texttt{pvars} \setminus \{\widehat{x}\}$,
   - $v'.o.\texttt{pvars} = v.o.\texttt{pvars} \cup \{\widehat{x}\}$,
   - $v'.i.\texttt{reachfrom} = v.i.\texttt{reachfrom} \setminus \{\widehat{x}\}$ if x is a global variable,
   - $v'.i.\texttt{reachto} = v.i.\texttt{reachto} \cup \{\widehat{x}\}$ if x is a global variable,
   - $v'.o.\texttt{reachfrom} = v.o.\texttt{reachfrom} \cup \{\widehat{x}\}$ if x is a global variable,
   - $v'.o.\texttt{reachto} = v.o.\texttt{reachto} \cup \{\widehat{x}\}$ if x is a global variable,
3. We perform analogous inclusions for fragments v with $v \xrightarrow{+}_V v_y$, $v_y \xrightarrow{*}_V$ v, $v_y \xleftrightarrow{*+}_V v$, and $v_y \xleftrightarrow{*o}_V v$. Here, we show only the case of $v_y \xleftrightarrow{*+}_V v$, in which case we let V' contain v' which is the same as v except that $\widehat{x}$ is removed from the sets $v'.i.\texttt{pvars}$, $v'.o.\texttt{pvars}$, $v'.i.\texttt{reachfrom}$, $v'.i.\texttt{reachto}$, $v'.o.\texttt{reachfrom}$, and $v'.o.\texttt{reachto}$.

The statement $x := y.\texttt{next}[1]$ is handled rather similarly to the case $x := y$. Let us therefore describe the postcondition computation for statements of the form $x.\texttt{next}[1] := y$. This is the most difficult statement, since it is a destructive update of the heap. It affects reachability relations for both x and y. The postcondition computation makes a case analysis on how a fragment in V is related to some pair of compatible fragments v_x, v_y in V such that $\widehat{x} \in v_x.i.\text{pvars}$, $\widehat{y} \in v_y.i.\text{pvars}$. Thus, for each pair of compatible fragments v_x, v_y in V such that $\widehat{x} \in v_x.i.\text{pvars}$ and $\widehat{y} \in v_y.i.\text{pvars}$, it is first checked whether the statement may form a cycle in the heap. This may happen if $v_y \xrightarrow{*}_V v_x$, in which case the postcondition computation reports a potential cycle. Otherwise, V' consists of

1. the fragment v_{new}, representing the new pair of neighbours formed by the statement, of form $v_{new} = \langle i, o, \phi \rangle$, such that $v_{new}.i.\text{tag} = v_x.i.\text{tag}$ and $v_{new}.o.\text{tag} = v_y.i.\text{tag}$ except that $v_{new}.o.\text{reachfrom} = v_y.i.\text{reachfrom} \cup v_x.i.\text{reachfrom}$ and $v_{new}.i.\text{reachto} = v_y.i.\text{reachto} \cup v_x.i.\text{pvars}$; the constraint represent by $v_{new}.\phi$ is obtained from the constraints represented by the data abstractions of $v_x.i$ and $v_y.i$, as well as the possible transitive closure-relations between v_x and v_y, some of which imply that the data fields of v_x and v_y are ordered, and

2. all possible fragments that can result from a transformation of some fragment $v \in V$. This is done by an exhaustive case analysis on the possible relationships between v, v_x and v_y. Let us consider an interesting case, in which $v_x \xrightarrow{*}_V v$ and either $v \xrightarrow{+}_V v_y$ or $v_y \xrightarrow{*+} v$. In this case,
   - for each subset **regset** of the observer registers in $v.i.\text{reachfrom} \cap v_x.i.\text{reachfrom}$, and for each subset **regset'** of the set of observer registers in $v.o.\text{reachfrom} \cap v_x.i.\text{reachfrom}$, we let V' contain a fragment v' which is the same as v except that $v'.i.\text{reachfrom} = (v.i.\text{reachfrom} \setminus v_x.i.\text{reachfrom}) \cup \textbf{regset}$ and $v'.o.\text{reachfrom} = (v.o.\text{reachfrom} \setminus v_x.i.\text{reachfrom}) \cup \textbf{regset'}$. An intuitive explanation for the rule for $v'.i.\text{reachfrom}$ is that the global variables that can reach $v_x.i$ should clearly be removed from $v'.i.\text{reachfrom}$ since $v_x \xrightarrow{*}_V v'$ is false after the statement. However, for an observer register x_i, an x_i-cell can still reach $v'.i$, if there are two x_i-cells, one which reaches $v_x.i$ and another which reaches $v'.i$; we cannot precisely determine for which x_i this may be the case, except that any such x_i must be in $v.i.\text{reachfrom} \cap v_x.i.\text{reachfrom}$. The intuition for the rule for $v'.o.\text{reachfrom}$ is analogous.

Construction of Higher-Level Fragments. Based on the above construction of level-1 fragments, the set of higher-level fragments in V' is obtained as follows. For each higher level-fragment $v \in V$, let v_1 and v_2 be level 1-fragments such that $v_1.i.\text{tag} = v.i.\text{tag}$ and $v_2.i.\text{tag} = v.o.\text{tag}$. For any fragments v_1' and v_2' that are derived from v_1 and v_2, respectively, V' contains a higher-level fragment v' which is the same as v except that (i) $v'.i.\text{pvars} = v_1'.i.\text{pvars}$ and $v'.o.\text{pvars} = v_2'.i.\text{pvars}$, (ii) $v'.i.\text{reachfrom} = v_1'.i.\text{reachfrom}$ and $v'.o.\text{reachfrom} = v_2'.i.\text{reachfrom}$, and (iii) $v'.i.\text{reachto} = v_1'.i.\text{reachto}$ and $v'.o.\text{reachto} = v_2'.i.\text{reachto}$. In addition, a statement of form $x.\text{next}[k] := y$ for $k \geq 2$ creates a new fragment. The formation of this fragment is simpler than for the statement $x.\text{next}[1] := y$, since reachability via $\text{next}[1]$-pointers is preserved.

Symbolic Postcondition Computation for Interference Steps. Here, the key step is the *intersection* operation, which takes two sets of fragments V_1 and V_2, and produces a set of joint fragments $V_{1,2}$, such that $c_{\mathcal{S}} \models^{heap}_{\mathtt{th}_1,\mathtt{th}_2} V_{1,2}$ for any configuration such that $c_{\mathcal{S}} \models^{heap}_{\mathtt{th}_i} V_i$ for $i = 1, 2$ (here $\models^{heap}_{\mathtt{th}_1,\mathtt{th}_2}$ is defined in the natural way). This means that for each heap cell accessible to either $\mathtt{th}_1$ or $\mathtt{th}_2$, the set $V_{1,2}$ contains a fragment v with $c \lhd^{cs}_{\{\mathtt{th}_1,\mathtt{th}_2\},k} v$ for each k which is at most the height of c (generalizing the notation $\lhd^{cs}_{\mathtt{th},k}$ to several threads). Note that a joint fragment represents local pointer variables of both $\mathtt{th}_1$ and $\mathtt{th}_2$. In order to distinguish between local variables of $\mathtt{th}_1$ and $\mathtt{th}_2$, we use x[i] to denote a local variable x of thread $\mathtt{th}_i$. Here, we describe the intersection operation for level-1 fragments. The intersection operation is analogous for higher-level fragments.

For a fragment v, define v.i.greachfrom as the set of global variables in v.i.reachfrom. Define v.i.greachto, v.o.greachfrom, v.o.greachto, v.i.gpvars, and v.o.gpvars analogously. Define v.i.gtag as the tuple $\langle$v.i.dabs, v.i.gpvars, v.i.greachfrom, v.i.greachto$\rangle$, and define v.o.gtag analogously. We must distinguish the following possibilities.

- If c is accessible to both $\mathtt{th}_1$ and $\mathtt{th}_2$, then there are fragments $v_1 \in V_1$ and $v_2 \in V_2$ such that $c \lhd^{cs}_{\mathtt{th}_1,1} v_1$ and $c \lhd^{cs}_{\mathtt{th}_2,1} v_2$. This can happen only if v_1.i.gtag $= v_2$.i.gtag, and v_1.o.gtag $= v_2$.o.gtag, and v_1.i.private $= v_2$.i.private $=$ false. Thus, for any such pair of fragments $v_1 \in V_1$ and $v_2 \in V_2$, we let $V_{1,2}$ contain a fragment v_{12} which is identical to v_1 except that
  - v_{12}.i.pvars $= v_1$.i.pvars $\cup v_2$.i.pvars,
  - v_{12}.o.pvars $= v_1$.o.pvars $\cup v_2$.o.pvars,
  - v_{12}.i.reachfrom $= v_1$.i.reachfrom $\cup v_2$.i.reachfrom, and
  - v_{12}.o.reachfrom $= v_1$.o.reachfrom $\cup v_2$.o.reachfrom.
- If c is accessible to $\mathtt{th}_1$, but not to $\mathtt{th}_2$, and c.next[1] is accessible also to $\mathtt{th}_2$, then there are fragments $v_1 \in V_1$ and $v_2 \in V_2$ such that $c \lhd^{cs}_{\mathtt{th}_1,1} v_1$ and c.next[1] $\lhd^{cs}_{\mathtt{th}_2,1} v_2$.o. This can happen only if v_1.i.greachfrom $= \emptyset$, and v_1.o.gtag $= v_2$.o.gtag, and v_1.o.private $= v_2$.o.private $=$ false. Thus, for any such pair of fragments $v_1 \in V_1$ and $v_2 \in V_2$, we let $V_{1,2}$ contain a fragment v_1' which is identical to v_1 except that
  - v_1'.o.pvars $= v_1$.o.pvars $\cup v_2$.o.pvars, and
  - v_1'.o.reachfrom $= v_1$.o.reachfrom $\cup v_2$.o.reachfrom.
- If neither c nor c.next[1] is accessible $\mathtt{th}_2$, then there is a fragment $v_1 \in V_1$ such that $c \lhd^{cs}_{\mathtt{th}_1,1} v_1$. This can happen only if v_1.o.greachfrom $= \emptyset$, in which case we let $V_{1,2}$ contain the fragment v_1.
- For each of the two last cases, there is also a symmetric case with the roles of $\mathtt{th}_1$ and $\mathtt{th}_2$ reversed.

5   Arrays of Singly-Linked Lists with Timestamps

In this section, we show how to apply fragment abstraction to concurrent programs that operate on a shared heap which represents an array of singly linked lists. We use this abstraction to provide the first automated verification of linearizability for the Timedstamped stack and Timestamped queue algorithms of [12] as reported in Sect. 6.

```
struct Node {
        int data;
        Timestamp ts;
        Node* next;
        boolean mark;
    }
```

```
init() :
Node* pools[maxThreads];
for(int i=1; i<=maxThreads; i++)
pools[i].next = null;
```

```
void push(int d):
1  Node* new := new Node(d,-1,null,false);
2  new.next = pools[myID];
3  pools[myID] = new;
4  Timestamp t = new Timestamp();
5  new.ts = t;
6  Node* next = new.next;
7  while (next.next != next & !next.mark)
8    next = next.next;
9  new.next = next;
10 return new;
```

```
int pop():
1  boolean success = false;
2  int maxTS = -1;
3  Node* youngest, myTop, n = null;
4  while (!success)
5    int k;
6    for(int i=1; i<=maxThreads; i++)
7      n = pools[i];
8      while (n.mark & n.next != n) n = n.next;
9      if(maxTS < n.ts)
10       maxTS = n.ts;
11       youngest = n;
12       k = i; myTop = pools[k];
13    if (youngest != null)
14      success = CAS(youngest.mark,false,true);
15      if (success)
16        CAS(pools[k], myTop, youngest);
17        if (myTop != youngest);
18          myTop.next = youngest;
19          pools[k].next = youngest.next;
20          Node* next=youngest.next
21          while (next.next != next & next.mark);
22            next = next.next;
23          youngest.next = next;
24 return youngest.data;
```

Fig. 8. Description of the Timestamped stack algorithm, with some simplifications.

Figure 8 shows a simplified version of the Timestamped Stack (TS stack) of [12], where we have omitted the check for emptiness in the pop method, and the optimization using push-pop elimination. These features are included in the full version of the algorithm, that we have verified automatically.

The algorithm uses an array of singly-linked lists (SLLs), one for each thread, accessed via the thread-indexed array pools[maxThreads] of pointers to the first cell of each list. The init method initializes each of these pointers to null. Each list cell contains a data value, a timestamp value, a next pointer, and a boolean flag mark which indicates whether the node is logically removed from the stack. Each thread pushes elements only to "its own" list, but can pop elements from any list.

A push method for inserting a data element d works as follows: first, a new cell with element d and minimal timestamp −1 is inserted at the beginning of the list indexed by the calling thread (line 1–3). After that, a new timestamp is created and assigned (via the variable t) to the ts field of the inserted cell (line 4–5). Finally, the method unlinks (i.e., physically removes) all cells that are reachable (through a sequence of next pointers) from the inserted cell and whose mark field is true; these cells are already logically removed. This is done by redirecting the next pointer of the inserted cell to the first cell with a false mark field, which is reachable from the inserted cell.

A pop method first traverses all lists, finding in each list the first cell whose mark field is false (line 8), and letting the variable youngest point to the most recent such cell (i.e., with the largest timestamp) (line 1–11). A compare-and-swap (CAS) is used to set the mark field of this youngest cell to true, thereby logically removing it. This procedure will restart if the CAS fails. After the youngest cell has been removed, the method will unlink all cells, whose mark field is true, that appear before (line 17–19) or after (line 20–23) the removed cell. Finally, the method returns the data value of the removed cell.

Fragment Abstraction. In our verification, we establish that the TS stack algorithm of Fig. 8 is correct in the sense that it is a linearizable implementation of a stack data structure. For stacks and queues, we specify linearizability by observers that synchronize on call and return actions of methods, as shown by [7]; this is done without any user-supplied annotation, hence the verification is fully automated.

The verification is performed analogously as for skiplists, as described in Sect. 4. Here we show how fragment abstraction is used for arrays of singly-linked lists. Figure 9 shows an example heap state of TS stack. The heap consists of a set of singly linked lists (SLLs), each of which is accessed from a pointer in the array pools[maxThreads] in a configuration when it is accessed concurrently by three threads th_1, th_2, and th_3. The heap consists of three SLLs accessed from the three pointers pools[1], pools[2], and pools[3] respectively. Each heap cell is shown with the values of its fields, using the layout shown to the right in Fig. 9. In addition, each cell is labeled by the pointer variables that point to it. We use lvar(i) to denote the local variable lvar of thread th_i.

In the heap state of Fig. 9, thread th_1 is trying to push a new node with data value 4, pointed by its local variable new, having reached line 3. Thread th_3 has just called the push method. Thread th_2 has reached line 12 in the execution of the pop method, and has just assigned youngest to the first node in the list pointed to by pools[3] which is not logically removed (in this case it is the last node of that list). The observer has two registers x_1 and x_2, which are assigned the values 4 and 2, respectively.

We verify the algorithm using a symbolic representation that is analogous to the one used for skiplists. There are two main differences.

– Since the array pools is global, all threads can reach all lists in the heap (the only cells that cannot be reached by all threads are new cells that are not yet inserted).
– We therefore represent the view of a thread by a thread-dependent abstraction of thread indices, which index the array pools. In the view of a thread, the index of the list where it is currently active is abstracted to me, and all other indices are abstracted to ot. The currently active index is taken to be the thread index for a thread performing a push, the value of i for a thread executing in the **for** loop of pop, and the value of k after that loop.

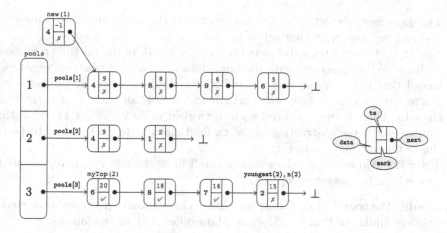

Fig. 9. A possible heap state of TS stack with three threads.

In the definition of tags, the only global variables that can occur in the fields **reachfrom** and **reachto** are therefore pools[me] and pools[other]. The data abstraction represents (i) for each cell, the set of observer registers, whose values are equal to the **datafield**, (ii) for each timestamp and observer register x_i, the possible orderings between this timestamp and the timestamp of an x_i-cell.

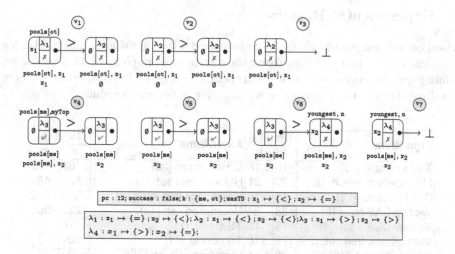

Fig. 10. Fragment abstraction

Figure 10 shows a set of fragments that is satisfied wrp. to th_2 by the configuration in Fig. 9. There are 7 fragments, named $v_1, \ldots, v_7$. Consider the tag which occurs in fragment v_7. This tag is an abstraction of the bottom-rightmost heap cell in Fig. 9. The different non-pointer fields are represented as follows.

- The data field of the tag (to the left) abstracts the data value 2 to the set of observer registers with that value: in this case x_2.
- The ts field (at the top) abstracts the timer value 15 to the possible relations with ts-fields of heap cells with the same data value as each observer registers. Recall that observer registers x_1 and x_2 have values 4 and 2, respectively. There are three heap cells with data field value 4, all with a ts value less than 15. There is one heap cell with data field value 2, having ts value 15. Consequently, the abstraction of the ts field maps x_1 to $\{>\}$ and x_2 to $\{=\}$: this is the mapping λ_4 in Fig. 10.
- The mark field assumes values from a small finite domain and is represented precisely as in concrete heap cells.

Symbolic Postcondition Computation. The symbolic postcondition computation is similar to that for skiplists. Main differences are as follows.

- Whenever a thread performing pop moves from one iteration of the for loop to the next, the abstraction must consider to swap between the abstractions me and ot.
- In interference steps, we must consider that the abstraction me for the interfering thread may have to be changed into ot. Furthermore, the abstractions me for two push methods cannot coincide, since each thread pushes only to its own list.

6   Experimental Results

Based on our framework, we have implemented a tool in OCaml, and used it for verifying various kinds of concurrent data structures implementation of stacks, priority queues, queues and sets. All of them are based on heap structures. There are three types of heap structures we consider in our experiments.

Algorithms	Time (s)		Algorithms	Time (s)	
	a	b		a	b
Treiber stack [35]	18	0.18	O'Hearn set [28]	88	12
MS lock-free queue [27]	22	21	HM lock-free set [19]	120	462
DGLM queue [13]	16	16	Harris lock-free set [15]	950	1512
Vechev-CAS set [40]	86	24	Unordered set [43]	1230	2301
Vechev-DCAS set [40]	16	16	TS stack [11]	176	
Michael lock-free set [25]	178	110	TS queue [11]	101	
Pessimistic set [19]	30	1.51	Lock-free skiplist [19]	1992	
Optimistic set [19]	25	60	Lock-based skiplist [18]	500	
Lazy set [17]	34	289	Priority queue skiplist 1 [23]	1320	
			Priority queue skiplist 2 [22]	599	

Fig. 11. Times for verifying concurrent data structure implementations. Column **a** shows the verification times for our tool based on fragment abstraction. Column **b** shows the verification times for the tool for SLLs in our previous work [3]

Singly-linked list benchmarks: These benchmarks include stacks, queues and sets algorithms which are the well-known in the literature. The challenge is that in some set implementation, the linearization points are not fixed, they depended on the future of each execution. The sets with non fixed linearization points are the lazy set [20], lock-free sets of *HM* [22], *Harris* [17], *Michael* [29], and unordered set of [48]. By using observers and controllers in our previous work [3]. Our approach is simple and strong enough to verify these singly-linked list benchmarks.

Skiplist benchmarks: We consider four skiplist algorithms including the lock-based skiplist set [31], the lock-free skiplist set which is described in Sect. 2 [22], and two skiplist-based priority queues [26,27]. One challenge for verifying these algorithms is to deal with unbounded number of levels. In addition, in the lock-free skiplist [22] and priority queue [26], the skiplist shape is not well formed, meaning that each higher level list need not be a sub-list of lower level lists. These algorithms have not been automatically verified in previous work. By applying our fragment abstraction, to the best of our knowledge, we provide first framework which can automatically verify these concurrent skiplists algorithms.

Arrays of singly-linked list benchmarks: We consider two challenging timestamp algorithms in [12]. There are two challenges when verifying these algorithm. The first challenge is how to deal with an unbounded number of SLLs, and the second challenge is that the linearization points of the algorithms are not fixed, but depend on the future of each execution. By combining our fragment abstraction with the observers for stacks and queues in [7], we are able to verify these two algorithms automatically. The observers are crucial for achieving automation, since they enforce the weakest possible ordering constraints that are necessary for proving linearizability, thereby making it possible to use a less precise abstraction.

Running Times. The experiments were performed on a desktop 2.8 GHz processor with 8 GB memory. The results are presented in Fig. 11, where running times are given in seconds. Column a shows the verification times of our tool, whereas column b shows the verification times for algorithms based on SLLs, using the technique in our previous work [3]. In our experiments, we run the tool together with an observer in [1,7] and controllers in [3] to verify linearizability of the algorithms. All experiments start from the initial heap, and end either when the analysis reaches a fixed point or when a violation of safety properties or linearizability is detected. As can be seen from the table, the verification times vary in the different examples. This is due to the types of shapes that are produced during the analysis. For instance, skiplist algorithms have much longer verification times. This is due to the number of pointer variables and their complicated shapes. In contrast, other algorithms produce simple shape patterns and hence they have shorter verification times.

Error Detection. In addition to establishing correctness of the original versions of the benchmark algorithms, we tested our tool with intentionally inserted bugs.

For example, we omitted setting time statement in line 5 of the push method in the TS stack algorithm, or we omitted the CAS statements in lock-free algorithms. The tool, as expected, successfully detected and reported the bugs.

7   Conclusions

We have presented a novel shape abstraction, called fragment abstraction, for automatic verification of concurrent data structure implementations that operate on different forms of dynamically allocated heap structures, including singly-linked lists, skiplists, and arrays of singly-linked lists. Our approach is the first framework that can automatically verify concurrent data structure implementations that employ skiplists and arrays of singly linked lists, at the same time as handling an unbounded number of concurrent threads, an unbounded domain of data values (including timestamps), and an unbounded shared heap. We showed fragment abstraction allows to combine local and global reachability information to allow verification of the functional behavior of a collection of threads.

As future work, we intend to investigate whether fragment abstraction can be applied also to other heap structures, such as concurrent binary search trees.

References

1. Abdulla, P.A., Haziza, F., Holík, L., Jonsson, B., Rezine, A.: An integrated specification and verification technique for highly concurrent data structures. In: Piterman, N., Smolka, S.A. (eds.) TACAS 2013. LNCS, vol. 7795, pp. 324–338. Springer, Heidelberg (2013). https://doi.org/10.1007/978-3-642-36742-7_23
2. Abdulla, P.A., Holík, L., Jonsson, B., Trinh, C.Q., et al.: Verification of heap manipulating programs with ordered data by extended forest automata. Acta Inf. **53**(4), 357–385 (2016)
3. Abdulla, P.A., Jonsson, B., Trinh, C.Q.: Automated verification of linearization policies. In: Rival, X. (ed.) SAS 2016. LNCS, vol. 9837, pp. 61–83. Springer, Heidelberg (2016). https://doi.org/10.1007/978-3-662-53413-7_4
4. Amit, D., Rinetzky, N., Reps, T., Sagiv, M., Yahav, E.: Comparison under abstraction for verifying linearizability. In: Damm, W., Hermanns, H. (eds.) CAV 2007. LNCS, vol. 4590, pp. 477–490. Springer, Heidelberg (2007). https://doi.org/10.1007/978-3-540-73368-3_49
5. Berdine, J., Lev-Ami, T., Manevich, R., Ramalingam, G., Sagiv, M.: Thread quantification for concurrent shape analysis. In: Gupta, A., Malik, S. (eds.) CAV 2008. LNCS, vol. 5123, pp. 399–413. Springer, Heidelberg (2008). https://doi.org/10.1007/978-3-540-70545-1_37
6. Bingham, J., Rakamarić, Z.: A logic and decision procedure for predicate abstraction of heap-manipulating programs. In: Emerson, E.A., Namjoshi, K.S. (eds.) VMCAI 2006. LNCS, vol. 3855, pp. 207–221. Springer, Heidelberg (2005). https://doi.org/10.1007/11609773_14
7. Bouajjani, A., Emmi, M., Enea, C., Hamza, J.: On reducing linearizability to state reachability. In: Halldórsson, M.M., Iwama, K., Kobayashi, N., Speckmann, B. (eds.) ICALP 2015, Part II. LNCS, vol. 9135, pp. 95–107. Springer, Heidelberg (2015). https://doi.org/10.1007/978-3-662-47666-6_8

8. Bouajjani, A., Emmi, M., Enea, C., Mutluergil, S.O.: Proving linearizability using forward simulations. In: Majumdar, R., Kunčak, V. (eds.) CAV 2017, Part II. LNCS, vol. 10427, pp. 542–563. Springer, Cham (2017). https://doi.org/10.1007/978-3-319-63390-9_28

9. Chakraborty, S., Henzinger, T.A., Sezgin, A., Vafeiadis, V.: Aspect-oriented linearizability proofs. Log. Methods Comput. Sci. **11**(1) (2015)

10. Chang, B.-Y.E., Rival, X., Necula, G.C.: Shape analysis with structural invariant checkers. In: Nielson, H.R., Filé, G. (eds.) SAS 2007. LNCS, vol. 4634, pp. 384–401. Springer, Heidelberg (2007). https://doi.org/10.1007/978-3-540-74061-2_24

11. Colvin, R., Groves, L., Luchangco, V., Moir, M.: Formal verification of a lazy concurrent list-based set algorithm. In: Ball, T., Jones, R.B. (eds.) CAV 2006. LNCS, vol. 4144, pp. 475–488. Springer, Heidelberg (2006). https://doi.org/10.1007/11817963_44

12. Dodds, M., Haas, A., Kirsch, C.: A scalable, correct time-stamped stack. In: POPL, pp. 233–246. ACM (2015)

13. Doherty, S., Detlefs, D., Groves, L., Flood, C., et al.: DCAS is not a silver bullet for nonblocking algorithm design. In: SPAA 2004, pp. 216–224. ACM (2004)

14. Doherty, S., Groves, L., Luchangco, V., Moir, M.: Formal verification of a practical lock-free queue algorithm. In: de Frutos-Escrig, D., Núñez, M. (eds.) FORTE 2004. LNCS, vol. 3235, pp. 97–114. Springer, Heidelberg (2004). https://doi.org/10.1007/978-3-540-30232-2_7

15. Dudka, K., Peringer, P., Vojnar, T.: Byte-precise verification of low-level list manipulation. In: Logozzo, F., Fähndrich, M. (eds.) SAS 2013. LNCS, vol. 7935, pp. 215–237. Springer, Heidelberg (2013). https://doi.org/10.1007/978-3-642-38856-9_13

16. Fomitchev, M., Ruppert, E.: Lock-free linked lists and skip lists. In: PODC 2004, pp. 50–59. ACM (2004)

17. Harris, T.L.: A pragmatic implementation of non-blocking linked-lists. In: Welch, J. (ed.) DISC 2001. LNCS, vol. 2180, pp. 300–314. Springer, Heidelberg (2001). https://doi.org/10.1007/3-540-45414-4_21

18. Haziza, F., Holík, L., Meyer, R., Wolff, S.: Pointer race freedom. In: Jobstmann, B., Leino, K.R.M. (eds.) VMCAI 2016. LNCS, vol. 9583, pp. 393–412. Springer, Heidelberg (2016). https://doi.org/10.1007/978-3-662-49122-5_19

19. Heinen, J., Noll, T., Rieger, S.: Juggrnaut: graph grammar abstraction for unbounded heap structures. ENTCS **266**, 93–107 (2010)

20. Heller, S., Herlihy, M., Luchangco, V., Moir, M., Scherer, W.N., Shavit, N.: A lazy concurrent list-based set algorithm. In: Anderson, J.H., Prencipe, G., Wattenhofer, R. (eds.) OPODIS 2005. LNCS, vol. 3974, pp. 3–16. Springer, Heidelberg (2006). https://doi.org/10.1007/11795490_3

21. Herlihy, M., Lev, Y., Luchangco, V., Shavit, N.: A simple optimistic skiplist algorithm. In: Prencipe, G., Zaks, S. (eds.) SIROCCO 2007. LNCS, vol. 4474, pp. 124–138. Springer, Heidelberg (2007). https://doi.org/10.1007/978-3-540-72951-8_11

22. Herlihy, M., Shavit, N.: The Art of Multiprocessor Programming. Morgan Kaufmann, San Francisco (2008)

23. Holík, L., Lengál, O., Rogalewicz, A., Šimáček, J., Vojnar, T.: Fully automated shape analysis based on forest automata. In: Sharygina, N., Veith, H. (eds.) CAV 2013. LNCS, vol. 8044, pp. 740–755. Springer, Heidelberg (2013). https://doi.org/10.1007/978-3-642-39799-8_52

24. Khyzha, A., Dodds, M., Gotsman, A., Parkinson, M.: Proving linearizability using partial orders. In: Yang, H. (ed.) ESOP 2017. LNCS, vol. 10201, pp. 639–667. Springer, Heidelberg (2017). https://doi.org/10.1007/978-3-662-54434-1_24
25. Liang, H., Feng, X.: Modular verification of linearizability with non-fixed linearization points. In: PLDI, pp. 459–470. ACM (2013)
26. Lindén, J., Jonsson, B.: A skiplist-based concurrent priority queue with minimal memory contention. In: Baldoni, R., Nisse, N., van Steen, M. (eds.) OPODIS 2013. LNCS, vol. 8304, pp. 206–220. Springer, Cham (2013). https://doi.org/10.1007/978-3-319-03850-6_15
27. Lotan, I., Shavit, N.: Skiplist-based concurrent priority queues. In: IPDPS, pp. 263–268. IEEE (2000)
28. Manevich, R., Yahav, E., Ramalingam, G., Sagiv, M.: Predicate abstraction and canonical abstraction for singly-linked lists. In: Cousot, R. (ed.) VMCAI 2005. LNCS, vol. 3385, pp. 181–198. Springer, Heidelberg (2005). https://doi.org/10.1007/978-3-540-30579-8_13
29. Michael, M.M.: High performance dynamic lock-free hash tables and list-based sets. In: SPAA, pp. 73–82 (2002)
30. Michael, M., Scott, M.: Correction of a memory management method for lock-free data structures. Technical report TR599, University of Rochester, Rochester, NY, USA (1995)
31. Michael, M., Scott, M.: Simple, fast, and practical non-blocking and blocking concurrent queue algorithms. In: PODC, pp. 267–275. ACM (1996)
32. O'Hearn, P.W., Rinetzky, N., Vechev, M.T., Yahav, E., Yorsh, G.: Verifying linearizability with hindsight. In: PODC, pp. 85–94 (2010)
33. Sagiv, S., Reps, T., Wilhelm, R.: Parametric shape analysis via 3-valued logic. ACM Trans. Program. Lang. Syst. 24(3), 217–298 (2002)
34. Sánchez, A., Sánchez, C.: Formal verification of skiplists with arbitrary many levels. In: Cassez, F., Raskin, J.-F. (eds.) ATVA 2014. LNCS, vol. 8837, pp. 314–329. Springer, Cham (2014). https://doi.org/10.1007/978-3-319-11936-6_23
35. Schellhorn, G., Derrick, J., Wehrheim, H.: A sound and complete proof technique for linearizability of concurrent data structures. ACM Trans. Comput. Log. 15(4), 31:1–37 (2014)
36. Segalov, M., Lev-Ami, T., Manevich, R., Ganesan, R., Sagiv, M.: Abstract transformers for thread correlation analysis. In: Hu, Z. (ed.) APLAS 2009. LNCS, vol. 5904, pp. 30–46. Springer, Heidelberg (2009). https://doi.org/10.1007/978-3-642-10672-9_5
37. Singh, V., Neamtiu, I., Gupta, R.: Proving concurrent data structures linearizable. In: ISSRE, pp. 230–240. IEEE (2016)
38. Sundell, H., Tsigas, P.: Fast and lock-free concurrent priority queues for multithread systems. J. Parallel Distrib. Comput. 65(5), 609–627 (2005)
39. Treiber, R.: Systems programming: Coping with parallelism. Technical report RJ5118, IBM Almaden Res. Ctr. (1986)
40. Turon, A.J., Thamsborg, J., Ahmed, A., Birkedal, L., Dreyer, D.: Logical relations for fine-grained concurrency. In: POPL 2013, pp. 343–356. ACM (2013)
41. Vafeiadis, V.: Modular fine-grained concurrency verification. Ph.D. thesis, University of Cambridge (2008)
42. Vafeiadis, V.: Automatically proving linearizability. In: Touili, T., Cook, B., Jackson, P. (eds.) CAV 2010. LNCS, vol. 6174, pp. 450–464. Springer, Heidelberg (2010). https://doi.org/10.1007/978-3-642-14295-6_40

43. Černý, P., Radhakrishna, A., Zufferey, D., Chaudhuri, S., Alur, R.: Model checking of linearizability of concurrent list implementations. In: Touili, T., Cook, B., Jackson, P. (eds.) CAV 2010. LNCS, vol. 6174, pp. 465–479. Springer, Heidelberg (2010). https://doi.org/10.1007/978-3-642-14295-6_41
44. Vechev, M.T., Yahav, E.: Deriving linearizable fine-grained concurrent objects. In: PLDI, pp. 125–135. ACM (2008)
45. Vechev, M., Yahav, E., Yorsh, G.: Experience with model checking linearizability. In: Păsăreanu, C.S. (ed.) SPIN 2009. LNCS, vol. 5578, pp. 261–278. Springer, Heidelberg (2009). https://doi.org/10.1007/978-3-642-02652-2_21
46. Wachter, B., Westphal, B.: The spotlight principle. In: Cook, B., Podelski, A. (eds.) VMCAI 2007. LNCS, vol. 4349, pp. 182–198. Springer, Heidelberg (2007). https://doi.org/10.1007/978-3-540-69738-1_13
47. Yang, H., Lee, O., Berdine, J., Calcagno, C., Cook, B., Distefano, D., O'Hearn, P.: Scalable shape analysis for systems code. In: Gupta, A., Malik, S. (eds.) CAV 2008. LNCS, vol. 5123, pp. 385–398. Springer, Heidelberg (2008). https://doi.org/10.1007/978-3-540-70545-1_36
48. Zhang, K., Zhao, Y., Yang, Y., Liu, Y., Spear, M.: Practical non-blocking unordered lists. In: Afek, Y. (ed.) DISC 2013. LNCS, vol. 8205, pp. 239–253. Springer, Heidelberg (2013). https://doi.org/10.1007/978-3-642-41527-2_17

Security

Reasoning About a Machine
with Local Capabilities
Provably Safe Stack and Return Pointer Management

Lau Skorstengaard[1]($\boxtimes$), Dominique Devriese[2], and Lars Birkedal[1]

[1] Aarhus University, Aarhus, Denmark
{lau,birkedal}@cs.au.dk
[2] imec-DistriNet, KU Leuven, Leuven, Belgium
dominique.devriese@cs.kuleuven.be

Abstract. Capability machines provide security guarantees at machine level which makes them an interesting target for secure compilation schemes that provably enforce properties such as control-flow correctness and encapsulation of local state. We provide a formalization of a representative capability machine with local capabilities and study a novel calling convention. We provide a logical relation that semantically captures the guarantees provided by the hardware (a form of capability safety) and use it to prove control-flow correctness and encapsulation of local state. The logical relation is not specific to our calling convention and can be used to reason about arbitrary programs.

1 Introduction

Compromising software security is often based on attacks that break programming language properties relied upon by software authors, such as control-flow correctness, local-state encapsulation, etc. Commodity processors offer little support for defending against such attacks: they offer security primitives with only coarse-grained memory protection and limited compartmentalization scalability. As a result, defenses against attacks on control-flow correctness and local-state encapsulation are either limited to only certain common forms of attacks (leading to an attack-defense arms race) and/or rely on techniques like machine code rewriting [1,2], machine code verification [3], virtual machines with a native stack [4] or randomization [5]. The latter techniques essentially emulate protection techniques on existing hardware, at the cost of performance, system complexity and/or security.

Capability machines are a type of processors that remediate these limitations with a better security model at the hardware level. They are based on old ideas [6–8], but have recently received renewed interest; in particular, the CHERI project has proposed new ideas and ways of tackling practical challenges like backwards compatibility and realistic OS support [9,10]. Capability machines tag every word (in the register file and in memory) to enforce a strict separation between numbers and capabilities (a kind of pointers that carry authority). Memory capabilities

© The Author(s) 2018
A. Ahmed (Ed.): ESOP 2018, LNCS 10801, pp. 475–501, 2018.
https://doi.org/10.1007/978-3-319-89884-1_17

carry the authority to read and/or write to a range of memory locations. There is also a form of *object capabilities*, which represent the authority to invoke a piece of code without exposing the code's encapsulated private state (e.g., the M-Machine's enter capabilities or CHERI's sealed code/data pairs).

Unlike commodity processors, capability machines lend themselves well to enforcing local-state encapsulation. Potentially, they will enable compilation schemes that enforce this property in an efficient but also 100% watertight way (ideally evidenced by a mathematical proof, guaranteeing that we do not end up in a new attack-defense arms race). However, a lot needs to happen before we get there. For example, it is far from trivial to devise a compilation scheme adapted to the details of a specific source language's notion of encapsulation (e.g., private member variables in OO languages often behave quite differently than private state in ML-like languages). And even if such a scheme were defined, a formal proof depends on a formalization of the encapsulation provided by the capability machine at hand.

A similar problem is the enforcement of control-flow correctness on capability machines. An interesting approach is taken in CheriBSD [9]: the standard contiguous C stack is split into a central, trusted stack, managed by trusted call and return instructions, and disjoint, private, per-compartment stacks. To prevent illegal use of stack references, the approach relies on *local capabilities*, a type of capabilities offered by CHERI to *temporarily* relinquish authority, namely for the duration of a function invocation whereafter the capability can be revoked. However, details are scarce (how does it work precisely? what features are supported?) and a lot remains to be investigated (e.g., combining disjoint stacks with cross-domain function pointers seems like it will scale poorly to large numbers of components?). Finally, there is no argument that the approach is watertight and it is not even clear what security property is targeted exactly.

In this paper, we make two main contributions: (1) an alternative calling convention that uses local capabilities to enforce stack frame encapsulation and well-bracketed control flow, and (2) perhaps more importantly, we adapt and apply the well-studied techniques of step-indexed Kripke logical relations for reasoning about code on a representative capability machine with local capabilities in general and correctness and security of the calling convention in particular. More specifically, we make the following contributions:

- We formalize a simple but representative capability machine featuring local capabilities and its operational semantics (Sect. 2).
- We define a novel calling convention enforcing control-flow correctness and encapsulation of stack frames (Sect. 3). It relies solely on local capabilities and does not require OS support (like a trusted stack or call/return instructions). It supports higher-order cross-component calls (e.g., cross-component function pointers) and can be efficient assuming only one additional piece of processor support: an efficient instruction for clearing a range of memory.
- We present a novel step-indexed Kripke logical relation for reasoning about programs on the capability machine. It is an untyped logical relation, inspired by previous work on object capabilities [11]. We prove an analogue of the

standard fundamental theorem of logical relations—to the best of our knowledge, our theorem is the most general and powerful formulation of the formal guarantees offered by a capability machine (a form of capability safety [11,12]), including the specific guarantees offered for local capabilities. It is very general and not tied to our calling convention or a specific way of using the system's capabilities. We are the first to apply these techniques for reasoning about capability machines and we believe they will prove useful for many other purposes than our calling convention.

- We introduce two novel technical ideas in the unary, step-indexed Kripke logical relation used to formulate the above theorem: the use of a *single* orthogonal closure (rather than the earlier used biorthogonal closure) and a variant of Dreyer et al. [13]'s public and private future worlds [13] to express the special nature of local capabilities. The logical relation and the fundamental theorem expressing capability safety are presented in Sect. 4.
- We demonstrate our results by applying them to challenging examples, specifically constructed to demonstrate local-state encapsulation and control-flow correctness guarantees in the presence of cross-component function pointers (Sect. 5). The examples demonstrate both the power of our formulation of capability safety and our calling convention.

For reasons of space, some details and all proofs have been omitted; please refer to the technical appendix [14] for those.

2   A Capability Machine with Local Capabilities

In this paper, we work with a formal capability machine with all the characteristics of real capability machines, as well as local capabilities much like CHERI's. Otherwise, it is kept as simple as possible. It is inspired by both the M-Machine [6] and CHERI [9]. To avoid uninteresting details, we assume an infinite address space and unbounded integers.

We define the syntax of our capability machine in Fig. 1. We assume an infinite set of addresses Addr and define machine words as either integers or capabilities of the form $((perm, g), base, end, a)$. Such a capability represents the authority to execute permissions $perm$ on the memory range $[base, end]$, together with a current address a and a locality tag g indicating whether the capability is global or local. There is no notion of pointers other than capabilities, so we will use the terms interchangeably. The available permissions and their ordering are depicted in Fig. 3: the permissions include null permission (O), readonly (RO), read/write (RW), read/execute (RX) and read/write/execute (RWX) permissions. Additionally, there are three special permissions: read/write-local (RWL), read/write-local/execute (RWLX) and enter (E), which we will explain below.

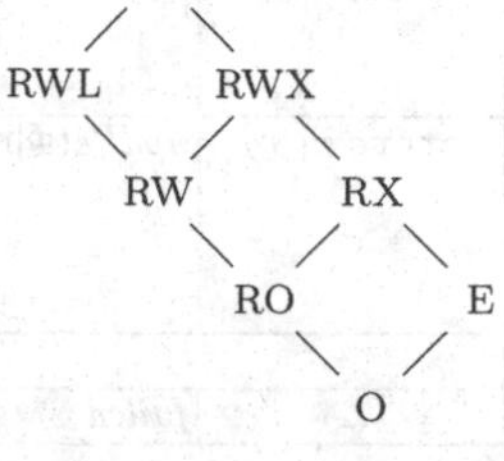

Fig. 3.   Permission hierarchy

$$a \in \text{Addr} \overset{\text{def}}{=} \mathbb{N}$$

$$w \in \text{Word} \overset{\text{def}}{=} \mathbb{Z} + \text{Cap}$$

$$perm \in \text{Perm} ::= \text{O} \mid \text{RO} \mid \text{RW} \mid \text{RWL} \mid$$
$$\text{RX} \mid \text{E} \mid \text{RWX} \mid \text{RWLX}$$

$$g \in \text{Global} ::= \text{global} \mid \text{local}$$
$$\text{Conf} ::= \text{ExecConf} + \{failed\} + \{halted\} \times \text{Mem}$$
$$\text{Cap} ::= \{((perm, g), b, e, a) \mid b, a \in \text{Addr}, e \in \text{Addr} \cup \{\infty\}\}$$

$$r \in \text{RegName} ::= \text{pc} \mid r_0 \mid r_1 \mid \ldots$$

$$reg \in \text{Reg} \overset{\text{def}}{=} \text{RegName} \to \text{Word}$$

$$m \in \text{Mem} \overset{\text{def}}{=} \text{Addr} \to \text{Word}$$

$$\Phi \in \text{ExecConf} \overset{\text{def}}{=} \text{Reg} \times \text{Mem}$$

$$ms \in \text{MemSeg} ::= \text{Addr} \rightharpoonup \text{Word}$$

$$r \in \mathbb{Z} + \text{RegName}$$
$$i ::= \text{jmp } r \mid \text{jnz } r \ r \mid \text{move } r \ r \mid \text{load } r \ r \mid \text{store } r \ r \mid \text{plus } r \ r \ r \mid \text{minus } r \ r \ r \mid$$
$$\text{lt } r \ r \ r \mid \text{lea } r \ r \mid \text{restrict } r \ r \mid \text{subseg } r \ r \ r \mid \text{isptr } r \ r \mid \text{getl } r \ r \mid$$
$$\text{getp } r \ r \mid \text{getb } r \ r \mid \text{gete } r \ r \mid \text{geta } r \ r \mid \text{fail} \mid \text{halt}$$

Fig. 1. The syntax of our capability machine assembly language.

$$\Phi \to \begin{cases} [\![decode(n)]\!] (\Phi) & \text{if } \Phi.\text{reg}(\text{pc}) = ((perm, g), b, e, a) \text{ and } b \le a \le e \\ & \text{and } perm \in \{\text{RX}, \text{RWX}, \text{RWLX}\} \text{ and } \Phi.\text{mem}(a) = n \\ failed & \text{otherwise} \end{cases}$$

$$updPc(\Phi) = \begin{cases} \Phi[\text{reg.pc} \mapsto newPc] & \text{if } \Phi.\text{reg}(\text{pc}) = ((perm, g), b, e, a) \\ & \text{and } newPc = ((perm, g), b, e, a+1) \\ failed & \text{otherwise} \end{cases}$$

i	$[\![i]\!] (\Phi)$	Conditions
fail	$failed$	
halt	$(halted, \Phi.\text{mem})$	
move r_1 r_2	$updPc(\Phi[\text{reg.}r_1 \mapsto w])$	$r_2 \in \text{Reg} \Rightarrow w = \Phi.\text{reg}(r_2)$ and $r_2 \in \mathbb{Z} \Rightarrow w = r_2$
load r_1 r_2	$updPc(\Phi[\text{reg.}r_1 \mapsto w])$	$\Phi.\text{reg}(r_2) = ((perm, g), b, e, a)$ and $w = \Phi.\text{mem}(a)$ and $b \le a \le e$ and $perm \in \{\text{RWX}, \text{RWLX}, \text{RX}, \text{RW}, \text{RWL}, \text{RO}\}$
restrict r_1 r_2	$updPc(\Phi[\text{reg.}r_1 \mapsto w])$	$\Phi.\text{reg}(r_2) = ((perm, g), b, e, a)$ and $(perm', g') = decodePermPair(\Phi.\text{reg}(r_2))$ and $(perm', g') \sqsubseteq (perm, g)$ and $w = ((perm', g'), b, e, a)$
geta r_1 r_2	$updPc(\Phi[\text{reg.}r_1 \mapsto a])$	$\Phi.\text{reg}(r_2) = ((\_,\_), \_, \_, a)$
jmp r	$\Phi[\text{reg.pc} \mapsto newPc]$	if $\Phi.\text{reg}(r) = ((\text{E}, g), b, e, a)$, then $newPc = ((\text{RX}, g), b, e, a)$ otherwise $newPc = \Phi.\text{reg}(r)$
store r_1 r_2	$updPc(\Phi[\text{mem.}a \mapsto w])$	$\Phi.\text{reg}(r_1) = ((perm, g), b, e, a)$ and $perm \in \{\text{RWX}, \text{RWLX}, \text{RW}, \text{RWL}\}$ and $b \le a \le e$ and $w = \Phi.\text{reg}(r_2)$ and if $w = ((\_, \text{local}), \_, \_, \_)$, then $perm \in \{\text{RWLX}, \text{RWL}\}$
	$\ldots$	
$-$	$failed$	otherwise

Fig. 2. An excerpt from the operational semantics.

We assume a finite set of register names RegName. We define register files *reg* and memories *ms* as functions mapping register names resp. addresses to words. The state of the entire machine is represented as a configuration that is either a running state $\Phi \in \text{ExecConf}$ containing a memory and a register file, or a failed or halted state, where the latter keeps hold of the final state of memory.

The machine's instruction set is rather basic. Instructions i include relatively standard jump (jmp), conditional jump (jnz) and move (move, copies words between registers) instructions. Also familiar are load and store instructions for reading from and writing to memory (load and store) and arithmetic addition operators (lt (less than), plus and minus, operating only on numbers). There are three instructions for modifying capabilities: lea (modifies the current address), restrict (modifies the permission and local/global tag) and subseg (modifies the range of a capability). Importantly, these instructions take care that the resulting capability always carries less authority than the original (e.g. restrict will only weaken a permission). Finally, the instruction isptr tests whether a word is a capability or a number and instructions getp, getl, getb, gete and geta provide access to a capability's permissions, local/global tag, base, end and current address, respectively.

Figure 2 shows an excerpt of the operational semantics for a few representative instructions. Essentially, a configuration Φ either decodes and executes the instruction at Φ.reg(pc) if it is executable and its address is in the valid range or otherwise fails. The table in the figure shows for instructions i the result of executing them in configuration Φ. fail and halt obviously fail and halt respectively. move simply modifies the register file as requested and updates the pc to the next instruction using the meta-function $updPc$.

The load instruction loads the contents of the requested memory location into a register, but only if the capability has appropriate authority (i.e. read permission and an appropriate range). restrict updates a capability's permissions and global/local tag in the register file, but only if the new permissions are weaker than the original. It also never turns local capabilities into global ones. geta queries the current address of a capability and stores it in a register.

The jmp instruction updates the program counter to a requested location, but it is complicated by the presence of *enter capabilities*, modeled after the M-Machine's [6]. Enter capabilities cannot be used to read, write or execute and their address and range cannot be modified. They can only be used to jump to, but when that happens, their permission changes to RX. They can be used to represent a kind of closures: an opaque package containing a piece of code together with local encapsulated state. Such a package can be built as an enter capability $c = ((\text{E}, g), b, e, a)$ where the range $[b, a - 1]$ contains local state (data or capabilities) and $[a, e]$ contains instructions. The package is opaque to an adversary holding c but when c is jumped to, the instructions can start executing and have access to the local data through the updated version of c that is then in pc.

Finally, the store instruction updates the memory to the requested value if the capability has write authority for the requested location. However, the instruction is complicated by the presence of *local capabilities*, modeled after the ones in the CHERI processor [9]. Basically, local capabilities are special in that they can only be kept in registers, i.e. they cannot be stored to memory. This means that local capabilities can be *temporarily* given to an adversary, for the duration of an invocation: if we take care to clear the capability from the register file after control is passed back to us, they will not have been able to store the capability. However, there is one exception to the rule above: local capabilities can be stored to memory for which we have a capability with write-local authority (i.e. permission RWL or RWLX). This is intended to accommodate a stack, where register contents can be stored, including local capabilities. As long as all capabilities with write-local authority are themselves local and the stack is cleared after control is passed back by the adversary, we will see that this does not break the intended behavior of local capabilities.

We point out that our local capabilities capture only a part of the semantics of local capabilities in CHERI. Specifically, in addition to the above, CHERI's default implementation of the CCall exception handler forbids local capabilities from being passed across module boundaries. Such a restriction fundamentally breaks our calling convention, since we pass around local return pointers and stack capabilities. However, CHERI's CCall is not implemented in hardware, but in software, precisely to allow experimenting with alternative models like ours.

In order to have a reasonably realistic system, we use a simple model of linking where a program has access to a linking table that contains capabilities for other programs. We also assume malloc to be part of the trusted computing base satisfying a certain specification. Malloc and linking tables are described further in the next section, but we refer to the technical appendix [14] for full details.

3   Stack and Return Pointer Management Using Local Capabilities

One of the contributions in this paper is a demonstration that local capabilities on a capability machine support a calling convention that enforces control-flow correctness in a way that is provably watertight, potentially efficient, does not rely on a trusted central stack manager and supports higher-order interfaces to an adversary, where an adversary is just some unknown piece of code. In this section, we explain this convention's high-level approach, the security measures to be taken in a number of situations (motivating each separately with a summary table at the end). After that, we define a number of reusable macro-instructions that can be used to conveniently apply the proposed convention in subsequent examples.

The basic idea of our approach is simple: we stick to a single, rather standard, C stack and register-passed stack and return pointers, much like a standard C calling convention. However, to prevent various ways of misusing this basic scheme, we put local capabilities to work and take a number of not-always-obvious safety measures. The safety measures are presented in terms of what *we* need to do to protect ourselves against an *adversary*, but this is only for presentation purposes as our code assumes no special status on the machine. In fact, an adversary can apply the same safety measures to protect themselves against us. In the next paragraphs, we will explain the issues to be considered in all the relevant situations: when (1) starting our program, (2) returning to the adversary, (3) invoking the adversary, (4) returning from the adversary, (5) invoking an adversary callback and (6) having a callback invoked by the adversary.

Program Start-Up. We assume that the language runtime initializes the memory as follows: a contiguous array of memory is reserved for the stack, for which we receive a stack pointer in a special register r_{stk}. We stress that the stack is not built-in, but merely an abstraction we put on this piece of the memory. The stack pointer is local and has RWLX permission. Note that this means that we will be placing and executing instructions on the stack. Crucially, the stack is the only part of memory for which the runtime (including malloc, loading, linking) will ever provide RWLX or RWL capabilities. Additionally, our examples typically also assume some memory to store instructions or static data. Another part of memory (called the heap) is initially governed by malloc and at program start-up, no other code has capabilities for this memory. Malloc hands out RWX capabilities for allocated regions as requested (no RWLX or RWL permissions). For simplicity, we assume that memory allocated through malloc cannot be freed.

Returning to the Adversary. Perhaps the simplest situation is returning to the adversary after they invoked our code. In this case, we have received a return pointer from them, and we just need to jump to it as usual. An obvious security measure to take care of is properly clearing the non-return-value registers before we jump (since they may contain data or capabilities that the adversary should not get access to). Additionally, we may have used the stack for various purposes (register spilling, storing local state when invoking other functions etc.), so we also need to clear that data before returning to the adversary.

However, if we are returning from a function that has itself invoked adversary code, then clearing the used part of the stack is not enough. The *unused* part of the stack may also contain data and capabilities, left there by the adversary, including local capabilities since the stack is write-local. As we will see later, we rely on the fact that the adversary cannot keep hold of local capabilities when they pass control to the trusted code and receive control back. In this case, the adversary could use the unused part of the stack to store local pointers and load them from there after they get control back. To prevent this, we need to clear (i.e. overwrite with zeros) the entire part of the stack that the adversary has had access to, not just the parts that we have used ourselves. Since we may be talking about a large part of memory, this requirement is the most problematic aspect of our calling convention for performance, but see Sect. 6 for how this might be mitigated.

Invoking the Adversary. A slightly more complex case is invoking the adversary. As above, we clear all the non-argument registers, as well as the part of the stack that we are not using (because, as above, it may contain local capabilities from previously executed code that the adversary could exploit in the same way). We leave a copy of the stack pointer in r_{stk}, but only after we have used the subseg instruction to shrink its authority to the part that we are not using ourselves.

In one of the registers, we also provide a return pointer, which must be a local capability. If it were global, the adversary would be able to store away the return pointer in a global data structure (i.e. there exists a global capability for it), and jump to it later, in circumstances where this should not be possible. For example, they could store the return pointer, legally jump to it a first time, wait to be invoked again and then jump to the old return pointer a second time, instead of the new return pointer received for the second invocation. Similarly, they could store the return pointer, invoke a function in our code, wait for us to invoke them again and then jump to the old return pointer rather than the new one, received for the second invocation. By making the return pointer local, we prevent such attacks: the adversary can only store local capabilities through write-local capabilities, which means (because of our assumptions above): on the stack. Since the stack pointer itself is also local, it can also only be stored on the stack. Because we clear the part of the stack that the adversary has had access to before we pass control back, there is no way for them to recover either of these local capabilities.

Note that storing stack pointers for use during future invocations would also be dangerous in itself, i.e. not just because it can be used to store return pointers. Imagine the adversary stores their stack pointer, invokes trusted code that uses part of the stack to store private data and then invokes the adversary again with a stack pointer restricted to exclude the part containing the private data. If the adversary had a way of keeping hold of their old stack pointer, it could access the private data stored there by the trusted code and break local-state encapsulation.

Returning from the Adversary. So return pointers must be passed as local capabilities. But what should their permissions be, what memory should they point to and what should that memory (the activation record) contain? Let us answer the last question first by considering what should happen when the adversary jumps to a return pointer. In that case, the program counter should be restored to the instruction after the jump to the adversary, so the activation record should store this old program counter. Additionally, the stack pointer should also be restored to its original value. Since the adversary has a more restricted authority over the stack than the code making the call, we cannot hope to reconstruct the original stack pointer from the stack pointer owned by the adversary. Instead, it should be stored as part of the activation record.

Clearly, neither of these capabilities should be accessible by the adversary. In other words, the return pointer provided to the adversary must be a capability that they can jump to but not read from, i.e. an enter capability. To make this work, we construct the activation record as depicted in Fig. 4. The E return pointer has authority over the entire activation record (containing the previous return and stack pointer), and its current address points to a number of restore instructions in the record, so that upon invocation, these instructions are executed and can load the old stack pointer and program counter back into the register file. As the return pointer is an enter pointer, the adversary cannot get

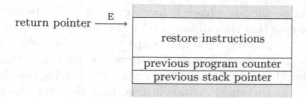

return pointer $\xrightarrow{\quad E \quad}$

restore instructions
previous program counter
previous stack pointer

Fig. 4. Structure of an activation record

hold of the activation record's contents, but after invocation, its permission is updated to RX, so the contents become available to the restore instructions.

The final question that remains is: where should we store this activation record? The attentive reader may already see that there is only one possibility: since the activation record contains the old stack pointer, which is local, the activation record can only be constructed in a part of memory where we have write-local access, i.e. on the stack. Note that this means we will be placing and executing instructions on the stack, i.e. it will not just contain code pointers and data. This means that our calling convention should be combined with protection against stack smashing attacks (i.e. buffer overflows on the stack overwriting activation records' contents). Luckily, the capability machine's fine-grained memory protection should make it reasonably easy for a compiler to implement such protection, by making sure that only appropriately bounded versions of the stack pointer are made available to source language code.

Invoking an Adversary Callback. If we have a higher-order interface to the adversary, we may need to invoke an adversary callback. In this case, not so much changes with respect to the situation where we invoke static adversary code. The adversary can provide a callback as a capability for us to jump to, either an E-capability if they want to protect themselves from us or just an RX capability if they are not worried about that. However, there is one scenario that we need to prevent: if they construct the callback capability to point into the stack, it may contain local capabilities that they should not have access to upon invocation of the callback. As before, this includes return and stack pointers from previous stack frames that they may be trying to illegally use inside the callback.

To prevent this, we only accept callbacks from the adversary in the form of global capabilities, which we dynamically check before invoking them (and we fail otherwise). This should not be an overly strict requirement: our own callbacks do not contain local data themselves, so there should be no need for the adversary to construct callbacks on the stack.[1]

Having a Callback Invoked by the Adversary. The above leaves us with perhaps the hardest scenario: how to provide a callback to the adversary. The

---

[1] Note that it does prevent a legitimate but non-essential scenario where the adversary wants to give us temporary access to a callback not allocated on the stack.

basic idea is that we allocate a block of memory using malloc that we fill with the capabilities and data that the callback needs, as well as some prelude instructions that load the data into registers and jumps to the right code. Note that this implies that no local capabilities can be stored as part of a closure. We can then provide the adversary with an enter-capability covering the allocated block and pointing to the contained prelude instructions. However, the question that remains in this setup is: from where do we get a stack pointer when the callback is invoked?

Our answer is that the adversary should provide it to us, just as we provide them with a stack pointer when we invoke their code. However, it is important that we do not just accept any capability as a stack pointer but check that it is safe to use. Specifically, we check that it is indeed an RWLX capability. Without this check, an adversary could potentially get control over our local stack frame during a subsequent callback by passing us a local RWX capability to a global data structure instead of a proper stack pointer and a global callback for our callback to invoke. If our local state contains no local capabilities, then, otherwise following our calling convention, the callback would not fail and the adversary could use a stored capability for the global data structure to access our local state. To prevent this from happening, we need to make sure the stack capability carries RWLX authority, since the system wide assumption then tells us that the adversary cannot have global capabilities to our local stack.

Calling Convention. With the security measures introduced and motivated, let us summarize our proposed calling convention: *At program start-up* A local RWLX stack pointer resides in register r_{stk}. No global write-local capabilities. *Before returning to the adversary* Clear non-return-value registers. Clear the part of the stack we had access to (not just the part we used). *Before invoking the adversary* Push activation record to the stack. Create return pointer as local E-capability to the instructions in the record. Restrict the stack capability to the unused part and clear it. Clear non-argument registers. *Before invoking an adversary callback* Make sure callback is global. *When invoked by an adversary* Make sure received stack pointer has permission RWLX.

Reusable Macro Instructions. We define a number of reusable macros capturing the calling convention and other conveniences. All macros that use the stack assume a stack pointer in register r_{stk}. The macro `fetch` r *name* fetches the capability related to *name* from the linking table and stores it in register r. The macros `push` r and `pop` r add and remove elements from the stack. The macro `prepstk` r is used when a callback is invoked by the adversary and prepares the received stack pointer by checking that it has permission RWLX. The macro `scall` $r(\overline{r_{args}}, \overline{r_{priv}})$ jumps to the capability in register r in the manner described above. That is, it pushes local state (the contents of registers $\overline{r_{priv}}$) and the activation record (return code, return pointer, stack pointer) to the stack, creates an E return pointer, restricts the stack pointer, clears the unused part of the stack, clears the necessary registers and jumps to r. Upon return, the private state is restored. The macro `mclear` r clears all the memory the capability in register r has authority over. The macro `rclear` *regSet* clears all the registers in *regSet*. The macro `reqglob` r checks whether the word in register r is a global capability. The macro `crtcls` $\overline{(x_i, r_i)}$ r allocates a closure where r points to the closure's code and a new environment is allocated (using malloc) where the contents of $\overline{r_i}$ is stored. In the code referred to by r, an implicit fetch happens when an instruction refers to x_i.

The technical appendix [14] contains detailed descriptions of all the macros.

4 Logical Relation

In this section, we formalize the guarantees provided by the capability machine, including the specific guarantees for local capabilities, by means of a step-indexed Kripke logical relation with recursively defined worlds. We use the logical relation in the following section to show local-state encapsulation and control-flow integrity properties for challenging example programs.

4.1 Worlds

A world is a finite map from region names, modeled as natural numbers, to regions that each correspond to an invariant of part of the memory. We have three types of regions: *permanent*, *temporary*, and *revoked*. Each permanent and temporary region contains a state transition system, with public and private transitions, to describe how the invariants are allowed to change over time. In other words, they are protocols for the region's memory. These are similar to what has been used in logical relations for high-level languages [11,13,15]. Protocols imposed by permanent regions stay in place indefinitely. Any capability, local or global, can depend on these protocols. Protocols imposed by temporary regions can be revoked in private future worlds. Doing this may break the safety of local capabilities but not global ones. This means that local capabilities can safely depend on the protocols imposed by temporary regions, but global capabilities cannot, since a global capability may outlive a temporary region that is revoked. This is illustrated in Fig. 5.

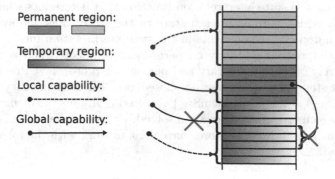

Fig. 5. The relation between local/global capabilities and temporary/permanent regions. The colored fields are regions governing parts of memory. Global capabilities cannot depend on temporary regions.

For technical reasons, we do not actually remove a revoked temporary region from the world, but we turn it into a special revoked region that exists for this purpose. Such a revoked region contains no state transition system and puts no requirements on the memory. It simply serves as a mask for a revoked temporary region. Masking a region like this goes back to earlier work of Ahmed [16] and was also used by Birkedal et al. [17].

Regions are used to define safe memory segments, but this set may itself be world-dependent. In other words, our worlds are defined recursively. Recursive worlds are common in Kripke models and the following lemma uses the method of Birkedal and Bizjak [18]; Birkedal et al. [19] for constructing them. The formulation of the lemma is technical, so we recommend that non-expert readers ignore the technicalities and accept that there exists a set of worlds Wor and two relations $\sqsupseteq^{priv}$ and $\sqsupseteq^{pub}$ satisfying the (recursive) equations in the theorem (where the $\blacktriangleright$ operator can be safely ignored).

Theorem 1. *There exists a c.o.f.e. (complete ordered family of equivalences)* Wor *and preorders* $\sqsupseteq^{priv}$ *and* $\sqsupseteq^{pub}$ *such that* (Wor, $\sqsupseteq^{priv}$) *and* (Wor, $\sqsupseteq^{pub}$) *are preordered c.o.f.e.'s, and there exists an isomorphism* ξ *such that*

$$\xi : \text{Wor} \cong \blacktriangleright(\mathbb{N} \xrightarrow{fin} \text{Region})$$

$$\text{Region} = \{\text{revoked}\} \uplus$$
$$\{\text{temp}\} \times \text{State} \times \text{Rels} \times (\text{State} \to (\text{Wor} \xrightarrow[\sqsupseteq^{pub}]{mon, \ ne} \text{UPred(MemSeg)}))\uplus$$
$$\{\text{perm}\} \times \text{State} \times \text{Rels} \times (\text{State} \to (\text{Wor} \xrightarrow[\sqsupseteq^{priv}]{mon, \ ne} \text{UPred(MemSeg)}))$$

and for $W, W' \in$ Wor.
$$W' \sqsupseteq^{priv} W \Leftrightarrow \xi(W') \sqsupseteq^{priv} \xi(W)$$
$$W' \sqsupseteq^{pub} W \Leftrightarrow \xi(W') \sqsupseteq^{pub} \xi(W)$$

In the above theorem, State $\times$ Rels corresponds to the aforementioned state transition system where Rels contains pairs of relations corresponding to the public and private transitions, and State is an unspecified set that we assume to contain at least the states we use in this paper. The last part of the temporary and permanent regions is a state interpretation function that determines what memory segments the region permits in each state of the state transition system. The different monotonicity requirements in the two interpretation functions reflects how permanent regions rely only on permanent protocols whereas temporary regions can rely on both temporary and permanent protocols. UPred(MemSeg) is the set of step-indexed, downwards closed predicates on memory segments: UPred(MemSeg) = $\{A \subseteq \mathbb{N} \times \text{MemSeg} \mid \forall(n, ms) \in A. \forall m \leq n. (m, ms) \in A\}$.

With the recursive domain equation solved, we could take Wor as our notion of worlds, but it is technically more convenient to work with the following definition instead:

$$\text{World} = \mathbb{N} \xrightarrow{fin} \text{Region}$$

Future Worlds. The future world relations model how memory may evolve over time. The *public future world* $W' \sqsupseteq^{pub} W$ requires that $\text{dom}(W') \supseteq \text{dom}(W)$ and $\forall r \in \text{dom}(W). W'(r) \sqsupseteq^{pub} W(r)$. That is, in a public future world, new regions may have been allocated, and existing regions may have evolved according to the public future region relation (defined below). The *private future world* relation $W' \sqsupseteq^{priv} W$ is defined similarly, using a private future region relation. The *public future* region relation is the simplest. It satisfies the following properties:

$$\frac{(s, s') \in \phi_{pub}}{(v, s', \phi_{pub}, \phi, H) \sqsupseteq^{pub} (v, s, \phi_{pub}, \phi, H)} \qquad \frac{(\text{temp}, s, \phi_{pub}, \phi, H) \in \text{Region}}{(\text{temp}, s, \phi_{pub}, \phi, H) \sqsupseteq^{pub} \text{revoked}}$$

$$\frac{}{\text{revoked} \sqsupseteq^{pub} \text{revoked}}$$

Both temporary and permanent regions are only allowed to transition according to the public part of their transition system. Additionally, revoked regions must either remain revoked or be replaced by a temporary region. This means that the public future world relations allows us to reinstate a region that has been revoked earlier. The *private future region* relation satisfies:

$$\frac{(s, s') \in \phi}{(v, s', \phi_{pub}, \phi, H) \sqsupseteq^{priv} (v, s, \phi_{pub}, \phi, H)} \qquad \frac{r \in \text{Region}}{r \sqsupseteq^{priv} (\text{temp}, s, \phi_{pub}, \phi, H)}$$

$$\frac{r \in \text{Region}}{r \sqsupseteq^{priv} \text{revoked}}$$

Here, revocation of temporary regions is allowed. In fact, temporary regions can be replaced by an arbitrary other region, not just the special revoked. Conversely, revoked regions may also be replaced by any other region. On the other hand, permanent regions cannot be masked away. They are only allowed to transition according to the private part of the transition system.

Notice that the public future region relation is a subset of the private future region relation.

World Satisfaction. A memory satisfies a world, written $ms :_n W$, if it can be partitioned into disjoint parts such that each part is accepted by an active (permanent or temporary) region. Revoked regions are not taken into account as their memory protocols are no longer in effect.

$$ms :_n W \quad \text{iff} \quad \begin{cases} \exists P : active(W) \to \text{MemSeg.} \ ms = \biguplus_{r \in active(W)} P(r) \ \text{and} \\ \forall r \in active(W). \\ \qquad \exists H, s. \ W(r) = (\_, s, \_, \_, H) \ \text{and} \ (n, P(r)) \in H(s)(\xi^{-1}(W)) \end{cases}$$

$\mathcal{O} : \text{World} \xrightarrow{ne} \text{UPred}(\text{Reg} \times \text{MemSeg})$

$$\mathcal{O}(W) \stackrel{def}{=} \left\{ (n, (reg, ms)) \;\middle|\; \begin{array}{l} \forall ms_f, mem', i \le n.\, (reg, ms \uplus ms_f) \to_i (halted, mem') \Rightarrow \\ \exists W' \sqsupseteq^{priv} W, ms_r, ms'. \\ \quad mem' = ms' \uplus ms_r \uplus ms_f \text{ and } ms' :_{n-i} W' \end{array} \right\}$$

$\mathcal{R} : \text{World} \xrightarrow[\sqsupseteq^{pub}]{mon,\, ne} \text{UPred}(\text{Reg})$

$$\mathcal{R}(W) \stackrel{def}{=} \{(n, reg) \mid \forall r \in \text{RegName} \setminus \{pc\}.\, (n, reg(r)) \in \mathcal{V}(W)\}$$

$\mathcal{E} : \text{World} \xrightarrow{ne} \text{UPred}(\text{Word})$

$$\mathcal{E}(W) \stackrel{def}{=} \left\{ (n, pc) \;\middle|\; \begin{array}{l} \forall n' \le n, (n', reg) \in \mathcal{R}(W), ms :_{n'} W. \\ (n', (reg[pc \mapsto pc], ms)) \in \mathcal{O}(W) \end{array} \right\}$$

$\mathcal{V} : \text{World} \xrightarrow[\sqsupseteq^{pub}]{mon,\, ne} \text{UPred}(\text{Word})$

$$\mathcal{V}(W) \stackrel{def}{=} \{(n, i) \mid i \in \mathbb{Z}\} \cup \{(n, ((\text{O}, g), b, e, a))\} \cup$$

$$\left\{ (n, ((\text{RW}, g), b, e, a)) \;\middle|\; \begin{array}{l} (n, (b, e)) \in readCond(g)(W) \text{ and} \\ (n, (b, e)) \in writeCond(\iota^{nwl}, g)(W) \end{array} \right\} \cup$$

$$\{(n, ((\text{E}, g), b, e, a)) \mid (n, (b, e, a)) \in enterCond(g)(W)\} \cup$$

$$\left\{ (n, ((\text{RWLX}, g), b, e, a)) \;\middle|\; \begin{array}{l} (n, (b, e)) \in readCond(g)(W) \text{ and} \\ (n, (b, e)) \in writeCond(\iota^{pwl}, g)(W) \text{ and} \\ (n, (\{\text{RWLX}, \text{RWX}, \text{RX}\}, b, e)) \in execCond(g)(W) \end{array} \right\}$$

$\cup \ldots$ *and so on for permissions* RO, RWL, RX, *and* RWX.

Fig. 6. The logical relation.

4.2   Logical Relation

The logical relation defines semantically when values, program counters, and configurations are capability safe. The definition is found in Figs. 6 and 7 and we provide some explanations in the following paragraphs. For space reasons, we omit some definitions and explain them only verbally, but precise definitions can be found in the technical appendix [14].

First, the *observation relation* $\mathcal{O}$ defines what configurations we consider safe. A configuration is safe with respect to a world, when the execution of said configuration does not break the memory protocols of the world. Roughly speaking, this means that when the execution of a configuration halts, then there is a private future world that the resulting memory satisfies. Notice that failing is considered safe behavior. In fact, the machine often resorts to failing when an unauthorized access is attempted, such as loading from a capability without read permission. This is similar to Devriese et al. [11]'s logical relation for an untyped language, but unlike typical logical relations for typed languages, which require that programs do not fail.

The *register-file relation* $\mathcal{R}$ defines safe register-files as those that contain safe words (i.e. words in $\mathcal{V}$) in all registers but pc. The *expression relation* $\mathcal{E}$ defines that a word is safe to use as a program counter if it can be plugged into

$$readCond(g)(W) = \left\{ (n,(b,e)) \; \middle| \; \begin{array}{l} \exists r \in localityReg(g,W). \\ \exists [b',e'] \supseteq [b,e].\, W(r) \overset{n}{\subsetneq} \iota^{pwl}_{b',e'} \end{array} \right\}$$

$$writeCond(\iota,g)(W) = \left\{ (n,(b,e)) \; \middle| \; \begin{array}{l} \exists r \in localityReg(g,W). \\ W(r) \text{ is address-stratified and} \\ \exists [b',e'] \supseteq [b,e].\, W(r) \overset{n-1}{\supseteq} \iota_{b',e'} \end{array} \right\}$$

$$execCond(g)(W) = \left\{ (n,(P,b,e)) \; \middle| \; \begin{array}{l} \forall n' < n, W' \sqsupseteq W, a \in [b,e], perm \in P. \\ (n',((perm,g),b,e,a)) \in \mathcal{E}(W') \end{array} \right\}$$

$$enterCond(g)(W) = \left\{ (n,(b,e,a)) \; \middle| \; \begin{array}{l} \forall n' < n.\, \forall W' \sqsupseteq W. \\ (n',((\text{RX},g),b,e,a)) \in \mathcal{E}(W') \end{array} \right\}$$

$$\text{where } g = \text{local} \Rightarrow \sqsupseteq = \sqsupseteq^{pub} \text{ and } g = \text{global} \Rightarrow \sqsupseteq = \sqsupseteq^{priv}$$

Fig. 7. Permission-based conditions

a safe register file (i.e. a register file in $\mathcal{R}$) and paired with a memory satisfying the world to become a safe configuration. Note that integers and non-executable capabilities (e.g. RO and E capabilities) are considered safe program counters because when they are plugged into a register file and paired with a memory, the execution will immediately fail, which is safe.

The *value relation* $\mathcal{V}$ defines when words are safe. We make the value relation as liberal as possible by considering what is the most we can allow an adversary to use a capability for without breaking the memory protocols. Non-capability data is always safe because it provides no authority. Capabilities give the authority to manipulate memory and potentially break memory protocols, so they need to satisfy certain conditions to be safe. In Fig. 7, we define such a condition for each kind of permission a capability can have.

For capabilities with read permission, the *readCond* ensures that it can only be used to read safe words, i.e. words in the value relation. To guarantee this, we require that the addressed memory is governed by a region $W(r)$ that imposes safety as a requirement on the values contained. This safety requirement is formulated in terms of a standard region $\iota^{pwl}_{b,e}$. The definition of that standard region is omitted for space reasons, but it simply requires all the words in the range $[b,e]$ to be safe, i.e. in the value relation. Requiring that $W(r) \overset{n}{\subsetneq} \iota^{pwl}_{b,e}$ means that $W(r)$ must accept only safe values like $\iota^{pwl}_{b,e}$, but can be even more restrictive if desired. The read condition also takes into account the locality of the capability because, generally speaking, global capabilities should only depend on permanent regions. Concretely, we use the function $localityReg(g,W)$, which projects out all active (non-revoked) regions when the locality g is local, but only the permanent regions when g is global. The definition of the standard region $\iota^{pwl}_{b,e}$ can be found in [14]; it makes use of the isomorphism from Theorem 1.

For a capability with write permission, *writeCond* must be satisfied for the capability's range of authority. An adversary can use such a capability to write any word they can get a hold of, and we can safely assume that they can only get a hold of safe words, so the region governing the relevant memory must allow any safe word to be written there. In order to make the logical relation as liberal as possible, we make this a lower bound of what the region may allow. For write capabilities, we also have to take into account the two flavours of write permissions: write and write-local. In the case of write-local capabilities, the region needs to allow (at least) any safe word to be written, but in the case of write capabilities, the capability cannot be used to write local capabilities, so the region only needs to allow safe non-local values. In the write condition, this is handled by parameterizing it with a region. For the write-local capabilities the write condition is applied with the standard region $\iota_{b,e}^{pwl}$ that we described previously. For the write capabilities we use a different standard region $\iota_{b,e}^{nwl}$ which requires that the words in $[b, e]$ are non-local and safe. As before, we use *localityReg* to pick an appropriate region based on the capability's locality. Finally, there is a technical requirement that the region must be *address-stratified*. Intuitively, this means that if a region accepts two memory segments, then it must also accept every memory segment "in between", that is every memory segment where each address contains a value from one of the two accepted memory segments. An interesting property of the write condition is that they prohibit global write-local capabilities which, as discussed in Sect. 3, is necessary for any safe use of local capabilities.

The conditions *enterCond* and *execCond* are very similar. Both require that the capability can be safely jumped to. However, executable capabilities can be updated to point anywhere in their range, so they must be safe as a program counter (in the $\mathcal{E}$-relation) no matter the current address. In contrast, enter capabilities are opaque and can only be used to jump to the address they point to. They also change permission when jumped to, so we require them to be safe as a program counter after the permission is changed to RX. Because the capabilities are not necessarily invoked immediately, this must be true in any future world, but it depends on the capability's locality which future worlds we consider. If it is global, then we require safety as a program counter in *private* future worlds (where temporary regions may be revoked). For local capabilities, it suffices to be safe in *public* future worlds, where temporary regions are still present.

In the technical appendix, we prove that safety of all values is preserved in public future worlds, and that safety of global values is also preserved in private future worlds:

Lemma 1 (Double monotonicity of value relation)

- *If $W' \sqsupseteq^{pub} W$ and $(n, w) \in \mathcal{V}(W)$, then $(n, w) \in \mathcal{V}(W')$.*
- *If $W' \sqsupseteq^{priv} W$ and $(n, w) \in \mathcal{V}(W)$ and $w = ((perm, \text{global}), b, e, a)$ (i.e. w is a global capability), then $(n, w) \in \mathcal{V}(W')$.*

4.3   Safety of the Capability Machine

With the logical relation defined, we can now state the fundamental theorem of our logical relation: a strong theorem that formalizes the guarantees offered by the capability machine. Essentially, it says a capability that only grants safe authority is capability safe as a program counter.

Theorem 2 (Fundamental theorem). *If one of the following holds:*

- $perm = \text{RX}$ *and* $(n, (b, e)) \in readCond(g)(W)$
- $perm = \text{RWX}$ *and* $(n, (b, e)) \in readCond(g)(W)$ *and*
  $(n, (b, e)) \in writeCond(\iota^{nwl}, g)(W)$
- $perm = \text{RWLX}$ *and* $(n, (b, e)) \in readCond(g)(W)$ *and*
  $(n, (b, e)) \in writeCond(\iota^{pwl}, g)(W),$

then $(n, ((perm, g), b, e, a)) \in \mathcal{E}(W)$

The permission based conditions of Theorem 2 make sure that the capability only provides safe authority in which case the capability must be in the $\mathcal{E}$ relation, i.e. it can safely be used as a program counter in an otherwise safe register-file.

The Fundamental Theorem can be understood as a general expression of the guarantees offered by the capability machine, an instance of a general property called capability safety [11, 12]. To understand this, consider that the theorem says the capability $((perm, g), b, e, a)$ is safe as a program counter, without any assumption about what instructions it actually points to (the only assumptions we have are about the read or write authority that it carries). As such, the theorem expresses the capability safety of the machine, which guarantees that *any* instruction is fine and will not be able to go beyond the authority of the values it has access to. We demonstrate this in Sect. 5 where Theorem 2 is used to reason about capabilities that point to arbitrary instructions. The relation between Theorem 2 and local-state encapsulation and control-flow correctness, will also be shown by example in Sect. 5 as the examples depend on these properties for correctness. See the technical appendix [14] for a detailed proof (by induction over the step-index n) of the theorem.

5   Examples

In this section, we demonstrate how our formalization of capability safety allows us to prove local-state encapsulation and control-flow correctness properties for challenging program examples. The security measures of Sect. 3 are deployed to ensure these properties. Since we are dealing with assembly language, there are many details to the formal treatment, and therefore we necessarily omit some details in the lemma statements. The examples may look deceivingly short, but it is because they use the macro instructions described in Sect. 3. The examples would be unintelligible without the macros, as each macro expands to multiple basic instructions. The interested reader can find all the technical details in the technical appendix [14].

```
f1: push 1                        f2: malloc r_l 1
    fetch r_1 adv                     store r_l 1
    scall r_1([],[])                 fetch r_1 adv
    pop r_1                          call r_1([],[r_l])
    assert r_1 1                     assert r_l 1
    halt                            halt
```

Fig. 8. Two example programs that rely on local-state encapsulation. f1 uses our stack-based calling convention. f2 does not rely on a stack.

5.1 Encapsulation of Local State

f1 and f2 in Fig. 8 demonstrate the capability machine's encapsulation of local state. They are very similar: both store some local state, call an untrusted piece of code (*adv*), and then test whether the local state is unchanged. They differ in the way they do this. Program f1 uses our stack-based calling convention (captured by scall) to call the adversary, so it can use the available stack to store its local state. On the other hand, f2 uses malloc to allocate memory for its local state and uses an activation-record based calling convention (described in the technical appendix) to run the adversarial code.

For both programs, we can prove that if they are linked with an adversary, *adv*, that is allowed to allocate memory but has no other capabilities, then the assertion will never fail during executing (see Lemmas 2 and 3 below). The two examples also illustrate the versatility of the logical relation. The logical relation is not specific to any calling convention, so we can use it to reason about both programs, even though they use different calling conventions.

In order to formulate results about f1 and f2, we need a way to observe whether the assertion fails. To this end, we assume they have access to a flag (an address in memory). If the assertion fails, then the flag is set to 1 and execution halts. The correctness lemma for f1 then states:

Lemma 2. *Let*

$$c_{adv} \stackrel{def}{=} ((\text{E}, \text{global}), \dots) \qquad c_{stk} \stackrel{def}{=} ((\text{RWLX}, \text{local}), \dots)$$
$$c_{f1} \stackrel{def}{=} ((\text{RWX}, \text{global}), \dots) \quad c_{link} \stackrel{def}{=} ((\text{RO}, \text{global}), \dots)$$
$$c_{malloc} \stackrel{def}{=} ((\text{E}, \text{global}), \dots) \qquad reg \in \text{Reg}$$
$$m \stackrel{def}{=} ms_{f1} \uplus ms_{flag} \uplus ms_{link} \uplus ms_{adv} \uplus ms_{malloc} \uplus ms_{stk} \uplus ms_{frame}$$

where each of the capabilities have an appropriate range of authority and pointer[2]. Furthermore

- ms_{f1} *contains* c_{link}, c_{flag} *and the code of f1*
- $ms_{flag}(flag) = 0$
- ms_{link} *contains* c_{adv} *and* c_{malloc}
- ms_{adv} *contains* c_{link} *and otherwise only instructions.*

If $(reg[\text{pc} \mapsto c_{f1}][r_{stk} \mapsto c_{stk}], m) \rightarrow^* (halted, m')$, *then* $m'(flag) = 0$

---

[2] These assumptions are kept intentionally vague for brevity. Full statements are in the technical appendix [14].

To prove Lemma 2, it suffices to show that the start configuration is safe (in the $\mathcal{O}$ relation) for a world with a permanent region that requires the assertion flag to be 0. By an anti-reduction lemma, it suffices to show that the configuration is safe after some reduction steps. We then use a general lemma for reasoning about scall, by which it suffices to show that (1) the configuration that scall will jump to is safe and (2) that the configuration just after scall is done cleaning up is safe. We use the Fundamental Theorem to reason about the unknown adversarial code, but notice that the adversary capability is an enter capability, which the Fundamental Theorem says nothing about. Luckily the enter capability becomes RX after the jump and then the Fundamental Theorem applies.

We have a similar lemma for f2:

Lemma 3. *Making similar assumptions about capabilities and linking as in Lemma 2 but assuming no stack pointer, if $(reg[\text{pc} \mapsto c_{f2}], m) \to^* (halted, m')$, then $m'(flag) = 0$.*

5.2   Well-Bracketed Control-Flow

Using the stack-based calling convention of scall, we get well-bracketed control-flow. To illustrate this, we look at two example programs f3 and g1 in Fig. 9.

In f3 there are two calls to an adversary and in order for the assertion in the middle to succeed, they need to be well-bracketed. If the adversary were able to store the return pointer from the first call and invoke it in the second call, then f3 would have 2 on top of its stack and the assertion would fail. However, the security measures in Sect. 3 prevent this attack: specifically, the return pointer is local, so it can only be stored on the stack, but the part of the stack that is accessible to the adversary is cleared before the second invocation. In fact, the following lemma shows that there are also no other attacks that can break well-bracketedness of this example, i.e. the assertion never fails. It is similar to the two previous lemmas:

Lemma 4. *Making similar assumptions about capabilities and linking as in Lemma 2 if $(reg[\text{pc} \mapsto c_{f3}][r_{stk} \mapsto c_{stk}], m) \to^* (halted, m')$, then $m'(flag) = 0$.*

The final example, g1 with f4, is a faithful translation of a tricky example known from the literature (known as the awkward example) [13,20]. It consists of two parts, g1 and f4. g1 is a closure generator that generates closures with one variable x set to 0 in its environment and f4 as the program (note we can omit some calling convention security measures because the stack is not used in the closure generator). f4 expects one argument, a callback. It sets x to 0 and calls the callback. When it returns, it sets x to 1 and calls the callback a second time. When it returns again, it asserts x is 1 and returns. This example is more complicated than the previous ones because it involves a closure invoked by the adversary and an adversary callback invoked by us. As explained in Sect. 3, this means that we need to check (1) that the stack pointer that the closure receives from the adversary has write-local permission and (2) that the adversary callback is global.

g1: malloc r_2 1
     store r_2 0
     move pc r_3
     lea r_3 *offset*
     crtcls $[(x, r_2)]$ r_3
     rclear RegName $\setminus \{$pc$, r_0, r_1\}$
     jmp r_0
f4: reqglob r_1
     prepstk r_{stk}
     (continues in next column)

(continued from previous column)
     store x 0
     scall $r_1([], [r_0, r_1, r_{env}])$
     store x 1
     scall $r_1([], [r_0, r_{env}])$
     load r_1 x
     assert r_1 1
     mclear r_{stk}
     rclear RegName $\setminus \{r_0,$ pc$\}$
     jmp r_0

f3: push 1
     fetch r_1 *adv*
     scall $r_1([], [r_1])$
     pop r_2
     assert r_2 1
     push 2
     scall $r_1([], [])$
     halt

Fig. 9. Two programs that rely on well-bracketedness of scalls to function correctly. *offset* is the offset to f4.

To illustrate how subtle this program is, consider how an adversary could try to make the assertion fail. In the second callback an adversary can get to the first callback by invoking the closure one more time. If there were any way for the adversary to transfer the return pointer from the point where it reinvokes the closure to where the closure reinvokes the callback, then the assertion could be made to fail. Similarly, if there were any way for the adversary to store a stack pointer or trick the trusted code into preserving it across an invocation, the assertion can likely be made to fail too. However, our calling convention prevents any of this from happening, as we prove in the following lemma.

Lemma 5. *Let*

$$c_{adv} \overset{def}{=} ((\text{RWX}, \text{global}), \dots) \quad c_{g1} \overset{def}{=} ((\text{E}, \text{global}), \dots)$$

and otherwise make assumptions about capabilities and linking similar to Lemma 2. Then if $(reg_0[\text{pc} \mapsto c_{adv}][r_{stk} \mapsto c_{stk}][r_1 \mapsto c_{g1}], m) \to^* (halted, m')$, then $m'(flag) = 0$.

As explained in Sect. 3, the macro-instruction reqglob r_1 checks that the callback is global, essentially to make sure it is not allocated on the stack where it might contain old stack pointers or return pointers. Otherwise, the encapsulation of our local stack frame could be broken. In the proof of Lemma 5, this requirement shows up because we invoke the callback in a world that is only a private future world of the one where we received the callback, precisely because we have invalidated the adversary's local state (particularly their old stack and return capabilities). The callback is still valid in this private future world, but only because we know that it is global.

In Lemma 5 the order of control has been inverted compared to the previous lemmas. In this lemma, the adversary assumes control first with a capability for the closure creator g1. Consequently, we need to check that all arguments are safe to use and that we clean up before returning in the end. The inversion of control poses an interesting challenge when it comes to reasoning about the adversary's local state during the execution of f4 and the callbacks where the adversary should not rely on the local state from before the call of f4. This is easily done by revoking all the temporary regions of the world given at the start of f4. However, when f4 returns, the adversary is again allowed to rely on its old local state so we need to guarantee that the local state is unchanged. This is important because the return pointer that f4 receives may be local, and the adversary is allowed to allocate the activation record on the stack (just like we do) so they can store and recover their old stack pointer after f4 returns. By utilizing the reinstation mechanism of the future world relation as well as our knowledge of the future worlds used, we can construct a world in which the adversary's invariants are preserved. The details of this and the proofs of the other lemmas are found in the technical appendix [14].

6 Discussion

Calling Convention

Formulating Control Flow Correctness. While we claim that our calling convention enforces control-flow correctness, we do not prove a general theorem that shows this, because it is not clear what such a theorem should look like. Formulations in terms of a control-flow graph, like the one by Abadi et al. [2], do not take into account temporal properties, like the well-bracketedness that Example g1 relies on. In fact, our examples show that our logical relation imply a stronger form of control-flow correctness than such formulations, although this is not made very explicit. As future work, we consider looking at a more explicit and useful way to formalize control-flow correctness. The idea would be to define a variant of our capability machine with call and return instructions and well-bracketed control flow built-in to the operational semantics, and then prove that compiling such code to our machine using our calling convention is fully abstract [21].

Performance and the Requirement for Stack Clearing. The additional security measures of the calling convention described in Sect. 3 impose an overhead compared to a calling convention without security guarantees. However, most of our security measures require only a few atomic checks or register clearings on boundary crossings between trusted code and adversary, which should produce an acceptable performance overhead. The only exception are the requirements for stack clearing that we have in two situations: when returning to the adversary and when invoking an adversary callback. As we have explained, we need to clear all of the stack that we are not using ourselves, not just the part that we have actually used. In other words, on every boundary cross between trusted code and adversary code, a potentially large region of memory must be cleared. We believe this is actually a common requirement for typical usage scenarios of local capabilities and capability machines like CHERI should consider to provide special support for this requirement, in the form of a highly-optimized instruction for erasing a large block of memory. Nevertheless, from a discussion with the designers of the CHERI capability machine, we gather that it is not immediately clear whether and how such a primitive could be implemented efficiently in the CHERI context.

Modularity. It is important that our calling convention is modular, i.e. we do not assume that our code is specially privileged w.r.t. the adversary, and they can apply the same measures to protect themselves from us as we do to protect ourselves from them. More concretely, the requirements we have on callbacks and return pointers received from the adversary are also satisfied by callbacks and return pointers that we pass to them. For example, our return pointers are local capabilities because they must point to memory where we can store the old stack pointer, but the adversary's return pointers are also allowed to be local. Adversary callbacks are required to be global but the callbacks we construct are allocated on the heap and also global.

Arguments and Local Capabilities. Local capabilities are a central part of the calling convention as they are used to construct stack and return pointers. The use of local capabilities for the calling convention unfortunately limits the extent to which local capabilities can be used for other things. Say we are using the calling convention and receive a local capability other than the stack and return pointer, then we need to be careful if we want to use it because it may be an alias to the stack pointer. That is, if we first push something to the stack and then write to the local capability, then we may be (tricked into) overwriting our own local state. The logical relation helps by telling us what we need to ascertain or check in such scenarios to guarantee safety and preserve our invariants, but such checks may be costly and it is not clear to us whether there are practical scenarios where this might be realistic.

We also need to be careful when we receive a capability from an adversary that we want to pass on to a different (instance of the) adversary. It turns out that the logical relation again tells us when this is safe. Namely, the logical relation says that we can only pass on safe arguments. For instance, when we receive a stack pointer from an adversary, then we may at some point want to pass on part of this stack pointer to, say, a callback. In order to do so, we need to make sure the stack pointer is safe which means that, if we have revoked temporary invariants, the stack must not directly or indirectly allow access to local values that we cannot guarantee safety of. When received from an adversary, we have to consider the contents of the stack unsafe, so before we pass it on, we have to clear it, or perform a dynamic safety analysis of the stack contents and anything it points to. Clearing everything is not always desirable and a dynamic safety analysis is hard to get right and potentially expensive.

In summary, the use of local capabilities for other things than stack and return pointers is likely only possible in very specific scenarios when using our calling convention. While this is unfortunate, it is not unheard of that processors have built-in constructs that are exclusively used for handling control flow, such as, for example, the call and return instructions that exist in some instruction sets.

Single Stack. A single stack is a good choice for the simple capability machine presented here, because it works well with higher-order functions. An alternative to a single stack would be to have a separate stack per component. The trouble with this approach is that, with multiple stacks and local stack pointers, it is not clear how components would retrieve their stack pointer upon invocation without compromising safety. A safe approach could be to have stack pointers stored by a central, trusted stack management component, but it is not clear how that could scale to large numbers of separate components. Handling large numbers of components is a requirement if we want to use capability machines to enforce encapsulation of, for example, every object in an object-oriented program or every closure in a functional program.

Logical Relation

Single Orthogonal Closure. The definitions of $\mathcal{E}$ and $\mathcal{V}$ in Fig. 6 apply a single orthogonal closure, a new variant of an existing pattern called biorthogonality. Biorthogonality is a pattern for defining logical relations [20, 22] in terms of an observation relation of safe configurations (like we do). The idea is to define safe evaluation contexts as the set of contexts that produce safe observations when plugging safe values and define safe terms as the set of terms that can be plugged into safe evaluation contexts to produce safe observations. This is an alternative to more direct definitions where safe terms are defined as terms that evaluate to safe values. An advantage of biorthogonality is that it scales better to languages with control effects like call/cc. Our definitions can be seen as a variant of biorthogonality, where we take only a single orthogonal closure: we do not define safe evaluation contexts but immediately define safe terms as those that produce safe observations when plugged with safe values. This is natural because we model arbitrary assembly code that does not necessarily respect a particular calling convention: return pointers are in principle values like all others and there is no reason to treat them specially in the logical relation.

Interestingly, Hur and Dreyer [23] also use a step-indexed, Kripke logical relation for an assembly language (for reasoning about correct compilation from ML to assembly), but because they only model non-adversarial code that treats return pointers according to a particular calling convention, they can use standard biorthogonality rather than a single orthogonal closure like us.

Public/Private Future Worlds. A novel aspect of our logical relation is how we model the temporary, revokable nature of local capabilities using public/private future worlds. The main insight is that this special nature generalizes that of the syntactically-enforced unstorable status of evaluation contexts in lambda calculi without control effects (of which well-bracketed control flow is a consequence). To reason about code that relies on this (particularly, the original awkward example), Dreyer et al. [13] (DNB) formally capture the special status of evaluation contexts using Kripke worlds with public and private future world relations. Essentially, they allow relatedness of evaluation contexts to be monotone with respect to a weaker future world relation (public) than relatedness of values, formalizing the idea that it is safe to make temporary internal state modifications (private world transitions, which invalidate the continuation, but not other values) while an expression is performing internal steps, as long as the code returns to a stable state (i.e. transitions to a public future world of the original) before returning. We generalize this idea to reason about local capabilities: validity of local capabilities is allowed to be monotone with respect to a weaker future-world relation than other values, which we can exploit to distinguish between state changes that are always safe (public future worlds) and changes that are only valid if we clear all local capabilities (private future worlds). Our future world relations are similar to DNB's (for example, our proof of the awkward example uses exactly the same state transition system), but they turn up in an entirely different place in the logical relation: rather than using public future worlds for the special syntactic category of evaluation contexts, they are used in the value relation depending on the locality of the capability at hand. Additionally, our worlds are a bit more complex because, to allow local memory capabilities and write-local capabilities, they can contain (revokable) temporary regions that are only monotonous w.r.t. public future worlds, while DNB's worlds are entirely permanent.

Local Capabilities in High-Level Languages. We point out that local capabilities are quite similar to a feature proposed for the high-level language Scala: Osvald et al. [24]'s second-class or local values. They are a kind of values that can be provided to other code for immediate use without allowing them to be stored in a closure or reference for later use. We believe reasoning about such values will require techniques similar to what we provide for local capabilities.

7   Related Work

Finally, we summarize how our work relates to previous work. We do not repeat the work we discussed in Sect. 6.

Capability machines originate with Dennis and Van Horn [7] and we refer to Levy [25] and Watson et al. [9] for an overview of previous work. The capability machine formalized in Sect. 2 is a simple but representative model, modeled mainly after the M-Machine [6] (the enter pointers resemble the M-Machine's) and CHERI [9,10] (the memory and local capabilities resemble CHERI's). The latter is a recent and relatively mature capability machine, which combines capabilities with a virtual memory approach, in the interest of backwards compatibility and gradual adoption. As discussed, our local capabilities can cross module boundaries, contrary to what is enforced by CHERI's default CCall implementation.

Plenty of other papers enforce well-bracketed control flow at a low level, but most are restricted to preventing particular types of attacks and enforce only partial correctness of control flow. This includes particularly the line of work on *control-flow integrity* [2]. Those use a quite different attacker model than us: they assume an attacker that is not able to execute code, but can overwrite arbitrary data at any time during execution (to model buffer overflows). By checking the address of every indirect jump and using memory access control to prevent overwriting code, this work enforces what they call control-flow integrity, formalized as the property that every jump will follow a legal path in the control-flow graph. As discussed in Sect. 6, such a property ignores temporal properties and seems hard to use for reasoning.

More closely related to our work are papers that use a trusted stack manager and some form of memory isolation to enforce control-flow correctness as part of a secure compilation result [26,27]. Our work differs from theirs in that we use a different form of low-level security primitive (a capability machine with local capabilities rather than a machine with a primitive notion of compartments) and we do not use a trusted stack manager, but a decentralized calling convention based on local capabilities. Also, both prove a secure compilation result from a high-level language, which clearly implies a general form of control-flow correctness, while we define a logical relation that can be used to reason about specific programs that rely on well-bracketed control flow.

Our logical relation is a unary, step-indexed Kripke logical relation with recursive worlds [16,18,20,28], closely related to the one used by Devriese et al. [11] to formulate capability safety in a high-level JavaScript-like lambda calculus. Our Fundamental Theorem is similar to theirs and expresses capability safety of the capability machine. Because we are not interested in externally observable side-effects (like console output or memory access traces), we do not require their notion of effect parametricity. Our logical relation uses several ideas from previous work, like Kripke worlds with regions containing state transition systems [15], public/private future worlds [13] (see Sect. 6 for a discussion), and biorthogonality [20,23,29].

Swasey et al. [30] have recently developed a *logic*, OCPL, for verification of object capability patterns. The logic is based on Iris [31–33], a state of the art higher-order concurrent separation logic and is formalized in Coq, building on the Iris Proof Mode for Coq [34]. OCPL gives a more abstract and modular way of proving capability safety for a lambda-calculus (with concurrency) compared to the earlier work by Devriese et al. [11].

El-Korashy also defined a formal model of a capability machine, namely CHERI, and uses it to prove a compartmentalization result [35] (not implying control-flow correctness). He also adapts control-flow integrity (see above) to the machine and shows soundness, seemingly without relying on capabilities.

Acknowledgements. This research was supported in part by the ModuRes Sapere Aude Advanced Grant from The Danish Council for Independent Research for the Natural Sciences (FNU). Dominique Devriese holds a Postdoctoral fellowship from the Research Foundation Flanders (FWO).

References

1. Wahbe, R., Lucco, S., Anderson, T.E., Graham, S.L.: Efficient software-based fault isolation. In: Symposium on Operating Systems Principles, pp. 203–216. ACM (1993)
2. Abadi, M., Budiu, M., Erlingsson, Ú., Ligatti, J.: Control-flow integrity. In: Conference on Computer and Communications Security, pp. 340–353. ACM (2005)
3. Morrisett, G., Walker, D., Crary, K., Glew, N.: From system F to typed assembly language. ACM Trans. Program. Lang. Syst. **21**(3), 527–568 (1999)
4. Lindholm, T., Yellin, F., Bracha, G., Buckley, A.: The Java Virtual Machine Specification. Pearson Education, London (2014)

5. Forrest, S., Somayaji, A., Ackley, D.H.: Building diverse computer systems. In: Hot Topics in Operating Systems, pp. 67–72, May 1997
6. Carter, N.P., Keckler, S.W., Dally, W.J.: Hardware support for fast capability-based addressing. In: Architectural Support for Programming Languages and Operating Systems, pp. 319–327. ACM (1994)
7. Dennis, J.B., Van Horn, E.C.: Programming semantics for multiprogrammed computations. Commun. ACM **9**(3), 143–155 (1966)
8. Shapiro, J.S., Smith, J.M., Farber, D.J.: EROS: a fast capability system. In: Symposium on Operating Systems Principles, SOSP 1999, pp. 170–185. ACM (1999)
9. Watson, R.N.M., Woodruff, J., Neumann, P.G., Moore, S.W., Anderson, J., Chisnall, D., Dave, N., Davis, B., Gudka, K., Laurie, B., Murdoch, S.J., Norton, R., Roe, M., Son, S., Vadera, M.: CHERI: a hybrid capability-system architecture for scalable software compartmentalization. In: IEEE Symposium on Security and Privacy, pp. 20–37 (2015)
10. Woodruff, J., Watson, R.N., Chisnall, D., Moore, S.W., Anderson, J., Davis, B., Laurie, B., Neumann, P.G., Norton, R., Roe, M.: The CHERI capability model: revisiting RISC in an age of risk. In: International Symposium on Computer Architecture, pp. 457–468. IEEE Press (2014)
11. Devriese, D., Birkedal, L., Piessens, F.: Reasoning about object capabilities using logical relations and effect parametricity. In: IEEE European Symposium on Security and Privacy. IEEE (2016)
12. Maffeis, S., Mitchell, J., Taly, A.: Object capabilities and isolation of untrusted web applications. In: S&P, pp. 125–140. IEEE (2010)
13. Dreyer, D., Neis, G., Birkedal, L.: The impact of higher-order state and control effects on local relational reasoning. J. Funct. Program. **22**(4–5), 477–528 (2012)
14. Skorstengaard, L., Devriese, D., Birkedal, L.: Reasoning about a machine with local capabilities: provably safe stack and return pointer management - technical appendix including proofs and details. Technical report, Department of Computer Science, Aarhus University (2018). https://cs.au.dk/~birke/papers/local-capabilities-conf-tr.pdf
15. Ahmed, A., Dreyer, D., Rossberg, A.: State-dependent representation independence. In: POPL, pp. 340–353. ACM (2009)
16. Ahmed, A.J.: Semantics of types for mutable state. Ph.D. thesis, Princeton University (2004)
17. Thamsborg, J., Birkedal, L.: A Kripke logical relation for effect-based program transformations. In: ICFP, pp. 445–456. ACM (2011)
18. Birkedal, L., Reus, B., Schwinghammer, J., Støvring, K., Thamsborg, J., Yang, H.: Step-indexed Kripke models over recursive worlds. In: POPL, pp. 119–132. ACM (2011)
19. Birkedal, L., Bizjak, A.: A Taste of Categorical Logic Tutorial Notes (2014). http://cs.au.dk/~birke/modures/tutorial/categorical-logic-tutorial-notes.pdf
20. Pitts, A.M., Stark, I.D.B.: Operational reasoning for functions with local state. In: Gordon, A.D., Pitts, A.M. (eds.) Higher Order Operational Techniques in Semantics, pp. 227–274. Cambridge University Press, New York (1998)
21. Abadi, M.: Protection in programming-language translations: mobile object systems. In: Demeyer, S., Bosch, J. (eds.) ECOOP 1998. LNCS, vol. 1543, p. 291. Springer, Heidelberg (1998). https://doi.org/10.1007/3-540-49255-0_70
22. Krivine, J.L.: Classical logic, storage operators and second-order lambda-calculus. Ann. Pure and Appl. Log. **68**(1), 53–78 (1994)

23. Hur, C.K., Dreyer, D.: A Kripke logical relation between ML and assembly. In: ACM SIGPLAN-SIGACT Symposium on Principles of Programming Languages, pp. 133–146. ACM (2011)
24. Osvald, L., Essertel, G., Wu, X., Alayón, L.I.G., Rompf, T.: Gentrification gone too far? Affordable 2nd-class values for fun and (co-)effect. In: Object-Oriented Programming, Systems, Languages, and Applications, pp. 234–251. ACM (2016)
25. Levy, H.M.: Capability-Based Computer Systems, vol. 12. Digital Press, Bedford (1984)
26. Patrignani, M., Devriese, D., Piessens, F.: On modular and fully-abstract compilation. In: Computer Security Foundations Symposium (CSF), pp. 17–30, June 2016
27. Juglaret, Y., Hritcu, C., Amorim, A.A.D., Eng, B., Pierce, B.C.: Beyond good and evil: formalizing the security guarantees of compartmentalizing compilation. In: Computer Security Foundations Symposium (CSF), pp. 45–60, June 2016
28. Appel, A.W., McAllester, D.: An indexed model of recursive types for foundational proof-carrying code. ACM Trans. Program. Lang. Syst. **23**(5), 657–683 (2001)
29. Benton, N., Hur, C.K.: Biorthogonality, step-indexing and compiler correctness. In: International Conference on Functional Programming, pp. 97–108. ACM (2009)
30. Swasey, D., Garg, D., Dreyer, D.: Robust and compositional verification of object capability patterns (2017, to appear)
31. Jung, R., Swasey, D., Sieczkowski, F., Svendsen, K., Turon, A., Birkedal, L., Dreyer, D.: Iris: monoids and invariants as an orthogonal basis for concurrent reasoning. In: POPL, pp. 637–650 (2015)
32. Jung, R., Krebbers, R., Birkedal, L., Dreyer, D.: Higher-order ghost state. In: ICFP, pp. 256–269 (2016)
33. Krebbers, R., Jung, R., Bizjak, A., Jourdan, J.-H., Dreyer, D., Birkedal, L.: The essence of higher-order concurrent separation logic. In: Yang, H. (ed.) ESOP 2017. LNCS, vol. 10201, pp. 696–723. Springer, Heidelberg (2017). https://doi.org/10.1007/978-3-662-54434-1_26
34. Krebbers, R., Timany, A., Birkedal, L.: Interactive proofs in higher-order concurrent separation logic. In: POPL (2017)
35. El-Korashy, A.: A formal model for capability machines: an illustrative case study towards secure compilation to CHERI. Master's thesis, Saarland University, September 2016

Modular Product Programs

Marco Eilers$^{(\boxtimes)}$ ⓘ, Peter Müller ⓘ, and Samuel Hitz

Department of Computer Science, ETH Zurich, Zurich, Switzerland
{marco.eilers,peter.mueller,samuel.hitz}@inf.ethz.ch

Abstract. Many interesting program properties like determinism or information flow security are hyperproperties, that is, they relate multiple executions of the same program. Hyperproperties can be verified using relational logics, but these logics require dedicated tool support and are difficult to automate. Alternatively, constructions such as self-composition represent multiple executions of a program by one product program, thereby reducing hyperproperties of the original program to trace properties of the product. However, existing constructions do not fully support procedure specifications, for instance, to derive the determinism of a caller from the determinism of a callee, making verification non-modular.

We present modular product programs, a novel kind of product program that permits hyperproperties in procedure specifications and, thus, can reason about calls modularly. We demonstrate its expressiveness by applying it to information flow security with advanced features such as declassification and termination-sensitivity. Modular product programs can be verified using off-the-shelf verifiers; we have implemented our approach to secure information flow using the Viper verification infrastructure.

1 Introduction

The past decades have seen significant progress in automated reasoning about program behavior. In the most common scenario, the goal is to prove trace properties of programs such as functional correctness or termination. However, important program properties such as information flow security, injectivity, and determinism cannot be expressed as properties of individual traces; these so-called *hyperproperties* relate different executions of the same program. For example, proving determinism of a program requires showing that any two executions from identical initial states will result in identical final states.

An important attribute of reasoning techniques about programs is *modularity*. A technique is modular if it allows reasoning about parts of a program in isolation, e.g., verifying each procedure separately and using only the *specifications* of other procedures. Modularity is vital for scalability and to verify libraries without knowing all of their clients. Fully modular reasoning about hyperproperties thus requires the ability to formulate *relational* specifications, which relate

A. Ahmed (Ed.): ESOP 2018, LNCS 10801, pp. 502–529, 2018.
https://doi.org/10.1007/978-3-319-89884-1_18

different executions of a procedure, and to apply those specifications where the procedure is called. As an example, the statement

```
if (x) then {y:=x} else {y:= call f(x)}
```

can be proved to be deterministic if f's relational specification guarantees that its result deterministically depends on its input.

Relational program logics [11,27,29] allow directly proving general hyperproperties, however, automating relational logics is difficult and requires building dedicated tools. Alternatively, self-composition [9] and product programs [6,7] reduce a hyperproperty to an ordinary trace property, thus making it possible to use off-the-shelf program verifiers for proving hyperproperties. Both approaches construct a new program that combines the behaviors of multiple runs of the original program. However, by the nature of their construction, neither approach supports modular verification based on relational specifications: Procedure calls in the original program will be duplicated, which means that there is no single program point at which a relational specification can be applied. For the aforementioned example, self-composition yields the following program:

```
if (x) then {y:=x} else {y:= call f(x)};
if (x') then {y':=x'} else {y':= call f(x')}
```

Determinism can now be verified by proving the trace property that identical values for x and x' in the initial state imply identical values for y and y' in the final state. However, such a proof cannot make use of a relational specification for procedure f (expressing that f is deterministic). Such a specification relates several executions of f, whereas each call in the self-composition belongs to a single execution. Instead, verification requires a *precise functional specification* of f, which *exactly* determines its result value in terms of the input. Verifying such precise functional specifications increases the verification effort and is at odds with data abstraction (for instance, a collection might not want to promise the exact iteration order); inferring them is beyond the state of the art for most procedures [28]. Existing product programs allow aligning or combining some statements and can thereby lift this requirement in some cases, but this requires manual effort during the construction, depends on the used specifications, and does not solve the problem in general.

In this paper, we present modular product programs, a novel kind of product programs that allows modular reasoning about hyperproperties. Modular product programs enable proving k-safety hyperproperties, i.e., hyperproperties that relate finite prefixes of k execution traces, for arbitrary values of k [12]. We achieve this via a transformation that, unlike existing products, does not duplicate loops or procedure calls, meaning that for any loop or call in the original program, there is exactly one statement in the k-product at which a relational specification can be applied. Like existing product programs, modular products can be reasoned about using off-the-shelf program verifiers.

We demonstrate the expressiveness of modular product programs by applying them to prove secure information flow, a 2-safety hyperproperty. We show

how modular products enable proving traditional non-interference using natural and concise information flow specifications, and how to extend our approach for proving the absence of timing or termination channels, and supporting declassification in an intuitive way.

To summarize, we make the following contributions:

- We introduce modular k-product programs, which enable modular proofs of arbitrary k-safety hyperproperties for sequential programs using off-the-shelf verifiers.
- We demonstrate the usefulness of modular product programs by applying them to secure information flow, with support for declassification and preventing different kinds of side channels.
- We implement our product-based approach for information flow verification in an automated verifier and show that our tool can automatically prove information flow security of challenging examples.

After giving an informal overview of our approach in Sect. 2 and introducing our programming and assertion language in Sect. 3, we formally define modular product programs in Sect. 4. We sketch a soundness proof in Sect. 5. Section 6 demonstrates how to apply modular products for proving secure information flow. We describe and evaluate our implementation in Sect. 7, discuss related work in Sect. 8, and conclude in Sect. 9.

2   Overview

In this section, we will illustrate the core concepts behind modular k-products on an example program. We will first show how modular products are constructed, and subsequently demonstrate how they allow using relational specifications to modularly prove hyperproperties.

2.1   Relational Specifications

Consider the example program in Fig. 1, which counts the number of female entries in a sequence of people. Now assume we want to prove that the program is deterministic, i.e., that its output state is completely determined by its input arguments. This can be expressed as a 2-safety hyperproperty which states that, for two terminating executions of the program with identical inputs, the outputs will be the same. This hyperproperty can be expressed by the *relational* (as opposed to *unary*) specification $\mathsf{main} : \overset{1}{\mathsf{people}} = \overset{2}{\mathsf{people}} \rightsquigarrow \overset{1}{\mathsf{count}} = \overset{2}{\mathsf{count}}$, where $\overset{i}{x}$ refers to the value of the variable x in the ith execution.

Intuitively, it is possible to prove this specification by giving is_female a precise functional specification like $\mathsf{is\_female} : true \rightsquigarrow \mathsf{res} = 1 - \mathsf{person}\ \mathbf{mod}\ 2$, meaning that is_female can be invoked in any state and that $\mathsf{res} = 1 - \mathsf{person}$ $\mathbf{mod}\ 2$ will hold if it returns. From this specification and an appropriate loop invariant, main can be shown to be deterministic. However, this specification

```
procedure main( people )              procedure is_female( person )
         returns ( count )                     returns ( res )
{                                     {
   i := 0;                               // gender encoded in first bit
   count := 0;                           gender := person mod 2;
   while ( i < | people |) {             if ( gender == 0 ) {
      current := people[ i ];               res := 1;
      f := is_female( current );         } else {
      count := count + f;                   res := 0;
      i := i + 1;                        }
   }                                  }
}
```

Fig. 1. Example program. The parameter people contains a sequence of integers that each encode attributes of a person; the main procedure counts the number of females in this sequence.

is unnecessarily strong. For proving determinism, it is irrelevant what exactly the final value of count is; it is only important that it is uniquely determined by the procedure's inputs. Proving hyperproperties using only unary specifications, however, critically depends on having exact specifications for every value returned by a called procedure, as well as all heap locations modified by it. Not only are such specifications difficult to infer and cumbersome to provide manually; this requirement also fundamentally removes the option of underspecifying program behavior, which is often desirable in practice. Because of these limitations, verification techniques that require precise functional specifications for proving hyperproperties often do not work well in practice, as observed by Terauchi and Aiken for the case of self-composition [28].

Proving determinism of the example program becomes much simpler if we are able to reason about two program executions at once. If both runs start with identical values for people then they will have identical values for people, i, and count when they reach the loop. Since the loop guard only depends on i and people, it will either be true for both executions or false for both. Assuming that is_female behaves deterministically, all three variables will again be equal in both executions at the end of the loop body. This means that the program establishes and preserves the relational loop invariant that people, i, and count have identical values in both executions, from which we can deduce the desired relational postcondition. Our modular product programs enable this modular and intuitive reasoning, as we explain next.

2.2 Modular Product Programs

Like other product programs, our modular k-product programs multiply the state space of the original program by creating k renamed versions of all original variables. However, unlike other product programs, they do *not* duplicate control structures like loops or procedure calls, while still allowing different executions to take different paths through the program.

Modular product programs achieve this as follows: The set of transitions made by the execution of a product is the union of the transitions made by

```
procedure main(p1, p2, people1, people2)        procedure is_female(p1, p2,
          returns (count1, count2)                                  person1,
{                                                                   person2)
  if (p1) { i1 := 0; }                                    returns (res1, res2)
  if (p2) { i2 := 0; }                           {
  if (p1) { count1 := 0; }                          if (p1) {
  if (p2) { count2 := 0; }                            gender1 := person1 mod 2;
  while ((p1 && i1 < |people1|) ||                  }
          (p2 && i2 < |people2|)) {                 if (p2) {
    l1 := p1 && i1 < |people1|;                       gender2 := person2 mod 2;
    l2 := p2 && i2 < |people2|;                     }
    if (l1) { current1 := people1[i1]; }            t1 := p1 && gender1 == 0;
    if (l2) { current2 := people2[i2]; }            t2 := p2 && gender2 == 0;
    if (l1 || l2) {                                 f1 := p1 && !(gender1 == 0);
      t1, t2 := is_female(l1, l2,                   f2 := p2 && !(gender2 == 0);
                  current1, current2);              if (t1) { res1 := 1; }
    }                                               if (t2) { res2 := 1; }
    if (l1) { f1 := t1; }                           if (f1) { res1 := 0; }
    if (l2) { f2 := t2; }                           if (f2) { res2 := 0; }
    if (l1) { count1 := count1 + f1; }            }
    if (l2) { count2 := count2 + f2; }
    if (l1) { i1 := i1 + 1; }
    if (l2) { i2 := i2 + 1; }
  }
}
```

Fig. 2. Modular 2-product of the program in Fig. 1 (slightly simplified). Parameters and local variables have been duplicated, but control flow statements have not. All statements are parameterized by activation variables.

the executions of the original program it represents. This means that if two executions of an if-then-else statement execute different branches, an execution of the product will execute the corresponding versions of *both* branches; however, it will be aware of the fact that each branch is taken by only one of the original executions, and the transformation of the statements *inside* each branch will ensure that the state of the other execution is not modified by executing it.

For this purpose, modular product programs use boolean *activation variables* that store, for each execution, the condition under which it is currently active. All activation variables are initially true. For every statement that directly changes the program state, the product performs the state change for all active executions. Control structures update which executions are active (for instance based on the loop condition) and pass this information down (into the branches of a conditional, the body of a loop, or the callee of a procedure call) to the level of atomic statements[1]. This representation avoids duplicating these control structures.

Figure 2 shows the modular 2-product of the program in Fig. 1. Consider first the main procedure. Its parameters have been duplicated, there are now two copies of all variables, one for each execution. This is analogous to self-composition or existing product programs. In addition, the transformed procedure has two boolean parameters p1 and p2; these variables are the initial

---

[1] The information stored in activation variables is similar to a path condition in symbolic execution, which is also updated every time a branch is taken. However, they differ for loops and calls.

activation variables of the procedure. Since main is the entry point of the program, the initial activation variables can be assumed to be true.

Consider what happens when the product is run with arbitrary input values for people1 and people2. The product will first initialize i1 and i2 to zero, like it does with i in the original program, and analogously for count1 and count2.

The loop in the original program has been transformed to a single loop in the product. Its condition is true if the original loop condition is true for any active execution. This means that the loop will iterate as long as at least one execution of the original program would. Inside the loop body, the fresh activation variables l1 and l2 represent whether the corresponding executions would execute the loop body. That is, for each execution, the respective activation variable will be true if the previous activation variable (p1 or p2, respectively) is true, meaning that this execution actually reaches the loop, and the loop guard is true for that execution. All statements in the loop body are then transformed using these new activation variables. Consequently, the loop will keep iterating while at least one execution executes the loop, but as soon as the loop guard is false for any execution, its activation variable will be false and the loop body will have no effect.

Conceptually, procedure calls are handled very similarly to loops. For the call to is_female in the original program, only a single call is created in the product. This call is executed if at least one activation variable is true, i.e., if at least one execution would perform the call in the original program. In addition to the (duplicated) arguments of the original call, the current activation variables are passed to the called procedure. In the transformed version of is_female, all statements are then made conditional on those activation variables. Therefore, like with loops, a call in the product will be performed if at least one execution would perform it in the original program, but it will have no effect on the state of the executions that are not active when the call is made.

The transformed version of is_female shows how conditionals are handled. We introduce four fresh activation variables t1, t2, f1, and f2, two for each execution. The first pair encodes whether the then-branch should be executed by either of the two executions; the second encodes the same for the else-branch. These activation variables are then used to transform the branches. Consequently, neither branch will have an effect for inactive executions, and exactly one branch has an effect for each active execution.

To summarize, our activation variables ensure that the sequence of state-changing statements executed by each execution is the same in the product and the original program. We achieve this without duplicating control structures or imposing restrictions on the control flow.

2.3 Interpretation of Relational Specifications

Since modular product programs do not duplicate calls, they provide a simple way of interpreting relational procedure specifications: If all executions call a procedure, its relational precondition is required to hold before the call and the relational postcondition afterwards. If a call is performed by some executions but not all, the relational specification are not meaningful, and thus cannot be required to hold. To encode this intuition, we transform every relational pre- or postcondition $\hat{Q}$ of the original program into an implication $(\bigwedge_{i=1}^{k} \mathsf{p}_i) \Rightarrow \hat{Q}$. In the transformed version, both pre- and postconditions are made conditional on the conjunction of all activation parameters p_i of the procedure. As a result, both will be trivially true if at least one execution is not active at the call site.

In our example, we give is_female the relational specification is_female : $true \rightsquigarrow \overset{1}{\mathsf{person}} = \overset{2}{\mathsf{person}} \Rightarrow \overset{1}{\mathsf{res}} = \overset{2}{\mathsf{res}}$, which expresses determinism. This specification will be transformed into a unary specification of the product program: is_female : $\mathsf{p1} \wedge \mathsf{p2} \Rightarrow true \rightsquigarrow \mathsf{p1} \wedge \mathsf{p2} \Rightarrow (\mathsf{person1} = \mathsf{person2} \Rightarrow \mathsf{res1} = \mathsf{res2})$.

Assume for the moment that is_female also has a unary precondition person $\geq$ 0. Such a specification should hold for *every* call, and therefore for every active execution, even if other executions are inactive. Therefore, its interpretation in the product program is $(\mathsf{p1} \Rightarrow \mathsf{person1} \geq 0) \wedge (\mathsf{p2} \Rightarrow \mathsf{person2} \geq 0)$. The translation of other unary assertions is analogous.

Note that it is possible (and useful) to give a procedure both a relational and a unary specification; in the product this is encoded by simply conjoining the transformed versions of the unary and the relational assertions.

2.4   Product Program Verification

We can now prove determinism of our example using the product program. Verifying is_female is simple. For main, we want to prove the transformed specification main : $(\mathsf{p1} \wedge \mathsf{p2} \Rightarrow \mathsf{people1} = \mathsf{people2}) \rightsquigarrow (\mathsf{p1} \wedge \mathsf{p2} \Rightarrow \mathsf{count1} = \mathsf{count2})$. We use the relational loop invariant $\overset{1}{\mathsf{i}} = \overset{2}{\mathsf{i}} \wedge \overset{1}{\mathsf{count}} = \overset{2}{\mathsf{count}} \wedge \overset{1}{\mathsf{people}} = \overset{2}{\mathsf{people}}$, encoded as $\mathsf{p1} \wedge \mathsf{p2} \Rightarrow \mathsf{i1} = \mathsf{i2} \wedge \mathsf{count1} = \mathsf{count2} \wedge \mathsf{people1} = \mathsf{people2}$. The loop invariant holds trivially if either $\mathsf{p1}$ or $\mathsf{p2}$ is false. Otherwise, it ensures $\mathsf{l1} = \mathsf{l2}$ and $\mathsf{current1} = \mathsf{current2}$. Using the specification of is_female, we obtain $\mathsf{t1} = \mathsf{t2}$, which implies that the loop invariant is preserved. The loop invariant implies the postcondition.

3   Preliminaries

We model our setting according to the relational logic by Banerjee, Naumann and Nikouei [5][2] and, like them, use a standard Hoare logic [4] to reason about single program executions. Figure 3 shows the language we use to define modular product programs. x ranges over the set of local integer variable names VAR. Note that this language is deterministic; non-determinism can for example be modelled via additional inputs, as is often done for modelling fairness in concurrent programs [16]. Program configurations have the form $\langle s, \sigma \rangle$, where $\sigma \in \Sigma$ maps variable names to values. The value of expression e in state σ is

---

[2] Our handling of procedure calls is slightly different, but amounts to restricting procedures to work only on local variables not used in the rest of the program (as opposed to having a global state on which all procedures work directly), and only interacting with the rest of the program via explicitly declared return parameters.

(*Programs*)	$Prog ::= \textbf{procedure } main(\overline{x}) \textbf{ returns } (\overline{y})\{s\} :: Nil \mid Proc :: Prog$
(*Procedures*)	$Proc ::= \textbf{procedure } m(\overline{x}) \textbf{ returns } (\overline{y})\{s\}$
(*Statements*)	$s ::= x{:}{=}e \mid s; s \mid \textbf{if } (e) \textbf{ then } \{s\} \textbf{ else } \{s\} \mid \textbf{while } (e) \textbf{ do } \{s\}$
	$\mid \overline{x}{:}{=}\textbf{ call } m(\overline{e})$
(*Expressions*)	$e ::= c \mid x \mid e \oplus e \text{ where } c \in \mathbb{Z} \text{ and } \oplus \in \{+, -, \times, \ldots\}$
(*Assertions*)	$P ::= P \wedge P \mid P \Rightarrow P \mid \forall x.\, P \mid e$
(*RelExpressions*)	$\hat{e} ::= c \mid \dot{x} \mid \hat{e} \oplus \hat{e}$
(*RelAssertions*)	$\hat{P} ::= \hat{P} \wedge \hat{P} \mid \hat{P} \Rightarrow \hat{P} \mid \forall \dot{x}, \ldots, \dot{x}.\, \hat{P} \mid \hat{e}$
(*MixAssertions*)	$\check{P} ::= P \mid \hat{P} \mid \check{P} \wedge \check{P}$

Fig. 3. Language.

denoted as $\sigma(e)$. The small-step transition relation for program configurations has the form $\langle s, \sigma \rangle \rightarrow \langle s', \sigma' \rangle$. A hypothesis context Φ maps procedure names to specifications.

The judgment $\Phi \vDash s : P \rightsquigarrow Q$ denotes that statement s, when executed in a state fulfilling the unary assertion P, will not fault, and if the execution terminates, the resulting state will fulfill the unary assertion Q. For an extensive discussion of the language and its operational and axiomatic semantics, see [5].

In addition to standard unary expressions and assertions, we define relational expressions and assertions. They differ from normal expressions and assertions in that they contain parameterized variable references of the form $\dot{x}$ and are evaluated over a tuple of states instead of a single one. A relational expression is k-relational if for all contained variable references $\dot{x}$, $1 \leq i \leq k$, and analogous for relational assertions. The value of a variable reference $\dot{x}$ with $1 \leq i \leq k$ in a tuple of states $(\sigma_1, \ldots, \sigma_k)$ is $\sigma_i(x)$; the evaluation of arbitrary relational expressions and the validity of relational assertions $(\sigma_1, \ldots, \sigma_k) \vDash \hat{P}$ are defined accordingly.

Definition 1. *A k-relational specification $s : \hat{P} \rightsquigarrow_k \hat{Q}$ holds iff $\hat{P}$ and $\hat{Q}$ are k-relational assertions, and for all $\sigma_1, \ldots, \sigma_k, \sigma_1', \ldots, \sigma_k'$, if $(\sigma_1, \ldots, \sigma_k) \vDash \hat{P}$ and $\forall i \in \{1, \ldots, k\}.\, \langle s, \sigma_i \rangle \rightarrow^* \langle \textbf{skip}, \sigma_i' \rangle$, then $(\sigma_1', \ldots, \sigma_k') \vDash \hat{Q}$.*

We write $s : \hat{P} \rightsquigarrow \hat{Q}$ for the most common case $s : \hat{P} \rightsquigarrow_2 \hat{Q}$.

4 Modular k-Product Programs

In this section, we define the construction of modular products for arbitrary k. We will subsequently define the transformation of both relational and unary specifications to modular products.

4.1 Product Construction

Assume as given a function $(\text{VAR}, \mathbb{N}) \rightarrow \text{VAR}$ that renames variables for different executions. We write $e^{(i)}$ for the renaming of expression e for execution i and require that $\forall x, y, i, j.\, i \neq j \Rightarrow x^{(i)} \neq y^{(j)}$. We write $fresh(x_1, x_2, \ldots)$ to denote that the variable names $x_1, x_2, \ldots$ are fresh names that do not occur in the program and have not yet been used during the transformation. $\mathring{e}$ is used to abbreviate $e^{(1)}, \ldots, e^{(k)}$.

We denote the modular k-product of a statement s that is parameterized by the activation variables $p^{(1)}, \ldots, p^{(k)}$ as $[\![s]\!]_k^{\mathring{p}}$. The product construction for procedures is defined as

$$[\![\textbf{procedure } m(x_1, \ldots, x_m) \textbf{ returns } (y_1, \ldots, y_n)\{s\}]\!]_k$$

$$= \textbf{procedure } m(p^{(1)}, \ldots, p^{(k)}, args) \textbf{ returns } (rets)\{[\![s]\!]_k^{\mathring{p}}\}$$

where

$$args = x_1^{(1)}, \ldots, x_1^{(k)}, \ldots, x_m^{(1)}, \ldots, x_m^{(k)}$$
$$rets = y_1^{(1)}, \ldots, y_1^{(k)}, \ldots, y_n^{(1)}, \ldots, y_n^{(k)}$$

Figure 4 shows the product construction rules for statements, which generalize the transformation explained in Sect. 2. We write $\textbf{if } (e) \textbf{ then } \{s\}$ as a shorthand for $\textbf{if } (e) \textbf{ then } \{s\} \textbf{ else } \{\texttt{skip}\}$, and $\bigodot_{i=1}^{k} s_i$ for the sequential composition of k statements $s_1; \ldots; s_k$.

The core principle behind our encoding is that statements that directly change the state are duplicated for each execution and made conditional under the respective activation variables, whereas control statements are not duplicated and instead manipulate the activation variables to pass activation information to their sub-statements. This enables us to assert or assume relational assertions before and after any statement from the original program. The only state-changing statements in our language, variable assignments, are therefore transformed to a sequence of conditional assignments, one for each execution. Each assignment is executed only if the respective execution is currently active.

Duplicating conditionals would also duplicate the calls and loops in their branches. To avoid that, modular products eliminate top-level conditionals; instead, new activation variables are created and assigned the values of the current activation variables conjoined with the guard for each branch. The branches are then sequentially executed based on their respective activation variables.

A while loop is transformed to a single while loop in the product program that iterates as long as the loop guard is true for *any* active execution. Inside the loop, fresh activation variables indicate whether an execution reaches the loop *and* its loop condition is true. The loop body will then modify the state of an execution only if its activation variable is true. The resulting construct affects the program state in the same way as a self-composition of the original loop would, but the fact that our product contains only a single loop enables us to use relational loop invariants instead of full functional specifications.

For procedure calls, it is crucial that the product contains a single call for every call in the original program, in order to be able to apply relational specifications at the call site. As explained before, initial activation parameters are added to every procedure declaration, and all parameters are duplicated k times.

$$[\![s_1; s_2]\!]_k^{\mathring{p}} \qquad\qquad\qquad = [\![s_1]\!]_k^{\mathring{p}}; [\![s_2]\!]_k^{\mathring{p}}$$

$$[\![\mathtt{skip}]\!]_k^{\mathring{p}} \qquad\qquad\qquad = \mathtt{skip}$$

$$[\![x:=e]\!]_k^{\mathring{p}} \qquad\qquad\qquad = \bigodot_{i=1}^{k} \mathtt{if}\ (p^{(i)})\ \mathtt{then}\ \{x^{(i)}:=e^{(i)}\}$$

$$[\![\mathtt{if}\ (e)\ \mathtt{then}\ \{s_1\}\ \mathtt{else}\ \{s_2\}]\!]_k^{\mathring{p}} = \bigodot_{i=1}^{k}(p_1^{(i)}:=p^{(i)} \wedge e^{(i)});$$

$$\qquad\qquad\qquad\qquad \bigodot_{i=1}^{k}(p_2^{(i)}:=p^{(i)} \wedge \neg e^{(i)});$$

$$\qquad\qquad\qquad\qquad [\![s_1]\!]_k^{\mathring{p}_1}; [\![s_2]\!]_k^{\mathring{p}_2}$$

$$\qquad\qquad\qquad\qquad \mathtt{where}$$

$$\qquad\qquad\qquad\qquad fresh(\mathring{p}_1) \wedge fresh(\mathring{p}_2)$$

$$[\![\mathtt{while}\ (e)\ \mathtt{do}\ \{s\}]\!]_k^{\mathring{p}} = \mathtt{while}\ (\bigvee_{i=1}^{k}(p^{(i)} \wedge e^{(i)}))\ \mathtt{do}\ \{$$

$$\qquad\qquad\qquad\qquad \bigodot_{i=1}^{k}(p_1^{(i)}:=p^{(i)} \wedge e^{(i)});$$

$$\qquad\qquad\qquad\qquad [\![s]\!]_k^{\mathring{p}_1}$$

$$\qquad\qquad\qquad\qquad \}$$

$$\qquad\qquad\qquad\qquad \mathtt{where}$$

$$\qquad\qquad\qquad\qquad fresh(\mathring{p}_1)$$

$$[\![x_1, \ldots, x_n := \mathtt{call}\ m(e_1, \ldots, e_m)]\!]_k^{\mathring{p}} = \mathtt{if}\ (\bigvee_{i=1}^{k} p^{(i)})\ \mathtt{then}\ \{$$

$$\qquad\qquad\qquad\qquad \bigodot_{i=1}^{k} \mathtt{if}\ (p^{(i)})\ \mathtt{then}\ \{\bigodot_{j=1}^{m}(a_j^{(i)}:=e_j^{(i)})\};$$

$$\qquad\qquad\qquad\qquad ts := \mathtt{call}\ m(p^{(1)}, \ldots, p^{(k)}, as);$$

$$\qquad\qquad\qquad\qquad \bigodot_{i=1}^{k} \mathtt{if}\ (p^{(i)})\ \mathtt{then}\ \{\bigodot_{j=1}^{n}(x_j^{(i)}:=t_j^{(i)})\}$$

$$\qquad\qquad\qquad\qquad \}$$

$$\qquad\qquad\qquad\qquad \mathtt{where}$$

$$\qquad\qquad\qquad\qquad fresh(\mathring{a}_1, \ldots, \mathring{a}_m) \wedge fresh(\mathring{t}_1, \ldots, \mathring{t}_n)$$

$$\qquad\qquad\qquad\qquad as = [a_1^{(1)}, \ldots, a_1^{(k)}, \ldots, a_m^{(1)}, \ldots, a_m^{(k)}]$$

$$\qquad\qquad\qquad\qquad ts = [t_1^{(1)}, \ldots, t_1^{(k)}, \ldots, t_n^{(1)}, \ldots, t_n^{(k)}]$$

Fig. 4. Construction rules for statement products.

Procedure calls are therefore transformed such that the values of the current activation variables are passed, and all arguments are passed once for each execution. The return values are stored in temporary variables and subsequently assigned to the actual target variables only for those executions that actually execute the call, so that for all other executions, the target variables are not affected.

The transformation wraps the call in a conditional so that the call is performed only if at least one execution is active. This prevents the transformation from introducing infinite recursion that is not present in the original program.

Note that for an inactive execution i, arbitrary argument values are passed in procedure calls, since the passed variables $a_j^{(i)}$ are not initialized. This is unproblematic because these values will not be used by the procedure. It is important to not evaluate $e_j^{(i)}$ for inactive executions, since this could lead to false alarms for languages where expression evaluation can fail.

4.2   Transformation of Assertions

We now define how to transform unary and relational assertions for use in a modular product.

Unary assertions such as ordinary procedure preconditions describe state properties that should hold for every single execution. When checking or assuming that a unary assertion holds at a specific point in the program, we need to take into account that it only makes sense to do so for executions that actually reach that program point. We can express this by making the assertion conditional on the activation variable of the respective execution; as a result, any unary assertion is trivially valid for all inactive executions.

A k-relational assertion, on the other hand, describes the relation between the states of all k executions. Checking or assuming a relational assertion at some point is meaningful only if *all* executions actually reach that point. This can be expressed by making relational assertions conditional on the conjunction of all current activation variables. If at least one execution does not reach the assertion, it holds trivially.

We formalize this idea by defining a function α that maps relational assertions $\hat{P}$ to unary assertions P of the product program such that $\alpha(\hat{P}) = \hat{P}[Var^{(1)}/\hat{Var}]\ldots[Var^{(k)}/\hat{Var}]$. Assertions can then be transformed for use in a k-product as follows:

- The transformation $\lfloor \hat{P} \rfloor_k^{\hat{p}}$ of a k-relational assertion $\hat{P}$ with the activation variables $p^{(1)}, \ldots, p^{(k)}$ is $(\bigwedge_{i=1}^{k} p^{(i)}) \Rightarrow \alpha(\hat{P})$.
- The transformation $\lfloor P \rfloor_k^{\hat{p}}$ of a unary assertion P is $\bigwedge_{i=1}^{k}(p^{(i)} \Rightarrow P^{(i)})$.

Importantly, our approach allows using *mixed* assertions and specifications, which represent conjunctions of unary and relational assertions. For example, it is common to combine a unary precondition that ensures that a procedure will not raise an error with a relational postcondition that states that it is deterministic.

A mixed assertion $\check{R}$ of the form $P \wedge \hat{Q}$ means that the unary assertion P holds for every single execution, and if all executions are currently active, the relational assertion $\hat{Q}$ holds as well. The transformation of mixed assertions is straightforward: $\lfloor \check{R} \rfloor_k^{\hat{p}} = \lfloor P \rfloor_k^{\hat{p}} \wedge \lfloor \hat{Q} \rfloor_k^{\hat{p}}$.

4.3   Heap-Manipulating Programs

The approach outlined so far can easily be extended to programs that work on a mutable heap, assuming that object references are opaque, i.e., they cannot be inspected or used in arithmetic. In order to create a distinct state space for each execution represented in the product, allocation statements are duplicated and made conditional like assignments, and therefore create a different object for each active execution. The renaming of a field dereference $e.f$ is then defined as $e^{(i)}.f$. As a result, the heap of a k-product will consist of k partitions that do not contain references to each other, and execution i will only ever interact with objects from its partition of the heap.

The verification of modular products of heap-manipulating programs does not depend on any specific way of achieving framing. Our implementation is based on implicit dynamic frames [25], but other approaches are feasible as well, provided that procedures can be specified in such a way that the caller knows the heap stays unmodified for all executions whose activation variables are false.

Since the handling of the heap is largely orthogonal to our main technique, we will not go into further detail here, but we do support heap-manipulating programs in our implementation.

5   Soundness and Completeness

A product construction is sound if an execution of a k-product mirrors k separate executions of the original program such that properties proved about the product entail hyperproperties of the original program. In this section, we sketch a soundness proof of our k-product construction in the presence of only unary procedure specifications. We also sketch a proof for relational specifications for the case $k = 2$, making use of the relational logic presented by Banerjee et al. [5]. Finally, we informally discuss the completeness of modular products.

5.1   Soundness with Unary Specifications

A modular k-product must soundly encode k executions of the original program. That is, if an encoded unary specification holds for a product program then the original specification holds for the original program.

We define a relation $\sigma \simeq_i \sigma'$ that denotes that σ contains a renamed version of all variables in σ', i.e., $\forall v \in dom(\sigma') : \sigma(v^{(i)}) = \sigma'(v)$. Without the index i, $\simeq$ denotes the same but without renaming, and is used to express equality modulo newly introduced activation variables.

Theorem 1. *Assume that for all procedures m in a hypothesis context Φ we have that $m : S \rightsquigarrow T \in dom(\Phi)$ if and only if $m : \lfloor S \rfloor_k^{\mathring{p}} \rightsquigarrow \lfloor T \rfloor_k^{\mathring{p}} \in dom(\Phi')$. Then $\Phi' \vDash [\![s]\!]_k^{\mathring{p}} : \lfloor P \rfloor_k^{\mathring{p}} \rightsquigarrow \lfloor Q \rfloor_k^{\mathring{p}}$ implies that $\Phi \vDash s : P \rightsquigarrow Q$.*

Proof (Sketch). We sketch a proof based on the operational semantics of our language. We show that the execution of the product program with exactly one active execution corresponds to a single execution of the original program.

Assume that $\Phi' \vDash [\![s]\!]_k^{\mathring{p}} : \lfloor P \rfloor_k^{\mathring{p}} \rightsquigarrow \lfloor Q \rfloor_k^{\mathring{p}}$, and that $\sigma \vDash \lfloor P \rfloor_k^{\mathring{p}}$. If $[\![s]\!]_k^{\mathring{p}}$ does not diverge when executed from σ we have that $\langle [\![s]\!]_k^{\mathring{p}}, \sigma \rangle \rightarrow^* \langle \texttt{skip}, \sigma' \rangle$ and $\sigma' \vDash \lfloor Q \rfloor_k^{\mathring{p}}$. We now prove that a run of the product with all but one execution being inactive reflects the states that occur in a run of the original program. Assume that $\sigma \vDash p^{(1)} \land \bigwedge_{i=2}^k (\neg p^{(i)})$ and $\langle s, \sigma_1 \rangle \rightarrow^* \langle \texttt{skip}, \sigma_1' \rangle$ and initially $\sigma \simeq_1 \sigma_1$, which implies $\sigma_1 \vDash P$. We prove by induction on the derivation of $\langle s, \sigma_1 \rangle \rightarrow^* \langle \texttt{skip}, \sigma_1' \rangle$ that $\langle [\![s]\!]_k^{\mathring{p}}, \sigma \rangle \rightarrow^* \langle \texttt{skip}, \sigma' \rangle$ and $\sigma' \simeq_1 \sigma_1'$, meaning that the product execution terminates, and subsequently by induction on the derivation of $\langle [\![s]\!]_k^{\mathring{p}}, \sigma \rangle \rightarrow^* \langle \texttt{skip}, \sigma' \rangle$ that $\sigma' \simeq_1 \sigma_1'$, from which we can derive that $\sigma_1' \vDash Q$. □

5.2 Soundness for Relational Specifications

The main advantage of modular product programs over other kinds of product programs is that it allows reasoning about procedure calls in terms of relational specifications. We therefore need to show the soundness of our approach in the presence of procedures with such specifications. In particular, we must establish that if a transformed relational specification holds for a modular product then the original relational specification will hold for a set of k executions of the original program.

Our proof sketch is phrased in terms of *biprograms* as introduced by Banerjee et al. [5]. Biprogram executions correspond to two partly aligned executions of their two underlying programs. A biprogram ss can have the form $(s_1|s_2)$ or $\|s\|$; the former represents the two executions of s_1 and s_2, whereas the latter represents an aligned execution of s by both executions, which enables using relational specifications for procedure calls[3]. We denote the small-step transition relation between biprogram configurations as $\langle ss, \sigma_1|\sigma_2\rangle \Rightarrow^* \langle ss', \sigma_1'|\sigma_2'\rangle$. We make use of a relation $\sigma \approx \sigma_1|\sigma_2$ that denotes that σ contains renamed versions of all variables in both σ_1 and σ_2 with the same values.

Biprograms do not allow mixed procedure specifications, meaning that a procedure can either have only a unary specification, or it can have only a relational specification, in which case it can only be invoked by both executions simultaneously. As mentioned before, our approach does not have this limitation, but we can artificially enforce it for the purposes of the soundness proof.

We can now state our theorem. Since biprograms represent the execution of two programs, we formulate soundness for $k = 2$ here.

Theorem 2. *Assume that hypothesis context Φ maps procedure names to relational specifications if all calls to the procedure in s can be aligned from any pair of states satisfying $\hat{P}$, and to unary specifications otherwise. Assume further that hypothesis context Φ' maps the same procedure names to their transformed specifications. Finally, assume that $\Phi' \vdash [\![s]\!]_2^{\hat{p}} : \lfloor \hat{P}\rfloor_2^{\hat{p}} \rightsquigarrow \lfloor\hat{Q}\rfloor_2^{\hat{p}}$ and $(\sigma_1, \sigma_2) \vDash \hat{P}$. If $\langle s, \sigma_1\rangle \rightarrow^* \langle \mathtt{skip}, \sigma_1'\rangle$ and $\langle s, \sigma_2\rangle \rightarrow^* \langle \mathtt{skip}, \sigma_2'\rangle$, then $(\sigma_1', \sigma_2') \vDash \hat{Q}$.*

Proof (Sketch). The proof follows the same basic outline as the one for Theorem 1 but reasons about the operational semantics of biprograms representing two executions of s.

Assume that $\Phi' \vdash [\![s]\!]_2^{\hat{p}} : \lfloor \hat{P}\rfloor_2^{\hat{p}} \rightsquigarrow \lfloor\hat{Q}\rfloor_2^{\hat{p}}$ and $\sigma = \lfloor\hat{P}\rfloor_2^{\hat{p}}$. If $[\![s]\!]_2^{\hat{p}}$ does not diverge when executed from σ we get that $\langle [\![s]\!]_2^{\hat{p}}, \sigma\rangle \rightarrow^* \langle \mathtt{skip}, \sigma'\rangle$ and $\sigma' \vDash \lfloor\hat{Q}\rfloor_2^{\hat{p}}$. Assume that initially $\sigma \approx \sigma_1|\sigma_2$, which implies that $(\sigma_1, \sigma_2) \vDash \hat{P}$. We prove by induction on the derivation of $\langle [\![s]\!]_2^{\hat{p}}, \sigma\rangle \rightarrow^* \langle \mathtt{skip}, \sigma'\rangle$ that (1) if $\sigma \vDash p^{(1)} \wedge p^{(2)}$, then there exists ss that represents two executions of s s.t. $\langle ss, \sigma_1|\sigma_2\rangle \Rightarrow^* \langle \|\mathtt{skip}\|, \sigma_1'|\sigma_2'\rangle$ and $\sigma' \approx \sigma_1'|\sigma_2'$; (2) if $\sigma \vDash p^{(1)} \wedge \neg p^{(2)}$, then $\langle s, \sigma_1\rangle \rightarrow^* \langle \mathtt{skip}, \sigma_1'\rangle$ and $\sigma' \approx \sigma_1'|\sigma_2$; (3) if $\sigma \vDash \neg p^{(1)} \wedge p^{(2)}$, then $\langle s, \sigma_2\rangle \rightarrow^* \langle \mathtt{skip}, \sigma_2'\rangle$ and $\sigma' \approx \sigma_1|\sigma_2'$; (4) if $\sigma \vDash \neg p^{(1)} \wedge \neg p^{(2)}$, then $\sigma \simeq \sigma'$. From the first point and semantic consistency

---

[3] We modified the original notation to avoid clashes with our own concepts introduced earlier.

of the relational logic, we can conclude that $(\sigma_1', \sigma_2') \vDash \hat{Q}$. Finally, we prove that $\langle [\![s]\!]_2^{\stackrel{\circ}{\beta}}, \sigma \rangle \rightarrow^* \langle \text{skip}, \sigma' \rangle$ by showing that non-termination of the product implies the non-termination of at least one of the two original program runs. If the condition of a loop in the product remains true forever, the loop condition of at least one encoded execution must be true after every iteration. We show that (1) this is not due to an interaction of multiple executions, since the condition for every execution will remain false if it becomes false once, and (2) since the encoded states of active executions progress as they do in the original program, the condition of a single execution in the product remains true forever only if it does in the original program. A similar argument shows that the product cannot diverge because of infinite recursive calls.   □

5.3 Completeness

We believe modular product programs to be complete, meaning that any hyper-property of multiple executions of a program can be proved about its modular product program. Since the product faithfully models the executions of the original program, the completeness of modular products is potentially limited only by the underlying verification logic and the assertion language, but not by the product construction itself.

6 Modular Verification of Secure Information Flow

In this section, we demonstrate the expressiveness of modular product programs by showing how they can be used to verify an important hyperproperty, information flow security. We first concentrate on secure information flow in the classical sense [9], and later demonstrate how the ability to check relational assertions at any point in the program can be exploited to prove advanced properties like the absence of timing and termination channels, and to encode declassification.

6.1 Non-interference

Secure information flow, i.e., the property that secret information is not leaked to the public outputs of a program, can be expressed as a relational 2-safety property of a program called *non-interference*. Non-interference states that, if a program is run twice, with the public (often called *low*) inputs being equal in both runs but the secret (or *high*) inputs possibly being different, the public outputs of the program must be equal in both runs [8]. This property guarantees that the high inputs do not influence the low outputs.

We can formalize non-interference as follows:

Definition 2. *A statement* s *that operates on a set of variables* $X = \{x_1, \ldots, x_n\}$, *of which some subset* $X_l \subseteq X$ *is low, satisfies non-interference iff for all* σ_1, σ_2 *and* σ_1', σ_2', *if* $\forall x \in X_l . \sigma_1(x) = \sigma_2(x)$ *and* $\langle s, \sigma_1 \rangle \rightarrow^* \langle \text{skip}, \sigma_1' \rangle$ *and* $\langle s, \sigma_2 \rangle \rightarrow^* \langle \text{skip}, \sigma_2' \rangle$ *then* $\forall x \in X_l . \sigma_1'(x) = \sigma_2'(x)$.

Since our definition of non-interference describes a hyperproperty, we can verify it using modular product programs:

Theorem 3. *A statement s that operates on a set of variables $X = \{x_1, \ldots, x_n\}$, of which some subset $X_l \subseteq X$ is low, satisfies non-interference under a unary precondition P if $\Phi \vdash [\![s]\!]_2^{\mathring{p}} : \lfloor P \rfloor_2^{\mathring{p}} \wedge (\forall x \in X_l . x^{(1)} = x^{(2)}) \rightsquigarrow \forall x \in X_l . x^{(1)} = x^{(2)}$*

Proof (Sketch). Since non-interference can be expressed using a 2-relational specification, the theorem follows directly from Theorem 2.   □

For non-deterministic programs whose behavior can be modelled by adding input parameters representing the non-deterministic choices, those parameters can be considered low if the choice is not influenced in any way by secret data.

An expanded notion of secure information flow considers observable *events* in addition to regular program outputs [17]. An event is a statement that has an effect that is visible to an outside observer, but may not necessarily affect the program state. The most important examples of events are output operations like printing a string to the console or sending a message over a network. Programs that cause events can be considered information flow secure only if the sequence of produced events is not influenced by high data. One way to verify this using our approach is to track the sequence of produced events in a ghost variable and verify that its value never depends on high data. This approach requires substantial amounts of additional specifications.

Modular product programs offer an alternative approach for preventing leaks via events, since they allow formulating assertions about the relation between the activation variables of different executions. In particular, if a given event has the precondition that all activation variables are equal when the event statement is reached then this event will either be executed by both executions or be skipped by both executions. As a result, the sequence of events produced by a program will be equal in all executions.

6.2   Information Flow Specifications

The relational specifications required for modularly proving non-interference with the previously described approach have a specific pattern: they can contain functional specifications meant to be valid for both executions (e.g., to make sure both executions run without errors), they may require that some information is low, which is equivalent to the two renamings of the same expression being equal, and, in addition, they may assert that the control flow at a specific program point is low.

We therefore introduce modular *information flow specifications*, which can express all properties required for proving secure information flow but are transparent w.r.t. the encoding or the verification methodology, i.e., they allow expressing that a given operation or value must not be secret without knowledge of the encoding of this fact into an assertion about two different program executions. We define information flow specifications as follows:

$(SIF\,Assertions)\ \tilde{P} ::= \tilde{P} \wedge \tilde{P} \mid e \mid low(e) \mid lowEvent \mid \tilde{P} \Rightarrow \tilde{P} \mid \forall x.\,\tilde{P}$

$low(e)$ and $lowEvent$ may be used on the left side of an implication only if the right side has the same form. $low(e)$ specifies that the value of the expression e is not influenced by high data. Note that e can be any expression and is not limited to variable references; this reflects the fact that our approach can label secrecy in a more fine-grained way than, e.g., a type system. One can, for example, declare to be public whether a number is odd while keeping its value secret.

$$\lceil e \rceil^{\tilde{p}} \qquad = (p^{(1)} \Rightarrow e^{(1)}) \wedge (p^{(2)} \Rightarrow e^{(2)})$$
$$\lceil low(e) \rceil^{\tilde{p}} = (p^{(1)} \wedge p^{(2)} \Rightarrow e^{(1)} = e^{(2)})$$
$$\lceil lowEvent \rceil^{\tilde{p}} = p^{(1)} = p^{(2)}$$
$$\lceil \tilde{P}_1 \wedge \tilde{P}_2 \rceil^{\tilde{p}} = \lceil \tilde{P}_1 \rceil^{\tilde{p}} \wedge \lceil \tilde{P}_2 \rceil^{\tilde{p}}$$
$$\lceil \tilde{P}_1 \Rightarrow \tilde{P}_2 \rceil^{\tilde{p}} = \lceil \tilde{P}_1 \rceil^{\tilde{p}} \Rightarrow \lceil \tilde{P}_2 \rceil^{\tilde{p}}$$
$$\lceil \forall x.\,\tilde{P} \rceil^{\tilde{p}} \quad = \forall x^{(1)}, x^{(2)}.\, x^{(1)} = x^{(2)} \Rightarrow \lceil \tilde{P} \rceil^{\tilde{p}}$$

Fig. 5. Translation of information flow specifications.

$lowEvent$ specifies that high data must not influence if and how often the current program point is reached by an execution, which is a sufficient precondition of any statement that causes an observable event. In particular, if a procedure outputs an expression e, the precondition $lowEvent \wedge low(e)$ guarantees that no high information will be leaked via this procedure.

Information flow specifications can express complex properties. $e_1 \Rightarrow low(e_2)$, for example, expresses that if e_1 is true, e_2 must not depend on high data; $e_1 \Rightarrow lowEvent$ says the same about the current control flow. A possible use case for these assertions is the precondition of a library function that prints e_2 to a low-observable channel if e_1 is true, and to a secure channel otherwise.

The encoding $\lceil \tilde{P} \rceil^{\tilde{p}}$ of an information flow assertion $\tilde{P}$ under the activation variables $p^{(1)}$ and $p^{(2)}$ is defined in Fig. 5. Note that high-ness of some expression is not modelled by its renamings being definitely unequal, but by leaving underspecified whether they are equal or not, meaning that high-ness is simply the absence of the knowledge of low-ness. As a result, it is never necessary to specify explicitly that an expression is high. This approach (which is also used in self-composition) is analogous to the way type systems encode security levels, where low is typically a subtype of high. For the example in Fig. 1, a possible, very precise information flow specification could say that the results of main are low if the first bit of all entries in people is low. We can write this as main : $low(|\mathsf{people}|) \wedge \forall i \in \{0, \ldots, |\mathsf{people}| - 1\}.\ low(\mathsf{people}[i]\ \mathbf{mod}\ 2) \rightsquigarrow low(\mathsf{count})$. In the product, this will be translated to main : $\mathsf{p1} \wedge \mathsf{p2} \Rightarrow |\mathsf{people1}| = |\mathsf{people2}| \wedge \forall i \in \{0, \ldots, |\mathsf{people1}| - 1\}.\ (\mathsf{people1}[i]\ \mathbf{mod}\ 2) = (\mathsf{people2}[i]\ \mathbf{mod}\ 2) \rightsquigarrow \mathsf{count1} = \mathsf{count2}$.

In this scenario, the loop in main could have the simple invariant $low(\mathsf{i}) \wedge low(\mathsf{count})$, and the procedure is_female could have the contract is_female : $true \rightsquigarrow (low(\mathsf{person}\ \mathbf{mod}\ 2) \Rightarrow low(\mathsf{res}))$. This contract follows a useful pattern

```
procedure check(password, input)
          returns (result)
{
  result := |password| == |input|;
  i := 0;
  while (i < min(|password|, |input|) {
    result := result && password[i] == input[i];
    i := i + 1;
  }
}
```

Fig. 6. Password check example: leaking secret data is desired.

where, instead of requiring an input to be low and promising that an output will be low for all calls, the output is decribed as *conditionally* low based on the level of the input, which is more permissive for callers.

The example shows that the information relevant for proving secure information flow can be expressed concisely, without requiring any knowledge about the methodology used for verification. Modular product programs therefore enable the verification of the information flow security of main based solely on modular, relational specifications, and without depending on functional specifications.

6.3   Secure Information Flow with Arbitrary Security Lattices

The definition of secure information flow used in Definition 2 is a special case in which there are exactly two possible classifications of data, high and low. In the more general case, classifications come from an arbitrary lattice $\langle \mathcal{L}, \sqsubseteq \rangle$ of security levels s.t. for some $l_1, l_2 \in \mathcal{L}$, information from an input with level l_1 may influence an output with level l_2 only if $l_1 \sqsubseteq l_2$. Instead of the specification $low(e)$, information flow assertions can therefore have the form $levelBelow(e, l)$, meaning that the security level of expression e is at most l.

It is well-known that techniques for verifying information flow security with two levels can conceptually be used to verify programs with arbitrary finite security lattices [23] by splitting the verification task into $|\mathcal{L}|$ different verification tasks, one for each element of $\mathcal{L}$. Instead, we propose to combine all these verification tasks into a single task by using a symbolic value for l, i.e., declaring an unconstrained global constant representing l. Specifications can then be translated as follows:

$$levelBelow(e, l') \mathrel{\hat{=}} l' \sqsubseteq l \Rightarrow e^{(1)} = e^{(2)}$$

Since no information about l is known, verification will only succeed if all assertions can be proven for all possible values of l, which is equivalent to proving them separately for each possible value of l.

6.4   Declassification

In practice, non-interference is too strong a property for many use cases. Often, some leakage of secret data is required for a program to work correctly. Consider

```
procedure main(h: Int)              procedure main(h: Int)
{                                   {
    while (h != 0) {                    i := 0;
        h := h - 1;                     while (i < h) {
    }                                       i := i + 1
}                                       }
                                        print(0)
                                    }
```

Fig. 7. Programs with a termination channel (left), and a timing channel (right). In both cases, h is high.

the case of a password check (see Fig. 6): A secret internal password is compared to a non-secret user input. While the password itself must not be leaked, the information whether the user input matches the password should influence the public outcome of the program, which is forbidden by non-interference.

To incorporate this intention, the relevant part of the secret information can be *declassified* [24], e.g., via a declassification statement declassify e that declares an arbitrary expression e to be low. With modular products, declassification can be encoded via a simple assumption stating that, if the declassification is executed in both executions, the expression is equal in both executions:

$$[\![\texttt{declassify } e]\!]_2^{\mathring{p}} = \texttt{assume } (p^{(1)} \wedge p^{(2)}) \Rightarrow e^{(1)} = e^{(2)}$$

Introducing an assumption of this form is sound if the information flow specifications from Sect. 6.2 are used to specify the program. Since high-ness is encoded as the absence of the knowledge that an expression is equal in both executions, not by the knowledge that they are different, there is no danger that assuming equality will contradict current knowledge and thereby cause unsoundness. As in the information flow specifications, the declassified expression can be arbitrarily complex, so that it is for example possible to declassify the sign of an integer while keeping all other information about it secret.

The example in Fig. 6 becomes valid if we add declassify result at the end of the procedure, or if we declassify a more complex expression by adding declassify *equal* (password, input) at some earlier point. The latter would arguably be safer because it specifies exactly the information that is intended to be leaked, and would therefore prevent accidentally leaking more if the implementation of the checking loop was faulty.

This kind of declassification has the following interesting properties: First, it is *imperative*, meaning that the declassified information may be leaked (e.g., via a **print** statement) after the execution of the declassification statement, but not before. Second, it is *semantic*, meaning that the declassification affects the value of the declassified expression as opposed to, e.g., syntactically the declassified variable. As a result, it will be allowed to leak any expression whose value contains the same (or a part of the) secret information which was declassified, e.g., the expression $f(e)$ if f is a deterministic function and e has been declassified.

6.5   Preventing Termination Channels

In Definition 2, we have considered only terminating program executions. In practice, however, termination is a possible side-channel that can leak secret information to an outside observer. Figure 7 (left) shows an example of a program that verifies under the methodology presented so far, but leaks information about the secret input h to an observer: If h is initially negative, the program will enter an endless loop. Anyone who can observe the termination behavior of the program can therefore conclude if h was negative or not.

To prevent leaking information via a termination side channel, it is necessary to verify that the termination of a program depends only on public data. We will show that modular product programs are expressive enough to encode and check this property. We will focus on preventing non-termination caused by infinite loops here; preventing infinite recursion works analogously. In particular, we want to prove that if a loop iterates forever in one execution, any other execution with the same low inputs will also reach this loop and iterate forever. More precisely, this means that

(A) if a loop does not terminate, then whether or not an execution reaches that loop must not depend on high data.
(B) whether a loop that is reached by both executions terminates must not depend on high data.

We propose to verify these properties by requiring additional specifications that state, for every loop, an exact condition under which it terminates. This condition may neither over- nor underapproximate the termination behavior; the loop must terminate if and only if the condition is true. For Fig. 7 (left) the condition is $h \geq 0$. We also require a ranking function for the cases when the termination condition is true. We can then prove the following:

(a) If the termination condition of a loop evaluates to false, then any two executions with identical low inputs either both reach the loop or both do not reach the loop (i.e., reaching the loop is a low event). This guarantees property (A) above.
(b) For loops executed by both executions, the loop's termination condition is low. This guarantees property (B) under the assumption that the termination condition is exact.
(c) The termination condition is sound, i.e., every loop terminates if its termination condition is true. We prove this by showing that if the termination condition is true, we can prove the termination of the loop using the supplied ranking function.
(d) The termination condition is complete, i.e., every loop terminates only if its termination condition is true. We prove this by showing that if the condition is false, the loop condition will always remain true. This check, along with the previous proof obligation, ensures that the termination condition is exact.
(e) Every statement in a loop body terminates if the loop's termination condition is true, i.e., the loop's termination condition implies the termination conditions of all statements in its body.

```
term(w, c) = cond:=e_c;
              assert ¬e_c ⇒ lowEvent;          // checks (a)
              assert low(e_c);                  // checks (b)
              assert e_c ⇒ e_r ≥ 0;             // checks (c)
              assert c ⇒ e_c;                   // checks (e)
              while (e)
              invariant ¬cond ⇒ e               // checks (d)
              do {
                  if (cond) then {rank:=e_r};
                  term(s, cond);
                  if (cond) then {              // checks (c)
                      assert 0 ≤ e_r ∧ e_r < rank
                  }
              }
```

Fig. 8. Program instrumentation for termination leak prevention. We abbreviate while (e) terminates(e_c, e_r) do $\{s\}$ as w.

We introduce an annotated while loop while (e) terminates(e_c, e_r) do $\{s\}$, where e_c is the exact termination condition and e_r is the ranking function, i.e., an integer expression whose value decreases with every loop iteration but never becomes negative if the termination condition is true. Based on these annotations, we present a program instrumentation $term\,(s, c)$ that inserts the checks outlined above for every while loop in s. c is the termination condition of the outside scope, i.e., for the instrumentation of a nested loop, it is the termination condition e_c of the outer loop. The instrumentation is defined for annotated while loops in Fig. 8; for all other statements, it does not make any changes except instrumenting all substatements. The instrumentation uses information flow assertions as defined in Sect. 6.2. Again, we make use of the fact that modular products allow checking relational assertions at arbitrary program points and formulating assertions about the control flow.

We now prove that if an instrumented statement verifies under some 2-relational precondition then any two runs from a pair of states fulfilling that precondition will either both terminate or both loop forever.

Theorem 4. *If $s' = term(s, false)$, and $[\![s']\!]_2^{\hat{p}}$ verifies under some precondition $P = \lfloor\hat{P}\rfloor_2^{\hat{p}}$, and for some $\sigma_1, \sigma_2, \sigma_1'$, $(\sigma_1, \sigma_2) \vDash \hat{P}$ and $\langle s, \sigma_1 \rangle \rightarrow^* \langle \texttt{skip}, \sigma_1' \rangle$, then there exists some σ_2' s.t. $\langle s, \sigma_2 \rangle \rightarrow^* \langle \texttt{skip}, \sigma_2' \rangle$.*

Proof (Sketch). We first establish that our instrumentation ensures that each statement terminates (1) if and (2) only if its termination condition is true, (1) by showing equivalence to a standard termination proof, and (2) by a contradiction if a loop which should not terminate does. Since the execution from σ_1 terminates, by the second condition, its termination condition must have been true before the loop. We case split on whether the other execution also reaches the loop or not. If it does then the termination condition before the loop is identical in both executions, so by the first condition, the other execution also terminates. If it does not then the loop is not executed at all by the other execution, and therefore cannot cause non-termination.   □

6.6   Preventing Timing Channels

A program has a *timing channel* if high input data influences the program's execution time, meaning that an attacker who can observe the time the program executes can gain information about those secrets. Timing channels can occur in combination with observable events; the time at which an event occurs may depend on a secret even if the overall execution time of a program does not.

Consider the example in Fig. 7 (right). Assuming main receives a positive secret h, both the **print** statement and the end of the program execution will be reached later for larger values of h.

Using modular product programs, we can verify the absence of timing side channels by adding ghost state to the program that tracks the time passed since the program has started; this could, for example, be achieved via a simple step counting mechanism, or by tracking the sequence of previously executed bytecode statements. This ghost state is updated separately for both executions. We can then assert anywhere in the program that the passed time does not depend on high data in the same way we do for program variables. In particular, we can enforce that the passed time is equal whenever an observable event occurs, and we can enable users to write relational specifications that compare the time passed in both executions of a loop or a procedure.

7   Implementation and Evaluation

We have implemented our approach for secure information flow in the Viper verification infrastructure [22] and applied it to a number of example programs from the literature. Both the implementation and examples are available at http://viper.ethz.ch/modularproducts/.

7.1   Implementation in Viper

Our implementation supports a version of the Viper language that adds the following features:

1. The assertions *low(e)* and *lowEvent* for information flow specifications
2. A **declassify** statement
3. Variations of the existing method declarations and while loops that include the termination annotations shown in Sect. 6.5

The implementation transforms a program in this extended language into a modular 2-product in the original language, which can then be verified by the (unmodified) Viper back-end verifiers. All specifications are provided as information flow specifications (see Sect. 6.2) such that users require no knowledge about the transformation or the methodology behind information flow verification. Error messages are automatically translated back to the original program.

Declassification is implemented as described in Sect. 6.4. Our implementation optionally verifies the absence of timing channels; the metric chosen for tracking execution time is simple step-counting. Viper uses implicit dynamic frames [25] to reason about heap-manipulating programs; our implementation uses quantified permissions [21] to support unbounded heap data structures.

For languages with opaque object references, secure information flow can require that pointers are low, i.e., equal up to a consistent renaming of addresses. Therefore, our approach to duplicating the heap state space in the implementation differs from that described in Sect. 4.3: Instead of duplicating objects, our implementation creates a single new statement for every new in the original program, but duplicates the fields each object has. As a result, if both executions execute the same new statement, the newly created object will be considered low afterwards (but the values of its fields might still be high).

7.2 Qualitative Evaluation

We have evaluated our implementation by verifying a number of examples in the extended Viper language. The examples are listed in Table 1 and include all code snippets shown in this paper as well as a number of examples from the literature [2,3,6,13,14,17,18,23,26,28]. They combine complex language features like mutable state on the heap, arrays and procedure calls, as well as timing and termination channels, declassification, and non-trivial information flows (e.g., flows whose legality depends on semantic information not available in a standard information flow type system). We manually added pre- and postconditions as well as loop invariants; for those that have forbidden flows and therefore should not verify, we also added a legal version that declassifies the leaked information. Our implementation returns the correct result for all examples.

In all cases but one, our approach allows us to express all information flow related assertions, i.e., procedure specifications and loop invariants, purely as relational specifications in terms of *low*-assertions (see Table 1). For all these examples, we completely avoid the need to specify the functional behavior of the program. Unlike the original product program paper [6], we also do not inline any procedure calls; verification is completely modular.

The only exception is an example that, depending on a high input, executes different loops with identical behavior, and for which we need to prove that the execution time is low. In this case we have to provide invariants for both loops that exactly specify their execution time in order to prove that the overall execution time after the conditional is low. Nevertheless, the specification of the procedure containing the loop is again expressed with a relational specification using only *low*. For all other examples, unary specifications were only needed to verify the absence of runtime errors (e.g., out-of-bounds array accesses), which Viper verifies by default. Consequently, a verified program cannot leak low data through such errors, which is typically not guaranteed by type systems or static analyses.

File	Event	Heap	Array	Decl.	Term.	Time	Call	LOC	Ann/SF/NI/TM/F	T_{VCG}	T_{SE}
antopolous1 [2]						x		25	7/3/3/0/2	0.78	1.10
antopolous2 [2]			x			x		61	14/0/14/0/0	0.72	0.91
banerjee [3]		x		x			x	76	17/11/6/0/0	1.02	0.61
constanzo [13]	x		x					22	7/2/5/0/0	0.67	0.28
darvas [14]		x		x				33	12/8/4/0/0	0.67	0.35
example		x					x	31	7/1/6/0/0	0.73	0.59
example_decl		x	x					19	5/2/3/0/0	0.72	0.77
example_term			x	x				31	8/4/2/2/0	0.77	0.43
example_time	x		x			x	x	32	9/0/9/0/0	0.70	0.38
joana_1_tl [17]	x			x			x	28	1/0/1/0/0	0.62	0.23
joana_2_bl [17]	x						x	18	2/0/2/0/0	0.63	0.25
joana_2_t [17]	x							15	1/0/1/0/0	0.62	0.20
joana_3_bl [17]	x			x	x		x	47	5/1/2/2/0	0.77	0.47
joana_3_br [17]	x			x	x		x	43	8/0/2/6/0	0.83	0.60
joana_3_tl [17]	x			x			x	33	8/2/2/4/0	0.75	0.53
joana_3_tr [17]	x			x	x		x	35	8/4/2/2/0	0.76	0.51
joana_13_l [17]							x	12	1/0/1/0/0	0.62	0.24
kusters [18]		x					x	29	9/6/3/0/0	0.64	0.44
naumann [23]		x	x					20	6/3/6/0/0	0.81	0.88
product [6]		x	x				x	65	30/21/21/0/0	5.47	15.73
smith [26]			x	x				43	12/6/8/0/0	0.87	0.89
terauchi1 [28]								14	2/0/2/0/0	0.62	0.26
terauchi2 [28]			x				x	21	4/0/4/0/0	0.63	0.30
terauchi3 [28]								24	5/1/4/0/0	0.66	0.40

Table 1. Evaluated examples. We show the used language features, lines of code including specifications, overall lines used for specifications (Ann), unary specifications for safety (SF), relational specifications for non-interference (NI), specifications for termination (TM), and functional specifications required for non-interference (F). Note that some lines contain specifications belonging to multiple categories. Columns T_{SE} and T_{VCG} show the running times of the verifiers for the SE backend and the VCG backend, respectively, in seconds.

7.3   Performance

For all but one example, the runtime (averaged over 10 runs on a Lenovo ThinkPad T450s running Ubuntu) with both the Symbolic Execution (SE) and the Verification Condition Generation (VCG) verifiers is under or around one second (see Table 1). The one exception, which makes extensive use of unbounded heap data structures, takes ca. five seconds when verified using VCG, and 15 in the SE verifier. This is likely a result of inefficiencies in our encoding: The created product has a high number of branching statements, and some properties have to be proved more than once, two issues which have a much larger performance impact for SE than for VCG. We believe that it is feasible to remove much of this overhead by optimizing the encoding; we leave this as future work.

8   Related Work

The notion of k-safety hyperproperties was originally introduced by Clarkson and Schneider [12]. Here, we focus on statically proving hyperproperties for imperative and object-oriented programs; much more work exists for testing or monitoring hyperproperties like secure information flow at runtime, or for reasoning about hyperproperties in different programming paradigms.

Relational logics such as Relational Hoare Logic [11], Relational Separation Logic [29] and others [1,10] allow reasoning directly about relational properties of two different program executions. Unlike our approach, they usually allow reasoning about the executions of two *different* programs; as a result, they do not give special support for two executions of the same program calling the same procedure with a relational specification. Recently, Banerjee et al. [5] introduced biprograms, which allow explicitly expressing alignment between executions and using relational specifications to reason about aligned calls; however, this approach requires that procedures with relational specifications are always called by both executions, which is for instance not the case if a call occurs under a high guard in secure information flow verification. We handle such cases by interpreting relational specifications as trivially true; one can then still resort to functional specifications to complete the proof. Their work also does not allow mixed specifications, which are easily supported in our product programs. Relational program logics are generally difficult to automate. Recent work by Sousa and Dillig [27] presents a logic that can be applied automatically by an algorithm that implicitly constructs different product programs that align *some* identical statements, but does not fully support relational specifications. Moreover, their approach requires dedicated tool support, whereas our modular product programs can be verified using off-the-shelf tools.

The approach of reducing hyperproperties to ordinary trace properties was introduced by self-composition [9]. While self-composition is theoretically complete, it does not allow modular reasoning with relational specifications. The resulting problem of having to fully specify program behavior was pointed out by Terauchi and Aiken [28]; since then, there have been a number of different attempts to solve this problem by allowing (parts of) programs to execute in lock-step. Terauchi and Aiken [28] did this for secure information flow by relying on information from a type system; other similar approaches exist [23].

Product programs [6,7] allow different interleavings of program executions. The initial product program approach [6] would in principle allow the use of relational specifications for procedure calls, but only under the restriction that both program executions always follow the same control flow. The generalized approach [7] allows combining different programs and arbitrary numbers of executions. This product construction is non-deterministic and usually interactive. In some (but not all) cases, programmers can manually construct product programs that avoid duplicated calls and loops and thereby allow using relational specifications. However, whether this is possible depends on the used specification, meaning that the product construction and verification are intertwined and a new product has to be constructed when specifications change. In contrast, our new product construction is fully deterministic and automatic, allows arbitrary control flows while still being able to use relational specifications for all loops and calls, and therefore avoids the issue of requiring full functional specifications.

Considerable work has been invested into proving specific hyperproperties like secure information flow. One popular approach is the use of type systems [26]; while those are modular and offer good performance, they overapproximate possible program behaviors and are therefore less precise than approaches using logics. In particular, they require labeling any single value as either high or low, and do not allow distinctions like the one we made for the example in Fig. 1, where only the first bits of a sequence of integers were low. In addition, type systems typically struggle to prevent information leaks via side channels like termination or program aborts. There have been attempts to create type systems that handle some of these limitations (e.g. [15]).

Static analyses [2,17] enable fully automatic reasoning. They are typically not modular and, similarly to type systems, need to abstract semantic information, which can lead to false positives. They strike a trade-off different from our solution, which requires specifications, but enables precise, modular reasoning.

A number of logic-based approaches to proving specific hyperproperties exist. As an example, Darvas et al. use dynamic logic for proving non-interference [14]; this approach offers some automation, but requires user interaction for most realistic programs. Leino et al. [19] verify determinism up to equivalence using self-composition, which suffers from the drawbacks explained above.

Different kinds of declassification have been studied extensively, Sabelfeld and Sands [24] provide a good overview. Li and Zdancewic [20] introduce downgrading policies that describe which information can be declassified and, similar to our approach, can do so for arbitrary expressions.

9 Conclusion and Future Work

We have presented modular product programs, a novel form of product programs that enable modular reasoning about k-safety hyperproperties using relational specifications with off-the-shelf verifiers. We showed that modular products are expressive enough to handle advanced aspects of secure information flow verification. They can prove the absence of termination and timing side channels and encode declassification. Our implementation shows that our technique works in practice on a number of challenging examples from the literature, and exhibits good performance even without optimizations.

For future work, we plan to infer relational properties by using standard program analysis techniques on the products. We also plan to generalize our technique to prove probabilistic secure information flow for concurrent program by combining our encoding with ideas from concurrent separation logic. Finally, we plan to optimize our encoding to further improve performance.

Acknowledgements. We would like to thank Toby Murray and David Naumann for various helpful discussions. We are grateful to the anonymous reviewes for their valuable comments. We also gratefully acknowledge support from the Zurich Information Security and Privacy Center (ZISC).

References

1. Aguirre, A., Barthe, G., Gaboardi, M., Garg, D., Strub, P.: A relational logic for higher-order programs. PACMPL **1**(ICFP), 21:1–21:29 (2017)
2. Antonopoulos, T., Gazzillo, P., Hicks, M., Koskinen, E., Terauchi, T., Wei, S.: Decomposition instead of self-composition for proving the absence of timing channels. In: Proceedings of the 38th ACM SIGPLAN Conference on Programming Language Design and Implementation, PLDI 2017, Barcelona, Spain, 18–23 June 2017, pp. 362–375 (2017)
3. Banerjee, A., Naumann, D.A., Secure information flow and pointer confinement in a java-like language. In: 15th IEEE Computer Security Foundations Workshop (CSFW-15 2002), 24–26 June 2002, Cape Breton, Nova Scotia, Canada, p. 253 (2002)
4. Banerjee, A., Naumann, D.A.: A logical analysis of framing for specifications with pure method calls. In: Giannakopoulou, D., Kroening, D. (eds.) VSTTE 2014. LNCS, vol. 8471, pp. 3–20. Springer, Cham (2014). https://doi.org/10.1007/978-3-319-12154-3_1
5. Banerjee, A., Naumann, D.A., Nikouei, M.: Relational logic with framing and hypotheses. In: 36th IARCS Annual Conference on Foundations of Software Technology and Theoretical Computer Science, FSTTCS 2016, Chennai, India, 13–15 December 2016, pp. 11:1–11:16 (2016)
6. Barthe, G., Crespo, J.M., Kunz, C.: Relational verification using product programs. In: Butler, M., Schulte, W. (eds.) FM 2011. LNCS, vol. 6664, pp. 200–214. Springer, Heidelberg (2011). https://doi.org/10.1007/978-3-642-21437-0_17
7. Barthe, G., Crespo, J.M., Kunz, C.: Beyond 2-safety: asymmetric product programs for relational program verification. In: Artemov, S., Nerode, A. (eds.) LFCS 2013. LNCS, vol. 7734, pp. 29–43. Springer, Heidelberg (2013). https://doi.org/10.1007/978-3-642-35722-0_3
8. Barthe, G., D'Argenio, P.R., Rezk, T.: Secure information flow by self-composition. In: 17th IEEE Computer Security Foundations Workshop, (CSFW-17 2004), 28–30 June 2004, Pacific Grove, CA, USA, pp. 100–114 (2004)
9. Barthe, G., D'Argenio, P.R., Rezk, T.: Secure information flow by self-composition. Math. Struct. Comput. Sci. **21**(6), 1207–1252 (2011)
10. Barthe, G., Grégoire, B., Béguelin, S.Z.: Formal certification of code-based cryptographic proofs. In: Proceedings of the 36th ACM SIGPLAN-SIGACT Symposium on Principles of Programming Languages, POPL 2009, Savannah, GA, USA, 21–23 January 2009, pp. 90–101 (2009)
11. Benton, N.: Simple relational correctness proofs for static analyses and program transformations. In: Proceedings of the 31st ACM SIGPLAN-SIGACT Symposium on Principles of Programming Languages, POPL 2004, Venice, Italy, 14–16 January 2004, pp. 14–25 (2004)
12. Clarkson, M.R., Schneider, F.B.: Hyperproperties. J. Comput. Secur. **18**(6), 1157–1210 (2010)
13. Costanzo, D., Shao, Z.: A separation logic for enforcing declarative information flow control policies. In: Abadi, M., Kremer, S. (eds.) POST 2014. LNCS, vol. 8414, pp. 179–198. Springer, Heidelberg (2014). https://doi.org/10.1007/978-3-642-54792-8_10
14. Darvas, Á., Hähnle, R., Sands, D.: A theorem proving approach to analysis of secure information flow. In: Hutter, D., Ullmann, M. (eds.) SPC 2005. LNCS, vol. 3450, pp. 193–209. Springer, Heidelberg (2005). https://doi.org/10.1007/978-3-540-32004-3_20

15. Deng, Z., Smith, G.: Lenient array operations for practical secure information flow. In: 17th IEEE Computer Security Foundations Workshop, (CSFW-17 2004), 28–30 June 2004, Pacific Grove, CA, USA, p. 115 (2004)
16. Francez, N.: Fairness. Springer-Verlag, New York Inc., New York (1986). https://doi.org/10.1007/978-1-4612-4886-6
17. Giffhorn, D., Snelting, G.: A new algorithm for low-deterministic security. Int. J. Inf. Sec. **14**(3), 263–287 (2015)
18. Küsters, R., Truderung, T., Beckert, B., Bruns, D., Kirsten, M., Mohr, M.: A hybrid approach for proving noninterference of java programs. In: IEEE 28th Computer Security Foundations Symposium, CSF 2015, Verona, Italy, 13–17 July 2015, pp. 305–319 (2015)
19. Leino, K.R.M., Müller, P.: Verification of equivalent-results methods. In: Drossopoulou, S. (ed.) ESOP 2008. LNCS, vol. 4960, pp. 307–321. Springer, Heidelberg (2008). https://doi.org/10.1007/978-3-540-78739-6_24
20. Li, P., Zdancewic, S.: Downgrading policies and relaxed noninterference. In: Proceedings of the 32nd ACM SIGPLAN-SIGACT Symposium on Principles of Programming Languages, POPL 2005, Long Beach, California, USA, 12–14 January 2005, pp. 158–170 (2005)
21. Müller, P., Schwerhoff, M., Summers, A.J.: Automatic verification of iterated separating conjunctions using symbolic execution. In: Chaudhuri, S., Farzan, A. (eds.) CAV 2016, Part I. LNCS, vol. 9779, pp. 405–425. Springer, Cham (2016). https://doi.org/10.1007/978-3-319-41528-4_22
22. Müller, P., Schwerhoff, M., Summers, A.J.: Viper: a verification infrastructure for permission-based reasoning. In: Jobstmann, B., Leino, K.R.M. (eds.) VMCAI 2016. LNCS, vol. 9583, pp. 41–62. Springer, Heidelberg (2016). https://doi.org/10.1007/978-3-662-49122-5_2
23. Naumann, D.A.: From coupling relations to mated invariants for checking information flow. In: Gollmann, D., Meier, J., Sabelfeld, A. (eds.) ESORICS 2006. LNCS, vol. 4189, pp. 279–296. Springer, Heidelberg (2006). https://doi.org/10.1007/11863908_18
24. Sabelfeld, A., Sands, D.: Dimensions and principles of declassification. In: 18th IEEE Computer Security Foundations Workshop, (CSFW-18 2005), 20–22 June 2005, Aix-en-Provence, France, pp. 255–269 (2005)
25. Smans, J., Jacobs, B., Piessens, F.: Implicit dynamic frames. ACM Trans. Program. Lang. Syst. **34**(1), 2:1–2:58 (2012)
26. Smith, G.: Principles of secure information flow analysis. In: Christodorescu, M., Jha, S., Maughan, D., Song, D., Wang, C. (eds.) Malware Detection. ADIS, vol. 27, pp. 291–307. Springer, Boston (2007). https://doi.org/10.1007/978-0-387-44599-1_13
27. Sousa, M., Dillig, I.: Cartesian hoare logic for verifying k-safety properties. In: Proceedings of the 37th ACM SIGPLAN Conference on Programming Language Design and Implementation, PLDI 2016, Santa Barbara, CA, USA, 13–17 June 2016, pp. 57–69 (2016)
28. Terauchi, T., Aiken, A.: Secure information flow as a safety problem. In: Hankin, C., Siveroni, I. (eds.) SAS 2005. LNCS, vol. 3672, pp. 352–367. Springer, Heidelberg (2005). https://doi.org/10.1007/11547662_24
29. Yang, H.: Relational separation logic. Theor. Comput. Sci. **375**(1–3), 308–334 (2007)

Program Verification

A Fistful of Dollars: Formalizing Asymptotic Complexity Claims via Deductive Program Verification

Armaël Guéneau[1], Arthur Charguéraud[1,2], and François Pottier[1(✉)]

[1] Inria, Paris, France
francois.pottier@inria.fr
[2] Université de Strasbourg, CNRS, ICube UMR 7357, Strasbourg, France

Abstract. We present a framework for simultaneously verifying the functional correctness and the worst-case asymptotic time complexity of higher-order imperative programs. We build on top of Separation Logic with Time Credits, embedded in an interactive proof assistant. We formalize the O notation, which is key to enabling modular specifications and proofs. We cover the subtleties of the multivariate case, where the complexity of a program fragment depends on multiple parameters. We propose a way of integrating complexity bounds into specifications, present lemmas and tactics that support a natural reasoning style, and illustrate their use with a collection of examples.

1 Introduction

A program or program component whose functional correctness has been verified might nevertheless still contain complexity bugs: that is, its performance, in some scenarios, could be much poorer than expected.

Indeed, many program verification tools only guarantee partial correctness, that is, do not even guarantee termination, so a verified program could run forever. Some program verification tools do enforce termination, but usually do not allow establishing an explicit complexity bound. Tools for automatic complexity inference can produce complexity bounds, but usually have limited expressive power.

In practice, many complexity bugs are revealed by testing. Some have also been detected during ordinary program verification, as shown by Filliâtre and Letouzey [14], who find a violation of the balancing invariant in a widely-distributed implementation of binary search trees. Nevertheless, none of these techniques can guarantee, with a high degree of assurance, the absence of complexity bugs in software.

To illustrate the issue, consider the binary search implementation in Fig. 1. Virtually every modern software verification tool allows proving that this OCaml

This research was partly supported by the French National Research Agency (ANR) under the grant ANR-15-CE25-0008.

A. Ahmed (Ed.): ESOP 2018, LNCS 10801, pp. 533–560, 2018.
https://doi.org/10.1007/978-3-319-89884-1_19

code (or analogous code, expressed in another programming language) satisfies the specification of a binary search and terminates on all valid inputs. This code might even pass a lightweight testing process, as some search queries will be answered very quickly, even if the array is very large. Yet, a more thorough testing process would reveal a serious issue: a search for a value that is stored in the second half of the range $[i, j)$ takes linear time. It would be embarrassing if such faulty code was deployed, as it would aggravate benevolent users and possibly allow malicious users to mount denial-of-service attacks.

```
(* Requires t to be a sorted array of integers.
   Returns k such that i <= k < j and t.(k) = v
   or -1 if there is no such k. *)
let rec bsearch t v i j =
  if j <= i then -1 else
    let k = i + (j - i) / 2 in
    if v = t.(k) then k
    else if v < t.(k) then bsearch t v i k
    else bsearch t v (i+1) j
```

Fig. 1. A flawed binary search. This code is provably correct and terminating, yet exhibits linear (instead of logarithmic) time complexity for some input parameters.

As illustrated above, complexity bugs can affect execution time, but could also concern space (including heap space, stack space, and disk space) or other resources, such as the network, energy, and so on. In this paper, for simplicity, we focus on execution time only. That said, much of our work is independent of which resource is considered. We expect that our techniques could be adapted to verify asymptotic bounds on the use of other non-renewable resources, such as the network.

We work with a simple model of program execution, where certain operations, such as calling a function or entering a loop body, cost one unit of time, and every other operation costs nothing. Although this model is very remote from physical running time, it is independent of the compiler, operating system, and hardware [18,24] and still allows establishing asymptotic time complexity bounds, and therefore, detecting complexity bugs—situations where a program is asymptotically slower than it should be.

In prior work [11], the second and third authors present a method for verifying that a program satisfies a specification that includes an explicit bound on the program's worst-case, amortized time complexity. They use Separation Logic with Time Credits, a simple extension of Separation Logic [23] where the assertion \$1 represents a permission to perform one step of computation, and is consumed when exercised. The assertion \$$n$ is a separating conjunction of n such time credits. Separation Logic with Time Credits is implemented in the second author's interactive verification framework, CFML [9,10], which is embedded in the Coq proof assistant.

Using CFML, the second and third authors verify the correctness and time complexity of an OCaml implementation of the Union-Find data structure [11]. However, their specifications involve *concrete* cost functions: for instance, the precondition of the function *find* indicates that calling *find* requires and consumes $\$(2\alpha(n) + 4)$, where n is the current number of elements in the data structure, and where α denotes an inverse of Ackermann's function. We would prefer the specification to give the *asymptotic* complexity bound $O(\alpha(n))$, which means that, for *some* function $f \in O(\alpha(n))$, calling *find* requires and consumes $\$f(n)$. This is the purpose of this paper.

We argue that the use of asymptotic bounds, such as $O(\alpha(n))$, is necessary for (verified or unverified) complexity analysis to be applicable at scale. At a superficial level, it reduces clutter in specifications and proofs: $O(mn)$ is more compact and readable than $3mn + 2n \log n + 5n + 3m + 2$. At a deeper level, it is crucial for stating modular specifications, which hide the details of a particular implementation. Exposing the fact that *find* costs $2\alpha(n) + 4$ is undesirable: if a tiny modification of the Union-Find module changes this cost to $2\alpha(n) + 5$, then all direct and indirect clients of the Union-Find module must be updated, which is intolerable. Furthermore, sometimes, the constant factors are unknown anyway. Applying the Master Theorem [12] to a recurrence equation only yields an order of growth, not a concrete bound. Finally, for most practical purposes, no critical information is lost when concrete bounds such as $2\alpha(n) + 4$ are replaced with asymptotic bounds such as $O(\alpha(n))$. Indeed, the number of computation steps that take place at the source level is related to physical time only up to a hardware- and compiler-dependent constant factor. The use of asymptotic complexity in the analysis of algorithms, initially advocated by Hopcroft and by Tarjan, has been widely successful and is nowadays standard practice.

One must be aware of several limitations of our approach. First, it is not a worst-case execution time (WCET) analysis: it does not yield bounds on actual physical execution time. Second, it is not fully automated. We place emphasis on expressiveness, as opposed to automation. Our vision is that verifying the functional correctness *and* time complexity of a program, at the same time, should not involve much more effort than verifying correctness alone. Third, we control only the growth of the cost as the parameters grow large. A loop that counts up from 0 to 2^{60} has complexity $O(1)$, even though it typically won't terminate in a lifetime. Although this is admittedly a potential problem, traditional program verification falls prey to analogous pitfalls: for instance, a program that attempts to allocate and initialize an array of size (say) 2^{48} can be proved correct, even though, on contemporary desktop hardware, it will typically fail by lack of memory. We believe that there is value in our approach in spite of these limitations.

Reasoning and working with asymptotic complexity bounds is not as simple as one might hope. As demonstrated by several examples in Sect. 2, typical paper proofs using the O notation rely on informal reasoning principles which can easily be abused to prove a contradiction. Of course, using a proof assistant steers us clear of this danger, but implies that our proofs cannot be quite as simple and perhaps cannot have quite the same structure as their paper counterparts.

A key issue that we run against is the handling of existential quantifiers. According to what was said earlier, the specification of a sorting algorithm, say *mergesort*, should be, roughly: "there exists a cost function $f \in O(\lambda n.n \log n)$ such that *mergesort* is content with $\$f(n)$, where n is the length of the input list." Therefore, the very first step in a naïve proof of *mergesort* must be to exhibit a witness for f, that is, a concrete cost function. An appropriate witness might be $\lambda n.2n \log n$, or $\lambda n.n \log n + 3$, who knows? This information is not available up front, at the very *beginning* of the proof; it becomes available only *during* the proof, as we examine the code of *mergesort*, step by step. It is not reasonable to expect the human user to guess such a witness. Instead, it seems desirable to *delay* the production of the witness and to *gradually* construct a cost expression as the proof progresses. In the case of a nonrecursive function, such as *insertionsort*, the cost expression, once fully synthesized, yields the desired witness. In the case of a recursive function, such as *mergesort*, the cost expression yields the body of a recurrence equation, whose solution is the desired witness.

We make the following contributions:

1. We formalize O as a binary *domination* relation between functions of type $A \to \mathbb{Z}$, where the type A is chosen by the user. Functions of several variables are covered by instantiating A with a product type. We contend that, in order to define what it means for $a \in A$ to "grow large", or "tend towards infinity", the type A must be equipped with a filter [6], that is, a quantifier $\mathbb{U}a.P$. (Eberl [13] does so as well.) We propose a library of lemmas and tactics that can prove nonnegativeness, monotonicity, and domination assertions (Sect. 3).
2. We propose a standard style of writing specifications, in the setting of the CFML program verification framework, so that they integrate asymptotic time complexity claims (Sect. 4). We define a predicate, specO, which imposes this style and incorporates a few important technical decisions, such as the fact that every cost function must be nonnegative and nondecreasing.
3. We propose a methodology, supported by a collection of Coq tactics, to prove such specifications (Sect. 5). Our tactics, which heavily rely on Coq metavariables, help gradually synthesize cost expressions for straight-line code and conditionals, and help construct the recurrence equations involved in the analysis of recursive functions, while delaying their resolution.
4. We present several classic examples of complexity analyses (Sect. 6), including: a simple loop in $O(n.2^n)$, nested loops in $O(n^3)$ and $O(nm)$, binary search in $O(\log n)$, and Union-Find in $O(\alpha(n))$.

Our code can be found online in the form of two standalone Coq libraries and a self-contained archive [16].

2   Challenges in Reasoning with the O Notation

When informally reasoning about the complexity of a function, or of a code block, it is customary to make assertions of the form "this code has asymptotic complexity $O(1)$", "that code has asymptotic complexity $O(n)$", and so on. Yet, these assertions are too informal: they do not have sufficiently precise meaning, and can be easily abused to produce flawed paper proofs.

A striking example appears in Fig. 2, which shows how one might "prove" that a recursive function has complexity $O(1)$, whereas its actual cost is $O(n)$. The flawed proof exploits the (valid) relation $O(1) + O(1) = O(1)$, which means that a sequence of two constant-time code fragments is itself a constant-time code fragment. The flaw lies in the fact that the O notation hides an existential quantification, which is inadvertently swapped with the universal quantification over the parameter n. Indeed, the claim is that "there exists a constant c such that, for every n, waste(n) runs in at most c computation steps". However, the proposed proof by induction establishes a much weaker result, to wit: "for every n, there exists a constant c such that waste(n) runs in at most c steps". This result is certainly true, yet does not entail the claim.

An example of a different nature appears in Fig. 3. There, the auxiliary function g takes two integer arguments n and m and involves two nested loops, over the intervals $[1, n]$ and $[1, m]$. Its asymptotic complexity is $O(n + nm)$, which, *under the hypothesis that m is large enough*, can be simplified to $O(nm)$. The reasoning, thus far, is correct. The flaw lies in our attempt to substitute 0 for m

Incorrect claim: The OCaml function waste has asymptotic complexity $O(1)$.

```
let rec waste n =
  if n > 0 then waste (n-1)
```

Flawed proof:
Let us prove by induction on n that waste(n) costs $O(1)$.
- **Case $n \leq 0$:** waste(n) terminates immediately. Therefore, its cost is $O(1)$.
- **Case $n > 0$:** A call to waste(n) involves constant-time processing, followed with a call to waste$(n - 1)$. By the induction hypothesis, the cost of the recursive call is $O(1)$. We conclude that the cost of waste(n) is $O(1) + O(1)$, that is, $O(1)$.

Fig. 2. A flawed proof that waste(n) costs $O(1)$, when its actual cost is $O(n)$.

Incorrect claim: The OCaml function f has asymptotic complexity $O(1)$.

```
let g (n, m) =
  for i = 1 to n do
    for j = 1 to m do () done
  done
let f n = g (n, 0)
```

Flawed proof:
- g(n, m) involves nm inner loop iterations, thus costs $O(nm)$.
- The cost of f(n) is the cost of g$(n, 0)$, plus $O(1)$. As the cost of g(n, m) is $O(nm)$, we find, by substituting 0 for m, that the cost of g$(n, 0)$ is $O(0)$. Thus, f(n) is $O(1)$.

Fig. 3. A flawed proof that f(n) costs $O(1)$, when its actual cost is $O(n)$.

Incorrect claim: The OCaml function h has asymptotic complexity $O(nm^2)$.

```
1    let h (m, n) =
2      for i = 0 to m−1 do
3        let p = (if i = 0 then pow2 n else n*i) in
4        for j = 1 to p do () done
5      done
```

Flawed proof:

- The body of the outer loop (lines 3-4) has asymptotic cost $O(ni)$. Indeed, as soon as $i > 0$ holds, the inner loop performs ni constant-time iterations. The case where $i = 0$ does not matter in an asymptotic analysis.
- The cost of $h(m,n)$ is the sum of the costs of the iterations of the outer loop:

$$\sum_{i=0}^{m-1} O(ni) = O\left(n \cdot \sum_{i=0}^{m-1} i\right) = O(nm^2).$$

Fig. 4. A flawed proof that $h(m,n)$ costs $O(nm^2)$, when its actual cost is $O(2^n + nm^2)$.

in the bound $O(nm)$. Because this bound is valid only for sufficiently large m, it does not make sense to substitute a specific value for m. In other words, from the fact that "$g(n,m)$ costs $O(nm)$ when n and m are sufficiently large", one *cannot* deduce anything about the cost of $g(n,0)$. To repair this proof, one must take a step back and prove that $g(n,m)$ has asymptotic complexity $O(n + nm)$ *for sufficiently large n and for every m*. This fact *can* be instantiated with $m = 0$, allowing one to correctly conclude that $g(n,0)$ costs $O(n)$. We come back to this example in Sect. 3.3.

One last example of tempting yet invalid reasoning appears in Fig. 4. We borrow it from Howell [19]. This flawed proof exploits the dubious idea that "the asymptotic cost of a loop is the sum of the asymptotic costs of its iterations". In more precise terms, the proof relies on the following implication, where $f(m,n,i)$ represents the true cost of the i-th loop iteration and $g(m,n,i)$ represents an asymptotic bound on $f(m,n,i)$:

$$f(m,n,i) \in O(g(m,n,i)) \quad \Rightarrow \quad \sum_{i=0}^{m-1} f(m,n,i) \in O\left(\sum_{i=0}^{m-1} g(m,n,i)\right)$$

As pointed out by Howell, this implication is in fact invalid. Here, $f(m,n,0)$ is 2^n and $f(m,n,i)$ when $i > 0$ is ni, while $g(m,n,i)$ is just ni. The left-hand side of the above implication holds, but the right-hand side does not, as $2^n + \sum_{i=1}^{m-1} ni$ is $O(2^n + nm^2)$, not $O(nm^2)$. The Summation lemma presented later on in this paper (Lemma 8) rules out the problem by adding the requirement that f be a nondecreasing function of the loop index i. We discuss in depth later on (Sect. 4.5) why cost functions should and can be monotonic.

The examples that we have presented show that the informal reasoning style of paper proofs, where the O notation is used in a loose manner, is unsound. One cannot hope, in a formal setting, to faithfully mimic this reasoning style. In this paper, we do assign O specifications to functions, because we believe that this style is elegant, modular and scalable. However, during the analysis of a function body, we abandon the O notation. We first synthesize a cost expression for the function body, then check that this expression is indeed dominated by the asymptotic bound that appears in the specification.

3   Formalizing the O Notation

3.1   Domination

In many textbooks, the fact that f is bounded above by g asymptotically, up to constant factor, is written "$f = O(g)$" or "$f \in O(g)$". However, the former notation is quite inappropriate, as it is clear that "$f = O(g)$" cannot be literally understood as an equality. Indeed, if it truly were an equality, then, by symmetry and transitivity, $f_1 = O(g)$ and $f_2 = O(g)$ would imply $f_1 = f_2$. The latter notation makes much better sense: $O(g)$ is then understood as a set of functions. This approach has in fact been used in formalizations of the O notation [3]. Yet, in this paper, we prefer to think directly in terms of a *domination* preorder between functions. Thus, instead of "$f \in O(g)$", we write $f \preceq g$.

Although the O notation is often defined in the literature only in the special case of functions whose domain is $\mathbb{N}$, $\mathbb{Z}$ or $\mathbb{R}$, we must define domination in the general case of functions whose domain is an arbitrary type A. By later instantiating A with a product type, such as $\mathbb{Z}^k$, we get a definition of domination that covers the multivariate case. Thus, let us fix a type A, and let f and g inhabit the function type $A \to \mathbb{Z}$.[1]

Fixing the type A, it turns out, is not quite enough. In addition, the type A must be equipped with a *filter* [6]. To see why that is the case, let us work towards the definition of domination. As is standard, we wish to build a notion of "growing large enough" into the definition of domination. That is, instead of requiring a relation of the form $|f(x)| \leq c\,|g(x)|$ to be "everywhere true", we require it to be "ultimately true", that is, "true when x is large enough".[2] Thus, $f \preceq g$ should mean, roughly:

"up to a constant factor, ultimately, $|f|$ is bounded above by $|g|$."

That is, somewhat more formally:

"for some c, for every sufficiently large x, $|f(x)| \leq c\,|g(x)|$"

In mathematical notation, we would like to write: $\exists c.\ \mathbb{U}x.\ |f(x)| \leq c\,|g(x)|$. For such a formula to make sense, we must define the meaning of the formula $\mathbb{U}x.P$, where x inhabits the type A. This is the reason why the type A must be

---

[1] At this time, we require the codomain of f and g to be $\mathbb{Z}$. Following Avigad and Donnelly [3], we could allow it to be an arbitrary nondegenerate ordered ring. We have not yet needed this generalization.

[2] When A is $\mathbb{N}$, provided $g(x)$ is never zero, requiring the inequality to be "everywhere true" is in fact the same as requiring it to be "ultimately true". Outside of this special case, however, requiring the inequality to hold everywhere is usually too strong.

equipped with a filter $\mathbb{U}$, which intuitively should be thought of as a quantifier, whose meaning is "ultimately". Let us briefly defer the definition of a filter (Sect. 3.2) and sum up what has been explained so far:

Definition 1 (Domination). *Let A be a filtered type, that is, a type A equipped with a filter $\mathbb{U}_A$.*
The relation $\preceq_A$ on $A \to \mathbb{Z}$ is defined as follows:

$$f \preceq_A g \quad \equiv \quad \exists c.\, \mathbb{U}_A\, x.\, |f(x)| \leq c\,|g(x)|$$

3.2   Filters

Whereas $\forall x.P$ means that P holds of *every* x, and $\exists x.P$ means that P holds of *some* x, the formula $\mathbb{U}x.P$ should be taken to mean that P holds of every *sufficiently large* x, that is, P *ultimately* holds.

The formula $\mathbb{U}x.P$ is short for $\mathbb{U}\,(\lambda x.P)$. If x ranges over some type A, then $\mathbb{U}$ must have type $\mathcal{P}(\mathcal{P}(A))$, where $\mathcal{P}(A)$ is short for $A \to \text{Prop}$. To stress this better, although Bourbaki [6] states that a filter is "a set of subsets of A", it is crucial to note that $\mathcal{P}(\mathcal{P}(A))$ is the type of a quantifier in higher-order logic.

Definition 2 (Filter). *A filter [6] on a type A is an object $\mathbb{U}$ of type $\mathcal{P}(\mathcal{P}(A))$ that enjoys the following four properties, where $\mathbb{U}x.P$ is short for $\mathbb{U}\,(\lambda x.P)$:*

(1)	$(P_1 \Rightarrow P_2) \Rightarrow \mathbb{U}x.P_1 \Rightarrow \mathbb{U}x.P_2$	*(covariance)*
(2a)	$\mathbb{U}x.P_1 \wedge \mathbb{U}x.P_2 \Rightarrow \mathbb{U}x.(P_1 \wedge P_2)$	*(stability under binary intersection)*
(2b)	$\mathbb{U}x.\,True$	*(stability under 0-ary intersection)*
(3)	$\mathbb{U}x.P \Rightarrow \exists x.P$	*(nonemptiness)*

Properties (1)–(3) are intended to ensure that the intuitive reading of $\mathbb{U}x.P$ as: "for sufficiently large x, P holds" makes sense. Property (1) states that if P_1 implies P_2 and if P_1 holds when x is large enough, then P_2, too, should hold when x is large enough. Properties (2a) and (2b), together, state that if each of $P_1, \ldots, P_k$ independently holds when x is large enough, then $P_1, \ldots, P_k$ should simultaneously hold when x is large enough. Properties (1) and (2b) together imply $\forall x.P \Rightarrow \mathbb{U}x.P$. Property (3) states that if P holds when x is large enough, then P should hold of some x. In classical logic, it would be equivalent to $\neg(\mathbb{U}x.\text{False})$.

In the following, we let the metavariable A stand for a *filtered type*, that is, a pair of a carrier type and a filter on this type. By abuse of notation, we also write A for the carrier type. (In Coq, this is permitted by an implicit projection.) We write $\mathbb{U}_A$ for the filter.

3.3   Examples of Filters

When $\mathbb{U}$ is a *universal filter*, $\mathbb{U}x.Q(x)$ is (by definition) equivalent to $\forall x.Q(x)$. Thus, a predicate Q is "ultimately true" if and only if it is "everywhere true". In other words, the universal quantifier is a filter.

Definition 3 (Universal filter). *Let T be a nonempty type. Then $\lambda Q.\forall x.Q(x)$ is a filter on T.*

When $\mathbb{U}$ is the *order filter* associated with the ordering $\leq$, the formula $\mathbb{U}x.Q(x)$ means that, when x becomes sufficiently large with respect to $\leq$, the property $Q(x)$ becomes true.

Definition 4 (Order filter). *Let $(T, \leq)$ be a nonempty ordered type, such that every two elements have an upper bound. Then $\lambda Q.\exists x_0.\forall x \geq x_0.\, Q(x)$ is a filter on T.*

The order filter associated with the ordered type $(\mathbb{Z}, \leq)$ is the most natural filter on the type $\mathbb{Z}$. Equipping the type $\mathbb{Z}$ with this filter yields a filtered type, which, by abuse of notation, we also write $\mathbb{Z}$. Thus, the formula $\mathbb{U}_\mathbb{Z}\, x.Q(x)$ means that $Q(x)$ becomes true "as x tends towards infinity".

By instantiating Definition 1 with the filtered type $\mathbb{Z}$, we recover the classic definition of domination between functions of $\mathbb{Z}$ to $\mathbb{Z}$:

$$f \preceq_\mathbb{Z} g \iff \exists c.\, \exists n_0.\, \forall n \geq n_0.\, |f(n)| \leq c\, |g(n)|$$

We now turn to the definition of a filter on a product type $A_1 \times A_2$, where A_1 and A_2 are filtered types. Such a filter plays a key role in defining domination between functions of several variables. The following *product filter* is the most natural construction, although there are others:

Definition 5 (Product filter). *Let A_1 and A_2 be filtered types. Then*

$$\lambda Q.\exists Q_1, Q_2. \begin{cases} \mathbb{U}_{A_1}\, x_1.\, Q_1 \\ \wedge\, \mathbb{U}_{A_2}\, x_2.\, Q_2 \\ \wedge\, \forall x_1, x_2.\, Q_1(x_1) \wedge Q_2(x_2) \Rightarrow Q(x_1, x_2) \end{cases}$$

is a filter on the product type $A_1 \times A_2$.

To understand this definition, it is useful to consider the special case where A_1 and A_2 are both $\mathbb{Z}$. Then, for $i \in \{1, 2\}$, the formula $\mathbb{U}_{A_i}\, x_i.\, Q_i$ means that the predicate Q_i contains an infinite interval of the form $[a_i, \infty)$. Thus, the formula $\forall x_1, x_2.\, Q_1(x_1) \wedge Q_2(x_2) \Rightarrow Q(x_1, x_2)$ requires the predicate Q to contain the infinite rectangle $[a_1, \infty) \times [a_2, \infty)$. Thus, a predicate Q on $\mathbb{Z}^2$ is "ultimately true" w.r.t. to the product filter if and only if it is "true on some infinite rectangle". In Bourbaki's terminology [6, Chap. 1, Sect. 6.7], the infinite rectangles form a *basis* of the product filter.

We view the product filter as the default filter on the product type $A_1 \times A_2$. Whenever we refer to $A_1 \times A_2$ in a setting where a filtered type is expected, the product filter is intended.

We stress that there are several filters on $\mathbb{Z}$, including the universal filter and the order filter, and therefore several filters on $\mathbb{Z}^k$. Therefore, it does not make sense to use the O notation without specifying which filter one considers. Consider again the function $\mathsf{g}(n, m)$ in Fig. 3 (Sect. 2). One can prove that

$g(n, m)$ has complexity $O(nm + n)$ with respect to the standard filter on $\mathbb{Z}^2$. With respect to *this filter*, this complexity bound is equivalent to $O(mn)$, as the functions $\lambda(m, n).mn + n$ and $\lambda(m, n).mn$ dominate each other. Unfortunately, this *does not allow* deducing anything about the complexity of $g(n, 0)$, since the bound $O(mn)$ holds only when n and m grow large. An alternate approach is to prove that $g(n, m)$ has complexity $O(nm + n)$ with respect to a stronger filter, namely the product of the standard filter on $\mathbb{Z}$ and the universal filter on $\mathbb{Z}$. With respect to *that filter*, the functions $\lambda(m, n).mn + n$ and $\lambda(m, n).mn$ are *not* equivalent. This bound *does allow* instantiating m with 0 and deducing that $g(n, 0)$ has complexity $O(n)$.

3.4   Properties of Domination

Many properties of the domination relation can be established with respect to an arbitrary filtered type A. Here are two example lemmas; there are many more. As before, f and g range over $A \to \mathbb{Z}$. The operators $f + g$, $\max(f, g)$ and $f.g$ denote pointwise sum, maximum, and product, respectively.

Lemma 6 (Sum and Max Are Alike). *Assume f and g are ultimately nonnegative, that is, $\mathbb{U}_A\, x.\ f(x) \geq 0$ and $\mathbb{U}_A\, x.\ g(x) \geq 0$ hold. Then, we have $\max(f, g) \preceq_A f + g$ and $f + g \preceq_A \max(f, g)$.*

Lemma 7 (Multiplication). $f_1 \preceq_A g_1$ *and* $f_2 \preceq_A g_2$ *imply* $f_1.f_2 \preceq_A g_1.g_2$.

Lemma 7 corresponds to Howell's Property 5 [19]. Whereas Howell states this property on $\mathbb{N}^k$, our lemma is polymorphic in the type A. As noted by Howell, this lemma is useful when the cost of a loop body is independent of the loop index. In the case where the cost of the i-th iteration may depend on the loop index i, the following, more complex lemma is typically used instead:

Lemma 8 (Summation). *Let f, g range over $A \to \mathbb{Z} \to \mathbb{Z}$. Let $i_0 \in \mathbb{Z}$. Assume the following three properties:*

1. $\mathbb{U}_A\, a.\ \forall i \geq i_0.\ f(a)(i) \geq 0$.
2. $\mathbb{U}_A\, a.\ \forall i \geq i_0.\ g(a)(i) \geq 0$.
3. *for every a, the function $\lambda i.f(a)(i)$ is nondecreasing on the interval $[i_0, \infty)$.*

Then,

$$\lambda(a, i).f(a)(i) \ \preceq_{A \times \mathbb{Z}} \ \lambda(a, i).g(a)(i)$$

implies

$$\lambda(a, n). \sum\nolimits_{i=i_0}^{n} f(a)(i) \ \preceq_{A \times \mathbb{Z}} \ \lambda(a, n). \sum\nolimits_{i=i_0}^{n} g(a)(i).$$

Lemma 8 uses the product filter on $A \times \mathbb{Z}$ in its hypothesis and conclusion. It corresponds to Howell's property 2 [19]. The variable i represents the loop index, while the variable a collectively represents all other variables in scope, so the type A is usually instantiated with a tuple type (an example appears in Sect. 6).

An important property is the fact that function composition is compatible, in a certain sense, with domination. This allows transforming the parameters under which an asymptotic analysis is carried out (examples appear in Sect. 6). Due to space limitations, we refer the reader to the Coq library for details [16].

3.5 Tactics

Our formalization of filters and domination forms a stand-alone Coq library [16]. In addition to many lemmas about these notions, the library proposes automated tactics that can prove nonnegativeness, monotonicity, and domination goals. These tactics currently support functions built out of variables, constants, sums and maxima, products, powers, logarithms. Extending their coverage is ongoing work. This library is not tied to our application to the complexity analysis of programs. It could have other applications in mathematics.

4   Specifications with Asymptotic Complexity Claims

In this section, we first present our existing approach to verified time complexity analysis. This approach, proposed by the second and third authors [11], does not use the O notation: instead, it involves explicit cost functions. We then discuss how to extend this approach with support for asymptotic complexity claims. We find that, even once domination (Sect. 3) is well-understood, there remain nontrivial questions as to the style in which program specifications should be written. We propose one style which works well on small examples and which we believe should scale well to larger ones.

4.1   CFML with Time Credits for Cost Analysis

CFML [9,10] is a system that supports the interactive verification of OCaml programs, using higher-order Separation Logic, inside Coq. It is composed of a trusted standalone tool and a Coq library. The CFML tool transforms a piece of OCaml code into a *characteristic formula*, a Coq formula that describes the semantics of the code. The characteristic formula is then exploited, inside Coq, to state that the code satisfies a certain specification (a Separation Logic triple) and to interactively prove this statement. The CFML library provides a set of Coq tactics that implement the reasoning rules of Separation Logic.

In prior work [11], the second and third authors extend CFML with time credits [2,22] and use it to simultaneously verify the functional correctness and the (amortized) time complexity of OCaml code. To illustrate the style in which they write specifications, consider a function that computes the length of a list:

```
let rec length l =
    match l with
    | []       -> 0
    | _ :: l -> 1 + length l
```

About this function, one can prove the following statement:

$$\forall (A : \mathsf{Type})(l : \mathsf{list}\,A). \ \{\, \$(|l| + 1) \,\} \ (\mathtt{length}\ l) \ \{\lambda y.\, [\,y = |l|\,]\}$$

This is a Separation Logic triple $\{H\}\,(t)\,\{Q\}$. The postcondition $\lambda y.\,[\,y = |l|\,]$ asserts that the call length l returns the length of the list l.[3] The precondition $\$(|l| + 1)$ asserts that this call requires $|l| + 1$ credits. This triple is proved in a variant of Separation Logic where every function call and every loop iteration consumes one credit. Thus, the above specification guarantees that the execution of length l involves no more than $|l| + 1$ function calls or loop iterations. Our previous paper [11, Definition 2] gives a precise definition of the meaning of triples.

As argued in prior work [11, Sect. 2.7], bounding the number of function calls and loop iterations is equivalent, up to a constant factor, to bounding the number of reduction steps of the program. Assuming that the OCaml compiler is complexity-preserving, this is equivalent, up to a constant factor, to bounding the number of instructions executed by the compiled code. Finally, assuming that the machine executes one instruction in bounded time, this is equivalent, up to a constant factor, to bounding the execution time of the compiled code. Thus, the above specification guarantees that length runs in linear time.

Instead of understanding Separation Logic with Time Credits as a variant of Separation Logic, one can equivalently view it as standard Separation Logic, applied to an instrumented program, where a pay() instruction has been inserted at the beginning of every function body and loop body. The proof of the program is carried out under the axiom $\{\$1\}\,(\text{pay}())\,\{\lambda\_.\top\}$, which imposes the consumption of one time credit at every pay() instruction. This instruction has no runtime effect: it is just a way of marking where credits must be consumed.

For example, the OCaml function length is instrumented as follows:

```
let rec length l =
    pay ();
    match l with [] -> 0 | _ :: l -> 1 + length l
```

Executing "length l" involves executing pay() exactly $|l| + 1$ times. For this reason, a valid specification of this instrumented code in ordinary Separation Logic must require at least $|l| + 1$ credits in its precondition.

4.2   A Modularity Challenge

The above specification of length guarantees that length runs in linear time, but does not allow predicting how much real time is consumed by a call to length. Thus, this specification is already rather abstract. Yet, it is still too precise. Indeed, we believe that it would not be wise for a list library to publish a specification of length whose precondition requires exactly $|l| + 1$ credits. Indeed, there are implementations of length that do not meet this specification. For example, the tail-recursive implementation found in the OCaml standard library, which in practice is more efficient than the naïve implementation shown

---

[3]   The square brackets denote a pure Separation Logic assertion. $|l|$ denotes the length of the Coq list l. CFML transparently reflects OCaml integers as Coq relative integers and OCaml lists as Coq lists.

above, involves exactly $|l| + 2$ function calls, therefore requires $|l| + 2$ credits. By advertising a specification where $|l| + 1$ credits suffice, one makes too strong a guarantee, and rules out the more efficient implementation.

After initially publishing a specification that requires $\$(|l| + 1)$, one could of course still switch to the more efficient implementation and update the published specification so as to require $\$(|l| + 2)$ instead of $\$(|l| + 1)$. However, that would in turn require updating the specification and proof of every (direct and indirect) client of the list library, which is intolerable.

To leave some slack, one should publish a more abstract specification. For example, one could advertise that the cost of length l is an affine function of the length of the list l, that is, the cost is $a \cdot |l| + b$, for some constants a and b:

$$\exists (a, b : \mathbb{Z}). \ \forall (A : \mathsf{Type})(l : \mathsf{list}\, A). \ \{\$(a \cdot |l| + b)\}\, (\mathtt{length}\ l)\, \{\lambda y. \, [\, y = |l|\,]\}$$

This is a better specification, in the sense that it is more modular. The naïve implementation of length shown earlier and the efficient implementation in OCaml's standard library both satisfy this specification, so one is free to choose one or the other, without any impact on the clients of the list library. In fact, any reasonable implementation of length should have linear time complexity and therefore should satisfy this specification.

That said, the style in which the above specification is written is arguably slightly too low-level. Instead of directly expressing the idea that the cost of length l is $O(|l|)$, we have written this cost under the form $a \cdot |l| + b$. It is preferable to state at a more abstract level that $cost$ is dominated by $\lambda n.n$: such a style is more readable and scales to situations where multiple parameters and nonstandard filters are involved. Thus, we propose the following statement:

$$\exists cost : \mathbb{Z} \to \mathbb{Z}. \ \begin{cases} cost \preceq_{\mathbb{Z}} \lambda n. \, n \\ \forall (A : \mathsf{Type})(l : \mathsf{list}\, A). \ \{\$cost(|l|)\}\, (\mathtt{length}\ l)\, \{\lambda y. \, [\, y = |l|\,]\} \end{cases}$$

Thereafter, we refer to the function $cost$ as the *concrete cost* of length, as opposed to the *asymptotic bound*, represented here by the function $\lambda n.\, n$. This specification asserts that there exists a concrete cost function $cost$, which is dominated by $\lambda n.\, n$, such that $cost(|l|)$ credits suffice to justify the execution of length l. Thus, $cost(|l|)$ is an upper bound on the actual number of pay() instructions that are executed at runtime.

The above specification informally means that length l has time complexity $O(n)$ where the parameter n represents $|l|$, that is, the length of the list l. The fact that n represents $|l|$ is expressed by applying $cost$ to $|l|$ in the precondition. The fact that this analysis is valid when n grows large enough is expressed by using the standard filter on $\mathbb{Z}$ in the assertion $cost \preceq_{\mathbb{Z}} \lambda n.n$.

In general, it is up to the user to choose what the parameters of the cost analysis should be, what these parameters represent, and which filter on these parameters should be used. The example of the Bellman-Ford algorithm (Sect. 6) illustrates this.

Record specO (A : filterType) (le : A → A → Prop)
                  (bound : A → Z) (P : (A → Z) → Prop)
  := { cost : A → Z;
       cost_spec : P cost;
       cost_dominated : dominated A cost bound;
       cost_nonneg : ∀x, 0 ≤ cost x;
       cost_monotonic : monotonic le Z.le cost; }.

Fig. 5. Definition of specO.

4.3 A Record for Specifications

The specifications presented in the previous section share a common structure. We define a record type that captures this common structure, so as to make specifications more concise and more recognizable, and so as to help users adhere to this specification pattern.

This type, specO, is defined in Fig. 5. The first three fields in this record type correspond to what has been explained so far. The first field asserts the existence of a function cost of A to $\mathbb{Z}$, where A is a user-specified filtered type. The second field asserts that a certain property P cost is satisfied; it is typically a Separation Logic triple whose precondition refers to cost. The third field asserts that cost is dominated by the user-specified function bound. The need for the last two fields is explained further on (Sects. 4.4 and 4.5).

Using this definition, our proposed specification of length (Sect. 4.2) is stated in concrete Coq syntax as follows:

Theorem length_spec:
    specO Z_filterType Z.le (fun n ⇒ n) (fun cost ⇒
      ∀A (l:list A), triple (length l)
        PRE ($ (cost |l|))
        POST (fun y ⇒ [y = |l|]))

The key elements of this specification are Z_filterType, which is $\mathbb{Z}$, equipped with its standard filter; the asymptotic bound fun n ⇒ n, which means that the time complexity of length is $O(n)$; and the Separation Logic triple, which describes the behavior of length, and refers to the concrete cost function cost.

One key technical point is that specO is a strong existential, whose witness can be referred to via to the first projection, cost. For instance, the concrete cost function associated with length can be referred to as cost length_spec. Thus, at a call site of the form length xs, the number of required credits is cost length_spec |xs|.

In the next subsections, we explain why, in the definition of specO, we require the concrete cost function to be nonnegative and monotonic. These are design decisions; although these properties may not be strictly necessary, we find that enforcing them greatly simplifies things in practice.

4.4 Why Cost Functions Must Be Nonnegative

There are several common occasions where one is faced with the obligation of proving that a cost expression is nonnegative. These proof obligations arise from several sources.

One source is the Separation Logic axiom for splitting credits, whose statement is $\$(m + n) = \$m \star \$n$, subject to the side conditions $m \geq 0$ and $n \geq 0$. Without these side conditions, out of \$0, one would be able to create $\$1 \star \$(-1)$. Because our logic is affine, one could then discard $\$(-1)$, keeping just \$1. In short, an unrestricted splitting axiom would allow creating credits out of thin air.[4] Another source of proof obligations is the Summation lemma (Lemma 8), which requires the functions at hand to be (ultimately) nonnegative.

Now, suppose one is faced with the obligation of proving that the expression `cost length_spec |xs|` is nonnegative. Because `length_spec` is an existential package (a `specO` record), this is impossible, unless this information has been recorded up front within the record. This is the reason why the field `cost_nonneg` in Fig. 5 is needed.

For simplicity, we require cost functions to be nonnegative everywhere, as opposed to within a certain domain. This requirement is stronger than necessary, but simplifies things, and can easily be met in practice by wrapping cost functions within "$\max(0, -)$". Our Coq tactics automatically insert "$\max(0, -)$" wrappers where necessary, making this issue mostly transparent to the user. In the following, for brevity, we write c^+ for $\max(0, c)$, where $c \in \mathbb{Z}$.

4.5 Why Cost Functions Must Be Monotonic

One key reason why cost functions should be monotonic has to do with the "avoidance problem". When the cost of a code fragment depends on a local variable x, can this cost be reformulated (and possibly approximated) in such a way that the dependency is removed? Indeed, a cost expression that makes sense outside the scope of x is ultimately required.

The problematic cost expression is typically of the form $E[|x|]$, where $|x|$ represents some notion of the "size" of the data structure denoted by x, and E is an arithmetic context, that is, an arithmetic expression with a hole. Furthermore, an upper bound on $|x|$ is typically available. This upper bound can be exploited if the context E is monotonic, i.e., if $x \leq y$ implies $E[x] \leq E[y]$. Because the hole in E can appear as an actual argument to an abstract cost function, we must record the fact that this cost function is monotonic.

To illustrate the problem, consider the following OCaml function, which counts the positive elements in a list of integers. It does so, in linear time, by first building a sublist of the positive elements, then computing the length of this sublist.

---

[4] Another approach would be to define $\$n$ only for $n \in \mathbb{N}$, in which case an unrestricted axiom would be sound. However, as we use $\mathbb{Z}$ everywhere, that would be inconvenient. A more promising idea is to view $\$n$ as linear (as opposed to affine) when n is negative. Then, $\$(-1)$ cannot be discarded, so unrestricted splitting is sound.

```
let count_pos l =
    let l' = List.filter (fun x -> x > 0) l in
    List.length l'
```

How would one go about proving that this code actually has linear time complexity? On paper, one would informally argue that the cost of the sequence pay(); filter; length is $O(1) + O(|l|) + O(|l'|)$, then exploit the inequality $|l'| \leq |l|$, which follows from the semantics of filter, and deduce that the cost is $O(|l|)$.

In a formal setting, though, the problem is not so simple. Assume that we have two specification lemmas length_spec and filter_spec for List.length and List.filter, which describe the behavior of these OCaml functions and guarantee that they have linear-time complexity. For brevity, let us write just g and f for the functions cost length_spec and cost filter_spec. Also, at the mathematical level, let us write $l\!\downarrow$ for the sublist of the positive elements of the list l. It is easy enough to check that the cost of the expression "pay(); let l' = ... in List.length l'" is $1 + f(|l|) + g(|l'|)$. The problem, now, is to *find an upper bound* for this cost *that does not depend on l'*, a local variable, and to verify that this upper bound, *expressed as a function of $|l|$*, is dominated by $\lambda n. n$. Indeed, this is required in order to establish a spec0 statement about count_pos.

What might this upper bound be? That is, which functions *cost* of $\mathbb{Z}$ to $\mathbb{Z}$ are such that (A) $1 + f(|l|) + g(|l'|) \leq cost(|l|)$ can be proved (in the scope of the local variable l') and (B) $cost \preceq_{\mathbb{Z}} \lambda n. n$ holds? Three potential answers come to mind:

1. Within the scope of l', the equality $l' = l\!\downarrow$ is available, as it follows from the postcondition of filter. Thus, within this scope, $1 + f(|l|) + g(|l'|)$ is provably equal to *let $l' = l\!\downarrow$ in* $1 + f(|l|) + g(|l'|)$, that is, $1 + f(|l|) + g(|l\!\downarrow|)$. This remark may seem promising, as this cost expression does not depend on l'. Unfortunately, this approach falls short, because this cost expression cannot be expressed as the application of a closed function *cost* to $|l|$. Indeed, the length of the filtered list, $|l\!\downarrow|$, is not a function of the length of l. In short, substituting local variables away in a cost expression does not always lead to a usable cost function.

2. Within the scope of l', the inequality $|l'| \leq |l|$ is available, as it follows from $l' = l\!\downarrow$. Thus, inequality (A) can be proved, provided we take:

$$cost = \lambda n. \max_{0 \leq n' \leq n} 1 + f(n) + g(n')$$

Furthermore, for this definition of *cost*, the domination assertion (B) holds as well. The proof relies on the fact the functions g and $\hat{g}$, where $\hat{g}$ is $\lambda n. \max_{0 \leq n' \leq n} g(n')$ [19], dominate each other. Although this approach seems viable, and does not require the function g to be monotonic, it is a bit more complicated than we would like.

3. Let us now assume that the function g is monotonic, that is, nondecreasing. As before, within the scope of l', the inequality $|l'| \leq |l|$ is available. Thus, the cost expression $1 + f(|l|) + g(|l'|)$ is bounded by $1 + f(|l|) + g(|l|)$. Therefore, inequalities (A) and (B) are satisfied, provided we take:

$$cost = \lambda n.\, 1 + f(n) + g(n)$$

We believe that approach 3 is the simplest and most intuitive, because it allows us to easily eliminate l', without giving rise to a complicated cost function, and without the need for a running maximum.

However, this approach requires that the cost function g, which is short for cost length_spec, be monotonic. This explains why we build a monotonicity condition in the definition of spec0 (Fig. 5, last line). Another motivation for doing so is the fact that some lemmas (such as Lemma 8, which allows reasoning about the asymptotic cost of an inner loop) also have monotonicity hypotheses.

The reader may be worried that, in practice, there might exist concrete cost functions that are not monotonic. This may be the case, in particular, of a cost function f that is obtained as the solution of a recurrence equation. Fortunately, in the common case of functions of $\mathbb{Z}$ to $\mathbb{Z}$, the "running maximum" function $\hat{f}$ can always be used in place of f: indeed, it is monotonic and has the same asymptotic behavior as f. Thus, we see that both approaches 2 and 3 above involve running maxima in some places, but their use seems less frequent with approach 3.

5   Interactive Proofs of Asymptotic Complexity Claims

To prove a specification lemma, such as length_spec (Sect. 4.3) or loop_spec (Sect. 4.4), one must construct a spec0 record. By definition of spec0 (Fig. 5), this means that one must exhibit a concrete cost function $cost$ and prove a number of properties of this function, including the fact that, when supplied with $\$(cost \ldots)$, the code runs correctly (cost_spec) and the fact that $cost$ is dominated by the desired asymptotic bound (cost_dominated).

Thus, the very first step in a naïve proof attempt would be to *guess* an appropriate cost function for the code at hand. However, such an approach would be painful, error-prone, and brittle. It seems much preferable, if possible, to enlist the machine's help in *synthesizing* a cost function *at the same time as we step through the code*—which we have to do anyway, as we must build a Separation Logic proof of the correctness of this code.

To illustrate the problem, consider the recursive function p, whose integer argument n is expected to satisfy $n \geq 0$. For the sake of this example, p calls an auxiliary function g, which we assume runs in constant time.

```
let rec p n =
    if n <= 1 then () else begin g(); p(n-1) end
```

Suppose we wish to establish that p runs in linear time. As argued at the beginning of the paper (Sect. 2, Fig. 2), it does not make sense to attempt a proof by induction on n that "p n runs in time $O(n)$". Instead, in a formal framework, we must exhibit a concrete cost function *cost* such that $cost(n)$ credits justify the call p n and *cost* grows linearly, that is, $cost \preceq_{\mathbb{Z}} \lambda n.\, n$.

Let us assume that a specification lemma g_spec for the function g has been established already, so the number of credits required by a call to g is cost g_spec (). In the following, we write G as a shorthand for this constant.

Because this example is very simple, it is reasonably easy to manually come up with an appropriate cost function for p. One valid guess is $\lambda n.\, 1 + \Sigma_{i=2}^{n}(1+G)$. Another valid guess, obtained via a simplification step, is $\lambda n.\, 1 + (1+G)(n-1)^{+}$. Another witness, obtained via an approximation step, is $\lambda n.\, 1 + (1 + G)n^{+}$. As the reader can see, there is in fact a spectrum of valid witnesses, ranging from verbose, low-level to compact, high-level mathematical expressions. Also, it should be evident that, as the code grows larger, it can become very difficult to guess a valid concrete cost function.

This gives rise to two questions. Among the valid cost functions, which one is preferable? Which ones can be systematically constructed, without guessing?

Among the valid cost functions, there is a tradeoff. At one extreme, a low-level cost function has exactly the same syntactic structure as the code, so it is easy to prove that it is an upper bound for the actual cost of the code, but a lot of work may be involved in proving that it is dominated by the desired asymptotic bound. At the other extreme, a high-level cost function can be essentially identical to the desired asymptotic bound, up to explicit multiplicative and additive constants, so the desired domination assertion is trivial, but a lot of accounting work may be involved in proving that this function represents enough credits to execute the code. Thus, by choosing a cost function, we shift some of the burden of the proof from one subgoal to another. From this point of view, no cost function seems inherently preferable to another.

From the point of view of systematic construction, however, the answer is more clear-cut. It seems fairly clear that it is possible to systematically build a cost function whose syntactic structure is the same as the syntactic structure of the code. This idea goes at least as far back as Wegbreit's work [26]. Coming up with a compact, high-level expression of the cost, on the other hand, seems to require human insight.

To provide as much machine assistance as possible, our system mechanically synthesizes a low-level cost expression for a piece of OCaml code. This is done transparently, at the same time as the user constructs a proof of the code in Separation Logic. Furthermore, we take advantage of the fact that we are using an interactive proof assistant: we allow the user to guide the synthesis process. For instance, the user controls how a local variable should be eliminated, how the cost of a conditional construct should be approximated (i.e., by a conditional or by a maximum), and how recurrence equations should be solved. In the following, we present this semi-interactive synthesis process. We first consider straight-line (nonrecursive) code (Sect. 5.1), then recursive functions (Sect. 5.2).

5.1 Synthesizing Cost Expressions for Straight-Line Code

The CFML library provides the user with interactive tactics that implement the reasoning rules of Separation Logic. We set things up in such a way that, as these rules are applied, a cost expression is automatically synthesized.

WEAKENCOST
$$\frac{\{\$\, c_2^+ \star H\}\,(e)\,\{Q\} \qquad c_2^+ \leq c_1}{\{\$\, c_1 \star H\}\,(e)\,\{Q\}}$$

SEQ
$$\frac{\{\$\, c_1^+ \star H\}\,(e_1)\,\{Q'\} \qquad \{\$\, c_2^+ \star Q'()\}\,(e_2)\,\{Q\}}{\{\$\,(c_1^+ + c_2^+)^+ \star H\}\,(e_1; e_2)\,\{Q\}}$$

LET
$$\frac{\{\$\, c_1^+ \star H\}\,(e_1)\,\{Q'\} \qquad \forall x.\,\{\$\, c_2^+ \star Q'(x)\}\,(e_2)\,\{Q\}}{\{\$\,(c_1^+ + c_2^+)^+ \star H\}\,(\text{let } x = e_1 \text{ in } e_2)\,\{Q\}}$$

VAL
$$\frac{H \Vdash Q(v)}{\{\$\, 0^+ \star H\}\,(v)\,\{Q\}}$$

IF
$$\frac{b = \text{true} \Rightarrow \{\$\, c_1^+ \star H\}\,(e_1)\,\{Q\} \qquad b = \text{false} \Rightarrow \{\$\, c_2^+ \star H\}\,(e_2)\,\{Q\}}{\{\$\,(\text{if } b \text{ then } c_1 \text{ else } c_2)^+ \star H\}\,(\text{if } b \text{ then } e_1 \text{ else } e_2)\,\{Q\}}$$

PAY
$$\frac{H \Vdash Q()}{\{\$\, 1^+ \star H\}\,(\text{pay}())\,\{Q\}}$$

FOR
$$\frac{\forall i.\, a \leq i < b \Rightarrow \{\$\, c(i)^+ \star I(i)\}\,(e)\,\{I(i+1)\} \qquad H \Vdash I(a) \star Q}{\{\$\,(\Sigma_{a \leq i < b}\, c(i)^+)^+ \star H\}\,(\text{for } i = a \text{ to } b - 1 \text{ do } e \text{ done})\,\{I(b) \star Q\}}$$

Fig. 6. The reasoning rules of Separation Logic, specialized for cost synthesis.

To this end, we use specialized variants of the reasoning rules, whose premises and conclusions take the form $\{\$\, n \star H\}\,(e)\,\{Q\}$. Furthermore, to simplify the nonnegativeness side conditions that must be proved while reasoning, we make all cost expressions obviously nonnegative by wrapping them in $\max(0, -)$. Recall that c^+ stands for $\max(0, c)$, where $c \in \mathbb{Z}$. Our reasoning rules work with triples of the form $\{\$\, c^+ \star H\}\,(e)\,\{Q\}$. They are shown in Fig. 6.

Because we wish to *synthesize* a cost expression, our Coq tactics maintain the following invariant: whenever the goal is $\{\$\, c^+ \star H\}\,(e)\,\{Q\}$, the cost c is *uninstantiated*, that is, it is represented in Coq by a metavariable, a placeholder. This metavariable is instantiated when the goal is proved by applying one of the reasoning rules. Such an application produces new subgoals, whose preconditions contain new metavariables. As this process is repeated, a cost expression is incrementally constructed.

The rule WEAKENCOST is a special case of the consequence rule of Separation Logic. It is typically used once at the root of the proof: even though the initial goal $\{\$\, c_1 \star H\}\,(e)\,\{Q\}$ may not satisfy our invariant, because it lacks a $-^+$ wrapper and because c_1 is not necessarily a metavariable, WEAKENCOST gives rise to a subgoal $\{\$\, c_2^+ \star H\}\,(e)\,\{Q\}$ that satisfies it. Indeed, when this rule is applied, a fresh metavariable c_2 is generated. WEAKENCOST can also be explicitly applied by the user when desired. It is typically used just before leaving the scope of a local variable x to approximate a cost expression c_2^+ that depends on x with an expression c_1 that does not refer to x.

The SEQ rule is a special case of the LET rule. It states that the cost of a sequence is the sum of the costs of its subexpressions. When this rule is applied to a goal of the form $\{\$\,c^+ \star H\}\,(e)\,\{Q\}$, where c is a metavariable, two new metavariables c_1 and c_2 are introduced, and c is instantiated with $c_1^+ + c_2^+$.

The LET rule is similar to SEQ, but involves an additional subtlety: the cost c_2 must not refer to the local variable x. Naturally, Coq enforces this condition: any attempt to instantiate the metavariable c_2 with an expression where x occurs fails. In such a situation, it is up to the user to use WEAKENCOST so as to avoid this dependency. The example of `count_pos` (Sect. 4.5) illustrates this issue.

The VAL rule handles values, which in our model have zero cost. The symbol $\Vdash$ denotes entailment between Separation Logic assertions.

The IF rule states that the cost of an OCaml conditional expression is a mathematical conditional expression. Although this may seem obvious, one subtlety lurks here. Using WEAKENCOST, the cost expression *if b then c_1 else c_2* can be approximated by $\max(c_1, c_2)$. Such an approximation can be beneficial, as it leads to a simpler cost expression, or harmful, as it causes a loss of information. In particular, when carried out in the body of a recursive function, it can lead to an unsatisfiable recurrence equation. We let the user decide whether this approximation should be performed.

The PAY rule handles the `pay()` instruction, which is inserted by the CFML tool at the beginning of every function and loop body (Sect. 4.1). This instruction costs one credit.

The FOR rule states that the cost of a `for` loop is the sum, over all values of the index i, of the cost of the i-th iteration of the body. In practice, it is typically used in conjunction with WEAKENCOST, which allows the user to simplify and approximate the iterated sum $\Sigma_{a \leq i < b}\, c(i)^+$. In particular, if the synthesized cost $c(i)$ happens to not depend on i, or can be approximated so as to not depend on i, then this iterated sum can be expressed under the form $c(b-a)^+$. A variant of the FOR rule, not shown, covers this common case. There is in principle no need for a primitive treatment of loops, as loops can be encoded in terms of higher-order recursive functions, and our program logic can express the specifications of these combinators. Nevertheless, in practice, primitive support for loops is convenient.

This concludes our exposition of the reasoning rules of Fig. 6. Coming back to the example of the OCaml function p (Sect. 5), under the assumption that the cost of the recursive call `p(n-1)` is $f(n-1)$, we are able, by repeated application of the reasoning rules, to automatically find that the cost of the OCaml expression:

```
if n <= 1 then () else begin g(); p(n-1) end
```

is: $1 + if\ n \leq 1\ then\ 0\ else\ (G + f(n-1))$. The initial 1 accounts for the implicit `pay()`. This may seem obvious, and it is. The point is that this cost expression is automatically constructed: its synthesis adds no overhead to an interactive proof of functional correctness of the function p.

5.2   Synthesizing and Solving Recurrence Equations

There now remains to explain how to deal with recursive functions. Suppose $S(f)$ is the Separation Logic triple that we wish to establish, where f stands for an as-yet-unknown cost function. Following common informal practice, we would like to do this in two steps. First, from the code, derive a "recurrence equation" $E(f)$, which in fact is usually not an equation, but a constraint (or a conjunction of constraints) bearing on f. Second, prove that this recurrence equation admits a solution that is dominated by the desired asymptotic cost function g. This approach can be formally viewed as an application of the following tautology:

$$\forall E.\ (\forall f.E(f) \to S(f)) \ \to\ (\exists f.E(f) \wedge f \preceq g) \ \to\ (\exists f.S(f) \wedge f \preceq g)$$

The conclusion $S(f) \wedge f \preceq g$ states that the code is correct and has asymptotic cost g. In Coq, applying this tautology gives rise to a new metavariable E, as the recurrence equation is initially unknown, and two subgoals.

During the proof of the first subgoal, $\forall f.E(f) \to S(f)$, the cost function f is abstract (universally quantified), but we are allowed to assume $E(f)$, where E is initially a metavariable. So, should the need arise to prove that f satisfies a certain property, this can be done just by instantiating E. In the example of the OCaml function p (Sect. 5), we prove $S(f)$ by induction over n, under the hypothesis $n \geq 0$. Thus, we assume that the cost of the recursive call p(n-1) is $f(n - 1)$, and must prove that the cost of p n is $f(n)$. We synthesize the cost of p n as explained earlier (Sect. 5.1) and find that this cost is $1 + if\ n \leq 1\ then\ 0\ else\ (G + f(n - 1))$. We apply WEAKENCOST and find that our proof is complete, provided we are able to prove the following inequation:

$$1 + if\ n \leq 1\ then\ 0\ else\ (G + f(n - 1)) \ \leq\ f(n)$$

We achieve that simply by instantiating E as follows:

$$E := \lambda f.\ \forall n.\ n \geq 0 \ \to\ 1 + if\ n \leq 1\ then\ 0\ else\ (G + f(n - 1)) \ \leq\ f(n)$$

This is our "recurrence equation"—in fact, a universally quantified, conditional inequation. We are done with the first subgoal.

We then turn to the second subgoal, $\exists f.E(f) \wedge f \preceq g$. The metavariable E is now instantiated. The goal is to solve the recurrence and analyze the asymptotic growth of the chosen solution. There are at least three approaches to solving such a recurrence.

First, one can guess a closed form that satisfies the recurrence. For example, the function $f := \lambda n.\ 1 + (1 + G)n^+$ satisfies $E(f)$ above. But, as argued earlier, guessing is in general difficult and tedious.

Second, one can invoke Cormen *et al.*'s Master Theorem [12] or the more general Akra-Bazzi theorem [1,21]. Unfortunately, at present, these theorems are not available in Coq, although an Isabelle/HOL formalization exists [13].

The last approach is Cormen *et al.*'s substitution method [12, Sect. 4]. The idea is to guess a parameterized *shape* for the solution; substitute this shape into the goal; gather a set of constraints that the parameters must satisfy for the goal to hold; finally, show that these constraints are indeed satisfiable. In the above example, as we expect the code to have linear time complexity, we propose that the solution f should have the shape $\lambda n.(an^+ + b)$, where a and b are parameters, about which we wish to gradually accumulate a set of constraints. From a formal point of view, this amounts to applying the following tautology:

$$\forall P. \forall C. \quad (\forall ab. \; C(a,b) \to P(\lambda n.(an^+ + b))) \; \to \; (\exists ab. \; C(a,b)) \; \to \; \exists f.P(f)$$

This application again yields two subgoals. During the proof of the first subgoal, C is a metavariable and can be instantiated as desired (possibly in several steps), allowing us to gather a conjunction of constraints bearing on a and b. During the proof of the second subgoal, C is fixed and we must check that it is satisfiable. In our example, the first subgoal is:

$$E(\lambda n.(an^+ + b)) \quad \wedge \quad \lambda n.(an^+ + b) \preceq_{\mathbb{Z}} \lambda n.n$$

The second conjunct is trivial. The first conjunct simplifies to:

$$\forall n. \quad n \geq 0 \; \to \; 1 + \mathit{if} \; n \leq 1 \; \mathit{then} \; 0 \; \mathit{else} \; (G + a(n-1)^+ + b) \; \leq \; an^+ + b$$

By distinguishing the cases $n = 0$, $n = 1$, and $n > 1$, we find that this property holds provided we have $1 \leq b$ and $1 \leq a + b$ and $1 + G \leq a$. Thus, we prove this subgoal by instantiating C with $\lambda(a,b).(1 \leq b \wedge 1 \leq a + b \wedge 1 + G \leq a)$.

There remains to check the second subgoal, that is, $\exists ab.C(a,b)$. This is easy; we pick, for instance, $a := 1 + G$ and $b := 1$. This concludes our use of Cormen et al.'s substitution method.

In summary, by exploiting Coq's metavariables, we are able to set up our proofs in a style that closely follows the traditional paper style. During a first phase, as we analyze the code, we synthesize a cost function and (if the code is recursive) a recurrence equation. During a second phase, we guess the shape of a solution, and, as we analyze the recurrence equation, we synthesize a constraint on the parameters of the shape. During a last phase, we check that this constraint is satisfiable. In practice, instead of explicitly building and applying tautologies as above, we use the first author's `procrastination` library [16], which provides facilities for introducing new parameters, gradually gathering constraints on these parameters, and eventually checking that these constraints are satisfiable.

6   Examples

Binary Search. We prove that binary search has time complexity $O(\log n)$, where $n = j - i$ denotes the width of the search interval $[i, j)$. The code is as in Fig. 1, except that the flaw is fixed by replacing i+1 with k+1 on the last line. As outlined earlier (Sect. 5), we synthesize the following recurrence equation on the cost function f:

$$f(0) + 3 \leq f(1) \quad \wedge \quad \forall n \geq 0. \; 1 \leq f(n) \quad \wedge \quad \forall n \geq 2. \; f(n/2) + 3 \leq f(n)$$

We apply the substitution method and search for a solution of the form $\lambda n.$ if $n \leq 0$ then 1 else $a \log n + b$, which is dominated by $\lambda n. \log n$. Substituting this shape into the above constraints, we find that they boil down to $(4 \leq b) \wedge (0 \leq a \wedge 1 \leq b) \wedge (3 \leq a)$. Finally, we guess a solution, namely $a := 3$ and $b := 4$.

Dependent Nested Loops. Many algorithms involve dependent nested `for` loops, that is, nested loops, where the bounds of the inner loop depend on the outer loop index, as in the following simplified example:

```
for i = 1 to n do
    for j = 1 to i do () done
done
```

For this code, the cost function $\lambda n.$ $\sum_{i=1}^{n}(1 + \sum_{j=1}^{i} 1)$ is synthesized. There remains to prove that it is dominated by $\lambda n.n^2$. We could recognize and prove that this function is equal to $\lambda n. \frac{n(n+3)}{2}$, which clearly is dominated by $\lambda n.n^2$. This works because this example is trivial, but, in general, computing explicit closed forms for summations is challenging, if at all feasible.

A higher-level approach is to exploit the fact that, if f is monotonic, then $\sum_{i=1}^{n} f(i)$ is less than $n.f(n)$. Applying this lemma twice, we find that the above cost function is less than $\lambda n. \sum_{i=1}^{n}(1 + i)$ which is less than $\lambda n.n(1 + n)$ which is dominated by $\lambda n.n^2$. This simple-minded approach, which does not require the Summation lemma (Lemma 8), is often applicable. The next example illustrates a situation where the Summation lemma is required.

A Loop Whose Body Has Exponential Cost. In the following simple example, the loop body is just a function call:

```
for i = 0 to n-1 do b(i) done
```

Thus, the cost of the loop body is not known exactly. Instead, let us assume that a specification for the auxiliary function b has been proved and that its cost is $O(2^i)$, that is, cost b $\preceq_{\mathbb{Z}} \lambda i.\ 2^i$ holds. We then wish to prove that the cost of the whole loop is also $O(2^n)$.

For this loop, the cost function $\lambda n.$ $\sum_{i=0}^{n}(1 + \text{cost b } (i))$ is automatically synthesized. We have an asymptotic bound for the cost of the loop body, namely: $\lambda i.\ 1 + \text{cost b } (i) \preceq_{\mathbb{Z}} \lambda i.\ 2^i$. The side conditions of the Summation lemma (Lemma 8) are met: in particular, the function $\lambda i.\ 1 + \text{cost b } (i)$ is monotonic. The lemma yields $\lambda n.$ $\sum_{i=0}^{n}(1 + \text{cost b } (i)) \preceq_{\mathbb{Z}} \lambda n.$ $\sum_{i=0}^{n} 2^i$. Finally, we have $\lambda n.$ $\sum_{i=0}^{n} 2^i = \lambda n.\ 2^{n+1} - 1 \preceq_{\mathbb{Z}} \lambda n.\ 2^n$.

The Bellman-Ford Algorithm. We verify the asymptotic complexity of an implementation of Bellman-Ford algorithm, which computes shortest paths in a weighted graph with n vertices and m edges. The algorithm involves an outer loop that is repeated $n - 1$ times and an inner loop that iterates over all m edges. The specification asserts that the asymptotic complexity is $O(nm)$:

$$\exists cost : \mathbb{Z}^2 \to \mathbb{Z}. \begin{cases} cost \preceq_{\mathbb{Z}^2} \lambda(m, n).\ nm \\ \{\$cost(\#edges(g), \#vertices(g))\}\,(\text{bellmanford } g)\,\{\ldots\} \end{cases}$$

By exploiting the fact that a graph without duplicate edges must satisfy $m \le n^2$, we prove that the complexity of the algorithm, viewed as a function of n, is $O(n^3)$.

$$\exists cost : \mathbb{Z} \to \mathbb{Z}. \begin{cases} cost \preceq_\mathbb{Z} \lambda n.\, n^3 \\ \{\$cost(\#vertices(g))\}\,(\texttt{bellmanford}\ g)\,\{\ldots\} \end{cases}$$

To prove that the former specification implies the latter, one instantiates m with n^2, that is, one exploits a composition lemma (Sect. 3.4). In practice, we publish both specifications and let clients use whichever one is more convenient.

Union-Find. Charguéraud and Pottier [11] use Separation Logic with Time Credits to verify the correctness and time complexity of a Union-Find implementation. For instance, they prove that the (amortized) concrete cost of `find` is $2\alpha(n) + 4$, where n is the number of elements. With a few lines of proof, we derive a specification where the cost of `find` is expressed under the form $O(\alpha(n))$:

```
specO Z_filterType Z.le (fun n ⇒ alpha n) (fun cost ⇒
    ∀D R V x, x \in D → triple (UnionFind_ml.find x)
    PRE (UF D R V ⋆ $(cost (card D)))
    POST (fun y ⇒ UF D R V ⋆ [R x = y ])).
```

Union-Find is a mutable data structure, whose state is described by the abstract predicate UF D R V. In particular, the parameter D represents the domain of the data structure, that is, the set of all elements created so far. Thus, its cardinal, card D, corresponds to n. This case study illustrates a situation where the cost of an operation depends on the current state of a mutable data structure.

7   Related Work

Our work builds on top of Separation Logic [23] with Time Credits [2], which has been first implemented in a verification tool and exploited by the second and third authors [11]. We refer the reader to their paper for a survey of the related work in the general area of formal reasoning about program complexity, including approaches based on deductive program verification and approaches based on automatic complexity analysis. In this section, we restrict our attention to informal and formal treatments of the O notation.

The O notation and its siblings are documented in several textbooks [7,15,20]. Out of these, only Howell [19,20] draws attention to the subtleties of the multi-variate case. He shows that one cannot take for granted that the properties of the O notation, which in the univariate case are well-known, remain valid in the multivariate case. He states several properties which, at first sight, seem natural and desirable, then proceeds to show that they are inconsistent, so no definition of the O notation can satisfy them all. He then proposes a candidate notion of domination between functions whose domain is $\mathbb{N}^k$. His notation, $f \in \hat{O}(g)$, is defined as the conjunction of $f \in O(g)$ and $\hat{f} \in O(\hat{g})$, where the function $\hat{f}$ is a "running maximum" of the function f, and is by construction monotonic. He shows that this notion satisfies all the desired properties, provided some of them are restricted by additional side conditions, such as monotonicity requirements.

In this work, we go slightly further than Howell, in that we consider functions whose domain is an arbitrary filtered type A, rather than necessarily $\mathbb{N}^k$. We give a standard definition of O and verify all of Howell's properties, again restricted with certain side conditions. We find that we do not need $\hat{O}$, which is fortunate, as it seems difficult to define $\hat{f}$ in the general case where f is a function of domain A. The monotonicity requirements that we impose are not exactly the same as Howell's, but we believe that the details of these administrative conditions do not matter much, as all of the functions that we manipulate in practice are everywhere nonnegative and monotonic.

Avigad and Donnelly [3] formalize the O notation in Isabelle/HOL. They consider functions of type $A \to B$, where A is arbitrary and B is an ordered ring. Their definition of "$f = O(g)$" requires $|f(x)| \leq c|g(x)|$ for every x, as opposed to "when x is large enough". Thus, they get away without equipping the type A with a filter. The price to pay is an overly restrictive notion of domination, except in the case where A is $\mathbb{N}$, where both $\forall x$ and $\mathbb{U}x$ yield the same notion of domination—this is Brassard and Bratley's "threshold rule" [7]. Avigad and Donnelly suggest defining "$f = O(g)$ eventually" as an abbreviation for $\exists f', (f' = O(g) \wedge \mathbb{U}x.f(x) = f'(x))$. In our eyes, this is less elegant than parameterizing O with a filter in the first place.

Eberl [13] formalizes the Akra-Bazzi method [1,21], a generalization of the well-known Master Theorem [12], in Isabelle/HOL. He creates a library of Landau symbols specifically for this purpose. Although his paper does not mention filters, his library in fact relies on filters, whose definition appears in Isabelle's Complex library. Eberl's definition of the O symbol is identical to ours. That said, because he is concerned with functions of type $\mathbb{N} \to \mathbb{R}$ or $\mathbb{R} \to \mathbb{R}$, he does not define product filters, and does not prove any lemmas about domination in the multivariate case. Eberl sets up a decision procedure for domination goals, like $x \in O(x^3)$, as well as a procedure that can simplify, say, $O(x^3 + x^2)$ to $O(x^3)$.

TiML [25] is a functional programming language where types carry time complexity annotations. Its type-checker generates proof obligations that are discharged by an SMT solver. The core type system, whose metatheory is formalized in Coq, employs concrete cost functions. The TiML implementation allows associating a O specification with each toplevel function. An unverified component recognizes certain classes of recurrence equations and automatically applies the Master Theorem. For instance, $mergesort$ is recognized to be $O(mn \log n)$, where n is the input size and m is the cost of a comparison. The meaning of the O notation in the multivariate case is not spelled out; in particular, which filter is meant is not specified.

Boldo *et al.* [4] use Coq to verify the correctness of a C program which implements a numerical scheme for the resolution of the one-dimensional acoustic wave equation. They define an ad hoc notion of "uniform O" for functions of type $\mathbb{R}^2 \to \mathbb{R}$, which we believe can in fact be viewed as an instance of our generic definition of domination, at an appropriate product filter. Subsequent work on the Coquelicot library for real analysis [5] includes general definitions of filters, limits, little-*o* and asymptotic equivalence. A few definitions and lemmas in Coquelicot are identical to ours, but the focus in Coquelicot is on various filters on $\mathbb{R}$, whereas we are more interested in filters on $\mathbb{Z}^k$.

The tools RAML [17] and Pastis [8] perform fully automated amortized time complexity analysis of OCaml programs. They can be understood in terms of Separation Logic with Time Credits, under the constraint that the number of credits that exist at each program point must be expressed as a polynomial over the variables in scope at this point. The a priori unknown coefficients of this polynomial are determined by an LP solver. Pastis produces a proof certificate that can be checked by Coq, so the trusted computing base of this approach is about the same as ours. RAML and Pastis offer much stronger automation than our approach, but have weaker expressive power. It would be very interesting to offer access to a Pastis-like automated system within our interactive system.

References

1. Akra, M.A., Bazzi, L.: On the solution of linear recurrence equations. Comput. Optim. Appl. **10**(2), 195–210 (1998). https://doi.org/10.1023/A:1018373005182
2. Atkey, R.: Amortised resource analysis with separation logic. Log. Methods Comput. Sci. **7**(2:17) (2011). http://bentnib.org/amortised-sep-logic-journal.pdf
3. Avigad, J., Donnelly, K.: Formalizing *O* notation in Isabelle/HOL. In: Basin, D., Rusinowitch, M. (eds.) IJCAR 2004. LNCS (LNAI), vol. 3097, pp. 357–371. Springer, Heidelberg (2004). https://doi.org/10.1007/978-3-540-25984-8_27
4. Boldo, S., Clément, F., Filliâtre, J.C., Mayero, M., Melquiond, G., Weis, P.: Wave equation numerical resolution: a comprehensive mechanized proof of a C program. J. Autom. Reason. **50**(4), 423–456 (2013). https://hal.inria.fr/hal-00649240
5. Boldo, S., Lelay, C., Melquiond, G.: Coquelicot: a user-friendly library of real analysis for Coq. Math. Comput. Sci. **9**(1), 41–62 (2015). https://hal.inria.fr/hal-00860648
6. Bourbaki, N.: General Topology, Chapters 1–4. Springer, Heidelberg (1995). https://doi.org/10.1007/978-3-642-61701-0
7. Brassard, G., Bratley, P.: Fundamentals of Algorithmics. Prentice Hall, Upper Saddle River (1996)
8. Carbonneaux, Q., Hoffmann, J., Reps, T., Shao, Z.: Automated resource analysis with Coq proof objects. In: Majumdar, R., Kunčak, V. (eds.) CAV 2017, Part II. LNCS, vol. 10427, pp. 64–85. Springer, Cham (2017). https://doi.org/10.1007/978-3-319-63390-9_4
9. Charguéraud, A.: Characteristic formulae for the verification of imperative programs. In: International Conference on Functional Programming (ICFP), pp. 418–430, September 2011. http://www.chargueraud.org/research/2011/cfml/main.pdf
10. Charguéraud, A.: The CFML tool and library (2016). http://www.chargueraud.org/softs/cfml/
11. Charguéraud, A., Pottier, F.: Verifying the correctness and amortized complexity of a union-find implementation in separation logic with time credits. J. Autom. Reason. September 2017. http://gallium.inria.fr/~fpottier/publis/chargueraud-pottier-uf-sltc.pdf

12. Cormen, T.H., Leiserson, C.E., Rivest, R.L., Stein, C.: Introduction to Algorithms, 3rd edn. MIT Press (2009). http://mitpress.mit.edu/catalog/item/default.asp?ttype=2&tid=11866

13. Eberl, M.: Proving divide and conquer complexities in Isabelle/HOL. J. Autom. Reason. **58**(4), 483–508 (2017). https://www21.in.tum.de/~Eeberlm/divide_and_conquer_isabelle.pdf

14. Filliâtre, J.-C., Letouzey, P.: Functors for proofs and programs. In: Schmidt, D. (ed.) ESOP 2004. LNCS, vol. 2986, pp. 370–384. Springer, Heidelberg (2004). https://doi.org/10.1007/978-3-540-24725-8_26

15. Graham, R.L., Knuth, D.E., Patashnik, O.: Concrete Mathematics: A Foundation for Computer Science. Addison-Wesley (1994). http://www-cs-faculty.stanford.edu/~knuth/gkp.html

16. Guéneau, A., Charguéraud, A., Pottier, F.: Electronic appendix, January 2018. http://gallium.inria.fr/~agueneau/bigO/

17. Hoffmann, J., Das, A., Weng, S.: Towards automatic resource bound analysis for OCaml. In: Principles of Programming Languages (POPL), pp. 359–373, January 2017. http://www.cs.cmu.edu/~janh/papers/HoffmannDW17.pdf

18. Hopcroft, J.E.: Computer science: the emergence of a discipline. Commun. ACM **30**(3), 198–202 (1987). http://doi.acm.org/10.1145/214748.214750

19. Howell, R.R.: On asymptotic notation with multiple variables. Technical report 2007–4, Kansas State University, January 2008. http://people.cs.ksu.edu/~rhowell/asymptotic.pdf

20. Howell, R.R.: Algorithms: a top-down approach, July 2012, draft. http://people.cs.ksu.edu/~rhowell/algorithms-text/text/

21. Leighton, T.: Notes on better master theorems for divide-and-conquer recurrences (1996). http://courses.csail.mit.edu/6.046/spring04/handouts/akrabazzi.pdf

22. Pilkiewicz, A., Pottier, F.: The essence of monotonic state. In: Types in Language Design and Implementation (TLDI), January 2011. http://gallium.inria.fr/~fpottier/publis/pilkiewicz-pottier-monotonicity.pdf

23. Reynolds, J.C.: Separation logic: a logic for shared mutable data structures. In: Logic in Computer Science (LICS), pp. 55–74 (2002). http://www.cs.cmu.edu/~jcr/seplogic.pdf

24. Tarjan, R.E.: Algorithm design. Commun. ACM **30**(3), 204–212 (1987). http://doi.acm.org/10.1145/214748.214752

25. Wang, P., Wang, D., Chlipala, A.: TiML: a functional language for practical complexity analysis with invariants. Proc. ACM Program. Lang. **1**(OOPSLA), 79:1–79:26 (2017). http://adam.chlipala.net/papers/TimlOOPSLA17/TimlOOPSLA17.pdf

26. Wegbreit, B.: Mechanical program analysis. Commun. ACM **18**(9), 528–539 (1975). http://doi.acm.org/10.1145/361002.361016

Verified Learning Without Regret
From Algorithmic Game Theory to Distributed Systems with Mechanized Complexity Guarantees

Samuel Merten[✉][iD], Alexander Bagnall[iD], and Gordon Stewart[iD]

Ohio University, Athens, OH, USA
{sm137907,ab667712,gstewart}@ohio.edu

Abstract. Multiplicative Weights (MW) is a simple yet powerful algorithm for learning linear classifiers, for ensemble learning à la boosting, for approximately solving linear and semidefinite systems, for computing approximate solutions to multicommodity flow problems, and for online convex optimization, among other applications. Recent work in algorithmic game theory, which applies a computational perspective to the design and analysis of systems with mutually competitive actors, has shown that no-regret algorithms like MW naturally drive games toward approximate Coarse Correlated Equilibria (CCEs), and that for certain games, approximate CCEs have bounded cost with respect to the optimal states of such systems.

In this paper, we put such results to practice by building distributed systems such as routers and load balancers with performance and convergence guarantees mechanically verified in Coq. The main contributions on which our results rest are (1) the first mechanically verified implementation of Multiplicative Weights (specifically, we show that our MW is no regret) and (2) a language-based formulation, in the form of a DSL, of the class of games satisfying Roughgarden smoothness, a broad characterization of those games whose approximate CCEs have cost bounded with respect to optimal. Composing (1) with (2) within Coq yields a new strategy for building distributed systems with mechanically verified complexity guarantees on the time to convergence to near-optimal system configurations.

Keywords: Multiplicative weights · Algorithmic game theory
Smooth games · Interactive theorem proving · Coq

1 Introduction

The Multiplicative Weights algorithm (MW, [1,25]) solves the general problem of "combining expert advice", in which an agent repeatedly chooses which action, or "expert", to play against an adaptive environment. The agent, after playing an action, learns from the environment both the cost of that action and of other actions it could have played in that round. The environment, in turn, may adapt

© The Author(s) 2018
A. Ahmed (Ed.): ESOP 2018, LNCS 10801, pp. 561–588, 2018.
https://doi.org/10.1007/978-3-319-89884-1_20

in order to minimize environment costs. MW works by maintaining a weighted distribution over the action space, in which each action initially has equal weight, and by updating weights with a linear or exponential loss function to penalize poorly performing actions.

MW is a *no-regret* algorithm: its expected cost approaches that of the best fixed action the agent could have chosen in hindsight (i.e., external regret tends to zero) as time $t \to \infty$. Moreover, this simple algorithm performs remarkably well: in number of rounds logarithmic in the size of the action space, MW's expected regret can be bounded by a small constant ϵ (MW has bounded external regret). In [1], Arora, Hazan, and Kale showed that MW has wide-ranging connections to numerous problems in computer science, including optimization, linear and semidefinite programming, and machine learning (cf. boosting [14]).

Our work targets another important application of MW: the approximate solution of multi-agent games, especially as such games relate to the construction of distributed systems. It is well known (cf. [30, Chapter 4]) that no-regret algorithms such as MW converge, when played by multiple independent agents, to a large equilibrium class known as Coarse Correlated Equilibria (CCEs). CCEs may not be socially optimal, but for some games, such as Roughgarden's smooth games [35], the social cost of such equilibrium states can be bounded by a constant factor of the optimal cost of the game (the game has bounded Price of Anarchy, or POA). Therefore, to drive the social cost of a smooth game to near optimal, it suffices simply to let each agent play a no-regret algorithm such as MW.

Moreover, a number of distributed systems can be encoded as games, especially when the task being distributed is viewed as an optimization problem. Consider, for example, distributed balancing of network flows over a set of web servers, an application we return to in Sect. 3. Assuming the set of flows is fixed, and that the cost of (or latency incurred by) assigning a flow to a particular web server increases as a function of the number of flows already assigned to that server (the traffic), then the load balancing application is encodable as a game in which each flow is a "player" attempting to optimize its cost (latency). An optimal solution of this game minimizes the total latency across all flows. Since the game is Roughgarden smooth (assuming affine cost functions), the social cost of its CCEs as induced by letting each player independently run MW is bounded with respect to that of an optimal solution.

1.1   Contributions

In this paper, we put such results to work by building the first verified implementation of the MW algorithm – which we use to drive all games to approximate CCEs – and by defining a language-based characterization of a subclass of games called Roughgarden smooth games that have robust Price of Anarchy guarantees extending even to approximate CCEs. Combining our verified MW with smooth games, we construct distributed systems for applications such as routing and load balancing that have verified convergence and correctness guarantees.

Specifically, our main contributions are:

- a new architecture, as embodied in the CAGE system (https://github.com/gstew5/cage), for the construction of distributed systems with verified complexity guarantees, by composition of verified Multiplicative Weights (MW) with robust Price of Anarchy bounds via Roughgarden smoothness;
- the first formally verified implementation of the MW algorithm;
- a language-based characterization of Roughgarden smooth games, in the form of a mechanized DSL for the construction of such games together with smoothness preservation theorems showing that each combinator in the language preserves smoothness;
- the application of the resulting system to distributed routing and load balancing.

By *verified*, we mean our MW implementation has mechanically checked convergence bounds and proof of correctness within an interactive theorem prover (specifically, Ssreflect [16], an extension of the Coq [5] system). By *convergence* and *correctness*, we mean that we prove both that MW produces the right answer (functional correctness with respect to a high-level functional specification), but also that it does so with external regret[1] bounded by a function of the number of iterations of the protocol (convergence). Convergence of MW in turn implies convergence to an approximate CCE. By composing this second convergence property with Roughgarden smoothness, we bound the social, or total, cost of the resulting system state with respect to the optimal.

As we've mentioned, MW has broad application across a number of subdisciplines of computer science, including linear programming, optimization, and machine learning. Although our focus in this paper is the use of MW to implement no-regret dynamics, a general strategy for computing the CCEs of multi-agent games, our implementation of MW (Sect. 5.3) could be used to build, e.g., a verified LP solver or verified implementation of boosting as well.

Limitations. The approach we outline above does not apply to all distributed systems, nor even to all distributed systems encodable as games. In particular, in order to prove POA guarantees in our approach, the game encoding a particular distributed system must first be shown Roughgarden smooth, a condition which does not always apply (e.g., to network formation games [35, Section 2]). More positively, the Smooth Games DSL we present in Sects. 3 and 4 provides one method by which to explore the combinatorial nature of Roughgarden smoothness, as we demonstrate with some examples in Sect. 3.

Relationship to Prior Work. Some of the ideas we present in this paper previously appeared in summary form in a 3-page brief announcement at PODC 2017 [4]. The current paper significantly expands on the architecture of the CAGE system, our verified implementation of Multiplicative Weights, the definition of the Smooth Games DSL, and the composition theorems of Sect. 6 proving that the pieces fit together to imply system-wide convergence and quality bounds.

---

[1] The expected (per-step) cost of the algorithm minus that of the best fixed action.

1.2   Organization

The following section provides background on games, algorithmic game theory, and smoothness. Section 3 presents an overview of the main components of the CAGE approach, via application to examples. Section 4 provides more detail on the combinators of our Smooth Games DSL. Section 5 presents our verified implementation of MW. Section 6 describes the composition theorems proving that multi-agent MW converges to near-optimal ϵ-CCEs. Sections 7 and 8 present related work and conclude.

2   Background

2.1   Games

Von Neumann, Morgenstern, and Nash [28, 29] (in the US) and Bachelier, Borel, and Zermelo [3, 8, 43] (in Europe) were the first to study the mathematical theory of strategic interaction, modern game theory. Nash's famous result [27] showed that in all finite games, mixed-strategy equilibria (those in which players are allowed to randomize) always exist. Since the 1950s, game theory has had huge influence in numerous fields, especially economics.

In our context, a game is a tuple of a finite type A (the strategy space) and a cost function C_i mapping tuples of strategies of type $A_1 \times A_2 \times \ldots \times A_N$ to values of type $\mathbb{R}$, the cost to player i of state $(a_1, \ldots, a_i, \ldots, a_N)$. For readers interested in formalization-related aspects, Listing 1 provides additional details.

Listing 1: Games in Ssreflect-Coq

In SSREFLECT-COQ, an extension of the standard Coq system, a finite type A : finType pairs the type A with an enumerator enum : list A such that for all $a : A$, count a enum = 1 (every element is included exactly once). To define games, we use operational type classes [38], which facilitate parameter sharing:

Class game (A : finType) (N : nat) ($\mathbb{R}$: realFieldType)
    '(costClass : CostClass N $\mathbb{R}$ A) : Type ≜ {}.

costClass declares the cost function C_i, and N is the number of players.

A state $s : A_1 \times A_2 \times \ldots \times A_N$ is a *Pure Nash Equilibrium (PNE)* when no player $i \in [1, N]$ has incentive to change its strategy: $\forall s_i'. \ C_i(s) \leq C_i(s_i', s_{-i})$. Here s_i' is an arbitrary strategy. Strategy s_i is player i's move in state s. By s_i', s_{-i} we denote the state in which player i's strategy is s_i' and all other players play s. In other words, no player can decrease its cost by unilateral deviation.

Pure-strategy Nash equilibria do not always exist. Mixed Nash Equilibria (MNE), which *do* exist in all finite games, permit players to randomize over the strategy space, by playing a distribution σ_i over A. The overall state is the product distribution over the player distributions. Every PNE is trivially an MNE, by letting players choose deterministic distributions σ_i.

Correlated Equilibria (CEs) generalize MNEs to situations in which players coordinate via a trusted third party. In what follows, we'll mostly be interested in a generalization of CEs, called *Coarse Correlated Equilibria (CCEs)*, and their approximate relaxations. Specifically, a distribution σ over A^N (Listing 2) is a CCE when $\forall i \forall s_i'$. $\mathbb{E}_{s \sim \sigma}[C_i(s)] \leq \mathbb{E}_{s \sim \sigma}[C_i(s_i', s_{-i})]$. $\mathbb{E}_{s \sim \sigma}[C_i(s)]$ is the expected cost to player i in distribution σ. The CCE condition states that there is no s_i' that could decrease player i's expected cost. CCEs are essentially a relaxation of MNEs which do not require σ to be a product distribution (i.e., the players' strategies may be correlated). CEs are a subclass of CCEs in which $\mathbb{E}_{s \sim \sigma}[C_i(s_i', s_{-i})]$ may be conditioned on s_i.

A distribution σ over states may only be *approximately* a CCE. Define as ϵ-approximate those CCEs σ for which $\forall i \forall s'$. $\mathbb{E}_{s \sim \sigma}[C_i(s)] \leq \mathbb{E}_{s \sim \sigma}[C_i(s_i', s_{-i})] + \epsilon$. Moving to s_i' can decrease player i's expected cost, but only by at most ϵ.

Listing 2: Discrete Distributions in Ssreflect-Coq

Since our games A are finite, discrete distributions suffice to formalize MNEs, CEs, and CCEs. We model such distributions as finite functions (those with finite domain) from the strategy space A to $\mathbb{R}$:

Record dist $(A : \text{finType})$: Type $\triangleq$
   mkDist { pmf :> {ffun $A \to \mathbb{R}$}; dist_ax : dist_axiom pmf }.

Here {ffun $A \to \mathbb{R}$} is Ssreflect syntax for the type of finite functions from A to $\mathbb{R}$. The second projection of the record, dist_ax, asserts that pmf represents a valid distribution: pmf is positive and $\sum_{a:A}$ pmf $a = 1$.
The Coq predicate eCCE:

Definition eCCE $(\epsilon : \mathbb{R})$ $(\sigma : \text{dist } A^N)$: Prop $\triangleq$
   $\forall (i : [0..N-1])$ $(s' : A)$,
   expectedCost i $\sigma \leq$ (expectedUnilateralCost i σ s') $+ \epsilon$.

states that distribution σ (over N-tuples of strategies A, one per player) is an ϵ-approximate CCE, or ϵ-CCE.

2.2 Algorithmic Game Theory

Equilibria are only useful if we're able to quantify, with respect to the game being analyzed:

1. How good equilibrium states are with respect to the optimal configurations of a game. By optimal, we usually mean states s^* that optimize the social cost: $\forall s$. $\sum_i C_i(s^*) \leq \sum_i C_i(s)$.
2. How "easy" (read computationally tractable) it is to drive competing players of the game toward an equilibrium state.

Algorithmic game theory and the related fields of mechanism design and distributed optimization provide excellent tools here.

Good Equilibria. The *Price of Anarchy*, or POA, of game (A, C) quantifies the cost of equilibrium states of (A, C) with respect to optimal configurations. Precisely, define POA as the ratio of the social cost of the worst equilibrium s to the social cost of an optimal state s^*. POA near 1 indicates high-quality equilibria: finding an equilibrium in such a game leads to overall social cost close to optimal. Prior work in algorithmic game theory has established nontrivial POA bounds for a number of game classes: on various classes of congestion and routing games [2,6,10], on facility location games [40], and others [11,32].

In the system of Sect. 3, we use the related concept of *Roughgarden smooth games* [35], or simply *smooth games*, which define a subclass of games with canonical POA proofs. To each smooth game are associated two constants, λ and μ. The precise definition of the smoothness condition is less relevant here than its consequences: if a cost-minimization game is (λ, μ)-smooth, then it has POA $\lambda/(1-\mu)$. Not all games are smooth, but for those that are, the POA bound above extends even to CCEs and their approximations, a particularly large (and therefore tractable) class of equilibria [35, Sects. 3 and 4].

Tractable Dynamics. Good equilibrium bounds are most useful when we know how quickly a particular game converges to equilibrium [7,9,12,13,17]. Certain classes of games, e.g. potential games [26], reach equilibria under a simple model of dynamics called best response. As we've mentioned, we use a different distributed learning algorithm in this work, variously called Multiplicative Weights (MW) [1] or sometimes Randomized Weighted Majority [25], which drives *all* games to CCEs, a larger class of equilibrium states than those achieved by potential games under best response.

3 Cage by Example

No-regret algorithms such as MW can be used to drive multi-agent systems toward the ϵ-CCEs of arbitrary games. Although the CCEs of general games may have high social cost, those of *smooth* games, as identified by Roughgarden [35], have robust Price of Anarchy (POA) bounds that extend even to ϵ-CCEs. Figure 1 depicts how these pieces fit together in the high-level architecture of our CAGE system, which formalizes the results of Sect. 2 in Coq. Shaded boxes are program-related components while white boxes are proof related.

3.1 Overview

At the top, we have a domain-specific language in Coq (DSL, box 1) that generates games with automatically verified POA bounds. To execute such games, we have verified (also in Coq) an implementation of the Multiplicative Weights algorithm (MW, 2). Correctness of MW implies convergence bounds on the games it executes: $O((\ln |A|)/\epsilon^2)$ iterations suffice to drive the game to an ϵ-CCE (here, $|A|$ is the size of the action space, or game type, A).

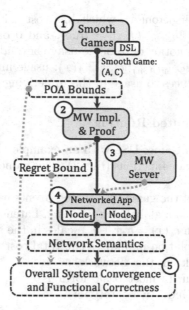

Fig. 1. System architecture

We compose N instances of multiplicative weights (4), one per agent, with a server (3) that facilitates communication, implemented in OCaml and modeled by an operational semantics in Coq. To actually execute games, we use Coq's code extraction mechanism to generate OCaml code that runs clients against the server, using an unverified OCaml shim to send and receive messages. We prove performance guarantees in Coq from POA bounds on the game and from the regret bound on MW.

3.2 Smooth Games DSL

The combinators exposed by the Smooth Games DSL operate over game types A, cost functions C, and smoothness parameters λ and μ. Basic combinators in this language include (i) Resource and (ii) Unit games, the first for coordinating access to shared resources under congestion and the second with fixed cost 0. Combinators that take other games as arguments include:

- the bias combinator Bias(A, b), which adds the fixed value b to the cost function associated with game A;
- the scalar combinator Scalar(A, m), which multiplies the output of the cost function C associated with game A by a fixed value m;
- the product combinator $A \times B$, corresponding to the parallel composition of two games A and B with cost equal to the sum of the costs in the two games;
- the subtype game $\{x : A, \ P(x)\}$, which constructs a new game over the dependent sum type $\Sigma x : A.P(x)$ (values x satisfying the predicate P);

– the singleton game Singleton(A), which has cost 1 if if player i "uses" the underlying resource ($\mathbb{B}_{\text{Resource}}(f\ i) = \text{true}$), and 0 otherwise. The function $\mathbb{B}_-(-)$ generalizes the notion of resource usage beyond the primitive Resource game. For example, $\mathbb{B}_{\text{Scalar}(A,m)}(x) = \mathbb{B}_A(x)$: usage in a game built from the scalar combinator reduces to usage in the underlying game.

3.3   Example: Distributed Routing

We illustrate the Smooth Games DSL with an example: distributed routing over networks with affine latency functions (Fig. 2). This game is known to have POA 5/2 [35].

In a simple version of the game, N routing agents each choose a path from a global source vertex s to a global sink vertex t. Latency over edge e, modeled by an affine cost function $c_e(x) = a_e x + b_e$, scales in the amount of traffic x over that edge. An optimal solution minimizes the total cost to all agents.

We model each link in the network as a Resource game, which in its most basic form is defined by the following inductive datatype:

Inductive Resource : Type $\triangleq$
| RYes : Resource
| RNo : Resource.

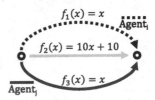

Fig. 2. Routing game with affine edge costs

RYes indicates the agent chose to use the resource (a particular edge) and RNo otherwise. The cost function for Resource is defined by:

Definition ResourceCostFun (i : $[0..N-1]$) (s : $[0..N-1] \to_{\text{fin}}$ Resource) : $\mathbb{R} \triangleq$
if s_i **is** RYes **then** traffic s **else** 0.

in which s is a map from agent labels to resource strategies and traffic s is the total number of agents that chose to use resource s. An agent pays traffic s if it uses the resource, otherwise 0. We implement Resource as a distinct inductive type, even though it's isomorphic to bool, to ensure that types in the Smooth Games DSL have unique game instances. To give each resource the more interesting cost function $c_e(x) = a_e x + b_e$, we compose Resource with a second combinator, Affine(a_e, b_e, Resource), which has cost 0 if an agent does not use the resource, and cost $a_e*(\text{traffic } s) + b_e$ otherwise. This combinator preserves (λ, μ)-smoothness assuming $\lambda + \mu \geq 1$, a side condition which holds for Resource games.

We encode m affine resources by applying Affine to Resource m times, then folding under product:

T $\triangleq$ Affine(a_1, b_1, Resource)
$\times$ Affine(a_2, b_2, Resource)
$\times$ ...
$\times$ Affine(a_m, b_m, Resource)

The associated cost function is the sum of the individual resource cost functions.

Values of type T may assign RYes to a subset of resources that doesn't correspond to a valid path in a graph $G = (V, E)$. To prevent this behavior, we apply to T the subtype combinator Σ, specialized to a predicate isValidPath(G, s, t) enforcing that strategies $(r_1, r_2, \ldots, r_{|E|})$ correspond to valid paths from s to t: T' $\triangleq \Sigma_{\text{isValidPath}(G,s,t)}(\text{T})$. The game T' is (5/3, 1/3)-smooth, just like the underlying Resource game, which implies POA of $(5/3)/(1 - 1/3) = 5/2$.

3.4   Example: Load Balancing

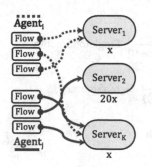

Fig. 3. Load balancing game

As a second example, consider the load balancing game depicted in Fig. 3, in which a number of network flows are distributed over several servers with affine cost functions. In general, N load balancing agents are responsible for distributing M flows over K servers. The cost of allocating a flow to a server is modeled by an affine cost function which scales in the total load (number of flows) on that server. Like routing, the load balancing game has POA 5/2. This is no coincidence; both are special cases of "finite congestion games", a class of games which have POA 5/2 when costs are linear [10]. The connection between them can be seen more concretely by observing that they are built up from the same primitive Resource game.

We model the system as an NM-player K-resource game in which each player corresponds to a single network flow. Each load balancing agent poses as multiple players (MW instances) in the game, one per flow, and composes the actions chosen by these players to form its overall strategy. The result of running the game is an approximate CCE with respect to the distribution of flows over servers.

Each server is defined as a Resource with an affine cost function, using the same data type and cost function as in the routing example. Instead of isValidPath, we use a new predicate exactlyOne to ensure that each network flow is assigned to exactly one server.

4   Smooth Games

Roughgarden smoothness [35] characterizes a subclass of games with canonical Price of Anarchy (POA) proofs. In [35], Roughgarden showed that smooth games have canonical POA bounds not only with respect to pure Nash equilibria but also with respect to mixed Nash equilibria, correlated equilibra, CCEs, and their approximate relaxations. In the context of CAGE, we use smoothness to bound the social cost of games executed by multiple clients each running MW. We show how the technical pieces fit together, in the form of bounds on an operational semantics of the entire CAGE system, in Sect. 6. This section introduces the technical definition of smoothness and the language of combinators,

Syntax

$$Scalars\ m, b;\quad Predicates\ P$$
$$Game\ types\ A, B ::= \mathsf{Resource}\ |\ \mathsf{Unit}\ |\ \mathsf{Bias}(A, b)\ |\ \mathsf{Scalar}(A, m)$$
$$|\ A \times B\ |\ \{x : A,\ P(x)\}\ |\ \mathsf{Singleton}(A)$$

Judgment $\boxed{\vdash_{(\lambda,\mu)} (A, C)}$ read "Game (A, C) is (λ, μ)-smooth."

$$\frac{}{\vdash_{(\frac{5}{3},\frac{1}{3})} (\mathsf{Resource, ResourceCostFun})}\ \mathsf{ResourceSmooth}$$

$$\frac{}{\vdash_{(1,0)} (\mathsf{Unit, fun}\ i\ f.\ 0)}\ \mathsf{UnitSmooth}$$

$$\frac{\vdash_{(\lambda,\mu)} (A, C)}{\vdash_{(1,0)} (\mathsf{Singleton}(A), \mathsf{fun}\ i\ f.\ \mathsf{if}\ \mathbb{B}_A(f\ i)\ \mathsf{then}\ 1\ \mathsf{else}\ 0)}\ \mathsf{SingletonSmooth}$$

$$\frac{\vdash_{(\lambda,\mu)} (A, C)}{\vdash_{(\lambda,\mu)} (\{x : A,\ P(x)\}, \mathsf{fun}\ i\ f.\ C_i\ (\mathsf{fun}\ j.\ (f\ j).1))}\ \mathsf{SigmaSmooth}$$

$$\frac{\vdash_{(\lambda,\mu)} (A, C)\quad 1 \le \lambda + \mu\quad 0 \le b}{\vdash_{(\lambda,\mu)} (\mathsf{Bias}(A, b), \mathsf{fun}\ i\ f.\ C_i\ f + b)}\ \mathsf{BiasSmooth}$$

$$\frac{\vdash_{(\lambda,\mu)} (A, C)\quad 0 \le m}{\vdash_{(\lambda,\mu)} (\mathsf{Scalar}(A, m), \mathsf{fun}\ i\ f.\ m * C_i\ f)}\ \mathsf{ScalarSmooth}$$

$$\frac{\vdash_{(\lambda_A,\mu_A)} (A, C^A)\quad \vdash_{(\lambda_B,\mu_B)} (B, C^B)}{\vdash_{(\max(\lambda_A,\lambda_B),\max(\mu_A,\mu_B))} (A \times B, \mathsf{fun}\ i\ f.\ C_i^A\ f + C_i^B\ f)}\ \mathsf{ProductSmooth}$$

Fig. 4. Smooth games DSL

or Smooth Games DSL of Sect. 3, that we use to build games that are smooth by construction.

Definition 1 (Smoothness). *A game (A, C) is (λ, μ)-smooth if for any two states $s, s^* : A^N$, the following inequality holds:*

$$\sum_{i=1}^{k} C_i(s_i^*, s_{-i}) \le \lambda \cdot C(s^*) + \mu \cdot C(s).$$

Here, $C_i(s_i^*, s_{-i})$ denotes the individual cost to player i in the mixed state where all other players follow their strategies from s, while player i follows the corresponding strategy from s^*. Smooth games bound the individual cost of players' unilateral deviations from state s to s^* by the weighted social costs of s and s^*. In essence, when λ and μ are small, the effect of any single player's deviation from a given state has minimal effect.

The smoothness inequality leads to natural proofs of POA for a variety of equilibrium classes. As an example, consider the following bound on the expected cost of ϵ-CCEs of (λ, μ)-smooth games:

Lemma smooth_eCCE $(d : \text{dist} (\text{state } N \ T))$ $(s' : \text{state } N \ T)$ $(\epsilon : \mathbb{R})$:
  eCCE ϵ d → optimal s' →
  ExpectedCost $d \leq \lambda *(\text{Cost } s') + \mu *(\text{ExpectedCost } d) + N * \epsilon$.

ExpectedCost d is the sum for all players i of the expected cost to player i of distribution d. N is the number of players in the game.

The smooth_eCCE bound implies the following Price of Anarchy bound on the expected cost, summed across all players, of distribution d:

Lemma smooth_POA ϵ $(d : \text{dist} (\text{state } N \ T))$ s' :
  eCCE ϵ d → optimal s' →
  ExpectedCost $d \leq \lambda/(1 - \mu)*(\text{Cost } s') + (N*\epsilon)/(1 - \mu)$.

If d is an ϵ-CCE, then its cost is no more than $\lambda/(1 - \mu)$ times the optimal cost of s', plus an additional term that scales in the number of players N. For example, for concrete values $\lambda = 5/3$, $\mu = 1/3$, $\epsilon = 0.0375$, and $N = 5$, we get multiplicative approximation factor $\lambda/(1 - \mu) = 5/2$ and additive factor 0.28. A value of $\epsilon = 0.0375$ is reasonable; as Sect. 5 will show, it takes fewer than $20,000$ iterations of the Multiplicative Weights algorithm, in a game with strategy space of size 1000, to produce $\epsilon \leq 0.0375$.

4.1 Combinators

Figure 4 lists the syntax and combinators of the Smooth Games DSL we used in Sect. 3 to build smooth routing and load balancing games.

The smoothness proof accompanying the judgment of Resource games is the least intuitive, and provides some insight into the behavior of smooth games. The structure of our proof borrows from a stronger result given by Roughgarden [35]: smoothness for resource games with affine cost functions and multiple resources. The key step is the following inequality first noted by Christodoulou and Koutsoupias [10]:

$$y(z + 1) \leq \frac{5}{3}y^2 + \frac{1}{3}z^2$$

for non-negative integers y and z. We derive $(\frac{5}{3}, \frac{1}{3})$-smoothness of Resource games from the following inequalities:

$$\sum_{i=0}^{N-1} C_i(s_i^*, s_{-i}) \leq (\text{traffic } s^*) \cdot (\text{traffic } s + 1) \tag{1}$$

$$(\text{traffic } s^*) \cdot (\text{traffic } s + 1) \leq \frac{5}{3} \cdot (\text{traffic } s^*)^2 + \frac{1}{3} \cdot (\text{traffic } s)^2 \tag{2}$$

$$(\text{traffic } s^*) \cdot (\text{traffic } s + 1) \leq \frac{5}{3} \cdot C(s^*) + \frac{1}{3} \cdot C(s) \tag{3}$$

$$\sum_{i=0}^{N-1} C_i(s_i^*, s_{-i}) \leq \frac{5}{3} \cdot C(s^*) + \frac{1}{3}\mu \cdot C(s) \tag{4}$$

The inequality in step 1 is due to the fact that the cost per player in state s^* is at most traffic $s + 1$, and there are exactly traffic s^* players incurring such cost. I.e., (traffic s^*) · (traffic $s + 1$) is the number of nonzero terms times the upper bound on each term. The substitution in step 3 comes from the fact that in any state s, $C(s) =$ (traffic s)^2; each of the m players using the resource incur cost m.

The proofs of smoothness for other combinators are straightforward. For example, since Unit games always have cost 0, all values of λ and μ satisfy the smoothness inequality: $0 \leq \lambda \cdot 0 + \mu \cdot 0$. We restrict the range of the cost function in SingletonSmooth games to $\{0, 1\}$ by applying the function $\mathbb{B}_A(\cdot)$, which generalizes the notion of "using a resource" to all the game types of Fig. 4. Smoothness of the Singleton game follows by case analysis on the results of $\mathbb{B}_A(\cdot)$ in the states s and s^* of the smoothness inequality. The games produced by the SigmaSmooth combinator have costs equal to those of the underlying games but restrict the domain to those states satisfying a predicate P. Since smoothness of the underlying bound holds for all states in A, the same bound holds of the restricted domain of states $a \in A$ drawn from P. Smoothness of product games relies on the fact that smoothness still holds if λ and μ are replaced with larger values. Thus, each of the argument games to ProductSmooth is $(\max(\lambda_A, \lambda_B), \max(\mu_A, \mu_B))$-smooth. The overall product game, which sums the costs of its argument games, is $(\max(\lambda_A, \lambda_B), \max(\mu_A, \mu_B))$-smooth as well.

It's possible to derive combinators from those defined in Fig. 4. For example, define as Affine(m, b, A) the game with cost function $mx + b$. We implement this game as $\{p : \text{Scalar}(m, A) \times \text{Scalar}(b, \text{Singleton}(A)), \ p.1 = p.2\}$, or the subset of product games over the scalar game Scalar(m, A) and the $\{0, 1\}$ scalar game over b such that the first and second projections of each strategy p are equal.

5   Multiplicative Weights (MW)

At the heart of the CAGE architecture of Sect. 3 lies our verified implementation of the Multiplicative Weights algorithm. In this section, we present the details of the algorithm and sketch its convergence proof. Section 5.3 presents our verified MW implementation and mechanized proof of convergence.

For all $a \in A$, client initializes $w_1(a) = 1$.

For time $t \in [1 \dots T]$:

Client	Environment
Let $\Gamma_t \triangleq \sum_{a \in A} w_t(a)$. Play strategy $p_t(a) = w_t(a)/\Gamma_t$.	
	Choose cost vector c_t.
Update weights $w_{t+1}(a) \triangleq w_t(a) * (1 - \eta * c_t(a))$	

Fig. 5. Multiplicative Weights (MW)

5.1   The Algorithm

The MW algorithm (Fig. 5) pits a client, or agent, against an adaptive environment. The agent maintains a weight distribution w over the action space, initialized to give each action equal weight. At each time step $t \in [1 \ldots T]$, the agent commits to the distribution $w_t / \sum_{a \in A} w_t(a)$, communicating this mixed strategy to the environment. After receiving a cost vector c_t from the environment, the agent updates its weights w_{t+1} to penalize high-cost actions, at a rate determined by a learning constant $\eta \in (0, 1/2]$. High η close to $1/2$ leads to higher penalties, and thus relatively less exploration of the action space.

The environment is typically adaptive, and may be implemented by a number of other agents also running instances of MW. The algorithm proceeds for a fixed number of epochs T, or until some bound on expected external regret (expected cost minus the cost of the best fixed action) is achieved. In what follows, we always assume that costs lie in the range $[-1, 1]$. Costs in an arbitrary but bounded range are also possible (with a concomitant relaxation of the algorithm's regret bounds), as are variations of MW to solve payoff maximization instead of cost minimization.

5.2   MW Is No Regret

The MW algorithm converges reasonably quickly: To achieve expected regret at most ϵ, it's sufficient to run the algorithm $O((ln\,|A|)/\epsilon^2)$ iterations, where $|A|$ is the size of the action space [36, Chapter 17]. Regret can be driven arbitrarily small as the number of iterations approaches infinity. Bounded regret suffices to prove convergence to an approximate CCE, as [36] also shows.

In this section, we present a high-level sketch of the proof that MW is no regret. We follow [36, Chapter 17], which has additional details. At the level of the mathematics, our formal proof makes no significant departures from Roughgarden.

Definition 2 (Per-Step External Regret). *Let a^* be the best fixed action in hindsight (i.e., the action with minimum cost given the cost vectors received from the environment) and let $OPT \triangleq \sum_{t=1}^{T} c_t(a^*)$. The expected per-step external regret of MW is*

$$\left(\sum_{t=1}^{T} \zeta_t - OPT \right) / T.$$

The summed term defines the cumulative expected cost of the algorithm for time $t \in [1 \ldots T]$, where by ζ_t we denote the expected cost at time t:

$$\zeta_t = \sum_{a \in A} p_t(a) \cdot c_t(a) = \sum_{a \in A} \frac{w_t(a)}{\Gamma_t} \cdot c_t(a)$$

To get per-step expected regret, we subtract the cumulative cost of a^* and divide by the number of time steps T.

Theorem 1 (MW Has Bounded Regret). *The algorithm of Fig. 5 has expected per-step external regret at most $\eta + ln\,|A|\,/\,\eta T$.*

Proof Sketch. The proof of Theorem 1 uses a potential-function argument, with potential Φ_t equal the sum of the weights $\Gamma_t = \sum_{a \in A} w_t(a)$ at time t. It proceeds by relating the cumulative expected cost $\sum_t \zeta_t$ of the algorithm to OPT, the cost of the best fixed action, through the intermediate quantity Γ_{T+1}.

The proof additionally relies on the following two facts derived from the Taylor expansion $ln(1 - x) = -x - \frac{x^2}{2} - \frac{x^3}{3} - \cdots$:

$$ln(1 - x) \leq -x, \qquad\qquad x < 1$$
$$-x - x^2 \leq ln(1 - x), \qquad\qquad x \leq 1/2$$

$\square$

By letting $\eta = \sqrt{ln\,|A|\,/\,T}$ (cf. [36, Chapter 17]), it's possible to restate the regret bound of Theorem 1 to the following arguably nicer bound:

Corollary 1 (MW Is No Regret)

$$\left(\sum_{t=1}^{T} \zeta_t - OPT \right) / T \leq 2\sqrt{ln\,|A|\,/\,T}$$

Here, the number of iterations T must be large enough to ensure that $\eta = \sqrt{ln\,|A|\,/\,T} \leq 1/2$, thus ensuring that $\eta \in (0, 1/2]$.

5.3 MW Architecture

Our implementation and proof of MW (Fig. 6) were designed to be extensible. At a high level, the proof structure follows the program refinement methodology, in which a high-level mathematical but inefficient specification of MW (High-Level Functional Specification) is gradually made more efficient by a series of refinements to various features of the program (for example, by

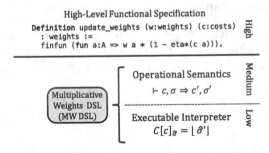

Fig. 6. MW architecture

replacing an inefficient implementation of a key-value map with a more efficient balanced binary tree).

For each such refinement, we prove that every behavior of the lower-level program is a possible behavior of the higher-level program it refines. Thus specifications proved for all behaviors of the high-level program also apply to each behavior at the low level. By behavior here, we mean the trace of action distributions output by MW as it interacts with, and receives cost vectors from, the environment.

We factor the lower implementation layers (Medium and Low) into an interpreter and operational semantics over a domain-specific language specialized to MW-style algorithms (MW DSL). The DSL defines commands for maintaining and updating weights tables as well as commands for interacting with the environment. We prove, for any DSL program c, that the interpretation of that program refines its behavior with respect to the small-step operational semantics (Medium). Our overall proof specializes this general refinement to an implementation of MW as a command in the DSL, in order to relate that command's interpreted behavior to the high-level functional specification.

5.4   MW DSL

The syntax and semantics of the MW DSL are given in Fig. 7. The small-step operational semantics $(\vdash c, \sigma \Rightarrow c', \sigma')$ is parameterized by an environment oracle that defines functions for sending action distributions to the environment (oracle_send) and for receiving the resulting cost vectors (oracle_recv). The oracle will in general be implemented by other clients also running MW (Sect. 6) but is left abstract here to facilitate abstraction and reuse. The oracle is stateful (the type T, of oracle states, may be updated both by oracle_send and oracle_recv).

Most of the operational semantics rules are straightforward. In the MW-STEP-WEIGHTS rule for updating the state's weights table, we make use of an auxiliary expression evaluation function $E_-[-]$ (standard and therefore not shown in Fig. 7). The only other interesting rules are those for send and recv, which call oracle_send and oracle_recv respectively. In the relation oracle_recv, the first two arguments are treated as inputs (the input oracle state of type T and the channel) while the second two are treated as outputs (the cost vector of type $A \to \mathbb{Q}$ and the output oracle state). In the relation oracle_send, the first three arguments are inputs while only the last (the output oracle state) is an output.

Multiplicative Weights. As an example of an MW DSL program, consider our implementation (Listing 1.1) of the high-level MW of Fig. 5. To the right of each program line, we give comments describing the effect of each command. The program is itself divided into three functions: mult_weights_init, which initializes the weights table to assign weight 1 to each action a in the action space A; mult_weights_body, which defines the body of the main loop of MW; and mult_weights, which simply composes mult_weights_init with mult_weights_body.

Listing 1.1. MW DSL Implementation of Multiplicative Weights

Definition mult_weights_init $(A : \text{Type}) \triangleq$
  update $(\lambda\ a : A \Rightarrow 1)$; (* For all $a \in A$, initialize $w_1(a) = 1$. *)
  send. (* Commit to the uniform distribution over actions. *)

Definition mult_weights_body $(A : \text{Type}) \triangleq$
  recv; (* Block until agent receives cost vector c_t from environment. *)
  update $(\lambda\ a : A \Rightarrow \text{weight}\ a * (1 - \eta * \text{cost}\ a))$; (* Update weights. *)
  send. (* Commit to distribution w_t/Γ_t. *)

Definition mult_weights $(A : \text{Type})\ (n : \text{N.t}) \triangleq$
  mult_weights_init A; (* Initialize weights and commit to initial mixed strategy. *)
  iter n (mult_weights_body A). (* Do n iterations of the MW main loop. *)

The MW DSL contains commands and expressions that are specialized to MW-style applications. Consider the function mult_weights_body (line 5). It first receives a cost vector from the environment using the specialized recv command. At the level of the MW DSL, recv is somewhat abstract. The program does not specify, e.g., which network socket to use. Implementation details such as these are resolved by the MW interpreter, which we discuss below in Sect. 5.5.

After recv, mult_weights_body implements an update to its weights table as defined by the command: update $(\lambda a : A \Rightarrow \text{weight}\ a * (1 - \eta * \text{cost}\ a))$. As an argument to the update, we embed a function from actions $a \in A$ to expressions that defines how the weight of each action a should change at this step (time $t + 1$). The expressions weight a and cost a refer to the weight and cost, respectively, of action a at time t. The anonymous function term is defined in SSREFLECT-COQ, the metalanguage in which the MW DSL is defined.

5.5 Interpreter

To run MW DSL programs, we wrote an executable interpreter in Coq with type:

  interp $(c : \text{com}\ A)\ (s : \text{cstate})$: option cstate.

The type cstate defines the state of the interpreter after each step, and in general maps quite closely to the type of states σ used in the MW DSL operational semantics. It is given by the record:

Syntax

> $Binary\ operators \oplus ::= + \mid - \mid *$
> $Expressions\ \ e ::= d \mid -e \mid \mathsf{weight}\ a \mid \mathsf{cost}\ a \mid \eta \mid e_1 \oplus e_2$
> $Commands\ \ c ::= \mathsf{skip} \mid \mathsf{update}\ (\lambda a : A \Rightarrow e) \mid c_1; c_2 \mid \mathsf{iter}\ n\ c \mid \mathsf{recv} \mid \mathsf{send}$

Environment Oracle

> $\mathsf{oracle\_recv} : T \rightarrow \mathsf{oracle\_chanty} \rightarrow (A \rightarrow \mathbb{Q}) \rightarrow T \rightarrow \mathsf{Prop}$
> $\mathsf{oracle\_send} : T \rightarrow \mathsf{dist}\ A \rightarrow \mathsf{oracle\_chanty} \rightarrow T \rightarrow \mathsf{Prop}$

States $\sigma \triangleq$

$\{\ \mathsf{SCosts} : A \rightarrow \mathbb{Q};\ \mathsf{SCostsOk} : \forall a.\ \lvert \mathsf{SCosts}\ a \rvert \leq 1$	Current cost vector
$;\ \mathsf{SPrevCosts} : \mathsf{seq}\ \{c : A \rightarrow \mathbb{Q} \mid \forall a.\ \lvert c\ a \rvert \leq 1\}$	Previous cost vectors
$;\ \mathsf{SWeights} : A \rightarrow \mathbb{Q}$	Weights table
$;\ \mathsf{SWeightsOk} : \forall a.\ 0 < \mathsf{SWeights}\ a$	
$;\ \mathsf{SEta} : \mathbb{Q};\ \mathsf{SEtaOk} : 0 < \mathsf{SEta} \leq 1/2$	The η parameter
$;\ \mathsf{SOutputs} : \mathsf{seq}\ (\mathsf{dist}\ A)$	Committed distributions
$;\ \mathsf{SChan} : \mathsf{oracle\_chanty}$	I/O channel
$;\ \mathsf{SOracleSt} : T\ \}.$	Environment/oracle state

Operational Semantics

$$\frac{\sigma' = \sigma\{\mathsf{SWeights} \triangleq \lambda a : A \Rightarrow E_\sigma[e[x \leftarrow a]]\}}{\vdash \mathsf{update}\ (\lambda x : A \Rightarrow e), \sigma \Rightarrow \mathsf{skip}, \sigma'}\ \text{MW-Step-Weights}$$

$$\frac{}{\vdash \mathsf{skip}; c_2, \sigma \Rightarrow c_2, \sigma} \qquad \frac{\vdash c_1, \sigma \Rightarrow c_1', \sigma'}{\vdash c_1; c_2, \sigma \Rightarrow c_1'; c_2, \sigma'}$$

$$\frac{}{\vdash \mathsf{iter}\ 1\ c, \sigma \Rightarrow c, \sigma} \qquad \frac{1 < n}{\vdash \mathsf{iter}\ n\ c, \sigma \Rightarrow c; \mathsf{iter}\ (n-1)\ c, \sigma}$$

$$\frac{\mathsf{oracle\_recv}\ (\mathsf{SOracleSt}\ \sigma)\ (\mathsf{SChan}\ \sigma)\ c\ t}{\vdash \mathsf{recv}, \sigma \Rightarrow \mathsf{skip}, \sigma\{\mathsf{SCosts} \triangleq c;\ \mathsf{SPrevCosts} \triangleq \mathsf{SCosts}\ \sigma :: \mathsf{SPrevCosts}\ \sigma;\ \mathsf{SOracleSt} \triangleq t\}}$$

$$\frac{\mathsf{oracle\_send}\ (\mathsf{SOracleSt}\ \sigma)\ d\ ch\ t}{\vdash \mathsf{send}, \sigma \Rightarrow \mathsf{skip}, \sigma\{\mathsf{SOutputs} \triangleq d :: \mathsf{SOutputs}\ \sigma;\ \mathsf{SChan} \triangleq ch;\ \mathsf{SOracleSt} \triangleq t\}}$$

Fig. 7. MW DSL syntax and operational semantics, parameterized by an environment oracle defining the type T of environment states and the functions oracle_recv and oracle_send for interacting with the environment. The type A is that of states in the underlying game.

Record cstate : Type $\triangleq$

$\{\ \mathsf{SCosts} : \mathsf{M.t}\ \mathbb{Q}$	Current cost vector
$;\ \mathsf{SPrevCosts} : \mathsf{list}\ (\mathsf{M.t}\ \mathbb{Q})$	Previous cost vectors
$;\ \mathsf{SWeights} : \mathsf{M.t}\ \mathbb{Q}$	Weights table
$;\ \mathsf{SEta} : \mathbb{Q}$	The η parameter
$;\ \mathsf{SOutputs} : \mathsf{list}\ (A \rightarrow \mathbb{Q})$	Committed distributions
$;\ \mathsf{SChan} : \mathsf{oracle\_chanty}$	I/O channel
$;\ \mathsf{SOracleSt} : T\ \}.$	Environment/oracle state

At the level of cstates, we use efficient purely functional data structures such as AVL trees. For example, the type M.t $\mathbb{Q}$ denotes an AVL-tree map from actions A to rational numbers $\mathbb{Q}$. In the small-step semantics state, by contrast, we model the weights table not as a balanced binary tree but as a SSREFLECT-COQ finite function, of type {ffun $A \to \mathbb{Q}$}, which directly maps actions of type A to values of type $\mathbb{Q}$.

To speed up computation on rationals, we use a dyadic representation $q = \frac{n}{2^d}$, which facilitates fast multiplication. We do exact arithmetic on dyadic $\mathbb{Q}$ instead of floating point arithmetic to avoid floating-point precision error. Verification of floating-point error bounds is an interesting but orthogonal problem (cf. [31,34]).

The field SOutputs in the cstate record, a list of functions mapping actions $a \in A$ to their probabilities, stores the history of weights distributions generated by the interpreter as send commands are executed. To implement commands such as send and recv, we parameterize our MW interpreter by an environment oracle, just as we did the operational semantics. The operations implemented by the interpreter environment oracle are functional versions of the operational semantics oracle_send and oracle_recv:

oracle_send' : $\forall A$:Type, $T \to A \to$ oracle_chanty $* T$
oracle_recv' : $\forall A$:Type, $T \to$ oracle_chanty $\to$ list $(A*\mathbb{Q}) * T$

The oracle state type T is provided by the implementation of the oracle, as in the operational semantics. The command oracle_send' takes a state of type T and a value of type A as arguments and returns a pair of a channel of type oracle_chanty (on which to listen for a response from the environment) and a new oracle state of type T. The command oracle_recv' takes as arguments the oracle state and channel and returns a list of (a, q) pairs, representing a cost vector over actions, along with the new oracle state.

5.6   Proof

The top-level theorem proved of our high-level functional specification of MW is:

Theorem perstep_weights_noregret :
(expCostsR $-$ OPTR)/T $\leq \eta +$ ln size_A $/ (\eta *T)$.

The expression expCostsR is the cumulative expected cost of MW on a sequence of cost vectors, or the sum, for each time t, of the expected cost of the MW algorithm at time t. OPTR is the cumulative cost over T rounds of the best fixed action. The number η (a dyadic rational required to lie in range $(0, 1/2]$) is the learning parameter provided to MW and ln size_A is the natural log of the size of the action space A. T is the number of time steps. In contrast to the interpreter and semantics of Sect. 5.3 (where we do exact arithmetic on dyadics), for reasoning and specification at the level of the proof we use Coq's real number library and real-valued functions such as square root and log.

By choosing η to equal $\sqrt{ln\ \text{size\_A} / T}$, Corollary 1 showed that it's possible to restate the right-hand side of the inequality in perstep_weights_noregret to

2 * sqrt (ln size_A / T), thus giving an arguably nicer bound. Since in our implementation of MW we require that η be a dyadic rational, we cannot implement $\eta = \sqrt{ln\ size\_A\ /\ T}$ directly (ln size_A is irrational). We do, however, prove the following tight approximation for all values of η approaching $\sqrt{ln\ size\_A\ /\ T}$:

Lemma perstep_weights_noregret' :
$\forall r : \mathbb{R}.\ r \neq -1 \rightarrow \eta = (1{+}r){*}(\text{sqrt (ln size\_A / T)}) \rightarrow$
$(\text{expCostsR} - \text{OPTR})/\text{T} \leq$
$(1{+}r){*}(\text{sqrt (ln size\_A / T)}) + (\text{sqrt (ln size\_A / T)})/(1{+}r).$

In the statement of this lemma, the r term quantifies the error (how far η is from its optimal value sqrt (ln size_A / T). We require that $r \neq -1$ to ensure that division by $1 + r$ is well-defined. The resulting bound approaches 2 * sqrt (ln size_A / T) as r approaches 0.

High-Level Functional Specification. Our high-level functional specification of MW closely models the mathematical specification of MW given in Fig. 5. For example, the following four definitions:

Definition weights : Type $\triangleq$ {ffun $A \rightarrow \mathbb{Q}$}.
Definition costs : Type $\triangleq$ {ffun $A \rightarrow \mathbb{Q}$}.
Definition init_weights : weights $\triangleq \lambda(\_ : A) \Rightarrow 1$.
Definition update_weights (w:weights) (c:costs) : weights $\triangleq$
$\lambda a : A \Rightarrow w\ a * (1 - \eta * c\ a).$

construct the types of weight (weights) and cost vectors (costs), represented as finite functions from A to $\mathbb{Q}$; define the initial weight vector (init_weights), which maps all actions to cost 1; and define the MW weight update rule (update_weights). The recursive function:

Fixpoint weights_of (cs : seq costs) (w : weights) : weights $\triangleq$
  if cs **is** $c :: cs'$ **then** update_weights (weights_of cs' w) c **else** w.

defines the vector that results from using update_weights to repeatedly update w with respect to cost vectors cs.

Adaptive Vs. Oblivious Adversaries. In our high-level specification of MW, we parameterize functions like weights_of by a fixed sequence of cost vectors cs rather than model interaction with the environment, as is done in Fig. 5. An execution of our low-level interpreted MW, even against an adaptive adversary, is always simulatable by the high-level functional specification by recording in the low-level execution the cost vectors produced by the adversary, as is done by the SPrevCosts field (Sect. 5.5), and then passing this sequence to weights_of. This strategy is quite similar to using backward induction to solve the MW game for an oblivious adversary.

Connecting the Dots. To connect the MW interpreter to the high-level specification, we prove a series of refinement theorems (technically, backward simulations). As example, consider:

Lemma interp_step_plus :
  $\forall (a_0 : A)\ (s : \text{state } A)\ (t\ t' : \text{cstate})\ (c : \text{com } A),$
  interp $c\ t = \text{Some } t' \rightarrow$
  match_states $s\ t \rightarrow$
  $\exists c'\ s',$ final_com $c' \wedge$
    $((c = \text{CSkip} \wedge s = s') \vee \text{step\_plus } a_0\ c\ s\ c'\ s') \wedge$
    match_states $s'\ t'.$

which relates the behavior of the interpreter (interp $c\ t$) when run on an arbitrary command c in cstate t to our model of MW DSL commands as specified by the operational semantics.

To prove that the operational semantics correctly refines our high-level functional specification of MW (and therefore satisfies the regret bounds given at the start of Sect. 5.6), we prove a similar series of refinements. Since backward simulations compose transitively, we prove regret bounds on our interpreted MW just by composing the refinements in series. The bounds we prove in this way are parametric in the environment oracle with which MW is instantiated. When the oracle state types differ from source to target in a particular simulation, as is the case in our proof that the MW DSL interpreter refines the operational semantics, we require that the oracles simulate as well.

6   Coordinated MW

A system of multiple agents each running MW yields an ϵ-CCE of the underlying game. If the game being played is smooth – for example, it was built using the combinators of the Smooth Games DSL of Sect. 4 – then the resulting ϵ-CCE has bounded social cost with respect to a globally optimal strategy. In this section, we put these results together by (1) defining an operational semantics of distributed interaction among multiple clients each running MW, and (2) proving that distributed executions of this semantics yield near-optimal solutions, as long as the underlying game being played is smooth.

6.1   Machine Semantics

We model the evolution of the distributed machine by the operational semantics in Fig. 8. Client states (client_state) bundle commands from the MW DSL (Sect. 5) with MW states parameterized by the ClientPkg oracle. The client oracle send and receive functions model single-element (pin) queues, represented as values of type option (dist A), storing values sent by an MW node, and of type option $(A \rightarrow Q)$, storing values received by an MW node.

States of the coordinated machine (type machine_state $N\ A$) map client indices in range $[0..N-1]$ to client states (type client_state A). Machine states also record, at each iteration of the distributed MW protocol, the history of distributions received from the clients in that round (type seq $([0..N-1] \rightarrow \text{dist } A)$), which will be used to prove Price of Anarchy bounds in the next section (Sect. 6.2). We say that all_clients_have_sent in a particular machine state m,

Client Oracle

ClientPkg $\triangleq$
$\{$ sent : option (dist A);
    received : option $(A \to \mathbb{Q})$;
    received_ok : $\forall v.$ received $=$ Some $v \to \forall a.\ 0 \leq v_a \leq 1\ \}$
client_oracle_recv A $(p$: ClientPkg) $(-$: unit) $(v$: $A \to \mathbb{Q})$ $(p'$: ClientPkg) $\triangleq$
p.received $=$ Some $v \land p'$.received $=$ None $\land p'$.sent $= p$.sent
client_oracle_send A $(p$: ClientPkg) $(d$: dist $A)$ $(-$: unit) $(p'$: ClientPkg) $\triangleq$
p.sent $=$ None $\land p'$.sent $=$ Some $d \land p'$.received $= p$.received

Machine States

client_state $A \ni \sigma \triangleq$ (com $A *$ state A ClientPkg unit)
machine_state N $A \ni m \triangleq$
$\{$ clients : $[0..N-1] \to$ client_state A;
    hist : seq $([0..N-1] \to$ dist $A)$ $\}$
all_clients_have_sent A $(m$: machine_state) $(f$: $[0..N-1] \to$ dist $A) \triangleq$
$\forall i$: $[0..N-1]$. let $(-, \sigma) \triangleq$ m.clients i in
(SOracleSt σ).received $=$ None $\land$ (SOracleSt σ).sent $=$ Some f_i.

Machine Step $\boxed{\vdash m \Longrightarrow m'}$

$$\text{cost\_vec } A\ i\ :\ A \to \mathbb{Q} \triangleq \lambda a.\ \sum_{(p:[0..N-1]\to A | p_i = a)} \prod_{(j | i \neq j)} f_j\ p_j * C_i\ p$$

$$\frac{\begin{array}{ccc} \text{m.clients } i = (c, \sigma) & \text{m'.clients } i = (c, \sigma') & \sigma \sim_o \sigma' \\ \text{(SOracleSt } \sigma).\text{sent} = \text{None} & \text{(SOracleSt } \sigma').\text{received} = \text{Some (cost\_vec } f\ i) \end{array}}{\text{server\_sent\_cost\_vector } i\ f\ m\ m'}$$

$$\frac{\text{m.clients } i = (c, \sigma) \qquad \text{(SOracleSt } \sigma).\text{sent} = \text{None} \qquad \vdash c, \sigma \Rightarrow c', \sigma'}{\vdash m \Longrightarrow m\{ \text{ clients} \triangleq \text{m.clients}[i \mapsto (c', \sigma')] \ \}} \ \text{ClientStep}$$

$$\frac{\begin{array}{c} \text{all\_clients\_have\_sent } m\ f \\ (\forall i.\ \text{server\_sent\_cost\_vector } i\ f\ m\ m') \qquad m'.\text{hist} = f :: m.\text{hist} \end{array}}{\vdash m \Longrightarrow m'} \ \text{ServerStep}$$

Fig. 8. Semantics of the distributed machine

committing to the set of distributions f, if each client's received buffer is empty and its sent buffer contains the distribution f_i, of type dist A.

The machine step relation models a server–client protocol, distinguishing server steps (ServerStep) from client steps (ClientStep). Client steps, which run commands in the language of Fig. 7, may interleave arbitrarily. Server steps are synchronized by the all_clients_have_sent relation to run only after all clients have completed the current round. The work done by the server is modeled by the auxiliary relation server_sent_cost_vector i f m m', which constructs and sends to client i the cost vector derived from the set of client distributions f. The relation $\sigma \sim_O \sigma'$ states that σ and σ' are equal up to their SOracleSt components.

In the distributed MW setting, the cost to player i of a particular action $a : A$ is defined as the expected value, over all N-player strategy vectors p in which player i chose action a ($p_i = a$), of the cost to player i of p, with the expectation over the $(N - 1)$-size product distribution induced by the players $j \neq i$.

6.2   Convergence and Optimality

Our proof that MW is no regret (Sect. 5) extends to system-wide convergence and optimality guarantees, with respect to the distributed execution model of Fig. 8 in which each client runs our MW implementation. The proof has three major steps:

1. Show that no-regret clients implementing MW are still no regret when interleaved in the distributed semantics of Fig. 8.
2. Prove that per-client regret bounds – one for each client running MW – imply system-wide convergence to an ϵ-CCE.
3. Use POA results for smooth games from Sect. 4 to bound the cost, with respect to that of an optimal state, of all such ϵ-CCEs.

Composing 1, 2, and 3 proves that the distributed machine of Fig. 8 – when instantiated to clients running MW – converges to near-optimal solutions to smooth games. We briefly describe each part in turn.

Part 1 : No-regret clients are still no regret when interleaved. That MW no-regret bounds lift to an MW client running in the context of the distributed operational semantics of Fig. 8 follows from the oracular structure of our implementation of MW (Sect. 5) – clients interact with other clients and with the server only through the oracle.

In particular, for any execution $\vdash m \Longrightarrow^+ m'$ of the machine of Fig. 8, and for any client i, there is a corresponding execution of client i with respect to a small nondeterministic oracle that simply "guesses" which cost vector to supply every time the MW client executes a recv operation. Because MW is no regret for all possible sequences of cost vectors, proving a refinement against the nondeterministic oracle implies a regret bound on client i's execution from state m_i to state m'_i.

We lift this argument to all the clients running in the Fig. 8 semantics by proving the following theorem:

> **Theorem** all_clients_bounded_regret A m m' T (ϵ : rat) :
> hist $m = $ nil $\to 0 < $ size (hist m') $\to$ final_state $m' \to$
> $\vdash m \Longrightarrow^+ m' \to$
> ($\forall i$, m.clients $i = $ (mult_weights A T, init_state A η tt (init_ClientPkg A))) $\to$
> $\eta + $ ln size_$A/(\eta * T) \leq \epsilon \to$
> machine_regret_eps m' ϵ.

The predicate machine_regret_eps holds in state s', against regret bound ϵ, if all clients have expected regret in state s' at most ϵ (with respect to the σ_T distribution we describe below), for any rational ϵ larger than $\eta + \ln \text{size\_}A/(\eta * T)$ (the regret bound we proved of MW in Sect. 5).

We assume that the history is empty in the initial state (hist $m = $ nil), and that at least one round was completed ($0 < $ size (hist m')). By final_state m', we mean that all clients have synchronized with the server (by receiving a cost vector and sending a distribution) and then have terminated in CSkip. All clients in state m are initialized to execute T steps of MW over game A (mult_weights A T), from an initial state and initial ClientPkg.

Part 2: System-wide convergence to an ϵ-CCE. The machine semantics of Fig. 8 converges to an approximate Coarse Correlated Equilibrium (ϵ-CCE).

More formally, consider an execution $\vdash m \Longrightarrow^+ m'$ of the Fig. 8 semantics that results in a state m' for which machine_regret_eps m' ϵ (all clients have regret at most ϵ, as established in Part I). The distribution σ_T, defined as the time-averaged history of the product of the distributions output by the MW clients at each round, is an ϵ-CCE:

$$\sigma_T \triangleq \lambda p. \ \frac{\sum_{i=1}^{T} \prod_{j=1}^{N} (\text{hist } m')_i^j \ p_j}{T}$$

By (hist m')$_i^j$ we mean the distribution associated to player j at time i, as recorded in the execution history stored in state m'. The value ((hist m')$_i^j$ p_j) is the probability that client j chose action p_j in round i.

We formalize this property in the following Coq theorem:

Theorem machine_regret_eCCE m' ϵ :
  machine_regret_eps m' ϵ $\rightarrow$
  eCCE ϵ σ_T.

which states that σ_T is an eCCE, with approximation factor ϵ, as long as each client's expected regret over σ_T is at most ϵ (machine_regret_eps m' ϵ) – exactly the property we proved in Part 1 above.

Part 3 System-wide regret bounds. The machine semantics of Fig. 8 converge to a state with expected cost bounded with respect to the optimal cost.

Consider an execution of the Fig. 8 semantics $\vdash m \Longrightarrow^+ m'$ and an ϵ satisfying the conditions of all_clients_bounded_regret. If the underlying game is smooth, the expected cost of the time-averaged distribution of the clients in m', σ_T, is bounded with respect to the cost of an optimal strategy profile s' by the following Coq theorem:

Theorem systemwide_POA_bound A m m' T (ϵ : rat) s' :
  hist $m = $ nil $\rightarrow \vdash m \Longrightarrow^+ m' \rightarrow 0 < $ size (hist m') $\rightarrow$ final_state $m' \rightarrow$
  ($\forall i$, m.clients $i = $ (mult_weights A T, init_state A η tt (init_ClientPkg A))) $\rightarrow$
  $\eta + \ln \text{size\_}A/(\eta * T) \leq \epsilon \rightarrow$
  optimal $s' \rightarrow$
  ExpectedCost $\sigma_T \leq \lambda/(1-\mu) * $ Cost $s' + (N * \epsilon/(1-\mu))$

In the above theorem, λ and μ are the smoothness parameters of the game A while N is the number of players. Cost s' is the social (total) cost of the optimal state s'.

7   Related Work

Reinforcement Learning, Bandits. There is extensive work on reinforcement learning [39], multi-agent reinforcement learning (MARL [19]), and multi-armed bandits (MAB, [15]), more than can be cited here. We note, however, that Q-learning [41], while similar in spirit to MW, addresses the more general scenario in which an agent's action space is modeled by an arbitrary Markov Decision Process (in MW, the action space is a single set A). Our verified MW implementation is most suitable, therefore, for use in the full-information analog of MAB problems, in which actions are associated with "arms" and each agent learns the cost of all arms – not just the one it pulled – at each time step. In this domain, MW has good convergence bounds, as we prove formally of our implementation in this paper. Relaxing our verified MW and formal proofs to the partial information Bandit setting is interesting future work.

Verified Distributed Systems. EventML [33] is a domain-specific language for specifying distributed algorithms in the Logic of Events, which can be mechanically verified within the Nuprl proof assistant. Work has been done to develop methods for formally verifying distributed systems in Isabelle [20]. Model checking has been used extensively (e.g., [21,24]) to test distributed systems for bugs.

Verdi [42] is a Coq framework for implementing verified distributed systems. A Verdi system is implemented as a collection of handler functions which exchange messages through the network or communicate with the "outside world" via input and output. Application-level safety properties of the system can be proved with respect to a simple, idealized network semantics. A verified system transformer (VST) can then be used to transform the executable system into one which is robust to network faults such as reordering, duplication, and dropping of packets. The safety properties of the system proved under the original network semantics are preserved under the new faulty semantics, with minimal additional proof effort required of the programmer.

The goals of Verdi are complementary to our own. We implement a verified no-regret MW algorithm, together with a language of Roughgarden smooth games, for constructing distributed systems with verified convergence and correctness guarantees. Verdi allows safety properties of a distributed system to be lifted to analogous systems which tolerate various network faults, and provides a robust runtime system for execution in a practical setting. It stands to reason, then, that Verdi (as well as follow-on related work such as [37]) may provide a natural avenue for building robust executable versions of our distributed applications. We leave this for future work.

Chapar [23] is a Coq framework for verifying causal consistency of distributed key-value stores as well as correctness of client programs with respect to causally consistent key-value stores. The implementation of a key-value store is proved correct with respect to a high-level specification using a program refinement method similar to ours. Although Chapar's goal isn't to verify robustness to network faults, node crashes and message losses are modeled by its abstract operational semantics.

IronFleet [18] is a framework and methodology for building verified distributed systems using a mix of TLA-style state machine refinement, Hoare logic, and automated theorem proving. An IronFleet system is comprised of three layers: a high-level state machine specification of the overall system, a more detailed distributed protocol layer which describes the behavior of each agent in the system as a state machine, and the implementation layer in which each agent is programmed using a variant of the Dafny [22] language extended with a trusted set of UDP networking operations. Correctness properties are proved with respect to the high-level specifications, and a series of refinements is used to prove that every behavior in the implementation layer is a refinement of some behavior in the high-level specification. IronFleet has been used to prove safety and liveness properties of IronRSL, a Paxos-based replicated state machine, as well as IronKV, a shared key-value store.

Alternative Proofs. Variant proofs of Theorem 1, such as the one via KL-divergence (cf. [1, Section 2.2]), could be formalized in our framework without modifying most parts of the MW implementation. In particular, because we have proved once and for all that our interpreted MW refines a high-level specification of MW, it would be sufficient to formalize the new proof just with respect to the high-level program of Sect. 5.6.

8   Conclusion

This paper reports on the first formally verified implementation of Multiplicative Weights (MW), a simple yet powerful algorithm for approximately solving Coarse Correlated Equilibria, among many other applications. We prove our MW implementation correct via a series of program refinements with respect to a high-level implementation of the algorithm. We present a DSL for building smooth games and show how to compose MW with smoothness to build distributed systems with verified Price of Anarchy bounds. Our implementation and proof are open source and available online.

Acknowledgments. This material is based on work supported by the National Science Foundation under Grant No. CCF-1657358. We thank the ESOP anonymous referees for their comments on an earlier version of this paper.

References

1. Arora, S., Hazan, E., Kale, S.: The multiplicative weights update method: a meta-algorithm and applications. Theor. Comput. **8**(1), 121–164 (2012)
2. Awerbuch, B., Azar, Y., Epstein, A.: The price of routing unsplittable flow. In: Proceedings of the thirty-seventh annual ACM Symposium on Theory of Computing, pp. 57–66. ACM (2005)
3. Bachelier, L.: Théorie mathématique du jeu. Annales Scientifiques de l'Ecole Normale Supérieure **18**, 143–209 (1901)
4. Bagnall, A., Merten, S., Stewart, G.: Brief announcement: certified multiplicative weights update: verified learning without regret. In: Proceedings of the ACM Symposium on Principles of Distributed Computing, PODC 2017. ACM (2017)
5. Bertot, Y., Castéran, P.: Interactive Theorem Proving and Program Development: Coq'Art: The Calculus of Inductive Constructions. Springer, Heidelberg (2013)
6. Bhawalkar, K., Gairing, M., Roughgarden, T.: Weighted congestion games: price of anarchy, universal worst-case examples, and tightness. In: de Berg, M., Meyer, U. (eds.) ESA 2010, Part II. LNCS, vol. 6347, pp. 17–28. Springer, Heidelberg (2010). https://doi.org/10.1007/978-3-642-15781-3_2
7. Blum, A., Monsour, Y.: Learning, regret minimization, and equilibria. In: Nisan, N., Roughgarden, T., Tardos, E., Vazirani, V.V. (eds.) Algorithmic Game Theory. Cambridge University Press, Cambridge (2007). Chapter 4
8. Borel, E.: La théorie du jeu et les équations intégrales à noyau symétrique. Comptes rendus de l'Académie des Sci. **173**(1304–1308), 58 (1921)
9. Borowski, H., Marden, J.R., Shamma, J.: Learning efficient correlated equilibrium. Submitted for journal publication (2015)
10. Christodoulou, G., Koutsoupias, E.: The price of anarchy of finite congestion games. In: Proceedings of the 37th Annual ACM Symposium on Theory of Computing, pp. 67–73. ACM (2005)
11. Demaine, E.D., Hajiaghayi, M., Mahini, H., Zadimoghaddam, M.: The price of anarchy in network creation games. In: Proceedings of the Twenty-sixth Annual ACM Symposium on Principles of Distributed Computing, pp. 292–298. ACM (2007)
12. Fanelli, A., Moscardelli, L., Skopalik, A.: On the impact of fair best response dynamics. In: Rovan, B., Sassone, V., Widmayer, P. (eds.) MFCS 2012. LNCS, vol. 7464, pp. 360–371. Springer, Heidelberg (2012). https://doi.org/10.1007/978-3-642-32589-2_33
13. Foster, D.P., Vohra, R.V.: Calibrated learning and correlated equilibrium. Games Econ. Behav. **21**(1), 40–55 (1997)
14. Freund, Y., Schapire, R.E.: A desicion-theoretic generalization of on-line learning and an application to boosting. In: Vitányi, P. (ed.) EuroCOLT 1995. LNCS, vol. 904, pp. 23–37. Springer, Heidelberg (1995). https://doi.org/10.1007/3-540-59119-2_166
15. Gittins, J.C.: Bandit processes and dynamic allocation indices. J. R. Stat. Soc. Ser. B (Methodol.) **41**(2), 148–177 (1979)
16. Gonthier, G., Mahboubi, A., Tassi, E.: A small scale reflection extension for the Coq system. Technical report, INRIA (2015)
17. Hart, S., Mas-Colell, A.: A simple adaptive procedure leading to correlated equilibrium. Econometrica **68**(5), 1127–1150 (2000)

18. Hawblitzel, C., Howell, J., Kapritsos, M., Lorch, J.R., Parno, B., Roberts, M.L., Setty, S., Zill, B.: IronFleet: proving practical distributed systems correct. In: Proceedings of the 25th Symposium on Operating Systems Principles, pp. 1–17. ACM (2015)
19. Hu, J., Wellman, M.P., et al.: Multiagent reinforcement learning: theoretical framework and an algorithm. In: ICML, vol. 98, pp. 242–250. Citeseer (1998)
20. Küfner, P., Nestmann, U., Rickmann, C.: Formal verification of distributed algorithms. In: Baeten, J.C.M., Ball, T., de Boer, F.S. (eds.) TCS 2012. LNCS, vol. 7604, pp. 209–224. Springer, Heidelberg (2012). https://doi.org/10.1007/978-3-642-33475-7_15
21. Lamport, L.: Specifying Systems: The TLA+ Language and Tools for Hardware and Software Engineers. Addison-Wesley Longman Publishing Co., Inc., Boston (2002)
22. Leino, K.R.M.: Dafny: an automatic program verifier for functional correctness. In: Clarke, E.M., Voronkov, A. (eds.) LPAR 2010. LNCS (LNAI), vol. 6355, pp. 348–370. Springer, Heidelberg (2010). https://doi.org/10.1007/978-3-642-17511-4_20
23. Lesani, M., Bell, C.J., Chlipala, A.: Chapar: certified causally consistent distributed key-value stores. In: ACM SIGPLAN Notices, vol. 51. ACM (2016)
24. Lin, H., Yang, M., Long, F., Zhang, L., Zhou, L.: MODIST: transparent model checking of unmodified distributed systems. In: Proceedings of the 6th USENIX Symposium on Networked Systems Design and Implementation (2009)
25. Littlestone, N., Warmuth, M.K.: The weighted majority algorithm. In: Proceedings of the 30th Annual Symposium on Foundations of Computer Science. IEEE (1989)
26. Monderer, D., Shapley, L.S.: Potential games. Games Econ. Behav. 14(1), 124–143 (1996)
27. Nash, J.: Non-cooperative games. Ann. Math. 54(2), 286–295 (1951)
28. Nash, J.F.: Equilibrium in n-player games. Proc. Natl. Acad. Sci. (PNAS) 36(1), 48–49 (1950)
29. von Neumann, J., Morgenstern, O.: Theory of Games and Economic Behavior, vol. 60. Princeton University Press, New Jersey (1944)
30. Nisan, N., Roughgarden, T., Tardos, E., Vazirani, V.V.: Algorithmic Game Theory, vol. 1. Cambridge University Press, New York (2007)
31. Panchekha, P., et al.: Automatically improving accuracy for floating point expressions. ACM SIGPLAN Not. 50(6), 1–11 (2015)
32. Perakis, G., Roels, G.: The price of anarchy in supply chains: quantifying the efficiency of price-only contracts. Manag. Sci. 53(8), 1249–1268 (2007)
33. Rahli, V.: Interfacing with proof assistants for domain specific programming using EventML. In: Proceedings of the 10th International Workshop on User Interfaces for Theorem Provers, Bremen, Germany (2012)
34. Ramananandro, T., et al.: A unified Coq framework for verifying C programs with floating-point computations. In: Proceedings of the 5th ACM SIGPLAN Conference on Certified Programs and Proofs. ACM (2016)
35. Roughgarden, T.: Intrinsic robustness of the price of anarchy. In: Proceedings of the 41st Annual ACM Symposium on Theory of Computing, pp. 513–522. ACM (2009)
36. Roughgarden, T.: Twenty Lectures on Algorithmic Game Theory. Cambridge University Press, New York (2016)
37. Sergey, I., Wilcox, J.R., Tatlock, Z.: Programming and proving with distributed protocols. In: Proceedings of the ACM on Programming Languages, vol. 2 (POPL), Article 28 (2018)

38. Spitters, B., Van der Weegen, E.: Type classes for mathematics in type theory. Math. Struct. Comput. Sci. **21**(04), 795–825 (2011)
39. Sutton, R.S., Barto, A.G.: Reinforcement Learning: An Introduction, vol. 1. MIT press, Cambridge (1998)
40. Vetta, A.: Nash equilibria in competitive societies, with applications to facility location, traffic routing and auctions. In: Proceedings of the 43rd Annual IEEE Symposium on Foundations of Computer Science, pp. 416–425. IEEE (2002)
41. Watkins, C.J., Dayan, P.: Q-learning. Mach. Learn. **8**(3–4), 279–292 (1992)
42. Wilcox, J.R., Woos, D., Panchekha, P., Tatlock, Z., Wang, X., Ernst, M.D., Anderson, T.: Verdi: a framework for implementing and formally verifying distributed systems. In: ACM SIGPLAN Notices, vol. 50, pp. 357–368. ACM (2015)
43. Zermelo, E.: Über eine anwendung der mengenlehre auf die theorie des schachspiels. In: Proceedings of the Fifth International Congress of Mathematicians, vol. 2, pp. 501–504. II, Cambridge University Press, Cambridge (1913)

Program Verification by Coinduction

Brandon Moore[1], Lucas Peña[2]([✉]), and Grigore Rosu[1,2]

[1] Runtime Verification, Inc., Urbana, IL, USA
[2] University of Illinois at Urbana-Champaign, Urbana, IL, USA
lpena7@illinois.edu

Abstract. We present a novel program verification approach based on coinduction, which takes as input an operational semantics. No intermediates like program logics or verification condition generators are needed. Specifications can be written using any state predicates. We implement our approach in Coq, giving a certifying language-independent verification framework. Our proof system is implemented as a single module imported unchanged into language-specific proofs. Automation is reached by instantiating a generic heuristic with language-specific tactics. Manual assistance is also smoothly allowed at points the automation cannot handle. We demonstrate the power and versatility of our approach by verifying algorithms as complicated as Schorr-Waite graph marking and instantiating our framework for object languages in several styles of semantics. Finally, we show that our coinductive approach subsumes reachability logic, a recent language-independent sound and (relatively) complete logic for program verification that has been instantiated with operational semantics of languages as complex as C, Java and JavaScript.

1 Introduction

Formal verification is a powerful technique for ensuring program correctness, but it requires a suitable verification framework for the target language. Standard approaches such as Hoare logic [1] (or verification condition generators) require significant effort to adapt and prove sound and relatively complete for a given language, with few or no theorems or tools that can be reused between languages. To use a software engineering metaphor, Hoare logic is a design pattern rather than a library. This becomes literal when we formalize it in a proof assistant.

We present instead a single language-independent program verification framework, to be used with an executable semantics of the target programming language given as input. The core of our approach is a simple theorem which gives a coinduction principle for proving partial correctness.

To trust a non-executable semantics of a desired language, an equivalence to an executable semantics is typically proved. Executable semantics of programming languages abound in the literature. Recently, executable semantics of several real languages have been proposed, e.g., of C [2], Java [3], JavaScript [4,5], Python [6], PHP [7], CAML [8], thanks to the development of executable semantics engineering frameworks like K [9], PLT-Redex [10], Ott [11], etc., which

© The Author(s) 2018
A. Ahmed (Ed.): ESOP 2018, LNCS 10801, pp. 589–618, 2018.
https://doi.org/10.1007/978-3-319-89884-1_21

make defining a formal semantics for a programming language almost as easy as implementing an interpreter, if not easier. Our coinductive program verification approach can be used with any of these executable semantics or frameworks, and is correct-by-construction: no additional "axiomatic semantics", "program logic", or "semantics suitable for verification" with soundness proofs needed.

As detailed in Sect. 6, we are not the first to propose a language-independent verification infrastructure that takes an operational semantics as input, nor the first to propose coinduction for proving isolated properties about some programs. However, we believe that coinduction can offer a fresh, promising and general approach as a language-independent verification infrastructure, with a high potential for automation that has not been fully explored yet. In this paper we make two steps in this direction, by addressing the following research questions:

RQ1 *Is it feasible to have a sound and (relatively) complete verification infrastructure based on coinduction, which is language-independent and versatile, i.e., takes an arbitrary language as input, given by its operational semantics?*

RQ2 *Is it possible to match, or even exceed, the capabilities of existing language-independent verification approaches based on operational semantics?*

To address RQ1, we make use of a key mathematical result, Theorem 1, which has been introduced in more general forms in the literature, e.g., in [12,13] and in [14]. We mechanized it in Coq in a way that allows us to instantiate it with a transition relation corresponding to any target language semantics, hereby producing certifying program verification for that language. Using the resulting coinduction principle to show that a program meets a specification produces a proof which depends only on the operational semantics. We demonstrate our proofs can be effectively automated, on examples including heap data structures and recursive functions, and describe the implemented proof strategy and how it can be reused across languages defined using a variety of operational styles.

To address RQ2, we show that our coinductive approach not only subsumes reachability logic [15], whose practicality has been demonstrated with languages like C, Java, and JavaScript, but also offers several specific advantages. Reachability logic consists of a sound and (relatively) complete proof system that takes a given language operational semantics as a *theory* and derives reachability properties about programs in that language. A mechanical procedure can translate any proof using reachability logic into a proof using our coinductive approach.

We first introduce our approach with a simple intuitive example, then prove its correctness. We then discuss mechanical verification experiments across different languages, show how reachability logic proofs can be translated into coinductive proofs, and conclude with related and future work. Our entire Coq formalization, proofs and experiments are available at [16].

2   Overview and Basic Notions

Section 4 will show the strengths of our approach by means of verifying rather complex programs. Here our objective is different, namely to illustrate it by verifying a trivial IMP (C-style) program: s=0; while (--n) {s=s+n;}. Let sum stand for the program and loop for its while loop. When run with a positive initial value n of n, it sets s to the sum of $1, \ldots, n-1$. To illustrate non-termination, we assume unbounded integers, so loop runs forever for non-positive n. An IMP language syntax sufficient for this example and a possible execution trace are given in Fig. 1. The exact step granularity is not critical for our approach, as long as diverging executions produce infinite traces.

$Pgm ::= Stmt$	$\langle$s=0; while (--n) {s=s+n;} $\| n \mapsto 4\rangle$
	$\langle$while (--n) {s=s+n;} $\| n \mapsto 4,$ s $\mapsto 0\rangle$
$Exp ::= Id$	$\langle$if (--n) {s=s+n; loop} else {skip} $\| n \mapsto 4,$ s $\mapsto 0\rangle$
$\| \quad Int$	$\langle$if (3) {s=s+n; loop} else {skip} $\| n \mapsto 3,$ s $\mapsto 0\rangle$
$\| \quad$ -- Id	$\langle$s=s+n; loop $\| n \mapsto 3,$ s $\mapsto 0\rangle$
$\| \quad Exp$ op Exp	$\langle$s=0+n; loop $\| n \mapsto 3,$ s $\mapsto 0\rangle$
	$\langle$s=0+3; loop $\| n \mapsto 3,$ s $\mapsto 0\rangle$
$Stmt ::=$ skip	$\langle$s=3; loop $\| n \mapsto 3,$ s $\mapsto 0\rangle$
$\| \quad Stmt\ Stmt$	$\langle$skip; loop $\| n \mapsto 3,$ s $\mapsto 3\rangle$
$\| \quad Id$ = Exp ;	$\langle$while (--n) {s=s+n;} $\| n \mapsto 3,$ s $\mapsto 3\rangle$
$\| \quad$ if Exp { $Stmt$ }	$\ldots \| \ldots$
else { $Stmt$ }	$\langle$while (--n) {s=s+n;} $\| n \mapsto 1,$ s $\mapsto 6\rangle$
$\| \quad$ while Exp { $Stmt$ }	$\langle$if (--n) {s=s+n; loop} else {skip} $\| n \mapsto 1,$ s $\mapsto 6\rangle$
	$\langle$if (0) {s=s+n; loop} else {skip} $\| n \mapsto 0,$ s $\mapsto 6\rangle$
	$\langle$skip $\| n \mapsto 0,$ s $\mapsto 6\rangle$

Fig. 1. Syntax of **IMP** (left) and sample execution of sum (right)

While our coinductive program verification approach is self-contained and thus can be presented without reliance on other verification approaches, we prefer to start by discussing the traditional Hoare logic approach, for two reasons. First, it will put our coinductive approach in context, showing also how it avoids some of the limitations of Hoare logic. Second, we highlight some of the subtleties of Hoare logic when related to operational semantics, which will help understand the reasons and motivations underlying our definitions and notations.

2.1   Intuitive Hoare Logic Proof

A Hoare logic specification/triple has the form $\{\!|\varphi_{pre}|\!\}$ code $\{\!|\varphi_{post}|\!\}$. The convenience of this notation depends on specializing to a particular target language, such as allowing variable names to be used directly in predicates to stand for their values, or writing only the current statement. This hides details of the environment/state representation, and some framing conventions or compositionality assumptions over the unmentioned parts. A Hoare triple specifies a set of (partial correctness) reachability claims about a program's behavior, and it is

(IMP statement rules)

$$\frac{}{\{\!|\varphi[e/x]|\!\} \; \texttt{x= e;} \; \{\!|\varphi|\!\}} \qquad \text{(HL-ASGN)}$$

$$\frac{\{\!|\varphi_1|\!\} \; \texttt{s}_1 \; \{\!|\varphi_2|\!\}, \quad \{\!|\varphi_2|\!\} \; \texttt{s}_2 \; \{\!|\varphi_3|\!\}}{\{\!|\varphi_1|\!\} \; \texttt{s}_1 \; \texttt{s}_2 \; \{\!|\varphi_3|\!\}} \qquad \text{(HL-SEQ)}$$

$$\frac{\{\!|\varphi \wedge e \neq 0|\!\} \; \texttt{s}_1 \; \{\!|\varphi'|\!\}, \quad \{\!|\varphi \wedge e = 0|\!\} \; \texttt{s}_2 \; \{\!|\varphi'|\!\}}{\{\!|\varphi|\!\} \; \texttt{if (e) then } \{\texttt{s}_1\} \texttt{ else } \{\texttt{s}_2\} \; \{\!|\varphi'|\!\}} \qquad \text{(HL-IF)}$$

$$\frac{\{\!|\varphi \wedge e \neq 0|\!\} \; \texttt{s} \; \{\!|\varphi|\!\}}{\{\!|\varphi|\!\} \; \texttt{while (e) } \{\texttt{s}\} \; \{\!|\varphi \wedge e = 0|\!\}} \qquad \text{(HL-WHILE)}$$

(Generic rule)

$$\frac{\models \psi \rightarrow \varphi, \quad \{\!|\varphi|\!\} \; \texttt{s} \; \{\!|\varphi'|\!\}, \quad \models \varphi' \rightarrow \psi'}{\{\!|\psi|\!\} \; \texttt{s} \; \{\!|\psi'|\!\}} \qquad \text{(HL-CONSEQ)}$$

Fig. 2. IMP program logic.

typically an over-approximation (i.e., it specifies more reachability claims than desired or feasible). Specifically, assume some formal language semantics of IMP defining an execution step relation $R \subseteq C \times C$ on a set C of configurations of the form $\langle \texttt{code} \,|\, \sigma \rangle$, like those in Fig. 1. We write $a \rightarrow_R b$ for $(a, b) \in R$. Section 2.3 (Fig. 3) discusses several operational semantics approaches we experimented with (Sect. 4), that yield such step relations R. A (partial correctness) *reachability claim* (c, P), relating an initial state $c \in C$ and a target set of states $P \subseteq C$, is *valid* (or *holds*) iff the initial state c can either reach a state in P or can take an infinite number of steps (with $\rightarrow_R$); we write $c \Rightarrow_R P$ to indicate that claim (c, P) is valid, and $a \rightarrow b$ or $c \Rightarrow P$ instead of $a \rightarrow_R b$ or $c \Rightarrow_R P$, resp., when R is understood. Then $\{\!|\varphi_{pre}|\!\}\texttt{code}\{\!|\varphi_{post}|\!\}$ specifies the set of reachability claims

$$\{((\langle \texttt{code} \,|\, \sigma_{pre} \rangle, \{\langle \texttt{skip} \,|\, \sigma_{post} \rangle \,|\, \sigma_{post} \models \varphi_{post}\}) \,|\, \sigma_{pre} \models \varphi_{pre}\}$$

and it is *valid* iff all of its reachability claims are valid. It is necessary for P in reachability claims (c, P) specified by Hoare triples to be a set of configurations (and thus an over-approximation): it is generally impossible for φ_{post} to determine exactly the possible final configuration or configurations.

While one can prove Hoare triples valid directly using the step relation $\rightarrow_R$ and induction, or coinduction like we propose in this paper, the traditional approach is to define a language-specific proof system for deriving Hoare triples from other triples, also known as *a* Hoare logic, or program logic, for the target programming language. Figure 2 shows such a program logic for IMP. Hoare logics are generally not executable, so testing cannot show whether they match the *intended* semantics of the language. Even for a simple language like IMP, if one mistakenly writes $e = 1$ instead of $e \neq 0$ in rule (HL-WHILE), then one gets an incorrect program logic. When trusted verification is desired, the program logic needs to be proved sound w.r.t. a reference executable semantics of the language, i.e, that each derivable Hoare triple is valid. This is a highly non-trivial task for complex languages (C, Java, JavaScript), in addition to defining a Hoare logic itself. Our coinductive approach completely avoids this difficulty by requiring no additional semantics of the programming language for verification purposes.

The property to prove is that sum (or more specifically loop) exits only when n is 0, with s as the sum $\sum_{i=1}^{n-1} i$ (or $\frac{n(n-1)}{2}$). In more detail, any configuration whose statement begins with sum and whose store defines n as n can run indefinitely or reach a state where it has just left the loop with $n \mapsto 0$, $s \mapsto \sum_{i=1}^{n-1} i$, and the store otherwise unchanged. As a Hoare logic triple, that specification is

$$\{\!| n = n |\!\} \; \texttt{s=0; while(--n)\{s=s+n;\}} \; \{\!| s = \sum_{i=1}^{n-1} i \wedge n{=}0 |\!\}$$

As seen, this Hoare triple asserts the validity of the set of reachability claims

$$S \equiv \{(c_{n,\sigma}, P_{n,\sigma}) \mid \forall n, \forall \sigma \text{ undefined in n}\} \tag{1}$$

where

$$c_{n,\sigma} \equiv \langle \texttt{s=0; while(--n)\{s=s+n;\}} \mid n \mapsto n, \; \sigma \rangle$$

$$P_{n,\sigma} \equiv \{\langle \texttt{skip} \mid n \mapsto 0, s \mapsto \sum_{i=1}^{n-1} i, \sigma' \rangle \mid \forall \sigma' \text{ undefined in n, s}\}$$

We added the σ and σ' state frames above for the sake of complete details about what Hoare triples actually specify, and to illustrate why P in claims (c, P) needs to be a set. Since the addition/removal of σ and σ' does not change the subsequent proofs, for the remainder of this section, for simplicity, we drop them.

Now let us assume, without proof, that the proof system in Fig. 2 is sound (for the executable step relation $\rightarrow_R$ of IMP discussed above), and let us use it to derive a proof of the sum example. Note that the proof system in Fig. 2 assumes that expressions have no side effects and thus can be used unchanged in state formulae, which is customary in Hoare logics, so the program needs to be first translated out into an equivalent one without the problematic --n where expressions have no side effects. We could have had more Hoare logic rules instead of needing to translate the code segment, but this would quickly make our program logics significantly more complicated. Either way, with even a simple imperative programming language like we have here, it is necessary to either add Hoare logic rules to Fig. 2 or to modify our code segment. These inconveniences are taken for granted in Hoare logic based verifiers, and they require non-negligible additional effort if trusted verification is sought. For comparison, our coinductive verification approach proposed in this paper requires no transformation of the original program. After modifying the above problematic expression, our code segment gets translated to the (hopefully) equivalent code:

$$\texttt{s=0; n=n-1; while (n) \{s=s+n; n=n-1;\}}$$

Let loop' be the new loop and let φ_{inv}, its invariant, be

$$\texttt{s} = \frac{((n-1) - \texttt{n}) \, (n + \texttt{n})}{2}$$

The program variable n stands for its current value, while the mathematical variable n stands for the initial (sometimes called "old") value of n. Next, using the assign and sequence Hoare logic rules in Fig. 2, as well as basic arithmetic via the (HL-CONSEQ) rule, we derive

$$\{n = n\} \text{ s=0; n=n-1; } \{\varphi_{inv}\} \qquad (2)$$

Similarly, we can derive $\{\varphi_{inv} \wedge n \neq 0\}$ s=s+n; n=n-1; $\{\varphi_{inv}\}$. Then, applying the while rule, we derive $\{\varphi_{inv}\}$ loop' $\{\varphi_{inv} \wedge n = 0\}$. The rest follows by the sequence rule with the above, (2), and basic arithmetic.

This example is not complicated, in fact it is very intuitive. However, it abstracts out a lot of details in order to make it easy for a human to understand. It is easy to see the potential difficulties that can arise in larger examples from needing to factor out the side effect, and from mixing both program variables and mathematical variables in Hoare logic specifications and proofs. With our coinduction verification framework, all of these issues are mitigated.

2.2 Intuitive Coinduction Proof

Since our coinductive approach is language-independent, we do not commit to any particular, language-specific formalism for specifying reachability claims, such as Hoare triples. Consequently, we will work directly with raw reachability claims/specifications $S \subseteq C \times \mathcal{P}(C)$ consisting of sets of pairs (c, P) with $c \in C$ and $P \subseteq C$ as seen above. We show how to coinductively prove the claim for the example sum program in the form given in (1), relying on nothing but a general language-independent coinductive machinery and the trusted execution step relation $\rightarrow_R$ of IMP. Recall that we drop the state frames (σ) in (1).

Intuitively, our approach consists of symbolic execution with the language step relation, plus coinductive reasoning for circular behaviors. Specifically, suppose that $S_{circ} \subseteq C \times \mathcal{P}(C)$ is a specification corresponding to some code with circular behavior, say some loop. Pairs $(c, P) \in S_{circ}$ with $c \in P$ are already valid, that is, $c \Rightarrow_R P$ for those. "Execute" the other pairs $(c, P) \in S_{circ}$ with the step relation $\rightarrow_R$, obtaining a new specification S' containing pairs of the form (d, P), where $c \rightarrow_R d$; since we usually have a mathematical description of the pairs in S_{circ} and S', this step has the feel of symbolic execution. Note that S_{circ} is valid if S' is valid. Do the same for S' obtaining a new specification S'', and so on and so forth. If at any moment during this (symbolic) execution process we reach a specification S that is included in our original S_{circ}, then simply assume that S is valid. While this kind of cyclic reasoning may not seem sound, it is in fact valid, and justified by *coinduction*, which captures the essence of partial correctness, *language-independently*. Reaching something from the original specification shows we have reached some fixpoint, and coinduction is directly related to greatest fixpoints. This is explained in detail in Sect. 3.

In many examples it is useful to chain together individual proofs, similar to (HL-SEQ). Thus, we introduce the following sequential composition construct:

Definition 1. *For $S_1, S_2 \subseteq C \times \mathcal{P}(C)$, let $S_1 \, {}_9 \, S_2 \equiv \{(c, P) \mid \exists Q \, . \, (c, Q) \in S_1 \wedge \forall d \in Q, (d, P) \in S_2\}$. Also, we define* $\mathrm{trans}(S)$ *as $S \, {}_9 \, S$ (trans can be thought of as a transitivity proof rule).*

If S_1 and S_2 are valid then $S_1 \, {}_9 \, S_2$ is also valid (Lemma 2).

Given n, let Q_n and T_n be the following sets of configurations, where Q_n and T_n represent the *invariant set* and *terminal set*, respectively:

$$Q_n \equiv \{\langle \texttt{loop} \mid \texttt{n} \mapsto n', \texttt{s} \mapsto \textstyle\sum_{i=n'}^{n-1} i \rangle \mid \forall n'\}$$

$$T_n \equiv \{\langle \texttt{skip} \mid \texttt{n} \mapsto 0, \texttt{s} \mapsto \textstyle\sum_{i=1}^{n-1} i \rangle\}$$

and let us define the following specifications:

$$S_1 \equiv \{(\langle \texttt{s=0; loop} \mid \texttt{n} \mapsto n \rangle, Q_n) \mid \forall n\}$$

$$S_2 \equiv \{(\langle \texttt{loop} \mid \texttt{n} \mapsto n', \texttt{s} \mapsto \textstyle\sum_{i=n'}^{n-1} i \rangle, T_n) \mid \forall n, n'\}$$

Our target S in (1) is included in $S_1 \, {}_9 \, S_2$, so it suffices to show that S_1 and S_2 are valid. S_1 clearly is: $\langle \texttt{s=0;loop} \mid \texttt{n} \mapsto n \rangle \rightarrow_R^+ \langle \texttt{loop} \mid \texttt{n} \mapsto n, \texttt{s} \mapsto 0 \rangle$ represents the (symbolic) execution step or steps taken to assign program variable $\texttt{s}$, and the set of specifications $\{(\langle \texttt{loop} \mid \texttt{n} \mapsto n, \texttt{s} \mapsto 0 \rangle, Q_n) \mid \forall n\}$ is vacuously valid (note $\sum_{i=n}^{n-1} i = 0$). For the validity of S_2, we partition it in two subsets, one where $n' = 1$ and another with $n' \neq 1$ (case analysis). The former holds same as S_1, noting that

$$\langle \texttt{loop} \mid \texttt{n} \mapsto 1, \texttt{s} \mapsto \textstyle\sum_{i=1}^{n-1} i \rangle \rightarrow_R^+ \langle \texttt{skip} \mid \texttt{n} \mapsto 0, \texttt{s} \mapsto \textstyle\sum_{i=1}^{n-1} i \rangle$$

The latter holds by coinduction (for S_2), because first

$$\langle \texttt{loop} \mid \texttt{n} \mapsto n', \texttt{s} \mapsto \textstyle\sum_{i=n'}^{n-1} i \rangle \rightarrow_R^+ \langle \texttt{loop} \mid \texttt{n} \mapsto n' - 1, \texttt{s} \mapsto \textstyle\sum_{i=n'-1}^{n-1} i \rangle$$

and second the following inclusion holds:

$$\{(\langle \texttt{loop} \mid \texttt{n} \mapsto n' - 1, \texttt{s} \mapsto \textstyle\sum_{i=n'-1}^{n-1} i \rangle, T_n) \mid \forall n, n'\} \subseteq S_2$$

The key part of the proof above was to show that the reachability claim about the loop (S_2) was stable under the language semantics. Everything else was symbolic execution using the (trusted) operational semantics of the language. By allowing desirable program properties to be uniformly specified as reachability claims about the (executable) language semantics itself, our approach requires no auxiliary formalization of the language for verification purposes, and thus no soundness or equivalence proofs and no transformations of the original program to make it fit the restrictions of the auxiliary semantics. Unlike for the Hoare logic proof, the main "proof rules" used were just performing execution steps using the operational semantics rules, as well as the generic coinductive principle. Section 3 provides all the technical details.

$$\boxed{\text{Structural Operational Semantics}}$$

$$\langle x \mid \sigma \rangle \to \langle \sigma(x) \mid \sigma \rangle$$

$$\langle \texttt{--}x \mid \sigma \rangle \to \langle i \mid \sigma[i/x] \rangle \quad \text{if } i = \sigma(x) -_{Int} 1$$

$$\frac{\langle e_1 \mid \sigma \rangle \to \langle e_1' \mid \sigma' \rangle}{\langle e_1 \text{ op } e_2 \mid \sigma \rangle \to \langle e_1' \text{ op } e_2 \mid \sigma' \rangle}$$

$$\frac{\langle e_2 \mid \sigma \rangle \to \langle e_2' \mid \sigma' \rangle}{\langle i_1 \text{ op } e_2 \mid \sigma \rangle \to \langle i_1 \text{ op } e_2' \mid \sigma' \rangle}$$

$$\langle i_1 \text{ op } i_2 \mid \sigma \rangle \to \langle i_1 \text{ op}_{Int} i_2 \mid \sigma \rangle$$

$$\frac{\langle s_1 \mid \sigma \rangle \to \langle s_1' \mid \sigma' \rangle}{\langle s_1 \ s_2 \mid \sigma \rangle \to \langle s_1' \ s_2 \mid \sigma' \rangle}$$

$$\langle \texttt{skip } s \mid \sigma \rangle \to \langle s \mid \sigma \rangle$$

$$\frac{\langle e \mid \sigma \rangle \to \langle e' \mid \sigma' \rangle}{\langle x := e \mid \sigma \rangle \to \langle x := e' \mid \sigma' \rangle}$$

$$\langle x := i \mid \sigma \rangle \to \langle \texttt{skip} \mid \sigma[i/x] \rangle$$

$$\frac{\langle e \mid \sigma \rangle \to \langle e' \mid \sigma' \rangle}{\langle \texttt{if } e \texttt{ then } \{s_1\} \texttt{ else } \{s_2\} \mid \sigma \rangle \to \langle \texttt{if } e' \texttt{ then } \{s_1\} \texttt{ else } \{s_2\} \mid \sigma' \rangle}$$

$$\langle \texttt{if } i \texttt{ then } \{s_1\} \texttt{ else } \{s_2\} \mid \sigma \rangle \to \langle s_1 \mid \sigma \rangle \quad \text{if } i \neq 0$$

$$\langle \texttt{if } 0 \texttt{ then } \{s_1\} \texttt{ else } \{s_2\} \mid \sigma \rangle \to \langle s_2 \mid \sigma \rangle$$

$$\langle \texttt{while } e \ \{s\} \mid \sigma \rangle \to \langle \texttt{if } e \texttt{ then } \{s \texttt{ while } e \ \{s\}\} \texttt{ else } \{\texttt{skip}\} \mid \sigma \rangle$$

$$\boxed{\text{Reduction Semantics}}$$
(evaluation contexts syntax omitted— [17])

$$\frac{r \to r'}{E[r] \to E[r']}$$

$$\langle E \mid \sigma \rangle[x] \to \langle E \mid \sigma \rangle[\sigma(x)]$$

$$\langle E \mid \sigma \rangle[\texttt{--}x] \to \langle E \mid \sigma[i/x] \rangle[i] \quad \text{if } i = \sigma(x) -_{Int} 1$$

$$\langle E \mid \sigma \rangle[x := i] \to \langle E \mid \sigma[i/x] \rangle[\texttt{skip}]$$

$$i_1 \text{ op } i_2 \to i_1 \text{ op}_{Int} i_2$$
$$\texttt{skip } s \to s$$
$$\texttt{if } i \texttt{ then } \{s_1\} \texttt{ else } \{s_2\} \to s_1 \quad \text{if } i \neq 0$$
$$\texttt{if } 0 \texttt{ then } \{s_1\} \texttt{ else } \{s_2\} \to s_2$$
$$\texttt{while } e \ \{s\} \to \texttt{if } e \texttt{ then } \{s \texttt{ while } e \ \{s\}\} \texttt{ else } \{\texttt{skip}\}$$

$$\boxed{\text{K Semantics}}$$
(configuration and strictness omitted— [9])

$$\frac{\langle x \ \dots \rangle_k}{i} \ \langle \dots x \mapsto i \ \dots \rangle_{state}$$

$$\frac{\langle \ \texttt{--} \ x \ \dots \rangle_k}{i -_{Int} 1} \ \langle \dots x \mapsto \frac{i}{i -_{Int} 1} \ \dots \rangle_{state}$$

$$\frac{\langle x := i \ \dots \rangle_k}{\texttt{skip}} \ \langle \dots x \mapsto \frac{\_}{i} \ \dots \rangle_{state}$$

(plus the last five simple rules under reduction semantics)

Fig. 3. Three different operational semantics of **IMP**, generating the same execution step relation R (or $\to_R$).

2.3   Defining Execution Step Relations

Since our coinductive verification framework is parametric in a step relation, which also becomes the only trust base when certified verification is sought, it is imperative for its practicality to support a variety of approaches to define step relations. Ideally, it should not be confined to any particular semantic style that ultimately defines a step relation, and it should simply take existing semantics "off-the-shelf" and turn them into sound and relatively complete program verifiers for the defined languages. We briefly recall three of the semantic approaches that we experimented with in our Coq formalization [16].

Small-step structural operational semantics [18] (Fig. 3 top) is one of the most popular semantic approaches. It defines the transition relation inductively. This semantic style is easy to use, though often inconvenient to define some features such as abrupt changes of control and true concurrency. Additionally, finding the next successor of a configuration may take longer than in other approaches. Reduction semantics with evaluation contexts [17], depicted in the middle of Fig. 3, is another popular approach. It allows us to elegantly and compactly define complex evaluation strategies and semantics of control intensive constructs (e.g., call/cc), and it avoids a recursive definition of the transition relation. On the other hand, it requires an auxiliary definition of contexts along with splitting and plugging functions.

As discussed in Sect. 1, several large languages have been given formal semantics using K [9] (Fig. 3 bottom). K is more involved and less conventional than the other approaches, so it is a good opportunity to evaluate our hypothesis that we can just "plug-and-play" operational semantics in our coinductive framework. A K-style semantics extends the code in the configuration to a list of terms, and evaluates within subterms by having a transition that extracts the term to the front of the list, where it can be examined directly. This allows a non-recursive definition of transition, whose cases can be applied by unification.

In practice, in our automation, we only need to modify how a successor for a configuration is found. Besides that, the proofs remain exactly the same.

3   Coinduction as Partial Correctness

The intuitive coinductive proof of the correctness of sum in Sect. 2.2 likely raised a lot of questions. We give formal details of that proof in this section as well go through some definitions and results of the underlying theory. All proofs, including our Coq formalization, are in [16].

3.1   Definitions and Main Theorem

First, we introduce a definition that we used intuitively in the previous section:

Definition 2. *If $R \subseteq C \times C$, let $valid_R \subseteq C \times \mathcal{P}(C)$ be defined as $valid_R = \{(c, P) \mid c \Rightarrow_R P \text{ holds}\}$.*

Recall from Sect. 2.1 that $c \Rightarrow_R P$ holds iff the initial state c can either reach a state in P or can take an infinite number of steps (with $\rightarrow_R$). Pairs $(c, P) \in C \times \mathcal{P}(C)$ are called *claims* or *specifications*, and our objective is to prove they hold, i.e., $c \Rightarrow_R P$. Sets of claims $S \subseteq C \times \mathcal{P}(C)$ are valid if $S \subseteq \text{valid}_R$. To show such inclusions by coinduction, we notice that valid_R is a greatest fixpoint, specifically of the following operator:

Definition 3. *Given* $R \subseteq C \times C$, *let* $\text{step}_R : \mathcal{P}(C \times \mathcal{P}(C)) \rightarrow \mathcal{P}(C \times \mathcal{P}(C))$ *be*

$$\text{step}_R(S) = \{(c, P) \mid c \in P \ \vee \ \exists d \,.\, c \rightarrow_R d \wedge (d, P) \in S\}$$

Therefore, to prove $(c, P) \in \text{step}_R(S)$, one must show either that $c \in P$ or that $(succ(c), P) \in S$, where $succ(c)$ is a resulting configuration after taking a step from c by the operational semantics.

Definition 4. *Given a monotone function* $F : \mathcal{P}(D) \rightarrow \mathcal{P}(D)$, *let its* F-*closure* $F^* : \mathcal{P}(D) \rightarrow \mathcal{P}(D)$ *be defined as* $F^*(X) = \mu Y . F(Y) \cup X$, *where* μ *is the least fixpoint operator. This is well-defined as* $Y \mapsto F(Y) \cup X$ *is monotone for any* X.

The following lemma suffices for reachability verification:

Lemma 1. *For any* $R \subseteq C \times C$ *and* $S \subseteq C \times \mathcal{P}(C)$, *we have* $S \subseteq \text{step}_R(\text{step}_R^*(S))$ *implies* $S \subseteq \text{valid}_R$.

The intuition behind this lemma is captured in Sect. 2.2: we continue taking steps and once we reach a set of states already seen, we know our claim is valid. This would not be valid if $\text{step}_R(\text{step}_R^*(S))$ was replaced simply with $\text{step}_R^*(S)$, as $X \subseteq F^*(X)$ hold trivially for any F and X. Lemma 1 (along with elementary set properties) replaces the entire program logic shown in Fig. 2. The only formal definition specific to the target language is the operational semantics. Lemma 1 does not need to be modified or re-proven to use it with other languages or semantics. It generalizes into a more powerful result, that can be used to derive a variety of coinductive proof principles:

Theorem 1. *If* $F, G : \mathcal{P}(D) \rightarrow \mathcal{P}(D)$ *are monotone and* $G(F(A)) \subseteq F(G^*(A))$ *for any* $A \subseteq D$, *then* $X \subseteq F(G^*(X))$ *implies* $X \subseteq \nu F$ *for any* $X \subseteq D$, *where* νF *is the greatest fixpoint of* F.

Proofs, including a verified proof in our Coq formulation are in [16]. The proof can also be derived from [12–14], though techniques from these papers had previously not been applied to program verification. Lemma 1 is an easy corollary, with both F and G instantiated as step_R, along with a proof that $\nu \text{step}_R = \text{valid}_R$ (see [16]). However, instantiating F and G to be the same function is not always best. An interesting and useful G is the transitivity function trans in Definition 1, which satisfies the hypothesis in Theorem 1 when F is step_R. [16] shows other sound instantiations of G.

We can also use Theorem 1 with other definitions of validity expressible as a greatest fixpoint, e.g., all-path validity. For nondeterministic languages we might prefer to say $c \Rightarrow^\forall P$ holds if no path from c reaches a stuck configuration without passing through P. This is the greatest fixpoint of

$$\text{step}_R^\forall(S) = \{(c, P) \mid c \in P \ \vee \exists d \,.\, c \rightarrow_R d \wedge \forall d \,.\, (c \rightarrow_R d \text{ implies } (d, P) \in S)\}$$

The universe of validity notions that can be expressed coinductively, and thus the universe of instances of Theorem 1 is virtually limitless. Below is another notion of validity that we experimented with in our Coq formalization [16]. When proving global program invariants or safety properties of non-deterministic programs, we want to state not only reachability claims $c \Rightarrow P$, but also that all the transitions from c to configurations in P respect some additional property, say T. For example, a global state invariant I can be captured by a T such that $(a, b) \in T$ iff $I(a)$ and $I(b)$, while an arbitrary safety property can be captured by a T that encodes a monitor for it. This notion of validity, which we call (all-path) "until" validity, is the greatest fixpoint of:

$$\text{until}_R^\forall(S) = \{(c, T, P) \mid c \in P \ \vee$$
$$\exists d \,.\, c \to_R d \wedge \forall d \,.\, (c \to_R d \text{ implies } (c, d) \in T \wedge (d, T, P) \in S)\}$$

This allows verification of properties that are not expressible using Hoare logic.

3.2 Example Proof: Sum

Now we demonstrate the results above by providing all the details that were skipped in our informal proof in Sect. 2.2. The property that we want to prove, expressed as a set of claims (c, P), is

$$S \equiv \{(\langle \texttt{s=0;while(--n)\{s=s+n;\}} \, T \mid \texttt{n} \mapsto n, \sigma[\bot/\texttt{s}]\rangle,$$
$$\{\langle T \mid \texttt{n} \mapsto 0, \texttt{s} \mapsto \textstyle\sum_{i=1}^{n-1} i, \sigma\rangle\}) \mid \forall n, T, \sigma\}$$

We have to prove $S \subseteq \text{valid}_R$. Note that this specification is more general than the specifications in Sect. 2.2. Here, T represents the remainder of the code to be executed, while σ represents the remainder of the store, with $\sigma[\bot/\texttt{s}]$ as σ restricted to $Dom(\sigma)/\{\texttt{s}\}$. Thus, we write out the entire configuration here, which gives us freedom in expressing more complex specifications if needed.

Instead of proving this directly, we will prove two subclaims valid and connect them via sequential composition (Definition 1). First, we need the following:

Lemma 2. $S_1 \, \fatsemi \, S_2 \subseteq \text{valid}_R$ if $S_1 \subseteq \text{valid}_R$ and $S_2 \subseteq \text{valid}_R$.

As before, let

$$Q_n \equiv \{\langle \texttt{loop;} \ T \mid \texttt{n} \mapsto n', \texttt{s} \mapsto \textstyle\sum_{i=n'}^{n-1} i, \sigma\rangle \mid \forall n'\}$$
$$T_n \equiv \{\langle T \mid \texttt{n} \mapsto 0, \texttt{s} \mapsto \textstyle\sum_{i=1}^{n-1} i\rangle\}$$

and define

$$S_1 \equiv \{(\langle \texttt{s=0; loop;} \ T \mid \texttt{n} \mapsto n, \sigma[\bot/\texttt{s}]\rangle, Q_n) \mid \forall n, T, \sigma\}$$
$$S_2 \equiv \{(\langle \texttt{loop;} \ T \mid \texttt{n} \mapsto n', \texttt{s} \mapsto \textstyle\sum_{i=n'}^{n-1} i, \sigma\rangle, T_n) \mid \forall n, n', T, \sigma\}$$

Since $S \subseteq S_1 \,\mathbin{;}\, S_2$ (by Q_n), it suffices to show $S_1 \cup S_2 \subseteq \text{valid}_R$. To prove $S_1 \subseteq \text{valid}_R$, by Lemma 1 we show $S_1 \subseteq \text{step}_R(\text{step}_R^*(S_1))$. Regardless of the employed executable semantics, this should hold:

$$\forall n, T, \sigma. \langle \texttt{s=0; loop;}\ T \mid \mathtt{n} \mapsto n, \sigma[\bot/\mathtt{s}] \rangle \to_R \langle \texttt{loop;}\ T \mid \mathtt{n} \mapsto n, \mathtt{s} \mapsto 0, \sigma \rangle$$

Choosing the second case of the disjunction in step_R with d matching this step, it suffices to show

$$\{(\langle \texttt{loop;}\ T \mid \mathtt{n} \mapsto n, \mathtt{s} \mapsto 0, \sigma \rangle, Q_n) \mid \forall n, T, \sigma\} \subseteq \text{step}_R^*(S_1)$$

Note that we can unfold any fixpoint $F^*(S)$ to get the following two equations:

$$F(F^*(S)) \subseteq F(F^*(S)) \cup S = F^*(S) \qquad S \subseteq F(F^*(S)) \cup S = F^*(S) \qquad (3)$$

We use the first equation to expose an application of step_R on the right hand side, so it suffices to show the above is a subset of $\text{step}_R(\text{step}_R^*(S))$. We then use the first case of the disjunction (showing $c \in P$) in step_R, and instantiating n' to n proves this goal, since $\sum_{i=n}^{n-1} i = 0$. Thus $S_1 \subseteq \text{valid}_R$.

Now we prove $S_2 \subseteq \text{valid}_R$, or $S_2 \subseteq \text{step}_R(\text{step}_R^*(S_2))$. First, note the operational semantics of IMP rewrites while loops to if statements. Then, by the definition of step_R, it suffices to show that

$$\{(\langle \texttt{if(--n)\{s=s+n;loop\};}\ T \mid \mathtt{n} \mapsto n', \mathtt{s} \mapsto \textstyle\sum_{i=n'}^{n-1} i, \sigma \rangle, T_n) \mid \forall n, n', T, \sigma\} \subseteq \text{step}_R^*(S_2)$$

Using the first unfolding from (3), it suffices to show the above is a subset of $\text{step}_R(\text{step}_R^*(S_2))$, i.e. we expose an application of step_R on the right hand side. The definition of step_R thus allows the left hand side to continue taking execution steps, as long as we keep unfolding the fixpoint. Continuing this, the if condition becomes a single, but symbolic, boolean value. Specifically, it suffices to show:

$$\{(\langle \texttt{if}(n'-1 \neq 0)\texttt{\{s=s+n;loop\};}\ T \mid \mathtt{n} \mapsto n'\text{-}1, \mathtt{s} \mapsto \textstyle\sum_{i=n'}^{n-1} i, \sigma \rangle, T_n) \mid \forall n, n', T, \sigma\} \subseteq \text{step}_R^*(S_2)$$

Further progress requires making a case distinction on whether $n' - 1 = 0$. A case distinction corresponds to observing that $A \cup B \subseteq X$ if both $A \subseteq X$ and $B \subseteq X$. Here we split the current set of claims into those with $n' - 1 = 0$ and $n' - 1 \neq 0$, and separately establish the following inclusions:

$$\{(\langle \texttt{if(false)\{s=s+n;loop\};}\ T \mid \mathtt{n} \mapsto 0, \mathtt{s} \mapsto \textstyle\sum_{i=1}^{n-1} i, \sigma \rangle, T_n) \mid \forall n, T, \sigma\} \subseteq \text{step}_R^*(S_2)$$

$$\{(\langle \texttt{if(true)\{s=s+n;loop\};}\ T \mid \mathtt{n} \mapsto n'\text{-}1, \mathtt{s} \mapsto \textstyle\sum_{i=n'}^{n-1} i, \sigma \rangle, T_n) \mid \forall n, n' \neq 1, T, \sigma\} \subseteq \text{step}_R^*(S_2)$$

Continuing symbolic execution and using $\sum_{i=n'}^{n-1} i + (n' - 1) = \sum_{i=n'-1}^{n-1} i$, we get

$$\{(\langle T \mid \mathtt{n} \mapsto 0, \mathtt{s} \mapsto \textstyle\sum_{i=1}^{n-1} i, \sigma \rangle, T_n) \mid \forall n, T, \sigma\} \subseteq \text{step}_R^*(S_2)$$

$$\{(\langle \texttt{loop;}\ T \mid \mathtt{n} \mapsto n' - 1, \mathtt{s} \mapsto \textstyle\sum_{i=n'-1}^{n-1} i, \sigma \rangle, T_n) \mid \forall n, n', T, \sigma, n' - 1 \neq 0\} \subseteq \text{step}_R^*(S_2)$$

In the $n' - 1 = 0$ case, the current configuration is already in the corresponding target set. To conclude, we expose another application of step_R as before, but use the clause $c \in P$ of the disjunction in step_R to leave the trivial goal $\forall n, T, \sigma. \langle T \mid \mathtt{n} \mapsto 0, \mathtt{s} \mapsto \frac{n(n-1)}{2}, \sigma \rangle \in \{\langle T \mid \mathtt{n} \mapsto 0, \mathtt{s} \mapsto \frac{n(n-1)}{2}, \sigma \rangle\}$. For the $n' - 1 \neq 0$ case, we have a set of claims that are contained in the initial specification S_2. We conclude by showing $S_2 \subseteq \text{step}_R^*(S_2)$ from the second equation in (3) by noting that $S \subseteq F^*(S)$ for any F. So this set of claims is contained in S_2 by instantiating the universally quantified variable n' in the definition of S_2 with $n' - 1$. Thus it is contained in $\text{step}_R^*(S_2)$ and thus it is a subset of valid_R.

3.3   Example Proof: Reverse

Consider now the following program to reverse a linked list, written in the HIMP language (Fig. 5a). We will discuss HIMP in more detail Sect. 4.

```
decl p; decl y; p := 0;
while (x<>0) { y := (x+1); *(x+1) := p; p := x; x := y; }
```

Call the above code **rev** and the loop **rev-loop**. We prove this program is correct following intuitions from separation logic [19,20] but using the exact same coinductive technical machinery as before. Assuming we have a predicate that matches a heap containing only a linked list starting at address x and representing the list l (which we will see in Sect. 4.2), our specification becomes:

$$ S \equiv \{(\langle \texttt{rev};\, T \mid \text{list}(l,x)\rangle, \{\langle T \mid \lambda r.\text{list}(rev(l),r)\rangle\}) \mid \forall l,x,T\} $$

where rev is the mathematical list reverse. We proceed as in the previous example, first using lemma then stepping with the semantics, but with Q_n as

$$ \{\langle \texttt{rev-loop};\, T \mid \text{list}(A,x) * \text{list}(B,p) * \texttt{x} \mapsto x * \texttt{p} \mapsto p * \texttt{y} \mapsto y * \lambda r.\text{list}(B\texttt{++}A,r)\rangle $$
$$ \mid \forall A,B,p,y\} $$

where **++** is list append. We continue as before to prove our original specification. S_1 and S_2 follow from our choice for Q_n, our "loop invariant." Specifically,

$$ S_1 \equiv \{(\langle \texttt{rev};\, T \mid \text{list}(l,x)\rangle, \{\langle \texttt{rev-loop};\, T \mid \text{list}(A,x) * \text{list}(B,p) * \texttt{x} \mapsto x * \texttt{p} \mapsto p * \texttt{y} \mapsto y $$
$$ * \lambda r.\text{list}(B\texttt{++}A,r)\rangle \mid \forall A,B,p,y\}) \mid \forall l,x,T\} $$
$$ S_2 \equiv \{(\langle \texttt{rev-loop};\, T \mid \text{list}(A,x) * \text{list}(B,p) * \texttt{x} \mapsto x * \texttt{p} \mapsto p * \texttt{y} \mapsto y * \lambda r.\text{list}(B\texttt{++}A,r)\rangle, $$
$$ \{\langle T \mid \lambda r.\text{list}(rev(l),r)\rangle\}) \mid \forall A,B,p,y,l,x,T\} $$

Then, the individual proofs for these specifications closely follow the same flavor as in the previous example: use step_R to execute the program via the operational semantics, use unions to case split as needed, and finish when we reach something in the target set or that was previously in our specification. The inherent similarity between these two examples hints that automation should not be too difficult. We go into detail regarding such automation in Sect. 4.

Reasoning with fixpoints and functions like step_R can be thought of as reasoning with proof rules, but ones which interact with the target programming language only through its operational semantics. The step_R operation corresponds, conceptually, to two such proof rules: taking an execution step and

HIMP

```
append(x, y)
  decl p;
  if (!x) return y;
  p := x;
  while(*(p+1)<>0) p := *(p+1);
  *(p+1) := y;
  return x;
```

Stack

```
: append over if over begin
1+ dup @ dup while nip repeat
drop ! else nip then ;
```

Lambda

```
(λ (λ IfNil 1 0
  ((λ (λ 0 0)
    (λ 1 (λ 1 1 0))) (λ
  (λ (λ (λ 0 1)) (Deref 0)
    (λ IfNil (Cdr 0)
     ((λ 5) (Assign 0
       (Cons (Car 0) 3)))
       (2 (Cdr 0)))))
1)))
```

Fig. 4. Destructive list append in three languages.

showing that the current configuration is in the target set. Sequential composition and the trans rule corresponds to a transitivity rule used to chain together separate proofs. Unions correspond to case analysis. The fixpoint in the closure definition corresponds to iterative uses of these proof rules or to referring back to claims in the original specification.

4   Experiments

Now that we have proved the correctness of our coinductive verification approach and have seen some simple examples, we must consider the following pragmatic question: "Can this simple approach really work?". We have implemented it in Coq, and specified and verified programs in a variety of languages, each language being defined as an operational semantics [16]. We show not only that coinductive program verification is feasible and versatile, but also that it is amenable to highly effective proof automation. The simplifications in the manual proof, such as taking many execution steps at once, translate easily into proof tactics.

We first discuss the example languages and programs, and the reusable elements in specifications, especially an effective style of representation predicates for heap-allocated data structures. Then we show how we wrote specifications for example programs. Next we describe our proof automation, which was based on an overall heuristic applied unchanged for each language, though parameterized over subroutines which required somewhat more customization. Finally, we conclude with discussion of our verification of the Schorr-Waite graph-marking example and a discussion of our support for verification of divergent programs.

4.1   Languages

We discuss three languages following different paradigms, each defined operationally. Many language semantics are available with the distributions of K [9],

PLT-Redex [10], and Ott [11], e.g., but we believe these three languages are sufficient to illustrate the language-independence of our approach. Figure 4 shows a destructive linked list append function in each of the three languages.

HIMP (IMP with Heap) is an imperative language with (recursive) functions and a heap. The heap addresses are integers, to demonstrate reasoning about low-level representations, and memory allocation/deallocation are primitives. The configuration is a 5-tuple of current code, local variable environment mapping identifiers to values, call stack with frames as pairs of code and environment, heap, and a collection of functions as a map from function name to definition.

Stack is a Forth-like stack based language, though, unlike in Forth, we do make control structures part of the grammar. A shared data stack is used both for local state and to communicate between function invocations, eliminating the store, formal parameters on function declarations, and the environment of stack frames. Stack's configuration is also a 5-tuple, but instead of a current environment there is a stack of values, and stack frames do not store an environment.

Lambda is a call-by-value lambda calculus, extended with primitive integers, pair and nil values, and primitive operations for heap access. Fixpoint combinators enable recursive definitions without relying on primitive support for named functions. We use De Bruijn indices instead of named variables. The semantics is based on a CEK/CESK machine [21,22], extended with a heap. Lambda's configuration is a 4-tuple: current expression, environment, heap, continuation.

$Pgm ::= FunDef^*$

$FunDef ::=$
  $Id \ (\ Id^*_, \ ) \ \{ \ Stmt \ \}$

$Exp ::= \ Id \ (\ Exp^*_, \ )$
  $| \ \texttt{alloc} \ | \ \texttt{load} \ Exp$
  $| \ Exp \ . \ Id$
  $| \ \texttt{build} \ Map$
  $| \ ...$

$Stmt ::= \ * \ Exp := Exp$
  $| \ \texttt{dealloc} \ Exp$
  $| \ Id \ (\ Exp^*_, \ ) \ | \ \texttt{decl} \ Id$
  $| \ \texttt{return} \ Exp \ ;$
  $| \ \texttt{return} \ ;$
  $| \ ...$

(a) **HIMP** syntax, extending the **IMP** syntax

$Pgm ::= \ FunDef^*$

$FunDef ::=$
  $name : Inst^*$

$Inst ::= \texttt{Dup} \ \texttt{n}$
  $| \ \texttt{Roll} \ \texttt{n}$
  $| \ \texttt{Pop} \ | \ \texttt{Push} \ \texttt{z}$
  $| \ \texttt{BinOp} \ \texttt{f}$
  $| \ \texttt{Load} \ | \ \texttt{Store}$
  $| \ \texttt{Call} \ name \ | \ \texttt{Ret}$
  $| \ \texttt{If} \ Inst^* \ Inst^*$
  $| \ \texttt{While}$
  $\quad Inst^* \ Inst^*$

(b) **Stack** syntax

$Pgm ::= \ Val$

$Val ::= \ Nat \ | \ \texttt{Inc} \ | \ \texttt{Dec} \ | \ \texttt{Add}$
  $| \ \texttt{Add1} \ Nat \ | \ \texttt{Eq} \ | \ \texttt{Eq} \ Val$
  $| \ \texttt{Nil} \ | \ \texttt{Cons} \ | \ \texttt{Cons1} \ Val$
  $| \ \texttt{Car} \ | \ \texttt{Cdr}$
  $| \ \texttt{Closure} \ (Exp, \ Env)$
  $| \ \texttt{Pair} \ (Val, \ Val)$

$Exp ::= \ Exp \ Exp \ | \ \lambda \ Exp$
  $| \ \texttt{Var} \ Nat$
  $| \ \texttt{if} \ Exp \ \texttt{then} \ Exp \ \texttt{else} \ Exp$
  $| \ Exp \ ; \ Exp \ | \ \texttt{Deref} \ Exp$
  $| \ \& \ Exp \ | \ * \ Exp \ | \ Exp := Exp$

$Env ::= \ Val^*$

(c) **Lambda** syntax

Fig. 5. Syntax of **HIMP**, **Stack**, and **Lambda**

4.2   Specifying Data Structures

Our coinductive verification approach is agnostic to how claims in $C \times \mathcal{P}(C)$ are specified. In Coq, we can specify sets using any definable predicates. Within this design space, we chose matching logic [23] for our experiments, which introduces patterns that concisely generalize the formulae of first order logic (FOL) and separation logic, as well as term unification. Symbols apply on patterns to build other patterns, just like terms, and patterns can be combined using FOL connectives, just like formulae. E.g., pattern $P \wedge Q$ matches a value if P and Q both match it, $[t]$ matches only the value t, $\exists x.P$ matches if there is any assignment of x under which P matches, and $\llbracket \varphi \rrbracket$ where φ is a FOL formula matches any value if φ holds, and no values otherwise (in [23] neither $[t]$ nor $\llbracket \varphi \rrbracket$ require a visible marker, but in Coq patterns are a distinct type, requiring explicit injections).

To specify programs manipulating heap data structures we use patterns matching subheaps that contain a data structure representing an abstract value. Following [24], we define representation predicates for data structures as functions from abstract values to more primitive patterns. The basic ingredients are primitive map patterns: pattern **emp** for the empty map, $k \mapsto v$ for the singleton map binding key k to value v, and $P * Q$ for maps which are a disjoint union of submaps matching P and, resp., Q. We use abbreviation $\langle \varphi \rangle \equiv \llbracket \varphi \rrbracket \wedge \mathbf{emp}$ to facilitate inline assertions, and $p \mapsto \{v_0, \dots, v_i\} \equiv p \mapsto v_0 * \dots * (p + i) \mapsto v_i$ to describe values at contiguous addresses. A heap pattern for a linked list starting at address p and holding list l is defined recursively by

$$\text{list}(\text{nil}, p) = \langle p = 0 \rangle$$
$$\text{list}(x : l, p) = \langle p \neq 0 \rangle * \exists p_l . p \mapsto \{x, p_l\} * \text{list}(l, p_l)$$

We also define list_seg(l, e, p) for list segments, useful in algorithms using pointers to the middle of a list, by generalizing the constant 0 (the pointer to the end of the list) to the trailing pointer parameter e. Also, simple binary trees:

$$\text{tree}(\text{leaf}, p) = \langle p = 0 \rangle$$
$$\text{tree}(\text{node}(x, l, r), p) = \langle p \neq 0 \rangle * \exists p_l, p_r.p \mapsto \{x, lp, rp\} * \text{tree}(l, lp) * \text{tree}(r, rp)$$

Given such patterns, specifications and proofs can be done in terms of the abstract values represented in memory. Moreover, such primitive patterns are widely reusable across different languages, and so is our proof automation that deals with primitive patterns. Specifically, our proof scripting specific to such pattern definitions is concerned exclusively with unfolding the definition when allowed, deciding what abstract value, if any, is represented at a given address in a partially unfolded heap. This is further used to decide how another claim applies to the current state when attempting a transitivity step.

4.3   Specifying Reachability Claims

As mentioned, claims in $C \times \mathcal{P}(C)$ can be specified using any logical formalism, here the full power of Coq. An explicit specification can be verbose and low-level,

Table 1. Example list specifications

$call(\text{Head}, [x], [H] \wedge \text{list}(v : l, x), \lambda r.\langle r = v \rangle * [H])$

$call(\text{Tail}, [x], [H] \wedge \text{list}(v : l, x), \lambda r.[H] \wedge \_ * \text{list}(l, r))$

$call(\text{Add}, [y, x], \text{list}(l, x), \lambda r.\text{list}(y : l, r))$

$call(\text{Add}', [y, x], [H] \wedge \text{list}(l, x), \lambda r.\text{list\_seg}([y], x, r) * [H])$

$call(\text{Swap}, [x], \text{list}(a : b : l, x), \lambda r.\text{list}(b : a : l, x))$

$call(\text{Dealloc}, [x], \text{list}(l, x), \lambda r.\textbf{emp})$

$call(\text{Length}, [x], [H] \wedge \text{list}(l, x), \lambda r.\langle r = len(l) \rangle * [H])$

$call(\text{Sum}, [x], [H] \wedge \text{list}(l, x), \lambda r.\langle r = sum(l) \rangle\rangle * [H])$

$call(\text{Reverse}, [x], \text{list}(l, x), \lambda r.\text{list}(rev(l), r))$

$call(\text{Append}, [x, y], \text{list}(a, x) * \text{list}(b, y), \lambda r.\text{list}(a+\!\!+b, r))$

$call(\text{Copy}, [x], [H] \wedge \text{list}(l, x), \lambda r.\text{list}(l, r) * [H])$

$call(\text{Delete}, [v, x], \text{list}(l, x), \lambda r.\text{list}(delete(v, l), r))$

especially when many semantic components in the configuration stay unchanged. However, any reasonable logic allows making definitions to reduce verbosity and redundancy. Our use of matching logic particularly facilitates framing conditions, allowing us to regain the compactness and elegance of Hoare logic or separation logic specifications with definable syntactic sugar. For example, defining

$$call(f(formals)\{body\}, args, P_{in}, P_{out}) =$$
$$\{((\langle f(args) \curvearrowright rest, env, stk, heap, funs\rangle, \{\langle r \curvearrowright rest, env, stk, heap', funs\rangle$$
$$\mid \forall r, heap'. \; heap' \vDash P_{out}(r) * [H_f]\})$$
$$\mid \forall rest, env, stk, heap, H_f, funs. \; heap \vDash P_{in} * [H_f] \wedge f \mapsto f(formals)\{body\} \in funs\}$$

gives the equivalent of the usual Hoare pre-/post-condition on function calls, including heap framing (in separation logic style). The notation $x \curvearrowright y$ represents the order of evaluation: evaluate x first followed by y. This is often used when y can depend on the value x takes after evaluation.

The first parameter is the function definition. The second is the arguments. The heap effect is described as a pattern P_{in} for the allowable initial states of the heap and function P_{out} from returned values to corresponding heap patterns. For example, we specify the definition D of append in Fig. 4 by writing $call(D, [x, y], (\text{list}(a, x) * \text{list}(b, y)), (\lambda r.\text{list}(a+\!\!+b, r)))$, which is as compact and elegant as it can be. More specifications are given in Table 1. A number of specifications assert that part of the heap is left entirely unchanged by writing $[H] \wedge \ldots$ in the precondition to bind a variable H to a specific heap, and using the variable in the postcondition (just repeating a representation predicate might permit a function to reallocate internal nodes in a data structure to different addresses). The specifications Add and Add' show that it can be a bit more complicated to assert that an input list is used undisturbed as a suffix of a result list. Specifications such as Length, Append, and Delete are written in terms of corresponding mathematical functions on the lists represented in the heap, separating those functional descriptions from details of memory layout.

When a function contains loops, proving that it meets a specification often requires making some additional claims about configurations which are just about to enter loops, as we saw in Sect. 2.2. We support this with another pattern that takes the current code at an intermediate point in the execution of a function, and a description of the environment:

$$stmt(code, env, P_{in}, P_{out}) =$$
$$\{(\langle code, (env, e_f), stk, heap, funs\rangle, \{\langle \texttt{return}\ r \curvearrowright rest, env', stk, heap', funs\rangle$$
$$|\ \forall r, rest, env', heap'.heap' \vDash P_{out}(r) * [H_f]\})$$
$$|\ \forall e_f, stk, heap, H_f, funs\ .\ heap \vDash P_{in} * [H_f]\}$$

Verifying the definition of append in Fig. 4 meets the call specification above requires an auxiliary claim about the loop, which can be written using *stmt* as

$$stmt(\texttt{while}\ (\texttt{*(p+1)<>0})\ldots, (\texttt{x}\mapsto x, \texttt{y}\mapsto y, \texttt{p}\mapsto p),$$
$$(\text{list\_seg}(l_x, p, x) * \text{list}(l_p, p) * \text{list}(l_y, y)), (\lambda r.\text{list}(l_x +\!\!+ l_p +\!\!+ l_y, r)))$$

The patterns above were described using HIMP's configurations; we defined similar ones for Stack and Lambda also.

4.4 Proofs and Automation

The basic heuristic in our proofs, which is also the basis of our proof automation, is to attack a goal by preferring to prove that the current configuration is in the target set if possible, then trying to use claims in the specification by transitivity, and only last resorting to taking execution steps according to the operational semantics or making case distinctions. Each of these operations begins, as in the example proofs, with certain manipulations of the definitions and fixpoints in the language-independent core. Our heuristic is reusable, as a proof tactic parameterized over sub-tactics for the more specific operations. A prelude to the main loop begins by applying the main theorem to move from claiming validity to showing a coinduction-style inclusion, and breaking down a specification with several classes of claims into a separate proof goal for each family of claims.

Additionally, our automation leverages support offered by the proof assistant, such as handling conjuncts by trying to prove each case, existentials by introducing a unification variable, equalities by unification, and so on. Moreover, we added tactics for map equalities and numerical formulae, which are shared among all languages involving maps and integers. The current proof goal after each step is always a reachability claim. So even in proofs which are not completely automatic, the proof automation can give up by leaving subgoals for the user, who can reinvoke the proof automation after making some proof steps of their own as long as they leave a proof goal in the same form.

Proving the properties in Table 1 sometimes required making additional claims about while loops or auxiliary recursive functions. All but the last four were proved automatically by invoking (an instance of) our heuristic proof tactic:

```
Proof. list_solver. Qed.
```

Append and copy needed to make use of associativity of list append. Reverse used a loop reversing the input list element by element onto an output list, which required relating the tail recursive $rev\_app(x : l, y) = rev\_app(l, x : y)$ with the Coq standard library definition $rev(x : l) = rev(l) + \!\!+ [x]$. Manually applying these lemmas merely modified the proof scripts to

```
list_solver. rewrite app_ass in * |- . list_run.
list_solver. rewrite <- rev_alt in * |- . list_run.
```

These proofs were used verbatim in each of our example languages. The only exceptions were append and copy for Lambda, for which the app_ass lemma was not necessary. For Delete, simple reasoning about $delete(v, l)$ when v is and is not at the head of the list is required, though the actual reasoning in Coq varies between our example languages. No additional lemmas or tactics equivalent to Hoare rules are needed in any of these proofs.

4.5 Other Data Structures

Matching logic allows us to concisely define many other important data structures. Besides lists, we also have proofs in Coq with trees, graphs, and stacks [16]. These data structures are all used for proving properties about the Schorr-Waite algorithm. In the next section we go into more detail about these data structures and how they are used in proving the Schorr-Waite algorithm.

4.6 Schorr-Waite

Our experiments so far demonstrate that our coinductive verification approach applies across languages in different paradigms, and can handle usual heap programs with a high degree of automation. Here we show that we can also handle the famous Schorr-Waite graph marking algorithm [25], which is a well-known verification challenge, "The Schorr-Waite algorithm is the first mountain that any formalism for pointer aliasing should climb" [26]. To give the reader a feel for what it takes to mechanically verify such an algorithm, previous proofs in [27] and [28] required manually produced proof scripts of about 470 and, respectively, over 1400 lines and they both used conventional Hoare logic. In comparison our proof is 514 lines. Line counts are a crude measure, but we can at least conclude that the language independence and generality of our approach did not impose any great cost compared to using language-specific program logics.

The version of Schorr-Waite that we verified is based on [29]. First, however, we verify a simpler property of the algorithm, showing that the given code correctly marks a tree, in the absence of sharing or cycles. Then we prove the same code works on general graphs by considering the tree resulting from a depth first traversal. We define graphs by extending the definition of trees to allow a child of a node in an abstract tree to be a reference back to some existing node, in addition to an explicit subtree or a null pointer for a leaf. To specify that graph nodes are at their original addresses after marking, we include an address along with the mark flag in the abstract data structure in the pattern

$$\mathrm{grph}(\mathrm{leaf}, m, p') = \langle p' = 0 \rangle$$
$$\mathrm{grph}(\mathrm{backref}(p), m, p') = \langle p' = p \rangle$$
$$\mathrm{grph}(\mathrm{node}(p, l, r), m, p') = \langle p'{=}p \rangle * \exists p_l, p_r \;.$$
$$p \mapsto \{m, p_l, p_r\} * \mathrm{grph}(l, m, p_l) * \mathrm{grph}(r, m, p_r)$$

The overall specification is $call(Mark, [p], \mathrm{grph}(G, 0, p), \lambda r.\mathrm{grph}(G, 3, p))$.

To describe the intermediate states in the algorithm, including the clever pointer-reversal trick used to encode a stack, we define another data structure for the context, in zipper style. A position into a tree is described by its immediate context, which is either the topmost context, or the point immediately left or right of a sibling tree, in a parent context. These are represented by nodes with intermediate values of the mark field, with one field pointing to the sibling subtree and the other pointing to the representation of the rest of the context.

$$\mathrm{stack}(\mathrm{Top}, p) = \langle p = 0 \rangle$$
$$\mathrm{stack}(\mathrm{LeftOf}(r, k), p) = \exists p_r, p_k \;.\; p \mapsto \{1, p_r, p_k\} * \mathrm{grph}(r, 0, p_r) * \mathrm{stack}(k, p_k)$$
$$\mathrm{stack}(\mathrm{RightOf}(l, k), p) = \exists p_l, p_k \;.\; p \mapsto \{2, p_k, p_l\} * \mathrm{stack}(k, p_k) * \mathrm{grph}(l, 3, p_l)$$

This is the second data structure needed to specify the main loop. When it is entered, there are only two live local variables, one pointing to the next address to visit and the other keeping context. The next node can either be the root of an unmarked subtree, with the context as stack, or the first node in the implicit stack when ascending after marking a tree, with the context pointing to the node that was just finished. For simplicity, we write a separate claim for each case.

$$stmt(Loop, (\mathsf{p} \mapsto p, \mathsf{q} \mapsto q), (\mathrm{grph}(G, 0, p) * \mathrm{stack}(S, q)), \lambda r.\mathrm{grph}(plug(G, S), 3))$$
$$stmt(Loop, (\mathsf{p} \mapsto p, \mathsf{q} \mapsto q), (\mathrm{stack}(S, p) * \mathrm{grph}(G, 3, q)), \lambda r.\mathrm{grph}(plug(G, S), 3))$$

The application of all the semantic steps was handled entirely automatically, the manual proof effort being entirely concerned with reasoning about the predicates above, for which no proof automation was developed.

4.7   Divergence

Our coinductive framework can also be used to verify a program is divergent. Such verification is often a topic that is given its own treatment, as in [30,31], though in our framework, no additional care is needed. To prove a program is divergent on all inputs, one verifies a set of claims of the form $(c, \emptyset)$, so that no configuration can be determined valid by membership in the final set of states. We have verified the divergence of a simple program under each style of IMP semantics in Fig. 3, as well as programs in each language from Sect. 4.1. These program include the omega combinator and the sum program from Sect. 3.2 with true replacing the loop guard.

4.8   Summary of Experiments

Statistics are shown in Table 2. For each example, size shows the amount of code to be verified, the size of the specification, and the size of the proof script. If verifying an example required auxiliary definitions or lemmas specific to that example, the size of those definitions were counted with the specification or proof. Many examples were verified by a single invocation of our automatic proof tactic, giving 1-line proofs. Other small proofs required human assistance only in the form of applying lemmas about the domain. Proofs are generally smaller than the specifications, which are usually about as large as the code. This is similar to the results for Bedrock [32], and good for a foundational verification system.

Table 2. Proof statistics

Example	Size (lines) Code	Spec	Proof	Time (s) Prove	Check	Example	Size (lines) Code	Spec	Proof	Time (s) Prove	Check
Simple						Lists: head	2	4	1	2.1	0.8
undefined	2	3	1	2.1	1.1	tail	2	4	1	2.2	0.9
average3	2	5	1	2.3	0.8	add	4	4	1	4.8	1.2
min	3	4	2	2.1	0.7	swap	6	4	1	19.6	3.6
max	3	4	2	2.1	0.7	dealloc	6	4	1	6.3	1.3
multiply	9	6	1	7.2	1.4	length(rec)	4	4	1	4.8	1.4
sum(rec)	6	7	6	4.2	1.0	length(iter)	4	8	1	7.2	1.5
sum(iter)	6	11	8	6.0	1.0	sum(rec)	4	4	1	8.2	2.0
Trees						sum(iter)	4	8	1	9.11	1.7
height	8	3	3	20.5	4.1	reverse	8	5	3	15.0	2.2
size	5	3	1	8.0	2.2	append	7	9	3	19.4	3.6
find	6	9	1	15.5	3.1	copy	14	11	3	55.0	9.3
mirror	7	6	1	19.0	4.2	delete	16	18	9	44.6	6.0
dealloc	15	7	1	19.6	4.1	Schorr-Waite					
flatten(rec)	12	10	1	30.9	6.8	tree	14	91	116	60.1	7.6
flatten(iter)	24	17	4	150.3	22.8	graph	14	91	203	133.6	18.2

The reported "Proof" time is the time for Coq to process the proof script, which includes running proof tactics and proof searches to construct a complete proof. If this run succeeds, it produces a proof certificate file which can be rechecked without that overhead. For an initial comparison with Bedrock we timed their SinglyLinkedList.v example, which verifies length, reverse, and append functions that closely resemble our example code. The total time to run the Bedrock proof script was 93 s, and 31 s to recheck the proof certificate, distinctly slower than our times in Table 2. To more precisely match the Bedrock examples we modified our programs to represent lists nodes with fields at successive addresses rather than using HIMP's records, but this only improved performance, down to 20 s to run the proof scripts, and 4 s to check the certificates.

5 Subsuming Reachability Logic

Reachability logic [33] is a closely related approach to program verification using operational semantics. In fact, our coinductive approach came about when trying to distill reachability logic into its mathematical essence. The practicality of reachability logic has recently been demonstrated, as the reachability logic proof system has been shown to work with several independently developed semantics of real-world languages, such as C, Java, and JavaScript [15].

5.1 Advantages of Coinduction

A mechanical proof of our soundness theorem gives a more usable verification framework, since reachability logic requires operational semantics to be given as a set of rewrite rules, while our approach does not. Further, reachability logic fixes a set of syntactic proof rules, while in our approach the mathematical fixpoints and functions act as proof rules without explicitly requiring any. In fact, the generality of our approach allows introductions of other derived rules that do not compromise the soundness result. Similarly, the generality allows higher-order verification, which reachability logic cannot handle.

Further, we saw in Sect. 3 that the general proof of our theorem is entirely mathematical. We instantiate it with the $step_R$ function to get a program verification framework. However, if we instantiate it with other functions, we could get frameworks for proving different properties, such as all-path validity or the "until" notion of validity previously mentioned. Reachability logic does not support any other notion of validity without changes to its proof system, which then require new proofs of soundness and relative

Axiom:
$$\frac{\varphi \Rightarrow \varphi' \in \mathcal{A}}{\mathcal{A} \vdash_C \varphi \Rightarrow \varphi'}$$

Reflexivity:
$$\mathcal{A} \vdash \varphi \Rightarrow \varphi$$

Transitivity:
$$\frac{\mathcal{A} \vdash_C \varphi_1 \Rightarrow^+ \varphi_2 \quad \mathcal{A} \cup C \vdash \varphi_2 \Rightarrow \varphi_3}{\mathcal{A} \vdash_C \varphi_1 \Rightarrow \varphi_3}$$

Logic Framing:
$$\frac{\mathcal{A} \vdash_C \varphi \Rightarrow \varphi' \quad \psi \text{ is a FOL formula}}{\mathcal{A} \vdash_C \varphi \wedge \psi \Rightarrow \varphi' \wedge \psi}$$

Consequence:
$$\frac{\models \varphi_1 \rightarrow \varphi_1' \quad \mathcal{A} \vdash_C \varphi_1' \Rightarrow \varphi_2' \quad \models \varphi_2' \rightarrow \varphi_2}{\mathcal{A} \vdash_C \varphi_1 \Rightarrow \varphi_2}$$

Case Analysis:
$$\frac{\mathcal{A} \vdash_C \varphi_1 \Rightarrow \varphi \quad \mathcal{A} \vdash_C \varphi_2 \Rightarrow \varphi}{\mathcal{A} \vdash_C \varphi_1 \vee \varphi_2 \Rightarrow \varphi}$$

Abstraction:
$$\frac{\mathcal{A} \vdash_C \varphi \Rightarrow \varphi' \quad X \cap FreeVars(\varphi') = \emptyset}{\mathcal{A} \vdash_C \exists X \varphi \Rightarrow \varphi'}$$

Circularity:
$$\frac{\mathcal{A} \vdash_{C \cup \{\varphi \Rightarrow \varphi'\}} \varphi \Rightarrow \varphi'}{\mathcal{A} \vdash_C \varphi \Rightarrow \varphi'}$$

Fig. 6. Reachability Logic proof system. Sequent $\mathcal{A} \vdash \varphi \Rightarrow \varphi'$ is a shorthand for $\mathcal{A} \vdash_\emptyset \varphi \Rightarrow \varphi'$.

completeness. For our framework, the proof of the main theorem does not need to be modified at all, and one only needs to prove that all-path validity is a greatest fixpoint (see Sect. 3). The same is true for any property. In this sense, this coinduction framework is much more general than the reachability logic proof system presented in [34].

5.2   Reachability Logic Proof System

The key construct in reachability logic is the notion of circularity. Circularities, represented as C in Fig. 6, intuitively represent claims that are conjectured to be true but have not yet been proved true. These claims are proved using the Circularity rule, which is analogous in our coinductive framework to referring back to claims previously seen. Most of the other rules in Fig. 6 are not as interesting. Transitivity requires progress before the circularities are flushed as axioms. This corresponds to the outer step$_R$ in our coinductive framework.

Clearly, there are obvious parallels between the Reachability Logic proof system and our coinductive framework. We have formalized and mechanically verified a detailed proof that reachability logic is an instance of our coinductive verification framework. One can refer to [16] for full details, but we briefly discuss the nature of the proof below.

5.3   Reachability Logic is Coinduction

To formalize what it means for reachability logic to be an instance of coinduction, we first need some definitions. First, we need a translation from a reachability rule to a set of coinductive claims. In a reachability rule $\varphi \Rightarrow \varphi'$, both φ and φ' are patterns which respectively describe (symbolically) the starting and the reached configurations. Both φ and φ' can have free variables. Let Var be the set of variables. Then, we define the set of claims

$$S_{\varphi \Rightarrow \varphi'} \equiv \{(c, \overline{\rho}(\varphi')) \mid c \in \overline{\rho}(\varphi), \ \forall \rho : Var \to Cfg\}$$

where Cfg is the model of configurations and $\overline{\rho}(\cdot)$ is the extension of the valuation ρ to patterns [15]. Also, let the claims derived from a set of reachability rules $X = \{\varphi_1 \Rightarrow \varphi'_1, \ldots, \varphi_n \Rightarrow \varphi'_n\}$ be:

$$\overline{X} \equiv \bigcup_{\varphi_i \Rightarrow \varphi'_i \in X} S_{\varphi_i \Rightarrow \varphi'_i}$$

In reachability logic, programming language semantics are defined as *theories*, that is, as sets of (one-step) reachability rules $\mathcal{A}$ with patterns over a given signature of symbols. Each theory $\mathcal{A}$ defines a transition relation over the configurations in Cfg, say $R_{\mathcal{A}}$, which is then used to define the semantic validity in reachability logic, $\mathcal{A} \models \varphi \Rightarrow \varphi'$. It is possible and easier to prove our main theorem more generally, for any transition relation R that satisfies $R \vDash^+ \mathcal{A}$.

$$R \vDash^+ \mathcal{A} \text{ if } R \vDash^+ \varphi \Rightarrow \varphi' \text{ for each } \varphi \Rightarrow \varphi' \in \mathcal{A}$$

where $R \vDash^+ \varphi \Rightarrow \varphi'$ if for each $\rho : Var \to Cfg$ and $\gamma : Cfg$ such that $(\rho, \gamma) \vDash \varphi$ [33], there is a γ' such that $\gamma \to_R \gamma'$ and $(\gamma', \overline{\rho}(\varphi'))$ is a valid reachability claim.

Lemma 3. $R_{\mathcal{A}} \vDash^+ \mathcal{A}$ and if $S_{\varphi \Rightarrow \varphi'} \subseteq \mathrm{valid}_{R_{\mathcal{A}}}$ then $\mathcal{A} \vDash \varphi \Rightarrow \varphi'$.

This lemma suggests what to do: take any reachability logic proof of $\mathcal{A} \vdash \varphi \Rightarrow \varphi'$ and any transition relation R such that $R \vDash^+ \mathcal{A}$, and produce a coinductive proof of $S_{\varphi \Rightarrow \varphi'} \subseteq \mathrm{valid}_R$. This gives us not only a procedure to associate coinductive proofs to reachability logic proofs, but also an alternative method to prove the soundness of reachability logic. This is what we do below:

Theorem 2. *If there is a reachability logic proof derivation for $\mathcal{A} \vdash \varphi \Rightarrow \varphi'$ and a transition relation R such that $R \vDash^+ \mathcal{A}$, then $S_{\varphi \Rightarrow \varphi'} \subseteq \mathrm{valid}_R$, and in particular this holds by applying Theorem 1 to an inclusion $\overline{\mathcal{C}} \subseteq \mathrm{step}_R(\mathrm{derived}^*_R(\overline{\mathcal{C}}))$. Here, $\mathrm{derived}_R$ is a particular function satisfying the conditions for G in Theorem 1 (see [16] for more details), and $\mathcal{C}$ is a set of reachability rules consisting of $\varphi \Rightarrow \varphi'$ along with those reachability rules which appear as conclusions of instances of the Circularity proof rule in the proof tree of $\mathcal{A} \vdash \varphi \Rightarrow \varphi'$.*

To prove Theorem 2, we apply the Set Circularity theorem of reachability logic [35], which states that any reachability logic claim $\mathcal{A} \vdash \varphi \Rightarrow \varphi'$ is provable iff there is some set of claims $\mathcal{C}$ such that $\varphi \Rightarrow \varphi' \in \mathcal{C}$ and for each $\varphi_i \Rightarrow \varphi'_i \in \mathcal{C}$ there is a proof of $\mathcal{A} \vdash_{\mathcal{C}} \varphi_i \Rightarrow \varphi'_i$ which does not use the Circularity proof rule. In the forward direction, we can take $\mathcal{C}$ as defined in the statement of Theorem 2. The main idea is to convert proof trees into inclusions of sets of claims:

Lemma 4. *Given a proof derivation of $\mathcal{A} \vdash_{\mathcal{C}} \varphi_a \Rightarrow \varphi_b$ which does not use the Circularity proof rule (last rule in Fig. 6), if $R \vDash^+ \mathcal{A}$ and $\mathcal{C}$ is nonempty then $S_{\varphi_a \Rightarrow \varphi_b} \subseteq \mathrm{step}_R(\mathrm{derived}^*_R(\overline{\mathcal{C}}))$.*

This lemma is proven by strengthening the inclusion into one that can be proven by structural induction over the Reachability Logic proof rules besides Circularity.

Combining this lemma with Set Circularity shows that $\overline{\mathcal{C}} = \cup_i S_{\varphi_i \Rightarrow \varphi'_i} \subseteq \mathrm{valid}_R$ which implies that $S_{\varphi \Rightarrow \varphi'} \subseteq \mathrm{valid}_R$ exactly as desired. We have mechanized the proofs of Lemmas 3 and 4 in Coq [16]. This is a major result, constituting an independent soundness proof for Reachability Logic, and helps demonstrate the strength of our coinductive framework, despite its simplicity. Moreover, this allows proofs done using reachability logic as in [15] to be translated to mechanically verified proofs in Coq, immediately allowing foundational verification of programs written in *any language*.

6   Other Related Work

Here we discuss work other than reachability logic that is related to our coinductive verification system. We discuss commonly used program verifiers, including approaches based on operational semantics and Iris [36], an approach with some language independence. We also discuss related coinduction schemata.

6.1 Current Verification Tools

A number of prominent tools such as Why [37], Boogie [38,39], and Bedrock [24,32] provide program verification for a fixed language, and support other languages by translation if at all. For example, Frama-C and Krakatoa, respectively, attempt to verify C and Java by translation through Why. Also, Spec# and Havoc, respectively, verify C# and C by translation through Boogie. We are not aware of soundness proofs for these translations. Such proofs would be highly non-trivial, requiring formal semantics of both source and target languages.

All of these systems are based on a verification condition (VC) generator for their programming language. Bedrock is closest in architecture and guarantees to our system, as it is implemented in Coq and verification results in a Coq proof certificate that the specification is sound with respect to a semantics of the object language. Bedrock supports dynamically created code, and modular verification of higher-order functions, for which our framework has preliminary support. Bedrock also makes more aggressive attempts at complete automation, which costs increased runtime. Most fundamentally, Bedrock is built around a VC generator for a fixed target language.

In sharp contrast to the above approaches, we demonstrated that a small-step operational semantics suffices for program verification, without a need to define any other semantics, or verification condition generators, for the same language. A language-independent, sound and (relatively) complete coinductive proof method then allows us to verify properties of programs using directly the operational semantics. As seen in Sect. 4.8 this language independence does not compromise other desirable properties. The required human effort and the performance of the verification task compare well with foundational program verifiers such as Bedrock, and we provide the same high confidence in correctness: the trust base consists of the operational semantics only.

6.2 Operational Semantics Based Approaches

Verifiable C [40] is a program verification tool for the C programming language based on an operational semantics for C defined in Coq. Hoare triples are then proved as lemmas about the operational semantics. However, in this approach and other similar approaches, it is necessary to prove such lemmas. Without them, verification of any nontrivial C program would be nearly impossible. In our approach, while we can also define and prove Hoare triples as lemmas, doing so is not needed to make program verification feasible, as demonstrated in the previous sections. We only need some additional domain reasoning in Coq, which logics like Verifiable C require *in addition* to Hoare logic reasoning. Thus, our approach automatically yields a program verification tool for any language with minimal additional reasoning, while approaches such as Verifiable C need over 40,000 lines of Coq to define the program logic. We believe this is completely unnecessary, and hope our coinductive framework will be the first step in eliminating such superfluous logics.

The work by the FLINT group [41–43] is another approach to program verification based on operational semantics. Languages developed use shallowly embedded state predicates in Coq, and inference rules are derived directly from the operational semantics. However, their work is not generic over operational semantics. For example, [43] is developed in the context of a particular machine model, with a fixed memory representation and register file. Even simple changes such as adding registers require updating soundness proofs. Our approach has a single soundness theorem that can be instantiated for *any* language.

Iris [36] is a concurrent separation logic that has language independence, with operational semantics formalized in Coq. Iris adds monoids and invariants to the program logic in order to facilitate verification. It also derives some Hoare-style rules for verification from the semantics of a language. However, there are still structural Hoare rules that depend on the language that must be added manually. Additionally, once proof rules are generated, they are specialized to that particular language. Further, the verification in the paper relies on Hoare style reasoning, while in our approach, we do not assume any such verification style, as we work directly with the mathematical specifications. Finally, the monoids used are not generated and are specific to the program language used.

6.3   Other Coinduction Schemata

A categorical generalization of our key theorem was presented as a recursion scheme in [12,13]. The titular result of the former is the dual of the λ-coiteration scheme of the latter, which specializes to preorder categories to give our Theorem 1. A more recent and more general result is [14], which also generalized other recent work on coinductive proofs such as [44]. Unlike these approaches, which were presented for showing bisimilarity, the novelty of our approach stems in the use of these techniques directly to show Hoare-style functional correctness claims, and in the development of the afferent machinery and automation that makes it work with a variety of languages, and not in advancing the already solid mathematical foundations of coinduction. Various weaker coinduction schemes are folklore, such as Isabelle/HOL's standard library's lemma coinduct3: $mono(f) \wedge A \subseteq f(\mu x.\, f(x) \cup A \cup \nu f) \implies A \subseteq \nu(f)$.

7   Conclusion and Future Work

We presented a language-independent program verification framework. Proofs can be as simple as with a custom Hoare logic, but only an operational semantics of the target language is required. We have mechanized a proof of the correctness of our approach in Coq. Combining this with a coinductive proof thus produces a Coq proof certificate concluding that the program meets the specification according to the provided semantics. Our approach is amenable to proof automation. Further automation may improve convenience and cannot compromise soundness of the proof system. A language designer need only give an authoritative semantics to enable program verification for a new language, rather than needing to have the experience and invest the effort to design and prove the soundness of a custom program logic.

One opportunity for future work is using our approach to provide proof certificates for reachability logic program verifiers such as K [9]. The K prover was used to verify programs in several real programming languages [15]. While the proof system is sound, trusting the results of these tools requires trusting the implementation of the K system. Our translation in Sect. 5 will allow us to produce proof objects in Coq for proofs done in K's backend, which will make it sufficient to trust only Coq's proof checker to rely on the results from K's prover.

Another area for future work is verifying programs with higher-order specifications, where a specification can make reachability claims about values quantified over in the specification. This allows higher-order functions to have specifications that require functional arguments to themselves satisfy some specification. We have begun preliminary work on proving validity of such specifications using the notions of compatibility up-to presented in [14]. Combining this with more general forms of claims may allow modular verification of concurrent programs, as in RGsep [45]. See [16] for initial work in these areas.

Other areas for future work are evaluating the reusability of proof automation between languages, and using the ability to easily verify programs under a modified semantics, e.g. adding time costs to allow proving real-time properties.

References

1. Hoare, C.A.R.: An axiomatic basis for computer programming. Commun. ACM 12(10), 576–580 (1969). https://doi.org/10.1145/363235.363259
2. Hathhorn, C., Ellison, C., Roşu, G.: Defining the undefinedness of C. In: PLDI, pp. 336–345. ACM (2015). https://doi.org/10.1145/2737924.2737979
3. Bogdănaş, D., Roşu, G.: K-Java: a complete semantics of Java. In: POPL, pp. 445–456. ACM (2015). https://doi.org/10.1145/2676726.2676982
4. Bodin, M., Chargueraud, A., Filaretti, D., Gardner, P., Maffeis, S., Naudziuniene, D., Schmitt, A., Smith, G.: A trusted mechanised JavaScript specification. In: POPL, pp. 87–100. ACM (2014). https://doi.org/10.1145/2535838.2535876
5. Park, D., Ştefănescu, A., Roşu, G.: KJS: a complete formal semantics of Javascript. In: PLDI, pp. 346–356. ACM (2015). https://doi.org/10.1145/2737924.2737991
6. Politz, J.G., Martinez, A., Milano, M., Warren, S., Patterson, D., Li, J., Chitipothu, A., Krishnamurthi, S.: Python: the full monty. In: OOPSLA, pp. 217–232. ACM (2013). https://doi.org/10.1145/2509136.2509536
7. Filaretti, D., Maffeis, S.: An executable formal semantics of PHP. In: Jones, R. (ed.) ECOOP 2014. LNCS, vol. 8586, pp. 567–592. Springer, Heidelberg (2014). https://doi.org/10.1007/978-3-662-44202-9_23
8. Owens, S.: A sound semantics for OCaml$_{light}$. In: Drossopoulou, S. (ed.) ESOP 2008. LNCS, vol. 4960, pp. 1–15. Springer, Heidelberg (2008). https://doi.org/10.1007/978-3-540-78739-6_1
9. Roşu, G., Şerbănuţă, T.F.: An overview of the K semantic framework. J. LAP 79(6), 397–434 (2010). https://doi.org/10.1016/j.jlap.2010.03.012

10. Klein, C., Clements, J., Dimoulas, C., Eastlund, C., Felleisen, M., Flatt, M., McCarthy, J.A., Rafkind, J., Tobin-Hochstadt, S., Findler, R.B.: Run your research: on the effectiveness of lightweight mechanization. In: POPL, pp. 285–296. ACM (2012). https://doi.org/10.1145/2103656.2103691

11. Sewell, P., Nardelli, F.Z., Owens, S., Peskine, G., Ridge, T., Sarkar, S., Strnisa, R.: Ott: effective tool support for the working semanticist. In: ICFP. ACM (2007). https://doi.org/10.1017/S0956796809990293

12. Uustalu, T., Vene, V., Pardo, A.: Recursion schemes from comonads. Nord. J. Comput. **8**(3), 366–390 (2001)

13. Bartels, F.: On generalised coinduction and probabilistic specification formats: distributive laws in coalgebraic modelling. Ph.D. thesis, Vrije Universiteit Amsterdam (2004)

14. Pous, D.: Coinduction all the way up. In: LICS, pp. 307–316. IEEE (2016). https://doi.org/10.1145/2933575.2934564

15. Ştefănescu, A., Park, D., Yuwen, S., Li, Y., Roşu, G.: Semantics-based program verifiers for all languages. In: OOPSLA, pp. 74–91. ACM (2016). https://doi.org/10.1145/2983990.2984027

16. Moore, B., Peña, L., Rosu, G.: GitHub repository (2017). https://github.com/Formal-Systems-Laboratory/coinduction. Source code

17. Wright, A.K., Felleisen, M.: A syntactic approach to type soundness. Inf. Comput. **115**(1), 38–94 (1992). https://doi.org/10.1006/inco.1994.1093

18. Plotkin, G.D.: A structural approach to operational semantics. J. Log. Algebraic Program. **60–61**, 17–139 (2004). https://doi.org/10.1016/j.jlap.2004.05.001

19. Reynolds, J.C.: Separation logic: a logic for shared mutable data structures. In: LICS, pp. 55–74. IEEE (2002). https://doi.org/10.1109/LICS.2002.1029817

20. O'Hearn, P.W., Pym, D.J.: The logic of bunched implications. Bull. Symbolic Log. **5**(2), 215–244 (1999). https://doi.org/10.2307/421090

21. Felleisen, M., Friedman, D.P.: A calculus for assignments in higher-order languages. In: POPL, p. 314. ACM (1987). https://doi.org/10.1145/41625.41654

22. Felleisen, M.: The calculi of Lambda-ν-cs conversion: a syntactic theory of control and state in imperative higher-order programming languages. Ph.D. thesis, Indiana University (1987)

23. Roşu, G.: Matching logic – extended abstract. In: RTA, LIPIcs, pp. 5–21. Schloss Dagstuhl-LZ I (2015). https://doi.org/10.4230/LIPIcs.RTA.2015.5

24. Chlipala, A.: Mostly-automated verification of low-level programs in computational separation logic. In: PLDI, pp. 234–245. ACM (2011). https://doi.org/10.1145/1993498.1993526

25. Schorr, H., Waite, W.M.: An efficient machine-independent procedure for garbage collection in various list structures. Commun. ACM **10**(8), 501–506 (1967). https://doi.org/10.1145/363534.363554

26. Bornat, R.: Proving pointer programs in Hoare logic. In: Backhouse, R., Oliveira, J.N. (eds.) MPC 2000. LNCS, vol. 1837, pp. 102–126. Springer, Heidelberg (2000). https://doi.org/10.1007/10722010_8

27. Mehta, F., Nipkow, T.: Proving pointer programs in higher-order logic. Inf. Comput. **199**(1–2), 200–227 (2005). https://doi.org/10.1016/j.ic.2004.10.007

28. Hubert, T., Marche, C.: A case study of C source code verification: the Schorr-Waite algorithm. In: SEFM, pp. 190–199. IEEE (2005). https://doi.org/10.1109/SEFM.2005.1

29. Gries, D.: The Schorr-Waite graph marking algorithm. Acta Informatica **11**(3), 223–232 (1979). https://doi.org/10.1007/BF00289068

30. Gupta, A., Henzinger, T.A., Majumdar, R., Rybalchenko, A., Xu, R.G.: Proving non-termination. In: POPL, pp. 147–158. ACM (2008). https://doi.org/10.1145/1328438.1328459

31. Chen, H.-Y., Cook, B., Fuhs, C., Nimkar, K., O'Hearn, P.: Proving nontermination via safety. In: Ábrahám, E., Havelund, K. (eds.) TACAS 2014. LNCS, vol. 8413, pp. 156–171. Springer, Heidelberg (2014). https://doi.org/10.1007/978-3-642-54862-8_11

32. Chlipala, A.: The Bedrock structured programming system: combining generative metaprogramming and Hoare logic in an extensible program verifier. In: ICFP, pp. 391–402. ACM (2013). https://doi.org/10.1145/2500365.2500592

33. Roşu, G., Ştefănescu, A., Ciobâcă, Ş., Moore, B.M.: One-path reachability logic. In: LICS, pp. 358–367. IEEE (2013). https://doi.org/10.1109/LICS.2013.42

34. Roşu, G., Ştefănescu, A.: From Hoare logic to matching logic reachability. In: Giannakopoulou, D., Méry, D. (eds.) FM 2012. LNCS, vol. 7436, pp. 387–402. Springer, Heidelberg (2012). https://doi.org/10.1007/978-3-642-32759-9_32

35. Roşu, G., Ştefănescu, A., Ciobâcă, c., Moore, B.M.: Reachability logic. Technical report, University of Illinois, July 2012. http://hdl.handle.net/2142/32952

36. Jung, R., Swasey, D., Sieczkowski, F., Svendsen, K., Turon, A., Birkedal, L., Dreyer, D.: Iris: monoids and invariants as an orthogonal basis for concurrent reasoning. In: POPL, pp. 637–650. ACM (2015). https://doi.org/10.1145/2775051.2676980

37. Filliâtre, J.-C., Paskevich, A.: Why3—where programs meet provers. In: Felleisen, M., Gardner, P. (eds.) ESOP 2013. LNCS, vol. 7792, pp. 125–128. Springer, Heidelberg (2013). https://doi.org/10.1007/978-3-642-37036-6_8

38. Leino, K.R.M.: This is Boogie 2. Technical report, Microsoft Research, June 2008

39. Barnett, M., Chang, B.-Y.E., DeLine, R., Jacobs, B., Leino, K.R.M.: Boogie: a modular reusable verifier for object-oriented programs. In: de Boer, F.S., Bonsangue, M.M., Graf, S., de Roever, W.-P. (eds.) FMCO 2005. LNCS, vol. 4111, pp. 364–387. Springer, Heidelberg (2006). https://doi.org/10.1007/11804192_17

40. Appel, A.W., Dockins, R., Hobor, A., Beringer, L., Dodds, J., Stewart, G., Blazy, S., Leroy, X.: Program Logics for Certified Compilers. Cambridge University Press, New York (2014)

41. Yu, D., Shao, Z.: Verification of safety properties for concurrent assembly code. In: ICFP, pp. 175–188. ACM (2004). https://doi.org/10.1145/1016850.1016875

42. Feng, X., Shao, Z., Vaynberg, A., Xiang, S., Ni, Z.: Modular verification of assembly code with stack-based control abstractions. In: PLDI, pp. 401–414. ACM (2006). https://doi.org/10.1145/1133981.1134028

43. Feng, X., Shao, Z., Guo, Y., Dong, Y.: Combining domain-specific and foundational logics to verify complete software systems. In: Shankar, N., Woodcock, J. (eds.) VSTTE 2008. LNCS, vol. 5295, pp. 54–69. Springer, Heidelberg (2008). https://doi.org/10.1007/978-3-540-87873-5_8

44. Hur, C.K., Neis, G., Dreyer, D., Vafeiadis, V.: The power of parameterization in coinductive proof. In: POPL, pp. 193–206. ACM (2013)

45. Vafeiadis, V.: Modular fine-grained concurrency verification. Ph.D. thesis, University of Cambridge (2008)

Velisarios: Byzantine Fault-Tolerant Protocols Powered by Coq

Vincent Rahli[✉], Ivana Vukotic, Marcus Völp, and Paulo Esteves-Verissimo

SnT, University of Luxembourg, Esch-sur-Alzette, Luxembourg
{vincent.rahli,ivana.vukotic,marcus.voelp,paulo.verissimo}@uni.lu

Abstract. Our increasing dependence on complex and critical information infrastructures and the emerging threat of sophisticated attacks,
ask for extended efforts to ensure the correctness and security of these
systems. Byzantine fault-tolerant state-machine replication (BFT-SMR)
provides a way to harden such systems. It ensures that they maintain
correctness and availability in an application-agnostic way, provided that
the replication protocol is correct and at least $n - f$ out of n replicas
survive arbitrary faults. This paper presents Velisarios, a logic-of-events
based framework implemented in Coq, which we developed to implement
and reason about BFT-SMR protocols. As a case study, we present the
first machine-checked proof of a crucial safety property of an implementation of the area's reference protocol: PBFT.

Keywords: Byzantine faults · State machine replication
Formal verification · Coq

1 Introduction

Critical information infrastructures such as the power grid or water supply systems assume an unprecedented role in our society. On one hand, our lives depend
on the correctness of these systems. On the other hand, their complexity has
grown beyond manageability. One state of the art technique to harden such critical systems is Byzantine fault-tolerant state-machine replication (BFT-SMR).
It is a generic technique that is used to turn any service into one that can tolerate *arbitrary* faults, by extensively replicating the service to mask the behavior
of a minority of possibly faulty replicas behind a majority of healthy replicas,
operating in consensus.[1] The total number of replicas n is a parameter over the
maximum number of faulty replicas f, which the system is configured to tolerate

---

This work is partially supported by the Fonds National de la Recherche Luxembourg
(FNR) through PEARL grant FNR/P14/8149128.

[1] For such techniques to be useful and in order to avoid persistent and shared vulnerabilities, replicas need to be rejuvenated periodically [17,76], they need to be
diverse enough [43], and ideally they need to be physically far apart. Diversity and
rejuvenation are not covered here.

© The Author(s) 2018
A. Ahmed (Ed.): ESOP 2018, LNCS 10801, pp. 619–650, 2018.
https://doi.org/10.1007/978-3-319-89884-1_22

at any point in time. Typically, $n = 3f + 1$ for classical protocols such as in [16], and $n = 2f + 1$ for protocols that rely on tamper-proof components such as in [82]. Because such protocols tolerate arbitrary faults, a faulty replica is one that does not behave according to its specification. For example it can be one that is controlled by an attacker, or simply one that contains a bug.

Ideally, we should guarantee the correctness and security of such replicated and distributed, hardened systems to the highest standards known to mankind today. That is, the proof of their correctness should be checked by a machine and their model refined down to machine code. Unfortunately, as pointed out in [29], most distributed algorithms, including BFT protocols, are published in pseudo-code or, in the best case, a formal but not executable specification, leaving their safety and liveness questionable. Moreover, Lamport, Shostak, and Pease wrote about such programs: "We know of no area in computer science or mathematics in which informal reasoning is more likely to lead to errors than in the study of this type of algorithm." [54]. Therefore, we focus here on developing a generic and extensible formal verification framework for systematically supporting the mechanical verification of BFT protocols and their implementations.[2]

Our framework provides, among other things, a model that captures the idea of arbitrary/Byzantine faults; a collection of standard assumptions to reason about systems with faulty components; proof tactics that capture common reasoning patterns; as well as a general library of distributed knowledge. All these parts can be reused to reason about any BFT protocol. For example, most BFT protocols share the same high-level structure (they essentially disseminate knowledge and vote on the knowledge they gathered), which we capture in our knowledge theory. We have successfully used this framework to prove a crucial safety property of an implementation of a complex BFT-SMR protocol called PBFT [14–16]. We handle all the functionalities of the base protocol, including garbage collection and view change, which are essential in practical protocols. Garbage collection is used to bound message logs and buffers. The view change procedure enables BFT protocols to make progress in case the *primary*—a distinguished replica used in some fault-tolerant protocols to coordinate votes—becomes faulty.

Contributions. Our contributions are as follows: (1) Section 3 presents Velisarios, our continuing effort towards a generic and extensible logic-of-events based framework for verifying implementations of BFT-SMR protocols using Coq [25]. (2) As discussed in Sect. 4, our framework relies on a library to reason about *distributed epistemic knowledge*. (3) We implemented Castro's landmark PBFT protocol, and proved its agreement safety property (see Sect. 5). (4) We implemented a runtime environment to run the OCaml code we extract from Coq (see Sect. 6). (5) We released Velisarios and our PBFT safety proof under an open source licence.[3]

---

[2] Ideally, both (1) the replication mechanism and (2) the instances of the replicated service should be verified. However, we focus here on (1), which has to be done only once, while (2) needs to be done for every service and for every replica instance.

[3] Available at: https://github.com/vrahli/Velisarios.

Why PBFT? We have chosen PBFT because several BFT-SMR protocols designed since then either use (part of) PBFT as one of their main building blocks, or are inspired by it, such as [6,8,26,45,46,82], to cite only a few. Therefore, a bug in PBFT could imply bugs in those protocols too. Castro provided a thorough study of PBFT: he described the protocol in [16], studied how to proactively rejuvenate replicas in [14], and provided a pen-and-paper proof of PBFT's safety in [15,17]. Even though we use a different model—Castro used I/O automata (see Sect. 7.1), while we use a logic-of-events model (see Sect. 3)—our mechanical proof builts on top of his pen-and-paper proof. One major difference is that here we verify actual running code, which we obtain thanks to Coq's extraction mechanism.

2 . PBFT Recap

This section provides a rundown of PBFT [14–16], which we use as running example to illustrate our model of BFT-SMR protocols presented in Sect. 3.

2.1 Overview of the Protocol

We describe here the public-key based version of PBFT, for which Castro provides a formal pen-and-paper proof of its safety. PBFT is considered the first practical BFT-SMR protocol. Compared to its predecessors, it is more efficient and it does not rely on unrealistic assumptions. It works with asynchronous, unreliable networks (i.e., messages can be dropped, altered, delayed, duplicated, or delivered out of order), and it tolerates independent network failures. To achieve this, PBFT assumes strong cryptography in the form of collision-resistant digests, and an existentially unforgeable signature scheme. It supports any deterministic state machine. Each state machine replica maintains the service state and implements the service operations. Clients send requests to all replicas and await $f+1$ matching replies from different replicas. PBFT ensures that healthy replicas execute the same operations in the same order.

To tolerate up to f faults, PBFT requires $|R| = 3f+1$ replicas. Replicas move trough a succession of configurations called *views*. In each view v, one replica $(p = v \bmod |R|)$ assumes the role of *primary* and the others become *backups*. The primary coordinates the votes, i.e., it picks the order in which client requests are executed. When a backup suspects the primary to be faulty, it requests a view-change to select another replica as new primary.

Normal-Case. During normal-case operation, i.e., when the primary is not suspected to be faulty by a majority of replicas, clients send requests to be executed, which trigger agreement among the replicas. Various kinds of messages have to be sent among clients and replicas before a client knows its request has been executed. Figure 1 shows the resulting message patterns for PBFT's normal-case operation and view-change protocol. Let us discuss here normal-case operation:

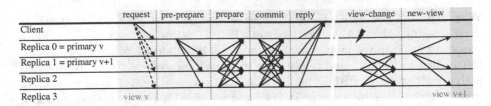

Fig. 1. PBFT normal-case (left) and view-change (right) operations

1. *Request:* To initiate agreement, a client c sends a request of the form $\langle \text{REQUEST}, o, t, c \rangle_{\sigma_c}$ to the primary, but is also prepared to broadcast it to all replicas if replies are late or primaries change. $\langle \text{REQUEST}, o, t, c \rangle_{\sigma_c}$ specifies the operation to execute o and a timestamp t that orders requests of the same client. Replicas will not re-execute requests with a lower timestamp than the last one processed for this client, but are prepared to resend recent replies.

2. *Pre-prepare:* The primary of view v puts the pending requests in a total order and initiates agreement by sending $\langle \text{PRE-PREPARE}, v, n, m \rangle_{\sigma_p}$ to all the backups, where m should be the nth executed request. The strictly monotonically increasing and contiguous sequence number n ensures preservation of this order despite message reordering.

3. *Prepare:* Backup i acknowledges the receipt of a pre-prepare message by sending the digest d of the client's request in $\langle \text{PREPARE}, v, n, d, i \rangle_{\sigma_i}$ to all replicas.

4. *Commit:* Replica i acknowledges the reception of $2f$ prepares matching a valid pre-prepare by broadcasting $\langle \text{COMMIT}, v, n, d, i \rangle_{\sigma_i}$. In this case, we say that the message is *prepared* at i.

5. *Execution & Reply:* Replicas execute client operations after receiving $2f + 1$ matching commits, and follow the order of sequence numbers for this execution. Once replica i has executed the operation o requested by client c, it sends $\langle \text{REPLY}, v, t, c, i, r \rangle_{\sigma_i}$ to c, where r is the result of applying o to the service state. Client c accepts r if it receives $f + 1$ matching replies from different replicas.

Client and replica authenticity, and message integrity are ensured through signatures of the form $\langle m \rangle_{\sigma_i}$. A replica accepts a message m only if: (1) m's signature is correct, (2) m's view number matches the current view, and (3) the sequence number of m is in the water mark interval (see below).

PBFT buffers pending client requests, processing them later in batches. Moreover, it makes use of checkpoints and water marks (which delimit sequence number intervals) to limit the size of all message logs and to prevent replicas from exhausting the sequence number space.

Garbage Collection. Replicas store all correct messages that were created or received in a log. Checkpoints are used to limit the number of logged messages by removing the ones that the protocol no longer needs. A replica starts checkpointing after executing a request with a sequence number divisible by some predefined constant, by multicasting the message $\langle \text{CHECKPOINT}, v, n, d, i \rangle_{\sigma_i}$ to all other replicas. Here n is the sequence number of the last executed request and d is the digest of the state. Once a replica received $f + 1$ different checkpoint messages[4] (possibly including its own) for the same n and d, it holds a proof of correctness of the log corresponding to d, which includes messages up to sequence number n. The checkpoint is then called *stable* and all messages lower than n (except view-change messages) are pruned from the log.

View Change. The view change procedure ensures progress by allowing replicas to change the leader so as to not wait indefinitely for a faulty primary. Each backup starts a timer when it receives a request and stops it after the request has been executed. Expired timers cause the backup to suspect the leader and request a view change. It then stops receiving normal-case messages, and multicasts $\langle \text{VIEW-CHANGE}, v + 1, n, s, C, P, i \rangle_{\sigma_i}$, reporting the sequence number n of the last stable checkpoint s, its proof of correctness C, and the set of messages P with sequence numbers greater than n that backup i prepared since then. When the new primary p receives $2f + 1$ view-change messages, it multicasts $\langle \text{NEW-VIEW}, v + 1, V, O, N \rangle_{\sigma_p}$, where V is the set of $2f + 1$ valid view-change messages that p received; O is the set of messages prepared since the latest checkpoint reported in V; and N contains only the special *null* request for which the execution is a no-op. N is added to the O set to ensure that there are no gaps between the sequence numbers of prepared messages sent by the new primary. Upon receiving this new-view message, replicas enter view $v + 1$ and re-execute the normal-case protocol for all messages in $O \cup N$.

We have proved a critical safety property of PBFT, including its garbage collection and view change procedures, which are essential in practical protocols. However, we have not yet developed generic abstractions to specifically reason about garbage collection and view changes, that can be reused in other protocols, which we leave as future work.

2.2 Properties

PBFT with $|R| = 3f + 1$ replicas is safe and live. Its safety boils down to linearizability [42], i.e., the replicated service behaves like a centralized implementation that executes operations atomically one at a time. Castro used a modified version of linearizability in [14] to deal with faulty clients. As presented in Sect. 5, we proved the crux of this property, namely the agreement property (we leave linearizability for future work).

As informally explained by Castro [14], assuming weak synchrony (which constrains message transmission delays), PBFT is live, i.e., clients will eventually receive replies to their requests. In the future, we plan to extend Velisarios to support liveness and mechanize PBFT's liveness proof.

---

[4] Castro first required $2f + 1$ checkpoint messages [16] but relaxed this requirement in [14].

2.3 Differences with Castro's Implementation

As mentioned above, besides the normal-case operation, our Coq implementation of PBFT handles garbage collection, view changes and request batching. However, we slightly deviated from Castro's implementation [14], primarily in the way checkpoints are handled: we always work around sending messages that are not between the water marks, and a replica always requires its own checkpoint before clearing its log. Assuming the reader is familiar with PBFT, we now detail these deviations and refer the reader to [14] for comparison.

(1) To the best of our knowledge, to ensure liveness, Castro's implementation requires replicas to resend prepare messages below the low water mark when adopting a new-view message and processing the pre-prepares in $O \cup N$. In contrast, our implementation never sends messages with sequence numbers lower than the low water mark. This liveness issue can be resolved by bringing late replicas up to date through a state transfer.

(2) We require a new leader to send its own view-change message updated with its latest checkpoint as part of its new-view message. If not, it may happen that a checkpoint stabilizes after the view-change message is sent and before the new-view message is prepared. This might result in a new leader sending messages in $O \cup N$ with a sequence number below its low water mark, which it avoids by updating its own view-change message to contain its latest checkpoint.

(3) We require replicas to wait for their own checkpoint message before stabilizing a checkpoint and garbage collecting logs. This avoids stabilizing a checkpoint that has not been computed locally. Otherwise, a replica could lose track of the last executed request if its sequence number is superseded by the one in the checkpoint. Once proven, a state transfer of the latest checkpoint state and an update of the last executed request would also resolve this point.

We slightly deviated from Castro's protocol to make our proofs go through. We leave it for future work to formally study whether we could do without these changes, or whether they are due to shortcomings of the original specification.

3 Velisarios Model

Using PBFT as a running example, we now present our Coq model for Byzantine fault-tolerant distributed systems, which relies on a logic of events—Fig. 2 outlines our formalization.

3.1 The Logic of Events

We adapt the Logic of Events (LoE) we used in EventML [9,11,71] to not only deal with crash faults, but arbitrary faults in general (including malicious

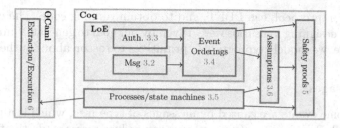

Fig. 2. Outline of formalization

faults). LoE, related to Lamport's notion of causal order [53] and to event structures [60,65], was developed to reason about events occurring in the execution of a distributed system. LoE has recently been used to verify consensus protocols [71,73] and cyber-physical systems [3]. Another standard model of distributed computing is Chandy and Lamport's *global state semantics* [19], where a distributed system is modeled as a single state machine: a state is the collection of all processes at a given time, and a transition takes a message in flight and delivers it to its recipient (a process in the collection). Each of these two models has advantages and disadvantages over the other. We chose LoE because in our experience it corresponds more closely to the way distributed system researchers and developers reason about protocols. As such, it provides a convenient communication medium between distributed systems and verification experts.

In LoE, an event is an abstract entity that corresponds either (1) to the handling of a received message, or (2) to some arbitrary activity about which no information is provided (see the discussion about trigger in Sect. 3.4). We use those arbitrary events to model arbitrary/Byzantine faults. An event happens at a specific point in space/time: the space coordinate of an event is called its location, and the time coordinate is given by a well-founded ordering on events that totally orders all events at the same location. Processes react to the messages that triggered the events happening at their locations one at a time, by transitioning through their states and creating messages to send out, which in turn might trigger other events. In order to reason about distributed systems, we use the notion of *event orderings* (see Sect. 3.4), which essentially are collections of ordered events and represent runs of a system. They are abstract entities that are never instantiated. Rather, when proving a property about a distributed system, one has to prove that the property holds for all event orderings corresponding to all possible runs of the system (see Sects. 3.5 and 5 for examples). Some runs/event orderings are not possible and therefore excluded through assumptions, such as the ones described in Sect. 3.6. For example, exists_at_most_f_faulty excludes event orderings where more than f out of n nodes could be faulty.

In the next few sections, we explain the different components (messages, authentication, event orderings, state machines, and correct traces) of Velisarios, and their use in our PBFT case study. Those components are parameterized by abstract types (parameters include the type of messages and the kind of authentication schemes), which we later have to instantiate in order to reason about a given protocol, e.g. PBFT, and to obtain running code. The choices we made when designing Velisarios were driven by our goal to generate running code. For example, we model cryptographic primitives to reason about authentication.

3.2 Messages

Model. Some events are caused by messages of type msg, which is a parameter of our model. Processes react to messages to produce message/destinations pairs (of type DirectedMsg), called *directed messages*. A directed message is typically handled by a message outbox, which sends the message to the listed destinations.[5] A destination is the name (of type name, which is a parameter of our model) of a node participating in the protocol.

PBFT. In our PBFT implementation, we instantiate the msg type using the following datatype (we only show some of the normal-case operation messages, leaving out for example the more involved pre-prepare messages—see Sect. 2.1):

```
Inductive PBFTmsg :=              Inductive Bare_Prepare :=
| REQUEST (r : Request)          | bare_prepare (v : View) (n : SeqNum) (d : digest) (i : Rep).
| PREPARE (p : Prepare)          Inductive Prepare :=
| REPLY (r : Reply) ...          | prepare (b : Bare_Prepare) (a : list Token).
```

As for prepares, all messages are defined as follows: we first define bare messages that do not contain authentication tokens (see Sect. 3.3), and then authenticated messages as pairs of a bare message and an authentication token. Views and sequence numbers are nats, while digests are parameters of the specification. PBFT involves two types of nodes: replicas of the form PBFTreplica(r), where r is of type Rep; and clients of the form PBFTclient(c), where c is of type Client. Both Rep and Client are parameters of our formalization, such that Rep is of arity 3f+1, where f is a parameter that stands for the number of tolerated faults.

3.3 Authentication

Model. Our model relies on an abstract concept of keys, which we use to implement and reason about authenticated communication. Capturing authenticity at the level of keys allows us to talk about impersonation through key leakage. Keys are divided into *sending keys* (of type sending_key) to authenticate a message for a target node, and *receiving keys* (of type receiving_key) to check the validity of a received message. Both sending_key and receiving_key are parameters of our model.[6] Each node maintains *local keys* (of type local_keys), which consists of two lists of *directed keys*: one for sending keys and one for receiving keys. Directed keys are pairs of a key and a list of node names identifying the processes that the holder of the key can communicate with.

---

[5] Message inboxes/outboxes are part of the runtime environment but not part of the model.

[6] Sending and receiving keys must be different when using asymmetric cryptography, and can be the same when using symmetric cryptography.

Sending keys are used to create *authentication tokens* of type Token, which we use to authenticate messages. Tokens are parameters of our model and abstract away from concrete concepts such as digital signatures or MACs. Typically, a message consists of some data plus some tokens that authenticates the data. Therefore, we introduce the following parameters: (1) the type data, for the kind of data that can be authenticated; (2) a create function to authenticate some data by generating authentication tokens using the sending keys; and (3) a verify function to verify the authenticity of some data by checking that it corresponds to some token using the receiving keys.

Once some data has been authenticated, it is typically sent over the network to other nodes, which in turn need to check the authenticity of the data. Typically, when a process sends an authenticated message to another process it includes its identity somewhere in the message. This identity is used to select the corresponding receiving key to check the authenticity of the data using verify. To extract this claimed identity we require users to provide a data_sender function.

It often happens in practice that a message contains more than one piece of authenticated data (e.g., in PBFT, pre-prepare messages contain authenticated client requests). Therefore, we require users to provide a get_contained_auth_data function that extracts all authenticated pieces of data contained in a message. Because we sometimes want to use different tokens to authenticate some data (e.g., when using MACs), an authenticated piece of data of type auth_data is defined as a pair of: (1) a piece of data, and (2) a list of tokens.

PBFT. Our PBFT implementation leaves keys and authentication tokens abstract because our safety proof is agnostic to the kinds of these elements. However, we turn them into actual asymmetric keys when extracting OCaml code (see Sect. 6 for more details). The create and verify functions are also left abstract until we extract the code to OCaml. Finally, we instantiate the data (the objects that can be authenticated, i.e., bare messages here), data_sender, and get_contained_auth_data parameters using:

```
Inductive PBFTdata := | PBFTdata_request (r : Bare_Request)
 | PBFTdata_prepare (p : Bare_Prepare) | PBFTdata_reply (r : Bare_Reply) ...

Definition PBFTdata_sender (m : data) : option name := match m with
 | PBFTdata_request (bare_request o t c) ⇒ Some (PBFTclient c)
 | PBFTdata_prepare (bare_prepare v n d i) ⇒ Some (PBFTreplica i)
 | PBFTdata_reply (bare_reply v t c i r) ⇒ Some (PBFTreplica i) ...

Definition PBFTget_contained_auth_data (m : msg) : list auth_data := match m with
 | REQUEST (request b a) ⇒ [(PBFTdata_request b,a)]
 | PREPARE (prepare b a) ⇒ [(PBFTdata_prepare b,a)]
 | REPLY (reply b a) ⇒ [(PBFTdata_reply b,a)] ...
```

3.4   Event Orderings

A typical way to reason about a distributed system is to reason about its possible runs, which are sometimes modeled as execution traces [72], and which are captured in LoE using *event orderings*. An *event ordering* is an abstract representation of a run of a distributed system; it provides a formal definition of a *message sequence diagram* as used by system designers (see for example Fig. 1). As opposed to [72], a trace here is not just one sequence of events but instead can be seen as a collection of local traces (one local trace per sequential process), where a local trace is a collection of events all happening at the same location and ordered in time, and such that some events of different local traces are causally ordered. Event orderings are never instantiated. Instead, we express system properties as predicates on event orderings. A system satisfies such a property if every possible execution of the system satisfies the predicate. We first formally define the components of an event ordering, and then present the axioms that these components have to satisfy.

Components.   An event ordering is formally defined as the tuple:[7]

```
Class EventOrdering :=
   { Event : Type;                    happenedBefore : Event → Event → Prop;
     loc : Event → name;              direct_pred : Event → option Event;
     trigger : Event → option msg;    keys : Event → local_keys; }
```

where (1) Event is an abstract type of events; (2) happenedBefore is an ordering relation on events; (3) loc returns the location at which events happen; (4) direct_pred returns the direct local predecessor of an event when one exists, i.e., for all events except initial events; (5) given an event e, trigger either returns the message that triggered e, or it returns None to indicate that no information is available regarding the action that triggered the event (see below); (6) keys returns the keys a node can use at a given event to communicate with other nodes. The event orderings presented here are similar to the ones used in [3,71], which we adapted to handle Byzantine faults by modifying the type of trigger so that events can be triggered by arbitrary actions and not necessarily by the receipt of a message, and by adding support for authentication through keys.

The trigger function returns None to capture the fact that nodes can sometimes behave arbitrarily. This includes processes behaving correctly, i.e., according to their specifications; as well as (possibly malicious) processes deviating from their specifications. Note that this does not preclude from capturing the behavior of correct processes because for all event orderings where trigger returns None for an event where the node behaved correctly, there is a similar event ordering, where trigger returns the triggering message at that event. To model that at most f nodes out of n can be faulty we use the exists_at_most_f_faulty assumption, which enforces that trigger returns None at most f nodes.

Moreover, even though non-syntactically valid messages do not trigger events because they are discarded by message boxes, a triggering message could be

---

[7] A Coq type class is essentially a dependent record.

syntactically valid, but have an invalid signature. Therefore, it is up to the programmer to ensure that processes only react to messages with valid signatures using the verify function. Our authenticated_messages_were_sent_non_byz and exists_at_most_f_faulty assumptions presented in Sect. 3.6 are there to constrain trigger to ensure that at most f nodes out of n can diverge from their specifications, for example, by producing valid signatures even though they are not the nodes they claim to be (using leaked keys of other nodes).

Axioms. The following axioms characterize the behavior of these components:

1. Equality between events is decidable. Events are abstract entities that correspond to points in space/time that can be seen as pairs of numbers (one for the space coordinate and one for the time coordinate), for which equality is decidable.
2. The happened before relation is transitive and well-founded. This allows us to prove properties by induction on causal time. We assume here that it is not possible to infinitely go back in time, i.e., that there is a beginning of (causal) time, typically corresponding to the time a system started.
3. The direct predecessor e_2 of e_1 happens at the same location and before e_1. This makes local orderings sub-orderings of the happenedBefore ordering.
4. If an event e does not have a direct predecessor (i.e., e is an initial event) then there is no event happening locally before e.
5. The direct predecessor function is injective, i.e., two different events cannot have the same direct predecessor.
6. If an event e_1 happens locally before e_2 and e is the direct predecessor of e_2, then either $e = e_1$ or e_1 happens before e. From this, it follows that the direct predecessor function can give us the complete local history of an event.

Notation. We use $a \prec b$ to stand for (happenedBefore a b); $a \preceq b$ to stand for $(a \prec b$ or $a=b)$; and $a \sqsubseteq b$ to stand for $(a \preceq b$ and loc $a=$loc $b)$. We also sometimes write EO instead of EventOrdering.

Some functions take an event ordering as a parameter. For readability, we sometimes omit those when they can be inferred from the context. Similarly, we will often omit type declarations of the form $(T : \mathsf{Type})$.

Correct Behavior. To prove properties about distributed systems, one only reasons about processes that have a correct behavior. To do so we only reason about events in event orderings that are correct in the sense that they were triggered by some message:

```
Definition isCorrect (e : Event) := match trigger e with Some m ⇒ True | None ⇒ False end.
Definition arbitrary (e : Event) := ∼ isCorrect e.
```

Next, we characterize correct replica histories as follows: (1) First we say that an event e has a correct trace if all local events prior to e are correct. (2) Then, we say that a node i has a correct trace before some event e, not necessarily happening at i, if all events happening before e at i have a correct trace:

Definition has_correct_bounded_trace $(e : \text{Event}) := \text{forall } e',\ e' \sqsubseteq e \to \text{isCorrect } e'$.
Definition has_correct_trace_before $(e : \text{Event})\ (i : \text{name}) :=$
  forall $e',\ e' \preceq e \to \text{loc } e' = i \to$ has_correct_bounded_trace e'.

3.5 Computational Model

Model. We now present our computational model, which we use when extracting OCaml programs. Unlike in EventML [71] where systems are first specified as *event observers* (abstract processes), and then later refined to executable code, we skip here event observers, and directly specify systems using executable state machines, which essentially consist of an update function and a current state. We define a system of distributed state machines as a function that maps names to state machines. Systems are parametrized by a function that associates state types with names in order to allow for different nodes to run different machines.

Definition Update $S\ I\ O := S \to I \to (\text{option } S * O)$.
Record StateMachine $S\ I\ O := \text{MkSM } \{ \text{ halted : bool; update : Update } S\ I\ O; \text{ state : } S \ \}$.
Definition System $(F : \text{name} \to \text{Type})\ I\ O := \text{forall } (i : \text{name}), \text{StateMachine } (F\ i)\ I\ O$.

where S is the type of the machine's state, I/O are the input/output types, and halted indicates whether the state machine is still running or not.

Let us now discuss how we relate state machines and events. We define state_sm_before_event and state_sm_after_event that compute a machine's state before and after a given event e. These states are computed by extracting the local history of events up to e using direct_pred, and then updating the state machine by running it on the triggering messages of those events. These functions return None if some arbitrary event occurs or the machine halts sometime along the way. Otherwise they return Some s, where s is the state of the machine updated according to the events. Therefore, assuming they return Some amounts to assuming that all events prior to e are correct, i.e., we can prove that if state_sm_after_event $sm\ e = \text{Some } s$ then has_correct_trace_before e (loc e). As illustrated below, we use these functions to adopt a Hoare-like reasoning style by stating pre/post-conditions on the state of a process prior and after some event.

PBFT. We implement PBFT replicas as state machines, which we derive from an update function that dispatches input messages to the corresponding handlers. Finally, we define PBFTsys as the function that associates PBFTsm with replicas and a halted machine with clients (because we do not reason here about clients).

Definition PBFTupdate $(i : \text{Rep}) := \text{fun } state\ msg \Rightarrow \text{match } msg \text{ with}$
  | REQUEST $r \Rightarrow$ PBFThandle_request $i\ state\ r$
  | PREPARE $p \Rightarrow$ PBFThandle_prepare $i\ state\ p \dots$
Definition PBFTsm $(i : \text{Rep}) := \text{MkSM false (PBFTupdate } i)\ (\text{initial\_state } i)$.
Definition PBFTsys $:= \text{fun } name \Rightarrow \text{match } name \text{ with}$
  | PBFTreplica $i \Rightarrow$ PBFTsm i | PBFTclient $c \Rightarrow$ haltedSM end.

Let us illustrate how we reason about state machines through a simple example that shows that they maintain a view that only increases over time. It shows a local property, while Sect. 5 presents the distributed agreement property that makes use of the assumptions presented in Sect. 3.6. As mentioned above we prove such properties for all possible event orderings, which means that they are true for all possible runs of the system. In this lemma, *s1* is the state prior to the event *e*, and *s2* is the state after handling *e*. It does not have pre-conditions, and its post-condition states that the view in *s1* is smaller than the view in *s2*.

```
Lemma current_view_increases : forall (eo : EO) (e : Event) i s1 s2,
    state_sm_before_event (PBFTsm i) e = Some s1
  → state_sm_after_event (PPBFTsm i) e = Some s2
  → current_view s1 ≤ current_view s2.
```

3.6 Assumptions

Model. Let us now turn to the assumptions we make regarding the network and the behavior of correct and faulty nodes.

Assumption 1. Proving safety properties of crash fault-tolerant protocols that only require reasoning about past events, such as agreement, does not require reasoning about faults and faulty replicas. To prove such properties, one merely has to follow the causal chains of events back in time, and if a message is received by a node then it must have been sent by some node that had not crashed at that time. The state of affairs is different when dealing with Byzantine faults.

One issue it that Byzantine nodes can deviate from their specifications or impersonate other nodes. However, BFT protocols are designed in such a way that nodes only react to collections of messages, called *certificates*, that are larger than the number of faults. This means that there is always at least one correct node that can be used to track down causal chains of events.

A second issue is that, in general, we cannot assume that some received message was sent as such by the designated (correct) sender of the message because messages can be manipulated while in flight. As captured by the authenticated_messages_were_sent_or_byz predicate defined below,[8] we can only assume that the authenticated parts of the received message were actually sent by the designated senders, possibly inside larger messages, provided the senders did not leak their keys. As usual, we assume that attackers cannot break the cryptographic primitives, i.e., that they cannot authenticate messages without the proper keys [14].

```
1.Definition authenticated_messages_were_sent_or_byz (P : AbsProcess) :=
2.  forall e (a : auth_data),
3.    In a (bind_op_list get_contained_auth_data (trigger e))
4.    → verify_auth_data (loc e) a (keys e) = true
```

---

[8] For readability, we show a slightly simplified version of this axiom. The full axiom can be found in https://github.com/vrahli/Velisarios/blob/master/model/EventOrdering.v.

5.　　→ exists e', $e' \prec e \wedge$ am_auth $a =$ authenticate (am_data a) (keys e')
6.　　　∧ ((exists dst m,
7.　　　　　In a (get_contained_auth_data m) ∧ In (m, dst) $(P\ eo\ e')$
8.　　　　　∧ data_sender (loc e) (am_data a) = Some (loc e'))
9.　　　　∨
10.　　　　(exists e'',
11.　　　　　$e'' \preceq e' \wedge$ arbitrary $e' \wedge$ arbitrary $e'' \wedge$ got_key_for (loc e) (keys e'') (keys e')
12.　　　　　∧ data_sender (loc e) (am_data a) = Some (loc e''))).

This assumption says that if the authenticated piece of data a is part of the message that triggered some event e (L.3), and a is verified (L.4), then there exists a prior event e' such that the data was authenticated while handling e' using the keys available at that time (L.5). Moreover, (1) either the sender of the data was correct while handling e' and sent the data as part of a message following the process described by P (L.6–8); or (2) the node at which e' occurred was Byzantine at that time, and either it generated the data itself (e.g. when $e''{=}e'$), or it impersonated some other replica (by obtaining the keys that some node leaked at event e'') (L.10–12).

We used a few undefined abstractions in this predicate: An AbsProcess is an abstraction of a process, i.e., a function that returns the collection of messages generated while handling a given event: (forall (eo : EO) (e : Event), list DirectedMsg). The bind_op_list function is wrapped around get_contained_auth_data to handle the fact that trigger might return None, in which case bind_op_list returns nil. The verify_auth_data function takes an authenticated message a and some keys and: (1) invokes data_sender (defined in Sect. 3.3) to extract the expected sender s of a; (2) searches among its keys for a receiving_key that it can use to verify that s indeed authenticated a; and (3) finally verifies the authenticity of a using that key and the verify function. The authenticate function simply calls create and uses the sending keys to create tokens. The got_key_for function takes a name i and two local_keys $lk1$ and $lk2$, and states that the sending keys for i in $lk1$ are all included in $lk2$.

However, it turns out that because we never reason about faulty nodes, we never have to deal with the right disjunct of the above formula. Therefore, this assumption about received messages can be greatly simplified when we know that the sender is a correct replica, which is always the case when we use this assumption because BFT protocols as designed so that there is always a correct node that can be used to track down causal chains of events. We now define the following simpler assumption, which we have proved to be a consequence of authenticated_messages_were_sent_or_byz:

Definition authenticated_messages_were_sent_non_byz (P : AbsProcess) :=
　　forall (e : Event) (a : auth_data) (c : name),
　　　In a (bind_op_list get_contained_auth_data (trigger e))
　　　→ has_correct_trace_before e c
　　　→ verify_auth_data (loc e) a (keys e) = true
　　　→ data_sender (loc e) (am_data a) = Some c
　　　→ exists e' dst m, $e' \prec e \wedge$ loc $e' = c$.
　　　　　∧ am_auth $a =$ authenticate (am_data a) (keys e')
　　　　　∧ In a (get_contained_auth_data m)
　　　　　∧ In (m, dst) $(P\ eo\ e')$

As opposed to the previous formula, this one assumes that the authenticated data was sent by a correct replica, which has a correct trace prior to the event e—the event when the message containing a was handled.

Assumption 2. Because processes need to store their keys to sign and verify messages, we must connect those keys to the ones in the model. We do this through the correct_keys assumption, which states that for each event e, if a process has a correct trace up to e, then the keys (keys e) from the model are the same as the ones stored in its state (which are computed using state_sm_before_event).

Assumption 3. Finally, we present our assumption regarding the number of faulty nodes. There are several ways to state that there can be at most f faulty nodes. One simple definition is (where node is a subset of name as discussed in Sect. 4.2):

```
Definition exists_at_most_f_faulty (E : list Event) (f : nat) :=
  exists (faulty : list node), length faulty ≤ f
    ∧ forall e1 e2, In e2 E → e1 ⪯ e2 → ~ In (loc e1) faulty
        → has_correct_bounded_trace e1.
```

This assumption says that at most f nodes can be faulty by stating that the events happening at nodes that are not in the list of faulty nodes *faulty*, of length f, are correct up to some point characterized by the partial cut E of a given event ordering (i.e., the collection of events happening before those in E).

PBFT Assumption 4. In addition to the ones above, we made further assumptions about PBFT. Replicas sometimes send message hashes instead of sending the entire messages. For example, pre-prepare messages contain client requests, but prepare and commit messages simply contain digests of client requests. Consequently, our PBFT formalization is parametrized by the following *create* and *verify* functions, and we assume that the create function is collision resistant:[9]

```
Class PBFThash := MkPBFThash {
  create_hash : list PBFTmsg → digest; verify_hash : list PBFTmsg → digest → bool; }.
Class PBFThash_axioms := MkPBFThash_axioms {
  create_hash_collision_resistant :
    forall msgs1 msgs2, create_hash msgs1 = create_hash msgs2 → msgs1 = msgs2; }.
```

The version of PBFT, called PBFT-PK in [14], that we implemented relies on digital signatures. However, we did not have to make any more assumptions regarding the cryptographic primitives than the ones presented above, and in particular we did not assume anything that is true about digital signatures and false about MACs. Therefore, our safety proof works when using either digital signatures or MAC vectors. As discussed below, this is true because we adapted the way messages are verified (we have not verified the MAC version of PBFT but a slight variant of PBFT-PK) and because we do not deal with liveness.

---

[9] Note that our current collision resistant assumption is too strong because it is always possible to find two distinct messages that are hashed to the same hash. We leave it to future work to turn it into a more realistic probabilistic assumption.

As Castro showed [14, Chap. 3], PBFT-PK has to be adapted when digital signatures are replaced by MAC vectors. Among other things, it requires "significant and subtle changes to the view change protocol" [14, Sect. 3.2]. Also, to the best of our knowledge, in PBFT-PK backups do not check the authenticity of requests upon receipt of pre-prepares. They only check the authenticity of requests before executing them [14, p. 42]. This works when using digital signatures but not when using MACs: one backup might not execute the request because its part of the MAC vector does not check out, while another backup executes the request because its part of the MAC vector checks out, which would lead to inconsistent states and break safety. Castro lists other problems related to liveness.

Instead, as in the MAC version of PBFT [14, p. 42], in our implementation we always check requests' validity when checking the validity of a pre-prepare. If we were to check the validity of requests only before executing them, we would have to assume that two correct replicas would either both be able to verify the data, or both would not be able to do so. This assumption holds for digital signatures but not for MAC vectors.

4   Methodology

Because distributed systems are all about exchanging information among nodes, we have developed a theory that captures abstractions and reasoning patterns to deal with knowledge dissemination (see Sect. 4.4). In the presence of faulty nodes, one has to ensure that this knowledge is reliable. Fault-tolerant state-machine replication protocols provide such guarantees by relying on certificates, which ensure that we can always get hold of a correct node to trace back information through the system. This requires reasoning about the past, i.e., reasoning by induction on causal time using the happenedBefore relation.

4.1   Automated Inductive Reasoning

We use induction on causal time to prove both distributed and local properties. As discussed here, we automated the typical reasoning pattern we use to prove local properties. As an example, in our PBFT formalization, we proved the following local property: if a replica has a prepare message in its log, then it either received or generated it. Moreover, as for any kinds of programs, using Velisarios we prove local properties about processes by reasoning about all possible paths they can take when reacting upon messages. Thus, a typical proof of such a lemma using Velisarios goes as follows: (1) we go by induction on events; (2) we split the code of a process into all possible execution paths; (3) we prune the paths that could not happen because they invalidate some hypotheses of the lemma being proved; and (4) we automatically prove some other cases by induction hypothesis. We packaged this reasoning as a Coq tactic, which in practice can significantly reduce the number of cases to prove, and used this automation technique to prove local properties of PBFT, such as Castro's A.1.2 local invariants [14]. Because of PBFT's complexity, our Coq tactic typically reduces the number of cases to prove from between 50 to 60 cases down to around 7 cases, sometimes less, as we show in this histogram of goals left to interactively prove after automation:

# of goals left to prove	0	1	2	3	4	5	6	7	8
# of lemmas		8	1	5	4	4	2	9	17	3

4.2 Quorums

As usual, we use quorum theory to trace back correct information between nodes. A (Byzantine) quorum w.r.t. a given set of nodes N, is a subset Q of N, such that $f + 1 \leq (2 * |Q|) - |N|$ (where $|X|$ is the size of X), i.e. every two quorums intersect [59,83] in sufficiently many replicas.[10] Typically, a quorum corresponds to a majority of nodes that agree on some property. In case of state machine replication, quorums are used to ensure that a majority of nodes agree to update the state using the same operation. If we know that two quorums intersect, then we know that both quorums agree, and therefore that the states cannot diverge. In order to reason about quorums, we have proved the following general lemma:[11]

Lemma overlapping_quorums :
    forall (*l1 l2* : NRlist node), exists *Correct*,
        (length *l1* + length *l2*) - num_nodes ≤ length *Correct*
        ∧ subset *Correct l1* ∧ subset *Correct l2* ∧ no_repeats *Correct*.

This lemma implies that if we have two sets of nodes *l1* and *l2* (NRlist ensures that the sets have no repeats), such that the sum of their length is greater than the total number of nodes (num_nodes), there must exist an overlapping subset of nodes (*Correct*). We use this result below in Sect. 4.4.

The node type parameter is the collection of nodes that can participate in quorums. For example, PBFT replicas can participate in quorums but clients cannot. This type comes with a node2name function to convert nodes into names.

4.3 Certificates

Lemmas that require reasoning about several replicas are much more complex than local properties. They typically require reasoning about some information computed by a collection of replicas (such as quorums) that vouch for the information. In PBFT, a collection of $2f + 1$ messages from different replicas is called

---

[10] We use here Castro's notation where quorums are *majority* quorums [79] (also called *write quorums*) that require intersections to be non-empty, as opposed to *read quorums* that are only required to intersect with write quorums [36].

[11] We present here a simplified version for readability.

a *strong (or quorum) certificate*, and a collection of $f+1$ messages from different replicas is called a *weak certificate*.

When working with strong certificates, one typically reasons as follows: (1) Because PBFT requires $3f+1$ replicas, two certificates of size $2f+1$ always intersect in $f+1$ replicas. (2) One message among those $f+1$ messages must be from a correct replica because at most f replicas can be faulty. (3) This correct replica can vouch for the information of both quorums—we use that replica to trace back the corresponding information to the point in space/time where/when it was generated. We will get back to this in Sect. 4.4.

When working with weak certificates, one typically reasons as follows: Because, the certificate has size $f+1$ and there are at most f faulty nodes, there must be one correct replica that can vouch for the information of the certificate.

4.4 Knowledge Theory

Model. Let us now present an excerpt of our distributed epistemic knowledge library. Knowledge is a widely studied concept [10,30,31,37–39,70]. It is often captured using possible-worlds models, which rely on Kripke structures: an agent knows a fact if that fact is true in all possible worlds. For distributed systems, agents are nodes and a possible world at a given node is essentially one that has the same local history as the one of the current world, i.e., it captures the current state of the node. As Halpern stresses, e.g. in [37], such a definition of knowledge is *external* in the sense that it cannot necessarily be computed, though some work has been done towards deriving programs from knowledge-based specifications [10]. We follow a different, more pragmatic and computational approach, and say that a node knows some piece of data if it is stored locally, as opposed to the external and logical notion of knowing facts mentioned above. This computational notion of knowledge relies on exchanging messages to propagate it, which is what is required to derive programs from knowledge-based specifications (i.e., to compute that some knowledge is gained [20,37]).

We now extend the model presented in Sect. 3 with two epistemic modal operators *know* and *learn* that express what it means for a process to know and learn some information, and which bear some resemblance with the *fact discovery* and *fact publication* notions discussed in [38]. Formally, we extend our model with the following parameters, which can be instantiated as many times as needed for all the pieces of known/learned data that one wants to reason about—see below for examples:

```
Class LearnAndKnow := MkLearnAndKnow {
    lak_data : Type;        lak_data2info : lak_data → lak_info;
    lak_info : Type;        lak_know : lak_data → lak_memory → Prop;
    lak_memory : Type;      lak_data2owner : lak_data → node;
                            lak_data2auth : lak_data → auth_data; }.
```

The lak_data type is the type of "raw" data that we have knowledge of; while lak_info is some distinct information that might be shared by different pieces of data. For example, PBFT replicas collect batches of $2f + 1$ (pre-)prepare messages from different replicas, that share the same view, sequence number, and digest. In that case, the (pre-)prepare messages are the raw data that contain the common information consisting of a view, a sequence number, and a digest. The lak_memory type is the type of objects used to store one's knowledge, such as a state machine state. One has to provide a lak_data2info function to extract the information embedded in some piece of data. The lak_know predicate explains what it means to know some piece of data. The lak_data2owner function extracts the "owner" of some piece of data, typically the node that generated the data. In order to authenticate pieces of data, the lak_data2auth function extracts some piece of authenticated data from some piece of raw data. For convenience, we define the following wrapper around lak_data2owner:

Definition lak_data2node (d : lak_data) : name := node2name (lak_data2owner d).

Let us now turn to the two main components of our theory, namely the know and learn epistemic modal operators. These operators provide an abstraction barrier: they allow us to abstract away from *how* knowledge is stored and computed, in order to focus on the mere *fact* that we have that knowledge.

Definition know (sm : node $\rightarrow$ StateMachine lak_memory) (e : Event) (d : lak_data) :=
  exists *mem* i, loc e = node2name i
  $\wedge$ state_sm_after_event ($sm\ i$) e = Some *mem*
  $\wedge$ lak_know d *mem*.

where we simply write (StateMachine S) for a state machine with a state of type S, that takes messages as inputs, and outputs lists of directed messages. This states that the state machine ($sm\ i$) knows the data d at event e if its state is *mem* at e and (lak_know d *mem*) is true. We define learn as follows:

Definition learn (e : Event) (d : lak_data) :=
  exists i, loc e = node2name i
  $\wedge$ In (lak_data2auth d) (bind_op_list get_contained_auth_data (trigger e))
  $\wedge$ verify_auth_data (loc e) (lak_data2auth d) (keys e) = true.

This states that a node learns d at some event e, if e was triggered by a message that contains the data d. Moreover, because we deal with Byzantine faults, we require that to learn some data one has to be able to verify its authenticity.

Next, we define a few predicates that are useful to track down knowledge. The first one is a local predicate that says that for a state machine to know about a piece of information it has to either have learned it or generated it.

Definition learn_or_know (sm : node $\rightarrow$ StateMachine lak_memory) :=
  forall (d : lak_data) (e : Event),
    know $sm\ e\ d \rightarrow$ (exists e', $e' \sqsubseteq e \wedge$ learn $e'\ d$) $\vee$ lak_data2node d = loc e.

The next one is a distributed predicate that states that if one learns some piece of information that is owned by a correct node, then that correct node must have known that piece of information:

Definition learn_if_know (sm : node → StateMachine lak_memory) :=
  forall (d : lak_data) (e : Event),
    (learn e d ∧ has_correct_trace_before e (lak_data2node d))
    → exists e', $e' \prec e$ ∧ loc e' = lak_data2node d ∧ know sm e' d.

Using these two predicates, we have proved this general lemma about knowledge propagating through nodes:

Lemma know_propagates :
  forall (e : Event) (sm : node → StateMachine lak_memory) (d : lak_data),
    (learn_or_know sm ∧ learn_if_know sm)
    → (know sm e d ∧ has_correct_trace_before e (lak_data2node d))
    → exists e', $e' \preceq e$ ∧ loc e' = lak_data2node d ∧ know sm e' d.

This lemma says that, assuming learn_or_know and learn_if_know, if one knows at some event e some data d that is owned by a correct node, then that correct node must have known that data at a prior event e'. We use this lemma to track down information through correct nodes.

As mentioned in Sect. 4.3, when reasoning about distributed systems, one often needs to reason about certificates, i.e., about collections of messages from different sources. In order to capture this, we introduce the following know_certificate predicate, which says that the state machine sm knows the information i at event e if there exists a list l of pieces of data of length at least k (the certificate size) that come from different sources, and such that sm knows each of these pieces of data, and each piece of data carries the common information nfo:

Definition know_certificate (sm : node → StateMachine lak_memory)
        (e : Event) (k : nat) (nfo : lak_info) (P : list lak_data → Prop) :=
  exists (l : list lak_data),
    $k \leq$ length l ∧ no_repeats (map lak_data2owner l) ∧ P l
    ∧ forall d, In d l → (know sm e d ∧ nfo = lak_data2info d).

Using this predicate, we can then combine the quorum and knowledge theories to prove the following lemma, which captures the fact that if there are two quorums for information $nfo1$ (known at $e1$) and $nfo2$ (known at $e2$), and the intersection of the two quorums is guaranteed to contain a correct node, then there must be a correct node (at which $e1'$ and $e2'$ happen) that owns and knows both $nfo1$ and $nfo2$—this lemma follows from know_propagates and overlapping_quorums:

Lemma know_in_intersection :
  forall (sm : node → StateMachine lak_memory) ($e1$ $e2$: Event) ($nfo1$ $nfo2$: lak_info)
        (k f : nat) (P : list lak_data → Prop) (E : list Event),
    (learn_or_know sm ∧ learn_if_know sm)
    → ($k \leq$ num_nodes ∧ num_nodes + f < 2 * k)
    → (exists_at_most_f_faulty E f ∧ In $e1$ E ∧ In $e2$ E)
    → (know_certificate sm $e1$ k $nfo1$ P ∧ know_certificate sm $e2$ k $nfo2$ P)
    → exists $e1'$ $e2'$ $d1$ $d2$, loc $e1'$ = loc $e2'$ ∧ $e1' \preceq e1$ ∧ $e2' \preceq e2$
        ∧ loc $e1'$ = lak_data2node $d1$ ∧ loc $e2'$ = lak_data2node $d2$
        ∧ know sm $e1'$ $d1$ ∧ know sm $e2'$ $d2$
        ∧ $i1$ = lak_data2info $d1$ ∧ $i2$ = lak_data2info $d2$.

Similarly, we proved the following lemma, which captures the fact that there is always a correct replica that can vouch for the information of a weak certificate:

```
Lemma know_weak_certificate :
  forall (e : Event) (k f : nat) (nfo : lak_info) (P : list lak_data → Prop) (E : list Event),
    (f < k ∧ exists_at_most_f_faulty E f ∧ In e E ∧ know_certificate e k nfo P)
  → exists d, has_correct_trace_before e (node2node d) ∧ know e d ∧ nfo = lak_data2info d.
```

PBFT. One of the key lemmas to prove PBFT's safety says that if two correct replicas have prepared some requests with the same sequence and view numbers, then the requests must be the same [14, Inv.A.1.4]. As mentioned in Sect. 2.1, a replica has prepared a request if it received pre-prepare and prepare messages from a quorum of replicas. To prove this lemma, we instantiated LearnAndKnow as follows: lak_data can either be a pre-prepare or a prepare message; lak_info is the type of triples view/sequence number/digest; lak_memory is the type of states maintained by replicas; lak_data2info extracts the view, sequence number and digest contained in pre-prepare and prepare messages; lak_know states that the pre-prepare or prepare message is stored in the state; lak_data2owner extracts the sender of the message; and lak_data2auth is similar to the PBFTget_contained_auth_data function presented in Sect. 3.6. The two predicates learn_or_know and learn_if_know, which we proved using the tactic discussed in Sect. 4.1, are true about this instance of LearnAndKnow. Inv.A.1.4 is then a straightforward consequence of know_in_intersection applied to the two quorums.

5   Verification of PBFT

Agreement. Velisarios is designed as a general, reusable, and extensible framework that can be instantiated to prove the correctness of any BFT protocol. We demonstrated its usability by proving that our PBFT implementation satisfies the standard agreement property, which is the crux of linearizability (we leave linearizability for future work—see Sect. 2.2 for a high-level definition). Agreement states that, regardless of the view, any two replies sent by correct replicas *i1* and *i2* at events *e1* and *e2* for the same timestamp *ts* to the same client *c* contain the same replies. We proved that this is true in any event ordering that satisfies the assumptions from Sect. 3.6:[12]

```
Lemma agreement :
  forall (eo : EventOrdering) (e1 e2 : Event) (v1 v2 : View) (ts : Timestamp)
        (c : Client) (i1 i2 : Rep) (r1 r2 : Request) (a1 a2 : list Token),
    authenticated_messages_were_sent_or_byz_sys eo PBFTsys ∧ correct_keys eo
  → (exists_at_most_f_faulty [e1,e2] f ∧ loc e1 = PBFTreplica i1 ∧ loc e2 = PBFTreplica i2)
  → In (send_reply v1 ts c i1 r1 a1) (output_system_on_event PBFTsys e1)
  → In (send_reply v2 ts c i2 r2 a2) (output_system_on_event PBFTsys e2)
  → r1 = r2.
```

---

[12] See   agreement   in   https://github.com/vrahli/Velisarios/blob/master/PBFT/ PBFTagreement.v.

where Timestamps are nats; authenticated_messages_were_sent_or_byz_sys is defined on systems using authenticated_messages_were_sent_or_byz; the function output_system_on_event is similar to state_sm_after_event (see Sect. 3.5) but returns the outputs of a given state machine at a given event instead of returning its state; and send_reply builds a reply message. To prove this lemma, we proved most of the invariants stated by Castro in [14, Appendix A]. In addition, we proved that if the last executed sequence number of two correct replicas is the same, then these two replicas have, among other things, the same service state.[13]

As mentioned above, because our model is based on LoE, we only ever prove such properties by induction on causal time. Similarly, Castro proved most of his invariants by induction on the length of the executions. However, he used other induction principles to prove some lemmas, such as Inv.A.1.9, which he proved by induction on views [14, p. 151]. This invariant says that prepared requests have to be consistent with the requests sent in pre-prepare messages by the primary. A straightforward induction on causal time was more natural in our setting.

Castro used a simulation method to prove PBFT's safety: he first proved the safety of a version without garbage collection and then proved that the version with garbage collection implements the one without. This requires defining two versions of the protocol. Instead, we directly prove the safety of the one with garbage collection. This involved proving further invariants about stored, received and sent messages, essentially that they are always within the water marks.

Proof Effort. In terms of proof effort, developing Velisarios and verifying PBFT's agreement property took us around 1 person year. Our generic Velisarios framework consists of around 4000 lines of specifications and around 4000 lines of proofs. Our verified implementation of PBFT consists of around 20000 lines of specifications and around 22000 lines of proofs.

6   Extraction and Evaluation

Extraction. To evaluate our PBFT implementation (i.e., PBFTsys defined in Sect. 3.5—a collection of state machines), we generate OCaml code using Coq's extraction mechanism. Most parameters, such as the number of tolerated faults, are instantiated before extraction. Note that not all parameters need to be instantiated. For example, as mentioned in Sect. 3.1, neither do we instantiate event orderings, nor do we instantiate our assumptions (such as exists_at_most_f_faulty), because they are not used in the code but are only used to prove that properties are true about all possible runs. Also, keys, signatures, and digests are only instantiated by stubs in Coq. We replace those stubs when extracting OCaml code by implementations provided by the nocrypto [66] library, which is the cryptographic library we use to hash, sign, and verify messages (we use RSA).

---

[13] See same_states_if_same_next_to_execute in https://github.com/vrahli/Velisarios/blob/master/PBFT/PBFTsame_states.v.

Evaluation. To run the extracted code in a real distributed environment, we implemented a small trusted runtime environment in OCaml that uses the Async library [5] to handle sender/receiver threads. We show among other things here that the average latency of our implementation is acceptable compared to the state of the art BFT-SMaRt [8] library. Note that because we do not offer a new protocol, but essentially a re-implementation of PBFT, we expect that on average the scale will be similar in other execution scenarios such as the ones studied by Castro in [14]. We ran our experiments using desktops with 16 GB of memory, and 8 i7-6700 cores running at 3.40 GHz. We report some of our experiments where we used a single client, and a simple state machine where the state is a number, and an operation is either adding or subtracting some value.

We ran a local simulation to measure the performance of our PBFT implementation without network and signatures: when 1 client sends 1 million requests, it takes on average $27.6\,\mu s$ for the client to receive $f + 1$ ($f = 1$) replies.

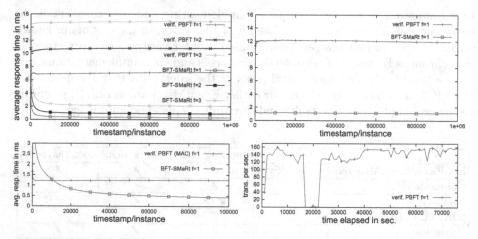

Fig. 3. (1) Single machine (top/left); (2) several machines (top/right); (3) single machine using MACs (bottom/left); (4) view change response time (bottom/right)

Top/left of Fig. 3 shows the experiment where we varied f from 1 to 3, and replicas sent messages, signed using RSA, through sockets, but on a single machine. As mentioned above, we implemented the digital signature-based version of PBFT, while BFT-SMaRt uses a more efficient MAC-based authentication scheme, which in part explains why BFT-SMaRt is around one order of magnitude faster than our implementation. As in [14, Table 8.9], we expect a similar improvement when using the more involved, and as of yet not formally verified, MAC-based version of PBFT (bottom/left of Fig. 3 shows the average response time when replacing digital signatures by MACs, without adapting the rest of the protocol). Top/right of Fig. 3 presents results when running our version of PBFT and BFT-SMaRt on several machines, for $f = 1$. Finally, bottom/right of Fig. 3 shows the response time of our view-change protocol. In this experiment, we killed the primary after 16 s of execution, and it took around 7 s for the system to recover.

Trusted Computing Base. The TCB of our system includes: (1) the fact that our LoE model faithfully reflects the behavior of distributed systems (see Sect. 3.4); (2) the validity of our assumptions: authenticated_messages_were_sent_or_byz; exists_at_most_f_faulty; correct_keys; and create_hash_collision_resistant (Sect. 3.6); (3) Coq's logic and implementation; (4) OCaml and the nocrypto and Async libraries we use in our runtime environment, and the runtime environment itself (Sect. 6); (5) the hardware and software on which our framework is running.

7   Related Work

Our framework is not the first one for implementing and reasoning about the correctness of distributed systems (see Fig. 4). However, to the best of our knowledge, (1) it is the first theorem prover based tool for verifying the correctness of asynchronous Byzantine fault-tolerant protocols and their implementations; and (2) we provide the first mechanical proof of the safety of a PBFT implementation. Velisarios has evolved from our earlier EventML framework [71], primarily to reason about Byzantine faults and distributed epistemic knowledge.

	Running code	Byz. (synch.)	Byz. (asynch.)
IronFleet/EventML/Verdi/Disel/PSync	✓	✗	✗
HO-model/PVS	✗	✓	✗
Event-B	✓/✗	✓	✗
IOA/TLA⁺/ByMC	✗	✓	✓
Velisarios	✓	✓	✓

Fig. 4. Comparison with related work

7.1   Logics and Models

IOA [33–35,78] is the model used by Castro [14] to prove PBFT's safety. It is a programming/specification language for describing asynchronous distributed systems as I/O automata [58] (labeled state transition systems) and stating their properties. While IOA is state-based, the logic we use in this paper is event-based. IOA can interact with a large range of tools such as type checkers, simulators, model checkers, theorem provers, and there is support for synthesis of Java code [78]. In contrast, our methodology allows us to both implement and verify protocols within the same tool, namely Coq.

TLA$^+$ [24,51] is a language for specifying and reasoning about systems. It combines: (1) TLA [52], which is a temporal logic for describing systems [51], and (2) set theory, to specify data structures. TLAPS [24] uses a collection of theorem provers, proof assistants, SMT solvers, and decision procedures to mechanically check TLA proofs. Model checker integration helps catch errors before verification attempts. TLA$^+$ has been used in a large number of projects (e.g., [12,18,44,56,63,64]) including proofs of safety and liveness of Multi-Paxos [18], and safety of a variant of an abstract model of PBFT [13]. To the best of our knowledge, TLA$^+$ does not perform program synthesis.

The Heard-Of (HO) Model [23] requires processes to execute in lock-step through rounds into which the distributed algorithms are divided. Asynchronous fault-tolerant systems are treated as synchronous systems with adversarial environments that cause messages to be dropped. The HO-model was implemented in Isabelle/HOL [22] and used, for example, to verify the EIGByz [7] Byzantine agreement algorithm for synchronous systems with reliable links. This formalization uses the notion of *global state of the system* [19], while our approach relies on Lamport's *happened before* relation [53], which does not require reasoning about a distributed system as a single entity (a global state). Model checking and the HO-model were also used in [21,80,81] for verifying the crash fault-tolerant consensus algorithms presented in [23]. To the best of our knowledge, there is no tool that allows generating code from algorithms specified using the HO-model.

Event-B [1] is a set-theory-based language for modeling reactive systems and for *refining* high-level abstract specifications into low-level concrete ones. It supports code generation [32,61], with some limitations (not all features are covered). The Rodin [2] platform for Event-B provides support for refinement, and automated and interactive theorem proving. Both have been used in a number of projects, such as: to prove the safety and liveness of self-$\star$ systems [4]; to prove the agreement and validity properties of the synchronous crash-tolerant Floodset consensus algorithm [57]; and to prove the agreement and validity of synchronous Byzantine agreement algorithms [50]. In [50], the authors assume that messages cannot be forged (using PBFT, at most f nodes can forge messages), and do not verify implementations of these algorithms.

7.2 Tools

Verdi [85,86] is a framework to develop and reason about distributed systems using Coq. As in our framework, Verdi leaves no gaps between verified and running code. Instead, OCaml code is extracted directly from the verified Coq implementation. Verdi provides a compositional way of specifying distributed systems. This is done by applying *verified system transformers*. For example, Raft [67]—an alternative to Paxos—transforms a distributed system into a crash-tolerant one. One difference between our respective methods is that they verify a system by reasoning about the evolution of its global state, while we use Lamport's happened before relation. Moreover, they do not deal with the full spectrum of arbitrary faults (e.g., malicious faults).

Disel [75,84] is a verification framework that implements a separation-style program logic, and that enables compositional verification of distributed systems.

IronFleet [40,41] is a framework for building and reasoning about distributed systems using Dafny [55] and the Z3 theorem prover [62]. Because systems are both implemented in and verified using Dafny, IronFleet also prevents gaps between running and verified code. It uses a combination of TLA-style state-machine refinements [51] to reason about the distributed aspects of protocols, and Floyd-Hoare-style imperative verification techniques to reason about local behavior. The authors have implemented, among other things, the Paxos-based state machine replication library IronRSL, and verified its safety and liveness.

PSync [28] is a domain specific language embedded in Scala, that enables executing and verifying fault-tolerant distributed algorithms in synchronous and partially asynchronous networks. PSync is based on the HO-model, and has been used to implement several crash fault-tolerant algorithms. Similar to the Verdi framework, PSync makes use of a notion of global state and supports reasoning based on the multi-sorted first-order *Consensus verification logic* (CL) [27]. To prove safety, users have to provide invariants, which CL checks for validity. Unlike Verdi, IronFleet and PSync, we focus on Byzantine faults.

ByMC is a model checker for verifying safety and liveness of fault-tolerant distributed algorithms [47–49]. It applies an automated method for model checking parametrized threshold-guarded distributed algorithms (e.g., processes waiting for messages from a majority of distinct senders). ByMC is based on a short counter-example property, which says that if a distributed algorithm violates a temporal specification then there is a counterexample whose length is bounded and independent of the parameters (e.g. the number of tolerated faults).

Ivy [69] allows debugging infinite-state systems using bounded verification, and formally verifying their safety by gradually building universally quantified inductive invariants. To the best of our knowledge, Ivy does not support faults.

Actor Services [77] allows verifying the distributed and functional properties of programs communicating via asynchronous message passing at the level of the source code (they use a simple Java-like language). It supports modular reasoning and proving liveness. To the best of our knowledge, it does not deal with faults.

PVS has been extensively used for verification of synchronous systems that tolerate malicious faults such as in [74], to the extent that its design was influenced by these verification efforts [68].

8   Conclusions and Future Work

We introduced Velisarios, a framework to implement and reason about BFT-SMR protocols using the Coq theorem prover, and described a methodology based on learn/know epistemic modal operators. We used this framework to prove the safety of a complex system, namely Castro's PBFT protocol. In the future, we plan to also tackle liveness/timeliness. Indeed, proving the safety of a distributed system is far from being enough: a protocol that does not run (which is not live) is useless. Following the same line of reasoning, we want to tackle timeliness because, for real world systems, it is not enough to prove that a system will *eventually reply*. One often desires that the system replies in a timely fashion.

References

1. Abrial, J.-R.: Modeling in Event-B - System and Software Engineering. Cambridge University Press, Cambridge (2010)
2. Abrial, J.-R., Butler, M.J., Hallerstede, S., Hoang, T.S., Mehta, F., Voisin, L.: Rodin: an open toolset for modelling and reasoning in Event-B. STTT **12**(6), 447–466 (2010)
3. Anand, A., Knepper, R.: ROSCoq: robots powered by constructive reals. In: Urban, C., Zhang, X. (eds.) ITP 2015. LNCS, vol. 9236, pp. 34–50. Springer, Cham (2015). https://doi.org/10.1007/978-3-319-22102-1_3
4. Andriamiarina, M.B., Méry, D., Singh, N.K.: Analysis of self-⋆ and P2P systems using refinement. In: Ait Ameur, Y., Schewe, K.D. (eds.) ABZ 2014. LNCS, vol. 8477, pp. 117–123. Springer, Heidelberg (2014). https://doi.org/10.1007/978-3-662-43652-3_9
5. Async. https://janestreet.github.io/guide-async.html
6. Aublin, P.-L., Mokhtar, S.B., Qéuma, V.: RBFT: redundant Byzantine fault tolerance. In: ICDCS 2013, pp. 297–306. IEEE Computer Society (2013)
7. Bar-Noy, A., Dolev, D., Dwork, C., Raymond Strong, H.: Shifting gears: changing algorithms on the fly to expedite Byzantine agreement. Inf. Comput. **97**(2), 205–233 (1992)
8. Bessani, A.N., Sousa, J., Alchieri, E.A.P.: State machine replication for the masses with BFT-SMART. In: DSN 2014, pp. 355–362. IEEE (2014)
9. Bickford, M.: Component specification using event classes. In: Lewis, G.A., Poernomo, I., Hofmeister, C. (eds.) CBSE 2009. LNCS, vol. 5582, pp. 140–155. Springer, Heidelberg (2009). https://doi.org/10.1007/978-3-642-02414-6_9
10. Bickford, M., Constable, R.C., Halpern, J.Y., Petride, S.: Knowledge-based synthesis of distributed systems using event structures. In: Baader, F., Voronkov, A. (eds.) LPAR 2005. LNCS (LNAI), vol. 3452, pp. 449–465. Springer, Heidelberg (2005). https://doi.org/10.1007/978-3-540-32275-7_30
11. Bickford, M., Constable, R.L., Rahli, V.: Logic of events, a framework to reason about distributed systems. In: Languages for Distributed Algorithms Workshop (2012)
12. Bolosky, W.J., Douceur, J.R., Howell, J.: The Farsite project: a retrospective. Oper. Syst. Rev. **41**(2), 17–26 (2007)
13. Mechanically Checked Safety Proof of a Byzantine Paxos Algorithm. http://lamport.azurewebsites.net/tla/byzpaxos.html
14. Castro, M.: Practical Byzantine Fault Tolerance. Also as Technical report MIT-LCS-TR-817. Ph.D. MIT, January 2001
15. Castro, M., Liskov, B.: A correctness proof for a practical Byzantine-fault-tolerant replication algorithm. Technical Memo MIT-LCS-TM-590. MIT, June 1999

16. Castro, M., Liskov, B.: Practical Byzantine fault tolerance. In: OSDI 1999, pp. 173–186. USENIX Association (1999)
17. Castro, M., Liskov, B.: Practical Byzantine fault tolerance and proactive recovery. ACM Trans. Comput. Syst. **20**(4), 398–461 (2002)
18. Chand, S., Liu, Y.A., Stoller, S.D.: Formal verification of multi-paxos for distributed consensus. In: Fitzgerald, J., Heitmeyer, C., Gnesi, S., Philippou, A. (eds.) FM 2016. LNCS, vol. 9995, pp. 119–136. Springer, Cham (2016). https://doi.org/10.1007/978-3-319-48989-6_8
19. Mani Chandy, K., Lamport, L.: Distributed snapshots: determining global states of distributed systems. ACM Trans. Comput. Syst. **3**(1), 63–75 (1985)
20. Mani Chandy, K., Misra, J.: How processes learn. Distrib. Comput. **1**(1), 40–52 (1986)
21. Chaouch-Saad, M., Charron-Bost, B., Merz, S.: A reduction theorem for the verification of round-based distributed algorithms. In: Bournez, O., Potapov, I. (eds.) RP 2009. LNCS, vol. 5797, pp. 93–106. Springer, Heidelberg (2009). https://doi.org/10.1007/978-3-642-04420-5_10
22. Charron-Bost, B., Debrat, H., Merz, S.: Formal verification of consensus algorithms tolerating malicious faults. In: Défago, X., Petit, F., Villain, V. (eds.) SSS 2011. LNCS, vol. 6976, pp. 120–134. Springer, Heidelberg (2011). https://doi.org/10.1007/978-3-642-24550-3_11
23. Charron-Bost, B., Schiper, A.: The Heard-Of model: computing in distributed systems with benign faults. Distrib. Comput. **22**(1), 49–71 (2009)
24. Chaudhuri, K., Doligez, D., Lamport, L., Merz, S.: Verifying safety properties with the TLA$^+$ proof system. In: Giesl, J., Hähnle, R. (eds.) IJCAR 2010. LNCS (LNAI), vol. 6173, pp. 142–148. Springer, Heidelberg (2010). https://doi.org/10.1007/978-3-642-14203-1_12
25. The Coq Proof Assistant. http://coq.inria.fr/
26. Distler, T., Cachin, C., Kapitza, R.: Resource-efficient Byzantine fault tolerance. IEEE Trans. Comput. **65**(9), 2807–2819 (2016)
27. Drăgoi, C., Henzinger, T.A., Veith, H., Widder, J., Zufferey, D.: A logic-based framework for verifying consensus algorithms. In: McMillan, K.L., Rival, X. (eds.) VMCAI 2014. LNCS, vol. 8318, pp. 161–181. Springer, Heidelberg (2014). https://doi.org/10.1007/978-3-642-54013-4_10
28. Dragoi, C., Henzinger, T.A., Zufferey, D.: PSync: a partially synchronous language for fault-tolerant distributed algorithms. In: POPL 2016, pp. 400–415. ACM (2016)
29. Dragoi, C., Henzinger, T.A., Zufferey, D.: The need for language support for fault-tolerant distributed systems. In: SNAPL 2015. LIPIcs, vol. 32, pp. 90–102. Schloss Dagstuhl - Leibniz-Zentrum fuerInformatik (2015)
30. Dwork, C., Moses, Y.: Knowledge and common knowledge in a Byzantine environment: crash failures. Inf. Comput. **88**(2), 156–186 (1990)
31. Fagin, R., Halpern, J.Y., Moses, Y., Vardi, M.Y.: Knowledge-based programs. Distrib. Comput. **10**(4), 199–225 (1997)
32. Fürst, A., Hoang, T.S., Basin, D., Desai, K., Sato, N., Miyazaki, K.: Code generation for Event-B. In: Albert, E., Sekerinski, E. (eds.) IFM 2014. LNCS, vol. 8739, pp. 323–338. Springer, Cham (2014). https://doi.org/10.1007/978-3-319-10181-1_20
33. Garland, S., Lynch, N., Tauber, J., Vaziri, M.: IOA user guide and reference manual. Technical report MIT/LCS/TR-961. Laboratory for Computer Science, Massachusetts Institute of Technology, Cambridge, MA (2004)

34. Garland, S.J., Lynch, N.: Using I/O automata for developing distributed systems. In: Foundations of Component Based Systems, pp. 285–312. Cambridge University Press, New York (2000)
35. Georgiou, C., Lynch, N., Mavrommatis, P., Tauber, J.A.: Automated implementation of complex distributed algorithms specified in the IOA language. Int. J. Softw. Tools Technol. Transf. **11**, 153–171 (2009)
36. Gifford, D.K.: Weighted voting for replicated data. In: SOSP 1979, pp. 150–162. ACM (1979)
37. Halpern, J.Y.: Using reasoning about knowledge to analyze distributed systems. Ann. Rev. Comput. Sci. **2**(1), 37–68 (1987). https://doi.org/10.1146/annurev.cs.02.060187.000345
38. Halpern, J.Y., Moses, Y.: Knowledge and common knowledge in a distributed environment. J. ACM **37**(3), 549–587 (1990)
39. Halpern, J.Y., Zuck, L.D.: A little knowledge goes a long way: knowledge-based derivations and correctness proofs for a family of protocols. J. ACM **39**(3), 449–478 (1992)
40. Hawblitzel, C., Howell, J., Kapritsos, M., Lorch, J.R., Parno, B., Roberts, M.L., Setty, S.T.V., Zill, B.: IronFleet: proving practical distributed systems correct. In: SOSP 2015, pp. 1–17. ACM (2015)
41. Hawblitzel, C., Howell, J., Kapritsos, M., Lorch, J.R., Parno, B., Roberts, M.L., Setty, S.T.V., Zill, B.: IronFleet: proving safety and liveness of practical distributed systems. Commun. ACM **60**(7), 83–92 (2017)
42. Herlihy, M., Wing, J.M.: Axioms for concurrent objects. In: POPL 1987, pp. 13–26. ACM Press (1987)
43. Jajodia, S., Ghosh, A.K., Swarup, V., Wang, C., Wang, X.S.: Moving Target Defense - Creating Asymmetric Uncertainty for Cyber Threats. Advances in Information Security, vol. 54. Springer, New York (2011). https://doi.org/10.1007/978-1-4614-0977-9
44. Joshi, R., Lamport, L., Matthews, J., Tasiran, S., Tuttle, M.R., Yuan, Y.: Checking cache-coherence protocols with TLA$^+$. Formal Methods Syst. Des. **22**(2), 125–131 (2003)
45. Kapitza, R., Behl, J., Cachin, C., Distler, T., Kuhnle, S., Mohammadi, S.V., Schröder-Preikschat, W., Stengel, K.: CheapBFT: resource-efficient Byzantine fault tolerance. In: EuroSys 2012, pp. 295–308. ACM (2012)
46. Kokoris-Kogias, E., Jovanovic, P., Gailly, N., Khoffi, I., Gasser, L., Ford, B.: Enhancing Bitcoin security and performance with strong consistency via collective signing. In: USENIX Security Symposium, pp. 279–296. USENIX Association (2016)
47. Konnov, I.V., Lazic, M., Veith, H., Widder, J.: A short counterexample property for safety and liveness verification of fault-tolerant distributed algorithms. In: POPL 2017, pp. 719–734. ACM (2017)
48. Konnov, I.V., Veith, H., Widder, J.: On the completeness of bounded model checking for threshold-based distributed algorithms: reachability. Inf. Comput. **252**, 95–109 (2017)
49. Konnov, I., Veith, H., Widder, J.: SMT and POR beat counter abstraction: parameterized model checking of threshold-based distributed algorithms. In: Kroening, D., Păsăreanu, C.S. (eds.) CAV 2015, Part I. LNCS, vol. 9206, pp. 85–102. Springer, Cham (2015). https://doi.org/10.1007/978-3-319-21690-4_6
50. Krenický, R., Ulbrich, M.: Deductive verification of a Byzantine agreement protocol. Technical report 2010-7. Karlsruhe Institute of Technology, Department of Computer Science (2010)

51. Lamport, L.: Specifying Systems: The TLA+ Language and Tools for Hardware and Software Engineers. Addison-Wesley, Boston (2004)
52. Lamport, L.: The temporal logic of actions. ACM Trans. Program. Lang. Syst. 16(3), 872–923 (1994)
53. Lamport, L.: Time, clocks, and the ordering of events in a distributed system. Commun. ACM 21(7), 558–565 (1978)
54. Lamport, L., Shostak, R.E., Pease, M.C.: The Byzantine generals problem. ACM Trans. Program. Lang. Syst. 4(3), 382–401 (1982)
55. Leino, K.R.M.: Dafny: an automatic program verifier for functional correctness. In: Clarke, E.M., Voronkov, A. (eds.) LPAR-16. LNCS (LNAI), vol. 6355, pp. 348–370. Springer, Heidelberg (2010). https://doi.org/10.1007/978-3-642-17511-4_20
56. Lu, T., Merz, S., Weidenbach, C.: Towards verification of the pastry protocol using TLA+. In: Bruni, R., Dingel, J. (eds.) FMOODS/FORTE 2011. LNCS, vol. 6722, pp. 244–258. Springer, Heidelberg (2011). https://doi.org/10.1007/978-3-642-21461-5_16
57. Lynch, N.A.: Distributed Algorithms. Morgan Kaufmann, San Francisco (1996)
58. Lynch, N.A., Tuttle, M.R.: Hierarchical correctness proofs for distributed algorithms. In: PODC 1987, pp. 137–151. ACM (1987)
59. Malkhi, D., Reiter, M.K.: Byzantine quorum systems. In: STOC 1997, pp. 569–578. ACM (1997)
60. Mattern, F.: Virtual time and global states of distributed systems. In: Proceedings of the Workshop on Parallel and Distributed Algorithms, pp. 215–226. North-Holland/Elsevier (1989). Reprinted. In: Yang, Z., Marsland, T.A. (eds.) Global States and Time in Distributed Systems, pp. 123–133. IEEE (1994)
61. Méry, D., Singh, N.K.: Automatic code generation from event-B models. In: Symposium on Information and Communication Technology, SoICT 2011, pp. 179–188. ACM (2011)
62. de Moura, L., Bjørner, N.: Z3: an efficient SMT solver. In: Ramakrishnan, C.R., Rehof, J. (eds.) TACAS 2008. LNCS, vol. 4963, pp. 337–340. Springer, Heidelberg (2008). https://doi.org/10.1007/978-3-540-78800-3_24
63. Newcombe, C.: Why Amazon chose TLA+. In: Ait Ameur, Y., Schewe, K.D. (eds.) ABZ 2014. LNCS, vol. 8477, pp. 25–39. Springer, Heidelberg (2014). https://doi.org/10.1007/978-3-662-43652-3_3
64. Newcombe, C., Rath, T., Zhang, F., Munteanu, B., Brooker, M., Deardeuff, M.: How Amazon web services uses formal methods. Commun. ACM 58(4), 66–73 (2015)
65. Nielsen, M., Plotkin, G.D., Winskel, G.: Petri Nets, event structures and domains, Part I. Theor. Comput. Sci. 13, 85–108 (1981)
66. nocrypto. https://github.com/mirleft/ocaml-nocrypto
67. Ongaro, D., Ousterhout, J.K.: In search of an understandable consensus algorithm. In: 2014 USENIX Annual Technical Conference, USENIX ATC 2014, Philadelphia, PA, USA, 19–20 June 2014, pp. 305–319. USENIX Association (2014)
68. Owre, S., Rushby, J.M., Shankar, N., von Henke, F.W.: Formal verification for fault-tolerant architectures: prolegomena to the design of PVS. IEEE Trans. Softw. Eng. 21(2), 107–125 (1995)
69. Padon, O., McMillan, K.L., Panda, A., Sagiv, M., Shoham, S.: Ivy: safety verification by interactive generalization. In: PLDI 2016, pp. 614–630. ACM (2016)
70. Panangaden, P., Taylor, K.: Concurrent common knowledge: defining agreement for asynchronous systems. Distrib. Comput. 6(2), 73–93 (1992)

71. Rahli, V., Guaspari, D., Bickford, M., Constable, R.L.: EventML: Specification, verification, and implementation of crash-tolerant state machine replication systems. In: SCP (2017)
72. Roscoe, A.W., Hoare, C.A.R., Bird, R.: The Theory and Practice of Concurrency. Prentice Hall PTR, Upper Saddle River (1997)
73. Schiper, N., Rahli, V., van Renesse, R., Bickford, M., Constable, R.L.: Developing correctly replicated databases using formal tools. In: DSN 2014, pp. 395–406. IEEE (2014)
74. Schmid, U., Weiss, B., Rushby, J.M.: Formally verified Byzantine agreement in presence of link faults. In: ICDCS, pp. 608–616 (2002)
75. Sergey, I., Wilcox, J.R., Tatlock, Z.: Programming and proving with distributed protocols. In: POPL 2018 (2018)
76. Sousa, P.: Proactive resilience. Ph.D. thesis. Faculty of Sciences, University of Lisbon, Lisbon, May 2007
77. Summers, A.J., Müller, P.: Actor services. In: Thiemann, P. (ed.) ESOP 2016. LNCS, vol. 9632, pp. 699–726. Springer, Heidelberg (2016). https://doi.org/10.1007/978-3-662-49498-1_27
78. Tauber, J.A.: Verifiable compilation of I/O automata without global synchronization. Ph.D. thesis. Department of Electrical Engineering and Computer Science, Massachusetts Institute of Technology, Cambridge, MA (2004)
79. Thomas, R.H.: A majority consensus approach to concurrency control for multiple copy databases. ACM Trans. Database Syst. **4**(2), 180–209 (1979)
80. Tsuchiya, T., Schiper, A.: Model checking of consensus algorithm. In: SRDS 2007, pp. 137–148. IEEE Computer Society (2007)
81. Tsuchiya, T., Schiper, A.: Using bounded model checking to verify consensus algorithms. In: Taubenfeld, G. (ed.) DISC 2008. LNCS, vol. 5218, pp. 466–480. Springer, Heidelberg (2008). https://doi.org/10.1007/978-3-540-87779-0_32
82. Veronese, G.S., Correia, M., Bessani, A.N., Lung, L.C., Veríssimo, P.: Efficient Byzantine fault-tolerance. IEEE Trans. Comput. **62**(1), 16–30 (2013)
83. Vukolic, M.: The origin of quorum systems. Bull. EATCS **101**, 125–147 (2010)
84. Wilcox, J.R., Sergey, I., Tatlock, Z.: Programming language abstractions for modularly verified distributed systems. In: SNAPL 2017. LIPIcs, vol. 71, pp. 19:1–19:12. Schloss Dagstuhl - Leibniz-Zentrum fuer Informatik (2017)
85. Wilcox, J.R., Woos, D., Panchekha, P., Tatlock, Z., Wang, X., Ernst, M.D., Anderson, T.E.: Verdi: a framework for implementing and formally verifying distributed systems. In: PLDI 2015, pp. 357–368. ACM (2015)
86. Woos, D., Wilcox, J.R., Anton, S., Tatlock, Z., Ernst, M.D., Anderson, T.E.: Planning for change in a formal verification of the raft consensus protocol. In: CPP 2016, pp. 154–165. ACM (2016)

Program Analysis and Automated Verification

Evaluating Design Tradeoffs in Numeric Static Analysis for Java

Shiyi Wei[1(✉)], Piotr Mardziel[2], Andrew Ruef[3], Jeffrey S. Foster[3],
and Michael Hicks[3]

[1] The University of Texas at Dallas, Richardson, USA
swei@utdallas.edu
[2] Carnegie Mellon University, Moffett Field, USA
piotrm@gmail.com
[3] University of Maryland, College Park, USA
{awruef,jfoster,mwh}@cs.umd.edu

Abstract. Numeric static analysis for Java has a broad range of potentially useful applications, including array bounds checking and resource usage estimation. However, designing a scalable numeric static analysis for real-world Java programs presents a multitude of design choices, each of which may interact with others. For example, an analysis could handle method calls via either a top-down or bottom-up interprocedural analysis. Moreover, this choice could interact with how we choose to represent aliasing in the heap and/or whether we use a relational numeric domain, e.g., convex polyhedra. In this paper, we present a family of abstract interpretation-based numeric static analyses for Java and systematically evaluate the impact of 162 analysis configurations on the DaCapo benchmark suite. Our experiment considered the precision and performance of the analyses for discharging array bounds checks. We found that top-down analysis is generally a better choice than bottom-up analysis, and that using access paths to describe heap objects is better than using summary objects corresponding to points-to analysis locations. Moreover, these two choices are the most significant, while choices about the numeric domain, representation of abstract objects, and context-sensitivity make much less difference to the precision/performance tradeoff.

1 Introduction

Static analysis of numeric program properties has a broad range of useful applications. Such analyses can potentially detect array bounds errors [50], analyze a program's resource usage [28,30], detect side channels [8,11], and discover vectors for denial of service attacks [10,26].

One of the major approaches to numeric static analysis is abstract interpretation [18], in which program statements are evaluated over an abstract domain until a fixed point is reached. Indeed, the first paper on abstract interpretation [18] used numeric intervals as one example abstract domain,

© The Author(s) 2018
A. Ahmed (Ed.): ESOP 2018, LNCS 10801, pp. 653–682, 2018.
https://doi.org/10.1007/978-3-319-89884-1_23

and many subsequent researchers have explored abstract interpretation-based numeric static analysis [13, 22–25, 31].

Despite this long history, applying abstract interpretation to real-world Java programs remains a challenge. Such programs are large, have many interacting methods, and make heavy use of heap-allocated objects. In considering how to build an analysis that aims to be sound but also precise, prior work has explored some of these challenges, but not all of them together. For example, several works have considered the impact of the choice of numeric domain (e.g., intervals vs. convex polyhedra) in trading off precision for performance but not considered other tradeoffs [24, 38]. Other works have considered how to integrate a numeric domain with analysis of the heap, but unsoundly model method calls [25] and/or focus on very precise properties that do not scale beyond small programs [23, 24]. Some scalability can be recovered by using programmer-specified pre- and post-conditions [22]. In all of these cases, there is a lack of consideration of the broader design space in which many implementation choices interact. (Sect. 7 considers prior work in detail.)

In this paper, we describe and then systematically explore a large design space of fully automated, abstract interpretation-based numeric static analyses for Java. Each analysis is identified by a choice of five configurable options—the numeric domain, the heap abstraction, the object representation, the interprocedural analysis order, and the level of context sensitivity. In total, we study 162 analysis configurations to asses both how individual configuration options perform overall and to study interactions between different options. To our knowledge, our basic analysis is one of the few fully automated numeric static analyses for Java, and we do not know of any prior work that has studied such a large static analysis design space.

We selected analysis configuration options that are well-known in the static analysis literature and that are key choices in designing a Java static analysis. For the numeric domain, we considered both intervals [17] and convex polyhedra [19], as these are popular and bookend the precision/performance spectrum. (See Sect. 2.)

Modeling the flow of data through the heap requires handling pointers and aliasing. We consider three different choices of *heap abstraction*: using *summary objects* [25, 27], which are *weakly updated*, to summarize multiple heap locations; *access paths* [21, 52], which are *strongly updated*; and a combination of the two.

To implement these abstractions, we use an ahead-of-time, global *points-to analysis* [44], which maps static/local variables and heap-allocated fields to abstract objects. We explore three variants of *abstract object representation*: the standard *allocation-site abstraction* (the most precise) in which each syntactic **new** in the program represents an abstract object; *class-based abstraction* (the least precise) in which each class represents all instances of that class; and a *smushed string abstraction* (intermediate precision) which is the same as allocation-site abstraction except strings are modeled using a class-based abstraction [9]. (See Sect. 3.)

We compare three choices in the *interprocedural analysis order* we use to model method calls: *top-down analysis*, which starts with `main` and analyzes callees as they are encountered; and *bottom-up analysis*, which starts at the leaves of the call tree and instantiates method summaries at call sites; and a hybrid analysis that is bottom-up for library methods and top-down for application code. In general, top-down analysis explores fewer methods, but it may analyze callees multiple times. Bottom-up analysis explores each method once but needs to create summaries, which can be expensive.

Finally, we compare three kinds of *context-sensitivity* in the points-to analysis: *context-insensitive* analysis, *1-CFA analysis* [46] in which one level of calling context is used to discriminate pointers, and *type-sensitive analysis* [49] in which the type of the receiver is the context. (See Sect. 4.)

We implemented our analysis using WALA [2] for its intermediate representation and points-to analyses and either APRON [33, 41] or ELINA [47, 48] for the interval or polyhedral, respectively, numeric domain. We then applied all 162 analysis configurations to the DaCapo benchmark suite [6], using the numeric analysis to try to prove array accesses are within bounds. We measured the analyses' performance and the number of array bounds checks they discharged. We analyzed our results by using a multiple linear regression over analysis features and outcomes, and by performing data visualizations.

We studied three research questions. First, we examined how analysis configuration affects performance. We found that using summary objects causes significant slowdowns, e.g., the vast majority of the analysis runs that timed out used summary objects. We also found that polyhedral analysis incurs a significant slowdown, but only half as much as summary objects. Surprisingly, bottom-up analysis provided little performance advantage generally, though it did provide some benefit for particular object representations. Finally, context-insensitive analysis is faster than context-sensitive analysis, as might be expected, but the difference is not great when combined with more approximate (class-based and smushed string) abstract object representations.

Second, we examined how analysis configuration affects precision. We found that using access paths is critical to precision. We also found that the bottom-up analysis has worse precision than top-down analysis, especially when using summary objects, and that using a more precise abstract object representation improves precision. But other traditional ways of improving precision do so only slightly (the polyhedral domain) or not significantly (context-sensitivity).

Finally, we looked at the precision/performance tradeoff for all programs. We found that using access paths is always a good idea, both for precision and performance, and top-down analysis works better than bottom-up. While summary objects, originally proposed by Fu [25], do help precision for some programs, the benefits are often marginal when considered as a percentage of all checks, so they tend not to outweigh their large performance disadvantage. Lastly, we found that the precision gains for more precise object representations and polyhedra are modest, and performance costs can be magnified by other analysis features.

Table 1. Analysis configuration options, and their possible settings.

Config. Option	Setting	Description
Numeric domain (ND)	INT	Intervals
	POL	Polyhedra
Heap abstraction (HA)	SO	Only summary objects
	AP	Only access paths
	AP+SO	Both access paths and summary objects
Abstract object	ALLO	Alloc-site abstraction
representation (OR)	CLAS	Class-based abstraction
	SMUS	Alloc-site except Strings
Inter-procedural analysis	TD	Top-down
order (AO)	BU	Bottom-up
	TD+BU	Hybrid top-down and bottom-up
Context sensitivity (CS)	CI	Context-insensitive
	1CFA	1-CFA
	1TYP	Type-sensitive

In summary, our empirical study provides a large, comprehensive evaluation of the effects of important numeric static analysis design choices on performance, precision, and their tradeoff; it is the first of its kind. Our code and data is available at https://github.com/plum-umd/JANA.

2 Numeric Static Analysis

A *numeric static analysis* is one that tracks numeric properties of memory locations, e.g., that $x \leqslant 5$ or $y > z$. A natural starting point for a numeric static analysis for Java programs is numeric abstract interpretation over program variables within a single procedure/method [18].

A standard abstract interpretation expresses numeric properties using a *numeric abstract domain*, of which the most common are *intervals* (also known as boxes) and *convex polyhedra*. Intervals [17] define abstract states using inequalities of the form $p \ relop \ n$ where p is a variable, n is a constant integer, and *relop* is a relational operator such as $\leqslant$. A variable such as p is sometimes called a *dimension*, as it describes one axis of a numeric space. Convex polyhedra [19] define abstract states using linear relationships between variables and constants, e.g., of the form $3p_1 - p_2 \leqslant 5$. Intervals are less precise but more efficient than polyhedra. Operation on intervals have time complexity linear in the number of dimensions whereas the time complexity for polyhedra operations is exponential in the number of dimensions.[1]

---

[1] Further, the time complexity of join is $O(d \cdot c^{2^{d+1}})$ where c is the number of constraints, and d is the number of dimensions [47].

Numeric abstract interpretation, including our own analyses, are usually flow-sensitive, i.e., each program point has an associated abstract state characterizing properties that hold at that point. Variable assignments are *strong updates*, meaning information about the variable is replaced by information from the right-hand side of the assignment. At merge points (e.g., after the completion of a conditional), the abstract states of the possible prior states are *joined* to yield properties that hold regardless of the branch taken. Loop bodies are reanalyzed until their constituent statements' abstract states reach a fixed point. Reaching a fixed point is accelerated by applying the numeric domain's standard *widening* operator [4] in place of join after a fixed number of iterations.

Scaling a basic numeric abstract interpreter to full Java requires making many design choices. Table 1 summarizes the key choices we study in this paper. Each configuration option has a range of settings that potentially offer different precision/performance tradeoffs. Different options may interact with each other to affect the tradeoff. In total, we study five options with two or three settings each. We have already discussed the first option, the numeric domain (ND), for which we consider intervals (INT) and polyhedra (POL). The next two options consider the heap, and are discussed in the next section, and the last two options consider method calls, and are discussed in Sect. 4.

For space reasons, our paper presentation focuses on the high-level design and tradeoffs. Detailed algorithms are given formally in the technical report [51] for the heap and interprocedural analysis.

3 The Heap

The numeric analysis described so far is sufficient only for analyzing code with local, numeric variables. To analyze numeric properties of heap-manipulating programs, we must also consider heap locations $x.f$, where x is a reference to a heap-allocated object, and f is a numeric field.[2] To do so requires developing a *heap abstraction* (HA) that accounts for aliasing. In particular, when variables x and y may point to the same heap object, an assignment to $x.f$ could affect $y.f$. Moreover, the referent of a pointer may be uncertain, e.g., the true branch of a conditional could assign location o_1 to x, while the false branch could assign o_2 to x. This uncertainty must be reflected in subsequent reads of $x.f$.

We use a *points-to analysis* to reason about aliasing. A points-to analysis computes a mapping Pt from variables x and access paths $x.f$ to (one or more) *abstract objects* [44]. If Pt maps two variables/paths p_1 and p_2 to a common abstract object o then p_1 and p_2 *may alias*. We also use points-to analysis to determine the call graph, i.e., to determine what method may be called by an expression $x.m(\ldots)$ (discussed in Sect. 4).

---

[2] In our implementation, statements such as $z = x.f.g$ are decomposed so that paths are at most length one, e.g., $w = x.f; z = w.g$.

3.1 Summary Objects (SO)

The first heap abstraction we study is based on Fu [25]: use a *summary object* (SO) to abstract information about multiple heap locations as a single abstract state "variable" [27]. As an example, suppose that $Pt(x) = \{o\}$ and we encounter the assignment $x.f := 5$. Then in this approach, we add a variable o_f to the abstract state, modeling the field f of object o, and we add constraint $o\_f = n$. Subsequent assignments to such summary objects must be *weak updates*, to respect the *may alias* semantics of the points-to analysis. For example, suppose $y.f$ may alias $x.f$, i.e., $o \in Pt(x) \cap Pt(y)$. Then after a later assignment $y.f := 7$ the analysis would weakly update o_f with 7, producing constraints $5 \leqslant o\_f \leqslant 7$ in the abstract state. These constraints conservatively model that either $o\_f = 5$ or $o\_f = 7$, since the assignment to $y.f$ may or may not affect $x.f$.

In general, weak updates are more expensive than strong updates, and reading a summary object is more expensive than reading a variable. A strong update to x is implemented by *forgetting* x in the abstract state,[3] and then re-adding it to be equal to the assigned-to value. Note that x cannot appear in the assigned-to value because programs are converted into static single assignment form (Sect. 5). A weak update—which is not directly supported in the numeric domain libraries we use—is implemented by copying the abstract state, strongly updating x in the copy, and then joining the two abstract states. Reading from a summary object requires "expanding" the abstract state with a copy o'_f of the summary object and its constraints, creating a constraint on o'_f, and then forgetting o'_f. Doing this ensures that operations on a variable into which a summary object is read do not affect prior reads. A normal read just references the read variable.

Fu [25] argues that this basic approach is better than ignoring heap locations entirely by measuring how often field reads are not unconstrained, as would be the case for a heap-unaware analysis. However, it is unclear whether the approach is sufficiently precise for applications such as array-bounds check elimination. Using the polyhedra numeric domain should help. For example, a `Buffer` class might store an array in one field and a conservative bound on an array's length in another. The polyhedral domain will permit relating the latter to the former while the interval domain will not. But the slowdown due to the many added summary objects may be prohibitive.

3.2 Access Paths (AP)

An alternative heap abstraction we study is to treat *access paths* (AP) as if they are normal variables, while still accounting for possible aliasing [21,52]. In particular, a path $x.f$ is modeled as a variable x_f, and an assignment $x.f := n$ strongly updates x_f to be n. At the same time, if there exists another path $y.f$ and x and y may alias, then we must weakly update y_f as possibly containing n. In general, determining which paths must be weakly updated depends on the abstract object representation and context-sensitivity of the points-to analysis.

---

[3] Doing so has the effect of "connecting" constraints that are transitive via x. For example, given $y \leqslant x \leqslant 5$, forgetting x would yield constraint $y \leqslant 5$.

Two key benefits of AP over SO are that (1) AP supports strong updates to paths $x.f$, which are more precise and less expensive than weak updates, and (2) AP may require fewer variables to be tracked, since, in our design, access paths are mostly local to a method whereas points-to sets are computed across the entire program. On the other hand, SO can do better at summarizing invariants about heap locations pointed to by other heap locations, i.e., not necessarily via an access path. Especially when performing an interprocedural analysis, such information can add useful precision.

Combined (AP+SO). A natural third choice is to combine AP and SO. Doing so sums both the costs and benefits of the two approaches. An assignment $x.f := n$ strongly updates x_f and weakly updates o_f for each o in $Pt(x)$ and each y_f where $Pt(x) \cap Pt(y) \neq \varnothing$. Reading from $x.f$ when it has not been previously assigned to is just a normal read, after first strongly updating x_f to be the join of the summary read of o_f for each $o \in Pt(x)$.

3.3   Abstract Object Representation (OR)

Another key precision/performance tradeoff is the *abstract object representation* (OR) used by the points-to analysis. In particular, when $Pt(x) = \{o_1, ..., o_n\}$, where do the names $o_1, ..., o_n$ come from? The answer impacts the naming of summary objects, the granularity of alias checks for assignments to access paths, and the precision of the call-graph, which requires aliasing information to determine which methods are targeted by a dynamic dispatch $x.m(...)$.

As shown in the third row of Table 1, we explore three representations for abstract objects. The first choice names abstract objects according to their *allocation site* (ALLO)—all objects allocated at the same program point have the same name. This is precise but potentially expensive, since there are many possible allocation sites, and each path $x.f$ could be mapped to many abstract objects. We also consider representing abstract objects using *class names* (CLAS), where all objects of the same class share the same abstract name, and a hybrid *smushed string* (SMUS) approach, where every `String` object has the same abstract name but objects of other types have allocation-site names [9]. The class name approach is the least precise but potentially more efficient since there are fewer names to consider. The smushed string analysis is somewhere in between. The question is whether the reduction in names helps performance enough, without overly compromising precision.

4   Method Calls

So far we have considered the first three options of Table 1, which handle integer variables and the heap. This section considers the last two options—interprocedural analysis order (AO) and context sensitivity (CS).

4.1 Interprocedural Analysis Order (AO)

We implement three styles of interprocedural analysis: top-down (TD), bottom-up (BU), and their combination (TD+BU). The TD analysis starts at the program entry point and, as it encounters method calls, analyzes the body of the callee (memoizing duplicate calls). The BU analysis starts at the leaves of the call graph and analyzes each method in isolation, producing a summary of its behavior [29,53]. (We discuss call graph construction in the next subsection.) This summary is then instantiated at each method call. The hybrid analysis works top-down for application code but bottom-up for any code from the Java standard library.

Top-Down (TD). Assuming the analyzer knows the method being called, a simple approach to top-down analysis would be to transfer the caller's state to the beginning of callee, analyze the callee in that state, and then transfer the state at the end of the callee back to the caller. Unfortunately, this approach is prohibitively expensive because the abstract state would accumulate all local variables and access paths across all methods along the call-chain.

We avoid this blowup by analyzing a call to method m while considering only relevant local variables and heap abstractions. Ignoring the heap for the moment, the basic approach is as follows. First, we make a copy C_m of the caller's abstract state C. In C_m, we set variables for m's formal numeric arguments to the actual arguments and then forget (as defined in Sect. 3.1) the caller's local variables. Thus C_m will only contain the portion of C relevant to m. We analyze m's body, starting in C_m, to yield the final state C_m'. Lastly, we merge C and C_m', strongly update the variable that receives the returned result, and forget the callee's local variables—thus avoiding adding the callee's locals to the caller's state.

Now consider the heap. If we are using summary objects, when we copy C to C_m we do not forget those objects that might be used by m (according to the points-to analysis). As m is analyzed, the summary objects will be weakly updated, ultimately yielding state C_m' at m's return. To merge C_m' with C, we first forget the summary objects in C not forgotten in C_m and then concatenate C_m' with C. The result is that updated summary objects from C_m' replace those that were in the original C.

If we are using access paths, then at the call we forget access paths in C because assignments in m's code might invalidate them. But if we have an access path $x.f$ in the caller and we pass x to m, then we retain $x.f$ in the callee but rename it to use m's parameter's name. For example, $x.f$ becomes $y.f$ if m's parameter is y. If y is never assigned to in m, we can map $y.f$ back to $x.f$ (in the caller) once m returns.[4] All other access paths in C_m are forgotten prior to concatenating with the caller's state.

Note that the above reasoning is only for numeric values. We take no particular steps for pointer values as the points-to analysis already tracks those across all methods.

---

[4] Assignments to $y.f$ in the callee are fine; only assignments to y are problematic.

Bottom Up (BU). In the BU analysis, we analyze a method m's body to produce a *method summary* and then instantiate the summary at calls to m. Ignoring the heap, producing a method summary for m is straightforward: start analyzing m in a state C_m in which its (numeric) parameters are unconstrained variables. When m returns, forget all variables in the final state except the parameters and return value, yielding a state C'_m that is the method summary. Then, when m is called, we concatenate C'_m with the current abstract state; add constraints between the parameters and their actual arguments; strongly update the variable receiving the result with the summary's returned value; and then forget those variables.

When using the polyhedral numeric domain, C'_m can express relationships between input and output parameters, e.g., `ret` $\leqslant$ z or `ret` = x+y. For the interval domain, which is non-relational, summaries are more limited, e.g., they can express `ret` $\leqslant$ 100 but not `ret` $\leqslant$ x. As such, we expect bottom-up analysis to be far more useful with the polyhedral domain than the interval domain.

Summary Objects. Now consider the heap. Recall that when using summary objects in the TD analysis, reading a path $x.f$ into z "expands" each summary object o_f when $o \in Pt(x)$ and strongly updates z with the join of these expanded objects, before forgetting them. This expansion makes a copy of each summary object's constraints so that later use of z does not incorrectly impact the summary. However, when analyzing a method bottom-up, we may not yet know all of a summary object's constraints. For example, if x is passed into the current method, we will not (yet) know if o_f is assigned to a particular numeric range in the caller.

We solve this problem by allocating a fresh, unconstrained *placeholder object* at each read of $x.f$ and include it in the initialization of the assigned-to variable z. The placeholder is also retained in m's method summary. Then at a call to m, we instantiate each placeholder with the constraints in the caller involving the placeholder's summary location. We also create a fresh placeholder in the caller and weakly update it to the placeholder in the callee; doing so allows for further constraints to be added from calls further up the call chain.

Access Paths. If we are using access paths, we treat them just as in TD—each $x.f$ is allocated a special variable that is strongly updated when possible, according to the points-to analysis. These are not kept in method summaries. When also using summary objects, at the first read to $x.f$ we initialize it from the summary objects derived from x's points-to set, following the above expansion procedure. Otherwise $x.f$ will be unconstrained.

Hybrid (TD+BU). In addition to TD or BU analysis (only), we implemented a hybrid strategy that performs TD analysis for the application, but BU analysis for code from the Java standard library. Library methods are analyzed first, bottom-up. Application method calls are analyzed top-down. When an application method calls a library method, it applies the BU method call approach.

TD+BU could potentially be better than TD because library methods, which are likely called many times, only need to be analyzed once. TD+BU could similarly be better than BU because application methods, which are likely not called as many times as library methods, can use the lower-overhead TD analysis.

Now, consider the interaction between the heap abstraction and the analysis order. The use of access paths (only) does not greatly affect the normal TD/BU tradeoff: TD may yield greater precision by adding constraints from the caller when analyzing the callee, while BU's lower precision comes with the benefit of analyzing method bodies less often. Use of summary objects complicates this tradeoff. In the TD analysis, the use of summary objects adds a relatively stable overhead to all methods, since they are included in every method's abstract state. For the BU analysis, methods further down in the call chain will see fewer summary objects used, and method bodies may end up being analyzed less often than in the TD case. On the other hand, placeholder objects add more dimensions overall (one per read) and more work at call sites (to instantiate them). But, instantiating a summary may be cheaper than reanalyzing the method.

4.2 Context Sensitivity (CS)

The last design choice we considered was context-sensitivity. A *context-insensitive* (CI) analysis conflates information from different call sites of the same method. For example, two calls to method m in which the first passes x_1, y_1 and the second passes x_2, y_2 will be conflated such that within m we will only know that either x_1 or x_2 is the first parameter, and either y_1 or y_2 is the second; we will miss the correlation between parameters. A context sensitive analysis provides some distinction among different call sites. A *1-CFA analysis* [46] (1CFA) distinguishes based on one level of calling context, i.e., two calls originating from different program points will be distinguished, but two calls from the same point, but in a method called from two different points will not. A *type-sensitive analysis* [49] (1TYP) uses the type of the receiver as the context.

Context sensitivity in the points-to analysis affects alias checks, e.g., when determining whether an assignment to $x.f$ might affect $y.f$. It also affects the abstract object representation and call graph construction. Due to the latter, context sensitivity also affects our interprocedural numeric analysis. In a context-sensitive analysis, a single method is essentially treated as a family of methods indexed by a calling context. In particular, our analysis keeps track of the current context as a *frame*, and when considering a call to method x.m(), the target methods to which m may refer differ depending on the frame. This provides more precision than a context-insensitive (i.e., frame-less) approach, but the analysis may consider the same method code many times, which adds greater precision but also greater expense. This is true both for TD and BU, but is perhaps more detrimental to the latter since it reduces potential method summary reuse. On the other hand, more precise analysis may reduce unnecessary work by pruning infeasible call graph edges. For example, when a call might dynamically dispatch to several different methods, the analysis must consider them all, joining their abstract states. A more precise analysis may consider fewer target methods.

5 Implementation

We have implemented an analysis for Java with all of the options described in the previous two sections. Our implementation is based on the intermediate representation in the T. J. Watson Libraries for Analysis (WALA) version 1.3.10 [2], which converts a Java bytecode program into static single assignment (SSA) form [20], which is then analyzed. We use APRON [33,41] trunk revision 1096 (published on 2016/05/31) implementation of intervals, and ELINA [47,48], snapshot as of October 4, 2017, for convex polyhedra. Our current implementation supports all non-floating point numeric Java values and comprises 14K lines of Scala code.

Next we discuss a few additional implementation details.

Preallocating Dimensions. In both APRON and ELINA, it is very expensive to perform join operations that combine abstract states with different variables. Thus, rather than add dimensions as they arise during abstract interpretation, we instead *preallocate* all necessary dimensions—including for local variables, access paths, and summary objects, when enabled—at the start of a method body. This ensures the abstract states have the same dimensions at each join point. We found that, even though this approach makes some states larger than they need to be, the overall performance savings is still substantial.

Arrays. Our analysis encodes an array as an object with two fields, `contents`, which represents the contents of the array, and `len`, representing the array's length. Each read/write from `a[i]` is modeled as a weak read/write of `contents` (because all array elements are represented with the same field), with an added check that `i` is between 0 and `len`. We treat `Strings` as a special kind of array.

Widening. As is standard in abstract interpretation, our implementation performs widening to ensure termination when analyzing loops. In a pilot study, we compared widening after between one and ten iterations. We found that there was little added precision when applying widening after more than three iterations when trying to prove array indexes in bounds (our target application, discussed next). Thus we widen at that point in our implementation.

Limitations. Our implementation is sound with a few exceptions. In particular, it ignores calls to native methods and uses of reflection. It is also unsound in its handling of recursive method calls. If the return value of a recursive method is numeric, it is regarded as unconstrained. Potential side effects of the recursive calls are not modeled.

6 Evaluation

In this section, we present an empirical study of our family of analyses, focusing on the following research questions:

RQ1: Performance. How does the configuration affect analysis running time?
RQ2: Precision. How does the configuration affect analysis precision?
RQ3: Tradeoffs. How does the configuration affect precision and performance?

To answer these questions, we chose an important analysis client, array index out-of-bound analysis, and ran it on the DaCapo benchmark suite [6]. We vary each of the analysis features listed in Table 1, yielding 162 total configurations. To understand the impact of analysis features, we used multiple linear regression and logistic regression to model precision and performance (the dependent variables) in terms of analysis features and across programs (the independent variables). We also studied per-program data directly.

Overall, we found that using access paths is a significant boon to precision but costs little in performance, while using summary objects is the reverse, to the point that use of summary objects is a significant source of timeouts. Polyhedra add precision compared to intervals, and impose some performance cost, though only half as much as summary objects. Interestingly, when both summary objects and polyhedra together would result in a timeout, choosing the first tends to provide better precision over the second. Finally, bottom-up analysis harms precision compared to top-down analysis, especially when only summary objects are enabled, but yields little gain in performance.

6.1   Experimental Setup

We evaluated our analyses by using them to perform array index out of bounds analysis. More specifically, for each benchmark program, we counted how many array access instructions (x[i]=y, y=x[i], etc.) an analysis configuration could verify were in bounds (i.e., i<x.length), and measured the time taken to perform the analysis.

Benchmarks. We analyzed all eleven programs from the DaCapo benchmark suite [6] version 2006-10-MR2. The first three columns of Table 2 list the programs' names, their size (number of IR instructions), and the number of array bounds checks they contain. The rest of the table indicates the fastest and most precise analysis configuration for each program; we discuss these results in Sect. 6.4. We ran each benchmark three times under each of the 162 analysis configurations. The experiments were performed on two 2.4 GHz single processor (with four logical cores) Intel Xeon E5-2609 servers, each with 128GB memory running Ubuntu 16.04 (LTS). On each server, we ran three analysis configurations in parallel, binding each process to a designated core.

Since many analysis configurations are time-intensive, we set a limit of 1 hour for running a benchmark under a particular configuration. All performance results reported are the median of the three runs. We also use the median precision result, though note the analyses are deterministic, so the precision does not vary except in the case of timeouts. Thus, we treat an analysis as not timing out as long as either two or three of the three runs completed, and otherwise it is a timeout. Among the 1782 median results (11 benchmarks, 162 configurations),

Table 2. Benchmarks and overall results.

Prog.	Size	# Checks	Best Performance			Best Precision		
			Time (min)	# Checks	Percent	Time (min)	# Checks	Percent
			BU-AP-CI-CLAS-INT			TD-AP+SO-1TYP-CLAS-INT		
antlr	55734	1526	0.6	1176	77.1%	18.5	1306	85.6%
			BU-AP-CI-CLAS-INT			TD-AP-1TYP-SMUS-POL		
bloat	150197	4621	4.0	2538	54.9%	17.2	2795	60.5%
			BU-AP-CI-CLAS-INT			TD-AP-1TYP-SMUS-INT		
chart	167621	7965	3.3	5593	70.2%	7.7	5654	71.0%
			BU-AP-CI-ALLO-INT			TD-AP+SO-1TYP-SMUS-POL		
eclipse	18938	1043	0.2	896	85.9%	3.3	977	93.7%
			BU-AP-CI-CLAS-INT			TD-AP+SO-1CFA-SMUS-INT		
fop	33243	1337	0.4	998	74.6%	2.6	1137	85.0%
			BU-AP-CI-SMUS-INT			TD-AP+SO-CI-SMUS-INT		
hsqldb	19497	1020	0.3	911	89.3%	1.4	975	95.6%
			BU-AP-CI-SMUS-INT			TD-AP-1CFA-CLAS-POL		
jython	127661	4232	1.3	2667	63.0%	33.6	2919	69.0%
			BU-AP-CI-SMUS-INT			TD-AP+SO-1TYP-ALLO-INT		
luindex	69027	2764	1.8	1682	60.9%	46.8	2015	72.9%
			BU-AP-CI-CLAS-INT			TD-AP+SO-1CFA-ALLO-POL		
lusearch	20242	1062	0.2	912	85.9%	54.2	979	92.2%
			BU-AP-CI-CLAS-INT			TD-AP+SO-CI-CLAS-INT		
pmd	116422	4402	1.7	3153	71.6%	49.5	3301	75.0%
			BU-AP-CI-CLAS-INT			TD-AP+SO-1CFA-SMUS-POL		
xalan	20315	1043	0.2	912	87.4%	3.8	981	94.1%

667 of them (37%) timed out. The percentage of the configurations that timed out analyzing a program ranged from 0% (xalan) to 90% (chart).

Statistical Analysis. To answer RQ1 and RQ2, we constructed a model for each question using multiple linear regression. Roughly put, we attempt to produce a model of performance (RQ1) and precision (RQ2)—the *dependent variables*—in terms of a linear combination of analysis configuration options (i.e., one choice from each of the five categories given in Table 1) and the benchmark program (i.e., one of the eleven subjects from DaCapo)—the *independent variables*. We include the programs themselves as independent variables, which allows us to roughly factor out program-specific sources of performance or precision gain/loss (which might include size, complexity, etc.); this is standard in this sort of regression [45]. Our models also consider all two-way interactions among analysis options. In our scenario, a significant interaction between two option settings suggests that the combination of them has a different impact on the analysis precision and/or performance compared to their independent impact.

To obtain a model that best fits the data, we performed variable selection via the Akaike Information Criterion (AIC) [12], a standard measure of model quality. AIC drops insignificant independent variables to better estimate the impact of analysis options. The R^2 values for the models are good, with the lowest of any model being 0.71.

After performing the regression, we examine the results to discover potential trends. Then we draw plots to examine how those trends manifest in the different programs. This lets us study the whole distribution, including outliers and any non-linear behavior, in a way that would be difficult if we just looked at the regression model. At the same time, if we only looked at plots it would be hard to see general trends because there is so much data.

Threats to Validity. There are several potential threats to the validity of our study. First, the benchmark programs may not be representative of programs that analysis users are interested in. That said, the programs were drawn from a well-studied benchmark suite, so they should provide useful insights.

Second, the insights drawn from the results of the array index out-of-bound analysis may not reflect the trends of other analysis clients. We note that array bounds checking is a standard, widely used analysis.

Third, we examined a design space of 162 analysis configurations, but there are other design choices we did not explore. Thus, there may be other independent variables that have important effects. In addition, there may be limitations specific to our implementation, e.g., due to precisely how WALA implements points-to analysis. Even so, we relied on time-tested implementations as much as possible, and arrived at our choices of analysis features by studying the literature and conversing with experts. Thus, we believe our study has value even if further variables are worth studying.

Fourth, for our experiments we ran each analysis configuration three times, and thus performance variation may not be fully accounted for. While more trials would add greater statistical assurance, each trial takes about a week to run on our benchmark machines, and we observed no variation in precision across the trials. We did observe variations in performance, but they were small and did not affect the broader trends. In more detail, we computed the variance of the running time among a set of three runs of a configuration as `(max-min)/median` to calculate the variance. The average variance across all configurations is only 4.2%. The maximum total time difference (`max-min`) is 32 min, an outlier from eclipse. All the other time differences are within 4 min.

6.2   RQ1: Performance

Table 3 summarizes our regression model for performance. We measure performance as the time to run both the core analysis and perform array index out-of-bounds checking. If a configuration timed out while analyzing a program, we set its running time as one hour, the time limit (characterizing a lower bound on the configuration's performance impact). Another option would have been to

Table 3. Model of run-time performance in terms of analysis configuration options (Table 1), including two-way interactions. Independent variables for individual programs not shown. R^2 of 0.72.

Option	Setting	Est. (min)	CI	p-value
AO	TD	-	-	-
	BU	-1.98	[-6.3, 1.76]	0.336
	TD+BU	1.97	[-1.78, 6.87]	0.364
HA	AP+SO	-	-	-
	AP	-37.6	[-42.36, -32.84]	<0.001
	SO	0.15	[-4.60, 4.91]	0.949
CS	1TYP	-	-	-
	CI	-7.09	[-10.89, -3.28]	<0.001
	1CFA	1.62	[-2.19, 5.42]	0.405
OR	ALLO	-	-	-
	CLAS	-11.00	[-15.44, -6.56]	<0.001
	SMUS	-7.15	[-11.59, -2.70]	0.002
ND	POL	-	-	-
	INT	-16.51	[-19.56, -13.46]	<0.001
AO:HA	TD:AP+SO	-	-	-
	BU:AP	-5.31	[-9.35, -1.27]	0.01
	TD+BU:AP	-3.13	[-7.38, 1.12]	0.15
	BU:SO	0.11	[-3.92, 4.15]	0.956
	TD+BU:SO	-0.08	[-4.33, 4.17]	0.97
AO:OR	TD:ALLO	-	-	-
	BU:CLAS	-8.87	[-12.91, -4.83]	<0.001
	BU:SMUS	-4.23	[-8.27, -0.19]	0.04
	TD+BU:CLAS	-4.07	[-8.32, 0.19]	0.06
	TD+BU:SMUS	-2.52	[-6.77, 1.74]	0.247
AO:ND	TD:POL	-	-	-
	BU:INT	8.04	[4.73, 11.33]	<0.001
	TD+BU:INT	2.35	[-1.12, 5.82]	0.185
HA:CS	AP+SO:1TYP	-	-	-
	AP:1CFA	7.01	[2.83, 11.17]	<0.001
	AP:CI	3.38	[-0.79, 7.54]	0.112
	SO:CI	-0.20	[-4.37, 3.96]	0.924
	SO:1CFA	-0.21	[-4.37, 3.95]	0.921
HA:OR	AP+SO:ALLO	-	-	-
	AP:CLAS	9.55	[5.37, 13.71]	<0.001
	AP:SMUS	6.25	[2.08, 10.42]	<0.001
	SO:SMUS	0.07	[-4.09, 4.24]	0.973
	SO:CLAS	-0.43	[-4.59, 3.73]	0.839
HA:ND	AP+SO:POL	-	-	-
	AP:INT	6.94	[3.53, 10.34]	<0.001
	SO:INT	0.08	[-3.32, 3.48]	0.964
CS:OR	1TYP:ALLO	-	-	-
	CI:CLAS	4.76	[0.59, 8.93]	0.025
	CI:SMUS	4.02	[-0.15, 8.18]	0.05
	1CFA:CLAS	-3.09	[-7.25, 1.08]	0.147
	1CFA:SMUS	-0.52	[-4.68, 3.64]	0.807

leave the configuration out of the regression, but doing so would underrepresent the important negative contribution to performance.

In the top part of the table, the first column shows the independent variables and the second column shows a setting. One of the settings, identified by dashes in the remaining columns, is the baseline in the regression. We use the following settings as baselines: TD, AP+SO, 1TYP, ALLO, and POL. We chose the baseline according to what we expected to be the most precise settings. For

Table 4. Model of timeout in terms of analysis configuration options (Table 1). Independent variables for individual programs not shown. R^2 of 0.77.

Option	Setting	Coef.	CI	Exp(coef.)	p-value
AO	TD	–	–	–	–
	BU	-1.47	[-2.04, -0.92]	0.23	<0.001
	TD+BU	0.09	[-0.46, 0.65]	1.09	0.73
HA	AP+SO	–	–	–	–
	AP	-10.6	[-12.29, -9.05]	2.49E-5	<0.001
	SO	0.03	[-0.46, 0.53]	1.03	0.899
CS	1TYP	–	–	–	–
	CI	-0.89	[-1.46, -0.34]	0.41	0.002
	1CFA	0.94	[0.39, 1.49]	2.56	0.001
OR	ALLO	–	–	–	–
	CLAS	-3.84	[-4.59, -3.15]	0.02	<0.001
	SMUS	-1.78	[-2.36, -1.23]	0.17	<0.001
ND	POL	–	–	–	–
	INT	-3.73	[-4.40, -3.13]	0.02	<0.001

the other settings, the third column shows the estimated effect of that setting with all other settings (including the choice of program, each an independent variable) held fixed. For example, the fifth row of the table shows that AP (only) decreases overall analysis time by 37.6 min compared to AP+SO (and the other baseline settings). The fourth column shows the 95% confidence interval around the estimate, and the last column shows the p-value. As is standard, we consider p-values less than 0.05 (5%) significant; such rows are highlighted green.

The bottom part of the table shows the additional effects of two-way combinations of options compared to the baseline effects of each option. For example, the BU:CLAS row shows a coefficient of –8.87. We add this to the individual effects of BU (–1.98) and CLAS (–11.0) to compute that BU:CLAS is 21.9 min faster (since the number is negative) than the baseline pair of TD:ALLO. Not all interactions are shown, e.g., AO:CS is not in the table. Any interactions not included were deemed not to have meaningful effect and thus were dropped by the model generation process [12].

Setting the running time of a timed-out configuration as one hour in Table 3 may under-report a configuration's (negative) performance impact. For a more complete view, we follow the suggestion of Arcuri and Briand [3], and construct a model of success/failure using logistic regression. We consider "if a configuration timed out" as the categorical dependent variable, and the analysis configuration options and the benchmark programs as independent variables.

Table 4 summarizes our logistic regression model for timeout. The coefficients in the third column represent the change in log likelihood associated with each configuration setting, compared to the baseline setting. Negative coefficients indicate lower likelihood of timeout. The exponential of the coefficient, Exp(coef) in the fifth column, indicates roughly how strongly that configuration setting being turned on affects the likelihood relative to the baseline setting. For example, the third row of the table shows that BU is roughly 5 times less likely to time out compared to TD, a significant factor to the model.

Tables 3 and 4 present several interesting performance trends.

Summary Objects Incur a Significant Slowdown. Use of summary objects results in a very large slowdown, with high significance. We can see this in the AP row in Table 3. It indicates that using *only* AP results in an average 37.6-min speedup compared to the baseline AP+SO (while SO only had no significant difference from the baseline). We observed a similar trend in Table 4; use of summary objects has the largest effect, with high significance, on the likelihood of timeout. Indeed, 624 out of the 667 analyses that timed out had summary objects enabled (i.e., SO or AP+SO). We investigated further and found the slowdown from summary objects is mostly due to significantly larger number of dimensions included in the abstract state. For example, analyzing jython with AP-TD-CI-ALLO-INT has, on average, 11 numeric variables when analyzing a method, and the whole analysis finished in 15 min. Switching AP to SO resulted in, on average, 1473 variables per analyzed method and the analysis ultimately timed out.

The Polyhedral Domain is Slow, But Not as Slow as Summary Objects. Choosing INT over baseline POL nets a speedup of 16.51 min. This is the second-largest performance effect with high significance, though it is half as large as the effect of SO. Moreover, per Table 4, turning on POL is more likely to result in timeout; 409 out of 667 analyses that timed out used POL.

Heavyweight CS and OR Settings Hurt Performance, Particularly When Using Summary Objects. For CS settings, CI is faster than baseline 1TYP by 7.1 min, while there is not a statistically significant difference with 1CFA. For the OR settings, we see that the more lightweight representations CLAS and SMUS are faster than baseline ALLO by 11.00 and 7.15 min, respectively, when using baseline AP+SO. This makes sense because these representations have a direct effect on reducing the number of summary objects. Indeed, when summary objects are disabled, the performance benefit disappears: AP:CLAS and AP:SMUS add back 9.55 and 6.25 min, respectively.

Bottom-up Analysis Provides No Substantial Performance Advantage. Table 4 indicates that a BU analysis is less likely to time out than a TD analysis. However, the performance model in Table 3 does not show a performance advantage of bottom-up analysis: neither BU nor TD+BU provide a statistically significant impact on running time over baseline TD. Setting one hour for the configurations that timed out in the performance model might fail to capture the negative performance of top-down analysis. This observation underpins the utility of constructing a success/failure analysis to complement the performance model. In any case, we might have expected bottom-up analysis to provide a real performance advantage (Sect. 4.1), but that is not what we have observed.

6.3   RQ2: Precision

Table 5 summarizes our regression model for precision, using the same format as Table 3. We measure precision as the number of array indexes proven to be in

Table 5. Model of precision, measured as # of array indexes proved in bounds, in terms of analysis configuration options (Table 1), including two-way interactions. Independent variables for individual programs not shown. R^2 of 0.98.

Option	Setting	Est. (#)	CI	p-value
AO	TD	-	-	-
	TD+BU	-134.22	[-184.93, -83.50]	<0.001
	BU	-129.98	[-180.24, -79.73]	<0.001
HA	AP+SO	-	-	-
	SO	-94.46	[-166.79, -22.13]	0.011
	AP	-5.24	[-66.47, 55.99]	0.866
OR	ALLO	-	-	-
	CLAS	-90.15	[-138.80, -41.5]	<0.001
	SMUS	35.47	[-14.72, 85.67]	0.166
ND	POL	-	-	-
	INT	5.11	[-28.77, 38.99]	0.767
AO:HA	TD:AP+SO	-	-	-
	BU:SO	-686.79	[-741.82, -631.76]	<0.001
	TD+BU:SO	-630.99	[-687.41, -574.56]	<0.001
	TD+BU:AP	63.59	[14.71, 112.47]	0.011
	BU:AP	58.92	[11.75, 106.1]	0.014
AO:OR	TD:ALLO	-	-	-
	TD+BU:CLAS	156.31	[107.78, 204.83]	<0.001
	BU:CLAS	141.46	[94.13, 188.80]	<0.001
	BU:SMUS	-29.16	[-77.69, 19.37]	0.238
	TD+BU:SMUS	-29.25	[-79.23, 20.72]	0.251
HA:OR	AP+SO:ALLO	-	-	-
	SO:CLAS	-351.01	[-408.35, -293.67]	<0.001
	SO:SMUS	-72.23	[-131.99, -12.47]	0.017
	AP:SMUS	-16.88	[-67.20, 33.44]	0.51
	AP:CLAS	-8.81	[-57.84, 40.20]	0.724
HA:ND	AP+SO:POL	-	-	-
	AP:INT	-58.87	[-99.39, -18.35]	0.004
	SO:INT	-61.96	[-109.08, -14.84]	0.01

bounds. As recommended by Arcuri and Briand [3], we omit from the regression those configurations that timed out.[5] We see several interesting trends.

Access Paths are Critical to Precision. Removing access paths from the configuration, by switching from AP+SO to SO, yields significantly lower precision. We see this in the SO (only) row in the table, and in all of its interactions (i.e., SO:*opt* and *opt*:SO rows). In contrast, AP on its own is not statistically worse than AP+SO, indicating that summary objects often add little precision. This is unfortunate, given their high performance cost.

Bottom-up Analysis Harms Precision Overall, Especially for SO (Only). BU has a strongly negative effect on precision: 129.98 fewer checks compared to TD. Coupled with SO it fares even worse: BU:SO nets 686.79 fewer checks, and TD+BU:SO nets 630.99 fewer. For example, for xalan the most precise configuration, which uses TD and AP+SO, discharges 981 checks, while all configurations

---

[5] The alternative of setting precision to be 0 would misrepresent the general power of a configuration, particularly when combined with runs that did not time out. Fewer runs might reduce statistical power, however, which is captured in the model.

that instead use BU and SO on xalan discharge close to zero checks. The same basic trend holds for just about every program.

The Relational Domain Only Slightly Improves Precision. The row for INT is not statistically different from the baseline POL. This is a bit of a surprise, since by itself POL is strictly more precise than INT. In fact, it does improve precision empirically when coupled with either AP or SO—the interaction AP:INT and SO:INT reduces the number of checks. This sets up an interesting performance tradeoff that we explore in Sect. 6.4: using AP+SO with INT vs. using AP with POL.

More Precise Abstract Object Representation Improves Precision, But Context Sensitivity Does Not. The table shows CLAS discharges 90.15 fewer checks compared to ALLO. Examining the data in detail, we found this occurred because CLAS conflates all arrays of the same type as one abstract object, thus imprecisely approximating those arrays' lengths, in turn causing some checks to fail.

Also notice that context sensitivity (CS) does not appear in the model, meaning it does not significantly increase or decrease the precision of array bounds checking. This is interesting, because context-sensitivity is known to reduce points-to set size [35, 49] (thus yielding more precise alias checks and dispatch targets). However, for our application this improvement has minimal impact.

6.4   RQ3: Tradeoffs

Finally, we examine how analysis settings affect the tradeoff between precision and performance. To begin out discussion, recall Table 2 (page 12), which shows the fastest configuration and the most precise configuration for each benchmark. Further, the table shows the configurations' running time, number of checks discharged, and percentage of checks discharged.

We see several interesting patterns in this table, though note the table shows just two data points and not the full distribution. First, the configurations in each column are remarkably consistent. The fastest configurations are all of the form BU-AP-CI-*-INT, only varying in the abstract object representation. The most precise configurations are more variable, but all include TD and some form of AP. The rest of the options differ somewhat, with different forms of precision benefiting different benchmarks. Finally, notice that, overall, the fastest configurations are much faster than the most precise configurations—often by an order of magnitude—but they are not that much less precise—typically by 5–10% points.

To delve further into the tradeoff, we examine, for each program, the overall performance and precision distribution for the analysis configurations, focusing on particular options (HA, AO, etc.). As settings of option HA have come up prominently in our discussion so far, we start with it and then move through the other options. Figure 1 gives per-benchmark scatter plots of this data. Each plotted point corresponds to one configuration, with its performance on the x-axis and number of discharged array bounds checks on the y-axis. We regard a configuration that times out as discharging no checks, so it is plotted at (60, 0).

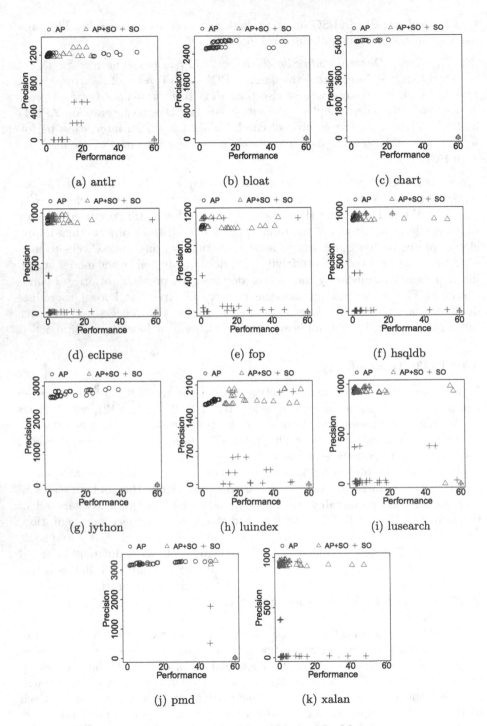

Fig. 1. Tradeoffs: AP vs. SO vs. AP+SO.

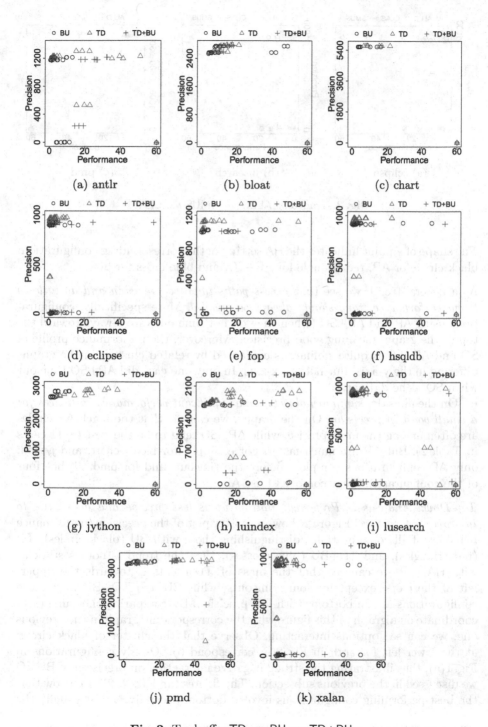

Fig. 2. Tradeoffs: TD vs. BU vs. TD+BU.

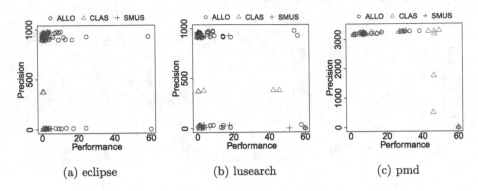

Fig. 3. Tradeoffs: ALLO vs. SMUS vs. CLAS.

The shape of a point indicates the HA setting of the corresponding configuration: black circle for AP, red triangle for AP+SO, and blue cross for SO.

As a general trend, we see that *access paths improve precision and do little to harm performance; they should always be enabled.* More specifically, configurations using AP and AP+SO (when they do not time out) are always toward the top of the graph, meaning good precision. Moreover, the performance profile of SO and AP+SO is quite similar, as evidenced by related clusters in the graphs differing in the y-axis, but not the x-axis. In only one case did AP+SO time out when SO alone did not.[6]

On the flip side, *summary objects are a significant performance bottleneck for a small boost in precision.* On the graphs, we can see that the black AP circles are often among the most precise, while AP+SO tend to be the best (8/11 cases in Table 2). But AP are much faster. For example, for bloat, chart, and jython, only AP configurations complete before the timeout, and for pmd, all but four of the configurations that completed use AP.

Top-Down Analysis is Preferred: Bottom-up is less precise and does little to improve performance. Figure 2 shows a scatter plot of the precision/performance behavior of all configurations, distinguishing those with BU (black circles), TD (red triangles), and TD+BU (blue crosses). Here the trend is not as stark as with HA, but we can see that the mass of TD points is towards the upper-left of the plots, except for some timeouts, while BU and TD+BU have more configurations at the bottom, with low precision. By comparing the same (x,y) coordinate on a graph in this figure with the corresponding graph in the previous one, we can see options interacting. Observe that the cluster of black circles at the lower left for antlr in Fig. 2(a) correspond to SO-only configurations in Fig. 1(a), thus illustrating the strong negative interaction on precision of BU:SO we discussed in the previous subsection. The figures (and Table 2) also show that the best-performing configurations involve bottom-up analysis, but usually the

---

[6] In particular, for eclipse, configuration TD+BU-SO-1CFA-ALLO-POL finished at 59 min, while TD+BU-AP+SO-1CFA-ALLO-POL timed out.

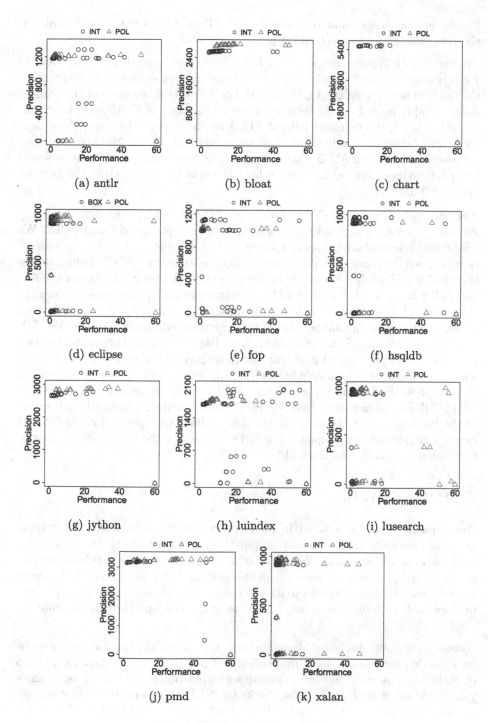

Fig. 4. Tradeoffs: INT vs. POL.

benefit is inconsistent and very small. And TD+BU does not seem to balance the precision/performance tradeoff particularly well.

Precise Object Representation Often Helps with Precision at a Modest Cost to Performance. Figure 3 shows a representative sample of scatter plots illustrating the tradeoff between ALLO, CLAS, and SMUS. In general, we see that the highest points tend to be ALLO, and these are more to the right of CLAS and SMUS. On the other hand, the precision gain of ALLO tends to be modest, and these usually occur (examining individual runs) when combining with AP+SO. However, summary objects and ALLO together greatly increase the risk of timeouts and low performance. For example, for eclipse the row of circles across the bottom are all SO-only.

The Precision Gains of POLY are More Modest than Gains Due to Using AP+SO (over AP). Figure 4 shows scatter plots comparing INT and POLY. We investigated several groupings in more detail and found an interesting interaction between the numeric domain and the heap abstraction: POLY is often better than INT for AP (only). For example, the points in the upper left of bloat use AP, and POLY is slightly better than INT. The same phenomenon occurs in luindex in the cluster of triangles and circles to the upper left. But INT does better further up and to the right in luindex. This is because these configurations use AP+SO, which times out when POLY is enabled. A similar phenomenon occurs for the two points in the upper right of pmd, and the most precise points for hsqldb. Indeed, when a configuration with AP+SO-INT terminates, it will be more precise than those with AP-POLY, but is likely slower. We manually inspected the cases where AP+SO-INT is more precise than AP-POLY, and found that it mostly is because of the limitation that access paths are dropped through method calls. AP+SO rarely terminates when coupled with POLY because of the very large number of dimensions added by summary objects.

7   Related Work

Our numeric analysis is novel in its focus on fully automatically identifying numeric invariants in real (heap-manipulating, method-calling) Java programs, while aiming to be sound. We know of no prior work that carefully studies precision and performance tradeoffs in this setting. Prior work tends to be much more imprecise and/or intentionally unsound, but scale better, or more precise, but not scale to programs as large as those in the DaCapo benchmark suite.

Numeric vs. Heap Analysis. Many abstract interpretation-based analyses focus on numeric properties or heap properties, but not both. For example, Calcagno et al. [13] uses separation logic to create a compositional, bottom-up heap analysis. Their client analysis for Java checks for NULL pointers [1], but not out-of-bounds array indexes. Conversely, the PAGAI analyzer [31] for LLVM explores abstract interpretation algorithms for precise invariants of numeric variables, but ignores the heap (soundly treating heap locations as $\top$).

Numeric Analysis in Heap-Manipulating Programs. Fu [25] first proposed the basic summary object heap abstraction we explore in this paper. The approach uses a points-to analysis [44] as the basis of generating abstract names for summary objects that are weakly updated [27]. The approach does not support strong updates to heap objects and ignores procedure calls, making unsound assumptions about effects of calls to or from the procedure being analyzed. Fu's evaluation on DaCapo only considered how often the analysis yields a non-$\top$ field, while ours considers how often the analysis can prove that an array index is in bounds, which is a more direct measure of utility. Our experiments strongly suggest that when modeled soundly and at scale, summary objects add enormous performance overhead while doing much less to assist precision when compared to strongly updatable access paths alone [21,52].

Some prior work focuses on inferring precise invariants about heap-allocated objects, e.g., relating the presence of an object in a collection to the value of one of the object's fields. Ferrera et al. [23,24] also propose a composed analysis for numeric properties of heap manipulating programs. Their approach is amenable to both points-to and shape analyses (e.g., TVLA [34]), supporting strong updates for the latter. DESKCHECK [39] and Chang and Rival [14,15] also aim to combine shape analysis and numeric analysis, in both cases requiring the analyst to specify predicates about the data structures of interest. Magill [37] automatically converts heap-manipulating programs into integer programs such that proving a numeric property of the latter implies a numeric shape property (e.g., a list's length) of the former. The systems just described support more precise invariants than our approach, but are less general or scalable: they tend to focus on much smaller programs, they do not support important language features (e.g., Ferrara's approach lacks procedures, DESKCHECK lacks loops), and may require manual annotation.

Clousot [22] also aims to check numeric invariants on real programs that use the heap. Methods are analyzed in isolation but require programmer-specified pre/post conditions and object invariants. In contrast, our interprocedural analysis is fully automated, requiring no annotations. Clousot's heap analysis makes local, optimistic (and unsound) assumptions about aliasing,[7] while our approach aims to be sound by using a global points-to analysis.

Measuring Analysis Parameter Tradeoffs. We are not aware of work exploring performance/precision tradeoffs of features in realistic abstract interpreters. Oftentimes, papers leave out important algorithmic details. The initial ASTRÉE paper [7] contains a wealth of ideas, but does not evaluate them systematically, instead reporting anecdotal observations about their particular analysis targets. More often, papers focus on one element of an analysis to evaluate, e.g., Logozzo [36] examines precision and performance tradeoffs useful for certain kinds of numeric analyses, and Ferrara [24] evaluates his technique using both intervals and octagons as the numeric domain. Regarding the latter, our paper shows that interactions with the heap abstraction can have a strong impact on

---

[7] Interestingly, Clousot's assumptions often, but not always, lead to sound results [16].

the numeric domain precision/performance tradeoff. Prior work by Smaragdakis et al. [49] investigates the performance/precision tradeoffs of various implementation decisions in points-to analysis. PADDLE [35] evaluates tradeoffs among different abstractions of heap allocation sites in a points-to analysis, but specifically only evaluates the heap analysis and not other analyses that use it.

8 Conclusion and Future Work

We presented a family of static numeric analyses for Java. These analyses implement a novel combination of techniques to handle method calls, heap-allocated objects, and numeric analysis. We ran the 162 resulting analysis configurations on the DaCapo benchmark suite, and measured performance and precision in proving array indexes in bounds. Using a combination of multiple linear regression and data visualization, we found several trends. Among others, we discovered that strongly updatable access paths are always a good idea, adding significant precision at very little performance cost. We also found that top-down analysis also tended to improve precision at little cost, compared to bottom-up analysis. On the other hand, while summary objects did add precision when combined with access paths, they also added significant performance overhead, often resulting in timeouts. The polyhedral numeric domain improved precision, but would time out when using a richer heap abstraction; intervals and a richer heap would work better.

The results of our study suggest several directions for future work. For example, for many programs, a much more expensive analysis often did not add much more in terms of precision; a pre-analysis that identifies the tradeoff would be worthwhile. Another direction is to investigate a more sparse representation of summary objects that retains their modest precision benefits, but avoids the overall blowup. We also plan to consider other analysis configuration options. Our current implementation uses an ahead-of-time points-to analysis to model the heap; an alternative solution is to analyze the heap along with the numeric analysis [43]. Concerning abstract object representation and context sensitivity, there are other potentially interesting choices, e.g., recency abstraction [5] and object sensitivity [40]. Other interesting dimensions to consider are field sensitivity [32] and widening, notably *widening with thresholds*. Finally, we plan to explore other effective ways to design hybrid top-down and bottom-up analysis [54], and investigate sparse inter-procedural analysis for better performance [42].

Acknowledgments. We thank Gagandeep Singh for his help in debugging ELINA. We thank Arlen Cox, Xavier Rival, and the anonymous reviewers for their detailed feedback and comments. This research was supported in part by DARPA under contracts FA8750-15-2-0104 and FA8750-16-C-0022.

References

1. Facebook Infer. http://fbinfer.com. Accessed 11 Nov 2016
2. Watson, T.J.: Libraries for Analysis (WALA). http://wala.sourceforge.net/, version 1.3
3. Arcuri, A., Briand, L.: A practical guide for using statistical tests to assess randomized algorithms in software engineering. In: ICSE (2011)
4. Bagnara, R., Hill, P.M., Ricci, E., Zaffanella, E.: Precise widening operators for convex polyhedra. In: Cousot, R. (ed.) SAS 2003. LNCS, vol. 2694, pp. 337–354. Springer, Heidelberg (2003). https://doi.org/10.1007/3-540-44898-5_19
5. Balakrishnan, G., Reps, T.: Recency-abstraction for heap-allocated storage. In: Yi, K. (ed.) SAS 2006. LNCS, vol. 4134, pp. 221–239. Springer, Heidelberg (2006). https://doi.org/10.1007/11823230_15
6. Blackburn, S.M., Garner, R., Hoffman, C., Khan, A.M., McKinley, K.S., Bentzur, R., Diwan, A., Feinberg, D., Frampton, D., Guyer, S.Z., Hirzel, M., Hosking, A., Jump, M., Lee, H., Moss, J.E.B., Phansalkar, A., Stefanović, D., VanDrunen, T., von Dincklage, D., Wiedermann, B.: The DaCapo benchmarks: java benchmarking development and analysis. In: OOPSLA (2006)
7. Blanchet, B., Cousot, P., Cousot, R., Feret, J., Mauborgne, L., Miné, A., Monniaux, D., Rival, X.: A static analyzer for large safety-critical software. In: PLDI (2003)
8. Bortz, A., Boneh, D.: Exposing private information by timing web applications. In: WWW (2007)
9. Bravenboer, M., Smaragdakis, Y.: Strictly declarative specification of sophisticated points-to analyses. In: OOPSLA (2009)
10. Brodkin, J.: Huge portions of the web vulnerable to hashing denial-of-service attack (2011). http://arstechnica.com/business/2011/12/huge-portions-of-web-vulnerable-to-hashing-denial-of-service-attack/
11. Brumley, D., Boneh, D.: Remote timing attacks are practical. In: USENIX Security (2003)
12. Burnham, K.P., Anderson, D.R., Huyvaert, K.P.: AIC model selection and multi-model inference in behavioral ecology: some background, observations, and comparisons. Behav. Ecol. Sociobiol. **65**(1), 23–25 (2011)
13. Calcagno, C., Distefano, D., O'Hearn, P.W., Yang, H.: Compositional shape analysis by means of bi-abduction. J. ACM **58**(6), 1–66 (2011)
14. Chang, B.Y.E., Rival, X.: Relational inductive shape analysis. In: POPL (2008)
15. Chang, B.Y.E., Rival, X.: Modular construction of shape-numeric analyzers. In: Semantics, Abstract Interpretation, and Reasoning about Programs: Essays Dedicated to David A. Schmidt on the Occasion of his Sixtieth Birthday (SAIRP) (2013)
16. Christakis, M., Müller, P., Wüstholz, V.: An experimental evaluation of deliberate unsoundness in a static program analyzer. In: D'Souza, D., Lal, A., Larsen, K.G. (eds.) VMCAI 2015. LNCS, vol. 8931, pp. 336–354. Springer, Heidelberg (2015). https://doi.org/10.1007/978-3-662-46081-8_19
17. Cousot, P., Cousot, R.: Static determination of dynamic properties of programs. In: Proceedings of the Second International Symposium on Programming (1976)
18. Cousot, P., Cousot, R.: Abstract interpretation: a unified lattice model for static analysis of programs by construction or approximation of fixpoints. In: POPL (1977)
19. Cousot, P., Halbwachs, N.: Automatic discovery of linear restraints among variables of a program. In: POPL (1978)

20. Cytron, R., Ferrante, J., Rosen, B.K., Wegman, M.N., Zadeck, F.K.: Efficiently computing static single assignment form and the control dependence graph. ACM Trans. Program. Lang. Syst. **13**(4), 451–490 (1991)

21. De, A., D'Souza, D.: Scalable flow-sensitive pointer analysis for java with strong updates. In: ECOOP (2012)

22. Fähndrich, M., Logozzo, F.: Static contract checking with abstract interpretation. In: Beckert, B., Marché, C. (eds.) FoVeOOS 2010. LNCS, vol. 6528, pp. 10–30. Springer, Heidelberg (2011). https://doi.org/10.1007/978-3-642-18070-5_2

23. Ferrara, P.: Generic combination of heap and value analyses in abstract interpretation. In: McMillan, K.L., Rival, X. (eds.) VMCAI 2014. LNCS, vol. 8318, pp. 302–321. Springer, Heidelberg (2014). https://doi.org/10.1007/978-3-642-54013-4_17

24. Ferrara, P., Müuller, P., Novacek, M.: Automatic inference of heap properties exploiting value domains. In: D'Souza, D., Lal, A., Larsen, K.G. (eds.) VMCAI 2015. LNCS, vol. 8931, pp. 393–411. Springer, Heidelberg (2015). https://doi.org/10.1007/978-3-662-46081-8_22

25. Fu, Z.: Modularly combining numeric abstract domains with points-to analysis, and a scalable static numeric analyzer for java. In: McMillan, K.L., Rival, X. (eds.) VMCAI 2014. LNCS, vol. 8318, pp. 282–301. Springer, Heidelberg (2014). https://doi.org/10.1007/978-3-642-54013-4_16

26. Goodin, D.: Long passwords are good, but too much length can be a dos hazard (2013). http://arstechnica.com/security/2013/09/long-passwords-are-good-but-too-much-length-can-be-bad-for-security/

27. Gopan, D., DiMaio, F., Dor, N., Reps, T., Sagiv, M.: Numeric domains with summarized dimensions. In: Jensen, K., Podelski, A. (eds.) TACAS 2004. LNCS, vol. 2988, pp. 512–529. Springer, Heidelberg (2004). https://doi.org/10.1007/978-3-540-24730-2_38

28. Gulwani, S., Jain, S., Koskinen, E.: Control-flow refinement and progress invariants for bound analysis. In: PLDI (2009)

29. Gulwani, S., Tiwari, A.: Computing procedure summaries for interprocedural analysis. In: De Nicola, R. (ed.) ESOP 2007. LNCS, vol. 4421, pp. 253–267. Springer, Heidelberg (2007). https://doi.org/10.1007/978-3-540-71316-6_18

30. Gulwani, S., Zuleger, F.: The reachability-bound problem. In: PLDI (2010)

31. Henry, J., Monniaux, D., Moy, M.: Pagai: a path sensitive static analyser. Electron. Notes Theor. Comput. Sci. **289**, 15–25 (2012)

32. Hind, M.: Pointer analysis: haven't we solved this problem yet? In: PASTE (2001)

33. Jeannet, B., Miné, A.: APRON: a library of numerical abstract domains for static analysis. In: Bouajjani, A., Maler, O. (eds.) CAV 2009. LNCS, vol. 5643, pp. 661–667. Springer, Heidelberg (2009). https://doi.org/10.1007/978-3-642-02658-4_52

34. Lev-Ami, T., Sagiv, M.: TVLA: a system for implementing static analyses. In: Palsberg, J. (ed.) SAS 2000. LNCS, vol. 1824, pp. 280–301. Springer, Heidelberg (2000). https://doi.org/10.1007/978-3-540-45099-3_15

35. Lhoták, O., Hendren, L.: Evaluating the benefits of context-sensitive points-to analysis using a BDD-based implementation. ACM Trans. Softw. Eng. Methodol. (TOSEM) **18**(1), 1–53 (2008)

36. Logozzo, F., Fähndrich, M.: Pentagons: a weakly relational abstract domain for the efficient validation of array accesses. In: SAC (2008)

37. Magill, S.: Instrumentation analysis: an automated method for producing numeric abstractions of heap-manipulating programs. Ph.D. thesis, School of Computer Science, Carnegie Mellon University (2010)

38. Mardziel, P., Magill, S., Hicks, M., Srivatsa, M.: Dynamic enforcement of knowledge-based security policies using probabilistic abstract interpretation. J. Comput. Secur. 21(4), 463–532 (2013)
39. McCloskey, B., Reps, T., Sagiv, M.: Statically inferring complex heap, array, and numeric invariants. In: Cousot, R., Martel, M. (eds.) SAS 2010. LNCS, vol. 6337, pp. 71–99. Springer, Heidelberg (2010). https://doi.org/10.1007/978-3-642-15769-1_6
40. Milanova, A., Rountev, A., Ryder, B.G.: Parameterized object sensitivity for points-to analysis for java. ACM Trans. Softw. Eng. Methodol. (TOSEM) 14(1), 1–14 (2005)
41. Miné, A.: APRON numerical abstract domain library. http://apron.cri.ensmp.fr/library/
42. Oh, H., Heo, K., Lee, W., Lee, W., Yi, K.: Design and implementation of sparse global analyses for c-like languages. In: PLDI (2012)
43. Pioli, A., Hind, M.: Combining interprocedural pointer analysis and conditional constant propagation. Technical report, IBM T. J. Watson Research Center (1999)
44. Ryder, B.G.: Dimensions of precision in reference analysis of object-oriented programming languages. In: Hedin, G. (ed.) CC 2003. LNCS, vol. 2622, pp. 126–137. Springer, Heidelberg (2003). https://doi.org/10.1007/3-540-36579-6_10
45. Seltman, H.: Experimental design and analysis (2015). http://www.stat.cmu.edu/~hseltman/309/Book/Book.pdf. e-book
46. Shivers, O.: Control-flow analysis of higher-order languages or taming lambda. Ph.D. thesis, School of Computer Science, Carnegie Mellon University (1991)
47. Singh, G., Püschel, M., Vechev, M.: ETH Library for Numerical Analysis. http://elina.ethz.ch and https://github.com/eth-srl/ELINA
48. Singh, G., Püschel, M., Vechev, M.T.: Fast polyhedra abstract domain. In: POPL (2017)
49. Smaragdakis, Y., Bravenboer, M., Lhoták, O.: Pick your contexts well: understanding object-sensitivity. In: POPL (2011)
50. Wagner, D., Foster, J.S., Brewer, E.A., Aiken, A.: A first step towards automated detection of buffer overrun vulnerabilities. In: NDSS (2000)
51. Wei, S., Mardziel, P., Ruef, A., Foster, J.S., Hicks, M.: Evaluating design tradeoffs in numeric static analysis for java (extended version). Technical report (2018). http://www.cs.umd.edu/~mwh/papers/jana-extended.pdf
52. Wei, S., Ryder, B.G.: State-sensitive points-to analysis for the dynamic behavior of javascript objects. In: Jones, R. (ed.) ECOOP 2014. LNCS, vol. 8586, pp. 1–26. Springer, Heidelberg (2014). https://doi.org/10.1007/978-3-662-44202-9_1
53. Whaley, J., Rinard, M.: Compositional pointer and escape analysis for java programs. In: OOPSLA (1999)
54. Zhang, X., Mangal, R., Naik, M., Yang, H.: Hybrid top-down and bottom-up interprocedural analysis. In: PLDI (2014)

An Abstract Interpretation Framework for Input Data Usage

Caterina Urban$^{(\boxtimes)}$ and Peter Müller

Department of Computer Science, ETH Zurich, Zurich, Switzerland
{caterina.urban,peter.mueller}@inf.ethz.ch

Abstract. Data science software plays an increasingly important role in critical decision making in fields ranging from economy and finance to biology and medicine. As a result, errors in data science applications can have severe consequences, especially when they lead to results that look plausible, but are incorrect. A common cause of such errors is when applications erroneously ignore some of their input data, for instance due to bugs in the code that reads, filters, or clusters it.

In this paper, we propose an abstract interpretation framework to automatically detect unused input data. We derive a program semantics that precisely captures data usage by abstraction of the program's operational trace semantics and express it in a constructive fixpoint form. Based on this semantics, we systematically derive static analyses that automatically detect unused input data by fixpoint approximation.

This clear design principle provides a framework that subsumes existing analyses; we show that secure information flow analyses and a form of live variables analysis can be used for data usage, with varying degrees of precision. Additionally, we derive a static analysis to detect single unused data inputs, which is similar to dependency analyses used in the context of backward program slicing. Finally, we demonstrate the value of expressing such analyses as abstract interpretation by combining them with an existing abstraction of compound data structures such as arrays and lists to detect unused chunks of the data.

1 Introduction

In the past few years, data science has grown considerably in importance and now heavily influences many domains, ranging from economy and finance to biology and medicine. As we rely more and more on data science for making decisions, we become increasingly vulnerable to programming errors.

Programming errors can cause frustration, especially when they lead to a program failure after hours of computation. However, programming errors that do not cause failures can have more serious consequences as code that produces an erroneous but plausible result gives no indication that something went wrong. A notable example is the paper "Growth in a Time of Debt" published in 2010 by economists Reinhart and Rogoff, which was widely cited in political debates and

A. Ahmed (Ed.): ESOP 2018, LNCS 10801, pp. 683–710, 2018.
https://doi.org/10.1007/978-3-319-89884-1_24

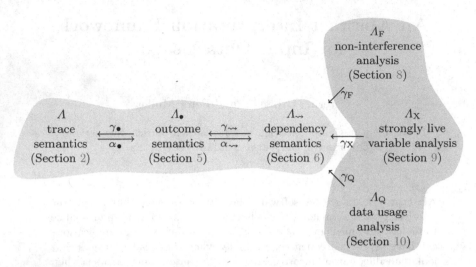

Fig. 1. Overview of the program semantics presented in the paper. The *dependency semantics*, derived by abstraction of the *trace semantics*, is sound and complete for data usage. Further sound but not complete abstractions are shown on the right.

was later demonstrated to be flawed. Notably, one of the flaws was a programming error, which *entirely excluded some data* from the analysis [23]. Its critics hold that this paper led to unjustified adoption of austerity policies for countries with various levels of public debt [30]. Programming errors in data analysis code for medical applications are even more critical [27]. It is thus paramount to achieve a high level of confidence in the correctness of data science code.

The likelihood that a programming error causes some input data to remain unused is particularly high for data science applications, where data goes through long pipelines of modules that acquire, filter, merge, and manipulate it. In this paper, we propose an abstract interpretation [14] framework to automatically detect *unused input data*. We characterize when a program uses (some of) its input data using the notion of *dependency* between the input data and the *outcome* of the program. Our notion of dependency accounts for non-determinism and non-termination. Thus, it encompasses notions of dependency that arise in many different contexts, such as secure information flow and program slicing [1], as well as provenance or lineage analysis [9], to name a few.

Following the theory of abstract interpretation [12], we systematically derive a new program semantics that precisely captures exactly the information needed to reason about input data usage, abstracting away from irrelevant details about the program behavior. Figure 1 gives an overview of our approach. The semantics is first expressed in a constructive fixpoint form over *sets of sets of traces*, by partitioning the operational trace semantics of a program based on its outcome (cf. *outcome semantics* in Fig. 1), and a further abstraction ignores intermediate state computations (cf. *dependency semantics* in Fig. 1). Starting the development of the semantics from the operational trace semantics enables a uniform mathematical reasoning about programs semantics and program properties (Sect. 3). In particular, since input data usage is not a trace property or a subset-closed property [11] (Sect. 4), we show that a formulation of the semantics using sets of sets of traces is necessary for a sound validation of input data usage via fixpoint approximation [28].

This clear design principle provides a unifying framework for reasoning about existing analyses based on dependencies. We survey existing analyses and identify key design decisions that limit or facilitate their applicability to input data usage, and we assess their precision. We show that non-interference analyses [6] are sound for proving that a *terminating* program does not use *any* of its input data; although this is too strong a property in general. We prove that strongly live variable analysis [20] is sound for data usage even for non-terminating programs, albeit it is imprecise with respect to implicit dependencies between program variables. We then derive a more precise static analysis similar to dependency analyses used in the context of backward program slicing [37]. Finally, we demonstrate the value of expressing these analyses as abstract interpretations by combining them with an existing abstraction of compound data structures such as arrays and lists [16]. This allows us to detect unused chunks of the input data, and thus apply our work to realistic data science applications.

2   Trace Semantics

The *semantics* of a program is a mathematical characterization of its behavior when executed for all possible input data. We model the operational semantics of a program as a *transition system* $\langle \Sigma, \tau \rangle$ where Σ is a (potentially infinite) set of program states and the transition relation $\tau \subseteq \Sigma \times \Sigma$ describes the possible transitions between states [12,14]. Note that this model allows representing programs with (possibly unbounded) non-determinism. The set $\Omega \stackrel{\text{def}}{=} \{s \in \Sigma \mid \forall s' \in \Sigma : \langle s, s' \rangle \notin \tau\}$ is the set of *final states* of the program.

In the following, let $\Sigma^n \stackrel{\text{def}}{=} \{s_0 \cdots s_{n-1} \mid \forall i < n : s_i \in \Sigma\}$ be the set of all sequences of exactly n program states. We write ε to denote the empty sequence, i.e., $\Sigma^0 \stackrel{\text{def}}{=} \{\varepsilon\}$. Let $\Sigma^\star \stackrel{\text{def}}{=} \bigcup_{n \in \mathbb{N}} \Sigma^n$ be the set of all finite sequences, $\Sigma^+ \stackrel{\text{def}}{=} \Sigma^\star \setminus \Sigma^0$ be the set of all non-empty finite sequences, Σ^ω be the set of all infinite sequences, $\Sigma^{+\infty} \stackrel{\text{def}}{=} \Sigma^+ \cup \Sigma^\omega$ be the set of all non-empty finite or infinite sequences and $\Sigma^{\star\infty} \stackrel{\text{def}}{=} \Sigma^\star \cup \Sigma^\omega$ be the set of all finite or infinite sequences of program states. In the following, we write $\sigma\sigma'$ for the concatenation of two sequences $\sigma, \sigma' \in \Sigma^{\star\infty}$ (with $\sigma\varepsilon = \varepsilon\sigma = \sigma$, and $\sigma\sigma' = \sigma$ when $\sigma \in \Sigma^\omega$), $T^+ \stackrel{\text{def}}{=} T \cap \Sigma^+$ and $T^\omega \stackrel{\text{def}}{=} T \cap \Sigma^\omega$ for the selection of the non-empty finite sequences and the infinite sequences of $T \in \mathcal{P}(\Sigma^{\star\infty})$, and $T \mathbin{;} T' \stackrel{\text{def}}{=} \{\sigma s \sigma' \mid s \in \Sigma \wedge \sigma s \in T \wedge s\sigma' \in T'\}$ for the merging of two sets of sequences $T \in \mathcal{P}(\Sigma^+)$ and $T' \in \mathcal{P}(\Sigma^{+\infty})$, when a finite sequence in T terminates with the initial state of a sequence in T'.

Given a transition system $\langle \Sigma, \tau \rangle$, a *trace* is a non-empty sequence of program states described by the transition relation τ, that is, $\langle s, s' \rangle \in \tau$ for each pair of

$$T_0 = \left\{ \rotatebox{0}{$\sim\!\!\sim\!\!\sim$}^{\Sigma^\omega} \right\}$$

$$T_1 = \left\{ \begin{array}{c} \Omega \\ \bullet \end{array} \right\} \cup \left\{ \underline{\quad\tau\quad} \rotatebox{0}{$\sim\!\!\sim\!\!\sim$}^{\Sigma^\omega} \right\}$$

$$T_2 = \left\{ \begin{array}{c} \Omega \\ \bullet \end{array} \right\} \cup \left\{ \underline{\quad\tau\quad}^{\Omega} \right\} \cup \left\{ \underline{\quad\tau\quad}\underline{\quad\tau\quad} \rotatebox{0}{$\sim\!\!\sim\!\!\sim$}^{\Sigma^\omega} \right\}$$

Fig. 2. First fixpoint iterates of the trace semantics Λ.

consecutive states $s, s' \in \Sigma$ in the sequence. The set of final states Ω and the transition relation τ can be understood as sets of traces of length one and length two, respectively. The *trace semantics* $\Lambda \in \mathcal{P}(\Sigma^{+\infty})$ generated by a transition system $\langle \Sigma, \tau \rangle$ is the union of all finite traces that are terminating with a final state in Ω, and all infinite traces. It can be expressed as a least fixpoint in the complete lattice $\langle \mathcal{P}(\Sigma^{+\infty}), \sqsubseteq, \sqcup, \sqcap, \Sigma^\omega, \Sigma^+ \rangle$ [12]:

$$\Lambda = \mathrm{lfp}^{\sqsubseteq} \Theta$$

$$\Theta(T) \stackrel{\text{def}}{=} \Omega \cup (\tau \,;\, T) \tag{1}$$

where the computational order is $T_1 \sqsubseteq T_2 \stackrel{\text{def}}{=} T_1^+ \subseteq T_2^+ \wedge T_1^\omega \supseteq T_2^\omega$. Figure 2 illustrates the first fixpoint iterates. The fixpoint iteration starts from the set of all infinite *sequences* of program states. At each iteration, the final program states in Ω are added to the set, and sequences already in the set are extended by prepending transitions to them. In this way, we *add* increasingly longer finite traces, and we *remove* infinite sequences of states with increasingly longer prefixes not forming traces. In particular, the i-th iterate builds all finite traces of length less than or equal to i, and selects all infinite sequences whose prefixes of length i form traces. At the limit we obtain all infinite traces and all finite traces that terminate in a final state in Ω. Note that Λ is *suffix-closed*.

The trace semantics Λ fully describes the behavior of a program. However, to reason about a particular property of a program, it is not necessary to consider all aspects of its behavior. In fact, reasoning is facilitated by the design of a semantics that abstracts away from irrelevant details about program executions. In the next sections, we define our property of interest and use abstract interpretation [14] to systematically derive, by successive abstractions of the trace semantics, a semantics that precisely captures such a property.

3   Input Data Usage

A *property* is specified by its extension, that is, the set of elements having such a property [14,15]. Thus, properties of program traces in $\Sigma^{+\infty}$ are sets of traces in

$\mathcal{P}(\Sigma^{+\infty})$, and properties of programs with trace semantics in $\mathcal{P}(\Sigma^{+\infty})$ are *sets of sets of traces* in $\mathcal{P}(\mathcal{P}(\Sigma^{+\infty}))$. Accordingly, a program P satisfies a property $\mathcal{H} \in \mathcal{P}(\mathcal{P}(\Sigma^{+\infty}))$ if and only if its semantics $[\![P]\!] \in \mathcal{P}(\Sigma^{+\infty})$ belongs to $\mathcal{H}$:

$$P \models \mathcal{H} \Leftrightarrow [\![P]\!] \in \mathcal{H} \tag{2}$$

Some program properties are defined in terms of individual program traces and can be equivalently expressed as trace properties. This is the case for the traditional safety [26] and liveness [4] properties of programs. In such a case, a program P satisfies a trace property $\mathcal{T}$ if and only if all traces in its semantics $[\![P]\!]$ belong to the property: $P \models \mathcal{T} \Leftrightarrow [\![P]\!] \subseteq \mathcal{T}$.

Program properties that establish a relation between different program traces cannot be expressed as trace properties [11]. Examples are security properties such as *non-interference* [21,35]. In this paper, we consider a closely related but more general property called *input data usage*, which expresses that *the outcome of a program does not depend on (some of) its input data*. The notion of *outcome* accounts for non-determinism as well as non-termination. Thus, our notion of dependency encompasses non-interference as well as notions of dependency that arise in many other contexts [1,9]. We further explore this in Sects. 8 to 10.

Let each program P with trace semantics $[\![P]\!]$ have a set I_P of input variables and a set O_P of output variables[1]. For simplicity, we can assume that these variables are all of the same type (e.g., boolean variables) and their values are all in a set V of possible values (e.g., $\mathrm{V} = \{\mathrm{T}, \mathrm{F}\}$ where T is the boolean value true and F is the boolean value false). Given a trace $\sigma \in [\![P]\!]$, we write $\sigma[0]$ to denote its initial state and $\sigma[\omega]$ to denote its outcome, that is, its final state if the trace is finite or $\bot$ if the trace is infinite. The input variables at the initial states of the traces of a program store the values of its input data: we write $\sigma[0](i)$ to denote the value of the input data stored in the input variable i at the initial state of the trace σ, and $\sigma_1[0] \neq_i \sigma_2[0]$ to denote that the initial states of two traces σ_1 and σ_2 disagree on the value of the input variable i but agree on the values of all other variables. The output variables at the final states of the finite traces of a program store its result: we write $\sigma[\omega](o)$ to denote the result stored in the output variable o at the final state of a finite trace σ. We can now formally define when an input variable $i \in \mathrm{I}_P$ is *unused* with respect to a program with trace semantics $[\![P]\!] \in \mathcal{P}(\Sigma^{+\infty})$:

$$\mathrm{UNUSED}_i([\![P]\!]) \overset{\mathrm{def}}{=} \forall \sigma \in [\![P]\!], v \in \mathrm{V} \colon \sigma[0](i) \neq v \Rightarrow \\ \exists \sigma' \in [\![P]\!] \colon \sigma'[0] \neq_i \sigma[0] \wedge \sigma'[0](i) = v \wedge \sigma[\omega] = \sigma'[\omega] \tag{3}$$

Intuitively, an input variable i is unused if all feasible program outcomes (e.g., the outcome $\sigma[\omega]$ of a trace σ) are feasible from all possible initial values of i (i.e., for all possible initial values v of i that differ from the initial value of i in σ, there exists a trace with initial value v for i that has the same outcome $\sigma[\omega]$). In other words, the outcome of the program is the same independently of

---

[1] The approach can be easily extended to infinite inputs and/or outputs via abstractions such as the one later presented in Sect. 11.

```
1  english = input ()
2  math = input ()
3  science = input ()
4  bonus = input ()
5
6  passing = True
7  if not english: english = False          # english should be passing
8  if not math: passing = bonus
9  if not math: passing = bonus             # math should be science
10
11 print ( passing )
```

Fig. 3. Simple program to check if a student has passed three school subjects. The programmer has made two mistakes at line 7 and at line 9, which cause the input data stored in the variables **english** and **science** to be unused.

the initial value of the input variable i. Note that this definition accounts for non-determinism (since it considers each program outcome independently) and non-termination (since a program outcome can be $\bot$).

Example 1. Let us consider the simple program P in Fig. 3. Based on the input variables **english**, **math**, and **science** (cf. lines 1–3), the program is supposed to check if a student has passed all three considered school subjects and store the result in the output variable **passing** (cf. line 11). For mathematics and science, the student is allowed a bonus based on the input variable **bonus** (cf. line 8 and 9). However, the programmer has made two mistakes at line 7 and at line 9, which cause the input variables **english** and **science** to be unused.

Let us now consider the input variable **science**. The trace semantics of the program (simplified to consider only the variables **science** and **passing**) is:

$$[\![P]\!]_{\text{science}} = \{(\text{T\_}) \dots (\text{TT}), (\text{T\_}) \dots (\text{TF}), (\text{F\_}) \dots (\text{FT}), (\text{F\_}) \dots (\text{FF})\}$$

where each state $(v_1 v_2)$ shows the boolean value v_1 of **science** and v_2 of **passing**, and $\_$ denotes any boolean value. We omitted the trace suffixes for brevity. The input variable **science** is *unused*, since each result value (T or F) for **passing** is feasible from all possible initial values of **science**. Note that all other outcomes of the program (i.e., non-termination) are not feasible.

Let us now consider the input variable **math**. The trace semantics of the program (now simplified to only consider **math** and **passing**) is the following:

$$[\![P]\!]_{\text{math}} = \{(\text{T\_}) \dots (\text{TT}), (\text{F\_}) \dots (\text{FT}), (\text{F\_}) \dots (\text{FF})\}$$

In this case, the input variable **math** is used since only the initial state (F_) yields the result value F for **passing** (in the final state (FF)). ∎

The input data usage property $\mathcal{N}$ can now be formally defined as follows:

$$\mathcal{N} \overset{\text{def}}{=} \{[\![P]\!] \in \mathcal{P}\left(\Sigma^{+\infty}\right) \mid \forall i \in \mathbb{I}_P : \text{UNUSED}_i([\![P]\!])\} \tag{4}$$

which states that the outcome of a program does not depend on *any* input data. In practice one is interested in weaker input data usage properties for a subset

J of the input variables, i.e., $\mathcal{N}_J \stackrel{\text{def}}{=} \{[\![P]\!] \in \mathcal{P}(\Sigma^{+\infty}) \mid \forall i \in J \subseteq I_P : \text{UNUSED}_i([\![P]\!])\}$.

In the following, we use abstract interpretation to reason about input data usage. In the next section, we discuss the challenges to the application of the standard abstract interpretation framework that emerge from the fact that input data usage cannot be expressed as a trace property.

4   Sound Input Data Usage Validation

In the standard framework of abstract interpretation, one defines a semantics that precisely captures a property S of interest by abstraction of the trace semantics Λ [12]. Then, further abstractions $\Lambda^\natural$ provide sound over-approximations $\gamma(\Lambda^\natural)$ of Λ (by means of a concretization function γ): $\Lambda \subseteq \gamma(\Lambda^\natural)$. For a *trace property*, an over-approximation $\gamma([\![P]\!]^\natural)$ of the semantics $[\![P]\!]$ of a program P allows a sound validation of the property: since $[\![P]\!] \subseteq \gamma([\![P]\!]^\natural)$, we have that $\gamma([\![P]\!]^\natural) \subseteq S \Rightarrow [\![P]\!] \subseteq S$ and so, if $\gamma([\![P]\!]^\natural) \subseteq S$, we can conclude that $P \models S$ (cf. Sect. 3). This conclusion is also valid for all other *subset-closed* properties [11]: since by definition $\gamma([\![P]\!]^\natural) \in S \Rightarrow \forall T \subseteq \gamma([\![P]\!]^\natural) : T \in S$, we have that $\gamma([\![P]\!]^\natural) \in S \Rightarrow [\![P]\!] \in S$ (and so we can conclude that $P \models S$). However, for program properties that are not subset-closed, we have that $\gamma([\![P]\!]^\natural) \in S \not\Rightarrow [\![P]\!] \in S$ [28] and so we cannot conclude that $P \models S$, even if $\gamma([\![P]\!]^\natural) \in S$ (cf. Eq. 2).

We have seen in the previous section that input data usage is not a trace property. The example below shows that it is *not* a subset-closed property either.

Example 2. Let us consider again the program P and its semantics $[\![P]\!]_{\text{science}}$ and $[\![P]\!]_{\text{math}}$ shown in Example 1. We have seen in Example 1 that the semantics $[\![P]\!]_{\text{science}}$ belongs to the data usage property $\mathcal{N}$: $[\![P]\!]_{\text{science}} \in \mathcal{N}$. Let us consider now the following subset T of $[\![P]\!]_{\text{science}}$:

$$T = \{(\text{T}_-)\dots(\text{TT}), (\text{F}_-)\dots(\text{FT}), (\text{F}_-)\dots(\text{FF})\}$$

In this case, the input variable science is used. Indeed, we can observe that T coincides with $[\![P]\!]_{\text{math}}$ (except for the considered input variable). Thus $T \notin \mathcal{N}$ even though $T \subseteq [\![P]\!]_{\text{science}}$.   ∎

Since input data usage is not subset-closed, we are in the unfortunate situation that we cannot use the standard abstract interpretation framework to soundly prove that a program does not use (some of) its input data using an over-approximation of the semantics of the program: $\gamma([\![P]\!]^\natural) \in \mathcal{N}_J \not\Rightarrow [\![P]\!] \in \mathcal{N}_J$.

We solve this problem in the next section, by lifting the trace semantics $[\![P]\!] \in \mathcal{P}(\Sigma^{+\infty})$ of a program P (i.e., a set of traces) to a set of sets of traces $([\![P]\!]) \in \mathcal{P}(\mathcal{P}(\Sigma^{+\infty}))$ [28]. In this setting, a program P satisfies a property $\mathcal{H}$ if and only if its semantics $([\![P]\!])$ is a subset of $\mathcal{H}$:

$$P \models \mathcal{H} \Leftrightarrow ([\![P]\!]) \subseteq \mathcal{H} \tag{5}$$

As we will explain in the next section, now an over-approximation $\gamma((\!|P|\!)^\natural)$ of $(\!|P|\!)$ allows again a sound validation of the property: since $(\!|P|\!) \subseteq \gamma((\!|P|\!)^\natural)$, we have that $\gamma((\!|P|\!)^\natural) \subseteq \mathcal{H} \Rightarrow (\!|P|\!) \subseteq \mathcal{H}$ (and so we can conclude that $P \models \mathcal{H}$).

More specifically, in the next section, we define a program semantics $(\!|P|\!)$ that precisely captures which subset J of the input variables is unused by a program P. In later sections, we present further abstractions $(\!|P|\!)^\natural$ that over-approximate the subset of the input variables that *may be used* by P, and thus allows a sound validation of an *under-approximation* $J^\natural$ of J: $\gamma((\!|P|\!)^\natural) \subseteq \mathcal{N}_{J^\natural} \Rightarrow (\!|P|\!) \subseteq \mathcal{N}_{J^\natural}$. In other words, this means that every input variable reported as unused by an abstraction is indeed not used by the program.

5   Outcome Semantics

We lift the trace semantics Λ to a set of sets of traces by *partitioning*. The *partitioning abstraction* $\alpha_Q \colon \mathcal{P}(\Sigma^{+\infty}) \to \mathcal{P}(\mathcal{P}(\Sigma^{+\infty}))$ of a set of traces T is:

$$\alpha_Q(T) \stackrel{\text{def}}{=} \{T \cap C \mid C \in Q\} \tag{6}$$

where $Q \in \mathcal{P}(\mathcal{P}(\Sigma^{+\infty}))$ is a *partition* of sequences of program states.

More specifically, to reason about input data usage of a program P, we lift the trace semantics $[\![P]\!]$ to $(\!|P|\!)$ by partitioning it into sets of traces that yield the same program outcome. The key insight behind this idea is that, given an input variable i, the initial states of all traces in a partition give all initial values for i that yield a program outcome; the variable i is unused if and only if these initial values are all the possible values for i (or the set of values is empty because the outcome is unfeasible, cf. Eq. 3). Thus, if the trace semantics $[\![P]\!]$ of a program P belongs to the input data usage property $\mathcal{N}_J$, then each partition in $(\!|P|\!)$ must also belong to $\mathcal{N}_J$, and vice versa: we have that $[\![P]\!] \in \mathcal{N}_J \Leftrightarrow (\!|P|\!) \subseteq \mathcal{N}_J$, which is precisely what we want (cf. Eq. 5).

Let $T^+_{o=v}$ denote the subset of the finite sequences of program states in $T \in \mathcal{P}(\Sigma^{+\infty})$ with value v for the output variable o in their outcome (i.e., their final state): $T^+_{o=v} \stackrel{\text{def}}{=} \{\sigma \in T^+ \mid \sigma[\omega](o) = v\}$. We define the *outcome partition* $O \in \mathcal{P}(\mathcal{P}(\Sigma^{+\infty}))$ of sequences of program states:

$$O \stackrel{\text{def}}{=} \{\Sigma^+_{o_1=v_1,\dots,o_k=v_k} \mid v_1,\dots,v_k \in \mathrm{V}\} \cup \{\Sigma^\omega\}$$

where V is the set of possible values of the output variables $o_1,\dots,o_k$ (cf. Sect. 3). The partition contains all sets of finite sequences that agree on the values of the output variables in their outcome, and all infinite sequences of program states (i.e., all sequences with outcome $\bot$). We instantiate α_Q above with the outcome partition to obtain the *outcome abstraction* $\alpha_\bullet \colon \mathcal{P}(\Sigma^{+\infty}) \to \mathcal{P}(\mathcal{P}(\Sigma^{+\infty}))$:

$$\alpha_\bullet(T) \stackrel{\text{def}}{=} \{T^+_{o_1=v_1,\dots,o_k=v_k} \mid v_1,\dots,v_k \in \mathrm{V}\} \cup \{T^\omega\} \tag{7}$$

Example 3. The program P of Example 1 has only one output variable `passing` with boolean value T or F. Let us consider again the trace semantics $[\![P]\!]_{\text{math}}$ shown in Example 1. Its outcome abstraction $\alpha_\bullet([\![P]\!]_{\text{math}})$ is:

$$\alpha_\bullet([\![P]\!]_{\text{math}}) = \{\emptyset, \{(\mathrm{F}_-)\dots(\mathrm{FF})\}, \{(\mathrm{T}_-)\dots(\mathrm{TT}), (\mathrm{F}_-)\dots(\mathrm{FT})\}\}$$

Note that all traces with different result values for the output variable `passing` belong to different sets of traces (i.e., partitions) in $\alpha_\bullet([\![P]\!]_{\text{math}})$. The empty set corresponds to the (unfeasible) non-terminating outcome of the program. ∎

We can now use the outcome abstraction $\alpha_\bullet$ to define the *outcome semantics* $\Lambda_\bullet \in \mathcal{P}(\mathcal{P}(\Sigma^{+\infty}))$ as an abstraction of the trace semantics Λ:

Definition 1. *The* outcome semantics $\Lambda_\bullet \in \mathcal{P}(\mathcal{P}(\Sigma^{+\infty}))$ *is defined as:*

$$\Lambda_\bullet \stackrel{\text{def}}{=} \alpha_\bullet(\Lambda) \tag{8}$$

where $\alpha_\bullet$ is the outcome abstraction (cf. Eq. 7) and $\Lambda \in \mathcal{P}(\Sigma^{+\infty})$ is the trace semantics (cf. Eq. 1).

The outcome semantics contains the set of all infinite traces and all sets of finite traces that agree on the value of the output variables in their outcome.

In the following, we express the outcome semantics $\Lambda_\bullet$ in a constructive fixpoint form. This allows us to later derive further abstractions of $\Lambda_\bullet$ by *fixpoint transfer* and *fixpoint approximation* [12]. Given a set of sets of traces S, we write $S_{o=v}^+ \stackrel{\text{def}}{=} \{T \in S \mid T = T_{o=v}^+\}$ for the selection of the sets of traces in S that agree on the value v of the output variable o in their outcome, and $S^\omega \stackrel{\text{def}}{=} \{T \in S \mid T = T^\omega\}$ for the selection of the sets of infinite traces in S. When $S_{o=v}^+$ (resp. S^ω) contains a single set of traces T, we abuse notation and write $S_{o=v}^+$ (resp. S^ω) to also denote T. The following result gives a fixpoint definition of $\Lambda_\bullet$ in the complete lattice $\langle \mathcal{P}(\mathcal{P}(\Sigma^{+\infty})), \sqsubseteq, \sqcup, \sqcap, \{\Sigma^\omega, \emptyset\}, \{\emptyset, \Sigma^+\}\rangle$, where the computational order $\sqsubseteq$ is defined (similarly to $\sqsubseteq$, cf. Sect. 2) as:

$$S_1 \sqsubseteq S_2 \stackrel{\text{def}}{=} \bigwedge_{v_1,\dots,v_k \in V} S_{1\,o_1=v_1,\dots,o_k=v_k}^+ \subseteq S_{2\,o_1=v_1,\dots,o_k=v_k}^+ \wedge S_1^\omega \supseteq S_2^\omega$$

Theorem 1. *The* outcome semantics $\Lambda_\bullet \in \mathcal{P}(\mathcal{P}(\Sigma^{+\infty}))$ *can be expressed as a least fixpoint in* $\langle \mathcal{P}(\mathcal{P}(\Sigma^{+\infty})), \sqsubseteq, \sqcup, \sqcap, \{\Sigma^\omega, \emptyset\}, \{\emptyset, \Sigma^+\}\rangle$ *as:*

$$\Lambda_\bullet = \text{lfp}^{\sqsubseteq} \Theta_\bullet$$

$$\Theta_\bullet(S) \stackrel{\text{def}}{=} \{\Omega_{o_1=v_1,\dots,o_k=v_k} \mid v_1,\dots,v_k \in V\} \cup \{\tau\,;T \mid T \in S\} \tag{9}$$

where $S_1 \uplus S_2 \stackrel{\text{def}}{=} \{S_{1\,o_1=v_1,\dots,o_k=v_k}^+ \cup S_{2\,o_1=v_1,\dots,o_k=v_k}^+ \mid v_1,\dots,v_k \in V\} \cup S_1^\omega \cup S_2^\omega.$

Figure 4 illustrates the first fixpoint iterates of the outcome semantics for a single output variable o. The fixpoint iteration starts from the partition containing the set of all infinite sequences of program states and the empty set (which

$$S_0 = \left\{ \left\{ \sim\hspace{-4pt}\sim\hspace{-4pt}\sim^{\Sigma^\omega} \right\}, \emptyset \right\}$$

$$S_1 = \left\{ \left\{ \stackrel{\Omega_{o=v}}{\bullet} \right\} \,\middle|\, v \in V \right\} \cup \left\{ \left\{ \stackrel{\tau}{\bullet\!-\!\!\!\!\sim\hspace{-4pt}\sim^{\Sigma^\omega}} \right\} \right\}$$

$$S_2 = \left\{ \left\{ \stackrel{\Omega_{o=v}}{\bullet} \right\} \cup \left\{ \stackrel{\tau}{\bullet\!-\!\!\!\bullet^{\Omega_{o=v}}} \right\} \,\middle|\, v \in V \right\} \cup \left\{ \left\{ \stackrel{\tau}{\bullet\!-\!\!\!\bullet\!-\!\!\!\!\sim\hspace{-4pt}\sim^{\Sigma^\omega}} \right\} \right\}$$

Fig. 4. First iterates of the outcome semantics $\Lambda_\bullet$ for a single output variable o.

represents an empty set of finite traces). At the first iteration, the empty set is replaced with a partition of the final states Ω based on the value v of the output variable o, while the infinite sequences are extended by prepending transitions to them (similarly to the trace semantics, cf. Eq. 1). At the next iterations, all sequences contained in each partition are further extended, and the final states that agree on the value v of o are again added to the matching set of traces that agree on v in their outcome. At the limit, we obtain a partition containing the set of all infinite traces and all sets of finite traces that agree on the value v of the output variable o in their outcome.

To prove Theorem 1 we first need to show that the outcome abstraction $\alpha_\bullet$ preserves least upper bounds of non-empty sets of sets of traces.

Lemma 1. *The outcome abstraction $\alpha_\bullet$ is Scott-continuous.*

Proof. We need to show that for any non-empty ascending chain C of sets of traces with least upper bound $\sqcup C$, we have that $\alpha_\bullet(\sqcup C) = \sqcup\{\alpha_\bullet(T) \mid T \in C\}$, that is, $\alpha_\bullet(\sqcup C)$ is the least upper bound of $\alpha_\bullet(C)$, the image of C via $\alpha_\bullet$.

First, we know that $\alpha_\bullet$ is monotonic, i.e., for any two sets of traces T_1 and T_2 we have $T_1 \sqsubseteq T_2 \Rightarrow \alpha_\bullet(T_1) \sqsubseteq \alpha_\bullet(T_2)$. Since $\sqcup C$ is the least upper bound of C, for any set T in C we have that $T \sqsubseteq \sqcup C$ and, since $\alpha_\bullet$ is monotonic, we have that $\alpha_\bullet(T) \sqsubseteq \alpha_\bullet(\sqcup C)$. Thus $\alpha(\sqcup C)$ is an upper bound of $\{\alpha_\bullet(T) \mid T \in C\}$.

To show that $\alpha(\sqcup C)$ is the least upper bound of $\alpha_\bullet(C)$, we need to show that for any other upper bound U of $\alpha_\bullet(C)$ we have $\alpha_\bullet(\sqcup C) \sqsubseteq U$. Let us assume by absurd that $\alpha_\bullet(\sqcup C) \not\sqsubseteq U$. Then, there exists $T_1 \in \alpha_\bullet(\sqcup C)$ and $T_2 \in U$ such that $T_1 \not\sqsubseteq T_2$: $T_1^+ \supset T_2^+$ or $T_1^\omega \subset T_2^\omega$. Let us assume that $T_1^+ \supset T_2^+$. By definition of $\alpha_\bullet$, we observe that T_1 is a partition of $\sqcup C$ and, since $\sqcup C$ is the least upper bound of C, U cannot be an upper bound of $\alpha_\bullet(C)$ (since T_2 does not contain enough finite traces). Similarly, if $T_1^\omega \subset T_2^\omega$, then U cannot be an upper bound of $\alpha_\bullet(C)$ (since T_2 contains too many infinite traces). Thus, we must have $\alpha_\bullet(\sqcup C) \sqsubseteq U$ and we can conclude that $\alpha(\sqcup C)$ is the least upper bound of $\alpha_\bullet(C)$. $\square$

We can now prove Theorem 1 by Kleenian fixpoint transfer [12].

Proof (Sketch). The proof follows by Kleenian fixpoint transfer. We have that $\langle \mathcal{P}(\mathcal{P}(\Sigma^{+\infty})), \sqsubseteq, \sqcup, \sqcap, \{\Sigma^\omega, \emptyset\}, \{\emptyset, \Sigma^+\} \rangle$ is a complete lattice and that $\phi^{+\infty}$ (cf. Eq. 1) and $\Theta_\bullet$ (cf. Eq. 8) are monotonic function. Additionally, we have that the outcome abstraction $\alpha_\bullet$ (cf. Eq. 7) is Scott-continuous (cf. Lemma 1) and such that $\alpha_\bullet(\Sigma^\omega) = \{\Sigma^\omega, \emptyset\}$ and $\alpha_\bullet \circ \phi^{+\infty} = \Theta_\bullet \circ \alpha_\bullet$. Then, by Kleenian fixpoint transfer, we have that $\alpha_\bullet(\Lambda) = \alpha_\bullet(\mathrm{lfp}^\sqsubseteq \phi^{+\infty}) = \mathrm{lfp}^\sqsubseteq \Theta_\bullet$. Thus, we can conclude that $\Lambda_\bullet = \mathrm{lfp}^\sqsubseteq \Theta_\bullet$. □

Finally, we show that the outcome semantics $\Lambda_\bullet$ is sound and complete for proving that a program does not use (a subset of) its input variables.

Theorem 2. *A program does not use a subset J of its input variables if and only if its outcome semantics $\Lambda_\bullet$ is a subset of $\mathcal{N}_J$:*

$$P \models \mathcal{N}_J \Leftrightarrow \Lambda_\bullet \subseteq \mathcal{N}_J$$

Proof (Sketch). The proof follows immediately from the definition of $\mathcal{N}_J$ (cf. Eq. 3 and Sect. 4) and the definition of $\Lambda_\bullet$ (cf. Eq. 8). □

Example 4. Let us consider again the program P and its semantics $[\![P]\!]_{\mathrm{science}}$ shown in Example 1. The corresponding outcome semantics $\alpha_\bullet([\![P]\!]_{\mathrm{science}})$ is:

$$\alpha_\bullet([\![P]\!]_{\mathrm{science}}) = \{\emptyset, \{(\mathrm{T\_}) \ldots (\mathrm{TF}), (\mathrm{F\_}) \ldots (\mathrm{FF})\}, \{(\mathrm{T\_}) \ldots (\mathrm{TT}), (\mathrm{F\_}) \ldots (\mathrm{FT})\}\}$$

Note that all sets of traces in $\alpha_\bullet([\![P]\!]_{\mathrm{science}})$ belong to $\mathcal{N}_{\{\mathrm{science}\}}$: the initial states of all traces in a non-empty partition contain all possible initial values (T or F) for the input variable science. Thus, P satisfies $\mathcal{N}_{\{\mathrm{science}\}}$ and, indeed, the input variable science is unused by P. ∎

As discussed in Sect. 4, we now can again use the standard framework of abstract interpretation to soundly over-approximate $\Lambda_\bullet$ and prove that a program does not use (some of) its input data. In the next section, we propose an abstraction that remains sound and complete for input data usage. Further sound but not complete abstractions are presented in later sections.

6 Dependency Semantics

We observe that, to reason about input data usage, it is not necessary to consider all intermediate state computations between the initial state of a trace and its outcome. Thus, we can further abstract the outcome semantics $\Lambda_\bullet$ into a set $\Lambda_{\leadsto}$ of (dependency) relations between initial states and outcomes of a set of traces.

We lift the abstraction defined for this purpose on sets of traces [12] to $\alpha_{\leadsto} : \mathcal{P}(\mathcal{P}(\Sigma^{+\infty})) \to \mathcal{P}(\mathcal{P}(\Sigma \times \Sigma_\perp))$ on sets of sets of traces:

$$\alpha_{\leadsto}(S) \stackrel{\text{def}}{=} \{\{\langle \sigma[0], \sigma[\omega] \rangle \in \Sigma \times \Sigma_\perp \mid \sigma \in T\} \mid T \in S\} \tag{10}$$

where $\Sigma_\perp \stackrel{\text{def}}{=} \Sigma \cup \{\perp\}$. The *dependency abstraction* $\alpha_{\leadsto}$ ignores all intermediate states between the initial state $\sigma[0]$ and the outcome $\sigma[\omega]$ of all traces σ in all partitions T of S. Observe that a trace σ that consists of a single state s is abstracted as a pair $\langle s, s \rangle$. The corresponding dependency concretization function $\gamma_{\rightsquigarrow} \colon \mathcal{P}\left(\mathcal{P}\left(\Sigma \times \Sigma_{\perp}\right)\right) \rightarrow \mathcal{P}\left(\mathcal{P}\left(\Sigma^{+\infty}\right)\right)$ over-approximates the original sets of traces by inserting arbitrary intermediate states:

$$\gamma_{\rightsquigarrow}(S) \stackrel{\text{def}}{=} \left\{ T \in \mathcal{P}\left(\Sigma^{+\infty}\right) \mid \{\langle \sigma[0], \sigma[\omega]\rangle \in \Sigma \times \Sigma_{\perp} \mid \sigma \in T\} \in S \right\} \qquad (11)$$

Example 5. Let us consider again the program of Example 1 and its outcome semantics $\alpha_{\bullet}(\llbracket P \rrbracket_{\text{math}})$ shown in Example 3. Its dependency abstraction is:

$$\alpha_{\rightsquigarrow}(\alpha_{\bullet}(\llbracket P \rrbracket_{\text{math}})) = \{\emptyset, \{\langle \text{F}_-, \text{FF}\rangle\}, \{\langle \text{T}_-, \text{TT}\rangle, \langle \text{F}_-, \text{FT}\rangle\}\}$$

which explicitly ignores intermediate program states. ∎

Using $\alpha_{\rightsquigarrow}$, we now define the *dependency semantics* $\Lambda_{\rightsquigarrow} \in \mathcal{P}\left(\mathcal{P}\left(\Sigma^{+\infty}\right)\right)$ as an abstraction of the outcome semantics $\Lambda_{\bullet}$.

Definition 2. *The* dependency semantics $\Lambda_{\rightsquigarrow} \in \mathcal{P}\left(\mathcal{P}\left(\Sigma^{+\infty}\right)\right)$ *is defined as:*

$$\Lambda_{\rightsquigarrow} \stackrel{\text{def}}{=} \alpha_{\rightsquigarrow}(\Lambda_{\bullet}) \qquad (12)$$

where $\Lambda_{\bullet} \in \mathcal{P}\left(\mathcal{P}\left(\Sigma^{+\infty}\right)\right)$ *is the outcome semantics (cf. Eq. 8) and* $\alpha_{\rightsquigarrow}$ *is the dependency abstraction (cf. Eq. 10).*

Neither the Kleenian fixpoint transfer nor the Tarskian fixpoint transfer can be used to obtain a fixpoint definition for the dependency semantics, but we have to proceed by union of disjoint fixpoints [12]. To this end, we observe that the outcome semantics $\Lambda_{\bullet}$ can be equivalently expressed as follows:

$$\Lambda_{\bullet} = \Lambda_{\bullet}^{+} \cup \Lambda_{\bullet}^{\omega} = \text{lfp}_{\emptyset}^{\sqsubseteq} \, \Theta_{\bullet}^{+} \cup \text{lfp}_{\{\Sigma^{\omega}\}}^{\sqsubseteq} \, \Theta_{\bullet}^{\omega}$$

$$\Theta_{\bullet}^{+}(S) \stackrel{\text{def}}{=} \left\{ \Omega_{o_1 = v_1, \ldots, o_k = v_k} \mid v_1, \ldots, v_k \in \text{V} \right\} \uplus \{\tau ; T \mid T \in S\} \qquad (13)$$

$$\Theta_{\bullet}^{\omega}(S) \stackrel{\text{def}}{=} \{\tau ; T \mid T \in S\}$$

where $\Lambda_{\bullet}^{+}$ and $\Lambda_{\bullet}^{\omega}$ separately compute the set of all sets of finite traces that agree on their outcome, and the set of all infinite traces, respectively.

In the following, given a set of traces $T \in \mathcal{P}\left(\Sigma^{+\infty}\right)$ and its dependency abstraction $\alpha_{\rightsquigarrow}(T)$, we abuse notation and write T^{+} (resp. T^{ω}) to also denote $\alpha_{\rightsquigarrow}(T)^{+} \stackrel{\text{def}}{=} \alpha_{\rightsquigarrow}(T) \cap (\Sigma \times \Sigma)$ (resp. $\alpha_{\rightsquigarrow}(T)^{\omega} \stackrel{\text{def}}{=} \alpha_{\rightsquigarrow}(T) \cap (\Sigma \times \{\perp\})$). Similarly, we reuse the symbols for the computational order $\sqsubseteq$, least upper bound $\sqcup$, and greatest lower bound $\sqcap$, instead of their abstractions. We can now use the Kleenian and Tarskian fixpoint transfer to separately derive fixpoint definitions of $\alpha_{\rightsquigarrow}(\Lambda_{\bullet}^{+})$ and $\alpha_{\rightsquigarrow}(\Lambda_{\bullet}^{\omega})$ in $\langle \mathcal{P}\left(\mathcal{P}\left(\Sigma \times \Sigma_{\perp}\right)\right), \sqsubseteq, \sqcup, \sqcap, \{\Sigma \times \{\perp\}, \emptyset\}, \{\emptyset, \Sigma \times \Sigma\}\rangle$.

Lemma 2. *The abstraction* $\Lambda_{\rightsquigarrow}^{+} \stackrel{\text{def}}{=} \alpha_{\rightsquigarrow}(\Lambda_{\bullet}^{+}) \in \mathcal{P}\left(\mathcal{P}\left(\Sigma \times \Sigma\right)\right)$ *can be expressed as a least fixpoint in* $\langle \mathcal{P}\left(\mathcal{P}\left(\Sigma \times \Sigma_{\perp}\right)\right), \sqsubseteq, \sqcup, \sqcap, \{\Sigma \times \{\perp\}, \emptyset\}, \{\emptyset, \Sigma \times \Sigma\}\rangle$ *as:*

$$\Lambda_{\rightsquigarrow}^{+} = \text{lfp}_{\{\emptyset\}}^{\sqsubseteq} \, \Theta_{\rightsquigarrow}^{+}$$

$$\Theta_{\rightsquigarrow}^{+}(S) \stackrel{\text{def}}{=} \left\{ \Omega_{o_1 = v_1, \ldots, o_k = v_k} \times \Omega_{o_1 = v_1, \ldots, o_k = v_k} \mid v_1, \ldots, v_k \in \text{V} \right\} \uplus \{\tau \circ R \mid R \in S\}$$
$$(14)$$

Proof (Sketch). By Kleenian fixpoint transfer (cf. Theorem 17 in [12]).   □

Lemma 3. *The abstraction* $\Lambda_{\rightsquigarrow}^{\omega} \overset{\text{def}}{=} \alpha_{\rightsquigarrow}(\Lambda_{\bullet}^{\omega}) \in \mathcal{P}(\mathcal{P}(\Sigma \times \Sigma))$ *can be expressed as a least fixpoint in* $\langle \mathcal{P}(\mathcal{P}(\Sigma \times \Sigma_{\perp})), \sqsubseteq, \sqcup, \sqcap, \{\Sigma \times \{\perp\}, \emptyset\}, \{\emptyset, \Sigma \times \Sigma\}\rangle$ *as:*

$$\Lambda_{\rightsquigarrow}^{\omega} = \text{lfp}_{\{\Sigma \times \{\perp\}\}}^{\sqsubseteq} \Theta_{\rightsquigarrow}^{\omega}$$

$$\Theta_{\rightsquigarrow}^{\omega}(S) \overset{\text{def}}{=} \{\tau \circ R \mid R \in S\} \tag{15}$$

Proof (Sketch). By Tarskian fixpoint transfer (cf. Theorem 18 in [12]).   □

The fixpoint iteration for $\Lambda_{\rightsquigarrow}^{+}$ starts from the set containing only the empty relation. At the first iteration, the empty relation is replaced by all relations between pairs of final states that agree on the values of the output variables. At each next iteration, all relations are combined with the transition relation to obtain relations between initial and final states of increasingly longer traces. At the limit, we obtain the set of all relations between the initial and the final states of a program that agree on the final value of the output variables. The fixpoint iteration for $\Lambda_{\rightsquigarrow}^{\omega}$ starts from the set containing (the set of) all pairs of states and the $\perp$ outcome, and each iteration discards more and more pairs with initial states that do not belong to infinite traces of the program.

Now we can use Lemmas 2 and 3 to express the dependency semantics $\Lambda_{\rightsquigarrow}$ in a constructive fixpoint form (as the union of $\Lambda_{\rightsquigarrow}^{+}$ and $\Lambda_{\rightsquigarrow}^{\omega}$).

Theorem 3. *The dependency semantics* $\Lambda_{\rightsquigarrow} \in \mathcal{P}(\mathcal{P}(\Sigma \times \Sigma_{\perp}))$ *can be expressed as a least fixpoint in* $\langle \mathcal{P}(\mathcal{P}(\Sigma \times \Sigma_{\perp})), \sqsubseteq, \sqcup, \sqcap, \{\Sigma \times \{\perp\}, \emptyset\}, \{\emptyset, \Sigma \times \Sigma\}\rangle$ *as:*

$$\Lambda_{\rightsquigarrow} = \Lambda_{\rightsquigarrow}^{+} \cup \Lambda_{\rightsquigarrow}^{\omega} = \text{lfp}_{\{\Sigma \times \{\perp\}, \emptyset\}}^{\sqsubseteq} \Theta_{\rightsquigarrow}$$

$$\Theta_{\rightsquigarrow}(S) \overset{\text{def}}{=} \{\Omega_{o_1 = v_1, \ldots, o_k = v_k} \times \Omega_{o_1 = v_1, \ldots, o_k = v_k} \mid v_1, \ldots, v_k \in \mathrm{V}\} \cup \{\tau \circ R \mid R \in S\} \tag{16}$$

Proof (Sketch). The proof follows immediately from Lemmas 2 and 3.   □

Finally, we show that the dependency semantics $\Lambda_{\rightsquigarrow}$ is sound and complete for proving that a program does not use (a subset of) its input variables.

Theorem 4. *A program does not use a subset J of its input variables if and only if the image via* $\gamma_{\rightsquigarrow}$ *of its dependency semantics* $\Lambda_{\rightsquigarrow}$ *is a subset of* $\mathcal{N}_J$:

$$P \models \mathcal{N}_J \Leftrightarrow \gamma_{\rightsquigarrow}(\Lambda_{\rightsquigarrow}) \subseteq \mathcal{N}_J$$

Proof (Sketch). The proof follows from the definition of $\Lambda_{\rightsquigarrow}$ (cf. Eq. 12) and $\gamma_{\rightsquigarrow}$ (cf. Eq. 11), and from Theorem 2.   □

Example 6. Let us consider again the program P and its outcome semantics $\alpha_{\bullet}(\llbracket P \rrbracket_{\text{science}})$ from Example 4. The corresponding dependency semantics is:

$$\alpha_{\rightsquigarrow}(\alpha_{\bullet}(\llbracket P \rrbracket_{\text{science}})) = \{\emptyset, \{\langle \mathrm{T}_-, \mathrm{TF}\rangle, \langle \mathrm{F}_-, \mathrm{FF}\rangle\}, \{\langle \mathrm{T}_-, \mathrm{TT}\rangle, \langle \mathrm{F}_-, \mathrm{FT}\rangle\}\}$$

and, by definition of $\gamma_{\leadsto}$, we have that its concretization $\gamma_{\leadsto}(\alpha_{\leadsto}(\alpha_{\bullet}(\llbracket P \rrbracket_{\text{science}})))$ is an over-approximation of $\alpha_{\bullet}(\llbracket P \rrbracket_{\text{science}})$. In particular, since intermediate state computations are irrelevant for deciding the input data usage property, all sets of traces in $\gamma_{\leadsto}(\alpha_{\leadsto}(\alpha_{\bullet}(\llbracket P \rrbracket_{\text{science}})))$ are over-approximations of exactly one set in $\alpha_{\bullet}(\llbracket P \rrbracket_{\text{science}})$ with the same set of initial states and outcome. Thus, in this case, we can observe that all sets of traces in $\gamma_{\leadsto}(\alpha_{\leadsto}(\alpha_{\bullet}(\llbracket P \rrbracket_{\text{science}})))$ belong to $\mathcal{N}_{\{\text{science}\}}$ and correctly conclude that P does not use the variable science. ∎

At this point we have a sound and complete program semantics that captures only the minimal information needed to decide which input variables are unused by a program. In the rest of the paper, we present various static analyses for input data usage by means of sound abstractions of this semantics, which *under-approximate* (resp. over-approximate) the subset of the input variables that are *unused* (resp. used) by a program.

7   Input Data Usage Abstractions

We introduce a simple sequential programming language with boolean variables, which we use for illustration throughout the rest of the paper:

$$e ::= v \mid x \mid \text{not } e \mid e \text{ and } e \mid e \text{ or } e \qquad \text{(expressions)}$$
$$s ::= \text{skip} \mid x = e \mid \text{if } e\colon s \text{ else}\colon s \mid \text{while } e\colon s \mid s\ s \qquad \text{(statements)}$$

where v ranges over boolean values, and x ranges over program variables. The skip statement, which does nothing, is a placeholder useful, for instance, for writing a conditional if statement without an else branch: if $e\colon s$ else: skip. In the following, we often simply write if $e\colon s$ instead of if $e\colon s$ else: skip. Note that our work is not limited by the choice of a particular programming language, as the formal treatment in previous sections is language independent.

In Sects. 8 and 9, we show that existing static analyses based on dependencies [6,20] are abstractions of the dependency semantics $\Lambda_{\leadsto}$. We define each abstraction $\Lambda^{\natural}$ over a partially ordered set $\langle \mathcal{A}, \sqsubseteq_{A} \rangle$ called *abstract domain*. More specifically, for each program statement s, we define a *transfer function* $\Theta^{\natural}[\![s]\!]\colon \mathcal{A} \to \mathcal{A}$, and the abstraction $\Lambda^{\natural}$ is the composition of the transfer functions of all statements in a program. We derive a more precise static analysis similar to dependency analyses used for program slicing [37] in Sect. 10. Finally, Sect. 11 demonstrates the value of expressing such analyses as abstract domains by combining them with an existing abstraction of compound data structures such as arrays and lists [16] to detect unused chunks of input data.

8   Secure Information Flow Abstractions

Secure information flow analysis [18] aims at proving that a program will not leak sensitive information. Most analyses focus on proving *non-interference* [35] by classifying program variables into different security levels [17], and ensuring the absence of information flow from variables with higher security level to variables with lower security level. The most basic classification comprises a low security level L, and a high security level H: program variables classified as L are public information, while variables classified as H are private information.

In our context, if we classify input variables as H and all other variables as L, possiblistic non-interference [21] coincides with the input data usage property $\mathcal{N}$ (cf. Eq. 4) *restricted to consider only terminating programs*. However, in general, (possibilistic) non-interference is too strong for our purposes as it requires that *none* of the input variables is used by a program. We illustrate this using as an example a non-interference analysis recently proposed by Assaf et al. [6] that is conveniently formalized in the framework of abstract interpretation. We briefly present here a version of the originally proposed analysis, simplified to consider only the security levels L and H, and we point out the significance of the definitions for input data usage.

Let $\mathcal{L} \stackrel{\text{def}}{=} \{L, H\}$ be the set of security levels, and let the set X of all program variables be partitioned into a set X_L of variables classified as L and a set X_H of variables classified as H (i.e., the input variables). A dependency constraint $L \rightsquigarrow x$ expresses that the current value of the variable x depends only on the initial values of variables having at most security level L (i.e., it does not depend on the initial value of any of the input variables). The non-interference analysis Λ_F proposed by Assaf et al. is a *forward analysis* in the lattice $\langle \mathcal{P}(F), \sqsubseteq_F, \sqcup_F \rangle$ where $F \stackrel{\text{def}}{=} \{L \rightsquigarrow x \mid x \in X\}$ is the set of all dependency constraints, $S_1 \sqsubseteq_F S_2 \stackrel{\text{def}}{=} S_1 \supseteq S_2$, and $S_1 \sqcup_F S_2 \stackrel{\text{def}}{=} S_1 \cap S_2$. The transfer function $\Theta_F[\![s]\!] \colon \mathcal{P}(F) \to \mathcal{P}(F)$ for each statement s in our simple programming language is defined as follows:

$$\Theta_F[\![\texttt{skip}]\!](S) \stackrel{\text{def}}{=} S$$

$$\Theta_F[\![x = e]\!](S) \stackrel{\text{def}}{=} \{L \rightsquigarrow y \in S \mid y \neq x\} \cup \{L \rightsquigarrow x \mid \mathcal{V}_F[\![e]\!]S\}$$

$$\Theta_F[\![\texttt{if } e\colon s_1 \texttt{ else: } s_2]\!](S) \stackrel{\text{def}}{=} \begin{cases} \Theta_F[\![s_1]\!](S) \sqcup_F \Theta_F[\![s_2]\!](S) & \text{if } \mathcal{V}_F[\![e]\!]S \\ \{L \rightsquigarrow x \in S \mid x \notin \mathrm{w}(s_1) \cup \mathrm{w}(s_2)\} & \text{otherwise} \end{cases}$$

$$\Theta_F[\![\texttt{while } e\colon s]\!](S) \stackrel{\text{def}}{=} \mathrm{lfp}_S^{\sqsubseteq_F} \Theta_F[\![\texttt{if } e\colon s \texttt{ else: skip}]\!]$$

$$\Theta_F[\![s_1\ s_2]\!](S) \stackrel{\text{def}}{=} \Theta_F[\![s_2]\!] \circ \Theta_F[\![s_1]\!](S)$$

where $\mathrm{w}(s)$ denotes the set of variables modified by the statement s, and $\mathcal{V}_F[\![e]\!]S$ determines whether a set of dependencies S guarantees that the expression e has a unique value independently of the initial value of the input variables. For a variable x, $\mathcal{V}_F[\![x]\!]S$ is true if and only if $L \rightsquigarrow x \in S$. Otherwise, $\mathcal{V}_F[\![e]\!]S$ is defined recursively on the structure of e, and it is always true for a boolean value v [6]. An assignment $x = e$ discards all dependency constraints related to the assigned variable x, and adds constraints $L \rightsquigarrow x$ if e has a unique value independently of the initial values of the input variables. This captures an *explicit flow* of information between e and x. A conditional statement if $e\colon s_1$ else: s_2 joins the dependency constraints obtained from s_1 and s_2, if e does not depend on the initial values of the input variables (i.e., $\mathcal{V}_F[\![e]\!]S$ is true). Otherwise, it discards all dependency constraints related to the variables modified in either of its branches. This captures an *implicit flow* of information from e. The initial set of dependencies contains a constraint $L \rightsquigarrow x$ for each variable x that is not an input variable. We exemplify the analysis below.

Example 7. Let us consider again the program P from Example 1 (stripped of the `input` and `print` statements, which are not present in our simple language):

```
1 passing = True
2 if not english: english = False         # english should be passing
3 if not math: passing = bonus
4 if not math: passing = bonus            # math should be science
```

The analysis begins from the set of dependency constraints $\{L \rightsquigarrow \texttt{passing}\}$, which classifies input variables as H and all other variables as L. The assignment at line 1 leaves the set unchanged as the value of the expression `True` on the right-hand side of the assignment does not depend on the initial value of the input variables. The set remains unchanged by the conditional statement at line 2, even though the boolean condition depends on the input variable `english`, because the variable `passing` is not modified. Finally, at line 3 and 4, the analysis captures an explicit flow of information from the input variable `bonus` and an implicit flow of information from the input variable `math`. Thus, the set of dependency constraints becomes empty at line 3, and remains empty at line 4.

Observe that, in this case, non-interference does not hold since the result of the program depends on some of the input variables. Therefore, the analysis is only able to conclude that at least one of the input variables may be used by the program, but it cannot determine which input variables are unused.   ■

The example shows that non-interference is too strong a property in general. Of course, one could determine which input variables are unused by running multiple instances of the non-interference analysis Λ_F, each one of them classifying a single different input variable as H and all other variables as L. However, this becomes cumbersome in a data science application where a program reads and manipulates a large amount of input data.

Moreover, we emphasize that our input data usage property is more general than (possibilistic) non-interference since it also considers non-termination. We are not aware of any work on termination-sensitive possibilistic non-interference.

Example 8. Let us modify the program P shown in Example 7 as follows:

```
1 passing = True
2 while not english: english = False
```

In this case, since the loop at line 2 does not modify the output variable `passing`, the non-interference analysis Λ_F will leave the initial set of dependency constraints $\{L \rightsquigarrow \texttt{passing}\}$ unchanged, meaning that the result of the program does not depend on any of its input variables. However, the input variable `english` is used since its value influences the outcome of the program: the program terminates if `english` is true, and does not terminate otherwise.   ■

The example demonstrates that the analysis is *unsound* for a non-terminating program.[2] We show that the non-interference analysis Λ_F is sound for proving that a program does not use any of its input variables, *only if the program is terminating.* We define the concretization function $\gamma_F \colon \mathcal{P}(F) \to \mathcal{P}(\mathcal{P}(\Sigma \times \Sigma))$:

$$\gamma_F(S) \stackrel{\text{def}}{=} \{R \in \mathcal{P}(\Sigma \times \Sigma) \mid \alpha_F(R) \sqsubseteq_F S\} \tag{17}$$

The abstraction function $\alpha_F \colon \mathcal{P}(\mathcal{P}(\Sigma \times \Sigma)) \to \mathcal{P}(F)$ maps each relation R between states of a program to the corresponding set of dependency constraints: $\alpha_F(R) \stackrel{\text{def}}{=} \{L \rightsquigarrow x \mid x \in X_L \wedge \forall i \in X_H \colon \text{UNUSED}_{i,x}(R)\}$, where $\text{UNUSED}_{i,x}$ is the relational abstraction of UNUSED_i (cf. Eq. 3) in which we compare only the result stored in the variable x (i.e., we compare $\sigma[\omega](o)$ and $\sigma'[\omega](o)$, instead of $\sigma[\omega]$ and $\sigma'[\omega]$ as in Eq. 3).

Theorem 5. *A terminating program does not use any of its input variables if the image via $\gamma_{\rightsquigarrow} \circ \gamma_F$ of its non-interference abstraction Λ_F is a subset of $\mathcal{N}$:*

$$\gamma_{\rightsquigarrow}(\gamma_F(\Lambda_F)) \subseteq \mathcal{N} \Rightarrow P \models \mathcal{N}$$

Proof. Let us assume that $\gamma_{\rightsquigarrow}(\gamma_F(\Lambda_F)) \subseteq \mathcal{N}$. By definition of γ_F (cf. Eq. 17), since the program is terminating, we have that $\Lambda_{\rightsquigarrow} \subseteq \gamma_F(\Lambda_F)$ and, by monotonicity of the concretization function $\gamma_{\rightsquigarrow}$ (cf. Eq. 11), we have that $\gamma_{\rightsquigarrow}(\Lambda_{\rightsquigarrow}) \subseteq \gamma_{\rightsquigarrow}(\gamma_F(\Lambda_F))$. Thus, since $\gamma_{\rightsquigarrow}(\gamma_F(\Lambda_F)) \subseteq \mathcal{N}$, we have that $\gamma_{\rightsquigarrow}(\Lambda_{\rightsquigarrow}) \subseteq \mathcal{N}$. The conclusion follows from Theorem 4. □

Note that the termination of the program is necessary for the proof of Theorem 5. Indeed, for a non-terminating program, we have that $\Lambda_{\rightsquigarrow} \not\subseteq \gamma_F(\Lambda_F)$ (since $\Lambda_{\rightsquigarrow}$ includes relational abstractions of infinite traces that are missing from $\gamma_F(\Lambda_F)$) and thus we cannot conclude the proof.

This result shows that the non-interference analysis Λ_F is an abstraction of the dependency semantics $\Lambda_{\rightsquigarrow}$ presented earlier. However, we remark that the same result applies to all other instances in this important class of analysis [5, 25, etc.], which are therefore subsumed by our framework.

9 Strongly Live Variable Abstraction

Strongly live variable analysis [20] is a variant of the classic live variable analysis [32] performed by compilers to determine, for each program point, which variables may be potentially used before they are assigned to. A variable is *strongly live* if it is used in an assignment to another strongly live variable, or if is used in a statement other than an assignment. Otherwise, a variable is considered *faint*.

---

[2] The case of a program using an input variable and then always diverging is not problematic because the analysis would be imprecise but still sound.

Strongly live variable analysis Λ_X is a *backward analysis* in the complete lattice $\langle \mathcal{P}(X), \subseteq, \cup, \cap, \emptyset, X \rangle$, where X is the set of all program variables. The transfer function $\Theta_X[\![s]\!]\colon \mathcal{P}(X) \to \mathcal{P}(X)$ for each statement s is defined as:

$$\Theta_X[\![\texttt{skip}]\!](S) \overset{\text{def}}{=} S$$

$$\Theta_X[\![x = e]\!](S) \overset{\text{def}}{=} \begin{cases} (S \setminus \{x\}) \cup \text{VARS}(e) & x \in S \\ S & \text{otherwise} \end{cases}$$

$$\Theta_X[\![\texttt{if } b\colon s_1 \texttt{ else: } s_2]\!](S) \overset{\text{def}}{=} \text{VARS}(b) \cup \Theta_X[\![s_1]\!](S) \cup \Theta_X[\![s_2]\!](S)$$

$$\Theta_X[\![\texttt{while } b\colon s]\!](S) \overset{\text{def}}{=} \text{VARS}(b) \cup \Theta_X[\![s]\!](S)$$

$$\Theta_X[\![s_1 \ s_2]\!](S) \overset{\text{def}}{=} \Theta_X[\![s_1]\!] \circ \Theta_X[\![s_2]\!](S)$$

where $\text{VARS}(e)$ is the set of variables in the expression e. For input data usage, the initial set of strongly live variables contains the output variables of the program.

Example 9. Let us consider again the program P shown in Example 7. The strongly live variable analysis begins from the set $\{\texttt{passing}\}$ containing the output variable $\texttt{passing}$. At line 3, the set of strongly live variables is $\{\texttt{math}, \texttt{bonus}\}$ since $\texttt{bonus}$ is used in an assignment to the strongly live variable $\texttt{passing}$, and $\texttt{math}$ is used in the condition of the $\texttt{if}$ statement. Finally, at line 1, the set of strongly live variables is $\{\texttt{english}, \texttt{math}, \texttt{bonus}\}$ because $\texttt{english}$ is used in the condition of the $\texttt{if}$ statement at line 2. Thus, strongly live variable analysis is able to conclude that the input variable $\texttt{science}$ is unused. However, it is not precise enough to determine that the variable $\texttt{english}$ is also unused. ∎

The imprecision of the analysis derives from the fact that it does not capture implicit flows of information precisely (cf. Sect. 8) but only over-approximates their presence. Thus, the analysis is unable to detect when a conditional statement, for instance, modifies only variables that have no impact on the outcome of a program; a situation likely to arise due to a programming error, as shown in the previous example. However, in virtue of this imprecise treatment of implicit flows, we can show that strongly live variable analysis is sound for input data usage, even for non-terminating programs.

We define the concretization function $\gamma_X\colon \mathcal{P}(X) \to \mathcal{P}(\mathcal{P}(\Sigma \times \Sigma_\perp))$ as:

$$\gamma_X(S) \overset{\text{def}}{=} \{R \in \Sigma \times \Sigma_\perp \mid \forall i \in X \setminus S\colon \text{UNUSED}_i(R)\} \tag{18}$$

where we abuse notation and use UNUSED_i (cf. Eq. 3) to also denote its dependency abstraction (cf. Eq. 10). We now show that strongly live variable analysis is sound for proving that a program does not use the faint variables.

Theorem 6. *A program does not use a subset J of its input variables if the image via $\gamma_{\leadsto} \circ \gamma_X$ of its strongly live variable abstraction Λ_X is a subset of $\mathcal{N}_J$:*

$$\gamma_{\leadsto}(\gamma_X(\Lambda_X)) \subseteq \mathcal{N}_J \Rightarrow P \models \mathcal{N}_J$$

Proof. Let us assume that $\gamma_{\leadsto}(\gamma_{\mathrm{X}}(\Lambda_{\mathrm{X}})) \subseteq \mathcal{N}_J$. By definition of γ_{X} (cf. Eq. 18), we have that $\Lambda_{\leadsto} \subseteq \gamma_{\mathrm{X}}(\Lambda_{\mathrm{X}})$ and, by monotonicity of $\gamma_{\leadsto}$ (cf. Eq. 11), we have that $\gamma_{\leadsto}(\Lambda_{\leadsto}) \subseteq \gamma_{\leadsto}(\gamma_{\mathrm{X}}(\Lambda_{\mathrm{X}}))$. Thus, since $\gamma_{\leadsto}(\gamma_{\mathrm{X}}(\Lambda_{\mathrm{X}})) \subseteq \mathcal{N}_J$, we have that $\gamma_{\leadsto}(\Lambda_{\leadsto}) \subseteq \mathcal{N}_J$. The conclusion follows from Theorem 4. $\qquad\square$

This result shows that also strongly live variable analysis is subsumed by our framework as it is an abstraction of the dependency semantics $\Lambda_{\leadsto}$.

10 Syntactic Dependency Abstractions

In the following, we derive a more precise data usage analysis based on *syntactic* dependencies between program variables. For simplicity, the analysis does not take program termination into account, but we discuss possible solutions at the end of the section. Due to space limitations, we only provide a terse description of the abstraction and refer to [36] for further details.

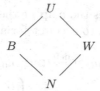

Fig. 5. Hasse diagram for the complete lattice $\langle \text{USAGE}, \sqsubseteq_{\text{USAGE}}, \sqcup_{\text{USAGE}}, \sqcap_{\text{USAGE}}, N, U \rangle$.

In order to capture implicit dependencies from variables appearing in boolean conditions of conditional and while statements, we track when the value of a variable is used or modified in a statement based on the level of nesting of the statement in other statements. More formally, each program variable maps to a value in the complete lattice shown in Fig. 5: the values U (*used*) and N (*not-used*) respectively denote that a variable may be used and is not used at the current nesting level; the values B (*below*) and W (*overwritten*) denote that a variable may be used at a lower nesting level, and the value W additionally indicates that the variable is modified at the current nesting level.

A variable is used (i.e., maps to U) if it is used in an assignment to another variable that is used in the current or a lower nesting level (i.e., a variable that maps to U or B). We define the operator $\text{ASSIGN}[\![x = e]\!]$ to compute the effect of an assignment on a map $m \colon \mathrm{X} \to \text{USAGE}$, where X is the set of all variables:

$$\text{ASSIGN}[\![x = e]\!](m) \stackrel{\text{def}}{=} \lambda y. \begin{cases} W & y = x \wedge y \notin \text{VARS}(e) \wedge m(x) \in \{U, B\} \\ U & y \in \text{VARS}(e) \wedge m(x) \in \{U, B\} \\ m(y) & \text{otherwise} \end{cases} \tag{19}$$

The assigned variable is overwritten (i.e., maps to W), unless it is used in e.

Another reason for a variable to be used is if it appears in the boolean condition e of a statement that uses another variable or modifies another used variable (i.e., there exists a variable x that maps to U or W):

$$\text{FILTER}[\![e]\!](m) \overset{\text{def}}{=} \lambda y. \begin{cases} U & y \in \text{VARS}(e) \wedge \exists x \in \text{X}: m(x) \in \{U, W\} \\ m(y) & \text{otherwise} \end{cases} \quad (20)$$

We maintain a *stack* of these maps that grows or shrinks based on the level of nesting of the currently analyzed statement. More formally, a stack is a tuple $\langle m_0, m_1, \ldots, m_k \rangle$ of mutable length k, where each element $m_0, m_1, \ldots, m_k$ is a map from X to USAGE. In the following, we use Q to denote the set of all stacks, and we abuse notation by writing $\text{ASSIGN}[\![x = e]\!]$ and $\text{FILTER}[\![e]\!]$ to also denote the corresponding operators on stacks:

$$\text{ASSIGN}[\![x = e]\!](\langle m_0, m_1, \ldots, m_k \rangle) \overset{\text{def}}{=} \langle \text{ASSIGN}[\![x = e]\!](m_0), m_1, \ldots, m_k \rangle$$

$$\text{FILTER}[\![e]\!](\langle m_0, m_1, \ldots, m_k \rangle) \overset{\text{def}}{=} \langle \text{FILTER}[\![e]\!](m_0), m_1, \ldots, m_k \rangle$$

The operator PUSH duplicates the map at the top of the stack and modifies the copy using the operator INC, to account for an increased nesting level:

$$\text{PUSH}(\langle m_0, m_1, \ldots, m_k \rangle) \overset{\text{def}}{=} \langle \text{INC}(m_0), m_0, m_1, \ldots, m_k \rangle$$

$$\text{INC}(m) \overset{\text{def}}{=} \lambda y. \begin{cases} B & m(y) \in \{U\} \\ N & m(y) \in \{W\} \\ m(y) & \text{otherwise} \end{cases} \quad (21)$$

A used variable (i.e., mapping to U) becomes used below (i.e., now maps to B), and a modified variable (i.e., mapping to W) becomes unused (i.e., now maps to N). The dual operator POP combines the two maps at the top of the stack:

$$\text{POP}(\langle m_0, m_1, \ldots, m_k \rangle) \overset{\text{def}}{=} \langle \text{DEC}(m_0, m_1), \ldots, m_k \rangle$$

$$\text{DEC}(m, k) \overset{\text{def}}{=} \lambda y. \begin{cases} k(y) & m(y) \in \{B, N\} \\ m(y) & \text{otherwise} \end{cases} \quad (22)$$

where the DEC operator restores the value a variable y mapped to before increasing the nesting level (i.e., $k(y)$) if it has not changed since (i.e., if the variable still maps to B or N), and otherwise retains the new value y maps to.

We can now define the data usage analysis Λ_Q, which is a *backward analysis* on the lattice $\langle Q, \sqsubseteq_Q, \sqcup_Q \rangle$. The partial order $\sqsubseteq_Q$ and the least upper bound $\sqcup_Q$ are the pointwise lifting, for each element of the stack, of the partial order and least upper bound between maps from X to USAGE (which in turn are the pointwise lifting of the partial order $\sqsubseteq_{\text{USAGE}}$ and least upper bound $\sqcup_{\text{USAGE}}$ of the USAGE lattice, cf. Fig. 5). We define the transfer function $\Theta_Q[\![s]\!]: Q \to Q$ for each statement s in our simple programming language as follows:

math, bonus $\mapsto U$, passing $\mapsto W \sqcup_Q$ passing $\mapsto U =$ math, bonus, passing $\mapsto U$
if not math:
    bonus $\mapsto U$, passing $\mapsto W$ | passing $\mapsto U$
    passing = bonus
    passing $\mapsto B$ | passing $\mapsto U$
passing $\mapsto U$

Fig. 6. Data usage analysis of the last statement of the program shown in Example 7. Stack elements are separated by | and, for brevity, variables mapping to N are omitted.

$$\Theta_Q[\![\texttt{skip}]\!](q) \overset{\text{def}}{=} q$$

$$\Theta_Q[\![x = e]\!](q) \overset{\text{def}}{=} \textsc{assign}[\![x = e]\!](q)$$

$$\Theta_Q[\![\texttt{if } b\colon s_1 \texttt{ else}\colon s_2]\!](q) \overset{\text{def}}{=} \textsc{pop} \circ \textsc{filter}[\![b]\!] \circ \Theta_Q[\![s_1]\!] \circ \textsc{push}(q)$$
$$\sqcup_Q \textsc{pop} \circ \textsc{filter}[\![b]\!] \circ \Theta_Q[\![s_2]\!] \circ \textsc{push}(q)$$

$$\Theta_Q[\![\texttt{while } b\colon s]\!](q) \overset{\text{def}}{=} \text{lfp}_t^{\sqsubseteq_Q} \Theta_Q[\![\texttt{if } b\colon s \texttt{ else}\colon \texttt{skip}]\!]$$

$$\Theta_Q[\![s_1\ s_2]\!](q) \overset{\text{def}}{=} \Theta_Q[\![s_1]\!] \circ \Theta_Q[\![s_2]\!](q)$$

The initial stack contains a single map, in which the output variables map to the value U, and all other variables map to N. We exemplify the analysis below.

Example 10. Let us consider again the program P shown in Example 7. The initial stack begins with a single map m, in which the output variable **passing** maps to U and all other variables map to N.

At line 4, before analyzing the body of the conditional statement, a modified copy of m is pushed onto the stack: this copy maps **passing** to B, meaning that **passing** is only used in a lower nesting level, and all other variables still map to N (cf. Eq. 21). As a result of the assignment (cf. Eq. 19), **passing** is overwritten (i.e., maps to W), and bonus is used (i.e., maps to U). Since the body of the conditional statement modifies a used variable and uses another variable, the analysis of its boolean condition makes **math** used as well (cf. Eq. 20). Finally, the maps at the top of the stack are merged and the result maps **math**, **bonus**, and **passing** to U, and all other variables to N (cf. Eq. 22). The analysis is visualized in Fig. 6.

The stack remains unchanged at line 3 and line 2, since the statement at line 3 is identical to line 4 and the body of the conditional statement at line 2 does not modify any used variable and does not use any other variable. Finally, at line 1 the variable **passing** is modified (i.e., it now maps to W), while **math** and **bonus** remain used (i.e., they map to U). Thus, the analysis is precise enough to conclude that the input variables **english** and **science** are unused. ∎

Note that, similarly to the non-interference analysis presented in Sect. 8, the data usage analysis Λ_Q does not consider non-termination. Indeed, for the program shown in Example 8, the analysis does not capture that the input variable english is used, even though the termination of the program depends on its value. We define the concretization function $\gamma_Q \colon Q \to \mathcal{P}\left(\mathcal{P}\left(\Sigma \times \Sigma\right)\right)$ as:

$$\gamma_Q(\langle m_0, \ldots, m_k \rangle) \stackrel{\text{def}}{=} \{R \in \Sigma \times \Sigma \mid \forall i \in X \colon m_0(i) \in \{N\} \Rightarrow \text{UNUSED}_i(R)\} \qquad (23)$$

where again we write UNUSED_i (cf. Eq. 3) to also denote its dependency abstraction. We now show that Λ_Q is sound for proving that a program does not use a subset of its input variables, *if the program is terminating*.

Theorem 7. *A terminating program does not use a subset J of its input variables if the image via $\gamma_{\rightsquigarrow} \circ \gamma_Q$ of its abstraction Λ_Q is a subset of $\mathcal{N}_J$:*

$$\gamma_{\rightsquigarrow}(\gamma_Q(\Lambda_Q)) \subseteq \mathcal{N}_J \Rightarrow P \models \mathcal{N}_J$$

Proof. Let us assume that $\gamma_{\rightsquigarrow}(\gamma_Q(\Lambda_Q)) \subseteq \mathcal{N}_J$. Since the program is terminating, we have that $\Lambda_{\rightsquigarrow} \subseteq \gamma_Q(\Lambda_Q)$, by definition of the concretization function γ_Q (cf. Eq. 23). Then, by monotonicity of $\gamma_{\rightsquigarrow}$ (cf. Eq. 11), we have that $\gamma_{\rightsquigarrow}(\Lambda_{\rightsquigarrow}) \subseteq \gamma_{\rightsquigarrow}(\gamma_Q(\Lambda_Q))$. Thus, since $\gamma_{\rightsquigarrow}(\gamma_Q(\Lambda_Q)) \subseteq \mathcal{N}_J$, we have that $\gamma_{\rightsquigarrow}(\Lambda_{\rightsquigarrow}) \subseteq \mathcal{N}_J$. The conclusion follows from Theorem 4. □

In order to take termination into account, one could map each variable appearing in the guard of a loop to the value U. Alternatively, one could run a termination analysis [3,33,34], along with the data usage analysis, and only map to U variables appearing in the loop guard of a possibly non-terminating loop.

11 Piecewise Abstractions

The static analyses presented so far can be used only to detect unused data stored in program variables. However, realistic data science applications read and manipulate data organized in data structures such as arrays, lists, and dictionaries. In the following, we demonstrate that having expressed the analyses as abstract domains allows us to easily lift the analyses to such a scenario. In particular, to detect unused chunks of the input data, we combine the more precise data usage analysis presented in the previous section with the array content abstraction proposed by Cousot et al. [16]. Due to space limitations, we provide only an informal description of the resulting abstract domain and refer to [36] for further details and examples. The analyses presented in earlier sections can be similarly combined with the array abstraction for the same purpose.

We extend our small programming language introduced in Sect. 7 with integer variables, arithmetic and boolean comparison expressions, and arrays:

$$e ::= \cdots \mid a[e] \mid \texttt{len}(a) \mid e \oplus e \mid e \bowtie e \qquad \text{(expressions)}$$
$$s ::= \cdots \mid a[e] = e \qquad \text{(statements)}$$

where $\oplus$ and $\bowtie$ respectively range over arithmetic and boolean comparison operators, a ranges over array variables, and $\texttt{len}(a)$ denotes the length of a.

Piecewise Array Abstraction. The array abstraction [16] divides an array into consecutive segments, each segment being a uniform abstraction of the array content in that segment. The bounds of the segments are specified by sets of side-effect free expressions restricted to a canonical normal form, all having the same (concrete) value. The abstraction is parametric in the choice of the abstract domains used to manipulate sets of expressions and to represent the array content within each segment. For our analysis, we use the octagon abstract domain [31] for the expressions, and the USAGE lattice presented in the previous section (cf. Fig. 5) for the segments. Thus, an array a is abstracted, for instance, as $\{0, i\} N \{j + 1\}?\ U \{\texttt{len}(a)\}$, where the symbol ? indicates that the segment $\{0, i\} N \{j + 1\}$ might be empty. The abstraction indicates that all array elements (if any) from index i (which is equal to zero) to index j (the bound $j + 1$ is exclusive) are unused, and all elements from $j + 1$ to $\texttt{len}(a) - 1$ may be used. Let A be the set of all such array abstractions. The initial segmentation of an array $a \in A$ is a single segment with unused content (i.e., $\{0\} N \{\texttt{len}(a)\}?$).

For our analysis, we augment the array abstraction with new backward assignment and filter operators. The operators $\text{ASSIGN}_A [\![a[i] = e]\!]$ and $\text{FILTER}_A [\![e]\!]$ split and fill segments to take into account assignments and accesses to array elements that influence the program outcome. For instance, an assignment to $a[i]$ with an expression containing a used variable modifies the segmentation $\{0\} N \{\texttt{len}(a)\}?$ into $\{0\} N \{i\}?\ U \{i + 1\} N \{\texttt{len}(a)\}?$, which indicates that the array element at index i is used by the program. An access $a[i]$ in a boolean condition guarding a statement that uses or modifies another used variables is handled analogously. Instead, the operator $\text{ASSIGN}_A [\![x = e]\!]$ modifies the segmentation of an array by replacing each occurrence of the assigned variable x with the canonical normal form of the expression e. For instance, an assignment $i = i + 1$ modifies the segmentation $\{0\} N \{i\}?\ U \{i + 1\} N \{\texttt{len}(a)\}?$ into $\{0\} N \{i + 1\}?\ U \{i + 2\} N \{\texttt{len}(a)\}?$. If e cannot be precisely put into a canonical normal form, the operator replaces the assigned variable with an approximation of e as an integer interval [13] computed using the underlying numerical domain, and possibly merges segments together as a result of the approximation. For instance, a non-linear assignment $i = i * j$ approximated as $i = [0, 1]$ modifies the segmentation $\{0\} N \{i\}?\ U \{i + 1\} N \{\texttt{len}(a)\}?$ into $\{0\} U \{2\} N \{\texttt{len}(a)\}?$, which loses the information that the initial segment of the array is unused.

When merging control flows, segmentations are compared or joined by means of a *unification algorithm* [16], which finds the coarsest common refinement of both segmentations. Then, the comparison $\sqsubseteq_A$ or the join $\sqcup_A$ is performed pointwise for each segment using the corresponding operators of the underlying abstract domain chosen to abstract the array content. For our analysis, we adapt and refine the originally proposed unification algorithm to take into account the knowledge of the numerical domain chosen to abstract the segment bounds. We refer to [36] for further details. A widening ∇_A limits the number of segments to enforce termination of the analysis.

Piecewise Data Usage Analysis. We can now map each scalar variable to an element of the USAGE lattice and each array variable to an array segmentation

```
1 failed = 0
2 i = 1                                        # 1 should be 0
3 while i < len(grades):
4     if grades[i] < 4: failed = failed + 1
5     i = i + 1
6 passing = 2 * failed < len(grades)
```

Fig. 7. Another program to check if a student has passed a number of exams based on their grades stored in the array **grades**. The programmer has made a mistake at line 2 that causes the program to ignore the grade stored at index 0 in **grades**.

$grades \mapsto \{0\}\, N\, \{i\}?\, U\, \{i+1\}?\, U\, \{\text{len(grades)}\}?$
$\text{while } i < \text{len(\textbf{grades})}:$
$\quad grades \mapsto \{0\}\, N\, \{i\}?\, U\, \{i+1\}?\, B\, \{i+2\}?\, B\, \{\text{len(grades)}\}?\,|\ldots$
$\quad \text{if \textbf{grades[i]}} < 4:$
$\qquad grades \mapsto \{0\}\, N\, \{i+1\}?\, B\, \{i+2\}?\, B\, \{\text{len(grades)}\}?\,|\cdots|\ldots$
$\qquad \textbf{failed} = \textbf{failed} + 1$
$\qquad grades \mapsto \{0\}\, N\, \{i+1\}?\, B\, \{i+2\}?\, B\, \{\text{len(grades)}\}?\,|\cdots|\ldots$
$\quad grades \mapsto \{0\}\, N\, \{i+1\}?\, B\, \{i+2\}?\, B\, \{\text{len(grades)}\}?\,|\ldots$
$\quad \textbf{i} = \textbf{i} + 1$
$\quad grades \mapsto \{0\}\, N\, \{i\}?\, B\, \{i+1\}?\, B\, \{\text{len(grades)}\}?\,|\ldots$
$grades \mapsto \{0\}\, N\, \{\text{len(grades)}\}?$

Fig. 8. Data usage analysis of the loop statement of the program shown in Example 11. Stack elements are separated by | and, for brevity, only array variables are shown.

in A, and use the data usage analysis Λ_Q presented in the previous section to identify unused input data stored in variables and portions of arrays.

Example 11. Let us consider the program shown in Fig. 7 where the array variable **grades** and the variable **passing** are the input and output variables, respectively. The initial stack contains a single map in which **passing** maps to U, all other scalar variables map to N, and **grades** maps to $\{0\}\, N\, \{\text{len(grades)}\}?$, indicating that all elements of the array (if any) are unused.

At line 6, the assignment modifies the variable **passing** (i.e., **passing** now maps to W) and uses the variable **failed** (i.e., **failed** now maps to U), while every other variable remains unchanged.

The result of the analysis of the loop statement at line 3 is shown in Fig. 8. The analysis of the loop begins by pushing (cf. Eq. 21) a map onto the stack in which **passing** becomes unused (i.e., maps to N) and **failed** is used only in a lower nesting level (i.e., maps to B), and every other variable still remains unchanged. At the first iteration of the analysis of the loop body, the assignment at line 4 uses **failed** and thus the access **grades[i]** at line 3 creates a used segment in the segmentation for **grades**, which becomes $\{0\}\, N\, \{i\}?\, U\, \{i+1\}\, N\, \{\text{len(grades)}\}?$. At the second iteration, the PUSH operator turns the used segment $\{i\}\, U\, \{i+1\}$ into $\{i\}\, B\, \{i+1\}$, and the assignment to i modifies the segment into $\{i+1\}\, B\, \{i+2\}$ (while the segmentation in the second stack element becomes

$\{0\}\,N\,\{\text{i}+1\}$? $U\,\{\text{i}+2\}$ $N\,\{\text{len}(\text{grades})\}$?). Then, the access to the array at line 3 creates again a used segment $\{\text{i}\}\,U\,\{\text{i}+1\}$ (in the first segmentation) and the analysis continues with the result of the POP operator (cf. Eq. 22): $\{0\}\,N\,\{\text{i}\}$? $U\,\{\text{i}+1\}$? $U\,\{\text{i}+2\}$? $N\,\{\text{len}(\text{grades})\}$?. After widening, the last two segments are merged into a single segment, and the analysis of the loop terminates with $\{0\}\,N\,\{\text{i}\}$? $U\,\{\text{i}+1\}$? $U\,\{\text{len}(\text{grades})\}$?.

Finally, the analysis of the assignment at line 2 produces the segmentation $\{0\}\,N\,\{1\}$? $U\,\{2\}$? $U\,\{\text{len}(\text{grades})\}$?, which correctly indicates that the first element of the array grades (if any) is unused by the program.   ∎

Implementation. The analyses presented in this and in the previous section are implemented in the prototype static analyzer LYRA and are available online[3].

The implementation is in PYTHON and, at the time of writing, accepts programs written in a limited subset of PYTHON without user-defined classes. A type inference is run before the analysis of a program. The analysis is performed backwards on the control flow graph of the program with a standard worklist algorithm [32], using widening at loop heads to enforce termination.

12   Related Work

The most directly relevant work has been discussed throughout the paper. The non-interference analysis proposed by Assaf et al. [6] (cf. Sect. 8) is similar to the logic of Amtoft and Banerjee [5] and the type system of Hunt and·Sands [25]. The data usage analysis proposed in Sect. 10 is similar to dependency analyses used for program slicing [37] (e.g., [24]). Both analyses as well as strongly live variable analysis (cf. Sect. 9) are based on the *syntactic* presence of a variable in the definition of another variable. To overcome this limitation, one should look further for *semantic* dependencies between *values* of program variables. In this direction, Giacobazzi, Mastroeni, and others [19,22,29] have proposed the notion of *abstract dependency*. However, note that an analysis based on abstract dependencies would over-approximate the subset of the input variables that are unused by a program. Indeed, the absence of an abstract dependency between variables (e.g., a dependency between the parity of the variables [19,29]) does not imply the absence of a (concrete) dependency between the variables (i.e., a dependency between the values of the variables). Thus, such an analysis could not be used to prove that a program *does not use* a subset of its input variables, but would be used to prove that a program *uses* a subset of its input variables.

Semantics formulations using *sets of sets of traces* have already been proposed in the literature [6,28]. Mastroeni and Pasqua [28] lift the hierarchy of semantics developed by Cousot [12] to sets of sets of traces to obtain a hierarchy of semantics suitable for verifying general program properties (i.e., properties that are not subset-closed, cf. Sect. 7). However, *none* of the semantics that they proposed is suitable for input data usage: all semantics in the hierarchy are abstractions of a semantics that contains sets with both finite and infinite traces

---

[3]   http://www.pm.inf.cthz.ch/research/lyra.html.

and thus, unlike our outcome semantics (cf. Sect. 5), cannot be used to reason about terminating and non-terminating outcomes of a program. Similarly, as observed in [28], the semantics proposed by Assaf et al. [6] can be used to verify only subset-closed properties. Thus, it cannot be used for input data usage.

Finally, to the best of our knowledge, our work is the first to aim at detecting programming errors in data science code using static analysis. Closely related are [7,10] which, however, focus on spreadsheet applications and target errors in the data rather than the code that analyzes it. Recent work [2] proposes an approach to repair *bias* in data science code. We believe that our work can be applied in this context to prove absence of bias, e.g., by showing that a program does not use gender information to decide whether to hire a person.

13   Conclusion and Future Work

In this paper, we have proposed an abstract interpretation framework to automatically detect input data that remains unused by a program. Additionally, we have shown that existing static analyses based on dependencies are subsumed by our unifying framework and can be used, with varying degrees of precision, for proving that a program does not use some of its input data. Finally, we have proposed a data usage analysis for more realistic data science applications that store input data in compound data structures such as arrays or lists.

As part of our future work, we plan to use our framework to guide the design of new, more precise static analyses for data usage. We also want to explore the complementary direction of proving that a program *uses* its input data by developing an analysis based on abstract dependencies [19,22,29] between program variables, as discussed above. Additionally, we plan to investigate other applications of our work such as provenance or lineage analysis [9] as well as proving absence of algorithmic bias [2]. Finally, we want to study other programming errors related to data usage such as accidental data duplication.

References

1. Abadi, M., Banerjee, A., Heintze, N., Riecke, J.G.: A core calculus of dependency. In: POPL, pp. 147–160 (1999)
2. Albarghouthi, A., D'Antoni, L., Drews, S.: Repairing decision-making programs under uncertainty. In: Majumdar, R., Kunčak, V. (eds.) CAV 2017. LNCS, vol. 10426, pp. 181–200. Springer, Cham (2017). https://doi.org/10.1007/978-3-319-63387-9_9
3. Alias, C., Darte, A., Feautrier, P., Gonnord, L.: Multi-dimensional rankings, program termination, and complexity bounds of flowchart programs. In: Cousot, R., Martel, M. (eds.) SAS 2010. LNCS, vol. 6337, pp. 117–133. Springer, Heidelberg (2010). https://doi.org/10.1007/978-3-642-15769-1_8
4. Alpern, B., Schneider, F.B.: Defining Liveness. Inf. Process. Lett. **21**(4), 181–185 (1985)
5. Amtoft, T., Banerjee, A.: Information flow analysis in logical form. In: Giacobazzi, R. (ed.) SAS 2004. LNCS, vol. 3148, pp. 100–115. Springer, Heidelberg (2004). https://doi.org/10.1007/978-3-540-27864-1_10

6. Assaf, M., Naumann, D.A., Signoles, J., Totel, E., Tronel, F.: Hypercollecting semantics and its application to static analysis of information flow. In: POPL, pp. 874–887 (2017)

7. Barowy, D.W., Gochev, D., Berger, E.D.: CheckCell: data debugging for spreadsheets. In: OOPSLA, pp. 507–523 (2014)

8. Binkley, D., Gallagher, K.B.: Program slicing. Adv. Comput. **43**, 1–50 (1996)

9. Cheney, J., Ahmed, A., Acar, U.A.: Provenance as dependency analysis. Math. Struct. Comput. Sci. **21**(6), 1301–1337 (2011)

10. Cheng, T., Rival, X.: Static analysis of spreadsheet applications for type-unsafe operations detection. In: Vitek, J. (ed.) ESOP 2015. LNCS, vol. 9032, pp. 26–52. Springer, Heidelberg (2015). https://doi.org/10.1007/978-3-662-46669-8_2

11. Clarkson, M.R., Schneider, F.B.: Hyperproperties. J. Comput. Secur. **18**(6), 1157–1210 (2010)

12. Cousot, P.: Constructive design of a hierarchy of semantics of a transition system by abstract interpretation. Theoret. Comput. Sci. **277**(1–2), 47–103 (2002)

13. Cousot, P., Cousot, R.: Static determination of dynamic properties of programs. In: Symposium on Programming, pp. 106–130 (1976)

14. Cousot, P., Cousot, R.: Abstract interpretation: a unified lattice model for static analysis of programs by construction or approximation of fixpoints. In: POPL, pp. 238–252 (1977)

15. Cousot, P., Cousot, R.: Systematic design of program analysis frameworks. In: POPL, pp. 269–282 (1979)

16. Cousot, P., Cousot, R., Logozzo, F.: A parametric segmentation functor for fully automatic and scalable array content analysis. In: POPL, pp. 105–118 (2011)

17. Denning, D.E.: A lattice model of secure information flow. Commun. ACM **19**(5), 236–243 (1976)

18. Denning, D.E., Denning, P.J.: Certification of programs for secure information flow. Commun. ACM **20**(7), 504–513 (1977)

19. Giacobazzi, R., Mastroeni, I.: Abstract non-interference: parameterizing non-interference by abstract interpretation. In POPL, pp. 186–197 (2004)

20. Giegerich, R., Möncke, U., Wilhelm, R.: Invariance of approximate semantics with respect to program transformations. In: Brauer, W. (ed.) GI - 11. Jahrestagung. Informatik-Fachberichte, vol. 50. Springer, Heidelberg (1981). https://doi.org/10.1007/978-3-662-01089-1_1

21. Goguen, J.A., Meseguer, J.: Security policies and security models. In: S & P, pp. 11–20 (1982)

22. Halder, R., Cortesi, A.: Abstract program slicing on dependence condition graphs. Sci. Comput. Program. **78**(9), 1240–1263 (2013)

23. Herndon, T., Ash, M., Pollin, R.: Does high public debt consistently stifle economic growth? A critique of Reinhart and Rogoff. Camb. J. Econ. **38**(2), 257–279 (2014)

24. Horwitz, S., Reps, T.W., Binkley, D.: Interprocedural slicing using dependence graphs. ACM Trans. Program. Lang. Syst. **12**(1), 26–60 (1990)

25. Hunt, S., Sands, D.: On flow-sensitive security types. In: POPL, pp. 79–90 (2006)

26. Lamport, L.: Proving the correctness of multiprocess programs. IEEE Trans. Softw. Eng. **3**(2), 125–143 (1977)

27. Leveson, N.G., Turner, C.S.: Investigation of the Therac-25 accidents. IEEE Comput. **26**(7), 18–41 (1993)

28. Mastroeni, I., Pasqua, M.: Hyperhierarchy of semantics - a formal framework for hyperproperties verification. In: Ranzato, F. (ed.) SAS 2017. LNCS, vol. 10422, pp. 232–252. Springer, Cham (2017). https://doi.org/10.1007/978-3-319-66706-5_12

29. Mastroeni, I., Zanardini, D.: Abstract program slicing: an abstract interpretation-based approach to program slicing. ACM Trans. Comput. Log. **18**(1), 7:1–7:58 (2017)

30. Mencinger, J., Aristovnik, A., Verbic, M.: The impact of growing public debt on economic growth in the European Union. Amfiteatru Econ. **16**(35), 403–414 (2014)

31. Miné, A.: The octagon abstract domain. High. Order Symb. Comput. **19**(1), 31–100 (2006)

32. Nielson, F., Nielson, H.R., Hankin, C.: Principles of Program Analysis. Springer, Heidelberg (1999)

33. Podelski, A., Rybalchenko, A.: A complete method for the synthesis of linear ranking functions. In: Steffen, B., Levi, G. (eds.) VMCAI 2004. LNCS, vol. 2937, pp. 239–251. Springer, Heidelberg (2004). https://doi.org/10.1007/978-3-540-24622-0_20

34. Urban, C.: The abstract domain of segmented ranking functions. In: Logozzo, F., Fähndrich, M. (eds.) SAS 2013. LNCS, vol. 7935, pp. 43–62. Springer, Heidelberg (2013). https://doi.org/10.1007/978-3-642-38856-9_5

35. Volpano, D.M., Irvine, C.E., Smith, G.: A sound type system for secure flow analysis. J. Comput. Secur. **4**(2/3), 167–188 (1996)

36. Wehrli, S.: Static program analysis of data usage properties. Master's thesis, ETH Zurich, Zurich, Switzerland (2017)

37. Weiser, M.: Program slicing. IEEE Trans. Softw. Eng. **10**(4), 352–357 (1984)

Higher-Order Program Verification
via HFL Model Checking

Naoki Kobayashi[⊠], Takeshi Tsukada, and Keiichi Watanabe

The University of Tokyo, Tokyo, Japan
koba@is.s.u-tokyo.ac.jp

Abstract. There are two kinds of higher-order extensions of model checking: HORS model checking and HFL model checking. Whilst the former has been applied to automated verification of higher-order functional programs, applications of the latter have not been well studied. In the present paper, we show that various verification problems for functional programs, including may/must-reachability, trace properties, and linear-time temporal properties (and their negations), can be naturally reduced to (extended) HFL model checking. The reductions yield a sound and complete logical characterization of those program properties. Compared with the previous approaches based on HORS model checking, our approach provides a more uniform, streamlined method for higher-order program verification.

1 Introduction

There are two kinds of higher-order extensions of model checking in the literature: HORS model checking [16,32] and HFL model checking [42]. The former is concerned about whether the tree generated by a given higher-order tree grammar called a higher-order recursion scheme (HORS) satisfies the property expressed by a given modal μ-calculus formula (or a tree automaton), and the latter is concerned about whether a given finite state system satisfies the property expressed by a formula of higher-order modal fixpoint logic (HFL), a higher-order extension of the modal μ-calculus. Whilst HORS model checking has been applied to automated verification of higher-order functional programs [17,18,22,26,33,41,43], there have been few studies on applications of HFL model checking to program/system verification. Despite that HFL has been introduced more than 10 years ago, we are only aware of applications to assume-guarantee reasoning [42] and process equivalence checking [28].

In the present paper, we show that various verification problems for higher-order functional programs can actually be reduced to (extended) HFL model checking in a rather natural manner. We briefly explain the idea of our reduction below.[1] We translate a program to an HFL formula that says "the program has a valid behavior" (where the *validity* of a behavior depends on each verification

---

[1] In this section, we use only a fragment of HFL that can be expressed in the modal μ-calculus. Some familiarity with the modal μ-calculus [25] would help.

© The Author(s) 2018
A. Ahmed (Ed.): ESOP 2018, LNCS 10801, pp. 711–738, 2018.
https://doi.org/10.1007/978-3-319-89884-1_25

problem). Thus, a program is actually mapped to a *property*, and a program property is mapped to a system to be verified; this has been partially inspired by the recent work of Kobayashi et al. [19], where HORS model checking problems have been translated to HFL model checking problems by switching the roles of models and properties.

For example, consider a simple program fragment $\mathtt{read}(x); \mathtt{close}(x)$ that reads and then closes a file (pointer) x. The transition system in Fig. 1 shows a valid access protocol to read-only files. Then, the property that a read operation is allowed in the current state can be expressed by a formula of the form $\langle\mathtt{read}\rangle\varphi$, which says that the current state has a $\mathtt{read}$-transition, after which φ is satisfied. Thus, the program $\mathtt{read}(x); \mathtt{close}(x)$ being valid is expressed as $\langle\mathtt{read}\rangle\langle\mathtt{close}\rangle\mathbf{true}$,[2] which is indeed satisfied by the initial state q_0 of the transition system in Fig. 1. Here, we have just replaced the operations $\mathtt{read}$ and $\mathtt{close}$ of the program with the corresponding modal operators $\langle\mathtt{read}\rangle$ and $\langle\mathtt{close}\rangle$. We can also naturally deal with branches and recursions. For example, consider the program $\mathtt{close}(x)\square(\mathtt{read}(x); \mathtt{close}(x))$, where $e_1\square e_2$ represents a non-deterministic choice between e_1 and e_2. Then the property that the program always accesses x in a valid manner can be expressed by $(\langle\mathtt{close}\rangle\mathbf{true}) \wedge (\langle\mathtt{read}\rangle\langle\mathtt{close}\rangle\mathbf{true})$. Note that we have just replaced the non-deterministic branch with the logical conjunction, as we wish here to require that the program's behavior is valid in *both* branches. We can also deal with conditional branches if HFL is extended with predicates; $\mathbf{if}\ b\ \mathbf{then}\ \mathtt{close}(x)\ \mathbf{else}\ (\mathtt{read}(x); \mathtt{close}(x))$ can be translated to $(b \Rightarrow \langle\mathtt{close}\rangle\mathbf{true}) \wedge (\neg b \Rightarrow \langle\mathtt{read}\rangle\langle\mathtt{close}\rangle\mathbf{true})$. Let us also consider the recursive function f defined by:

$$f\,x = \mathtt{close}(x)\square(\mathtt{read}(x); \mathtt{read}(x); f\,x),$$

Then, the program $f\,x$ being valid can be represented by using a (greatest) fixpoint formula:

$$\nu F.(\langle\mathtt{close}\rangle\mathbf{true}) \wedge (\langle\mathtt{read}\rangle\langle\mathtt{read}\rangle F).$$

If the state q_0 satisfies this formula (which is indeed the case), then we know that all the file accesses made by $f\,x$ are valid. So far, we have used only the modal μ-calculus formulas. If we wish to express the validity of higher-order programs, we need HFL formulas; such examples are given later.

Fig. 1. File access protocol

We generalize the above idea and formalize reductions from various classes of verification problems for simply-typed higher-order functional programs with recursion, integers and non-determinism – including verification of may/must-reachability, trace properties, and linear-time temporal properties (and their negations) – to (extended) HFL model checking where HFL is extended with integer predicates, and prove soundness and completeness of the reductions. Extended HFL model checking problems obtained by the reductions are (necessarily) undecidable in general, but for finite-data programs (i.e., programs that consist of only functions and data from finite data domains such as Booleans), the reductions yield *pure* HFL model checking problems, which are decidable [42].

Our reductions provide sound and complete logical characterizations of a wide range of program properties mentioned above. Nice properties of the logical characterizations include: (i) (like verification conditions for Hoare triples,) once the logical characterization is obtained as an HFL formula, purely logical reasoning can be used to prove or disprove it (without further referring to the program semantics); for that purpose, one may use theorem provers with various degrees of automation, ranging from interactive ones like Coq, semi-automated ones requiring some annotations, to fully automated ones (though the latter two are yet to be implemented), (ii) (unlike the standard verification condition generation for Hoare triples using invariant annotations) the logical characterization can *automatically* be computed, without any annotations,[3] (iii) standard logical reasoning can be applied based on the semantics of formulas; for example, co-induction and induction can be used for proving ν- and μ-formulas respectively, and (iv) thanks to the completeness, the set of program properties characterizable by HFL formula is closed under negations; for example, from a formula characterizing may-reachability, one can obtain a formula characterizing non-reachability by just taking the De Morgan dual.

Compared with previous approaches based on HORS model checking [18, 22, 26, 33, 37], our approach based on (extended) HFL model checking provides more uniform, streamlined methods for higher-order program verification. HORS model checking provides sound and complete verification methods for *finite-data* programs [17, 18], but for infinite-data programs, other techniques such as predicate abstraction [22] and program transformation [27, 31] had to be combined to obtain sound (but incomplete) reductions to HORS model checking. Furthermore, the techniques were different for each of program properties, such as reachability [22], termination [27], non-termination [26], fair termination [31], and fair non-termination [43]. In contrast, our reductions are sound and complete even for infinite-data programs. Although the obtained HFL model checking problems are undecidable in general, the reductions allow us to treat various program properties uniformly; all the verifications are boiled down to the issue of how to prove μ- and ν-formulas (and as remarked above, we can use induction and co-induction to deal with them). Technically, our reduction to HFL model

---

[3] This does not mean that invariant discovery is unnecessary; invariant discovery is just postponed to the later phase of discharging verification conditions, so that it can be uniformly performed among various verification problems.

checking may actually be considered an extension of HORS model checking in the following sense. HORS model checking algorithms [21,32] usually consist of two phases, one for computing a kind of higher-order "procedure summaries" in the form of variable profiles [32] or intersection types [21], and the other for nested least/greatest fixpoint computations. Our reduction from program verification to extended HFL model checking (the reduction given in Sect. 7, in particular) can be regarded as an extension of the first phase to deal with infinite data domains, where the problem for the second phase is expressed in the form of extended HFL model checking: see [23] for more details.

The rest of this paper is structured as follows. Section 2 introduces HFL extended with integer predicates and defines the HFL model checking problem. Section 3 informally demonstrates some examples of reductions from program verification problems to HFL model checking. Section 4 introduces a functional language used to formally discuss the reductions in later sections. Sections 5, 6, and 7 consider may/must-reachability, trace properties, and temporal properties respectively, and present (sound and complete) reductions from verification of those properties to HFL model checking. Section 8 discusses related work, and Sect. 9 concludes the paper. Proofs are found in an extended version [23].

2   (Extended) HFL

In this section, we introduce an extension of higher-order modal fixpoint logic (HFL) [42] with integer predicates (which we call $HFL_{\mathbf{Z}}$; we often drop the subscript and write HFL, as in Sect. 1), and define the $HFL_{\mathbf{Z}}$ model checking problem. The set of integers can actually be replaced by another infinite set X of data (like the set of natural numbers or the set of finite trees) to yield HFL_X.

2.1   Syntax

For a map f, we write $dom(f)$ and $codom(f)$ for the domain and codomain of f respectively. We write $\mathbf{Z}$ for the set of integers, ranged over by the meta-variable n below. We assume a set $\mathbf{Pred}$ of primitive predicates on integers, ranged over by p. We write $\mathtt{arity}(p)$ for the arity of p. We assume that $\mathbf{Pred}$ contains standard integer predicates such as $=$ and $<$, and also assume that, for each predicate $p \in \mathbf{Pred}$, there also exists a predicate $\neg p \in \mathbf{Pred}$ such that, for any integers $n_1, \ldots, n_k$, $p(n_1, \ldots, n_k)$ holds if and only if $\neg p(n_1, \ldots, n_k)$ does not hold; thus, $\neg p(n_1, \ldots, n_k)$ should be parsed as $(\neg p)(n_1, \ldots, n_k)$, but can semantically be interpreted as $\neg(p(n_1, \ldots, n_k))$.

The syntax of $HFL_{\mathbf{Z}}$ *formulas* is given by:

$$\varphi \text{ (formulas)} ::= n \mid \varphi_1 \text{ op } \varphi_2 \mid \mathbf{true} \mid \mathbf{false} \mid p(\varphi_1, \ldots, \varphi_k) \mid \varphi_1 \vee \varphi_2 \mid \varphi_1 \wedge \varphi_2$$
$$\mid X \mid \langle a \rangle \varphi \mid [a]\varphi \mid \mu X^\tau.\varphi \mid \nu X^\tau.\varphi \mid \lambda X : \sigma.\varphi \mid \varphi_1 \varphi_2$$
$$\tau \text{ (types)} ::= \bullet \mid \sigma \rightarrow \tau \qquad \sigma \text{ (extended types)} ::= \tau \mid \mathtt{int}$$

Here, op ranges over a set of binary operations on integers, such as $+$, and X ranges over a denumerable set of variables. We have extended the original HFL [42] with integer expressions (n and φ_1 op φ_2), and atomic formulas

$p(\varphi_1, \ldots, \varphi_k)$ on integers (here, the arguments of integer operations or predicates will be restricted to integer expressions by the type system introduced below). Following [19], we have omitted negations, as any formula can be transformed to an equivalent negation-free formula [30].

We explain the meaning of each formula informally; the formal semantics is given in Sect. 2.2. Like modal μ-calculus [10,25], each formula expresses a property of a labeled transition system. The first line of the syntax of formulas consists of the standard constructs of predicate logics. On the second line, as in the standard modal μ-calculus, $\langle a \rangle \varphi$ means that there exists an a-labeled transition to a state that satisfies φ. The formula $[a]\varphi$ means that after any a-labeled transition, φ is satisfied. The formulas $\mu X^\tau.\varphi$ and $\nu X^\tau.\varphi$ represent the least and greatest fixpoints respectively (the least and greatest X that $X = \varphi$) respectively; unlike the modal μ-calculus, X may range over not only propositional variables but also higher-order predicate variables (of type τ). The λ-abstractions $\lambda X{:}\sigma.\varphi$ and applications $\varphi_1\,\varphi_2$ are used to manipulate higher-order predicates. We often omit type annotations in $\mu X^\tau.\varphi$, $\nu X^\tau.\varphi$ and $\lambda X:\sigma.\varphi$, and just write $\mu X.\varphi$, $\nu X.\varphi$ and $\lambda X.\varphi$.

Example 1. Consider $\varphi_{\mathsf{ab}}\,\varphi$ where $\varphi_{\mathsf{ab}} = \mu X^{\bullet \to \bullet}.\lambda Y : \bullet.Y \vee \langle \mathsf{a} \rangle(X(\langle \mathsf{b} \rangle Y))$. We can expand the formula as follows:

$$\varphi_{\mathsf{ab}}\,\varphi = (\lambda Y. \bullet .Y \vee \langle \mathsf{a} \rangle(\varphi_{\mathsf{ab}}(\langle \mathsf{b} \rangle Y)))\varphi = \varphi \vee \langle \mathsf{a} \rangle(\varphi_{\mathsf{ab}}(\langle \mathsf{b} \rangle \varphi))$$
$$= \varphi \vee \langle \mathsf{a} \rangle(\langle \mathsf{b} \rangle \varphi \vee \langle \mathsf{a} \rangle(\varphi_{\mathsf{ab}}(\langle \mathsf{b} \rangle \langle \mathsf{b} \rangle \varphi))) = \cdots,$$

and obtain $\varphi \vee (\langle \mathsf{a} \rangle \langle \mathsf{b} \rangle \varphi) \vee (\langle \mathsf{a} \rangle \langle \mathsf{a} \rangle \langle \mathsf{b} \rangle \langle \mathsf{b} \rangle \varphi) \vee \cdots$. Thus, the formula means that there is a transition sequence of the form $\mathsf{a}^n \mathsf{b}^n$ for some $n \geq 0$ that leads to a state satisfying φ.

Following [19], we exclude out unmeaningful formulas such as $(\langle a \rangle \mathbf{true})+1$ by using a simple type system. The types $\bullet$, $\mathtt{int}$, and $\sigma \to \tau$ describe propositions, integers, and (monotonic) functions from σ to τ, respectively. Note that the integer type $\mathtt{int}$ may occur only in an argument position; this restriction is required to ensure that least and greatest fixpoints are well-defined. The typing rules for formulas are given in Fig. 2. In the figure, Δ denotes a type environment, which is a finite map from variables to (extended) types. Below we consider only well-typed formulas.

2.2 Semantics and HFL$_\mathbf{Z}$ Model Checking

We now define the formal semantics of HFL$_\mathbf{Z}$ formulas. A *labeled transition system* (LTS) is a quadruple $\mathsf{L} = (U, A, \longrightarrow, \mathsf{s}_{\mathsf{init}})$, where U is a finite set of states, A is a finite set of actions, $\longrightarrow \subseteq U \times A \times U$ is a labeled transition relation, and $\mathsf{s}_{\mathsf{init}} \in U$ is the initial state. We write $\mathsf{s}_1 \xrightarrow{a} \mathsf{s}_2$ when $(\mathsf{s}_1, a, \mathsf{s}_2) \in \longrightarrow$.

For an LTS $\mathsf{L} = (U, A, \longrightarrow, \mathsf{s}_{\mathsf{init}})$ and an extended type σ, we define the partially ordered set $(\mathcal{D}_{\mathsf{L},\sigma}, \sqsubseteq_{\mathsf{L},\sigma})$ inductively by:

$$\mathcal{D}_{\mathsf{L},\bullet} = 2^U \qquad \sqsubseteq_{\mathsf{L},\bullet} = \subseteq \qquad \mathcal{D}_{\mathsf{L},\mathtt{int}} = \mathbf{Z} \qquad \sqsubseteq_{\mathsf{L},\mathtt{int}} = \{(n,n) \mid n \in \mathbf{Z}\}$$
$$\mathcal{D}_{\mathsf{L},\sigma \to \tau} = \{f \in \mathcal{D}_{\mathsf{L},\sigma} \to \mathcal{D}_{\mathsf{L},\tau} \mid \forall x, y.(x \sqsubseteq_{\mathsf{L},\sigma} y \Rightarrow f\,x \sqsubseteq_{\mathsf{L},\tau} f\,y)\}$$
$$\sqsubseteq_{\mathsf{L},\sigma \to \tau} = \{(f,g) \mid \forall x \in \mathcal{D}_{\mathsf{L},\sigma}.f(x) \sqsubseteq_{\mathsf{L},\tau} g(x)\}$$

$$\frac{}{\Delta \vdash_{\mathrm{H}} n : \mathtt{int}} \quad \text{(HT-Int)}$$

$$\frac{\Delta \vdash_{\mathrm{H}} \varphi_i : \bullet \text{ for each } i \in \{1,2\}}{\Delta \vdash_{\mathrm{H}} \varphi_1 \wedge \varphi_2 : \bullet} \quad \text{(HT-And)}$$

$$\frac{\Delta \vdash_{\mathrm{H}} \varphi_i : \mathtt{int} \text{ for each } i \in \{1,2\}}{\Delta \vdash_{\mathrm{H}} \varphi_1 \text{ op } \varphi_2 : \mathtt{int}} \quad \text{(HT-Op)}$$

$$\frac{\Delta \vdash_{\mathrm{H}} \varphi : \bullet}{\Delta \vdash_{\mathrm{H}} \langle a \rangle \varphi : \bullet} \quad \text{(HT-Some)}$$

$$\frac{}{\Delta \vdash_{\mathrm{H}} \mathbf{true} : \bullet} \quad \text{(HT-True)}$$

$$\frac{\Delta \vdash_{\mathrm{H}} \varphi : \bullet}{\Delta \vdash_{\mathrm{H}} [a]\varphi : \bullet} \quad \text{(HT-All)}$$

$$\frac{}{\Delta \vdash_{\mathrm{H}} \mathbf{false} : \bullet} \quad \text{(HT-False)}$$

$$\frac{\Delta, X : \tau \vdash_{\mathrm{H}} \varphi : \tau}{\Delta \vdash_{\mathrm{H}} \mu X^\tau. \; \varphi : \tau} \quad \text{(HT-Mu)}$$

$$\frac{\mathtt{arity}(p) = k \qquad \Delta \vdash_{\mathrm{H}} \varphi_i : \mathtt{int} \text{ for each } i \in \{1,\dots,k\}}{\Delta \vdash_{\mathrm{H}} p(\varphi_1,\dots,\varphi_k) : \bullet} \quad \text{(HT-Pred)}$$

$$\frac{\Delta, X : \tau \vdash_{\mathrm{H}} \varphi : \tau}{\Delta \vdash_{\mathrm{H}} \nu X^\tau. \; \varphi : \tau} \quad \text{(HT-Nu)}$$

$$\frac{}{\Delta, X : \sigma \vdash_{\mathrm{H}} X : \sigma} \quad \text{(HT-Var)}$$

$$\frac{\Delta, X : \sigma \vdash_{\mathrm{H}} \varphi : \tau}{\Delta \vdash_{\mathrm{H}} \lambda X : \sigma. \; \varphi : \sigma \rightarrow \tau} \quad \text{(HT-Abs)}$$

$$\frac{\Delta \vdash_{\mathrm{H}} \varphi_i : \bullet \text{ for each } i \in \{1,2\}}{\Delta \vdash_{\mathrm{H}} \varphi_1 \vee \varphi_2 : \bullet} \quad \text{(HT-Or)}$$

$$\frac{\Delta \vdash_{\mathrm{H}} \varphi_1 : \sigma \rightarrow \tau \qquad \Delta \vdash_{\mathrm{H}} \varphi_2 : \sigma}{\Delta \vdash_{\mathrm{H}} \varphi_1 \; \varphi_2 : \tau} \quad \text{(HT-App)}$$

Fig. 2. Typing rules for HFL$_\mathbf{Z}$ formulas

Note that $(\mathcal{D}_{\mathrm{L},\tau}, \sqsubseteq_{\mathrm{L},\tau})$ forms a complete lattice (but $(\mathcal{D}_{\mathrm{L},\mathtt{int}}, \sqsubseteq_{\mathrm{L},\mathtt{int}})$ does not). We write $\perp_{\mathrm{L},\tau}$ and $\top_{\mathrm{L},\tau}$ for the least and greatest elements of $\mathcal{D}_{\mathrm{L},\tau}$ (which are $\lambda\widetilde{x}.\emptyset$ and $\lambda\widetilde{x}.U$) respectively. We sometimes omit the subscript L below. Let $[\![\Delta]\!]_{\mathrm{L}}$ be the set of functions (called *valuations*) that maps X to an element of $\mathcal{D}_{\mathrm{L},\sigma}$ for each $X : \sigma \in \Delta$. For an HFL formula φ such that $\Delta \vdash_{\mathrm{H}} \varphi : \sigma$, we define $[\![\Delta \vdash_{\mathrm{H}} \varphi : \sigma]\!]_{\mathrm{L}}$ as a map from $[\![\Delta]\!]_{\mathrm{L}}$ to $\mathcal{D}_\sigma$, by induction on the derivation[4] of $\Delta \vdash_{\mathrm{H}} \varphi : \sigma$, as follows.

$$[\![\Delta \vdash_{\mathrm{H}} n : \mathtt{int}]\!]_{\mathrm{L}}(\rho) = n \qquad [\![\Delta \vdash_{\mathrm{H}} \mathbf{true} : \bullet]\!]_{\mathrm{L}}(\rho) = U \qquad [\![\Delta \vdash_{\mathrm{H}} \mathbf{false} : \bullet]\!]_{\mathrm{L}}(\rho) = \emptyset$$

$$[\![\Delta \vdash_{\mathrm{H}} \varphi_1 \text{ op } \varphi_2 : \mathtt{int}]\!]_{\mathrm{L}}(\rho) = ([\![\Delta \vdash_{\mathrm{H}} \varphi_1 : \mathtt{int}]\!]_{\mathrm{L}}(\rho))[\![\text{op}]\!]([\![\Delta \vdash_{\mathrm{H}} \varphi_2 : \mathtt{int}]\!]_{\mathrm{L}}(\rho))$$

$$[\![\Delta \vdash_{\mathrm{H}} p(\varphi_1,\dots,\varphi_k) : \bullet]\!]_{\mathrm{L}}(\rho) =$$
$$\begin{cases} U \text{ if } ([\![\Delta \vdash_{\mathrm{H}} \varphi_1 : \mathtt{int}]\!]_{\mathrm{L}}(\rho),\dots,[\![\Delta \vdash_{\mathrm{H}} \varphi_k : \mathtt{int}]\!]_{\mathrm{L}}(\rho)) \in [\![p]\!] \\ \emptyset \text{ otherwise} \end{cases}$$

$$[\![\Delta, X : \sigma \vdash_{\mathrm{H}} X : \sigma]\!]_{\mathrm{L}}(\rho) = \rho(X)$$

$$[\![\Delta \vdash_{\mathrm{H}} \varphi_1 \vee \varphi_2 : \bullet]\!]_{\mathrm{L}}(\rho) = [\![\Delta \vdash_{\mathrm{H}} \varphi_1 : \bullet]\!]_{\mathrm{L}}(\rho) \cup [\![\Delta \vdash_{\mathrm{H}} \varphi_2 : \bullet]\!]_{\mathrm{L}}(\rho)$$

$$[\![\Delta \vdash_{\mathrm{H}} \varphi_1 \wedge \varphi_2 : \bullet]\!]_{\mathrm{L}}(\rho) = [\![\Delta \vdash_{\mathrm{H}} \varphi_1 : \bullet]\!]_{\mathrm{L}}(\rho) \cap [\![\Delta \vdash_{\mathrm{H}} \varphi_2 : \bullet]\!]_{\mathrm{L}}(\rho)$$

$$[\![\Delta \vdash_{\mathrm{H}} \langle a \rangle \varphi : \bullet]\!]_{\mathrm{L}}(\rho) = \{\mathbf{s} \mid \exists \mathbf{s}' \in [\![\Delta \vdash_{\mathrm{H}} \varphi : \bullet]\!]_{\mathrm{L}}(\rho). \; \mathbf{s} \xrightarrow{a} \mathbf{s}'\}$$

$$[\![\Delta \vdash_{\mathrm{H}} [a]\varphi : \bullet]\!]_{\mathrm{L}}(\rho) = \{\mathbf{s} \mid \forall \mathbf{s}' \in U. \; (\mathbf{s} \xrightarrow{a} \mathbf{s}' \text{ implies } \mathbf{s}' \in [\![\Delta \vdash_{\mathrm{H}} \varphi : \bullet]\!]_{\mathrm{L}}(\rho))\}$$

$$[\![\Delta \vdash_{\mathrm{H}} \mu X^\tau.\varphi : \tau]\!]_{\mathrm{L}}(\rho) = \mathbf{lfp}_{\mathrm{L},\tau}([\![\Delta \vdash_{\mathrm{H}} \lambda X : \tau. \; \varphi : \tau \rightarrow \tau]\!]_{\mathrm{L}}(\rho))$$

$$[\![\Delta \vdash_{\mathrm{H}} \nu X^\tau.\varphi : \tau]\!]_{\mathrm{L}}(\rho) = \mathbf{gfp}_{\mathrm{L},\tau}([\![\Delta \vdash_{\mathrm{H}} \lambda X : \tau. \; \varphi : \tau \rightarrow \tau]\!]_{\mathrm{L}}(\rho))$$

$$[\![\Delta \vdash_{\mathrm{H}} \lambda X : \sigma. \; \varphi : \sigma \rightarrow \tau]\!]_{\mathrm{L}}(\rho) = \{(v, [\![\Delta, X : \sigma \vdash_{\mathrm{H}} \varphi : \tau]\!]_{\mathrm{L}}(\rho[X \mapsto v])) \mid v \in \mathcal{D}_{\mathrm{L},\sigma}\}$$

$$[\![\Delta \vdash_{\mathrm{H}} \varphi_1 \; \varphi_2 : \tau]\!]_{\mathrm{L}}(\rho) = [\![\Delta \vdash_{\mathrm{H}} \varphi_1 : \sigma \rightarrow \tau]\!]_{\mathrm{L}}(\rho)([\![\Delta \vdash_{\mathrm{H}} \varphi_2 : \sigma]\!]_{\mathrm{L}}(\rho))$$

---

[4] Note that the derivation of each judgment $\Delta \vdash_{\mathrm{H}} \varphi : \sigma$ is unique if there is any.

Here, $\llbracket \mathsf{op} \rrbracket$ denotes the binary function on integers represented by op and $\llbracket p \rrbracket$ denotes the k-ary relation on integers represented by p. The least/greatest fixpoint operators $\mathbf{lfp}_{\mathrm{L},\tau}$ and $\mathbf{gfp}_{\mathrm{L},\tau}$ are defined by $\mathbf{lfp}_{\mathrm{L},\tau}(f) = \bigcap_{\mathrm{L},\tau}\{x \in \mathcal{D}_{\mathrm{L},\tau} \mid f(x) \sqsubseteq_{\mathrm{L},\tau} x\}$ and $\mathbf{gfp}_{\mathrm{L},\tau}(f) = \bigsqcup_{\mathrm{L},\tau}\{x \in \mathcal{D}_{\mathrm{L},\tau} \mid x \sqsubseteq_{\mathrm{L},\tau} f(x)\}$. Here, $\bigsqcup_{\mathrm{L},\tau}$ and $\bigcap_{\mathrm{L},\tau}$ respectively denote the least upper bound and the greatest lower bound with respect to $\sqsubseteq_{\mathrm{L},\tau}$. We often omit the subscript L and write $\llbracket \Delta \vdash_{\mathrm{H}} \varphi : \sigma \rrbracket$ for $\llbracket \Delta \vdash_{\mathrm{H}} \varphi : \sigma \rrbracket_{\mathrm{L}}$. For a closed formula, i.e., a formula well-typed under the empty type environment $\emptyset$, we often write $\llbracket \varphi \rrbracket_{\mathrm{L}}$ or just $\llbracket \varphi \rrbracket$ for $\llbracket \emptyset \vdash_{\mathrm{H}} \varphi : \sigma \rrbracket_{\mathrm{L}}(\emptyset)$.

Example 2. For the LTS L_{file} in Fig. 1, we have:

$$\llbracket \nu X^{\bullet}.(\langle \mathsf{close}\rangle \mathbf{true} \wedge \langle \mathsf{read}\rangle X) \rrbracket =$$
$$\mathbf{gfp}_{\mathrm{L},\bullet}(\lambda x \in \mathcal{D}_{\mathrm{L},\bullet}.\llbracket X : \bullet \vdash \langle \mathsf{close}\rangle \mathbf{true} \wedge \langle \mathsf{read}\rangle X : \bullet \rrbracket(\{X \mapsto x\})) = \{q_0\}.$$

In fact, $x = \{q_0\} \in \mathcal{D}_{\mathrm{L},\bullet}$ satisfies the equation: $\llbracket X : \bullet \vdash \langle \mathsf{close}\rangle \mathbf{true} \wedge \langle \mathsf{read}\rangle X : \bullet \rrbracket_{\mathrm{L}}(\{X \mapsto x\}) = x$, and $x = \{q_0\} \in \mathcal{D}_{\mathrm{L},\bullet}$ is the greatest such element.

Consider the following LTS L_1:

$$q_0 \xrightarrow{a} q_1 \underset{c}{\overset{b}{\rightleftarrows}} q_2$$

and $\varphi_{\mathsf{ab}}(\langle c \rangle \mathbf{true})$ where φ_{ab} is the one introduced in Example 1. Then, $\llbracket \varphi_{\mathsf{ab}}(\langle c \rangle \mathbf{true}) \rrbracket_{\mathrm{L}_1} = \{q_0, q_2\}$.

Definition 1 (HFL$_{\mathbf{Z}}$ model checking). *For a closed formula φ of type $\bullet$, we write $\mathrm{L}, \mathbf{s} \models \varphi$ if $\mathbf{s} \in \llbracket \varphi \rrbracket_{\mathrm{L}}$, and write $\mathrm{L} \models \varphi$ if $\mathbf{s}_{\mathrm{init}} \in \llbracket \varphi \rrbracket_{\mathrm{L}}$. HFL$_{\mathbf{Z}}$ model checking is the problem of, given L and φ, deciding whether $\mathrm{L} \models \varphi$ holds.*

The HFL$_{\mathbf{Z}}$ model checking problem is *undecidable*, due to the presence of integers; in fact, the semantic domain $\mathcal{D}_{\mathrm{L},\sigma}$ is not finite for σ that contains int. The undecidability is obtained as a corollary of the soundness and completeness of the reduction from the may-reachability problem to HFL model checking discussed in Sect. 5. For the fragment of pure HFL (i.e., HFL$_{\mathbf{Z}}$ without integers, which we write HFL$_{\emptyset}$ below), the model checking problem is decidable [42].

The *order* of an HFL$_{\mathbf{Z}}$ model checking problem $\mathrm{L} \overset{?}{\models} \varphi$ is the highest order of types of subformulas of φ, where the order of a type is defined by: $\mathtt{order}(\bullet) = \mathtt{order}(\mathsf{int}) = 0$ and $\mathtt{order}(\sigma \to \tau) \doteq \max(\mathtt{order}(\sigma) + 1, \mathtt{order}(\tau))$. The complexity of order-k HFL$_{\emptyset}$ model checking is k-EXPTIME complete [1], but polynomial time in the size of HFL formulas under the assumption that the other parameters (the size of LTS and the largest size of types used in formulas) are fixed [19].

Remark 1. Though we do not have quantifiers on integers as primitives, we can encode them using fixpoint operators. Given a formula $\varphi : \mathsf{int} \to \bullet$, we can express $\exists x : \mathsf{int}.\varphi(x)$ and $\forall x : \mathsf{int}.\varphi(x)$ by $(\mu X^{\mathsf{int}\to\bullet}.\lambda x : \mathsf{int}.\varphi(x) \vee X(x - 1) \vee X(x + 1))0$ and $(\nu X^{\mathsf{int}\to\bullet}.\lambda x : \mathsf{int}.\varphi(x) \wedge X(x - 1) \wedge X(x + 1))0$ respectively.

2.3 HES

As in [19], we often write an HFL$_\mathbf{Z}$ formula as a sequence of fixpoint equations, called a *hierarchical equation system* (HES).

Definition 2. *An (extended) hierarchical equation system (HES) is a pair* $(\mathcal{E}, \varphi)$ *where* $\mathcal{E}$ *is a sequence of fixpoint equations, of the form:* $X_1^{\tau_1} =_{\alpha_1} \varphi_1; \cdots; X_n^{\tau_n} =_{\alpha_n} \varphi_n$, *where* $\alpha_i \in \{\mu, \nu\}$. *We assume that* $X_1 : \tau_1, \ldots, X_n : \tau_n \vdash_H \varphi_i : \tau_i$ *holds for each* $i \in \{1, \ldots, n\}$, *and that* $\varphi_1, \ldots, \varphi_n, \varphi$ *do not contain any fixpoint operators.*

The HES $\Phi = (\mathcal{E}, \varphi)$ represents the HFL$_\mathbf{Z}$ formula $toHFL(\mathcal{E}, \varphi)$ defined inductively by: $toHFL(\epsilon, \varphi) = \varphi$ and $toHFL(\mathcal{E}; X^\tau =_\alpha \varphi', \varphi) = toHFL([\alpha X^\tau.\varphi'/X]\mathcal{E}, [\alpha X^\tau.\varphi'/X]\varphi)$. Conversely, every HFL$_\mathbf{Z}$ formula can be easily converted to an equivalent HES. In the rest of the paper, we often represent an HFL$_\mathbf{Z}$ formula in the form of HES, and just call it an HFL$_\mathbf{Z}$ formula. We write $[\![\Phi]\!]$ for $[\![toHFL(\Phi)]\!]$. An HES $(X_1^{\tau_1} =_{\alpha_1} \varphi_1; \cdots; X_n^{\tau_n} =_{\alpha_n} \varphi_n, \varphi)$ can be normalized to $(X_0^{\tau_0} =_\nu \varphi; X_1^{\tau_1} =_{\alpha_1} \varphi_1; \cdots; X_n^{\tau_n} =_{\alpha_n} \varphi_n, X_0)$ where τ_0 is the type of φ. Thus, we sometimes call just a sequence of equations $X_0^{\tau_0} =_\nu \varphi; X_1^{\tau_1} =_{\alpha_1} \varphi_1; \cdots; X_n^{\tau_n} =_{\alpha_n} \varphi_n$ an HES, with the understanding that "the main formula" is the first variable X_0. Also, we often write $X^\tau x_1 \cdots x_k =_\alpha \varphi$ for the equation $X^\tau =_\alpha \lambda x_1. \cdots \lambda x_k.\varphi$. We often omit type annotations and just write $X =_\alpha \varphi$ for $X^\tau =_\alpha \varphi$.

Example 3. The formula $\nu X.\mu Y.\langle \mathbf{b}\rangle X \vee \langle \mathbf{a}\rangle Y$ (which means that the current state has a transition sequence of the form $(\mathbf{a}^*\mathbf{b})^\omega$) is expressed as the following HES:

$$((X =_\nu Y; Y =_\mu \langle \mathbf{b}\rangle X \vee \langle \mathbf{a}\rangle Y), \quad X).$$

3 Warming Up

To help readers get more familiar with HFL$_\mathbf{Z}$ and the idea of reductions, we give here some variations of the examples of verification of file-accessing programs in Sect. 1, which are instances of the "resource usage verification problem" [15]. General reductions will be discussed in Sects. 5, 6 and 7, after the target language is set up in Sect. 4.

Consider the following OCaml-like program, which uses exceptions.

```
let readex x = read x; (if * then () else raise Eof) in
let rec f x = readex x; f x in
let d = open_in "foo" in try f d with Eof -> close d
```

Here, $*$ represents a non-deterministic boolean value. The function `readex` reads the file pointer x, and then non-deterministically raises an end-of-file (`Eof`) exception. The main expression (on the third line) first opens file "foo", calls `f` to read the file repeatedly, and closes the file upon an end-of-file exception. Suppose, as in the example of Sect. 1, we wish to verify that the file "foo" is accessed following the protocol in Fig. 1.

First, we can remove exceptions by representing an exception handler as a special continuation [6]:

```
let readex x h k = read x; (if * then k() else h()) in
let rec f x h k = readex x h (fun _ -> f x h k) in
let d = open_in "foo" in f d (fun _ -> close d) (fun _ -> ())
```

Here, we have added to each function two parameters h and k, which represent an exception handler and a (normal) continuation respectively.

Let Φ be $(\mathcal{E}, F\,\mathbf{true}\,(\lambda r.\langle\mathbf{close}\rangle\mathbf{true})\,(\lambda r.\mathbf{true}))$ where $\mathcal{E}$ is:

$$Readex\ x\ h\ k =_{\nu} \langle\mathbf{read}\rangle(k\,\mathbf{true} \wedge h\,\mathbf{true});$$
$$F\ x\ h\ k =_{\nu} Readex\ x\ h\ (\lambda r.F\ x\ h\ k).$$

Here, we have just replaced read/close operations with the modal operators $\langle\mathbf{read}\rangle$ and $\langle\mathbf{close}\rangle$, non-deterministic choice with a logical conjunction, and the unit value ( ) with $\mathbf{true}$. Then, $\mathsf{L}_{file} \models \Phi$ if and only if the program performs only valid accesses to the file (e.g., it does not access the file after a close operation), where L_{file} is the LTS shown in Fig. 1. The correctness of the reduction can be informally understood by observing that there is a close correspondence between reductions of the program and those of the HFL formula above, and when the program reaches a read command read x, the corresponding formula is of the form $\langle\mathbf{read}\rangle\cdots$, meaning that the read operation is valid in the current state; a similar condition holds also for close operations. We will present a general translation and prove its correctness in Sect. 6.

Let us consider another example, which uses integers:

```
let rec f y x k = if y=0 then (close x; k())
                 else (read x; f (y-1) x k) in
let d = open_in "foo" in f n d (fun _ -> ())
```

Here, n is an integer constant. The function f reads x y times, and then calls the continuation k. Let L'_{file} be the LTS obtained by adding to L_{file} a new state q_2 and the transition $q_1 \xrightarrow{\mathbf{end}} q_2$ (which intuitively means that a program is allowed to terminate in the state q_1), and let Φ' be $(\mathcal{E}', F\,n\,\mathbf{true}\,(\lambda r.\langle\mathbf{end}\rangle\mathbf{true}))$ where $\mathcal{E}'$ is:

$$F\ y\ x\ k =_{\mu} (y = 0 \Rightarrow \langle\mathbf{close}\rangle(k\,\mathbf{true})) \wedge (y \neq 0 \Rightarrow \langle\mathbf{read}\rangle(F\ (y-1)\ x\ k)).$$

Here, $p(\varphi_1, \ldots, \varphi_k) \Rightarrow \varphi$ is an abbreviation of $\neg p(\varphi_1, \ldots, \varphi_k) \vee \varphi$. Then, $\mathsf{L}'_{file} \models \Phi'$ if and only if (i) the program performs only valid accesses to the file, (ii) it eventually terminates, and (iii) the file is closed when the program terminates. Notice the use of μ instead of ν above; by using μ, we can express liveness properties. The property $\mathsf{L}'_{file} \models \Phi'$ indeed holds for $n \geq 0$, but not for $n < 0$. In fact, $F\ n\ x\ k$ is equivalent to $\mathbf{false}$ for $n < 0$, and $\langle\mathbf{read}\rangle^n\langle\mathbf{close}\rangle(k\,\mathbf{true})$ for $n \geq 0$.

4   Target Language

This section sets up, as the target of program verification, a call-by-name[5] higher-order functional language extended with events. The language is essentially the same as the one used by Watanabe et al. [43] for discussing fair non-termination.

4.1   Syntax and Typing

We assume a finite set **Ev** of names called *events*, ranged over by a, and a denumerable set of variables, ranged over by $x, y, \ldots$. Events are used to express temporal properties of programs. We write $\tilde{x}$ ($\tilde{t}$, resp.) for a sequence of variables (terms, resp.), and write $|\tilde{x}|$ for the length of the sequence.

A *program* is a pair (D, t) consisting of a set D of function definitions $\{f_1 \, \tilde{x}_1 = t_1, \ldots, f_n \, \tilde{x}_n = t_n\}$ and a term t. The set of *terms*, ranged over by t, is defined by:

$$t ::= () \mid x \mid n \mid t_1 \text{ op } t_2 \mid \textbf{event } a; t \mid \textbf{if } p(t'_1, \ldots, t'_k) \textbf{ then } t_1 \textbf{ else } t_2$$
$$\mid t_1 t_2 \mid t_1 \square t_2.$$

Here, n and p range over the sets of integers and integer predicates as in HFL formulas. The expression **event** $a; t$ raises an event a, and then evaluates t. Events are used to encode program properties of interest. For example, an assertion **assert**(b) can be expressed as **if** b **then** () **else** (**event fail**; Ω), where **fail** is an event that expresses an assertion failure and Ω is a non-terminating term. If program termination is of interest, one can insert "**event end**" to every termination point and check whether an **end** event occurs. The expression $t_1 \square t_2$ evaluates t_1 or t_2 in a non-deterministic manner; it can be used to model, e.g., unknown inputs from an environment. We use the meta-variable P for programs. When $P = (D, t)$ with $D = \{f_1 \, \tilde{x}_1 = t_1, \ldots, f_n \, \tilde{x}_n = t_n\}$, we write **funs**$(P)$ for $\{f_1, \ldots, f_n\}$ (i.e., the set of function names defined in P). Using λ-abstractions, we sometimes write $f = \lambda\tilde{x}.t$ for the function definition $f \, \tilde{x} = t$. We also regard D as a map from function names to terms, and write $dom(D)$ for $\{f_1, \ldots, f_n\}$ and $D(f_i)$ for $\lambda\tilde{x}_i.t_i$.

Any program (D, t) can be normalized to $(D \cup \{\textbf{main} = t\}, \textbf{main})$ where **main** is a name for the "main" function. We sometimes write just D for a program $(D, \textbf{main})$, with the understanding that D contains a definition of **main**.

We restrict the syntax of expressions using a type system. The set of *simple types*, ranged over by κ, is defined by:

$$\kappa ::= \star \mid \eta \to \kappa \qquad\qquad \eta ::= \kappa \mid \texttt{int}.$$

The types $\star$, $\texttt{int}$, and $\eta \to \kappa$ describe the unit value, integers, and functions from η to κ respectively. Note that $\texttt{int}$ is allowed to occur only in argument

---

[5] Call-by-value programs can be handled by applying the CPS transformation before applying the reductions to HFL model checking.

positions. We defer typing rules to [23], as they are standard, except that we require that the righthand side of each function definition must have type $\star$; this restriction, as well as the restriction that int occurs only in argument positions, does not lose generality, as those conditions can be ensured by applying CPS transformation. We consider below only well-typed programs.

4.2 Operational Semantics

We define the labeled transition relation $t \xrightarrow{\ell}_D t'$, where ℓ is either ϵ or an event name, as the least relation closed under the rules in Fig. 3. We implicitly assume that the program (D, t) is well-typed, and this assumption is maintained throughout reductions by the standard type preservation property. In the rules for if-expressions, $[\![t'_i]\!]$ represents the integer value denoted by t'_i; note that the well-typedness of (D, t) guarantees that t'_i must be arithmetic expressions consisting of integers and integer operations; thus, $[\![t'_i]\!]$ is well defined. We often omit the subscript D when it is clear from the context. We write $t \xrightarrow{\ell_1 \cdots \ell_k}_D^* t'$ if $t \xrightarrow{\ell_1}_D \cdots \xrightarrow{\ell_k}_D t'$. Here, ϵ is treated as an empty sequence; thus, for example, we write $t \xrightarrow{ab}_D^* t'$ if $t \xrightarrow{a}_D \xrightarrow{\epsilon}_D \xrightarrow{b}_D \xrightarrow{\epsilon}_D t'$.

$$
\frac{}{\text{event } a; t \xrightarrow{a}_D t} \qquad \frac{f\widetilde{x} = u \in D \quad |\widetilde{x}| = |\widetilde{t}|}{f\,\widetilde{t} \xrightarrow{\epsilon}_D [\widetilde{t}/\widetilde{x}]u} \qquad \frac{([\![t'_1]\!], \ldots, [\![t'_k]\!]) \in [\![p]\!]}{\textbf{if } p(t'_1, \ldots, t'_k) \textbf{ then } t_1 \textbf{ else } t_2 \xrightarrow{\epsilon}_D t_1}
$$

$$
\frac{i \in \{1, 2\}}{t_1 \Box t_2 \xrightarrow{\epsilon}_D t_i} \qquad \frac{([\![t'_1]\!], \ldots, [\![t'_k]\!]) \notin [\![p]\!]}{\textbf{if } p(t'_1, \ldots, t'_k) \textbf{ then } t_1 \textbf{ else } t_2 \xrightarrow{\epsilon}_D t_2}
$$

Fig. 3. Labeled transition semantics

For a program $P = (D, t_0)$, we define the set $\textbf{Traces}(P)(\subseteq \textbf{Ev}^* \cup \textbf{Ev}^\omega)$ of *traces* by:

$$
\textbf{Traces}(D, t_0) = \{\ell_0 \cdots \ell_{n-1} \in (\{\epsilon\} \cup \textbf{Ev})^* \mid \forall i \in \{0, \ldots, n-1\}.t_i \xrightarrow{\ell_i}_D t_{i+1}\}
$$
$$
\cup \{\ell_0 \ell_1 \cdots \in (\{\epsilon\} \cup \textbf{Ev})^\omega \mid \forall i \in \omega.t_i \xrightarrow{\ell_i}_D t_{i+1}\}.
$$

Note that since the label ϵ is regarded as an empty sequence, $\ell_0 \ell_1 \ell_2 = aa$ if $\ell_0 = \ell_2 = a$ and $\ell_1 = \epsilon$, and an element of $(\{\epsilon\} \cup \textbf{Ev})^\omega$ is regarded as that of $\textbf{Ev}^* \cup \textbf{Ev}^\omega$. We write $\textbf{FinTraces}(P)$ and $\textbf{InfTraces}(P)$ for $\textbf{Traces}(P) \cap \textbf{Ev}^*$ and $\textbf{Traces}(P) \cap \textbf{Ev}^\omega$ respectively. The set of *full traces* $\textbf{FullTraces}(D, t_0)(\subseteq \textbf{Ev}^* \cup \textbf{Ev}^\omega)$ is defined as:

$$
\{\ell_0 \cdots \ell_{n-1} \in (\{\epsilon\} \cup \textbf{Ev})^* \mid t_n = (\,) \wedge \forall i \in \{0, \ldots, n-1\}.t_i \xrightarrow{\ell_i}_D t_{i+1}\}
$$
$$
\cup \{\ell_0 \ell_1 \cdots \in (\{\epsilon\} \cup \textbf{Ev})^\omega \mid \forall i \in \omega.t_i \xrightarrow{\ell_i}_D t_{i+1}\}.
$$

Example 4. The last example in Sect. 1 is modeled as $P_{file} = (D, f\,())$, where $D = \{f\,x = (\textbf{event close};\,())\square(\textbf{event read}; \textbf{event read}; f\,x)\}$. We have:

$\textbf{Traces}(P) = \{\textbf{read}^n \mid n \geq 0\} \cup \{\textbf{read}^{2n}\textbf{close} \mid n \geq 0\} \cup \{\textbf{read}^\omega\}$
$\textbf{FinTraces}(P) = \{\textbf{read}^n \mid n \geq 0\} \cup \{\textbf{read}^{2n}\textbf{close} \mid n \geq 0\}$
$\textbf{InfTraces}(P) = \{\textbf{read}^\omega\}\ \ \textbf{FullTraces}(P) = \{\textbf{read}^{2n}\textbf{close} \mid n \geq 0\} \cup \{\textbf{read}^\omega\}$.

5   May/Must-Reachability Verification

Here we consider the following problems:

- May-reachability: "Given a program P and an event a, may P raise a?"
- Must-reachability: "Given a program P and an event a, must P raise a?"

Since we are interested in a particular event a, we restrict here the event set **Ev** to a singleton set of the form $\{a\}$. Then, the may-reachability is formalized as $a \overset{?}{\in} \textbf{Traces}(P)$, whereas the must-reachability is formalized as "does every trace in $\textbf{FullTraces}(P)$ contain a?" We encode both problems into the validity of HFL$_\textbf{Z}$ formulas (without any modal operators $\langle a\rangle$ or $[a]$), or the HFL$_\textbf{Z}$ model checking of those formulas against a trivial model (which consists of a single state without any transitions). Since our reductions are sound and complete, the characterizations of their negations –non-reachability and may-non-reachability– can also be obtained immediately. Although these are the simplest classes of properties among those discussed in Sects. 5, 6 and 7, they are already large enough to accommodate many program properties discussed in the literature, including lack of assertion failures/uncaught exceptions [22] (which can be characterized as non-reachability; recall the encoding of assertions in Sect. 4), termination [27,29] (characterized as must-reachability), and non-termination [26] (characterized as may-non-reachability).

5.1   May-Reachability

As in the examples in Sect. 3, we translate a program to a formula that says "the program may raise an event a" in a compositional manner. For example, **event** $a; t$ can be translated to **true** (since the event will surely be raised immediately), and $t_1\square t_2$ can be translated to $t_1^\dagger \vee t_2^\dagger$ where $t_i^\dagger$ is the result of the translation of t_i (since only one of t_1 and t_2 needs to raise an event).

Definition 3. *Let $P = (D, t)$ be a program. $\Phi_{P,may}$ is the HES $(D^{\dagger may}, t^{\dagger may})$, where $D^{\dagger may}$ and $t^{\dagger may}$ are defined by:*

$\{f_1\,\widetilde{x}_1 = t_1, \ldots, f_n\,\widetilde{x}_n = t_n\}^{\dagger may} = (f_1\,\widetilde{x}_1 =_\mu t_1{}^{\dagger may}; \cdots; f_n\,\widetilde{x}_n =_\mu t_n{}^{\dagger may})$
$()^{\dagger may} = \textbf{false} \qquad x^{\dagger may} = x \qquad n^{\dagger may} = n \qquad (t_1\ \textbf{op}\ t_2)^{\dagger may} = t_1{}^{\dagger may}\ \textbf{op}\ t_2{}^{\dagger may}$
$(\textbf{if}\ p(t'_1, \ldots, t'_k)\ \textbf{then}\ t_1\ \textbf{else}\ t_2)^{\dagger may} =$
$\qquad (p(t'_1{}^{\dagger may}, \ldots, t'_k{}^{\dagger may}) \wedge t_1{}^{\dagger may}) \vee (\neg p(t'_1{}^{\dagger may}, \ldots, t'_k{}^{\dagger may}) \wedge t_2{}^{\dagger may})$
$(\textbf{event}\ a; t)^{\dagger may} = \textbf{true} \qquad (t_1 t_2)^{\dagger may} = t_1{}^{\dagger may} t_2{}^{\dagger may} \qquad (t_1\square t_2)^{\dagger may} = t_1{}^{\dagger may} \vee t_2{}^{\dagger may}$.

Note that, in the definition of $D^{\dagger may}$, the order of function definitions in D does not matter (i.e., the resulting HES is unique up to the semantic equality), since all the fixpoint variables are bound by μ.

Example 5. Consider the program:

$$P_{loop} = (\{loop\ x = loop\ x\}, loop(\mathbf{event}\ a; (\ ))).$$

It is translated to the HES $\Phi_{loop} = (loop\ x =_\mu loop\ x, loop(\mathbf{true}))$. Since $loop \equiv \mu loop.\lambda x.loop\ x$ is equivalent to $\lambda x.\mathbf{false}$, Φ_{loop} is equivalent to $\mathbf{false}$. In fact, P_{loop} never raises an event a (recall that our language is call-by-name).

Example 6. Consider the program $P_{sum} = (D_{sum}, \mathbf{main})$ where D_{sum} is:

$$\mathbf{main} = sum\ n\ (\lambda r.\mathbf{assert}(r \geq n))$$
$$sum\ x\ k = \mathbf{if}\ x = 0\ \mathbf{then}\ k\,0\ \mathbf{else}\ sum\ (x - 1)\ (\lambda r.k(x + r))$$

Here, n is some integer constant, and $\mathbf{assert}(b)$ is the macro introduced in Sect. 4. We have used λ-abstractions for the sake of readability. The function sum is a CPS version of a function that computes the summation of integers from 1 to x. The main function computes the sum $r = 1 + \cdots + n$, and asserts $r \geq n$. It is translated to the HES $\Phi_{P_2,may} = (\mathcal{E}_{sum}, \mathbf{main})$ where $\mathcal{E}_{sum}$ is:

$$\mathbf{main} =_\mu sum\ n\ (\lambda r.(r \geq n \wedge \mathbf{false}) \vee (r < n \wedge \mathbf{true}));$$
$$sum\ x\ k =_\mu (x = 0 \wedge k\,0) \vee (x \neq 0 \wedge sum\ (x - 1)\ (\lambda r.k(x + r))).$$

Here, n is treated as a constant. Since the shape of the formula does not depend on the value of n, the property "an assertion failure may occur for some n" can be expressed by $\exists n.\Phi_{P_2,may}$. $\qquad\square$

The following theorem states that $\Phi_{P,may}$ is a complete characterization of the may-reachability of P.

Theorem 1. *Let P be a program. Then, $a \in \mathbf{Traces}(P)$ if and only if $\mathsf{L}_0 \models \Phi_{P,may}$ for $\mathsf{L}_0 = (\{\mathsf{s}_\star\}, \emptyset, \emptyset, \mathsf{s}_\star)$.*

A proof of the theorem above is found in [23]. We only provide an outline. We first show the theorem for recursion-free programs and then lift it to arbitrary programs by using the continuity of functions represented in the fixpoint-free fragment of $\mathrm{HFL_Z}$ formulas. To show the theorem for recursion-free programs, we define the reduction relation $t \longrightarrow_D t'$ by:

$$\frac{f\widetilde{x} = u \in D \qquad |\widetilde{x}| = |\widetilde{t}|}{E[f\ \widetilde{t}] \longrightarrow_D E[[\widetilde{t}/\widetilde{x}]u]} \qquad \frac{([\![t'_1]\!], \ldots, [\![t'_k]\!]) \in [\![p]\!]}{E[\mathbf{if}\ p(t'_1, \ldots, t'_k)\ \mathbf{then}\ t_1\ \mathbf{else}\ t_2] \longrightarrow_D E[t_1]}$$

$$\frac{([\![t'_1]\!], \ldots, [\![t'_k]\!]) \notin [\![p]\!]}{E[\mathbf{if}\ p(t'_1, \ldots, t'_k)\ \mathbf{then}\ t_1\ \mathbf{else}\ t_2] \longrightarrow_D E[t_2]}$$

Here, E ranges over the set of evaluation contexts given by $E ::= [\ ]\ |\ E\square t\ |\ t\square E\ |\ \mathbf{event}\ a; E$. The reduction relation differs from the labeled transition relation given in Sect. 4, in that $\square$ and **event** $a; \cdots$ are not eliminated. By the definition of the translation, the theorem holds for programs in normal form (with respect to the reduction relation), and the semantics of translated HFL formulas is preserved by the reduction relation; thus the theorem holds for recursion-free programs, as they are strongly normalizing.

5.2   Must-Reachability

The characterization of must-reachability can be obtained by an easy modification of the characterization of may-reachability: we just need to replace branches with logical conjunction.

Definition 4. *Let* $P = (D, t)$ *be a program.* $\Phi_{P,must}$ *is the HES* $(D^{\dagger must}, t^{\dagger must})$, *where* $D^{\dagger must}$ *and* $t^{\dagger must}$ *are defined by:*

$$\{f_1 \widetilde{x}_1 = t_1, \ldots, f_n \widetilde{x}_n = t_n\}^{\dagger must} = \left(f_1 \widetilde{x}_1 =_\mu t_1{}^{\dagger must}; \cdots ; f_n \widetilde{x}_n =_\mu t_n{}^{\dagger must}\right)$$
$$()^{\dagger must} = \textbf{false} \qquad x^{\dagger must} = x \qquad n^{\dagger must} = n \qquad (t_1 \textbf{ op } t_2)^{\dagger must} = t_1{}^{\dagger must} \textbf{ op } t_2{}^{\dagger must}$$
$$(\textbf{if } p(t'_1, \ldots, t'_k) \textbf{ then } t_1 \textbf{ else } t_2)^{\dagger must} =$$
$$\qquad (p(t'_1{}^{\dagger must}, \ldots, t'_k{}^{\dagger must}) \Rightarrow t_1{}^{\dagger must}) \wedge (\neg p(t'_1{}^{\dagger must}, \ldots, t'_k{}^{\dagger must}) \Rightarrow t_2{}^{\dagger must})$$
$$(\textbf{event } a; t)^{\dagger must} = \textbf{true} \quad (t_1 t_2)^{\dagger must} = t_1{}^{\dagger must} t_2{}^{\dagger must} \quad (t_1 \square t_2)^{\dagger must} = t_1{}^{\dagger must} \wedge t_2{}^{\dagger must}.$$

Here, $p(\varphi_1, \ldots, \varphi_k) \Rightarrow \varphi$ *is a shorthand for* $\neg p(\varphi_1, \ldots, \varphi_k) \vee \varphi$.

Example 7. Consider $P_{\texttt{loop}} = (D, \texttt{loop } m\, n)$ where D is:

$$\texttt{loop } x\, y = \textbf{if } x \leq 0 \vee y \leq 0 \textbf{ then } (\textbf{event end}; ())$$
$$\textbf{else } (\texttt{loop } (x-1)\, (y*y)) \square (\texttt{loop } x\, (y-1))$$

Here, the event **end** is used to signal the termination of the program. The function `loop` non-deterministically updates the values of x and y until either x or y becomes non-positive. The must-termination of the program is characterized by $\Phi_{P_{\texttt{loop}},must} = (\mathcal{E}, \texttt{loop } m\, n)$ where $\mathcal{E}$ is:

$$\texttt{loop } x\, y =_\mu (x \leq 0 \vee y \leq 0 \Rightarrow \textbf{true})$$
$$\wedge (\neg (x \leq 0 \vee y \leq 0) \Rightarrow (\texttt{loop } (x-1)\, (y*y)) \wedge (\texttt{loop } x\, (y-1))).$$

We write $\textbf{Must}_a(P)$ if every $\pi \in \textbf{FullTraces}(P)$ contains a. The following theorem, which can be proved in a manner similar to Theorem 1, guarantees that $\Phi_{P,must}$ is indeed a sound and complete characterization of the must-reachability.

Theorem 2. *Let* P *be a program. Then,* $\textbf{Must}_a(P)$ *if and only if* $\mathsf{L}_0 \models \Phi_{P,must}$ *for* $\mathsf{L}_0 = (\{\mathsf{s}_\star\}, \emptyset, \emptyset, \mathsf{s}_\star)$.

6   Trace Properties

Here we consider the verification problem: "Given a (non-ω) regular language L and a program P, does *every* finite event sequence of P belong to L? (i.e. $\textbf{FinTraces}(P) \overset{?}{\subseteq} L$)" and reduce it to an HFL$_{\textbf{Z}}$ model checking problem. The verification of file-accessing programs considered in Sect. 3 may be considered an instance of the problem.

Here we assume that the language L is closed under the prefix operation; this does not lose generality because $\textbf{FinTraces}(P)$ is also closed under the prefix operation. We write $A_L = (Q, \Sigma, \delta, q_0, F)$ for the minimal, deterministic automaton with no dead states (hence the transition function δ may be partial). Since L is prefix-closed and the automaton is minimal, $w \in L$ if and only if $\hat{\delta}(q_0, w)$ is defined (where $\hat{\delta}$ is defined by: $\hat{\delta}(q, \epsilon) = q$ and $\hat{\delta}(q, aw) = \hat{\delta}(\delta(q, a), w)$). We use the corresponding LTS $\textsf{L}_L = (Q, \Sigma, \{(q, a, q') \mid \delta(q, a) = q'\}, q_0)$ as the model of the reduced HFL$_{\textbf{Z}}$ model checking problem.

Given the LTS $\textsf{L}_L$ above, whether an event sequence $a_1 \cdots a_k$ belongs to L can be expressed as $\textsf{L}_L \models \langle a_1 \rangle \cdots \langle a_k \rangle \textbf{true}$. Whether all the event sequences in $\{a_{j,1} \cdots a_{j,k_j} \mid j \in \{1, \ldots, n\}\}$ belong to L can be expressed as $\textsf{L}_L \overset{?}{\models} \bigwedge_{j \in \{1, \ldots, n\}} \langle a_{j,1} \rangle \cdots \langle a_{j,k_j} \rangle \textbf{true}$. We can lift these translations for event sequences to the translation from a program (which can be considered a description of a set of event sequences) to an HFL$_{\textbf{Z}}$ formula, as follows.

Definition 5. *Let* $P = (D, t)$ *be a program.* $\Phi_{P,path}$ *is the HES* $(D^{\dagger path}, t^{\dagger path})$, *where* $D^{\dagger path}$ *and* $t^{\dagger path}$ *are defined by:*

$$\{f_1 \, \widetilde{x}_1 = t_1, \ldots, f_n \, \widetilde{x}_n = t_n\}^{\dagger path} = \left(f_1 \, \widetilde{x}_1 =_\nu t_1{}^{\dagger path}; \cdots ; f_n \, \widetilde{x}_n =_\nu t_n{}^{\dagger path}\right)$$
$$()^{\dagger path} = \textbf{true} \qquad x^{\dagger path} = x \qquad n^{\dagger path} = n \qquad (t_1 \, \text{op} \, t_2)^{\dagger path} = t_1{}^{\dagger path} \, \text{op} \, t_2{}^{\dagger path}$$
$$(\textbf{if } p(t_1', \ldots, t_k') \textbf{ then } t_1 \textbf{ else } t_2)^{\dagger path} =$$
$$\left(p(t_1'{}^{\dagger path}, \ldots, t_k'{}^{\dagger path}) \Rightarrow t_1{}^{\dagger path}\right) \wedge \left(\neg p(t_1'{}^{\dagger path}, \ldots, t_k'{}^{\dagger path}) \Rightarrow t_2{}^{\dagger path}\right)$$
$$(\textbf{event } a; t)^{\dagger path} = \langle a \rangle t^{\dagger path} \qquad (t_1 t_2)^{\dagger path} = t_1{}^{\dagger path} t_2{}^{\dagger path} \qquad (t_1 \Box t_2)^{\dagger path} = t_1{}^{\dagger path} \wedge t_2{}^{\dagger path}.$$

Example 8. The last program discussed in Sect. 3 is modeled as $P_2 = (D_2, f \, m \, g)$, where m is an integer constant and D_2 consists of:

$$f \, y \, k = \textbf{if } y = 0 \textbf{ then } (\textbf{event close}; k\,(\,)) \textbf{ else } (\textbf{event read}; f \, (y - 1) \, k)$$
$$g \, r = \textbf{event end}; (\,)$$

Here, we have modeled accesses to the file, and termination as events. Then, $\Phi_{P_2,path} = (\mathcal{E}_{P_2,path}, f \, m \, g)$ where $\mathcal{E}_{P_2,path}$ is:[6]

$$f \, n \, k =_\nu (n = 0 \Rightarrow \langle \text{close} \rangle (k \, \textbf{true})) \wedge (n \neq 0 \Rightarrow \langle \text{read} \rangle (f \, (n - 1) \, k))$$
$$g \, r =_\nu \langle \text{end} \rangle \textbf{true}.$$

Let L be the prefix-closure of $\textbf{read}^* \cdot \textbf{close} \cdot \textbf{end}$. Then $\textsf{L}_L$ is $\textsf{L}'_{file}$ in Sect. 3, and $\textbf{FinTraces}(P_2) \subseteq L$ can be verified by checking $\textsf{L}_L \models \Phi_{P_2,path}$.   □

---

[6] Unlike in Sect. 3, the variables are bound by ν since we are not concerned with the termination property here.

Theorem 3. *Let P be a program and L be a regular, prefix-closed language. Then,* $\mathbf{FinTraces}(P) \subseteq L$ *if and only if* $\mathsf{L}_L \models \Phi_{P,path}$.

As in Sect. 5, we first prove the theorem for programs in normal form, and then lift it to recursion-free programs by using the preservation of the semantics of $\mathrm{HFL_Z}$ formulas by reductions, and further to arbitrary programs by using the (co-)continuity of the functions represented by fixpoint-free $\mathrm{HFL_Z}$ formulas. See [23] for a concrete proof.

7   Linear-Time Temporal Properties

This section considers the following problem: "Given a program P and an ω-regular word language L, does $\mathbf{InfTraces}(P) \cap L = \emptyset$ hold?". From the viewpoint of program verification, L represents the set of "bad" behaviors. This can be considered an extension of the problems considered in the previous sections.

The reduction to HFL model checking is more involved than those in the previous sections. To see the difficulty, consider the program P_0:

$$(\{f = \mathbf{if}\ c\ \mathbf{then}\ (\mathbf{event}\ \mathsf{a}; f)\ \mathbf{else}\ (\mathbf{event}\ \mathsf{b}; f)\},\quad f),$$

where c is some boolean expression. Let L be the complement of $(\mathsf{a^*b})^\omega$, i.e., the set of infinite sequences that contain only finitely many b's. Following Sect. 6 (and noting that $\mathbf{InfTraces}(P) \cap L = \emptyset$ is equivalent to $\mathbf{InfTraces}(P) \subseteq (\mathsf{a^*b})^\omega$ in this case), one may be tempted to prepare an LTS like the one in Fig. 4 (which corresponds to the transition function of a (parity) word automaton accepting $(\mathsf{a^*b})^\omega$), and translate the program to an HES Φ_{P_0} of the form:

$$(f =_\alpha (c \Rightarrow \langle \mathsf{a} \rangle f) \wedge (\neg c \Rightarrow \langle \mathsf{b} \rangle f),\quad f),$$

where α is μ or ν. However, such a translation would not work. If $c = \mathbf{true}$, then $\mathbf{InfTraces}(P_0) = \mathsf{a}^\omega$, hence $\mathbf{InfTraces}(P_0) \cap L \neq \emptyset$; thus, α should be μ for Φ_{P_0} to be unsatisfied. If $c = \mathbf{false}$, however, $\mathbf{InfTraces}(P_0) = \mathsf{b}^\omega$, hence $\mathbf{InfTraces}(P_0) \cap L = \emptyset$; thus, α must be ν for Φ_{P_0} to be satisfied.

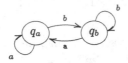

Fig. 4. LTS for $(a^*b)^\omega$

The example above suggests that we actually need to distinguish between the two occurrences of f in the body of f's definition. Note that in the then- and else-clauses respectively, f is called after different events a and b. This difference is important, since we are interested in whether b occurs infinitely often. We thus duplicate f, and replace the program with the following program P_{dup}:

$$(\{f_b = \textbf{if } c \textbf{ then } (\textbf{event a; } f_a) \textbf{ else } (\textbf{event b; } f_b),$$
$$f_a = \textbf{if } c \textbf{ then } (\textbf{event a; } f_a) \textbf{ else } (\textbf{event b; } f_b)\}, f_b).$$

For checking $\textbf{InfTraces}(P_0) \cap L = \emptyset$, it is now sufficient to check that f_b is recursively called infinitely often. We can thus obtain the following HES:

$$((f_b =_\nu (c \Rightarrow \langle a \rangle f_a) \wedge (\neg c \Rightarrow \langle b \rangle f_b); \quad f_a =_\mu (c \Rightarrow \langle a \rangle f_a) \wedge (\neg c \Rightarrow \langle b \rangle f_b)), f_b).$$

Note that f_b and f_a are bound by ν and μ respectively, reflecting the fact that b should occur infinitely often, but a need not. If $c = \textbf{true}$, the formula is equivalent to $\nu f_b.\langle a \rangle \mu f_a.\langle a \rangle f_a$, which is false. If $c = \textbf{false}$, then the formula is equivalent to $\nu f_b.\langle b \rangle f_b$, which is satisfied by by the LTS in Fig. 4.

The general translation is more involved due to the presence of higher-order functions, but, as in the example above, the overall translation consists of two steps. We first replicate functions according to what events may occur between two recursive calls, and reduce the problem $\textbf{InfTraces}(P) \cap L \stackrel{?}{=} \emptyset$ to a problem of analyzing which functions are recursively called infinitely often, which we call a *call-sequence analysis*. We can then reduce the call-sequence analysis to HFL model checking in a rather straightforward manner (though the proof of the correctness is non-trivial). The resulting HFL formula actually does not contain modal operators.[7] So, as in Sect. 5, the resulting problem is the validity checking of HFL formulas without modal operators.

In the rest of this section, we first introduce the call-sequence analysis problem and its reduction to HFL model checking in Sect. 7.1. We then show how to reduce the temporal verification problem $\textbf{InfTraces}(P) \cap L \stackrel{?}{=} \emptyset$ to an instance of the call-sequence analysis problem in Sect. 7.2.

7.1   Call-Sequence Analysis

We define the call-sequence analysis and reduce it to an HFL model-checking problem. As mentioned above, in the call-sequence analysis, we are interested in analyzing which functions are *recursively called* infinitely often. Here, we say that g is *recursively called from* f, if $f \, \widetilde{s} \xrightarrow{\epsilon}_D [\widetilde{s}/\widetilde{x}] t_f \xrightarrow{\widetilde{\ell}}^*_D g \, \widetilde{t}$, where $f \, \widetilde{x} = t_f \in D$ and g "originates from" t_f (a more formal definition will be given in Definition 6 below). For example, consider the following program P_{app}, which is a twisted version of P_{dup} above.

$(\{\textbf{app } h \, x = h \, x,$
$\quad f_b \, x = \textbf{if } x > 0 \textbf{ then } (\textbf{event a; app } f_a \, (x - 1)) \textbf{ else } (\textbf{event b; app } f_b \, 5),$
$\quad f_a \, x = \textbf{if } x > 0 \textbf{ then } (\textbf{event a; app } f_a \, (x - 1)) \textbf{ else } (\textbf{event b; app } f_b \, 5)\}, f_b \, 5).$

---

[7] In the example above, we can actually remove $\langle a \rangle$ and $\langle b \rangle$, as information about events has been taken into account when f was duplicated.

Then f_a is "recursively called" from f_b in $f_b\, 5 \xrightarrow{a}{}^*_D \mathsf{app}\, f_a\, 4 \xrightarrow{\epsilon}{}^*_D f_a\, 4$ (and so is app). We are interested in infinite chains of recursive calls $f_0 f_1 f_2 \cdots$, and which functions may occur infinitely often in each chain. For instance, the program above has the unique infinite chain $(f_b f_a^5)^\omega$, in which both f_a and f_b occur infinitely often. (Besides the infinite chain, the program has finite chains like $f_b\, \mathsf{app}$; note that the chain cannot be extended further, as the body of app does not have any occurrence of recursive functions: app, f_a and f_b.)

We define the notion of "recursive calls" and call-sequences formally below.

Definition 6 (Recursive call relation, call sequences). *Let* $P = (D, f_1\, \tilde{s})$ *be a program, with* $D = \{f_i\, \tilde{x}_i = u_i\}_{1 \le i \le n}$. *We define* $D^\sharp := D \cup \{f_i^\sharp\, \tilde{x} = u_i\}_{1 \le i \le n}$ *where* $f_1^\sharp, \ldots, f_n^\sharp$ *are fresh symbols. (Thus,* $D^\sharp$ *has two copies of each function symbol, one of which is marked by* $\sharp$.) *For the terms* $\tilde{t}_i$ *and* $\tilde{t}_j$ *that do not contain marked symbols, we write* $f_i\, \tilde{t}_i \leadsto_D f_j\, \tilde{t}_j$ *if (i)* $[\tilde{t}_i/\tilde{x}_i][f_1^\sharp/f_1, \ldots, f_n^\sharp/f_n] u_i \xrightarrow{\ell}{}^*_{D^\sharp} f_j^\sharp\, \tilde{t}'_j$ *and (ii)* $\tilde{t}_j$ *is obtained by erasing all the marks in* $\tilde{t}'_j$. *We write* **Callseq**(P) *for the set of (possibly infinite) sequences of function symbols:*

$$\{f_1\, g_1\, g_2 \cdots \mid f_1\, \tilde{s} \leadsto_D g_1\, \tilde{t}_1 \leadsto_D g_2\, \tilde{t}_2 \leadsto_D \cdots\}.$$

We write **InfCallseq**(P) *for the subset of* **Callseq**(P) *consisting of infinite sequences, i.e.,* **Callseq**$(P) \cap \{f_1, \ldots, f_n\}^\omega$.

For example, for P_{app} above, **Callseq**(P) is the prefix closure of $\{(f_b f_a^5)^\omega\} \cup \{s \cdot \mathsf{app} \mid s$ is a non-empty finite prefix of $(f_b f_a^5)^\omega\}$, and **InfCallseq**(P) is the singleton set $\{(f_b f_a^5)^\omega\}$.

Definition 7 (Call-sequence analysis). *A priority assignment for a program* P *is a function* $\Omega : \mathsf{funs}(P) \to \mathbb{N}$ *from the set of function symbols of* P *to the set* $\mathbb{N}$ *of natural numbers. We write* $\models_{csa} (P, \Omega)$ *if every infinite call-sequence* $g_0 g_1 g_2 \cdots \in$ **InfCallseq**(P) *satisfies the parity condition w.r.t.* Ω, *i.e., the largest number occurring infinitely often in* $\Omega(g_0)\Omega(g_1)\Omega(g_2)\ldots$ *is even. Call-sequence analysis is the problem of, given a program* P *with a priority assignment* Ω, *deciding whether* $\models_{csa} (P, \Omega)$ *holds.*

For example, for P_{app} and the priority assignment $\Omega_{app} = \{\mathsf{app} \mapsto 3, f_a \mapsto 1, f_b \mapsto 2\}$, $\models_{csa} (P_{app}, \Omega_{app})$ holds.

The call-sequence analysis can naturally be reduced to HFL model checking against the trivial LTS $\mathsf{L}_0 = (\{\mathsf{s}_*\}, \emptyset, \emptyset, \mathsf{s}_*)$ (or validity checking).

Definition 8. *Let* $P = (D, t)$ *be a program and* Ω *be a priority assignment for* P. *The HES* $\Phi_{(P,\Omega),csa}$ *is* $(D^{\dagger csa}, t^{\dagger csa})$, *where* $D^{\dagger csa}$ *and* $t^{\dagger csa}$ *are defined by:*

$$\{f_1\, \tilde{x}_1 = t_1, \ldots, f_n\, \tilde{x}_n = t_n\}^{\dagger csa} = (f_1\, \tilde{x}_1 =_{\alpha_1} t_1^{\dagger csa}; \cdots; f_n\, \tilde{x}_n =_{\alpha_n} t_n^{\dagger csa})$$

$$()^{\dagger csa} = \mathbf{true} \qquad x^{\dagger csa} = x \qquad n^{\dagger csa} = n \qquad (t_1\ \mathsf{op}\ t_2)^{\dagger csa} = t_1^{\dagger csa}\ \mathsf{op}\ t_2^{\dagger csa}$$

$(\mathbf{if}\ p(t'_1, \ldots, t'_k)\ \mathbf{then}\ t_1\ \mathbf{else}\ t_2)^{\dagger csa} =$

$\qquad (p(t_1'^{\dagger csa}, \ldots, t_k'^{\dagger csa}) \Rightarrow t_1^{\dagger csa}) \wedge (\neg p(t_1'^{\dagger csa}, \ldots, t_k'^{\dagger csa}) \Rightarrow t_2^{\dagger csa})$

$(\mathbf{event}\ a; t)^{\dagger csa} = t^{\dagger csa} \qquad (t_1\, t_2)^{\dagger csa} = t_1^{\dagger csa}\, t_2^{\dagger csa} \qquad (t_1 \Box t_2)^{\dagger csa} = t_1^{\dagger csa} \wedge t_2^{\dagger csa}.$

Here, we assume that $\Omega(f_i) \geq \Omega(f_{i+1})$ *for each* $i \in \{1, \ldots, n-1\}$, *and* $\alpha_i = \nu$ *if* $\Omega(f_i)$ *is even and* μ *otherwise.*

The following theorem states the soundness and completeness of the reduction. See [23] for a proof.

Theorem 4. *Let* P *be a program and* Ω *be a priority assignment for* P. *Then* $\models_{csa} (P, \Omega)$ *if and only if* $\mathsf{L}_0 \models \Phi_{(P,\Omega),csa}$.

Example 9. For P_{app} and Ω_{app} above, $(P_{app}, \Omega_{app})^{\dagger_{csa}} = (\mathcal{E}, f_b\,5)$, where: $\mathcal{E}$ is:

$$\mathsf{app}\,h\,x =_\mu h\,x; \quad f_b\,x =_\nu (x > 0 \Rightarrow \mathsf{app}\,f_a\,(x-1)) \wedge (x \leq 0 \Rightarrow \mathsf{app}\,f_b\,5);$$
$$f_a\,x =_\mu (x > 0 \Rightarrow \mathsf{app}\,f_a\,(x-1)) \wedge (x \leq 0 \Rightarrow \mathsf{app}\,f_b\,5).$$

Note that $\mathsf{L}_0 \models (P_{app}, \Omega_{app})^{\dagger_{csa}}$ holds.

7.2 From Temporal Verification to Call-Sequence Analysis

This subsection shows a reduction from the temporal verification problem **InfTraces**$(P) \cap L \overset{?}{=} \emptyset$ to a call-sequence analysis problem $\models_{csa}^{?} (P', \Omega)$.

For the sake of simplicity, we assume without loss of generality that every program $P = (D, t)$ in this section is non-terminating and every infinite reduction sequence produces infinite events, so that **FullTraces**$(P) = $ **InfTraces**(P) holds. We also assume that the ω-regular language L for the temporal verification problem is specified by using a non-deterministic, parity word automaton [10]. We recall the definition of non-deterministic, parity word automata below.

Definition 9 (Parity automaton). *A non-deterministic parity word automaton is a quintuple* $\mathcal{A} = (Q, \Sigma, \delta, q_I, \Omega)$ *where (i)* Q *is a finite set of states; (ii)* Σ *is a finite alphabet; (iii)* δ, *called a transition function, is a total map from* $Q \times \Sigma$ *to* 2^Q; *(iv)* $q_I \in Q$ *is the initial state; and (v)* $\Omega \in Q \to \mathbb{N}$ *is the priority function. A run of* $\mathcal{A}$ *on an* ω*-word* $a_0 a_1 \cdots \in \Sigma^\omega$ *is an infinite sequence of states* $\rho = \rho(0)\rho(1)\cdots \in Q^\omega$ *such that (i)* $\rho(0) = q_I$, *and (ii)* $\rho(i+1) \in \delta(\rho(i), a_i)$ *for each* $i \in \omega$. *An* ω*-word* $w \in \Sigma^\omega$ *is accepted by* $\mathcal{A}$ *if, there exists a run* ρ *of* $\mathcal{A}$ *on* w *such that* $\max\{\Omega(q) \mid q \in \mathbf{Inf}(\rho)\}$ *is even, where* $\mathbf{Inf}(\rho)$ *is the set of states that occur infinitely often in* ρ. *We write* $\mathcal{L}(\mathcal{A})$ *for the set of* ω*-words accepted by* $\mathcal{A}$.

For technical convenience, we assume below that $\delta(q, a) \neq \emptyset$ for every $q \in Q$ and $a \in \Sigma$; this does not lose generality since if $\delta(q, a) = \emptyset$, we can introduce a new "dead" state q_{dead} (with priority 1) and change $\delta(q, a)$ to $\{q_{dead}\}$. Given a parity automaton $\mathcal{A}$, we refer to each component of $\mathcal{A}$ by $Q_\mathcal{A}, \Sigma_\mathcal{A}, \delta_\mathcal{A}, q_{I,\mathcal{A}}$ and $\Omega_\mathcal{A}$.

Example 10. Consider the automaton $\mathcal{A}_{ab} = (\{q_a, q_b\}, \{\mathsf{a}, \mathsf{b}\}, \delta, q_a, \Omega)$, where δ is as given in Fig. 4, $\Omega(q_a) = 0$, and $\Omega(q_b) = 1$. Then, $\mathcal{L}(\mathcal{A}_{ab}) = \overline{(\mathsf{a^*b})^\omega} = (\mathsf{a^*b})^* \mathsf{a}^\omega$.

The goal of this subsection is, given a program P and a parity word automaton $\mathcal{A}$, to construct another program P' and a priority assignment Ω for P', such that $\mathbf{InfTraces}(P) \cap \mathcal{L}(\mathcal{A}) = \emptyset$ if and only if $\models_{csa} (P', \Omega)$.

Note that a necessary and sufficient condition for $\mathbf{InfTraces}(P) \cap \mathcal{L}(\mathcal{A}) = \emptyset$ is that no trace in $\mathbf{InfTraces}(P)$ has a run whose priority sequence satisfies the parity condition; in other words, for every sequence in $\mathbf{InfTraces}(P)$, and for every run for the sequence, the largest priority that occurs in the associated priority sequence is odd. As explained at the beginning of this section, we reduce this condition to a call sequence analysis problem by appropriately duplicating functions in a given program. For example, recall the program P_0:

$$(\{f = \mathbf{if}\ c\ \mathbf{then}\ (\mathbf{event}\ a; f)\ \mathbf{else}\ (\mathbf{event}\ b; f)\}, f).$$

It is translated to P_0':

$$(\{f_b = \mathbf{if}\ c\ \mathbf{then}\ (\mathbf{event}\ a; f_a)\ \mathbf{else}\ (\mathbf{event}\ b; f_b),$$
$$f_a = \mathbf{if}\ c\ \mathbf{then}\ (\mathbf{event}\ a; f_a)\ \mathbf{else}\ (\mathbf{event}\ b; f_b)\}, f_b),$$

where c is some (closed) boolean expression. Since the largest priorities encountered before calling f_a and f_b (since the last recursive call) respectively are 0 and 1, we assign those priorities plus 1 (to flip odd/even-ness) to f_a and f_b respectively. Then, the problem of $\mathbf{InfTraces}(P_0) \cap \mathcal{L}(\mathcal{A}) = \emptyset$ is reduced to $\models_{csa} (P_0', \{f_a \mapsto 1, f_b \mapsto 2\})$. Note here that the priorities of f_a and f_b represent *summaries* of the priorities (plus one) that occur in the run of the automaton until f_a and f_b are respectively called since the last recursive call; thus, the largest priority of states that occur infinitely often in the run for an infinite trace is equivalent to the largest priority that occurs infinitely often in the sequence of summaries $(\Omega(f_1) - 1)(\Omega(f_2) - 1)(\Omega(f_3) - 1) \cdots$ computed from a corresponding call sequence $f_1 f_2 f_3 \cdots$.

Due to the presence of higher-order functions, the general reduction is more complicated than the example above. First, we need to replicate not only function symbols, but also arguments. For example, consider the following variation P_1 of P_0 above:

$$(\{g\ k = \mathbf{if}\ c\ \mathbf{then}\ (\mathbf{event}\ a; k)\ \mathbf{else}\ (\mathbf{event}\ b; k),\quad f = g\ f\},\quad f).$$

Here, we have just made the calls to f indirect, by preparing the function g. Obviously, the two calls to k in the body of g must be distinguished from each other, since different priorities are encountered before the calls. Thus, we duplicate the argument k, and obtain the following program P_1':

$$(\{g\ k_a\ k_b = \mathbf{if}\ c\ \mathbf{then}\ (\mathbf{event}\ a; k_a)\ \mathbf{else}\ (\mathbf{event}\ b; k_b), f_a = g\ f_a\ f_b, f_b = g\ f_a\ f_b\}, f_a).$$

Then, for the priority assignment $\Omega = \{f_a \mapsto 1, f_b \mapsto 2, g \mapsto 1\}$, $\mathbf{InfTraces}(P_1) \cap \mathcal{L}(\mathcal{A}_{ab}) = \emptyset$ if and only if $\models_{csa} (P_1', \Omega)$. Secondly, we need to take into account not only the priorities of states visited by $\mathcal{A}$, but also the states themselves. For example, if we have a function definition $f\ h = h(\mathbf{event}\ a; f\ h)$, the largest priority encountered before f is recursively called in the body of f depends on the priorities encountered inside h, *and also* the state of $\mathcal{A}$ when h uses the argument **event** a; f (because the state after the a event depends on the previous state in general). We, therefore, use *intersection types* (a la Kobayashi and Ong's intersection types for HORS model checking [21]) to represent summary information on how each function traverses states of the automaton, and replicate each function and its arguments for each type. We thus formalize the translation as an intersection-type-based program transformation; related transformation techniques are found in [8,11,12,20,38].

Definition 10. *Let* $\mathcal{A} = (Q, \Sigma, \delta, q_I, \Omega)$ *be a non-deterministic parity word automaton. Let q and m range over Q and the set $codom(\Omega)$ of priorities respectively. The set* **Types**$_{\mathcal{A}}$ *of intersection types, ranged over by θ, is defined by:*

$$\theta :: = q \mid \rho \to \theta \qquad\qquad \rho :: = \text{int} \mid \bigwedge_{1 \leq i \leq k}(\theta_i, m_i)$$

We assume a certain total order $<$ on **Types**$_{\mathcal{A}} \times \mathbb{N}$, *and require that in* $\bigwedge_{1 \leq i \leq k}(\theta_i, m_i)$, $(\theta_i, m_i) < (\theta_j, m_j)$ *holds for each $i < j$.*

We often write $(\theta_1, m_1) \wedge \cdots \wedge (\theta_k, m_k)$ for $\bigwedge_{1 \leq i \leq k}(\theta_i, m_i)$, and $\top$ when $k = 0$. Intuitively, the type q describes expressions of simple type $\star$, which may be evaluated when the automaton $\mathcal{A}$ is in the state q (here, we have in mind an execution of the *product* of a program and the automaton, where the latter takes events produced by the program and changes its states). The type $(\bigwedge_{1 \leq i \leq k}(\theta_i, m_i)) \to \theta$ describes functions that take an argument, use it according to types $\theta_1, \ldots, \theta_k$, and return a value of type θ. Furthermore, the part m_i describes that the argument may be used as a value of type θ_i only when the largest priority visited since the function is called is m_i. For example, given the automaton in Example 10, the function $\lambda x.(\textbf{event a}; x)$ may have types $(q_a, 0) \to q_a$ and $(q_a, 0) \to q_b$, because the body may be executed from state q_a or q_b (thus, the return type may be any of them), but x is used only when the automaton is in state q_a and the largest priority visited is 1. In contrast, $\lambda x.(\textbf{event b}; x)$ have types $(q_b, 1) \to q_a$ and $(q_b, 1) \to q_b$.

Using the intersection types above, we shall define a type-based transformation relation of the form $\Gamma \vdash_{\mathcal{A}} t : \theta \Rightarrow t'$, where t and t' are the source and target terms of the transformation, and Γ, called an *intersection type environment*, is a finite set of type bindings of the form $x : \text{int}$ or $x : (\theta, m, m')$. We allow multiple type bindings for a variable x except for $x : \text{int}$ (i.e. if $x : \text{int} \in \Gamma$, then this must be the unique type binding for x in Γ). The binding $x : (\theta, m, m')$ means that x should be used as a value of type θ when the largest priority visited is m; m' is auxiliary information used to record the largest priority encountered so far.

The transformation relation $\Gamma \vdash_{\mathcal{A}} t : \theta \Rightarrow t'$ is inductively defined by the rules in Fig. 5. (For technical convenience, we have extended terms with λ-abstractions; they may occur only at top-level function definitions.) In the figure, $[k]$ denotes the set $\{i \in \mathbb{N} \mid 1 \leq i \leq k\}$. The operation $\Gamma \uparrow m$ used in the figure is defined by:

$$\Gamma \uparrow m = \{x : \text{int} \mid x : \text{int} \in \Gamma\} \cup \{x : (\theta, m_1, \textbf{max}(m_2, m)) \mid x : (\theta, m_1, m_2) \in \Gamma\}$$

The operation is applied when the priority m is encountered, in which case the largest priority encountered is updated accordingly. The key rules are IT-VAR, IT-EVENT, IT-APP, and IT-ABS. In IT-VAR, the variable x is replicated for each type; in the target of the translation, $x_{\theta,m}$ and $x_{\theta',m'}$ are treated as different variables if $(\theta, m) \neq (\theta', m')$. The rule IT-EVENT reflects the state change caused by the event a to the type and the type environment. Since the state change may be non-deterministic, we transform t for each of the next states $q_1, \ldots, q_n$, and combine the resulting terms with non-deterministic choice. The rule IT-APP and IT-ABS replicates function arguments for each type. In addition, in IT-APP, the operation $\Gamma \uparrow m_i$ reflects the fact that t_2 is used as a value of type θ_i after the priority m_i is encountered. The other rules just transform terms in a compositional manner. If target terms are ignored, the entire rules are close to those of Kobayashi and Ong's type system for HORS model checking [21].

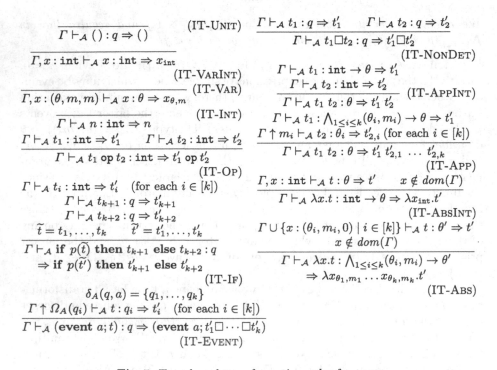

Fig. 5. Type-based transformation rules for terms

We now define the transformation for programs. A *top-level type environment* $\varXi$ is a finite set of type bindings of the form $x : (\theta, m)$. Like intersection type environments, $\varXi$ may have more than one binding for each variable. We write $\varXi \vdash_{\mathcal{A}} t : \theta$ to mean $\{x : (\theta, m, 0) \mid x : (\theta, m) \in \varXi\} \vdash_{\mathcal{A}} t : \theta$. For a set D of function definitions, we write $\varXi \vdash_{\mathcal{A}} D \Rightarrow D'$ if $dom(D') = \{f_{\theta,m} \mid f : (\theta, m) \in \varXi\}$ and $\varXi \vdash_{\mathcal{A}} D(f) : \theta \Rightarrow D'(f_{\theta,m})$ for every $f : (\theta, m) \in \varXi$. For a program $P = (D, t)$, we write $\Xi \vdash_\mathcal{A} P \Rightarrow (P', \Omega')$ if $P' = (D', t')$, $\Xi \vdash_\mathcal{A} D \Rightarrow D'$ and $\Xi \vdash_\mathcal{A} t : q_I \Rightarrow t'$, with $\Omega'(f_{\theta,m}) = m+1$ for each $f_{\theta,m} \in dom(D')$. We just write $\vdash_\mathcal{A} P \Rightarrow (P', \Omega')$ if $\Xi \vdash_\mathcal{A} P \Rightarrow (P', \Omega')$ holds for some Ξ.

Example 11. Consider the automaton $\mathcal{A}_{ab}$ in Example 10, and the program $P_2 = (D_2, f\,5)$ where D_2 consists of the following function definitions:

$$g\,k = (\textbf{event a}; k) \Box (\textbf{event b}; k),$$
$$f\,x = \textbf{if } x > 0 \textbf{ then } g\,(f(x-1)) \textbf{ else } (\textbf{event b}; f\,5).$$

Let Ξ be: $\{g : ((q_a, 0) \wedge (q_b, 1) \to q_a, 0), g : ((q_a, 0) \wedge (q_b, 1) \to q_b, 0), f : (\textbf{int} \to q_a, 0), f : (\textbf{int} \to q_b, 1)\}$. Then, $\Xi \vdash_\mathcal{A} P_1 \Rightarrow ((D_2', f_{\textbf{int} \to q_a, 0}\,5), \Omega)$ where:

$$D_2' = \{g_{(q_a,0) \wedge (q_b,1) \to q_a, 0}\,k_{q_a, 0}\,k_{q_b, 1} = t_g, \quad g_{(q_a,0) \wedge (q_b,1) \to q_b, 0}\,k_{q_a, 0}\,k_{q_b, 1} = t_g,$$
$$f_{\textbf{int} \to q_a, 0}\,x_{\textbf{int}} = t_{f, q_a}, \quad f_{\textbf{int} \to q_b, 1}\,x_{\textbf{int}} = t_{f, q_b}\}$$
$$t_g = (\textbf{event a}; k_{q_a, 0}) \Box (\textbf{event b}; k_{q_b, 1}),$$
$$t_{f, q} = \textbf{if } x_{\textbf{int}} > 0 \textbf{ then}$$
$$g_{(q_a,0) \wedge (q_b,1) \to q, 0}\,(f_{\textbf{int} \to q_a, 0}(x_{\textbf{int}} - 1))\,(f_{\textbf{int} \to q_b, 1}(x_{\textbf{int}} - 1))$$
$$\textbf{else } (\textbf{event b}; f_{\textbf{int} \to q_b, 1}\,5), \qquad (\text{for each } q \in \{q_a, q_b\})$$
$$\Omega = \{g_{(q_a,0) \wedge (q_b,1) \to q_a, 0} \mapsto 1, g_{(q_a,0) \wedge (q_b,1) \to q_b, 0} \mapsto 1, f_{\textbf{int} \to q_a, 0} \mapsto 1, f_{\textbf{int} \to q_b, 1} \mapsto 2\}.$$

Notice that f, g, and the arguments of g have been duplicated. Furthermore, whenever $f_{\theta,m}$ is called, the largest priority that has been encountered since the last recursive call is m. For example, in the then-clause of $f_{\textbf{int} \to q_a, 0}$, $f_{\textbf{int} \to q_b, 1}(x-1)$ may be called through $g_{(q_a,0) \wedge (q_b,1) \to q_a, 0}$. Since $g_{(q_a,0) \wedge (q_b,1) \to q_a, 0}$ uses the second argument only after an event b, the largest priority encountered is 1. This property is important for the correctness of our reduction.

The following theorems below claim that our reduction is sound and complete, and that there is an effective algorithm for the reduction: see [23] for proofs.

Theorem 5. *Let P be a program and $\mathcal{A}$ be a parity automaton. Suppose that $\Xi \vdash_\mathcal{A} P \Rightarrow (P', \Omega)$. Then $\textbf{InfTraces}(P) \cap \mathcal{L}(\mathcal{A}) = \emptyset$ if and only if $\models_{csa} (P', \Omega)$.*

Theorem 6. *For every P and $\mathcal{A}$, one can effectively construct Ξ, P' and Ω such that $\Xi \vdash_\mathcal{A} P \Rightarrow (P', \Omega)$.*

The proof of Theorem 6 above also implies that the reduction from temporal property verification to call-sequence analysis can be performed in polynomial time. Combined with the reduction from call-sequence analysis to HFL model checking, we have thus obtained a polynomial-time reduction from the temporal verification problem $\textbf{InfTraces}(P) \overset{?}{\subseteq} \mathcal{L}(\mathcal{A})$ to HFL model checking.

8 Related Work

As mentioned in Sect. 1, our reduction from program verification problems to HFL model checking problems has been partially inspired by the translation of

Kobayashi et al. [19] from HORS model checking to HFL model checking. As in their translation (and unlike in previous applications of HFL model checking [28, 42]), our translation switches the roles of properties and models (or programs) to be verified. Although a combination of their translation with Kobayashi's reduction from program verification to HORS model checking [17,18] yields an (indirect) translation from *finite-data* programs to pure HFL model checking problems, the combination does not work for infinite-data programs. In contrast, our translation is sound and complete even for infinite-data programs. Among the translations in Sects. 5, 6 and 7, the translation in Sect. 7.2 shares some similarity to their translation, in that functions and their arguments are replicated for each priority. The actual translations are however quite different; ours is type-directed and optimized for a given automaton, whereas their translation is not. This difference comes from the difference of the goals: the goal of [19] was to clarify the relationship between HORS and HFL, hence their translation was designed to be independent of an automaton. The proof of the correctness of our translation in Sect. 7 is much more involved due to the need for dealing with integers. Whilst the proof of [19] could reuse the type-based characterization of HORS model checking [21], we had to generalize arguments in both [19,21] to work on infinite-data programs.

Lange et al. [28] have shown that various process equivalence checking problems (such as bisimulation and trace equivalence) can be reduced to (pure) HFL model checking problems. The idea of their reduction is quite different from ours. They reduce processes to LTSs, whereas we reduce programs to HFL formulas.

Major approaches to automated or semi-automated higher-order program verification have been HORS model checking [17,18,22,27,31,33,43], (refinement) type systems [14,24,34–36,39,41,44], Horn clause solving [2,7], and their combinations. As already discussed in Sect. 1, compared with the HORS model checking approach, our new approach provides more uniform, streamlined methods. Whilst the HORS model checking approach is for fully automated verification, our approach enables various degrees of automation: after verification problems are automatically translated to $\text{HFL}_{\mathbb{Z}}$ formulas, one can prove them (i) interactively using a proof assistant like Coq (see [23]), (ii) semi-automatically, by letting users provide hints for induction/co-induction and discharging the rest of proof obligations by (some extension of) an SMT solver, or (iii) fully automatically by recasting the techniques used in the HORS-based approach; for example, to deal with the ν-only fragment of $\text{HFL}_{\mathbb{Z}}$, we can reuse the technique of predicate abstraction [22]. For a more technical comparison between the HORS-based approach and our HFL-based approach, see [23].

As for type-based approaches [14,24,34–36,39,41,44], most of the refinement type systems are (i) restricted to safety properties, and/or (ii) incomplete. A notable exception is the recent work of Unno et al. [40], which provides a relatively complete type system for the classes of properties discussed in Sect. 5. Our approach deals with a wider class of properties (cf. Sects. 6 and 7). Their "relative completeness" property relies on Godel coding of functions, which cannot be exploited in practice.

The reductions from program verification to Horn clause solving have recently been advocated [2–4] or used [34, 39] (via refinement type inference problems) by a number of researchers. Since Horn clauses can be expressed in a fragment of HFL without modal operators, fixpoint alternations (between ν and μ), and higher-order predicates, our reductions to HFL model checking may be viewed as extensions of those approaches. Higher-order predicates and fixpoints over them allowed us to provide sound and complete characterizations of properties of higher-order programs for a wider class of properties. Bjørner et al. [4] proposed an alternative approach to obtaining a complete characterization of safety properties, which defunctionalizes higher-order programs by using algebraic data types and then reduces the problems to (first-order) Horn clauses. A disadvantage of that approach is that control flow information of higher-order programs is also encoded into algebraic data types; hence even for finite-data higher-order programs, the Horn clauses obtained by the reduction belong to an undecidable fragment. In contrast, our reductions yield pure HFL model checking problems for finite-data programs. Burn et al. [7] have recently advocated the use of *higher-order* (constrained) Horn clauses for verification of safety properties (i.e., which correspond to the negation of may-reachability properties discussed in Sect. 5.1 of the present paper) of higher-order programs. They interpret recursion using the least fixpoint semantics, so their higher-order Horn clauses roughly corresponds to a fragment of the $\text{HFL}_{\mathbf{Z}}$ without modal operators and fixpoint alternations. They have not shown a general, concrete reduction from safety property verification to higher-order Horn clause solving.

The characterization of the reachability problems in Sect. 5 in terms of formulas without modal operators is a reminiscent of predicate transformers [9, 13] used for computing the weakest preconditions of imperative programs. In particular, [5] and [13] respectively used least fixpoints to express weakest preconditions for while-loops and recursions.

9   Conclusion

We have shown that various verification problems for higher-order functional programs can be naturally reduced to (extended) HFL model checking problems. In all the reductions, a program is mapped to an HFL formula expressing the property that the behavior of the program is correct. For developing verification tools for higher-order functional programs, our reductions allow us to focus on the development of (automated or semi-automated) $\text{HFL}_{\mathbf{Z}}$ model checking tools (or, even more simply, theorem provers for $\text{HFL}_{\mathbf{Z}}$ without modal operators, as the reductions of Sects. 5 and 7 yield HFL formulas without modal operators). To this end, we have developed a prototype model checker for pure HFL (without integers), which will be reported in a separate paper. Work is under way to develop $\text{HFL}_{\mathbf{Z}}$ model checkers by recasting the techniques [22, 26, 27, 43] developed for the HORS-based approach, which, together with the reductions presented in this paper, would yield fully automated verification tools. We have also started building a Coq library for interactively proving $\text{HFL}_{\mathbf{Z}}$ formulas, as briefly discussed in [23]. As a final remark, although one may fear that our reductions may map program verification problems to "harder" problems due to the expressive power of HFL_Z, it is actually not the case at least for the classes of problems in Sects. 5 and 6, which use the only alternation-free fragment of HFL_Z. The model checking problems for μ-only or ν-only HFL_Z are semi-decidable and co-semi-decidable respectively, like the source verification problems of may/must-reachability and their negations of closed programs.

Acknowledgment. We would like to thank anonymous referees for useful comments. This work was supported by JSPS KAKENHI Grant Number JP15H05706 and JP16K16004.

References

1. Axelsson, R., Lange, M., Somla, R.: The complexity of model checking higher-order fixpoint logic. Logical Methods Comput. Sci. **3**(2), 1–33 (2007)
2. Bjørner, N., Gurfinkel, A., McMillan, K., Rybalchenko, A.: Horn clause solvers for program verification. In: Beklemishev, L.D., Blass, A., Dershowitz, N., Finkbeiner, B., Schulte, W. (eds.) Fields of Logic and Computation II. LNCS, vol. 9300, pp. 24–51. Springer, Cham (2015). https://doi.org/10.1007/978-3-319-23534-9_2
3. Bjørner, N., McMillan, K.L., Rybalchenko, A.: Program verification as satisfiability modulo theories. In: SMT 2012, EPiC Series in Computing, vol. 20, pp. 3–11. EasyChair (2012)
4. Bjørner, N., McMillan, K.L., Rybalchenko, A.: Higher-order program verification as satisfiability modulo theories with algebraic data-types. CoRR, abs/1306.5264 (2013)
5. Blass, A., Gurevich, Y.: Existential fixed-point logic. In: Börger, E. (ed.) Computation Theory and Logic. LNCS, vol. 270, pp. 20–36. Springer, Heidelberg (1987). https://doi.org/10.1007/3-540-18170-9_151
6. Blume, M., Acar, U.A., Chae, W.: Exception handlers as extensible cases. In: Ramalingam, G. (ed.) APLAS 2008. LNCS, vol. 5356, pp. 273–289. Springer, Heidelberg (2008). https://doi.org/10.1007/978-3-540-89330-1_20
7. Burn, T.C., Ong, C.L., Ramsay, S.J.: Higher-order constrained horn clauses for verification. PACMPL **2**(POPL), 11:1–11:28 (2018)
8. Carayol, A., Serre, O.: Collapsible pushdown automata and labeled recursion schemes: equivalence, safety and effective selection. In: LICS 2012, pp. 165–174. IEEE (2012)
9. Dijkstra, E.W.: Guarded commands, nondeterminacy and formal derivation of programs. Commun. ACM **18**(8), 453–457 (1975)
10. Grädel, E., Thomas, W., Wilke, T. (eds.): Automata Logics, and Infinite Games: A Guide to Current Research. LNCS, vol. 2500. Springer, Heidelberg (2002). https://doi.org/10.1007/3-540-36387-4
11. Grellois, C., Melliès, P.: Relational semantics of linear logic and higher-order model checking. In: Proceedings of CSL 2015, LIPIcs, vol. 41, pp. 260–276 (2015)
12. Haddad, A.: Model checking and functional program transformations. In: Proceedings of FSTTCS 2013, LIPIcs, vol. 24, pp. 115–126 (2013)
13. Hesselink, W.H.: Predicate-transformer semantics of general recursion. Acta Inf. **26**(4), 309–332 (1989)

14. Hofmann, M., Chen, W.: Abstract interpretation from Büchi automata. In: Proceedings of CSL-LICS 2014, pp. 51:1–51:10. ACM (2014)
15. Igarashi, A., Kobayashi, N.: Resource usage analysis. ACM Trans. Prog. Lang. Syst. **27**(2), 264–313 (2005)
16. Knapik, T., Niwiński, D., Urzyczyn, P.: Higher-order pushdown trees are easy. In: Nielsen, M., Engberg, U. (eds.) FoSSaCS 2002. LNCS, vol. 2303, pp. 205–222. Springer, Heidelberg (2002). https://doi.org/10.1007/3-540-45931-6_15
17. Kobayashi, N.: Types and higher-order recursion schemes for verification of higher-order programs. In: Proceedings of POPL, pp. 416–428. ACM Press (2009)
18. Kobayashi, N.: Model checking higher-order programs. J. ACM **60**(3), 1–62 (2013)
19. Kobayashi, N., Lozes, É., Bruse, F.: On the relationship between higher-order recursion schemes and higher-order fixpoint logic. In: Proceedings of POPL 2017, pp. 246–259 (2017)
20. Kobayashi, N., Matsuda, K., Shinohara, A., Yaguchi, K.: Functional programs as compressed data. High.-Order Symbolic Comput. **25**(1), 39–84 (2013)
21. Kobayashi, N., Ong, C.H.L.: A type system equivalent to the modal mu-calculus model checking of higher-order recursion schemes. In: Proceedings of LICS 2009, pp. 179–188 (2009)
22. Kobayashi, N., Sato, R., Unno, H.: Predicate abstraction and CEGAR for higher-order model checking. In: Proceedings of PLDI, pp. 222–233. ACM Press (2011)
23. Kobayashi, N., Tsukada, T., Watanabe, K.: Higher-order program verification via HFL model checking. CoRR abs/1710.08614 (2017). http://arxiv.org/abs/1710.08614
24. Koskinen, E., Terauchi, T.: Local temporal reasoning. In: Proceedings of CSL-LICS 2014, pp. 59:1–59:10. ACM (2014)
25. Kozen, D.: Results on the propositional μ-calculus. Theor. Comput. Sci. **27**, 333–354 (1983)
26. Kuwahara, T., Sato, R., Unno, H., Kobayashi, N.: Predicate abstraction and CEGAR for disproving termination of higher-order functional programs. In: Kroening, D., Păsăreanu, C.S. (eds.) CAV 2015. LNCS, vol. 9207, pp. 287–303. Springer, Cham (2015). https://doi.org/10.1007/978-3-319-21668-3_17
27. Kuwahara, T., Terauchi, T., Unno, H., Kobayashi, N.: Automatic termination verification for higher-order functional programs. In: Shao, Z. (ed.) ESOP 2014. LNCS, vol. 8410, pp. 392–411. Springer, Heidelberg (2014). https://doi.org/10.1007/978-3-642-54833-8_21
28. Lange, M., Lozes, É., Guzmán, M.V.: Model-checking process equivalences. Theor. Comput. Sci. **560**, 326–347 (2014)
29. Ledesma-Garza, R., Rybalchenko, A.: Binary reachability analysis of higher order functional programs. In: Miné, A., Schmidt, D. (eds.) SAS 2012. LNCS, vol. 7460, pp. 388–404. Springer, Heidelberg (2012). https://doi.org/10.1007/978-3-642-33125-1_26
30. Lozes, É.: A type-directed negation elimination. In: Proceedings FICS 2015, EPTCS, vol. 191, pp. 132–142 (2015)
31. Murase, A., Terauchi, T., Kobayashi, N., Sato, R., Unno, H.: Temporal verification of higher-order functional programs. In: Proceedings of POPL 2016, pp. 57–68 (2016)
32. Ong, C.H.L.: On model-checking trees generated by higher-order recursion schemes. In: LICS 2006, pp. 81–90. IEEE Computer Society Press (2006)
33. Ong, C.H.L., Ramsay, S.: Verifying higher-order programs with pattern-matching algebraic data types. In: Proceedings of POPL, pp. 587–598. ACM Press (2011)

34. Rondon, P.M., Kawaguchi, M., Jhala, R.: Liquid types. PLDI **2008**, 159–169 (2008)
35. Skalka, C., Smith, S.F., Horn, D.V.: Types and trace effects of higher order programs. J. Funct. Program. **18**(2), 179–249 (2008)
36. Terauchi, T.: Dependent types from counterexamples. In: Proceedings of POPL, pp. 119–130. ACM (2010)
37. Tobita, Y., Tsukada, T., Kobayashi, N.: Exact flow analysis by higher-order model checking. In: Schrijvers, T., Thiemann, P. (eds.) FLOPS 2012. LNCS, vol. 7294, pp. 275–289. Springer, Heidelberg (2012). https://doi.org/10.1007/978-3-642-29822-6_22
38. Tsukada, T., Ong, C.L.: Compositional higher-order model checking via ω-regular games over Böhm trees. In: Proceedings of CSL-LICS 2014, pp. 78:1–78:10. ACM (2014)
39. Unno, H., Kobayashi, N.: Dependent type inference with interpolants. In: PPDP 2009, pp. 277–288. ACM (2009)
40. Unno, H., Satake, Y., Terauchi, T.: Relatively complete refinement type system for verification of higher-order non-deterministic programs. PACMPL **2**(POPL), 12:01–12:29 (2018)
41. Unno, H., Terauchi, T., Kobayashi, N.: Automating relatively complete verification of higher-order functional programs. In: POPL 2013. pp. 75–86. ACM (2013)
42. Viswanathan, M., Viswanathan, R.: A higher order modal fixed point logic. In: Gardner, P., Yoshida, N. (eds.) CONCUR 2004. LNCS, vol. 3170, pp. 512–528. Springer, Heidelberg (2004). https://doi.org/10.1007/978-3-540-28644-8_33
43. Watanabe, K., Sato, R., Tsukada, T., Kobayashi, N.: Automatically disproving fair termination of higher-order functional programs. In: Proceedings of ICFP 2016, pp. 243–255. ACM (2016)
44. Zhu, H., Nori, A.V., Jagannathan, S.: Learning refinement types. In: Proceedings of ICFP 2015, pp. 400–411. ACM (2015)

Quantitative Analysis of Smart Contracts

Krishnendu Chatterjee[1], Amir Kafshdar Goharshady[1(✉)], and Yaron Velner[2]

[1] IST Austria (Institute of Science and Technology Austria), Klosterneuburg, Austria
{krishnendu.chatterjee,amir.goharshady}@ist.ac.at
[2] Hebrew University of Jerusalem, Jerusalem, Israel
yaron.welner@mail.huji.ac.il

Abstract. Smart contracts are computer programs that are executed
by a network of mutually distrusting agents, without the need of an
external trusted authority. Smart contracts handle and transfer assets of
considerable value (in the form of crypto-currency like Bitcoin). Hence,
it is crucial that their implementation is bug-free. We identify the utility (or expected payoff) of interacting with such smart contracts as the
basic and canonical quantitative property for such contracts. We present
a framework for such quantitative analysis of smart contracts. Such a
formal framework poses new and novel research challenges in programming languages, as it requires modeling of game-theoretic aspects to analyze incentives for deviation from honest behavior and modeling utilities
which are not specified as standard temporal properties such as safety
and termination. While game-theoretic incentives have been analyzed in
the security community, their analysis has been restricted to the very special case of stateless games. However, to analyze smart contracts, stateful
analysis is required as it must account for the different program states
of the protocol. Our main contributions are as follows: we present (i) a
simplified programming language for smart contracts; (ii) an automatic
translation of the programs to state-based games; (iii) an abstraction-
refinement approach to solve such games; and (iv) experimental results
on real-world-inspired smart contracts.

1 Introduction

In this work we present a quantitative stateful game-theoretic framework for
formal analysis of smart-contracts.

Smart Contracts. Hundreds of crypto-currencies are in use today, and invest-
ments in them are increasing steadily [24]. These currencies are not controlled
by any central authority like governments or banks, instead they are governed
by the *blockchain* protocol, which dictates the rules and determines the outcomes, e.g., the validity of money transactions and account balances. Blockchain
was initially used for peer-to-peer Bitcoin payments [43], but recently it is also
used for running programs (called smart contracts). A *smart contract* is a program that runs on the blockchain, which enforces its correct execution (i.e., that

---

A longer version of this article is available in [19].

© The Author(s) 2018
A. Ahmed (Ed.): ESOP 2018, LNCS 10801, pp. 739–767, 2018.
https://doi.org/10.1007/978-3-319-89884-1_26

it is running as originally programmed). This is done by encoding semantics in crypto-currency transactions. For example, Bitcoin transaction scripts allow users to specify conditions, or contracts, which the transactions must satisfy prior to acceptance. Transaction scripts can encode many useful functions, such as validating that a payer owns a coin she is spending or enforcing rules for multi-party transactions. The Ethereum crypto-currency [16] allows arbitrary stateful Turing-complete conditions over the transactions which gives rise to smart contracts that can implement a wide range of applications, such as financial instruments (e.g., financial derivatives or wills) or autonomous governance applications (e.g., voting systems). The protocols are globally specified and their implementation is decentralized. Therefore, there is no central authority and they are immutable. Hence, the economic consequences of bugs in a smart contract cannot be reverted.

Types of Bugs. There are two types of bugs with monetary consequences:

1. *Coding errors.* Similar to standard programs, bugs could arise from coding mistakes. At one reported case [33], mistakenly replacing += operation with =+ enabled loss of tokens that were backed by $800,000 of investment.
2. *Dishonest interaction incentives.* Smart contracts do not fully dictate the behavior of participants. They only specify the outcome (e.g., penalty or rewards) of the behaviors. Hence, a second source for bugs is the high level *interaction aspects* that could give a participant unfair advantage and incentive for dishonest behavior. For example, a naive design of rock-paper-scissors game [29] allows playing sequentially, rather than concurrently, and gives advantage to the second player who can see the opponent's move.

DAO Attack: Interaction of Two Types of Bugs. Quite interestingly a coding bug can incentivize dishonest behavior as in the famous DAO attack [48]. The Decentralized Autonomous Organization (DAO) [38] is an Ethereum smart contract [51]. The contract consists of investor-directed venture capital fund. On June 17, 2016 an attacker exploited a bug in the contract to extract $80 million [48]. Intuitively, the root cause was that the contract allowed users to first get hold of their funds, and only then updated their balance records while a semantic detail allowed the attacker to withdraw multiple times before the update.

Necessity of Formal Framework. Since bugs in smart contracts have direct economic consequences and are irreversible, they have the same status as safety-critical errors for programs and reactive systems and must be detected before deployment. Moreover, smart contracts are deployed rapidly. There are over a million smart contracts in Ethereum, holding over 15 billion dollars at the time of writing [31]. It is impossible for security researchers to analyze all of them, and lack of automated tools for programmers makes them error prone. Hence, a formal analysis framework for smart contract bugs is of great importance.

Utility Analysis. In verification of programs, specifying objectives is non-trivial and a key goal is to consider specification-less verification, where basic properties are considered canonical. For example, termination is a basic property in program analysis; and data-race freedom or serializability are basic properties in concurrency. Given these properties, models are verified wrt them without considering any other specification. For smart contracts, describing the correct specification that prevents dishonest behavior is more challenging due to the presence of game-like interactions. We propose to consider the expected user utility (or payoff) that is guaranteed even in presence of adversarial behavior of other agents as a canonical property. Considering malicious adversaries is standard in game theory. For example, the expected utility of a fair lottery is 0. An analysis reporting a different utility signifies a bug.

New Research Challenges. Coding bugs are detected by classic verification, program analysis, and model checking tools [23,39]. However, a formal framework for incentivization bugs presents a new research challenge for the programming language community. Their analysis must overcome two obstacles: (a) the framework will have to handle game-theoretic aspects to model interactions and incentives for dishonest behavior; and (b) it will have to handle properties that cannot be deduced from standard temporal properties such as safety or termination, but require analysis of monetary gains (i.e., quantitative properties).

   While game-theoretic incentives are widely analyzed by the security community (e.g., see [13]), their analysis is typically restricted to the very special case of one-shot games that do not consider different states of the program, and thus the consequences of decisions on the next state of the program are ignored. In addition their analysis is typically ad-hoc and stems from brainstorming and special techniques. This could work when very few protocols existed (e.g., when bitcoin first emerged) and deep thought was put into making them elegant and analyzable. However, the fast deployment of smart contracts makes it crucial to automate the process and make it accessible to programmers.

Our Contribution. In this work we present a formal framework for quantitative analysis of utilities in smart contracts. Our contributions are as follows:

1. We present a simplified (loop-free) programming language that allows game-theoretic interactions. We show that many classical smart contracts can be easily described in our language, and conversely, a smart contract programmed in our language can be easily translated to Solidity [30], which is the most popular Ethereum smart contract language.
2. The underlying mathematical model for our language is stateful concurrent games. We automatically translate programs in our language to such games.
3. The key challenge to analyze such game models automatically is to tackle the state-space explosion. While several abstraction techniques have been considered for programs [14,35,45], they do not work for game-theoretic models with quantitative objectives. We present an approach based on interval-abstraction for reducing the states, establish soundness of our abstraction, and present a refinement process. This is our core technical contribution.
4. We present experimental results on several classic real-world smart contracts. We show that our approach can handle contracts that otherwise give rise to games with up to 10^{23} states. While special cases of concurrent games

(namely, turn-based games) have been studied in verification and reactive synthesis, there are no practical methods to solve general concurrent quantitative games. To the best of our knowledge, there are no tools to solve quantitative concurrent games other than academic examples of few states, and we present the first practical method to solve quantitative concurrent games that scales to real-world smart contract analysis.

In summary, our contributions range from (i) modeling of smart contracts as state-based games, to (ii) an abstraction-refinement approach to solve such games, to (iii) experimental results on real-world smart contracts.

2   Background on Ethereum Smart Contracts

2.1   Programmable Smart Contracts

Ethereum [16] is a decentralized virtual machine, which runs programs called contracts. Contracts are written in a Turing-complete bytecode language, called Ethereum Virtual Machine (EVM) bytecode [53]. A contract is invoked by calling one of its functions, where each function is defined by a sequence of instructions. The contract maintains a persistent internal state and can receive (transfer) currency from (to) users and other contracts. Users send transactions to the Ethereum network to invoke functions. Each transaction may contain input parameters for the contract and an associated monetary amount, possibly 0, which is transferred from the user to the contract.

Upon receiving a transaction, the contract collects the money sent to it, executes a function according to input parameters, and updates its internal state. All transactions are recorded on a decentralized ledger, called blockchain. A sequence of transactions that begins from the creation of the network uniquely determines the state of each contract and balances of users and contracts. The blockchain does not rely on a trusted central authority, rather, each transaction is processed by a large network of mutually untrusted peers called miners. Users constantly broadcast transactions to the network. Miners add transactions to the blockchain via a proof-of-work consensus protocol [43].

Subtleties. In this work, for simplicity, we ignore some details in the underlying protocol of Ethereum smart contract. We briefly describe these details below:

- *Transaction fees.* In exchange for including her transactions in the blockchain, a user pays transaction fees to the miners, proportionally to the execution time of her transaction. This fact could slightly affect the monetary analysis of the user gain, but could also introduce bugs in a program, as there is a bound on execution time that cannot be exceeded. Hence, it is possible that some functions could never be called, or even worse, a user could actively give input parameters that would prevent other users from invoking a certain function.

- *Recursive invocation of contracts.* A contract function could invoke a function in another contract, which in turn can have a call to the original contract. The underling Ethereum semantic in recursive invocation was the root cause for the notorious DAO hack [27].
- *Behavior of the miners.* Previous works have suggested that smart contracts could be implemented to encourage miners to deviate from their honest behavior [50]. This could in theory introduce bugs into a contract, e.g., a contract might give unfair advantage for a user who is a big miner.

2.2 Tokens and User Utility

A user's utility is determined by the Ether she spends and receives, but could also be affected by the state of the contract. Most notably, smart contracts are used to issue *tokens*, which can be viewed as a stake in a company or an organization, in return to an Ether (or tokens) investment (see an example in Fig. 1). These tokens are *transferable* among users and are traded in exchanges in return to Ether, Bitcoin and Fiat money. At the time of writing, smart contracts instantiate tokens worth billions of dollars [32]. Hence, gaining or losing tokens has clear utility for the user. At a larger scope, user utility could also be affected by more abstract storage changes. Some users would be willing to pay to have a contract declare them as Kings of Ether [4], while others could gain from registering their domain name in a smart contract storage [40]. In the examples provided in this work we mainly focus on utility that arises from Ether, tokens and the like. However, our approach is general and can model any form of utility by introducing auxiliary utility variables and definitions.

```
1 contract Token {
2     mapping(address=>uint) balances;
3     function buy() payable {
4         balances[msg.sender] += msg.value;
5     }
6     function transfer( address to, uint amount ) {
7         if(balances[msg.sender]>=amount) {
8             balances[msg.sender] -= amount;
9             balances[to] += amount;
10  }}}
```

Fig. 1. Token contract example.

3 Programming Language for Smart Contracts

In this section we present our programming language for smart contracts that supports concurrent interactions between parties. A party denotes an agent that decides to interact with the contract. A contract is a tuple $C = (N, I, M, R, X_0, F, T)$ where $X := N \cup I \cup M$ is a set of variables, R describes the range of values that can be stored in each variable, X_0 is the initial values stored in variables, F is a list of functions and T describes for each function, the time segment in which it can be invoked. We now formalize these concepts.

Variables. There are three distinct and disjoint types of variables in X:

- N contains "numeric" variables that can store a single integer.
- I contains "identification" ("id") variables capable of pointing to a party in the contract by her address or storing NULL. The notion of ids is quite flexible in our approach: The only dependence on ids is that they should be distinct and an id should not act on behalf of another id. We simply use different integers to denote distinct ids and assume that a "faking of identity" does not happen. In Ethereum this is achieved by digital signatures.
- M is the set of "mapping" variables. Each $m \in M$ maps parties to integers.

Bounds and Initial Values. The tuple $R = (\underline{R}, \overline{R})$ where $\underline{R}, \overline{R} : N \cup M \rightarrow \mathbb{Z}$ represent lower and upper bounds for integer values that can be stored in a variable. For example, if $n \in N$, then n can only store integers between $\underline{R}(n)$ and $\overline{R}(n)$. Similarly, if $m \in M$ is a mapping and $i \in I$ stores an address to a party in the contract, then $m[i]$ can save integers between $\underline{R}(m)$ and $\overline{R}(m)$. The function $X_0 : X \rightarrow \mathbb{Z} \cup \{\text{NULL}\}$ assigns an initial value to every variable. The assigned value is an integer in case of numeric and mapping variables, i.e., a mapping variable maps everything to its initial value by default. Id variables can either be initialized by NULL or an id used by one of the parties.

Functions and Timing. The sequence $F = \langle f_1, f_2, \ldots, f_n \rangle$ is a list of functions and $T = (\underline{T}, \overline{T})$, where $\underline{T}, \overline{T} : F \rightarrow \mathbb{N}$. The function f_i can only be invoked in time-frame $T(f_i) = [\underline{T}(f_i), \overline{T}(f_i)]$. The contract uses a global clock, for example the current block number in the blockchain, to keep track of time.

Note that we consider a single contract, and interaction between multiple contracts is a subject of future work.

3.1 Syntax

We provide a simple overview of our contract programming language. Our language is syntactically similar to Solidity [30], which is a widely used language for writing Ethereum contracts. A translation mechanism for different aspects is discussed in [19]. An example contract, modeling a game of rock-paper-scissors, is given in Fig. 2. Here, a party, called **issuer** has issued the contract and taken the role of **Alice**. Any other party can join the contract by registering as **Bob** and then playing rock-paper-scissors. To demonstrate our language, we use a bidding mechanism.

Declaration of Variables. The program begins by declaring variables[1], their type, name, range and initial value. For example, **Bids** is a map variable that assigns a value between 0 and 100 to every id. This value is initially 0. Line numbers (labels) are defined in Sect. 3.2 below and are not part of the syntax.

Declaration of Functions. After the variables, the functions are defined one-by-one. Each function begins with the keyword **function** followed by its name and

---

[1] For simplicity, we demonstrate our method with global variables only. However, the method is applicable to general variables as long as their ranges are well-defined at each point of the program.

```
(0)  contract RPS {
map  Bids[0, 100] = 0;
id Alice = issuer;
id Bob = null;                              (11)  if(BobsMove==0 and AlicesMove!=0)
numeric played[0,1] = 0;                    (12)      AliceWon = 1;
numeric AliceWon[0,1] = 0;                  (13)  else if(AlicesMove==0 and BobsMove!=0)
numeric BobWon[0,1] = 0;                     (14)      BobWon = 1;
numeric bid[0, 100] = 0;                    (15)  else if(AlicesMove==0 and BobsMove==0)
numeric AlicesMove[0,3] = 0;                      {
numeric BobsMove[0,3] = 0;                  (16)      AliceWon = 0;
//0 denotes no choice,                      (17)      BobWon = 0;
//1 rock, 2 paper,                                }
//3 scissors                                (18)  else if(AlicesMove==BobsMove+1 or
                                                       AlicesMove==BobsMove-2)
(1)  function registerBob[1,10]             (19)      AliceWon = 1;
        (payable bid : caller) {                  else
(2)      if(Bob==null) {                     (20)      BobWon = 1;
(3)          Bob = caller;                  (21)  }
(4)          Bids[Bob]=bid;
         }                                  (22)  function getReward[16,20]() {
         else{                              (23)      if(caller==Alice and AliceWon==1
(5)          payout(caller, bid);                    or caller==Bob and BobWon==1)
         }                                            {
(6)  }                                      (24)         payout(caller,
(7)  function play[11, 15]                                    Bids[Alice] + Bids[Bob]);
        (AlicesMove:Alice = 0,              (25)      Bids[Alice] = 0;
        BobsMove:Bob = 0,                   (26)      Bids[Bob] = 0;
        payable Bids[Alice]: Alice){              }
(8)  if(played==1)                          (27)  }
(9)      return;                            }
     else
(10)     played = 1;
```

Fig. 2. A rock-paper-scissors contract.

the time interval in which it can be called by parties. Then comes a list of input parameters. Each parameter is of the form variable : party which means that the designated party can choose a value for that variable. The chosen value is required to be in the range specified for that variable. The keyword caller denotes the party that has invoked this function and payable signifies that the party should not only decide a value, but must also pay the amount she decides. For example, registerBob can be called in any time between 1 and 10 by any of the parties. At each such invocation the party that has called this function must pay some amount which will be saved in the variable bid. After the decisions and payments are done, the contract proceeds with executing the function.

Types of Functions. There are essentially two types of functions, depending on their parameters. *One-party functions*, such as registerBob and getReward require parameters from caller only, while *multi-party functions*, such as play ask several, potentially different, parties for input. In this case all parties provide their input decisions and payments concurrently and without being aware of the choices made by other parties, also a default value is specified for every decision in case a relevant party does not take part.

Summary. Putting everything together, in the contract specified in Fig. 2, any party can claim the role of Bob between time 1 and time 10 by paying a bid to the contract, if the role is not already occupied. Then at time 11 one of the parties calls `play` and both parties have until time 15 to decide which choice (rock, paper, scissors or none) they want to make. Then the winner can call `getReward` and collect her prize.

3.2 Semantics

In this section we present the details of the semantics. In our programming language there are several key aspects which are non-standard in programming languages, such as the notion of time progress, concurrency, and interactions of several parties. Hence we present a detailed description of the semantics. We start with the requirements.

Requirements. In order for a contract to be considered valid, other than following the syntax rules, a few more requirements must be met, which are as follows:

- We assume that no division by zero or similar undefined behavior happens.
- To have a well-defined message passing, we also assume that no multi-party function has an associated time interval intersecting that of another function.
- Finally, for each non-id variable v, it must hold that $\underline{R}(v) \leq X_0(v) \leq \overline{R}(v)$ and similarly, for every function f_i, we must have $\underline{T}(f_i) < \overline{T}(f_i)$.

Overview of Time Progress. Initially, the time is 0. Let F_t be the set of functions executable at time t, i.e., $F_t = \{f_i \in F | t \in T(f_i)\}$, then F_t is either empty or contains one or more one-party functions or consists of a single multi-party function. We consider the following cases:

- F_t *empty.* If F_t is empty, then nothing can happen until the clock ticks.
- *Execution of one-party functions.* If F_t contains one or more one-party functions, then each of the parties can call any subset of these functions at time t. If there are several calls at the same time, the contract might run them in any order. While a function call is being executed, all parties are able to see the full state of the contract, and can issue new calls. When there are no more requests for function calls, the clock ticks and the time is increased to $t + 1$. When a call is being executed and is at the beginning part of the function, its caller can send messages or payments to the contract. Values of these messages and payments will then be saved in designated variables and the execution continues. If the caller fails to make a payment or specify a value for a decision variable or if her specified values/payments are not in the range of their corresponding variables, i.e. they are too small or too big, the call gets canceled and the contract reverts any changes to variables due to the call and continues as if this call had never happened.
- *Execution of multi-party functions.* If F_t contains a single multi-party function f_i and $t < \overline{T}(f_i)$, then any party can send messages and payments to the contract to specify values for variables that are designated to be paid or decided by her. These choices are hidden and cannot be observed by other participants. She can also change her decisions as many times as she sees fit.

The clock ticks when there are no more valid requests for setting a value for a variable or making a payment. This continues until we reach time $\overline{T}(f_i)$. At this time parties can no longer change their choices and the choices become visible to everyone. The contract proceeds with execution of the function. If a party fails to make a payment/decision or if NULL is asked to make a payment or a decision, default behavior will be enforced. Default value for payments is 0 and default behavior for other variables is defined as part of the syntax. For example, in function play of Fig. 2, if a party does not choose, a default value of 0 is enforced and given the rest of this function, this will lead to a definite loss.

Given the notion of time progress we proceed to formalize the notion of "runs" of the contract. This requires the notion of labels, control-flow graphs, valuations, and states, which we describe below.

Labels. Starting from 0, we give the contract, beginning and end points of every function, and every command a label. The labels are given in order of appearance. As an example, see the labels in parentheses in Fig. 2.

Entry and Exit Labels. We denote the first (beginning point) label in a function f_i by $\square_i$ and its last (end point) label by $\blacksquare_i$.

Control Flow Graphs (CFGs). We define the control flow graph CFG_i of the function f_i in the standard manner, i.e. $CFG_i = (V, E)$, where there is a vertex corresponding to every labeled entity inside f_i. Each edge $e \in E$ has a condition $cond(e)$ which is a boolean expression that must be true when traversing that edge. For more details see [19].

Valuations. A valuation is a function val, assigning a value to every variable. Values for numeric variables must be integers in their range, values for identity variables can be party ids or NULL and a value assigned to a map variable m must be a function $val(m)$ such that for each identity i, we have $\underline{R}(m) \leq val(m)(i) \leq \overline{R}(m)$. Given a valuation, we extend it to expressions containing mathematical operations in the straight-forward manner.

States. A state of the contract is a tuple $s = (t, b, l, val, c)$, where t is a time stamp, $b \in \mathbb{N} \cup \{0\}$ is the current balance of the contract, i.e., the total amount of payment to the contract minus the total amount of payouts, l is a label (that is being executed), val assigns values to variables and $c \in P \cup \{\bot\}$, is the caller of the current function. $c = \bot$ corresponds to the case where the caller is undefined, e.g., when no function is being executed. We use S to denote the set of all states that can appear in a run of the contract as defined below.

Runs. A run ρ of the contract is a finite sequence $\{\rho_j = (t_j, b_j, l_j, val_j, c_j)\}_{j=0}^r$ of states, starting from $(0, 0, 0, X_0, \bot)$, that follows all rules of the contract and ends in a state with time-stamp $t_r > \max_{f_i} \overline{T}(f_i)$. These rules must be followed when switching to a new state in a run:

– The clock can only tick when there are no valid pending requests for running a one-party function or deciding or paying in multi-party functions.

- Transitions that happen when the contract is executing a function must follow its control flow graph and update the valuation correctly.
- No variable can contain an out-of-bounds value. If an overflow or underflow happens, the closest possible value will be saved. This rule also ensures that the contract will not create new money, given that paying more than the current balance of the contract results in an underflow.
- Each party can call any set of the functions at any time.

Remark 1. Note that in our semantics each function body completes its execution in a single tick of the clock. However, ticks might contain more than one function call and execution.

Run Prefixes. We use H to mean the set of all prefixes of runs and denote the last state in $\eta \in H$ by $end(\eta)$. A run prefix η' is an extension of η if it can be obtained by adding one state to the end of η.

Probability Distributions. Given a finite set $\mathcal{X}$, a probability distribution on $\mathcal{X}$ is a function $\delta : \mathcal{X} \to [0,1]$ such that $\sum_{x \in \mathcal{X}} \delta(x) = 1$. Given such a distribution, its support, $Supp(\delta)$, is the set of all $x \in \mathcal{X}$ such that $\delta(x) > 0$. We denote the set of all probability distributions on $\mathcal{X}$ by $\Delta(\mathcal{X})$.

Typically for programs it suffices to define runs for the semantics. However, given that there are several parties in contracts, their semantics depends on the possible choices of the parties. Hence we need to define policies for parties, and such policies will define probability distribution over runs, which constitute the semantics for contracts. To define policies we first define moves.

Moves. We use $\mathcal{M}$ for the set of all moves. The moves that can be taken by parties in a contract can be summarized as follows:

- Calling a function f_i, we denote this by $call(f_i)$.
- Making a payment whose amount, y is saved in x, we denote this by $pay(x,y)$.
- Deciding the value of x to be y, we denote this by $decide(x,y)$.
- Doing none of the above, we denote this by $\boxtimes$.

Permitted Moves. We define $P_i : S \to \mathcal{M}$, so that $P_i(s)$ is the set of permitted moves for the party with identity i if the contract is in state $s = (t, b, l, val, p_j)$. It is formally defined as follows:

- If f_k is a function that can be called at state s, then $call(f_k) \in P_i(s)$.
- If $l = \square_q$ is the first label of a function f_q and x is a variable that can be decided by i at the beginning of the function f_q, then $decide(x,y) \in P_i(s)$ for all permissible values of y. Similarly if x can be paid by i, $pay(x,y) \in P_i(s)$.
- $\boxtimes \in P_i(s)$.

Policies and Randomized Policies. A policy π_i for party i is a function $\pi_i : H \to A$, such that for every $\eta \in H$, $\pi_i(\eta) \in P_i(end(\eta))$. Intuitively, a policy is a way of deciding what move to use next, given the current run prefix. A policy profile

$\pi = (\pi_i)$ is a sequence assigning one policy to each party i. The policy profile π defines a unique run ρ^π of the contract which is obtained when parties choose their moves according to π. A randomized policy ξ_i for party i is a function $\xi_i : H \to \Delta(\mathcal{M})$, such that $Supp(\xi_i(s)) \subseteq P_i(s)$. A randomized policy assigns a probability distribution over all possible moves for party i given the current run prefix of the contract, then the party can follow it by choosing a move randomly according to the distribution. We use Ξ to denote the set of all randomized policy profiles, Ξ_i for randomized policies of i and Ξ_{-i} to denote the set of randomized policy profiles for all parties except i. A randomized policy profile ξ is a sequence (ξ_i) assigning one randomized policy to each party. Each such randomized policy profile induces a unique probability measure on the set of runs, which is denoted as $\mathsf{Prob}^\xi [\cdot]$. We denote the expectation measure associated to $\mathsf{Prob}^\xi [\cdot]$ by $\mathbb{E}^\xi [\cdot]$.

3.3 Objective Function and Values of Contracts

As mentioned in the introduction we identify expected payoff as the canonical property for contracts. The previous section defines expectation measure given randomized policies as the basic semantics. Given the expected payoff, we define values of contracts as the worst-case guaranteed payoff for a given party. We formalize the notion of objective function (the payoff function).

Objective Function. An objective o for a party p is in one of the following forms:

- $(p^+ - p^-)$, where p^+ is the total money received by party p from the contract (by "payout" statements) and p^- is the total money paid by p to the contract (as "payable" parameters).
- An expression containing mathematical and logical operations (addition, multiplication, subtraction, integer division, and, or, not) and variables chosen from the set $N \cup \{m[i] \mid m \in M, i \in I\}$. Here N is the set of numeric variables, $m[i]$'s are the values that can be saved inside maps.[2]
- A sum of the previous two cases.

Informally, p is trying to choose her moves so as to maximize o.

Run Outcomes. Given a run ρ of the program and an objective o for party p, the outcome $\kappa(\rho, o, p)$ is the value of o computed using the valuation at $end(\rho)$ for all variables and accounting for payments in ρ to compute p^+ and p^-.

Contract Values. Since we consider worst-case guaranteed payoff, we consider that there is an objective o for a single party p which she tries to maximize and all other parties are adversaries who aim to minimize o. Formally, given a contract C and an objective o for party p, we define the value of contract as:

$$V(C, o, p) := \sup_{\xi_p \in \Xi_p} \inf_{\xi_{-p} \in \Xi_{-p}} \mathbb{E}^{(\xi_p, \xi_{-p})} [\kappa(\rho, o, p)],$$

---

[2] We are also assuming, as in many programming languages, that TRUE = 1 and FALSE = 0.

This corresponds to p trying to maximize the expected value of o and all other parties maliciously colluding to minimize it. In other words, it provides the worst-case guarantee for party p, irrespective of the behavior of the other parties, which in the worst-case is adversarial to party p.

3.4   Examples

One contribution of our work is to present the simplified programming language, and to show that this simple language can express several classical smart contracts. To demonstrate the applicability, we present several examples of classical smart contracts in this section. In each example, we present a contract and a "buggy" implementation of the same contract that has a different value. In Sect. 6 we show that our automated approach to analyze the contracts can compute contract values with enough precision to differentiate between the correct and the buggy implementation. All of our examples are motivated from well-known bugs that have happened in real life in Ethereum.

Rock-Paper-Scissors. Let our contract be the one specified in Fig. 2 and assume that we want to analyze it from the point of view of the issuer p. Also, let the objective function be $(p^+ - p^- + 10 \cdot \texttt{AliceWon})$. Intuitively, this means that winning the rock-paper-scissors game is considered to have an additional value of 10, other than the spending and earnings. The idea behind this is similar to the case with chess tournaments, in which players not only win a prize, but can also use their wins to achieve better "ratings", so winning has extra utility.

A common bug in writing rock-paper-scissors is allowing the parties to move sequentially, rather than concurrently [29]. If parties can move sequentially and the issuer moves after Bob, then she can ensure a utility of 10, i.e. her worst-case expected reward is 10. However, in the correct implementation as in Fig. 2, the best strategy for both players is to bid 0 and then Alice can win the game with probability 1/3 by choosing each of the three options with equal probability. Hence, her worst-case expected reward is 10/3.

Auction. Consider an open auction, in which during a fixed time interval everyone is allowed to bid for the good being sold and everyone can see others' bids. When the bidding period ends a winner emerges and every other participant can get their money back. Let the variable `HighestBid` store the value of the highest bid made at the auction. Then for a party p, one can define the objective as:

$$p^+ - p^- + (\texttt{Winner==}p) \times \texttt{HighestBid}.$$

This is of course assuming that the good being sold is worth precisely as much as the highest bid. A correctly written auction should return a value of 0 to every participant, because those who lose the auction must get their money back and the party that wins pays precisely the highest bid. The contract in Fig. 3 (left) is an implementation of such an auction. However, it has a slight problem. The function bid allows the winner to reduce her bid. This bug is fixed in the contract on the right.

```
contract BuggyAuction {
map Bids[0,1000] = 0;
numeric HighestBid[0,1000] = 0;
id Winner = null;
numeric bid[0,1000] = 0;

function bid[1,10]
(payable bid : caller) {
  payout(caller, Bids[caller]);
  Bids[caller]=bid;
  if(bid>HighestBid)
  {
    HighestBid = bid;
    Winner = caller;
  }
}

function withdraw[11,20]()
{
  if(caller!=Winner)
  {
    payout(caller, Bids[caller]);
    Bids[caller]=0;
  }
}}
```

```
contract Auction {
map Bids[0,1000] = 0;
numeric HighestBid[0,1000] = 0;
id Winner = null;
numeric bid[0,1000] = 0;

function bid[1,10]
(payable bid : caller) {
  if(bid<Bids[caller])
    return;
  payout(caller, Bids[caller]);
  Bids[caller]=bid;
  if(bid>HighestBid)
  {
    HighestBid = bid;
    Winner = caller;
  }
}

function withdraw[11,20]()
{
  if(caller!=Winner)
  {
    payout(caller, Bids[caller]);
    Bids[caller]=0;
  }
}}
```

Fig. 3. A buggy auction contract (left) and its fixed version (right).

Three-Way Lottery. Consider a three-party lottery contract issued by a party p. The other two players can sign up by buying tickets worth 1 unit each. Then each of the players is supposed to randomly and uniformly choose a nonce. A combination of these nonces produces the winner with equal probability for all three parties. If a person does not make a choice or pay the fees, she will certainly lose the lottery. The rules are such that if the other two parties choose the same nonce, which is supposed to happen with probability $\frac{1}{3}$, then the issuer wins. Otherwise the winner is chosen according to the parity of sum of nonces. This gives everyone a winning probability of $\frac{1}{3}$ if all sides play uniformly at random. However, even if one of the sides refuses to play uniformly at random, the resulting probabilities of winning stays the same because each side's probability of winning is independent of her own choice assuming that others are playing randomly. We assume that the issuer p has objective $p^+ - p^-$. This is because the winner can take other players' money. In a bug-free contract we will expect the value of this objective to be 0, given that winning has a probability of $\frac{1}{3}$. However, the bug here is due to the fact that other parties can collude. For example, the same person might register as both players and then opt for different nonces. This will ensure that the issuer loses. The bug can be solved by ensuring one's probability of winning is $\frac{1}{3}$ if she honestly plays uniformly at random, no matter what other parties do. For more details about this contract see [19].

Token Sale. Consider a contract that sells *tokens* modeling some aspect of the real world, e.g. shares in a company. At first anyone can buy tokens at a fixed price of 1 unit per token. However, there are a limited number of tokens

available and at most 1000 of them are meant to be sold. The tokens can then
be transferred between parties, which is the subject of our next example. For
now, Fig. 4 (left) is an implementation of the selling phase. However, there is
a big problem here. The problem is that one can buy any number of tokens as
long as there is at least one token remaining. For example, one might first buy
999 tokens and then buy another 1000. If we analyze the contract from the point
of view of a solo party p with objective $balance[p]$, then it must be capped by
1000 in a bug-free contract, while the process described above leads to a value
of 1999. The fixed contract is in Fig. 4 (right). This bug is inspired by a very
similar real-world bug described in [52].

Token Transfer. Consider the same bug-free token sale as in the previous
example, we now add a function for transferring tokens. An owner can choose
a recipient and an amount less than or equal to her balance and transfer that
many tokens to the recipient. Figure 5 (left) is an implementation of this concept.
Taking the same approach and objective as above, we expect a similar result.
However, there is again an important bug in this code. What happens if a party
transfers tokens to herself? She gets free extra tokens! This has been fixed in the
contract on the right. This example models a real-world bug as in [42].

```
contract BuggySale {              contract Sale {
map balance[0,2000] = 0;          map balance[0,2000] = 0;
numeric remaining[0,2000] = 1000; numeric remaining[0,2000] = 1000;
numeric payment[0,2000] = 0;      numeric payment[0,2000] = 0;

function buy[1,10]                function buy[1,10]
  (payable payment:caller)          (payable payment:caller)
{                                 {
  if(remaining<=0){                 if(remaining-payment<0){
    payout(caller, payment);          payout(caller, payment);
    return;                           return;
  }                                 }
  balance[caller] += payment;       balance[caller] += payment;
  remaining -= payment;             remaining -= payment;
}}                                }}
```

Fig. 4. A buggy token sale (left) and its fixed version (right).

Translation to Solidity. All aspects of our programming language are already
present in Solidity, except for the global clock and concurrent interactions. The
global clock can be modeled by the number of the current block in the blockchain
and concurrent interactions can be implemented using commitment schemes. For
more details see [19].

4   Bounded Analysis and Games

Since smart contracts can be easily described in our programming language,
and programs in our programming language can be translated to Solidity, the

```
contract BuggyTransfer {                  contract Transfer {
map balance[0,2000] = 0;                  map balance[0,2000] = 0;
numeric remaining[0,2000] = 1000;         numeric remaining[0,2000] = 1000;
numeric payment[0,2000] = 0;              numeric payment[0,2000] = 0;
numeric amount[0,2000] = 0;               numeric amount[0,2000] = 0;
numeric fromBalance[0,2000] = 0;
numeric toBalance[0,2000] = 0;
id recipient = null;                      id recipient = null;

function buy[1,10]...                      function buy[1,10]...

function transfer[1,10](                   function transfer[1,10](
  recipient : caller                         recipient : caller
  amount : caller) {                         amount : caller) {
    fromBalance = balance[caller];
    toBalance = balance[recipient];
    if(fromBalance<amount)                     if(balance[caller]<amount)
      return;                                    return;
    fromBalance -= amount;                     balance[caller] -= amount;
    toBalance += amount;                       balance[recipient] += amount;
    balance[caller] = fromBalance;
    balance[recipient] = toBalance;
}}                                         }}
```

Fig. 5. A buggy transfer function (left) and its fixed version (right).

main aim to automatically compute values of contracts (i.e., compute guaranteed payoff for parties). In this section, we introduce the bounded analysis problem for our programming language framework, and present concurrent games which is the underlying mathematical framework for the bounded analysis problem.

4.1 Bounded Analysis

As is standard in verification, we consider the bounded analysis problem, where the number of parties and the number of function calls are bounded. In standard program analysis, bugs are often detected with a small number of processes, or a small number of context switches between concurrent threads. In the context of smart contracts, we analogously assume that the number of parties and function calls are bounded.

Contracts with Bounded Number of Parties and Function Calls. Formally, a contract with bounded number of parties and function calls is as follows:

- Let C be a contract and $k \in \mathbb{N}$, we define C_k as an equivalent contract that can have at most k parties. This is achieved by letting $\mathbb{P} = \{\mathbb{p}_1, \mathbb{p}_2, \ldots, \mathbb{p}_k\}$ be the set of all possible ids in the contract. The set $\mathbb{P}$ must contain all ids that are in the program source, therefore k is at least the number of such ids. Note that this does not restrict that ids are controlled by unique users, and a real-life user can have several different ids. We only restrict the analysis to bounded number of parties interacting with the smart contract.
- To ensure runs are finite, number of function calls by each party is also bounded. Specifically, each party can call each function at most once during each time frame, i.e. between two consecutive ticks of the clock. This

closely resembles real-life contracts in which one's ability to call many functions is limited by the capacity of a block in the blockchain, given that the block must save all messages.

4.2   Concurrent Games

The programming language framework we consider has interacting agents that act simultaneously, and we have the program state. We present the mathematical framework of concurrent games, which are games played on finite state spaces with concurrent interaction between the players.

Concurrent Game Structures. A concurrent two-player game structure is a tuple $G = (S, s_0, A, \Gamma_1, \Gamma_2, \delta)$, where S is a finite set of states, $s_0 \in S$ is the start state, A is a finite set of actions, $\Gamma_1, \Gamma_2 : S \to 2^A \setminus \emptyset$ such that Γ_i assigns to each state $s \in S$, a non-empty set $\Gamma_i(s) \subseteq A$ of actions available to player i at s, and finally $\delta : S \times A \times A \to S$ is a transition function that assigns to every state $s \in S$ and action pair $a_1 \in \Gamma_1(s), a_2 \in \Gamma_2(s)$ a successor state $\delta(s, a_1, a_2) \in S$.

Plays and Histories. The game starts at state s_0. At each state $s_i \in S$, player 1 chooses an action $a_1^i \in \Gamma_1(s_i)$ and player 2 chooses an action $a_2^i \in \Gamma_2(s_i)$. The choices are made simultaneously and independently. The game subsequently transitions to the new state $s_{i+1} = \delta(s_i, a_1, a_2)$ and the same process continues. This leads to an infinite sequence of tuples $p = \left(s_i, a_1^i, a_2^i\right)_{i=0}^{\infty}$ which is called a *play* of the game. We denote the set of all plays by $\mathscr{P}$. Every finite prefix $p[..r] := \left((s_0, a_1^0, a_2^0), (s_1, a_1^1, a_2^1), \ldots, (s_r, a_1^r, a_2^r)\right)$ of a play is called a *history* and the set of all histories is denoted by $\mathscr{H}$. If $h = p[..r]$ is a history, we denote the last state appearing according to h, i.e. $s_{r+1} = \delta(s_r, a_1^r, a_2^r)$, by $last(h)$. We also define $p[.. - 1]$ as the empty history.

Strategies and Mixed Strategies. A strategy is a recipe that describes for a player the action to play given the current game history. Formally, a strategy φ_i for player i is a function $\varphi_i : \mathscr{H} \to A$, such that $\varphi_i(h) \in \Gamma_i(last(h))$. A pair $\varphi = (\varphi_1, \varphi_2)$ of strategies for the two players is called a strategy profile. Each such φ induces a unique play. A mixed strategy $\sigma_i : \mathscr{H} \to \Delta(A)$ for player i given the history of the game. Intuitively, such a strategy suggests a distribution of actions to player i at each step and then she plays one of them randomly according to that distribution. Of course it must be the case that $Supp(\sigma_i(h)) \subseteq \Gamma_i(last(h))$. A pair $\sigma = (\sigma_1, \sigma_2)$ of mixed strategies for the two players is called a mixed strategy profile. Note that mixed strategies generalize strategies with randomization. Every mixed strategy profile $\sigma = (\sigma_1, \sigma_2)$ induces a unique probability measure on the set of plays, which is denoted as $\mathsf{Prob}^\sigma[\cdot]$, and the associated expectation measure is denoted by $\mathbb{E}^\sigma[\cdot]$.

State and History Utilities. In a game structure G, a state utility function u for player 1 is of the form $u : S \to \mathbb{R}$. Intuitively, this means that when the game enters state s, player 1 receives a reward of $u(s)$. State utilities can be extended to history utilities. We define the utility of a history to be the sum of utilities of all the states included in that history. Formally, if $h = \left(s_i, a_1^i, a_2^i\right)_{i=0}^{r}$, then

$u(h) = \sum_{i=0}^{r} u(s_i)$. Given a play $p \in \mathscr{P}$, we denote the utility of its prefix of length L by $u_L(p)$.

Games. A game is a pair (G, u) where G is a game structure and u is a utility function for player 1. We assume that player 1 is trying to maximize u, while player 2's goal is to minimize it.

Values. The L-step finite-horizon value of a game (G, u) is defined as

$$\upsilon_L(G, u) := \sup_{\sigma_1} \inf_{\sigma_2} \mathbb{E}^{(\sigma_1, \sigma_2)}[u_L(p)], \tag{1}$$

where σ_i iterates over all possible mixed strategies of player i. This models the fact that player 1 is trying to maximize the utility in the first L steps of the run, while player 2 is minimizing it. The values of games can be computed using the value-iteration algorithm or dynamic programming, which is standard. A more detailed overview of the algorithms for games is provided in [19].

Remark 2. Note that in (1), limiting player 2 to pure strategies does not change the value of the game. Hence, we can assume that player 2 is an arbitrarily powerful nondeterministic adversary and get the exact same results.

4.3   Translating Contracts to Games

The translation from bounded smart contracts to games is straightforward, where the states of the concurrent game encodes the states of the contract. Correspondences between objects in the contract and game are as follows: (a) moves in contracts with actions in games; (b) run prefixes in contracts with histories in games; (c) runs in contracts with plays in games; and (d) policies (resp., randomized policies) in contracts with strategies (resp., mixed strategies) in games. Note that since all runs of the bounded contract are finite and have a limited length, we can apply finite horizon analysis to the resulting game, where L is the maximal length of a run in the contract. This gives us the following theorem:

Theorem 1 (Correspondence). *Given a bounded contract C_k for a party $\mathbb{p}$ with objective o, a concurrent game can be constructed such that value of this game, $\upsilon_L(G, u)$, is equal to the value of the bounded contract, $V(C_k, o, \mathbb{p})$.*

For details of the translation of smart contracts to games and proof of the theorem above see [19].

Remark 3. In standard programming languages, there are no parties to interact and hence the underlying mathematical models are graphs. In contrast, for smart contracts programming languages, where parties interact in a game-like manner, we have to consider games as the mathematical basis of our analysis.

5   Abstraction for Quantitative Concurrent Games

Abstraction is a key technique to handle large-scale systems. In the previous section we described that smart contracts can be translated to games, but due to state-space explosion (since we allow integer variables), the resulting state space of the game is huge. Hence, we need techniques for abstraction, as well as refinement of abstraction, for concurrent games with quantitative utilities. In this section we present such abstraction refinement for quantitative concurrent games, which is our main technical contribution in this paper. We show the soundness of our approach and its completeness in the limit. Then, we introduce a specific method of abstraction, called interval abstraction, which we apply to the games obtained from contracts and show that soundness and refinement are inherited from the general case. We also provide a heuristic for faster refining of interval abstractions for games obtained from contracts.

5.1   Abstraction for Quantitative Concurrent Games

Abstraction considers a partition of the state space, and reduces the number of states by taking each partition set as a state. In case of transition systems (or graphs) the standard technique is to consider existential (or universal) abstraction to define transitions between the partition sets. However, for game-theoretic interactions such abstraction ideas are not enough. We now describe the key intuition for abstraction in concurrent games with quantitative objectives and formalize it. We also provide a simple example for illustration.

Abstraction Idea and Key Intuition. In an abstraction the state space of the game (G, u) is partitioned into several abstract states, where an abstract state represents a set of states of the original game. Intuitively, an abstract state represents a set of similar states of the original game. Given an abstraction our goal is to define two games that can provide lower and upper bound on the value of the original game. This leads to the concepts of lower and upper abstraction.

– *Lower abstraction.* The lower abstraction $(G^{\downarrow}, u^{\downarrow})$ represents a lower bound on the value. Intuitively, the utility is assigned as minimal utility among states in the partition, and when an action profile can lead to different abstract states, then the adversary, i.e. player 2, chooses the transition.
– *Upper abstraction.* The upper abstraction $(G^{\uparrow}, u^{\uparrow})$ represents an upper bound on the value. Intuitively, the utility is assigned as maximal utility among states in the partition, and when an action profile can lead to different abstract states, then player 1 is chooses between the possible states.

Informally, the lower abstraction gives more power to the adversary, player 2, whereas the upper abstraction is favorable to player 1.

General Abstraction for Concurrent Games. Given a game (G, u) consisting of a game structure $G = (S, s_0, A, \Gamma_1, \Gamma_2, \delta)$ and a utility function u, and a partition Π of S, the lower and upper abstractions, $(G^{\downarrow} = (S^{\mathrm{a}}, s_0^{\mathrm{a}}, A^{\mathrm{a}}, \Gamma_1^{\downarrow}, \Gamma_2^{\downarrow}, \delta^{\downarrow}), u^{\downarrow})$ and $(G^{\uparrow} = (S^{\mathrm{a}}, s_0^{\mathrm{a}}, A^{\mathrm{a}}, \Gamma_1^{\uparrow}, \Gamma_2^{\uparrow}, \delta^{\uparrow}), u^{\uparrow})$, of (G, u) with respect to Π are defined as:

- $S^a = \Pi \cup D$, where $D = \Pi \times A \times A$ is a set of dummy states for giving more power to one of the players. Members of S^a are called abstracted states.
- The start state of G is in the start state of $G^\uparrow$ and $G^\downarrow$, i.e. $s_0 \in s_0^a \in \Pi$.
- $A^a = A \cup \Pi$. Each action in abstracted games either corresponds to an action in the original game or to a choice of the next state.
- If two states $s_1, s_2 \in S$, are in the same abstracted state $s^a \in \Pi$, then they must have the same set of available actions for both players, i.e. $\Gamma_1(s_1) = \Gamma_1(s_2)$ and $\Gamma_2(s_1) = \Gamma_2(s_2)$. Moreover, s^a inherits these action sets. Formally, $\Gamma_1^\downarrow(s^a) = \Gamma_1^\uparrow(s^a) = \Gamma_1(s_1) = \Gamma_1(s_2)$ and $\Gamma_2^\downarrow(s^a) = \Gamma_2^\uparrow(s^a) = \Gamma_2(s_1) = \Gamma_2(s_2)$.
- For all $\pi \in \Pi$ and $a_1 \in \Gamma_1^\downarrow(\pi)$ and $a_2 \in \Gamma_2^\downarrow(\pi)$, we have $\delta^\downarrow(\pi, a_1, a_2) = (\pi, a_1, a_2) \in D$. Similarly for $a_1 \in \Gamma_1^\uparrow(\pi)$ and $a_2 \in \Gamma_2^\uparrow(\pi)$, $\delta^\uparrow(\pi, a_1, a_2) = (\pi, a_1, a_2) \in D$. This means that all transitions from abstract states in Π go to the corresponding dummy abstract state in D.
- If $d = (\pi, a_1, a_2) \in D$ is a dummy abstract state, then let $X_d = \{\pi' \in \Pi \mid \exists\ s \in \pi\ \ \delta(s, a_1, a_2) \in \pi'\}$ be the set of all partition sets that can be reached from π by a_1, a_2 in G. Then in $G^\downarrow$, $\Gamma_1^\downarrow(d)$ is a singleton, i.e., player 1 has no choice, and $\Gamma_2^\downarrow(d) = X_d$, i.e., player 2 can choose which abstract state is the next. Conversely, in $G^\uparrow$, $\Gamma_2^\uparrow(d)$ is a singleton and player 2 has no choice, while $\Gamma_1^\uparrow(d) = X_d$ and player 1 chooses the next abstract state.
- In line with the previous point, $\delta^\downarrow(d, a_1, a_2) = a_2$ and $\delta^\uparrow(d, a_1, a_2) = a_1$ for all $d \in D$ and available actions a_1 and a_2.
- We have $u^\downarrow(s^a) = \min_{s \in s^a}\{u(s)\}$ and $u^\uparrow(s^a) = \max_{s \in s^a}\{u(s)\}$. The utility of a non-dummy abstracted state in $G^\downarrow$, resp. $G^\uparrow$, is the minimal, resp. maximal, utility among the normal states included in it. Also, for each dummy state $d \in D$, we have $u^\downarrow(d) = u^\uparrow(d) = 0$.

Given a partition Π of S, either (i) there is no lower or upper abstraction corresponding to it because it puts states with different sets of available actions together; or (ii) there is a unique lower and upper abstraction pair. Hence we will refer to the unique abstracted pair of games by specifying Π only.

Remark 4. Dummy states are introduced for conceptual clarity in explaining the ideas because in lower abstraction all choices are assigned to player 2 and upper abstraction to player 1. However, in practice, there is no need to create them, as the choices can be allowed to the respective players in the predecessor state.

Example. Figure 6 (left) shows a concurrent game with (G, u) with 4 states. The utilities are denoted in red. The edges correspond to transitions in δ and each edge is labeled with its corresponding action pair. Here $A = \{a, b\}$, $\Gamma_1(s_0) = \Gamma_2(s_0) = \Gamma_2(s_1) = \Gamma_1(s_2) = \Gamma_2(s_2) = \Gamma_2(s_3) = A$ and $\Gamma_1(s_1) = \Gamma_1(s_3) = \{a\}$. Given that action sets for s_0 and s_2 are equal, we can create abstracted games using the partition $\Pi = \{\pi_0, \pi_1, \pi_2\}$ where $\pi_1 = \{s_0, s_2\}$ and other sets are singletons. The resulting game structure is depicted in Fig. 6 (center). Dummy states are shown by circles and whenever a play reaches a dummy state in $G^\downarrow$, player 2 chooses which red edge should be taken. Conversely, in $G^\uparrow$ player 1 makes this choice. Also, $u^\uparrow(\pi_0) = \max\{u(s_0), u(s_2)\} = 10, u^\downarrow(\pi_0) = \min\{u(s_0), u(s_2)\} = 0$

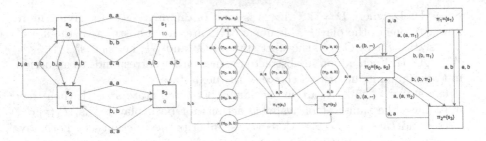

Fig. 6. An example concurrent game (left), abstraction process (center) and the corresponding $G^{\downarrow}$ without dummy states (right).

and $u^{\uparrow}(\pi_1)u^{\downarrow}(\pi_1) = u(s_1) = 10, u^{\uparrow}(\pi_2) = u^{\downarrow}(\pi_2) = u(s_3) = 0$. The final abstracted $G^{\downarrow}$ of the example above, without dummy states, is given in Fig. 6 (right).

5.2 Abstraction: Soundness, Refinement, and Completeness in Limit

For an abstraction we need three key properties: (a) soundness, (b) refinement of the abstraction, and (c) completeness in the limit. The intuitive description is as follows: (a) soundeness requires that the value of the games is between the value of the lower and upper abstraction; (b) refinement requires that if the partition is refined, then the values of lower and upper abstraction becomes closer; and (c) completeness requires that if the partitions are refined enough, then the value of the original game can be approximated. We present each of these results below.

Soundness. Soundness means that when we apply abstraction, value of the original game must lie between values of the lower and upper abstractions. Intuitively, this means abstractions must provide us with some interval containing the value of the game. We expect the value of $(G^{\downarrow}, u^{\downarrow})$ to be less than or equal to the value of the original game because in $(G^{\downarrow}, u^{\downarrow})$, the utilities are less than in (G, u) and player 2 has more power, given that she can choose which transition to take. Conversely, we expect $(G^{\uparrow}, u^{\uparrow})$ to have a higher value than (G, u).

Formal Requirement for Soundness. An abstraction of a game (G, u) leading to abstraction pair $(G^{\uparrow}, u^{\uparrow}), (G^{\downarrow}, u^{\downarrow})$ is sound if for every L, we have $\upsilon_{2\text{L}}(G^{\downarrow}, u^{\downarrow}) \leq \upsilon_{\text{L}}(G, u) \leq \upsilon_{2\text{L}}(G^{\uparrow}, u^{\uparrow})$. The factor 2 in the inequalities above is due to the fact that each transition in the original game is modeled by two transitions in abstracted games, one to a dummy state and a second one out of it. We now present our soundness result.

Theorem 2 (Soundness, Proof in [19]). *Given a game (G, u) and a partition Π of its state space, if $G^{\uparrow}$ and $G^{\downarrow}$ exist, then the abstraction is sound, i.e. for all L, it is the case that $\upsilon_{2\text{L}}(G^{\downarrow}, u^{\downarrow}) \leq \upsilon_{\text{L}}(G, u) \leq \upsilon_{2\text{L}}(G^{\uparrow}, u^{\uparrow})$.*

Refinement. We say that a partition Π_2 is a refinement of a partition Π_1, and write $\Pi_2 \sqsubseteq \Pi_1$, if every $\pi \in \Pi_1$ is a union of several π_i's in Π_2, i.e. $\pi = \bigcup_{i \in \mathcal{I}} \pi_i$ and for all $i \in \mathcal{I}$, $\pi_i \in \Pi_2$. Intuitively, this means that Π_2 is obtained by further subdividing the partition sets in Π_1. It is easy to check that $\sqsubseteq$ is a partial order over partitions. We expect that if $\Pi_2 \sqsubseteq \Pi_1$, then the abstracted games resulting from Π_2 give a better approximation of the value of the original game in comparison with abstracted games resulting from Π_1. This is called the refinement property.

Formal Requirement for the Refinement Property. Two abstractions of a game (G, u) using two partitions Π_1, Π_2, such that $\Pi_2 \sqsubseteq \Pi_1$, and leading to abstracted games $(G_i^\uparrow, u_i^\uparrow), (G_i^\downarrow, u_i^\downarrow)$ corresponding to each Π_i satisfy the refinement property if for every L, we have $\upsilon_{2L}(G_1^\downarrow, u_1^\downarrow) \leq \upsilon_{2L}(G_2^\downarrow, u_2^\downarrow) \leq \upsilon_{2L}(G_2^\uparrow, u_2^\uparrow) \leq \upsilon_{2L}(G_1^\uparrow, u_1^\uparrow)$.

Theorem 3 (Refinement Property, Proof in [19]). *Let $\Pi_2 \sqsubseteq \Pi_1$ be two partitions of the state space of a game (G, u), then the abstractions corresponding to Π_1, Π_2 satisfy the refinement property.*

Completeness in the Limit. We say that an abstraction is complete in the limit, if by refining it enough the values of upper and lower abstractions get as close together as desired. Equivalently, this means that if we want to approximate the value of the original game within some predefined threshold of error, we can do so by repeatedly refining the abstraction.

Formal Requirement for Completeness in the Limit. Given a game (G, u), a fixed finite-horizon L and an abstracted game pair corresponding to a partition Π_1, the abstraction is said to be complete in the limit, if for every $\epsilon \geq 0$ there exists $\Pi_2 \sqsubseteq \Pi_1$, such that if $(G_2^\downarrow, u_2^\downarrow), (G_2^\uparrow, u_2^\uparrow)$ are the abstracted games corresponding to Π_2, then $\upsilon_L(G_2^\uparrow, u_2^\uparrow) - \upsilon_L(G_2^\downarrow, u_2^\downarrow) \leq \epsilon$.

Theorem 4 (Completeness in the Limit, Proof in [19]). *Every abstraction on a game (G, u) using a partition Π is complete in the limit for all values of L.*

5.3   Interval Abstraction

In this section, we turn our focus to games obtained from contracts and provide a specific method of abstraction that can be applied to them.

Intuitive Overview. Let (G, u) be a concurrent game obtained from a contract as in the Sect. 4.3. Then the states of G, other than the unique dummy state, correspond to states of the contract C_k. Hence, they are of the form $s = (t, b, l, val, p)$, where t is the time, b the contract balance, l is a label, p is the party calling the current function and val is a valuation. In an abstraction, one cannot put states with different times or labels or callers together, because they might have different moves and hence different action sets in the corresponding game. The main idea in interval abstraction is to break the states according to intervals over their balance and valuations. We can then refine the abstraction by making the intervals smaller. We now formalize this concept.

Objects. Given a contract C_k, let $\mathcal{O}$ be the set of all objects that can have an integral value in a state s of the contract. This consists of the contract balance, numeric variables and $m[\mathbb{p}]$'s where m is a map variable and $\mathbb{p}$ is a party. More precisely, $\mathcal{O} = \{\beta\} \cup N \cup \{m[\mathbb{p}]|m \in M, \mathbb{p} \in \mathbb{P}\}$ where β denotes the balance. For an $o \in \mathcal{O}$, the value assigned to o at state s is denoted by o_s.

Interval Partition. Let C_k be a contract and (G, u) its corresponding game. A partition Π of the state space of G is called an interval partition if:

- The dummy state is put in a singleton set π_d.
- Each $\pi \in \Pi$ except π_d has associated values, $t_\pi, l_\pi, \mathbb{p}_\pi$ and for each $o \in \mathcal{O}$, $\bar{o}_\pi, \underline{o}_\pi$, such that $\pi = \{s \in S | s = (t_\pi, b, l_\pi, val, \mathbb{p}_\pi)$ and for all $o \in \mathcal{O}, \ \underline{o}_\pi \leq s_o \leq \bar{o}_\pi\}$. Basically, each partition set includes states with the same time, label and caller in which the value of every object o is in an interval $[\underline{o}_\pi, \bar{o}_\pi]$.

We call an abstraction using an interval partition, an interval abstraction.

Refinement Heuristic. We can start with big intervals and continually break them into smaller ones to get refined abstractions and a finer approximation of the game value. We use the following heuristic to choose which intervals to break: Assume that the current abstracted pair of games are $(G^\downarrow, u^\downarrow)$ and $(G^\uparrow, u^\uparrow)$ corresponding to an interval partition Π. Let $d = (\pi_d, a_1, a_2)$ be a dummy state in $G^\uparrow$ and define the skewness of d as $\upsilon(G_d^\uparrow, u^\uparrow) - \upsilon(G_d^\downarrow, u^\downarrow)$. Intuitively, skewness of d is a measure of how different the outcomes of the games $G^\uparrow$ and $G^\downarrow$ are, from the point when they have reached d. Take a label l with maximal average skewness among its corresponding dummy states and cut all non-unit intervals of it in more parts to get a new partition Π'. Continue the same process until the approximation is as precise as desired. Intuitively, it tries to refine parts of the abstraction that show the most disparity between $G^\downarrow$ and $G^\uparrow$ with the aim to bring their values closer. Our experiments show its effectiveness.

Soundness and Completeness in the Limit. If we restrict our attention to interval abstractions, soundness is inherited from general abstractions and completeness in the limit holds because Π_* is an interval partition. Therefore, using interval abstractions is both sound and complete in the limit.

Interval Refinement. An interval partition Π' is interval refinement of a given interval partition Π if $\Pi' \sqsubseteq \Pi$. Refinement property is inherited from general abstractions. This intuitively means that Π' is obtained by breaking the intervals in some sets of Π into smaller intervals.

Conclusion. We devised a sound abstraction-refinement method for approximating values of contracts. Our method is also complete in the limit. It begins by converting the contract to a game, then applies interval abstraction to the resulting game and repeatedly refines the abstraction using a heuristic until the desired precision is reached.

6   Experimental Results

Implementation and Optimizations. The state-space of the games corresponding to the smart contracts is huge. Hence the original game corresponding to the contract is computationally too expensive to construct. Therefore, we do not first construct the game and then apply abstraction, instead we first apply the interval abstraction, and construct the lower and upper abstraction and compute values in them. We optimized our implementation by removing dummy states and exploiting acyclicity using backward-induction. More details are provided in [19].

Experimental Results. We present our experimental results (Table 1) for the five examples mentioned in Sect. 3.4. In each of the examples, the original game is quite large, and the size of the state space is calculated without creating them. In our experimental results we show the abstracted game size, the refinement of games to larger sizes, and how the lower and upper bound on the values change. We used an Ubuntu machine with 3.2 GHz Intel i7-5600U CPU and 12 GB RAM.

Interpretation of the Experimental Results. Our results demonstrate the effectiveness of our approach in automatically approximating values of large games and real-world smart contracts. Concretely, the following points are shown:

- *Refinement Property.* By repeatedly refining the abstractions, values of lower and upper abstractions get closer at the expense of a larger state space.
- *Distinguishing Correct and Buggy Programs.* Values of the lower and upper abstractions provide an approximation interval containing the contract value. These intervals shrink with refinement until the intervals for correct and buggy programs become disjoint and distinguishable.
- *Bug Detection.* One can anticipate a sensible value for the contract, and an approximation interval not containing the value shows a bug. For example, in token sale, the objective (number of tokens sold) is at most 1000, while results show the buggy program has a value between 1741 and 2000.
- *Quantification of Economic Consequences.* Abstracted game values can also be seen as a method to quantify and find limits to the economic gain or loss of a party. For example, our results show that if the buggy auction contract is deployed, a party can potentially gain no more than 1000 units from it.

7   Comparison with Related Work

Blockchain Security Analysis. The first security analysis of Bitcoin protocol was done by Nakamoto [43] who showed resilience of the blockchain against double-spending. A stateful analysis was done by Sapirshtein et al. [47] and by Sompolinsky and Zohar [49] in which states of the blockchain were considered. It was done using MDPs where only the attacker decides on her actions and the victim follows a predefined protocol. Our paper is the first work that is using two-player and concurrent games to analyze contracts and the first to use stateful analysis on arbitrary smart contracts, rather than a specific protocol.

Table 1. Experimental results for correct and buggy contracts. $l := \upsilon(G^\downarrow, u^\downarrow)$ denotes the lower value and $u := \upsilon(G^\uparrow, u^\uparrow)$ is the upper value. Times are in seconds.

Rock-Paper-Scissors							
Size	Abstractions						
	Correct Program				Buggy Variant		
	states	$[l$,	$u]$	time	states	$[l$,	$u]$	time
$> 2.5 \cdot 10^{14}$	19440	[0.00 ,	10.00]	367	25200	[0.00 ,	10.00]	402
	135945	[1.47 ,	6.10]	2644	258345	[8.01 ,	10.00]	4815
	252450	[1.83 ,	5.59]	3381				

Auction							
Size	Abstractions						
	Correct Program				Buggy Variant		
	states	$[l$,	$u]$	time	states	$[l$,	$u]$	time
$> 5.2 \cdot 10^{14}$	3360	[0 ,	1000]	68	2880	[0 ,	1000]	38
	22560	[0 ,	282]	406	27360	[565 ,	1000]	552
	272160	[0 ,	227]	4237	233280	[748 ,	1000]	3780

Lottery							
Size	Abstractions						
	Correct Program				Buggy Variant		
	states	$[l$,	$u]$	time	states	$[l$,	$u]$	time
$> 2.5 \cdot 10^{8}$	1539	[−1 ,	1]	17	1701	[−1 ,	1]	22
	2457600	[0 ,	0]	13839	2457600	[−1 ,	−1]	13244

Sale							
Size	Abstractions						
	Correct Program				Buggy Variant		
	states	$[l$,	$u]$	time	states	$[l$,	$u]$	time
$> 4.6 \cdot 10^{22}$	17010	[0 ,	2000]	226	17010	[0 ,	2000]	275
	75762	[723 ,	1472]	1241	81202	[1167 ,	2000]	1733
	131250	[792 ,	1260]	2872	124178	[1741 ,	2000]	2818

Transfer							
Size	Abstractions						
	Correct Program				Buggy Variant		
	states	$[l$,	$u]$	time	states	$[l$,	$u]$	time
$> 10^{23}$	1040	[0 ,	2000]	20	6561	[0 ,	2000]	237
	32880	[844 ,	1793]	562	131520	[1716 ,	2000]	3979
	148311	[903 ,	1352]	3740				

Smart Contract Security. Delmolino et al. [29] held a contract programming workshop and showed that even simple contracts can contain incentive misalignment bugs. Luu et al. [41] introduced a symbolic model checker with which they could detect specific erroneous patterns. However the use of model checker cannot be extended to game-theoretic analysis. Bhargavan et al. [9] translated solidity programs to F^* and then used standard verification tools to detect vulnerable code patterns. See [7] for a survey of the known causes for Solidity bugs that result in security vulnerabilities.

Games and Verification. Abstraction for concurrent games has been considered wrt qualitative temporal objectives [3,22,28,44]. Several works considered concurrent games with only pure strategies [28,36,37]. Concurrent games with pure strategies are extremely restrictive and effectively similar to turn-based games. The min-max theorem (determinacy) does not hold for them even in special cases of one-shot games or games with qualitative objectives.

Quantitative analysis with games is studied in [12,17,21]. However these approaches either consider games without concurrent interactions or do not consider any abstraction-refinement. A quantitative abstraction-refinement framework has been considered in [18]; however, there is no game-theoretic interaction. Abstraction-refinement for games has also been considered [20,36]; however, these works neither consider games with concurrent interaction, nor quantitative objectives. Moreover, [20,36] start with a finite-state model without variables, and interval abstraction is not applicable to these game-theoretic frameworks. In contrast, our technical contribution is an abstraction-refinement approach for quantitative games and its application to analysis of smart contracts.

Formal Methods in Security. There is a huge body of work on program analysis for security; see [1,46] for survey. Formal methods are used to create safe programming languages (e.g., [34,46]) and to define new logics that can express security properties (e.g., [5,6,15]). They are also used to automatically verify security and cryptographic protocols, e.g., [2,8,11] for a survey. However, all of these works aimed to formalize qualitative properties such as privacy violation and information leakage. To the best of our knowledge, our framework is the first attempt to use formal methods as a tool for reasoning about monetary loses and identifying them as security errors.

Bounded Model Checking (BMC). BMC was proposed by Biere et al. in 1999 [10]. The idea in BMC is to search for a counterexample in executions whose length is at most k. If no bug is found then one increases k until either a bug is found, the problem becomes intractable, or some pre-known upper bound is reached.

Interval Abstraction. The first infinite abstract domain was introduced in [25]. This was later used to prove that infinite abstract domains can lead to effective static analysis for a given programming language [26]. However, none of the standard techniques is applicable to game analysis.

8   Conclusion

In this work we present a programming language for smart contracts, and an abstraction-refinement approach for quantitative concurrent games to automatically analyze (i.e., compute worst-case guaranteed utilities of) such contracts. This is the first time a quantitative stateful game-theoretic framework is studied for formal analysis of smart contracts. There are several interesting directions of future work. First, we present interval-based abstraction techniques for such games, and whether different abstraction techniques can lead to more scalability or other classes of contracts is an interesting direction of future work. Second, since we consider worst-case guarantees, the games we obtain are two-player zero-sum games. The extension to study multiplayer games and compute values for rational agents is another interesting direction of future work. Finally, in this work we do not consider interaction between smart contracts, and an extension to encompass such study will be a subject of its own.

Acknowledgments. The research was partially supported by Vienna Science and Technology Fund (WWTF) Project ICT15-003, Austrian Science Fund (FWF) NFN Grant No S11407-N23 (RiSE/SHiNE), and ERC Starting grant (279307: Graph Games).

References

1. Abadi, M.: Software security: a formal perspective. In: Giannakopoulou, D., Méry, D. (eds.) FM 2012. LNCS, vol. 7436, pp. 1–5. Springer, Heidelberg (2012). https://doi.org/10.1007/978-3-642-32759-9_1
2. Abadi, M., Rogaway, P.: Reconciling two views of cryptography. In: van Leeuwen, J., Watanabe, O., Hagiya, M., Mosses, P.D., Ito, T. (eds.) TCS 2000. LNCS, vol. 1872, pp. 3–22. Springer, Heidelberg (2000). https://doi.org/10.1007/3-540-44929-9_1
3. Alur, R., Henzinger, T.A., Kupferman, O., Vardi, M.Y.: Alternating refinement relations. In: Sangiorgi, D., de Simone, R. (eds.) CONCUR 1998. LNCS, vol. 1466, pp. 163–178. Springer, Heidelberg (1998). https://doi.org/10.1007/BFb0055622
4. Anonymous Author: King of the ether (2017). www.kingoftheether.com
5. Arden, O., Liu, J., Myers, A.C.: Flow-limited authorization. In: CSF, pp. 569–583 (2015)
6. Arden, O., Myers, A.C.: A calculus for flow-limited authorization. In: CSF (2016)
7. Atzei, N., Bartoletti, M., Cimoli, T.: A survey of attacks on ethereum smart contracts. IACR Cryptology ePrint Archive, 1007 (2016)
8. Avalle, M., Pironti, A., Sisto, R.: Formal verification of security protocol implementations: a survey. Formal Aspects Comput. **26**(1), 99–123 (2014)
9. Bhargavan, K., et al.: Formal verification of smart contracts: short paper. In: PLAS. ACM (2016)
10. Biere, A., Cimatti, A., Clarke, E., Zhu, Y.: Symbolic model checking without BDDs. In: Cleaveland, W.R. (ed.) TACAS 1999. LNCS, vol. 1579, pp. 193–207. Springer, Heidelberg (1999). https://doi.org/10.1007/3-540-49059-0_14
11. Blanchet, B., Chaudhuri, A.: Automated formal analysis of a protocol for secure file sharing on untrusted storage. In: SP, pp. 417–431. IEEE (2008)

12. Bloem, R., Chatterjee, K., Henzinger, T.A., Jobstmann, B.: Better quality in synthesis through quantitative objectives. In: Bouajjani, A., Maler, O. (eds.) CAV 2009. LNCS, vol. 5643, pp. 140–156. Springer, Heidelberg (2009). https://doi.org/10.1007/978-3-642-02658-4_14

13. Bonneau, J., Miller, A., Clark, J., Narayanan, A., Kroll, J.A., Felten, E.W.: Sok: research perspectives and challenges for bitcoin and cryptocurrencies. In: SP, pp. 104–121. IEEE (2015)

14. Burch, J., Clarke, E., McMillan, K., Dill, D., Hwang, L.J.: Symbolic model checking: 1020 states and beyond. Inf. Comput. **98**(2), 142–170 (1992)

15. Burrows, M., Abadi, M., Needham, R.M.: A logic of authentication. In: Proceedings of the Royal Society of London A: Mathematical, Physical and Engineering Sciences, pp. 233–271. The Royal Society (1989)

16. Buterin, V., et al.: Ethereum white paper (2013)

17. Černý, P., Chatterjee, K., Henzinger, T.A., Radhakrishna, A., Singh, R.: Quantitative synthesis for concurrent programs. In: Gopalakrishnan, G., Qadeer, S. (eds.) CAV 2011. LNCS, vol. 6806, pp. 243–259. Springer, Heidelberg (2011). https://doi.org/10.1007/978-3-642-22110-1_20

18. Cerný, P., Henzinger, T.A., Radhakrishna, A.: Quantitative abstraction refinement. In: POPL (2013)

19. Chatterjee, K., Goharshady, A.K., Velner, Y.: Quantitative analysis of smart contracts (2018). arXiv preprint: arXiv:1801.03367

20. Chatterjee, K., Henzinger, T.A., Jhala, R., Majumdar, R.: Counterexample-guided planning. In: UAI, pp. 104–111 (2005)

21. Chatterjee, K., Ibsen-Jensen, R.: Qualitative analysis of concurrent mean-payoff games. Inf. Comput. **242**, 2–24 (2015)

22. Church, A.: Logic, arithmetic, and automata. In: Proceedings of the International Congress of Mathematicians, pp. 23–35. Institut Mittag-Leffler (1962)

23. Clarke, E., Grumberg, O., Peled, D.: Model Checking. MIT Press, Cambridge (1999)

24. CoinMarketCap: Crypto-currency market capitalizations (2017). coinmarketcap.com

25. Cousot, P., Cousot, R.: Static determination of dynamic properties of generalized type unions. In: ACM Conference on Language Design for Reliable Software, vol. 12, pp. 77–94. ACM (1977)

26. Cousot, P., Cousot, R.: Comparing the Galois connection and widening/narrowing approaches to abstract interpretation. In: Bruynooghe, M., Wirsing, M. (eds.) PLILP 1992. LNCS, vol. 631, pp. 269–295. Springer, Heidelberg (1992). https://doi.org/10.1007/3-540-55844-6_142

27. Daian, P.: Analysis of the DAO exploit (2016). hackingdistributed.com/2016/06/18/analysis-of-the-dao-exploit

28. de Alfaro, L., Godefroid, P., Jagadeesan, R.: Three-valued abstractions of games: uncertainty, but with precision. In: LICS. IEEE (2004)

29. Delmolino, K., Arnett, M., Kosba, A.E., Miller, A., Shi, E.: Step by step towards creating a safe smart contract: Lessons and insights from a cryptocurrency lab. IACR Cryptology ePrint Archive 2015, 460 (2015)

30. Ethereum Foundation: Solidity language documentation (2017)

31. Etherscan: Contract accounts (2017). etherscan.io/accounts/c

32. Etherscan: Token information (2017). etherscan.io/tokens

33. ETHNews: Hkg token has a bug and needs to be reissued (2017). ethnews.com/ethercamps-hkg-token-has-a-bug-and-needs-to-be-reissued

34. Fuchs, A.P., Chaudhuri, A., Foster, J.S.: Scandroid: automated security certification of android. Technical report (2009)
35. Godefroid, P. (ed.): Partial-Order Methods for the Verification of Concurrent Systems: An Approach to the State-Explosion Problem. LNCS, vol. 1032. Springer, Heidelberg (1996). https://doi.org/10.1007/3-540-60761-7
36. Henzinger, T.A., Jhala, R., Majumdar, R.: Counterexample-guided control. In: ICALP (2003)
37. Henzinger, T.A., Majumdar, R., Mang, F., Raskin, J.-F.: Abstract interpretation of game properties. In: Palsberg, J. (ed.) SAS 2000. LNCS, vol. 1824, pp. 220–239. Springer, Heidelberg (2000). https://doi.org/10.1007/978-3-540-45099-3_12
38. Jentzsch, C.: Decentralized autonomous organization to automate governance (2016). download.slock.it/public/DAO/WhitePaper.pdf
39. Jhala, R., Majumdar, R.: Software model checking. ACM Comput. Surv. **41**(4), 21:1–21:54 (2009)
40. Johnson, N.: A beginner's guide to buying an ENS domain (2017)
41. Luu, L., Chu, D.H., Olickel, H., Saxena, P., Hobor, A.: Making smart contracts smarter. In: CCS; pp. 254–269 (2016)
42. Luu, L., Velner, Y.: Audit report for digix's smart contract platform (2017)
43. Nakamoto, S.: Bitcoin: a peer-to-peer electronic cash system (2008)
44. Pnueli, A., Rosner, R.: On the synthesis of a reactive module. In: POPL, pp. 179–190 (1989)
45. Queille, J.P., Sifakis, J.: Specification and verification of concurrent systems in CESAR. In: Dezani-Ciancaglini, M., Montanari, U. (eds.) International Symposium on Programming. LNCS, vol. 137, pp. 337–351. Springer, Heidelberg (1982). https://doi.org/10.1007/3-540-11494-7_22
46. Sabelfeld, A., Myers, A.C.: Language-based information-flow security. IEEE J. Sel. Areas Commun. **21**(1), 5–19 (2003)
47. Sapirshtein, A., Sompolinsky, Y., Zohar, A.: Optimal selfish mining strategies in bitcoin (2015). arXiv preprint: arXiv:1507.06183
48. Simonite, T.: $80 million hack shows the dangers of programmable money, June 2016. www.technologyreview.com
49. Sompolinsky, Y., Zohar, A.: Bitcoin's security model revisited. CoRR abs/1605.09193 (2016)
50. Teutsch, J., Jain, S., Saxena, P.: When cryptocurrencies mine their own business? In: Grossklags, J., Preneel, B. (eds.) FC 2016. LNCS, vol. 9603, pp. 499–514. Springer, Heidelberg (2017). https://doi.org/10.1007/978-3-662-54970-4_29
51. Toobin, A.: The DAO, Ethereum's $150 million blockchain investment fund, has a logic problem (2016). www.inverse.com/article/16314-the-dao-ethereum-s-150-million-blockchain
52. Tran, V., Velner, Y.: Coindash audit report (2017)
53. Wood, G.: Ethereum yellow paper (2014)

Session Types and Concurrency

Session-Typed Concurrent Contracts

Hannah Gommerstadt[✉], Limin Jia, and Frank Pfenning

Carnegie Mellon University, Pittsburgh, PA, USA
{hgommers,fp}@cs.cmu.edu, liminjia@cmu.edu

Abstract. In sequential languages, dynamic contracts are usually expressed as boolean functions without externally observable effects, written within the language. We propose an analogous notion of concurrent contracts for languages with session-typed message-passing concurrency. Concurrent contracts are partial identity processes that monitor the bidirectional communication along channels and raise an alarm if a contract is violated. Concurrent contracts are session-typed in the usual way and must also satisfy a transparency requirement, which guarantees that terminating compliant programs with and without the contracts are observationally equivalent. We illustrate concurrent contracts with several examples. We also show how to generate contracts from a refinement session-type system and show that the resulting monitors are redundant for programs that are well-typed.

Keywords: Contracts · Session types · Monitors

1 Introduction

Contracts, specifying the conditions under which software components can safely interact, have been used for ensuring key properties of programs for decades. Recently, contracts for distributed processes have been studied in the context of session types [15,17]. These contracts can enforce the communication protocols, specified as session types, between processes. In this setting, we can assign each channel a monitor for detecting whether messages observed along the channel adhere to the prescribed session type. The monitor can then detect any deviant behavior the processes exhibit and trigger alarms. However, contracts based solely on session types are inherently limited in their expressive power. Many contracts that we would like to enforce cannot even be stated using session types alone. As a simple example, consider a "factorization service" which may be sent a (possibly large) integer x and is supposed to respond with a list of prime factors. Session types can only express that the request is an integer and the response is a list of integers, which is insufficient.

In this paper, we show that by generalizing the class of monitors beyond those derived from session types, we can enforce, for example, that multiplying the numbers in the response yields the original integer x. This paper focuses on monitoring more expressive contracts, specifically those that cannot be expressed with session types, or even refinement types.

A. Ahmed (Ed.): ESOP 2018, LNCS 10801, pp. 771–798, 2018.
https://doi.org/10.1007/978-3-319-89884-1_27

To handle these contracts, we have designed a model where our monitors execute as transparent processes alongside the computation. They are able to maintain internal state which allows us to check complex properties. These monitoring processes act as partial identities, which do not affect the computation except possibly raising an alarm, and merely observe the messages flowing through the system. They then perform whatever computation is needed, for example, they can compute the product of the factors, to determine whether the messages are consistent with the contract. If the message is not consistent, they stop the computation and blame the process responsible for the mistake. To show that our contracts subsume refinement-based contracts, we encode refinement types in our model by translating refinements into monitors. This encoding is useful because we can show a blame (safety) theorem stating that monitors that enforce a less precise refinement type than the type of the process being monitored will not raise alarms. Unfortunately, the blame theory for the general model is challenging because the contracts cannot be expressed as types.

The main contributions of this paper are:

- A novel approach to contract checking via partial-identity monitors
- A method for verifying that monitors are partial identities, and a proof that the method is correct
- Examples showing the breadth of contracts that our monitors can enforce
- A translation from refinement types to our monitoring processes and a blame theorem for this fragment

The rest of this paper is organized as follows. We first review the background on session types in Sect. 2. Next, we show a range of example contracts in Sect. 3. In Sect. 4, we show how to check that a monitor process is a partial identity and prove the method correct. We then show how we can encode refinements in our system in Sect. 5. We discuss related work in Sect. 6. Due to space constraints, we only present the key theorems. Detailed proofs can be found in our companion technical report [12].

2   Session Types

Session types prescribe the communication behavior of message-passing concurrent processes. We approach them here via their foundation in intuitionistic linear logic [4,5,22]. The key idea is that an intuitionistic linear sequent

$$A_1, \ldots, A_n \vdash C$$

is interpreted as the interface to a *process expression* P. We label each of the antecedents with a channel name a_i and the succedent with a channel name c. The a_i are the channels *used* and c is the channel *provided* by P.

$$a_1 : A_1, \ldots, a_n : A_n \vdash P :: (c : C)$$

We abbreviate the antecedents by Δ. All the channels a_i and c must be distinct, and bound variables may be silently renamed to preserve this invariant in the rules. Furthermore, the antecedents are considered modulo exchange. Cut corresponds to parallel composition of two processes that communicate along a private channel x, where P is the *provider* along x and Q the *client*.

$$\frac{\Delta \vdash P :: (x : A) \quad x : A, \Delta' \vdash Q :: (c : C)}{\Delta, \Delta' \vdash x{:}A \leftarrow P \,;\, Q :: (c : C)} \text{ cut}$$

Operationally, the process $x \leftarrow P \,;\, Q$ spawns P as a new process and continues as Q, where P and Q communicate along a fresh channel a, which is substituted for x. We sometimes omit the type A of x in the syntax when it is not relevant.

In order to define the operational semantics rigorously, we use *multiset rewriting* [6]. The configuration of executing processes is described as a collection $\mathcal{C}$ of propositions $\mathsf{proc}(c, P)$ (process P is executing, providing along c) and $\mathsf{msg}(c, M)$ (message M is sent along c). All the channels c provided by processes and messages in a configuration must be distinct.

A cut spawns a new process, and is in fact the only way new processes are spawned. We describe a transition $\mathcal{C} \longrightarrow \mathcal{C}'$ by defining how a subset of $\mathcal{C}$ can be rewritten to a subset of $\mathcal{C}'$, possibly with a freshness condition that applies to all of $\mathcal{C}$ in order to guarantee the uniqueness of each channel provided.

$$\mathsf{proc}(c, x{:}A \leftarrow P \,;\, Q) \longrightarrow \mathsf{proc}(a, [a/x]P), \mathsf{proc}(c, [a/x]Q) \quad (a \text{ } fresh)$$

Each of the connectives of linear logic then describes a particular kind of communication behavior which we capture in similar rules. Before we move on to that, we consider the identity rule, in logical form and operationally.

$$\overline{A \vdash A} \text{ id} \qquad \overline{b : A \vdash a \leftarrow b :: (a : A)} \text{ id} \qquad \mathsf{proc}(a, a \leftarrow b), \mathcal{C} \longrightarrow [b/a]\mathcal{C}$$

Operationally, it corresponds to identifying the channels a and b, which we implement by substituting b for a in the remainder $\mathcal{C}$ of the configuration (which we make explicit in this rule). The process offering a terminates. We refer to $a \leftarrow b$ as *forwarding* since any messages along a are instead "forwarded" to b.

We consider each class of session type constructors, describing their process expression, typing, and asynchronous operational semantics. The linear logical semantics can be recovered by ignoring the process expressions and channels.

Internal and External Choice. Even though we distinguish a *provider* and its *client*, this distinction is orthogonal to the direction of communication: both may either send or receive along a common private channel. Session typing guarantees that both sides will always agree on the direction and kind of message that is sent or received, so our situation corresponds to so-called *binary session types*.

First, the *internal choice* $c : A \oplus B$ requires the provider to send a token inl or inr along c and continue as prescribed by type A or B, respectively. For practical programming, it is more convenient to support n-ary labelled choice $\oplus\{\ell : A_\ell\}_{\ell \in L}$ where L is a set of labels. A process providing $c : \oplus\{\ell : A_\ell\}_{\ell \in L}$ sends a label $k \in L$ along c and continues with type A_k. The client will operate dually, branching on a label received along c.

$$\dfrac{k \in L \quad \Delta \vdash P :: (c : A_k)}{\Delta \vdash c.k \; ; \; P :: (c : \oplus\{\ell : A_\ell\}_{\ell \in L})} \; \oplus R \qquad \dfrac{\Delta, c : A_\ell \vdash Q_\ell :: (d : D) \quad \text{for every } \ell \in L}{\Delta, c : \oplus\{\ell : A_\ell\}_{\ell \in L} \vdash \text{case } c \; (\ell \Rightarrow Q_\ell)_{\ell \in L} :: (d : D)} \; \oplus L$$

The operational semantics is somewhat tricky, because we communicate asynchronously. We need to spawn a message carrying the label ℓ, but we also need to make sure that the *next* message sent along the same channel does not overtake the first (which would violate session fidelity). Sending a message therefore creates a fresh continuation channel c' for further communication, which we substitute in the continuation of the process. Moreover, the recipient also switches to this continuation channel after the message is received.

$$\text{proc}(c, c.k \; ; \; P) \longrightarrow \text{proc}(c', [c'/c]P), \text{msg}(c, c.k \; ; \; c \leftarrow c') \quad (c' \; fresh)$$
$$\text{msg}(c, c.k \; ; \; c \leftarrow c'), \text{proc}(d, \text{case } c \; (\ell \Rightarrow Q_\ell)_{\ell \in L}) \longrightarrow \text{proc}(d, [c'/c]Q_k)$$

It is interesting that the message along c, followed by its continuation c' can be expressed as a well-typed process expression using forwarding $c.k \; ; \; c \leftarrow c'$. This pattern will work for all other pairs of send/receive operations.

External choice reverses the roles of client and provider, both in the typing and the operational rules. Below are the semantics and the typing is in Fig. 6.

$$\text{proc}(d, c.k \; ; \; Q) \longrightarrow \text{msg}(c', c.k \; ; \; c' \leftarrow c), \text{proc}(d, [c'/c]Q) \quad (c' \; fresh)$$
$$\text{proc}(c, \text{case } c \; (\ell \Rightarrow P_\ell)_{\ell \in L}), \text{msg}(c', c.k \; ; \; c' \leftarrow c) \longrightarrow \text{proc}(c', [c'/c]P_k)$$

Sending and Receiving Channels. Session types are *higher-order* in the sense that we can send and receive channels along channels. Sending a channel is perhaps less intuitive from the logical point of view, so we show that and just summarize the rules for receiving.

If we provide $c : A \otimes B$, we send a channel $a : A$ along c and continue as B. From the typing perspective, it is a restricted form of the usual two-premise $\otimes R$ rule by requiring the first premise to be an identity. This restriction separates spawning of new processes from the sending of channels.

$$\dfrac{\Delta \vdash P :: B}{\Delta, a : A \vdash \text{send } c \; a \; ; \; P :: (c : A \otimes B)} \; \otimes R^* \qquad \dfrac{\Delta, x : A, c : B \vdash Q :: (d : D)}{\Delta, c : A \otimes B \vdash x \leftarrow \text{recv } c \; ; \; Q :: (d : D)} \; \otimes L$$

The operational rules follow the same patterns as the previous case.

$$\text{proc}(c, \text{send } c \; a \; ; \; P) \longrightarrow \text{proc}(c', [c'/c]P), \text{msg}(\text{send } c \; a \; ; \; c \leftarrow c') \quad (c' \; fresh)$$
$$\text{msg}(c, \text{send } c \; a \; ; \; c \leftarrow c'), \text{proc}(d, x \leftarrow \text{recv } c \; ; \; Q) \longrightarrow \text{proc}(d, [c'/c][a/x]Q)$$

Receiving a channel (written as a linear implication $A \multimap B$) works symmetrically. Below are the semantics and the typing is shown in Fig. 6.

$$\text{proc}(d, \text{send } c \; a \; ; \; Q) \longrightarrow \text{msg}(c', \text{send } c \; a \; ; \; c' \leftarrow c), \text{proc}(d, [c'/c]Q) \quad (c' \; fresh)$$
$$\text{proc}(c, x \leftarrow \text{recv } c \; ; \; P), \text{msg}(c', \text{send } c \; a \; ; \; c' \leftarrow c) \longrightarrow \text{proc}(c', [c'/c][a/x]P)$$

Termination. We have already seen that a process can terminate by forwarding. Communication along a channel ends explicitly when it has type $\mathbf{1}$ (the unit of $\otimes$) and is closed. By linearity there must be no antecedents in the right rule.

$$\dfrac{}{\cdot \vdash \text{close } c :: (c : \mathbf{1})} \; 1R \qquad \dfrac{\Delta \vdash Q :: (d : D)}{\Delta, c : \mathbf{1} \vdash \text{wait } c \; ; \; Q :: (d : D)} \; 1L$$

Since there cannot be any continuation, the message takes a simple form.

$$\mathsf{proc}(c, \mathsf{close}\ c) \longrightarrow \mathsf{msg}(c, \mathsf{close}\ c)$$
$$\mathsf{msg}(c, \mathsf{close}\ c), \mathsf{proc}(d, \mathsf{wait}\ c\ ;\ Q) \longrightarrow \mathsf{proc}(d, Q)$$

Quantification. First-order quantification over elements of domains such as integers, strings, or booleans allows ordinary basic data values to be sent and received. At the moment, since we have no type families indexed by values, the quantified variables cannot actually appear in their scope. This will change in Sect. 5 so we anticipate this in these rules.

The proof of an existential quantifier contains a witness term, whose value is what is sent. In order to track variables ranging over values, a new context Ψ is added to all judgments and the preceding rules are modified accordingly. All value variables n declared in context Ψ must be distinct. Such variables are not linear, but can be arbitrarily reused, and are therefore propagated to all premises in all rules. We write $\Psi \vdash v : \tau$ to check that value v has type τ in context Ψ.

$$\frac{\Psi \vdash v : \tau \quad \Psi\ ;\ \Delta \vdash P :: (c : [v/n]A)}{\Psi\ ;\ \Delta \vdash \mathsf{send}\ c\ v\ ;\ P :: (c : \exists n{:}\tau.\ A)}\ \exists R \qquad \frac{\Psi, n{:}\tau\ ;\ \Delta, c : A \vdash Q :: (d : D)}{\Psi\ ;\ \Delta, c : \exists n{:}\tau.\ A \vdash n \leftarrow \mathsf{recv}\ c\ ;\ Q :: (d : D)}\ \exists L$$

$$\mathsf{proc}(c, \mathsf{send}\ c\ v\ ;\ P) \longrightarrow \mathsf{proc}(c', [c'/c]P), \mathsf{msg}(c, \mathsf{send}\ c\ v\ ;\ c \leftarrow c')$$
$$\mathsf{msg}(c, \mathsf{send}\ c\ v\ ;\ c \leftarrow c'), \mathsf{proc}(d, n \leftarrow \mathsf{recv}\ c\ ;\ Q) \longrightarrow \mathsf{proc}(d, [c'/c][v/n]Q)$$

The situation for universal quantification is symmetric. The semantics are given below and the typing is shown in Fig. 6.

$$\mathsf{proc}(d, \mathsf{send}\ c\ v\ ;\ Q) \longrightarrow \mathsf{msg}(c', \mathsf{send}\ c\ v\ ;\ c' \leftarrow c), \mathsf{proc}(d, [c'/c]Q)$$
$$\mathsf{proc}(c, x \leftarrow \mathsf{recv}\ c\ ;\ P), \mathsf{msg}(c', \mathsf{send}\ c\ v\ ;\ c' \leftarrow c) \longrightarrow \mathsf{proc}(c', [c'/c][v/n]P)$$

Processes may also make internal transitions while computing ordinary values, which we don't fully specify here. Such a transition would have the form

$$\mathsf{proc}(c, P[e]) \longrightarrow \mathsf{proc}(c, P[e'])\quad \text{if}\ \ e \mapsto e'$$

where $P[e]$ would denote a process with an ordinary value expression in evaluation position and $e \mapsto e'$ would represent a step of computation.

Shifts. For the purpose of monitoring, it is important to track the direction of communication. To make this explicit, we *polarize* the syntax and use *shifts* to change the direction of communication (for more detail, see prior work [18]).

Negative types A^-, B^-	$::=$	$\&\{\ell : A_\ell^-\}_{\ell \in L} \mid A^+ \multimap B^- \mid \forall n{:}\tau.\ A^- \mid {\uparrow}A^+$
Positive types A^+, B^+	$::=$	$\oplus\{\ell : A_\ell^+\}_{\ell \in L} \mid A^+ \otimes B^+ \mid 1 \mid \exists n{:}\tau.\ A^+ \mid {\downarrow}A^-$
Types	$A, B, C, D ::=$	$A^- \mid A^+$

From the perspective of the provider, all negative types receive and all positive types send. It is then clear that ${\uparrow}A$ must receive a shift message and then start sending, while ${\downarrow}A$ must send a shift message and then start receiving.

For this restricted form of shift, the logical rules are otherwise uninformative. The semantics are given below and the typing is shown in Fig. 6.

$$\mathsf{proc}(c, \mathsf{send}\ c\ \mathsf{shift}\ ;\ P) \longrightarrow \mathsf{proc}(c', [c'/c]P), \mathsf{msg}(c, \mathsf{send}\ c\ \mathsf{shift}\ ;\ c \leftarrow c') \quad (c'\ \mathsf{fresh})$$
$$\mathsf{msg}(c, \mathsf{send}\ c\ \mathsf{shift}\ ;\ c \leftarrow c'), \mathsf{proc}(d, \mathsf{shift} \leftarrow \mathsf{recv}\ d\ ;\ Q) \longrightarrow \mathsf{proc}(d, [c'/c]Q)$$
$$\mathsf{proc}(d, \mathsf{send}\ d\ \mathsf{shift}\ ;\ Q) \longrightarrow \mathsf{msg}(c', \mathsf{send}\ c\ \mathsf{shift}\ ;\ c' \leftarrow c), \mathsf{proc}(d, [c'/c]Q)$$
$$\mathsf{proc}(c, \mathsf{shift} \leftarrow \mathsf{recv}\ c\ ;\ P), \mathsf{msg}(c', \mathsf{send}\ c\ \mathsf{shift}\ ;\ c' \leftarrow c) \longrightarrow \mathsf{proc}(c', [c'/c]P)$$

Recursive Types. Practical programming with session types requires them to be recursive, and processes using them also must allow recursion. For example, lists with elements of type int can be defined as the purely positive type list^+.

$$\mathsf{list}^+ = \oplus\{\ \mathsf{cons} : \exists n{:}\mathsf{int}.\,\mathsf{list}^+\ ;\ \mathsf{nil} : \mathbf{1}\ \}$$

A provider of type $c : \mathsf{list}$ is required to send a sequence such as $\mathsf{cons}{\cdot}v_1{\cdot}\mathsf{cons}{\cdot}v_2\cdots$ where each v_i is an integer. If it is finite, it must be terminated with $\mathsf{nil} \cdot \mathsf{end}$. In the form of a grammer, we could write

$$From ::= \mathsf{cons} \cdot v \cdot From \mid \mathsf{nil} \cdot \mathsf{end}$$

A second example is a multiset (bag) of integers, where the interface allows inserting and removing elements, and testing if it is empty. If the bag is empty when tested, the provider terminates after responding with the empty label.

$$\mathsf{bag}^- = \&\{\ \mathsf{insert} : \forall n{:}\mathsf{int}.\,\mathsf{bag}^-,\ \mathsf{remove} : \forall n{:}\mathsf{int}.\,\mathsf{bag}^-,$$
$$\mathsf{is\_empty} : {\uparrow}\oplus\{\mathsf{empty} : \mathbf{1}, \mathsf{nonempty} : {\downarrow}\,\mathsf{bag}^-\}\ \}$$

The protocol now describes the following grammar of exchanged messages, where *To* goes to the provider, *From* comes from the provider, and v stands for integers.

$$To \quad ::= \mathsf{insert} \cdot v \cdot To \mid \mathsf{remove} \cdot v \cdot To \mid \mathsf{is\_empty} \cdot \mathsf{shift} \cdot From$$
$$From ::= \mathsf{empty} \cdot \mathsf{end} \mid \mathsf{nonempty} \cdot \mathsf{shift} \cdot To$$

For these protocols to be realized in this form and support rich subtyping and refinement types without change of protocol, it is convenient for recursive types to be *equirecursive*. This means a defined type such as list^+ is viewed as *equal* to its definition $\oplus\{\ldots\}$ rather than *isomorphic*. For this view to be consistent, we require type definitions to be *contractive* [11], that is, they need to provide at least one send or receive interaction before recursing.

The most popular formalization of equirecursive types is to introduce an explicit μ-constructor. For example, $\mathsf{list} = \mu\alpha. \oplus\{\ \mathsf{cons} : \exists n{:}\mathsf{int}.\,\alpha, \mathsf{nil} : \mathbf{1}\ \}$ with rules unrolling the type $\mu\alpha.\,A$ to $[(\mu\alpha.\,A)/\alpha]A$. An alternative (see, for example, Balzers and Pfenning 2017 [3]) is to use an explicit definition just as we stated, for example, list and bag, and consider the left-hand side *equal* to the right-hand side in our discourse. In typing, this works without a hitch. When we consider subtyping explicitly, we need to make sure we view inference systems on types as being defined *co-inductively*. Since a co-inductively defined judgment essentially expresses the absence of a counterexample, this is exactly what we need for the operational properties like progress, preservation, or absence of blame. We therefore adopt this view.

Recursive Processes. In addition to recursively defined types, we also need recursively defined processes. We follow the general approach of Toninho et al. [23] for the integration of a (functional) data layer into session-typed communication. A process can be named p, ascribed a type, and be defined as follows.

$$p : \forall n_1{:}\tau_1. \ldots, \forall n_k{:}\tau_k.\{A \leftarrow A_1, \ldots, A_m\}$$
$$x \leftarrow p\, n_1 \ldots n_k \leftarrow y_1, \ldots, y_m = P$$

where we check $(n_1{:}\tau_1, \ldots, n_k{:}\tau_k) \,;\, (y_1{:}A_1, \ldots, y_m{:}A_m) \vdash P :: (x : A)$

We use such process definitions when spawning a new process with the syntax

$$c \leftarrow p\, e_1 \ldots, e_k \leftarrow d_1, \ldots, d_m \,;\, P$$

which we check with the rule

$$\frac{(\Psi \vdash e_i : \tau_i)_{i \in \{1, \ldots, k\}} \quad \Delta' = (d_1{:}A_1, \ldots, d_m{:}A_m) \quad \Psi \,;\, \Delta, c : A \vdash Q :: (d : D)}{\Psi \,;\, \Delta, \Delta' \vdash c \leftarrow p\, e_1 \ldots e_k \leftarrow d_1, \ldots, d_m \,;\, Q :: (d : D)} \; \text{pdef}$$

After evaluating the value arguments, the call consumes the channels d_j (which will not be available to the continuation Q, due to linearity). The continuation Q will then be the (sole) client of c and The new process providing c will execute $[c/x][d_1/y_1] \ldots [d_m/y_m]P$.

One more quick shorthand used in the examples: a tail-call $c \leftarrow p\, \overline{e} \leftarrow \overline{d}$ in the definition of a process that provides along c is expanded into $c' \leftarrow p\, \overline{e} \leftarrow \overline{d}$; $c \leftarrow c'$ for a fresh c'. Depending on how forwarding is implemented, however, it may be much more efficient [13].

Stopping Computation. Finally, in order to be able to successfully monitor computation, we need the capability to stop the computation. We add an abort l construct that aborts on a particular label. We also add assert blocks to check conditions on observable values. The semantics are given below and the typing is in Fig. 6.

$$\text{proc}(c, \text{assert}\ l\ \text{True}; Q) \longrightarrow \text{proc}(c, Q) \qquad \text{proc}(c, \text{assert}\ l\ \text{False}; Q) \longrightarrow \text{abort}(l)$$

Progress and preservation were proven for the above system, with the exception of the abort and assert rules, in prior work [18]. The additional proof cases do not change the proof significantly.

3   Contract Examples

In this section, we present monitoring processes that can enforce a variety of contracts. The examples will mainly use lists as defined in the previous section. Our monitors are transparent, that is, they do not change the computation. We accomplish this by making them act as partial identities (described in more detail in Sect. 4). Therefore, any monitor that enforces a contract on a list must peel off each layer of the type one step at a time (by sending or receiving over the channel as dictated by the type), perform the required checks on values or labels, and then reconstruct the original type (again, by sending or receiving as appropriate).

Refinement. The simplest kind of monitoring process we can write is one that models a refinement of an integer type; for example, a process that checks whether every element in the list is positive. This is a recursive process that receives the head of the list from channel b, checks whether it is positive (if yes, it continues to the next value, if not it aborts), and then sends the value along to reconstruct the monitored list a. We show three refinement monitors in Fig. 1. The process pos implements the refinement mentioned above.

```
pos : {list ← list}
a ← pos_mon ← b =
  case b of
  | nil ⇒ a.nil ; wait b ; close a
  | cons ⇒ x ← recv b ;
    assert(x > 0)^ρ ;
    a.cons ; send a x ;
    a ← pos_mon ← b; ;
```

```
empty : {list ← list}
a ← empty ← b =
  case b of
  | nil ⇒ wait b ;
    a.nil ; close a
  | cons ⇒ abort^ρ; ;
```

```
nempty : {list ← list}
a ← nempty ← b =
  case b of
  | nil ⇒ abort^ρ
  | cons ⇒ a.cons ;
    x ← recv b ;
    send a x ; a ← b; ;
```

Fig. 1. Refinement examples

Our monitors can also exploit information that is contained in the labels in the external and internal choices. The empty process checks whether the list b is empty and aborts if b sends the label cons. Similarly, the nempty monitor checks whether the list b is not empty and aborts if b sends the label nil. These two monitors can then be used by a process that zips two lists and aborts if they are of different lengths. These two monitors enforce the refinements {nil} ⊆ {nil, cons} and {cons} ⊆ {nil, cons}. We discuss how to generate monitors from refinement types in more detail in Sect. 5.

Monitors with Internal State. We now move beyond refinement contracts, and model contracts that have to maintain some internal state (Fig. 2).

We first present a monitor that checks whether the given list is sorted in ascending order (ascending). The monitor's state consists of a lower bound on the subsequent elements in the list. This value has an option type, which can either be None if no bound has yet been set, or Some b if b is the current bound.

If the list is empty, there is no bound to check, so no contract failure can happen. If the list is nonempty, we check to see if a bound has already been set. If not, we set the bound to be the first received element. If there is already a bound in place, then we check if the received element is greater or equal to the bound. If it is not, then the list must be unsorted, so we abort with a contract

```
                                        match : int → {list ← list}; ;
ascending : option int → {list ← list}; ;    a ← match count ← b =
m ← ascending bound ← n =                    case b of
  case n of                                  | nil ⇒ assert (count = 0)ᵖ ;
  | nil ⇒ m.nil ; wait n ; close m             a.nil ; wait b ; close a
  | cons ⇒ x ← recv n ;                      | cons ⇒ a.cons ; x ← recv b ;
    case bound of                              if (x = 1) then send a x ;
    | None ⇒ m.cons ; send m x ;                 a ← match (count + 1) ← b;
      m ← ascending (Some x) ← n               else if (x = −1)
    | Some a ⇒ assert (x ≥ a)ᵖ ;                 then assert(count > 0)ᵖ ;
      m.cons ; send m x ;                        send a x ;
      m ← ascending (Some x) ← n; ;             a ← match (count−1) ← b ;
                                             else abortᵖ   //invalid input
```

Fig. 2. Monitors using internal state

failure. Note that the output list m is the same as the input list n because every element that we examine is then passed along unchanged to m.

We can use the **ascending** monitor to verify that the output list of a sorting procedure is in sorted order. To take the example one step further, we can verify that the elements in the output list are in fact a permutation of the elements in the input list of the sorting procedure as follows. Using a reasonable hash function, we hash each element as it is sent to the sorting procedure. Our monitor then keeps track of a running total of the sum of the hashes, and as elements are received from the sorting procedure, it computes their hash and subtracts it from the total. After all of the elements are received, we check that the total is 0 – if it is, with high probability, the two lists are permutations of each other. This example is an instance of *result checking*, inspired by Wasserman and Blum [26]. The monitor encoding is straightforward and omitted from the paper.

Our next example **match** validates whether a set of right and left parentheses match. The monitor can use its internal state to push every left parenthesis it sees on its stack and to pop it off when it sees a right parenthesis. For brevity, we model our list of parentheses by marking every left parenthesis with a 1 and right parenthesis with a -1. So the sequence ()(()) would look like $1, -1, 1, -1, -1$. As we can see, this is not a proper sequence of parenthesis because adding all of the integer representations does not yield 0. In a similar vein, we can implement a process that checks that a tree is serialized correctly, which is related to recent work on context-free session types by Thiemann and Vasconcelos [21].

Mapper. Finally, we can also define monitors that check higher-order contracts, such as a contract for a mapping function (Fig. 3). Consider the mapper which takes an integer and doubles it, and a function **map** that applies this mapper to a list of integers to produce a new list of integers. We can see that any integer that the mapper has produced will be strictly larger than the original integer, assuming the original integer is positive. In order to monitor this contract, it makes sense to impose a contract on the mapper itself. This **mapper_mon** process enforces both the precondition, that the original integer is positive, and the

```
mapper_tp : {&{done : 1 ; next : ∀n : int.∃n : int.mapper_tp}}
m ← mapper =
  case m of
  | done ⇒ close m
  | next ⇒ x ← recv m ; send m (2 * x) ; m ← mapper
map : {list ← mapper_tp ; list}
k ← map ← m l =
  case l of
  | nil ⇒ m.done ; k.nil ; wait l ; close k
  | cons ⇒ m' ← mapper_mon ← m;    //run monitor
      x ← recv l ; send m' x ; y ← recv m' ; k.cons ; send k y ; k ← map m' l;;
mapper_mon : {mapper_tp ← mapper_tp}
n ← mapper_mon ← m =
  case n of
  | done ⇒ m.done ; wait m ; close n
  | next ⇒ x ← recv n ; assert(x > 0)^{ρ₁}    //checks precondition
      m.next ; send m x ; y ← recv m ; assert(y > x)^{ρ₂}    //checks postcondition
      send n y ; n ← mapper_mon ← m
```

Fig. 3. Higher-order monitor

postcondition, that the resulting integer is greater than the original. We can now run the monitor on the mapper, in the map process, before applying the mapper to the list l.

4   Monitors as Partial Identity Processes

In the literature on contracts, they are often depicted as guards on values sent to and returned from functions. In our case, they really *are* processes that monitor message-passing communications between processes. For us, a central property of contracts is that a program may be executed with or without contract checking and, unless an alarm is raised, the observable outcome should be the same. This means that contract monitors should be *partial identity processes* passing messages back and forth along channels while testing properties of the messages.

This may seem very limiting at first, but session-typed processes can maintain local state. For example, consider the functional notion of a *dependent contract*, where the contract on the result of a function depends on its input. Here, a function would be implemented by a process to which you send the arguments and which sends back the return value *along the same channel*. Therefore, a monitor can remember any (non-linear) "argument values" and use them to validate the "result value". Similarly, when a list is sent element by element, properties that can be easily checked include constraints on its length, or whether it is in ascending order. Moreover, local state can include additional (private) concurrent processes.

This raises a second question: how can we guarantee that a monitor really is a partial identity? The criterion should be general enough to allow us to naturally express the contracts from a wide range of examples. A key constraint is that *contracts are expressed as session-typed processes*, just like functional contracts should be expressed within the functional language, or object contracts within the object oriented language, etc.

The purpose of this section is to present and prove the correctness of a criterion on session-typed processes that guarantees that they are observationally equivalent to partial identity processes. All the contracts in this paper can be verified to be partial identities under our definition.

4.1 Buffering Values

As a first simple example let's take a process that receives one positive integer n and factors it into two integers p and q that are sent back where $p \leq q$. The part of the specification that is *not* enforced is that if n is not prime, p and q should be proper factors, but we at least enforce that all numbers are positive and $n = p * q$. We are being very particular here, for the purpose of exposition, marking the place where the direction of communication changes with a shift ($\uparrow$). Since a minimal number of shifts can be inferred during elaboration of the syntax [18], we suppress it in most examples.

> factor_t $= \forall n$:int. $\uparrow \exists p$:int. $\exists q$:int. $\mathbf{1}$
> factor_monitor : {factor_t $\leftarrow$ factor_t}
> $c \leftarrow$ factor_monitor $\leftarrow d =$
> $\quad n \leftarrow$ recv c ; assert $(n > 0)^{\rho_1}$; shift $\leftarrow$ recv c ; send $d\,n$; send d shift ;
> $\quad p \leftarrow$ recv d ; assert$(p > 0)^{\rho_2}$; $q \leftarrow$ recv d ; assert$(q > 0)^{\rho_3}$; assert$(p \leq q)^{\rho_4}$;
> $\quad$ assert$(n = p * q)^{\rho_5}$; send $c\,p$; send $c\,q$; $c \leftarrow d$

This is a one-time interaction (the session type factor_t is not recursive), so the monitor terminates. It terminates here by forwarding, but we could equally well have replaced it by its identity-expanded version at type $\mathbf{1}$, which is wait d ; close c.

The contract could be invoked by the provider or by the client. Let's consider how a provider factor might invoke it:

> factor : {factor_t}
> $c \leftarrow$ factor $=$
> $\quad c' \leftarrow$ factor_raw ; $c' \leftarrow$ factor_monitor $\leftarrow c'$; $c \leftarrow c'$

To check that factor_monitor is a partial identity we need to track that p and q are received from the provider, in this order. In general, for any received message, we need to enter it into a message queue q and we need to check that the messages are passed on in the correct order. As a first cut (to be generalized several times), we write for negative types:

$$[q](b : B^-) \; ; \Psi \vdash P :: (a : A^-)$$

which expresses that the two endpoints of the monitor are $a : A^-$ and $b : B^-$ (both negative), and we have already received the messages in q along a. The context Ψ declares types for local variables.

A monitor, at the top level, is defined with

$$mon : \tau_1 \to \cdots \to \tau_n \to \{A \leftarrow A\}$$
$$a \leftarrow mon \; x_1 \ldots x_n \leftarrow b = P$$

where context Ψ declares value variables x. The body P here is type-checked as one of (depending on the polarity of A)

$$[\,](b : A^-) \, ; \, \Psi \vdash P :: (a : A^-) \quad \text{or} \quad (b : A^+) \, ; \, \Psi \vdash P :: [\,](a : A^+)$$

where $\Psi = (x_1{:}\tau_1) \cdots (x_n{:}\tau_n)$. A use such as

$$c \leftarrow mon \; e_1 \ldots e_n \leftarrow c$$

is transformed into

$$c' \leftarrow mon \; e_1 \ldots e_n \leftarrow c \, ; \, c \leftarrow c'$$

for a fresh c' and type-checked accordingly.

In general, queues have the form $q = m_1 \cdots m_n$ with

$$
\begin{array}{llll}
m ::= l_k & \text{labels} & \oplus, \& & \\
\mid \;\; c & \text{channels} & \otimes, \multimap & \mid n \quad \text{value variables} \; \exists, \forall \\
\mid \;\; \text{end} & \text{close} & \mathbf{1} & \mid \text{shift} \quad \text{shifts} \qquad\quad \uparrow, \downarrow
\end{array}
$$

where m_1 is the front of the queue and m_n the back.

When a process P receives a message, we add it to the end of the queue q. We also need to add it to Ψ context, marked as *unrestricted* (non-linear) to remember its type. In our example $\tau = \text{int}$.

$$\frac{[q \cdot n](b : B) \, ; \, \Psi, n{:}\tau \vdash P :: (a : A^-)}{[q](b : B) \, ; \, \Psi \vdash n \leftarrow \text{recv } a \, ; \, P :: (a : \forall n{:}\tau. \, A^-)} \; \forall R$$

Conversely, when we *send* along b the message must be equal to the one at the front of the queue (and therefore it must be a variable). The m is a value variable and remains in the context so it can be reused for later assertion checks. However, it could never be sent again since it has been removed from the queue.

$$\frac{[q](b : [m/n]B) \, ; \, \Psi, m{:}\tau \vdash P :: (a : A)}{[m \cdot q](b : \forall n{:}\tau. \, B) \, ; \, \Psi, m{:}\tau \vdash \text{send } b \; m \, ; \, Q :: (a : A)} \; \forall L$$

All the other send and receive rules for negative types ($\forall$, $\multimap$, $\&$) follow exactly the same pattern. For positive types, a queue must be associated with the channel along which the monitor provides (the succedent of the sequent judgment).

$$(b : B^+) \, ; \, \Psi \vdash Q :: [q](a : A^+)$$

Moreover, when end has been received along b the corresponding process has terminated and the channel is closed, so we generalize the judgment to

$$\omega \, ; \, \Psi \vdash Q :: [q](a : A^+) \qquad \text{with } \omega = \cdot \mid (b : B).$$

The shift messages change the direction of communication. They therefore need to switch between the two judgments and also ensure that the queue has been emptied before we switch direction. Here are the two rules for $\uparrow$, which appears in our simple example:

$$\frac{[q \cdot \mathsf{shift}](b : B^-) \,;\, \Psi \vdash P :: (a : A^+)}{[q](b : B^-) \,;\, \Psi \vdash \mathsf{shift} \leftarrow \mathsf{recv}\ a \,;\, P :: (a : \uparrow A^+)} \ \uparrow R$$

We notice that after receiving a shift, the channel a already changes polarity (we now have to send along it), so we generalize the judgment, allowing the succedent to be either positive or negative. And conversely for the other judgment.

$$[q](b : B^-) \,;\, \Psi \vdash P :: (a : A)$$
$$\omega \,;\, \Psi \vdash Q :: [q](a : A^+) \quad \text{where } \omega = \cdot \mid (b : B)$$

When we *send* the final shift, we initialize a new empty queue. Because the queue is empty the two sides of the monitor must have the same type.

$$\frac{(b : B^+) \,;\, \Psi \vdash Q :: [\,](a : B^+)}{[\mathsf{shift}](b : \uparrow B^+) \,;\, \Psi \vdash \mathsf{send}\ b\ \mathsf{shift} \,;\, Q :: (a : B^+)} \ \uparrow L$$

The rules for forwarding are also straightforward. Both sides need to have the same type, and the queue must be empty. As a consequence, the immediate forward is always a valid monitor at a given type.

$$\frac{}{(b : A^+) \,;\, \Psi \vdash a \leftarrow b :: [\,](a : A^+)} \ \mathsf{id}^+ \qquad \frac{}{[\,](b : A^-) \,;\, \Psi \vdash a \leftarrow b :: (a : A^-)} \ \mathsf{id}^-$$

4.2   Rule Summary

The current rules allow us to communicate *only along the channels a and b that are being monitored*. If we send channels along channels, however, these channels must be recorded in the typing judgment, but we are not allowed to communicate along them directly. On the other hand, if we spawn internal (local) channels, say, as auxiliary data structures, we should be able to interact with them since such interactions are not externally observable. Our judgment thus requires two additional contexts: Δ for channels internal to the monitor, and Γ for externally visible channels that may be sent along the monitored channels. Our full judgments therefore are

$$[q](b : B^-) \,;\, \Psi \,;\, \Gamma \,;\, \Delta \vdash P :: (a : A)$$
$$\omega \,;\, \Psi \,;\, \Gamma \,;\, \Delta \vdash Q :: [q](a : A^+) \quad \text{where } \omega = \cdot \mid (b : B)$$

So far, it is given by the following rules

$$\frac{(\forall \ell \in L) \quad (b : B_\ell) \,;\, \Psi \,;\, \Gamma \,;\, \Delta \vdash Q_\ell :: [q \cdot \ell](a : A^+)}{(b : \oplus\{\ell : B_\ell\}_{\ell \in L}) \,;\, \Psi \,;\, \Gamma \,;\, \Delta \vdash \mathsf{case}\ b\ (\ell \Rightarrow Q_\ell)_{\ell \in L} :: [q](a : A^+)} \ \oplus L$$

$$\frac{\omega \,;\, \Psi \,;\, \Gamma \,;\, \Delta \vdash P :: [q](a : B_k) \quad (k \in L)}{\omega \,;\, \Psi \,;\, \Gamma \,;\, \Delta \vdash a.k \,;\, P :: [k \cdot q](a : \oplus\{\ell : B_\ell\}_{\ell \in L})} \ \oplus R$$

$$\cfrac{(\forall \ell \in L) \quad [q \cdot \ell](b:B) \; ; \; \Psi \; ; \; \Gamma \; ; \; \Delta \vdash P_\ell :: (a:A_\ell)}{[q](b:B) \; ; \; \Psi \; ; \; \Gamma \; ; \; \Delta \vdash \mathsf{case}\ a\ (\ell \Rightarrow P_\ell)_{\ell \in L} :: (a : \&\{\ell : A_\ell\}_{\ell \in L})} \&R$$

$$\cfrac{[q](b:B_k) \; ; \; \Psi \; ; \; \Gamma \; ; \; \Delta \vdash P :: (a:A) \quad (k \in L)}{[k \cdot q](b : \oplus\{\ell : B_\ell\}_{\ell \in L}) \; ; \; \Psi \; ; \; \Gamma \; ; \; \Delta \vdash b.k \; ; \; P :: (a:A)} \&L$$

$$\cfrac{(b:B) \; ; \; \Psi \; ; \; \Gamma, x{:}C \; ; \; \Delta \vdash Q :: [q \cdot x](a:A)}{(b : C \otimes B) \; ; \; \Psi \; ; \; \Gamma \; ; \; \Delta \vdash x \leftarrow \mathsf{recv}\ b \; ; \; Q :: [q](a:A)} \otimes L$$

$$\cfrac{\omega \; ; \; \Psi \; ; \; \Gamma \; ; \; \Delta \vdash P :: [q](a:A)}{\omega \; ; \; \Psi \; ; \; \Gamma, x{:}C \; ; \; \Delta \vdash \mathsf{send}\ a\ x \; ; \; P :: [x \cdot q](a : C \otimes A)} \otimes R$$

$$\cfrac{[q \cdot x](b:B) \; ; \; \Psi \; ; \; \Gamma, x{:}C \; ; \; \Delta \vdash P :: (a:A)}{[q](b:B) \; ; \; \Psi \; ; \; \Gamma \; ; \; \Delta \vdash x \leftarrow \mathsf{recv}\ a \; ; \; P :: (a : C \multimap A)} \multimap R$$

$$\cfrac{[q](b:B) \; ; \; \Psi \; ; \; \Gamma \; ; \; \Delta \vdash Q :: (a:A)}{[x \cdot q](b : C \multimap B) \; ; \; \Psi \; ; \; \Gamma, x{:}C \; ; \; \Delta \vdash \mathsf{send}\ b\ x \; ; \; Q :: (a:A)} \multimap L$$

$$\cfrac{\cdot \; ; \; \Psi \; ; \; \Gamma \; ; \; \Delta \vdash Q :: [q \cdot \mathsf{end}](a:A)}{(b:\mathbf{1}) \; ; \; \Psi \; ; \; \Gamma \; ; \; \Delta \vdash \mathsf{wait}\ b \; ; \; Q :: [q](a:A)} \mathbf{1}L$$

$$\cfrac{}{\cdot \; ; \; \Psi \; ; \; \cdot \; ; \; \cdot \vdash \mathsf{close}\ a :: [\mathsf{end}](a:\mathbf{1})} \mathbf{1}R$$

$$\cfrac{(b:B) \; ; \; \Psi, n{:}\tau \; ; \; \Gamma \; ; \; \Delta \vdash Q :: [q \cdot n](a:A)}{(b : \exists n{:}\tau.\, B) \; ; \; \Psi \; ; \; \Gamma \; ; \; \Delta \vdash n \leftarrow \mathsf{recv}\ b \; ; \; Q :: [q](a:A)} \exists L$$

$$\cfrac{\omega \; ; \; \Psi, m{:}\tau \; ; \; \Gamma \; ; \; \Delta \vdash P :: [q](a : [m/n]A)}{\omega \; ; \; \Psi, m{:}\tau \; ; \; \Gamma \; ; \; \Delta \vdash \mathsf{send}\ a\ m \; ; \; P :: [m \cdot q](a : \exists n{:}\tau.\, A)} \exists R$$

$$\cfrac{[q \cdot n](b:B) \; ; \; \Psi, n{:}\tau \; ; \; \Gamma \; ; \; \Delta \vdash P :: (a : A^-)}{[q](b:B) \; ; \; \Psi \; ; \; \Gamma \; ; \; \Delta \vdash v \leftarrow \mathsf{recv}\ a \; ; \; P :: (a : \forall n{:}\tau.\, A^-)} \forall R$$

$$\cfrac{[q](b : [m/n]B) \; ; \; \Psi, m{:}\tau \; ; \; \Gamma \; ; \; \Delta \vdash P :: (a:A)}{[m \cdot q](b : \forall n{:}\tau.\, B) \; ; \; \Psi, m{:}\tau \; ; \; \Gamma \; ; \; \Delta \vdash \mathsf{send}\ b\ m \; ; \; Q :: (a:A)} \forall L$$

$$\cfrac{(b : B^-) \; ; \; \Psi \; ; \; \Gamma \; ; \; \Delta \vdash Q :: [q \cdot \mathsf{shift}](a : A^+)}{(b : {\downarrow}B^-) \; ; \; \Psi \; ; \; \Gamma \; ; \; \Delta \vdash \mathsf{shift} \leftarrow \mathsf{recv}\ b \; ; \; Q :: [q](a : A^+)} {\downarrow}L$$

$$\cfrac{[\,](b : A^-) \; ; \; \Psi \; ; \; \Gamma \; ; \; \Delta \vdash P :: (a : A^-)}{(b : A^-) \; ; \; \Psi \; ; \; \Gamma \; ; \; \Delta \vdash \mathsf{send}\ a\ \mathsf{shift} \; ; \; P :: [\mathsf{shift}](a : {\downarrow}A^-)} {\downarrow}R$$

$$\cfrac{[q \cdot \mathsf{shift}](b : B^-) \; ; \; \Psi \; ; \; \Gamma \; ; \; \Delta \vdash P :: (a : A^+)}{[q](b : B^-) \; ; \; \Psi \; ; \; \Gamma \; ; \; \Delta \vdash \mathsf{shift} \leftarrow \mathsf{recv}\ a \; ; \; P :: (a : {\uparrow}A^+)} {\uparrow}R$$

$$\cfrac{(b : B^+) \; ; \; \Psi \; ; \; \Gamma \; ; \; \Delta \vdash Q :: [\,](a : B^+)}{[\mathsf{shift}](b : {\uparrow}B^+) \; ; \; \Psi \; ; \; \Gamma \; ; \; \Delta \vdash \mathsf{send}\ b\ \mathsf{shift} \; ; \; Q :: (a : B^+)} {\uparrow}L$$

4.3 Spawning New Processes

The most complex part of checking that a process is a valid monitor involves spawning new processes. In order to be able to spawn and use local (private) processes, we have introduced the (so far unused) context Δ that tracks such channels. We use it here only in the following two rules:

$$\frac{\Psi \;;\; \Delta \vdash P :: (c : C) \quad \omega \;;\; \Psi \;;\; \Gamma \;;\; \Delta', c{:}C \vdash Q :: [q](a : A^+)}{\omega \;;\; \Psi \;;\; \Gamma \;;\; \Delta, \Delta' \vdash (c : C) \leftarrow P \;;\; Q :: [q](a : A^+)} \; \text{cut}_1^+$$

$$\frac{\Psi \;;\; \Delta \vdash P :: (c : C) \quad [q](b : B^-) \;;\; \Psi \;;\; \Gamma \;;\; \Delta', c{:}C \vdash Q :: (a : A)}{[q](b : B^-) \;;\; \Psi \;;\; \Gamma \;;\; \Delta, \Delta' \vdash (c : C) \leftarrow P \;;\; Q :: (a : A)} \; \text{cut}_1^-$$

The second premise (that is, the continuation of the monitor) remains the monitor, while the first premise corresponds to a freshly spawned local progress accessible through channel c. All the ordinary left rules for sending or receiving along channels in Δ are also available for the two monitor validity judgments. By the strong ownership discipline of intuitionistic session types, none of this information can flow out of the monitor.

It is also possible for a single monitor to decompose into two monitors that operate concurrently, in sequence. In that case, the queue q may be split anywhere, as long as the intermediate type has the right polarity. Note that Γ must be chosen to contain all channels in q_2, while Γ' must contain all channels in q_1.

$$\frac{\omega \;;\; \Psi \;;\; \Gamma \;;\; \Delta \vdash P :: [q_2](c : C^+) \quad (c : C^+) \;;\; \Psi \;;\; \Gamma' \;;\; \Delta' \vdash Q :: [q_1](a : A^+)}{\omega \;;\; \Psi \;;\; \Gamma, \Gamma' \;;\; \Delta, \Delta' \vdash c : C^+ \leftarrow P \;;\; Q :: [q_1 \cdot q_2](a : A^+)} \; \text{cut}_2^+$$

Why is this correct? The first messages sent along a will be the messages in q_1. If we receive messages along c in the meantime, they will be first the messages in q_2 (since P is a monitor), followed by any messages that P may have received along b if $\omega = (b : B)$. The second rule is entirely symmetric, with the flow of messages in the opposite direction.

$$\frac{[q_1](b : B^-) \;;\; \Psi \;;\; \Gamma \;;\; \Delta \vdash P :: (c : C^-) \quad [q_2](c : C^-) \;;\; \Psi' \;;\; \Gamma' \;;\; \Delta' \vdash Q :: (a : A)}{[q_1 \cdot q_2](b : B^-) \;;\; \Psi \;;\; \Gamma, \Gamma' \;;\; \Delta, \Delta' \vdash c : C^- \leftarrow P \;;\; Q :: (a : A)} \; \text{cut}_2^-$$

The next two rules allow a monitor to be attached to a channel x that is passed between a and b. The monitored version of x is called x', where x' is chosen fresh. This apparently violates our property that we pass on all messages exactly as received, because here we pass on a monitored version of the original. However, if monitors are partial identities, then the original x and the new x' are indistinguishable (unless a necessary alarm is raised), which will be a tricky part of the correctness proof.

$$\frac{(x : C^+) \;;\; \Psi \;;\; \cdot \;;\; \Delta \vdash P :: [\,](x' : C^+) \quad \omega \;;\; \Psi \;;\; \Gamma, x'{:}C^+ \;;\; \Delta' \vdash Q :: [q_1 \cdot x' \cdot q_2](a : A^+)}{\omega \;;\; \Psi \;;\; \Gamma, x{:}C^+ \;;\; \Delta, \Delta' \vdash x' \leftarrow P \;;\; Q :: [q_1 \cdot x \cdot q_2](a : A^+)} \; \text{cut}_3^{++}$$

$$\frac{[\,](x : C^-) \;;\; \Psi \;;\; \cdot \;;\; \Delta \vdash P :: (x' : C^-) \quad [q_1 \cdot x' \cdot q_2](b : B^-) \;;\; \Psi \;;\; \Gamma, x'{:}C^- \;;\; \Delta' \vdash Q :: (a : A)}{[q_1 \cdot x \cdot q_2](b : B^-) \;;\; \Psi \;;\; \Gamma \;;\; \Delta, \Delta' \vdash x' \leftarrow P \;;\; Q :: (a : A)} \; \text{cut}_3^{--}$$

There are two more versions of these rules, depending on whether the types of x and the monitored types are positive or negative. These rules play a critical role in monitoring higher-order processes, because monitoring $c : A^+ \multimap B^-$ may require us to monitor the continuation $c : B^-$ (already covered) but also communication along the channel $x : A^+$ received along c.

In actual programs, we mostly use cut $x \leftarrow P \; ; \; Q$ in the form $x \leftarrow p \, \overline{e} \leftarrow \overline{d} \; ; \; Q$ where p is a defined process. The rules are completely analogous, except that for those rules that require splitting a context in the conclusion, the arguments $\overline{d}$ will provide the split for us. When a new sub-monitor is invoked in this way, we remember and eventually check that the process p must also be a partial identity process, unless we are already checking it. This has the effect that recursively defined monitors with proper recursive calls are in fact allowed. This is important, because monitors for recursive types usually have a recursive structure. An illustration of this can be seen in pos in Fig. 1.

4.4   Transparency

We need to show that monitors are *transparent*, that is, they are indeed observationally equivalent to partial identity processes. Because of the richness of types and process expressions and the generality of the monitors allowed, the proof has some complexities. First, we define the configuration typing, which consists of just three rules. Because we also send and receive ordinary values, we also need to type (closed) substitutions $\sigma = (v_1/n_1, \ldots, v_k/n_k)$ using the judgment $\sigma :: \Psi$.

$$\frac{}{(\cdot) :: (\cdot)} \qquad \frac{\cdot \vdash v : \tau}{(v/n) :: (n : \tau)} \qquad \frac{\sigma_1 :: \Psi_1 \quad \sigma_2 :: \Psi_2}{(\sigma_1, \sigma_2) :: (\Psi_1, \Psi_2)}$$

For configurations, we use the judgment

$$\Delta \vdash \mathcal{C} :: \Delta'$$

which expresses that process configuration $\mathcal{C}$ *uses* the channels in Δ and *provides* the channels in Δ'. Channels that are neither used nor offered by $\mathcal{C}$ are "passed through". Messages are just a restricted form of processes, so they are typed exactly the same way. We write *pred* for either proc or msg.

$$\frac{}{\Delta \vdash (\cdot) :: \Delta} \qquad \frac{\Delta_0 \vdash \mathcal{C}_1 :: \Delta_1 \quad \Delta_1 \vdash \mathcal{C}_2 :: \Delta_2}{\Delta_0 \vdash \mathcal{C}_1, \mathcal{C}_2 :: \Delta_2}$$

$$\frac{\Psi \, ; \, \Delta \vdash P :: (c : A) \quad \sigma : \Psi}{\Delta', \Delta[\sigma] \vdash pred(c, P[\sigma]) :: (\Delta', c : A[\sigma])} \qquad pred ::= \mathsf{proc} \mid \mathsf{msg}$$

To characterize observational equivalence of processes, we need to first characterize the possible messages and the direction in which they flow: towards the client (channel type is positive) or towards the provider (channel type is negative). We summarize these in the following table. In each case, c is the channel along with the message is transmitted, and c' is the continuation channel.

Message to client of c		Message to provider of c	
$\mathsf{msg}^+(c, c.k \; ; \; c \leftarrow c')$	$(\oplus)$	$\mathsf{msg}^-(c', c.k \; ; \; c' \leftarrow c)$	$(\&)$
$\mathsf{msg}^+(c, \mathsf{send}\ c\ d \; ; \; c \leftarrow c')$	$(\otimes)$	$\mathsf{msg}^-(c', \mathsf{send}\ c\ d \; ; \; c' \leftarrow c)$	$(\multimap)$
$\mathsf{msg}^+(c, \mathsf{close}\ c)$	$(\mathbf{1})$		
$\mathsf{msg}^+(c, \mathsf{send}\ c\ v \; ; \; c \leftarrow c')$	$(\exists)$	$\mathsf{msg}^-(c', \mathsf{send}\ c\ v \; ; \; c' \leftarrow c)$	$(\forall)$
$\mathsf{msg}^+(c, \mathsf{send}\ c\ \mathsf{shift} \; ; \; c \leftarrow c')$	$(\downarrow)$	$\mathsf{msg}^-(c', \mathsf{send}\ c\ \mathsf{shift} \; ; \; c' \leftarrow c)$	$(\uparrow)$

The notion of observational equivalence we need does not observe "nontermination", that is, it only compares messages that are actually received. Since messages can flow in two directions, we need to observe messages that arrive at either end. We therefore do *not* require, as is typical for bisimulation, that if one configuration takes a step, another configuration can also take a step. Instead we say if both configurations send an externally visible message, then the messages must be equivalent.

Supposing $\Gamma \vdash \mathcal{C} : \Delta$ and $\Gamma \vdash \mathcal{D} :: \Delta$, we write $\Gamma \vdash \mathcal{C} \sim \mathcal{D} :: \Delta$ for our notion of observational equivalence. It is the largest relation satisfying that $\Gamma \vdash \mathcal{C} \sim \mathcal{D} : \Delta$ implies

1. If $\Gamma' \vdash \mathsf{msg}^+(c, P) :: \Gamma$ then $\Gamma' \vdash (\mathsf{msg}^+(c, P), \mathcal{C}) \sim (\mathsf{msg}^+(c, P), \mathcal{D}) :: \Delta$.
2. If $\Delta \vdash \mathsf{msg}^-(c, P) :: \Delta'$ then $\Gamma \vdash (\mathcal{C}, \mathsf{msg}^-(c, P)) \sim (\mathcal{D}, \mathsf{msg}^-(c, P)) :: \Delta'$.
3. If $\mathcal{C} = (\mathcal{C}', \mathsf{msg}^+(c, P))$ with $\Gamma \vdash \mathcal{C}' :: \Delta_1'$ and $\Delta_1' \vdash \mathsf{msg}^+(c, P) :: \Delta$
   and $\mathcal{D} = (\mathcal{D}', \mathsf{msg}^+(c, Q))$ with $\Gamma \vdash \mathcal{D}' :: \Delta_2'$ and $\Delta_2' \vdash \mathsf{msg}^+(c, Q) :: \Delta$
   then $\Delta_1' = \Delta_2' = \Delta'$ and $P = Q$ and $\Gamma \vdash \mathcal{C}' \sim \mathcal{D}' :: \Delta'$.
4. If $\mathcal{C} = (\mathsf{msg}^-(c, P), \mathcal{C}')$ with $\Gamma \vdash \mathsf{msg}^-(c, P) :: \Gamma_1'$ and $\Gamma_1' \vdash \mathcal{C}' :: \Delta$
   and $\mathcal{D} = (\mathsf{msg}^-(c, Q), \mathcal{D}')$ with $\Gamma \vdash \mathsf{msg}^-(c, Q) :: \Gamma_2'$ and $\Gamma_2' \vdash \mathcal{D}' :: \Delta$
   then $\Gamma_1' = \Gamma_2' = \Gamma'$ and $P = Q$ and $\Gamma' \vdash \mathcal{C}' \sim \mathcal{D}' :: \Delta$.
5. If $\mathcal{C} \longrightarrow \mathcal{C}'$ then $\Gamma \vdash \mathcal{C}' \sim \mathcal{D} :: \Delta$.
6. If $\mathcal{D} \longrightarrow \mathcal{D}'$ then $\Gamma \vdash \mathcal{C} \sim \mathcal{D}' :: \Delta$.

Clauses (1) and (2) correspond to absorbing a message into a configuration, which may later be received by a process according to clauses (5) and (6).

Clauses (3) and (4) correspond to observing messages, either by a client (clause (3)) or provider (clause (4)).

In clause (3) we take advantage of the property that a new continuation channel in the message P (one that does not appear already in Γ) is always chosen fresh when created, so we can consistently (and silently) rename it in $\mathcal{C}'$, Δ_1', and P (and $\mathcal{D}'$, Δ_2', and Q, respectively). This slight of hand allows us to match up the context and messages exactly. An analogous remark applies to clause (4). A more formal description would match up the contexts and messages modulo two renaming substitution which allow us to leave Γ and Δ fixed.

Clauses (5) and (6) make sense because a transition never changes the interface to a configuration, except when executing a forwarding $\mathsf{proc}(a, a \leftarrow b)$ which substitutes b for a in the remaining configuration. We can absorb this renaming into the renaming substitution. Cut creates a new channel, which remains internal since it is linear and will have one provider and one client within the new configuration. Unfortunately, our notation is already somewhat unwieldy and carrying additional renaming substitutions further obscures matters. We therefore omit them in this presentation.

We now need to define a relation $\sim_M$ such that (a) it satisfies the closure conditions of $\sim$ and is therefore an observational equivalence, and (b) allows us to conclude that monitors satisfying our judgment are partial identities. Unfortunately, the theorem is rather complex, so we will walk the reader through a sequence of generalizations that account for various phenomena.

The $\oplus, \&$ Fragment. For this fragment, we have no value variables, nor are we passing channels. Then the top-level properties we would like to show are

(1^+) If $(y : A^+) ; \cdot ; \cdot \vdash P :: (x : A^+)[\,]$
 then $y : A^+ \vdash \mathsf{proc}(x, x \leftarrow y) \sim_M P :: (x : A^+)$
(1^-) If $[\,](y : A^-) ; \cdot ; \cdot \vdash P :: (x : A^-)$
 then $y : A^- \vdash \mathsf{proc}(x, x \leftarrow y) \sim_M P :: (x : A^-)$

Of course, asserting that $\mathsf{proc}(x, x \leftarrow y) \sim_M P$ will be insufficient, because this relation is not closed under the conditions of observational equivalence. For example, if we add a message along y to both sides, P will change its state once it receives the message, and the queue will record that this message still has to be sent. To generalize this, we need to define the queue that corresponds to a sequence of messages. First, a single message:

Message to client of c			Message to provider of c		
$\langle\!\langle \mathsf{msg}^+(c, c.k \; ; c \leftarrow c')\rangle\!\rangle$	$= k$	$(\oplus)$	$\langle\!\langle \mathsf{msg}^-(c', c.k \; ; c' \leftarrow c)\rangle\!\rangle$	$= k$	$(\&)$
$\langle\!\langle \mathsf{msg}^+(c, \mathsf{send}\; c\, d \; ; c \leftarrow c')\rangle\!\rangle$	$= d$	$(\otimes)$	$\langle\!\langle \mathsf{msg}^-(c', \mathsf{send}\; c\, d \; ; c' \leftarrow c)\rangle\!\rangle$	$= d$	$(\multimap)$
$\langle\!\langle \mathsf{msg}^+(c, \mathsf{close}\; c)\rangle\!\rangle$	$= \mathsf{end}$	(1)			
$\langle\!\langle \mathsf{msg}^+(c, \mathsf{send}\; c\, v \; ; c \leftarrow c')\rangle\!\rangle$	$= v$	$(\exists)$	$\langle\!\langle \mathsf{msg}^-(c', \mathsf{send}\; c\, v \; ; c' \leftarrow c)\rangle\!\rangle$	$= v$	$(\forall)$
$\langle\!\langle \mathsf{msg}^+(c, \mathsf{send}\; c\, \mathsf{shift} \; ; c \leftarrow c')\rangle\!\rangle = \mathsf{shift}$		$(\downarrow)$	$\langle\!\langle \mathsf{msg}^-(c', \mathsf{send}\; c\, \mathsf{shift} \; ; c' \leftarrow c)\rangle\!\rangle = \mathsf{shift}$		$(\uparrow)$

We extend this to message sequences with $\langle\!\langle\;\rangle\!\rangle = (\cdot)$ and $\langle\!\langle \mathcal{E}_1, \mathcal{E}_2 \rangle\!\rangle = \langle\!\langle \mathcal{E}_1 \rangle\!\rangle \cdot \langle\!\langle \mathcal{E}_2 \rangle\!\rangle$, provided $\Delta_0 \vdash \mathcal{E}_1 : \Delta_1$ and $\Delta_1 \vdash \mathcal{E}_2 :: \Delta_2$.

Then we build into the relation that sequences of messages correspond to the queue.

(2^+) If $(y{:}B^+) ; \cdot ; \cdot ; \cdot \vdash P :: (x{:}A^+)[\langle\!\langle \mathcal{E} \rangle\!\rangle]$ then $y : B^+ \vdash \mathcal{E} \sim_M \mathsf{proc}(x, P) ::$
 $(x : A^+)$.
(2^-) If $[\langle\!\langle \mathcal{E} \rangle\!\rangle](y{:}B^-) \cdot \; ; \cdot \; ; \cdot \vdash P :: (x{:}A^-)$ then $y{:}B^- \vdash \mathcal{E} \sim_M \mathsf{proc}(x, P) ::$
 $(x{:}A^-)$.

When we add shifts the two propositions become mutually dependent, but otherwise they remain the same since the definition of $\langle\!\langle \mathcal{E} \rangle\!\rangle$ is already general enough. But we need to generalize the type on the opposite side of queue to be either positive or negative, because it switches polarity after a shift has been received. Similarly, the channel might terminate when receiving 1, so we also need to allow ω, which is either empty or of the form $y : B$.

(3^+) If $\omega ; \cdot ; \cdot ; \cdot \vdash P :: (x{:}A^+)[\langle\!\langle \mathcal{E} \rangle\!\rangle]$ then $\omega \vdash \mathcal{E} \sim_M \mathsf{proc}(x, P) :: (x{:}A^+)$.
(3^-) If $[\langle\!\langle \mathcal{E} \rangle\!\rangle](y{:}B^-) ; \cdot ; \cdot ; \cdot \vdash P :: (x{:}A)$ then $y{:}B^- \vdash \mathcal{E} \sim_M \mathsf{proc}(x, P) ::$
 $(x{:}xA)$.

Next, we can permit local state in the monitor (rules cut_1^+ and cut_1^-). The fact that neither of the two critical endpoints y and x, nor any (non-local) channel,s can appear in the typing of the local process is key. That local process will evolve to a local configuration, but its interface will not change and it cannot access externally visible channels. So we generalize to allow a configuration $\mathcal{D}$ that does not use any channels, and any channels it offers are used by P.

(4^+) If ω ; $\cdot$; $\cdot$; $\Delta \vdash P :: [\langle\!\langle\mathcal{E}\rangle\!\rangle](x : A^+)$ and $\cdot \vdash \mathcal{D} :: \Delta$ then $\omega \vdash \mathcal{E} \sim_M$ $\mathcal{D}, \text{proc}(x, P) :: [q](x : A^+)$.

(4^-) If $[\langle\!\langle\mathcal{E}\rangle\!\rangle](y : B^-)$; $\cdot$; $\cdot$; $\Delta \vdash P :: (x : A)$ and $\cdot \vdash \mathcal{D} :: \Delta$ then $\Gamma, y : B^- \vdash$ $\mathcal{E} \sim_M \mathcal{D}, \text{proc}(x, P) :: (x : A)$.

Next, we can allow value variables necessitated by the universal and existential quantifiers. Since they are potentially dependent, we need to apply the closing substitution σ to a number of components in our relation.

(5^+) If ω ; Ψ ; $\cdot$; $\Delta \vdash P :: [q](x : A^+)$ and $\sigma : \Psi$ and $q[\sigma] = \langle\!\langle\mathcal{E}\rangle\!\rangle$ and $\cdot \vdash \mathcal{D} :: \Delta[\sigma]$ then $\omega[\sigma] \vdash \mathcal{E} \sim_M \mathcal{D}, \text{proc}(x, P[\sigma]) :: (x : A^+[\sigma])$.

(5^-) If $[q](y : B^-)$; Ψ ; $\cdot$; $\Delta \vdash P :: (x : A)$ and $\sigma : \Psi$ and $q[\sigma] = \mathcal{E}$ and $\cdot \vdash \mathcal{D} :: \Delta[\sigma]$ then $y : B^-[\sigma] \vdash \mathcal{E} \sim_M \mathcal{D}, \text{proc}(x, P[\sigma]) :: (x : A[\sigma])$.

Breaking up the queue by spawning a sequence of monitors (rule cut_2^+ and cut_2^-) just comes down to the compositionality of the partial identity property. This is a new and separate way that two configurations might be in the $\sim_M$ relation, rather than a replacement of a previous definition.

(6) If $\omega \vdash \mathcal{E}_1 \sim_M \mathcal{D}_1 :: (z : C)$ and $(z : C) \vdash \mathcal{E}_2 \sim_M \mathcal{D}_2 :: (x : A)$ then $\omega \vdash (\mathcal{E}_1, \mathcal{E}_2) \sim_M (\mathcal{D}_1, \mathcal{D}_2) :: (x : A)$.

At this point, the only types that have not yet accounted for are $\otimes$ and $\multimap$. If these channels were only "passed through" (without the four cut3 rules), this would be rather straightforward. However, for higher-order channel-passing programs, a monitor must be able to spawn a monitor on a channel that it receives before sending on the monitored version. First, we generalize properties (5) to allow the context Γ of channels that may occur in the queue q and the process P, but that P may not interact with.

(7^+) If ω ; Ψ ; Γ ; $\Delta \vdash P :: [q](x : A^+)$ and $\sigma : \Psi$ and $q[\sigma] = \langle\!\langle\mathcal{E}\rangle\!\rangle$ and $\cdot \vdash \mathcal{D} :: \Delta[\sigma]$ then $\Gamma[\sigma], \omega[\sigma] \vdash \mathcal{E} \sim_M \mathcal{D}, \text{proc}(x, P[\sigma]) :: (x : A^+[\sigma])$.

(7^-) If $[q](y : B^-)$; Ψ ; Γ ; $\Delta \vdash P :: (x : A)$ and $\sigma : \Psi$ and $q[\sigma] = \mathcal{E}$ and $\cdot \vdash \mathcal{D} :: \Delta[\sigma]$ then $\Gamma[\sigma], y : B^-[\sigma] \vdash \mathcal{E} \sim_M \mathcal{D}, \text{proc}(x, P[\sigma]) :: (x : A[\sigma])$.

In addition we need to generalize property (6) into (8) and (9) to allow multiple monitors to run concurrently in a configuration.

(8) If $\Gamma \vdash \mathcal{E} \sim_M \mathcal{D} :: \Delta$ then $(\Gamma', \Gamma) \vdash \mathcal{E} \sim_M \mathcal{D} :: (\Gamma', \Delta)$.

(9) If $\Gamma_1 \vdash \mathcal{E}_1 \sim_M \mathcal{D}_1 :: \Gamma_2$ and $\Gamma_2 \vdash \mathcal{E}_2 \sim_M \mathcal{D}_2 :: \Gamma_3$ then $\Gamma_1 \vdash (\mathcal{E}_1, \mathcal{E}_2) \sim_M$ $(\mathcal{D}_1, \mathcal{D}_2) :: \Gamma_3$.

At this point we can state the main theorem regarding monitors.

Theorem 1. *If* $\Gamma \vdash \mathcal{E} \sim_M \mathcal{D} :: \Delta$ *according to properties* $(7^+), (7^-), (8), and (9)$ *then* $\Gamma \vdash \mathcal{E} \sim \mathcal{D} :: \Delta$.

Proof. By closure under conditions 1–6 in the definition of $\sim$.

By applying it as in equations (1^+) and (1^-), generalized to include value variables as in (5^+) and (5^-) we obtain:

Corollary 1. *If* $[\,](b : A^-) ; \Psi \vdash P :: (a : A^-)$ *or* $(b : A^+) ; \Psi \vdash P :: [\,](a : A^+)$ *then* P *is a partial identity process.*

5   Refinements as Contracts

In this section we show how to check refinement types dynamically using our contracts. We encode refinements as type casts, which allows processes to remain well-typed with respect to the non-refinement type system (Sect. 2). These casts are translated at run time to monitors that validate whether the cast expresses an appropriate refinement. If so, the monitors behave as identity processes; otherwise, they raise an alarm and abort. For refinement contracts, we can prove a safety theorem, analogous to the classic "Well-typed Programs Can't be Blamed" [25], stating that if a monitor enforces a contract that casts from type A to type B, where A is a subtype of B, then this monitor will never raise an alarm.

5.1   Syntax and Typing Rules

We first augment messages and processes to include casts as follows. We write $\langle A \Leftarrow B \rangle^\rho$ to denote a cast from type B to type A, where ρ is a unique label for the cast. The cast for values is written as $(\langle \tau \Leftarrow \tau' \rangle^\rho)$. Here, the types τ' and τ are refinement types of the form $\{n{:}t \mid b\}$, where b is a boolean expression that expresses simple properties of the value n.

$$P ::= \cdots \mid x \leftarrow \langle \tau \Leftarrow \tau' \rangle^\rho \, v \; ; \, Q \mid a{:}A \leftarrow \langle A \Leftarrow B \rangle^\rho \, b$$

Adding casts to forwarding is expressive enough to encode a more general cast $\langle A \Leftarrow B \rangle^\rho P$. For instance, the process $x{:}A \leftarrow \langle A \Leftarrow B \rangle^\rho P \; ; \, Q_x$ can be encoded as: $y{:}B \leftarrow P; x{:}A \leftarrow \langle A \Leftarrow B \rangle^\rho \, y \; ; \, Q_x$.

One of the additional rules to type casts is shown below (both rules can be found in Fig. 6). We only allow casts between two types that are compatible with each other (written $A \sim B$), which is co-inductively defined based on the structure of the types (the full definition is omitted from the paper).

$$\frac{A \sim B}{\Psi \, ; \, b : B \vdash a \leftarrow \langle A \Leftarrow B \rangle^\rho \, b :: (a : A)} \; \text{id\_cast}$$

5.2   Translation to Monitors

At run time, casts are translated into monitoring processes. A cast $a \leftarrow \langle A \Leftarrow B \rangle^\rho \, b$ is implemented as a monitor. This monitor ensures that the process that offers a service on channel b behaves according to the prescribed type A. Because of the typing rules, we are assured that channel b must adhere to the type B.

Figure 4 is a summary of all the translation rules, except recursive types. The translation is of the form: $[\![\langle A \Leftarrow B \rangle^\rho]\!]_{a,b} = P$, where A, B are types; the channels a and b are the offering channel and monitoring channel (respectively) for the resulting monitoring process P; and ρ is a label of the monitor (i.e., the contract).

Note that this differs from blame labels for high-order functions, where the monitor carries two labels, one for the argument, and one for the body of the function. Here, the communication between processes is bi-directional. Though the blame is always triggered by processes sending messages to the monitor, our contracts may depend on a set of the values received so far, so it does not make sense to blame one party. Further, in the case of forwarding, the processes at either end of the channel are behaving according to the types (contracts) assigned to them, but the cast may forcefully connect two processes that have incompatible types. In this case, it is unfair to blame either one of the processes. Instead, we raise an alarm of the label of the failed contract.

The translation is defined inductively over the structure of the types. The tensor rule generates a process that first receives a channel (x) from the channel being monitored (b). It then spawns a new monitor (denoted by the @monitor keyword) to monitor channel x, making sure that it behaves as type A_1, and passes the new monitor's offering channel y to channel a. Finally, the monitor continues to monitor b to make sure that it behaves as type A_2. The lolli rule is similar to the tensor rule, except that the monitor first receives a channel from its offering channel. Similar to the higher-order function case, the argument position is contravariant, so the newly spawned monitor checks that the received channel behaves as type B_1. The exists rule generates a process that first receives a value from the channel b, then checks the boolean condition e to validate the contract. The forall rule is similar, except the argument position is contravariant, so the boolean expression e' is checked on the offering channel a. The with rule generates a process that checks that all of the external choices promised by the type $\&\{\ell : A_\ell\}_{\ell \in I}$ are offered by the process being monitored. If a label in the set I is not implemented, then the monitor aborts with the label ρ. The plus rule requires that, for internal choices, the monitor checks that the monitored process only offers choices within the labels in the set $\oplus\{\ell : A_\ell\}_{\ell \in I}$.

For ease of explanation, we omit details for translating casts involving recursive types. Briefly, these casts are translated into recursive processes. For each pair of compatible recursive types A and B, we generate a unique monitor name f and record its type $f : \{A \leftarrow B\}$ in a context Ψ. The translation algorithm needs to take additional arguments, including Ψ to generate and invoke the appropriate recursive process when needed. For instance, when generating the monitor process for $f : \{\mathsf{list} \leftarrow \mathsf{list}\}$, we follow the rule for translating internal

$$\frac{}{[\![\langle 1 \Leftarrow 1 \rangle^\rho]\!]_{a,b} = \text{wait } b; \text{close } a} \; \text{one}$$

$$\frac{}{\begin{array}{l}[\![\langle A_1 \multimap A_2 \Leftarrow B_1 \multimap B_2 \rangle^\rho]\!]_{a,b} = \\ x \leftarrow \text{recv } a; \\ @\text{monitor } y \leftarrow [\![\langle B_1 \Leftarrow A_1 \rangle^\rho]\!]_{y,x} \leftarrow x \\ \text{send } b \; y; \\ [\![\langle A_2 \Leftarrow B_2 \rangle^\rho]\!]_{a,b}\end{array}} \multimap \qquad \frac{}{\begin{array}{l}[\![\langle A_1 \otimes A_2 \Leftarrow B_1 \otimes B_2 \rangle^\rho]\!]_{a,b} = \\ x \leftarrow \text{recv } b; \\ @\text{monitor } y \leftarrow [\![\langle A_1 \Leftarrow B_1 \rangle^\rho]\!]_{y,x} \leftarrow x \\ \text{send } a \; y; \\ [\![\langle A_2 \Leftarrow B_2 \rangle^\rho]\!]_{a,b}\end{array}} \otimes$$

$$\frac{}{\begin{array}{l}[\![\langle \forall\{n : \tau \mid e\}. A \Leftarrow \forall\{n : \tau' \mid e'\}. B \rangle^\rho]\!]_{a,b} = x \leftarrow \text{recv } a; \\ \qquad\qquad\qquad\qquad \text{assert } \rho \, e'(x) \, (\text{send } b \; x; [\![\langle A \Leftarrow B \rangle^\rho]\!]_{a,b})\end{array}} \forall$$

$$\frac{}{\begin{array}{l}[\![\langle \exists\{n : \tau \mid e\}. A \Leftarrow \exists\{n : \tau' \mid e'\}. B \rangle^\rho]\!]_{a,b} = x \leftarrow \text{recv } b; \\ \qquad\qquad\qquad\qquad \text{assert } \rho \, e(x) \, (\text{send } a \; x; [\![\langle A \Leftarrow B \rangle^\rho]\!]_{a,b})\end{array}} \exists$$

$$\frac{\forall \ell, \ell \in I \cap J, \; a.\ell \; ; [\![\langle A_\ell \Leftarrow B_\ell \rangle^\rho]\!]_{a,b} = Q_\ell \quad \forall \ell, \ell \in J \wedge \ell \notin I, \; Q_\ell = \text{abort } \rho}{[\![\langle \oplus\{\ell : A_\ell\}_{\ell \in I} \Leftarrow \oplus\{\ell : B_\ell\}_{\ell \in J} \rangle^\rho]\!]_{a,b} = \text{case } b \; (\ell \Rightarrow Q_\ell)_{\ell \in I}} \oplus$$

$$\frac{\forall \ell, \ell \in I \cap J, \; b.\ell \; ; [\![\langle A_\ell \Leftarrow B_\ell \rangle^\rho]\!]_{a,b} = Q_\ell \quad \forall \ell, \ell \in I \wedge \ell \notin J, \; Q_\ell = \text{abort } \rho}{[\![\langle \&\{\ell : A_\ell\}_{\ell \in I} \Leftarrow \&\{\ell : B_\ell\}_{\ell \in J} \rangle^\rho]\!]_{a,b} = \text{case } a \; (\ell \Rightarrow Q_\ell)_{\ell \in I}} \&$$

$$\frac{}{\begin{array}{l}[\![\langle \uparrow A \Leftarrow \uparrow B \rangle^\rho]\!]_{a,b} = \\ \text{shift} \leftarrow \text{recv } b; \\ \text{send } a \; \text{shift} \; ; [\![\langle A \Leftarrow B \rangle^\rho]\!]_{a,b}\end{array}} \uparrow \qquad \frac{}{\begin{array}{l}[\![\langle \downarrow A \Leftarrow \downarrow B \rangle^\rho]\!]_{a,b} = \\ \text{shift} \leftarrow \text{recv } a; \\ \text{send } b \; \text{shift} \; ; [\![\langle A \Leftarrow B \rangle^\rho]\!]_{a,b}\end{array}} \downarrow$$

Fig. 4. Cast translation

choices. For $[\![\langle \text{list} \Leftarrow \text{list} \rangle^\rho]\!]_{y,x}$ we apply the cons case in the translation to get $@\text{monitor } y \leftarrow f \leftarrow x$.

5.3   Metatheory

We prove two formal properties of cast-based monitors: safety and transparency.

Because of the expressiveness of our contracts, a general safety (or blame) theorem is difficult to achieve. However, for cast-based contracts, we can prove that a cast which enforces a subtyping relation, and the corresponding monitor, will not raise an alarm. We first define our subtyping relation in Fig. 5. In addition to the subtyping between refinement types, we also include label subtyping for our session types. A process that offers more external choices can always be used as a process that offers fewer external choices. Similarly, a process that offers fewer internal choices can always be used as a process that offers more internal choices (e.g., non-empty list can be used as a list). The subtyping rules for internal and external choices are drawn from work by Acay and Pfenning [1].

$$\frac{}{1 \leq 1} \, 1 \qquad \frac{A \leq A' \quad B \leq B'}{A \otimes B \leq A' \otimes B'} \, \otimes \qquad \frac{A' \leq A \quad B \leq B'}{A \multimap B \leq A' \multimap B'} \, \multimap$$

$$\frac{A_k \leq A'_k \text{ for } k \in J \quad J \subseteq I}{\oplus\{lab_k : A_k\}_{k \in J} \leq \oplus\{lab_k : A'_k\}_{k \in I}} \, \oplus \qquad \frac{A_k \leq A'_k \text{ for } k \in J \quad I \subseteq J}{\&\{lab_k : A_k\}_{k \in J} \leq \&\{lab_k : A'_k\}_{k \in I}} \, \&$$

$$\frac{A \leq B}{\downarrow A \leq \downarrow B} \, \downarrow \qquad \frac{A \leq B}{\uparrow A \leq \uparrow B} \, \uparrow \qquad \frac{A \leq B \quad \tau_1 \leq \tau_2}{\exists n : \tau_1.A \leq \exists n : \tau_2.B} \, \exists \qquad \frac{A \leq B \quad \tau_2 \leq \tau_1}{\forall n : \tau_1.A \leq \forall n : \tau_2.B} \, \forall$$

$$\frac{\mathsf{def}(A) \leq \mathsf{def}(B)}{A \leq B} \, \mathsf{def} \qquad \frac{\forall v{:}\tau, [v/x]b_1 \mapsto^* \mathsf{true} \text{ implies } [v/x]b_2 \mapsto^* \mathsf{true}}{\{x{:}\tau \mid b_1\} \leq \{x{:}\tau \mid b_2\}} \, \mathsf{refine}$$

Fig. 5. Subtyping

For recursive types, we directly examine their definitions. Because of these recursive types, our subtyping rules are co-inductively defined.

We prove a safety theorem (i.e., well-typed casts do not raise alarms) via the standard preservation theorem. The key is to show that the monitor process generated from the translation algorithm in Fig. 4 is well-typed under a typing relation which guarantees that no abort state can be reached. We refer to the type system presented thus far in the paper as T, where monitors that may evaluate to abort can be typed. We define a stronger type system S which consists of the rules in T with the exception of the abort rule and we replace the assert rule with the assert_strong rule. The new rule for assert, which semantically verifies that the condition b is true using the fact that the refinements are stored in the context Ψ, is shown below. The two type systems are summarized in Fig. 6.

Theorem 2 (Monitors are well-typed). *Let Ψ be the context containing the type bindings of all recursive processes.*

1. $\Psi \, ; b : B \vdash_T [\![\langle A \Leftarrow B \rangle^\rho]\!]^\Psi_{a,b} :: (a : A)$.
2. *If $B \leq A$, then $\Psi \, ; b : B \vdash_S [\![\langle A \Leftarrow B \rangle^\rho]\!]^\Psi_{a,b} :: (a : A)$.*

Proof. The proof is by induction over the monitor translation rules. For 2, we need to use the sub-typing relation to show that (1) for the internal and external choice cases, no branches that include abort are generated; and (2) for the forall and exists cases, the assert never fails (i.e., the assert_strong rule applies). □

As a corollary, we can show that when executing in a well-typed context, a monitor process translated from a well-typed cast will never raise an alarm.

Corollary 2 (Well-typed casts cannot raise alarms). $\vdash \mathcal{C} :: b : B$ *and* $B \leq A$ *implies* $\mathcal{C}, \mathsf{proc}(a, [\![\langle A \Leftarrow B \rangle^\rho]\!]_{a,b}) \not\longmapsto^* \mathsf{abort}(\rho)$.

Finally, we prove that monitors translated from casts are partial identify processes.

Both System T and S

$$\frac{}{\Psi \;;\; b : A \vdash a \leftarrow b :: (a : A)} \; id \qquad \frac{\Psi \;;\; \Delta \vdash P :: (x : A) \quad x : A, \Delta' \vdash Q :: (c : C)}{\Psi \;;\; \Delta, \Delta' \vdash x{:}A \leftarrow P \;;\; Q :: (c : C)} \; cut$$

$$\frac{\Psi \;;\; \Delta \vdash P :: (c : A^+)}{\Psi \;;\; \Delta \vdash \text{shift} \leftarrow \text{recv } c \;;\; P :: (c : \uparrow A^+)} \; \uparrow R \qquad \frac{\Psi \;;\; \Delta, c : A^+ \vdash Q :: (d : D)}{\Psi \;;\; \Delta, c : \uparrow A^+ \vdash \text{send } c \text{ shift} \;;\; Q :: (d : D)} \; \uparrow L$$

$$\frac{\Psi \;;\; \Delta \vdash P :: (c : A^-)}{\Psi \;;\; \Delta \vdash \text{send } c \text{ shift} \;;\; P :: (c : \downarrow A^-)} \; \downarrow R \qquad \frac{\Psi \;;\; \Delta, c : A^- \vdash Q :: (d : D)}{\Psi \;;\; \Delta, c : \downarrow A^- \vdash \text{shift} \leftarrow \text{recv } c \;;\; Q :: (d : D)} \; \downarrow L$$

$$\frac{}{\cdot \vdash \text{close } c :: (c : \mathbf{1})} \; 1R \qquad \frac{\Psi ; \Delta \vdash Q :: (d : D)}{\Psi; \Delta, c : \mathbf{1} \vdash \text{wait } c \;;\; Q :: (d : D)} \; 1L$$

$$\frac{\Psi \;;\; \Delta \vdash P :: (c : B)}{\Psi \;;\; \Delta, a : A \vdash \text{send } c \; a \;;\; P :: (c : A \otimes B)} \; \otimes R \qquad \frac{\Psi; \Delta, x : A, c : B \vdash Q :: (d : D)}{\Psi; \Delta, c : A \otimes B \vdash x \leftarrow \text{recv } c \;;\; Q :: (d : D)} \; \otimes L$$

$$\frac{\Psi; \Delta, x : A \vdash P :: (c : B)}{\Psi; \Delta \vdash x \leftarrow \text{recv } c \;;\; P :: (c : A \multimap B)} \; \multimap R \qquad \frac{\Psi \;;\; \Delta, c : B \vdash Q :: (d : D)}{\Psi \;;\; \Delta, a : A, c : A \multimap B \vdash \text{send } c \; a \;;\; Q :: (d : D)} \; \multimap L$$

$$\frac{\Psi; \Delta \vdash P_\ell :: (c : A_\ell) \quad \text{for every } \ell \in L}{\Psi; \Delta \vdash \text{case } c \; (\ell \Rightarrow P_\ell)_{\ell \in L} :: (c : \&\{\ell : A_\ell\}_{\ell \in L})} \; \&R \qquad \frac{k \in L \quad \Psi; \Delta, c : A_k \vdash Q :: (d : D)}{\Psi; \Delta, c : \&\{\ell : A_\ell\}_{\ell \in L} \vdash c.k \;;\; Q :: (d : D)} \; \&L$$

$$\frac{k \in L \quad \Psi; \Delta \vdash P :: (c : A_k)}{\Psi; \Delta \vdash c.k \;;\; P :: (c : \oplus\{\ell : A_\ell\}_{\ell \in L})} \; \oplus R \qquad \frac{\Psi; \Delta, c : A_\ell \vdash Q_\ell :: (d : D) \quad \text{for every } \ell \in L}{\Psi; \Delta, c : \oplus\{\ell : A_\ell\}_{\ell \in L} \vdash \text{case } c \; (\ell \Rightarrow Q_\ell)_{\ell \in L} :: (d : D)} \; \oplus L$$

$$\frac{\Psi \vdash v : \tau \quad \Psi; \Delta \vdash P :: (c : [v/n]A)}{\Psi \;;\; \Delta \vdash \text{send } c \, v \;;\; P :: (c : \exists n{:}\tau. \, A)} \; \exists R \qquad \frac{\Psi, n{:}\tau \;;\; \Delta, c : A \vdash Q :: (d : D)}{\Psi \;;\; \Delta, c : \exists n{:}\tau. \, A \vdash n \leftarrow \text{recv } c \;;\; Q :: (d : D)} \; \exists L$$

$$\frac{\Psi, n{:}\tau \;;\; \Delta \vdash P :: (c : A)}{\Psi \;;\; \Delta \vdash n \leftarrow \text{recv } c \;;\; P :: (c : \forall n{:}\tau. A)} \; \forall R \qquad \frac{\Psi \vdash v : \tau \quad \Psi; \Delta, c : [v/n]A \vdash Q :: (d : D)}{\Psi \;;\; \Delta, c : \forall n{:}\tau. A \vdash \text{send } c \, v \;;\; Q :: (d : D)} \; \forall L$$

$$\frac{\Psi \vdash v : \tau' \quad \Psi, x : \tau \;;\; \Delta \vdash Q :: (c : C) \quad \tau \sim \tau'}{\Psi \;;\; \Delta \vdash x \leftarrow \langle \tau \Leftarrow \tau' \rangle^\rho \, v \;;\; Q :: (c : C)} \; \text{val\_cast} \qquad \frac{A \sim B}{\Psi \;;\; b : B \vdash a \leftarrow \langle A \Leftarrow B \rangle^\rho \, b :: (a : A)} \; \text{id\_cast}$$

System T only

$$\frac{\Psi \vdash b : \text{bool} \quad \Psi \;;\; \Delta \vdash Q :: (x : A)}{\Psi \;;\; \Delta \vdash \text{assert } \rho \; b; Q :: (x : A)} \; \text{assert} \qquad \frac{}{\Psi \;;\; \Delta \vdash \text{abort } \rho :: (x : A)} \; \text{abort}$$

System S only

$$\frac{\Psi \Vdash b \text{ true} \quad \Psi \;;\; \Delta \vdash Q :: (x : A)}{\Psi \;;\; \Delta \vdash \text{assert } \rho \; b; Q :: (x : A)} \; \text{assert\_strong}$$

Fig. 6. Typing process expressions

Theorem 3 (Casts are transparent).
$b : B \vdash \text{proc}(b, a \leftarrow b) \sim \text{proc}(a, [\![\langle A \Leftarrow B \rangle^\rho]\!]_{a,b}) :: (a : A)$.

Proof. We just need to show that the translated process passes the partial identity checks. We can show this by induction over the translation rules and by applying the rules in Sect. 4. We note that rules in Sect. 4 only consider identical types; however, our casts only cast between two compatible types. Therefore, we can lift A and B to their super types (i.e., insert abort cases for mismatched labels), and then apply the checking rules. This does not change the semantics of the monitors.

6   Related Work

There is a rich body of work on higher-order contracts and the correctness of blame assignments in the context of the lambda calculus [2,7,8,10,16,24,25]. The contracts in these papers are mostly based on refinement or dependent types. Our contracts are more expressive than the above, and can encode refinement-based contracts. While our monitors are similar to reference monitors (such as those described by Schneider [19]), they have a few features that are not inherent to reference monitors such as the fact that our monitors are written in the target language. Our monitors are also able to monitor contracts in a higher-order setting by spawning a separate monitor for the sent/received channel.

Disney et al.'s [9] work, which investigates behavioral contracts that enforce temporal properties for modules, is closely related to our work. Our contracts (i.e., session types) also enforce temporal properties; the session types specify the order in which messages are sent and received by the processes. Our contracts can also make use of internal state, as those of Disney et al, but our system is concurrent, while their system does not consider concurrency.

Recently, gradual typing for two-party session-type systems has been developed [14,20]. Even though this formalism is different from our contracts, the way untyped processes are gradually typed at run time resembles how we monitor type casts. Because of dynamic session types, their system has to keep track of the linear use of channels, which is not needed for our monitors.

Most recently, Melgratti and Padovani have developed chaperone contracts for higher-order session types [17]. Their work is based on a classic interpretation of session types, instead of an intuitionistic one like ours, which means that they do not handle spawning or forwarding processes. While their contracts also inspect messages passed between processes, unlike ours, they cannot model contracts which rely on the monitor making use of internal state (e.g., the parenthesis matching). They proved a blame theorem relying on the notion of locally correct modules, which is a semantic categorization of whether a module satisfies the contract. We did not prove a general blame theorem; instead, we prove a somewhat standard safety theorem for cast-based contracts.

The Whip system [27] addresses a similar problem as our prior work [15], but does not use session types. They use a dependent type system to implement a contract monitoring system that can connect services written in different languages. Their system is also higher order, and allows processes that are monitored by Whip to interact with unmonitored processes. While Whip can express dependent contacts, Whip cannot handle stateful contracts. Another distinguishing feature of our monitors is that they are partial identity processes encoded in the same language as the processes to be monitored.

7 Conclusion

We have presented a novel approach for contract-checking for concurrent processes. Our model uses partial identity monitors which are written in the same language as the original processes and execute transparently. We define what it means to be a partial identity monitor and prove our characterization correct. We provide multiple examples of contracts we can monitor including ones that make use of the monitor's internal state, ones that make use of the idea of probabilistic result checking, and ones that cannot be expressed as dependent or refinement types. We translate contracts in the refinement fragment into monitors, and prove a safety theorem for that fragment.

Acknowledgment. This research was supported in part by NSF grant CNS1423168 and a Carnegie Mellon University Presidential Fellowship.

References

1. Acay, C., Pfenning, F.: Intersections and unions of session types. In: Proceedings Eighth Workshop on Intersection Types and Related Systems, ITRS 2016, Porto, Portugal, pp. 4–19, 26 June 2016. https://dx.doi.org/10.4204/EPTCS.242.3
2. Ahmed, A., Findler, R.B., Siek, J.G., Wadler, P.: Blame for all. In: 38th ACM SIGPLAN-SIGACT Symposium on Principles of Programming Languages (POPL 2011) (2011). https://doi.acm.org/10.1145/1570506.1570507
3. Balzer, S., Pfenning, F.: Manifest sharing with session types. Proc. ACM Program. Lang. **1**(ICFP), 37:1–37:29 (2017). https://doi.org/10.1145/3110281
4. Caires, L., Pfenning, F.: Session types as intuitionistic linear propositions. In: Gastin, P., Laroussinie, F. (eds.) CONCUR 2010. LNCS, vol. 6269, pp. 222–236. Springer, Heidelberg (2010). https://doi.org/10.1007/978-3-642-15375-4_16
5. Caires, L., Pfenning, F., Toninho, B.: Linear logic propositions as session types. Math. Struct. Comput. Sci. **26**(3), 367–423 (2016)
6. Cervesato, I., Scedrov, A.: Relating state-based and process-based concurrency through linear logic. Inf. Comput. **207**(10), 1044–1077 (2009). https://doi.org/10.1016/j.ic.2008.11.006
7. Dimoulas, C., Findler, R.B., Flanagan, C., Felleisen, M.: Correct blame for contracts: no more scapegoating. In: Proceedings of the 38th Annual ACM SIGPLAN-SIGACT Symposium on Principles of Programming Languages, POPL 2011, pp. 215–226. ACM, New York (2011). https://doi.acm.org/10.1145/1926385.1926410
8. Dimoulas, C., Tobin-Hochstadt, S., Felleisen, M.: Complete monitors for behavioral contracts. In: Seidl, H. (ed.) ESOP 2012. LNCS, vol. 7211, pp. 214–233. Springer, Heidelberg (2012). https://doi.org/10.1007/978-3-642-28869-2_11
9. Disney, T., Flanagan, C., McCarthy, J.: Temporal higher-order contracts. In: 16th ACM SIGPLAN International Conference on Functional Programming (ICFP 2011) (2011). https://doi.acm.org/10.1145/2034773.2034800
10. Findler, R.B., Felleisen, M.: Contracts for higher-order functions. In: Proceedings of the Seventh ACM SIGPLAN International Conference on Functional Programming, ICFP 2002, pp. 48–59. ACM, New York (2002). https://doi.acm.org/10.1145/581478.581484

11. Gay, S.J., Hole, M.: Subtyping for session types in the π-calculus. Acta Informatica **42**(2–3), 191–225 (2005). https://doi.org/10.1007/s00236-005-0177-z
12. Gommerstadt, H., Jia, L., Pfenning, F.: Session-typed concurrent contracts. Technical report CMU-CyLab-17-004, CyLab, Carnegie Mellon University, February 2018
13. Griffith, D.: Polarized Substructural Session Types. Ph.D. thesis, University of Illinois at Urbana-Champaign, April 2016
14. Igarashi, A., Thiemann, P., Vasconcelos, V.T., Wadler, P.: Gradual session types. Proc. ACM Program. Lang. **1**(ICFP), 38:1–38:28 (2017). https://doi.org/10.1145/3110282
15. Jia, L., Gommerstadt, H., Pfenning, F.: Monitors and blame assignment for higher-order session types. In: Proceedings of the 43rd Annual ACM SIGPLAN-SIGACT Symposium on Principles of Programming Languages, POPL 2016, pp. 582–594. ACM, New York (2016). https://doi.acm.org/10.1145/2837614.2837662
16. Keil, M., Thiemann, P.: Blame assignment for higher-order contracts with intersection and union. In: 20th ACM SIGPLAN International Conference on Functional Programming (ICFP 2015) (2015). https://doi.acm.org/10.1145/2784731.2784737
17. Melgratti, H., Padovani, L.: Chaperone contracts for higher-order sessions. Proc. ACM Program. Lang. **1**(ICFP), 35:1–35:29 (2017). https://doi.org/10.1145/3110279
18. Pfenning, F., Griffith, D.: Polarized substructural session types. In: Pitts, A. (ed.) FoSSaCS 2015. LNCS, vol. 9034, pp. 3–22. Springer, Heidelberg (2015). https://doi.org/10.1007/978-3-662-46678-0_1
19. Schneider, F.B.: Enforceable security policies. ACM Trans. Inf. Syst. Secur. **3**(1), 30–50 (2000). https://doi.org/10.1145/353323.353382
20. Thiemann, P.: Session types with gradual typing. In: Maffei, M., Tuosto, E. (eds.) TGC 2014. LNCS, vol. 8902, pp. 144–158. Springer, Heidelberg (2014). https://doi.org/10.1007/978-3-662-45917-1_10
21. Thiemann, P., Vasconcelos, V.T.: Context-free session types. In: Proceedings of the 21st ACM SIGPLAN International Conference on Functional Programming, ICFP 2016, pp. 462–475. ACM, New York (2016). https://acm.doi.org/10.4230/LIPIcs.ECOOP.2016.9
22. Toninho, B.: A Logical Foundation for Session-based Concurrent Computation. Ph.D. thesis, Carnegie Mellon University and New University of Lisbon (2015)
23. Toninho, B., Caires, L., Pfenning, F.: Higher-order processes, functions, and sessions: a monadic integration. In: Felleisen, M., Gardner, P. (eds.) ESOP 2013. LNCS, vol. 7792, pp. 350–369. Springer, Heidelberg (2013). https://doi.org/10.1007/978-3-642-37036-6_20
24. Wadler, P.: A complement to blame. In: 1st Summit on Advances in Programming Languages (SNAPL 2015) (2015). https://doi.acm.org/10.4230/LIPIcs.SNAPL.2015.309
25. Wadler, P., Findler, R.B.: Well-typed programs can't be blamed. In: Castagna, G. (ed.) ESOP 2009. LNCS, vol. 5502, pp. 1–16. Springer, Heidelberg (2009). https://doi.org/10.1007/978-3-642-00590-9_1
26. Wasserman, H., Blum, M.: Software reliability via run-time result-checking. J. ACM **44**(6), 826–849 (1997). https://doi.org/10.1145/268999.269003
27. Waye, L., Chong, S., Dimoulas, C.: Whip: higher-order contracts for modern services. Proc. ACM Program. Lang. **1**(ICFP), 36:1–36:28 (2017). https://doi.org/10.1145/3110280

A Typing Discipline for Statically Verified Crash Failure Handling in Distributed Systems

Malte Viering[1]($\boxtimes$), Tzu-Chun Chen[1], Patrick Eugster[1,2,3], Raymond Hu[4], and Lukasz Ziarek[5]

[1] Department of Computer Science, TU Darmstadt, Darmstadt, Germany
viering@dsp.tu-darmstadt.de
[2] Faculty of Informatics, Università della Svizzera italiana, Lugano, Switzerland
[3] Department of Computer Science, Purdue University, West Lafayette, USA
[4] Department of Computing, Imperial College London, London, UK
[5] Department of Computer Science and Engineering, SUNY Buffalo, Buffalo, USA

Abstract. A key requirement for many distributed systems is to be resilient toward partial failures, allowing a system to progress despite the failure of some components. This makes programming of such systems daunting, particularly in regards to avoiding inconsistencies due to failures and asynchrony. This work introduces a formal model for crash failure handling in asynchronous distributed systems featuring a lightweight coordinator, modeled in the image of widely used systems such as ZooKeeper and Chubby. We develop a typing discipline based on multiparty session types for this model that supports the specification and static verification of multiparty protocols with explicit failure handling. We show that our type system ensures subject reduction and progress in the presence of failures. In other words, in a well-typed system even if some participants crash during execution, the system is guaranteed to progress in a consistent manner with the remaining participants.

1 Introduction

Distributed Programs, Partial Failures, and Coordination. Developing programs that execute across a set of physically remote, networked processes is challenging. The correct operation of a *distributed program* requires correctly designed protocols by which concurrent processes interact asynchronously, and correctly implemented processes according to their roles in the protocols. This becomes particularly challenging when distributed programs have to be resilient to *partial failures*, where some processes crashes while others remain operational. Partial failures affect both *safety* and *liveness* of applications. Asynchrony is the key

Financially supported by ERC grant FP7-617805 "LiVeSoft - Lightweight Verification of Software", NSF grants CNS-1405614 and IIS-1617586, and EPSRC EP/K034413/1 and EP/K011715/1.

A. Ahmed (Ed.): ESOP 2018, LNCS 10801, pp. 799–826, 2018.
https://doi.org/10.1007/978-3-319-89884-1_28

issue, resulting in the inability to distinguish slow processes from failed ones. In general, this makes it impossible for processes to reach agreement, even when only a single process can crash [19].

In practice, such impasses are overcome by making appropriate assumptions for the considered infrastructure and applications. One common approach is to assume the presence of a highly available *coordination service* [26] – realized using a set of replicated processes large enough to survive common rates of process failures (e.g., 1 out of 3, 2 out of 5) – and delegating critical decisions to this service. While this *coordinator model* has been in widespread use for many years (cf. *consensus service* [22]), the advent of cloud computing has recently brought it further into the mainstream, via instances like Chubby [4] and ZooKeeper [26]. Such systems are used not only by end applications but also by a variety of frameworks and middleware systems across the layers of the protocol stack [11, 20,31,40].

Typing Disciplines for Distributed Programs. Typing disciplines for distributed programs is a promising and active research area towards addressing the challenges in the correct development of distributed programs. See Hüttel et al. [27] for a broad survey. *Session types* are one of the established typing disciplines for message passing systems. Originally developed in the π-calculus [23], these have been later successfully applied to a range of practical languages, e.g., Java [25,41], Scala [39], Haskell [34,38], and OCaml [28,37]. *Multiparty* session types (MPSTs) [15,24] generalize session types beyond two participants. In a nutshell, a standard MPST framework takes (1) a specification of the whole multiparty message protocol as a *global type*; from which (2) *local types*, describing the protocol from the perspective of each participant, are derived; these are in turn used to (3) statically *type check* the I/O actions of endpoint programs implementing the session participants. A well-typed system of session endpoint programs enjoys important safety and liveness properties, such as *no reception errors* (only expected messages are received) and *session progress*. A basic intuition behind MPSTs is that the design (i.e., restrictions) of the type language constitutes a class of distributed protocols for which these properties can be statically guaranteed by the type system.

Unfortunately, *no* MPST work supports protocols for asynchronous distributed programs dealing with *partial failures due to process crashes*, so the aforementioned properties no longer hold in such an event. Several MPST works have treated communication patterns based on *exception messages* (or *interrupts*) [6,7,16]. In these works, such messages may convey exceptional states in an *application* sense; from a protocol compliance perspective, however, these messages are the same as any other message communicated during a *normal* execution of the session. This is in contrast to *process* failures, which may invalidate already in-transit (*orphan*) messages, and where the task of agreeing on the concerted handling of a crash failure is itself prone to such failures.

Outside of session types and other type-based approaches, there have been a number of advances on verifying fault tolerant distributed protocols and applications (e.g., based on model checking [29], proof assistants [44]); however, little work exists on providing direct compile-time support for *programming* such applications in the spirit of MPSTs.

Contributions and Challenges. This paper puts forward a new typing discipline for safe specification and implementation of distributed programs prone to process crash failures based on MPSTs. The following summarizes the key challenges and contributions.

Multiparty session calculus with coordination service. We develop an extended multiparty session calculus as a formal model of processes prone to crash failures in asynchronous message passing systems. Unlike standard session calculi that reflect only "minimal" networking infrastructures, our model introduces a practically-motivated *coordinator* artifact and explicit, asynchronous messages for run-time crash notifications and failure handling.

MPSTs with explicit failure handling. We introduce new global and local type constructs for *explicit failure handling*, designed for specifying protocols tolerating partial failures. Our type system carefully reworks many of the key elements in standard MPSTs to manage the intricacies of handling crash failures. These include the well-formedness of failure-prone global types, and the crucial *coherence* invariant on MPST typing environments to reflect the notion of system consistency in the presence of crash failures and the resulting errors. We show safety and progress for a well-typed MPST session despite potential failures.

To fit our model to practice, we introduce programming constructs similar to well-known and intuitive exception handling mechanisms, for handling concurrent and asynchronous process crash failures in sessions. These constructs serve to integrate user-level session control flow in endpoint processes and the underlying communications with the coordination service, used by the target applications of our work to outsource critical failure management decisions (see Fig. 1). It is important to note that the coordinator does *not* magically solve all problems. Key design challenges are to ensure that communication with it is fully asynchronous as in real-life, and that it is involved only in a "minimal" fashion. Thus we treat the coordinator as a first-class, asynchronous network artifact, as opposed to a convenient but impractical global "oracle" (cf. [6]), and our operational semantics of multiparty sessions remains primarily *choreographic* in the original spirit of distributed MPSTs, unlike works that resort to a centralized *orchestrator* to conduct all actions [5,8]. As depicted in Fig. 1, application-specific communication does not involve the coordinator. Our model lends itself to common practical scenarios where processes monitor each other in a peer-based fashion to detect failures, and rely on a coordinator only to establish agreement on which processes have failed, and when.

A long version of this paper is available online [43]. The long version contains: full formal definitions, full proofs, and a prototype implementation in Scala.

Example. As a motivating example, Fig. 2 gives a global formal specification for a big data streaming task between a distributed file system (DFS) *dfs*, and two

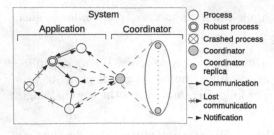

$$[dfs]G = \mathsf{t}(\mu t.$$
$$dfs{\to}w_1\ l_{d_1}(S).dfs{\to}w_2\ l_{d_2}(S).$$
$$w_1{\to}dfs\ l_{r_1}(S').w_2{\to}dfs\ l_{r_2}(S').t$$
$$)\mathsf{h}($$
$$\{w_1\}:\mu t'.dfs{\to}w_2\ l'_{d_1}(S).$$
$$w_2{\to}dfs\ l'_{r_1}(S').t',$$
$$\{w_2\}:...,\{w_1,w_2\}:\mathsf{end})$$

Fig. 1. Coordinator model for asynchronous distributed systems. The coordinator is implemented by replicated processes (internals omitted).

Fig. 2. Global type for a big data streaming task with failure handling capabilities.

workers $w_{1,2}$. The DFS streams data to two workers, which process the data and write the result back. Most DFSs have built-in fault tolerance mechanisms [20], so we consider *dfs* to be *robust*, denoted by the annotation [*dfs*]; the workers, however, may individually fail. In the *try-handle* construct t(...)h(...), the *try-block* t(...) gives the *normal* (i.e., failure-free) flow of the protocol, and h(...) contains the explicit *handlers* for potential crashes. In the try-block, the workers receive data from the DFS ($dfs{\to}w_i$), perform local computations, and send back the result ($w_i{\to}dfs$). If a worker crashes ($\{w_i\}:$ ...), the other worker will also take over the computation of the crashed worker, allowing the system to still produce a valid result. If both workers crash (by any interleaving of their concurrent crash events), the global type specifies that the DFS should safely terminate its role in the session.

We shall refer to this basic example, that focuses on the new failure handling constructs, in explanations in later sections. We also give many further examples throughout the following sections to illustrate the potential session errors due to failures exposed by our model, and how our framework resolves them to recover MPST safety and progress.

Roadmap. Section 2 describes the adopted system and failure model. Section 3 introduces global types for guiding failure handling. Section 4 introduces our process calculus with failure handling capabilities and a coordinator. Section 5 introduces local types, derived from global types by projection. Section 6 describes typing rules, and defines *coherence* of session environments with respect to endpoint crashes. Section 7 states properties of our model. Section 8 discusses related work. Sect. 9 draws conclusions.

2   System and Failure Model

In distributed systems care is required to avoid partial failures affecting liveness (e.g., waiting on messages from crashed processes) or safety (e.g., when processes manage to communicate with some peers but not others before crashing) properties of applications. Based on the nature of the infrastructure and application, appropriate *system and failure models* are chosen along with judiciously made assumptions to overcome such impasses in practice.

We pinpoint the key characteristics of our model, according to our practical motivations and standard distributed systems literature, that shape the design choices we make later for the process calculus and types. As it is common we augment our system with a *failure detector* (FD) to allow for distinguishing slow and failed processes. The advantage of the FD (1) in terms of reasoning is that it concentrates all assumptions to solve given problems and (2) implementation-wise it yields a single main module where time-outs are set and used.

Concretely we make the following assumptions on failures and the system:

(1) **Crash-stop failures**: Application processes fail by crashing (halting), and do not recover.
(2) **Asynchronous system**: Application processes and the network are asynchronous, meaning that there are no upper bounds on processes' relative speeds or message transmission delays.
(3) **Reliable communication**: Messages transmitted between correct (i.e., non-failed) participants are eventually received.
(4) **Robust coordinator**: The coordinator (coordination service) is permanently available.
(5) **Asynchronous reliable failure detection**: Application processes have access to local FDs which eventually detect all failed peers and do not falsely suspect peers.

(1)–(3) are standard in literature on fault-tolerant distributed systems [19].

Note that processes can still recover but will not do so *within* sessions (or will not be re-considered for those). Other failure models, e.g., network partitions [21] or Byzantine failures [32], are subject of future work. The former are not tolerated by ZooKeeper et al., and the latter have often been argued to be a too generic failure model (e.g., [3]).

The assumption on the coordinator (4) implicitly means that the number of concomitant failures among the coordinator replicas is assumed to remain within a minority, and that failed replicas are replaced in time (to tolerate further failures). Without loss of validity, the coordinator internals can be treated as a blackbox. The final assumption (5) on failure detection is backed in practice by the concept of *program-controlled* crash [10], which consists in communicating decisions to disregard supposedly failed processes also to those processes, prompting them to reset themselves upon false suspicion. In practice systems can be configured to minimize the probability of such events, and by a "two-level" membership consisting in evicting processes from *individual* sessions (cf. recovery above) more quickly than from a system as a whole; several authors have also proposed network support to entirely avoid false suspicions (e.g., [33]).

These assumptions do not make handling of failures trivial, let alone mask them. For instance, the network can arbitrarily delay messages and thus reorder them with respect to their real sending times, and so different processes can detect failures at different points in time and in different orders.

(Basic type)	$S ::= \mathsf{bool} \mid \mathsf{str} \mid \mathsf{int}$
(Global type)	$G ::= p \to q\{l_i(S_i).G_i\}_{i \in I} \mid \mu t.G \mid t \mid \mathsf{end} \mid \mathsf{t}(G_1)\mathsf{h}(H)^\kappa.G_2$
(Handling env.)	$H ::= F{:}G \mid H, H$ (Handler sig.) $F ::= \{p_i\}_{i \in I}$

Fig. 3. Syntax of global types with explicit handling of partial failures.

3   Global Types for Explicit Handling of Partial Failures

Based on the foundations of MPSTs, we develop *global types* to formalize specifications of distributed protocols with explicit handling of *partial failures due to role crashes*, simply referred to as *failures*. We present global types before introducing the process calculus to provide a high-level intuition of how failure handling works in our model.

The syntax of *global types* is depicted in Fig. 3. We use the following base notations: $p, q, \ldots$ for *role* (i.e., participant) names; $l_1, l_2, \ldots$ for message *labels*; and $t, t', \ldots$ for type variables. *Base types* S may range over, bool, int, etc.

Global types are denoted by G. We first summarize the constructs from standard MPST [15,24]. A *branch* type $p \to q\{l_i(S_i).G_i\}_{i \in I}$ means that p can send to q *one* of the messages of type S_k with label l_k, where k is a member of the non-empty index set I. The protocol then proceeds according to the continuation G_k. When I is a singleton, we may simply write $p \to q\, l(S).G$. We use t for type variables and take an equi-recursive view, i.e., $\mu t.G$ and its unfolding $[\mu t.G/t]$ are equivalent. We assume type variable occurrences are bound and guarded (e.g., $\mu t.t$ is not permitted). end is for termination.

We now introduce our extensions for partial failure handling. A *try-handle* $\mathsf{t}(G_1)\mathsf{h}(H)^\kappa.G_2$ describes a "failure-atomic" protocol unit: all *live* (i.e., non-crashed) roles will eventually reach a consistent protocol state, despite any concurrent and asynchronous role crashes. The try-block G_1 defines the *default* protocol flow, and H is a *handling environment*. Each element of H maps a *handler signature* F, that specifies a set of *failed* roles $\{p_i\}_{i \in I}$, to a *handler body* specified by a G. The handler body G specifies how the live roles should proceed given the failure of roles F. The protocol then proceeds (for live roles) according to the continuation G_2 after the default block G_1 or failure handling defined in H has been completed as appropriate.

To simplify later technical developments, we annotate each try-handle term in a given G by a unique $\kappa \in \mathbb{N}$ that lexically identifies the term within G. These annotations may be assigned mechanically. As a short hand, we refer to the try-block and handling environment of a particular try-handle by its annotation; e.g., we use κ to stand for $\mathsf{t}(G_1)\mathsf{h}(H)^\kappa$. In the running examples (e.g., Fig. 2), if there exists only one try-handle, we omit κ for simplicity.

Top-Level Global Types and Robust Roles. We use the term *top-level* global type to mean the source protocol specified by a user, following a typical top-down interpretation of MPST frameworks [15,24]. We allow top-level global types to be optionally annotated $[\tilde{p}]G$, where $[\tilde{p}]$ specifies a set of *robust* roles—i.e., roles that can be assumed to never fail. In practice, a participant may be robust if it is replicated or is made inherently fault tolerant by other means (e.g., the participant that represents the distributed file system in Fig. 2).

Well-Formedness. The first stage of validation in standard MPSTs is to check that the top-level global type satisfies the supporting criteria used to ensure the desired properties of the type system. We first list basic syntactic conditions which we assume on any given G: (i) each F is non-empty; (ii) a role in a F cannot occur in the corresponding handler body (a failed role cannot be involved in the handling of its own failure); and (iii) every occurrence of a non-robust role p must be contained within a, possibly outer, try-handle that has a handler signature $\{p\}$ (the protocol must be able to handle its potential failure). Lastly, to simplify the presentation without loss of generality, we impose that separate branch types *not* defined in the same default block or handler body must have disjoint label sets. This can be implicitly achieved by combining label names with try-handle annotations.

Assuming the above, we define *well-formedness* for our extended global types. We write $G' \in G$ to mean that G' syntactically occurs in G ($\in$ is reflexive); similarly for the variations $\kappa \in G$ and $\kappa \in \kappa'$. Recall κ is shorthand for $\mathsf{t}(G_1)\mathsf{h}(H)^\kappa$. We use a lookup function $outer_G(\kappa)$ for the set of all try-handles in G that enclose a given κ, including κ itself, defined by $outer_G(\kappa) = \{\kappa' \mid \kappa \in \kappa' \land \kappa' \in G\}$.

Definition 1 (Well-formedness). Let κ stand for $\mathsf{t}(G_1)\mathsf{h}(H)^\kappa$, and κ' for $\mathsf{t}(G'_1)\mathsf{h}(H')^{\kappa'}$. A global type G is *well-formed* if both of the following conditions hold. For all $\kappa \in G$:

1. $\forall F_1 \in dom(H).\forall F_2 \in dom(H).\exists \kappa' \in outer_G(\kappa)$ s.t. $F_1 \cup F_2 \in dom(H')$
2. $\nexists F \in dom(H).\exists \kappa' \in outer_G(\kappa).\exists F' \in dom(H')$ s.t. $\kappa' \neq \kappa \land F' \subseteq F$

The first condition asserts that for any two separate handler signatures of a handling environment of κ, there always exists a handler whose handler signature matches the union of their respective failure sets – this handler is either inside the handling environment of κ itself, or in the handling environment of an outer try-handle. This ensures that if roles are active in different handlers of the same try-handle then there is a handler whose signature corresponds to the union over the signatures of those different handlers. Example 2 together with Example 3 in Sect. 4 illustrate a case where this condition is needed. The second condition asserts that if the handling environment of a try-handle contains a handler for F, then there is no outer try-handle with a handler for F' such that $F' \subseteq F$. The reason for this condition is that in the case of *nested* try-handles, our communication model allows separate try-handles to start failure handling independently (the operational semantics will be detailed in the next section; see (**TryHdl**) in Fig. 6). The aim is to have the relevant roles eventually converge on performing the handling of the outermost try-handle, possibly by interrupting the handling of an inner try-handle. Consider the following example:

Example 1. $G = \mathsf{t}(\mathsf{t}(G')\mathsf{h}(\{p_1, p_2\} : G_1)^2)\mathsf{h}(\{p_1\} : G_1')^1$ violates condition 2 because, when p_1 and p_2 both failed, the handler signature $\{p_1\}$ will still be triggered (i.e., the outer try-handle will eventually take over). It is not sensible to run G_1' instead of G_1 (which is for the crashes of p_1 and p_2).

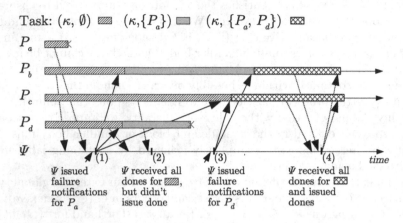

Fig. 4. Challenges under pure asynchronous interactions with a coordinator. Between time (1) and time (2), the task $\phi = (\kappa, \emptyset)$ is interrupted by the crash of P_a. Between time (3) and time (4), due to asynchrony and multiple crashes, P_c starts handling the crash of $\{P_a, P_d\}$ without handling the crash of $\{P_a\}$. Finally after (4) P_b and P_c finish their common task.

4   A Process Calculus for Coordinator-Based Failure Handling

Figure 4 depicts a scenario that can occur in practical asynchronous systems with coordinator-based failure handling through frameworks such as ZooKeeper (Sect. 2). Using this scenario, we first illustrate challenges, formally define our model, and then develop a safe type system.

The scenario corresponds to a global type of the form $\mathsf{t}(G)\mathsf{h}(\{P_a\} : G_a, \{P_a, P_d\} : G_{ad}, ...)^\kappa$, with processes $P_{a..d}$ and a coordinator Ψ. We define a *task* to mean a unit of interactions, which includes failure handling behaviors. Initially all processes are collaborating on a task ϕ, which we label $(\kappa, \emptyset)$ (identifying the task context, and the set of failed processes). The shaded boxes signify which task each process is working on. Dotted arrows represent notifications between processes and Ψ related to task completion, and solid arrows for failure notifications from Ψ to processes. During the scenario, P_a first fails, then P_d fails: the execution proceeds through failure handling for $\{P_a\}$ and $\{P_a, P_d\}$.

(I)   When P_b reaches the end of its part in ϕ, the application has P_b notify Ψ. P_b then remains in the context of ϕ (the continuation of the box after notifying) in consideration of other non-robust participants still working on ϕ—P_b may yet need to handle their potential failure(s).

(Expression)	$e ::= v \mid x \mid e + e \mid -e \mid \ ...$	(Channel)	$c ::= s[p] \mid y$
(Process)	$P ::= a[p](y).P \mid c : \eta$	(Level)	$\phi ::= (\kappa, F)$
(Statement)	$\eta ::= t(\eta)h(H)^\phi.\eta \mid \underline{0} \mid 0 \mid p!\,l(e).\eta$	(Declaration)	$D ::= X(x) = \eta$
	$\mid p?\{l_i(x_i).\eta_i\}_{i \in I} \mid X\langle e \rangle$	(Handling)	$H ::= F: \eta \mid H, H$
	$\mid\ \mathsf{def}\ D\ \mathsf{in}\ \eta \mid \mathsf{if}\ e\ \eta\ \mathsf{else}\ \eta$		
(Application)	$N ::= P \mid N \mid N \mid s : h$	(Queue)	$h ::= \emptyset \mid h \cdot m$
(Message)	$m ::= \langle p, q, l(v) \rangle \mid \langle\!\langle p, \mathsf{crash}\ F \rangle\!\rangle \mid dn$	(Done)	$dn ::= \langle p, q \rangle^\phi$
(System)	$S ::= \Psi \blacklozenge N \mid (\nu s)S \mid S \mid S$	(Coordinator)	$\Psi ::= G : (F, d)$
(Context)	$E ::= t(E)h(H)^\phi.\eta \mid \mathsf{def}\ D\ \mathsf{in}\ E \mid [\ ]$	(Done Queue)	$d ::= \emptyset \mid d \cdot dn$

Fig. 5. Grammar for processes, applications, systems, and evaluation contexts.

(II) The processes of synchronizing on the completion of a task or performing failure handling *are themselves subject to failures* that may arise concurrently. In Fig. 4, all processes reach the end of ϕ (i.e., four dotted arrows from ϕ), but P_a fails. Ψ determines this failure and it initiates failure handling at time (1), while *done* notifications for ϕ continue to arrive asynchronously at time (2). The failure handling for crash of P_a is itself interrupted by the second failure at time (3).

(III) Ψ can receive notifications that are no longer relevant. For example, at time (2), Ψ has received all *done* notifications for ϕ, but the failure of P_a has already triggered failure handling from time (1).

(IV) Due to multiple concurrent failures, interacting participants may end up in different tasks: around time (2), P_b and P_d are in task $\phi' = (\kappa, \{P_a\})$, whereas P_c is still in ϕ (and asynchronously sending or receiving messages with the others). Moreover, P_c never executes ϕ' because of delayed notifications, so it goes from ϕ directly to $(\kappa, \{P_a, P_d\})$.

Processes. Figure 5 defines the grammar of processes and (distributed) applications. Expressions $e, e_i, ..$ can be values $v, v_i, ...$, variables $x, x_i, ...$, and standard operations. (Application) processes are denoted by $P, P_i, ...$ An initialization $a[p](y).P$ agrees to play role p via shared name a and takes actions defined in P; actions are executed on a session channel $c : \eta$, where c ranges over $s[p]$ (session name and role name) and session variables y; η represents action statements.

A try-handle $t(\eta)h(H)^\phi$ attempts to execute the local action η, and can handle failures occurring therein as defined in the handling environment H, analogously to global types. H thus also maps a handler signature F to a handler body η defining how to handle F. Annotation $\phi = (\kappa, F)$ is composed of two elements: an identity κ of a *global* try-handle, and an indication of the *current* handler signature which can be empty. $F = \emptyset$ means that the default try-block is executing, whereas $F \neq \emptyset$ means that the handler body for F is executing. Term $\underline{0}$ only occurs in a try-handle during runtime. It denotes a *yielding* for a *notification* from a *coordinator* (introduced shortly).

Other statements are similar to those defined in [15,24]. Term 0 represents an *idle* action. For convention, we omit 0 at the end of a statement. Action $p!\,l(e).\eta$ represents a sending action that sends p a label l with content e, then it continues as η. Branching $p?\{l_i(x_i).\eta_i\}_{i \in I}$ represents a receiving action from p with several possible branches. When label l_k is selected, the transmitted value v is saved in x_k, and $\eta_k\{v/x_k\}$ continues. For convenience, when there is only one branch, the curly brackets are omitted, e.g., $c : p?l(x).P$ means there is only one branch $l(x)$. $X\langle e \rangle$ is for a statement variable with one parameter e, and def D in η is for recursion, where declaration D defines the recursive body that can be called in η. The conditional statement is standard.

The structure of processes ensures that failure handling is not interleaved between different sessions. However, we note that in standard MPSTs [15,24], session interleaving must anyway be prohibited for the basic progress property. Since our aim will be to show progress, we disallow session interleaving within process bodies. Our model does allow parallel sessions at the top-level, whose actions may be concurrently interleaved during execution.

(Distributed) Systems. A (distributed) *system* in our programming framework is a composition of an application, which contains more than one process, and a coordinator (cf. Fig. 1). A system can be running within a private session s, represented by $(\nu s)\mathcal{S}$, or $\mathcal{S} \mid \mathcal{S}'$ for systems running in different sessions independently and in parallel (i.e., no session interleaving). The job of the coordinator is to ensure that even in the presence of failures there is consensus on whether all participants in a given try-handle completed their local actions, or whether failures need to be handled, and which ones. We use $\Psi = G : (F, d)$ to denote a (robust) coordinator for the global type G, which stores in (F, d) the failures F that occurred in the application, and in d done notifications sent to the coordinator. The coordinator is denoted by ψ when viewed as a role.

A (distributed) *application*[1] is a process P, a parallel composition $N \mid N'$, or a global queue carrying messages $s : h$. A global queue $s : h$ carries a sequence of messages m, sent by participants in session s. A message is either a regular message $\langle p, q, l(v) \rangle$ with label l and content v sent from p to q or a *notification*. A notification may contain the role of a coordinator. There are *done* and *failure* notifications with two kinds of done notifications dn used for coordination: $\langle p, \psi \rangle^\phi$ notifies ψ that p has finished its local actions of the try-handle ϕ; $\langle \psi, p \rangle^\phi$ is sent from ψ to notify p that ψ has received all done notifications for the try-handle ϕ so that p shall end its current try-handle and move to its next task. For example, in Fig. 4 at time (4) the coordinator will inform P_b and P_c via $\langle \psi, P_b \rangle^{(\kappa, \{P_a, P_d\})}.\langle \psi, P_c \rangle^{(\kappa, \{P_a, P_d\})}$ that they can finish the try-handle $(\kappa, \{P_a, P_d\})$. Note that the appearance of $\langle \psi, p \rangle^\phi$ implies that the coordinator has been informed that all participants in ϕ have completed their local actions. We define two kinds of *failure* notifications: $\langle\!\langle \psi, \mathsf{crash}\ F \rangle\!\rangle$ notifies ψ that F occurred, e.g., $\{q\}$ means q has failed; $\langle\!\langle p, \mathsf{crash}\ F \rangle\!\rangle$ is sent from ψ to notify p about the failure F for possible handling. We write $\langle\!\langle \widetilde{p}, \mathsf{crash}\ F \rangle\!\rangle$, where $\widetilde{p} = p_1, ..., p_n$ short for $\langle\!\langle p_1, \mathsf{crash}\ F \rangle\!\rangle \cdot ... \cdot \langle\!\langle p_n, \mathsf{crash}\ F \rangle\!\rangle$; similarly for $\langle \psi, \widetilde{p} \rangle^\phi$.

---

[1] Other works use the term *network* which is the reason why we use N instead of, e.g., A. We call it application to avoid confusion with the physical network which interconnects all processes as well as the coordinator.

$$a[p_1](y_1).P_1 \mid ... \mid a[p_n](y_n).P_n \rightarrow$$
$$(\nu s)(G : (\emptyset, \emptyset) \blacklozenge P_1\{s[p_1]/y_1\} \mid ... \mid P_n\{s[p_n]/y_n\} \mid s : \emptyset) \quad a : G \quad \textbf{(Link)}$$

$$s[p] : E[q! \; l(e).\eta] \mid s : h \rightarrow s[p] : E[\eta] \mid s : h \cdot \langle p, q, l(v) \rangle \quad e \Downarrow v \quad \textbf{(Snd)}$$

$$s[p] : E[q?\{l_i(x_i).\eta_i\}_{i \in I}] \mid s : \langle q, p, l_k(v_k) \rangle \cdot h \rightarrow$$
$$s[p] : E[\eta_k\{v_k/x_k\}] \mid s : h \quad k \in I \quad \textbf{(Rcv)}$$

$$s[p] : E[\text{def } X(x) = \eta \text{ in } X\langle e \rangle] \rightarrow s[p] : E[\text{def } X(x) = \eta \text{ in } \eta\{v/x\}] \quad e \Downarrow v \quad \textbf{(Rec)}$$

$$\frac{N_1 \equiv N_3 \rightarrow N_4 \equiv N_2}{N_1 \rightarrow N_2} \qquad \frac{N_1 \rightarrow N_2}{N_1|N \rightarrow N_2|N} \qquad \textbf{(Str, Par)}$$

$$\frac{N_1 \rightarrow N_2}{\psi \blacklozenge N_1 \rightarrow \psi \blacklozenge N_2} \qquad \frac{\mathcal{S} \rightarrow \mathcal{S}'}{(\nu s)\mathcal{S} \rightarrow (\nu s)\mathcal{S}'} \qquad \textbf{(Sys, New)}$$

$$N \mid s : h \rightarrow N \setminus s[p] : \eta \mid s : remove(h, p) \cdot \langle\!| \psi, \text{crash } \{p\} |\!\rangle$$
$$s[p] : \eta \text{ non-robust } \textbf{(Crash)}$$

Fig. 6. Operational semantics of distributed applications, for local actions.

Following the tradition of other MPST works the global queue provides an abstraction for multiple FIFO queues, each queue being between two endpoints (cf. TCP) with no global ordering. Therefore $m_i \cdot m_j$ can be permuted to $m_j \cdot m_i$ in the global queue if the sender or the receiver differ. For example the following messages are permutable: $\langle p, q, l(v) \rangle \cdot \langle p, q', l(v) \rangle$ if $q \neq q'$ and $\langle p, q, l(v) \rangle \cdot \langle\!| \psi, p |\!\rangle^\phi$ and $\langle p, q, l(v) \rangle \cdot \langle\!| q, \text{crash } F |\!\rangle$. But $\langle\!| \psi, p |\!\rangle^\phi \cdot \langle\!| p, \text{crash } F |\!\rangle$ is not permutable, both have the same sender and receiver (ψ is the sender of $\langle\!| p, \text{crash } F |\!\rangle$).

Basic Dynamic Semantics for Applications. Figure 6 shows the operational semantics of applications. We use evaluation contexts as defined in Fig. 5. Context E is either a hole [ ], a default context $t(E)h(H)^\phi.\eta$, or a recursion context def D in E. We write $E[\eta]$ to denote the action statement obtained by filling the hole in $E[\cdot]$ with η.

Rule (**Link**) says that (local) processes who agree on shared name a, obeying to some protocol (global type), playing certain roles p_i represented by $a[p_i](y_i).P$, together will start a private session s; this will result in replacing every variable y_i in P_i and, at the same time, creating a new global queue $s : \emptyset$, and appointing a coordinator $G : (\emptyset, \emptyset)$, which is novel in our work.

Rule (**Snd**) in Fig. 6 reduces a sending action $q! \; l(e)$ by emitting a message $\langle p, q, l(v) \rangle$ to the global queue $s : h$. Rule (**Rcv**) reduces a receiving action if the message arriving at its end is sent from the expected sender with an expected label. Rule (**Rec**) is for recursion. When the recursive body, defined inside η, is called by $X\langle e \rangle$ where e is evaluated to v, it reduces to the statement $\eta\{v/x\}$ which will again implement the recursive body. Rule (**Str**) says that processes which are structurally congruent have the same reduction. Processes, applications, and systems are considered modulo structural congruence, denoted by $\equiv$, along with α-renaming. Rule (**Par**) and (**Str**) together state that a parallel composition has a reduction if its sub-application can reduce. Rule (**Sys**) states that a system has a reduction if its application has a reduction, and (**New**)

says a reduction can proceed under a session. Rule (**Crash**) states that a process
on channel $s[p]$ can fail at any point in time. (**Crash**) also adds a notification
$\langle\!\langle \psi, \mathsf{crash}\ F\rangle\!\rangle$ which is sent to ψ (the coordinator). This is an abstraction for
the failure detector described in Sect. 2 (5), the notification $\langle\!\langle \psi, \mathsf{crash}\ F\rangle\!\rangle$ is the
first such notification issued by a participant based on its local failure detector.
Adding the notification into the global queue instead of making the coordinator
immediately aware of it models that failures are only detected eventually. Note
that a failure is not annotated with a level because failures transcend all levels,
and asynchrony makes it impossible to identify "where" exactly they occurred.
As a failure is permanent it can affect multiple try-handles. The (**Crash**) rule
does not apply to participants which are robust, i.e., that conceptually cannot fail
(e.g., *dfs* in Fig. 2). Rule (**Crash**) removes channel $s[p]$ (the failed process) from
application N, and removes messages and notifications delivered from, or heading
to, the failed p by function $remove(h, p)$. Function $remove(h, p)$ returns a new
queue after removing all regular messages and notifications that contain p, e.g.,
let $h = \langle p_2, p_1, l(v)\rangle \cdot \langle p_3, p_2, l'(v')\rangle \cdot \langle p_3, p_4, l'(v')\rangle \cdot \langle p_2, \psi\rangle^\phi \cdot \langle\!\langle p_2, \mathsf{crash}\ \{p_3\}\rangle\!\rangle \cdot$
$\langle \psi, p_2\rangle^\phi$ then $remove(h, p_2) = \langle p_3, p_4, l'(v')\rangle$. Messages are removed to model
that in a real system send/receive does *not* constitute an atomic action.

Handling at Processes. Failure handling, defined in Fig. 7, is based on the observations that (i) a process that fails stays down, and (ii) multiple processes
can fail. As a consequence a failure can trigger multiple failure handlers either
because these handlers are in different (subsequent) try-handles or because of
additional failures. Therefore a process needs to retain the information of *who*
failed. For simplicity we do not model state at processes, but instead processes
read but do not remove failure notifications from the global queue. We define
$Fset(h, p)$ to return the union of failures for which there are notifications head-
ing to p, i.e., $\langle\!\langle p, \mathsf{crash}\ F\rangle\!\rangle$, issued by the coordinator in queue h *up to the first
done notification heading to p*:

Definition 2 (Union of Existing Failures $Fset(h, p)$)

$$Fset(\emptyset, p) = \emptyset \quad Fset(h, p) = \begin{cases} F \cup Fset(h', p) & \text{if } h = \langle\!\langle p, \mathsf{crash}\ F\rangle\!\rangle \cdot h' \\ \emptyset & \text{if } h = \langle \psi, p\rangle^\phi \cdot h' \\ Fset(h', p) & \text{otherwise} \end{cases}$$

In short, if the global queue is $\emptyset$, then naturally there are no failure notifications.
If the global queue contains a failure notification sent from the coordinator, say
$\langle\!\langle p, \mathsf{crash}\ F\rangle\!\rangle$, we collect the failure. If the global queue contains done notification
$\langle \psi, p\rangle^\phi$ sent from the coordinator then *all* participants in ϕ have finished their
local actions, which implies that the try-handle ϕ can be completed. Our failure
handling semantics, (**TryHdl**), allows a try-handle $\phi = (\kappa, F)$ to handle different
failures or sets of failures by allowing a try-handle to switch between different
handlers. F thus denotes the current set of handled failures. For simplicity we
refer to this as the *current(ly handled) failure set*. This is a slight abuse of
terminology, done for brevity, as obviously failures are only detected with a

$$\frac{F' = \cup\{A \mid A \in dom(\mathsf{H}) \wedge F \subset A \subseteq Fset(h,p)\} \quad F'{:}\eta' \in \mathsf{H}}{\mathsf{s}[p] : E[\mathsf{t}(\eta)\mathsf{h}(\mathsf{H})^{(\kappa,F)}.\eta''] \mid \mathsf{s} : h \rightarrow \mathsf{s}[p] : E[\mathsf{t}(\eta')\mathsf{h}(\mathsf{H})^{(\kappa,F')}.\eta''] \mid \mathsf{s} : h} \quad \textbf{(TryHdl)}$$

$$\mathsf{s}[p] : E[\mathsf{t}(0)\mathsf{h}(\mathsf{H})^{\phi}.\eta] \mid \mathsf{s} : h \rightarrow \mathsf{s}[p] : E[\mathsf{t}(\underline{0})\mathsf{h}(\mathsf{H})^{\phi}.\eta] \mid \mathsf{s} : h \cdot \langle p, \psi \rangle^{\phi} \quad \textbf{(SndDone)}$$

$$\frac{\langle \psi, p \rangle^{\phi} \in h}{\mathsf{s}[p] : E[\mathsf{t}(\underline{0})\mathsf{h}(\mathsf{H})^{\phi}.\eta] \mid \mathsf{s} : h \rightarrow \mathsf{s}[p] : E[\eta] \mid \mathsf{s} : h \setminus \{\langle \psi, p \rangle^{\phi}\}} \quad \textbf{(RcvDone)}$$

$$\mathsf{s}[p] : E[\eta] \mid \mathsf{s} : \langle q, p, l(v) \rangle \cdot h \rightarrow \mathsf{s}[p] : E[\eta] \mid \mathsf{s} : h \quad l \notin labels(E[\eta]) \quad \textbf{(Cln)}$$

$$\frac{\langle \psi, p \rangle^{\phi} \in h \quad \phi \notin E[\eta]}{\mathsf{s}[p] : E[\eta] \mid \mathsf{s} : h \rightarrow \mathsf{s}[p] : E[\eta] \mid \mathsf{s} : h \setminus \langle \psi, p \rangle^{\phi}} \quad \textbf{(ClnDone)}$$

Fig. 7. Operational semantics of distributed applications, for endpoint handling.

certain lag. The handling strategy for a process is to handle the—currently—largest set of failed processes that this process has been informed of and is able to handle. This largest set is calculated by $\cup\{A \mid A \in dom(\mathsf{H}) \wedge F \subset A \subseteq Fset(h,p)\}$, that selects all failure sets which are larger than the current one ($A \in dom(\mathsf{H}) \wedge F \subset A$) if they are also triggered by known failures ($A \subseteq Fset(h,p)$). Condition $F' : \eta' \in \mathsf{H}$ in (**TryHdl**) ensures that there exists a handler for F'. The following example shows how (**TryHdl**) is applied to switch handlers.

Example 2. Take h such that $Fset(h,p) = \{p_1\}$ and $\mathsf{H} = \{p_1\} : \eta_1, \{p_2\} : \eta_2, \{p_1, p_2\} : \eta_{12}$ in process $P = \mathsf{s}[p] : \mathsf{t}(\eta_1)\mathsf{h}(\mathsf{H})^{(\kappa,\{p_1\})}$, which indicates that P is handling failure $\{p_1\}$. Assume now one more failure occurs and results in a new queue h' such that $Fset(h',p) = \{p_1, p_2\}$. By (**TryHdl**), the process acting at $\mathsf{s}[p]$ is handling the failure set $\{p_1, p_2\}$ such that $P = \mathsf{s}[p] : \mathsf{t}(\eta_{12})\mathsf{h}(\mathsf{H})^{(\kappa,\{p_1,p_2\})}$ (also notice the η_{12} inside the try-block). A switch to only handling $\{p_2\}$ does not make sense, since, e.g., η_2 can contain p_1. Figure 2 shows a case where the handling strategy differs according to the number of failures.

In Sect. 3 we formally define well-formedness conditions, which guarantee that if there exist two handlers for two different handler signatures in a try-handle, then a handler exists for their union. The following example demonstrates why such a guarantee is needed.

Example 3. Assume a slightly different P compared to the previous examples (no handler for the union of failures): $P = \mathsf{s}[p] : E[\mathsf{t}(\eta)\mathsf{h}(\mathsf{H})^{(\kappa,\emptyset)}]$ with $\mathsf{H} = \{p_1\} : \eta_1, \{p_2\} : \eta_2$. Assume also that $Fset(h,p) = \{p_1, p_2\}$. Here (**TryHdl**) will not apply since there is no failure handling for $\{p_1, p_2\}$ in P. If we would allow a handler for either $\{p_1\}$ or $\{p_2\}$ to be triggered we would have no guarantee that other participants involved in this try-handle will all select the same failure set. Even with a deterministic selection, i.e., all participants in that try-handle selecting the same handling activity, there needs to be a handler with handler signature $= \{p_1, p_2\}$ since it is possible that p_1 is involved in η_2. Therefore the type system will ensure that there is a handler for $\{p_1, p_2\}$ either at this level or at an outer level.

(1) explains that a process finishing its default action (P_b) cannot leave its current try-handle ($\kappa, \emptyset$) immediately because other participants may fail (P_a failed). Below Eq. 1 also shows this issue from the perspective of semantics:

$$s[p] : t(0)h(F : q!l(10).q?l'(x))^{(\kappa,\emptyset)}.\eta' \mid s[q] : t(p?l(x').p!l'(x' + 10))h(H)^{(\kappa,F)}.\eta''$$
$$\mid s : \langle\!\langle q, \text{crash } F \rangle\!\rangle \cdot \langle\!\langle p, \text{crash } F \rangle\!\rangle \cdot h \tag{1}$$

In Eq. 1 the process acting on $s[p]$ ended its try-handle (i.e., the action is 0 in the try-block), and if $s[p]$ finishes its try-handle the participant acting on $s[q]$ which started handling F would be stuck.

To solve the issue, we use (**SndDone**) and (**RcvDone**) for completing a local try-handle with the help of a coordinator. The rule (**SndDone**) sends out a done notification $\langle p, \psi \rangle^\phi$ if the current action in ϕ is 0 and sets the action to $\underline{0}$, indicating that a done notification from the coordinator is needed for ending the try-handle.

Assume process on channel $s[p]$ finished its local actions in the try-block (i.e., as in Eq. 1 above), then by (**SndDone**), we have

$$(1) \rightarrow s : \langle\!\langle q, \text{crash } F \rangle\!\rangle \cdot \langle\!\langle p, \text{crash } F \rangle\!\rangle \cdot \langle p, \psi \rangle^{(\kappa,\emptyset)} \cdot h \mid$$
$$s[p] : t(\underline{0})h(F : q!l(10).q?l'(x))^{(\kappa,\emptyset)}.\eta' \mid s[q] : t(p?l(x').p!l'(x' + 10))h(H)^{(\kappa,F)}.\eta''$$

where notification $\langle p, \psi \rangle^{(\kappa,\emptyset)}$ is added to inform the coordinator. Now the process on channel $s[p]$ can still handle failures defined in its handling environment. This is similar to the case described in (II).

Rule (**RcvDone**) is the counterpart of (**SndDone**). Once a process receives a done notification for ϕ from the coordinator it can finish the try-handle ϕ and reduces to the continuation η. Consider Eq. 2 below, which is similar to Eq. 1 but we take a case where the try-handle can be reduced with (**RcvDone**). In Eq. 2 (**SndDone**) is applied:

$$s[p] : t(\underline{0})h(F : q!l(10).q?l'(x))^{(\kappa,\emptyset)}.\eta' \mid$$
$$s[q] : t(\underline{0})h(F : p?l(x').p!l'(x' + 10))^{(\kappa,\emptyset)}.\eta'' \mid s : h \tag{2}$$

With $h = \langle \psi, q \rangle^{(\kappa,\emptyset)} \cdot \langle \psi, p \rangle^{(\kappa,\emptyset)} \cdot \langle\!\langle q, \text{crash } F \rangle\!\rangle \cdot \langle\!\langle p, \text{crash } F \rangle\!\rangle$ both processes can apply (**RcvDone**) and safely terminate the try-handle ($\kappa, \emptyset$). Note that $Fset(h, p) = Fset(h, q) = \emptyset$ (by Definition 2), i.e., rule (**TryHdl**) can not be applied since a done notification suppresses the failure notification. Thus Eq. 2 will reduce to:

$$(2) \rightarrow^* s[p] : \eta' \mid s[q] : \eta'' \mid s : \langle\!\langle q, \text{crash } F \rangle\!\rangle \cdot \langle\!\langle p, \text{crash } F \rangle\!\rangle$$

It is possible that η' or η'' have handlers for F. Note that once a queue contains $\langle \psi, p \rangle^{(\kappa,\emptyset)}$, all non-failed process in the try-handle ($\kappa, \emptyset$) have sent done notifications to ψ (i.e. applied rule (**SndDone**)). The coordinator which will be introduced shortly ensures this.

$$\frac{\tilde{p} = roles(G) \setminus F' \quad F' = F \cup \{p\} \quad m = \langle\!\langle\tilde{p}, \mathsf{crash}\ \{p\}\rangle\!\rangle}{G : (F,d)\blacklozenge N \mid s : \langle\!\langle\psi, \mathsf{crash}\ \{p\}\rangle\!\rangle \cdot h \to G : (F',d)\blacklozenge N \mid s : h \cdot m} \ (\mathbf{F})$$

$$\frac{d' = d \cdot \langle p, \psi\rangle^\phi}{G : (F,d)\blacklozenge s : \langle p, \psi\rangle^\phi \cdot h \to G : (F,d')\blacklozenge s : h} \ (\mathbf{CollectDone})$$

$$\frac{roles(d,\phi) \supseteq roles(G,\phi) \setminus F \quad \forall F' \in hdl(G,\phi).(F' \not\subseteq F)}{G : (F,d)\blacklozenge s : h \to G : (F, remove(d,\phi))\blacklozenge s : h \cdot \langle\psi, roles(G,\phi) \setminus F\rangle^\phi} (\mathbf{IssueDone})$$

Fig. 8. Operational semantics for the coordinator.

Rule (**Cln**) removes a normal message from the queue if the label in the message does not exist in the target process, which can happen when a failure handler was triggered. The function $labels(\eta)$ returns all labels of receiving actions in η which are able to receive messages now or possible later. This removal based on the syntactic process is safe because in a global type separate branch types *not* defined in the same default block or handler body must have disjoint sets of labels (c.f., Sect. 3). Let $\phi \in P$ if try-handle ϕ appears inside P. Rule (**ClnDone**) removes a done notification of ϕ from the queue if no try-handle ϕ exists, which can happen in case of nesting when a handler of an outer try-handle is triggered.

Handling at Coordinator. Figure 8 defines the semantics of the coordinator. We firstly give the auxiliary definition of $roles(G)$ which gives the set of *all* roles appearing in G.

In rule (**F**), F represents the failures that the coordinator is aware of. This rule states that the coordinator collects and removes a failure notification $\langle\!\langle\psi, \mathsf{crash}\ p\rangle\!\rangle$ heading to it, retains this notification by $G : (F',d)$, $F' = F \cup \{p\}$, and issues failure notifications to all non-failed participants.

Rules (**CollectDone, IssueDone**), in short inform all participants in $\phi = (\kappa, F)$ to finish their try-handle ϕ if the coordinator has received sufficient done notifications of ϕ and did not send out failure notifications that interrupt the task (κ, F) (e.g. see (III)). Rule (**CollectDone**) collects done notifications, i.e., $\langle p, \psi\rangle^\phi$, from the queue and retains these notification; they are used in (**IssueDone**). For introducing (**IssueDone**), we first introduce $hdl(G, (\kappa, F))$ to return a set of handler signatures which can be triggered with respect to the current handler:

Definition 3. $hdl(G, (\kappa, F)) = dom(H) \setminus \mathcal{P}(F)$ if $\mathsf{t}(G_0)\mathsf{h}(H)^\kappa \in G$ where $\mathcal{P}(F)$ represents a powerset of F.

Also, we abuse the function $roles$ to collect the non-coordinator roles of ϕ in d, written $roles(d, \phi)$; similarly, we write $roles(G, \phi)$ where $\phi = (\kappa, F)$ to collect the roles appearing in the handler body F in the try-handle of κ in G. Remember that d only contains done notifications sent by participants.

Rule (**IssueDone**) is applied for some ϕ when conditions $\forall F' \in hdl(G, \phi).(F' \not\subseteq F)$ and $roles(d, \phi) \supseteq roles(G, \phi) \setminus F$ are both satisfied, where F contains all failures the coordinator is aware of. Intuitively, these two conditions ensure that (1) the coordinator only issues done notifications to the participants in the try-handle ϕ if it did not send failure notifications which will trigger a handler of the try-handle ϕ; (2) the coordinator has received all done notifications from all non-failed participants of ϕ. We further explain both conditions in the following examples, starting from condition $\forall F' \in hdl(G, \phi).(F' \not\subseteq F)$, which ensures no handler in ϕ can be triggered based on the failure notifications F sent out by the coordinator.

Example 4. Assume a process playing role p_i is $P_i = s[p_i] : t(\eta_i)h(H_i)^{\phi_i}$. Where $i \in \{1, 2, 3\}$ and $H_i = \{p_2\} : \eta_{i2}, \{p_3\} : \eta_{i3}, \{p_2, p_3\} : \eta_{i23}$ and the coordinator is $G : (\{p_2, p_3\}, d)$ where $t(...)h(H)^\kappa \in G$ and $dom(H) = dom(H_i)$ for any $i \in \{1, 2, 3\}$ and $d = \langle p_1, \psi \rangle^{(\kappa, \{p_2\})} \cdot \langle p_1, \psi \rangle^{(\kappa, \{p_2, p_3\})} \cdot d'$. For any ϕ in d, the coordinator checks if it has issued any failure notification that can possibly trigger a new handler of ϕ:

1. For $\phi = (\kappa, \{p_2\})$ the coordinator issued failure notifications that can interrupt a handler since

$$hdl(G, (\kappa, \{p_2\})) = dom(H) \setminus \mathcal{P}(\{p_2\}) = \{\{p_3\}, \{p_2, p_3\}\}$$

   and $\{p_2, p_3\} \subseteq \{p_2, p_3\}$. That means the failure notifications issued by the coordinator, i.e., $\{p_2, p_3\}$, can trigger the handler with signature $\{p_2, p_3\}$. Thus the coordinator will not issue done notifications for $\phi = (\kappa, \{p_2\})$. A similar case is visualized in Fig. 4 at time (2).
2. For $\phi = (\kappa, \{p_2, p_3\})$ the coordinator did not issue failure notifications that can interrupt a handler since

$$hdl(G, (\kappa, \{p_2, p_3\})) = dom(H) \setminus \mathcal{P}(\{p_2, p_3\}) = \emptyset$$

   so that $\forall F' \in hdl(G, (\kappa, \{p_2, p_3\})).(F' \not\subseteq \{p_2, p_3\})$ is true. The coordinator will issue done notifications for $\phi = (\kappa, \{p_2, p_3\})$.

Another condition $roles(d, \phi) \supseteq roles(G, \phi) \setminus F$ states that only when the coordinator sees sufficient done notifications (in d) for ϕ, it issues done notifications to *all* non-failed participants in ϕ, i.e., $\langle \psi, roles(G, \phi) \setminus F \rangle^\phi$. Recall that $roles(d, \phi)$ returns all roles which have sent a done notification for the handling of ϕ and $roles(G, \phi)$ returns all roles involving in the handling of ϕ. Intuitively one might expect the condition to be $roles(d, \phi) = roles(G, \phi)$; the following example shows why this would be wrong.

Example 5. Consider a process P acting on channel $s[p]$ and $\{q\} \notin dom(H)$:

$$P = s[p] : t(...t(...)h(\{q\} : \eta, H')^{\phi'} . \eta')h(H)^\phi$$

Assume P has already reduced to:

$$P = s[p] : t(\underline{0})h(H)^\phi$$

We show why $roles(d, \phi) \supseteq roles(G, \phi) \setminus F$ is necessary. We start with the simple cases and then move to the more involving ones.

$$T ::= p!\{l_i(S_i).T_i\}_{i\in I} \mid p?\{l_i(S_i).T_i\}_{i\in I} \mid t \mid \mu t.T \mid \mathsf{end} \mid \underline{\mathsf{end}} \mid \mathsf{t}(T)\mathsf{h}(\mathcal{H}_j)^*.T$$
$$\mathcal{H} ::= F\!:\!T \mid \mathcal{H}, \mathcal{H}$$

Fig. 9. The grammar of local types.

(a) Assume q did not fail, the coordinator is $G : (\emptyset, d)$, and all roles in ϕ issued a done notification. Then $roles(d, \phi) = roles(G, \phi)$ and $F = \emptyset$.

(b) Assume q failed in the try-handle ϕ', the coordinator is $G : (\{q\}, d)$, and all roles except q in ϕ issued a done notification. $roles(d, \phi) \neq roles(G, \phi)$ however $roles(d, \phi) = roles(G, \phi) \setminus \{q\}$. Cases like this are the reason why (**IssueDone**) only requires done notifications from non-failed roles.

(c) Assume q failed after it has issued a done notification for ϕ (i.e., q finished try-handle ϕ') and the coordinator collected it (by (**CollectDone**)), so we have $G : (\{q\}, d)$ and $q \in roles(d, \phi)$. Then $roles(d, \phi) \supset roles(G, \phi) \setminus \{q\}$. i.e. (**IssueDone**) needs to consider done notifications from failed roles.

Thus rule (**IssueDone**) has the condition $roles(d, \phi) \supseteq roles(G, \phi) \setminus F$ because of cases like (b) and (c).

The interplay between issuing of done notification (**IssueDone**) and issuing of failure notifications (**F**) is non-trivial. The following proposition clarifies that the participants in the same try-handle ϕ will never get confused with handling failures or completing the try-handle ϕ.

Proposition 1. *Given* $s : h$ *with* $h = h' \cdot \langle \psi, p \rangle^\phi \cdot h''$ *and* $Fset(h, p) \neq \emptyset$, *the rule (**TryHdl**) is not applicable for the try-handle* ϕ *at the process playing role* p.

5   Local Types

Figure 9 defines local types for typing behaviors of endpoint processes with failure handling. Type $p!$ is the primitive for a sending type, and $p?$ is the primitive for a receiving type, derived from global type $p \to q\{l_i(S_i).G_i\}_{i\in I}$ by projection. Others correspond straightforwardly to process terms. Note that type $\underline{\mathsf{end}}$ only appears in *runtime* type checking. Below we define $G{\restriction}p$ to project a global type G on p, thus generating p's local type.

Definition 4 (Projection). Consider a well-formed top-level global type $[\tilde{q}]G$. Then $G{\restriction}p$ is defined as follows:

(1) $G{\restriction}p$ where $G = \mathsf{t}(G_0)\mathsf{h}(F_1\!:\!G_1, ..., F_n\!:\!G_n)^\kappa.G' =$
$$\begin{cases} \mathsf{t}(G_0{\restriction}p)\mathsf{h}(\Gamma_1\!:\!G_1{\restriction}p, ..., F_n\!:\!G_n{\restriction}p)^{(\kappa, \emptyset)}.G'{\restriction}p & \text{if } p \in roles(G) \\ G'{\restriction}p & \text{otherwise} \end{cases}$$

(2) $p_1 \to p_2\{l_i(S_i).G_i\}_{i\in I}{\restriction}p = \begin{cases} p_2!\{l_i(S_i).G_i{\restriction}p\}_{i\in I} & \text{if } p = p_1 \\ p_1?\{l_i(S_i).G_i{\restriction}p\}_{i\in I} & \text{if } p = p_2 \\ G_1{\restriction}p & \text{if } \forall i, j \in I.G_i{\restriction}p = G_j{\restriction}p \end{cases}$

(3) $(\mu t.G')\!\restriction\! p = \mu t.(G\!\restriction\! p)$ if $\nexists t(G')\mathsf{h}(H) \in G$ and $G\!\restriction\! p \neq t'$ for any t'

(4) $t\!\restriction\! p = t$ (5) $\mathsf{end}\!\restriction\! p = \mathsf{end}$

Otherwise it is undefined.

The main rule is (1): if p appears somewhere in the target try-handle global type then the endpoint type has a try-handle annotated with κ and the default logic (i.e., $F = \emptyset$). Note that even if $G_0\!\restriction\! p = \mathsf{end}$ the endpoint still gets such a try-handle because it needs to be ready for (possible) failure handling; if p does not appear anywhere in the target try-handle global type, then the projection skips to the continuation.

Rule (2) produces local types for interaction endpoints. If the endpoint is a sender (i.e., $p = p_1$), then its local type abstracts that it will send something from one of the possible internal choices defined in $\{l_i(S_i)\}_{i \in I}$ to p_2, then continue as $G_k\!\restriction\! p$, gained from the projection, if $k \in I$ is chosen. If the endpoint is a receiver (i.e., $p = p_2$), then its local type abstracts that it will receive something from one of the possible external choices defined in $\{l_i(S_i)\}_{i \in I}$ sent by p_1; the rest is similarly as for the sender. However, if p is not in this interaction, then its local type starts from the next interaction which p is in; moreover, because p does not know what choice that p_1 has made, every path $G_i\!\restriction\! p$ lead by branch l_i shall be the same for p to ensure that interactions are consistent. For example, in $G = p_1 \to p_2\{l_1(S_1).p_3 \to p_1\ l_3(S),\ l_2(S_2).p_3 \to p_1\ l_4(S)\}$, interaction $p_3 \to p_1$ continues after $p_1 \to p_2$ takes place. If $l_3 \neq l_4$, then G is not projectable for p_3 because p_3 does not know which branch that p_1 has chosen; if p_1 chose branch l_1, but p_3 (blindly) sends out label l_4 to p_1, for p_1 it is a mistake (but it is not a mistake for p_3) because p_1 is expecting to receive label l_3. To prevent such inconsistencies, we adopt the projection algorithm proposed in [24]. Other session type works [17,39] provide ways to weaken the classical restriction on projection of branching which we use.

Rule (3) forbids a try-handle to appear in a recursive body, e.g., $\mu t.$ $\mathsf{t}(F : t)^{\kappa}.G$ is not allowed, but $\mathsf{t}(\mu t.G)\mathsf{h}(H)^{\kappa}$ and $\mathsf{t}(G)\mathsf{h}(F : \mu t.G', H)^{\kappa}$ are allowed. This is because κ is used to avoid confusion of messages from different try-handles. If a recursive body contains a try-handle, we have to dynamically generate different levels to maintain interaction consistency, so static type checking does not suffice. We are investigating alternative runtime checking mechanisms, but this is beyond the scope of this paper. Other rules are straightforward.

Example 6. Recall the global type G from Fig. 2 in Sect. 1. Applying projection rules defined in Definition 4 to G on every role in G we obtain the following:

$$
\begin{aligned}
T_{dfs} = G\!\restriction\! dfs &= \mathsf{t}(\mu t.w_1!l_{d_1}(S).w_2!l_{d_2}(S).w_1?l_{r_1}(S').w_2?l_{r_2}(S').t)\mathsf{h}(\mathcal{H}_{dfs})^{(1,\emptyset)}\\
\mathcal{H}_{dfs} &= \{w_1\}\!:\!\mu t'.w_2!l'_{d_1}(S).w_2?l'_{r_1}(S').t',\\
&\quad \{w_2\}\!:\!\mu t''.w_1!l'_{d_2}(S).w_1?l'_{r_2}(S').t'', \{w_1, w_2\}\!:\!\mathsf{end}\\
T_{w_1} = G\!\restriction\! w_1 &= \mathsf{t}(\mu t.dfs?l_{d_1}(S).dfs!l_{r_1}(S').t)\mathsf{h}(\mathcal{H}_{w_1})^{(1,\emptyset)}\\
\mathcal{H}_{w_1} &= \{w_1\}\!:\!\mathsf{end}, \{w_2\}\!:\!\mu t'.dfs?l'_{d_2}(S).dfs!l'_{r_2}(S').t', \{w_1, w_2\}\!:\!\mathsf{end}\\
T_{w_2} = G\!\restriction\! w_2 &= \mathsf{t}(\mu t.dfs?l_{d_2}(S).dfs!l_{r_2}(S').t)\mathsf{h}(\mathcal{H}_{w_2})^{(1,\emptyset)}\\
\mathcal{H}_{w_2} &= \{w_1\}\!:\!\mu t''.dfs?l'_{d_1}(S).dfs!l'_{r_1}(S').t'', \{w_2\}\!:\!\mathsf{end}, \{w_1, w_2\}\!:\!\mathsf{end}
\end{aligned}
$$

$$\frac{\Gamma \vdash a : \langle G \rangle \qquad \qquad k \in I \quad \Gamma \vdash e : S_k}{\Gamma \vdash P \rhd \ \{c : G\!\restriction\! p\} \qquad \qquad \Gamma \vdash c : \eta_k \rhd \ \{c : T_k\}}{\Gamma \vdash a[p].P \rhd \ \emptyset \qquad \Gamma \vdash c : p!\, l_k(e).\eta_k \rhd \ \{c : p!\, \{l_i(S_i).T_i\}_{i \in I}\}} \quad \lfloor \texttt{T-ini/T-snd} \rfloor$$

$$\frac{\forall i \in I.\ \Gamma, x_i : S_i \ \vdash c : \eta_i \rhd \ \{c : T_i\}}{\Gamma \ \vdash c : p?\, \{l_i(x_i).\eta_i\}_{i \in I} \rhd \ \{c : p?\, \{l_i(S_i).T_i\}_{i \in I}\}} \quad \lfloor \texttt{T-rcv} \rfloor$$

$$\frac{\Delta \ \text{end-only} \qquad \Gamma \vdash c : \eta \rhd \ \{c : \text{end}\}}{\Gamma \vdash c : 0 \rhd \ \Delta \qquad \Gamma \vdash c : \underline{0}.\eta \rhd \ \{c : \underline{\text{end}}.\text{end}\}} \quad \lfloor \texttt{T-0/T-yd} \rfloor$$

$$\frac{\begin{array}{c} \Gamma \vdash e : \text{bool} \\ \forall i \in \{1,2\}.\ \Gamma \ \vdash c : \eta_i \rhd \ \Delta \end{array} \qquad \qquad \Gamma \vdash e : S}{\Gamma \ \vdash c : \text{if } e\ \eta_1 \text{ else } \eta_2 \rhd \ \Delta \qquad \Gamma, X : S\, T \ \vdash c : X\langle e \rangle \rhd \ \{c : T\}} \quad \lfloor \texttt{T-if/T-var} \rfloor$$

$$\frac{\begin{array}{c} \Gamma, X : S\ t, x : S \ \vdash c : \eta_1 \rhd \ \{c : T'\} \\ \Gamma, X : S\ \mu t.T' \ \vdash c : \eta_2 \rhd \ \{c : T\} \end{array}}{\Gamma \ \vdash c : \text{def } X(x) = \eta_1 \text{ in } \eta_2 \rhd \ \{c : T\}} \quad \lfloor \texttt{T-def} \rfloor$$

$$\frac{\Gamma \ \vdash c : \eta \rhd \ \{c : T\} \quad \Gamma \ \vdash c : \eta' \rhd \ \{c : T'\} \quad dom(\text{H}) = dom(\mathcal{H}) \quad \forall F \in dom(\text{H}).\ \Gamma \ \vdash c : \text{H}(F) \rhd \ \{c : \mathcal{H}(F)\}}{\Gamma \ \vdash c : t(\eta)h(\text{H})^\phi.\eta' \rhd \ \{c : t(T)h(\mathcal{H})^\phi.T'\}} \quad \lfloor \texttt{T-th} \rfloor$$

Fig. 10. Typing rules for processes

6   Type System

Next we introduce our type system for typing processes. Figures 10 and 11 present typing rules for endpoints processes, and typing judgments for applications and systems respectively.

We define shared environments Γ to keep information on variables and the coordinator, and session environments Δ to keep information on endpoint types:

$$\Gamma ::= \emptyset \mid \Gamma, X : S\ T \mid \Gamma, x : S \mid \Gamma, a : G \mid \Gamma, \Psi \qquad \Delta ::= \emptyset \mid \Delta, c : T \mid \Delta, s : h$$
$$m ::= \langle p, q, l(S) \rangle \mid \langle\!\langle p, \text{crash } F \rangle\!\rangle \mid \langle p, q \rangle^\phi \qquad \qquad h ::= \emptyset \mid h \cdot m$$

Γ maps process variables X and content variables x to their types, shared names a to global types G, and a coordinator $\Psi = G : (F, d)$ to failures and done notifications it has observed. Δ maps session channels c to local types and session queues to queue types. We write $\Gamma, \Gamma' = \Gamma \cup \Gamma'$ when $dom(\Gamma) \cap dom(\Gamma') = \emptyset$; same for Δ, Δ'. Queue types h are composed of message types m. Their permutation is defined analogously to the permutation for messages. The typing judgment for local processes $\Gamma \vdash P \rhd \Delta$ states that process P is well-typed by Δ under Γ.

Since we do not define sequential composition for processes, our type system implicitly forbids session interleaving by $\lfloor \texttt{T-ini} \rfloor$. This is different from other session type works [15,24], where session interleaving is prohibited for the progress property; here the restriction is inherent to the type system.

Figure 10 lists our typing rules for endpoint processes. Rule $\lfloor \texttt{T-ini} \rfloor$ says that if a process's set of actions is well-typed by $G\!\restriction\! p$ on some c, this process can play role p in a, which claims to have interactions obeying behaviors defined in G. $\langle G \rangle$ means that G is closed, i.e., devoid of type variables. This rule forbids

$$\Gamma \vdash \mathsf{s} : \emptyset \rhd \{\mathsf{s} : \emptyset\} \qquad \frac{\Gamma \vdash \mathsf{s} : h \rhd \{\mathsf{s} : \mathsf{h}\} \quad \Gamma \vdash e : S}{\Gamma \vdash \mathsf{s} : h \cdot \langle p, q, l(e) \rangle \rhd \{\mathsf{s} : \mathsf{h} \cdot \langle p, q, l(S) \rangle\}} \qquad \lfloor \text{T-}\emptyset/\text{T-m} \rfloor$$

$$\frac{(p_1, p_2) \in \{(p, \psi), (\psi, p)\} \quad \Gamma \vdash \mathsf{s} : h \rhd \{\mathsf{s} : \mathsf{h}\}}{\Gamma \vdash \mathsf{s} : h \cdot \langle p_1, p_2 \rangle^\phi \rhd \{\mathsf{s} : \mathsf{h} \cdot \langle p_1, p_2 \rangle^\phi\}} \qquad \lfloor \text{T-D} \rfloor$$

$$\frac{\begin{array}{c} p \in \{q, \psi\} \quad \mathsf{m} = \langle p, \mathsf{crash}\ F \rangle \\ \Gamma \vdash \mathsf{s} : h \rhd \{\mathsf{s} : \mathsf{h}\} \end{array}}{\Gamma \vdash \mathsf{s} : h \cdot \langle p, \mathsf{crash}\ F \rangle \rhd \{\mathsf{s} : \mathsf{h} \cdot \mathsf{m}\}} \quad \frac{\begin{array}{c} \Gamma \vdash N_1 \rhd \Delta_1 \quad \Gamma \vdash N_2 \rhd \Delta_2 \\ dom(\Delta_1) \cap dom(\Delta_2) = \emptyset \end{array}}{\Gamma \vdash N_1 \mid N_2 \rhd \Delta_1, \Delta_2} \qquad \lfloor \text{T-}F/\text{T-pa} \rfloor$$

$$\frac{\begin{array}{c} \Gamma \vdash \mathcal{S} \rhd \Delta \\ \Gamma \vdash \Delta_\mathsf{s}\ \text{coherent} \end{array}}{\Gamma \vdash (\nu\mathsf{s})\mathcal{S} \rhd \Delta \setminus \Delta_\mathsf{s}} \quad \frac{\Gamma' = \Gamma, \Psi \quad \Gamma \vdash N \rhd \Delta}{\Gamma' \vdash \Psi \blacklozenge N \rhd \Delta} \qquad \lfloor \text{T-s/T-sys} \rfloor$$

Fig. 11. Typing rules for applications and systems.

$a[p].b[q].P$ because a process can only use one session channel. Rule $\lfloor \text{T-snd} \rfloor$ states that an action for sending is well-typed to a sending type if the label and the type of the content are expected; $\lfloor \text{T-rcv} \rfloor$ states that an action for branching (i.e., for receiving) is well-typed to a branching type if all labels and the types of contents are as expected. Their follow-up actions shall also be well-typed. Rule $\lfloor \text{T-0} \rfloor$ types an idle process. Predicate end-only Δ is defined as stating whether all endpoints in Δ have type end:

Definition 5 (End-only Δ). We say Δ is end-only if and only if $\forall \mathsf{s}[p] \in dom(\Delta), \Delta(\mathsf{s}[p]) = \mathsf{end}$.

Rule $\lfloor \text{T-yd} \rfloor$ types yielding actions, which only appear at runtime. Rule $\lfloor \text{T-if} \rfloor$ is standard in the sense that the process is well-typed by Δ if e has boolean type and its sub-processes (i.e., η_1 and η_2) are well-typed by Δ. Rules $\lfloor \text{T-var}, \text{T-def} \rfloor$ are based on a recent summary of MPSTs [14]. Note that $\lfloor \text{T-def} \rfloor$ forbids the type $\mu t.t$. Rule $\lfloor \text{T-th} \rfloor$ states that a try-handle is well-typed if it is annotated with the expected level ϕ, its default statement is well-typed, $\mathcal{H}$ and H have the same handler signatures, and all handling actions are well-typed.

Figure 11 shows typing rules for applications and systems. Rule $\lfloor \text{T-}\emptyset \rfloor$ types an empty queue. Rules $\lfloor \text{T-m}, \text{T-D}, \text{T-}F \rfloor$ simply type messages based on their shapes. Rule $\lfloor \text{T-pa} \rfloor$ says two applications composed in parallel are well-typed if they do not share any session channel. Rule $\lfloor \text{T-s} \rfloor$ says a part of a system $\mathcal{S}$ can start a private session, say s, if $\mathcal{S}$ is well-typed according to a $\Gamma \vdash \Delta_\mathsf{s}$ that is *coherent* (defined shortly). The system $(\nu\mathsf{s})\mathcal{S}$ with a part becoming private in s is well-typed to $\Delta \setminus \Delta_\mathsf{s}$, that is, Δ after removing Δ_s.

Definition 6 (A Session Environment Having s Only: Δ_s)

$$\Delta_\mathsf{s} = \{\mathsf{s}[p] : T \mid \mathsf{s}[p] \in dom(\Delta)\} \cup \{\mathsf{s} : h \mid \mathsf{s} \in dom(\Delta)\}$$

Rule $\lfloor \text{T-sys} \rfloor$ says that a system $\Psi \blacklozenge N$ is well-typed if application N is well-typed and there exists a coordinator Ψ for handling this application. We say $\Gamma \vdash \Delta$ is coherent under Γ if the local types of all endpoints are dual to each other after their local types are updated because of messages or notifications in $\mathsf{s} : h$.

Coherence. We say that a session environment is coherent if, at any time, given a session with its latest messages and notifications, every endpoint participating in it is able to find someone to interact with (i.e., its dual party exists) right now or afterwards.

Example 7. Continuing with Example 6 – the session environment $\Gamma \vdash \Delta$ is coherent even if w_2 will not receive any message from *dfs* at this point. The only possible action to take in Δ is that *dfs* sends out a message to w_1. When this action fires, Δ is reduced to Δ' under a coordinator. (The reduction relation $\Gamma \vdash \Delta \to_T \Gamma' \vdash \Delta'$, where $\Gamma = \Gamma_0, \Psi$ and $\Gamma' = \Gamma_0, \Psi'$, is defined based on the rules of operational semantics of applications in Sect. 4, Figs. 6 and 7). In Δ', which abstracts the environment when *dfs* sends a message to w_1, w_2 will be able to receive this message.

$$\Delta = \mathsf{s}[dfs] : T_{dfs},\ \mathsf{s}[w_1] : T_{w_1},\ \mathsf{s}[w_2] : T_{w_2}, \mathsf{s} : \emptyset$$
$$\Delta' = \mathsf{s}[dfs] : \mathsf{t}(w_2!l_{d_2}(S).w_1?l_{r_1}(S').w_2?l_{r_2}(S').T)\mathsf{h}(\mathcal{H})^{(1,\emptyset)},$$
$$\mathsf{s}[w_1] : T_{w_1},\ \mathsf{s}[w_2] : T_{w_2}, \mathsf{s} : \langle dfs, w_1, l_{d_1}(S)\rangle$$
$$\text{where } T = \mu t.w_1!l_{d_1}(S).w_2!l_{d_2}(S).w_1?l_{r_1}(S').w_2?l_{r_2}(S').t$$

We write $\mathsf{s}[p] : T \bowtie \mathsf{s}[q] : T'$ to state that actions of the two types are *dual*:

Definition 7 (Duality). We define $\mathsf{s}[p] : T \bowtie \mathsf{s}[q] : T'$ as follows:

$$\mathsf{s}[p] : \mathsf{end} \bowtie \mathsf{s}[q] : \mathsf{end} \quad \mathsf{s}[p] : \underline{\mathsf{end}} \bowtie \mathsf{s}[q] : \underline{\mathsf{end}} \quad \mathsf{s}[p] : \mathsf{end} \bowtie \mathsf{s}[q] : \underline{\mathsf{end}}$$

$$\mathsf{s}[p] : \underline{\mathsf{end}} \bowtie \mathsf{s}[q] : \mathsf{end} \quad \mathsf{s}[p] : t \bowtie \mathsf{s}[q] : t \quad \frac{\mathsf{s}[p] : T \bowtie \mathsf{s}[q] : T'}{\mathsf{s}[p] : \mu t.T \bowtie \mathsf{s}[q] : \mu t.T'}$$

$$\frac{\forall i \in I.\ \mathsf{s}[p] : T_i \bowtie \mathsf{s}[q] : T_i'}{\mathsf{s}[p] : q!\ \{l_i(S_i).T_i\}_{i\in I} \bowtie \mathsf{s}[q] : p?\ \{l_i(S_i).T_i'\}_{i\in I}}$$

$$\frac{\mathsf{s}[p] : T_1 \bowtie \mathsf{s}[q] : T_2 \quad \mathsf{s}[p] : T_1' \bowtie \mathsf{s}[q] : T_2' \quad dom(\mathcal{H}_1) = dom(\mathcal{H}_2)}{\forall F \in dom(\mathcal{H}_1).\ \mathsf{s}[p] : \mathcal{H}_1(F) \bowtie \mathsf{s}[q] : \mathcal{H}_2(F)}$$
$$\frac{}{\mathsf{s}[p] : \mathsf{t}(T_1)\mathsf{h}(\mathcal{H}_1)^\phi.T_1' \bowtie \mathsf{s}[q] : \mathsf{t}(T_2)\mathsf{h}(\mathcal{H}_2)^\phi.T_2'}$$

Operation $T \downarrow p$ is to filter T to get the partial type which only contains actions of p. For example, $p_1!l'(S').p_2!l(S) \downarrow p_2 = p_2!l(S)$ and $p_1!\{T_1, T_2\} \downarrow p_2 = p_2?l(S)$ where $T_1 = l_1(S_1).p_2?l(S)$ and $T_2 = l_2(S_2).p_2?l(S)$. Next we define $(\mathsf{h})_{p\to q}$ to filter h to generate (1) the normal message types sent from p heading to q, and (2) the notifications heading to q. For example $(\langle p, q, l(S)\rangle \cdot \langle\!\langle q, \mathsf{crash}\ F \rangle\!\rangle \cdot \langle \psi, q \rangle^\phi \cdot \langle\!\langle p, \mathsf{crash}\ F \rangle\!\rangle)_{p\to q} = p?l(S) \cdot \langle\!\langle F \rangle\!\rangle \cdot \langle \psi \rangle^\phi$. The message types are abbreviated to contain only necessary information.

We define T−ht to mean the effect of ht on T. Its concept is similar to the *session remainder* defined in [35], which returns new local types of participants after participants consume messages from the global queue. Since failure notifications will not be consumed in our system, and we only have to observe the change of a participant's type after receiving or being triggered by some message types in ht, we say that T−ht represents the effect of ht on T. The behaviors follows our operational semantics of applications and systems defined in Figs. 6, 7, and 8.

For example $\mathsf{t}(q?\{l_i(S_i).T_i\}_{i\in I})\mathsf{h}(\mathcal{H})^\phi.T'-q?l_k(S_k)\cdot\mathsf{ht} \;=\; \mathsf{t}(T_k)\mathsf{h}(\mathcal{H})^\phi.T'-\mathsf{ht}$ where $k \in I$.

Now we define what it means for Δ to be coherent under Γ:

Definition 8 (Coherence). $\Gamma \vdash \Delta$ coherent if the following conditions hold:

1. If $\mathsf{s} : \mathsf{h} \in \Delta$, then $\exists G : (F, d) \in \Gamma$ and $\{p \mid \mathsf{s}[p] \in dom(\Delta)\} \subseteq roles(G)$ and G is well-formed and $\forall p \in roles(G), G{\restriction}p$ is defined.
2. $\forall \mathsf{s}[p] : T, \mathsf{s}[q] : T' \in \Delta$ we have $\mathsf{s}[p] : T \restriction q - (\mathsf{h})_{q\to p} \bowtie \mathsf{s}[q] : T' \restriction p - (\mathsf{h})_{p\to q}$.

In condition 1, we require a coordinator for every session so that when a failure occurs, the coordinator can announce failure notifications to ask participants to handle the failure. Condition 2 requires that, for any two endpoints, say $\mathsf{s}[p]$ and $\mathsf{s}[q]$, in Δ, equation $\mathsf{s}[p] : T \restriction q - (\mathsf{h})_{q\to p} \bowtie \mathsf{s}[q] : T' \restriction p - (\mathsf{h})_{p\to q}$, must hold. This condition asserts that interactions of non-failed endpoints are dual to each other after the effect of h; while failed endpoints are removed from Δ, thus the condition is satisfied immediately.

7 Properties

We show that our type system ensures properties of subject congruence, subject reduction, and progress. All auxiliary definitions and proofs are in the long version [43].

The property of subject congruence states that if $\mathcal{S}$ (a system containing an application and a coordinator) is well-typed by some session environment, then a $\mathcal{S}'$ that is structurally congruent to it is also well-typed by the same session environment:

Theorem 1 (Subject Congruence). $\Gamma \vdash \mathcal{S} \rhd \Delta$ and $\mathcal{S} \equiv \mathcal{S}'$ imply $\Gamma \vdash \mathcal{S}' \rhd \Delta$.

Subject reduction states that a well-typed $\mathcal{S}$ (coherent session environment respectively) is always well-typed (coherent respectively) after reduction:

Theorem 2 (Subject Reduction)

- $\Gamma \vdash \mathcal{S} \rhd \Delta$ with $\Gamma \vdash \Delta$ coherent and $\mathcal{S} \to^* \mathcal{S}'$ imply that $\exists \Delta', \Gamma'$ such that $\Gamma' \vdash \mathcal{S}' \rhd \Delta'$ and $\Gamma \vdash \Delta \to_T^* \Gamma' \vdash \Delta'$ or $\Delta \equiv \Delta'$ and $\Gamma' \vdash \Delta'$ coherent.
- $\Gamma \vdash \mathcal{S} \rhd \emptyset$ and $\mathcal{S} \to^* \mathcal{S}'$ imply that $\Gamma' \vdash \mathcal{S}' \rhd \emptyset$ for some Γ'.

We allow sessions to run in parallel at the top level, e.g., $\mathcal{S} = (\nu \mathsf{s}_1)(\Psi_1 \blacklozenge N_1) \mid \dots \mid (\nu \mathsf{s}_n)(\Psi_n \blacklozenge N_n)$. Assume we have $\mathcal{S}$ with $a[p].P \in \mathcal{S}$. If we cannot apply rule (**Link**), $\mathcal{S}$ cannot reduce. To prevent this kind of situation, we require $\mathcal{S}$ to be *initializable* such that, $\forall a[p].P \in \mathcal{S}$, (**Link**) is applicable.

The following property states that $\mathcal{S}$ never gets stuck (property of progress):

Theorem 3 (Progress). If $\Gamma \vdash \mathcal{S} \rhd \emptyset$ and $\mathcal{S}$ is initializable, then either $\mathcal{S} \to^* \mathcal{S}'$ and $\mathcal{S}'$ is initializable or $\mathcal{S}' = \Psi \blacklozenge \mathsf{s} : h \mid \dots \mid \Psi' \blacklozenge \mathsf{s}' : h'$ and $h, \dots, h'$ only contain failure notifications sent by coordinators and messages heading to failed participants.

After all processes in S terminate, failure notifications sent by coordinators are left; thus the final system can be of the form $\Psi \blacklozenge \mathsf{s} : h \mid ... \mid \Psi' \blacklozenge \mathsf{s}' : h'$, where $h, ..., h'$ have failure notifications sent by coordinators and thus reduction rules (**CollectDone**), (**IssueDone**), and (**F**) will not be applied.

Minimality. The following proposition points out that, when all roles defined in a global type, say G, are robust, then the application obeying to G will never have interaction with a coordinator (i.e., interactions of the application are equivalent to those without a coordinator). This is an important property, as it states that our model does not incur coordination overhead when all participants are robust, or in failure-agnostic contexts as considered in previous MPST works.

Proposition 2. Assume $\forall p \in roles(G) = \{p_1, ..., p_n\}$, p is robust and $P_i = \mathsf{s}[p_i] : \eta_i$ for $i \in \{1..n\}$ and $S = (\nu\ \mathsf{s})(\Psi \blacklozenge P_1|...|P_n|\mathsf{s} : h)$ where $P_i, i \in \{1..n\}$ contains no try-handle. Then we have $\Gamma \vdash S \rhd \emptyset$ and whenever $S \rightarrow^* S'$ we have $\Psi \in S'$, $\Psi = G : (\emptyset, \emptyset)$.

Proof. Immediately by typing rules $\lfloor \mathtt{T\text{-}ini}, \mathtt{T\text{-}s}, \mathtt{T\text{-}sys} \rfloor$, Definition 4 (Projection), and the operational semantics defined in Figs. 6, 7, and 8.

8   Related Work

Several session type works study exception handling [7,9,16,30]. However, to the best of our knowledge this is the first theoretical work to develop a formalism and typing discipline for the coordinator-based model of *crash failure* handling in practical asynchronous distributed systems.

Structured interactional exceptions [7] study exception handling for binary sessions. The work extends session types with a *try-catch* construct and a *throw* instruction, allowing participants to raise runtime exceptions. Global escape [6] extends previous works on exception handling in binary session types to MPSTs. It supports nesting and sequencing of try-catch blocks with restrictions. Reduction rules for exception handling are of the form $\Sigma \vdash P \rightarrow \Sigma' \vdash P'$, where Σ is the *exception environment*. This central environment at the core of the semantics is updated synchronously and atomically. Furthermore, the reduction of a try-catch block to its continuation is done in a synchronous reduction step involving all participants in a block. Lastly this work can only handle exceptions, i.e., explicitly raised application-level failures. These do not affect communication channels [6], unlike participant crashes.

Similarly, our previous work [13] only deals with exceptions. An interaction $p \rightarrow q : S \vee F$ defines that p can send a message of type S to q. If F is not empty then instead of sending a message p can throw F. If a failure is thrown only participants that have casual dependencies to that failure are involved in the failure handling. No concurrent failures are allowed therefore all interactions which can raise failures are executed in a lock step fashion. As a consequence, the model can not be used to deal with crash failures.

Adameit et al. [1] propose session types for link failures, which extend session types with an optional block which surrounds a process and contains default values. The default values are used if a link failure occurs. In contrast to our work, the communication model is overall synchronous whereas our model is asynchronous; the optional block returns default values in case of a failure but it is still the task of the developer to do something useful with it.

Demangeon et al. study interrupts in MPSTs [16]. This work introduces an interruptible block $\{|G|\}^c \langle l$ by $r \rangle; G'$ identified by c; here the protocol G can be interrupted by a message l from r and is continued by G' after either a normal or an interrupted completion of G. Interrupts are more a control flow instruction like exceptions than an actual failure handling construct, and the semantics can not model participant crashes.

Neykova and Yoshida [36] show that MPSTs can be used to calculate safe global states for a safe recovery in Erlang's *let it crash* model [2]. That work is well suited for recovery of lightweight processes in an actor setting. However, while it allows for elaborate failure handling by connecting (endpoint) processes with runtime monitors, the model does not address the fault tolerance of runtime monitors themselves. As monitors can be interacting in complex manners replication does not seem straightforwardly applicable, at least not without potentially hampering performance (just as with *straightforward* replication of entire applications).

Failure handling is studied in several process calculi and communication-centered programming languages without typing discipline. The conversation calculus [42] models exception behavior in abstract service-based systems with message-passing based communication. The work does not use channel types but studies the behavioral theory of bisimilarity. Error recovery is also studied in a concurrent object setting [45]; interacting objects are grouped into coordinated atomic actions (CAs) which enable safe error recovery. CAs can however not be nested. PSYNC [18] is a domain specific language based on the *heard-of* model of distributed computing [12]. Programs written in PSYNC are structured into rounds which are executed in a lock step manner. PSYNC comes with a state-based verification engine which enables checking of safety and liveness properties; for that programmers have to define non-trivial inductive invariants and ranking functions. In contrast to the coordinator model, the heard-of model is not widely deployed in practice. Verdi [44] is a framework for implementing and verifying distributed systems in Coq. It provides the possibility to verify the system against different network models. Verdi enables the verification of properties in an idealized fault model and then transfers the guarantees to more realistic fault models by applying transformation functions. Verdi supports safety properties but no liveness properties.

9   Final Remarks

Implementation. Based on our presented calculus we developed a domain-specific language and corresponding runtime system in Scala, using ZooKeeper as the coordinator. Specifically our implementation provides mechanisms for (1) interacting with ZooKeeper as coordinator, (2) done and failure notification delivery and routing, (3) practical failure detection and dealing with false suspicions and (4) automatically inferring try-handle levels.

Conclusions. This work introduces a formal model of verified crash failure handling featuring a lightweight coordinator as common in many real-life systems. The model carefully exposes potential problems that may arise in distributed applications due to partial failures, such as inconsistent endpoint behaviors and orphan messages. Our typing discipline addresses these challenges by building on the mechanisms of MPSTs, e.g., global type well-formedness for sound failure handling specifications, modeling asynchronous permutations between regular messages and failure notifications in sessions, and the type-directed mechanisms for determining correct and orphaned messages in the event of failure. We adapt coherence of session typing environments (i.e., endpoint consistency) to consider failed roles and orphan messages, and show that our type system statically ensures subject reduction and progress in the presence of failures.

Future Work. We plan to expand our implementation and develop further applications. We believe dynamic role participation and role parameterization would be valuable for failure handling. Also, we are investigating options to enable addressing the coordinator as part of the protocol so that pertinent runtime information can be persisted by the coordinator. We plan to add support to our language and calculus for solving various explicit agreement tasks (e.g., consensus, atomic commit) via the coordinator.

References

1. Adameit, M., Peters, K., Nestmann, U.: Session types for link failures. In: Bouajjani, A., Silva, A. (eds.) FORTE 2017. LNCS, vol. 10321, pp. 1–16. Springer, Cham (2017). https://doi.org/10.1007/978-3-319-60225-7_1
2. Armstrong, J.: Making reliable distributed systems in the presence of software errors. Ph.D. thesis, Royal Institute of Technology, Stockholm, Sweden (2003)
3. Birman, K.P.: Byzantine Clients (2017). https://goo.gl/1Qbc4r
4. Burrows, M.: The Chubby lock service for loosely-coupled distributed systems. In: OSDI 2006, pp. 335–350. USENIX Association (2006)
5. Caires, L., Pérez, J.A.: Multiparty session types within a canonical binary theory, and beyond. In: Albert, E., Lanese, I. (eds.) FORTE 2016. LNCS, vol. 9688, pp. 74–95. Springer, Cham (2016). https://doi.org/10.1007/978-3-319-39570-8_6
6. Capecchi, S., Giachino, E., Yoshida, N.: Global escape in multiparty sessions. MSCS **26**(2), 156–205 (2016)
7. Carbone, M., Honda, K., Yoshida, N.: Structured interactional exceptions in session types. In: van Breugel, F., Chechik, M. (eds.) CONCUR 2008. LNCS, vol. 5201, pp. 402–417. Springer, Heidelberg (2008). https://doi.org/10.1007/978-3-540-85361-9_32

8. Carbone, M., Lindley, S., Montesi, F., Schürmann, C., Wadler, P.: Coherence generalises duality: a logical explanation of multiparty session types. In: CONCUR 2016. LIPIcs, vol. 59, pp. 33:1–33:15. Schloss Dagstuhl - Leibniz-Zentrum fuer Informatik (2016)

9. Carbone, M., Yoshida, N., Honda, K.: Asynchronous session types: exceptions and multiparty interactions. In: Bernardo, M., Padovani, L., Zavattaro, G. (eds.) SFM 2009. LNCS, vol. 5569, pp. 187–212. Springer, Heidelberg (2009). https://doi.org/10.1007/978-3-642-01918-0_5

10. Chandra, T.D., Hadzilacos, V., Toueg, S., Charron-Bost, B.: On the impossibility of group membership. In: PODC 1996, pp. 322–330. ACM (1996)

11. Chang, F., Dean, J., Ghemawat, S., Hsieh, W.C., Wallach, D.A., Burrows, M., Chandra, T., Fikes, A., Gruber, R.: Bigtable: a distributed storage system for structured data. In: OSDI 2006, pp. 205–218. USENIX Association (2006)

12. Charron-Bost, B., Schiper, A.: The Heard-Of model: computing in distributed systems with benign faults. Distrib. Comput. 22(1), 49–71 (2009)

13. Chen, T.-C., Viering, M., Bejleri, A., Ziarek, L., Eugster, P.: A type theory for robust failure handling in distributed systems. In: Albert, E., Lanese, I. (eds.) FORTE 2016. LNCS, vol. 9688, pp. 96–113. Springer, Cham (2016). https://doi.org/10.1007/978-3-319-39570-8_7

14. Coppo, M., Dezani-Ciancaglini, M., Padovani, L., Yoshida, N.: A gentle introduction to multiparty asynchronous session types. In: Bernardo, M., Johnsen, E.B. (eds.) SFM 2015. LNCS, vol. 9104, pp. 146–178. Springer, Cham (2015). https://doi.org/10.1007/978-3-319-18941-3_4

15. Coppo, M., Dezani-Ciancaglini, M., Yoshida, N., Padovani, L.: Global progress for dynamically interleaved multiparty sessions. MSCS 26(2), 238–302 (2016)

16. Demangeon, R., Honda, K., Hu, R., Neykova, R., Yoshida, N.: Practical interruptible conversations. Formal Methods Syst. Des. 46(3), 197–225 (2015)

17. Deniélou, P.M., Yoshida, N.: Dynamic multirole session types. In: POPL 2011, pp. 435–446. ACM (2011)

18. Dragoi, C., Henzinger, T., Zufferey, D.: PSync: a partially synchronous language for fault-tolerant distributed algorithms. In: POPL 2016, pp. 400–415. ACM (2016)

19. Fischer, M.J., Lynch, N.A., Paterson, M.S.: Impossibility of distributed consensus with one faulty process. J. ACM 32(2), 374–382 (1985)

20. Ghemawat, S., Gobioff, H., Leung, S.T.: The Google file system. In: SOSP 2003, pp. 29–43. ACM (2003)

21. Gilbert, S., Lynch, N.: Brewer's conjecture and the feasibility of consistent, available, partition-tolerant web services. SIGACT News 33(2), 51–59 (2002)

22. Guerraoui, R., Schiper, A.: The generic consensus service. IEEE Trans. Softw. Eng. 27(1), 29–41 (2001)

23. Honda, K., Vasconcelos, V.T., Kubo, M.: Language primitives and type discipline for structured communication-based programming. In: Hankin, C. (ed.) ESOP 1998. LNCS, vol. 1381, pp. 122–138. Springer, Heidelberg (1998). https://doi.org/10.1007/BFb0053567

24. Honda, K., Yoshida, N., Carbone, M.: Multiparty asynchronous session types. J. ACM 63(1), 9:1–9:67 (2016)

25. Hu, R., Yoshida, N.: Hybrid session verification through endpoint API generation. In: Stevens, P., Wąsowski, A. (eds.) FASE 2016. LNCS, vol. 9633, pp. 401–418. Springer, Heidelberg (2016). https://doi.org/10.1007/978-3-662-49665-7_24

26. Hunt, P.: ZooKeeper: wait-free coordination for internet-scale systems. In: USENIX 2010. USENIX Association (2010)

27. Hüttel, H., et al.: Foundations of session types and behavioural contracts. ACM Comput. Surv. **49**(1), 3:1–3:36 (2016)
28. Imai, K., Yoshida, N., Yuen, S.: Session-ocaml: a session-based library with polarities and lenses. In: Jacquet, J.-M., Massink, M. (eds.) COORDINATION 2017. LNCS, vol. 10319, pp. 99–118. Springer, Cham (2017). https://doi.org/10.1007/978-3-319-59746-1_6
29. Killian, C.E., Anderson, J.W., Braud, R., Jhala, R., Vahdat, A.M.: Mace: language support for building distributed systems. In: PLDI 2007, vol. 42, pp. 179–188. ACM (2007)
30. Kouzapas, D., Yoshida, N.: Globally governed session semantics. LMCS **10**(4), 1–45 (2014)
31. Kreps, J., Narkhede, N., Rao, J.: Kafka: a distributed messaging system for log processing. In: NetDB 2011 (2011)
32. Lamport, L., Shostak, R., Pease, M.: The Byzantine generals problem. ACM Trans. Program. Lang. Syst. **4**(3), 382–401 (1982)
33. Leners, J.B., Wu, H., Hung, W.L., Aguilera, M.K., Walfish, M.: Detecting failures in distributed systems with the FALCON spy network. In: SOSP 2011, pp. 279–294. ACM (2011)
34. Lindley, S., Morris, J.G.: embedding session types in haskell. In: Haskell 2016, pp. 133–145. ACM (2016)
35. Mostrous, D., Yoshida, N.: Session typing and asynchronous subtyping for the higher-order π-calculus. Inf. Comput. **241**, 227–263 (2015)
36. Neykova, R., Yoshida, N.: Let it recover: multiparty protocol-induced recovery. In: CC 2017, pp. 98–108. ACM (2017)
37. Padovani, L.: A simple library implementation of binary sessions. J. Funct. Program. **27**, e4 (2017)
38. Pucella, R., Tov, J.A.: Haskell session types with (almost) no class. In: Haskell 2008, pp. 25–36. ACM (2008)
39. Scalas, A., Dardha, O., Hu, R., Yoshida, N.: A linear decomposition of multiparty sessions for safe distributed programming. In: ECOOP 2017. LIPIcs, vol. 74, pp. 24:1–24:31. Schloss Dagstuhl - Leibniz-Zentrum fuer Informatik (2017)
40. Shvachko, K., Kuang, H., Radia, S., Chansler, R.: The Hadoop distributed file system. In: MSST 2010, pp. 1–10. IEEE Computer Society (2010)
41. Sivaramakrishnan, K.C., Qudeisat, M., Ziarek, L., Nagaraj, K., Eugster, P.: Efficient sessions. Sci. Comput. Program. **78**(2), 147–167 (2013)
42. Vieira, H.T., Caires, L., Seco, J.C.: The conversation calculus: a model of service-oriented computation. In: Drossopoulou, S. (ed.) ESOP 2008. LNCS, vol. 4960, pp. 269–283. Springer, Heidelberg (2008). https://doi.org/10.1007/978-3-540-78739-6_21
43. Viering, M., Chen, T.C., Eugster, P., Hu, R., Ziarek, L.: Technical appendix: a typing discipline for statically verified crash failure handling in distributed systems. http://distributed-systems-programming-group.github.io/paper/2018/esop_long.pdf
44. Wilcox, J.R., Woos, D., Panchekha, P., Tatlock, Z., Wang, X., Ernst, M.D., Anderson, T.E.: Verdi: a framework for implementing and formally verifying distributed systems. In: PLDI 2015, pp. 357–368. ACM (2015)
45. Xu, J., Randell, B., Romanovsky, A.B., Rubira, C.M.F., Stroud, R.J., Wu, Z.: Fault tolerance in concurrent object-oriented software through coordinated error recovery. In: FTCS 1995, pp. 499–508. IEEE Computer Society (1995)

On Polymorphic Sessions and Functions
A Tale of Two (Fully Abstract) Encodings

Bernardo Toninho[1,2]([⊠]) [iD] and Nobuko Yoshida[2] [iD]

[1] NOVA-LINCS, Departamento de Informática, FCT, Universidade Nova de Lisboa,
Lisbon, Portugal
btoninho@fct.unl.pt
[2] Department of Computing, Imperial College London, London, UK

Abstract. This work exploits the logical foundation of session types to
determine what kind of type discipline for the π-calculus can exactly
capture, and is captured by, λ-calculus behaviours. Leveraging the proof
theoretic content of the soundness and completeness of sequent calculus
and natural deduction presentations of linear logic, we develop the first
mutually inverse and *fully abstract* processes-as-functions and functions-
as-processes encodings between a polymorphic session π-calculus and a
linear formulation of System F. We are then able to derive results of
the session calculus from the theory of the λ-calculus: (1) we obtain
a characterisation of inductive and coinductive session types via their
algebraic representations in System F; and (2) we extend our results to
account for *value* and *process* passing, entailing strong normalisation.

1 Introduction

Dating back to Milner's seminal work [29], encodings of λ-calculus into π-calculus
are seen as essential benchmarks to examine expressiveness of various extensions
of the π-calculus. Milner's original motivation was to demonstrate the power of
link mobility by decomposing higher-order computations into pure name passing. Another goal was to analyse functional behaviours in a broad computational universe of concurrency and non-determinism. While *operationally* correct encodings of many higher-order constructs exist, it is challenging to obtain
encodings that are precise wrt behavioural equivalence: the semantic distance
between the λ-calculus and the π-calculus typically requires either restricting
process behaviours [45] (e.g. via typed equivalences [5]) or enriching the λ-
calculus with constants that allow for a suitable characterisation of the term
equivalence induced by the behavioural equivalence on processes [43].

Encodings in π-calculi also gave rise to new typing disciplines: Session types
[20,22], a typing system that is able to ensure deadlock-freedom for communication protocols between two or more parties [23], were originally motivated
"from process encodings of various data structures in an asynchronous version of
the π-calculus" [21]. Recently, a propositions-as-types correspondence between
linear logic and session types [8,9,54] has produced several new developments

© The Author(s) 2018
A. Ahmed (Ed.): ESOP 2018, LNCS 10801, pp. 827–855, 2018.
https://doi.org/10.1007/978-3-319-89884-1_29

and logically-motivated techniques [7,26,49,54] to augment both the theory and practice of session-based message-passing concurrency. Notably, parametric session polymorphism [7] (in the sense of Reynolds [41]) has been proposed and a corresponding abstraction theorem has been shown.

Our work expands upon the proof theoretic consequences of this propositions-as-types correspondence to address the problem of how to *exactly* match the behaviours induced by session π-calculus encodings of the λ-calculus with those of the λ-calculus. We develop *mutually inverse* and *fully abstract* encodings (up to typed observational congruences) between a polymorphic session-typed π-calculus and the polymorphic λ-calculus. The encodings arise from the proof theoretic content of the equivalence between sequent calculus (i.e. the session calculus) and natural deduction (i.e. the λ-calculus) for *second-order* intuitionistic linear logic, greatly generalising [49]. While fully abstract encodings between λ-calculi and π-calculi have been proposed (e.g. [5,43]), our work is the first to consider a two-way, *both* mutually inverse *and* fully abstract embedding between the two calculi by crucially exploiting the linear logic-based session discipline. This also sheds some definitive light on the nature of concurrency in the (logical) session calculi, which exhibit "don't care" forms of non-determinism (e.g. processes may race on stateless replicated servers) rather than "don't know" non-determinism (which requires less harmonious logical features [2]).

In the spirit of Gentzen [14], we use our encodings as a tool to study nontrivial properties of the session calculus, deriving them from results in the λ-calculus: We show the existence of inductive and coinductive sessions in the polymorphic session calculus by considering the representation of initial F-algebras and final F-coalgebras [28] in the polymorphic λ-calculus [1,19] (in a linear setting [6]). By appealing to full abstraction, we are able to derive processes that satisfy the necessary algebraic properties and thus form adequate *uniform* representations of inductive and coinductive session types. The derived algebraic properties enable us to reason about standard data structure examples, providing a logical justification to typed variations of the representations in [30].

We systematically extend our results to a session calculus with λ-term and process passing (the latter being the core calculus of [50], inspired by Benton's LNL [4]). By showing that our encodings naturally adapt to this setting, we prove that it is possible to encode higher-order process passing in the first-order session calculus fully abstractly, providing a typed and proof-theoretically justified re-envisioning of Sangiorgi's encodings of higher-order π-calculus [46]. In addition, the encoding instantly provides a strong normalisation property of the higher-order session calculus.

Contributions and the outline of our paper are as follows:

§ **3.1** develops a functions-as-processes encoding of a linear formulation of System F, Linear-F, using a logically motivated polymorphic session π-calculus, Polyπ, and shows that the encoding is operationally sound and complete.

§ **3.2** develops a processes-as-functions encoding of Polyπ into Linear-F, arising from the completeness of the sequent calculus wrt natural deduction, also operationally sound and complete.

§ **3.3** studies the relationship between the two encodings, establishing they are *mutually inverse* and *fully abstract* wrt typed congruence, the first two-way embedding satisfying *both* properties.

§ **4** develops a *faithful* representation of inductive and coinductive session types in Polyπ via the encoding of initial and final (co)algebras in the polymorphic λ-calculus. We demonstrate a use of these algebraic properties via examples.

§ **4.2** and **4.3** study term-passing and process-passing session calculi, extending our encodings to provide embeddings into the first-order session calculus. We show full abstraction and mutual inversion results, and derive strong normalisation of the higher-order session calculus from the encoding.

In order to introduce our encodings, we first overview Polyπ, its typing system and behavioural equivalence (§ **2**). We discuss related work and conclude with future work (§ **5**). Detailed proofs can be found in [52].

2   Polymorphic Session π-Calculus

This section summarises the polymorphic session π-calculus [7], dubbed Polyπ, arising as a process assignment to second-order linear logic [15], its typing system and behavioural equivalences.

2.1   Processes and Typing

Syntax. Given an infinite set Λ of names x, y, z, u, v, the grammar of processes P, Q, R and session types A, B, C is defined by:

$$P, Q, R ::= x\langle y\rangle.P \mid x(y).P \mid P \mid Q \mid (\nu y)P \mid [x \leftrightarrow y] \mid \mathbf{0}$$
$$\mid x\langle A\rangle.P \mid x(Y).P \mid x.\mathsf{inl}; P \mid x.\mathsf{inr}; P \mid x.\mathsf{case}(P, Q) \mid !x(y).P$$
$$A, B ::= 1 \mid A \multimap B \mid A \otimes B \mid A \& B \mid A \oplus B \mid !A \mid \forall X.A \mid \exists X.A \mid X$$

$x\langle y\rangle.P$ denotes the output of channel y on x with continuation process P; $x(y).P$ denotes an input along x, bound to y in P; $P \mid Q$ denotes parallel composition; $(\nu y)P$ denotes the restriction of name y to the scope of P; $\mathbf{0}$ denotes the inactive process; $[x \leftrightarrow y]$ denotes the linking of the two channels x and y (implemented as renaming); $x\langle A\rangle.P$ and $x(Y).P$ denote the sending and receiving of a *type A* along x bound to Y in P of the receiver process; $x.\mathsf{inl}; P$ and $x.\mathsf{inr}; P$ denote the emission of a selection between the left or right branch of a receiver $x.\mathsf{case}(P, Q)$ process; $!x(y).P$ denotes an input-guarded replication, that spawns replicas upon receiving an input along x. We often abbreviate $(\nu y)x\langle y\rangle.P$ to $\overline{x}\langle y\rangle.P$ and omit trailing $\mathbf{0}$ processes. By convention, we range over linear channels with x, y, z and shared channels with u, v, w.

(out) $\qquad$ (in) $\qquad\qquad$ (outT) $\qquad$ (inT)

$$x\langle y\rangle.P \xrightarrow{\overline{x\langle y\rangle}} P \quad x(y).P \xrightarrow{x(z)} P\{z/y\} \quad x\langle A\rangle.P \xrightarrow{\overline{x\langle A\rangle}} P \quad x(Y).P \xrightarrow{x(B)} P\{B/Y\}$$

(lout) $\qquad\qquad\qquad$ (id)

$$x.\mathsf{inl}; P \xrightarrow{\overline{x.\mathsf{inl}}} P \quad (\nu x)([x \leftrightarrow y] \mid P) \xrightarrow{\tau} P\{y/x\}$$

(lin) $\qquad\qquad\qquad$ (rep) $\qquad\qquad\qquad$ (open)

$$x.\mathsf{case}(P,Q) \xrightarrow{x.\mathsf{inl}} P \quad !x(y).P \xrightarrow{x(z)} P\{z/y\} \;\; !x(y).P \quad (\nu y)P \xrightarrow{\overline{(\nu y)x\langle y\rangle}} Q$$

$$\dfrac{P \xrightarrow{\overline{x\langle y\rangle}} Q}{} $$

(close) $\qquad\qquad\qquad\qquad$ (par) $\qquad\qquad$ (com) $\qquad\qquad$ (res)

$$\dfrac{P \xrightarrow{\overline{(\nu y)x\langle y\rangle}} P' \;\; Q \xrightarrow{x(y)} Q'}{P \mid Q \xrightarrow{\tau} (\nu y)(P' \mid Q')} \quad \dfrac{P \xrightarrow{\alpha} Q}{P \mid R \xrightarrow{\alpha} Q \mid R} \quad \dfrac{P \xrightarrow{\overline{\alpha}} P' \;\; Q \xrightarrow{\alpha} Q'}{P \mid Q \xrightarrow{\tau} P' \mid Q'} \quad \dfrac{P \xrightarrow{\alpha} Q}{(\nu y)P \xrightarrow{\alpha} (\nu y)Q}$$

Fig. 1. Labelled transition system.

The syntax of session types is that of (intuitionistic) linear logic propositions which are assigned to channels according to their usages in processes: $\mathbf{1}$ denotes the type of a channel along which no further behaviour occurs; $A \multimap B$ denotes a session that waits to receive a channel of type A and will then proceed as a session of type B; dually, $A \otimes B$ denotes a session that sends a channel of type A and continues as B; $A \;\&\; B$ denotes a session that offers a choice between proceeding as behaviours A or B; $A \oplus B$ denotes a session that internally chooses to continue as either A or B, signalling appropriately to the communicating partner; $!A$ denotes a session offering an unbounded (but finite) number of behaviours of type A; $\forall X.A$ denotes a polymorphic session that receives a type B and behaves uniformly as $A\{B/X\}$; dually, $\exists X.A$ denotes an existentially typed session, which emits a type B and behaves as $A\{B/X\}$.

Operational Semantics. The operational semantics of our calculus is presented as a standard labelled transition system (Fig. 1) in the style of the *early* system for the π-calculus [46].

In the remainder of this work we write $\equiv$ for a standard π-calculus structural congruence extended with the clause $[x \leftrightarrow y] \equiv [y \leftrightarrow x]$. In order to streamline the presentation of observational equivalence [7,36], we write $\equiv_!$ for structural congruence extended with the so-called sharpened replication axioms [46], which capture basic equivalences of replicated processes (and are present in the proof dynamics of the exponential of linear logic). A transition $P \xrightarrow{\alpha} Q$ denotes that P may evolve to Q by performing the action represented by label α. An action α ($\overline{\alpha}$) requires a matching $\overline{\alpha}$ (α) in the environment to enable progress. Labels include: the silent internal action τ, output and bound output actions ($\overline{x\langle y\rangle}$ and $\overline{(\nu z)x\langle z\rangle}$); input action $x(y)$; the binary choice actions ($x.\mathsf{inl}$, $\overline{x.\mathsf{inl}}$, $x.\mathsf{inr}$, and $\overline{x.\mathsf{inr}}$); and output and input actions of types ($\overline{x\langle A\rangle}$ and $x(A)$).

The labelled transition relation is defined by the rules in Fig. 1, subject to the side conditions: in rule (res), we require $y \notin fn(\alpha)$; in rule (par), we require $bn(\alpha) \cap fn(R) = \emptyset$; in rule (close), we require $y \notin fn(Q)$. We omit the symmetric versions of (par), (com), (lout), (lin), (close) and closure under α-conversion. We write $\rho_1\rho_2$ for the composition of relations ρ_1, ρ_2. We write $\rightarrow$ to stand for $\xrightarrow{\tau}\equiv$.

$$(\multimap\mathsf{R}) \; \frac{\Omega;\Gamma;\Delta,x{:}A \vdash P :: z{:}B}{\Omega;\Gamma;\Delta \vdash z(x).P :: z{:}A \multimap B} \qquad (\otimes\mathsf{R}) \; \frac{\Omega;\Gamma;\Delta_1 \vdash P :: y{:}A \quad \Omega;\Gamma;\Delta_2 \vdash Q :: z{:}B}{\Omega;\Gamma;\Delta_1,\Delta_2 \vdash (\nu x)z\langle y\rangle.(P \mid Q) :: z{:}A \otimes B}$$

$$(\forall\mathsf{R}) \; \frac{\Omega,X;\Gamma;\Delta \vdash P :: z{:}A}{\Omega;\Gamma;\Delta \vdash z(X).P :: z{:}\forall X.A} \qquad (\forall\mathsf{L}) \; \frac{\Omega \vdash B\,\mathsf{type} \quad \Omega;\Gamma;\Delta,x{:}A\{B/X\} \vdash P :: z{:}C}{\Omega;\Gamma;\Delta,x{:}\forall X.A \vdash x\langle B\rangle.P :: z{:}C}$$

$$(\exists\mathsf{R}) \; \frac{\Omega \vdash B\,\mathsf{type} \quad \Omega;\Gamma;\Delta \vdash P :: z{:}A\{B/X\}}{\Omega;\Gamma;\Delta \vdash z\langle B\rangle.P :: z{:}\exists X.A} \qquad (\exists\mathsf{L}) \; \frac{\Omega,X;\Gamma;\Delta,x{:}A \vdash P :: z{:}C}{\Omega;\Gamma;\Delta,x{:}\exists X.A \vdash x(X).P :: z{:}C}$$

$$(\mathsf{id}) \; \frac{}{\Omega;\Gamma;x{:}A \vdash [x \leftrightarrow z] :: z{:}A} \qquad (\mathsf{cut}) \; \frac{\Omega;\Gamma;\Delta_1 \vdash P :: x{:}A \quad \Omega;\Gamma;\Delta_2,x{:}A \vdash Q :: z{:}C}{\Omega;\Gamma;\Delta_1,\Delta_2 \vdash (\nu x)(P \mid Q) :: z{:}C}$$

Fig. 2. Typing rules (abridged – see [52] for all rules).

Weak transitions are defined as usual: we write $\Longrightarrow$ for the reflexive, transitive closure of $\xrightarrow{\tau}$ and $\rightarrow^+$ for the transitive closure of $\xrightarrow{\tau}$. Given $\alpha \neq \tau$, notation $\overset{\alpha}{\Longrightarrow}$ stands for $\Longrightarrow \xrightarrow{\alpha} \Longrightarrow$ and $\overset{\tau}{\Longrightarrow}$ stands for $\Longrightarrow$.

Typing System. The typing rules of Polyπ are given in Fig. 2, following [7]. The rules define the judgment $\Omega;\Gamma;\Delta \vdash P :: z{:}A$, denoting that process P offers a session of type A along channel z, using the *linear* sessions in Δ, (potentially) using the unrestricted or *shared* sessions in Γ, with polymorphic type variables maintained in Ω. We use a well-formedness judgment $\Omega \vdash A\,\mathsf{type}$ which states that A is well-formed wrt the type variable environment Ω (i.e. $fv(A) \subseteq \Omega$). We often write T for the right-hand side typing $z{:}A$, $\cdot$ for the empty context and Δ, Δ' for the union of contexts Δ and Δ', only defined when Δ and Δ' are disjoint. We write $\cdot \vdash P :: T$ for $\cdot;\cdot;\cdot \vdash P :: T$.

As in [8,9,36,54], the typing discipline enforces that channel outputs always have as object a *fresh* name, in the style of the internal mobility π-calculus [44]. We clarify a few of the key rules: Rule $\forall$R defines the meaning of (impredicative) universal quantification over session types, stating that a session of type $\forall X.A$ inputs a type and then behaves uniformly as A; dually, to use such a session (rule $\forall$L), a process must output a type B which then warrants the use of the session as type $A\{B/X\}$. Rule $\multimap$R captures session input, where a session of type $A \multimap B$ expects to receive a session of type A which will then be used to produce a session of type B. Dually, session output (rule $\otimes$R) is achieved by producing a fresh session of type A (that uses a disjoint set of sessions to those of the continuation) and outputting the fresh session along z, which is then a session of type B. Linear composition is captured by rule cut which enables a process that offers a session $x{:}A$ (using linear sessions in Δ_1) to be composed with a process that *uses* that session (amongst others in Δ_2) to offer $z{:}C$. As shown in [7], typing entails Subject Reduction, Global Progress, and Termination.

Observational Equivalences. We briefly summarise the typed congruence and logical equivalence with polymorphism, giving rise to a suitable notion of relational parametricity in the sense of Reynolds [41], defined as a contextual logical relation on typed processes [7]. The logical relation is reminiscent of a typed bisimulation. However, extra care is needed to ensure well-foundedness due to impredicative type instantiation. As a consequence, the logical relation allows us to reason about process equivalences where type variables are not instantiated with *the same*, but rather *related* types.

Typed Barbed Congruence ($\cong$). We use the typed contextual congruence from [7], which preserves *observable* actions, called barbs. Formally, *barbed congruence*, noted $\cong$, is the largest equivalence on well-typed processes that is τ-closed, barb preserving, and contextually closed under typed contexts; see [7,52] for the full definition.

Logical Equivalence ($\approx_L$). The definition of logical equivalence is no more than a typed contextual bisimulation with the following intuitive reading: given two open processes P and Q (i.e. processes with non-empty left-hand side typings), we define their equivalence by inductively closing out the context, composing with equivalent processes offering appropriately typed sessions. When processes are closed, we have a single distinguished session channel along which we can perform observations, and proceed inductively on the structure of the offered session type. We can then show that such an equivalence satisfies the necessary fundamental properties (Theorem 2.3).

The logical relation is defined using the candidates technique of Girard [16]. In this setting, an *equivalence candidate* is a relation on typed processes satisfying basic closure conditions: an equivalence candidate must be compatible with barbed congruence and closed under forward and converse reduction.

Definition 2.1 (Equivalence Candidate). An *equivalence candidate* $\mathcal{R}$ at $z{:}A$ and $z{:}B$, noted $\mathcal{R} :: z{:}A \Leftrightarrow B$, is a binary relation on processes such that, for every $(P, Q) \in \mathcal{R} :: z{:}A \Leftrightarrow B$ both $\cdot \vdash P :: z{:}A$ and $\cdot \vdash Q :: z{:}B$ hold, together with the following (we often write $(P, Q) \in \mathcal{R} :: z{:}A \Leftrightarrow B$ as $P \mathcal{R} Q :: z{:}A \Leftrightarrow B$):

1. If $(P, Q) \in \mathcal{R} :: z{:}A \Leftrightarrow B$, $\cdot \vdash P \cong P' :: z{:}A$, and $\cdot \vdash Q \cong Q' :: z{:}B$ then $(P', Q') \in \mathcal{R} :: z{:}A \Leftrightarrow B$.
2. If $(P, Q) \in \mathcal{R} :: z{:}A \Leftrightarrow B$ then, for all P_0 such that $\cdot \vdash P_0 :: z{:}A$ and $P_0 \Longrightarrow P$, we have $(P_0, Q) \in \mathcal{R} :: z{:}A \Leftrightarrow B$. Symmetrically for Q.

To define the logical relation we rely on some auxiliary notation, pertaining to the treatment of type variables arising due to impredicative polymorphism. We write $\omega : \Omega$ to denote a mapping ω that assigns a closed type to the type variables in Ω. We write $\omega(X)$ for the type mapped by ω to variable X. Given two mappings $\omega : \Omega$ and $\omega' : \Omega$, we define an equivalence candidate assignment η between ω and ω' as a mapping of equivalence candidate $\eta(X) :: -{:}\omega(X) \Leftrightarrow \omega'(X)$ to the type variables in Ω, where the particular choice of a distinguished right-hand side channel is *delayed* (i.e. to be instantiated later on). We write $\eta(X)(z)$ for the instantiation of the (delayed) candidate with the name z. We write $\eta : \omega \Leftrightarrow \omega'$ to denote that η is a candidate assignment between ω and ω'; and $\hat{\omega}(P)$ to denote the application of mapping ω to P.

We define a sequent-indexed family of process relations, that is, a set of pairs of processes (P, Q), written $\Gamma; \Delta \vdash P \approx_L Q :: T[\eta : \omega \Leftrightarrow \omega']$, satisfying some conditions, typed under $\Omega; \Gamma; \Delta \vdash T$, with $\omega : \Omega$, $\omega' : \Omega$ and $\eta : \omega \Leftrightarrow \omega'$. Logical equivalence is defined inductively on the size of the typing contexts and then on the structure of the right-hand side type. We show only select cases (see [52] for the full definition).

Definition 2.2 (Logical Equivalence). (Base Case) Given a type A and mappings ω, ω', η, we define *logical equivalence*, noted $P \approx_L Q :: z{:}A[\eta : \omega \Leftrightarrow \omega']$, as the smallest symmetric binary relation containing all pairs of processes (P, Q) such that (i) $\cdot \vdash \hat{\omega}(P) :: z{:}\hat{\omega}(A)$; (ii) $\cdot \vdash \hat{\omega}'(Q) :: z{:}\hat{\omega}'(A)$; and (iii) satisfies the conditions given below:

- $P \approx_L Q :: z{:}X[\eta : \omega \Leftrightarrow \omega']$ iff $(P, Q) \in \eta(X)(z)$
- $P \approx_L Q :: z{:}A \multimap B[\eta : \omega \Leftrightarrow \omega']$ iff $\forall P', y. \ (P \xrightarrow{z(y)} P') \Rightarrow \exists Q'.Q \xRightarrow{z(y)} Q'$ s.t. $\forall R_1, R_2. R_1 \approx_L R_2 :: y{:}A[\eta : \omega \Leftrightarrow \omega'](\nu y)(P' \mid R_1) \approx_L (\nu y)(Q' \mid R_2) :: z{:}B[\eta : \omega \Leftrightarrow \omega']$
- $P \approx_L Q :: z{:}A \otimes B[\eta : \omega \Leftrightarrow \omega']$ iff $\forall P', y. \ (P \xrightarrow{(\nu y)z\langle y \rangle} P') \Rightarrow \exists Q'.Q \xRightarrow{(\nu y)z\langle y \rangle} Q'$ s.t. $\exists P_1, P_2, Q_1, Q_2. \ P' \equiv_! P_1 \mid P_2 \wedge Q' \equiv_! Q_1 \mid Q_2 \wedge P_1 \approx_L Q_1 :: y{:}A[\eta : \omega \Leftrightarrow \omega'] \wedge P_2 \approx_L Q_2 :: z{:}B[\eta : \omega \Leftrightarrow \omega']$
- $P \approx_L Q :: z{:}\forall X.A[\eta : \omega \Leftrightarrow \omega']$ iff $\forall B_1, B_2, P', \mathcal{R} :: -{:}B_1 \Leftrightarrow B_2. \ (P \xrightarrow{z(B_1)} P')$ implies $\exists Q'.Q \xRightarrow{z(B_2)} Q'$, $P' \approx_L Q' :: z{:}A[\eta[X \mapsto \mathcal{R}] : \omega[X \mapsto B_1] \Leftrightarrow \omega'[X \mapsto B_2]]$

(Inductive Case). Let Γ, Δ be non empty. Given $\Omega; \Gamma; \Delta \vdash P :: T$ and $\Omega; \Gamma; \Delta \vdash Q :: T$, the binary relation on processes $\Gamma; \Delta \vdash P \approx_L Q :: T[\eta : \omega \Leftrightarrow \omega']$ (with $\omega, \omega' : \Omega$ and $\eta : \omega \Leftrightarrow \omega'$) is inductively defined as:

$\Gamma; \Delta, y : A \vdash P \approx_L Q :: T[\eta : \omega \Leftrightarrow \omega']$ iff $\forall R_1, R_2.$ s.t. $R_1 \approx_L R_2 :: y{:}A[\eta : \omega \Leftrightarrow \omega']$,
$\qquad\qquad \Gamma; \Delta \vdash (\nu y)(\hat{\omega}(P) \mid \hat{\omega}(R_1)) \approx_L (\nu y)(\hat{\omega}'(Q) \mid \hat{\omega}'(R_2)) :: T[\eta : \omega \Leftrightarrow \omega']$
$\Gamma, u{:}A; \Delta \vdash P \approx_L Q :: T[\eta : \omega \Leftrightarrow \omega']$ iff $\forall R_1, R_2.$ s.t. $R_1 \approx_L R_2 :: y{:}A[\eta : \omega \Leftrightarrow \omega']$,
$\qquad\qquad \Gamma; \Delta \vdash (\nu u)(\hat{\omega}(P) \mid !u(y).\hat{\omega}(R_1)) \approx_L (\nu u)(\hat{\omega}'(Q) \mid !u(y).\hat{\omega}'(R_2)) :: T[\eta : \omega \Leftrightarrow \omega']$

For the sake of readability we often omit the $\eta : \omega \Leftrightarrow \omega'$ portion of $\approx_L$, which is henceforth implicitly universally quantified. Thus, we write $\Omega; \Gamma; \Delta \vdash P \approx_L Q :: z{:}A$ (or $P \approx_L Q$) iff the two given processes are logically equivalent for all consistent instantiations of its type variables.

It is instructive to inspect the clause for type input $(\forall X.A)$: the two processes must be able to match inputs of any pair of *related* types (i.e. types related by a candidate), such that the continuations are related at the open type A with the appropriate type variable instantiations, following Girard [16]. The power of this style of logical relation arises from a combination of the extensional flavour of the equivalence and the fact that polymorphic equivalences do not require the same type to be instantiated in both processes, but rather that the types are *related* (via a suitable equivalence candidate relation).

Theorem 2.3 (Properties of Logical Equivalence [7]**)**

Parametricity: *If* $\Omega; \Gamma; \Delta \vdash P :: z{:}A$ *then, for all* $\omega, \omega' : \Omega$ *and* $\eta : \omega \Leftrightarrow \omega'$, *we have* $\Gamma; \Delta \vdash \hat{\omega}(P) \approx_L \hat{\omega}'(P) :: z{:}A[\eta : \omega \Leftrightarrow \omega']$.

Soundness: *If* $\Omega; \Gamma; \Delta \vdash P \approx_L Q :: z{:}A$ *then* $\mathcal{C}[P] \cong \mathcal{C}[Q] :: z{:}A$, *for any closing* $\mathcal{C}[-]$.

Completeness: *If* $\Omega; \Gamma; \Delta \vdash P \cong Q :: z{:}A$ *then* $\Omega; \Gamma; \Delta \vdash P \approx_L Q :: z{:}A$.

3   To Linear-F and Back

We now develop our mutually inverse and fully abstract encodings between Polyπ and a linear polymorphic λ-calculus [55] that we dub Linear-F. We first introduce the syntax and typing of the linear λ-calculus and then proceed to detail our encodings and their properties (we omit typing ascriptions from the existential polymorphism constructs for readability).

Definition 3.1 (Linear-F). The syntax of terms M, N and types A, B of Linear-F is given below.

$$M, N \ ::= \ \lambda x{:}A.M \mid M\,N \mid \langle M \otimes N \rangle \mid \mathsf{let}\,x \otimes y = M\,\mathsf{in}\,N \mid \,!M \mid \mathsf{let}\,!u = M\,\mathsf{in}\,N \mid \Lambda X.M$$
$$\mid \ M[A] \mid \mathsf{pack}\,A\,\mathsf{with}\,M \mid \mathsf{let}\,(X, y) = M\,\mathsf{in}\,N \mid \mathsf{let}\,\mathbf{1} = M\,\mathsf{in}\,N \mid \langle\rangle \mid \mathsf{T} \mid \mathsf{F}$$

$$A, B \ ::= \ A \multimap B \mid A \otimes B \mid \,!A \mid \forall X.A \mid \exists X.A \mid X \mid \mathbf{1} \mid \mathbf{2}$$

The syntax of types is that of the multiplicative and exponential fragments of second-order intuitionistic linear logic: $\lambda x{:}A.M$ denotes linear λ-abstractions; $M\,N$ denotes the application; $\langle M \otimes N \rangle$ denotes the multiplicative pairing of M and N, as reflected in its elimination form $\mathsf{let}\,x \otimes y = M\,\mathsf{in}\,N$ which simultaneously deconstructs the pair M, binding its first and second projection to x and y in N, respectively; $!M$ denotes a term M that does not use any linear variables and so may be used an arbitrary number of times; $\mathsf{let}\,!u = M\,\mathsf{in}\,N$ binds the underlying exponential term of M as u in N; $\Lambda X.M$ is the type abstraction former; $M[A]$ stands for type application; $\mathsf{pack}\,A\,\mathsf{with}\,M$ is the existential type introduction form, where M is a term where the existentially typed variable is instantiated with A; $\mathsf{let}\,(X, y) = M\,\mathsf{in}\,N$ unpacks an existential package M, binding the representation type to X and the underlying term to y in N; the multiplicative unit $\mathbf{1}$ has as introduction form the nullary pair $\langle\rangle$ and is eliminated by the construct $\mathsf{let}\,\mathbf{1} = M\,\mathsf{in}\,N$, where M is a term of type $\mathbf{1}$. Booleans (type $\mathbf{2}$ with values T and F) are the basic observable.

The typing judgment in Linear-F is given as $\Omega; \Gamma; \Delta \vdash M : A$, following the DILL formulation of linear logic [3], stating that term M has type A in a linear context Δ (i.e. bindings for linear variables $x{:}B$), intuitionistic context Γ (i.e. binding for intuitionistic variables $u{:}B$) and type variable context Ω. The typing rules are standard [7]. The operational semantics of the calculus are the expected call-by-name semantics with commuting conversions [27]. We write $\Downarrow$ for the evaluation relation. We write $\cong$ for the largest typed congruence that is consistent with the observables of type $\mathbf{2}$ (i.e. a so-called Morris-style equivalence as in [5]).

3.1 Encoding Linear-F into Session π-Calculus

We define a translation from Linear-F to Polyπ generalising the one from [49], accounting for polymorphism and multiplicative pairs. We translate typing derivations of λ-terms to those of π-calculus terms (we omit the full typing derivation for the sake of readability).

Proof theoretically, the λ-calculus corresponds to a proof term assignment for natural deduction presentations of logic, whereas the session π-calculus from § 2 corresponds to a proof term assignment for sequent calculus. Thus, we obtain a translation from λ-calculus to the session π-calculus by considering the proof theoretic content of the constructive proof of soundness of the sequent calculus wrt natural deduction. Following Gentzen [14], the translation from natural deduction to sequent calculus maps introduction rules to the corresponding right rules and elimination rules to a combination of the corresponding left rule, cut and/or identity.

Since typing in the session calculus identifies a distinguished channel along which a process offers a session, the translation of λ-terms is parameterised by a "result" channel along which the behaviour of the λ-term is implemented. Given a λ-term M, the process $[\![M]\!]_z$ encodes the behaviour of M along the session channel z. We enforce that the type $\mathbf{2}$ of booleans and its two constructors are consistently translated to their polymorphic Church encodings before applying the translation to Polyπ. Thus, type $\mathbf{2}$ is first translated to $\forall X.!X \multimap !X \multimap X$, the value T to $\Lambda X.\lambda u{:}!X.\lambda v{:}!X.\mathsf{let}\,!x = u\,\mathsf{in}\,\mathsf{let}\,!y = v\,\mathsf{in}\,x$ and the value F to $\Lambda X.\lambda u{:}!X.\lambda v{:}!X.\mathsf{let}\,!x = u\,\mathsf{in}\,\mathsf{let}\,!y = v\,\mathsf{in}\,y$. Such representations of the booleans are adequate up to parametricity [6] and suitable for our purposes of relating the session calculus (which has no primitive notion of value or result type) with the λ-calculus precisely due to the tight correspondence between the two calculi.

Definition 3.2 (From Linear-F to Polyπ). $[\![\Omega]\!]; [\![\Gamma]\!]; [\![\Delta]\!] \vdash [\![M]\!]_z :: z{:}A$ denotes the translation of contexts, types and terms from Linear-F to the polymorphic session calculus. The translations on contexts and types are the identity function. Booleans and their values are first translated to their Church encodings as specified above. The translation on λ-terms is given below:

$$
\begin{aligned}
&[\![x]\!]_z &&\triangleq [x \leftrightarrow z] & &[\![M\,N]\!]_z \triangleq (\nu x)([\![M]\!]_x \mid (\nu y)x\langle y\rangle.([\![N]\!]_y \mid [x \leftrightarrow z])) \\
&[\![u]\!]_z &&\triangleq (\nu x)u\langle x\rangle.[x \leftrightarrow z] & &[\![\mathsf{let}\,!u = M\,\mathsf{in}\,N]\!]_z \triangleq (\nu x)([\![M]\!]_x \mid [\![N]\!]_z\{x/u\}) \\
&[\![\lambda x{:}A.M]\!]_z &&\triangleq z(x).[\![M]\!]_z & &[\![\langle M \otimes N\rangle]\!]_z \triangleq (\nu y)z\langle y\rangle.([\![M]\!]_y \mid [\![N]\!]_z) \\
&[\![!M]\!]_z &&\triangleq !z(x).[\![M]\!]_x & &[\![\mathsf{let}\,x \otimes y = M\,\mathsf{in}\,N]\!]_z \triangleq (\nu w)([\![M]\!]_y \mid y(x).[\![N]\!]_z) \\
&[\![\Lambda X.M]\!]_z &&\triangleq z(X).[\![M]\!]_z & &[\![M[A]]\!]_z \triangleq (\nu x)([\![M]\!]_x \mid x\langle A\rangle.[x \leftrightarrow z]) \\
&[\![\mathsf{pack}\,A\,\mathsf{with}\,M]\!]_z &&\triangleq z\langle A\rangle.[\![M]\!]_z & &[\![\mathsf{let}\,(X,y) = M\,\mathsf{in}\,N]\!]_z \triangleq (\nu x)([\![M]\!]_y \mid y(X).[\![N]\!]_z) \\
&[\![\langle\rangle]\!]_z &&\triangleq \mathbf{0} & &[\![\mathsf{let}\,\mathbf{1} = M\,\mathsf{in}\,N]\!]_z \triangleq (\nu x)([\![M]\!]_x \mid [\![N]\!]_z)
\end{aligned}
$$

To translate a (linear) λ-abstraction $\lambda x{:}A.M$, which corresponds to the proof term for the introduction rule for $\multimap$, we map it to the corresponding $\multimap$R rule, thus obtaining a process $z(x).[\![M]\!]_z$ that inputs along the result channel z a channel x which will be used in $[\![M]\!]_z$ to access the function argument. To encode the application $M\,N$, we compose (i.e. cut) $[\![M]\!]_x$, where x is a fresh name, with a process that provides the (encoded) function argument by outputting along x

a channel y which offers the behaviour of $[\![N]\!]_y$. After the output is performed, the type of x is now that of the function's codomain and thus we conclude by forwarding (i.e. the id rule) between x and the result channel z.

The encoding for polymorphism follows a similar pattern: To encode the abstraction $\Lambda X.M$, we receive along the result channel a type that is bound to X and proceed inductively. To encode type application $M[A]$ we encode the abstraction M in parallel with a process that sends A to it, and forwards accordingly. Finally, the encoding of the existential package pack A with M maps to an output of the type A followed by the behaviour $[\![M]\!]_z$, with the encoding of the elimination form let $(X, y) = M$ in N composing the translation of the term of existential type M with a process performing the appropriate type input and proceeding as $[\![N]\!]_z$.

Example 3.3 (Encoding of Linear-F). Consider the following λ-term corresponding to a polymorphic pairing function (recall that we write $\overline{z}\langle w\rangle.P$ for $(\nu w)z\langle w\rangle.P$):

$$M \triangleq \Lambda X.\Lambda Y.\lambda x{:}X.\lambda y{:}Y.\langle x \otimes y\rangle \text{ and } N \triangleq ((M[A][B]\,M_1)\,M_2)$$

Then we have, with $\tilde{x} = x_1x_2x_3x_4$:

$$
\begin{aligned}
[\![N]\!]_z &\equiv (\nu\tilde{x})([\![M]\!]_{x_1} \mid x_1\langle A\rangle.[x_1 \leftrightarrow x_2] \mid x_2\langle B\rangle.[x_2 \leftrightarrow x_3] \mid \\
&\quad\quad \overline{x_3}\langle x\rangle.([\![M_1]\!]_x \mid [x_3 \leftrightarrow x_4]) \mid \overline{x_4}\langle y\rangle.([\![M_2]\!]_y \mid [x_4 \leftrightarrow z])) \\
&\equiv (\nu\tilde{x})(x_1(X).x_1(Y).x_1(x).x_1(y).\overline{x_1}\langle w\rangle.([x \leftrightarrow w] \mid [y \leftrightarrow x_1]) \mid x_1\langle A\rangle.[x_1 \leftrightarrow x_2] \mid \\
&\quad\quad x_2\langle B\rangle.[x_2 \leftrightarrow x_3] \mid \overline{x_3}\langle x\rangle.([\![M_1]\!]_x \mid [x_3 \leftrightarrow x_4]) \mid \overline{x_4}\langle y\rangle.([\![M_2]\!]_y \mid [x_4 \leftrightarrow z]))
\end{aligned}
$$

We can observe that $N \rightarrow^+ (((\lambda x{:}A.\lambda y{:}B.\langle x \otimes y\rangle)\,M_1)\,M_2) \rightarrow^+ \langle M_1 \otimes M_2\rangle$. At the process level, each reduction corresponding to the redex of type application is simulated by two reductions, obtaining:

$$
\begin{aligned}
[\![N]\!]_z \rightarrow^+ &(\nu x_3, x_4)(x_3(x).x_3(y).\overline{x_3}\langle w\rangle.([x \leftrightarrow w] \mid [y \leftrightarrow x_3]) \mid \\
&\overline{x_3}\langle x\rangle.([\![M_1]\!]_x \mid [x_3 \leftrightarrow x_4]) \mid \overline{x_4}\langle y\rangle.([\![M_2]\!]_y \mid [x_4 \leftrightarrow z])) = P
\end{aligned}
$$

The reductions corresponding to the β-redexes clarify the way in which the encoding represents substitution of terms for variables via fine-grained name passing. Consider $[\![\langle M_1 \otimes M_2\rangle]\!]_z \triangleq \overline{z}\langle w\rangle.([\![M_1]\!]_w \mid [\![M_2]\!]_z)$ and

$$P \rightarrow^+ (\nu x, y)([\![M_1]\!]_x \mid [\![M_2]\!]_y \mid \overline{z}\langle w\rangle.([x \leftrightarrow w] \mid [y \leftrightarrow z]))$$

The encoding of the pairing of M_1 and M_2 outputs a fresh name w which will denote the behaviour of (the encoding of) M_1, and then the behaviour of the encoding of M_2 is offered on z. The reduct of P outputs a fresh name w which is then identified with x and thus denotes the behaviour of $[\![M_1]\!]_w$. The channel z is identified with y and thus denotes the behaviour of $[\![M_2]\!]_z$, making the two processes listed above equivalent. This informal reasoning exposes the insights that justify the operational correspondence of the encoding. Proof-theoretically, these equivalences simply map to commuting conversions which push the processes $[\![M_1]\!]_x$ and $[\![M_2]\!]_z$ under the output on z.

Theorem 3.4 (Operational Correspondence)

- *If $\Omega; \Gamma; \Delta \vdash M : A$ and $M \rightarrow N$ then $[\![M]\!]_z \Longrightarrow P$ such that $[\![N]\!]_z \approx_L P$*
- *If $[\![M]\!]_z \rightarrow P$ then $M \rightarrow^+ N$ and $[\![N]\!]_z \approx_L P$*

3.2 Encoding Session π-calculus to Linear-F

Just as the proof theoretic content of the soundness of sequent calculus wrt natural deduction induces a translation from λ-terms to session-typed processes, the *completeness* of the sequent calculus wrt natural deduction induces a translation from the session calculus to the λ-calculus. This mapping identifies sequent calculus right rules with the introduction rules of natural deduction and left rules with elimination rules combined with (type-preserving) substitution. Crucially, the mapping is defined on *typing derivations*, enabling us to consistently identify when a process uses a session (i.e. left rules) or, dually, when a process offers a session (i.e. right rules).

$$\left((\multimap R) \frac{\Delta, x{:}A \vdash P :: z{:}B}{\Delta \vdash z(x).P :: z{:}A \multimap B} \right) \triangleq (\multimap I) \frac{\Delta, x{:}A \vdash (\!|P|\!)_{\Delta, x{:}A \vdash z{:}B} : B}{\Delta \vdash \lambda x{:}A.(\!|P|\!)_{\Delta, x{:}A \vdash z{:}B} : A \multimap B}$$

$$\left((\multimap L) \frac{\Delta_1 \vdash P :: y{:}A \quad \Delta_2, x{:}B \vdash Q :: z{:}C}{\Delta_1, \Delta_2, x{:}A \multimap B \vdash (\nu y)x\langle y\rangle.(P \mid Q) :: z{:}C} \right) \triangleq$$

(SUBST)

$$\frac{\Delta_2, x{:}B \vdash (\!|Q|\!)_{\Delta_2, x{:}B \vdash z{:}C} : C \quad \dfrac{x{:}A \multimap B \vdash x{:}A \multimap B \quad \Delta_1 \vdash (\!|P|\!)_{\Delta_1 \vdash y{:}A} : B}{\Delta_1, x{:}A \multimap B \vdash x\,(\!|P|\!)_{\Delta_1 \vdash y{:}A} : B}}{\Delta_1, \Delta_2, x{:}A \multimap B \vdash (\!|Q|\!)_{\Delta_2, x{:}B \vdash z{:}C}\{(x\,(\!|P|\!)_{\Delta_1 \vdash y{:}A})/x\} : C}$$

Fig. 3. Translation on typing derivations (excerpt – see [52])

Definition 3.5 (From Polyπ to Linear-F). We write $(\!|\Omega|\!); (\!|\Gamma|\!); (\!|\Delta|\!) \vdash (\!|P|\!) : A$ for the translation from typing derivations in Polyπ to derivations in Linear-F. The translations on types and contexts are the identity function. The translation on processes is given below, where the leftmost column indicates the typing rule at the root of the derivation (see Fig. 3 for an excerpt of the translation on typing derivations, where we write $(\!|P|\!)_{\Omega;\Gamma;\Delta \vdash z{:}A}$ to denote the translation of $\Omega; \Gamma; \Delta \vdash P :: z{:}A$. We omit Ω and Γ when unchanged).

(1R)	$(\!|\mathbf{0}|\!)$	$\triangleq \langle\rangle$	$(\multimap L)$	$(\!|(\nu y)x\langle y\rangle.(P \mid Q)|\!)$	$\triangleq (\!|Q|\!)\{(x\,(\!|P|\!))/x\}$
(id)	$(\!|[x \leftrightarrow y]|\!)$	$\triangleq x$	$(\multimap R)$	$(\!|z(x).P|\!)$	$\triangleq \lambda x{:}A.(\!|P|\!)$
(1L)	$(\!|P|\!)$	$\triangleq \mathsf{let}\,\mathbf{1} = x\,\mathsf{in}\,(\!|P|\!)$	$(\otimes R)$	$(\!|(\nu x)z\langle x\rangle.(P \mid Q)|\!)$	$\triangleq \langle(\!|P|\!) \otimes (\!|Q|\!)\rangle$
(!R)	$(\!|!z(x).P|\!)$	$\triangleq !(\!|P|\!)$	$(\otimes L)$	$(\!|x(y).P|\!)$	$\triangleq \mathsf{let}\,x \otimes y = x\,\mathsf{in}\,(\!|P|\!)$
(!L)	$(\!|P\{u/x\}|\!)$	$\triangleq \mathsf{let}\,!u = x\,\mathsf{in}\,(\!|P|\!)$	(copy)	$(\!|(\nu x)u\langle x\rangle.P|\!)$	$\triangleq (\!|P|\!)\{u/x\}$
($\forall$R)	$(\!|z(X).P|\!)$	$\triangleq \Lambda X.(\!|P|\!)$	($\forall$L)	$(\!|x\langle B\rangle.P|\!)$	$\triangleq (\!|P|\!)\{(x[B])/x\}$
($\exists$R)	$(\!|z\langle B\rangle.P|\!)$	$\triangleq \mathsf{pack}\,B\,\mathsf{with}\,(\!|P|\!)$	($\exists$L)	$(\!|x(Y).P|\!)$	$\triangleq \mathsf{let}\,(Y, x) = x\,\mathsf{in}\,(\!|P|\!)$
(cut)	$(\!|(\nu x)(P \mid Q)|\!)$	$\triangleq (\!|Q|\!)\{(\!|P|\!)/x\}$	(cut')	$(\!|(\nu u)(!u(x).P \mid Q)|\!)$	$\triangleq (\!|Q|\!)\{(\!|P|\!)/u\}$

For instance, the encoding of a process $z(x).P :: z:A \multimap B$, typed by rule $\multimap$R, results in the corresponding $\multimap I$ introduction rule in the λ-calculus and thus is $\lambda x{:}A.(\!|P|\!)$. To encode the process $(\nu y)x\langle y\rangle.(P \mid Q)$, typed by rule $\multimap$L, we make use of substitution: Given that the sub-process Q is typed as $\Omega; \Gamma; \Delta', x{:}B \vdash Q :: z{:}C$, the encoding of the full process is given by $(\!|Q|\!)\{(x\,(\!|P|\!))/x\}$. The term $x\,(\!|P|\!)$ consists of the application of x (of function type) to the argument $(\!|P|\!)$, thus ensuring that the term resulting from the substitution is of the appropriate type. We note that, for instance, the encoding of rule $\otimes$L does not need to appeal to substitution – the λ-calculus let style rules can be mapped directly. Similarly, rule $\forall$R is mapped to type abstraction, whereas rule $\forall$L which types a process of the form $x\langle B\rangle.P$ maps to a substitution of the type application $x[B]$ for x in $(\!|P|\!)$. The encoding of existential polymorphism is simpler due to the let-style elimination. We also highlight the encoding of the cut rule which embodies parallel composition of two processes sharing a linear name, which clarifies the use/offer duality of the intuitionistic calculus – the process that offers P is encoded and substituted into the encoded user Q.

Theorem 3.6. *If $\Omega; \Gamma; \Delta \vdash P :: z:A$ then $(\!|\Omega|\!); (\!|\Gamma|\!); (\!|\Delta|\!) \vdash (\!|P|\!) : A$.*

Example 3.7 (Encoding of Polyπ). Consider the following processes

$$P \triangleq z(X).z(Y).z(x).z(y).\overline{z}\langle w\rangle.([x \leftrightarrow w] \mid [y \leftrightarrow z]) \quad Q \triangleq z\langle 1\rangle.z\langle 1\rangle.\overline{z}\langle x\rangle.\overline{z}\langle y\rangle.z(w).[w \leftrightarrow r]$$

with $\vdash P :: z{:}\forall X.\forall Y.X \multimap Y \multimap X \otimes Y$ and $z{:}\forall X.\forall Y.X \multimap Y \multimap X \otimes Y \vdash Q :: r{:}\mathbf{1}$. Then: $(\!|P|\!) = \Lambda X.\Lambda Y.\lambda x{:}X.\lambda y{:}Y.\langle x \otimes y\rangle \quad (\!|Q|\!) = \mathsf{let}\, x \otimes y = z[1][1]\,\langle\rangle\,\langle\rangle\,\mathsf{in}\,\mathsf{let}\,\mathbf{1} = y\,\mathsf{in}\,x$
$(\!|(\nu z)(P \mid Q)|\!) = \mathsf{let}\, x \otimes y = (\Lambda X.\Lambda Y.\lambda x{:}X.\lambda y{:}Y.\langle x \otimes y\rangle)[1][1]\,\langle\rangle\,\langle\rangle\,\mathsf{in}\,\mathsf{let}\,\mathbf{1} = y\,\mathsf{in}\,x$

By the behaviour of $(\nu z)(P \mid Q)$, which consists of a sequence of cuts, and its encoding, we have that $(\!|(\nu z)(P \mid Q)|\!) \to^+ \langle\rangle$ and $(\nu z)(P \mid Q) \to^+ \mathbf{0} = (\!|\langle\rangle|\!)$.

In general, the translation of Definition 3.5 can introduce some distance between the immediate operational behaviour of a process and its corresponding λ-term, insofar as the translations of cuts (and left rules to non let-form elimination rules) make use of substitutions that can take place deep within the resulting term. Consider the process at the root of the following typing judgment $\Delta_1, \Delta_2, \Delta_3 \vdash (\nu x)(x(y).P_1 \mid (\nu y)x\langle y\rangle.(P_2 \mid w(z).\mathbf{0})) :: w{:}\mathbf{1} \multimap \mathbf{1}$, derivable through a cut on session x between instances of $\multimap$R and $\multimap$L, where the continuation process $w(z).\mathbf{0}$ offers a session $w{:}\mathbf{1} \multimap \mathbf{1}$ (and so must use rule 1L on x). We have that: $(\nu x)(x(y).P_1 \mid (\nu y)x\langle y\rangle.(P_2 \mid w(z).\mathbf{0})) \to (\nu x, y)(P_1 \mid P_2 \mid w(z).\mathbf{0})$. However, the translation of the process above results in the term $\lambda z{:}\mathbf{1}.\mathsf{let}\,\mathbf{1} = ((\lambda y{:}A.(\!|P_1|\!))\,(\!|P_2|\!))\,\mathsf{in}\,\mathsf{let}\,\mathbf{1} = z\,\mathsf{in}\,\langle\rangle$, where the redex that corresponds to the process reduction is present but hidden under the binder for z (corresponding to the input along w). Thus, to establish operational completeness we consider full β-reduction, denoted by $\to_\beta$, i.e. enabling β-reductions under binders.

Theorem 3.8 (Operational Completeness). *Let $\Omega; \Gamma; \Delta \vdash P :: z:A$. If $P \to Q$ then $(\!|P|\!) \to_\beta^* (\!|Q|\!)$.*

In order to study the soundness direction it is instructive to consider typed process $x{:}1 \multimap 1 \vdash \overline{x}\langle y\rangle.(\nu z)(z(w).\mathbf{0} \mid \overline{z}\langle w\rangle.\mathbf{0}) :: v{:}1$ and its translation:

$$(\![\overline{x}\langle y\rangle.(\nu z)(z(w).\mathbf{0} \mid \overline{z}\langle w\rangle.\mathbf{0})]\!) = (\![(\nu z)(z(w).\mathbf{0} \mid \overline{z}\langle w\rangle.\mathbf{0})]\!)\{(x\,\langle\rangle)/x\}$$
$$= \mathsf{let}\,1 = (\lambda w{:}1.\mathsf{let}\,1 = w\,\mathsf{in}\,\langle\rangle)\,\langle\rangle\,\mathsf{in}\,\mathsf{let}\,1 = x\,\langle\rangle\,\mathsf{in}\,\langle\rangle$$

The process above cannot reduce due to the output prefix on x, which cannot synchronise with a corresponding input action since there is no provider for x (i.e. the channel is in the left-hand side context). However, its encoding can exhibit the β-redex corresponding to the synchronisation along z, hidden by the prefix on x. The corresponding reductions hidden under prefixes in the encoding can be *soundly* exposed in the session calculus by appealing to the commuting conversions of linear logic (e.g. in the process above, the instance of rule $\multimap$L corresponding to the output on x can be commuted with the cut on z).

As shown in [36], commuting conversions are sound wrt observational equivalence, and thus we formulate operational soundness through a notion of *extended* process reduction, which extends process reduction with the reductions that are induced by commuting conversions. Such a relation was also used for similar purposes in [5] and in [26], in a classical linear logic setting. For conciseness, we define extended reduction as a relation on *typed* processes modulo $\equiv$.

Definition 3.9 (Extended Reduction [5]). We define $\mapsto$ as the type preserving relations on typed processes modulo $\equiv$ generated by:

1. $C[(\nu y)x\langle y\rangle.P] \mid x(y).Q \mapsto C[(\nu y)(P \mid Q)]$;
2. $C[(\nu y)x\langle y\rangle.P] \mid !x(y).Q \mapsto C[(\nu y)(P \mid Q)] \mid !x(y).Q$; and
3. $(\nu x)(!x(y).Q) \mapsto \mathbf{0}$

where C is a (typed) process context which does not capture the bound name y.

Theorem 3.10 (Operational Soundness). *Let* $\Omega; \Gamma; \Delta \vdash P :: z{:}A$ *and* $(\![P]\!) \to M$, *there exists* Q *such that* $P \mapsto^* Q$ *and* $(\![Q]\!) =_\alpha M$.

3.3 Inversion and Full Abstraction

Having established the operational preciseness of the encodings to-and-from Polyπ and Linear-F, we establish our main results for the encodings. Specifically, we show that the encodings are mutually inverse up-to behavioural equivalence (with *fullness* as its corollary), which then enables us to establish *full abstraction* for *both* encodings.

Theorem 3.11 (Inverse). *If* $\Omega; \Gamma; \Delta \vdash M : A$ *then* $\Omega; \Gamma; \Delta \vdash (\![[M]\!]_z]\!) \cong M :$ A. *Also, if* $\Omega; \Gamma; \Delta \vdash P :: z{:}A$ *then* $\Omega; \Gamma; \Delta \vdash [\![(\![P]\!)]\!]_z \approx_{\mathsf{L}} P :: z{:}A$.

Corollary 3.12 (Fullness). *Let* $\Omega; \Gamma; \Delta \vdash P :: z{:}A$. $\exists M$ *s.t.* $\Omega; \Gamma; \Delta \vdash M : A$ *and* $\Omega; \Gamma; \Delta \vdash [\![M]\!]_z \approx_{\mathsf{L}} P :: z{:}A$ *Also, let* $\Omega; \Gamma; \Delta \vdash M : A$. $\exists P$ *s.t.* $\Omega; \Gamma; \Delta \vdash$ $P :: z{:}A$ *and* $\Omega; \Gamma; \Delta \vdash (\![P]\!) \cong M : A$.

We now state our full abstraction results. Given two Linear-F terms of the same type, equivalence in the image of the $[\![-]\!]_z$ translation can be used as a proof technique for contextual equivalence in Linear-F. This is called the *soundness* direction of full abstraction in the literature [18] and proved by showing the relation generated by $[\![M]\!]_z \approx_\mathsf{L} [\![N]\!]_z$ forms $\cong$; we then establish the *completeness* direction by contradiction, using fullness.

Theorem 3.13 (Full Abstraction). $\Omega; \Gamma; \Delta \vdash M \cong N : A$ *iff* $\Omega; \Gamma; \Delta \vdash [\![M]\!]_z \approx_\mathsf{L} [\![N]\!]_z :: z{:}A$.

We can straightforwardly combine the above full abstraction with Theorem 3.11 to obtain full abstraction of the $(\!|-|\!)$ translation.

Theorem 3.14 (Full Abstraction). $\Omega; \Gamma; \Delta \vdash P \approx_\mathsf{L} Q :: z{:}A$ *iff* $\Omega; \Gamma; \Delta \vdash (\!|P|\!) \cong (\!|Q|\!) : A$.

4   Applications of the Encodings

In this section we develop applications of the encodings of the previous sections. Taking advantage of full abstraction and mutual inversion, we apply non-trivial properties from the theory of the λ-calculus to our session-typed process setting.

In § 4.1 we study inductive and coinductive sessions, arising through encodings of initial F-algebras and final F-coalgebras in the polymorphic λ-calculus.

In § 4.2 we study encodings for an extension of the core session calculus with term passing, where terms are derived from a simply-typed λ-calculus. Using the development of § 4.2 as a stepping stone, we generalise the encodings to a *higher-order* session calculus (§ 4.3), where processes can send, receive and execute other processes. We show full abstraction and mutual inversion theorems for the encodings from higher-order to first-order. As a consequence, we can straightforwardly derive a strong normalisation property for the higher-order process-passing calculus.

4.1   Inductive and Coinductive Session Types

The study of polymorphism in the λ-calculus [1,6,19,40] has shown that parametric polymorphism is expressive enough to encode both inductive and coinductive types in a precise way, through a faithful representation of initial and final (co)algebras [28], without extending the language of terms nor the semantics of the calculus, giving a logical justification to the Church encodings of inductive datatypes such as lists and natural numbers. The polymorphic session calculus can express fairly intricate communication behaviours, including generic protocols through both existential and universal polymorphism (i.e. protocols that are parametric in their sub-protocols). Using our fully abstract encodings between the two calculi, we show that session polymorphism is expressive enough to encode inductive and coinductive sessions, "importing" the results for the λ-calculus, which may then be instantiated to provide a session-typed formulation of the encodings of data structures in the π-calculus of [30].

Inductive and Coinductive Types in System F. Exploring an algebraic interpretation of polymorphism where types are interpreted as functors, it can be shown that given a type F with a free variable X that occurs only positively (i.e. occurrences of X are on the left-hand side of an even number of function arrows), the polymorphic type $\forall X.((F(X) \to X) \to X)$ forms an initial F-algebra [1,42] (we write $F(X)$ to denote that X occurs in F). This enables the representation of *inductively* defined structures using an algebraic or categorical justification. For instance, the natural numbers can be seen as the initial F-algebra of $F(X) = 1 + X$ (where 1 is the unit type and $+$ is the coproduct), and are thus *already present* in System F, in a precise sense, as the type $\forall X.((1 + X) \to X) \to X$ (noting that both 1 and $+$ can also be encoded in System F). A similar story can be told for *coinductively* defined structures, which correspond to final F-coalgebras and are representable with the polymorphic type $\exists X.(X \to F(X)) \times X$, where $\times$ is a product type. In the remainder of this section we assume the positivity requirement on F mentioned above.

While the complete formal development of the representation of inductive and coinductive types in System F would lead us to far astray, we summarise here the key concepts as they apply to the λ-calculus (the interested reader can refer to [19] for the full categorical details).

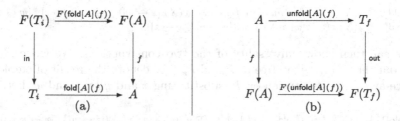

Fig. 4. Diagrams for initial F-algebras and final F-coalgebras

To show that the polymorphic type $T_i \triangleq \forall X.((F(X) \to X) \to X)$ is an initial F-algebra, one exhibits a pair of λ-terms, often dubbed fold and in, such that the diagram in Fig. 4(a) commutes (for any A, where $F(f)$, where f is a λ-term, denotes the functorial action of F applied to f), and, crucially, that fold is *unique*. When these conditions hold, we are justified in saying that T_i is a least fixed point of F. Through a fairly simple calculation, it is easy to see that:

$$\mathsf{fold} \triangleq \Lambda X.\lambda x{:}F(X) \to X.\lambda t{:}T_i.t[X](x)$$
$$\mathsf{in} \triangleq \lambda x{:}F(T_i).\Lambda X.\lambda y{:}F(X) \to X.y\,(F(\mathsf{fold}[X](x))(x))$$

satisfy the necessary equalities. To show uniqueness one appeals to *parametricity*, which allows us to prove that any function of the appropriate type is equivalent to fold. This property is often dubbed initiality or universality.

The construction of final F-coalgebras and their justification as *greatest* fixed points is dual. Assuming products in the calculus and taking $T_f \triangleq \exists X.(X \to$

$F(X)) \times X$, we produce the λ-terms

$$\mathsf{unfold} \triangleq \Lambda X.\lambda f{:}X \to F(X).\lambda x{:}T_f.\mathsf{pack}\, X \text{ with } (f, x)$$
$$\mathsf{out} \triangleq \lambda t : T_f.\mathsf{let}\,(X, (f, x)) = t \text{ in } F(\mathsf{unfold}[X](f))\,(f(x))$$

such that the diagram in Fig. 4(b) commutes and unfold is unique (again, up to parametricity). While the argument above applies to System F, a similar development can be made in Linear-F [6] by considering $T_i \triangleq \forall X.!(F(X) \multimap X) \multimap X$ and $T_f \triangleq \exists X.!(X \multimap F(X)) \otimes X$. Reusing the same names for the sake of conciseness, the associated *linear* λ-terms are:

$$\mathsf{fold} \triangleq \Lambda X.\lambda u{:}!(F(X) \multimap X).\lambda y{:}T_i.(y[X]\,u) : \forall X.!(F(X) \multimap X) \multimap T_i \multimap X$$
$$\mathsf{in} \triangleq \lambda x{:}F(T_i).\Lambda X.\lambda y{:}!(F(X) \multimap X).\mathsf{let}\,!u = y \text{ in } k\,(F\,(\mathsf{fold}[X](!u))(x)) : F(T_i) \multimap T_i$$
$$\mathsf{unfold} \triangleq \Lambda X.\lambda u{:}!(X \multimap F(X)).\lambda x{:}X.\mathsf{pack}\, X \text{ with } \langle u \otimes x \rangle : \forall X.!(X \multimap F(X)) \multimap X \multimap T_f$$
$$\mathsf{out} \triangleq \lambda t : T_f.\mathsf{let}\,(X, (u, x)) = t \text{ in let }!f = u \text{ in } F(\mathsf{unfold}[X](!f))\,(f(x)) : T_f \multimap F(T_f)$$

Inductive and Coinductive Sessions for Free. As a consequence of full abstraction we may appeal to the $[\![-]\!]_z$ encoding to derive representations of fold and unfold that satisfy the necessary algebraic properties. The derived processes are (recall that we write $\overline{x}\langle y \rangle.P$ for $(\nu y)x\langle y \rangle.P$):

$$[\![\mathsf{fold}]\!]_z \triangleq z(X).z(u).z(y).(\nu w)((\nu x)([y \leftrightarrow x] \mid x\langle X \rangle.[x \leftrightarrow w]) \mid \overline{w}\langle v \rangle.([u \leftrightarrow v] \mid [w \leftrightarrow z]))$$
$$[\![\mathsf{unfold}]\!]_z \triangleq z(X).z(u).z(x).z\langle X \rangle.\overline{z}\langle y \rangle.([u \leftrightarrow y] \mid [x \leftrightarrow z])$$

We can then show universality of the two constructions. We write $P_{x,y}$ to single out that x and y are free in P and $P_{z,w}$ to denote the result of employing capture-avoiding substitution on P, substituting x and y by z and w. Let:

$$\mathsf{foldP}(A)_{y_1,y_2} \triangleq (\nu x)([\![\mathsf{fold}]\!]_x \mid x\langle A \rangle.\overline{x}\langle v \rangle.(\overline{u}\langle y \rangle.[y \leftrightarrow v] \mid \overline{x}\langle z \rangle.([z \leftrightarrow y_1] \mid [x \leftrightarrow y_2])))$$
$$\mathsf{unfoldP}(A)_{y_1,y_2} \triangleq (\nu x)([\![\mathsf{unfold}]\!]_x \mid x\langle A \rangle.\overline{x}\langle v \rangle.(\overline{u}\langle y \rangle.[y \leftrightarrow v] \mid \overline{x}\langle z \rangle.([z \leftrightarrow y_1] \mid [x \leftrightarrow y_2])))$$

where $\mathsf{foldP}(A)_{y_1,y_2}$ corresponds to the application of fold to an F-algebra A with the associated morphism $F(A) \multimap A$ available on the shared channel u, consuming an ambient session $y_1{:}T_i$ and offering $y_2{:}A$. Similarly, $\mathsf{unfoldP}(A)_{y_1,y_2}$ corresponds to the application of unfold to an F-coalgebra A with the associated morphism $A \multimap F(A)$ available on the shared channel u, consuming an ambient session $y_1{:}A$ and offering $y_2{:}T_f$.

Theorem 4.1 (Universality of foldP). $\forall Q$ such that $X; u{:}F(X) \multimap X; y_1{:}T_i \vdash Q :: y_2{:}X$ we have $X; u{:}F(X) \multimap X; y_1{:}T_i \vdash Q \approx_{\mathrm{L}} \mathsf{foldP}(X)_{y_1,y_2} :: y_2{:}X$

Theorem 4.2 (Universality of unfoldP). $\forall Q$ and F-coalgebra A s.t $\cdot; \cdot; y_1{:}A \vdash Q :: y_2{:}T_f$ we have that $\cdot; u{:}F(A) \multimap A; y_1{:}A \vdash Q \approx_{\mathrm{L}} \mathsf{unfoldP}(A)_{y_1,y_2} :: y_2{::}T_f$.

Example 4.3 (Natural Numbers). We show how to represent the natural numbers as an inductive session type using $F(X) = 1 \oplus X$, making use of in:

$$\mathsf{zero}_x \triangleq (\nu z)(z.\mathsf{inl}; \mathbf{0} \mid [\![\mathsf{in}(z)]\!]_x) \qquad \mathsf{succ}_{y,x} \triangleq (\nu s)(s.\mathsf{inr}; [y \leftrightarrow s] \mid [\![\mathsf{in}(s)]\!]_x)$$

with $\mathsf{Nat} \triangleq \forall X.!((\mathbf{1} \oplus X) \multimap X) \multimap X$ where $\vdash \mathsf{zero}_x :: x{:}\mathsf{Nat}$ and $y{:}\mathsf{Nat} \vdash \mathsf{succ}_{y,x} :: x{:}\mathsf{Nat}$ encode the representation of 0 and successor, respectively. The natural 1 would thus be represented by $\mathsf{one}_x \triangleq (\nu y)(\mathsf{zero}_y \mid \mathsf{succ}_{y,x})$. The behaviour of type Nat can be seen as a that of a sequence of internal choices of arbitrary (but finite) length. We can then observe that the foldP process acts as a recursor. For instance consider:

$$\mathsf{stepDec}_d \triangleq d(n).n.\mathsf{case}(\mathsf{zero}_d, [n \leftrightarrow d]) \quad \mathsf{dec}_{x,z} \triangleq (\nu u)(!u(d).\mathsf{stepDec}_d \mid \mathsf{foldP}(\mathsf{Nat})_{x,z})$$

with $\mathsf{stepDec}_d :: d{:}(\mathbf{1} \oplus \mathsf{Nat}) \multimap \mathsf{Nat}$ and $x{:}\mathsf{Nat} \vdash \mathsf{dec}_{x,z} :: z{:}\mathsf{Nat}$, where dec decrements a given natural number session on channel x. We have that:

$$(\nu x)(\mathsf{one}_x \mid \mathsf{dec}_{x,z}) \equiv (\nu x, y.u)(\mathsf{zero}_y \mid \mathsf{succ}_{y,x}!u(d).\mathsf{stepDec}_d \mid \mathsf{foldP}(\mathsf{Nat})_{x,z}) \approx_L \mathsf{zero}_z$$

We note that the resulting encoding is reminiscent of the encoding of lists of [30] (where zero is the empty list and succ the cons cell). The main differences in the encodings arise due to our primitive notions of labels and forwarding, as well as due to the generic nature of in and fold.

Example 4.4 (Streams). We build on Example 4.3 by representing *streams* of natural numbers as a coinductive session type. We encode infinite streams of naturals with $F(X) = \mathsf{Nat} \otimes X$. Thus: $\mathsf{NatStream} \triangleq \exists X.!(X \multimap (\mathsf{Nat} \otimes X)) \otimes X$. The behaviour of a session of type $\mathsf{NatStream}$ amounts to an infinite sequence of outputs of channels of type Nat. Such an encoding enables us to construct the stream of all naturals nats (and the stream of all non-zero naturals oneNats):

$$\begin{aligned}
\mathsf{genHdNext}_z &\triangleq z(n).\overline{z}\langle y\rangle.(\overline{n}\langle n'\rangle.[n' \leftrightarrow y] \mid !z(w).\overline{n}\langle n'\rangle.\mathsf{succ}_{n',w}) \\
\mathsf{nats}_y &\triangleq (\nu x, u)(\mathsf{zero}_x \mid !u(z).\mathsf{genHdNext}_z \mid \mathsf{unfoldP}(!\mathsf{Nat})_{x,y}) \\
\mathsf{oneNats}_y &\triangleq (\nu x, u)(\mathsf{one}_x \mid !u(z).\mathsf{genHdNext}_z \mid \mathsf{unfoldP}(!\mathsf{Nat})_{x,y})
\end{aligned}$$

with $\mathsf{genHdNext}_z :: z{:}!\mathsf{Nat} \multimap \mathsf{Nat} \otimes !\mathsf{Nat}$ and both nats_y and $\mathsf{oneNats} :: y{:}\mathsf{NatStream}$. $\mathsf{genHdNext}_z$ consists of a helper that generates the current head of a stream and the next element. As expected, the following process implements a session that "unrolls" the stream once, providing the head of the stream and then behaving as the rest of the stream (recall that $\mathsf{out} : T_f \multimap F(T_f)$).

$$(\nu x)(\mathsf{nats}_x \mid \llbracket \mathsf{out}(x) \rrbracket_y) :: y{:}\mathsf{Nat} \otimes \mathsf{NatStream}$$

We note a peculiarity of the interaction of linearity with the stream encoding: a process that begins to deconstruct a stream has no way of "bottoming out" and stopping. One cannot, for instance, extract the first element of a stream of naturals and stop unrolling the stream in a well-typed way. We can, however, easily encode a "terminating" stream of all natural numbers via $F(X) = (\mathsf{Nat} \otimes !X)$ by replacing the $\mathsf{genHdNext}_z$ with the generator given as:

$$\mathsf{genHdNextTer}_z \triangleq z(n).\overline{z}\langle y\rangle.(\overline{n}\langle n'\rangle.[n' \leftrightarrow y] \mid !z(w).!w(w').\overline{n}\langle n'\rangle.\mathsf{succ}_{n',w'})$$

It is then easy to see that a usage of $\llbracket \mathsf{out}(x) \rrbracket_y$ results in a session of type $\mathsf{Nat} \otimes !\mathsf{NatStream}$, enabling us to discard the stream as needed. One can replay this argument with the operator $F(X) = (!\mathsf{Nat} \otimes X)$ to enable discarding of stream elements. Assuming such modifications, we can then show:

$$(\nu y)((\nu x)(\mathsf{nats}_x \mid [\![\mathsf{out}(x)]\!]_y) \mid y(n).[y \leftrightarrow z]) \approx_{\mathrm{L}} \mathsf{oneNats}_z :: z{:}\mathsf{NatStream}$$

4.2 Communicating Values – Sess$\pi\lambda$

We now consider a session calculus extended with a data layer obtained from a λ-calculus (whose terms are ranged over by M, N and types by τ, σ). We dub this calculus Sess$\pi\lambda$.

$$P, Q \;::= \cdots \mid x\langle M\rangle.P \mid x(y).P \qquad A, B \;::= \cdots \mid \tau \wedge A \mid \tau \supset A$$
$$M, N \;::= \lambda x{:}\tau.M \mid M\,N \mid x \qquad\quad \tau, \sigma \;::= \cdots \mid \tau \to \sigma$$

Without loss of generality, we consider the data layer to be simply-typed, with a call-by-name semantics, satisfying the usual type safety properties. The typing judgment for this calculus is $\Psi \vdash M : \tau$. We omit session polymorphism for the sake of conciseness, restricting processes to communication of data and (session) channels. The typing judgment for processes is thus modified to $\Psi; \Gamma; \Delta \vdash P :: z{:}A$, where Ψ is an intuitionistic context that accounts for variables in the data layer. The rules for the relevant process constructs are (all other rules simply propagate the Ψ context from conclusion to premises):

$$\frac{\Psi \vdash M : \tau \quad \Psi; \Gamma; \Delta \vdash P :: z{:}A}{\Psi; \Gamma; \Delta \vdash z\langle M\rangle.P :: z{:}\tau \wedge A} \; (\wedge\mathrm{R}) \qquad \frac{\Psi, y{:}\tau; \Gamma; \Delta, x{:}A \vdash Q :: z{:}C}{\Psi; \Gamma; \Delta, x{:}\tau \wedge A \vdash x(y).Q :: z{:}C} \; (\wedge\mathrm{L})$$

$$\frac{\Psi, x{:}\tau; \Gamma; \Delta \vdash P :: z{:}A}{\Psi; \Gamma; \Delta \vdash z(x).P :: z{:}\tau \supset A} \; (\supset\mathrm{R}) \qquad \frac{\Psi \vdash M : \tau \quad \Psi; \Gamma; \Delta, x{:}A \vdash Q :: z{:}C}{\Psi; \Gamma; \Delta, x{:}\tau \supset A \vdash x\langle M\rangle.Q :: z{:}C} \; (\supset\mathrm{L})$$

With the reduction rule given by:[1] $x\langle M\rangle.P \mid x(y).Q \to P \mid Q\{M/y\}$. With a simple extension to our encodings we may eliminate the data layer by encoding the data objects as processes, showing that from an expressiveness point of view, data communication is orthogonal to the framework. We note that the data language we are considering is *not* linear, and the usage discipline of data in processes is itself also not linear.

To First-Order Processes. We now introduce our encoding for Sess$\pi\lambda$, defined inductively on session types, processes, types and λ-terms (we omit the purely inductive cases on session types and processes for conciseness). As before, the encoding on processes is defined on *typing derivations*, where we indicate the typing rule at the root of the typing derivation.

$$[\![\tau \wedge A]\!] \triangleq ![\![\tau]\!] \otimes [\![A]\!] \qquad [\![\tau \supset A]\!] \triangleq ![\![\tau]\!] \multimap [\![A]\!] \qquad [\![\tau \to \sigma]\!] \triangleq ![\![\tau]\!] \multimap [\![\sigma]\!]$$

$(\wedge\mathrm{R})\;\; [\![z\langle M\rangle.P]\!] \triangleq \overline{z}\langle x\rangle.(!x(y).[\![M]\!]_y \mid [\![P]\!]) \;\; (\wedge\mathrm{L})\;\; [\![x(y).P]\!] \triangleq x(y).[\![P]\!]$
$(\supset\mathrm{R})\;\; [\![z(x).P]\!] \triangleq z(x).[\![P]\!] \qquad\qquad\qquad\quad (\supset\mathrm{L})\;\; [\![x\langle M\rangle.P]\!] \triangleq \overline{x}\langle y\rangle.(!y(w).[\![M]\!]_w \mid [\![P]\!])$

---

[1] For simplicity, in this section, we define the process semantics through a reduction relation.

$$[\![x]\!]_z \triangleq \overline{x}\langle y\rangle.[y \leftrightarrow z] \qquad [\![\lambda x{:}\tau.M]\!]_z \triangleq z(x).[\![M]\!]_z$$
$$[\![M\,N]\!]_z \triangleq (\nu y)([\![M]\!]_y \mid \overline{y}\langle x\rangle.(!x(w).[\![N]\!]_w \mid [y \leftrightarrow z]))$$

The encoding addresses the non-linear usage of data elements in processes by encoding the types $\tau \wedge A$ and $\tau \supset A$ as $![\![\tau]\!] \otimes [\![A]\!]$ and $![\![\tau]\!] \multimap [\![A]\!]$, respectively. Thus, sending and receiving of data is codified as the sending and receiving of channels of type !, which therefore can be used non-linearly. Moreover, since data terms are themselves non-linear, the $\tau \to \sigma$ type is encoded as $![\![\tau]\!] \multimap [\![\sigma]\!]$, following Girard's embedding of intuitionistic logic in linear logic [15].

At the level of processes, offering a session of type $\tau \wedge A$ (i.e. a process of the form $z\langle M\rangle.P$) is encoded according to the translation of the type: we first send a *fresh* name x which will be used to access the encoding of the term M. Since M can be used an arbitrary number of times by the receiver, we guard the encoding of M with a replicated input, proceeding with the encoding of P accordingly. Using a session of type $\tau \supset A$ follows the same principle. The input cases (and the rest of the process constructs) are completely homomorphic.

The encoding of λ-terms follows Girard's decomposition of the intuitionistic function space [49]. The λ-abstraction is translated as input. Since variables in a λ-abstraction may be used non-linearly, the case for variables and application is slightly more intricate: to encode the application $M\,N$ we compose M in parallel with a process that will send the "reference" to the function argument N which will be encoded using replication, in order to handle the potential for 0 or more usages of variables in a function body. Respectively, a variable is encoded by performing an output to trigger the replication and forwarding accordingly. Without loss of generality, we assume variable names and their corresponding replicated counterparts match, which can be achieved through α-conversion before applying the translation. We exemplify our encoding as follows:

$$[\![z(x).z\langle x\rangle.z\langle(\lambda y{:}\sigma.x)\rangle.\mathbf{0}]\!] = z(x).\overline{z}\langle w\rangle.(!w(u).[\![x]\!]_u \mid \overline{z}\langle v\rangle.(!v(i).[\![\lambda y{:}\sigma.x]\!]_i \mid \mathbf{0}))$$
$$= z(x).\overline{z}\langle w\rangle.(!w(u).\overline{x}\langle y\rangle.[y \leftrightarrow u] \mid \overline{z}\langle v\rangle.(!v(i).i(y).\overline{x}\langle t\rangle.[t \leftrightarrow i] \mid \mathbf{0}))$$

Properties of the Encoding. We discuss the correctness of our encoding. We can straightforwardly establish that the encoding preserves typing.

To show that our encoding is operationally sound and complete, we capture the interaction between substitution on λ-terms and the encoding into processes through logical equivalence. Consider the following reduction of a process:

$$(\nu z)(z(x).z\langle x\rangle.z\langle(\lambda y{:}\sigma.x)\rangle.\mathbf{0} \mid z\langle\lambda w{:}\tau_0.w\rangle.P)$$
$$\to (\nu z)(z\langle\lambda w{:}\tau_0.w\rangle.z\langle(\lambda y{:}\sigma.\lambda w{:}\tau_0.w)\rangle.\mathbf{0} \mid P) \qquad (1)$$

Given that substitution in the target session π-calculus amounts to renaming, whereas in the λ-calculus we replace a variable for a term, the relationship between the encoding of a substitution $M\{N/x\}$ and the encodings of M and N corresponds to the composition of the encoding of M with that of N, but where the encoding of N is guarded by a replication, codifying a form of explicit non-linear substitution.

Lemma 4.5 (Compositionality). *Let* $\Psi, x{:}\tau \vdash M : \sigma$ *and* $\Psi \vdash N : \tau$. *We have that* $[\![M\{N/x\}]\!]_z \approx_L (\nu x)([\![M]\!]_z \mid !x(y).[\![N]\!]_y)$

Revisiting the process to the left of the arrow in Eq. 1 we have:

$$[\![(\nu z)(z(x).z\langle x\rangle.z\langle(\lambda y{:}\sigma.x)\rangle.\mathbf{0} \mid z\langle\lambda w{:}\tau_0.w\rangle.P)]\!]$$
$$= (\nu z)([\![z(x).z\langle x\rangle.z\langle(\lambda y{:}\sigma.x)\rangle.\mathbf{0}]\!]_z \mid \overline{z}\langle x\rangle.(!x(b).[\![\lambda w{:}\tau_0.w]\!]_b \mid [\![P]\!]))$$
$$\rightarrow (\nu z, x)(\overline{z}\langle w\rangle.(!w(u).\overline{x}\langle y\rangle.[y \leftrightarrow u] \mid \overline{z}\langle v\rangle.(!v(i).[\![\lambda y{:}\sigma.x]\!]_i \mid \mathbf{0}) \mid !x(b).[\![\lambda w{:}\tau_0.w]\!]_b \mid [\![P]\!]))$$

whereas the process to the right of the arrow is encoded as:

$$[\![(\nu z)(z\langle\lambda w{:}\tau_0.w\rangle.z\langle(\lambda y{:}\sigma.\lambda w{:}\tau_0.w)\rangle.\mathbf{0} \mid P)]\!]$$
$$= (\nu z)(\overline{z}\langle w\rangle.(!w(u).[\![\lambda w{:}\tau_0.w]\!]_u \mid \overline{z}\langle v\rangle.(!v(i).[\![\lambda y{:}\sigma.\lambda w{:}\tau_0.w]\!]_i \mid [\![P]\!])))$$

While the reduction of the encoded process and the encoding of the reduct differ syntactically, they are observationally equivalent – the latter inlines the replicated process behaviour that is accessible in the former on x. Having characterised substitution, we establish operational correspondence for the encoding.

Theorem 4.6 (Operational Correspondence)

1. *If* $\Psi \vdash M : \tau$ *and* $[\![M]\!]_z \rightarrow Q$ *then* $M \rightarrow^+ N$ *such that* $[\![N]\!]_z \approx_L Q$
2. *If* $\Psi; \Gamma; \Delta \vdash P :: z{:}A$ *and* $[\![P]\!] \rightarrow Q$ *then* $P \rightarrow^+ P'$ *such that* $[\![P']\!] \approx_L Q$
3. *If* $\Psi \vdash M : \tau$ *and* $M \rightarrow N$ *then* $[\![M]\!]_z \Longrightarrow P$ *such that* $P \approx_L [\![N]\!]_z$
4. *If* $\Psi; \Gamma; \Delta \vdash P :: z{:}A$ *and* $P \rightarrow Q$ *then* $[\![P]\!] \rightarrow^+ R$ *with* $R \approx_L [\![Q]\!]$

The process equivalence in Theorem 4.6 above need not be extended to account for data (although it would be relatively simple to do so), since the processes in the image of the encoding are fully erased of any data elements.

Back to λ-Terms. We extend our encoding of processes to λ-terms to Sess$\pi\lambda$. Our extended translation maps processes to linear λ-terms, with the session type $\tau \wedge A$ interpreted as a pair type where the first component is replicated. Dually, $\tau \supset A$ is interpreted as a function type where the domain type is replicated. The remaining session constructs are translated as in § **3.2**.

$$(\!|\tau \wedge A|\!) \triangleq !(\!|\tau|\!) \otimes (\!|A|\!) \qquad (\!|\tau \supset A|\!) \triangleq !(\!|\tau|\!) \multimap (\!|A|\!) \qquad (\!|\tau \rightarrow \sigma|\!) \triangleq !(\!|\tau|\!) \multimap (\!|\sigma|\!)$$

$$(\wedge\mathrm{L}) \;\; (\!|x(y).P|\!) \triangleq \text{let } y \otimes x = x \text{ in let } !y = y \text{ in } (\!|P|\!) \quad (\wedge\mathrm{R}) \;\; (\!|z\langle M\rangle.P|\!) \triangleq \langle !(\!|M|\!) \otimes (\!|P|\!)\rangle$$
$$(\supset\mathrm{R}) \;\; (\!|x(y).P|\!) \triangleq \lambda x{:}!(\!|\tau|\!).\text{let } !x = x \text{ in } (\!|P|\!) \qquad (\supset\mathrm{L}) \;\; (\!|x\langle M\rangle.P|\!) \triangleq (\!|P|\!)\{(x\,!(\!|M|\!))/x\}$$

$$(\!|\lambda x{:}\tau.M|\!) \triangleq \lambda x{:}!(\!|\tau|\!).\text{let } !x = x \text{ in } (\!|M|\!) \qquad (\!|M\,N|\!) \triangleq (\!|M|\!)\,!(\!|N|\!) \qquad (\!|x|\!) \triangleq x$$

The treatment of non-linear components of processes is identical to our previous encoding: non-linear functions $\tau \rightarrow \sigma$ are translated to linear functions of type $!\tau \multimap \sigma$; a process offering a session of type $\tau \wedge A$ (i.e. a process of the form $z\langle M\rangle.P$, typed by rule $\wedge$R) is translated to a pair where the first component is the encoding of M prefixed with ! so that it may be used non-linearly, and the second is the encoding of P. Non-linear variables are handled at the respective binding sites: a process using a session of type $\tau \wedge A$ is encoded using the elimination form for the pair and the elimination form for the exponential; similarly, a process offering a session of type $\tau \supset A$ is encoded as a λ-abstraction where the bound variable is of type $!(\!|\tau|\!)$. Thus, we use the elimination form for the exponential, ensuring that the typing is correct. We illustrate our encoding:

$$
\begin{aligned}
(\!|z(x).z\langle x\rangle.z\langle(\lambda y{:}\sigma.x)\rangle.0|\!) &= \lambda x{:}!(\!|\tau|\!).\mathsf{let}\, !x = x\,\mathsf{in}\,\langle !x \otimes \langle !(\!|\lambda y{:}\sigma.x|\!) \otimes \langle\rangle\rangle\rangle \\
&= \lambda x{:}!(\!|\tau|\!).\mathsf{let}\, !x = x\,\mathsf{in}\,\langle !x \otimes \langle !(\lambda y{:}!(\!|\sigma|\!).\mathsf{let}\, !y = y\,\mathsf{in}\,x) \otimes \langle\rangle\rangle\rangle
\end{aligned}
$$

Properties of the Encoding. Unsurprisingly due to the logical correspondence between natural deduction and sequent calculus presentations of logic, our encoding satisfies both type soundness and operational correspondence (c.f. Theorems 3.6, 3.8 and 3.10). The full development can be found in [52].

Relating the Two Encodings. We prove the two encodings are mutually inverse and preserve the full abstraction properties (we write $=_\beta$ and $=_{\beta\eta}$ for β- and $\beta\eta$-equivalence, respectively).

Theorem 4.7 (Inverse). *If* $\Psi; \Gamma; \Delta \vdash P :: z{:}A$ *then* $[\![(\!|P|\!)]\!]_z \approx_{\mathrm{L}} [\![P]\!]$. *Also, if* $\Psi \vdash M : \tau$ *then* $(\!|[\![M]\!]_z|\!) =_\beta (\!|M|\!)$.

The equivalences above are formulated between the composition of the encodings applied to P (resp. M) and the process (resp. λ-term) *after* applying the translation embedding the non-linear components into their linear counterparts. This formulation matches more closely that of § **3.3**, which applies to linear calculi for which the *target* languages of this section are a strict subset (and avoids the formalisation of process equivalence with terms). We also note that in this setting, observational equivalence and $\beta\eta$-equivalence coincide [3,31]. Moreover, the extensional flavour of $\approx_{\mathrm{L}}$ includes η-like principles at the process level.

Theorem 4.8. *Let* $\cdot \vdash M : \tau$ *and* $\cdot \vdash N : \tau$. $(\!|M|\!) =_{\beta\eta} (\!|N|\!)$ *iff* $[\![M]\!]_z \approx_{\mathrm{L}} [\![N]\!]_z$. *Also, let* $\cdot \vdash P :: z{:}A$ *and* $\cdot \vdash Q :: z{:}A$. *We have that* $[\![P]\!] \approx_{\mathrm{L}} [\![Q]\!]$ *iff* $(\!|P|\!) =_{\beta\eta} (\!|Q|\!)$.

We establish full abstraction for the encoding of λ-terms into processes (Theorem 4.8) in two steps: The completeness direction (i.e. from left-to-right) follows from operational completeness and strong normalisation of the λ-calculus. The soundness direction uses operational soundness. The proof of Theorem 4.8 uses the same strategy of Theorem 3.14, appealing to the inverse theorems.

4.3   Higher-Order Session Processes – Sess$\pi\lambda^+$

We extend the value-passing framework of the previous section, accounting for process-passing (i.e. the higher-order) in a session-typed setting. As shown in [50], we achieve this by adding to the data layer a *contextual monad* that encapsulates (open) session-typed processes as data values, with a corresponding elimination form in the process layer. We dub this calculus Sess$\pi\lambda^+$.

$$
\begin{aligned}
P, Q &::= \cdots \mid x \leftarrow M \leftarrow \overline{y_i}; Q \qquad M.N ::= \cdots \mid \{x \leftarrow P \leftarrow \overline{y_i{:}A_i}\} \\
\tau, \sigma &::= \cdots \mid \{\overline{x_j{:}A_j} \vdash z{:}A\}
\end{aligned}
$$

The type $\{\overline{x_j{:}A_j} \vdash z{:}A\}$ is the type of a term which encapsulates an open process that uses the linear channels $\overline{x_j{:}A_j}$ and offers A along channel z. This formulation has the added benefit of formalising the integration of session-typed processes in a functional language and forms the basis for the concurrent programming language SILL [37,50]. The typing rules for the new constructs are (for simplicity we assume no shared channels in process monads):

$$\frac{\Psi;\cdot;\overline{x_i{:}A_i} \vdash P :: z{:}A}{\Psi \vdash \{z \leftarrow P \leftarrow \overline{x_i{:}A_i}\} : \{\overline{x_i{:}A_i} \vdash z{:}A\}} \ \{\}I$$

$$\frac{\Psi \vdash M : \{\overline{x_i{:}A_i} \vdash x{:}A\} \quad \Delta_1 = \overline{y_i{:}A_i} \quad \Psi;\Gamma;\Delta_2, x{:}A \vdash Q :: z{:}C}{\Psi;\Gamma;\Delta_1,\Delta_2 \vdash x \leftarrow M \leftarrow \overline{y_i}; Q :: z{:}C} \ \{\}E$$

Rule $\{\}I$ embeds processes in the term language by essentially quoting an open process that is well-typed according to the type specification in the monadic type. Dually, rule $\{\}E$ allows for processes to use monadic values through composition that *consumes* some of the ambient channels in order to provide the monadic term with the necessary context (according to its type). These constructs are discussed in substantial detail in [50]. The reduction semantics of the process construct is given by (we tacitly assume that the names $\overline{y}$ and c do not occur in P and omit the congruence case):

$$(c \leftarrow \{z \leftarrow P \leftarrow \overline{x_i{:}A_i}\} \leftarrow \overline{y_i}; Q) \to (\nu c)(P\{\overline{y}/\overline{x_i}\{c/z\}\} \mid Q)$$

The semantics allows for the underlying monadic term M to evaluate to a (quoted) process P. The process P is then executed in parallel with the continuation Q, sharing the linear channel c for subsequent interactions. We illustrate the higher-order extension with following typed process (we write $\{x \leftarrow P\}$ when P does not depend on any linear channels and assume $\vdash Q :: d{:}\mathsf{Nat} \wedge \mathbf{1}$):

$$P \triangleq (\nu c)(c\langle\{d \leftarrow Q\}\rangle.c(x).\mathbf{0} \mid c(y).d \leftarrow y; d(n).c\langle n\rangle.\mathbf{0}) \tag{2}$$

Process P above gives an abstract view of a communication idiom where a process (the left-hand side of the parallel composition) sends another process Q which potentially encapsulates some complex computation. The receiver then *spawns* the execution of the received process and inputs from it a result value that is sent back to the original sender. An execution of P is given by:

$$P \to (\nu c)(c(x).\mathbf{0} \mid d \leftarrow \{d \leftarrow Q\}; d(n).c\langle n\rangle.\mathbf{0}) \quad \to \quad (\nu c)(c(x).\mathbf{0} \mid (\nu d)(Q \mid d(n).c\langle n\rangle.\mathbf{0}))$$
$$\to^+ (\nu c)(c(x).\mathbf{0} \mid c\langle 42\rangle.\mathbf{0}) \to \mathbf{0}$$

Given the seminal work of Sangiorgi [46], such a representation naturally begs the question of whether or not we can develop a *typed* encoding of higher-order processes into the first-order setting. Indeed, we can achieve such an encoding with a fairly simple extension of the encoding of § **4.2** to $\mathsf{Sess}\pi\lambda^+$ by observing that monadic values are processes that need to be potentially provided with extra sessions in order to be executed correctly. For instance, a term of type $\{x{:}A \vdash y{:}B\}$ denotes a process that given a session x of type A will then offer $y{:}B$. Exploiting this observation we encode this type as the session $A \multimap B$, ensuring subsequent usages of such a term are consistent with this interpretation.

$$[\![\{\overline{x_j{:}A_j} \vdash z{:}A\}]\!] \triangleq \overline{[\![A_j]\!]} \multimap [\![A]\!]$$
$$[\![\{x \leftarrow P \to \overline{y_i}\}]\!]_z \triangleq z(y_0)\ldots\ldots z(y_n).[\![P\{z/x\}]\!] \quad (z \notin fn(P))$$
$$[\![x \leftarrow M \leftarrow \overline{y_i}; Q]\!] \triangleq (\nu x)([\![M]\!]_x \mid \overline{x}\langle a_0 \rangle.([a_0 \leftrightarrow y_0] \mid \cdots \mid x\langle a_n \rangle.([a_n \leftrightarrow y_n] \mid [\![Q]\!]) \ldots))$$

To encode the monadic type $\{\overline{x_j{:}A_j} \vdash z{:}A\}$, denoting the type of process P that is typed by $\overline{x_j{:}A_j} \vdash P :: z{:}A$, we require that the session in the image of the translation specifies a sequence of channel inputs with behaviours $\overline{A_j}$ that make up the linear context. After the contextual aspects of the type are encoded, the session will then offer the (encoded) behaviour of A. Thus, the encoding of the monadic type is $[\![A_0]\!] \multimap \ldots \multimap [\![A_n]\!] \multimap [\![A]\!]$, which we write as $\overline{[\![A_j]\!]} \multimap [\![A]\!]$. The encoding of monadic expressions adheres to this behaviour, first performing the necessary sequence of inputs and then proceeding inductively. Finally, the encoding of the elimination form for monadic expressions behaves dually, composing the encoding of the monadic expression with a sequence of outputs that instantiate the consumed names accordingly (via forwarding). The encoding of process P from Eq. 2 is thus:

$$[\![P]\!] = (\nu c)([\![c\langle\{d \leftarrow Q\}\rangle.c(x).0]\!] \mid [\![c(y).d \leftarrow y; d(n).c\langle n\rangle.0]\!])$$
$$= (\nu c)(\overline{c}\langle w\rangle.(!w(d).[\![Q]\!] \mid c(x).0)c(y).(\nu d)(\overline{y}\langle b\rangle.[b \leftrightarrow d] \mid d(n).\overline{c}\langle m\rangle.(\overline{n}\langle e\rangle.[e \leftrightarrow m] \mid 0)))$$

Properties of the Encoding. As in our previous development, we can show that our encoding for $\text{Sess}\pi\lambda^+$ is type sound and satisfies operational correspondence. The full development is omitted but can be found in [52].

We encode $\text{Sess}\pi\lambda^+$ into λ-terms, extending § **4.2** with:

$$(\!(\{\overline{x_i{:}A_i} \vdash z{:}A\})\!) \triangleq \overline{(\!(A_i)\!)} \multimap (\!(A)\!)$$
$$(\!(x \leftarrow M \leftarrow \overline{y_i}; Q)\!) \triangleq (\!(Q)\!)\{((\!(M)\!)\,\overline{y_i})/x\} \quad (\!(\{x \leftarrow P \leftarrow \overline{w_i}\})\!) \triangleq \lambda w_0.\ldots\ldots\lambda w_n.(\!(P)\!)$$

The encoding translates the monadic type $\{\overline{x_i{:}A_i} \vdash z{:}A\}$ as a linear function $\overline{(\!(A_i)\!)} \multimap (\!(A)\!)$, which captures the fact that the underlying value must be provided with terms satisfying the requirements of the linear context. At the level of terms, the encoding for the monadic term constructor follows its type specification, generating a nesting of λ-abstractions that closes the term and proceeding inductively. For the process encoding, we translate the monadic application construct analogously to the translation of a linear cut, but applying the appropriate variables to the translated monadic term (which is of function type). We remark the similarity between our encoding and that of the previous section, where monadic terms are translated to a sequence of inputs (here a nesting of λ-abstractions). Our encoding satisfies type soundness and operational correspondence, as usual. Further showcasing the applications of our development, we obtain a novel strong normalisation result for this higher-order session-calculus "for free", through encoding to the λ-calculus.

Theorem 4.9 (Strong Normalisation). *Let $\Psi; \Gamma; \Delta \vdash P :: z{:}A$. There is no infinite reduction sequence starting from P.*

Theorem 4.10 (Inverse Encodings). *If $\Psi; \Gamma; \Delta \vdash P :: z{:}A$ then $[\![(\!(P)\!)]\!]_z \approx_L [\![P]\!]$. Also, if $\Psi \vdash M : \tau$ then $(\!([\![M]\!]_z)\!) =_\beta (\!(M)\!)$.*

Theorem 4.11. *Let* $\vdash M : \tau,\ \vdash N : \tau,\ \vdash P :: z{:}A$ *and* $\vdash Q :: z{:}A.$ $(\!|M|\!) =_{\beta\eta} (\!|N|\!)$ *iff* $[\![M]\!]_z \approx_{\mathsf{L}} [\![N]\!]_z$ *and* $[\![P]\!] \approx_{\mathsf{L}} [\![Q]\!]$ *iff* $(\!|P|\!) =_{\beta\eta} (\!|Q|\!).$

5   Related Work and Concluding Remarks

Process Encodings of Functions. Toninho et al. [49] study encodings of the simply-typed λ-calculus in a logically motivated session π-calculus, via encodings to the linear λ-calculus. Our work differs since they do not study polymorphism nor reverse encodings; and we provide deeper insights through applications of the encodings. Full abstraction or inverse properties are not studied.

Sangiorgi [43] uses a fully abstract compilation from the higher-order π-calculus (HOπ) to the π-calculus to study full abstraction for Milner's encodings of the λ-calculus. The work shows that Milner's encoding of the lazy λ-calculus can be recovered by restricting the semantic domain of processes (the so-called *restrictive* approach) or by enriching the λ-calculus with suitable constants. This work was later refined in [45], which does not use HOπ and considers an operational equivalence on λ-terms called *open applicative bisimulation* which coincides with Lévy-Longo tree equality. The work [47] studies general conditions under which encodings of the λ-calculus in the π-calculus are fully abstract wrt Lévy-Longo and Böhm Trees, which are then applied to several encodings of (call-by-name) λ-calculus. The works above deal with *untyped calculi*, and so reverse encodings are unfeasible. In a broader sense, our approach takes the restrictive approach using linear logic-based session typing and the induced observational equivalence. We use a λ-calculus with booleans as observables and reason with a Morris-style equivalence instead of tree equalities. It would be an interesting future work to apply the conditions in [47] in our typed setting.

Wadler [54] shows a correspondence between a linear functional language with session types GV and a session-typed process calculus with polymorphism based on classical linear logic CP. Along the lines of this work, Lindley and Morris [26], in an exploration of inductive and coinductive session types through the addition of least and greatest fixed points to CP and GV, develop an encoding from a linear λ-calculus with session primitives (Concurrent μGV) to a pure linear λ-calculus (Functional μGV) via a CPS transformation. They also develop translations between μCP and Concurrent μGV, extending [25]. Mapping to the terminology used in our work [17], their encodings are shown to be operationally complete, but no results are shown for the operational soundness directions and neither full abstraction nor inverse properties are studied. In addition, their operational characterisations do not compose across encodings. For instance, while strong normalisation of Functional μGV implies the same property for Concurrent μGV through their operationally complete encoding, the encoding from μCP to μGV does not necessarily preserve this property.

Types for π-calculi delineate sequential behaviours by restricting composition and name usages, limiting the contexts in which processes can interact. Therefore typed equivalences offer a *coarser* semantics than untyped semantics. Berger et al. [5] study an encoding of System F in a polymorphic linear π-calculus, showing it to be fully abstract based on game semantics techniques. Their typing system and proofs are more complex due to the fine-grained constraints from game semantics. Moreover, they do not study a reverse encoding. Orchard and Yoshida [33] develop embeddings to-and-from PCF with parallel effects and a session-typed π-calculus, but only develop operational correspondence and semantic soundness results, leaving the full abstraction problem open.

Polymorphism and Typed Behavioural Semantics. The work of [7] studies parametric session polymorphism for the intuitionistic setting, developing a behavioural equivalence that captures parametricity, which is used (denoted as $\approx_L$) in our paper. The work [39] introduces a typed bisimilarity for polymorphism in the π-calculus. Their bisimilarity is of an intensional flavour, whereas the one used in our work follows the extensional style of Reynolds [41]. Their typing discipline (originally from [53], which also develops type-preserving encodings of polymorphic λ-calculus into polymorphic π-calculus) differs significantly from the linear logic-based session typing of our work (e.g. theirs does not ensure deadlock-freedom). A key observation in their work is the coarser nature of typed equivalences with polymorphism (in analogy to those for IO-subtyping [38]) and their interaction with channel aliasing, suggesting a use of typed semantics and encodings of the π-calculus for fine-grained analyses of program behaviour.

F-Algebras and Linear-F. The use of initial and final (co)algebras to give a semantics to inductive and coinductive types dates back to Mendler [28], with their strong definability in System F appearing in [1,19]. The definability of inductive and coinductive types using parametricity also appears in [40] in the context of a logic for parametric polymorphism and later in [6] in a linear variant of such a logic. The work of [55] studies parametricity for the polymorphic linear λ-calculus of this work, developing encodings of a few inductive types but not the initial (or final) algebraic encodings in their full generality. Inductive and coinductive session types in a logical process setting appear in [26,51]. Both works consider a calculus with built-in recursion – the former in an intuitionistic setting where a process that offers a (co)inductive protocol is composed with another that consumes the (co)inductive protocol and the latter in a classical framework where composed recursive session types are dual each other.

Conclusion and Future Work. This work answers the question of what kind of type discipline of the π-calculus can exactly capture and is captured by λ-calculus behaviours. Our answer is given by showing the first mutually inverse and fully abstract encodings between two calculi with polymorphism, one being the Polyπ session calculus based on intuitionistic linear logic, and the other (a linear) System F. This further demonstrates that the linear logic-based articulation of name-passing interactions originally proposed by [8] (and studied extensively thereafter e.g. [7,9,25,36,50,51,54]) provides a clear and applicable tool for message-passing concurrency. By exploiting the proof theoretic equivalences between natural deduction and sequent calculus we develop mutually inverse and fully abstract encodings, which naturally extend to more intricate settings such as process passing (in the sense of HOπ). Our encodings also enable us to derive properties of the π-calculi "for free". Specifically, we show how to obtain adequate representations of least and greatest fixed points in Polyπ through the encoding of initial and final (co)algebras in the λ-calculus. We also straightforwardly derive a strong normalisation result for the higher-order session calculus, which otherwise involves non-trivial proof techniques [5,7,12,13,36]. Future work includes extensions to the classical linear logic-based framework, including multiparty session types [10,11]. Encodings of session π-calculi to the λ-calculus have been used to implement session primitives in functional languages such as Haskell (see a recent survey [32]), OCaml [24,34,35] and Scala [48]. Following this line of work, we plan to develop encoding-based implementations of this work as embedded DSLs. This would potentially enable an exploration of algebraic constructs beyond initial and final co-algebras in a session programming setting. In particular, we wish to further study the meaning of functors, natural transformations and related constructions in a session-typed setting, both from a more fundamental viewpoint but also in terms of programming patterns.

Acknowledgements. The authors thank Viviana Bono, Dominic Orchard and the reviewers for their comments, suggestions and pointers to related works. This work is partially supported by EPSRC EP/K034413/1, EP/K011715/1, EP/L00058X/1, EP/N027833/1, EP/N028201/1 and NOVA LINCS (UID/CEC/04516/2013).

References

1. Bainbridge, E.S., Freyd, P.J., Scedrov, A., Scott, P.J.: Functorial polymorphism. Theor. Comput. Sci. **70**(1), 35–64 (1990)
2. Balzer, S., Pfenning, F.: Manifest sharing with session types. In: ICFP (2017)
3. Barber, A.: Dual intuitionistic linear logic. Technical report ECS-LFCS-96-347. School of Informatics, University of Edinburgh (1996)
4. Benton, P.N.: A mixed linear and non-linear logic: proofs, terms and models. In: Pacholski, L., Tiuryn, J. (eds.) CSL 1994. LNCS, vol. 933, pp. 121–135. Springer, Heidelberg (1995). https://doi.org/10.1007/BFb0022251
5. Berger, M., Honda, K., Yoshida, N.: Genericity and the π-calculus. Acta Inf. **42**(2–3), 83–141 (2005)
6. Birkedal, L., Møgelberg, R.E., Petersen, R.L.: Linear abadi and plotkin logic. Log. Methods Comput. Sci. **2**(5), 1–48 (2006)
7. Caires, L., Pérez, J.A., Pfenning, F., Toninho, B.: Behavioral polymorphism and parametricity in session-based communication. In: Felleisen, M., Gardner, P. (eds.) ESOP 2013. LNCS, vol. 7792, pp. 330–349. Springer, Heidelberg (2013). https://doi.org/10.1007/978-3-642-37036-6_19
8. Caires, L., Pfenning, F.: Session types as intuitionistic linear propositions. In: Gastin, P., Laroussinie, F. (eds.) CONCUR 2010. LNCS, vol. 6269, pp. 222–236. Springer, Heidelberg (2010). https://doi.org/10.1007/978-3-642-15375-4_16
9. Caires, L., Pfenning, F., Toninho, B.: Linear logic propositions as session types. Math. Struct. Comput. Sci. **26**(3), 367–423 (2016)
10. Carbone, M., Lindley, S., Montesi, F., Schuermann, C., Wadler, P.: Coherence generalises duality: a logical explanation of multiparty session types. In: CONCUR 2016, vol. 59, pp. 33:1–33:15. Sch. Dag. (2016)

11. Carbone, M., Montesi, F., Schurmann, C., Yoshida, N.: Multiparty session types as coherence proofs. In: CONCUR 2015, vol. 42, pp. 412–426. Sch. Dag. (2015)
12. Demangeon, R., Hirschkoff, D., Sangiorgi, D.: Mobile processes and termination. In: Palsberg, J. (ed.) Semantics and Algebraic Specification. LNCS, vol. 5700, pp. 250–273. Springer, Heidelberg (2009). https://doi.org/10.1007/978-3-642-04164-8_13
13. Demangeon, R., Hirschkoff, D., Sangiorgi, D.: Termination in higher-order concurrent calculi. J. Log. Algebr. Program. **79**(7), 550–577 (2010)
14. Gentzen, G.: Untersuchungen über das logische schließen. Math. Z. **39**, 176–210 (1935)
15. Girard, J.: Linear logic. Theor. Comput. Sci. **50**, 1–102 (1987)
16. Girard, J., Lafont, Y., Taylor, P.: Proofs and Types. CUP, Cambridge (1989)
17. Gorla, D.: Towards a unified approach to encodability and separation results for process calculi. Inf. Comput. **208**(9), 1031–1053 (2010)
18. Gorla, D., Nestmann, U.: Full abstraction for expressiveness: history, myths and facts. Math. Struct. Comput. Sci. **26**(4), 639–654 (2016)
19. Hasegawa, R.: Categorical data types in parametric polymorphism. Math. Struct. Comput. Sci. **4**(1), 71–109 (1994)
20. Honda, K.: Types for dyadic interaction. In: Best, E. (ed.) CONCUR 1993. LNCS, vol. 715, pp. 509–523. Springer, Heidelberg (1993). https://doi.org/10.1007/3-540-57208-2_35
21. Honda, K.: Session types and distributed computing. In: Czumaj, A., Mehlhorn, K., Pitts, A., Wattenhofer, R. (eds.) ICALP 2012. LNCS, vol. 7392, pp. 23–23. Springer, Heidelberg (2012). https://doi.org/10.1007/978-3-642-31585-5_4
22. Honda, K., Vasconcelos, V.T., Kubo, M.: Language primitives and type discipline for structured communication-based programming. In: Hankin, C. (ed.) ESOP 1998. LNCS, vol. 1381, pp. 122–138. Springer, Heidelberg (1998). https://doi.org/10.1007/BFb0053567
23. Honda, K., Yoshida, N., Carbone, M.: Multiparty asynchronous session types. In: POPL 2008, pp. 273–284 (2008)
24. Imai, K., Yoshida, N., Yuen, S.: `Session-ocaml`: a session-based library with polarities and lenses. In: Jacquet, J.-M., Massink, M. (eds.) COORDINATION 2017. LNCS, vol. 10319, pp. 99–118. Springer, Cham (2017). https://doi.org/10.1007/978-3-319-59746-1_6
25. Lindley, S., Morris, J.G.: A semantics for propositions as sessions. In: Vitek, J. (ed.) ESOP 2015. LNCS, vol. 9032, pp. 560–584. Springer, Heidelberg (2015). https://doi.org/10.1007/978-3-662-46669-8_23
26. Lindley, S., Morris, J.G.: Talking bananas: structural recursion for session types. In: ICFP 2016, pp. 434–447 (2016)
27. Maraist, J., Odersky, M., Turner, D.N., Wadler, P.: Call-by-name, call-by-value, call-by-need and the linear lambda calculus. T. C. S. **228**(1–2), 175–210 (1999)
28. Mendler, N.P.: Recursive types and type constraints in second-order lambda calculus. In: LICS 1987, pp. 30–36 (1987)
29. Milner, R.: Functions as processes. In: Paterson, M.S. (ed.) ICALP 1990. LNCS, vol. 443, pp. 167–180. Springer, Heidelberg (1990). https://doi.org/10.1007/BFb0032030
30. Milner, R., Parrow, J., Walker, D.: A calculus of mobile processes I and II. Inf. Comput. **100**(1), 1–77 (1992)
31. Ohta, Y., Hasegawa, M.: A terminating and confluent linear lambda calculus. In: Pfenning, F. (ed.) RTA 2006. LNCS, vol. 4098, pp. 166–180. Springer, Heidelberg (2006). https://doi.org/10.1007/11805618_13

32. Orchard, D., Yoshida, N.: Session types with linearity in Haskell. In: Gay, S., Ravara, A. (eds.) Behavioural Types: From Theory to Tools. River Publishers, Gistrup (2017)
33. Orchard, D.A., Yoshida, N.: Effects as sessions, sessions as effects. In: POPL 2016, pp. 568–581 (2016)
34. Padovani, L.: A Simple Library Implementation of Binary Sessions. JFP **27** (2016)
35. Padovani, L.: Context-free session type inference. In: Yang, H. (ed.) ESOP 2017. LNCS, vol. 10201, pp. 804–830. Springer, Heidelberg (2017). https://doi.org/10.1007/978-3-662-54434-1_30
36. Pérez, J.A., Caires, L., Pfenning, F., Toninho, B.: Linear logical relations for session-based concurrency. In: Seidl, H. (ed.) ESOP 2012. LNCS, vol. 7211, pp. 539–558. Springer, Heidelberg (2012). https://doi.org/10.1007/978-3-642-28869-2_27
37. Pfenning, F., Griffith, D.: Polarized substructural session types. In: Pitts, A. (ed.) FoSSaCS 2015. LNCS, vol. 9034, pp. 3–22. Springer, Heidelberg (2015). https://doi.org/10.1007/978-3-662-46678-0_1
38. Pierce, B.C., Sangiorgi, D.: Typing and subtyping for mobile processes. Math. Struct. Comput. Sci. **6**(5), 409–453 (1996)
39. Pierce, B.C., Sangiorgi, D.: Behavioral equivalence in the polymorphic pi-calculus. J. ACM **47**(3), 531–584 (2000)
40. Plotkin, G., Abadi, M.: A logic for parametric polymorphism. In: Bezem, M., Groote, J.F. (eds.) TLCA 1993. LNCS, vol. 664, pp. 361–375. Springer, Heidelberg (1993). https://doi.org/10.1007/BFb0037118
41. Reynolds, J.C.: Types, abstraction and parametric polymorphism. In: IFIP Congress, pp. 513–523 (1983)
42. Reynolds, J.C., Plotkin, G.D.: On functors expressible in the polymorphic typed lambda calculus. Inf. Comput. **105**(1), 1–29 (1993)
43. Sangiorgi, D.: An investigation into functions as processes. In: Brookes, S., Main, M., Melton, A., Mislove, M., Schmidt, D. (eds.) MFPS 1993. LNCS, vol. 802, pp. 143–159. Springer, Heidelberg (1994). https://doi.org/10.1007/3-540-58027-1_7
44. Sangiorgi, D.: Π-calculus, internal mobility, and agent-passing calculi. Theor. Comput. Sci. **167**(1&2), 235–274 (1996)
45. Sangiorgi, D.: Lazy functions and mobile processes. In: Proof, Language, and Interaction: Essays in Honour of Robin Milner, pp. 691–720 (2000)
46. Sangiorgi, D., Walker, D.: The π-Calculus: A Theory of Mobile Processes. Cambridge University Press, Cambridge (2001)
47. Sangiorgi, D., Xu, X.: Trees from functions as processes. In: Baldan, P., Gorla, D. (eds.) CONCUR 2014. LNCS, vol. 8704, pp. 78–92. Springer, Heidelberg (2014). https://doi.org/10.1007/978-3-662-44584-6_7
48. Scalas, A., Dardha, O., Hu, R., Yoshida, N.: A linear decomposition of multiparty sessions for safe distributed programming. In: ECOOP 2017 (2017)
49. Toninho, B., Caires, L., Pfenning, F.: Functions as session-typed processes. In: Birkedal, L. (ed.) FoSSaCS 2012. LNCS, vol. 7213, pp. 346–360. Springer, Heidelberg (2012). https://doi.org/10.1007/978-3-642-28729-9_23
50. Toninho, B., Caires, L., Pfenning, F.: Higher-order processes, functions, and sessions: a monadic integration. In: Felleisen, M., Gardner, P. (eds.) ESOP 2013. LNCS, vol. 7792, pp. 350–369. Springer, Heidelberg (2013). https://doi.org/10.1007/978-3-642-37036-6_20

51. Toninho, B., Caires, L., Pfenning, F.: Corecursion and non-divergence in session-typed processes. In: Maffei, M., Tuosto, E. (eds.) TGC 2014. LNCS, vol. 8902, pp. 159–175. Springer, Heidelberg (2014). https://doi.org/10.1007/978-3-662-45917-1_11

52. Toninho, B., Yoshida, N.: On polymorphic sessions and functions: a tale of two (fully abstract) encodings (long version). CoRR abs/1711.00878 (2017)

53. Turner, D.: The polymorphic pi-calculus: Theory and implementation. Technical report ECS-LFCS-96-345. School of Informatics, University of Edinburgh (1996)

54. Wadler, P.: Propositions as sessions. J. Funct. Program. **24**(2–3), 384–418 (2014)

55. Zhao, J., Zhang, Q., Zdancewic, S.: Relational parametricity for a polymorphic linear lambda calculus. In: Ueda, K. (ed.) APLAS 2010. LNCS, vol. 6461, pp. 344–359. Springer, Heidelberg (2010). https://doi.org/10.1007/978-3-642-17164-2_24

Concurrent Kleene Algebra: Free Model and Completeness

Tobias Kappé[✉], Paul Brunet, Alexandra Silva, and Fabio Zanasi

University College London, London, UK
tkappe@cs.ucl.ac.uk

Abstract. Concurrent Kleene Algebra (CKA) was introduced by Hoare, Moeller, Struth and Wehrman in 2009 as a framework to reason about concurrent programs. We prove that the axioms for CKA with bounded parallelism are complete for the semantics proposed in the original paper; consequently, these semantics are the free model for this fragment. This result settles a conjecture of Hoare and collaborators. Moreover, the technique developed to this end allows us to establish a Kleene Theorem for CKA, extending an earlier Kleene Theorem for a fragment of CKA.

1 Introduction

Concurrent Kleene Algebra (CKA) [8] is a mathematical formalism which extends Kleene Algebra (KA) with a parallel composition operator, in order to express concurrent program behaviour.[1] In spite of such a seemingly simple addition, extending the existing KA toolkit (notably, completeness) to the setting of CKA turned out to be a challenging task. A lot of research happened since the original paper, both foundational [13,20] and on how CKA could be used to reason about important verification tasks in concurrent systems [9,11]. However, and despite several conjectures [9,13], the question of the characterisation of the free CKA and the completeness of the axioms remained open, making it impractical to use CKA in verification tasks. This paper settles these two open questions. We answer positively the conjecture that the free model of CKA is formed by series parallel pomset languages, downward-closed under Gischer's subsumption order [6]—a generalisation of regular languages to sets of partially ordered words. To this end, we prove that the original axioms proposed in [8] are indeed complete.

Our proof of completeness is based on extending an existing completeness result that establishes series-parallel rational pomset languages as the free Bi-Kleene Algebra (BKA) [20]. The extension to the existing result for BKA provides a clear understanding of the difficulties introduced by the presence of the exchange axiom and shows how to separate concerns between CKA and BKA, a technique which is also useful elsewhere. For one, our construction also provides

---

[1] In its original formulation, CKA also features an operator (*parallel star*) for unbounded parallelism: in harmony with several recent works [13,14], we study the variant of CKA without parallel star, sometimes called "weak" CKA.

© The Author(s) 2018
A. Ahmed (Ed.): ESOP 2018, LNCS 10801, pp. 856–882, 2018.
https://doi.org/10.1007/978-3-319-89884-1_30

an extension of (half of) Kleene's theorem for BKA [14] to CKA, establishing pomset automata as an operational model for CKA and opening the door to decidability procedures similar to those previously studied for KA. Furthermore, it reduces deciding the equational theory of CKA to deciding the equational theory of BKA.

BKA is defined as CKA with the only (but significant) omission of the *exchange law*, $(e \parallel f) \cdot (g \parallel h) \leq_{CKA} (e \cdot g) \parallel (f \cdot h)$. The exchange law is the core element of CKA as it softens true concurrency: it states that when two sequentially composed programs (i.e., $e \cdot g$ and $f \cdot h$) are composed in parallel, they can be implemented by running their heads in parallel, followed by running their tails in parallel (i.e., $e \parallel f$, then $g \parallel h$). The exchange law allows the implementer of a CKA expression to interleave threads at will, without violating the specification.

To illustrate the use of the exchange law, consider a protocol with three actions: query a channel c, collect an answer from the same channel, and print an unrelated message m on screen. The specification for this protocol requires the query to happen before reception of the message, but the printing action being independent, it may be executed concurrently. We will write this specification as $(q(c) \cdot r(c)) \parallel p(m)$, with the operator $\cdot$ denoting sequential composition. However, if one wants to implement this protocol in a sequential programming language, a total ordering of these events has to be introduced. Suppose we choose to implement this protocol by printing m while we wait to receive an answer. This implementation can be written $q(c) \cdot p(m) \cdot r(c)$. Using the laws of CKA, we can prove that $q(c) \cdot p(m) \cdot r(c) \leq_{CKA} (q(c) \cdot r(c)) \parallel p(m)$, which we interpret as the fact that this implementation respects the specification. Intuitively, this means that the specification lists the necessary dependencies, but the implementation can introduce more.

Having a complete axiomatisation of CKA has two main benefits. First, it allows one to get certificates of correctness. Indeed, if one wants to use CKA for program verification, the decision procedure presented in [3] may be used to test program equivalence. If the test gives a negative answer, this algorithm provides a counter-example. However if the answer is positive, no meaningful witness is produced. With the completeness result presented here, that is constructive in nature, one could generate an axiomatic proof of equivalence in these cases. Second, it gives one a simple way of checking when the aforementioned procedure applies. By construction, we know that two terms are semantically equivalent whenever they are equal in every concurrent Kleene algebra, that is any model of the axioms of CKA. This means that if we consider a specific semantic domain, one simply needs to check that the axioms of CKA hold in there to know that the decision procedure of [3] is sound in this model.

While this paper was in writing, a manuscript with the same result appeared [19]. Among other things, the proof presented here is different in that it explicitly shows how to syntactically construct terms that express certain pomset languages, as opposed to showing that such terms must exist by reasoning on a semantic level. We refer to Sect. 5 for a more extensive comparison.

The remainder of this paper is organised as follows. In Sect. 2, we give an informal overview of the completeness proof. In Sect. 3, we introduce the necessary concepts, notation and lemmas. In Sect. 4, we work out the proof. We discuss the result in a broader perspective and outline further work in Sect. 5.

2   Overview of the Completeness Proof

We start with an overview of the steps necessary to arrive at the main result. As mentioned, our strategy in tackling CKA-completeness is to build on the existing BKA-completeness result. Following an observation by Laurence and Struth, we identify *downward-closure* (under Gischer's subsumption order [6]) as the feature that distinguishes the pomsets giving semantics to BKA-expressions from those associated with CKA-expressions. In a slogan,

$$\text{CKA-semantics} = \text{BKA-semantics} + \text{downward-closure.}$$

This situation is depicted in the upper part of the commuting diagram in Fig. 1. Intuitively, downward-closure can be thought of as the semantic outcome of adding the exchange axiom, which distinguishes CKA from BKA. Thus, if a and b are events that can happen in parallel according to the BKA-semantics of a term, then a and b may also be ordered in the CKA-semantics of that same term.

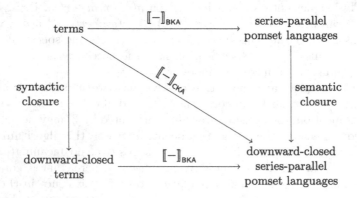

Fig. 1. The connection between BKA and CKA semantics mediated by closure.

The core of our CKA-completeness proof will be to construct a syntactic counterpart to the semantic closure. Concretely, we shall build a function that maps a CKA term e to an equivalent term $e{\downarrow}$, called the (syntactic) *closure* of e. The lower part of the commuting diagram in Fig. 1 shows the property that $e{\downarrow}$ must satisfy in order to deserve the name of closure: its BKA semantics has to be the same as the CKA semantics of e.

Example 2.1. Consider $e = a \parallel b$, whose CKA-semantics prescribe that a and b are events that may happen in parallel. One closure of this term would be $e{\downarrow} = a \parallel b + a \cdot b + b \cdot a$, whose BKA-semantics stipulate that either a and b execute purely in parallel, or a precedes b, or b precedes a—thus matching the optional parallelism of a and b. For a more non-trivial example, take $e = a^\star \parallel b^\star$, which represents that finitely many repetitions of a and b occur, possibly in parallel. A closure of this term would be $e{\downarrow} = (a^\star \parallel b^\star)^\star$: finitely many repetitions of a and b occur truly in parallel, which is repeated indefinitely.

In order to find $e{\downarrow}$ systematically, we are going to construct it in stages, through a completely syntactic procedure where each transformation has to be valid according to the axioms. There are three main stages.

(i) We note that, not unexpectedly, the hardest case for computing the closure of a term is when e is a parallel composition, i.e., when $e = e_0 \parallel e_1$ for some CKA terms e_0 and e_1. For the other operators, the closure of the result can be obtained by applying the same operator to the closures of its arguments. For instance, $(e + f){\downarrow} = e{\downarrow} + f{\downarrow}$. This means that we can focus on calculating the closure for the particular case of parallel composition.

(ii) We construct a *preclosure* of such terms e, whose BKA semantics contains all but possibly the sequentially composed pomsets of the CKA semantics of e. Since every sequentially composed pomset decomposes (uniquely) into non-sequential pomsets, we can use the preclosure as a basis for induction.

(iii) We extend this preclosure of e to a proper closure, by leveraging the fixpoint axioms of KA to solve a system of linear inequations. This system encodes "stringing together" non-sequential pomsets to build all pomsets in e.

As a straightforward consequence of the closure construction, we obtain a completeness theorem for CKA, which establishes the set of closed series-rational pomset languages as the free CKA.

3 Preliminaries

We fix a finite set of symbols Σ, the *alphabet*. We use the symbols a, b and c to denote elements of Σ. The two-element set $\{0, 1\}$ is denoted by 2. Given a set S, the set of subsets (*powerset*) of S is denoted by 2^S.

In the interest of readability, the proofs for technical lemmas in this section can be found in the full version [15].

3.1 Pomsets

A trace of a sequential program can be modelled as a word, where each letter represents an atomic event, and the order of the letters in the word represents the order in which the events took place. Analogously, a trace of a concurrent program can be thought of as word where letters are partially ordered, i.e., there need not be a causal link between events. In literature, such a partially ordered word is commonly called a *partial word* [7], or *partially ordered multiset* (*pomset*, for short) [6]; we use the latter term.

A formal definition of pomsets requires some work, because the partial order should order *occurrences* of events rather than the events themselves. For this reason, we first define a labelled poset.

Definition 3.1. *A labelled poset is a tuple* $\langle S, \leq, \lambda \rangle$, *where* $\langle S, \leq \rangle$ *is a partially ordered set (i.e.,* S *is a set and* $\leq$ *is a partial order on* S*), in which* S *is called the* carrier *and* $\leq$ *is the* order; $\lambda : S \to \Sigma$ *is a function called the* labelling.

We denote labelled posets with lower-case bold symbols $\mathbf{u}$, $\mathbf{v}$, et cetera. Given a labelled poset $\mathbf{u}$, we write $S_{\mathbf{u}}$ for its carrier, $\leq_{\mathbf{u}}$ for its order and $\lambda_{\mathbf{u}}$ for its labelling. We write $\mathbf{1}$ for the empty labelled poset. We say that two labelled posets are *disjoint* if their carriers are disjoint.

Disjoint labelled posets can be composed parallelly and sequentially; parallel composition simply juxtaposes the events, while sequential composition imposes an ordering between occurrences of events originating from the left operand and those originating from the right operand.

Definition 3.2. *Let* $\mathbf{u}$ *and* $\mathbf{v}$ *be disjoint. We write* $\mathbf{u} \parallel \mathbf{v}$ *for the* parallel composition *of* $\mathbf{u}$ *and* $\mathbf{v}$*, which is the labelled poset with the carrier* $S_{\mathbf{u} \cup \mathbf{v}} = S_{\mathbf{u}} \cup S_{\mathbf{v}}$*, the order* $\leq_{\mathbf{u} \parallel \mathbf{v}} = \leq_{\mathbf{u}} \cup \leq_{\mathbf{v}}$ *and the labeling* $\lambda_{\mathbf{u} \parallel \mathbf{v}}$ *defined by*

$$\lambda_{\mathbf{u} \parallel \mathbf{v}}(x) = \begin{cases} \lambda_{\mathbf{u}}(x) & x \in S_{\mathbf{u}}; \\ \lambda_{\mathbf{v}}(x) & x \in S_{\mathbf{v}}. \end{cases}$$

Similarly, we write $\mathbf{u} \cdot \mathbf{v}$ *for the* sequential composition *of* $\mathbf{u}$ *and* $\mathbf{v}$*, that is, labelled poset with the carrier* $S_{\mathbf{u} \cup \mathbf{v}}$ *and the partial order*

$$\leq_{\mathbf{u} \cdot \mathbf{v}} = \leq_{\mathbf{u}} \cup \leq_{\mathbf{v}} \cup (S_{\mathbf{u}} \times S_{\mathbf{v}}),$$

as well as the labelling $\lambda_{\mathbf{u} \cdot \mathbf{v}} = \lambda_{\mathbf{u} \parallel \mathbf{v}}$.

Note that $\mathbf{1}$ is neutral for sequential and parallel composition, in the sense that we have $\mathbf{1} \parallel \mathbf{u} = \mathbf{1} \cdot \mathbf{u} = \mathbf{u} = \mathbf{u} \cdot \mathbf{1} = \mathbf{u} \parallel \mathbf{1}$.

There is a natural ordering between labelled posets with regard to concurrency.

Definition 3.3. *Let* $\mathbf{u}, \mathbf{v}$ *be labelled posets. A* subsumption *from* $\mathbf{u}$ *to* $\mathbf{v}$ *is a bijection* $h : S_{\mathbf{u}} \to S_{\mathbf{v}}$ *that preserves order and labels, i.e.,* $u \leq_{\mathbf{u}} u'$ *implies that* $h(u) \leq_{\mathbf{v}} h(u')$*, and* $\lambda_{\mathbf{v}} \circ h = \lambda_{\mathbf{u}}$*. We simplify and write* $h : \mathbf{u} \to \mathbf{v}$ *for a subsumption from* $\mathbf{u}$ *to* $\mathbf{v}$*. If such a subsumption exists, we write* $\mathbf{v} \sqsubseteq \mathbf{u}$*. Furthermore,* h *is an* isomorphism *if both* h *and its inverse* h^{-1} *are subsumptions. If there exists an isomorphism from* $\mathbf{u}$ *to* $\mathbf{v}$ *we write* $\mathbf{u} \cong \mathbf{v}$.

Intuitively, if $\mathbf{u} \sqsubseteq \mathbf{v}$, then $\mathbf{u}$ and $\mathbf{v}$ both order the same set of (occurrences of) events, but $\mathbf{u}$ has more causal links, or "is more sequential" than $\mathbf{v}$. One easily sees that $\sqsubseteq$ is a preorder on labelled posets of finite carrier.

Since the actual contents of the carrier of a labelled poset do not matter, we can abstract from them using isomorphism. This gives rise to pomsets.

Definition 3.4. *A pomset is an isomorphism class of labelled posets, i.e., the class* $[\mathbf{v}] \triangleq \{\mathbf{u} : \mathbf{u} \cong \mathbf{v}\}$ *for some labelled poset* $\mathbf{v}$. *Composition lifts to pomsets: we write* $[\mathbf{u}] \parallel [\mathbf{v}]$ *for* $[\mathbf{u} \parallel \mathbf{v}]$ *and* $[\mathbf{u}] \cdot [\mathbf{v}]$ *for* $[\mathbf{u} \cdot \mathbf{v}]$. *Similarly, subsumption also lifts to pomsets: we write* $[\mathbf{u}] \sqsubseteq [\mathbf{v}]$, *precisely when* $\mathbf{u} \sqsubseteq \mathbf{v}$.

We denote pomsets with upper-case symbols U, V, et cetera. The *empty pomset*, i.e., $[\mathbf{1}] = \{\mathbf{1}\}$, is denoted by 1; this pomset is neutral for sequential and parallel composition. To ensure that $[\mathbf{v}]$ is a set, we limit the discussion to labelled posets whose carrier is a subset of some set $\mathbb{S}$. The labelled posets in this paper have finite carrier; it thus suffices to choose $\mathbb{S} = \mathbb{N}$ to represent all pomsets with finite (or even countably infinite) carrier.

Composition of pomsets is well-defined: if $\mathbf{u}$ and $\mathbf{v}$ are not disjoint, we can find $\mathbf{u}', \mathbf{v}'$ disjoint from $\mathbf{u}, \mathbf{v}$ respectively such that $\mathbf{u} \cong \mathbf{u}'$ and $\mathbf{v} \cong \mathbf{v}'$. The choice of representative does not matter, for if $\mathbf{u} \cong \mathbf{u}'$ and $\mathbf{v} \cong \mathbf{v}'$, then $\mathbf{u} \cdot \mathbf{v} \cong \mathbf{u}' \cdot \mathbf{v}'$. Subsumption of pomsets is also well-defined: if $\mathbf{u}' \cong \mathbf{u} \sqsubseteq \mathbf{v} \cong \mathbf{v}'$, then $\mathbf{u}' \sqsubseteq \mathbf{v}'$. One easily sees that $\sqsubseteq$ is a partial order on finite pomsets, and that sequential and parallel composition are monotone with respect to $\sqsubseteq$, i.e., if $U \sqsubseteq W$ and $V \sqsubseteq X$, then $U \cdot V \sqsubseteq W \cdot X$ and $U \parallel V \sqsubseteq W \parallel X$. Lastly, we note that both types of composition are associative, both on the level of pomsets and labelled posets; we therefore omit parentheses when no ambiguity is likely.

Series-Parallel Pomsets. If $a \in \Sigma$, we can construct a labelled poset with a single element labelled by a; indeed, since any labelled poset thus constructed is isomorphic, we also use a to denote this isomorphism class; such a pomset is called a *primitive pomset*. A pomset built from primitive pomsets and sequential and parallel composition is called *series-parallel*; more formally:

Definition 3.5. *The set of* series-parallel *pomsets, denoted* $\mathsf{SP}(\Sigma)$, *is the smallest set such that* $1 \in \mathsf{SP}(\Sigma)$ *as well as* $a \in \mathsf{SP}(\Sigma)$ *for every* $a \in \Sigma$, *and is closed under parallel and sequential composition.*

We elide the sequential composition operator when we explicitly construct a pomset from primitive pomsets, i.e., we write ab instead of $a \cdot b$ for the pomset obtained by sequentially composing the (primitive) pomsets a and b. In this notation, sequential composition takes precedence over parallel composition.

All pomsets encountered in this paper are series-parallel. A useful feature of series-parallel pomsets is that we can deconstruct them in a standard fashion [6].

Lemma 3.1. *Let* $U \in \mathsf{SP}(\Sigma)$. *Then exactly one of the following is true: either (i)* $U = 1$, *or (ii)* $U = a$ *for some* $a \in \Sigma$, *or (iii)* $U = U_0 \cdot U_1$ *for* $U_0, U_1 \in \mathsf{SP}(\Sigma) \setminus \{1\}$, *or (iv)* $U = U_0 \parallel U_1$ *for* $U_0, U_1 \in \mathsf{SP}(\Sigma) \setminus \{1\}$.

In the sequel, it will be useful to refer to pomsets that are *not* of the third kind above, i.e., cannot be written as $U_0 \cdot U_1$ for $U_0, U_1 \in \mathsf{SP}(\Sigma) \setminus \{1\}$, as *nonsequential* pomsets. Lemma 3.1 gives a normal form for series-parallel pomsets, as follows.

Corollary 3.1. *A pomset* $U \in \mathsf{SP}(\Sigma)$ *can be uniquely decomposed as* $U = U_0 \cdot U_1 \cdots U_{n-1}$, *where for all* $0 \leq i < n$, U_i *is series parallel and non-sequential.*

Factorisation. We now go over some lemmas on pomsets that will allow us to factorise pomsets later on. First of all, one easily shows that subsumption is irrelevant on empty and primitive pomsets, as witnessed by the following lemma.

Lemma 3.2. *Let U and V be pomsets such that $U \sqsubseteq V$ or $V \sqsubseteq U$. If U is empty or primitive, then $U = V$.*

We can also consider how pomset composition and subsumption relate. It is not hard to see that if a pomset is subsumed by a sequentially composed pomset, then this sequential composition also appears in the subsumed pomset. A similar statement holds for pomsets that subsume a parallel composition.

Lemma 3.3 (Factorisation). *Let U, V_0, and V_1 be pomsets such that U is subsumed by $V_0 \cdot V_1$. Then there exist pomsets U_0 and U_1 such that:*

$$U = U_0 \cdot U_1, \ U_0 \sqsubseteq V_0, \ and \ U_1 \sqsubseteq V_1.$$

Also, if U_0, U_1 and V are pomsets such that $U_0 \parallel U_1 \sqsubseteq V$, then there exist pomsets V_0 and V_1 such that:

$$V = V_0 \parallel V_1, \ U_0 \sqsubseteq V_0, \ and \ U_1 \sqsubseteq V_1.$$

The next lemma can be thought of as a generalisation of Levi's lemma [21], a well-known statement about words, to pomsets. It says that if a sequential composition is subsumed by another (possibly longer) sequential composition, then there must be a pomset "in the middle", describing the overlap between the two; this pomset gives rise to a factorisation.

Lemma 3.4. *Let U and V be pomsets, and let $W_0, W_1, \ldots, W_{n-1}$ with $n > 0$ be non-empty pomsets such that $U \cdot V \sqsubseteq W_0 \cdot W_1 \cdots W_{n-1}$. There exists an $m < n$ and pomsets Y, Z such that:*

$$Y \cdot Z \sqsubseteq W_m, \ U \sqsubseteq W_0 \cdot W_1 \cdots W_{m-1} \cdot Y, \ and \ V \sqsubseteq Z \cdot W_{m+1} \cdot W_{m+2} \cdots W_n.$$

Moreover, if U and V are series-parallel, then so are Y and Z.

Levi's lemma also has an analogue for parallel composition.

Lemma 3.5. *Let U, V, W, X be pomsets such that $U \parallel V = W \parallel X$. There exist pomsets Y_0, Y_1, Z_0, Z_1 such that*

$$U = Y_0 \parallel Y_1, \ V = Z_0 \parallel Z_1, \ W = Y_0 \parallel Z_0, \ and \ X = Y_1 \parallel Z_1.$$

The final lemma is useful when we have a sequentially composed pomset subsumed by a parallelly composed pomset. It tells us that we can factor the involved pomsets to find subsumptions between smaller pomsets. This lemma first appeared in [6], where it is called the interpolation lemma.

Lemma 3.6 (Interpolation). *Let U, V, W, X be pomsets such that $U \cdot V$ is subsumed by $W \parallel X$. Then there exist pomsets W_0, W_1, X_0, X_1 such that*

$$W_0 \cdot W_1 \sqsubseteq W, \; X_0 \cdot X_1 \sqsubseteq X, \; U \sqsubseteq W_0 \parallel X_0, \; \text{and} \; V \sqsubseteq W_1 \parallel X_1.$$

Moreover, if W and X are series-parallel, then so are W_0, W_1, X_0 and X_1.

On a semi-formal level, the interpolation lemma can be understood as follows. If $U \cdot V \sqsubseteq W \parallel X$, then the events in W are partitioned between those that end up in U, and those that end up in V; these give rise to the "sub-pomsets" W_0 and W_1 of W, respectively. Similarly, X partitions into "sub-pomsets" X_0 and X_1. We refer to Fig. 2 for a graphical depiction of this situation.

Now, if y precedes z in $W_0 \parallel X_0$, then y must precede z in $W \parallel X$, and therefore also in $U \cdot V$. Since y and z are both events in U, it then follows that y precedes z in U, establishing that $U \sqsubseteq W_0 \parallel X_0$. Furthermore, if y precedes z in W, then we can exclude the case where y is in W_1 and z in W_0, for then z precedes y in $U \cdot V$, contradicting that y precedes z in $U \cdot V$. Accordingly, either y and z both belong to W_0 or W_1, or y is in W_0 while z is in W_1; in all of these cases, y must precede z in $W_0 \cdot W_1$. The other subsumptions hold analogously.

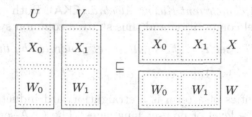

Fig. 2. Splitting pomsets in the interpolation lemma

Pomset Languages. The semantics of BKA and CKA are given in terms of sets of series-parallel pomsets.

Definition 3.6. *A subset of* $\mathsf{SP}(\Sigma)$ *is referred to as a* pomset language.

As a convention, we denote pomset languages by the symbols $\mathcal{U}, \mathcal{V}$, et cetera. Sequential and parallel composition of pomsets extends to pomset languages in a pointwise manner, i.e.,

$$\mathcal{U} \cdot \mathcal{V} \triangleq \{U \cdot V : U \in \mathcal{U}, V \in \mathcal{V}\}$$

and similarly for parallel composition. Like languages of words, pomset languages have a Kleene star operator, which is similarly defined, i.e., $\mathcal{U}^\star \triangleq \bigcup_{n \in \mathbb{N}} \mathcal{U}^n$, where the nth power of $\mathcal{U}$ is inductively defined as $\mathcal{U}^0 \triangleq \{1\}$ and $\mathcal{U}^{n+1} \triangleq \mathcal{U}^n \cdot \mathcal{U}$.

A pomset language $\mathcal{U}$ is *closed under subsumption* (or simply *closed*) if whenever $U \in \mathcal{U}$ with $U' \sqsubseteq U$ and $U' \in \mathsf{SP}(\Sigma)$, it holds that $U' \in \mathcal{U}$. The *closure under subsumption* (or simply *closure*) of a pomset language $\mathcal{U}$, denoted $\mathcal{U}{\downarrow}$, is defined as the smallest pomset language that contains $\mathcal{U}$ and is closed, i.e.,

$$\mathcal{U}{\downarrow} \triangleq \{U' \in \mathsf{SP}(\Sigma) : \exists U \in \mathcal{U}.\ U' \sqsubseteq U\}$$

Closure relates to union, sequential composition and iteration as follows.

Lemma 3.7. *Let $\mathcal{U}, \mathcal{V}$ be pomset languages; then:*

$$(\mathcal{U} \cup \mathcal{V})\!\downarrow \;=\; \mathcal{U}\!\downarrow \cup\, \mathcal{V}\!\downarrow, \;\; (\mathcal{U} \cdot \mathcal{V})\!\downarrow \;=\; \mathcal{U}\!\downarrow \cdot\, \mathcal{V}\!\downarrow, \;\; \text{and}\; \mathcal{U}^{\star}\!\downarrow \;=\; \mathcal{U}\!\downarrow^{\star}.$$

Proof. The first claim holds for infinite unions, too, and follows immediately from the definition of closure.

For the second claim, suppose that $U \in \mathcal{U}$ and $V \in \mathcal{V}$, and that $W \sqsubseteq U \cdot V$. By Lemma 3.3, we find pomsets W_0 and W_1 such that $W = W_0 \cdot W_1$, with $W_0 \sqsubseteq U$ and $W_1 \sqsubseteq V$. It then holds that $W_0 \in \mathcal{U}\!\downarrow$ and $W_1 \in \mathcal{V}\!\downarrow$, meaning that $W = W_0 \cdot W_1 \in \mathcal{U}\!\downarrow \cdot \mathcal{V}\!\downarrow$. This shows that $(\mathcal{U} \cdot \mathcal{V})\!\downarrow \sqsubseteq \mathcal{U}\!\downarrow \cdot \mathcal{V}\!\downarrow$. Proving the reverse inclusion is a simple matter of unfolding the definitions.

For the third claim, we can calculate directly using the first and second parts of this lemma:

$$\mathcal{U}^{\star}\!\downarrow = \Big(\bigcup_{n \in \mathbb{N}} \underbrace{\mathcal{U} \cdot \mathcal{U} \cdots \mathcal{U}}_{n \text{ times}} \Big)\!\downarrow = \bigcup_{n \in \mathbb{N}} \Big(\underbrace{\mathcal{U} \cdot \mathcal{U} \cdots \mathcal{U}}_{n \text{ times}} \Big)\!\downarrow = \bigcup_{n \in \mathbb{N}} \underbrace{\mathcal{U}\!\downarrow \cdot \mathcal{U}\!\downarrow \cdots \mathcal{U}\!\downarrow}_{n \text{ times}} = \mathcal{U}\!\downarrow^{\star} \qquad \square$$

3.2   Concurrent Kleene Algebra

We now consider two extensions of Kleene Algebra (KA), known as *Bi-Kleene Algebra* (BKA) and *Concurrent Kleene Algebra* (CKA). Both extend KA with an operator for parallel composition and thus share a common syntax.

Definition 3.7. *The set $\mathcal{T}$ is the smallest set generated by the grammar*

$$e, f ::= 0 \mid 1 \mid a \in \Sigma \mid e + f \mid e \cdot f \mid e \parallel f \mid e^{\star}\qquad .$$

The BKA-semantics of a term is a straightforward inductive application of the operators on the level of pomset languages. The CKA-semantics of a term is the BKA-semantics, downward-closed under the subsumption order; the CKA-semantics thus includes all possible sequentialisations.

Definition 3.8. *The function $[\![-]\!]_{\mathsf{BKA}} : \mathcal{T} \to 2^{\mathsf{SP}(\Sigma)}$ is defined as follows:*

$$[\![0]\!]_{\mathsf{BKA}} \triangleq \emptyset \qquad\quad [\![e + f]\!]_{\mathsf{BKA}} \triangleq [\![e]\!]_{\mathsf{BKA}} \cup [\![f]\!]_{\mathsf{BKA}} \qquad\quad [\![e^{\star}]\!]_{\mathsf{BKA}} \triangleq [\![e]\!]_{\mathsf{BKA}}^{\star}$$

$$[\![1]\!]_{\mathsf{BKA}} \triangleq \{1\} \qquad\quad [\![e \cdot f]\!]_{\mathsf{BKA}} \triangleq [\![e]\!]_{\mathsf{BKA}} \cdot [\![f]\!]_{\mathsf{BKA}}$$

$$[\![a]\!]_{\mathsf{BKA}} \triangleq \{a\} \qquad\quad [\![e \parallel f]\!]_{\mathsf{BKA}} \triangleq [\![e]\!]_{\mathsf{BKA}} \parallel [\![f]\!]_{\mathsf{BKA}}$$

Finally, $[\![-]\!]_{\mathsf{CKA}} : \mathcal{T} \to 2^{\mathsf{SP}(\Sigma)}$ *is defined as* $[\![e]\!]_{\mathsf{CKA}} \triangleq [\![e]\!]_{\mathsf{BKA}}\!\downarrow$.

Following Lodaya and Weil [22], if $\mathcal{U}$ is a pomset language such that $\mathcal{U} = [\![e]\!]_{\mathsf{BKA}}$ for some $e \in \mathcal{T}$, we say that the language $\mathcal{U}$ is *series-rational*. Note that if $\mathcal{U}$ is such that $\mathcal{U} = [\![e]\!]_{\mathsf{CKA}}$ for some term $e \in \mathcal{T}$, then $\mathcal{U}$ is closed by definition.

To axiomatise semantic equivalence between terms, we build the following relations, which match the axioms proposed in [20]. The axioms of CKA as defined in [8] come from a double quantale structure mediated by the exchange law; these imply the ones given here. The converse implication does not hold; in particular, our syntax does not include an infinitary greatest lower bound operator. However, BKA (as defined in this paper) does have a *finitary* greatest lower bound [20], and by the existence of closure, so does CKA.

Definition 3.9. *The relation* $\equiv_{\mathsf{BKA}}$ *is the smallest congruence on* $\mathcal{T}$ *(with respect to all operators) such that for all* $e, f, g \in \mathcal{T}$:

$$e + 0 \equiv_{\mathsf{BKA}} e \qquad e + e \equiv_{\mathsf{BKA}} e \qquad e + f \equiv_{\mathsf{BKA}} f + e \qquad e + (f + g) \equiv_{\mathsf{BKA}} (f + g) + h$$

$$e \cdot 1 \equiv_{\mathsf{BKA}} e \qquad 1 \cdot e \equiv_{\mathsf{BKA}} e \qquad e \cdot (f \cdot g) \equiv_{\mathsf{BKA}} (e \cdot f) \cdot g$$

$$e \cdot 0 \equiv_{\mathsf{BKA}} 0 \equiv_{\mathsf{BKA}} 0 \cdot e \qquad e \cdot (f + g) \equiv_{\mathsf{BKA}} e \cdot f + e \cdot h \qquad (e + f) \cdot g \equiv_{\mathsf{BKA}} e \cdot g + f \cdot g$$

$$e \parallel f \equiv_{\mathsf{BKA}} f \parallel e \qquad e \parallel 1 \equiv_{\mathsf{BKA}} e \qquad e \parallel (f \parallel g) \equiv_{\mathsf{BKA}} (e \parallel f) \parallel g$$

$$e \parallel 0 \equiv_{\mathsf{BKA}} 0 \qquad e \parallel (f + g) \equiv_{\mathsf{BKA}} e \parallel f + e \parallel g \qquad 1 + e \cdot e^{\star} \equiv_{\mathsf{BKA}} e^{\star}$$

$$e + f \cdot g \leq_{\mathsf{BKA}} g \implies f^{\star} \cdot e \leq_{\mathsf{BKA}} g$$

in which we use $e \leq_{\mathsf{BKA}} f$ *as a shorthand for* $e + f \equiv_{\mathsf{BKA}} f$. *The final (conditional) axiom is referred to as the* least fixpoint axiom.

The relation $\equiv_{\mathsf{CKA}}$ *is the smallest congruence on* $\mathcal{T}$ *that satisfies the rules of* $\equiv_{\mathsf{BKA}}$, *and furthermore satisfies the* exchange law *for all* $e, f, g, h \in \mathcal{T}$:

$$(e \parallel f) \cdot (g \parallel h) \leq_{\mathsf{CKA}} (e \cdot g) \parallel (f \cdot h)$$

where we similarly use $e \leq_{\mathsf{CKA}} f$ *as a shorthand for* $e + f \equiv_{\mathsf{CKA}} f$.

We can see that $\equiv_{\mathsf{BKA}}$ includes the familiar axioms of KA, and stipulates that $\parallel$ is commutative and associative with unit 1 and annihilator 0, as well as distributive over $+$. When using CKA to model concurrent program flow, the exchange law models sequentialisation: if we have two programs, the first of which executes e followed by g, and the second of which executes f followed by h, then we can sequentialise this by executing e and f in parallel, followed by executing g and h in parallel.

We use the symbol T in statements that are true for $\mathsf{T} \in \{\mathsf{BKA}, \mathsf{CKA}\}$. The relation $\equiv_{\mathsf{T}}$ is sound for equivalence of terms under T [13].

Lemma 3.8. *Let* $e, f \in \mathcal{T}$. *If* $e \equiv_{\mathsf{T}} f$, *then* $\llbracket e \rrbracket_{\mathsf{T}} = \llbracket f \rrbracket_{\mathsf{T}}$.

Since all binary operators are associative (up to $\equiv_{\mathsf{T}}$), we drop parentheses when writing terms like $e + f + g$—this does not incur ambiguity with regard to $\llbracket - \rrbracket_{\mathsf{T}}$. We furthermore consider $\cdot$ to have precedence over $\parallel$, which has precedence over $+$; as usual, the Kleene star has the highest precedence of all operators. For instance, when we write $e + f \cdot g^{\star} \parallel h$, this should be read as $e + ((f \cdot (g^{\star})) \parallel h)$.

In case of BKA, the implication in Lemma 3.8 is an equivalence [20], and thus gives a complete axiomatisation of semantic BKA-equivalence of terms.[2]

Theorem 3.1. *Let* $e, f \in \mathcal{T}$. *Then* $e \equiv_{\mathsf{BKA}} f$ *if and only if* $\llbracket e \rrbracket_{\mathsf{BKA}} = \llbracket f \rrbracket_{\mathsf{BKA}}$.

Given a term $e \in \mathcal{T}$, we can determine syntactically whether its (BKA or CKA) semantics contains the empty pomset, using the function defined below.

---

[2] Strictly speaking, the proof in [20] includes the parallel star operator in BKA. Since this is a conservative extension of BKA, this proof applies to BKA as well.

Definition 3.10. *The* nullability function $\epsilon : \mathcal{T} \to 2$ *is defined as follows:*

$$\epsilon(0) \triangleq 0 \qquad\qquad \epsilon(e+f) \triangleq \epsilon(e) \vee \epsilon(f) \qquad\qquad \epsilon(e^\star) \triangleq 1$$

$$\epsilon(1) \triangleq 1 \qquad\qquad \epsilon(e \cdot f) \triangleq \epsilon(e) \wedge \epsilon(f)$$

$$\epsilon(a) \triangleq 0 \qquad\qquad \epsilon(e \parallel f) \triangleq \epsilon(e) \wedge \epsilon(f)$$

in which $\vee$ *and* $\wedge$ *are understood as the usual lattice operations on* 2.

That ϵ encodes the presence of 1 in the semantics is witnessed by the following.

Lemma 3.9. *Let* $e \in \mathcal{T}$. *Then* $\epsilon(e) \leq_{\mathsf{T}} e$ *and* $1 \in [\![e]\!]_{\mathsf{T}}$ *if and only if* $\epsilon(e) = 1$.

In the sequel, we need the *(parallel) width* of a term. This is defined as follows.

Definition 3.11. *Let* $e \in \mathcal{T}$. *The* (parallel) width *of* e, *denoted by* $|e|$, *is defined as* 0 *when* $e \equiv_{\mathsf{BKA}} 0$; *for all other cases, it is defined inductively, as follows:*

$$|1| \triangleq 0 \qquad\qquad |e+f| \triangleq \max(|e|, |f|) \qquad\qquad |e \parallel f| \triangleq |e| + |f|$$

$$|a| \triangleq 1 \qquad\qquad |e \cdot f| \triangleq \max(|e|, |f|) \qquad\qquad |e^\star| \triangleq |e|$$

The width of a term is invariant with respect to equivalence of terms.

Lemma 3.10. *Let* $e, f \in \mathcal{T}$. *If* $e \equiv_{\mathsf{BKA}} f$, *then* $|e| = |f|$.

The width of a term is related to its semantics as demonstrated below.

Lemma 3.11. *Let* $e \in \mathcal{T}$, *and let* $U \in [\![e]\!]_{\mathsf{BKA}}$ *be such that* $U \neq 1$. *Then* $|e| > 0$.

3.3   Linear Systems

KA is equipped to find the least solutions to linear inequations. For instance, if we want to find X such that $e \cdot X + f \leq_{\mathsf{KA}} X$, it is not hard to show that $e^\star \cdot f$ is the *least solution* for X, in the sense that this choice of X satisfies the inequation, and for any choice of X that also satisfies this inequation it holds that $e^\star \cdot f \leq_{\mathsf{KA}} X$. Since KA is contained in BKA and CKA, the same constructions also apply there. These axioms generalise to systems of linear inequations in a straightforward manner; indeed, Kozen [18] exploited this generalisation to axiomatise KA. In this paper, we use systems of linear inequations to construct particular expressions. To do this, we introduce vectors and matrices of terms.

For the remainder of this section, we fix I as a finite set.

Definition 3.12. *An* I-vector *is a function from* I *to* $\mathcal{T}$. *Addition of* I-vectors *is defined pointwise, i.e., if* p *and* q *are* I-vectors, *then* $p + q$ *is the* I-vector *defined for* $i \in I$ *by* $(p+q)(i) \triangleq p(i) + q(i)$.

An I-matrix *is a function from* I^2 *to* $\mathcal{T}$. *Left-multiplication of an* I-vector *by an* I-matrix *is defined in the usual fashion, i.e., if* M *is an* I-matrix *and* p *is an* I-vector, *then* $M \cdot p$ *is the* I-vector *defined for* $i \in I$ *by*

$$(M \cdot p)(i) \triangleq \sum_{j \in I} M(i,j) \cdot p(j)$$

Equivalence between terms extends pointwise to I-vectors. More precisely, we write $p \equiv_\mathsf{T} q$ for I-vectors p and q when $p(i) \equiv_\mathsf{T} q(i)$ for all $i \in I$, and $p \leq_\mathsf{T} q$ when $p + q \equiv_\mathsf{T} q$.

Definition 3.13. *An I-linear system $\mathfrak{L}$ is a pair $\langle M, p \rangle$ where M is an I-matrix and p is an I-vector. A solution to $\mathfrak{L}$ in T is an I-vector s such that $M \cdot s + p \leq_\mathsf{T} s$. A least solution to $\mathfrak{L}$ in T is a solution s in T such that for any solution t in T it holds that $s \leq_\mathsf{T} t$.*

It is not very hard to show that least solutions of a linear system are unique, up to $\equiv_\mathsf{T}$; we therefore speak of *the* least solution of a linear system.

Interestingly, *any* I-linear system has a least solution, and one can construct this solution using only the operators of KA. The construction proceeds by induction on $|I|$. In the base, where I is empty, the solution is trivial; for the inductive step it suffices to reduce the problem to finding the least solution of a strictly smaller linear system. This construction is not unlike Kleene's procedure to obtain a regular expression from a finite automaton [17]. Alternatively, we can regard the existence of least solutions as a special case of Kozen's proof of the fixpoint for matrices over a KA, as seen in [18, Lemma 9].

As a matter of fact, because this construction uses the axioms of KA exclusively, the least solution that is constructed is the same for both BKA and CKA.

Lemma 3.12. *Let $\mathfrak{L}$ be an I-linear system. One can construct a single I-vector x that is the least solution to $\mathfrak{L}$ in both BKA and CKA.*

We include a full proof of the lemma above using the notation of this paper in the full version of this paper [15].

4 Completeness of CKA

We now turn our attention to proving that $\equiv_\mathsf{CKA}$ is complete for CKA-semantic equivalence of terms, i.e., that if $e, f \in \mathcal{T}$ are such that $[\![e]\!]_\mathsf{CKA} = [\![f]\!]_\mathsf{CKA}$, then $e \equiv_\mathsf{CKA} f$. In the interest of readability, proofs of technical lemmas in this section can be found in the full version of this paper [15].

As mentioned before, our proof of completeness is based on the completeness result for BKA reproduced in Theorem 3.1. Recall that $[\![e]\!]_\mathsf{CKA} = [\![e]\!]_\mathsf{BKA}{\downarrow}$. To reuse completeness of BKA, we construct a syntactic variant of the closure operator, which is formalised below.

Definition 4.1. *Let $e \in \mathcal{T}$. We say that $e{\downarrow}$ is a' closure of e if both $e \equiv_\mathsf{CKA} e{\downarrow}$ and $[\![e{\downarrow}]\!]_\mathsf{BKA} = [\![e]\!]_\mathsf{BKA}{\downarrow}$ hold.*

Example 4.1. Let $e = a \parallel b$; as proposed in Sect. 2, we claim that $e{\downarrow} = a \parallel b + b \cdot a + a \cdot b$ is a closure of e. To see why, first note that $e \leq_\mathsf{CKA} e{\downarrow}$ by construction. Furthermore,

$$ab \equiv_\mathsf{CKA} (a \parallel 1) \cdot (1 \parallel b) \leq_\mathsf{CKA} (a \cdot 1) \parallel (1 \cdot b) \equiv_\mathsf{CKA} a \parallel b$$

and similarly $ba \leq_\mathsf{CKA} e$; thus, $e =_\mathsf{CKA} e{\downarrow}$. Lastly, the pomsets in $[\![e]\!]_\mathsf{BKA}{\downarrow}$ and $[\![e{\downarrow}]\!]_\mathsf{BKA}$ are simply $a \parallel b$, ab and ba, and therefore $[\![e{\downarrow}]\!]_\mathsf{BKA} = [\![e]\!]_\mathsf{BKA}{\downarrow}$.

Laurence and Struth observed that the existence of a closure for every term implies a completeness theorem for CKA, as follows.

Lemma 4.1. *Suppose that we can construct a closure for every element of $\mathcal{T}$. If $e, f \in \mathcal{T}$ such that $[\![e]\!]_{\mathsf{CKA}} = [\![f]\!]_{\mathsf{CKA}}$, then $e \equiv_{\mathsf{CKA}} f$.*

Proof. Since $[\![e]\!]_{\mathsf{CKA}} = [\![e]\!]_{\mathsf{BKA}}{\downarrow} = [\![e{\downarrow}]\!]_{\mathsf{BKA}}$ and similarly $[\![f]\!]_{\mathsf{CKA}} = [\![f{\downarrow}]\!]_{\mathsf{BKA}}$, we have $[\![e{\downarrow}]\!]_{\mathsf{BKA}} = [\![f{\downarrow}]\!]_{\mathsf{BKA}}$. By Theorem 3.1, we get $e{\downarrow} \equiv_{\mathsf{BKA}} f{\downarrow}$, and thus $e{\downarrow} \equiv_{\mathsf{CKA}} f{\downarrow}$, since all axioms of BKA are also axioms of CKA. By $e \equiv_{\mathsf{CKA}} e{\downarrow}$ and $f{\downarrow} \equiv_{\mathsf{CKA}} f$, we can then conclude that $e \equiv_{\mathsf{CKA}} f$. $\qquad\square$

The remainder of this section is dedicated to showing that the premise of Lemma 4.1 holds. We do this by explicitly constructing a closure $e{\downarrow}$ for every $e \in \mathcal{T}$. First, we note that closure can be constructed for the base terms.

Lemma 4.2. *Let $e \in 2$ or $e = a$ for some $a \in \Sigma$. Then e is a closure of itself.*

Furthermore, closure can be constructed compositionally for all operators except parallel composition, in the following sense.

Lemma 4.3. *Suppose that $e_0, e_1 \in \mathcal{T}$, and that e_0 and e_1 have closures $e_0{\downarrow}$ and $e_1{\downarrow}$. Then (i) $e_0{\downarrow} + e_1{\downarrow}$ is a closure of $e_0 + e_1$, (ii) $e_0{\downarrow} \cdot e_1{\downarrow}$ is a closure of $e_0 \cdot e_1$, and (iii) $(e_0{\downarrow})^*$ is a closure of e_0^*.*

Proof. Since $e_0{\downarrow} \equiv_{\mathsf{CKA}} e_0$ and $e_1{\downarrow} \equiv_{\mathsf{CKA}} e_1$, by the fact that $\equiv_{\mathsf{CKA}}$ is a congruence we obtain $e_0{\downarrow} + e_1{\downarrow} \equiv_{\mathsf{CKA}} e_0 + e_1$. Similar observations hold for the other operators. We conclude using Lemma 3.7. $\qquad\square$

It remains to consider the case where $e = e_0 \parallel e_1$. In doing so, our induction hypothesis is that any $f \in \mathcal{T}$ with $|f| < |e_0 \parallel e_1|$ has a closure, as well as any strict subterm of $e_0 \parallel e_1$.

4.1 Preclosure

To get to a closure of a parallel composition, we first need an operator on terms that is not a closure quite yet, but whose BKA-semantics is "closed enough" to cover the non-sequential elements of the CKA-semantics of the term.

Definition 4.2. *Let $e \in \mathcal{T}$. A preclosure of e is a term $\tilde{e} \in \mathcal{T}$ such that $\tilde{e} \equiv_{\mathsf{CKA}} e$. Moreover, if $U \in [\![e]\!]_{\mathsf{CKA}}$ is non-sequential, then $U \in [\![\tilde{e}]\!]_{\mathsf{BKA}}$.*

Example 4.2. Suppose that $e_0 \parallel e_1 = (a \parallel b) \parallel c$. A preclosure of $e_0 \parallel e_1$ could be

$$\tilde{e} = a \parallel b \parallel c + (a \cdot b + b \cdot a) \parallel c + (b \cdot c + c \cdot b) \parallel a + (a \cdot c + c \cdot a) \parallel b$$

To verify this, note that $e \leq_{\mathsf{CKA}} \tilde{e}$ by construction; remains to show that $\tilde{e} \leq_{\mathsf{CKA}} e$. This is fairly straightforward: since $a \cdot b + b \cdot a \leq_{\mathsf{CKA}} a \parallel b$, we have $(a \cdot b + b \cdot a) \parallel c \leq_{\mathsf{CKA}} e$; the other terms are treated similarly. Consequently, $e \equiv_{\mathsf{CKA}} \tilde{e}$. Furthermore, there are seven non-sequential pomsets in $[\![e]\!]_{\mathsf{CKA}}$; they are

$$a \parallel b \parallel c \qquad ab \parallel c \qquad ba \parallel c \qquad bc \parallel a \qquad cb \parallel a \qquad ac \parallel b \qquad ca \parallel b$$

Each of these pomsets is found in $[\![\tilde{e}]\!]_{\mathsf{BKA}}$. It should be noted that $\tilde{e}$ is *not* a closure of e; to see this, consider for instance that $abc \in [\![e]\!]_{\mathsf{CKA}}$, while $abc \notin [\![\tilde{e}]\!]_{\mathsf{BKA}}$.

The remainder of this section is dedicated to showing that, under the induction hypothesis, we can construct a preclosure for any parallelly composed term. This is not perfectly straightforward; for instance, consider the term $e_0 \parallel e_1$ discussed in Example 4.2. At first glance, one might be tempted to choose $e_0{\downarrow} \parallel e_1{\downarrow}$ as a preclosure, since $e_0{\downarrow}$ and $e_1{\downarrow}$ exist by the induction hypothesis. In that case, $e_0{\downarrow} = a \parallel b + a \cdot b + b \cdot a$ is a closure of e_0. Furthermore, $e_1{\downarrow} = c$ is a closure of e_1, by Lemma 4.2. However, $e_0{\downarrow} \parallel e_1{\downarrow}$ is not a preclosure of $e_0 \parallel e_1$, since $(a \cdot c) \parallel b$ is non-sequential and found in $[\![e_0 \parallel e_1]\!]_{\mathsf{CKA}}$, but not in $[\![e_0{\downarrow} \parallel e_1{\downarrow}]\!]_{\mathsf{BKA}}$.

The problem is that the preclosure of e_0 and e_1 should also allow (partial) sequentialisation of *parallel parts* of e_0 and e_1; in this case, we need to sequentialise the a part of $a \parallel b$ with c, and leave b untouched. To do so, we need to be able to *split* $e_0 \parallel e_1$ into pairs of constituent terms, each of which represents a possible way to divvy up its parallel parts. For instance, we can split $e_0 \parallel e_1 = (a \parallel b) \parallel c$ parallelly into $a \parallel b$ and c, but also into a and $b \parallel c$, or into $a \parallel c$ and b. The definition below formalises this procedure.

Definition 4.3. *Let $e \in \mathcal{T}$; Δ_e is the smallest relation on $\mathcal{T}$ such that*

$$\frac{}{1\,\Delta_e\,e} \qquad \frac{}{e\,\Delta_e\,1} \qquad \frac{\ell\,\Delta_{e_0}\,r}{\ell\,\Delta_{e_1+e_0}\,r} \qquad \frac{\ell\,\Delta_{e_1}\,r}{\ell\,\Delta_{e_0+e_1}\,r} \qquad \frac{\ell\,\Delta_e\,r}{\ell\,\Delta_{e^\star}\,r}$$

$$\frac{\ell\,\Delta_{e_0}\,r \quad \epsilon(e_1)=1}{\ell\,\Delta_{e_0 \cdot e_1}\,r} \qquad \frac{\ell\,\Delta_{e_1}\,r \quad \epsilon(e_0)=1}{\ell\,\Delta_{e_0 \cdot e_1}\,r} \qquad \frac{\ell_0\,\Delta_{e_0}\,r_0 \quad \ell_1\,\Delta_{e_1}\,r_1}{\ell_0 \parallel \ell_1\,\Delta_{e_0 \parallel e_1}\,r_0 \parallel r_1}$$

Given $e \in \mathcal{T}$, we refer to Δ_e as the *parallel splitting relation* of e, and to the elements of Δ_e as *parallel splices* of e. Before we can use Δ_e to construct the preclosure of e, we go over a number of properties of the parallel splitting relation. The first of these properties is that a given $e \in \mathcal{T}$ has only finitely many parallel splices. This will be useful later, when we involve *all* parallel splices of e in building a new term, i.e., to guarantee that the constructed term is finite.

Lemma 4.4. *For $e \in \mathcal{T}$, Δ_e is finite.*

We furthermore note that the parallel composition of any parallel splice of e is ordered below e by $\leq_{\mathsf{BKA}}$. This guarantees that parallel splices never contain extra information, i.e., that their semantics do not contain pomsets that do not occur in the semantics of e. It also allows us to bound the width of the parallel splices by the width of the term being split, as a result of Lemma 3.10.

Lemma 4.5. *Let $e \in \mathcal{T}$. If $\ell\,\Delta_e\,r$, then $\ell \parallel r \leq_{\mathsf{BKA}} e$.*

Corollary 4.1. *Let $e \in \mathcal{T}$. If $\ell\,\Delta_e\,r$, then $|\ell| + |r| \leq |e|$.*

Finally, we show that Δ_e is *dense* when it comes to parallel pomsets, meaning that if we have a parallelly composed pomset in the semantics of e, then we can find a parallel splice where one parallel component is contained in the semantics of one side of the pair, and the other component in that of the other.

Lemma 4.6. *Let $e \in \mathcal{T}$, and let V, W be pomsets such that $V \parallel W \in \llbracket e \rrbracket_{\mathsf{BKA}}$. Then there exist $\ell, r \in \mathcal{T}$ with $\ell \Delta_e r$ such that $V \in \llbracket \ell \rrbracket_{\mathsf{BKA}}$ and $W \in \llbracket r \rrbracket_{\mathsf{BKA}}$.*

Proof. The proof proceeds by induction on e. In the base, we can discount the case where $e = 0$, for then the claim holds vacuously. This leaves us two cases.

- If $e = 1$, then $V \parallel W \in \llbracket e \rrbracket_{\mathsf{BKA}}$ entails $V \parallel W = 1$. By Lemma 3.1, we find that $V = W = 1$. Since $1 \Delta_e 1$ by definition of Δ_e, the claim follows when we choose $\ell = r = 1$.
- If $e = a$ for some $a \in \Sigma$, then $V \parallel W \in \llbracket e \rrbracket_{\mathsf{BKA}}$ entails $V \parallel W = a$. By Lemma 3.1, we find that either $V = 1$ and $W = a$, or $V = a$ and $W = 1$. In the former case, we can choose $\ell = 1$ and $r = a$, while in the latter case we can choose $\ell = a$ and $r = 1$. It is then easy to see that our claim holds in either case.

For the inductive step, there are four cases to consider.

- If $e = e_0 + e_1$, then $U_0 \parallel U_1 \in \llbracket e_i \rrbracket_{\mathsf{BKA}}$ for some $i \in 2$. But then, by induction, we find $\ell, r \in \mathcal{T}$ with $\ell \Delta_{e_i} r$ such that $V \in \llbracket \ell \rrbracket_{\mathsf{BKA}}$ and $W \in \llbracket r \rrbracket_{\mathsf{BKA}}$. Since this implies that $\ell \Delta_e r$, the claim follows.
- If $e = e_0 \cdot e_1$, then there exist pomsets U_0, U_1 such that $V \parallel W = U_0 \cdot U_1$, and $U_i \in \llbracket e_i \rrbracket_{\mathsf{BKA}}$ for all $i \in 2$. By Lemma 3.1, there are two cases to consider.
  - Suppose that $U_i = 1$ for some $i \in 2$, meaning that $V \parallel W = U_0 \cdot U_1 = U_{1-i} \in \llbracket e_{1-i} \rrbracket_{\mathsf{BKA}}$ for this i. By induction, we find $\ell, r \in \mathcal{T}$ with $\ell \Delta_{e_{1-i}} r$, and $V \in \llbracket \ell \rrbracket_{\mathsf{BKA}}$ as well as $W \in \llbracket r \rrbracket_{\mathsf{BKA}}$. Since $U_i = 1 \in \llbracket e_i \rrbracket_{\mathsf{BKA}}$, we have that $\epsilon(e_i) = 1$ by Lemma 3.9, and thus $\ell \Delta_e r$.
  - Suppose that $V = 1$ or $W = 1$. In the former case, $V \parallel W = W = U_0 \cdot U_1 \in \llbracket e \rrbracket_{\mathsf{CKA}}$. We then choose $\ell = 1$ and $r = e$ to satisfy the claim. In the latter case, we can choose $\ell = e$ and $r = 1$ to satisfy the claim analogously.
- If $e = e_0 \parallel e_1$, then there exist pomsets U_0, U_1 such that $V \parallel W = U_0 \parallel U_1$, and $U_i \in \llbracket e_i \rrbracket_{\mathsf{BKA}}$ for all $i \in 2$. By Lemma 3.5, we find pomsets V_0, V_1, W_0, W_1 such that $V = V_0 \parallel V_1$, $W = W_0 \parallel W_1$, and $U_i = V_i \parallel W_i$ for $i \in 2$. For $i \in 2$, we then find by induction $\ell_i, r_i \in \mathcal{T}$ with $\ell_i \Delta_{e_i} r_i$ such that $V_i \in \llbracket \ell_i \rrbracket_{\mathsf{BKA}}$ and $W_i \in \llbracket r_i \rrbracket_{\mathsf{BKA}}$. We then choose $\ell = \ell_0 \parallel \ell_1$ and $r = r_0 \parallel r_1$. Since $V = V_0 \parallel V_1$, it follows that $V \in \llbracket \ell \rrbracket_{\mathsf{BKA}}$, and similarly we find that $W \in \llbracket r \rrbracket_{\mathsf{BKA}}$. Since $\ell \Delta_e r$, the claim follows.
- If $e = e_0^\star$, then there exist $U_0, U_1, \ldots, U_{n-1} \in \llbracket e_0 \rrbracket_{\mathsf{BKA}}$ such that $V \parallel W = U_0 \cdot U_1 \cdots U_{n-1}$. If $n = 0$, i.e., $V \parallel W = 1$, then $V = W = 1$. In that case, we can choose $\ell = e$ and $r = 1$ to find that $\ell \Delta_e r$, $V \in \llbracket \ell \rrbracket_{\mathsf{BKA}}$ and $W \in \llbracket r \rrbracket_{\mathsf{BKA}}$, satisfying the claim.
  If $n > 0$, we can assume without loss of generality that, for $0 \le i < n$, it holds that $U_i \ne 1$. By Lemma 3.1, there are two subcases to consider.
  - Suppose that $V, W \ne 1$; then $n = 1$ (for otherwise $U_j = 1$ for some $0 \le j < n$ by Lemma 3.1, which contradicts the above). Since $V \parallel W = U_0 \in \llbracket e_0 \rrbracket_{\mathsf{BKA}}$, we find by induction $\ell, r \in \mathcal{T}$ with $\ell \Delta_{e_0} r$ such that $V \in \llbracket \ell \rrbracket_{\mathsf{BKA}}$ and $W \in \llbracket r \rrbracket_{\mathsf{BKA}}$. The claim then follows by the fact that $\ell \Delta_e r$.

- Suppose that $V = 1$ or $W = 1$. In the former case, $V \parallel W = W = U_0 \cdot U_1 \cdots U_{n-1} \in \llbracket e \rrbracket_{\mathsf{CKA}}$. We then choose $\ell = 1$ and $r = e$ to satisfy the claim. In the latter case, we can choose $\ell = e$ and $r = 1$ to satisfy the claim analogously. □

Example 4.3. Let $U = a \parallel c$ and $V = b$, and note that $U \parallel V \in \llbracket e_0 \parallel e_1 \rrbracket_{\mathsf{CKA}}$. We can then find that $a \, \Delta_a \, 1$ and $1 \, \Delta_b \, b$, and thus $a \parallel 1 \, \Delta_{e_0} \, 1 \parallel b$. Since also $c \, \Delta_c \, 1$, it follows that $(a \parallel 1) \parallel c \, \Delta_{e_0 \parallel e_1} \, (1 \parallel b) \parallel 1$. We can then choose $\ell = (a \parallel 1) \parallel c$ and $r = (1 \parallel b) \parallel 1$ to find that $U \in \llbracket \ell \rrbracket_{\mathsf{BKA}}$ and $V \in \llbracket r \rrbracket_{\mathsf{BKA}}$, while $\ell \, \Delta_{e_0 \parallel e_1} \, r$.

With parallel splitting in hand, we can define an operator on terms that combines all parallel splices of a parallel composition in a way that accounts for all of their downward closures.

Definition 4.4. *Let $e, f \in \mathcal{T}$, and suppose that, for every $g \in \mathcal{T}$ such that $|g| < |e| + |f|$, there exists a closure $g{\downarrow}$. The term $e \odot f$ is defined as follows:*

$$e \odot f \triangleq e \parallel f + \sum_{\substack{\ell \Delta_{e \parallel f} r \\ |\ell|, |r| < |e \parallel f|}} \ell{\downarrow} \parallel r{\downarrow}$$

Note that $e \odot f$ is well-defined: the sum is finite since $\Delta_{e \parallel f}$ is finite by Lemma 4.4, and furthermore $\ell{\downarrow}$ and $r{\downarrow}$ exist, as we required that $|\ell|, |r| < |e \parallel f|$.

Example 4.4. Let us compute $e_0 \odot e_1$ and verify that we obtain a preclosure of $e_0 \parallel e_1$. Working through the definition, we see that $\Delta_{e_0 \parallel e_1}$ consists of the pairs

$\langle (1 \parallel 1) \parallel 1, (a \parallel b) \parallel c \rangle$	$\langle (1 \parallel 1) \parallel c, (a \parallel b) \parallel 1 \rangle$	$\langle (1 \parallel b) \parallel 1, (a \parallel 1) \parallel c \rangle$
$\langle (1 \parallel b) \parallel c, (a \parallel 1) \parallel 1 \rangle$	$\langle (a \parallel 1) \parallel 1, (1 \parallel b) \parallel c \rangle$	$\langle (a \parallel 1) \parallel c, (1 \parallel b) \parallel 1 \rangle$

Since closure is invariant with respect to $\equiv_{\mathsf{CKA}}$, we can simplify these terms by applying the axioms of CKA. After folding the unit subterms, we are left with

$$\langle 1, a \parallel b \parallel c \rangle \qquad \langle c, a \parallel b \rangle \qquad \langle b, a \parallel c \rangle \qquad \langle b \parallel c, a \rangle \qquad \langle a, b \parallel c \rangle \qquad \langle a \parallel c, b \rangle$$

Recall that $a \parallel b + a \cdot b + b \cdot a$ is a closure of $a \parallel b$. Now, we find that

$$\begin{aligned} e_0 \odot e_1 = \; & (a \parallel b) \parallel c + c \parallel (a \parallel b + a \cdot b + b \cdot a) \\ & + b \parallel (a \parallel c + a \cdot c + c \cdot a) + (b \parallel c + b \cdot c + c \cdot b) \parallel a \\ & + a \parallel (b \parallel c + b \cdot c + c \cdot b) + (a \parallel c + a \cdot c + c \cdot a) \parallel b \\ \equiv_{\mathsf{CKA}} \; & a \parallel b \parallel c + a \parallel (b \cdot c + c \cdot b) + b \parallel (a \cdot c + c \cdot a) + c \parallel (a \cdot b + b \cdot a) \end{aligned}$$

which was shown to be a preclosure of $e_0 \parallel e_1$ in Example 4.2.

The general proof of correctness for $\odot$ as a preclosure plays out as follows.

Lemma 4.7. *Let $e, f \in \mathcal{T}$, and suppose that, for every $g \in \mathcal{T}$ with $|g| < |e| + |f|$, there exists a closure $g{\downarrow}$. Then $e \odot f$ is a preclosure of $e \parallel f$.*

Proof. We start by showing that $e \odot f \equiv_{\mathsf{CKA}} e \parallel f$. First, note that $e \parallel f \leq_{\mathsf{BKA}} e \odot f$ by definition of $e \odot f$. For the other direction, suppose that $\ell, r \in \mathcal{T}$ are such that $\ell \, \Delta_{e \parallel f} \, r$. By definition of closure, we know that $\ell{\downarrow} \parallel r{\downarrow} \equiv_{\mathsf{CKA}} \ell \parallel r$. By Lemma 4.5, we have $\ell \parallel r \leq_{\mathsf{BKA}} e \parallel f$. Since every subterm of $e \odot f$ is ordered below $e \parallel f$ by $\leq_{\mathsf{CKA}}$, we have that $e \odot f \leq_{\mathsf{CKA}} e \parallel f$. It then follows that $e \parallel f \equiv_{\mathsf{CKA}} e \odot f$.

For the second requirement, suppose that $X \in [\![e \parallel f]\!]_{\mathsf{CKA}}$ is non-sequential. We then know that there exists a $Y \in [\![e \parallel f]\!]_{\mathsf{BKA}}$ such that $X \sqsubseteq Y$. This leaves us two cases to consider.

- If X is empty or primitive, then $Y = X$ by Lemma 3.2, thus $X \in [\![e \parallel f]\!]_{\mathsf{BKA}}$. By the fact that $e \parallel f \leq_{\mathsf{BKA}} e \odot f$ and by Lemma 3.8, we find $X \in [\![e \odot f]\!]_{\mathsf{BKA}}$.
- If $X = X_0 \parallel X_1$ for non-empty pomsets X_0 and X_1, then by Lemma 3.3 we find non-empty pomsets Y_0 and Y_1 with $Y = Y_0 \parallel Y_1$ such that $X_i \sqsubseteq Y_i$ for $i \in 2$. By Lemma 4.6, we find $\ell, r \in \mathcal{T}$ with $\ell \, \Delta_{e \parallel f} \, r$ such that $Y_0 \in [\![\ell]\!]_{\mathsf{BKA}}$ and $Y_1 \in [\![r]\!]_{\mathsf{BKA}}$. By Lemma 3.11, we find that $|\ell|, |r| \geq 1$. Corollary 4.1 then allows us to conclude that $|\ell|, |r| < |e \parallel f|$.
  This means that $\ell{\downarrow} \parallel r{\downarrow} \leq_{\mathsf{BKA}} e \odot f$. Since $X_0 \in [\![\ell{\downarrow}]\!]_{\mathsf{BKA}}$ and $X_1 \in [\![r{\downarrow}]\!]_{\mathsf{BKA}}$ by definition of closure, we can derive by Lemma 3.8 that

$$X = X_0 \parallel X_1 \in [\![\ell{\downarrow} \parallel r{\downarrow}]\!]_{\mathsf{BKA}} \subseteq [\![e \odot f]\!]_{\mathsf{BKA}} \qquad \square$$

4.2 Closure

The preclosure operator discussed above covers the non-sequential pomsets in the language $[\![e \parallel f]\!]_{\mathsf{CKA}}$; it remains to find a term that covers the sequential pomsets contained in $[\![e \parallel f]\!]_{\mathsf{CKA}}$.

To better give some intuition to the construction ahead, we first explore the observations that can be made when a sequential pomset $W \cdot X$ appears in the language $[\![e \parallel f]\!]_{\mathsf{CKA}}$; without loss of generality, assume that W is non-sequential. In this setting, there must exist $U \in [\![e]\!]_{\mathsf{BKA}}$ and $V \in [\![f]\!]_{\mathsf{BKA}}$ such that $W \cdot X \sqsubseteq U \parallel V$. By Lemma 3.6, we find pomsets U_0, U_1, V_0, V_1 such that

$$W \sqsubseteq U_0 \parallel V_0 \qquad X \sqsubseteq U_1 \parallel V_1 \qquad U_0 \cdot U_1 \sqsubseteq U \qquad V_0 \cdot V_1 \sqsubseteq V$$

This means that $U_0 \cdot U_1 \in [\![e]\!]_{\mathsf{CKA}}$ and $V_0 \cdot V_1 \in [\![f]\!]_{\mathsf{CKA}}$. Now, suppose we could find $e_0, e_1, f_0, f_1 \in \mathcal{T}$ such that

$$e_0 \cdot e_1 \leq_{\mathsf{CKA}} e \qquad U_0 \in [\![e_0]\!]_{\mathsf{CKA}} \qquad U_1 \in [\![e_1]\!]_{\mathsf{CKA}}$$

$$f_0 \cdot f_1 \leq_{\mathsf{CKA}} f \qquad V_0 \in [\![f_0]\!]_{\mathsf{CKA}} \qquad V_1 \in [\![f_1]\!]_{\mathsf{CKA}}$$

Then we have $W \in [\![e_0 \odot f_0]\!]_{\mathsf{BKA}}$, and $X \in [\![e_1 \parallel f_1]\!]_{\mathsf{CKA}}$. Thus, if we can find a closure of $e_1 \parallel f_1$, then we have a term whose BKA-semantics contains $W \cdot X$.

There are two obstacles that need to be resolved before we can use the observations above to find the closure of $e \parallel f$. The first problem is that we need to be sure that this process of splitting terms into sequential components is at all possible, i.e., that we can split e into e_0 and e_1 with $e_0 \cdot e_1 \lesssim_{\mathsf{CKA}} e$ and $U_i \in [\![e_i]\!]_{\mathsf{CKA}}$ for $i \in 2$. We do this by designing a sequential analogue to the parallel splitting relation seen before. The second problem, which we will address later in this section, is whether this process of splitting a parallel term $e \parallel f$ according to the exchange law and finding a closure of remaining term $e_1 \parallel f_1$ is well-founded, i.e., if we can find "enough" of these terms to cover all possible ways of sequentialising $e \parallel f$. This will turn out to be possible, by using the fixpoint axioms of KA as in Sect. 3.3 with linear systems.

We start by defining the sequential splitting relation.[3]

Definition 4.5. *Let* $e \in \mathcal{T}$; ∇_e *is the smallest relation on* $\mathcal{T}$ *such that*

$$\frac{}{1 \nabla_1 1} \qquad \frac{}{a \nabla_a 1} \qquad \frac{}{1 \nabla_a a} \qquad \frac{}{1 \nabla_{e_0^*} 1} \qquad \frac{\ell \nabla_{e_0} r}{\ell \nabla_{e_0 + e_1} r} \qquad \frac{\ell \nabla_{e_1} r}{\ell \nabla_{e_0 + e_1} r}$$

$$\frac{\ell \nabla_{e_0} r}{\ell \nabla_{e_0 \cdot e_1} r \cdot e_1} \qquad \frac{\ell \nabla_{e_1} r}{e_0 \cdot \ell \nabla_{e_0 \cdot e_1} r} \qquad \frac{\ell_0 \nabla_{e_0} r_0 \quad \ell_1 \nabla_{e_1} r_1}{\ell_0 \parallel \ell_1 \nabla_{e_0 \parallel e_1} r_0 \parallel r_1} \qquad \frac{\ell \nabla_{e_0} r}{e_0^* \cdot \ell \nabla_{e_0^*} r \cdot e_0^*}$$

Given $e \in \mathcal{T}$, we refer to ∇_e as the *sequential splitting relation* of e, and to the elements of ∇_e as *sequential splices* of e. We need to establish a few properties of the sequential splitting relation that will be useful later on. The first of these properties is that, as for parallel splitting, ∇_e is finite.

Lemma 4.8. *For* $e \in \mathcal{T}$, ∇_e *is finite.*

We also have that the sequential composition of splices is provably below the term being split. Just like the analogous lemma for parallel splitting, this guarantees that our sequential splices never give rise to semantics not contained in the split term. This lemma also yields an observation about the width of sequential splices when compared to the term being split.

Lemma 4.9. *Let* $e \in \mathcal{T}$. *If* $\ell, r \in \mathcal{T}$ *with* $\ell \nabla_e r$, *then* $\ell \cdot r \lesssim_{\mathsf{CKA}} e$.

Corollary 4.2. *Let* $e \in \mathcal{T}$. *If* $\ell, r \in \mathcal{T}$ *with* $\ell \nabla_e r$, *then* $|\ell|, |r| \leq |e|$.

Lastly, we show that the splices cover every way of (sequentially) splitting up the semantics of the term being split, i.e., that ∇_e is dense when it comes to sequentially composed pomsets.

Lemma 4.10. *Let* $e \in \mathcal{T}$, *and let* V *and* W *be pomsets such that* $V \cdot W \in [\![e]\!]_{\mathsf{CKA}}$. *Then there exist* $\ell, r \in \mathcal{T}$ *with* $\ell \nabla_e r$ *such that* $V \in [\![\ell]\!]_{\mathsf{CKA}}$ *and* $W \in [\![r]\!]_{\mathsf{CKA}}$.

Proof. The proof proceeds by induction on e. In the base, we can discount the case where $e = 0$, for then the claim holds vacuously. This leaves us two cases.

---

[3] The contents of this relation are very similar to the set of *left- and right-spines* of a NetKAT expression as used in [5].

- If $e = 1$, then $V \cdot W = 1$; by Lemma 3.1, we find that $V = W = 1$. Since $1 \, \nabla_e \, 1$ by definition of ∇_e, the claim follows when we choose $\ell = r = 1$.
- If $e = a$ for some $a \in \Sigma$, then $V \cdot W = a$; by Lemma 3.1, we find that either $V = a$ and $W = 1$ or $V = 1$ and $W = a$. In the former case, we can choose $\ell = a$ and $r = 1$ to satisfy the claim; the latter case can be treated similarly.

For the inductive step, there are four cases to consider.

- If $e = e_0 + e_1$, then $V \cdot W \in [\![e_i]\!]_{\mathrm{CKA}}$ for some $i \in 2$. By induction, we find $\ell, r \in \mathcal{T}$ with $\ell \, \nabla_{e_i} \, r$ such that $V \in [\![\ell]\!]_{\mathrm{CKA}}$ and $W \in [\![r]\!]_{\mathrm{CKA}}$. Since $\ell \, \nabla_e \, r$ in this case, the claim follows.
- If $e = e_0 \cdot e_1$, then there exist $U_0 \in [\![e_0]\!]_{\mathrm{CKA}}$ and $U_1 \in [\![e_1]\!]_{\mathrm{CKA}}$ such that $V \cdot W = U_0 \cdot U_1$. By Lemma 3.4, we find a series-parallel pomset X such that either $V \sqsubseteq U_0 \cdot X$ and $X \cdot W \sqsubseteq U_1$, or $V \cdot X \sqsubseteq U_0$ and $W \sqsubseteq X \cdot U_1$. In the former case, we find that $X \cdot W \in [\![e_1]\!]_{\mathrm{CKA}}$, and thus by induction $\ell', r \in \mathcal{T}$ with $\ell' \, \nabla_{e_1} \, r$ such that $X \in [\![\ell']\!]_{\mathrm{CKA}}$ and $W \in [\![r]\!]_{\mathrm{CKA}}$. We then choose $\ell = e_0 \cdot \ell'$ to find that $\ell \, \nabla_e \, r$, as well as $V \sqsubseteq U_0 \cdot X \in [\![e_0]\!]_{\mathrm{CKA}} \cdot [\![\ell']\!]_{\mathrm{CKA}} = [\![\ell]\!]_{\mathrm{CKA}}$ and thus $V \in [\![\ell]\!]_{\mathrm{CKA}}$. The latter case can be treated similarly; here, we use the induction hypothesis on e_0.
- If $e = e_0 \parallel e_1$, then there exist $U_0 \in [\![e_0]\!]_{\mathrm{CKA}}$ and $U_1 \in [\![e_1]\!]_{\mathrm{CKA}}$ such that $V \cdot W \sqsubseteq U_0 \parallel U_1$. By Lemma 3.6, we find series-parallel pomsets V_0, V_1, W_0, W_1 such that $V \sqsubseteq V_0 \parallel V_1$ and $W \sqsubseteq W_0 \parallel W_1$, as well as $V_i \cdot W_i \sqsubseteq U_i$ for all $i \in 2$. In that case, $V_i \cdot W_i \in [\![e_i]\!]_{\mathrm{CKA}}$ for all $i \in 2$, and thus by induction we find $\ell_i, r_i \in \mathcal{T}$ with $\ell_i \, \nabla_{e_i} \, r_i$ such that $V_i \in [\![\ell_i]\!]_{\mathrm{CKA}}$ and $W_i \in [\![r_i]\!]_{\mathrm{CKA}}$. We choose $\ell = \ell_0 \parallel \ell_1$ and $r = r_0 \parallel r_1$ to find that $V \in [\![\ell_0 \parallel r_0]\!]_{\mathrm{CKA}}$ and $W \in [\![\ell_1 \parallel r_1]\!]_{\mathrm{CKA}}$, as well as $\ell \, \nabla_e \, r$.
- If $e = e_0^\star$, then there exist $U_0, U_1, \ldots, U_{n-1} \in [\![e_0]\!]_{\mathrm{CKA}}$ such that $V \cdot W = U_0 \cdot U_1 \cdots U_{n-1}$. Without loss of generality, we can assume that for $0 \le i < n$ it holds that $U_i \ne 1$. In the case where $n = 0$ we have that $V \cdot W = 1$, thus $V = W = 1$, we can choose $\ell = r = 1$ to satisfy the claim.
  For the case where $n > 0$, we find by Lemma 3.4 an $0 \le m < n$ and series-parallel pomsets X, Y such that $X \cdot Y \sqsubseteq U_m$, and $V \sqsubseteq U_0 \cdot U_1 \cdots U_{m-1} \cdot X$ and $W \sqsubseteq Y \cdot U_{m+1} \cdot U_{m+2} \cdots U_n$. Since $X \cdot Y \sqsubseteq U_m \in [\![e_0]\!]_{\mathrm{CKA}}$ and thus $X \cdot Y \in [\![e_0]\!]_{\mathrm{CKA}}$, we find by induction $\ell', r' \in \mathcal{T}$ with $\ell' \, \nabla_{e_0} \, r'$ and $X \in [\![\ell']\!]_{\mathrm{CKA}}$ and $Y \in [\![r']\!]_{\mathrm{CKA}}$. We can then choose $\ell = e_0^\star \cdot \ell'$ and $r = r' \cdot e_0^\star$ to find that $V \sqsubseteq U_0 \cdot U_1 \cdots U_{m-1} \cdot X \in [\![e_0^\star]\!]_{\mathrm{CKA}} \cdot [\![\ell']\!]_{\mathrm{CKA}} = [\![\ell]\!]_{\mathrm{CKA}}$ and $W \sqsubseteq Y \cdot U_{m+1} \cdot U_{m+2} \cdots U_n \in [\![r']\!]_{\mathrm{CKA}} \cdot [\![e_0^\star]\!]_{\mathrm{CKA}} = [\![r]\!]_{\mathrm{CKA}}$, and thus that $V \in [\![\ell]\!]_{\mathrm{CKA}}$ and $W \in [\![r]\!]_{\mathrm{CKA}}$. Since $\ell \, \nabla_e \, r$ holds, the claim follows. □

Example 4.5. Let U be the pomset ca and let V be bc. Furthermore, let e be the term $(a \cdot b + c)^\star$, and note that $U \cdot V \in [\![e]\!]_{\mathrm{CKA}}$. We then find that $a \, \nabla_a \, 1$, and thus $a \, \nabla_{a \cdot b} \, 1 \cdot b$. We can now choose $\ell = (a \cdot b + c)^\star \cdot a$ and $r = (1 \cdot b) \cdot (a \cdot b + c)^\star$ to find that $U \in [\![\ell]\!]_{\mathrm{CKA}}$ and $V \in [\![r]\!]_{\mathrm{CKA}}$, while $\ell \, \nabla_e \, r$.

We know how to split a term sequentially. To resolve the second problem, we need to show that the process of splitting terms repeatedly ends somewhere. This is formalised in the notion of *right-hand remainders*, which are the terms that can appear as the right hand of a sequential splice of a term.

Definition 4.6. *Let $e \in \mathcal{T}$. The set of* (right-hand) remainders *of e, written $R(e)$, is the smallest satisfying the rules*

$$\frac{}{e \in R(e)} \qquad \frac{f \in R(e) \quad \ell \, \nabla_f \, r}{r \in R(e)}$$

Lemma 4.11. *Let $e \in \mathcal{T}$. $R(e)$ is finite.*

With splitting and remainders we are in a position to define the linear system that will yield the closure of a parallel composition. Intuitively, we can think of this system as an automaton: every variable corresponds to a state, and every row of the matrix describes the "transitions" of the corresponding state, while every element of the vector describes the language "accepted" by that state without taking a single transition. Solving the system for a least fixpoint can be thought of as finding an expression that describes the language of the automaton.

Definition 4.7. *Let $e, f \in \mathcal{T}$, and suppose that, for every $g \in \mathcal{T}$ such that $|g| < |e| + |f|$, there exists a closure $g{\downarrow}$. We choose*

$$I_{e,f} = \{g \parallel h : g \in R(e), h \in R(f)\}$$

The $I_{e,f}$-vector $p_{e,f}$ and $I_{e,f}$-matrix $M_{e,f}$ are chosen as follows.

$$p_{e,f}(g \parallel h) \triangleq g \parallel f \qquad M_{e,f}(g \parallel h, g' \parallel h') \triangleq \sum_{\substack{\ell_g \nabla_g g' \\ \ell_h \nabla_h h'}} \ell_g \odot \ell_h$$

$I_{e,f}$ is finite by Lemma 4.11. We write $\mathfrak{L}_{e,f}$ for the $I_{e,f}$-linear system $\langle M_{e,f}, p_{e,f} \rangle$.

We can check that $M_{e,f}$ is well-defined. First, the sum is finite, because ∇_g and ∇_h are finite by Lemma 4.8. Second, if $g \parallel h \in I$ and $\ell_g, r_g, \ell_h, r_h \in \mathcal{T}$ such that $\ell_g \, \nabla_g \, r_g$ and $\ell_h \, \nabla_h \, r_h$, then $|\ell_g| \le |g| \le |e|$ and $|\ell_h| \le |h| \le |f|$ by Corollary 4.2, and thus, if $d \in \mathcal{T}$ such that $|d| < |\ell_g| + |\ell_h|$, then $|d| < |e| + |f|$, and therefore a closure of d exists, meaning that $\ell_g \odot \ell_h$ exists, too.

The least solution to $\mathfrak{L}_{e,f}$ obtained through Lemma 3.12 is the I-vector denoted by $s_{e,f}$. We write $e \otimes f$ for $s_{e,f}(e \parallel f)$, i.e., the least solution at $e \parallel f$.

Using the previous lemmas, we can then show that $e \otimes f$ is indeed a closure of $e \parallel f$, provided that we have closures for all terms of strictly lower width. The intuition of this proof is that we use the uniqueness of least fixpoints to show that $e \parallel f \equiv_{\mathsf{CKA}} e \otimes f$, and then use the properties of preclosure and the normal form of series-parallel pomsets to show that $[\![e \parallel f]\!]_{\mathsf{CKA}} = [\![e \otimes f]\!]_{\mathsf{BKA}}$.

Lemma 4.12. *Let $e, f \in \mathcal{T}$, and suppose that, for every $g \in \mathcal{T}$ with $|g| < |e| + |f|$, there exists a closure $g{\downarrow}$. Then $e \otimes f$ is a closure of $e \parallel f$.*

Proof. We begin by showing that $e \parallel f \equiv_{\mathrm{CKA}} e \otimes f$. We can see that $p_{e,f}$ is a solution to $\mathfrak{L}_{e,f}$, by calculating for $g \parallel h \in I_{e,f}$:

$$(p_{e,f} + M_{e,f} \cdot p_{e,f})(g \parallel h)$$
$$= g \parallel h + \sum_{r_g \parallel r_h \in I} \Big(\sum_{\substack{\ell_g \nabla_g r_g \\ \ell_h \nabla_h r_h}} \ell_g \odot \ell_h \Big) \cdot (r_g \parallel r_h) \qquad \text{(def. } M_{e,f}, p_{e,f})$$

$$\equiv_{\mathrm{CKA}} g \parallel h + \sum_{r_g \parallel r_h \in I} \sum_{\substack{\ell_g \nabla_g r_g \\ \ell_h \nabla_h r_h}} (\ell_g \odot \ell_h) \cdot (r_g \parallel r_h) \qquad \text{(distributivity)}$$

$$\equiv_{\mathrm{CKA}} g \parallel h + \sum_{r_g \parallel r_h \in I} \sum_{\substack{\ell_g \nabla_g r_g \\ \ell_h \nabla_h r_h}} (\ell_g \parallel \ell_h) \cdot (r_g \parallel r_h) \qquad \text{(Lemma 4.7)}$$

$$\leq_{\mathrm{CKA}} g \parallel h + \sum_{r_g \parallel r_h \in I} \sum_{\substack{\ell_g \nabla_g r_g \\ \ell_h \nabla_h r_h}} (\ell_g \cdot r_g) \parallel (\ell_h \cdot r_h) \qquad \text{(exchange)}$$

$$\leq_{\mathrm{CKA}} g \parallel h + \sum_{r_g \parallel r_h \in I} \sum_{\substack{\ell_g \nabla_g r_g \\ \ell_h \nabla_h r_h}} g \parallel h \qquad \text{(Lemma 4.9)}$$

$$\equiv_{\mathrm{CKA}} g \parallel h \qquad \text{(idempotence)}$$
$$= p_{e,f}(g \parallel h) \qquad \text{(def. } p_{e,f})$$

To see that $p_{e,f}$ is the *least* solution to $\mathfrak{L}_{e,f}$, let $q_{e,f}$ be a solution to $\mathfrak{L}_{e,f}$. We then know that $M_{e,f} \cdot q_{e,f} + p_{e,f} \leq_{\mathrm{CKA}} q_{e,f}$; thus, in particular, $p_{e,f} \leq_{\mathrm{CKA}} q_{e,f}$. Since the least solution to a linear system is unique up to $\equiv_{\mathrm{CKA}}$, we find that $s_{e,f} \equiv_{\mathrm{CKA}} p_{e,f}$, and therefore that $e \otimes f = s_{e,f}(e \parallel f) \equiv_{\mathrm{CKA}} p_{e,f}(e \parallel f) = e \parallel f$.

It remains to show that if $U \in [\![e \parallel f]\!]_{\mathrm{CKA}}$, then $U \in [\![e \otimes f]\!]_{\mathrm{BKA}}$. To show this, we show the more general claim that if $g \parallel h \in I$ and $U \in [\![g \parallel h]\!]_{\mathrm{CKA}}$, then $U \in [\![s_{e,f}(g \parallel h)]\!]_{\mathrm{BKA}}$. Write $U = U_0 \cdot U_1 \cdots U_{n-1}$ such that for $0 \leq i < n$, U_i is non-sequential (as in Corollary 3.1). The proof proceeds by induction on n. In the base, we have that $n = 0$. In this case, $U = 1$, and thus $U \in [\![g \parallel h]\!]_{\mathrm{BKA}}$ by Lemma 3.2. Since $g \parallel h = p_{e,f}(g \parallel h) \leq_{\mathrm{BKA}} s_{e,f}(g \parallel h)$, it follows that $U \in [\![s_{e,f}(g \parallel h)]\!]_{\mathrm{BKA}}$ by Lemma 3.8.

For the inductive step, assume the claim holds for $n-1$. We write $U = U_0 \cdot U'$, with $U' = U_1 \cdot U_2 \cdots U_{n-1}$. Since $U_0 \cdot U' \in [\![g \parallel h]\!]_{\mathrm{CKA}}$, there exist $W \in [\![g]\!]_{\mathrm{CKA}}$ and $X \in [\![h]\!]_{\mathrm{CKA}}$ such that $U_0 \cdot U' \sqsubseteq W \parallel X$. By Lemma 3.6, we find pomsets W_0, W_1, X_0, X_1 such that $W_0 \cdot W_1 \sqsubseteq W$ and $X_0 \cdot X_1 \sqsubseteq X$, as well as $U_0 \sqsubseteq W_0 \parallel X_0$ and $U' \sqsubseteq W_1 \parallel X_1$. By Lemma 4.10, we find $\ell_g, r_g, \ell_h, r_h \in \mathcal{T}$ with $\ell_g \nabla_g r_g$ and $\ell_h \nabla_h r_h$, such that $W_0 \in [\![\ell_g]\!]_{\mathrm{CKA}}$, $W_1 \in [\![r_g]\!]_{\mathrm{CKA}}$, $X_0 \in [\![\ell_h]\!]_{\mathrm{CKA}}$ and $X_1 \in [\![r_h]\!]_{\mathrm{CKA}}$.

From this, we know that $U_0 \in [\![\ell_g \parallel \ell_h]\!]_{\mathrm{CKA}}$ and $U' \in [\![r_g \parallel r_h]\!]_{\mathrm{CKA}}$. Since U_0 is non-sequential, we have that $U_0 \in [\![\ell_g \odot \ell_h]\!]_{\mathrm{BKA}}$. Moreover, by induction we find that $U' \in [\![s_{e,f}(r_g \parallel r_h)]\!]_{\mathrm{BKA}}$. Since $\ell_g \odot \ell_h \leq_{\mathrm{BKA}} M_{e,f}(g \parallel h, r_g \parallel r_h)$ by definition of $M_{e,f}$, we furthermore find that

$$(\ell_g \odot \ell_h) \cdot s_{e,f}(r_g \parallel r_h) \leq_{\mathrm{BKA}} M_{e,f}(g \parallel h, r_g \parallel r_h) \cdot s_{e,f}(r_g \parallel r_h)$$

Since $r_g \parallel r_h \in I$, we find by definition of the solution to a linear system that

$$M_{e,f}(g \parallel h, r_g \parallel r_h) \cdot s_{e,f}(r_g \parallel r_h) \leq_{\mathrm{BKA}} s_{e,f}(g \parallel h)$$

By Lemma 3.8 and the above, we conclude that $U = U_0 \cdot U' \in [\![s_{e,f}(g \parallel h)]\!]_{\mathrm{BKA}}$. □

For a concrete example where we find a closure of a (non-trivial) parallel composition by solving a linear system, we refer to Appendix A.

With closure of parallel composition, we can construct a closure for any term and therefore conclude completeness of CKA.

Theorem 4.1. *Let $e \in \mathcal{T}$. We can construct a closure $e{\downarrow}$ of e.*

Proof. The proof proceeds by induction on $|e|$ and the structure of e, i.e., by considering f before g if $|f| < |g|$, or if f is a strict subterm of g (in which case $|f| \leq |g|$ also holds). It is not hard to see that this induces a well-ordering on $\mathcal{T}$.

Let e be a term of width n, and suppose that the claim holds for all terms of width at most $n - 1$, and for all strict subterms of e. There are three cases.

- If $e = 0$, $e = 1$ or $e = a$ for some $a \in \Sigma$, the claim follows from Lemma 4.2.
- If $e = e_0 + e_1$, or $e = e_0 \cdot e_1$, or $e = e_0^*$, the claim follows from Lemma 4.3.
- If $e = e_0 \parallel e_1$, then $e_0 \otimes e_1$ exists by the induction hypothesis. By Lemma 4.12, we then find that $e_0 \otimes e_1$ is a closure of e. $\qquad\square$

Corollary 4.3. *Let $e, f \in \mathcal{T}$. If $[\![e]\!]_{\mathsf{CKA}} = [\![f]\!]_{\mathsf{CKA}}$, then $e \equiv_{\mathsf{CKA}} f$.*

Proof. Follows from Theorem 4.1 and Lemma 4.1. $\qquad\square$

5 Discussion and Further Work

By building a syntactic closure for each series-rational expression, we have shown that the standard axiomatisation of CKA is complete with respect to the CKA-semantics of series-rational terms. Consequently, the algebra of closed series-rational pomset languages forms the free CKA.

Our result leads to several decision procedures for the equational theory of CKA. For instance, one can compute the closure of a term as described in the present paper, and use an existing decision procedure for BKA [3,12,20]. Note however that although this approach seems suited for theoretical developments (such as formalising the results in a proof assistant), its complexity makes it less appealing for practical use. More practically, one could leverage recent work by Brunet et al. [3], which provides an algorithm to compare closed series-rational pomset languages. Since this is the free concurrent Kleene algebra, this algorithm can now be used to decide the equational theory of CKA. We also obtain from the latter paper that this decision problem is EXPSPACE-complete.

We furthermore note that the algorithm to compute downward closure can be used to extend half of the result from [14] to a Kleene theorem that relates the CKA-semantics of expressions to the pomset automata proposed there: if $e \in \mathcal{T}$, we can construct a pomset automaton A with a state q such that $L_A(q) = [\![e]\!]_{\mathsf{CKA}}$.

Having established pomset automata as an operational model of CKA, a further question is whether these automata are amenable to a bisimulation-based equivalence algorithm, as is the case for finite automata [10]. If this is the case, optimisations such as those in [2] might have analogues for pomset automata that can be found using the coalgebraic method [23].

While this work was in development, an unpublished draft by Laurence and Struth [19] appeared, with a first proof of completeness for CKA. The general outline of their proof is similar to our own, in that they prove that closure of pomset languages preserves series-rationality, and hence there exists a syntactic closure for every series-rational expression. However, the techniques used to establish this fact are quite different from the developments in the present paper. First, we build the closure via syntactic methods: explicit splitting relations and solutions of linear systems. Instead, their proof uses automata theoretic constructions and algebraic closure properties of regular languages; in particular, they rely on congruences of finite index and language homomorphisms. We believe that our approach leads to a substantially simpler and more transparent proof. Furthermore, even though Laurence and Struth do not seem to use any fundamentally non-constructive argument, their proof does not obviously yield an algorithm to effectively compute the closure of a given term. In contrast, our proof is explicit enough to be implemented directly; we wrote a simple Python script (under six hundred lines) to do just that [16].

A crucial ingredient in this work was the computation of least solutions of linear systems. This kind of construction has been used on several occasions for the study of Kleene algebras [1,4,18], and we provide here yet another variation of such a result. We feel that linear systems may not have yet been used to their full potential in this context, and could still lead to interesting developments.

A natural extension of the work conducted here would be to turn our attention to the signature of concurrent Kleene algebra that includes a "parallel star" operator $e^{\|}$. The completeness result of Laurence and Struth [20] holds for BKA with the parallel star, so in principle one could hope to extend our syntactic closure construction to include this operator. Unfortunately, using the results of Laurence and Struth, we can show that this is not possible. They defined a notion of *depth* of a series-parallel pomset, intuitively corresponding to the nesting of parallel and sequential components. An important step in their development consists of proving that for every series-parallel-rational language there exists a finite upper bound on the depth of its elements. However, the language $[\![a^{\|}]\!]_{CKA}$ does not enjoy this property: it contains every series-parallel pomset exclusively labelled with the symbol a. Since we can build such pomsets with arbitrary depth, it follows that there does not exist a syntactic closure of the term $a^{\|}$. New methods would thus be required to tackle the parallel star operator.

Another aspect of CKA that is not yet developed to the extent of KA is the coalgebraic perspective. We intend to investigate whether the coalgebraic tools developed for KA can be extended to CKA, which will hopefully lead to efficient bisimulation-based decision procedures [2,5].

Acknowledgements. We thank the anonymous reviewers for their insightful comments. This work was partially supported by the ERC Starting Grant ProFoundNet (grant code 679127).

A   Worked Example: A Non-trivial Closure

In this appendix, we solve an instance of a linear system as defined in Definition 4.7 for a given parallel composition. For the sake of brevity, the steps are somewhat coarse-grained; the reader is encouraged to reproduce the steps by hand.

Consider the expression $e \parallel f = a^* \parallel b$. The linear system $\mathfrak{L}_{e,f}$ that we obtain from this expression consists of six inequations; in matrix form (with zeroes omitted), this system is summarised as follows:[4]

$$
\begin{array}{c}
1 \parallel 1 \\
1 \parallel b \\
a \cdot a^* \parallel 1 \\
a^* \parallel 1 \\
a \cdot a^* \parallel b \\
a^* \parallel b
\end{array}
\left(
\begin{array}{cccccc:c}
1 & & & & & & 1 \\
b & 1 & & & & & b \\
a & & a^* & a \cdot a^* & & & a \cdot a^* \\
1 & & a^* & a^* \cdot a & & & a^* \\
a \parallel b & a & a^* \parallel b & a \cdot a^* \parallel b & a^* & a \cdot a^* & a \cdot a^* \parallel b \\
b & 1 & a^* \parallel b & a \cdot a^* \parallel b & a^* & a \cdot a^* & a^* \parallel b
\end{array}
\right)
$$

Let us proceed under the assumption that x is a solution to the system; the constraint imposed on x by the first two rows is given by the inequations

$$x(1 \parallel 1) + 1 \leqq_{\mathsf{CKA}} x(1 \parallel 1) \tag{1}$$

$$b \cdot x(1 \parallel 1) + x(1 \parallel b) + b \leqq_{\mathsf{CKA}} x(1 \parallel b) \tag{2}$$

Because these inequations do not involve the other positions of the system, we can solve them in isolation, and use their solutions to find solutions for the remaining positions; it turns out that choosing $x(1 \parallel 1) = 1$ and $x(1 \parallel b) = b$ suffices here.

We carry on to fill these values into the inequations given by the third and fourth row of the linear system. After some simplification, these work out to be

$$a \cdot a^* + a \cdot a^* \cdot x(a^* \parallel 1) + a^* \cdot x(a \cdot a^* \parallel 1) \leqq_{\mathsf{CKA}} x(a \cdot a^* \parallel 1) \tag{3}$$

$$a^* + a^* \cdot a \cdot x(a^* \parallel 1) + a^* \cdot x(a \cdot a^* \parallel 1) \leqq_{\mathsf{CKA}} x(a^* \parallel 1) \tag{4}$$

Applying the least fixpoint axiom to (3) and simplifying, we obtain

$$a \cdot a^* + a \cdot a^* \cdot x(a^* \parallel 1) \leqq_{\mathsf{CKA}} x(a \cdot a^* \parallel 1) \tag{5}$$

Substituting this into (4) and simplifying, we find that

$$a^* + a \cdot a^* \cdot x(a^* \parallel 1) \leqq_{\mathsf{CKA}} x(a^* \parallel 1) \tag{6}$$

This inequation, in turn, gives us that $a^* \leqq_{\mathsf{CKA}} x(a^* \parallel 1)$ by the least fixpoint axiom. Plugging this back into (3) and simplifying, we find that

$$a \cdot a^* + a^* \cdot x(a \cdot a^* \parallel 1) \leqq_{\mathsf{CKA}} x(a \cdot a^* \parallel 1) \tag{7}$$

---

[4] Actually, the system obtained from $a^* \parallel b$ as a result of Definition 4.7 is slightly larger; it also contains rows and columns labelled by $1 \cdot a^* \parallel 1$ and $1 \cdot a^* \parallel b$; these turn out to be redundant. We omit these rows from the example for simplicity.

Again by the least fixpoint axiom, this tells us that $a \cdot a^\star \leq_{\mathsf{CKA}} x(a \cdot a^\star \parallel 1)$. One easily checks that $x(a \cdot a^\star \parallel 1) = a \cdot a^\star$ and $x(a^\star \parallel 1) = a^\star$ are solutions to (3) and (4); by the observations above, they are also the least solutions.

It remains to find the least solutions for the final two positions. Filling in the values that we already have, we find the following for the fifth row:

$$a \parallel b + a \cdot b + (a^\star \parallel b) \cdot a \cdot a^\star + (a \cdot a^\star \parallel b) \cdot a^\star$$
$$+ a^\star \cdot x(a \cdot a^\star \parallel b) + a \cdot a^\star \cdot x(a^\star \parallel b) + a \cdot a^\star \parallel b \leq_{\mathsf{CKA}} x(a \cdot a^\star \parallel b) \qquad (8)$$

Applying the exchange law[5] to the first three terms, we find that they are contained in $(a \cdot a^\star \parallel b) \cdot a^\star$, as is the last term; (8) thus simplifies to

$$(a \cdot a^\star \parallel b) \cdot a^\star + a^\star \cdot x(a \cdot a^\star \parallel b) + a \cdot a^\star \cdot x(a^\star \parallel b) \leq_{\mathsf{CKA}} x(a \cdot a^\star \parallel b) \qquad (9)$$

By the least fixpoint axiom, we find that

$$a^\star \cdot (a \cdot a^\star \parallel b) \cdot a^\star + a \cdot a^\star \cdot x(a^\star \parallel b) \leq_{\mathsf{CKA}} x(a \cdot a^\star \parallel b) \qquad (10)$$

For the sixth row, we find that after filling in the solved positions, we have

$$b + b + (a^\star \parallel b) \cdot a \cdot a^\star + (a \cdot a^\star \parallel b) \cdot a^\star$$
$$+ a^\star \cdot x(a \cdot a^\star \parallel b) + a \cdot a^\star \cdot x(a^\star \parallel b) + a^\star \parallel b \leq_{\mathsf{CKA}} x(a^\star \parallel b) \qquad (11)$$

Simplifying and applying the exchange law as before, it follows that

$$(a^\star \parallel b) \cdot a^\star + a^\star \cdot x(a \cdot a^\star \parallel b) + a \cdot a^\star \cdot x(a^\star \parallel b) \leq_{\mathsf{CKA}} x(a^\star \parallel b) \qquad (12)$$

We then subsitute (10) into (12) to find that

$$(a^\star \parallel b) \cdot a^\star + a \cdot a^\star \cdot x(a^\star \parallel b) \leq_{\mathsf{CKA}} x(a^\star \parallel b) \qquad (13)$$

which, by the least fixpoint axiom, tells us that $a^\star \cdot (a^\star \parallel b) \cdot a^\star \leq_{\mathsf{CKA}} x(a^\star \parallel b)$. Plugging the latter back into (9), we find that

$$a^\star \cdot (a \cdot a^\star \parallel b) \cdot a^\star + a \cdot a^\star \cdot a^\star \cdot (a^\star \parallel b) \cdot a^\star \leq_{\mathsf{CKA}} x(a \cdot a^\star \parallel b) \qquad (14)$$

which can, using the exchange law, be reworked into

$$a^\star \cdot (a \cdot a^\star \parallel b) \cdot a^\star \leq_{\mathsf{CKA}} x(a \cdot a^\star \parallel b) \qquad (15)$$

Now, if we choose $x(a \cdot a^\star \parallel b) = a^\star \cdot (a \cdot a^\star \parallel b) \cdot a^\star$ and $x(a^\star \parallel b) = a^\star \cdot (a^\star \parallel b) \cdot a^\star$, we find that these choices satisfy (9) and (12)—making them part of a solution; by construction, they are also the least solutions.

In summary, x is a solution to the linear system, and by construction it is also the least solution. The reader is encouraged to verify that our choice of $x(a^\star \parallel b)$ is indeed a closure of $a^\star \parallel b$.

---

[5] A caveat here is that applying the exchange law indiscriminately may lead to a term that is not a closure (specifically, it may violate the semantic requirement in Definition 4.1). The algorithm used to solve arbitrary linear systems in Lemma 3.12 does not make use of the exchange law to simplify terms, and thus avoids this pitfall.

References

1. Backhouse, R.: Closure algorithms and the star-height problem of regular languages. Ph.D. thesis, University of London (1975)
2. Bonchi, F., Pous, D.: Checking NFA equivalence with bisimulations up to congruence. In: Proceedings of the Principles of Programming Languages (POPL), pp. 457–468 (2013)
3. Brunet, P., Pous, D., Struth, G.: On decidability of concurrent Kleene algebra. In: Proceedings of the Concurrency Theory (CONCUR), pp. 28:1–28:15 (2017)
4. Conway, J.H.: Regular Algebra and Finite Machines. Chapman and Hall Ltd., London (1971)
5. Foster, N., Kozen, D., Milano, M., Silva, A., Thompson, L.: A coalgebraic decision procedure for NetKAT. In: Proceedings of the Principles of Programming Languages (POPL), pp. 343–355 (2015)
6. Gischer, J.L.: The equational theory of pomsets. Theor. Comput. Sci. **61**, 199–224 (1988)
7. Grabowski, J.: On partial languages. Fundam. Inform. **4**(2), 427 (1981)
8. Hoare, T., Möller, B., Struth, G., Wehrman, I.: Concurrent Kleene algebra. In: Proceedings of the Concurrency Theory (CONCUR), pp. 399–414 (2009)
9. Hoare, T., van Staden, S., Möller, B., Struth, G., Zhu, H.: Developments in concurrent Kleene algebra. J. Log. Algebr. Meth. Program. **85**(4), 617–636 (2016)
10. Hopcroft, J.E., Karp, R.M.: A linear algorithm for testing equivalence of finite automata. Technical report, TR71-114, December 1971
11. Horn, A., Kroening, D.: On partial order semantics for SAT/SMT-based symbolic encodings of weak memory concurrency. In: Graf, S., Viswanathan, M. (eds.) FORTE 2015. LNCS, vol. 9039, pp. 19–34. Springer, Cham (2015). https://doi.org/10.1007/978-3-319-19195-9_2
12. Jategaonkar, L., Meyer, A.R.: Deciding true concurrency equivalences on safe, finite nets. Theor. Comput. Sci. **154**(1), 107–143 (1996)
13. Jipsen, P., Moshier, M.A.: Concurrent Kleene algebra with tests and branching automata. J. Log. Algebr. Methods Program. **85**(4), 637–652 (2016)
14. Kappé, T., Brunet, P., Luttik, B., Silva, A., Zanasi, F.: Brzozowski goes concurrent—a Kleene theorem for pomset languages. In: Proceedings of the Concurrency Theory (CONCUR), pp. 25:1–25:16 (2017)
15. Kappé, T., Brunet, P., Silva, A., Zanasi, F.: Concurrent Kleene algebra: free model and completeness. https://arxiv.org/abs/1710.02787
16. Kappé, T., Brunet, P., Silva, A., Zanasi, F.: Tools for concurrent Kleene algebra, Sep 2017. https://doi.org/10.5281/zenodo.926823
17. Kleene, S.C.: Representation of events in nerve nets and finite automata. In: Shannon, C.E., McCarthy, J. (eds.) Automata Studies, pp. 3–41. Princeton University Press, Princeton (1956)
18. Kozen, D.: A completeness theorem for Kleene algebras and the algebra of regular events. Inf. Comput. **110**(2), 366–390 (1994)
19. Laurence, M.R., Struth, G.: Completeness theorems for pomset languages and concurrent Kleene algebras. https://arxiv.org/abs/1705.05896
20. Laurence, M.R., Struth, G.: Completeness theorems for Bi-Kleene algebras and series-parallel rational pomset languages. In: Höfner, P., Jipsen, P., Kahl, W., Müller, M.E. (eds.) RAMICS 2014. LNCS, vol. 8428, pp. 65–82. Springer, Cham (2014). https://doi.org/10.1007/978-3-319-06251-8_5
21. Levi, F.W.: On semigroups. Bull. Calcutta Math. Soc. **36**(141–146), 82 (1944)

882   T. Kappé et al.

22. Lodaya, K., Weil, P.: Series-parallel languages and the bounded-width property. Theor. Comput. Sci. **237**(1), 347–380 (2000)
23. Rot, J., Bonsangue, M., Rutten, J.: Coalgebraic bisimulation-up-to. In: van Emde Boas, P., Groen, F.C.A., Italiano, G.F., Nawrocki, J., Sack, H. (eds.) SOFSEM 2013. LNCS, vol. 7741, pp. 369–381. Springer, Heidelberg (2013). https://doi.org/10.1007/978-3-642-35843-2_32

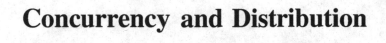
Concurrency and Distribution

Correctness of a Concurrent Object Collector for Actor Languages

Juliana Franco[1]([✉]), Sylvan Clebsch[2], Sophia Drossopoulou[1], Jan Vitek[3,4], and Tobias Wrigstad[5]

[1] Imperial College London, London, UK
j.vicente-franco@imperial.ac.uk
[2] Microsoft Research Cambridge, Cambridge, UK
[3] Northeastern University, Boston, USA
[4] CVUT, Prague, Czech Republic
[5] Uppsala University, Uppsala, Sweden

Abstract. ORCA is a garbage collection protocol for actor-based programs. Multiple actors may mutate the heap while the collector is running without any dedicated synchronisation. ORCA is applicable to any actor language whose type system prevents data races and which supports causal message delivery. We present a model of ORCA which is parametric to the host language and its type system. We describe the interplay between the host language and the collector. We give invariants preserved by ORCA, and prove its soundness and completeness.

1 Introduction

Actor-based systems are massively parallel programs in which individual actors communicate by exchanging messages. In such systems it is essential to be able to manage data automatically with as little synchronisation as possible. In previous work [9,12], we introduced the ORCA protocol for garbage collection in actor-based systems. ORCA is language-agnostic, and it allows for concurrent collection of objects in actor-based programs with no additional locking or synchronisation, no copying on message passing and no stop-the-world steps. ORCA can be implemented in any actor-based system or language that has a type system which prevents data races and that supports causal message delivery. There are currently two instantiations of ORCA, one is for Pony [8,11] and the other for Encore [5]. We hypothesise that ORCA could be applied to other actor-based systems that use static types to enforce isolation [7,21,28,36]. For libraries, such as Akka, which provide actor-like facilities, pluggable type systems could be used to enforce isolation [20].

This paper develops a formal model of ORCA. More specifically, the paper contributions are:

1. Identification of the requirements that the host language must statically guarantee;

© The Author(s) 2018
A. Ahmed (Ed.): ESOP 2018, LNCS 10801, pp. 885–911, 2018.
https://doi.org/10.1007/978-3-319-89884-1_31

2. Description and model of ORCA at a language-agnostic level;
3. Identification of invariants that ensure global consistency without synchronisation;
4. Proofs of *soundness*, *i.e.* live objects will not be collected, and proofs of *completeness*, *i.e.* all garbage will be identified as such.

A formal model facilitates the understanding of how ORCA can be applied to different languages. It also allows us to explore extensions such as shared mutable state across actors [40], reduction of tracing of immutable references [12], or incorporation of borrowing [4]. Alternative implementations of ORCA that rely on deep copying (*e.g.*, to reduce type system complexity) across actors on different machines can also be explored through our formalism.

Developing a formal model of ORCA presents challenges:

Can the model be parametric in the host language? We achieved parametricity by concentrating on the effects rather than the mechanisms of the language. We do not model language features, instead, we model actor behaviour through non-deterministic choice between heap mutation and object creation. All other actions, such as method call, conditionals, loops etc., are irrelevant.

Can the model be parametric in the host type system? We achieved parametricity by concentrating on the guarantees rather than the mechanism afforded by the type system. We do not define judgments, but instead, assume the existence of judgements which determines whether a path is readable or writeable from a given actor. Through an (uninterpreted) precondition to any heap mutation, we require that no aliasing lets an object writeable from an actor be readable/writeable from any other actor.

How to relax atomicity? ORCA relies on a global invariant that relates the number of references to any data object and the number of messages with a path to that object. This invariant only holds if actors execute atomically. Since we desire actors to run in parallel, we developed a more subtle, and weaker, definition of the invariant.

The full proofs and omitted definitions are available in appendix [16].

2   Host Language Requirements

ORCA makes some assumptions about its host language, we describe them here.

2.1   Actors and Objects

Actors are active entities with a thread of control, while objects are data structures. Both actors and objects may have fields and methods. Method calls on objects are synchronous, whereas method calls on actors amount to asynchronous message sends—they all called *behaviours*. Messages are stored in a FIFO queue. When idle, an actor processes the top message from its queue. At any given point of time an actor may be either idle, executing a behaviour, or collecting garbage.

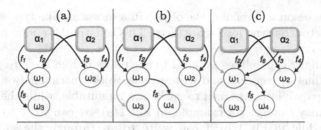

Fig. 1. Actors and objects. Full arrows are references, grey arrows are overwritten references: references that no longer exist.

Actor	Path	Capapability		Actor	Path	Capability
	this.f_1	write			this.f_2	tag
	this.f_1.f_5	write			this.f_2.f_5	$\perp$
α_1	this.f_3	read		α_2	this.f_4	read
					this.f_6	write
					this.f_6.f_5	write

Fig. 2. Capabilities. Heap mutation may modify what object is reachable through a path, but not the path's capability.

Figure 1 shows actors α_1 and α_2, objects ω_1 to ω_4. In [16] we show how to create this object graph in Pony. In Fig. 1(a), actor α_1 points to object ω_1 through field f_1 to ω_2 through field f_3, and object ω_1 points to ω_3 through field f_5. In Fig. 1(b), actor α_1 creates ω_4 and assigns it to this.f_1.f_5. In Fig. 1(c), α_1 has given up its reference to ω_1 and sent it to act_2 which stored it in field f_6. Note that the process of sending sent not only ω_1 but also implicitily ω_4.

2.2 Mutation, Transfer and Accessibility

Message passing is the only way to share objects. This falls out of the capability system. If an actor shares an object with another actor, then either it gives up the object or neither actor has a write capability to that object. For example, after α_1 sends ω_1 to α_2, it cannot mutate ω_1. As a consequence, heap mutation only decreases accessibility, while message sends can transfer accessibility from sender to receiver. When sending immutable data the sender does not need to transfer accessibility. However, when it sends a mutable object it cannot keep the ability to read or to write the object. Thus, upon message send of a mutable object, the actor must consume, or destroy, its reference to that object.

2.3 Capabilities and Accessibility

ORCA assumes that a host language's type system assigns *access rights* to paths. A path is a sequence of field names. We call these access rights *capabilities*.

We expect the following three capabilities: read, write, tag. The first two allow reading and writing an object's fields respectively. The tag capability only allows identity comparison and sending the object in a message. The type system must ensure that actors have no read-write races. This is natural for actor languages [5, 7,11,21].

Figure 2 shows capabilities assigned to the paths in Fig. 1: $\alpha_1.f_1.f_5$ has capability write, thus α_1 can read and write to the object reachable from that path. Note that capapabilities assigned to paths are immutable, while the contents of those paths may change. For example, in Fig. 1(a), α_1 can write to ω_3 through path $f_1.f_5$, while in Fig. 1(b) it can write to ω_4 through the same path. In Fig. 1(a) and (b), α_2 can use the address of ω_1 but cannot read or write it, due to the tag capability, and therefore cannot access ω_3 (in Fig. 1(a)) nor ω_4 (in Fig. 1(b)). However, in Fig. 1(c) the situation reverses: α_2, which received ω_1 with write capability is now able to reach it through field f_6, and therefore ω_4. Notice that the existence of a path from an actor to an object does not imply that the object is accessible to the actor: In Fig. 1(a), there is a path from α_2 to ω_3, but α_2 cannot access ω_3. Capabilities protect against data races by ensuring that if an object can be mutated by an actor, then no other actor can access its fields.

2.4 Causality

ORCA uses messages to deliver protocol-related information, it thus requires causal delivery. Messages must be delivered after any and all messages that caused them. Causality is the smallest transitive relation, such that if a message m' is sent by some actor after it received or sent m, then m is a cause of m'. Causal delivery entails that m' be delivered after m.

For example, if actor α_1 sends m_1 to actor α_2, then sends m_2 to actor α_3, and α_3 receives m_2 and sends m_3 to α_2, then m_1 is a cause of m_2, and m_2 is a cause of m_3. Causal delivery requires that α_2 receive m_1 before receiving m_3. No requirements are made on the order of delivery to different actors.

3   Overview of ORCA

We introduce ORCA and discuss how to localise the necessary information to guarantee safe deallocation of objects in the presence of sharing. Every actor has a local heap in which it allocates objects. An actor *owns* the objects it has allocated, and ownership is fixed for an object's life-time, but actors are free to reference objects that they do not own. Actors are obligated to collect their own objects once these are no longer needed. While collecting, an actor must be able to determine whether an object can be deallocated using only local information. This allows all other actors to make progress at any point.

3.1 Mutation and Collection

ORCA relies on capabilities for actors to reference objects owned by other actors and to support concurrent mutation to parts of the heap that are not being concurrently collected. Capabilities avoid the need for barriers.

I₁ An object accessible with write capability from an actor is not accessible with read or write capability from any other actor.

This invariant ensures an actor, while executing garbage collection, can safely trace any object to which it has read or write access without the need to protect against concurrent mutation from other actors.

3.2 Local Collection

An actor can collect its objects based on local information without consulting other actors. For this to be safe, the actor must know that an owned, locally inaccessible, object is also globally inaccessible (*i.e.*, inaccessible from any other actors or messages)[1]. Shared objects are reference counted by their owner to ensure:

I₂ An object accessible from a message queue or from a non-owning actor has reference count larger than zero in the owning actor.

Thus, a locally inaccessible object with a reference count of 0 can be collected.

3.3 Messages and Collection

I₁ and **I₂** are sufficient to ensure that local collection is safe. Maintaining **I₂** is not trivial as accessibility is affected by message sends. Moreover, it is possible for an actor to share a read object with another actor through a message. What if that actor drops its reference to the object? The object's owner should be informed so it can decrease its reference count. What happens when an actor receives an object in a message? The object's owner should be infomed, so that it can increase its reference count. To reduce message traffic, ORCA uses *distributed, weighted, deferred* reference counts. Each actor maintains reference counts that tracks the sharing of its objects. It also maintains counts for "foreign objects", tracking references to objects owned by other actors. This reference count for non-owning actors is what allows sending/receiving objects without having to inform their owner while maintaining **I₂**. For any object or actor ι, we denote with $\mathrm{LRC}(\iota)$ the reference count for ι in ι's owner, and with $\mathrm{FRC}(\iota)$ we denote the sum of the reference counts for ι in all other actors. The counts do not reflect the number of references, rather the existence of references:

I₃ If a non-owning actor can access an object through a path from its fields or call stack, its reference count for this object is greater than 0.

An object is globally accessible if it is accessible from any actor or from a message in some queue. Messages include reference increment or decrement messages—these are ORCA-level messages and they are not visible to applications. We introduce two logical counters: $\mathrm{AMC}(\iota)$ to account for the number of application

---

[1] For example, in Fig. 1(c) ω_4 in is locally inaccessible, but globally accessible.

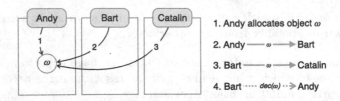

Fig. 3. Black arrows are references, numbered in creation order. Blue solid arrows are application messages and blue dashed arrows ORCA-level message. (Color figure online)

messages with paths to ι, and $OMC(\iota)$ to account for ORCA-level messages with reference count increment and decrement requests. These counters are not present at run-time, but they will be handy for reasoning about ORCA. The owner's view of an object is described by the LRC and the OMC, while the foreign view is described by the FRC and the AMC. These two views must agree:

I₄ $\forall\, \iota.\ LRC(\iota) + OMC(\iota) = AMC(\iota) + FRC(\iota)$

I₂, **I₃** and **I₄** imply that a locally inaccessible object with $LRC = 0$ can be reclaimed.

3.4   Example

Consider actors Andy, Bart and Catalin, and steps from Fig. 3.

Initial State. Let ω be a newly allocated object. As it is only accessible to its owning actor, Andy, there is no entry for it in any RC.

Sharing ω. When Andy shares ω with Bart, ω is placed on Bart's message queue, meaning that $AMC(\omega) = 1$. This is reflected by setting $RC_{Andy}(\omega)$ to 1. This preserves **I₄** and the other invariants. When Bart takes the message with ω from his queue, $AMC(\omega)$ becomes zero, and Bart sets his foreign reference count for ω to 1, that is, $RC_{Bart}(\omega) = 1$. When Bart shares ω with Catalin, we get $AMC(\omega) = 1$. To preserve **I₄**, Bart could set $RC_{Bart}(\omega)$ to 0, but this would break **I₃**. Instead, Bart sends an ORCA-level message to Andy, asking him to increment his (local) reference count by some n, and sets his own $RC_{Bart}(\omega)$ to n.[2] This preserves **I₄** and the other invariants. When Catalin receives the message later on, she will behave similarly to Bart in step 2, and set $RC_{Catalin}(\omega)=1$.

The general rule is that when an actor sends one of its objects, it increments the corresponding (local) RC by 1 (reflecting the increasing number of foreign references) but when it sends a non-owned object, it decrements the corresponding (foreign) RC (reflecting a transfer of some of its stake in the object). Special care needs to be taken when the sender's RC is 1.

---

[2] This step can be understood as if Bart "borrowed" n units from Andy, added $n-1$ to his own RC, and gave 1 to the AMC, to reach Catalin eventually.

Further note that if Andy, the owner of ω, received ω, he would decrease his counter for ω rather than increase it, as his reference count denotes foreign references to ω. When an actor receives one of its owned objects, it *decrements* the corresponding (local) RC by 1 but when it receives a non-owned object, it *increments* the corresponding (foreign) RC by 1.

Dropping References to ω. Subsequent to sharing ω with Catalin, Bart performs GC, and traces his heap without reaching ω (maybe because it did not store ω in a field). This means that Bart has given up his stake in ω. This is reflected by sending a message to Andy to decrease his RC for ω by n, and setting Bart's RC for ω to 0. Andy's local count of the foreign references to ω are decreased piecemeal like this, until LRC(ω) reaches zero. At this point, tracing Andy's local heap can determine if ω should be collected.

Further Aspects. We briefly outline further aspects which play a role in ORCA.

Concurrency. Actors execute concurrently. For example, sharing of ω by Bart and Catalin can happen in parallel. As long as Bart and Catalin have foreign references to ω, they may separately, and in parallel cause manipulation of the global number of references to ω. These manipulations will be captured locally at each site through FRC, and through increment and decrement messages to Andy (OMC).

Causality. Increment and decrement messages may arrive in any order. Andy's queue will serialise them, *i.e.* concurrent asynchronous reference count manipulations will be ordered and executed sequentially. Causality is key here, as it prevents ORCA-level messages to be overtaken by application messages which cause RCs to be decremented; thus causality keeps counters non-negative.

Composite Objects. Objects message must be traced to find the transitive closure of accessible data. For example, when passing ω_1 in a message in Fig. 1(c), objects accessible through it, *e.g.*, ω_4 will be traced. This is mandated by $\mathbf{I_3}$ and $\mathbf{I_4}$.

Finally, we reflect on the nature of reference counts: they are *distributed*, in the sense that an object's owner and every actor referencing it keep separate counts; *weighted*, in that they do not reflect the number of aliases; and *deferred*, in that they are not manipulated immediately on alias creation or destruction, and that non-local increments/decrements are handled asynchronously.

4   The ORCA Protocol

We assume enumerable, disjoint sets *ActorAddr* and *ObjAddr*, for addresses of actors and objects. The union of the two is the set of addresses including null. We require a mapping *Class* that gives the name of the class of each actor in a given configuration, and a mapping $\mathcal{O}$ that returns the owner of an address

$$Addr = ActorAddr \uplus ObjAddr \uplus \{\mathsf{null}\}$$
$$Class: \; Config \times ActorAddr \rightarrow ClassId$$
$$\mathcal{O}: Addr \rightarrow ActorAddr$$

such that the owner of an actor is the actor itself, $i.e.$, $\forall \alpha \in ActorAddr.\ \mathcal{O}(\alpha) = \alpha$.

Definition 1 describes run-time configurations, $\mathcal{C}$. They consist of a heap, χ, which maps addresses and field identifiers to addresses,[3] and an actor map, as, from actor addresses to actors. Actors consist of a frame, a queue, a reference count table, a state, a working set, marks, and a program counter. Frames are either empty, or consist of the identifier for the currently executing behaviour, and a mapping from variables to addresses. Queues are sequences of messages. A message is either an $application\ message$ of the form $\mathsf{app}(\phi)$ denoting a high-level language message with the frame ϕ, or an ORCA message, of the form $\mathsf{orca}(\iota : z)$, denoting an in-flight request for a reference count change for ι by z. The state distinguishes whether the actor is idle, or executing some behaviour, or performing garbage collection. We discuss states, working sets, marks, and program counters in Sect. 4.3. We use naming conventions: $\alpha \in ActorAddr$; $\omega \in ObjAddr$; $\iota \in Addr$; $z \in \mathbb{Z}$; $n \in \mathbb{N}$; $b \in BId$; $x \in VarId$; $A \in ClassId$; and ιs for a sequence of addresses $\iota_1...\iota_n$. We write $\mathcal{C}.\mathsf{heap}$ for $\mathcal{C}$'s heap; and $\alpha.\mathsf{qu}_\mathcal{C}$, or $\alpha.\mathsf{rc}_\mathcal{C}$, or $\alpha.\mathsf{frame}_\mathcal{C}$, or $\alpha.\mathsf{st}_\mathcal{C}$ for the queue, reference count table, frame or state of actor α in configuration $\mathcal{C}$, respectively.

Definition 1 (Runtime entities and notation)

$$\mathcal{C} \in Config = Heap \times Actors$$
$$\chi \in Heap = (Addr \setminus \{\mathsf{null}\}) \times FId \rightarrow Addr$$
$$as \in Actors = ActorAddr \rightharpoonup Actor$$
$$a \in Actor = Frame \times Queue \times ReferenceCounts$$
$$\times\ State \times Workset \times Marks \times PC$$
$$\phi \in Frame = \emptyset\ \cup\ (BId \times LocalMap)$$
$$\psi \in LocalMap = VarId \rightarrow Addr$$
$$q \in Queue = Message^\star$$
$$m \in Message ::= \mathsf{orca}(\iota : z)\ \mid\ \mathsf{app}(\phi)$$
$$\mathsf{rc} \in ReferenceCounts = Addr \rightarrow \mathbb{N}$$

$State$, $Workset$, $Marks$, and PC described in Definition 7.

Example: Figure 4 shows $\mathcal{C}_0$, our running example for a runtime configuration. It has three actors: α_1–α_3, represented by light grey boxes, and eight objects, ω_1–ω_8, represented by circles. We show ownership by placing the objects in square boxes, $e.g.$ $\mathcal{O}(\omega_7) = \alpha_1$. We show references through arrows, $e.g.$ ω_6 references ω_8 through field f_7, that is, $\mathcal{C}_0.\mathsf{heap}(\omega_6, f_7) = \omega_8$. The frame of α_2 contains behaviour identifier b', and maps x' to ω_8. All other frames are empty. The message queue of α_1 contains an application message for behaviour b and argument ω_5 for x, the queue of α_2 is empty, and the queue of α_3 an ORCA message for ω_7. The bottom part shows reference count tables: $\alpha_1.\mathsf{rc}_{\mathcal{C}_0}(\alpha_1) = 21$,

---

[3] Note that we omitted the class of objects. As our model is parametric with the type system, we can abstract from classes, and simplify our model.

and $\alpha_1.\mathrm{rc}_{\mathcal{C}_0}(\omega_7) = 50$. Entries of owned addresses are shaded. Since α_2 owns α_2 and ω_2, the entries for $\alpha_2.\mathrm{rc}_{\mathcal{C}_0}(\alpha_2)$ and $\alpha_2.\mathrm{rc}_{\mathcal{C}_0}(\omega_2)$ are shaded. Note that α_1 has a non-zero entry for ω_7, even though there is no path from α_1 to ω_7. There is no entry for ω_1; no such entry is needed, because no actor except for its owner has a path to it. The 0 values indicate potentially non-existent entries in the corresponding tables; for example, the reference count table for actor α_3 needs only to contain entries for α_1, α_3, ω_3, and ω_4. Ownership does not restrict access to an address: *e.g.* actor α_1 does not own object ω_3, yet may access it through the path $\mathsf{this}.f_1.f_2.f_3$, may read its field through $\mathsf{this}.f_1.f_2.f_3.f_4$, and may mutate it, *e.g.* by $\mathsf{this}.f_1.f_2.f_3 = \mathsf{this}.f_1$.

Lookup of fields in a configuration is defined in the obvious way, *i.e.*

Definition 2. $\mathcal{C}(\iota.f) \equiv \mathcal{C}.\mathsf{heap}(\iota, f)$, and $\mathcal{C}(\iota.\overline{f}.f') \equiv \mathcal{C}.\mathsf{heap}(\mathcal{C}(\iota.\overline{f}, f'))$

4.1   Capabilities and Accessibility

ORCA considers three capabilities:

$$\kappa \in Capability = \{\mathsf{read}, \mathsf{write}, \mathsf{tag}\},$$

where read allows reading, write allows reading and writing, and tag forbids both read and write, but allows the use of an object's address. To describe the capability at which objects are visible from actors we use the concepts of *static* and *dynamic paths*.

Static paths consist of the keyword this (indicating a path starting at the current actor), or the name of a behaviour, b, and a variable, x, (indicating a path starting at local variable x from a frame of b), followed by any number of fields, f.

$$sp ::= \mathsf{this} \mid b.x \mid sp.f$$

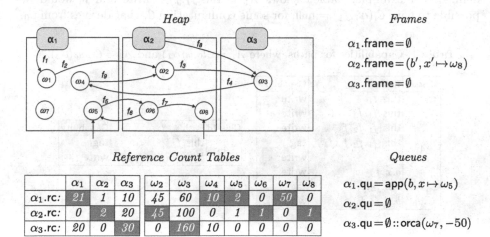

Fig. 4. Configuration $\mathcal{C}_0$. ω_1 is absent in the ref. counts, it has not been shared.

The host language must assign these capabilities to static paths. Thus, we assume it provides a static judgement of the form

$$A \vdash sp : \kappa \qquad \text{where } A \in ClassId$$

meaning that a static path sp has capability *capability* when "seen" from a class A. We highlight static judgments, *i.e.*, those provided by the type system in blue.

We expect the type system to guarantee that read and write access rights are "deep", meaning that all paths to a read capability must go through other read or write capabilities (**A1**), and all paths to a write capability must go through write capabilities (**A2**).

Axiom 1 *For class identifier A, static path sp, field f, capability κ, we assume:*
A1 $A \vdash sp.f : \kappa \qquad \longrightarrow \quad \exists \kappa' \neq \mathsf{tag}. \ A \vdash sp : \kappa'.$
A2 $A \vdash sp.f : \mathsf{write} \quad \longrightarrow \quad A \vdash sp : \mathsf{write}.$

Such requirements are satisfied by many type systems with read-only references or immutability (*e.g.* [7,11,18,23,29,33,37,41]). An implication of **A1** and **A2** is that capabilities degrade with growing paths, *i.e.*, the prefix of a path has more rights than its extensions. More precisely: $A \vdash sp : \kappa$ and $A \vdash sp.f : \kappa'$ imply that $\kappa \leq \kappa'$, where we define $\mathsf{write} < \mathsf{read} < \mathsf{tag}$, and $\kappa \leq \kappa'$ *iff* $\kappa = \kappa'$ or $\kappa < \kappa'$.

Example: Table 1 shows capabilities for some paths from Fig. 4. Thus, $A_1 \vdash \mathsf{this}.f_1 : \mathsf{write}$, and $A_2 \vdash b'.x' : \mathsf{write}$, and $A_2 \vdash \mathsf{this}.f_8 : \mathsf{tag}$. The latter, together with **A1** gives that $A_2 \nvdash \mathsf{this}.f_8.f : \kappa$ for all κ and f.

As we shall see later, the existence of a path does not imply that the path may be navigated. For example, $\mathcal{C}_0(\alpha_2.f_8.f_4) = \omega_4$, but actor α_2 cannot access ω_4 because of $A_2 \vdash \mathsf{this}.f_8 : \mathsf{tag}$.

Moreover, it is possible for a path to have a capability, while not being defined. For example, Table 1 shows $A_1 \vdash \mathsf{this}.f_1.f_2 : \mathsf{write}$ and it would be possible to have $\mathcal{C}_i(\alpha_1.f_1) = \mathsf{null}$, for some configuration $\mathcal{C}_i$ that derives from $\mathcal{C}_0$.

Table 1. Capabilities for paths, where $A_1 = Class(\alpha_1)$ and $A_2 = Class(\alpha_2)$.

ClassId	Path	Capability
A_1	$\mathsf{this}.f_1$	write
	$\mathsf{this}.f_1.f_2$	write
	$\mathsf{this}.f_1.f_2.f_3$	write
	$\mathsf{this}.f_1.f_2.f_3.f_4$	tag
	$b.x$	write
	$b.x.f_5$	write
	$b.x.f_5.f_7$	tag
	$b.x.f_5.f_6$	write

ClassId	Path	Capability
A_2	$\mathsf{this}.f_8$	tag
	$b'.x'$	write

Dynamic paths (in short paths p) start at the actor's fields, or frame, or at some pending message in an actor's queue (the latter cannot be navigated yet, but will be able to be navigated later on when the message is taken off the queue). Dynamic paths may be local paths (lp) or message paths. Local paths consist of this or a variable x followed by any number of fields f. In such paths, this is the current actor, and x is a local variable from the current frame. Message paths consist of $k.x$ followed by a sequence of fields. If $k \geq 0$, then $k.x$ indicates the local variable x from the k-th message from the queue; $k = -1$ indicates variables from either (a) a message that has been popped from the queue, but whose frame has not yet been pushed onto the stack, or (b) a message whose frame has been created but not yet been pushed onto the queue. Thus, $k = -1$ indicates that either (a) a frame will be pushed onto the stack, during message receiving, or (b) a message will be pushed onto the queue during message sending.

$$p \in Path ::= lp \mid mp \qquad lp ::= \text{this} \mid x \mid lp.f \qquad mp ::= k.x \mid mp.f$$

We define accessibility as the lookup of a path provided that the capability for this path is defined. The *partial* function $\mathcal{A}$ returns a pair: the address accessible from actor α following path p, and the capability of α on p. A path of the form p.owner returns the owner of the object accessible though p and capability tag.

Definition 3 (accessibility). *The partial function*
$$\mathcal{A} : Config \times ActorAddr \times Path \to (Addr \times Capability)$$
is defined as

$$
\begin{aligned}
\mathcal{A}_C(\alpha, \text{this}.\overline{f}) = (\iota, \kappa) \quad & iff \quad C(\alpha.\overline{f}) = \iota \;\wedge\; Class(\alpha) \vdash \text{this}.\overline{f} : \kappa \\
\mathcal{A}_C(\alpha, x.\overline{f}) = (\iota, \kappa) \quad & iff \quad \exists b.\psi. \,[\; \alpha.\text{frame}_C = (b, \psi) \;\wedge\; C(\psi(x).\overline{f}) = \iota \\
& \qquad\qquad\quad \wedge\; Class(\alpha) \vdash b.x.\overline{f} : \kappa \;] \\
\mathcal{A}_C(\alpha, k.x.\overline{f}) = (\iota, \kappa) \quad & iff \quad k \geq 0 \;\wedge\; \exists b.\psi. \,[\; \alpha.\text{qu}_C[k] = app(b, \psi) \;\wedge\; \\
& \qquad C(\psi(x).\overline{f}) = \iota \;\wedge\; Class(\alpha) \vdash b.x.\overline{f} : \kappa \;] \\
\mathcal{A}_C(\alpha, -1.x.\overline{f}) = (\iota, \kappa) \quad & iff \quad \alpha \text{ is executing Sending or Receiving, and } \dots \\
& \qquad \text{continued in Definition 9.} \\
\mathcal{A}_C(\alpha, p.\text{owner}) = (\alpha', \text{tag}) \quad & iff \quad \exists \iota.[\mathcal{A}_C(\alpha, p) = (\iota, \_) \wedge \mathcal{O}(\iota) = \alpha']
\end{aligned}
$$

We use $\mathcal{A}_C(\alpha, p) = \iota$ as shorthand for $\exists \kappa. \mathcal{A}_C(\alpha, p) = (\iota, \kappa)$. The second and third case above ensure that the capability of a message path is the same as when the message has been taken off the queue and placed on the frame.

Example: We obtain that $\mathcal{A}_{C_0}(\alpha_1, \text{this}.f_1.f_2.f_3) = (\omega_3, \text{write})$, from the fact that Fig. 4 says that $C_0(\alpha_1.f_1.f_2.f_3) = \omega_3$ and from the fact that Table 1 says that $A_1 \vdash \text{this}.f_1.f_2.f_3 : \text{write}$. Similarly, $\mathcal{A}_{C_0}(\alpha_2, \text{this}.f_8) = (\omega_3, \text{tag})$, and $\mathcal{A}_{C_0}(\alpha_2, x') = (\omega_8, \text{write})$, and $\mathcal{A}_{C_0}(\alpha_1, 0.x.f_5.f_7) = (\omega_8, \text{tag})$.

Both $\mathcal{A}_{C_0}(\alpha_1, \text{this}.f_1.f_2.f_3)$, and $\mathcal{A}_{C_0}(\alpha_2, \text{this}.f_8)$ describe paths from actors' fields, while $\mathcal{A}_{C_0}(\alpha_2, x')$ describes a path from the actor's frame, and finally $\mathcal{A}_{C_0}(\alpha_1, 0.x.f_5.f_7)$ is a path from the message queue.

Accessibility describes what may be read or written to: $\mathcal{A}_{C_0}(\alpha_1, \text{this}.f_1.f_2.f_3) = (\omega_3, \text{write})$, therefore actor α_1 may mutate object ω_3. However, this mutation is not visible by α_2, even though $\mathcal{C}_0(\alpha_2.f_8) = \omega_3$, because $\mathcal{A}_{\mathcal{C}_0}(\alpha_2, \text{this}.f_8) = (\omega_3, \text{tag})$, which means that actor α_2 has only opaque access to ω_3.

Accessibility plays a role in collection: If the reference f_3 were to be dropped it would be safe to collect ω_4; even though there exists a path from α_2 to ω_4; object ω_4 is not accessible to α_2: the path $\text{this}.f_8.f_4$ leads to ω_4 but will never be navigated ($\mathcal{A}_{\mathcal{C}_0}(\alpha_2, \text{this}.f_8.f_4)$ is undefined). Also, $\mathcal{A}_{\mathcal{C}}(\alpha_2, \text{this}.f_8.\text{owner}) = (\alpha_3, \text{tag})$; thus, as long as ω_4 is accessible from some actor, *e.g.* through $\mathcal{C}(\alpha_2.f_8) = \omega_4$, actor α_3 will not be collected.

Because the class of an actor as well as the capability attached to a static path are constant throughout program execution, the capabilities of paths starting from an actor's fields or from the same frame are also constant.

Lemma 1. *For actor α, fields $\overline{f}$, behaviour b, variable x, fields $\overline{f}$, capabilities κ, κ', configurations $\mathcal{C}$ and $\mathcal{C}'$, such that $\mathcal{C}$ reduces to $\mathcal{C}'$ in one or more steps:*

- $\mathcal{A}_{\mathcal{C}}(\alpha, \text{this}.\overline{f}) = (\iota, \kappa) \ \wedge \ \mathcal{A}_{\mathcal{C}'}(\alpha, \text{this}.\overline{f}) = (\iota', \kappa') \ \longrightarrow \ \kappa = \kappa'$
- $\mathcal{A}_{\mathcal{C}}(\alpha, x.\overline{f}) = (\iota, \kappa) \ \wedge \ \mathcal{A}_{\mathcal{C}'}(\alpha, x.\overline{f}) = (\iota', \kappa') \ \wedge$
  $\alpha.\text{frame}_{\mathcal{C}} = (b, \_) \ \wedge \ \alpha.\text{frame}_{\mathcal{C}'} = (b, \_) \qquad\qquad \longrightarrow \ \kappa = \kappa'$

4.2 Well-Formed Configurations

We characterise data-race free configurations ($\models \mathcal{C} \ \Diamond$):

Definition 4 (Data-race freedom). $\models \mathcal{C} \ \Diamond$ *iff*
$\forall \alpha, \alpha', p, p', \kappa, \kappa'.$
$$\alpha \neq \alpha' \ \wedge \ \mathcal{A}_{\mathcal{C}}(\alpha, p) = (\iota, \kappa) \ \wedge \ \mathcal{A}_{\mathcal{C}}(\alpha', p') = (\iota, \kappa')$$
$$\longrightarrow$$
$$\kappa \sim \kappa'$$
where we define
$$\kappa \sim \kappa' \ \text{iff} \ [\ (\kappa = \text{write} \longrightarrow \kappa' = \text{tag}) \ \wedge \ (\kappa' = \text{write} \longrightarrow \kappa = \text{tag})\ ]$$

This definition captures invariant $\mathbf{I_1}$. The remaining invariants depend on the four derived counters introduced in Sect. 3. Here we define LRC and FRC, and give a preliminary definition of AMC and OMC.

Definition 5 (Derived counters—preliminary for AMC and*ss* OMC)

$$\text{LRC}_{\mathcal{C}}(\iota) \ \equiv \ \mathcal{O}(\iota).\text{rc}_{\mathcal{C}}(\iota)$$

$$\text{FRC}_{\mathcal{C}}(\iota) \ \equiv \ \sum_{\alpha \neq \mathcal{O}(\iota)} \alpha.\text{rc}_{\mathcal{C}}(\iota)$$

$$\text{OMC}_{\mathcal{C}}(\iota) \equiv \ \sum_j \begin{cases} z & \text{if } \mathcal{O}(\iota).\text{qu}_{\mathcal{C}}[j] = \text{orca}(\iota : z) \\ 0 & \text{otherwise} \end{cases} + \ ...c.f.Definition \ 12$$

$$\text{AMC}_{\mathcal{C}}(\iota) \equiv \ \#\{\ (\alpha, k) \mid k > 0 \wedge \exists x.\overline{f}.\mathcal{A}_{\mathcal{C}}(\alpha, k.x.\overline{f}) = \iota\ \} + \ ...c.f.Definition \ 12$$

where $\#$ denotes cardinality.

For the time being, we will be reading this preliminary definition as if ... stood for 0. This works under the assumption the procedures are atomic. However Sect. 5.3, when we consider fine-grained concurrency, will refine the definition of AMC and OMC so as to also consider whether an actor is currently in the process of sending or receiving a message from which the address is accessible. For the time being, we continue with the preliminary reading.

Example: Assuming that in C_0 none of the actors is sending or receiving, we have $\mathrm{LRC}_{C_0}(\omega_3) = 160$, and $\mathrm{FRC}_{C_0}(\omega_3) = 160$, and $\mathrm{OMC}_{C_0}(\omega_3) = 0$, and $\mathrm{AMC}_{C_0}(\omega_3) = 0$. Moreover, $\mathrm{AMC}_{C_0}(\omega_6) = \mathrm{AMC}_{C_0}(\alpha_2) = 1$: neither ω_6 nor α_2 are arguments in application messages, but they are indirectly reachable through the first message on α_1's queue.

A well-formed configuration requires: $\mathbf{I_1}$–$\mathbf{I_4}$: introduced in Sect. 3; $\mathbf{I_5}$: the RC's are non-negative; $\mathbf{I_6}$: accessible paths are not dangling; $\mathbf{I_7}$: processing message queues will not turn RC's negative; $\mathbf{I_8}$: actors' contents is in accordance with their state. The latter two will be described in Definition 14.

Definition 6 (Well-formed configurations—preliminary). $\vDash C$, iff *for all* $\alpha,\ \alpha_o,\ \iota,\ \iota',\ p,\ lp,\ and\ mp,\ such\ that\ \alpha_o = \mathcal{O}(\iota) \neq \alpha$:

$\mathbf{I_1}$ $\vDash C \ \Diamond$
$\mathbf{I_2}$ $[\ \ \mathcal{A}_C(\alpha,p)=\iota \ \ \vee \mathcal{A}_C(\alpha_o,mp)=\iota\ ] \longrightarrow \mathrm{LRC}_C(\iota)>0$
$\mathbf{I_3}$ $\mathcal{A}_C(\alpha,lp) = \iota \longrightarrow \alpha.\mathsf{rc}_C(\iota) > 0$
$\mathbf{I_4}$ $\mathrm{LRC}_C(\iota) + \mathrm{OMC}_C(\iota) = \mathrm{FRC}_C(\iota) + \mathrm{AMC}_C(\iota)$
$\mathbf{I_5}$ $\alpha.\mathsf{rc}_C(\iota') \geq 0$
$\mathbf{I_6}$ $\mathcal{A}_C(\alpha,p)=\iota \longrightarrow C.\mathsf{heap}(\iota) \neq \bot$
$\mathbf{I_7}, \mathbf{I_8}$ *description in Definition 14.*

For ease of notation, we take $\mathbf{I_5}$ to mean that if $\alpha.\mathsf{rc}_C(\iota')$ is defined, then it is positive. And we take any undefined entry of $\alpha.\mathsf{rc}_C(\iota)$ to be 0.

4.3 Actor States

We now complete the definition of runtime entities (Definition 1), and describe the states of an actor, the worksets, the marks, and program counters. (Definition 7). We distinguish the following states: idle (IDLE), collecting (COLLECT), receiving (RECEIVE), sending a message (SEND), or executing the synchronous part of a behaviour (EXECUTE). We discuss these states in more detail next.

Except for the idle state, IDLE, all states use auxiliary data structures: *worksets*, denoted by ws, which stores a set of addresses; *marks* maps, denoted by ms, from addresses to R (reachable) or U (unreachable), and program counters. Frames are relevant when in states EXECUTE, or SEND, and otherwise are assumed to be empty. Worksets are used to store all addresses traced from a message or from the actor itself, and are relevant when in states SEND, or RECEIVE, or COLLECT, and otherwise are empty. Marks are used to calculate reachability and are used in state COLLECT, and are ignored otherwise. The program counters record the instruction an actor will execute next; they range between 4 and 27 and are ghost state, *i.e.* only used in the proofs.

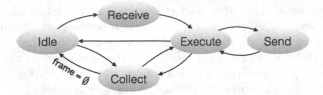

Fig. 5. State transitions diagram for an actor.

Definition 7 (Actor States, Working sets, and Marks)

$$
\begin{aligned}
\mathsf{st} \in \mathit{State} &::= \mathit{IDLE} \mid \mathit{EXECUTE} \mid \mathit{SEND} \mid \mathit{RECEIVE} \mid \mathit{COLLECT} \\
\mathsf{ws} \in \mathit{Workset} &= \mathcal{P}(\mathit{Addr}) \\
\mathsf{ms} \in \mathit{Marks} &= \mathit{Addr} \to \{\mathsf{R}, \mathsf{U}\} \\
\mathsf{pc} \in \mathit{PC} &= [4..27]
\end{aligned}
$$

We write $\alpha.\mathsf{st}_\mathcal{C}$, or $\alpha.\mathsf{ws}_\mathcal{C}$, or $\alpha.\mathsf{ms}_\mathcal{C}$, or $\alpha.\mathsf{pc}_\mathcal{C}$ for the state, working set, marks, or the program counter of α in $\mathcal{C}$, respectively.

Actors may transition between states. The state transitions are depicted in Fig. 5. For example, an actor in the idle state (IDLE) may receive an orca message (remaining in the same state), receive an app message (moving to the RECEIVE state), or start garbage collection (moving to the COLLECT state).

In the following sections we describe the actions an actor may perform. Following the style of [17, 26, 27] we describe actors' actions through pseudo-code procedures, which have the form:

procedure_name$\langle \alpha \rangle$:
$\underset{\rightarrow}{\text{condition}}$
{ instructions }

We let α denote the executing actor, and the left-hand side of the arrow describes the condition that must be satisfied in order to execute the instructions on the arrow's right-hand side. Any actor may execute concurrently with other actors. To simplify notation, we assume an implicit, globally accessible configuration $\mathcal{C}$. Thus, instruction $\alpha.\mathsf{state}:=\mathsf{EXECUTE}$ is short for updating the state of α in $\mathcal{C}$ to be EXECUTE. We elide configurations when obvious, *e.g.* $\alpha.\mathsf{frame} = \phi$ is short for requiring that in $\mathcal{C}$ the frame of α is ϕ, but we mention them when necessary—*e.g.* $\vDash \mathcal{C}[\iota_1, f \mapsto \iota_2] \; \Diamond$ expresses that the configuration that results from updating field f in ι_1 is data-race free.

Tracing Function. Both garbage collection, and application message sending/receiving need to find all objects accessible from the current actor and/or from the message arguments. We define two functions: trace_this finds all addresses which are accessible from the current actor, and trace_frame finds all addresses which are accessible through a stack frame (but not from the current actor, this).

```
1  GarbageCollection⟨α⟩:
2    α.st = IDLE ∨ α.st = EXECUTE
3  →
4  {
5    α.st := COLLECT
6    α.ms := ∅
7
8    // marking as unreachable
9    forall ι with α = O(ι) ∨ α.rc(ι) > 0 do α.ms := α.ms[ι ↦ U]
10
11   // tracing and marking locally accessible as reachable
12   forall ι ∈ trace_this(α) ∪ trace_frame(α.frame) do α.ms := α.ms[ι ↦ R]
13
14   // marking owned and globally accessible as reachable
15   forall ι with α = O(ι) ∧ α.rc(ι) > 0 do α.ms := α.ms[ι ↦ R]
16
17   // collecting
18   forall ι with α.ms(ι) = U do
19     if O(ι) = α then
20       C.heap := C.heap[ι ↦ ⊥]
21       α.rc := α.rc[ι ↦ ⊥]
22     else
23       O(ι).qu.push(orca(ι:−α.rc(ι)))
24       α.rc := α.rc[ι ↦ ⊥]
25
26   if α.frame=∅ then α.st := IDLE else α.st := EXECUTE
27 }
```

Fig. 6. Pseudo-code for garbage collection.

Definition 8 (Tracing). *We define the functions*
  trace_this : $Config \times ActorAddr \to \mathcal{P}(Addr)$
  trace_frame : $Config \times ActorAddr \times Frame \to \mathcal{P}(Addr)$
as follows
  $\text{trace\_this}_C(\alpha) \quad \equiv \{ι \mid \exists \overline{f}.\ \mathcal{A}_C(\alpha, \text{this}.\overline{f}) = ι\}$
  $\text{trace\_frame}_C(\alpha, \phi) \equiv \{ι \mid \exists x \in dom(\phi), \overline{f}.\ \mathcal{A}_C(\alpha, x.\overline{f}) = ι\}$

4.4 Garbage Collection

We describe garbage collection in Fig. 6. An idle, or an executing actor (pre-condition on line 2) may start collecting at any time. Then, it sets its state to COLLECT (line 5), and initialises the marks, ms, to empty (line 6).

The main idea of ORCA collection is that the requirement for global unreachability of owned objects can be weakened to the local requirement to local unreachability and a $LRC = 0$. Therefore, the actor marks all owned objects, and all addresses with a RC > 0 as U (line 9). After that, it traces the actor's fields, and also the actor's frame if it happens not to be empty (as we shall see later, idle actors have empty frames) and marks all accessible addresses as R (line 12). Then, the actor marks all owned objects with RC > 0 as R (line 15). Thus we expect that: (*) *Any ι with* ms(ι) = U *is locally unreachable, and if owned by the current actor, then its LRCis 0.* For each address with ms(ι) = U, if the actor owns ι, then it collects it (line 20)—this is sound because of $\mathbf{I_2}$, $\mathbf{I_3}$, $\mathbf{I_4}$ and (*). If the actor does not own ι, then it asks ι's owner to decrement its reference count by the current actor's reference count, and deletes its own reference count to it (thus becoming 0) (line 24)—this preserves $\mathbf{I_2}$, $\mathbf{I_3}$ and $\mathbf{I_4}$.

There is no need for special provision for cycles across actor boundaries. Rather, the corresponding objects will be collected by each actor separately, when it is the particular actor's turn to perform GC.

Example: Look at the cycle ω_5–ω_6, and assume that the message $\mathsf{app}(b, \omega_5)$ had finished execution without any heap mutation, and that $\alpha_1.\mathsf{rc}_\mathcal{C}(\omega_5) = \alpha_1.\mathsf{rc}_\mathcal{C}(\omega_6) = 1 = \alpha_2.\mathsf{rc}_\mathcal{C}(\omega_5) = \alpha_2.\mathsf{rc}_\mathcal{C}(\omega_6)$—this will be the outcome of the example in Sect. 4.5. Now, the objects ω_5 and ω_6 are globally unreachable. Assume that α_1 performs GC: it will *not* be able to collect any of these objects, but it will send a $\mathsf{orca}(\omega_6 : -1)$ to α_2. Some time later, α_2 will pop this message, and some time later it will enter a GC cycle: it will collect ω_6, and send a $\mathsf{orca}(\omega_5 : -1)$ to α_1. When, later on, α_1 pops this message, and later enters a GC cycle, it will collect ω_5.

At the end of the GC cycle, the actor sets is state back to what it was before (line 26). If the frame is empty, then the actor had been IDLE, otherwise it had been in state EXECUTE.

4.5   Receiving and Sending Messages

Through message send or receive, actors share addresses with other actors. This changes accessibility. Therefore, action is needed to re-establish $\mathbf{I_3}$ and $\mathbf{I_4}$ for all the objects accessible from the message's arguments.

Receiving application messages is described by Receiving in Fig. 7. It requires that the actor α is in the IDLE state and has an application message on top of its queue. The actor sets its state to RECEIVE (line 5), traces from the message arguments and stores all accessible addresses into ws (line 7). Since accessibility is not affected by other actors' actions, *c.f., last paragraph in Sect.* 4.6 it is legitimate to consider the calculation of trace_frame as one single step. It then pops the message from its queue (line 8), and thus the AMC for all the addresses in ws will decrease by 1. To preserve $\mathbf{I_4}$, for each ι in its ws, the actor:

- if it is ι's owner, then it *decrements* its reference count for ι by 1, thus decreasing $\mathsf{LRC}_\mathcal{C}(\iota)$ (line 12).
- if it is *not* ι's owner, then it *increments* its reference count for ι by 1, thus increasing $\mathsf{FRC}_\mathcal{C}(\iota)$ (line 14).

After that, the actor sets its frame to that from the message (line 17), and goes to the EXECUTE state (line 18).

Example: Actor α_1 has an application message in its queue. Assuming that it is IDLE, it may execute Receiving: It will trace ω_5 and as a result store

```
1  Receiving⟨α⟩:
2    α.st = IDLE ∧ α.qu.top() = app(φ)
3  →
4  {
5    α.st := RECEIVE
6
7    α.ws := trace_frame(α, φ)
8    pop(α.qu)
9
10   foreach ι ∈ α.ws do
11     if α = 𝒪(ι) then
12        α.rc(ι) −= 1
13     else
14        α.rc(ι) += 1;
15     α.ws := α.ws \ {ι}
16
17   α.frame := φ
18   α.st := EXECUTE
19 }
```

```
1  ReceiveORCA⟨α⟩:
2    α.state = IDLE ∧ α.qu.top() = ORCA(ι : z)
3  →
4  {
5    α.rc(ι) += z
6    α.qu.pop()
7  }
```

Fig. 7. Receiving application and ORCA messages.

$\{\omega_5, \omega_6, \omega_8, \alpha_1, \alpha_2\}$ in its ws. It will then decrement its reference count for ω_5 and α_1 (the owned addresses) and increment it for the others. It will then pop the message from its queue, create the appropriate frame, and go to state EXECUTE.

Receiving ORCA messages is described in Fig. 7. An actor in the IDLE state with an ORCA message at the top, pops the message from its queue, and adds the value z to the reference count for ι, and stays in the IDLE state.

Sending application messages is described in Fig. 8. The actor must be in the EXECUTE state for some behaviour b and must have local variables which can be split into ψ and ψ'—the latter will form part of the message to be sent. As the AMC for all the addresses reachable through the message increases by 1, in order to preserve $\mathbf{I}_4$ for each address ι in ws, the actor:

- increments its reference count for ι by 1, if it owns it (line 14);
- decrements its reference count for ι if it does not own it (line 16). But special care is needed if the actor's (foreign) reference count for ι is 1, because then a simple decrement would break $\mathbf{I}_5$. Instead, the actor set its reference count for ι by 256 (line 18) and sends an ORCA message to ι's owner with 256 as argument.

After this, it removes ψ' from its frame (line 22), pushes the message app(b', ψ') onto α''s queue, and transitions to the EXECUTE state.

```
 1  Sending⟨α⟩:
 2    α.st = EXECUTE  ∧   α.frame = (b, ψ · ψ')  ∧
 3    ∀x ∈ dom(ψ), x' ∈ dom(ψ').∀κ, κ'.∀f̄, f̄'. [
 4        [  [ A_C(α, x.f̄) = (ι, κ) ∧ A_C(α, x'.f̄') = (ι, κ')  ⟶  κ' ∼ κ ] ∧
 5           [ Class(α) ⊢ b.x'.f̄' : κ' ⟷ Class(α') ⊢ b'.x'.f̄' : κ' ]    ]
 6    →
 7  {
 8    α.st := SEND
 9
10    α.ws := trace_frame(α, (b, ψ'))
11
12    foreach ι ∈ α.ws do
13      if α = O(ι) then
14        α.rc(ι) += 1
15      elseif α.rc(ι) > 1 then
16        α.rc(ι) -= 1
17      else
18        α.rc(ι) := 256
19        O(ι).qu.push(orca(ι : 256))
20      α.ws := α.ws\{ι}
21
22    α.frame := (b, ψ)
23    α'.qu.push(app(b', ψ'))
24
25    α.st := EXECUTE
26  }
```

Fig. 8. Pseudo-code for message sending.

We now discuss the preconditions. These ensure that sending the message $app(b, ψ')$ will not introduce data races: Line 4 ensures that there are no data races between paths starting at $ψ$ and paths starting at $ψ'$, while Line 5 ensures that the sender, $α$, and the receiver, $α'$ see all the paths sent, i.e. those starting from $(b', ψ')$, at the same capability. We express our expectation that the source language compiler produces code only if it satisfies this property by adding this static requirement as a precondition. These static requirements imply that after the message has been sent, there will be no races between paths starting at the sender's frame and those starting at the last message in the receiver's queue. In more detail, after the sender's frame has been reduced to $(b, ψ)$, and $app(b', ψ')$ has been added to the receiver's queue (at location k), we will have a new configuration $C' = C[α, \text{frame} \mapsto (b, ψ)][α', \text{queue} \mapsto α'.\text{queue}_C :: (b', ψ')]$. In this new configuration lines 4 and 5 ensure that $A_{C'}(α, x.f̄) = (ι, κ) ∧ A_{C'}(α', k.x'.f̄') = (ι, κ') \longrightarrow κ' ∼ κ$, which means that if there were no data races in C, there will be no data races in C' either. Formally: $\vDash C \Diamond \longrightarrow \vDash C' \Diamond$.

We can now complete Definition 3 for the receiving and the sending cases, to take into account paths that do not exist yet, but which will exist when the message receipt or message sending has been completed.

Definition 9 (accessibility—receiving and sending). *Completing Definition 3:* $\mathcal{A}_C(\alpha, -1.x.\overline{f}) = (\iota, \kappa)$ *iff*

$\quad \alpha.\mathsf{st}_C = Receiving \ \wedge \ 9 \leq \alpha.\mathsf{pc}_C < 18 \ \wedge \ C(\psi(x).\overline{f}) = \iota \ \wedge \ Class(\alpha) \vdash b.x.\overline{f} : \kappa$
$\qquad where \ (b, \psi) is \ the \ frame \ popped \ at \ line \ 8,$

or

$\quad \alpha.\mathsf{st}_C = Sending \ \wedge \ \alpha.\mathsf{pc}_C = 23 \ \wedge \ C(\psi'(x).\overline{f}) = \iota \ \wedge \ Class(\alpha') \vdash b'.x.\overline{f} : \kappa$
$\qquad where \ \alpha' \ is \ the \ actor \ to \ receive \ the \ app\text{-}message, \ and$
$\qquad (b', \psi') \ is \ the \ frame \ to \ be \ sent \ in \ line \ 23.$

Example: When actor α_1 executes Receiving, and its program counter is between 9 and 18, then $\mathcal{A}_{C_0}(\alpha_1, -1.x.f_5) = (\omega_6, \mathsf{write})$, even though x is not yet on the stack frame. As soon as the frame is pushed on the stack, and we reach program counter 20, then t $\mathcal{A}_{C_0}(\alpha_1, -1.x.f_5)$ is undefined, but $\mathcal{A}_{C_0}(\alpha_1, x.f_5) = (\omega_6, \mathsf{write})$.

4.6   Actor Behaviour

As our model is parametric with the host language, we do not aim to describe any of the actions performed while executing behaviours, such as synchronous method calls and pushing frames onto stacks, conditionnals, loops etc. Instead, we concentrate on how behaviour execution may affect GC; this happens only when the heap is mutated either by object creation or by mutation of objects' fields (since this affects accessibility). In particular, our model does not accommodate for recursive calls; we claim that the result from the current model would easily be extended to a model with recursion in synchronous behaviour, but would require a considerable notation overhead.

Figure 9 shows the actions of an actor α while in the EXECUTE state, *i.e.* while it executes behaviours synchronously. The description is nondeterministic: the procedures Goldle, or Create, or MutateHeap, may execute when the corresponding preconditions hold. Thus, we do not describe the execution of a given program, rather we describe all possible executions for any program. In Goldle, the actor α simply passes from the execution state to the idle state; the only condition is that its state is EXECUTE (line 2). It deletes the frame, and sets the actor's state to IDLE (line 4). Create creates a new object, initialises its fields to null, and stores its address into local variable x.

The most interesting procedure is field assignment, MutateHeap. line 8 modifies the object at address ι_1, reachable through local path $lp1$, and stores in its field f the address ι_2 which was reachable through local path $lp2$. We require that the type system makes the following two guarantees: line 2, second conjunct, requires that $lp1$ should be writable, while line 3 requires that $lp2$ should be accessible. Line 4 and line 5 requite that capabilities of objects do not increase through heap mutation: any address that is accessible with a capability κ after the field update was accessible with the same or more permissive capability κ' before the field update. This requirment guarantees preservation of data race freedom, *i.e.* that $\vDash C \diamondsuit$ implies $\vDash C[\iota_1, f \mapsto \iota_2] \diamondsuit$.

```
1  Goldle⟨α⟩:
2    α.st = EXECUTE
3  →
4  { α.frame := ∅; α.st := IDLE; }
5
6  Create⟨α⟩:
7    α.st = EXECUTE   ∧   fresh ω ∧ O(ω) = α
8  →
9  {
10   heap :=
11     heap[ω ↦ (f_1 ↦ null, ..., f_n ↦ null)]
12   α.frame := α.frame[x ↦ ω]
13 }
```

```
1  MutateHeap⟨α⟩:
2    α.st = EXECUTE ∧  A_C(α, lp1) = (ι_1, write)
3    ∧  A_C(α, lp2) = ι_2
4    ∧  ∀ι, κ, lp [ A_C[ι_1, f↦ι_2](α, lp) = (ι, κ)  ⟶
5          (∃κ', lp' A_C(α, lp') = (ι, κ') ∧ κ' ≤ κ ])
6  →
7  {
8      heap := heap[ι_1, f ↦ ι_2]
9  }
```

Fig. 9. Pseudo-code for synchronous operations.

Heap Mutation Does not Affect Accessibility in Other Actors. Heap mutation either creates new objects, which will not be accessible to other actors, or modifies objects to which the current actor has write access. By ⊨ C ◇ all other actors have only tag access to the modified object. Therefore, because of *capabilities' degradation with growing paths (as in* **A1** *and* **A2***)*, no other actor will be able to access objects reachable through paths that go through the modified object.

5   Soundness and Completeness

In this section we show soundness and completeness of ORCA.

5.1 I_1 and I_2 Support Safe Local GC

As we said earlier, I_1 and I_2 support safe local GC. Namely, I_1 guarantees that as long as GC only traces objects to which the actor has read or write access, there will be no data races with other actors' behaviour or GC. And I_2 guarantees that collection can take place based on local information only:

Definition 10. *For a configuration C, and object address $ω$ we say that*

– $ω$ *is globally inaccessible in C, iff* $\forall α, p. A_C(α, p) \neq ω$
– $ω$ *is collectable, iff* $\text{LRC}_C(ω) = 0$, *and* $\forall lp. A_C(O(ω), lp) \neq ω$.

Lemma 2. *If I_2 holds, then every collectable object is globally inaccessible.*

5.2 Completeness

In [16] we show that globally inaccessible objects remain so, and that for any globally inaccessible object there exists a sequence of steps which will collect it.

Theorem 1 (Inaccessibility is monotonic). *For any configurations C, and C', if C' is the outcome of the execution of any single line of code from any of the procedures from Figs. 6, 7, 8 and 9, and ω is globally inaccessible in C, then ω is globally inaccessible in C'.*

Theorem 2 (Completeness of ORCA). *For any configuration C, and object address ω which is globally inaccessible in C, there exists a finite sequence of steps which lead to C' in which $\omega \notin dom(C')$.*

5.3 Dealing with Fine-Grained Concurrency

So far, we have discussed actions under an assumption atomicity. However, ORCA needs to work under fine-grained concurrency, whereby several actors may be executing concurrently, each of them executing a behaviour, or sending or receiving a message, or collecting garbage. With fine-grained concurrency, and with the preliminary definitions of AMC and OMC, the invariants are no longer preserved. In fact, they need never hold!

Example: Consider Fig. 4, and assume that actor α_1 was executing Receiving. Then, at line 7 and before popping the message off the queue, we have $\text{LRC}(\omega_5) = 2$, $\text{FRC}(\omega_5) = 1$, $\text{AMC}^p(\omega_5) = 1$, where $\text{AMC}^p(\_)$ stands for the preliminary definition of AMC; thus $\mathbf{I_4}$ holds. After popping and before updating the RC for ω_5, *i.e.* between lines 9 and 11, we have $\text{AMC}^p(\omega_5) = 0$—thus $\mathbf{I_4}$ is broken. At first sight, this might not seem a big problem, because the update of RC at line 12 will set $\text{LRC}(\omega_5) = 1$, and thus restore $\mathbf{I_4}$. However, if there was another message containing ω_5 in α_2's queue, and consider a snapshot where α_2 had just finished line 8 and α_1 had just finished line 12, then the update of α_1's RC will *not* restore $\mathbf{I_4}$.

The reason for this problem is, that with the preliminary definition $\text{AMC}^p(\_)$, upon popping at line 8, the AMC is decremented in one atomic step for all objects accessible from the message, while the RC is updated later on (at line 12 or line 14), and one object at a time. In other words, the updates to AMC and LRC are not in sync. Instead, we give the full definition of AMC so, that AMC is in sync LRC; namely it is not affected by popping the message, and is reduced one object at a time once we reach program counter line 15. Similarly, because updating the RC's takes place in a separate step from the removal of the ORCA-message from its queue, we refine the definition of OMC:

Definition 11 (Auxiliary Counters for AMC, and OMC)

$$\text{AMC}^{rcv}_C(\iota) \equiv \#\{\alpha \mid \alpha.\text{st}_C = RECEIVE \ \land \ 9 \leq \alpha.\text{pc}_C \ \land$$
$$\iota \in \alpha.\text{ws} \setminus CurrAddrRcv_C(\alpha)\}$$

$$CurrAddrRcv_C(\alpha) \equiv \begin{cases} \{\iota_{10}\} & \text{if } \alpha.\text{pc}_C = 15 \\ \emptyset & \text{otherwise} \end{cases}$$

In the above α.ws *refers to the contents of the variable* ws *while the actor* α *is executing the pseudocode from* Receiving, *and* ι_{10} *refers to the contents of the variable* ι *arbitrarily chosen in line 10 of the code.*

We define $\text{AMC}_{\mathcal{C}}^{snd}(\iota)$, $\text{OMC}_{\mathcal{C}}^{rcv}(\iota)$, and $\text{OMC}_{\mathcal{C}}^{snd}(\iota)$ *similarly in [16].*

The counters AMC^{rcv} and AMC^{snd} are zero except for actors which are in the process of receiving or sending application messages. Also, the counters OMC^{rcv} and AMC^{snd} are zero except for actors which are in the process of receiving or sending ORCA-messages. All these counters are always ≥ 0. We can now complete the definition of AMC and OMC:

Definition 12 (AMC and OMC – full definition)

$$\text{OMC}_{\mathcal{C}}(\iota) \equiv \sum_j \begin{cases} z & \text{if } \mathcal{O}(\iota).\text{qu}_{\mathcal{C}}[j] = \text{orca}(\iota : z) \\ 0 & \text{otherwise} \end{cases} + \text{OMC}_{\mathcal{C}}^{snd}(\iota) - \text{OMC}_{\mathcal{C}}^{rcv}(\iota)$$

$$\text{AMC}_{\mathcal{C}}(\iota) \equiv \#\{ (\alpha, k) \mid k > 0 \wedge \exists x.\overline{f}.\mathcal{A}_{\mathcal{C}}(\alpha, k.x.\overline{f}) = \iota \} + \text{AMC}_{\mathcal{C}}^{snd}(\iota) + \text{AMC}_{\mathcal{C}}^{rcv}(\iota)$$

where # *denotes cardinality.*

Example: Let us again consider that α_1 was executing Receiving. Then, at line 10 we have ws $= \{\iota_5, \iota_6\}$ and $\text{AMC}(\omega_5) = 1 = \text{AMC}(\omega_6)$. Assume at the first iteration, at line 10 we chose ι_5, then right before reaching line 15 we have $\text{AMC}(\omega_5) = 0$ and $\text{AMC}(\omega_6) = 1$. At the second iteration, at line 10 we will chose ι_6, and then right before reaching 15 we have $\text{AMC}(\omega_6) = 0$.

5.4   Soundness

To complete the definition of well-formed configurations, we need to define what it means for an actor or a queue to be well-formed.

Well-Formed Queues - I_7. The owner's reference count for any live address (*i.e.* any address reachable from a message path, or foreign actor, or in an ORCA message) should be greater than 0 at the current configuration, as well as, at all configurations which arise from receiving pending, but no new, messages from the owner's queue. Thus, in order to ensure that ORCA decrement messages do not make the local reference count negative, I_7 requires that the effect of any prefix of the message queue leaves the reference count for any object positive. To formulate I_7 we use the concept of $QueueEffect_{\mathcal{C}}(\alpha, \iota, n)$, which describes the contents of LRC after the actor α has consumed and reacted to the first n messages in its queue—*i.e.* is about "looking into the future". Thus, for actor α, address ι, and number n we define the effect of the n-prefix of the queue on the reference count as follows:

$$QueueEffect_{\mathcal{C}}(\alpha, \iota, n) \equiv \text{LRC}_{\mathcal{C}}(\iota) - z + \sum_{j=0}^{n} Weight_{\mathcal{C}}(\alpha, \iota, j)$$

where $z = k$, if α is in the process of executing ReceiveORCA, and $\alpha.\text{pc}_{\mathcal{C}} = 6$, and $\alpha.\text{qu.top} = \text{orca} (\iota : k)$, and otherwise $z = 0$.

And where,

$$Weight_C(\alpha, \iota, j) \equiv \begin{cases} z' & \text{if } \alpha.\mathsf{qu}_C[j] = \mathsf{orca}(\iota : z') \\ -1 & \text{if } \exists x.\exists \overline{f}.\ \mathcal{A}_C(\alpha, k.x.\overline{f}) = \iota \wedge \mathcal{O}(\iota) = \alpha \\ 0 & \text{otherwise} \end{cases}$$

I_7 makes the following four guarantees: [a] The effect of any prefix of the message queue leaves the LRC non-negative. [b] If ι is accessible from the j-th message in its owner's queue, then the LRC for ι will remain >0 during execution of the current message queue up to, and including, the j-th message. [c] If ι is accessible from an ORCA-message, then the LRC will remain >0 during execution of the current message queue, up to and excluding execution of the ORCA-message itself. [d] If ι is globally accessible (*i.e.* reachable from a local path or from a message in a non-owning actor) then $LRC(\iota)$ is currently >0, and will remain so after during popping of all the entries in the current queue.

Definition 13 (I_7). $\models_{Queues} C$, *iff for all* $j \in \mathbb{N}$, *for all addresses* ι, *actors* α, α', *where* $\mathcal{O}(\iota) = \alpha \neq \alpha'$, *the following conditions hold:*

a $\forall n.\ QueueEffect_C(\alpha, \iota, n) \geq 0$
b $\exists x.\ \exists \overline{f}.\ \mathcal{A}_C(\alpha, j.x.\overline{f}) = \iota \longrightarrow \forall k \leq j.\ QueueEffect_C(\alpha, \iota, k) > 0.$
c $\alpha.\mathsf{qu}_C[j] = \mathsf{orca}(\iota : z) \longrightarrow \forall k < j.\ QueueEffect_C(\alpha, \iota, k) > 0.$
d $\exists p.\mathcal{A}_C(\alpha', p) = \iota \longrightarrow \forall k \in \mathbb{N}.\ QueueEffect_C(\alpha, \iota, k) > 0.$

For example, in a configuration with $LRC(\iota) = 2$, and a queue with $\mathsf{orca}(\iota : -2) :: \mathsf{orca}(\iota : -1) :: \mathsf{orca}(\iota : 256)$ is illegal by $I_7.[a]$. Similarly, in a configuration with $LRC(\iota) = 2$, and a queue with $\mathsf{orca}(\iota : -2) :: \mathsf{orca}(\iota : 256)$, the owning actor could collect ι before popping the message $\mathsf{orca}(\iota : 256)$ from its queue. Such a configuration is also deemed illegal by $I_7.[c]$.

I_8-Well-Formed Actor. In [16] we define well-formedness of an actor α through the judgement $C, \alpha \vdash \mathsf{st}$. This judgement depends on α's current state st, and requires, among other things, that the contents of the local variables ws, ms are consistent with the contents of the pc and RC. Remember also, that because Receiving and Sending modify the ws or send ORCA-messages before updating the frame or sending the application message, in the definition of AMC and OMC we took into account the internal state of actors executing such procedures.

Well-Formed Configuration. The following completes Definition 6 from Sect. 4.2.

Definition 14 (Well-formed configurations—full). *A configuration C is well-formed,* $\models C$, *iff* I_1-I_6 *(Definition 6) for C, if its queues are well-formed* ($\models_{Queues} C$, I_7), *as well as, all its actors* ($C, \alpha \vdash \alpha.\mathsf{st}_C$, I_8).

In [16] we consider the execution of each line in the codes from Sect. 4, and prove:

Theorem 3 (Soundness of ORCA). *For any configurations C and C': If $\models C$, and C' is the outcome of the execution of any single line of code from any of the procedures from Figs. 6, 7, 8 and 9, then $\models C'$.*

This theorem together with I_6 implies that ORCA never leaves accessible paths dangling. Note that the theorem is stated so as to be applicable for a fine interleaving of the execution. Even though we expressed ORCA through procedures, in our proof we cater for an execution where one line of any of these procedures is executed interleaved with any other procedures in the other actors.

6   Related Work

The challenges faced when developing and debugging concurrent garbage collectors have motivated the development of formal models and proofs of correctness [6, 13, 19, 30, 35]. However, most work considers a global heap where mutator and collector threads *race* for objects and relies on synchronisation mechanisms (or atomic reduction steps), such as read or write barriers, in contrast to ORCA which considers many local heaps, no atomicity or synchronization, and relies on the properties of the type system. McCreight et al. [25] introduced a framework to reason about and build certified garbage collectors, verifying independently both mutator and collector threads. Their work focuses mainly on garbage collectors similar to those that run on Java programs, such as STW mark-and-sweep, STW copying and incremental copying. Vechev et al. [39] specified concurrent mark-and-sweep collectors with write barriers for synchronisation. The authors also present a parametric garbage collector from which other collectors can be derived. Hawblitzel and Petrank [22] mechanized proofs of two real-world collectors (copying and mark-and-sweep) and their respective allocators. The assembly code was instrumented with pre- and post-conditions, invariants and assertions, which were then verified using Z3 and Boogie. Ugawa et al. [38] extended a copying, on-the-fly, concurrent garbage collector to process reference types. The authors model-checked their algorithm using a model that limited the number of objects and threads. Gamie et al. [17] machine-checked a state-of-the-art, on-the-fly, concurrent, mark-and-sweep garbage collector [32]. They modelled one collector thread and many mutator threads. ORCA does not limit the number of actors running concurrently.

Local heaps have been used in the context of garbage collection to reduce the amount of synchronisation required before [1–3, 13, 15, 24, 31, 34], where different threads have their own heap and share a global heap. However, only two of these have been proved correct. Doligez and Gonthier [13] proved a collector [14] which splits the heap into many local heaps and one global heap, and uses mark-and-sweep for individual collection of local heaps. The algorithm imposes restrictions on the object graph, that is, a thread cannot access objects in other threads' local heaps. ORCA allows for references across heaps. Raghunathan et al. [34] proved correct a hierarchical model of local heaps for functional programming languages. The work restricted objects graphs and prevented mutation.

As for collectors that rely on message passing, Moreau et al. [26] revisited the Birrell's reference listing algorithm, which also uses message passing to update reference counts in a distributed system, and presented its formalisation and proofs or soundness and completeness. Moreover, Clebsch and Drossopoulou [10] proved correct MAC, a concurrent collector for actors.

7   Conclusions

We have shown the soundness and completeness of the ORCA actor memory reclamation protocol. The ORCA model is not tied to a particular programming language and is parametric in the host language. Instead it relies on a number of invariants and properties which can be met by a combination of language and static checks. The central property that is required is the absence of data races on objects shared between actors.

We developed a formal model of ORCA and identified requirements for the host language, its type system, or associated tooling. We described ORCA at a language-agnostic level and identified eight invariants that capture how global consistency is obtained in the absence of synchronisation. We proved that ORCA will not prematurely collect objects (soundness) and that all garbage will be identified as such (completeness).

Acknowledgements. We are deeply grateful to Tim Wood for extensive discussions and suggestions about effective communication of our ideas. We thank Rakhilya Mekhtieva for her contributions to the formal proofs, Sebastian Blessing and Andy McNeil for their contributions to the implementation, as well as the anonymous reviewers for their insightful comments. This work was initially funded by Causality Ltd, and has also received funding from the European Research Council (ERC) under the European Union's Horizon 2020 research and innovation programme (grant agreement 695412) and the FP7 project UPSCALE, the Swedish Research council through the grant Structured Aliasing and the UPMARC Linneaus Centre of Excellence, the EPSRC (grant EP/K011715/1), the NSF (award 1544542) and ONR (award 503353).

References

1. Armstrong, J.: A history of Erlang. In: HOPL III (2007)
2. Auerbach, J., Bacon, D.F., Guerraoui, R., Spring, J.H., Vitek, J.: Flexible task graphs: a unified restricted thread programming model for Java. In: LCTES (2008)
3. Auhagen, S., Bergstrom, L., Fluet, M., Reppy, J.: Garbage collection for multicore NUMA machines. In: MSPC (2011). https://doi.org/10.1145/1988915.1988929
4. Boyland, J., Noble, J., Retert, W.: Capabilities for sharing: a generalisation of uniqueness and read-only. In: ECOOP (2001). https://doi.org/10.1007/3-540-45337-7_2
5. Brandauer, S., et al.: Parallel objects for multicores: a glimpse at the parallel language ENCORE. In: Bernardo, M., Johnsen, E.B. (eds.) SFM 2015. LNCS, vol. 9104, pp. 1–56. Springer, Cham (2015). https://doi.org/10.1007/978-3-319-18941-3_1
6. Cheng, P.S.D.: Scalable real-time paralllel garbage collection for symmetric multiprocessors. Ph.D. thesis, Carnegie Mellon University (2001)
7. Clarke, D., Wrigstad, T., Östlund, J., Johnsen, E.B.: Minimal ownership for active objects. In: Ramalingam, G. (ed.) APLAS 2008. LNCS, vol. 5356, pp. 139–154. Springer, Heidelberg (2008). https://doi.org/10.1007/978-3-540-89330-1_11
8. Clebsch, S.: Pony: co-designing a type system and a runtime. Ph.D. thesis, Imperial College London (2018, to be published)

9. Clebsch, S., Blessing, S., Franco, J., Drossopoulou, S.: Ownership and reference counting based garbage collection in the actor world. In: ICOOOLPS (2015)
10. Clebsch, S., Drossopoulou, S.: Fully concurrent garbage collection of actors on many-core machines. In: OOPSLA (2013). https://doi.org/10.1145/2544173.2509557
11. Clebsch, S., Drossopoulou, S., Blessing, S., McNeil, A.: Deny capabilities for safe, fast actors. In: AGERE! (2015). https://doi.org/10.1145/2824815.2824816
12. Clebsch, S., Franco, J., Drossopoulou, S., Yang, A., Wrigstad, T., Vitek, J.: Orca: GC and type system co-design for actor languages. In: OOPSLA (2017). https://doi.org/10.1145/3133896
13. Doligez, D., Gonthier, G.: Portable, unobtrusive garbage collection for multiprocessor systems. In: POPL (1994). https://doi.org/10.1145/174675.174673
14. Doligez, D., Leroy, X.: A concurrent, generational garbage collector for a multithreaded implementation of ML. In: POPL (1993). https://doi.org/10.1145/158511.158611
15. Domani, T., Goldshtein, G., Kolodner, E.K., Lewis, E., Petrank, E., Sheinwald, D.: Thread-local heaps for Java. In: ISMM (2002). https://doi.org/10.1145/512429.512439
16. Franco, J., Clebsch, S., Drossopoulou, S., Vitek, J., Wrigstad, T.: Soundness of a concurrent collector for actors (extended version). Technical report, Imperial College London (2018). https://www.doc.ic.ac.uk/research/technicalreports/2018/
17. Gamie, P., Hosking, A., Engelhard, K.: Relaxing safely: verified on-the-fly garbage collection for x86-TSO. In: PLDI (2015). https://doi.org/10.1145/2737924.2738006
18. Gordon, C.S., Parkinson, M.J., Parsons, J., Bromfield, A., Duffy, J.: Uniqueness and reference immutability for safe parallelism. In: OOPSLA (2012). https://doi.org/10.1145/2384616.2384619
19. Gries, D.: An exercise in proving parallel programs correct. Commun. ACM **20**(12), 921–930 (1977). https://doi.org/10.1145/359897.359903
20. Haller, P., Loiko, A.: LaCasa: lightweight affinity and object capabilities in Scala. In: OOPSLA (2016). https://doi.org/10.1145/2983990.2984042
21. Haller, P., Odersky, M.: Capabilities for uniqueness and borrowing. In: D'Hondt, T. (ed.) ECOOP 2010. LNCS, vol. 6183, pp. 354–378. Springer, Heidelberg (2010). https://doi.org/10.1007/978-3-642-14107-2_17
22. Hawblitzel, C., Petrank, E.: Automated verification of practical garbage collectors. In: POPL (2009). https://doi.org/10.1145/1480881.1480935
23. Kniesel, G., Theisen, D.: JAC-access right based encapsulation for Java. Softw. Pract. Exp. **31**(6), 555–576 (2001)
24. Marlow, S., Peyton Jones, S.: Multicore garbage collection with local heaps. In: ISMM (2011). https://doi.org/10.1145/1993478.1993482
25. McCreight, A., Shao, Z., Lin, C., Li, L.: A general framework for certifying garbage collectors and their mutators. In: PLDI (2007). https://doi.org/10.1145/1250734.1250788
26. Moreau, L., Dickman, P., Jones, R.: Birrell's distributed reference listing revisited. ACM Trans. Program. Lang. Syst. (TOPLAS) **27**(6), 1344–1395 (2005). https://doi.org/10.1145/1108970.1108976
27. Moreau, L., Duprat, J.: A construction of distributed reference counting. Acta Informatica **37**(8), 563–595 (2001). https://doi.org/10.1007/PL00013315
28. Östlund, J.: Language constructs for safe parallel programming on multi-cores. Ph.D. thesis, Department of Information Technology, Uppsala University (2016)

29. Östlund, J., Wrigstad, T., Clarke, D., Åkerblom, B.: Ownership, uniqueness, and immutability. In: Paige, R.F., Meyer, B. (eds.) TOOLS EUROPE 2008. LNBIP, vol. 11, pp. 178–197. Springer, Heidelberg (2008). https://doi.org/10.1007/978-3-540-69824-1_11

30. Owicki, S., Gries, D.: An axiomatic proof technique for parallel programs I. Acta Informatica **6**(4), 319–340 (1976)

31. Pizlo, F., Hosking, A.L., Vitek, J.: Hierarchical Real-Time Garbage Collection (2007). https://doi.org/10.1145/1254766.1254784

32. Pizlo, F., Ziarek, L., Maj, P., Hosking, A.L., Blanton, E., Vitek, J.: Schism: fragmentation-tolerant real-time garbage collection. In: PLDI (2010). https://doi.org/10.1145/1806596.1806615

33. Potanin, A., Östlund, J., Zibin, Y., Ernst, M.D.: Immutability. In: Clarke, D., Noble, J., Wrigstad, T. (eds.) Aliasing in Object-Oriented Programming. Types, Analysis and Verification. LNCS, vol. 7850, pp. 233–269. Springer, Heidelberg (2013). https://doi.org/10.1007/978-3-642-36946-9_9

34. Raghunathan, R., Muller, S.K., Acar, U.A., Blelloch, G.: Hierarchical memory management for parallel programs. In: ICFP (2016). https://doi.org/10.1145/2951913.2951935

35. Ramesh, S., Mehndiratta, S.: The liveness property of on-the-fly garbage collector - a proof. Inf. Process. Lett. **17**(4), 189–195 (1983)

36. Srinivasan, S., Mycroft, A.: Kilim: isolation-typed actors for Java. In: Vitek, J. (ed.) ECOOP 2008. LNCS, vol. 5142, pp. 104–128. Springer, Heidelberg (2008). https://doi.org/10.1007/978-3-540-70592-5_6

37. Tschantz, M.S., Ernst, M.D.: Javari: adding reference immutability to Java. In: OOPSLA (2005). https://doi.org/10.1145/1094811.1094828

38. Ugawa, T., Jones, R.E., Ritson, C.G.: Reference object processing in on-the-fly garbage collection. In: ISMM (2014). https://doi.org/10.1145/2602988.2602991

39. Vechev, M.T., Yahav, E., Bacon, D.F.: Correctness-preserving derivation of concurrent garbage collection algorithms. In: PLDI (2006). https://doi.org/10.1145/1133981.1134022

40. Yang, A.M., Wrigstad, T.: Type-assisted automatic garbage collection for lock-free data structures. In: ISMM (2017). https://doi.org/10.1145/3092255.3092274

41. Zibin, Y., Potanin, A., Li, P., Ali, M., Ernst, M.D.: Ownership and immutability in generic Java. In: OOPSLA (2010). https://doi.org/10.1145/1932682.1869509

Paxos Consensus, Deconstructed and Abstracted

Álvaro García-Pérez[1]([✉]) ⓘ, Alexey Gotsman[1], Yuri Meshman[1],
and Ilya Sergey[2] ⓘ

[1] IMDEA Software Institute, Madrid, Spain
{alvaro.garcia.perez,alexey.gotsman,yuri.meshman}@imdea.org
[2] University College London, London, UK
i.sergey@ucl.ac.uk

Abstract. Lamport's Paxos algorithm is a classic consensus protocol
for state machine replication in environments that admit crash failures.
Many versions of Paxos exploit the protocol's intrinsic properties for
the sake of gaining better run-time performance, thus widening the gap
between the original description of the algorithm, which was proven correct, and its real-world implementations. In this work, we address the
challenge of specifying and verifying complex Paxos-based systems by (a)
devising composable specifications for implementations of Paxos's single-
decree version, and (b) engineering disciplines to reason about protocol-
aware, semantics-preserving optimisations to single-decree Paxos. In a
nutshell, our approach elaborates on the deconstruction of single-decree
Paxos by Boichat et al. We provide novel non-deterministic specifications
for each module in the deconstruction and prove that the implementations refine the corresponding specifications, such that the proofs of the
modules that remain unchanged can be reused across different implementations. We further reuse this result and show how to obtain a verified
implementation of Multi-Paxos from a verified implementation of single-
decree Paxos, by a series of novel protocol-aware transformations of the
network semantics, which we prove to be behaviour-preserving.

1 Introduction

Consensus algorithms are an essential component of the modern fault-tolerant
deterministic services implemented as message-passing distributed systems. In
such systems, each of the distributed nodes contains a replica of the system's
state (*e.g.*, a database to be accessed by the system's clients), and certain nodes
may propose values for the next state of the system (*e.g.*, requesting an update
in the database). Since any node can crash at any moment, all the replicas have
to keep copies of the state that are consistent with each other. To achieve this,
at each update to the system, all the non-crashed nodes run an instance of a
consensus protocol, uniformly deciding on its outcome. The safety requirements
for consensus can be thus stated as follows: "only a single value is decided uniformly by all non-crashed nodes, it never changes in the future, and the decided
value has been proposed by some node participating in the protocol" [16].

© The Author(s) 2018
A. Ahmed (Ed.): ESOP 2018, LNCS 10801, pp. 912–939, 2018.
https://doi.org/10.1007/978-3-319-89884-1_32

The Paxos algorithm [15,16] is the classic consensus protocol, and its single-decree version (SD-Paxos for short) allows a set of distributed nodes to reach an agreement on the outcome of a *single* update. Optimisations and modifications to SD-Paxos are common. For instance, the multi-decree version, often called Multi-Paxos [15,27], considers multiple slots (*i.e.*, multiple positioned updates) and decides upon a result for *each* slot, by running a slot-specific instance of an SD-Paxos. Even though it is customary to think of Multi-Paxos as of a series of independent SD-Paxos instances, in reality the implementation features multiple protocol-aware optimisations, exploiting intrinsic dependencies between separate single-decree consensus instances to achieve better throughput. To a great extent, these and other optimisations to the algorithm are pervasive, and verifying a modified version usually requires to devise a new protocol definition and a proof from scratch. New versions are constantly springing (*cf.* Sect. 5 of [27] for a comprehensive survey) widening the gap between the description of the algorithms and their real-world implementations.

We tackle the challenge of *specifying* and *verifying* these distributed algorithms by contributing two verification techniques for consensus protocols.

Our first contribution is a family of composable specifications for Paxos' core subroutines. Our starting point is the deconstruction of SD-Paxos by Boichat *et al.* [2,3], allowing one to consider a distributed consensus instance as a *shared-memory concurrent program*. We introduce novel specifications for Boichat *et al.*'s modules, and let them be non-deterministic. This might seem as an unorthodox design choice, as it *weakens* the specification. To show that our specifications are still *strong enough*, we restore the top-level *deterministic* abstract specification of the consensus, which is convenient for client-side reasoning. The weakness introduced by the non-determinism in the specifications has been impelled by the need to prove that the implementations of Paxos' components *refine* the specifications we have ascribed [9]. We prove the refinements modularly via the Rely/Guarantee reasoning with prophecy variables and explicit linearisation points [11,26]. On the other hand, this weakness becomes a virtue when better understanding the volatile nature of Boichat *et al.*'s abstractions and of the Paxos algorithm, which may lead to newer modifications and optimisations.

Our second contribution is a methodology for verifying composite consensus protocols by reusing the proofs of their constituents, targeting specifically Multi-Paxos. We distill protocol-aware system optimisations into a separate semantic layer and show how to obtain the realistic Multi-Paxos implementation from SD-Paxos by a *series of transformations* to the *network semantics* of the system, as long as these transformations preserve the behaviour observed by clients. We then provide a family of such transformations along with the formal conditions allowing one to compose them in a behaviour-preserving way.

We validate our approach for construction of modularly verified consensus protocols by providing an executable proof-of-concept implementation of Multi-Paxos with a high-level shared memory-like interface, obtained via a series of behaviour-preserving network transformations. The full proofs of lemmas and

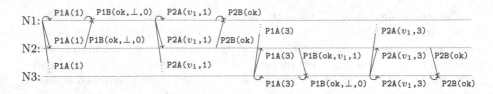

Fig. 1. A run of SD-Paxos.

theorems from our development, as well as some boilerplate definitions, are given in the appendices of the supplementary extended version of this paper.[1]

2   The Single-Decree Paxos Algorithm

We start with explaining SD-Paxos through an intuitive scenario. In SD-Paxos, each node in the system can adopt the roles of *proposer* or *acceptor*, or both. A value is decided when a *quorum* (*i.e.*, a majority of acceptors) accepts the value proposed by some proposer. Now consider a system with three nodes N1, N2 and N3, where N1 and N3 are both proposers and acceptors, and N2 is an acceptor, and assume N1 and N3 propose values v_1 and v_3, respectively.

The algorithm works in two phases. In Phase 1, a proposer polls every acceptor in the system and tries to convince a quorum to promise that they will later accept its value. If the proposer succeeds in Phase 1 then it moves to Phase 2, where it requests the acceptors to fulfil their promises in order to get its value decided. In our example, it would seem in principle possible that N1 and N3 could respectively convince two different quorums—one consisting of N1 and N2, and the other consisting of N2 and N3—to go through both phases and to respectively accept their values. This would happen if the communication between N1 and N3 gets lost and if N2 successively grants the promise and accepts the value of N1, and then does the same with N3. This scenario breaks the safety requirements for consensus because both v_1 and v_3—which can be different—would get decided. However, this cannot happen. Let us explain why.

The way SD-Paxos enforces the safety requirements is by distinguishing each attempt to decide a value with a unique *round*, where the rounds are totally ordered. Each acceptor stores its current round, initially the least one, and only grants a promise to proposers with a round greater or equal than its current round, at which moment the acceptor switches to the proposer's round. Figure 1 depicts a possible run of the algorithm. Assume that rounds are natural numbers, that the acceptors' current rounds are initially 0, and that the nodes N1 and N3 attempt to decide their values with rounds 1 and 3 respectively. In Phase 1, N1 tries to convince a quorum to switch their current round to 1 (messages P1A(1)). The message to N3 gets lost and the quorum consisting of N1 and N2 switches round and promises to only accept values at a round greater or

---

[1] Find the extended version online at https://arxiv.org/abs/1802.05969.

Paxos
Round-Based Consensus
Round-Based Register

```
1  val vP := undef;
2  proposeP(val v0) {
3    ⟨ assume(!(v0 = undef));
4    if (vP = undef) {
5      vP := v0;
6    } return vP; ⟩ }
```

Fig. 2. Deconstruction of SD-Paxos (left) and specification of module *Paxos* (right).

equal than 1. Each acceptor that switches to the proposer's round sends back to the proposer its stored value and the round at which this value was accepted, or an undefined value if the acceptor never accepted any value yet (messages P1B(ok, $\perp$, 0), where $\perp$ denotes a default undefined value). After Phase 1, N1 picks as a candidate value the one accepted at the greatest round from those returned by the acceptors in the quorum, or its proposed value if all acceptors returned an undefined value. In our case, N1 picks its value v_1. In Phase 2, N1 requests the acceptors to accept the candidate value v_1 at round 1 (messages P2A(v_1, 1)). The message to N3 gets lost, and N1 and N2 accept value v_1, which gets decided (messages P2B(ok)).

Now N3 goes through Phase 1 with round 3 (messages P1A(3)). Both N2 and N3 switch to round 3. N2 answers N3 with its stored value v_1 and with the round 1 at which v_1 was accepted (message P1B(ok, v_1, 1)), and N3 answers itself with an undefined value, as it has never accepted any value yet (message P1B(ok, $\perp$, 0)). This way, if some value has been already decided upon, *any* proposer that convinces a quorum to switch to its round would receive the decided value from some of the acceptors in the quorum (recall that two quorums have a non-empty intersection). That is, N3 picks the v_1 returned by N2 as the candidate value, and in Phase 2 it manages that the quorum N2 and N3 accepts v_1 at round 3 (messages P2A(v_1, 3) and P2B(ok)). N3 succeeds in making a new decision, but the decided value remains the same, and, therefore, the safety requirements of a consensus protocol are satisfied.

3 The Faithful Deconstruction of SD-Paxos

We now recall the faithfull deconstruction of SD-Paxos in [2,3], which we take as the reference architecture for the implementations that we aim to verify. We later show how each module of the deconstruction can be verified separately.

The deconstruction is depicted on the left of Fig. 2, which consists of modules *Paxos*, *Round-Based Consensus* and *Round-Based Register*. These modules correspond to the ones in Fig. 4 of [2], with the exception of *Weak Leader Election*. We assume that a correct process that is trusted by every other correct process always exists, and omit the details of the leader election. Leaders take the role of proposers and invoke the interface of *Paxos*. Each module uses the interface provided by the module below it.

```
1   read(int k) {                        18   write(int k, val vW) {
2     int j; val v; int kW; val maxV;    19     int j; set of int Q; msg m;
3     int maxKW; set of int Q; msg m;    20     for (j := 1, j <= n, j++)
4     for (j := 1, j <= n, j++)          21     { send(j, [WR, k, vW]); }
5     { send(j, [RE, k]); }              22     Q := {};
6     maxKW := 0; maxV := undef; Q := {};  23    do { (j, m) := receive();
7     do { (j, m) := receive();          24       switch (m) {
8         switch (m) {                   25         case [ackWR, @k]:
9           case [ackRE, @k, v, kW]:     26           Q := Q ∪ {j};
10            Q := Q ∪ {j};              27         case [nackWR, @k]:
11            if (kW >= maxKW)           28           return false;
12            { maxKW := kW; maxV := v; } 29       } if (|Q| = ⌈(n+1)/2⌉)
13          case [nackRE, @k]:           30         { return true; } }
14            return (false, _);         31    while (true); }
15        } if (|Q| = ⌈(n+1)/2⌉)
16          { return (true, maxV); } }
17    while (true); }
```

Fig. 3. Implementation of *Round-Based Register* (**read** and **write**).

The entry module *Paxos* implements SD-Paxos. Its specification (right of Fig. 2) keeps a variable vP that stores the decided value (initially undefined) and provides the operation **proposeP** that takes a proposed value v0 and returns vP if some value was already decided, or otherwise it returns v0. The code of the operation runs *atomically*, which we emphasise via angle brackets $\langle \ldots \rangle$. We define this specification so it meets the safety requirements of a consensus, therefore, any implementation whose entry point refines this specification will have to meet the same safety requirements.

In this work we present both specifications and implementations in pseudo-code for an imperative WHILE-like language with basic arithmetic and primitive types, where **val** is some user-defined type for the values decided by Paxos, and **undef** is a literal that denotes an undefined value. The pseudo-code is self-explanatory and we restraint ourselves from giving formal semantics to it, which could be done in standard fashion if so wished [30]. At any rate, the pseudo-code is ultimately a vehicle for illustration and we stick to this informal presentation.

The implementation of the modules is depicted in Figs. 3, 4 and 5. We describe the modules following a bottom-up approach, which better fits the purpose of conveying the connection between the deconstruction and SD-Paxos. We start with module *Round-Based Register*, which offers operations **read** and **write** (Fig. 3) and implements the replicated processes that adopt the role of acceptors (Fig. 4). We adapt the wait-free, crash-stop implementation of *Round-Based Register* in Fig. 5 of [2] by adding loops for the explicit reception of each individual message and by counting acknowledgement messages one by one. Processes are identified by integers from 1 to n, where n is the number of processes in the system. Proposers and acceptors exchange read and write requests, and their corresponding acknowledgements and non/acknowledgements. We assume a type **msg** for messages and let the message vocabulary to be as follows.

```
1    process Acceptor(int j) {
2      val v := undef; int r := 0; int w := 0;
3      start() {
4        int i; msg m; int k;
5        do { (i, m) := receive();
6          switch (m) {
7            case [RE, k]:
8              if (k < r) { send(i, [nackRE, k]); }
9              else { ⟨ r := k; send(i, [ackRE, k, v, w]); ⟩ }
10           case [WR, k, vW]:
11             if (k < r) { send(i, [nackWR, k]); }
12             else { ⟨ r := k; w := k; v := vW; send(i, [ackWR, k]); ⟩ }
13         } }
14     while (true); } }
```

Fig. 4. Implementation of *Round-Based Register* (acceptor).

Read requests [RE, k] carry the proposer's round k. Write requests [WR, k, v] carry the proposer's round k and the proposed value v. Read acknowledgements [ackRE, k, v, k'] carry the proposer's round k, the acceptor's value v, and the round k' at which v was accepted. Read non-acknowledgements [nackRE, k] carry the proposer's round k, and so do carry write acknowledgements [ackWR, k] and write non/acknowledgements [nackWR, K].

In the pseudo-code, we use _ for a wildcard that could take any literal value. In the pattern-matching primitives, the literals specify the pattern against which an expression is being matched, and operator @ turns a variable into a literal with the variable's value. Compare the case [ackRE, @k, v, kW]: in Fig. 3, where the value of k specifies the pattern and v and kW get some values assigned, with the case [RE, k]: in Fig. 4, where k gets some value assigned.

We assume the network ensures that messages are neither created, modified, deleted, nor duplicated, and that they are always delivered but with an arbitrarily large transmission delay.[2] Primitive send takes the destination j and the message m, and its effect is to send m from the current process to the process j. Primitive receive takes no arguments, and its effect is to receive at the current process a message m from origin i, after which it delivers the pair (i, m) of identifier and message. We assume that send is non-blocking and that receive blocks and suspends the process until a message is available, in which case the process awakens and resumes execution.

Each acceptor (Fig. 4) keeps a value v, a current round r (called the *read round*), and the round w at which the acceptor's value was last accepted (called the *write round*). Initially, v is **undef** and both r and w are 0.

Phase 1 of SD-Paxos is implemented by operation read on the left of Fig. 3. When a proposer issues a read, the operation requests each acceptor's promise to only accept values at a round greater or equal than k by sending [RE, k]

---

[2] We allow creation and duplication of [RE, k] messages in Sect. 5, where we obtain Multi-Paxos from SD-Paxos by a series of transformations of the network semantics.

```
1   proposeRC(int k, val v0) {          1   proposeP(val v0) {
2     bool res; val v;                   2     int k; bool res; val v;
3     (res, v) := read(k);               3     k := pid();
4     if (res) {                         4     do { (res, v) :=
5       if (v = undef) { v := v0; }      5           proposeRC(k, v0);
6       res := write(k, v);              6       k := k + n;
7       if (res) { return (true, v); } } 7     } while (!res);
8     return (false, _); }               8     return v; }
```

Fig. 5. Implementation of *Round-Based Consensus* (left) and *Paxos* (right)

(lines 4–5). When an acceptor receives a [RE, k] (lines 5–7 of Fig. 4) it acknowledges the promise depending on its read round. If k is strictly less than r then the acceptor has already made a promise to another proposer with greater round and it sends [nackRE, k] back (line 8). Otherwise, the acceptor updates r to k and acknowledges by sending [ackRE, k, v, w] (line 9). When the proposer receives an acknowledgement (lines 8–10 of Fig. 3) it counts acknowledgements up (line 10) and calculates the greatest write round at which the acceptors acknowledging so far accepted a value, and stores this value in maxV (lines 11–12). If a majority of acceptors acknowledged, the operation succeeds and returns (true, maxV) (lines 15–16). Otherwise, if the proposer received some [nackRE, k] the operation fails, returning (false, _) (lines 13–14).

Phase 2 of SD-Paxos is implemented by operation write on the right of Fig. 3. After having collected promises from a majority of acceptors, the proposer picks the candidate value vW and issues a write. The operation requests each acceptor to accept the candidate value by sending [WR, k, vW] (lines 20–21). When an acceptor receives [WR, k, vW] (line 10 of Fig. 4) it accepts the value depending on its read round. If k is strictly less than r, then the acceptor never promised to accept at such round and it sends [nackWR, k] back (line 11). Otherwise, the acceptor fullfils its promise and updates both w and r to k and assigns vW to its value v, and acknowledges by sending [ackWR, k] (line 12). Finally, when the proposer receives an acknowledgement (lines 23–25 of Fig. 3) it counts acknowledgements up (line 26) and checks whether a majority of acceptors acknowledged, in which case vW is decided and the operation succeeds and returns true (lines 29–30). Otherwise, if the proposer received some [nackWR, k] the operation fails and returns false (lines 27–28).[3]

Next, we describe module *Round-Based Consensus* on the left of Fig. 5. The module offers an operation proposeRC that takes a round k and a proposed value v0, and returns a pair (res, v) of Boolean and value, where res informs of the success of the operation and v is the decided value in case res is true. We have taken the implementation from Fig. 6 in [2] but adapted to our pseudo-code conventions. *Round-Based Consensus* carries out Phase 1 and Phase 2 of

---

[3] For the implementation to be correct with our shared-memory-concurrency approach, the update of the data in acceptors must happen atomically with the sending of acknowledgements in lines 9 and 12 of Fig. 4.

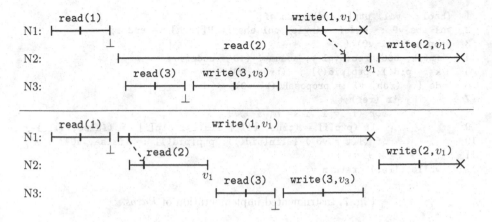

Fig. 6. Two histories in which a failing `write` contaminates some acceptor.

SD-Paxos as explained in Sect. 2. The operation `proposeRC` calls `read` (line 3) and if it succeeds then chooses a candidate value between the proposed value v0 or the value v returned by `read` (line 5). Then, the operation calls `write` with the candidate value and returns `(true, v)` if `write` succeeds, or fails and returns `(false, _)` (line 8) if either the `read` or the `write` fails.

Finally, the entry module *Paxos* on the right of Fig. 5 offers an operation `proposeP` that takes a proposed value v0 and returns the decided value. We assume that the system primitive `pid()` returns the process identifier of the current process. We have come up with this straightforward implementation of operation `proposeP`, which calls `proposeRC` with increasing round until the call succeeds, starting at a round equal to the process identifier `pid()` and increasing it by the number of processes n in each iteration. This guarantees that the round used in each invocation to `proposeRC` is unique.

The Challenge of Verifying the Deconstruction of Paxos. Verifying each module of the deconstruction separately is cumbersome because of the distributed character of the algorithm and the nature of a linearisation proof. A process may not be aware of the information that will flow from itself to other processes, but this future information flow may dictate whether some operation has to be linearised at the present. Figure 6 illustrates this challenge.

Let N1, N2 and N3 adopt both the roles of acceptors and proposers, which propose values v_1, v_2 and v_3 with rounds 1, 2 and 3 respectively. Consider the history on the top of the figure. N2 issues a read with round 2 and gets acknowledgements from all but one acceptors in a quorum. (Let us call this one acceptor A.) None of these acceptors have accepted anything yet and they all return $\perp$ as the last accepted value at round 0. In parallel, N3 issues a read with round 3 (third line in the figure) and gets acknowledgements from a quorum in which A does not occur. This read succeeds as well and returns $(true, undef)$.

```
1   (bool × val) ptp[1..n] := undef;
2   val abs_vP := undef; single bool abs_resP[1..n] := undef;
3   proposeP(val v0) {
4     int k; bool res; val v; assume(!(v0 = undef));
5     k := pid(); ptp[pid()] := (true, v0);
6     do { ⟨ (res, v) := proposeRC(k, v0);
7         if (res) {
8           for (i := 1, i <= n, i++) {
9             if (ptp[i] = (true, v)) { lin(i); ptp[i] := (false, v); } }
10            if (!(v = v0)) { lin(pid()); ptp[pid()] := (false, v0); } } ⟩
11        k := k + n; }
12    while (!res); return v; }
```

Fig. 7. Instrumented implementation of *Paxos*.

Then N3 issues a write with round 3 and value v_3. Again, it gets acknowledgements from a quorum in which A does not occur, and the write succeeds deciding value v_3 and returns **true**. Later on, and in real time order with the write by N3 but in parallel with the read by N2, node N1 issues a write with round 1 and value v_1 (first line in the figure). This write is to fail because the value v_3 was already decided with round 3. However, the write manages to "contaminate" acceptor A with value v_1, which now acknowledges N2 and sends v_1 as its last accepted value at round 1. Now N2 has gotten acknowledgements from a quorum, and since the other acceptors in the quorum returned 0 as the round of their last accepted value, the read will catch value v_1 accepted at round 1, and the operation succeeds and returns (true, v_1). This history linearises by moving N2's read after N1's write, and by respecting the real time order for the rest of the operations. (The linearisation ought to respect the information flow order between N1 and N2 as well, *i.e.*, N1 contaminates A with value v_1, which is read by N2.)

In the figure, a segment ending in an × indicates that the operation fails. The value returned by a successful read operation is depicted below the end of the segment. The linearisation points are depicted with a thick vertical line, and the dashed arrow indicates that two operations are in the information flow order.

The variation of this scenario on the bottom of Fig. 6 is also possible, where N1's write and N2's read happen concurrently, but where N2's read is shifted backwards to happen before in real time order with N3's read and write. Since N1's write happens before N2's read in the information flow order, then N1's write has to inexorably linearise before N3's operations, which are the ones that will "steal" N1's valid round.

These examples give us three important hints for designing the specifications of the modules. First, after a decision is committed it is *not enough* to store only the decided value, since a posterior write may contaminate some acceptor with a value different from the decided one. Second, a read operation *may succeed* with some round even if by that time other operation has already succeeded with a higher round. And third, a write with a valid round *may fail* if its round will be "stolen" by a concurrent operation. The non-deterministic specifications that we introduce next allow one to model execution histories as the ones in Fig. 6.

4   Modularly Verifying SD-Paxos

In this section, we provide non-deterministic specifications for *Round-Based Consensus* and *Round-Based Register* and show that each implementation refines its specification [9]. To do so, we instrument the implementations of all the modules with *linearisation-point* annotations and use Rely/Guarantee reasoning [26].

This time we follow a top-down order and start with the entry module *Paxos*.

Module *Paxos*. In order to prove that the implementation on the right of Fig. 5 refines its specification on the right of Fig. 2, we introduce the instrumented implementation in Fig. 7, which uses the helping mechanism for external linearisation points of [18]. We assume that each proposer invokes proposeP with a unique proposed value. The auxiliary pending thread pool ptp[n] is an array of pairs of Booleans and values of length n, where n is the number of processes in the system. A cell ptp[i] containing a pair (true, v) signals that the process i proposed value v and the invocation proposeP(v) by process i awaits to be linearised. Once this invocation is linearised, the cell ptp[i] is updated to the pair (false, v). A cell ptp[i] containing undef signals that the process i never proposed any value yet. The array abs_resP[n] of Boolean single-assignment variables stores the abstract result of each proposer's invocation. A linearisation-point annotation lin(i) takes a process identifier i and performs atomically the abstract operation invoked by proposer i and assigns its result to abs_resP[i]. The abstract state is modelled by variable abs_vP, which corresponds to variable vP in the specification on the right of Fig. 2. One invocation of proposeP may help linearise other invocations as follows. The linearisation point is together with the invocation to proposeRC (line 6). If proposeRC committed with some value v, the instrumented implementation traverses ptp and linearises all the proposers which were proposing value v (the proposer may linearise itself in this traversal) (lines 8–9). Then, the current proposer linearises itself if its proposed value v0 is different from v (line 10), and the operation returns v (line 12). All the annotations and code in lines 6–10 are executed inside an atomic block, together with the invocation to proposeRC(k, v0).

Theorem 1. *The implementation of Paxos on the right of Fig. 5 linearises with respect to its specification on the right of Fig. 2.*

Module *Round-Based Consensus*. The top of Fig. 8 shows the non-deterministic module's specification. Global variable vRC is the decided value, initially undef. Global variable roundRC is the highest round at which some value was decided, initially 0; a global set of values valsRC (initially empty) contains values that may have been proposed by proposers. The specification is non-deterministic in that local value vD and Boolean b are unspecified, which we model by assigning random values to them. We assume that the current process identifier is $((k-1) \bmod n) + 1$, which is consistent with how rounds are assigned to each process and incremented in the code of proposeP on the right of Fig. 5. If the unspecified value vD is neither in the set valsRC nor equal to v0 then the operation returns (false, _) (line 11). This models that the operation fails

```
1    val vRC := undef; int roundRC := 0; set of val valsRC := {};
2    proposeRC(int k, val v0) {
3      ⟨ val vD := random(); bool b := random();
4        assume(!(v0 = undef)); assume(pid() = ((k - 1) mod n) + 1);
5        if (vD ∈ (valsRC ∪ {v0})) {
6          valsRC := valsRC ∪ {vD};
7          if (b && (k >= roundRC)) { roundRC := k;
8                                     if (vRC = undef) { vRC := vD; }
9                                     return (true, vRC); }
10         else { return (false, _); } }
11       else { return (false, _); } ⟩ }
```

```
1    val abs_vRC := undef; int abs_roundRC := 0;
2    set of val abs_valsRC := {};
3    proposeRC(int k, val v0) {
4      single (bool × val) abs_resRC := undef; bool res; val v;
5      assume(!(v0 = undef)); assume(pid() = ((k - 1) mod n) + 1);
6      ⟨ (res, v) := read(k); if (res = false) { linRC(undef, _); } ⟩
7      if (res) { if (v = undef) { v := v0; }
8               ⟨ res := write(k, v); if (res) { linRC(v, true); }
9                                     else { linRC(v, false); } ⟩
10               if (res) { return (true, v); } }
11     return (false, _); }
```

Fig. 8. Specification (top) and instrumented implementation (bottom) of *Round-Based Consensus*.

without contaminating any acceptor. Otherwise, the operation may contaminate some acceptor and the value vD is added to the set valsRC (line 6). Now, if the unspecified Boolean b is false, then the operation returns (false, _) (lines 7 and 10), which models that the round will be stolen by a posterior operation. Finally, the operation succeeds if k is greater or equal than roundRC (line 7), and roundRC and vRC are updated and the operation returns (true, vRC) (lines 7–9).

In order to prove that the implementation in Fig. 5 linearises with respect to the specification on the top of Fig. 8, we use the instrumented implementation on the bottom of the same figure, where the abstract state is modelled by variables abs_vRC, abs_roundRC and abs_valsRC in lines 1–2, the local single-assignment variable abs_resRC stores the result of the abstract operation, and the linearisation-point annotations linRC(vD, b) take a value and a Boolean parameters and invoke the non-deterministic abstract operation and disambiguate it by assigning the parameters to the unspecified vD and b of the specification. There are two linearisation points together with the invocations of read (line 6) and write (line 8). If read fails, then we linearise forcing the unspecified vD to be undef (line 6), which ensures that the abstract operation fails without adding any value to abs_valsRC nor updating the round abs_roundRC. Otherwise, if write succeeds with value v, then we linearise forcing the unspecified value vD and Boolean b to be v and true respectively (line 8). This ensures that

```
1   read(int k) {                      16   val vRR := undef;
2     ⟨ val vD := random();            17   int roundRR := 0;
3       bool b := random(); val v;     18   set of val valsRR := {undef};
4       assume(vD ∈ valsRR);           19
5       assume(pid() =                 20   write(int k, val vW) {
6         ((k - 1) mod n) + 1);        21     ⟨ bool b := random();
7       if (b) {                       22       assume(!(vW = undef));
8         if (k >= roundRR) {          23       assume(pid() =
9           roundRR := k;              24         ((k - 1) mod n) + 1);
10          if (!(vRR = undef)) {      25       valsRR := valsRR ∪ {vW};
11            v := vRR; }              26       if (b && (k >= roundRR)) {
12          else { v := vD; } }        27         roundRR := k;
13        else { v := vD; }            28         vRR := vW;
14        return (true, v); }          29         return true; }
15      else { return (false, _); } ⟩ } 30      else { return false; } ⟩ }
```

Fig. 9. Specification of *Round-Based Register*.

the abstract operation succeeds and updates the round `abs_roundRC` to k and assigns v to the decided value `abs_vRC`. If `write` fails then we linearise forcing the unspecified vD and b to be v and `false` respectively (line 9). This ensures that the abstract operation fails.

Theorem 2. *The implementation of Round-Based Consensus in Fig. 5 linearises with respect to its specification on the top of Fig. 8.*

Module _Round-Based Register_. Figure 9 shows the module's nondeterministic specification. Global variable vRR represents the decided value, initially undef. Global variable roundRR represents the current round, initially 0, and global set of values valsRR, initially containing undef, stores values that may have been proposed by some proposer. The specification is non-deterministic in that method read has unspecified local Boolean b and local value vD (we assume that vD is valsRR), and method write has unspecified local Boolean b. We assume the current process identifier is $((k - 1) \bmod n) + 1$.

Let us explain the specification of the read operation. The operation can succeed regardless of the proposer's round k, depending on the value of the unspecified Boolean b. If b is true and the proposer's round k is valid (line 8), then the read round is updated to k (line 9) and the operation returns (true, v) (line 14), where v is the read value, which coincides with the decided value if some decision was committed already or with vD otherwise. Now to the specification of operation write. The value vW is always added to the set valsRR (line 25). If the unspecified Boolean b is false (the round will be stolen by a posterior operation) or if the round k is non-valid, then the operation returns false (lines 26 and 30). Otherwise, the current round is updated to k, and the decided value vRR is updated to vW and the operation returns true (lines 27–29).

In order to prove that the implementation in Figs. 3 and 4 linearises with respect to the specification in Fig. 9, we use the instrumented implementation in

Figs. 10 and 11, which uses prophecy variables [1,26] that "guess" whether the execution of the method will reach a particular program location or not. The instrumented implementation also uses external linearisation points. In particular, the code of the acceptors may help to linearise some of the invocations to `read` and `write`, based on the prophecies and on auxiliary variables that count the number of acknowledgements sent by acceptors after each invocation of a `read` or a `write`. The next paragraphs elaborate on our use of prophecy variables and on our helping mechanism.

Variables `abs_vRR`, `abs_roundRR` and `abs_valsRR` in Fig. 10 model the abstract state. They are initially set to `undef`, 0 and the set containing `undef` respectively. Variable `abs_res_r[k]` is an infinite array of single-assignment pairs of Boolean and value that model the abstract results of the invocations to `read`. (Think of an infinite array as a map from integers to some type; we use the array notation for convenience.) Similarly, variable `abs_res_w[k]` is an infinite array of single-assignment Booleans that models the abstract results of the invocations to `write`. All the cells in both arrays are initially `undef` (e.g. the initial maps are empty). Variables `count_r[k]` and `count_w[k]` are infinite arrays of integers that model the number of acknowledgements sent (but not necessarily received yet) from acceptors in response to respectively read or write requests. All cells in both arrays are initially 0. The variable `proph_r[k]` is an infinite array of single-assignment pairs `bool × val`, modelling the prophecy for the invocations of `read`, and variable `proph_w[k]` is an infinite array of single-assignment Booleans modelling the prophecy for the invocations of `write`.

The linearisation-point annotations `linRE(k, vD, b)` for `read` take the proposer's round `k`, a value `vD` and a Boolean `b`, and they invoke the abstract operation and disambiguate it by assigning the parameters to the unspecified `vD` and `b` of the specification on the left of Fig. 9. At the beginning of a `read(k)` (lines 11–14 of Fig. 10), the prophecy `proph_r[k]` is set to (true, v) if the invocation reaches `PL: RE_SUCC` in line 26. The v is defined to coincide with `maxV` at the time when that location is reached. That is, v is the value accepted at the greatest round by the acceptors acknowledging so far, or undefined if no acceptor ever accepted any value. If the operation reaches `PL: RE_FAIL` in line 24 instead, the prophecy is set to $(\text{false}, \_)$. (If the method never returns, the prophecy is left `undef` since it will never linearise.) A successful `read(k)` linearises in the code of the acceptor in Fig. 11, when the $\lceil (n+1)/2 \rceil$th acceptor sends `[ackRE, k, v, w]`, and only if the prophecy is (true, v) and the operation was not linearised before (lines 10–14). We force the unspecified `vD` and `b` to be v and `true` respectively, which ensures that the abstract operation succeeds and returns (true, v). A failing `read(k)` linearises at the `return` in the code of `read` (lines 23–24 of Fig. 10), after the reception of `[nackRE, k]` from one acceptor. We force the unspecified `vD` and `b` to be `undef` and `false` respectively, which ensures that the abstract operation fails.

The linearisation-point annotations `linWR(k, vW, b)` for `write` take the proposer's round `k` and value `vW`, and a Boolean `b`, and they invoke the abstract operation and disambiguate it by assigning the parameter to the unspecified `b`

```
1   val abs_vRR := undef; int abs_roundRR := 0;
2   set of val abs_valsRR := {undef};
3   single val abs_res_r[1..∞] := undef;
4   single val abs_res_w[1..∞] := undef;
5   int count_r[1..∞] := 0; int count_w[1..∞] := 0;
6   single (bool × val) proph_r[1..∞] := undef;
7   single bool proph_w[i..∞] := undef;
8   read(int k) {
9     int j; val v; set of int Q; int maxKW; val maxV; msg m;
10    assume(pid() = ((k - 1) mod n) + 1);
11    ⟨ if (operation reaches PL: RE_SUCC and define v = maxV at that time) {
12        proph_r[k] := (true, v); }
13      else { if (operation reaches PL: RE_FAIL) {
14              proph_r[k] := (false, _); } } ⟩
15    for (j := 1, j <= n, j++) { send(j, [RE, k]); }
16    maxKW := 0; maxV := undef; Q := {};
17    do { (j, m) := receive();
18        switch (m) {
19          case [ackRE, @k, v, kW]:
20            Q := Q ∪ {j};
21            if (kW >= maxKW) { maxKW := kW; maxV := v; }
22          case [nackRE, @k]:
23            ⟨ linRE(k, undef, false); proph_r[k] := undef;
24              return (false, _); ⟩ // PL: RE_FAIL
25        } if (|Q| = ⌈(n+1)/2⌉) {
26              return (true, maxV); } } // PL: RE_SUCC
27    while (true); }
28  write(int k, val vW) {
29    int j; set of int Q; msg m;
30    assume(!(vW = undef)); assume(pid() = ((k - 1) mod n) + 1);
31    ⟨ if (operation reaches PL: WR_SUCC) { proph_w[k] := true; }
32      else { if (operation reaches PL: WR_FAIL) {
33              proph_w[k] := false; } } ⟩
34    for (j := 1, j <= n, j++) { send(j, [WR, k, vW]); }
35    Q := {};
36    do { (j, m) := receive();
37        switch (m) {
38          case [ackWR, @k]:
39            Q := Q ∪ {j};
40          case [nackWR, @k]:
41            ⟨ if (count_w[k] = 0) {
42                linWR(k, vW, false); proph_w[k] := undef; }
43              return false; ⟩ // PL: WR_FAIL
44        } if (|Q| = ⌈(n+1)/2⌉) {
45              return true; } } // PL: WR_SUCC
46    while (true); }
```

Fig. 10. Instrumented implementation of **read** and **write** methods.

```
1   process Acceptor(int j) {
2     val v := undef; int r := 0; int w := 0;
3     start() {
4       int i; msg m; int k;
5       do { (i, m) := receive();
6           switch (m) {
7             case [RE, k]:
8               if (k < r) { send(i, [nackRE, k]); }
9               else { ⟨ r := k;
10                    if (abs_res_r[k] = undef) {
11                       if (proph_r[k] = (true, v)) {
12                          if (count_r[k] = ⌈(n+1)/2⌉ - 1) {
13                             linRE(k, v, true); } } }
14                    count_r[k]++; send(i, [ackRE, k, v, w]); ⟩ }
15            case [WR, k, vW]:
16               if (k < r) { send(j, i, [nackWR, k]); }
17               else { ⟨ r := k; w := k; v := vW;
18                    if (abs_res_w[k] = undef) {
19                       if (!(proph_w[k] = undef)) {
20                          if (proph_w[k]) {
21                             if (count_w[k] = ⌈(n+1)/2⌉ - 1) {
22                                linWR(k, vW, true); } }
23                          else { linWR(k, vW, false); } } }
24                    count_w[k]++; send(j, i, [ackWR, k]); ⟩ }
25        } }
26    while (true); } }
```

Fig. 11. Instrumented implementation of acceptor processes.

of the specification on the right of Fig. 9. At the beginning of a write(k, vW) (lines 31–33 of Fig. 10), the prophecy proph_r[k] is set to true if the invocation reaches PL: WR_SUCC in line 45, or to false if it reaches PL: WR_FAIL in line 43 (or it is left undef if the method never returns). A successfully write(k, vW) linearises in the code of the acceptor in Fig. 11, when the $\lceil(n+1)/2\rceil$th acceptor sends [ackWR, k], and only if the prophecy is true and the operation was not linearised before (lines 17–24). We force the unspecified b to be true, which ensures that the abstract operation succeeds deciding value vW and updates roundRR to k. A failing write(k, vW) may linearise either at the return in its own code (lines 41–43 of Fig. 10) if the proposer received one [nackWR, k] and no acceptor sent any [ackWR, k] yet, or at the code of the acceptor, when the first acceptor sends [ackWR, k], and only if the prophecy is false and the operation was not linearised before. In both cases, we force the unspecified b to be false, which ensures that the abstract operation fails.

Theorem 3. *The implementation of Round-Based Register in Figs. 10 and 11 linearises with respect to its specification in Fig. 9.*

5   Multi-Paxos via Network Transformations

We now turn to more complicated distributed protocols that build upon the idea of Paxos consensus. Our ultimate goal is to reuse the verification result from the Sects. 3 and 4, as well as the high-level round-based register interface. In this section, we will demonstrate how to reason about an implementation of Multi-Paxos as of an array of *independent* instances of the *Paxos* module defined previously, despite the subtle dependencies between its sub-components, as present in Multi-Paxos's "canonical" implementations [5,15,27]. While an abstraction of Multi-Paxos to an array of independent shared "single-shot" registers is almost folklore, what appears to be inherently difficult is to verify a Multi-Paxos-based consensus (*wrt.* to the array-based abstraction) by means of *reusing* the proof of a SD-Paxos. All proofs of Multi-Paxos we are aware of are, thus, *non-modular* with respect to underlying SD-Paxos instances [5,22,24], *i.e.*, they require one to redesign the invariants of the *entire* consensus protocol.

This proof modularity challenge stems from the optimised nature of a classical Multi-Paxos protocol, as well as its real-world implementations [6]. In this part of our work is to distil such protocol-aware optimisations into a separate *network semantics layer*, and show that each of them refines the semantics of a Cartesian product-based view, *i.e.*, exhibits the very same client-observable behaviours. To do so, we will establishing the refinement between the optimised implementations of Multi-Paxos and a simple Cartesian product abstraction, which will allow to extend the register-based abstraction, explored before in this paper, to what is considered to be a canonical amortised Multi-Paxos implementation.

5.1   Abstract Distributed Protocols

We start by presenting the formal definitions of encoding distributed protocols (including Paxos), their message vocabularies, protocol-based network semantics, and the notion of an observable behaviours.

Protocols and Messages. Figure 12 provides basic definitions of the distributed protocols and their components. Each protocol p is a tuple $\langle \Delta, \mathcal{M}, \mathcal{S}_{int}, \mathcal{S}_{rcv}, \mathcal{S}_{snd} \rangle$. Δ is a set of local states, which can be assigned to each of the participating nodes, also determining the node's role via an additional tag,[4] if necessary (*e.g.*, an acceptor and a proposer states in Paxos are

Protocols	$\mathcal{P} \ni p \triangleq \langle \Delta, \mathcal{M}, \mathcal{S} \rangle$
Configurations	$\Sigma \ni \sigma \triangleq \text{Nodes} \rightharpoonup \Delta$
Internal steps	$\mathcal{S}_{int} \in \Delta \times \Delta$
Receive-steps	$\mathcal{S}_{rcv} \in \Delta \times \mathcal{M} \times \Delta$
Send-steps	$\mathcal{S}_{snd} \in \Delta \times \Delta \times \wp(\mathcal{M})$

Fig. 12. States and transitions.

different). $\mathcal{M}$ is a "message vocabulary", determining the set of messages that can be used for communication between the nodes.

---

[4] We leave out implicit the consistency laws for the state, that are protocol-specific.

StepInt
$$n \in \mathsf{dom}(\sigma) \qquad \delta = \sigma(n)$$
$$\langle \delta, \delta' \rangle \in p.\mathcal{S}_{\mathrm{int}} \qquad \sigma' = \sigma[n \mapsto \delta']$$
$$\overline{\langle \sigma, M \rangle \xRightarrow[\mathrm{int}]{p} \langle \sigma', M \rangle}$$

StepSend
$$n \in \mathsf{dom}(\sigma) \qquad \delta = \sigma(n) \qquad \langle \delta, \delta', \mathsf{ms} \rangle \in p.\mathcal{S}_{\mathrm{snd}}$$
$$\sigma' = \sigma[n \mapsto \delta'] \qquad M' = M \cup \mathsf{ms}$$
$$\overline{\langle \sigma, M \rangle \xRightarrow[\mathrm{snd}]{p} \langle \sigma', M' \rangle}$$

StepReceive
$$m \in M \qquad m.\mathit{active} \qquad m.\mathit{to} \in \mathsf{dom}(\sigma) \qquad \delta = \sigma(m.\mathit{to}) \qquad \langle \delta, m, \delta' \rangle \in p.\mathcal{S}_{\mathrm{rcv}}$$
$$m' = m[\mathit{active} \mapsto \mathsf{False}] \qquad \sigma' = \sigma[n \mapsto \delta'] \qquad M' = M \setminus \{m\} \cup \{m'\}$$
$$\overline{\langle \sigma, M \rangle \xRightarrow[\mathrm{rcv}]{p} \langle \sigma', M' \rangle}$$

Fig. 13. Transition rules of the simple protocol-aware network semantics

Messages can be thought of as JavaScript-like dictionaries, pairing unique fields (isomorphic to strings) with their values. For the sake of a uniform treatment, we assume that each message $m \in \mathcal{M}$ has at least two fields, *from* and *to* that point to the source and the destination node of a message, correspondingly. In addition to that, for simplicity we will assume that each message carries a Boolean field *active*, which is set to True when the message is sent and is set to False when the message is received by its destination node. This flag is required to keep history information about messages sent in the past, which is customary in frameworks for reasoning about distributed protocols [10,23,28]. We assume that a "message soup" M is a multiset of messages (*i.e.* a set with zero or more copies of each message) and we consider that each copy of the same message in the multiset has its own "identity", and we write $m \neq m'$ to represent that m and m' are not the same copy of a particular message.

Finally, $\mathcal{S}_{\{\mathrm{int},\mathrm{rcv},\mathrm{snd}\}}$ are step-relations that correspond to the internal changes in the local state of a node ($\mathcal{S}_{\mathrm{int}}$), as well as changes associated with sending ($\mathcal{S}_{\mathrm{snd}}$) and receiving ($\mathcal{S}_{\mathrm{rcv}}$) messages by a node, as allowed by the protocol. Specifically, $\mathcal{S}_{\mathrm{int}}$ relates a local node state before and after the allowed internal change; $\mathcal{S}_{\mathrm{rcv}}$ relates the initial state and an incoming message $m \in \mathcal{M}$ with the resulting state; $\mathcal{S}_{\mathrm{snd}}$ relates the internal state, the output state and the set of atomically sent messages. For simplicity we will assume that $\mathsf{id} \subseteq \mathcal{S}_{\mathrm{int}}$.

In addition, we consider $\Delta_0 \subseteq \Delta$—the set of the allowed *initial* states, in which the system can be present at the very beginning of its execution. The global state of the network $\sigma \in \Sigma$ is a map from node identifiers ($n \in \mathsf{Nodes}$) to local states from the set of states Δ, defined by the protocol.

Simple Network Semantics. The simple initial operational semantics of the network ($\xRightarrow{p} \subseteq (\Sigma \times \wp(\mathcal{M})) \times (\Sigma \times \wp(\mathcal{M}))$) is parametrised by a protocol p and relates the initial *configuration* (*i.e.*, the global state and the set of messages) with the resulting configuration. It is defined via as a reflexive closure of the union of three relations $\xRightarrow[\mathrm{int}]{p} \cup \xRightarrow[\mathrm{rcv}]{p} \cup \xRightarrow[\mathrm{snd}]{p}$, their rules are given in Fig. 13.

The rule STEPINT corresponds to a node n picked non-deterministically from the domain of a global state σ, executing an internal transition, thus changing its local state from δ to δ'. The rule STEPRECEIVE non-deterministically picks a m message from a message soup $M \subseteq \mathcal{M}$, changes the state using the protocol's receive-step relation $p.\mathcal{S}_{\text{rcv}}$ at the corresponding host node to, and updates its local state accordingly in the common mapping ($\sigma[to \mapsto \delta']$). Finally, the rule STEPSEND, non-deterministically picks a node n, executes a send-step, which results in updating its local state emission of a set of messages ms, which is added to the resulting soup. In order to "bootstrap" the execution, the initial states from the set $\Delta_0 \subseteq \Delta$ are assigned to the nodes.

We next define the observable protocol behaviours *wrt.* the simple network semantics as the prefix-closed set of all system's configuration traces.

Definition 1. (Protocol behaviours)

$$\mathcal{B}_p = \bigcup_{m \in \mathbb{N}} \left\{ \langle \langle \sigma_0, M_0 \rangle, \ldots, \langle \sigma_m, M_m \rangle \rangle \;\middle|\; \begin{array}{c} \exists \delta_0^{n \in N} \in \Delta_0, \, \sigma_0 = \biguplus_{n \in N} [n \mapsto \delta_0^n] \wedge \\ \langle \sigma_0, M_0 \rangle \xRightarrow{p} \ldots \xRightarrow{p} \langle \sigma_m, M_m \rangle \end{array} \right\}$$

That is, the set of behaviours captures all possible configurations of initial states for a fixed set of nodes $N \subseteq \mathsf{Nodes}$. In this case, the set of nodes N is an implicit parameter of the definition, which we fix in the remainder of this section.

Example 1 (Encoding SD-Paxos). An abstract distributed protocol for SD-Paxos can be extracted from the pseudo-code of Sect. 3 by providing a suitable small-step operational semantics à la Winskel [30]. We restrain ourselves from giving such formal semantics, but in Appendix D of the extended version of the paper we outline how the distributed protocol would be obtained from the given operational semantics and from the code in Figs. 3, 4 and 5.

5.2 Out-of-Thin-Air Semantics

We now introduce an intermediate version of a simple protocol-aware semantics that generates messages "out of thin air" according to a certain predicate $\mathcal{P} \subseteq \Delta \times \mathcal{M}$, which determines whether the network generates a certain message without exercising the corresponding send-transition. The rule is as follows:

$$\frac{\text{OTASEND}}{n \in \mathsf{dom}(\sigma) \qquad \delta = \sigma(n) \qquad \mathcal{P}(\delta, m) \qquad M' = M \cup \{m\}}{\langle \sigma, M \rangle \xRightarrow[\text{ota}]{p, \mathcal{P}} \langle \sigma, M' \rangle}$$

That is, a random message m can be sent at any moment in the semantics described by $\xRightarrow{p} \cup \xRightarrow[\text{ota}]{p, \mathcal{P}}$, given that the node n, "on behalf of which" the message is sent is in a state δ, such that $\mathcal{P}(\delta, m)$ holds.

Example 2. In the context of Single-Decree Paxos, we can define $\mathcal{P}$ as follows:

$$\mathcal{P}(\delta, m) \triangleq m.content = [\mathtt{RE}, k] \wedge \delta.\mathtt{pid} = n \wedge \delta.\mathtt{role} = Proposer \wedge k \leq \delta.\mathtt{kP}$$

In other words, if a node n is a *Proposer* currently operating with a round $\delta.\mathtt{kP}$, the network semantics can always send another request "on its behalf", thus generating the message "out-of-thin-air". Importantly, the last conjunct in the definition of $\mathcal{P}$ is in terms of $\leq$, rather than equality. This means that the predicate is intentionally loose, allowing for sending even "stale" messages, with expired rounds that are smaller than what n currently holds (no harm in that!).

By definition of single-decree Paxos protocol, the following lemma holds:

Lemma 1 (OTA refinement). $\mathcal{B}_{\xRightarrow{p}\cup\xRightarrow[ota]{p,\mathcal{P}}} \subseteq \mathcal{B}_p$, *where p is an instance of the module Paxos, as defined in Sect. 3 and in Example 1.*

5.3 Slot-Replicating Network Semantics

With the basic definitions at hand, we now proceed to describing alternative network behaviours that make use of a specific protocol $p = \langle \Delta, \mathcal{M}, \mathcal{S}_{int}, \mathcal{S}_{rcv}, \mathcal{S}_{snd} \rangle$, which we will consider to be fixed for the remainder of this section, so we will be at times referring to its components (*e.g.*, $\mathcal{S}_{int}$, $\mathcal{S}_{rcv}$, *etc.*) without a qualifier.

SRStepInt
$$\frac{i \in I \qquad n \in \mathsf{dom}(\sigma) \\ \delta = \sigma(n)[i] \qquad \langle \delta, \delta' \rangle \in p.\mathcal{S}_{int} \\ \sigma' = \sigma[n[i] \mapsto \delta']}{\langle \sigma, M \rangle \xRightarrow[int]{\times} \langle \sigma', M \rangle}$$

SRStepSend
$$\frac{i \in I \qquad n \in \mathsf{dom}(\sigma) \\ \delta = \sigma(n)[i] \qquad \langle \delta, \delta', \mathsf{ms} \rangle \in p.\mathcal{S}_{snd} \\ \sigma' = \sigma[n[i] \mapsto \delta'] \qquad M' = M \cup \mathsf{ms}[slot \mapsto i]}{\langle \sigma, M \rangle \xRightarrow[snd]{\times} \langle \sigma', M' \rangle}$$

SRStepReceive
$$\frac{m \in M \quad m.active \quad m.to \in \mathsf{dom}(\sigma) \quad \delta = \sigma(m.to)[m.slot] \quad \langle \delta, m, \delta' \rangle \in p.\mathcal{S}_{rcv} \\ m' = m[active \mapsto \mathsf{False}] \qquad \sigma' = \sigma(n)[m.slot \mapsto \delta'] \qquad M' = M \setminus \{m\} \cup \{m'\}}{\langle \sigma, M \rangle \xRightarrow[rcv]{\times} \langle \sigma', M' \rangle}$$

Fig. 14. Transition rules of the slot-replicating network semantics.

Figure 14 describes a semantics of a *slot-replicating* (SR) network that exercises multiple copies of the *same* protocol instance p_i for $i \in I$, some, possibly infinite, set of indices, to which we will be also referring as *slots*. Multiple copies of the protocol are incorporated by enhancing the messages from p's vocabulary $\mathcal{M}$ with the corresponding indices, and implementing the on-site dispatch of the indexed messages to corresponding protocol instances at each node. The local protocol state of each node is, thus, no longer a single element being updated, but rather an *array*, mapping $i \in I$ into δ_i—the corresponding local state component. The small-step relation for SR semantics is denoted by $\overset{x}{\Rightarrow}$. The rule SRSTEPINT is similar to STEPINT of the simple semantics, with the difference that it picks not only a node but also an index i, thus referring to a specific component $\sigma(n)[i]$ as δ and updating it correspondingly $(\sigma(n)[i] \mapsto \delta')$. For the remaining transitions, we postulate that the messages from p's vocabulary $p.\mathcal{M}$ are enhanced to have a dedicated field *slot*, which indicates a protocol copy at a node, to which the message is directed. The receive-rule SRSTEPRECEIVE is similar to STEPRECEIVE but takes into the account the value of $m.slot$ in the received message m, thus redirecting it to the corresponding protocol instance and updating the local state appropriately. Finally, the rule SRSTEPSEND can be now executed for any slot $i \in I$, reusing most of the logic of the initial protocol and otherwise mimicking its simple network semantic counterpart STEPSEND.

Importantly, in this semantics, for two different slots i, j, such that $i \neq j$, the corresponding "projections" of the state behave *independently* from each other. Therefore, transitions and messages in the protocol instances indexed by i at different nodes *do not interfere* with those indexed by j. This observation can be stated formally. In order to do so we first defined the behaviours of slot-replicating networks and their projections as follows:

Definition 2 (Slot-replicating protocol behaviours).

$$\mathcal{B}_{\times} = \bigcup_{m \in \mathbb{N}} \left\{ \langle\langle\sigma_0, M_0\rangle, \ldots, \langle\sigma_m, M_m\rangle\rangle \;\middle|\; \begin{array}{l} \exists \delta_0^{n \in N} \in \Delta_0, \\ \sigma_0 = \biguplus_{n \in N}[n \mapsto \{i \mapsto \delta_0^n \mid i \in I\}] \wedge \\ \langle\sigma_0, M_0\rangle \overset{p}{\Rightarrow} \ldots \overset{p}{\Rightarrow} \langle\sigma_m, M_m\rangle \end{array} \right\}$$

That is, the slot-replicated behaviours are merely behaviours with respect to networks, whose nodes hold *multiple instances* of the same protocol, indexed by slots $i \in I$. For a slot $i \in I$, we define *projection* $\mathcal{B}_{\times}|_i$ as a set of global state traces, where each node's local states is restricted only to its ith component. The following simulation lemma holds naturally, connecting the state-replicating network semantics and simple network semantics.

Lemma 2 (Slot-replicating simulation).   *For all $I, i \in I$, $\mathcal{B}_{\times}|_i = \mathcal{B}_p$.*

Example 3 (Slot-replicating semantics and Paxos). Given our representation of Paxos using roles (acceptors/proposers) encoded via the corresponding parts of the local state δ, we can construct a "naïve" version of Multi-Paxos by using the SR semantics for the protocol. In such, every slot will correspond to a SD-Paxos instance, not interacting with any other slots. From the practical perspective, such an implementation is rather non-optimal, as it does not exploit dependencies between rounds accepted at different slots.

5.4 Widening Network Semantics

We next consider a version of the SR semantics, extended with a new rule for handling received messages. In the new semantics, dubbed *widening*, a node, upon receiving a message $m \in T$, where $T \subseteq p.\mathcal{M}$, for a slot i, *replicates* it for all slots from the index set I, for the very same node. The new rule is as follows:

WStepReceiveT

$$\frac{\begin{array}{llll} m \in M & m.active & m.to \in \mathsf{dom}(\sigma) & \delta = \sigma(m.to)[m.slot] \\ \langle \delta, m, \delta' \rangle \in p.\mathcal{S}_{rcv} & m' = m[active \mapsto \mathsf{False}] & \sigma' = \sigma(n)[m.slot \mapsto \delta'] \\ \mathsf{ms} = \text{if } (m \in T) \text{ then } \{m' \mid m' = m[slot \mapsto j], j \in I\} \text{ else } \emptyset \end{array}}{\langle \sigma, M \rangle \xRightarrow[rcv]{\nabla} \langle \sigma', (M \setminus \{m\}) \cup \{m'\} \cup \mathsf{ms} \rangle}$$

At first, this semantics seems rather unreasonable: it might create more messages than the system can "consume". However, it is possible to prove that, under certain conditions on the protocol p, the set of behaviours observed under this semantics (*i.e.*, with SRStepReceive replaced by WStepReceiveT) is *not larger* than $\mathcal{B}_\times$ as given by Definition 2. To state this formally we first relate the set of "triggering" messages T from WStepReceiveT to a specific predicate $\mathcal{P}$.

Definition 3 (OTA-compliant message sets). The set of messages $T \subseteq p.\mathcal{M}$ is OTA-compliant with the predicate $\mathcal{P}$ iff for any $b \in \mathcal{B}_p$ and $\langle \sigma, M \rangle \in b$, if $m \in M$, then $\mathcal{P}(\sigma(m.\mathtt{from}), m)$.

In other words, the protocol p is relaxed enough to "justify" the presence of m in the soup at *any* execution, by providing the predicate $\mathcal{P}$, relating the message to the corresponding sender's state. Next, we use this definition to slot-replicating and widening semantics via the following definition.

Definition 4 ($\mathcal{P}$-monotone protocols). A protocol p is $\mathcal{P}$-monotone iff for any, $b \in \mathcal{B}_\times$, $\langle \sigma, M \rangle \in b$, m, $i = m.slot$, and $j \neq i$, if $\mathcal{P}(\sigma(m.\mathtt{from})[i], \natural m)$ then we have that $\mathcal{P}(\sigma(m.\mathtt{from})[j], \natural m)$, where $\natural m$ "removes" the *slot* field from m.

Less formally, Definition 4 ensures that in a slot-replicated product $\times$ of a protocol p, different components cannot perform "out of sync" *wrt.* $\mathcal{P}$. Specifically, if a node in ith projection is related to a certain message $\natural m$ via $\mathcal{P}$, then any other projection j of the same node will be $\mathcal{P}$-related to this message, as well.

Example 4. This is a "non-example". A version of slot-replicated SD-Paxos, where we allow for arbitrary increments of the round *per-slot* at a same proposer node (*i.e.*, out of sync), would not be monotone *wrt.* $\mathcal{P}$ from Example 2. In contrast, a slot-replicated product of SD-Paxos instances with fixed rounds is monotone *wrt.* the same $\mathcal{P}$.

Lemma 3. *If T from* WStepReceiveT *is OTA-compliant with predicate $\mathcal{P}$, such that $\mathcal{B}_{\xRightarrow{p}\cup\xRightarrow[ota]{p,\mathcal{P}}} \subseteq \mathcal{B}_{\xRightarrow{p}}$ and p is $\mathcal{P}$-monotone, then $\mathcal{B}_{\xRightarrow{\nabla}} \subseteq \mathcal{B}_{\xRightarrow{\times}}$.*

Example 5 (Widening semantics and Paxos). The SD-Paxos instance as described in Sect. 3 satisfies the refinement condition from Lemma 3. By taking $T = \{m \mid m = \{content = [\mathtt{RE}, \mathtt{k}]; \ldots\}\}$ and using Lemma 3, we obtain the refinement between widened semantics and SR semantics of Paxos.

5.5   Optimised Widening Semantics

Our next step towards a realistic implementation of Multi-Paxos out of SD-Paxos instances is enabled by an observation that in the widening semantics, the replicated messages are *always* targeting the same node, to which the initial message $m \in T$ was addressed. This means that we can optimise the receive-step, making it possible to execute multiple receive-transitions of the core protocol in batch. The following rule OWSTEPRECEIVET captures this intuition formally:

$$\frac{\text{OWStepReceiveT}}{m \in M \qquad m.active \qquad m.to \in \text{dom}(\sigma) \qquad \langle \sigma', \text{ms} \rangle = \text{receiveAndAct}(\sigma, n, m)}{\langle \sigma, M \rangle \xrightarrow[\text{rcv}]{\nabla^*} \langle \sigma', M \setminus \{m\} \cup \{m[active \mapsto \text{False}]\} \cup \text{ms} \rangle}$$

where $\text{receiveAndAct}(\sigma, n, m) \triangleq \langle \sigma', \text{ms} \rangle$, such that $\text{ms} = \bigcup_j \{m[slot \mapsto j] \mid m \in \text{ms}_j\}$, $\forall j \in I, \delta = \sigma(m.to)[j] \wedge \langle \delta_j, \natural m, \delta_j^1 \rangle \in p.\mathcal{S}_{\text{rcv}} \wedge \langle \delta_j^1, \delta_j^2 \rangle \in p.\mathcal{S}_{\text{int}}^* \wedge \langle \delta_j^2, \delta_j^3, \text{ms}_j \rangle \in p.\mathcal{S}_{\text{snd}}$, $\forall j \in I, \sigma'(m.to)[j] = \delta_j^3$.

In essence, the rule OWSTEPRECEIVET blends several steps of the widening semantics together for a single message: (a) it first receives the message and replicates it for all slots at a destination node; (b) performs receive-steps for the message's replicas at each slot; (c) takes a number of internal steps, allowed by the protocol's $\mathcal{S}_{\text{int}}$; and (d) takes a send-transition, eventually sending all emitted message, instrumented with the corresponding slots.

Example 6. Continuing Example 5, with the same parameters, the optimising semantics will execute the transitions of an acceptor, *for all slots*, triggered by receiving a single [RE, k] message for a particular slot, sending back *all* the results for all the slots, which might either agree to accept the value or reject it.

The following lemma relates the optimising and the widening semantics.

Lemma 4 (Refinement for OW semantics). *For any $b \in \mathcal{B}_{\xRightarrow{\nabla^*}}$ there exists $b' \in \mathcal{B}_{\xRightarrow{\nabla}}$, such that b can be obtained from b' by replacing sequences of configurations $[\langle \sigma_k, M_k \rangle, \ldots, \langle \sigma_{k+m}, M_{k+m} \rangle]$ that have just a single node n, whose local state is affected in $\sigma_k, \ldots, \sigma_{k+m}$, by $[\langle \sigma_k, M_k \rangle, \langle \sigma_{k+m}, M_{k+m} \rangle]$.*

That is, behaviours in the optimised semantics are the same as in the widening semantics, modulo some sequences of locally taken steps that are being "compressed" to just the initial and the final configurations.

5.6   Bunching Semantics

As the last step towards Multi-Paxos, we introduce the final network semantics that optimises executions according to $\xRightarrow{\nabla^*}$ described in previous section even further by making a simple addition to the message vocabulary of a slot-replicated SD-Paxos—*bunched messages*. A bunched message simply packages

BStepRecvB

$$\frac{\begin{array}{c} m \in M \quad m.active \quad m.to \in \mathsf{dom}(\sigma) \\ \langle \sigma', \mathsf{ms} \rangle = receiveAndAct(\sigma, n, m) \\ M' = M \setminus \{m\} \cup \{m[active \mapsto \mathsf{False}]\} \\ m' = bunch(\mathsf{ms}, m.to, m.from) \end{array}}{\langle \sigma, M \rangle \xRightarrow[rcv]{B} \langle \sigma', M' \cup \{m'\} \rangle}$$

BStepRecvU

$$\frac{m \in M \quad m.active \quad m.to \in \mathsf{dom}(\sigma) \quad m.msgs = \mathsf{ms} \quad M' = M \setminus \{m\} \cup \mathsf{ms}}{\langle \sigma, M \rangle \xRightarrow[rcv]{B} \langle \sigma, M' \rangle}$$

where $bunch(\mathsf{ms}, n_1, n_2) = \{msgs = \mathsf{ms}; from = n_1; to = n_2; active = \mathsf{True}\}$.

Fig. 15. Added rules of the Bunching Semantics

together several messages, obtained typically as a result of a "compressed" execution via the optimised semantics from Sect. 5.5. We define two new rules for packaging and "unpackaging" certain messages in Fig. 15. The two new rules can be added to enhance either of the versions of the slot-replicating semantics shown before. In essence, the only effect they have is to combine the messages resulting in the execution of the corresponding steps of an optimised widening (via BStepRecvB), and to unpackage the messages ms from a bunching message, adding them back to the soup (BStepRecvU). The following natural refinement result holds:

Lemma 5. *For any $b \in \mathcal{B}_{\xRightarrow{B}}$ there exists $b' \in \mathcal{B}_{\xRightarrow{\nabla^*}}$, such that b' can be obtained from b by replacing all bunched messages in b by their msgs-component.*

The rule BStepRecvU enables effective local caching of the bunched messages, so they are processed *on demand* on the recipient side (*i.e.*, by the per-slot proposers), allowing the implementation to *skip* an entire round of Phase 1.

$$
\begin{array}{ccccc}
(\xRightarrow{B}) & & (\xRightarrow[ota]{p}) & \text{via Lm 1 refines} & (\xRightarrow{p}) \\
\text{via Lm 5 refines} & & \text{sim. via Lm 2} & & \text{sim. via Lm 2} \\
(\xRightarrow{\nabla^*}) & \text{via Lm 4 refines} & (\xRightarrow{\nabla}) & \text{via Lm 3 refines} & (\xRightarrow{x})
\end{array}
$$

Fig. 16. Refinement between different network semantics.

```
1  proposeM(val^ v, val v0) {          5  val vM[1..∞]  := undef;
2    ⟨ assume(!(v0 = undef));          6  getR(int s) { return &(vM[s]); }
3     if (*v = undef) { *v := v0; }    7  proposeM(getR(1), v);
4     return *v; ⟩ }                    8  proposeM(getR(2), v);
```

Fig. 17. Specification of *Multi-Paxos* and interaction via a *register provider*.

5.7   The Big Picture

What exactly have we achieved by introducing the described above family of semantics? As illustrated in Fig. 16, all behaviours of the leftmost-topmost, bunching semantics, which corresponds precisely to an implementation of Multi-Paxos with an "amortised" Phase 1, can be transitively related to the corresponding behaviours in the rightmost, vanilla slot-replicated version of a simple semantics (via the correspondence from Lemma 1) by constructing the corresponding refinement mappings [1], delivered by the proofs of Lemmas 3–5.

From the perspective of Rely/Guarantee reasoning, which was employed in Sect. 4, the refinement result from Fig. 16 justifies the replacement of a semantics on the right of the diagram by one to the left of it, as all program-level assertions will remain substantiated by the corresponding system configurations, as long as they are *stable* (*i.e.*, resilient *wrt.* transitions taken by nodes different from the one being verified), which they are in our case.

6   Putting It All Together

We culminate our story of faithfully deconstructing and abstracting Paxos via a round-based register, as well as recasting Multi-Paxos via a series of network transformations, by showing how to *implement* the register-based abstraction from Sect. 3 in tandem with the network semantics from Sect. 5 in order to deliver provably correct, yet efficient, implementation of Multi-Paxos.

The crux of the composition of the two results—a register-based abstraction of SD-Paxos and a family of semantics-preserving network transformations—is a convenient interface for the end client, so she could interact with a consensus instance via the `proposeM` method in lines 1–4 of Fig. 17, no matter with which particular slot of a Multi-Paxos implementation she is interacting. To do so, we propose to introduce a *register provider*—a service that would give a client a "reference" to the consensus object to interact with. Lines 6–7 of Fig. 17 illustrate the interaction with the service provider, where the client requests two specific slots, 1 and 2, of Multi-Paxos by invoking `getR` and providing a slot parameter. In both cases the client proposes the very same value v in the two instances that run the same machinery. (Notice that, except for the reference to the consensus object, `proposeM` is identical to the `proposeP` on the right of Fig. 2, which we have verified *wrt.* linearisability in Sect. 3.)

The implementation of Multi-Paxos that we have in mind resembles the one in Figs. 3, 4 and 5 of Sect. 3, but where all the global data is provided by the register provider and passed by reference. What differs in this implementation with respect to the one in Sect. 3 and is hidden from the client is the semantics of the network layer used by the bottom layer (*cf.* left part of Fig. 2) of the register-based implementation. The Multi-Paxos instances run (without changing the register's code) over this network layer, which "overloads" the meaning of the `send/receive` primitives from Figs. 3 and 4 to follow the bunching network semantics, described in Sect. 5.6.

Theorem 4. *The implementation of Multi-Paxos that uses a register provider and bunching network semantics refines the specification in Fig. 17.*

We implemented the register/network semantics in a proof-of-concept prototype written in Scala/Akka.[5] We relied on the abstraction mechanisms of Scala, allowing us to implement the register logic, verified in Sect. 4, separately from the network middle-ware, which has provided a family of Semantics from Sect. 5. Together, they provide a family of provably correct, modularly verified *distributed* implementations, coming with a simple *shared memory-like* interface.

7   Related Work

Proofs of Linearisability via Rely/Guarantee. Our work builds on the results of Boichat *et al.* [3], who were first to propose to a systematic deconstruction of Paxos into read/write operations of a *round-based register* abstraction. We extend and harness those abstractions, by intentionally introducing more non-determinism into them, which allows us to provide the first modular (*i.e.*, mutually independent) proofs of Proposer and Acceptor using Rely/Guarantee with linearisation points and prophecies. While several logics have been proposed recently to prove linearisability of concurrent implementations using Rely/Guarantee reasoning [14,18,19,26], none of them considers message-passing distributed systems or consensus protocols.

Verification of Paxos-Family Algorithms. Formal verification of different versions of Paxos-family protocols *wrt.* inductive invariants and liveness has been a focus of multiple verification efforts in the past fifteen years. To name just a few, Lamport has specified and verified Fast Paxos [17] using TLA+ and its accompanying model checker [32]. Chand *et al.* used TLA+ to specify and verify Multi-Paxos implementation, similar to the one we considered in this work [5]. A version of SD-Paxos has been verified by Kellomaki using the PVS theorem prover [13]. Jaskelioff and Merz have verified Disk Paxos in Isabelle/HOL [12]. More recently, Rahli *et al.* formalised an executable version of Multi-Paxos in EventML [24], a dialect of NuPRL. Dragoi *et al.* [8] implemented and verified SD-Paxos in the PSYNC framework, which implements a partially synchronised model [7], supporting automated proofs of system invariants. Padon *et al.* have proved the system invariants and the consensus property of both simple Paxos and Multi-Paxos using the verification tool IVY [22,23].

Unlike all those verification efforts that consider (Multi-/Disk/Fast/...)Paxos as a *single monolithic protocol*, our approach provides the first *modular* verification of single-decree Paxos using Rely/Guarantee framework, as well as the first verification of Multi-Paxos that directly reuses the proof of SD-Paxos.

---

[5] The code is available at https://github.com/certichain/protocol-combinators.

Compositional Reasoning about Distributed Systems. Several recent works have partially addressed modular formal verification of distributed systems. The IronFleet framework by Hawblitzel *et al.* has been used to verify both safety and liveness of a real-world implementation of a Paxos-based replicated state machine library and a lease-based shared key-value store [10]. While the proof is structured in a modular way by composing specifications in a way similar to our decomposition in Sects. 3 and 4, that work does not address the linearisability and does not provide composition of proofs about complex protocols (*e.g.*, Multi-Paxos) from proofs about its subparts

The Verdi framework for deductive verification of distributed systems [29,31] suggests the idea of *Verified System Transformers* (VSTs), as a way to provide *vertical composition* of distributed system implementation. While Verdi's VSTs are similar in its purpose and idea to our network transformations, they *do not* exploit the properties of the protocol, which was crucial for us to verify Multi-Paxos's implementation.

The DISEL framework [25,28] addresses the problem of *horizontal composition* of distributed protocols and their client applications. While we do not compose Paxos with any clients in this work, we believe its register-based specification could be directly employed for verifying applications that use Paxos as its subcomponent, which is what is demonstrated by our prototype implementation.

8   Conclusion and Future Work

We have proposed and explored two complementary mechanisms for modular verification of Paxos-family consensus protocols [15]: (a) non-deterministic register-based specifications in the style of Boichat *et al.* [3], which allow one to decompose the proof of protocol's linearisability into separate independent "layers", and (b) a family of protocol-aware transformations of network semantics, making it possible to reuse the verification efforts. We believe that the applicability of these mechanisms spreads beyond reasoning about Paxos and its variants and that they can be used for verifying other consensus protocols, such as Raft [21] and PBFT [4]. We are also going to employ network transformations to verify implementations of Mencius [20], and accommodate more protocol-specific optimisations, such as implementation of master leases and epoch numbering [6].

Acknowledgements. We thank the ESOP 2018 reviewers for their feedback. This work by was supported by ERC Starting Grant H2020-EU 714729 and EPSRC First Grant EP/P009271/1.

References

1. Abadi, M., Lamport, L.: The existence of refinement mappings. In: LICS, pp. 165–175. IEEE Computer Society (1988)
2. Boichat, R., Dutta, P., Frølund, S., Guerraoui, R.: Deconstructing Paxos (2001). OAIPMH server at infoscience.epfl.ch, record 52373. http://infoscience.epfl.ch/record/52373

3. Boichat, R., Dutta, P., Frølund, S., Guerraoui, R.: Deconstructing Paxos. SIGACT News **34**(1), 47–67 (2003)
4. Castro, M., Liskov, B.: Practical Byzantine fault tolerance. In: OSDI, pp. 173–186. USENIX Association (1999)
5. Chand, S., Liu, Y.A., Stoller, S.D.: Formal verification of multi-Paxos for distributed consensus. In: Fitzgerald, J., Heitmeyer, C., Gnesi, S., Philippou, A. (eds.) FM 2016. LNCS, vol. 9995, pp. 119–136. Springer, Cham (2016). https://doi.org/10.1007/978-3-319-48989-6_8
6. Chandra, T., Griesemer, R., Redstone, J.: Paxos made live: an engineering perspective. In: PODC, pp. 398–407. ACM (2007)
7. Charron-Bost, B., Merz, S.: Formal verification of a consensus algorithm in the heard-of model. Int. J. Softw. Inform. **3**(2–3), 273–303 (2009)
8. Dragoi, C., Henzinger, T.A., Zufferey, D.: PSync: a partially synchronous language for fault-tolerant distributed algorithms. In: POPL, pp. 400–415. ACM (2016)
9. Filipovic, I., O'Hearn, P.W., Rinetzky, N., Yang, H.: Abstraction for concurrent objects. Theor. Comput. Sci. **411**(51–52), 4379–4398 (2010)
10. Hawblitzel, C., Howell, J., Kapritsos, M., Lorch, J.R., Parno, B., Roberts, M.L., Setty, S.T.V., Zill, B.: IronFleet: proving practical distributed systems correct. In: SOSP, pp. 1–17. ACM (2015)
11. Herlihy, M., Wing, J.M.: Linearizability: a correctness condition for concurrent objects. ACM Trans. Program. Lang. Syst. **12**(3), 463–492 (1990)
12. Jaskelioff, M., Merz, S.: Proving the correctness of disk Paxos. Archive of Formal Proofs (2005)
13. Kellomäki, P.: An annotated specification of the consensus protocol of Paxos using superposition in PVS. Technical report 36, Tampere University of Technology, Institute of Software Systems (2004)
14. Khyzha, A., Gotsman, A., Parkinson, M.: A generic logic for proving linearizability. In: Fitzgerald, J., Heitmeyer, C., Gnesi, S., Philippou, A. (eds.) FM 2016. LNCS, vol. 9995, pp. 426–443. Springer, Cham (2016). https://doi.org/10.1007/978-3-319-48989-6_26
15. Lamport, L.: The part-time parliament. ACM Trans. Comput. Syst. **16**(2), 133–169 (1998)
16. Lamport, L.: Paxos made simple. SIGACT News **32**, 18–25 (2001)
17. Lamport, L.: Fast Paxos. Distrib. Comput. **19**(2), 79–103 (2006)
18. Liang, H., Feng, X.: Modular verification of linearizability with non-fixed linearization points. In: PLDI, pp. 459–470. ACM (2013)
19. Liang, H., Feng, X.: A program logic for concurrent objects under fair scheduling. In: POPL, pp. 385–399. ACM (2016)
20. Mao, Y., Junqueira, F.P., Marzullo, K.: Mencius: building efficient replicated state machine for WANs. In: OSDI, pp. 369–384. USENIX Association (2008)
21. Ongaro, D., Ousterhout, J.K.: In search of an understandable consensus algorithm. In: 2014 USENIX Annual Technical Conference, pp. 305–319 (2014)
22. Padon, O., Losa, G., Sagiv, M., Shoham, S.: Paxos made EPR: decidable reasoning about distributed protocols. PACMPL **1**(OOPSLA), 108:1–108:31 (2017)
23. Padon, O., McMillan, K.L., Panda, A., Sagiv, M., Shoham, S.: Ivy: safety verification by interactive generalization. In: PLDI, pp. 614–630. ACM (2016)
24. Rahli, V., Guaspari, D., Bickford, M., Constable, R.L.: Formal specification, verification, and implementation of fault-tolerant systems using EventML. In: AVOCS. EASST (2015)
25. Sergey, I., Wilcox, J.R., Tatlock, Z.: Programming and proving with distributed protocols. PACMPL **2**(POPL), 28:1–28:30 (2018)

26. Vafeiadis, V.: Modular fine-grained concurrency verification. Ph.D. thesis, University of Cambridge (2007)
27. van Renesse, R., Altinbuken, D.: Paxos made moderately complex. ACM Comput. Surv. **47**(3), 42:1–42:36 (2015)
28. Wilcox, J.R., Sergey, I., Tatlock, Z.: Programming language abstractions for modularly verified distributed systems. In: SNAPL. LIPIcs, vol. 71, pp. 19:1–19:12. Schloss Dagstuhl (2017)
29. Wilcox, J.R., Woos, D., Panchekha, P., Tatlock, Z., Wang, X., Ernst, M.D., Anderson, T.E.: Verdi: a framework for implementing and formally verifying distributed systems. In: PLDI, pp. 357–368. ACM (2015)
30. Winskel, G.: The Formal Semantics of Programming Languages. The MIT Press, Cambridge (1993)
31. Woos, D., Wilcox, J.R., Anton, S., Tatlock, Z., Ernst, M.D., Anderson, T.E.: Planning for change in a formal verification of the Raft consensus protocol. In: CPP, pp. 154–165. ACM (2016)
32. Yu, Y., Manolios, P., Lamport, L.: Model checking TLA$^+$ specifications. In: Pierre, L., Kropf, T. (eds.) CHARME 1999. LNCS, vol. 1703, pp. 54–66. Springer, Heidelberg (1999). https://doi.org/10.1007/3-540-48153-2_6

On Parallel Snapshot Isolation
and Release/Acquire Consistency

Azalea Raad[1(✉)], Ori Lahav[2], and Viktor Vafeiadis[1]

[1] MPI-SWS, Kaiserslautern, Germany
{azalea,viktor}@mpi-sws.org
[2] Tel Aviv University, Tel Aviv, Israel
orilahav@tau.ac.il

Abstract. Parallel snapshot isolation (PSI) is a standard transactional consistency model used in databases and distributed systems. We argue that PSI is also a useful formal model for software transactional memory (STM) as it has certain advantages over other consistency models. However, the formal PSI definition is given declaratively by acyclicity axioms, which most programmers find hard to understand and reason about.

To address this, we develop a simple lock-based reference implementation for PSI built on top of the release-acquire memory model, a well-behaved subset of the C/C++11 memory model. We prove that our implementation is sound and complete against its higher-level declarative specification.

We further consider an extension of PSI allowing transactional and non-transactional code to interact, and provide a sound and complete reference implementation for the more general setting. Supporting this interaction is necessary for adopting a transactional model in programming languages.

1 Introduction

Following the widespread use of transactions in databases, *software transactional memory* (STM) [19,35] has been proposed as a programming language abstraction that can radically simplify the task of writing correct and efficient concurrent programs. It provides the illusion of blocks of code, called *transactions*, executing atomically and in isolation from any other such concurrent blocks.

In theory, STM is great for programmers as it allows them to concentrate on the high-level algorithmic steps of solving a problem and relieves them of such concerns as the low-level details of enforcing mutual exclusion. In practice, however, the situation is far from ideal as the semantics of transactions in the context of non-transactional code is not at all settled. Recent years have seen a plethora of different STM implementations [1–3,6,17,20], each providing a slightly different—and often unspecified—semantics to the programmer.

Simple models in the literature are lock-based, such as *global lock atomicity* (GLA) [28] (where a transaction must acquire a global lock prior to execution and

© The Author(s) 2018
A. Ahmed (Ed.): ESOP 2018, LNCS 10801, pp. 940–967, 2018.
https://doi.org/10.1007/978-3-319-89884-1_33

release it afterwards) and *disjoint lock atomicity* (DLA) [28] (where a transaction must acquire all locks associated with the locations it accesses prior to execution and release them afterwards), which provide *serialisable* transactions. That is, all transactions appear to have executed atomically one after another in some total order. The problem with these models is largely their implementation cost, as they impose too much synchronisation between transactions.

The database community has long recognised this performance problem and has developed weaker transactional models that do not guarantee serialisability. The most widely used such model is *snapshot isolation* (SI) [10], implemented by major databases, both centralised (e.g. Oracle and MS SQL Server) and distributed [16,30,33], as well as in STM [1,11,25,26]. In this article, we focus on a closely related model, *parallel snapshot isolation* (PSI) [36], which is known to provide better scalability and availability in large-scale geo-replicated systems. SI and PSI allow conflicting transactions to execute concurrently and to commit successfully, so long as they do not have a write-write conflict. This in effect allows reads of SI/PSI transactions to read from an earlier memory snapshot than the one affected by their writes, and permits outcomes such as the following:

$$\text{Initially, } x = y = 0$$

$$\textbf{T1:} \begin{bmatrix} x := 1; \\ a := y; \text{ // reads } 0 \end{bmatrix} \quad \Big\| \quad \textbf{T2:} \begin{bmatrix} y := 1; \\ b := x; \text{ // reads } 0 \end{bmatrix} \qquad \text{(SB+txs)}$$

The above is also known as the *write skew* anomaly in the database literature [14]. Such outcomes are analogous to those allowed by weak memory models, such as x86-TSO [29,34] and C11 [9], for non-transactional programs. In this article, we consider—to the best of our knowledge for the first time—PSI as a possible model for STM, especially in the context of a concurrent language such as C/C++ with a weak memory model. In such contexts, programmers are already familiar with weak behaviours such as that exhibited by SB+txs above.

A key reason why PSI is more suitable for a programming language than SI (or other stronger models) is *performance*. This is analogous to why C/C++ adopted non-multi-copy-atomicity (allowing two different threads to observe a write by a third thread at different times) as part of their concurrency model. Consider the following "IRIW" (independent reads of independent writes) litmus test:

$$\text{Initially, } x = y = 0$$

$$\textbf{T1:} \begin{bmatrix} x := 1; \end{bmatrix} \Big\| \begin{array}{l} \textbf{T2:} \\ \begin{bmatrix} a := x; \text{ // reads } 0 \\ b := y; \text{ // reads } 0 \end{bmatrix} \end{array} \Big\| \begin{array}{l} \textbf{T3:} \\ \begin{bmatrix} c := y; \text{ // reads } 0 \\ d := x; \text{ // reads } 0 \end{bmatrix} \end{array} \Big\| \begin{array}{l} \textbf{T4:} \\ \begin{bmatrix} y := 1; \end{bmatrix} \end{array} \quad \text{(IRIW+txs)}$$

In the annotated behaviour, transactions T2 and T3 disagree on the relative order of transactions T1 and T4. Under PSI, this behaviour (called the *long fork anomaly*) is allowed, as T1 and T4 are not ordered—they commit in parallel—but it is disallowed under SI. This intuitively means that SI must impose ordering guarantees even on transactions that do not access a common location, and can be rather costly in the context of a weakly consistent system.

A second reason why PSI is much more suitable than SI is that it has better properties. A key intuitive property a programmer might expect of transactions is *monotonicity*. Suppose, in the (SB+txs) program we split the two transactions into four smaller ones as follows:

$$\text{Initially, } x = y = 0$$

T1: $[x := 1;$ **T2:** $[y := 1;$ (SB+txs+chop)
T3: $[a := y;$ *// reads 0*   **T4:** $[b := x;$ *// reads 0*

One might expect that if the annotated behaviour is allowed in (SB+txs), it should also be allowed in (SB+txs+chop). This indeed is the case for PSI, but not for SI! In fact, in the extreme case where every transaction contains a single access, SI provides serialisability. Nevertheless, PSI currently has two significant drawbacks, preventing its widespread adoption. We aim to address these here.

The first PSI drawback is that its formal semantics can be rather daunting for the uninitiated as it is defined declaratively in terms of acyclicity constraints. What is missing is perhaps a simple lock-based reference implementation of PSI, similar to the lock-based implementations of GLA and DLA, that the programmers can readily understand and reason about. As an added benefit, such an implementation can be viewed as an operational model, forming the basis for developing program logics for reasoning about PSI programs.

Although Cerone et al. [15] proved their declarative PSI specification equivalent to an implementation strategy of PSI in a distributed system with replicated storage over causal consistency, their implementation is not suitable for reasoning about *shared-memory* programs. In particular, it cannot help the programmers determine how transactional and non-transactional accesses may interact.

As our first contribution, in Sect. 4 we address this PSI drawback by providing a simple lock-based reference implementation that we prove equivalent to its declarative specification. Typically, one proves that an implementation is *sound* with respect to a declarative specification—i.e. every behaviour observable in the implementation is accounted for in the declarative specification. Here, we also want the other direction, known as *completeness*, namely that every behaviour allowed by the specification is actually possible in the implementation. Having a (simple) complete implementation is very useful for programmers, as it may be easier to understand and experiment with than the declarative specification.

Our reference implementation is built in the *release-acquire* fragment of the C/C++ memory model [8, 9, 21], using sequence locks [13, 18, 23, 32] to achieve the correct transactional semantics.

The second PSI drawback is that its study so far has not accounted for the subtle effects of non-transactional accesses and how they interact with transactional accesses. While this scenario does not arise in 'closed world' systems such as databases, it is crucially important in languages such as C/C++ and Java, where one cannot afford the implementation cost of making every access transactional so that it is "strongly isolated" from other concurrent transactions.

Therefore, as our second contribution, in Sect. 5 we extend our basic reference implementation to make it robust under uninstrumented non-transactional accesses, and characterise declaratively the semantics we obtain. We call this extended model RPSI (for "robust PSI") and show that it gives reasonable semantics even under scenarios where transactional and non-transactional accesses are mixed.

Outline. The remainder of this article is organised as follows. In Sect. 2 we present an overview of our contributions and the necessary background information. In Sect. 3 we provide the formal model of the C11 release/acquire fragment and describe how we extend it to specify the behaviour of STM programs. In Sect. 4 we present our PSI reference implementation (without non-transactional accesses), demonstrating its soundness and completeness against the declarative PSI specification. In Sect. 5 we formulate a declarative specification for RPSI as an extension of PSI accounting for non-transactional accesses. We then present our RPSI reference implementation, demonstrating its soundness and completeness against our proposed declarative specification. We conclude and discuss future work in Sect. 6.

2   Background and Main Ideas

One of the main differences between the specification of database transactions and those of STM is that STM specifications must additionally account for the interactions between *mixed-mode* (both transactional and non-transactional) accesses to the same locations. To characterise such interactions, Blundell et al. [12,27] proposed the notions of *weak* and *strong atomicity*, often referred to as weak and strong isolation. Weak isolation guarantees isolation only amongst transactions: the intermediate state of a transaction cannot affect or be affected by other transactions, but no such isolation is guaranteed with respect to non-transactional code (e.g. the accesses of a transaction may be interleaved by those of non-transactional code.). By contrast, strong isolation additionally guarantees full isolation from non-transactional code. Informally, each non-transactional access is considered as a transaction with a single access. In what follows, we explore the design choices for implementing STMs under each isolation model (Sect. 2.1), provide an intuitive account of the PSI model (Sect. 2.2), and describe the key requirements for implementing PSI and how we meet them (Sect. 2.3).

2.1   Implementing Software Transactional Memory

Implementing STMs under either strong or weak isolation models comes with a number of challenges. Implementing strongly isolated STMs requires a conflict detection/avoidance mechanism between transactional and non-transactional code. That is, unless non-transactional accesses are instrumented to adhere to the same access policies, conflicts involving non-transactional code cannot be detected. For instance, in order to guarantee strong isolation under the GLA model [28] discussed earlier, non-transactional code must be modified to acquire the global lock prior to each shared access and release it afterwards.

Implementing weakly-isolated STMs requires a careful handling of aborting transactions as their intermediate state may be observed by non-transactional code. Ideally, the STM implementation must ensure that the intermediate state of aborting transactions is not leaked to non-transactional code. A transaction may abort either because it failed to commit (e.g. due to a conflict), or because it encountered an explicit abort instruction in the transactional code. In the former case, leaks to non-transactional code can be avoided by pessimistic concurrency control (e.g. locks), pre-empting conflicts. In the latter case, leaks can be prevented either by lazy version management (where transactional updates are stored locally and propagated to memory only upon committing), or by disallowing explicit abort instructions altogether – an approach taken by the (weakly isolated) relaxed transactions of the C++ memory model [6].

As mentioned earlier, our aim in this work is to build an STM with PSI guarantees in the RA fragment of C11. As such, instrumenting non-transactional accesses is not feasible and thus our STM guarantees weak isolation. For simplicity, throughout our development we make a few simplifying assumptions: (i) transactions are not nested; (ii) the transactional code is without explicit abort instructions (as with the weakly-isolated transactions of C++ [6]); and (iii) the locations accessed by a transaction can be statically determined. For the latter, of course, a static over-approximation of the locations accessed suffices for the soundness of our implementations.

2.2   Parallel Snapshot Isolation (PSI)

The initial model of PSI introduced in [36] is described informally in terms of a multi-version concurrent algorithm as follows. A transaction T at a replica r proceeds by taking an initial *snapshot* S of the shared objects in r. The execution of T is then carried out locally: read operations query S and write operations similarly update S. Once the execution of T is completed, it attempts to *commit* its changes to r and it succeeds *only if* it is not *write-conflicted*. Transaction T is write-conflicted if another *committed* transaction T' has written to a location in r also written to by T, since it recorded its snapshot S. If T fails the conflict check it aborts and may restart the transaction; otherwise, it commits its changes to r, at which point its changes become visible to all other transactions that take a snapshot of replica r thereafter. These committed changes are later propagated to other replicas asynchronously.

The main difference between SI and PSI is in the way the committed changes at a replica r are propagated to other sites in the system. Under the SI model, committed transactions are *globally* ordered and the changes at each replica are propagated to others in this global order. This ensures that all concurrent transactions are observed in the same order by all replicas. By contrast, PSI does not enforce a global order on committed transactions: transactional effects are propagated between replicas in *causal* order. This ensures that, if replica r_1 commits a message m which is later read at replica r_2, and r_2 posts a response m', no replica can see m' without having seen the original message m. However, causal propagation allows two replicas to observe concurrent events as if occurring in different orders: if r_1 and r_2 concurrently commit messages m and m', then replica r_3 may initially see m but not m', and r_4 may see m' but not m. This is best illustrated by the (IRIW+txs) example in Sect. 1.

2.3 Towards a Lock-Based Reference Implementation for PSI

While the description of PSI above is suitable for understanding PSI, it is not very useful for integrating the PSI model in languages such as C, C++ or Java. From a programmer's perspective, in such languages the various threads directly access the shared memory; they do not access their own replicas, which are loosely related to the replicas of other threads. What we would therefore like is an equivalent description of PSI in terms of unreplicated accesses to shared memory and a synchronisation mechanism such as locks.

In effect, we want a definition similar in spirit to *global lock atomicity* (GLA) [28], which is arguably the simplest TM model, and models committed transactions as acquiring a global mutual exclusion lock, then accessing and updating the data in place, and finally releasing the global lock. Naturally, however, the implementation of PSI cannot be that simple.

A first observation is that PSI cannot be simply implemented over sequentially consistent (SC) shared memory.[1] To see this, consider the IRIW+txs program from the introduction. Although PSI allows the annotated behaviour, SC forbids it for the corresponding program without transactions. The point is that under SC, either the $x := 1$ or the $y := 1$ write first reaches memory. Suppose, without loss of generality, that $x := 1$ is written to memory before $y := 1$. Then, the possible atomic snapshots of memory are $x = y = 0$, $x = 1 \wedge y = 0$, and $x = y = 1$. In particular, the snapshot read by T3 is impossible.

To implement PSI we therefore resort to a weaker memory model. Among weak memory models, the "multi-copy-atomic" ones, such as x86-TSO [29,34], SPARC PSO [37,38] and ARMv8-Flat [31], also forbid the weak outcome of (IRIW+txs) in the same way as SC, and so are unsuitable for our purpose. We thus consider *release-acquire consistency* (RA) [8,9,21], a simple and well-behaved non-multi-copy-atomic model. It is readily available as a subset of the C/C++11 memory model [9] with verified compilation schemes to all major architectures.

RA provides a crucial property that is relied upon in the earlier description of PSI, namely *causality*. In terms of RA, this means that if thread A observes a write w of thread B, then it also observes all the previous writes of thread B as well as any other writes B observed before performing w.

A second observation is that using a single lock to enforce mutual exclusion does not work as we need to allow transactions that access disjoint sets of locations to complete in parallel. An obvious solution is to use multiple locks—one

---

[1] *Sequential consistency* (SC) [24] is the standard model for shared memory concurrency and defines the behaviours of a multi-threaded program as those arising by executing sequentially some interleaving of the accesses of its constituent threads.

per location—as in the *disjoint lock atomicity* (DLA) model [28]. The question remaining is how to implement taking a snapshot at the beginning of a transaction.

A naive attempt is to use reader/writer locks, which allow multiple readers (taking the snapshots) to run in parallel, as long as no writer has acquired the lock. In more detail, the idea is to acquire reader locks for all locations read by a transaction, read the locations and store their values locally, and then release the reader locks. However, as we describe shortly, this approach does not work. Consider the (IRIW+txs) example in Sect. 1. For T2 to get the annotated outcome, it must release its reader lock for y before T4 acquires it. Likewise, since T3 observes $y = 1$, it must acquire its reader lock for y after T4 releases it. By this point, however, it is transitively after the release of the y lock by T2, and so, because of causality, it must have observed all the writes observed by T2 by that point—namely, the $x := 1$ write. In essence, the problem is that reader-writer locks over-synchronise. When two threads acquire the same reader lock, they synchronise, whereas two read-only transactions should never synchronise in PSI.

To resolve this problem, we use *sequence locks* [13,18,23,32]. Under the sequence locking protocol, each location x is associated with a sequence (version) number vx, initialised to zero. Each write to x increments vx before and after its update, provided that vx is even upon the first increment. Each read from x checks vx before and after reading x. If both values are the same and even, then there cannot have been any concurrent increments, and the reader must have seen a consistent value. That is, `read(x)` $\triangleq$ `do{v:=vx; s:=x} while(is-odd(v) || vx!=v)`. Under SC, sequence locks are equivalent to reader-writer locks; however, under RA, they are weaker exactly because readers do not synchronise.

Handling Non-transactional Accesses. Let us consider what happens if some of the data accessed by a transaction is modified concurrently by an atomic non-transactional write. Since non-transactional accesses do not acquire any locks, the snapshots taken can include values written by non-transactional accesses. The result of the snapshot then depends on the order in which the variables are read. Consider for example the following litmus test:

$$x := 1; \quad \left\| \quad \mathbf{T:} \begin{bmatrix} a := y; & /\!/ \, reads \ 1 \\ b := x; & /\!/ \, reads \ 0 \end{bmatrix} \right.$$

In our implementation, if the transaction's snapshot reads y before x, then the annotated weak behaviour is not possible, because the underlying model (RA) disallows the weak "message passing" behaviour. If, however, x is read before y by the snapshot, then the weak behaviour is possible. In essence, this means that the PSI implementation described so far is of little use, when there are races between transactional and non-transactional code.

Another problem is the lack of *monotonicity*. A programmer might expect that wrapping some code in a transaction block will never yield additional behaviours not possible in the program without transactions. Yet, in this example, removing the T block and unwrapping its code gets rid of the annotated weak behaviour!

To get monotonicity, it seems that snapshots must read the variables in the same order they are accessed by the transactions. How can this be achieved for transactions that say read x, then y, and then x again? Or transactions that depending on some complex condition, access first x and then y or vice versa? The key to solving this conundrum is surprisingly simple: *read each variable twice*. In more detail, one takes two snapshots of the locations read by the transaction, and checks that both snapshots return the same values for each location. This ensures that every location is read both before and after every other location in the transaction, and hence all the high-level happens-before orderings in executions of the transactional program are also respected by its implementation.

There is however one caveat: since equality of values is used to determine whether the two snapshots are the same, we will miss cases where different non-transactional writes to a variable write the same value. In our formal development (see Sect. 5), we thus assume that if multiple non-transactional writes write the same value to the same location, they cannot race with the same transaction. This assumption is necessary for the soundness of our implementation and cannot be lifted without instrumenting non-transactional accesses.

3 The Release-Acquire Memory Model for STM

We present the notational conventions used in the remainder of this article and proceed with the declarative model of the *release-acquire* (RA) fragment [21] of the C11 memory model [9], in which we implement our STM. In Sect. 3.1 we describe how we extend this formal model to specify the behaviour of STM programs.

Notation. Given a relation r on a set A, we write $r^?$, r^+ and r^* for the reflexive, transitive and reflexive-transitive closure of r, respectively. We write r^{-1} for the inverse of r; $r|_A$ for $r \cap A^2$; $[A]$ for the identity relation on A, i.e. $\{(a,a) \mid a \in A\}$; irreflexive(r) for $\neg \exists a.\ (a,a) \in r$; and acyclic(r) for irreflexive(r^+). Given two relations r_1 and r_2, we write $r_1; r_2$ for their (left) relational composition, i.e. $\{(a,b) \mid \exists c.\ (a,c) \in r_1 \wedge (c,b) \in r_2\}$. Lastly, when r is a strict partial order, we write $r|_{imm}$ for the *immediate* edges in r: $\{(a,b) \in r \mid \neg \exists c.\ (a,c) \in r \wedge (c,b) \in r\}$.

The RA model is given by the fragment of the C11 memory model, where all read accesses are acquire (`acq`) reads, all writes are release (`rel`) writes, and all atomic updates (i.e. RMWs) are acquire-release (`acqrel`) updates. The semantics of a program under RA is defined as a set of *consistent executions*.

Definition 1 (Executions in RA). Assume a finite set of *locations* LOC; a finite set of *values* VAL; and a finite set of *thread identifiers* TID. Let x, y, z range over locations, v over values and τ over thread identifiers. An *RA execution graph of an STM implementation*, G, is a tuple of the form $(E, \mathsf{po}, \mathsf{rf}, \mathsf{mo})$ with its nodes given by E and its edges given by the po, rf and mo relations such that:

- $E \subset \mathbb{N}$ is a finite set of *events*, and is accompanied with the functions $\mathtt{tid}(.) : E \to \mathrm{TID}$ and $\mathtt{lab}(.) : E \to \mathrm{LABEL}$, returning the thread identifier and the label of an event, respectively. We typically use a, b, and e to range over events. The label of an event is a tuple of one of the following three forms: (i) $\mathtt{R}(x,v)$ for *read* events; (ii) $\mathtt{W}(x,v)$ for *write* events; or (iii) $\mathtt{U}(x,v,v')$ for *update* events. The $\mathtt{lab}(.)$ function induces the functions $\mathtt{typ}(.)$, $\mathtt{loc}(.)$, $\mathtt{val_r}(.)$ and $\mathtt{val_w}(.)$ that respectively project the type ($\mathtt{R}$, $\mathtt{W}$ or $\mathtt{U}$), location, and read/written values of an event, where applicable. The set of *read events* is denoted by $\mathcal{R} \triangleq \{e \in E \mid \mathtt{typ}(e) \in \{\mathtt{R},\mathtt{U}\}\}$; similarly, the set of *write events* is denoted by $\mathcal{W} \triangleq \{e \in E \mid \mathtt{typ}(e) \in \{\mathtt{W},\mathtt{U}\}\}$ and the set of *update events* is denoted by $\mathcal{U} \triangleq \mathcal{R} \cap \mathcal{W}$.
  We further assume that E always contains a set E_0 of initialisation events consisting of a write event with label $\mathtt{W}(x,0)$ for every $x \in \mathrm{LOC}$.
- $\mathsf{po} \subseteq E \times E$ denotes the *'program-order'* relation, defined as a disjoint union of strict total orders, each orders the events of one thread, together with $E_0 \times (E \setminus E_0)$ that places the initialisation events before any other event.
- $\mathsf{rf} \subseteq \mathcal{W} \times \mathcal{R}$ denotes the *'reads-from'* relation, defined as a relation between write and read events of the same location and value; it is total and functional on reads, i.e. every read event is related to exactly one write event;
- $\mathsf{mo} \subseteq \mathcal{W} \times \mathcal{W}$ denotes the *'modification-order'* relation, defined as a disjoint union of strict orders, each of which totally orders the write events to one location.

We often use "$G.$" as a prefix to project the various components of G (e.g. $G.E$). Given a relation $\mathsf{r} \subseteq E \times E$, we write r_{loc} for $\mathsf{r} \cap \{(a,b) \mid \mathtt{loc}(a) = \mathtt{loc}(b)\}$. Analogously, given a set $A \subseteq E$, we write A_x for $A \cap \{a \mid \mathtt{loc}(a) = x\}$. Lastly, given the rf and mo relations, we define the 'reads-before' relation $\mathsf{rb} \triangleq \mathsf{rf}^{-1}; \mathsf{mo} \setminus [E]$.

Executions of a given program represent traces of shared memory accesses generated by the program. We only consider "partitioned" programs of the form $\|_{\tau \in \mathrm{TID}} \ c_\tau$, where $\|$ denotes parallel composition, and each c_i is a sequential program. The set of executions associated with a

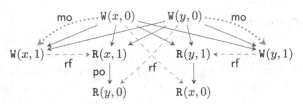

Fig. 1. An RA-consistent execution of a transaction-free variant of (IRIW+txs) in Sect. 1, with program outcome $a = c = 1$ and $b = d = 0$.

given program is then defined by induction over the structure of sequential programs. We do not define this construction formally as it depends on the syntax of the implementation programming language. Each execution of a program P has a particular program *outcome*, prescribing the final values of local variables in each thread (see example in Fig. 1).

In this initial stage, the execution outcomes are unrestricted in that there are no constraints on the rf and mo relations. These restrictions and thus the permitted outcomes of a program are determined by the set of *consistent* executions:

Definition 2 (RA-consistency). A program execution G is *RA-consistent*, written RA-consistent(G), if acyclic($\mathsf{hb}_{loc} \cup \mathsf{mo} \cup \mathsf{rb}$) holds, where $\mathsf{hb} \triangleq (\mathsf{po} \cup \mathsf{rf})^+$ denotes the 'RA-happens-before' relation.

Among all executions of a given program P, only the *RA-consistent* ones define the allowed outcomes of P.

3.1 Software Transactional Memory in RA: Specification

Our goal in this section is to develop a declarative framework that allows us to specify the behaviour of mixed-mode STM programs under weak isolation guarantees. Whilst the behaviour of transactional code is dictated by the particular isolation model considered (e.g. PSI), the behaviour of non-transactional code and its interaction with transactions is guided by the underlying memory model. As we build our STM in the RA fragment of C11, we assume the behaviour of non-transactional code to conform to the RA memory model. More concretely, we build our specification of a program P such that (i) in the absence of transactional code, the behaviour of P is as defined by the RA model; (ii) in the absence of non-transactional code, the behaviour of P is as defined by the PSI model.

Definition 3 (Specification Executions). Assume a finite set of *transaction identifiers* TXID. An *execution graph of an STM specification*, Γ, is a tuple of the form $(E, \mathsf{po}, \mathsf{rf}, \mathsf{mo}, \mathcal{T})$ where:

- $E \triangleq \mathcal{R} \cup \mathcal{W} \cup \mathcal{B} \cup \mathcal{E}$, denotes the set of *events* with $\mathcal{R}$ and $\mathcal{W}$ defined as the sets of read and write events as described above; and the $\mathcal{B}$ and $\mathcal{E}$ respectively denote the set of events marking the *beginning* and *end of transactions*. For each event $a \in \mathcal{B} \cup \mathcal{E}$, the $\mathtt{lab}(.)$ function is extended to return B when $a \in \mathcal{B}$, and E when $a \in \mathcal{E}$. The $\mathtt{typ}(.)$ function is accordingly extended to return a type in $\{\mathtt{R}, \mathtt{W}, \mathtt{U}, \mathtt{B}, \mathtt{E}\}$, whilst the remaining functions are extended to return default (dummy) values for events in $\mathcal{B} \cup \mathcal{E}$.
- po, rf and mo denote the *'program-order'*, *'reads-from'* and *'modification-order'* relations as described above;
- $\mathcal{T} \subseteq E$ denotes the set of *transactional events* with $\mathcal{B} \cup \mathcal{E} \subseteq \mathcal{T}$. For transactional events in $\mathcal{T}$, event labels are extended to carry an additional component, namely the associated transaction identifier. As such, a specification graph is additionally accompanied with the function $\mathtt{tx}(.) : \mathcal{T} \to \mathrm{TXID}$, returning the transaction identifier of transactional events. The derived *'same-transaction'* relation, $\mathsf{st} \in \mathcal{T} \times \mathcal{T}$, is the equivalence relation given by $\mathsf{st} \triangleq \big\{(a, b) \in \mathcal{T} \times \mathcal{T} \mid \mathtt{tx}(a) = \mathtt{tx}(b)\big\}$.

We write $\mathcal{T}/\mathsf{st}$ for the set of equivalence classes of $\mathcal{T}$ induced by st; $[a]_{\mathsf{st}}$ for the equivalence class that contains a; and $\mathcal{T}_\xi$ for the equivalence class of transaction

$\xi \in \text{TXID}: \mathcal{T}_\xi \triangleq \{a \mid \text{tx}(a){=}\xi\}$. We write $\mathcal{NT}$ for non-transactional events: $\mathcal{NT} \triangleq E \setminus \mathcal{T}$. We often use "$\Gamma$." as a prefix to project the Γ components.

Specification Consistency. The consistency of specification graphs is model-specific in that it is dictated by the guarantees provided by the underlying model. In the upcoming sections, we present two consistency definitions of PSI in terms of our specification graphs that lack cycles of certain shapes. In doing so, we often write r_T for lifting a relation $r \subseteq E \times E$ to transaction classes: $r_T \triangleq \text{st}; (r \setminus \text{st}); \text{st}$. Analogously, we write r_I to restrict r to the internal events of a transaction: $r \cap \text{st}$.

Comparison to Dependency Graphs. Adya et al. proposed *dependency graphs* for declarative specification of transactional consistency models [5,7]. Dependency graphs are similar to our specification graphs in that they are constructed from a set of nodes and a set of edges (relations) capturing certain dependencies. However, unlike our specification graphs, the nodes in dependency graphs denote entire transactions and not individual events. In particular, Adya et al. propose three types of dependency edges: (i) a *read dependency* edge, $T_1 \xrightarrow{WR} T_2$, denotes that transaction T_2 reads a value written by T_1; (ii) a *write dependency* edge $T_1 \xrightarrow{WW} T_2$ denotes that T_2 overwrites a value written by T_1; and (iii) an *anti-dependency* edge $T_1 \xrightarrow{RW} T_2$ denotes that T_2 overwrites a value read by T_1. Adya's formalism does not allow for *non-transactional* accesses and it thus suffices to define the dependencies of an execution as edges between transactional classes. In our specification graphs however, we account for both transactional and non-transactional accesses and thus define our relational dependencies between individual events of an execution. However, when we need to relate an entire transaction to another with relation r, we use the transactional lift (r_T) defined above. In particular, Adya's dependency edges correspond to ours as follows. Informally, the WR corresponds to our rf_T; the WW corresponds to our mo_T; and the RW corresponds to our rb_T. Adya's dependency graphs have been used to develop declarative specifications of the PSI consistency model [14]. In Sect. 4, we revisit this model, redefine it as specification graphs in our setting, and develop a reference lock-based implementation that is sound and complete with respect to this abstract specification. The model in [14] does not account for non-transactional accesses. To remedy this, later in Sect. 5, we develop a declarative specification of PSI that allows for both transactional and non-transactional accesses. We then develop a reference lock-based implementation that is sound and complete with respect to our proposed model.

4   Parallel Snapshot Isolation (PSI)

We present a declarative specification of PSI (Sect. 4.1), and develop a lock-based reference implementation of PSI in the RA fragment (Sect. 4.2). We then demonstrate that our implementation is both sound (Sect. 4.3) and complete (Sect. 4.4) with respect to the PSI specification. Note that the PSI model in this section accounts for transactional code only; that is, throughout this section we assume that $\Gamma.E = \Gamma.\mathcal{T}$. We lift this assumption later in Sect. 5.

4.1   A Declarative Specification of PSI STMs in RA

In order to formally characterise the weak behaviour and anomalies admitted by PSI, Cerone and Gotsman [14,15] formulated a declarative PSI specification. (In fact, they provide two equivalent specifications: one using dependency graphs proposed by Adya et al. [5,7]; and the other using abstract executions.) As is standard, they characterise the set of executions admitted under PSI as graphs that lack certain cycles. We present an equivalent declarative formulation of PSI, adapted to use our notation as discussed in Sect. 3. It is straightforward to verify that our definition coincides with the dependency graph specification in [15]. As with [14,15], throughout this section, we take PSI execution graphs to be those in which $E = \mathcal{T} \subseteq (\mathcal{R} \cup \mathcal{W}) \setminus \mathcal{U}$. That is, the PSI model handles transactional code only, consisting solely of read and write events (excluding updates).

PSI Consistency. A PSI execution graph $\Gamma = (E, \mathsf{po}, \mathsf{rf}, \mathsf{mo}, \mathcal{T})$ is *consistent*, written psi-consistent(Γ), if the following hold:

- $\mathsf{rf}_I \cup \mathsf{mo}_I \cup \mathsf{rb}_I \subseteq \mathsf{po}$ (INT)
- irreflexive$((\mathsf{po}_\mathsf{T} \cup \mathsf{rf}_\mathsf{T} \cup \mathsf{mo}_\mathsf{T})^+ ; \mathsf{rb}_\mathsf{T}^?)$ (EXT)

Informally, INT ensures the consistency of each transaction internally, while EXT provides the synchronisation guarantees among transactions. In particular, we note that the two conditions together ensure that if two read events in the same transaction read from the same location x, and no write to x is po-between them, then they must read from the same write (known as 'internal read consistency').

Next, we provide an alternative formulation of PSI-consistency that is closer in form to RA-consistency. This formulation is the basis of our extension in Sect. 5 with non-transactional accesses.

Lemma 1. *A PSI execution graph* $\Gamma = (E, \mathsf{po}, \mathsf{rf}, \mathsf{mo}, \mathcal{T})$ *is consistent if and only if* acyclic(psi-hb$_{loc}$ $\cup$ mo $\cup$ rb) *holds, where* psi-hb *denotes the 'PSI-happens-before' relation, defined as* psi-hb $\triangleq$ (po $\cup$ rf $\cup$ rf$_\mathsf{T}$ $\cup$ mo$_\mathsf{T}$)$^+$.

Proof. The full proof is provided in the technical appendix [4].

Note that this acyclicity condition is rather close to that of RA-consistency definition presented in Sect. 3, with the sole difference being the definition of 'happens-before' relation by replacing hb with psi-hb. The relation psi-hb is a strict extension of hb with rf$_\mathsf{T}$ $\cup$ mo$_\mathsf{T}$, which captures additional synchronisation guarantees resulting from transaction orderings, as described shortly. As in RA-consistency, the po and rf are included in the 'PSI-happens-before' relation psi-hb. Additionally, the rf$_\mathsf{T}$ and mo$_\mathsf{T}$ also contribute to psi-hb.

Intuitively, the rf$_\mathsf{T}$ corresponds to synchronisation due to causality between transactions. A transaction T_1 is causally-ordered before transaction T_2, if T_1 writes to x and T_2 later (in 'happens-before' order) reads x. The inclusion of rf$_\mathsf{T}$ ensures that T_2 cannot read from T_1 without observing its entire effect. This in turn ensures that transactions exhibit an atomic 'all-or-nothing' behaviour. In particular, transactions cannot mix-and-match the values they read.

0. for (x ∈ WS) lock vx;
 1. for (x ∈ RS) {
 2.   a := vx;
 3.   if (is-odd(a) && x ∉ WS) continue;
 4.   if (x ∉ WS) v[x] := a;
 5.   s[x] := x; }
 6. for (x ∈ RS)
 7.   if (¬valid(x)) goto line 1;
 8. [[T]];
 9. for (x ∈ WS) unlock vx;
	lock vx ≜
	   retry: v[x] := vx;
	      if (is-odd(v[x]))
	       goto retry;
	      if (!CAS(vx,v[x],v[x]+1))
	       goto retry;
	
	 unlock vx ≜ vx := v[x]+2
	
	 valid(x) ≜ vx == v[x]
	 valid$_{RPSI}$(x) ≜ vx == v[x] && x == s[x]
	
	 [[a := x]] ≜ a := s[x]
	 [[x := a]] ≜ x := a; s[x] := a
	 [[S$_1$; S$_2$]] ≜ [[S$_1$]]; [[S$_2$]]
	 [[while(e) S]] ≜ while(e) [[S]]
	 ... and so on ...

Fig. 2. PSI implementation of transaction T given RS, WS; the RPSI implementation (Sect. 5) is obtained by replacing valid on line 7 with valid$_{RPSI}$.

For instance, if T_1 writes to both x and y, transaction T_2 may not read the value of x from T_1 but read the value of y from an earlier (in 'happens-before' order) transaction T_0.

The mo$_T$ corresponds to synchronisation due to conflicts between transactions. Its inclusion enforces the write-conflict-freedom of PSI transactions. In other words, if two transactions T_1 and T_2 both write to the same location x via events w_1 and w_2 such that $w_1 \overset{mo}{\rightarrow} w_2$, then T_1 must commit before T_2, and thus the entire effect of T_1 must be visible to T_2.

4.2   A Lock-Based PSI Implementation in RA

We present an operational model of PSI that is both sound and complete with respect to the declarative semantics in Sect. 4.1. To this end, in Fig. 2 we develop a pessimistic (lock-based) reference implementation of PSI using sequence locks [13,18,23,32], referred to as *version locks* in our implementation. In order to avoid taking a snapshot of the *entire* memory and thus decrease the locking overhead, we assume that a transaction T is supplied with its *read set*, RS, containing those locations that are read by T. Similarly, we assume T to be supplied with its *write set*, WS, containing the locations updated by T.[2]

The implementation of T proceeds by exclusively acquiring the version locks on all locations in its write set (line 0). It then obtains a snapshot of the locations in its read set by inspecting their version locks, as described shortly, and subsequently recording their values in a thread-local array s (lines 1–7). Once a snapshot is recorded, the execution of T proceeds locally (via [[T]] on line 8) as

---

[2] A conservative estimate of RS and WS can be obtained by simple syntactic analysis.

follows. Each read operation consults the local snapshot in s; each write operation updates the memory eagerly (in-place) and subsequently updates its local snapshot to ensure correct lookup for future reads. Once the execution of T is concluded, the version locks on the write set are released (line 9). Observe that as the writer locks are acquired pessimistically, we do not need to check for write-conflicts in the implementation.

To facilitate our locking implementation, we assume that each location x is associated with a version lock at address x+1, written vx. The value held by a version lock vx may be in one of two categories: (i) an even number, denoting that the lock is free; or (ii) an odd number, denoting that the lock is exclusively held by a writer. For a transaction to write to a location x in its write set WS, the x version lock (vx) must be acquired exclusively by calling lock vx. Each call to lock vx reads the value of vx and stores it in v[x], where v is a thread-local array. It then checks if the value read is even (vx is free) and if so it atomically increments it by 1 (with a 'compare-and-swap' operation), thus changing the value of vx to an odd number and acquiring it exclusively; otherwise it repeats this process until the version lock is successfully acquired. Conversely, each call to unlock vx updates the value of vx to v[x]+2, restoring the value of vx to an even number and thus releasing it. Note that deadlocks can be avoided by imposing an ordering on locks and ensuring their in-order acquisition by all transactions. For simplicity however, we have elided this step as we are not concerned with progress or performance issues here and our main objective is a reference implementation of PSI in RA.

Analogously, for a transaction to read from the locations in its read set RS, it must record a snapshot of their values (lines 1–7). To obtain a snapshot of location x, the transaction must ensure that x is not currently being written to by another transaction. It thus proceeds by reading the value of vx and recording it in v[x]. If vx is free (the value read is even) or x is in its write set WS, the value of x can be freely read and tentatively stored in s[x]. In the latter case, the transaction has already acquired the exclusive lock on vx and is thus safe in the knowledge that no other transaction is currently updating x. Once a *tentative* snapshot of all locations is obtained (lines 1–5), the transaction must *validate* it by ensuring that it reflects the values of the read set at a single point in time (lines 6–7). To do this, it revisits the version locks, inspecting whether their values have changed (by checking them against v) since it recorded its snapshot. If so, then an intermediate update has intervened, potentially invalidating the obtained snapshot; the transaction thus restarts the snapshot process. Otherwise, the snapshot is successfully validated and returned in s.

4.3   Implementation Soundness

The PSI implementation in Fig. 2 is *sound*: for each RA-consistent implementation graph G, a corresponding specification graph Γ can be constructed such that psi-consistent(Γ) holds. In what follows we state our soundness theorem and briefly describe our construction of consistent specification graphs. We refer the reader to the technical appendix [4] for the full soundness proof.

Theorem 1 (Soundness). *For all RA-consistent implementation graphs G of the implementation in Fig. 2, there exists a PSI-consistent specification graph Γ of the corresponding transactional program that has the same program outcome.*

Constructing Consistent Specification Graphs. Observe that given an execution of our implementation with t transactions, the trace of each transaction $i \in \{1 \cdots t\}$ is of the form $\theta_i = Ls_i \overset{\text{po}}{\to} FS_i \overset{\text{po}}{\to} S_i \overset{\text{po}}{\to} Ts_i \overset{\text{po}}{\to} Us_i$, where Ls_i, FS_i, S_i, Ts_i and Us_i respectively denote the sequence of events acquiring the version locks, attempting but failing to obtain a valid snapshot, recording a valid snapshot, performing the transactional operations, and releasing the version locks. For each transactional trace θ_i of our implementation, we thus construct a corresponding trace of the specification as $\theta_i' = B_i \overset{\text{po}}{\to} Ts_i' \overset{\text{po}}{\to} E_i$, where B_i and E_i denote the transaction begin and end events ($\mathtt{lab}(B_i){=}\mathtt{B}$ and $\mathtt{lab}(E_i){=}\mathtt{E}$). When Ts_i is of the form $t_1 \overset{\text{po}}{\to} \cdots \overset{\text{po}}{\to} t_n$, we construct Ts_i' as $t_1' \overset{\text{po}}{\to} \cdots \overset{\text{po}}{\to} t_n'$ with each t_j' defined either as $t_j' \triangleq \mathtt{R}(\mathtt{x}, v)$ when $t_j = \mathtt{R}(\mathtt{s[x]}, v)$ (i.e. the corresponding implementation event is a read event); or as $t_j' \triangleq \mathtt{W}(\mathtt{x}, v)$ when $t_j{=}\mathtt{W}(\mathtt{x}, v) \overset{\text{po}}{\to} \mathtt{W}(\mathtt{s[x]}, v)$.

For each specification trace θ_i' we construct the 'reads-from' relation as:

$$
\mathsf{RF}_i \triangleq \left\{ (w, t_j') \left|
\begin{array}{l}
t_j' \in Ts_i' \wedge \exists \mathtt{x}, v.\ t_j'{=}\mathtt{R}(\mathtt{x}, v) \wedge w{=}\mathtt{W}(\mathtt{x}, v) \\
\wedge (w \in Ts_i' \Rightarrow w \overset{\text{po}}{\to} t_j' \wedge \\
\quad (\forall e \in Ts_i'.\ w \overset{\text{po}}{\to} e \overset{\text{po}}{\to} t_j' \Rightarrow (\mathtt{loc}(e){\neq}\mathtt{x} \vee e{\notin}\mathcal{W}))) \\
\wedge (w \notin Ts_i' \Rightarrow (\forall e \in Ts_i'.\ (e \overset{\text{po}}{\to} t_j' \Rightarrow (\mathtt{loc}(e) \neq \mathtt{x} \vee e \notin \mathcal{W})) \\
\quad \wedge \exists r' \in S_i.\ \mathtt{loc}(r'){=}\mathtt{x} \wedge (w, r') \in G.\mathsf{rf})
\end{array}
\right. \right\}
$$

That is, we construct our graph such that each read event t_j' from location $\mathtt{x}$ in Ts_i' either (i) is preceded by a write event w to $\mathtt{x}$ in Ts_i' without an intermediate write in between them and thus 'reads-from' w (lines two and three); or (ii) is not preceded by a write event in Ts_i' and thus 'reads-from' the write event w from which the initial snapshot read r' in S_i obtained the value of $\mathtt{x}$ (last two lines).

Given a consistent implementation graph $G = (E, \mathsf{po}, \mathsf{rf}, \mathsf{mo})$, we construct a consistent specification graph $\Gamma = (E, \mathsf{po}, \mathsf{rf}, \mathsf{mo}, \mathcal{T})$ such that:

- $\Gamma.E \triangleq \bigcup_{i \in \{1 \cdots t\}} \theta_i'.E$ – the events of $\Gamma.E$ is the union of events in each transaction trace θ_i' of the specification constructed as above;
- $\Gamma.\mathsf{po} \triangleq G.\mathsf{po}|_{\Gamma.E}$ – the $\Gamma.\mathsf{po}$ is that of $G.\mathsf{po}$ limited to the events in $\Gamma.E$;
- $\Gamma.\mathsf{rf} \triangleq \bigcup_{i \in \{1 \cdots t\}} \mathsf{RF}_i$ – the $\Gamma.\mathsf{rf}$ is the union of RF_i relations defined above;
- $\Gamma.\mathsf{mo} \triangleq G.\mathsf{mo}|_{\Gamma.E}$ – the $\Gamma.\mathsf{mo}$ is that of $G.\mathsf{mo}$ limited to the events in $\Gamma.E$;
- $\Gamma.\mathcal{T} \triangleq \Gamma.E$, where for each $e \in \Gamma.\mathcal{T}$, we define $\mathtt{tx}(e) = i$ when $e \in \theta_i'$.

4.4 Implementation Completeness

The PSI implementation in Fig. 2 is *complete*: for each consistent specification graph Γ a corresponding implementation graph G can be constructed such that RA-consistent(G) holds. We next state our completeness theorem and describe our construction of consistent implementation graphs. We refer the reader to the technical appendix [4] for the full completeness proof.

Theorem 2 (Completeness). *For all PSI-consistent specification graphs Γ of a transactional program, there exists an RA-consistent execution graph G of the implementation in Fig. 2 that has the same program outcome.*

Constructing Consistent Implementation Graphs. In order to construct an execution graph of the implementation G from the specification Γ, we follow similar steps as those in the soundness construction, in reverse order. More concretely, given each trace θ_i' of the specification, we construct an analogous trace of the implementation by inserting the appropriate events for acquiring and inspecting the version locks, as well as obtaining a snapshot. For each transaction class $T_i \in T/\text{st}$, we must first determine its read and write sets and subsequently decide the order in which the version locks are acquired (for locations in the write set) and inspected (for locations in the read set). This then enables us to construct the 'reads-from' and 'modification-order' relations for the events associated with version locks.

Given a consistent execution graph of the specification $\Gamma = (E, \text{po}, \text{rf}, \text{mo}, T)$, and a transaction class $T_i \in \Gamma.T/\text{st}$, we write WS_{T_i} for the set of locations written to by T_i. That is, $\text{WS}_{T_i} \triangleq \bigcup_{e \in T_i \cap W} \text{loc}(e)$. Similarly, we write RS_{T_i} for the set of locations read from by T_i, *prior to* being written to by T_i. For each location x read from by T_i, we additionally record the first read event in T_i that retrieved the value of x. That is,

$$\text{RS}_{T_i} \triangleq \left\{ (x, r) \,\middle|\, r \in T_i \cap \mathcal{R}_x \wedge \neg \exists e \in T_i \cap E_x.\, e \xrightarrow{\text{po}} r \right\}$$

Note that transaction T_i may contain several read events reading from x, prior to subsequently updating it. However, the internal-read-consistency property ensures that all such read events read from the same write event. As such, as part of the read set of T_i we record the first such read event (in program-order).

Determining the ordering of lock events hinges on the following observation. Given a consistent execution graph of the specification $\Gamma = (E, \text{po}, \text{rf}, \text{mo}, T)$, let for each location x the total order mo be given as: $w_1 \xrightarrow{\text{mo}|\text{imm}} \cdots \xrightarrow{\text{mo}|\text{imm}} w_{n_x}$. Observe that this order can be broken into adjacent segments where the events of each segment belong to the *same* transaction. That is, given the transaction classes $\Gamma.T/\text{st}$, the order above is of the following form where $T_1, \cdots, T_m \in \Gamma.T/\text{st}$ and for each such T_i we have $x \in \text{WS}_{T_i}$ and $w_{(i,1)} \cdots w_{(i,n_i)} \in T_i$:

$$\underbrace{w_{(1,1)} \xrightarrow{\text{mo}|\text{imm}} \cdots \xrightarrow{\text{mo}|\text{imm}} w_{(1,n_1)}}_{T_1} \xrightarrow{\text{mo}|\text{imm}} \cdots \xrightarrow{\text{mo}|\text{imm}} \underbrace{w_{(m,1)} \xrightarrow{\text{mo}|\text{imm}} \cdots \xrightarrow{\text{mo}|\text{imm}} w_{(m,n_m)}}_{T_m}$$

Were this not the case and we had $w_1 \xrightarrow{\text{mo}} w \xrightarrow{\text{mo}} w_2$ such that $w_1, w_2 \in T_i$ and $w \in T_j \neq T_i$, we would consequently have $w_1 \xrightarrow{\text{mo}_T} w \xrightarrow{\text{mo}_T} w_1$, contradicting the assumption that Γ is consistent. Given the above order, let us then define

$\Gamma.\mathsf{MO_x} = [\mathcal{T}_1 \cdots \mathcal{T}_m]$. We write $\Gamma.\mathsf{MO_x}|_i$ for the ith item of $\Gamma.\mathsf{MO_x}$. As we describe shortly, we use $\Gamma.\mathsf{MO_x}$ to determine the order of lock events.

Note that the execution trace for each transaction $\mathcal{T}_i \in \Gamma.\mathcal{T}/\text{st}$ is of the form $\theta'_i = B_i \xrightarrow{\text{po}} Ts'_i \xrightarrow{\text{po}} E_i$, where B_i is a transaction-begin (B) event, E_i is a transaction-end (E) event, and $Ts'_i = t'_1 \xrightarrow{\text{po}} \cdots \xrightarrow{\text{po}} t'_n$ for some n, where each t'_j is either a read or a write event. As such, we have $\Gamma.E = \Gamma.\mathcal{T} = \bigcup_{\mathcal{T}_i \in \Gamma.\mathcal{T}/\text{st}} \mathcal{T}_i = \theta'_i.E$.

For each trace θ'_i of the specification, we construct a corresponding trace of our implementation θ_i as follows. Let $\mathsf{RS}_{\mathcal{T}_i} = \{(\mathsf{x}_1, r_1) \cdots (\mathsf{x}_p, r_p)\}$ and $\mathsf{WS}_{\mathcal{T}_i} = \{\mathsf{y}_1 \cdots \mathsf{y}_q\}$. We then construct $\theta_i = Ls_i \xrightarrow{\text{po}} S_i \xrightarrow{\text{po}} Ts_i \xrightarrow{\text{po}} Us_i$, where

- $Ls_i = L_i^{\mathsf{y}_1} \xrightarrow{\text{po}} \cdots \xrightarrow{\text{po}} L_i^{\mathsf{y}_q}$ and $Us_i = U_i^{\mathsf{y}_1} \xrightarrow{\text{po}} \cdots \xrightarrow{\text{po}} U_i^{\mathsf{y}_q}$ denote the sequence of events acquiring and releasing the version locks, respectively. Each $L_i^{\mathsf{y}_j}$ and $U_i^{\mathsf{y}_j}$ are defined as follows, the first event $L_i^{\mathsf{y}_1}$ has the same identifier as that of B_i, the last event $U_i^{\mathsf{y}_q}$ has the same identifier as that of E_i, and the identifiers of the remaining events are picked fresh:

$$L_i^{\mathsf{y}_j} = \mathsf{U}(\mathsf{vy}_j, 2a, 2a+1) \quad U_i^{\mathsf{y}_j} = \mathsf{W}(\mathsf{vy}_j, 2a+2) \quad \text{where } \mathsf{MO_{y_j}}\Big|_a = \mathcal{T}_i$$

We then define the mo relation for version locks such that if transaction $\mathcal{T}_i$ writes to y immediately after $\mathcal{T}_j$ (i.e. $\mathcal{T}_i$ is $\mathsf{MO_y}$-ordered immediately after $\mathcal{T}_j$), then $\mathcal{T}_i$ acquires the vy version lock immediately after $\mathcal{T}_j$ has released it. On the other hand, if $\mathcal{T}_i$ is the first transaction to write to y, then it acquires vy immediately after the event initialising the value of vy, written $init_{\mathsf{vy}}$. Moreover, each vy release event of $\mathcal{T}_i$ is mo-ordered immediately after the corresponding vy acquisition event in $\mathcal{T}_i$:

$$\mathsf{IMO}_i \triangleq \bigcup_{\mathsf{y} \in \mathsf{WS}_{\mathcal{T}_i}} \left\{ \begin{matrix} (L_i^{\mathsf{y}}, U_i^{\mathsf{y}}), \\ (w, L_i^{\mathsf{y}}) \end{matrix} \,\middle|\, \begin{matrix} (\Gamma.\mathsf{MO_x}|_0 = \mathcal{T}_i \Rightarrow w = init_{\mathsf{vy}}) \wedge \\ (\exists \mathcal{T}_j, a > 0. \ \Gamma.\mathsf{MO_y}|_a = \mathcal{T}_i \wedge \Gamma.\mathsf{MO_y}|_{a-1} = \mathcal{T}_j \\ \Rightarrow w = U_j^{\mathsf{y}}) \end{matrix} \right\}$$

This partial mo order on lock events of $\mathcal{T}_i$ also determines the rf relation for its lock acquisition events: $\mathsf{IRF}_i^1 \triangleq \bigcup_{\mathsf{y} \in \mathsf{WS}_{\mathcal{T}_i}} \{(w, L_i^{\mathsf{y}}) \,|\, (w, L_i^{\mathsf{y}}) \in \mathsf{IMO}_i\}$.

- $S_i = tr_i^{\mathsf{x}_1} \xrightarrow{\text{po}} \cdots \xrightarrow{\text{po}} tr_i^{\mathsf{x}_p} \xrightarrow{\text{po}} vr_i^{\mathsf{x}_1} \xrightarrow{\text{po}} \cdots \xrightarrow{\text{po}} vr_i^{\mathsf{x}_p}$ denotes the sequence of events obtaining a tentative snapshot $(tr_i^{\mathsf{x}_j})$ and subsequently validating it $(vr_i^{\mathsf{x}_j})$. Each $tr_i^{\mathsf{x}_j}$ sequence is defined as $ir_i^{\mathsf{x}_j} \xrightarrow{\text{po}} r_i^{\mathsf{x}_j} \xrightarrow{\text{po}} s_i^{\mathsf{x}_j}$ (reading the version lock vx_j, reading x_j and recoding it in s), with $ir_i^{\mathsf{x}_j}$, $r_i^{\mathsf{x}_j}$, $s_i^{\mathsf{x}_j}$ and $vr_i^{\mathsf{x}_j}$ events defined as follows (with fresh identifiers). We then define the rf relation for each of these read events in S_i. For each $(\mathsf{x}, r) \in \mathsf{RS}_{\mathcal{T}_i}$, when r (i.e. the read event in the specification class $\mathcal{T}_i$ that reads the value of x) reads from an event w in the specification graph $((w, r) \in \Gamma.\mathsf{rf})$, we add (w, r_i^{x}) to the rf relation of G (the first line of IRF_i^2 below). For version locks, if transaction $\mathcal{T}_i$ also writes to x_j, then $ir_i^{\mathsf{x}_j}$ and $vr_i^{\mathsf{x}_j}$ events (reading and validating the value of version lock vx_j), read from the lock event in $\mathcal{T}_i$ that acquired vx_j, namely $L_i^{\mathsf{x}_j}$. On the other hand, if transaction $\mathcal{T}_i$ does not write to $\mathtt{x}_j$ and it reads the value of $\mathtt{x}_j$ written by T_j, then $ir_i^{\mathtt{x}_j}$ and $vr_i^{\mathtt{x}_j}$ read the value written to $\mathtt{vx}_j$ by T_j when releasing it ($U_j^{\mathtt{x}}$). Lastly, if T_i does not write to $\mathtt{x}_j$ and it reads the value of $\mathtt{x}_j$ written by the initial write, $init_{\mathtt{x}}$, then $ir_i^{\mathtt{x}_j}$ and $vr_i^{\mathtt{x}_j}$ read the value written to $\mathtt{vx}_j$ by the initial write to $\mathtt{vx}$, $init_{\mathtt{vx}}$.

$$\mathsf{IRF}_i^2 \triangleq \bigcup_{(\mathtt{x},r)\in\mathsf{RS}_{T_i}} \left\{ \begin{array}{l|l} (w,r_i^{\mathtt{x}}), & (w,r)\in\Gamma.\mathsf{rf} \\ (w',ir_i^{\mathtt{x}}), & \wedge\,(\mathtt{x}\in\mathsf{WS}_{T_i} \Rightarrow w'{=}L_i^{\mathtt{x}}) \\ (w',vr_i^{\mathtt{x}}) & \wedge\,(\mathtt{x}\notin\mathsf{WS}_{T_i} \wedge \exists T_j.\,w\in T_j \Rightarrow w'{=}U_j^{\mathtt{x}}) \\ & \wedge\,(\mathtt{x}\notin\mathsf{WS}_{T_i} \wedge w{=}init_{\mathtt{x}} \Rightarrow w'{=}init_{\mathtt{vx}}) \end{array} \right\}$$

$$r_i^{\mathtt{x}_j}{=}\mathtt{R}(\mathtt{x}_j,v) \quad s_i^{\mathtt{x}_j}{=}\mathtt{W}(\mathtt{s[x}_j],v) \qquad \text{s.t. } \exists w.\,(w,r_i^{\mathtt{x}_j})\in\mathsf{IRF}_i^2 \wedge \mathtt{val}_{\mathtt{w}}(w){=}v$$

$$ir_i^{\mathtt{x}_j}{=}vr_i^{\mathtt{x}_j}{=}\mathtt{R}(\mathtt{vx}_j,v) \qquad\qquad \text{s.t. } \exists w.\,(w,ir_i^{\mathtt{x}_j})\in\mathsf{IRF}_i^2 \wedge \mathtt{val}_{\mathtt{w}}(w){=}v$$

- $Ts_i = t_1 \xrightarrow{\mathsf{po}} \cdots \xrightarrow{\mathsf{po}} t_n$ (when $Ts_i' = t_1' \xrightarrow{\mathsf{po}} \cdots \xrightarrow{\mathsf{po}} t_n'$), with t_j defined as follows:

$$t_j = \mathtt{R}(\mathtt{s[x]},v) \text{ when } t_j' = \mathtt{R}(\mathtt{x},v)$$
$$t_j = \mathtt{W}(\mathtt{x},v) \xrightarrow{\mathsf{po}|_{\mathsf{imm}}} \mathtt{W}(\mathtt{s[x]},v) \text{ when } t_j' = \mathtt{W}(\mathtt{x},v)$$

When t_j' is a read event, the t_j has the same identifier as that of t_j'. When t_j' is a write event, the first event in t_j has the same identifier as that of t_j and the identifier of the second event is picked fresh.

We are now in a position to construct our implementation graph. Given a consistent execution graph Γ of the specification, we construct an execution graph $G = (E, \mathsf{po}, \mathsf{rf}, \mathsf{mo})$ of the implementation as follows.

- $G.E = \bigcup_{T_i \in \Gamma.T/\mathsf{st}} \theta_i.E$ – note that $G.E$ is an extension of $\Gamma.E$: $\Gamma.E \subseteq G.E$.
- $G.\mathsf{po}$ is defined as $\Gamma.\mathsf{po}$ extended by the po for the additional events of G, given by the θ_i traces defined above.
- $G.\mathsf{rf} = \bigcup_{T_i \in \Gamma.T/\mathsf{st}} (\mathsf{IRF}_i^1 \cup \mathsf{IRF}_i^2)$
- $G.\mathsf{mo} = \Gamma.\mathsf{mo} \cup \left(\bigcup_{T_i \in \Gamma.T/\mathsf{st}} \mathsf{IMO}_i \right)^+$

5   Robust Parallel Snapshot Isolation (RPSI)

In the previous section we adapted the PSI semantics in [14] to STM settings, in the *absence* of non-transactional code. However, a reasonable STM should account for mixed-mode code where shared data is accessed by both transactional and non-transactional code. To remedy this, we explore the semantics of PSI STMs in the presence of non-transactional code with *weak isolation* guarantees (see Sect. 2.1). We refer to the weakly isolated behaviour of such PSI STMs as *robust parallel snapshot isolation* (RPSI), due to its ability to provide PSI guarantees between transactions even in the presence of non-transactional code.

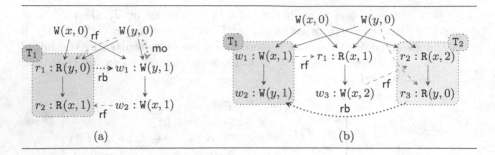

Fig. 3. RPSI-inconsistent executions due to NT-RF (a); and T-RF (b)

In Sect. 5.1 we propose the first declarative specification of RPSI STM programs. Later in Sect. 5.2 we develop a lock-based reference implementation of our RPSI specification in the RA fragment. We then demonstrate that our implementation is both sound (Sect. 5.3) and complete (Sect. 5.4) with respect to our proposed specification.

5.1   A Declarative Specification of RPSI STMs in RA

We formulate a declarative specification of RPSI semantics by adapting the PSI semantics presented in Sect. 4.1 to account for non-transactional accesses. As with the PSI specification in Sect. 4.1, throughout this section, we take RPSI execution graphs to be those in which $\mathcal{T} \subseteq (\mathcal{R} \cup \mathcal{W}) \setminus \mathcal{U}$. That is, RPSI transactions consist solely of read and write events (excluding updates). As before, we characterise the set of executions admitted by RPSI as graphs that lack cycles of certain shapes. More concretely, as with the PSI specification, we consider an RPSI execution graph to be *consistent* if acyclic(rpsi-hb$_{loc}$ ∪ mo ∪ rb) holds, where rpsi-hb denotes the *'RPSI-happens-before'* relation, extended from that of PSI psi-hb.

Definition 4 (RPSI consistency). An RPSI execution graph $\Gamma = (E, \text{po}, \text{rf}, , \text{mo}, \mathcal{T})$ is consistent, written rpsi-consistent(Γ), if acyclic(rpsi-hb$_{loc}$ ∪ mo ∪ rb) holds, where rpsi-hb denotes the *'RPSI-happens-before'* relation, defined as the smallest relation that satisfies the following conditions:

$$\text{rpsi-hb}; \text{rpsi-hb} \subseteq \text{rpsi-hb} \qquad (\text{TRANS})$$
$$\text{po} \cup \text{rf} \cup \text{mo}_\text{T} \subseteq \text{rpsi-hb} \qquad (\text{PSI-HB})$$
$$[E \setminus \mathcal{T}]; \text{rf}; \text{st} \subseteq \text{rpsi-hb} \qquad (\text{NT-RF})$$
$$\text{st}; ([\mathcal{W}]; \text{st}; (\text{rpsi-hb} \setminus \text{st}); \text{st}; [\mathcal{R}])_{loc}; \text{st} \subseteq \text{rpsi-hb} \qquad (\text{T-RF})$$

The TRANS and PSI-HB ensure that rpsi-hb is transitive and that it includes po, rf and mo$_\text{T}$ as with its PSI counterpart. The NT-RF ensures that if a value written by a non-transactional write w is observed (read from) by a read event r in a transaction T, then its effect is observed by *all* events in T. That is, the w *happens-before* all events in T and not just r. This allows us to rule out executions such as the one depicted in Fig. 3a, which we argue must be disallowed by RPSI.

Consider the execution graph of Fig. 3a, where transaction T_1 is denoted by the dashed box labelled T_1, comprising the read events r_1 and r_2. Note that as r_1 and r_2 are transactional reads without prior writes by the transaction, they constitute a *snapshot* of the memory at the time T_1 started. That is, the values read by r_1 and r_2 must reflect a valid snapshot of the memory at the time it was taken. As such, since we have $(w_2, r_2) \in$ rf, any event preceding w_2 by the 'happens-before' relation must also be observed by (synchronise with) T_1. In particular, as w_1 happens-before w_2 $((w_1, w_2) \in$ po$)$, the w_1 write must also be observed by T_1. The NT-RF thus ensures that a non-transactional write read from by a transaction (i.e. a snapshot read) synchronises with the entire transaction.

Recall from Sect. 4.1 that the PSI psi-hb relation includes rf$_T$ which has not yet been included in rpsi-hb through the first three conditions described. As we describe shortly, the T-RF is indeed a strengthening of rf$_T$ to account for the presence of non-transactional events. In particular, note that rf$_T$ is included in the left-hand side of T-RF: when rpsi-hb in $([\mathcal{W}];$ st$; ($rpsi-hb $\setminus$ st$);$ st$; [\mathcal{R}])$ is replaced with rf $\subseteq$ rpsi-hb, the left-hand side yields rf$_T$. As such, in the absence of non-transactional events, the definitions of psi-hb and rpsi-hb coincide.

Recall that inclusion of rf$_T$ in psi-hb ensured transactional synchronisation due to causal ordering: if T_1 writes to x and T_2 later (in psi-hb order) reads x, then T_1 must synchronise with T_2. This was achieved in PSI because either (i) T_2 reads x directly from T_1 in which case T_1 synchronises with T_2 via rf$_T$; or (ii) T_2 reads x from another later (mo-ordered) transactional write in T_3, in which case T_1 synchronises with T_3 via mo$_T$, T_3 synchronises with T_2 via rf$_T$, and thus T_1 synchronises with T_2 via mo$_T$; rf$_T$. How are we then to extend rpsi-hb to guarantee transactional synchronisation due to causal ordering in the presence of non-transactional events?

To justify T-RF, we present an execution graph that does not guarantee synchronisation between causally ordered transactions and is nonetheless deemed RPSI-consistent *without* the T-RF condition on rpsi-hb. We thus argue that this execution must be precluded by RPSI, justifying the need for T-RF. Consider the execution in Fig. 3b. Observe that as transaction T_1 writes to x via w_1, transaction T_2 reads x via r_2, and $(w_1, r_2) \in$ rpsi-hb $(w_1 \xrightarrow{\text{rf}} r_1 \xrightarrow{\text{po}} w_3 \xrightarrow{\text{rf}} r_2)$, T_1 is causally ordered before T_2 and hence T_1 must synchronise with T_2. As such, the r_3 in T_2 must observe w_2 in T_1: we must have $(w_2, r_3) \in$ rpsi-hb, rendering the above execution RPSI-inconsistent. To enforce the rpsi-hb relation between such causally ordered transactions with intermediate non-transactional events, T-RF stipulates that if a transaction T_1 writes to a location (e.g. x via w_1 above), another transaction T_2 reads from the same location (r_2), and the two events are related by 'RPSI-happens-before' $((w_1, r_2) \in$ rpsi-hb$)$, then T_1 must synchronise with T_2. That is, all events in T_1 must 'RPSI-happen-before' those in T_2. Effectively, this allows us to transitively close the causal ordering between transactions, spanning transactional and non-transactional events in between.

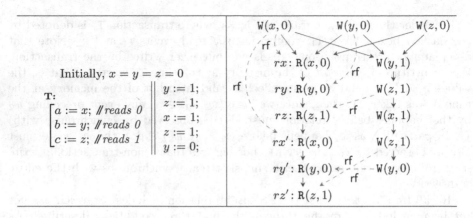

Initially, $x = y = z = 0$

T:
$$\begin{bmatrix} a := x; \text{ // reads } 0 \\ b := y; \text{ // reads } 0 \\ c := z; \text{ // reads } 1 \end{bmatrix}$$

$y := 1;$
$z := 1;$
$x := 1;$
$z := 1;$
$y := 0;$

Fig. 4. A mixed-mode program with its annotated behaviour disallowed by RPSI (left); an RA-consistent execution graph of its RPSI implementation (right)

5.2 A Lock-Based RPSI Implementation in RA

We present a lock-based reference implementation of RPSI in the RA fragment (Fig. 2) by using sequence locks [13,18,23,32]. Our implementation is both sound and complete with respect to our declarative RPSI specification in Sect. 5.1.

The RPSI implementation in Fig. 2 is rather similar to its PSI counterpart. The main difference between the two is in how they *validate* the tentative snapshot recorded in s. As before, in order to ensure that no intermediate *transactional* writes have intervened since s was recorded, for each location x in RS, the validation phase revisits vx, inspecting whether its value has changed from that recorded in v[x]. If this is the case, the snapshot is deemed invalid and the process is restarted. However, checking against intermediate transactional writes alone is not sufficient as it does not preclude the intervention of *non-transactional* writes. This is because unlike transactional writes, non-transactional writes do not update the version locks and as such their updates may go unnoticed. In order to rule out the possibility of intermediate non-transactional writes, for each location x the implementation checks the value of x against that recorded in s[x]. If the values do not agree, an intermediate non-transactional write has been detected: the snapshot fails validation and the process is restarted. Otherwise, the snapshot is successfully validated and returned in s. Observe that checking the value of x against s[x] does not entirely preclude the presence of non-transactional writes, in cases where the same value is written (nontransactionally) to x twice.

To understand this, consider the mixed-mode program on the left of Fig. 4 comprising a transaction in the left-hand thread and a non-transactional program in the right-hand thread writing the same value (1) to z twice. Note that the annotated behaviour is disallowed under RPSI: all execution graphs of the program with the annotated behaviour yield RPSI-inconsistent execution graphs. Intuitively, this is because the values read by the transaction ($x : 0, y : 0, z : 1$)

do not constitute a valid *snapshot*: at *no* point during the execution of this program, are the values of x, y and z as annotated.

Nevertheless, it is possible to find an RA-consistent execution of the RPSI implementation in Fig. 2 that reads the annotated values as its snapshot. Consider the execution graph on the right-hand side of Fig. 4, depicting a particular execution of the RPSI implementation (Fig. 2) of the program on the left. The rx, ry and rz denote the events reading the initial snapshot of x, y and z and recording them in s (line 5), respectively. Similarly, the rx', ry' and rz' denote the events validating the snapshots recorded in s (line 7). As T is the only transaction in the program, the version numbers vx, vy and vz remain unchanged throughout the execution and we have thus omitted the events reading (line 2) and validating (line 7) their values from the execution graph. Note that this execution graph is RA-consistent even though we cannot find a corresponding RPSI-consistent execution with the same outcome. To ensure the soundness of our implementation, we must thus rule out such scenarios.

To do this, we assume that if multiple non-transactional writes write the same value to the same location, they cannot race with the same transaction. More concretely, we assume that *every* RPSI-consistent execution graph of a given program satisfies the following condition:

$$\forall \mathtt{x}.\ \forall r \in \mathcal{T} \cap \mathcal{R}_{\mathtt{x}}.\ \forall w, w' \in \mathcal{NT} \cap \mathcal{W}_{\mathtt{x}}.$$
$$w \neq w' \wedge \mathtt{val_w}(w) = \mathtt{val_w}(w') \wedge (r, w) \notin \mathsf{rpsi\text{-}hb} \wedge (r, w') \notin \mathsf{rpsi\text{-}hb} \qquad (*)$$
$$\Rightarrow (w, r) \in \mathsf{rpsi\text{-}hb} \wedge (w', r) \in \mathsf{rpsi\text{-}hb}$$

That is, given a transactional read r from location $\mathtt{x}$, and any two distinct non-transactional writes w, w' of the same value to $\mathtt{x}$, either (i) at least one of the writes RPSI-happen-after r; or (ii) they both RPSI-happen-before r.

Observe that this does not hold of the program in Fig. 2. Note that this stipulation does not prevent two *transactions* to write the same value to a location $\mathtt{x}$. As such, in the absence of non-transactional writes, our RPSI implementation is equivalent to that of PSI in Sect. 4.2.

5.3 Implementation Soundness

The RPSI implementation in Fig. 2 is *sound*: for each consistent implementation graph G, a corresponding specification graph Γ can be constructed such that rpsi-consistent(Γ) holds. In what follows we state our soundness theorem and briefly describe our construction of consistent specification graphs. We refer the reader to the technical appendix [4] for the full soundness proof.

Theorem 3 (Soundness). *Let P be a program that possibly mixes transactional and non-transactional code. If every RPSI-consistent execution graph of P satisfies the condition in $(*)$, then for all RA-consistent implementation graphs G of the implementation in Fig. 2, there exists an RPSI-consistent specification graph Γ of the corresponding transactional program with the same program outcome.*

Constructing Consistent Specification Graphs. Constructing an RPSI-consistent specification graph from the implementation graph is similar to the corresponding PSI construction described in Sect. 4.3. More concretely, the events associated with non-transactional events remain unchanged and are simply added to the specification graph. On the other hand, the events associated with transactional events are adapted in a similar way to those of PSI in Sect. 4.3. In particular, observe that given an execution of the RPSI implementation with t transactions, as with the PSI implementation, the trace of each transaction $i \in \{1 \cdots t\}$ is of the form $\theta_i = Ls_i \xrightarrow{\text{po}} FS_i \xrightarrow{\text{po}} S_i \xrightarrow{\text{po}} Ts_i \xrightarrow{\text{po}} Us_i$, with Ls_i, FS_i, S_i, Ts_i and Us_i denoting analogous sequences of events to those of PSI. The difference between an RPSI trace θ_i and a PSI one is in the FS_i and S_i sequences, obtaining the snapshot. In particular, the validation phases of FS_i and S_i in RPSI include an additional read for each location to rule out intermediate non-transactional writes. As in the PSI construction, for each transactional trace θ_i of our implementation, we construct a corresponding trace of the specification as $\theta'_i = B_i \xrightarrow{\text{po}} Ts'_i \xrightarrow{\text{po}} E_i$, with B_i, E_i and Ts'_i as defined in Sect. 4.3.

Given a consistent RPSI implementation graph $G = (E, \mathsf{po}, \mathsf{rf}, \mathsf{mo})$, let $G.\mathcal{NT} \triangleq G.E \setminus \bigcup_{i \in \{1 \cdots t\}} \theta.E$ denote the non-transactional events of G. We construct a consistent RPSI specification graph $\Gamma = (E, \mathsf{po}, \mathsf{rf}, \mathsf{mo}, \mathcal{T})$ such that:

- $\Gamma.E \triangleq G.\mathcal{NT} \cup \bigcup_{i \in \{1 \cdots t\}} \theta'_i.E$ – the $\Gamma.E$ events comprise the non-transactional events in G and the events in each transactional trace θ'_i of the specification;
- $\Gamma.\mathsf{po} \triangleq G.\mathsf{po}|_{\Gamma.E}$ – the $\Gamma.\mathsf{po}$ is that of $G.\mathsf{po}$ restricted to the events in $\Gamma.E$;
- $\Gamma.\mathsf{rf} \triangleq \bigcup_{i \in \{1 \cdots t\}} \mathsf{RF}_i \cup G.\mathsf{rf}; [G.\mathcal{NT}]$ – the $\Gamma.\mathsf{rf}$ is the union of RF_i relations for transactional reads as defined in Sect. 4.3, together with the $G.\mathsf{rf}$ relation for non-transactional reads;
- $\Gamma.\mathsf{mo} \triangleq G.\mathsf{mo}|_{\Gamma.E}$ – the $\Gamma.\mathsf{mo}$ is that of $G.\mathsf{mo}$ restricted to the events in $\Gamma.E$;
- $\Gamma.\mathcal{T} \triangleq \bigcup_{i \in \{1 \cdots t\}} \theta'_i.E$, where for each $e \in \theta'_i.E$, we define $\mathsf{tx}(e) = i$.

We refer the reader to the technical appendix [4] for the full proof demonstrating that the above construction of Γ yields a consistent specification graph.

5.4   Implementation Completeness

The RPSI implementation in Fig. 2 is *complete*: for each consistent specification graph Γ a corresponding implementation graph G can be constructed such that RA-consistent(G) holds. We next state our completeness theorem and describe our construction of consistent implementation graphs. We refer the reader to the technical appendix [4] for the full completeness proof.

Theorem 4 (Completeness). *For all RPSI-consistent specification graphs Γ of a program, there exists an RA-consistent execution graph G of the implementation in Fig. 2 that has the same program outcome.*

Constructing Consistent Implementation Graphs. In order to construct an execution graph of the implementation G from the specification Γ, we follow similar steps as those in the corresponding PSI construction in Sect. 4.4. More concretely, the events associated with non-transactional events are unchanged and simply added to the implementation graph. For transactional events, given each trace θ_i' of a transaction in the specification, as before we construct an analogous trace of the implementation by inserting the appropriate events for acquiring and inspecting the version locks, as well as obtaining a snapshot. For each transaction class $\mathcal{T}_i \in \mathcal{T}/\mathsf{st}$, we first determine its read and write sets as before and subsequently decide the order in which the version locks are acquired and inspected. This then enables us to construct the 'reads-from' and 'modification-order' relations for the events associated with version locks.

Given a consistent execution graph of the specification $\Gamma = (E, \mathsf{po}, \mathsf{rf}, \mathsf{mo}, \mathcal{T})$, and a transaction class $\mathcal{T}_i \in \Gamma.\mathcal{T}/\mathsf{st}$, we define $\mathsf{WS}_{\mathcal{T}_i}$ and $\mathsf{RS}_{\mathcal{T}_i}$ as described in Sect. 4.4. Determining the ordering of lock events hinges on a similar observation as that in the PSI construction. Given a consistent execution graph of the specification $\Gamma = (E, \mathsf{po}, \mathsf{rf}, \mathsf{mo}, \mathcal{T})$, let for each location x the total order mo be given as: $w_1 \overset{\mathsf{mo|imm}}{\rightarrow} \cdots \overset{\mathsf{mo|imm}}{\rightarrow} w_{n_\mathsf{x}}$. This order can be broken into adjacent segments where the events of each segment are *either* non-transactional writes *or* belong to the *same* transaction. That is, given the transaction classes $\Gamma.\mathcal{T}/\mathsf{st}$, the order above is of the following form where $\mathcal{T}_1, \cdots, \mathcal{T}_m \in \Gamma.\mathcal{T}/\mathsf{st}$ and for each such $\mathcal{T}_i$ we have $\mathsf{x} \in \mathsf{WS}_{\mathcal{T}_i}$ and $w_{(i,1)} \cdots w_{(i,n_i)} \in \mathcal{T}_i$:

$$\underbrace{w_{(1,1)} \overset{\mathsf{mo|imm}}{\rightarrow} \cdots \overset{\mathsf{mo|imm}}{\rightarrow} w_{(1,n_1)}}_{\Gamma.\mathcal{NT} \cup \mathcal{T}_1} \overset{\mathsf{mo|imm}}{\rightarrow} \cdots \overset{\mathsf{mo|imm}}{\rightarrow} \underbrace{w_{(m,1)} \overset{\mathsf{mo|imm}}{\rightarrow} \cdots \overset{\mathsf{mo|imm}}{\rightarrow} w_{(m,n_m)}}_{\Gamma.\mathcal{NT} \cup \mathcal{T}_m}$$

Were this not the case and we had $w_1 \overset{\mathsf{mo}}{\rightarrow} w \overset{\mathsf{mo}}{\rightarrow} w_2$ such that $w_1, w_2 \in \mathcal{T}_i$ and $w \in \mathcal{T}_j \neq \mathcal{T}_i$, we would consequently have $w_1 \overset{\mathsf{mo}\mathcal{T}}{\rightarrow} w \overset{\mathsf{mo}\mathcal{T}}{\rightarrow} w_1$, contradicting the assumption that Γ is consistent. We thus define $\Gamma.\mathsf{MO}_\mathsf{x} = [\mathcal{T}_1 \cdots \mathcal{T}_m]$.

Note that each transactional execution trace of the specification is of the form $\theta_i' = B_i \overset{\mathsf{po}}{\rightarrow} Ts_i' \overset{\mathsf{po}}{\rightarrow} E_i$, with B_i, E_i and Ts_i' as described in Sect. 4.4. For each such θ_i', we construct a corresponding trace of our implementation as $\theta_i = Ls_i \overset{\mathsf{po}}{\rightarrow} S_i \overset{\mathsf{po}}{\rightarrow} Ts_i \overset{\mathsf{po}}{\rightarrow} Us_i$, where Ls_i, Ts_i and Us_i are as defined in Sect. 4.4, and $S_i = tr_i^{\mathsf{x}_1} \overset{\mathsf{po}}{\rightarrow} \cdots \overset{\mathsf{po}}{\rightarrow} tr_i^{\mathsf{x}_p} \overset{\mathsf{po}}{\rightarrow} vr_i^{\mathsf{x}_1} \overset{\mathsf{po}}{\rightarrow} \cdots \overset{\mathsf{po}}{\rightarrow} vr_i^{\mathsf{x}_p}$ denotes the sequence of events obtaining a tentative snapshot $(tr_i^{\mathsf{x}_j})$ and subsequently validating it $(vr_i^{\mathsf{x}_j})$. Each $tr_i^{\mathsf{x}_j}$ sequence is of the form $ivr_i^{\mathsf{x}_j} \overset{\mathsf{po}}{\rightarrow} ir_i^{\mathsf{x}_j} \overset{\mathsf{po}}{\rightarrow} s_i^{\mathsf{x}_j}$, with $ivr_i^{\mathsf{x}_j}$, $ir_i^{\mathsf{x}_j}$ and $s_i^{\mathsf{x}_j}$ defined below (with fresh identifiers). Similarly, each $vr_i^{\mathsf{x}_j}$ sequence is of the form $fr_i^{\mathsf{x}_j} \overset{\mathsf{po}}{\rightarrow} fvr_i^{\mathsf{x}_j}$, with $fr_i^{\mathsf{x}_j}$ and $fvr_i^{\mathsf{x}_j}$ defined as follows (with fresh identifiers). We then define the rf relation for each of these read events in S_i in a similar way.

For each $(\mathsf{x}, r) \in \mathsf{RS}_{\mathcal{T}_i}$, when r (the event in the specification class $\mathcal{T}_i$ that reads the value of x) reads from w in the specification graph $((w, r) \in \Gamma.\mathsf{rf})$, we add (w, ir_i^x) and (w, fr_i^x) to the rf of G (the first line of IRF_i^2 below). For version locks, as before if transaction $\mathcal{T}_i$ also writes to x_j, then $ivr_i^{\mathsf{x}_j}$ and $fvr_i^{\mathsf{x}_j}$ events (reading and validating vx_j), read from the lock event in $\mathcal{T}_i$ that acquired vx_j, namely $L_i^{\mathsf{x}_j}$. Similarly, if $\mathcal{T}_i$ does not write to x_j and it reads the value of x_j

written by the initial write, $init_x$, then $ivr_i^{x_j}$ and $fvr_i^{x_j}$ read the value written to vx_j by the initial write to vx, $init_{vx}$. Lastly, if transaction $\mathcal{T}_i$ does not write to x_j and it reads x_j from a write other than $init_x$, then $ir_i^{x_j}$ and $vr_i^{x_j}$ read from the unlock event of a transaction $\mathcal{T}_j$ (i.e. U_j^x), who has x in its write set and whose write to x, w_x, maximally 'RPSI-happens-before' r. That is, for all other such writes that 'RPSI-happen-before' r, then w_x 'RPSI-happens-after' them.

$$\mathsf{IRF}_i^2 \triangleq \bigcup_{(x,r)\in\mathsf{RS}_{\mathcal{T}_i}} \left\{ \begin{matrix} (w, ir_i^x), \\ (w, fr_i^x), \\ (w', ivr_i^x), \\ (w', fvr_i^x) \end{matrix} \;\middle|\; \begin{matrix} (w,r) \in \Gamma.\mathsf{rf} \wedge (x \in \mathsf{WS}_{\mathcal{T}_i} \Rightarrow w'{=}L_i^x) \\ \wedge\, (x \notin \mathsf{WS}_{\mathcal{T}_i} \wedge w{=}init_x \Rightarrow w'{=}init_{vx}) \\ \wedge\, (x \notin \mathsf{WS}_{\mathcal{T}_i} \wedge w{\neq}init_x \Rightarrow \\ \exists w_x, \mathcal{T}_j.\ w_x \in \mathcal{T}_j \cap \mathcal{W}_x \wedge w_x \overset{\mathsf{rpsi\text{-}hb}}{\rightarrow} r \wedge w'{=}U_j^x \\ \wedge [\forall w_x', \mathcal{T}_k.\ w_x' {\in} \mathcal{T}_k \cap \mathcal{W}_x \wedge w_x' \overset{\mathsf{rpsi\text{-}hb}}{\rightarrow} r \Rightarrow w_x' \overset{\mathsf{rpsi\text{-}hb}}{\rightarrow} w_x]) \end{matrix} \right\}$$

$ir_i^{x_j} {=} fr_i^{x_j} {=} \mathsf{R}(x_j, v) \quad s_i^{x_j} {=} \mathsf{W}(\mathsf{s}[x_j], v) \quad$ s.t. $\exists w.\ (w, ir_i^{x_j}) \in \mathsf{IRF}_i^2 \wedge \mathsf{val}_w(w){=}v$

$ivr_i^{x_j} {=} fvr_i^{x_j} {=} \mathsf{R}(vx_j, v)$ s.t. $\exists w.\ (w, ivr_i^{x_j}) \in \mathsf{IRF}_i^2 \wedge \mathsf{val}_w(w){=}v$

We are now in a position to construct our implementation graph. Given a consistent execution graph Γ of the specification, we construct an execution graph of the implementation, $G = (E, \mathsf{po}, \mathsf{rf}, \mathsf{mo})$, such that:

- $G.E = \displaystyle\bigcup_{\mathcal{T}_i \in \Gamma.\mathcal{T}/\mathsf{st}} \theta_i.E \cup \Gamma.\mathcal{N}\mathcal{T}$;
- $G.\mathsf{po}$ is defined as $\Gamma.\mathsf{po}$ extended by the po for the additional events of G, given by the θ_i traces defined above;
- $G.\mathsf{rf} = \displaystyle\bigcup_{\mathcal{T}_i \in \Gamma.\mathcal{T}/\mathsf{st}} (\mathsf{IRF}_i^1 \cup \mathsf{IRF}_i^2)$, with IRF_i^1 as in Sect. 4.4 and IRF_i^2 defined above;
- $G.\mathsf{mo} = \Gamma.\mathsf{mo} \cup \Big(\displaystyle\bigcup_{\mathcal{T}_i \in \Gamma.\mathcal{T}/\mathsf{st}} \mathsf{IMO}_i \Big)^+$, with IMO_i as defined in Sect. 4.4.

6   Conclusions and Future Work

We studied PSI, for the first time to our knowledge, as a consistency model for STMs as it has several advantages over other consistency models, thanks to its performance and monotonic behaviour. We addressed two significant drawbacks of PSI which prevent its widespread adoption. First, the absence of a simple lock-based reference implementation to allow the programmers to readily understand and reason about PSI programs. To address this, we developed a lock-based reference implementation of PSI in the RA fragment of C11 (using sequence locks), that is both sound and complete with respect to its declarative specification. Second, the absence of a formal PSI model in the presence of mixed-mode accesses. To this end, we formulated a declarative specification of RPSI (robust PSI) accounting for both transactional and non-transactional accesses. Our RPSI specification is an extension of PSI in that in the absence of non-transactional accesses it coincides with PSI. To provide a more intuitive account of RPSI, we developed a simple lock-based RPSI reference implementation by adjusting our PSI implementation. We established the soundness and completeness of our RPSI implementation against its declarative specification.

As directions of future work, we plan to build on top of the work presented here in three ways. First, we plan to explore possible lock-based reference implementations for PSI and RPSI in the context of other weak memory models, such as the full C11 memory models [9]. Second, we plan to study other weak transactional consistency models, such as SI [10], ALA (asymmetric lock atomicity), ELA (encounter-time lock atomicity) [28], and those of ANSI SQL, including RU (read-uncommitted), RC (read-committed) and RR (repeatable reads), in the STM context. We aim to investigate possible lock-based reference implementations for these models that would allow the programmers to understand and reason about STM programs with such weak guarantees. Third, taking advantage of the operational models provided by our simple lock-based reference implementations (those presented in this article as well as those in future work), we plan to develop reasoning techniques that would allow us to verify properties of STM programs. This can be achieved by either extending existing program logics for weak memory, or developing new program logics for currently unsupported models. In particular, we can reason about the PSI models presented here by developing custom proof rules in the existing program logics for RA such as [22,39].

Acknowledgments. We thank the ESOP 2018 reviewers for their constructive feedback. This research was supported in part by a European Research Council (ERC) Consolidator Grant for the project "RustBelt", under the European Union's Horizon 2020 Framework Programme (grant agreement no. 683289). The second author was additionally partly supported by Len Blavatnik and the Blavatnik Family foundation.

References

1. The Clojure Language: Refs and Transactions. http://clojure.org/refs
2. Haskell STM. http://hackage.haskell.org/package/stm-2.2.0.1/docs/Control-Concurrent-STM.html
3. Software transactional memory (Scala). https://doc.akka.io/docs/akka/1.2/scala/stm.html
4. Technical appendix for this paper. http://plv.mpi-sws.org/transactions/
5. Generalized isolation level definitions. In: Proceedings of the 16th International Conference on Data Engineering (2000)
6. Technical specification for C++ extensions for transactional memory (2015). http://www.open-std.org/jtc1/sc22/wg21/docs/papers/2015/n4514.pdf
7. Adya, A.: Weak consistency: a generalized theory and optimistic implementations for distributed transactions. Ph.D. thesis, MIT (1999)
8. Alglave, J., Maranget, L., Tautschnig, M.: Herding cats: modelling, simulation, testing, and data mining for weak memory. ACM Trans. Program. Lang. Syst. **36**(2), 7:1–7:74 (2014)
9. Batty, M., Owens, S., Sarkar, S., Sewell, P., Weber, T.: Mathematizing C++ concurrency. In: Proceedings of the 38th Annual ACM SIGPLAN-SIGACT Symposium on Principles of Programming Languages, pp. 55–66 (2011)
10. Berenson, H., Bernstein, P., Gray, J., Melton, J., O'Neil, E., O'Neil, P.: A critique of ANSI SQL isolation levels. In: Proceedings of the 1995 ACM SIGMOD International Conference on Management of Data, pp. 1–10 (1995)

11. Bieniusa, A., Fuhrmann, T.: Consistency in hindsight: a fully decentralized STM algorithm. In: Proceedings of the 2010 IEEE International Symposium on Parallel and Distributed Processing, IPDPS 2010, pp. 1–12 (2010)
12. Blundell, C., Lewis, E.C., Martin, M.M.K.: Deconstructing transactions: the subtleties of atomicity. In: 4th Annual Workshop on Duplicating, Deconstructing, and Debunking (2005)
13. Boehm, H.J.: Can seqlocks get along with programming language memory models? In: Proceedings of the 2012 ACM SIGPLAN Workshop on Memory Systems Performance and Correctness, pp. 12–20 (2012)
14. Cerone, A., Gotsman, A.: Analysing snapshot isolation. In: Proceedings of the 2016 ACM Symposium on Principles of Distributed Computing, pp. 55–64 (2016)
15. Cerone, A., Gotsman, A., Yang, H.: Transaction chopping for parallel snapshot isolation. In: Moses, Y. (ed.) DISC 2015. LNCS, vol. 9363, pp. 388–404. Springer, Heidelberg (2015). https://doi.org/10.1007/978-3-662-48653-5_26
16. Daudjee, K., Salem, K.: Lazy database replication with snapshot isolation. In: Proceedings of the 32nd International Conference on Very Large Data Bases, pp. 715–726 (2006)
17. Harris, T., Marlow, S., Peyton-Jones, S., Herlihy, M.: Composable memory transactions. In: Proceedings of the Tenth ACM SIGPLAN Symposium on Principles and Practice of Parallel Programming, pp. 48–60 (2005)
18. Hemminger, S.: Fast reader/writer lock for gettimeofday 2.5.30. http://lwn.net/Articles/7388/
19. Herlihy, M., Moss, J.E.B.: Transactional memory: architectural support for lock-free data structures. In: Proceedings of the 20th Annual International Symposium on Computer Architecture, pp. 289–300 (1993)
20. Hickey, R.: The Clojure programming language. In: Proceedings of the 2008 Symposium on Dynamic Languages, p. 1:1 (2008)
21. Lahav, O., Giannarakis, N., Vafeiadis, V.: Taming release-acquire consistency. In: Proceedings of the 43rd Annual ACM SIGPLAN-SIGACT Symposium on Principles of Programming Languages, pp. 649–662 (2016)
22. Lahav, O., Vafeiadis, V.: Owicki-Gries reasoning for weak memory models. In: Halldórsson, M.M., Iwama, K., Kobayashi, N., Speckmann, B. (eds.) ICALP 2015, Part II. LNCS, vol. 9135, pp. 311–323. Springer, Heidelberg (2015). https://doi.org/10.1007/978-3-662-47666-6_25
23. Lameter, C.: Effective synchronization on Linux/NUMA systems (2005). http://www.lameter.com/gelato2005.pdf
24. Lamport, L.: How to make a multiprocessor computer that correctly executes multiprocess programs. IEEE Trans. Comput. 28(9), 690–691 (1979)
25. Litz, H., Cheriton, D., Firoozshahian, A., Azizi, O., Stevenson, J.P.: SI-TM: reducing transactional memory abort rates through snapshot isolation. SIGPLAN Not. 42(1), 383–398 (2014)
26. Litz, H., Dias, R.J., Cheriton, D.R.: Efficient correction of anomalies in snapshot isolation transactions. ACM Trans. Archit. Code Optim. 11(4), 65:1–65:24 (2015)
27. Martin, M., Blundell, C., Lewis, E.: Subtleties of transactional memory atomicity semantics. IEEE Comput. Archit. Lett. 5(2), 17 (2006)
28. Menon, V., Balensiefer, S., Shpeisman, T., Adl-Tabatabai, A.R., Hudson, R.L., Saha, B., Welc, A.: Single global lock semantics in a weakly atomic STM. SIGPLAN Not. 43(5), 15–26 (2008)
29. Owens, S., Sarkar, S., Sewell, P.: A better x86 memory model: x86-TSO. In: Proceedings of the 22nd International Conference on Theorem Proving in Higher Order Logics, pp. 391–407 (2009)

30. Peng, D., Dabek, F.: Large-scale incremental processing using distributed transactions and notifications. In: Proceedings of the 9th USENIX Conference on Operating Systems Design and Implementation, pp. 251–264 (2010)

31. Pulte, C., Flur, S., Deacon, W., French, J., Sarkar, S., Sewell, P.: Simplifying ARM concurrency: multicopy-atomic axiomatic and operational models for ARMv8. Proc. ACM Program. Lang. 2(POPL), 19:1–19:29 (2017). http://doi.acm.org/10.1145/3158107

32. Rajwar, R., Goodman, J.R.: Speculative lock elision: enabling highly concurrent multithreaded execution. In: Proceedings of the 34th Annual ACM/IEEE International Symposium on Microarchitecture, pp. 294–305 (2001)

33. Serrano, D., Patino-Martinez, M., Jimenez-Peris, R., Kemme, B.: Boosting database replication scalability through partial replication and 1-copy-snapshot-isolation. In: Proceedings of the 13th Pacific Rim International Symposium on Dependable Computing, pp. 290–297 (2007)

34. Sewell, P., Sarkar, S., Owens, S., Zappa Nardelli, F., Myreen, M.O.: x86-TSO: a rigorous and usable programmer's model for x86 multiprocessors. Commun. ACM 53(7), 89–97 (2010)

35. Shavit, N., Touitou, D.: Software transactional memory. In: Proceedings of the Fourteenth Annual ACM Symposium on Principles of Distributed Computing, pp. 204–213 (1995)

36. Sovran, Y., Power, R., Aguilera, M.K., Li, J.: Transactional storage for geo-replicated systems. In: Proceedings of the Twenty-Third ACM Symposium on Operating Systems Principles, pp. 385–400 (2011)

37. CORPORATE SPARC International Inc.: The SPARC Architecture Manual: Version 8 (1992)

38. CORPORATE SPARC International Inc.: The SPARC Architecture Manual (Version 9) (1994)

39. Vafeiadis, V., Narayan, C.: Relaxed separation logic: a program logic for c11 concurrency. In: Proceedings of the 2013 ACM SIGPLAN International Conference on Object Oriented Programming Systems Languages and Applications, pp. 867–884 (2013)

Eventual Consistency for CRDTs

Radha Jagadeesan and James Riely$^{(\boxtimes)}$ (iD)

DePaul University, Chicago, USA
{rjagadeesan,jriely}@cs.depaul.edu

Abstract. We address the problem of *validity* in eventually consistent (EC) systems: In what sense does an EC data structure satisfy the sequential specification of that data structure? Because EC is a very weak criterion, our definition does not describe every EC system; however it is expressive enough to describe any Convergent or Commutative Replicated Data Type (CRDT).

1 Introduction

In a replicated implementation of a data structure, there are two impediments to requiring that all replicas achieve consensus on a global total order of the operations performed on the data structure (Lamport 1978): (a) the associated serialization bottleneck negatively affects performance and scalability (*e.g.* see (Ellis and Gibbs 1989)), and (b) the CAP theorem imposes a tradeoff between consistency and partition-tolerance (Gilbert and Lynch 2002).

In systems based on *optimistic replication* (Vogels 2009; Saito and Shapiro 2005), a replica may execute an operation without synchronizing with other replicas. If the operation is a mutator, the other replicas are updated asynchronously. Due to the vagaries of the network, the replicas could receive and apply the updates in possibly different orders.

For sequential systems, the correctness problem is typically divided into two tasks: proving *termination* and proving *partial correctness*. Termination requires that the program eventually halt on all inputs, whereas partial correctness requires that the program only returns results that are allowed by the specification.

For replicated systems, the analogous goals are *convergence* and *validity*. Convergence requires that all replicas eventually agree. Validity requires that they agree on something sensible. In a replicated list, for example, if the only value put into the list is 1, then convergence ensures that all replicas eventually see the same value for the head of the list; validity requires that the value be 1.

Convergence has been well-understood since the earliest work on replicated systems. Convergence is typically defined as *eventual consistency*, which requires that once all messages are delivered, all replicas have the same state. *Strong eventual consistency* (SEC) additionally requires convergence for all subsets of messages: replicas that have seen the same messages must have the same state.

© The Author(s) 2018
A. Ahmed (Ed.): ESOP 2018, LNCS 10801, pp. 968–995, 2018.
https://doi.org/10.1007/978-3-319-89884-1_34

Perhaps surprisingly, finding an appropriate definition of validity for replicated systems remains an open problem. There are solutions which use concurrent specifications, discussed below. But, as Shavit (2011) noted:

"It is infinitely easier and more intuitive for us humans to specify how abstract data structures behave in a sequential setting, where there are no interleavings. Thus, the standard approach to arguing the safety properties of a concurrent data structure is to specify the structure's properties sequentially, and find a way to map its concurrent executions to these 'correct' sequential ones."

In this paper we give the first definition of validity that is both (1) derived from standard sequential specifications and (2) validates the examples of interest.

We take the "examples of interest" to be *Convergent/Commutative Replicated Data Types* (CRDTs). These are replicated structures that obey certain monotonicity or commutativity properties. As an example of a CRDT, consider the *add-wins set*, also called an "observed remove" set in Shapiro et al. (2011a). The add-wins set behaves like a sequential set if add and remove operations on the same element are ordered. The concurrent execution of an add and remove result in the element being added to the set; thus the remove is ignored and the "add wins." This concurrent specification is very simple, but as we will see in the next section, it is quite difficult to pin down the relationship between the CRDT and the sequential specification used in the CRDT's definition. This paper is the first to successfully capture this relationship.

Many replicated data types are CRDTs, but not all (Shapiro et al. 2011a). Notably, Amazon's Dynamo (DeCandia et al. 2007) is not a CRDT. Indeed, interest in CRDTs is motivated by a desire to avoid the well-know concurrency anomalies suffered by Dynamo and other ad hoc systems (Bieniusa et al. 2012).

Shapiro et al. (2011b) introduced the notion of CRDT and proved that every CRDT has an SEC implementation. Their definition of SEC includes convergence, but not validity.

The validity requirement can be broken into two components. We describe these below using the example of a list data type that supports only two operations: the mutator put, which adds an element to the end of the list, and the query q, which returns the state of the list. This structure can be specified as a set of strings such as "put(1); put(3); q=[1,3]" and "put(1); put(2); put(3); q=[1,2,3]".

- *Linearization* requires that a response be consistent with some specification string. A state that received put(1) and put(3), may report q=[1,3] or q=[3,1], but not q=[2,1,3], since 2 has not been put into the list.
- *Monotonicity* requires that states evolve in a sensible way. We might permit the state q=[1,3] to evolve into q=[1,2,3], due to the arrival of action put(2). But we would not expect that q=[1,3] could evolve into q=[3,1], since the data type does not support deletion or reordering.

Burckhardt et al. (2012) provide a formal definition of validity using partial orders over events: linearizations respect the partial order on events; monotonicity is ensured by requiring that evolution extends the partial order. Similar definitions can be found in Jagadeesan and Riely (2015) and Perrin et al. (2015). Replicated data structures that are sound with respect to this definition enjoy many good properties, which we discuss throughout this paper. However, this notion of correctness is not general enough to capture common CRDTs, such as the add-wins set.

This lack of expressivity lead Burckhardt et al. (2014) to abandon notions of validity that appeal directly to a sequential specification. Instead they work directly with *concurrent* specifications, formalizing the style of specification found informally in Shapiro et al. (2011b). This has been a fruitful line of work, leading to proof rules (Gotsman et al. 2016) and extensions (Bouajjani et al. 2014). See (Burckhardt 2014; Viotti and Vukolic 2016) for a detailed treatment.

Positively, concurrent specifications can be used to validate any replicated structure, including CRDTs as well as anomalous structures such as Dynamo. Negatively, concurrent specifications have no the clear connection to their sequential counterparts. In this paper, we restore this connection. We arrive at a definition of SEC that admits CRDTs, but rejects Dynamo.

The following "corner cases" are a useful sanity-check for any proposed notion of validity.

- The principle of *single threaded semantics* (PSTS) (Haas et al. 2015) states that if an execution uses only a single replica, it should behave according to the sequential semantics.
- The principle of *single master* (PSM) (Budhiraja et al. 1993) states that if all mutators in an execution are initiated at a single replica, then the execution should be linearizable (Herlihy and Wing 1990).
- The principle of *permutation equivalence* (PPE) (Bieniusa et al. 2012) states that "if all sequential permutations of updates lead to equivalent states, then it should also hold that concurrent executions of the updates lead to equivalent states."

PSTS and PSM say that a replicated structure should behave sequentially when replication is not used. PPE says that the order of independent operations should not matter. Our definition implies all three conditions. Dynamo fails PPE (Bieniusa et al. 2012), and thus fails to pass our definition of SEC.

In the next section, we describe the validity problem and our solution in detail, using the example of a binary set. The formal definitions follow in Sect. 3. We state some consequences of the definition and prove that the add-wins set satisfies our definition. In Sect. 4, we describe a collaborative text editor and prove that it is SEC. In Sect. 5 we characterize the programmer's view of a CRDT by defining the *most general* CRDT that satisfies a given sequential specification. We show that any program that is correct using the most general CRDT will be correct using a more restricted CRDT. We also show that our validity criterion for SEC is *local* in the sense of Herlihy and Wing (1990): independent structures can be verified independently. In Sect. 6, we apply these results to prove the correctness of a graph that is implemented using two SEC sets.

Our work is inspired by the study of relaxed memory, such as (Alglave 2012). In particular, we have drawn insight from the RMO model of Higham and Kawash (2000).

2   Understanding Replicated Sets

In this section, we motivate the definition of SEC using replicated sets as an example. The final definition is quite simple, but requires a fresh view of both executions and specifications. We develop the definition in stages, each of which requires a subtle shift in perspective. Each subsection begins with an example and ends with a summary.

2.1   Mutators and Non-mutators

An *implementation* is a set of *executions*. We model executions abstractly as labelled partial orders (LPOs). The ordering of the LPO captures the history that precedes an event, which we refer to as *visibility*.

$$(1)$$

Here the events are a through j, with labels +0, +1, etc., and order represented by arrows. The LPO describes an execution with two replicas, shown horizontally, with time passing from left to right. Initially, the top replica receives a request to add 0 to the set ($+0^a$). Concurrently, the bottom replica receives a request to add 1 ($+1^b$). Then each replica is twice asked to report on the items contained in the set. At first, the top replica replies that 0 is present and 1 is absent ($\checkmark 0^b \mathsf{X} 1^c$), whereas the bottom replica answers with the reverse ($\mathsf{X} 0^g \checkmark 1^h$). Once the add operations are visible at all replicas, however, the replicas give the same responses ($\checkmark 0^d \checkmark 1^e$ and $\checkmark 0^i \checkmark 1^j$).

LPOs with non-interacting replicas can be denoted compactly using sequential and parallel composition. For example, the prefix of (1) that only includes the first three events at each replica can be written $(+0^a; \checkmark 0^b; \mathsf{X} 1^c) \parallel (+1^f; \mathsf{X} 0^g; \checkmark 1^h)$.

A *specification* is a set of *strings*. Let SET be the specification of a sequential set with elements 0 and 1. Then we expect that SET includes the string "+0$\checkmark$0X1", but not "+0X0$\checkmark$1". Indeed, each specification string can uniquely be extended with either $\checkmark$0 or X0 and either $\checkmark$1 or X1.

There is an isomorphism between strings and labelled *total* orders. Thus, specification strings correspond to the restricted class of LPOs where the visibility relation provides a total order.

Linearizability (Herlihy and Wing 1990) is the gold standard for concurrent correctness in tightly coupled systems. Under linearizability, an execution is valid if there exists a linearization τ of the events in the execution such that for every event e, the prefix of e in τ is a valid specification string.

Execution (1) is not linearizable. The failure can already be seen in the sub-LPO $(+0^a; X1^c) \parallel (+1^f; X0^g)$. Any linearization must have either $+1^f$ before $X1^c$ or $+0^a$ before $X0^g$. In either case, the linearization is invalid for SET.

Although it is not linearizable, execution (1) is admitted by every CRDT SET in Shapiro et al. (2011a). To validate such examples, Burckhardt et al. (2012) develop a weaker notion of validity by dividing labels into *mutators* and *accessors* (also known as non-mutators). Similar definitions appear in Jagadeesan and Riely (2015) and Perrin et al. (2015). Mutators change the state of a replica, and accessors report on the state without changing it. For SET, the mutators M and non-mutators $\overline{M}$ are as follows.

$M = \{+0, -0, +1, -1\}$, representing addition and removal of bits 0 and 1.

$\overline{M} = \{X0, \checkmark 0, X1, \checkmark 1\}$, representing membership tests returning false or true.

Define the *mutator prefix* of an event e to include e and the *mutators* visible to e. An execution is valid if there exists a linearization of the execution, τ, such that for every event e, the *mutator prefix* of e in τ is a valid specification string.

It is straightforward to see that execution (1) satisfies this weaker criterion. For both $\checkmark 0^b$ and $X1^c$, the mutator prefix is $+0^a$. This includes $+0^a$ but not $+1^f$, and thus their answers are validated. Symmetrically, the mutator prefixes of $X0^g$ and $\checkmark 1^h$ only include $+1^f$. The mutator prefixes for the final four events include both $+0^a$ and $+1^f$, but none of the prior accessors.

Summary: Convergent states must agree on the final order of mutators, but intermediate states may see incompatible subsequences of this order. By restricting attention to mutator prefixes, the later states need not linearize these incompatible views of the partial past.

This relaxation is analogous to the treatment of non-mutators in update serializability (Hansdah and Patnaik 1986; Garcia-Molina and Wiederhold 1982), which requires a global serialization order for mutators, ignoring non-mutators.

2.2 Dependency

The following LPO is admitted by the add-wins SET discussed in the introduction.

$$\begin{array}{c} \boxed{+0}^a \rightarrow \boxed{+1}^b \rightarrow \boxed{-1}^c \searrow \\ \boxed{\checkmark 0}^g \rightarrow \boxed{\checkmark 1}^h \\ \boxed{+1}_d \rightarrow \boxed{+0}_e \rightarrow \boxed{-0}_f \nearrow \end{array} \qquad (2)$$

In any CRDT implementation, the effect of $+1^b$ is negated by the subsequent -1^c The same reasoning holds for $+0^e$ and -0^f. In an add-wins set, however, the *concurrent* adds, $+0^a$ and $+1^d$, win over the deletions. Thus, in the final state both 0 and 1 are present.

This LPO is not valid under the definition of the previous subsection: Since $\checkmark 0^g$ and $\checkmark 1^h$ see the same mutators, they must agree on a linearization of $(+0^a; +1^b; -1^c) \parallel (+1^d; +0^e; -0^f)$. Any linearization must end in either -1^c or -0^f; thus it is not possible for both $\checkmark 0^g$ and $\checkmark 1^h$ to be valid.

Similar issues arise in relaxed memory models, where program order is often relaxed between uses of independent variables (Alglave et al. 2014). Generalizing, we write $m \mathbin{\#} n$ to indicate that labels m and n are dependent. Dependency is a property of a *specification*, not an implementation. Our results only apply to specifications that support a suitable notion of dependency, as detailed in Sect. 3. For SET, $\#$ is an equivalence relation with two equivalence classes, corresponding to actions on the independent values 0 and 1.

$$\# = \{+0,\ -0,\ \text{X0},\ \checkmark 0\}^2 \cup \{+1,\ -1,\ \text{X1},\ \checkmark 1\}^2, \text{ where } D^2 = D \times D.$$

While the dependency relation for SET is an equivalence, this is not required: In Sect. 4 we establish the correctness of collaborative text editing protocol with an intransitive dependency relation.

The *dependent restriction* of (2) is as follows.

$$\tag{3}$$

In the previous subsection, we defined validity using the *mutator prefix* of an event. We arrive at a weaker definition by restricting attention to the *mutator prefix of the dependent restriction*.

Under this definition, execution (2) is validated: Any interleaving of the strings $+0^e\text{-}0^f+0^a\checkmark 0^g$ and $+1^b\text{-}1^c+1^d\checkmark 1^h$ linearizes the dependent restriction of (2) given in (3).

Summary: CRDTs allow independent mutators to commute. We formalize this intuition by restricting attention to mutator prefixes of the dependent restriction. The CRDT must respect program order between dependent operations, but is free to reorder independent operations.

This relaxation is analogous to the distinction between *program order* and *preserved* program order (PPO) in relaxed memory models (Higham and Kawash 2000; Alglave 2012). Informally, PPO is the suborder of program order that removes order between independent memory actions, such as successive reads on different locations without an intervening memory barrier.

2.3 Puns

The following LPO is admitted by the add-wins SET.

$$\tag{4}$$

As in execution (2), the add $+0^a$ is undone by the following remove -0^b, but the concurrent add $+0^e$ wins over -0^b, allowing $\checkmark 0^c$. In effect, $\checkmark 0^c$ sees the order of the mutators as $+0^a\,\text{-}0^b+0^e$. Symmetrically, $\checkmark 0^g$ sees the order as $+0^e\,\text{-}0^f+0^a$.

While this is very natural from the viewpoint of a CRDT, there is no linearization of the events that includes both $+0^a -0^b +0^e$ and $+0^e -0^f +0^a$, since $+0^a$ and $+0^e$ must appear in different orders.

Indeed, this LPO is not valid under the definition of the previous subsection. First note that all events are mutually dependent. To prove validity we must find a linearization that satisfies the given requirements. Any linearization of the mutators must end in either -0^b or -0^f. Suppose we choose $+0^a -0^b +0^e -0^f$ and look for a mutator prefix to satisfy $\checkmark 0^g$. (All other choices lead to similar problems.) Since -0^f precedes $\checkmark 0^g$ and is the last mutator in our chosen linearization, every possible witness for $\checkmark 0^g$ must end with mutator -0^f. Indeed the only possible witness is $+0^a +0^e -0^f \checkmark 0^g$. However, this is not a valid specification string.

The problem is that we are linearizing *events*, rather than *labels*. If we shift to linearizing labels, then execution (4) is allowed. Fix the final order for the mutators to be $+0 -0 +0 -0$. The execution is allowed if we can find a subsequence that linearizes the labels visible at each event. It suffices to choose the witnesses as follows. In the table, we group events with a common linearization together.

$$+0^a, +0^e: \ +0 \qquad\qquad \checkmark 0^c, \checkmark 0^g: \ +0-0+0\checkmark 0$$
$$-0^b, -0^f: \ +0-0 \qquad\qquad \cancel{X}0^d, \cancel{X}0^h: \ +0-0+0-0\cancel{X}0$$

Each of these is a valid specification string. In addition, looking only at mutators, each is a subsequence of $+0 -0 +0 -0$.

In execution (4), each of the witnesses is actually a *prefix* of the final mutator order, but, in general, it is necessary to allow *subsequences*.

$$(5)$$

Execution (5) is admitted by the add-wins SET. It is validated by the final mutator sequence $-0 +0$. The mutator prefix $+0$ of b is a subsequence of $-0 +0$, but not a prefix.

Summary: While dependent events at a single replica must be linearized in order, concurrent events may slip anywhere into the linearization. A CRDT may *pun* on concurrent events with same label, using them in different positions at different replicas. Thus a CRDT may establish a final total over the labels of an execution even when there is no linearization of the events.

2.4 Frontiers

In the introduction, we mentioned that the validity problem can be decomposed into the separate concerns of *linearizability* and *monotonicity*. The discussion thus far has centered on the appropriate meaning of linearizability for CRDTs. In this subsection and the next, we look at the constraints imposed by monotonicity.

Consider the prefix $\{+0^a, -0^b, +0^e, \checkmark 0^c, -0^f\}$ of execution (4), extended with action $\chi 0^x$, with visibility order as follows.

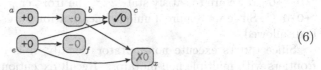

$$(6)$$

This execution is *not strong* EC, since $\checkmark 0^c$ and $\chi 0^x$ see exactly the same mutators, yet provide incompatible answers.

Unfortunately, execution (6) is valid by the definition given in the previous section: The witnesses for a–f are as before. In particular, the witness for $\checkmark 0^c$ is "+0-0+0$\checkmark$0". The witness for $\chi 0^x$ is "+0+0-0χ0". In each case, the mutator prefix is a subsequence of the global mutator order "+0-0+0-0".

It is well known that punning can lead to bad jokes. In this case, the problem is that $\chi 0^x$ is punning on a concurrent -0 that cannot be matched by a visible -0 in its history: the execution -0 that is visible to $\chi 0^x$ must appear *between* the two +0 operations; the specification -0 that is used by $\chi 0^x$ must appear *after*. The final states of execution (4) have seen both remove operations, therefore the pun is harmless there. But $\checkmark 0^c$ and $\chi 0^x$ have seen only one remove. They must agree on how it is used.

Up to now, we have discussed the linearization of each event in isolation. We must also consider the relationship between these linearizations. When working with linearizations of *events*, it is sufficient to require that the linearization chosen for each event be a subsequence for the linearization chosen for each visible predecessor; since events are unique, there can be no confusion in the lineariza tion about which event is which. Execution (6) shows that when working with linearizations of *labels*, it is insufficient to consider the relationship between individual events. The linearization "+0+0-0χ0" chosen for $\chi 0^x$ is a supersequence of those chosen for its predecessors: "+0" for $+0^e$ and "+0-0" for -0^b. The linearization "+0-0+0$\checkmark$0" chosen for $\checkmark 0^c$ is also a supersequence for the same predecessors. And yet, $\checkmark 0^c$ and $\chi 0^x$ are incompatible states.

Sequential systems have a single state, which evolves over time. In distributed systems, each replica has its own state, and it is this *set* of states that evolves. Such a set of states is called a *(consistent) cut* (Chandy and Lamport 1985).

A *cut* of an LPO is a sub-LPO that is down-closed with respect to visibility. The *frontier* of cut is the set of maximal elements. For example, there are 14 frontiers of execution (6): the singletons $\{+0^a\}$, $\{-0^b\}$, $\{\checkmark 0^c\}$, $\{+0^e\}$, $\{-0^f\}$, $\{\chi 0^x\}$, the pairs $\{+0^a, +0^e\}$, $\{+0^a, -0^f\}$, $\{-0^b, +0^e\}$, $\{-0^b, -0^f\}$, $\{\checkmark 0^c, -0^f\}$, $\{\checkmark 0^c, \chi 0^x\}$, $\{\chi 0^x, -0^f\}$, and the triple $\{\checkmark 0^c, \chi 0^x, -0^f\}$. As we explain below, we consider non-mutators in isolation. Thus we do not consider the last four cuts, which include a non-mutator with other events. That leaves 10 frontiers. The definition of the previous section only considered the 6 singletons. Singleton frontiers are generated by *pointed cuts*, with a single maximal element.

When applied to frontiers, the monotonicity requirement invalidates execu tion (6). Monotonicity requires that the linearization chosen for a frontier be a subsequence of the linearization chosen for any extension of that frontier. If we are to satisfy state $\checkmark 0^c$ in execution (6), the frontier $\{-0^b, +0^e\}$ must linearize to "+0-0+0". If we are to satisfy state $\chi 0^x$, the frontier $\{-0^b, +0^e\}$ must linearize to "+0+0-0". Since we require a unique linearization for each frontier, the execution is disallowed.

Since CRDTs execute non-mutators locally, it is important that we ignore frontiers with multiple non-mutators. Recall execution (4):

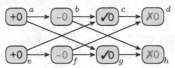

There is no specification string that linearizes the cut with frontier $\{\checkmark 0^c, \checkmark 0^g\}$, since we cannot have $\checkmark 0$ immediately after -0. If we consider only pointed cuts for non-mutators, then the execution is SEC, with witnesses as follows.

$\{+0^a\}, \{+0^e\}$	: +0	$\{\checkmark 0^c\}, \{\checkmark 0^g\}$:	+0-0+0$\checkmark 0$
$\{+0^a, +0^e\}$	: +0+0	$\{-0^b, -0^f\}$:	+0-0+0-0
$\{-0^b\}, \{-0^f\}$	: +0-0	$\{\chi 0^d\}, \{\chi 0^h\}$:	+0-0+0-0$\chi 0$
$\{-0^b, +0^e\}, \{+0^a, -0^f\}$:	+0-0+0		

In order to validate non-mutators, we *must* consider singleton non-mutator frontiers. The example shows that we *must not* consider frontiers with multiple non-mutators. There is some freedom in the choices otherwise. For SET, we can "saturate" an execution with accessors by augmenting the execution with accessors that witness each cut of the mutators. In a saturated execution, it is sufficient to consider only the *pointed accessor* cuts, which end in a maximal accessor. For non-saturated executions, we are forced to examine each mutator cut: it is possible that a future accessor extension may witness that cut. The status of "mixed" frontiers, which include mutators with a single maximal non-mutator, is open for debate. We choose to ignore them, but the definition does not change if they are included.

Summary: A CRDT must have a strategy for linearizing all mutator labels, even in the face of partitions. In order to ensure *strong* EC, the definition must consider sets of events across multiple replicas. Because non-mutators are resolved locally, SEC must ignore frontiers with multiple non-mutators.

Cuts and frontiers are well-known concepts in the literature of distributed systems (Chandy and Lamport 1985). It is natural to consider frontiers when discussing the evolving correctness of a CRDT.

2.5   Stuttering

Consider the following execution.

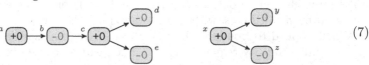

(7)

This LPO represents a partitioned system with events a–e in one partition and x–z in the other. As the partition heals, we must be able to account for the intermediate states. Because of the large number of events in this example, we have elided all accessors. We will present the example using the semantics of the add-wins set. Recall that the add-wins set validates ✓0 if and only if there is a maximal +0 beforehand. Thus, a replica that has seen the cut with frontier $\{+0^a, -0^y, -0^z\}$ must answer ✓0, whereas a replica that has seen $\{-0^b, -0^y, -0^z\}$ must answer ✗0.

Any linearization of $\{+0^a, -0^y, -0^z\}$ must end in +0, since the add-win set must reply ✓0: the only possibility is "+0-0-0+0". The linearization of $\{-0^b, -0^y, -0^z\}$ must end in -0. If it must be a supersequence, the only possibility is "+0-0-0+0-0". Taking one more step on the left, $\{+0^c, -0^y, -0^z\}$ must linearize to "+0-0-0+0-0+0". Thus the final state $\{-0^d, -0^e, -0^y, -0^z\}$ must linearize to "+0-0-0+0-0+0-0-0". Reasoning symmetrically, the linearization of $\{-0^d, -0^e, +0^x\}$ must be "+0-0+0-0-0+0", and thus the final $\{-0^d, -0^e, -0^y, -0^z\}$ must linearize to "+0-0+0-0-0+0-0-0". The constraints on the final state are incompatible. Each of these states can be verified in isolation; it is the relation between them that is not satisfiable.

Recall that monotonicity requires that the linearization chosen for a frontier be a *subsequence* of the linearization chosen for any extension of that frontier. The difficulty here is that subsequence relation ignores the similarity between "+0-0-0+0-0+0-0-0" and "+0-0+0-0-0+0-0-0". Neither of these is a subsequence of the other, yet they capture exactly the same sequence of *states*, each with six alternations between ✗0 and ✓0. The canonical state-based representative for these sequences is "+0-0+0-0+0-0".

CRDTs are defined in terms of states. In order to relate CRDTs to sequential specifications, it is necessary to extract information about states from the specification itself. Adapting Brookes (1996), we define strings as *stuttering equivalent* (notation $\sigma \sim \tau$) if they pass through the same states. So +0+1+0 $\sim$ +0+1 but +0-0+0 $\nsim$ +0. If we consider subsequences up to stuttering, then execution (7) is SEC, with witnesses as follow:

$$\begin{array}{ll}
\{a\}, \{x\}, \{a, x\} & : +0 \\
\{b\}, \{y\}, \{y, z\}, \{z\} & : +0\text{-}0 \\
\{a, y\}, \{a, y, z\}, \{a, z\}, \{b, x\} & : +0\text{-}0+0 \\
\{b, y\}, \{b, y, z\}, \{b, z\}, \{d\}, \{d, e\}, \{e\} & : +0\text{-}0+0\text{-}0 \\
\{c, y\}, \{c, y, z\}, \{c, z\}, \{d, x\}, \{d, e, x\}, \{e, x\} & : +0\text{-}0+0\text{-}0+0 \\
\{d, y\}, \{d, y, z\}, \{d, z\}, & \\
\{e, y\}, \{e, y, z\}, \{e, z\}, \{d, e, y\}, \{d, e, y, z\}, \{d, e, z\} & : +0\text{-}0+0\text{-}0+0\text{-}0
\end{array}$$

Recall that without stuttering, we deduced that $\{+0^c, -0^y, -0^z\}$ must linearize to "+0-0-0+0-0+0" and $\{-0^d, -0^e, +0^x\}$ must linearize to "+0-0+0-0-0+0". Under stuttering equivalence, these are the same, with canonical representative "+0-0+0-0+0". Thus, monotonicity under stuttering allows both linearizations to be extended to satisfy the final state $\{-0^d, -0^e, -0^y, -0^z\}$, which has canonical representative "+0-0+0-0+0-0".

Summary: CRDTs are described in terms of convergent states, whereas specifications are described as strings of actions. Actions correspond to labels in the LPO of an execution. Many strings of actions may lead to equivalent states. For example, idempotent actions can be applied repeatedly without modifying the state.

The stuttering equivalence of Brookes (1996) addresses this mismatch. In order to capture the validity of CRDTs, the definition of subsequence must change from a definition over individual specification strings to a definition over *equivalence classes* of strings *up to stuttering*.

3   Eventual Consistency for CRDTs

This section formalizes the intuitions developed in Sect. 2. We define executions, specifications and strong eventual consistency (SEC). We discuss properties of eventual consistency and prove that the add-wins set is SEC.

3.1   Executions

An execution realizes *causal delivery* if, whenever an event is received at a replica, all predecessors of the event are also received. Most of the CRDTs in Shapiro et al. (2011a) assume causal delivery, and we assumed it throughout the introductory section. There are costs to maintaining causality, however, and not all CRDTs assume that executions incur these costs. In the formal development, we allow non-causal executions.

Shapiro et al. (2011a) draw executions as timelines, explicitly showing the delivery of remote mutators. Below left, we give an example of such a timeline.

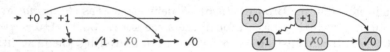

This is a non-causal execution: at the bottom replica, +1 is received before +0, even though +0 precedes +1 at the top replica.

Causal executions are naturally described as Labelled Partial Orders (LPOs), which are transitive and antisymmetric. Section 2 presented several examples of LPOs. To capture non-causal systems, we move to *Labelled Visibility Orders* (LVOs), which are merely acyclic. Acyclicity ensures that the transitive closure of an LVO is an LPO. The right picture above shows the LVO corresponding to the timeline on the left. The zigzag arrow represents an intransitive communication. When drawing executions, we use straight lines for "transitive" edges, with the intuitive reading that "this and all preceding actions are delivered".

LVOs arise directly due to non-causal implementations. As we will see in Sect. 4, they also arise via projection from an LPO.

LVOs are unusual in the literature. To make this paper self-contained, we define the obvious generalizations of concepts familiar from LPOs, including isomorphism, suborder, restriction, maximality, downclosure and cut.

Fix a set **L** of labels. A *Labelled Visibility Order* (LVO, also known as an *execution*) is a triple $u = \langle E_u, \lambda_u, \leadsto_u \rangle$ where E_u is a finite set of events, $\lambda_u \in (E_u \mapsto \mathbf{L})$ and $\leadsto_u \subseteq (E_u \times E_u)$ is reflexive and acyclic.

Let u, v range over LVOs. Many concepts extend smoothly from LPOs to LVOs.

- *Isomorphism:* Write $u =_{\mathsf{iso}} v$ when u and v differ only in the carrier set. We are often interested in the isomorphism class of an LVO.
- *Pomset:* We refer to the isomorphism class of an LVO as a *pomset*. Pomset abbreviates *Partially Ordered Multiset* (Plotkin and Pratt 1997). We stick with the name "pomset" here, since "vomset" is not particularly catchy.
- *Suborder:* Write $u \subseteq v$ when $E_u \subseteq E_v$, $\lambda_u \subseteq \lambda_v$, $\rho_u \subseteq \rho_v$, and $(\leadsto_v) \subseteq (\leadsto_u)$.
- *Restriction:*[1] When $D \subseteq E_v$, define $v \restriction D = \langle D, \lambda_v \restriction D, \leadsto_v \restriction D \rangle$. Restriction lifts subsets to suborders: $v \restriction D$ denotes the sub-LVO derived from a subset D of events. See Sect. 2.2 for an example of restriction.
- *Maximal elements:* $\mathsf{max}(v) = \{d \in E_v \mid \nexists e \in (E_v \setminus \{d\}). \ d \leadsto_v e\}$. We say that d is maximal for v when if $d \in \mathsf{max}(v)$.
- *Non-maximal suborder:* $\overline{\mathsf{max}}(v) = v \restriction (E_v \setminus \mathsf{max}(v))$. $\overline{\mathsf{max}}(v)$ is the suborder with the maximal elements removed.
- *Downclosure:* D is *downclosed* for v if $D \subseteq \{e \in E_v \mid \exists d \in D. \ d \leadsto_v e\}$.
- *Cut:* u is a *cut* of v if $u \subseteq v$ and E_u is downclosed for v. Let $\mathsf{cuts}(v)$ be the set of all cuts of v. A cut is the sub-LVO corresponding to a downclosed set. Cuts are also known as prefixes. See Sect. 2.4 for an example. A cut is determined by its maximal elements: if $u \in \mathsf{cuts}(v)$ then $u = v \restriction \{d \in E_v \mid \exists e \in \mathsf{max}(v). \ d \leadsto_v e\}$.
- *Linearization:* For $a_i \in \mathbf{L}$, we say that $a_1 \dots a_n$ is a *linearization* of $E \subseteq E_v$ if there exists a bijection $\alpha : E \to [1, n]$ such that $\forall e \in E. \ \lambda_v(e) = a_{\alpha(e)}$ and $\forall d, e \in E. \ d \leadsto_v e$ implies $\alpha(d) \leq \alpha(e)$.

Replica-Specific Properties. In the literature on replicated data types, some properties of interest (such as "read your writes" (Tanenbaum and Steen 2007)) require the concept of "session" or a distinction between local and remote events. These can be accommodated by augmenting LVOs with a replica labelling $\rho_u \in (E_u \mapsto \mathbf{R})$, which maps events to a set $\mathbf{R}$ of *replica identifiers*.

Executions can be generated operationally as follows: Replicas receive mutator and accessor events from the local client; they also receive mutator events that are forwarded from other replicas. Each replica maintains a set of *seen* events: an event that is received is added to this set. When an event is received from the local client, the event is additionally added to the execution, with the predecessors in the visibility relation corresponding to the current *seen* set. If we wish to restrict attention to causal executions, then we require that replicas forward all the mutators in their *seen* sets, rather than individual events, and, thus, the visibility relation is transitive over mutators.

All executions that are operationally generated satisfy the additional property that $\leadsto_u$ is per-replica total: if $\rho(d) = \rho(e)$ then either $d \leadsto_u e$ or $e \leadsto_u d$.

---

[1] We use the standard definitions for restriction on functions and relations. Given a function $f : E \to X, \mathcal{R} : E \times E$ and $D \subseteq E$, define $f \restriction D = \{\langle d, f(d) \rangle \mid d \in D\}$ and $\mathcal{R} \restriction D = \{\langle d_1, d_2 \rangle \mid d_1, d_2 \in D \text{ and } d_1 \ \mathcal{R} \ d_2\}$.

We do not demand per-replica totality because our results do not rely on replica-specific information.

3.2   Specifications and Stuttering Equivalence

Specifications are sets of strings, equipped with a distinguished set of mutators and a dependency relation between labels. Specifications are subject to some constraints to ensure that the mutator set and dependency relations are sensible; these are inspired by the conditions on Mazurkiewicz executions (Diekert and Rozenberg 1995). Every specification set yields a derived notion of stuttering equivalence. This leads to the definition of *observational subsequence* ($\leq_{obs}$).

We use standard notation for strings: Let σ and τ range over strings. Then $\sigma\tau$ denotes concatenation, σ^* denotes Kleene star, $\sigma \parallel \tau$ denotes the set of interleavings, ε denotes the empty string and σ^i denotes the ith element of σ. These notations lift to sets of strings via set union.

A *specification* is a quadruple $\langle \mathbf{L}, \mathbf{M}, \#, \Sigma \rangle$ where

- $\mathbf{L}$ is a set of *actions* (also known as *labels*),
- $\mathbf{M} \subseteq \mathbf{L}$ is a distinguished set of *mutator* actions,
- $\# \subseteq (\mathbf{L} \times \mathbf{L})$ is a symmetric and reflexive *dependency* relation, and
- $\Sigma \subseteq \mathbf{L}^*$ is a set of *valid strings*.

Let $\overline{\mathbf{M}} = \mathbf{L} \setminus \mathbf{M}$ be the sets of *non-mutators*.

A specification must satisfy the following properties:

(a) prefix closed: $\sigma\tau \in \Sigma$ implies $\sigma \in \Sigma$
(b) non-mutators are closed under stuttering, and commutation:
$\forall a \in \overline{\mathbf{M}} .\ \sigma a\tau \in \Sigma$ implies $\sigma a^*\tau \subseteq \Sigma$
$\forall a, b \in \overline{\mathbf{M}} .\ \{\sigma a, \sigma b\} \subseteq \Sigma$ implies $\{\sigma ab, \sigma ba\} \subseteq \Sigma$
(c) independent actions commute:
$\forall a, b \in \mathbf{L} .\ \neg(a \# b)$ implies $(\sigma ab\tau \in \Sigma$ iff $\sigma ba\tau \in \Sigma)$

Property (b) ensures that non-mutators do not affect the state of the data structure. Property (c) ensures that commuting of independent actions does not affect the state of the data structure.

Recall that the SET specification takes $\mathbf{M} = \{\text{+0, -0, +1, -1}\}$, representing addition and removal of bits 0 and 1, and $\overline{\mathbf{M}} = \{\mathsf{X}0, \checkmark0, \mathsf{X}1, \checkmark1\}$, representing membership tests returning false or true. The dependency relation is $\# = \{\text{+0,}$ $\text{-0,}\ \mathsf{X}0,\ \checkmark0\}^2 \cup \{\text{+1, -1,}\ \mathsf{X}1,\ \checkmark1\}^2$, where $D^2 = D \times D$.

The dependency relation for SET is an equivalence, but this need not hold generally. We will see an example in Sect. 4.

The definitions in the rest of the paper assume that we have fixed a specification $\langle \mathbf{L}, \mathbf{M}, \#, \Sigma \rangle$. In the examples of this section, we use SET.

State and Stuttering Equivalence. Specification strings σ and τ are *state equivalence* (notation $\sigma \approx \tau$) if every valid extension of σ is also a valid extension of τ, and vice versa. For example, +0+1+0 $\approx$ +0+1 and +0-0+0 $\approx$ +0, but +0-0 $\not\approx$ +0.

In particular, state equivalent strings agree on the valid accessors that can immediately follow them: either $\checkmark 0$ or $\chi 0$ and either $\checkmark 1$ or $\chi 1$. Formally, we define state equivalence, $\approx\, \subseteq \mathbf{L}^* \times \mathbf{L}^*$, as follows[2].

$$(\sigma \approx \sigma') \triangleq (\sigma = \sigma') \text{ or } (\{\sigma, \sigma'\} \subseteq \Sigma \text{ and } \forall \tau \in \mathbf{L}^*.\ \sigma\tau \in \Sigma \text{ iff } \sigma'\tau \in \Sigma).$$

From specification property (b), we know that non-mutators do not affect the state. Thus we have that $ua \approx u$ whenever $a \in \overline{\mathbf{M}}$ and $ua \in \Sigma$. From specification property (c), we know that independent actions commute. Thus we have that $\sigma ab \approx \sigma ba$ whenever $\neg(a \mathbin{\#} b)$ and $\{\sigma ab, \sigma ba\} \subseteq \Sigma$.

Two strings are *stuttering equivalent*[3] if they only differ in operations that have no effect on the state of the data structure, as given by Σ. Adapting Brookes (1996) to our notion of state equivalence, we define stuttering equivalence, $\sim\, \subseteq \mathbf{L}^* \times \mathbf{L}^*$, to be the least equivalence relation generated by the following rules, where a ranges over $\mathbf{L}$.

$$\frac{}{\varepsilon \sim \varepsilon} \qquad \frac{\sigma \sim \sigma'}{\sigma a \sim \sigma' a} \qquad \frac{\sigma \approx \sigma a}{\sigma \sim \sigma a} \qquad \frac{\sigma b \sim \sigma \quad \neg(a \mathbin{\#} b)}{\sigma ab \sim \sigma a}$$

The first rule above handles the empty string. The second rule allows stuttering in any context. The third rule motivates the name stuttering equivalence, for example, allowing $+0+0 \sim +0$. The last case captures the equivalence generated by independent labels, for example, allowing $+0+1+0 \sim +0+1$ but not $+0-0+0 \sim +0-0$. Using the properties of $\approx$ discussed above, we can conclude, for example, that $+0\checkmark0\checkmark0+0-0\chi0 \sim +0-0$.

Consider specification strings for a unary SET over value 0. Since stuttering equivalence allows us to remove both accessors and adjacent mutators with the same label we deduce that the *canonical representatives* of the equivalence classes induced by $\sim$ are generated by the regular expression $(+0)^?(-0+0)^*(-0)^?$.

Observational Subsequence. Recall that ac is a *subsequence* of abc, although it is not a *prefix*. We write $\leq_{\mathsf{seq}}$ for subsequence and $\leq_{\mathsf{obs}}$ for *observational subsequence*, defined as follows.

$$\sigma_1 \cdots \sigma_n \leq_{\mathsf{seq}} \tau_0 \sigma_1 \tau_1 \cdots \sigma_n \tau_n \qquad \sigma \leq_{\mathsf{obs}} \tau \text{ if } \exists \sigma' \sim \sigma.\ \exists \tau' \sim \tau.\ \sigma' \leq_{\mathsf{seq}} \tau'$$

Note that observational subsequence includes both subsequence and stuttering equivalence $(\leq_{\mathsf{obs}}) \subseteq (\leq_{\mathsf{seq}}) \cup (\sim)$.

$\leq_{\mathsf{seq}}$ can be understood in isolation, whereas $\leq_{\mathsf{obs}}$ can only be understood with respect to a given specification. In the remainder of the paper, the implied specification will be clear from context. $\leq_{\mathsf{seq}}$ is a partial order, whereas $\leq_{\mathsf{obs}}$ is only a preorder, since it is not antisymmetric.

Let σ and τ be strings over the unary SET with canonical representatives $a\sigma'$ and $b\tau'$. Then we have that $\sigma \leq_{\mathsf{obs}} \tau$ exactly when either $a = b$ and $|\sigma'| \leq |\tau'|$

---

[2] To extend the definition to non-specification strings, we allow $\sigma \approx \sigma'$ when $\sigma = \sigma'$.

[3] Readers of Brookes (1996) should note that mumbling is not relevant here, since all mutators are visible.

or $a \neq b$ and $|\sigma'| < |\tau'|$. Thus, observational subsequence order is determined by the number of alternations between the mutators.

Specification strings for the binary SET, then, are stuttering equivalent exactly when they yield the same canonical representatives when restricted to 0 and to 1. Thus, observational subsequence order is determined by the number of alternations between the mutators, when restricted to each dependent subsequence. (The final rule in the definition of stuttering, which allows stuttering across independent labels, is crucial to establishing this canonical form.)

3.3   Eventual Consistency

Eventual consistency is defined using the *cuts* of an execution and the *observational subsequence order* of the specification. As noted in Sects. 2.2 and 2.4, it is important that we not consider all cuts. Thus, before we define SEC, we must define *dependent cuts*.

The *dependent restriction* of an execution is defined: $v \downharpoonright \# = \langle \mathsf{E}_v, \lambda_v, \overset{\#}{\leadsto}_v \rangle$, where $d \overset{\#}{\leadsto}_v e$ when $\lambda_v(d) \# \lambda_v(e)$ and $d \leadsto_v e$. See Sect. 2.2 for an example of dependent restriction.

The *dependent cuts* of v are cuts of the dependent restriction. As discussed in Sect. 2.4, we only consider pointed cuts (with a single maximal element) for non-mutators. See Sect. 2.4 for an example.

$$\mathsf{cuts}_{\#}(v) = \big\{ u \in \mathsf{cuts}(v \downharpoonright \#) \ \big| \ \forall e \in \mathsf{E}_u. \text{ if } \lambda_u(e) \in \overline{\mathbf{M}} \text{ then } \max(u) = \{e\} \big\}$$

An execution v is *Eventually Consistent* (SEC) for specification $\langle \mathbf{L}, \mathbf{M}, \#, \Sigma \rangle$ iff there exists a function $\tau : \mathsf{cuts}_{\#}(v) \to \Sigma$ that satisfies the following.

Linearization: $\forall p \in \mathsf{cuts}_{\#}(v).\ p$ linearizes to $\tau(p)$, and
Monotonicity: $\forall p, q \in \mathsf{cuts}_{\#}(v).\ p \subseteq q$ implies $\tau(p) \leq_{\mathsf{obs}} \tau(q)$.

A data structure implementation is SEC if all of its executions are SEC.

In Sect. 2, we gave several examples that are SEC. See Sects. 2.4 and 2.5 for examples where τ is given explicitly. Section 2.4 also includes an example that is not SEC.

The concerns raised in Sect. 2 are reflected in the definition.

- Non-mutators are ignored by the dependent restriction of other non-mutators. As discussed in Sect. 2.1, this relaxation is similar that of update-serializability (Hansdah and Patnaik 1986; Garcia-Molina and Wiederhold 1982).
- Independent events are ignored by the dependent restriction of an event. As discussed in Sect. 2.2, this relaxation is similar to preserved program order in relaxed memory models (Higham and Kawash 2000; Alglave 2012).
- As discussed in Sect. 2.3, punning is allowed: each cut p is linearized separately to a specification string $\tau(p)$.
- As discussed in Sect. 2.4, we constrain the power puns by considering cuts of the distributed system (Chandy and Lamport 1985).

– Monotonicity ensures that the system evolves in a sensible way: new order may be introduced, but old order cannot be forgotten. As discussed in Sect. 2.5, the preserved order is captured in the observational subsequence relation, which allows stuttering (Brookes 1996).

3.4   Properties of Eventual Consistency

We discuss some basic properties of SEC. For further analysis, see Sect. 5.

An important property of CRDTs is *prefix closure*: If an execution is valid, then every prefix of the execution should also be valid. Prefix closure follows immediately from the definition, since whenever u is a prefix of v we have that $\mathsf{cuts}_{\#}(u) \subseteq \mathsf{cuts}_{\#}(v)$.

Prefix closure looks back in time. It is also possible to look forward: A system satisfies *eventual delivery* if every valid execution can be extended to a valid execution with a maximal element that sees every mutator. If one assumes that every specification string can be extended to a longer specification string by adding non-mutators, then eventual delivery is immediate.

The properties PSTS, PSM and PPE are discussed in the introduction. An SEC implementation must satisfies PPE since every dependent set of mutators is linearized: SEC enforces the stronger property that there are no new intermediate states, even when executing all mutators in parallel. For causal systems, where $\leadsto_u$ is transitive, PSTS and PSM follow by observing that if there is a total order on the mutators of u then any linearization of u is a specification string.

Burckhardt (2014, Sect. 5) provides a taxonomy of correctness criteria for replicated data types. Our definition implies NOCIRCULARCAUSALITY and CAUSALARBITRATION, but does not imply either CONSISTENTPREFIX or CAUSALVISIBILITY. For LPOs, which model causal systems, our definition implies CAUSALVISIBILITY. READMYWRITES and MONOTONICREADS require a distinction between local and remote events. If one assumes the replica-specific constraints given in Sect. 3.1, then our definition satisfies these properties; without them, our definition is too abstract.

3.5   Correctness of the Add-Wins Set

The add-wins set is defined to answer ✓k for a cut u exactly when

$$\exists d \in u.\ \lambda_u(d) = \text{+k} \quad \wedge \quad (\nexists e \in u.\ \lambda_u(e) = \text{-k} \wedge d \leadsto_u e).$$

It answers ✗k otherwise. The add-wins set is called the "observed-remove" set.

We show that any LPO that meets this specification is SEC with respect to SET. We restrict attention to LPOs since causal delivery is assumed for the add-wins set in (Shapiro et al. 2011a).

For SET, the dependency relation is an equivalence. For an equivalence relation R, let $\mathbf{L}/R \subseteq 2^{\mathbf{L}}$ denote the set of (disjoint) equivalence classes for R. For SET, $\mathbf{L}/\# = \{\{+0, -0, ✗0, ✓0\}, \{+1, -1, ✗1, ✓1\}\}$. When dependency is an equivalence, then *every* interleaving of independent actions is valid if *any* interleaving is valid. Formally, we have the following, where ⫴ denotes interleaving.

$$\forall D \in (\mathbf{L}/\#).\ \forall \sigma \in D^*.\ \forall \tau \in (\mathbf{L} \setminus D)^*.\ (\sigma \ \|\| \ \tau) \cap \Sigma \neq \emptyset \ \text{implies} \ (\sigma \ \|\| \ \tau) \subseteq \Sigma$$

Using the forthcoming composition result (Theorem 2), it suffices for us to address the case when u only involves operations on a single element, say 0. For any such LVO u, we choose a linearization $\tau(u) \in (\text{-0}|\text{+0})^*$ that has a maximum number of alternations between -0 and +0. If there is a linearization that begins with -0, then we choose one of these. Below, we summarize some of the key properties of such a linearization.

- $\tau(u)$ ends with +0 iff there is an +0 that is not followed by any -0 in u.
- For any LPO $v \subseteq u$, $\tau(v)$ has at most as many alternations as $\tau(u)$.

The first property above ensures that the accessors are validated correctly, *i.e.*, 0 is deemed to be present iff there is an +0 that is not followed by any -0.

We are left with proving monotonicity, *i.e.*, if $u \subseteq v$, then $\tau(u) \leq_{\mathsf{obs}} \tau(v)$. Consider $\tau(u) = a\sigma$ and $\tau(v) = b\rho$.

- If $b = a$, the second property above ensures that $\tau(u) \leq_{\mathsf{obs}} \tau(v)$.
- In the case that $b \neq a$, we deduce by construction that $b = \text{-0}$ and $a = \text{+0}$. In this case, ρ starts with +0 and has at least as many alternations as $\tau(u)$. So, we deduce that $\tau(u) \leq_{\mathsf{obs}} \rho$. The required result follows since $\rho \leq_{\mathsf{obs}} \tau(v)$.

4   A Collaborative Text Editing Protocol

In this section we consider a variant of the collaborative text editing protocol defined by Attiya et al. (2016). After stating the sequential specification, TEXT, we sketch a correctness proof with respect to our definition of eventual consistency. This example is interesting formally: the dependency relation is not an equivalence, and therefore the dependent projection does not preserve transitivity. The generality of intransitive LVOs is necessary to understand TEXT, even assuming a causal implementation.

Specification. Let a, b range over *nodes*, which contain some text, a unique identifier, and perhaps other information. Labels have the following forms:

- Mutator !a initializes the text to node a.
- Mutator +a<b adds node a immediately before node b.
- Mutator +a>b adds node a immediately after node b.
- Mutator -b removes node b.
- Non-mutator query ?$b_1 \cdots b_n$ returns the current state of the document.

We demonstrate the correct answers to queries by example. Initially, the document is empty, whereas after initialization, the document contains a single node; thus the specification contains strings such as "?ε !c ?c", where ε represents the empty document. Nodes can be added either before or after other nodes; thus

"!c +b<c +d>c" results in the document ?bcd. Nodes are always added adjacent to the target; thus, order matters in "!c +e>c +d>c" which results in ?cde rather than ?ced. Removal does what one expects; thus "!c +e>c +d>c -c" results in ?de.

Attiya et al. (2016) define the interface for TEXT using integer indices as targets, rather than nodes. Using the unique correspondence between the nodes and it indices (since node are unique), one can easily adapt an implementation that satisfies our specification to their interface.

We say that node a is a *added* in the actions !a, +a<b and +a>b. Node b is a *target* in +a<b and +a>b. In addition to correctly answering queries, specifications must satisfy the following constraints:

- Initialization may occur at most once,
- each node may be added at most once,
- a node may be removed only after it is added, and
- a node may be used as a target only if it has been added and not removed.

These constraints forbid adding to a target that has been removed; thus "!c +d>c -c" is a valid string, but "!c -c +d>c" is not. It also follows that initialization must precede any other mutators.

Because add operations use unique identifiers, punning and stuttering play little role in this example. In order to show the implementation correct, we need only choose an appropriate notion of dependency. As we will see, it is necessary that removes be independent of adds with disjoint label sets, but otherwise all actions may be dependent. Let $\mathbf{L}_{!+?}$ be the set of add and query labels, and let nodes return the set of nodes that appear in a label. Then we define dependency as follows.

$$\ell \mathrel{\#} k \text{ iff } \{\ell, k\} \subseteq \mathbf{L}_{!+?} \text{ or } \mathsf{nodes}(\ell) \cap \mathsf{nodes}(k) \neq \emptyset$$

Implementation. We consider executions that satisfy the same four conditions above imposed on specifications. We refer the reader to the algorithm of Attiya et al. (2016) that provides timestamps for insertions that are monotone with respect to causality.

As an example, Attiya et al. (2016) allow the execution given on the left below. In this case, the dependent restriction is an intransitive LVO, even though the underlying execution is an LPO: in particular, !b does not precede -d in the dependent restriction. We give the order considered by dependent cuts on the right—this is a restriction of the dependent restriction: since we only consider pointed accessor cuts, we can safely ignore order out of non-mutators.

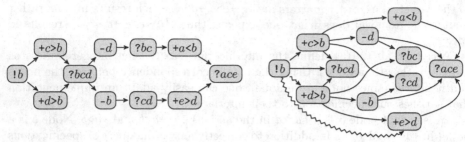

This execution is not linearizable, but it is SEC, choosing witnesses to be subsequences of the mutator string "!b +d>b +c>b +a<b +e>d -b -d". Here, the document is initialized to b, then c and d are added after b, resulting in ?bcd. The order of c and d is determined by their timestamps. Afterwards, the top replica removes d and adds a; the bottom replica removes b and adds e, resulting in the final state ?ace. In the right execution, the removal of order out of the non-mutators shows the "update serializability" effect; the removal of order between -b and +e>d (and between -d and +a<b) shows the "preserved program order" effect.

Correctness. Given an execution, we can find a specification string $s_1 s_2$ that linearizes the mutators in the dependent restriction of the execution such that s_1 contains only adds and s_2 contains only removes. Such a specification string exists because by the conditions on executions, deletes do not have any outgoing edges to other mutators in the dependent restriction; so, they can be moved to the end in the matching specification string. In order to find s_1 that linearizes the add events, any linearization that respects causality and timestamps (yielded by the algorithm of Attiya et al. (2016)) suffices for our purposes. The conditions required by SEC follow immediately.

5   Compositional Reasoning

The aim of this section is to establish compositional methods to reason about replicated data structures. We do so using *Labelled Transition Systems* (LTSs), where the transitions are labelled by dependent cuts. We show how to derive an LTS from an execution, lts(u). We also define an LTS for the *most general* CRDT that validates a specification, lts(Σ). We show that u is SEC for Σ exactly when lts(u) is a refinement of lts(Σ). We use this alternative characterization to establish composition and abstraction results.

LTSs. An LTS is a triple consisting of a set a states, an initial state and a labelled transition function between states. We first define the LTSs for executions and specifications, then provide examples and discussion.

For both executions and specifications, the labels of the LTS are dependent cuts: for executions, these are dependent cuts of the execution itself; for specifications, they are drawn from the set $\mathcal{L}_\# = \bigcup_{v \in \mathcal{L}} \mathsf{cuts}_\#(v)$ of all possible dependent cuts. We compare LTS labels up to isomorphism, rather than identity. Thus it is safe to think of LTS labels as (potentially intransitive) pomsets (Plotkin and Pratt 1997).

The states of the LTS are different for the execution and specification. For executions, the states are cuts of the execution u itself, $\mathsf{cuts}(u)$; these are general cuts, not just dependent cuts. For specifications, the states are the stuttering equivalence classes of strings allowed by the specification, $\Sigma/\sim$.

There is an isomorphism between strings and total orders. We make use of this in the definition, treating strings as totally-ordered LVOs.

Define $\mathsf{lts}(u) = \langle \mathsf{cuts}(u), \emptyset, \longmapsto_i \rangle$, where $p \overset{v}{\longmapsto}_i q$ if $v \in \mathsf{cuts}_\#(q)$ and

$$p \subseteq q \qquad\qquad \mathsf{E}_{\mathrm{max}(v)} \cup \mathsf{E}_p = \mathsf{E}_q \qquad\qquad \overline{\mathrm{max}}(v) \subseteq p$$
$$v \subseteq q \qquad\qquad \mathsf{E}_{\mathrm{max}(v)} \cap \mathsf{E}_p = \emptyset \qquad\qquad \mathsf{E}_{\mathrm{max}(v)} \subseteq \mathsf{E}_{\mathrm{max}(q)}$$

Define $\mathsf{lts}(\Sigma) = \langle \Sigma/\sim, \varepsilon, \longmapsto_s \rangle$, where $[\sigma] \overset{v}{\longmapsto}_s [\rho]$ if $v \in \mathcal{L}_\#$ and

$$\sigma \subseteq \rho \qquad\qquad \mathsf{E}_{\mathrm{max}(v)} \cup \mathsf{E}_\sigma = \mathsf{E}_\rho \qquad\qquad \overline{\mathrm{max}}(v) \subseteq \sigma$$
$$v \subseteq \rho \qquad\qquad \mathsf{E}_{\mathrm{max}(v)} \cap \mathsf{E}_\sigma = \emptyset$$

We explain the definitions using examples from SET, first for executions, then for specifications. Consider the execution on the left below. The derived LTS is given on the right.

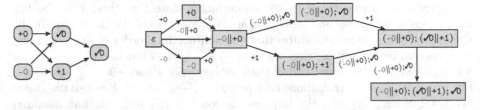

The states of the LTS are cuts of the execution. The labels on transitions are *dependent* cuts. The requirements for execution transitions relate the source p, target q and label v. The leftmost requirements state that the target state must extend both the source and the label; thus the target state must be a combination of events and order from source and label. The middle requirements state that the maximal elements of the label must be new in the target; only the maximal elements of the label are added when moving from source to target. The upper right requirement states that the non-maximal order of the label must be respected by the source; thus the causal history reported by the label cannot contradict the causal history of the source. The lower right requirement ensures that maximal elements of the label are also maximal in the target. The restriction to dependent cuts explains the labels on transitions $(-0\|+0) \overset{+1}{\longmapsto}_i (-0\|+0); +1$ and $(-0\|+0); (\checkmark0\|+1); \checkmark0 \overset{(-0\|+0);\checkmark0}{\longmapsto}_i (-0\|+0); (\checkmark0\|+1)$. By definition, there is a self-transition labelled with the empty LVO at every state; we elide these transitions in drawings.

The specification LTS for SET is infinite, of course. To illustrate, below we give two sub-LTSs with limitations on mutators. On the left, we only allow +0 and ⏐1. On the right, we only allow +0 and −0 and only consider the case in which there is at most one alternation between them. The states are shown using their canonical representatives. Because of the number of transitions, we show all dependent accessors as a single transition, with labels separated by commas.

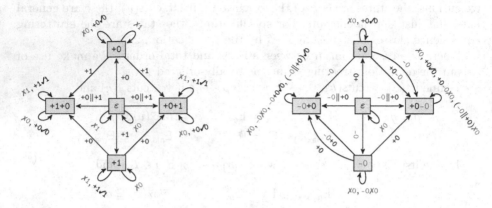

The requirements for specification transitions are similar to those for implementations, but the states are equivalence classes over specification strings: with source $[\sigma]$ and target $[\tau]$. There is a transition between the states if there are members of the equivalence classes, σ and τ, that satisfy the requirements. Since these are total orders, the leftmost requirements state that there must be linearizations of the source and label that are subsequences of the target. Similarly, the upper right requirement states that the non-maximal order of the label must be respected by the source; thus we have $+0 \xmapsto{+0\text{-}0}_s +0\text{-}0$ but not $+0 \xmapsto{-0+0}_s \sigma$, for any σ. The use of sub-order rather than subsequence allows $+0\text{-}0 \xmapsto{+0\text{-}0}_s +0\text{-}0\text{-}0$ but prevents nonsense transitions such as $+0\text{-}0 \xmapsto{+0\text{-}0}_s -0+0\text{-}0$. Because the states are total orders, we drop the implementation LTS requirement that maximal events of the label must be maximal in the target. If we were to impose this restriction, we would disallow $-0 \xmapsto{+0}_s +0\text{-}0$.

It is worth noting that the specification of the add-wins set removes exactly three edges from the right LTS: $\varepsilon \xmapsto{-0|+0}_s +0\text{-}0$, $+0 \xmapsto{-0}_s +0\text{-}0$, and $-0 \xmapsto{+0}_s +0\text{-}0$.

Refinement. Refinement is a functional form of simulation (Hoare 1972; Lamport 1983; Lynch and Vaandrager 1995). Let $P = \langle S_P, p_0, \mapsto_P \rangle$ and $Q = \langle S_Q, q_0, \mapsto_Q \rangle$ be LTSs. A function $f : S_P \to S_Q$ is a *(strong) refinement* if $p \xmapsto{v}_P p'$ and $f(p) = q$ imply that there exist $w =_{\text{iso}} v$ and $q' \in S_Q$ such that $q \xmapsto{w}_Q q'$ and $f(p') = q'$. Then P *refines* Q (notation $P \sqsubseteq Q$) if there exists a refinement $f : S_P \to S_Q$ such that the initial states are related, *i.e.*, $f(p_0) = q_0$.

We now prove that SEC can be characterized as a refinement. We write $p_0 \xmapsto{*}_P p_n$ when p_n is reachable from p_0 via a finite sequence of steps $p_i \xmapsto{u_i}_P p_{i+1}$.

Theorem 1. *u is EC for the specification Σ iff* $\mathsf{lts}(u) \sqsubseteq \mathsf{lts}(\Sigma)$.

Proof. For the forward direction, assume u is *EC* and therefore there exists a function $\tau : \mathsf{cuts}_\#(u) \to \Sigma$ such that $\forall E \in \mathsf{cuts}_\#(u).\ \tau(E)$ is a linearization of E. For each cut $p \in \mathsf{cuts}(u)$, we start with the dependent restriction, $p \restriction \#$. We further restriction attention to mutators, $p \mathbin{\lfloor} \# \mathbin{\lfloor} \mathbf{M}$. The required refinement maps p to the equivalence class of the linearization of $p \mathbin{\lfloor} \# \mathbin{\lfloor} \mathbf{M}$ chosen by τ: $f(p) \triangleq [\tau(p \mathbin{\lfloor} \# \mathbin{\lfloor} \mathbf{M})]$. We abuse notation below by identifying each equivalence class with a canonical element of the class.

We show that $p \xmapsto{v}_i q$ implies $f(p) \leq_{\mathsf{obs}} f(q)$. Since $p \subseteq q$, we deduce that $p \mathbin{\lfloor} \# \mathbin{\lfloor} \mathbf{M} \subseteq q \mathbin{\lfloor} \# \mathbin{\lfloor} \mathbf{M}$ and by monotonicity, $f(p) = \tau(p \mathbin{\lfloor} \# \mathbin{\lfloor} \mathbf{M}) \leq_{\mathsf{obs}} \tau(q \mathbin{\lfloor} \# \mathbin{\lfloor} \mathbf{M}) = f(q)$.

We show that $p \xmapsto{v}_i q$ implies $\tau(v) \leq_{\mathsf{obs}} f(q)$. Suppose v only contains mutators. Since $v \subseteq q$, we deduce that $v \subseteq q \mathbin{\lfloor} \# \mathbin{\lfloor} \mathbf{M}$ and by monotonicity, $\tau(v) \leq_{\mathsf{obs}} \tau(q \mathbin{\lfloor} \# \mathbin{\lfloor} \mathbf{M}) = f(v)$. On the other hand, suppose v contains the non-mutator a. Let $A = \mathbf{M} \cup \{a\}$. Since $v \subseteq q$, we deduce that $v \mathbin{\lfloor} \mathbf{M} \subseteq q \mathbin{\lfloor} \# \mathbin{\lfloor} A$. By monotonicity, $\tau(v \mathbin{\lfloor} \mathbf{M}) \leq_{\mathsf{obs}} \tau(q \mathbin{\lfloor} A)$. Since $\tau(q \mathbin{\lfloor} A) = \tau(q \mathbin{\lfloor} \mathbf{M})$, we have $\tau(v \mathbin{\lfloor} \mathbf{M}) \leq_{\mathsf{obs}} \tau(q \mathbin{\lfloor} \mathbf{M}) = f(q)$, as required.

Thus $f(p) \xmapsto{v}_s f(q)$, completing this direction of the proof.

For the reverse direction, we are given a refinement $f : \mathsf{cuts}(u) \to \Sigma/{\sim}$. For any $p \in \mathsf{cuts}_\#(u)$, define $\tau(p)$ to be a string in the equivalence class $f(p)$ that includes any non-mutator found in p.

We first prove that $\tau(p)$ is a linearization of p. A simple inductive proof demonstrates that for any $p \in \mathsf{cuts}_\#(u)$, there is a transition sequence of the form $\emptyset \xmapsto{\;*\;}_i \xmapsto{p}_i p$. Thus, we deduce from the label on the final transition into p that the $\tau(p)$ related to p is a linearization of p.

We now establish monotonicity. A simple inductive proof shows that for any $p, q \in \mathsf{cuts}(u)$, $p \subseteq q$ implies $p \xmapsto{\;*\;} q$. Thus $\tau(p) \leq_{\mathsf{obs}} \tau(q)$, by the properties of f and the definition of τ.

Composition. Given two *non-interacting* data structures whose replicated implementations satisfy their sequential specifications, the implementation that combines them satisfies the interleaving of their specifications. We formalize this as a composition theorem in the style of Herlihy and Wing (1990).

Given an execution u and $L \subseteq \mathbf{L}$, write $u \mathbin{\lfloor} L$ for the execution that results by restricting u to events with labels in L: $u \mathbin{\lfloor} L = u \mathbin{\lfloor} \{e \in \mathsf{E}_u \mid \lambda_u(e) \in L\}$. This notation lifts to sets in the standard way: $U \mathbin{\lfloor} L = \bigcup_{u \in U} \{u \mathbin{\lfloor} L\}$. Write $u \vDash_{\mathsf{sec}} \Sigma$ to indicate that u is SEC for Σ.

Theorem 2 (Composition). *Let L_1 and L_2 be mutually independent subsets of $\mathbf{L}$. For $i \in \{1, 2\}$, let Σ_i be a specification with labels chosen from L_i, such that $\Sigma_1 \parallel\!\parallel \Sigma_2$ is also a specification. If $(U \mathbin{\lfloor} L_1) \vDash_{\mathsf{sec}} \Sigma_1$ and $(U \mathbin{\lfloor} L_2) \vDash_{\mathsf{sec}} \Sigma_2$ then $U \vDash_{\mathsf{sec}} (\Sigma_1 \parallel\!\parallel \Sigma_2)$ (equivalently $\mathsf{lts}(\Sigma_1 \parallel\!\parallel \Sigma_2) \approx \mathsf{lts}(\Sigma_1) \parallel\!\parallel \mathsf{lts}(\Sigma_2)$).*

The proof is immediate. Since L_1 and L_2 are mutually independent, any interleaving of the labels will satisfy the definition.

Abstraction. We describe a process algebra with parallel composition and restriction and establish congruence results. We ignore syntactic details and work directly with LTSs. Replica identities do not play a role in the definition; thus, we permit implicit mobility of the client amongst replicas with the only constraint being that the replica has at least as much history on the current item of interaction as the client. This constraint is enforced by the synchronization of the labels, defined below. While the definition includes the case where the client itself is replicated, it does not provide for out-of-band interaction between the clients at different replicas: All interaction is assumed to happen through the data structure.

The relation $\|$ is defined between LTSs so that $P \| Q$ describes the system that results when client P interacts with data structure Q. For LTSs P and Q, define $\longmapsto_\times$ inductively, as follows, where $\emptyset$ represents the empty LVO.

$$\frac{q \overset{v}{\longmapsto}_Q q'}{\langle p, q \rangle \overset{v}{\longmapsto}_\times \langle p, q' \rangle} \qquad \frac{p \overset{v}{\longmapsto}_P p' \quad q \overset{w}{\longmapsto}_Q q'}{\langle p, q \rangle \overset{\emptyset}{\longmapsto}_\times \langle p', q' \rangle} \ \exists v' =_{\mathsf{iso}} v. \ v' \subseteq w \text{ and } \mathsf{max}(v') = \mathsf{max}(w)$$

Let $S_\times = \{\langle p, q \rangle \mid \exists \langle p', q' \rangle. \langle p, q \rangle \longmapsto_\times^* \langle p', q' \rangle \text{ and } \nexists v, p''. \ p' \overset{v}{\longrightarrow}_P p'' \}$

$$P \| Q = \begin{cases} \{\langle S_\times, \langle p_0, q_0 \rangle, \longmapsto_\times \rangle\} & \text{if } S_\times \text{ is non-empty} \\ \emptyset & \text{otherwise} \end{cases}$$

The $\|$ operator is asymmetric between the client and data structure in two ways. First, note that every action of the client must be matched by the data structure. The condition of client quiescence in the definition of $S_\times$, that all of the actions of the client P must be matched by Q; otherwise $P \| Q = \emptyset$. However, the first rule for $\longmapsto_\times$ explicitly permits actions of the data structure that may not be matched by the client. This asymmetry permits the composition of the data structure with multiple clients to be described incrementally, one client at a time. Thus, we expect that $(P_1 \mid P_2) \| Q \approx P_1 \| (P_2 \| Q)$.

Second, note that right rule for $\longmapsto_\times$ interaction permits the data structure Q to introduce order not found in the clients. This is clearly necessary to ensure that that the composition of client ✓0|+0 with the SET data structure is nonempty. In this case, the client has no order between +0 and ✓0 whereas the data structure orders ✓0 after +0. In this paper, we do not permit the client to introduce order that is not seen in the data structure. For a discussion of this issue, see (Jagadeesan and Riely 2015).

We can also define restriction for some set $A \subseteq \mathbf{L}$ of labels, a lá CCS. $P \backslash A = \langle S_P, p_0, \{\langle p, v, q \rangle \mid \langle p, v, q \rangle \in (\longmapsto_P) \text{ and } \mathsf{labels}(v) \cap A = \emptyset\}\rangle$. The definitions lift to sets: $\mathcal{P} \| \mathcal{Q} = \bigcup_{P \in \mathcal{P}, Q \in \mathcal{Q}} P \| Q$ and $\mathcal{P} \backslash A = \{(P \backslash A) \mid P \in \mathcal{P}\}$.

Lemma 3. *If $\mathcal{P} \sqsubseteq_\sim \mathcal{P}'$ and $\mathcal{Q} \sqsubseteq_\sim \mathcal{Q}'$ then $\mathcal{P} \| \mathcal{Q} \sqsubseteq_\sim \mathcal{P}' \| \mathcal{Q}'$ and $\mathcal{P} \backslash A \sqsubseteq_\sim \mathcal{P}' \backslash A$.* $\square$

It suffices to show that: $P \sqsubseteq_\sim \mathsf{lts}(u)$ implies $\mathcal{P} \| \mathsf{lts}(u) \sqsubseteq_\sim \mathcal{P} \| \mathsf{lts}(\Sigma)$. The proof proceeds in the traditional style of such proofs in process algebra. We illustrate by sketching the case for client parallel composition. Let f be the witness for $P \sqsubseteq_\sim \mathsf{lts}(u)$. The proof proceeds by constructing a "product" refinement S relation of the identity on the states of P with f, i.e.: $f(q) = q'$ implies $\langle p, q \rangle \ S \ \langle p, q' \rangle$.

Thus, an SEC implementation can be replaced by the specification.

Theorem 4 (Abstraction). *If u is SEC for Σ, then $\mathcal{P} \| \mathsf{lts}(u) \sqsubseteq_\sim \mathcal{P} \| \mathsf{lts}(\Sigma)$.*

6   A Replicated Graph Algorithm

We describe a graph implemented with sets for vertices and edges, as specified by Shapiro et al. (2011a). The graph maintains the invariant that the vertices of an edge are also part of the graph. Thus, an edge may be added only if the corresponding vertices exist; conversely, a vertex may be removed only if it supports no edge. In the case of a concurrent addition of an edge with the deletion of either of its vertices, the deletion takes precedence.

The vertices $v, w, \ldots$ are drawn from some universe $\mathcal{U}$. An edge $e, e', \ldots$ is a pair of vertices. Let $\mathsf{vert}(e) = \{v, w\}$ be the vertices of edge $e = (v, w)$. The vocabulary of the set specification includes mutators for the addition and removal of vertices and edges and non-mutators for membership tests.

$$\mathbf{M} = \{+v, -v, +(v,w), -(v,w) \mid v, w \in \mathcal{U}\}$$

$$\overline{\mathbf{M}} = \{\checkmark v, \boldsymbol{X} v, \checkmark(v,w), \boldsymbol{X}(v,w) \mid v, w \in \mathcal{U}\}$$

$$\# = \{(e,v), (v,e) \mid v \in \mathsf{vert}(e)\} \cup \{(e,e') \mid \mathsf{vert}(e) \cap \mathsf{vert}(e') \neq \emptyset\}$$

Valid graph specification strings answer queries like sets. In addition, we require the following.

- Vertices and edges added at most once: Each add label is unique.
- Removal of a vertex or edge is preceded by a corresponding add.
- Vertices are added before they are mentioned in any edges: If $\sigma^j = +(v,w)$, or $\sigma^j = -(v,w)$ there exists $i, i' < j$ such that: $\sigma^i = +v$, $\sigma^{i'} = +w$.
- Vertices are removed only after they are mentioned in edges: If $\sigma^j = +(v,w)$, or $\sigma^j = -(v,w)$, then for all $i < j$: $\sigma^i \neq -v$ and $\sigma^i \neq -w$.

Graph Implementation. We rewrite the graph program of Shapiro et al. (2011a) in a more abstract form. Our distributed graph implementation is written as a client of two replicate set: for vertices (V) and for edges (E). The implementation uses USETs, which require that an element be added at most once and that each remove causally follow the corresponding add. Here we show the graph implementation for various methods as client code that runs at each replica. At each replica, the code accesses its local copy of the USETs. All the message passing needed to propagate the updates is handled by the USET implementations of the sets V, E. For several methods, we list preconditions, which prescribe the natural assumptions that need to satisfied when these client methods are invoked. For example, an edge operation requires the presence of the vertices at the current replica.

```
addVertex(v)            removeVertex(v)           bool ?(v)
  Pre: fresh(v)           Pre: V.?(v)               return V.?(v)
  V.add(v)                V.remove(v)


addEdge(v,w)            removeEdge(v,w)           bool ?(v,w)
  Pre: V.?(v),V?(w)       Pre: V.?(v),V?(w)         if V.?(v)
  Pre: fresh((v,w))       Pre: E.?((v,w))           then return E.?((v,w))
  E.add((v,w))            E.remove((v,w))           else return false
```

We assume a causal transition system (as needed in Shapiro et al. (2011a)).

Correctness Using the Set Specification. We first show the correctness of the graph algorithm, using the SET specification for the vertex and edge sets. We then apply the abstraction and composition theorems to show the correctness of the algorithm using a set implementation.

Let u be a LVO generated in an execution of the graph implementation. The preconditions ensure that u has the following properties:

(a) For any v, $+v$ is never ordered after $-v$, and likewise for e.
(b) $-(v,w)$ or $+(v,w)$ is never ordered after $-v$ or $-w$.
(c) $-(v,w)$ or $+(v,w)$ is always ordered after some $+v$ and $+w$.

Define σ_1, σ_2 and σ_3 as follows.

- All elements of σ_1 are of the form $+v$. σ_1 exists by (c) above.
- All elements of σ_3 are of the form $-v$. σ_3 exists by (b) above.
- For each edge (v, w) that is accessed in u, let $\sigma_{(v,w)}$ be any interleaving of the events involving (v, w) in u such that no $+(v,w)$ occurs after any $-(v,w)$ in $\sigma_{(v,w)}$. $\sigma_{(v,w)}$ exists by (a) above. σ_2 is any interleaving of all the $s_{(v,w)}$.

Then u is SEC with witness $\sigma_u = \sigma_1 \sigma_2 \sigma_3$.

Full Correctness of the Implementation. We now turn to proving the correctness of the algorithm when the two sets are replaced by their implementations.

Consider two (distributed implementations of) separate and independent sets for vertices and edges, *i.e.* $\mathbf{L}_{\Sigma_1} \cap \mathbf{L}_{\Sigma_2} = \emptyset$. Suppose we have two implementations, each of which is correct individually: $\mathsf{lts}(U_i) \sqsubseteq \mathsf{lts}(\Sigma_i)$. By composition, we have that they are correct when composed together: $U_1 ||| U_2 \sqsubseteq \Sigma_1 ||| \Sigma_2$. Let $\mathcal{P}$ be the graph implementation, which is a client of the two sets. By abstraction, we know that $\mathcal{P} \,|\!|\!|\, (\Sigma_1 ||| \Sigma_2) \sqsubseteq T$ implies $\mathcal{P} \,|\!|\!|\, (U_1 ||| U_2) \sqsubseteq T$. By congruence, we deduce:

$$(\mathcal{P} \,|\!|\!|\, (\Sigma_1 ||| \Sigma_2)) \backslash (\mathbf{L}_{\Sigma_1} \cup \mathbf{L}_{\Sigma_2}) \sqsubseteq T \text{ implies } (\mathcal{P} \,|\!|\!|\, (U_1 ||| U_2)) \backslash (\mathbf{L}_{\Sigma_1} \cup \mathbf{L}_{\Sigma_2}) \sqsubseteq T.$$

Thus, in order to validate the full graph implementation, it is sufficient to establish the correctness of the graph client when interacting with the *specification* of the two independent SETs for edges and vertices, which we have already done in the previous treatment of abstract correctness.

7   Conclusions

We have provided a definition of *strong eventual consistency* that captures *validity* with respect to a *sequential specification*. Our definition reflects an attempt to resolve the tension between expressivity (cover the extant examples in the literature) and facilitating reasoning (by retaining a direct relationship with the sequential specification). The notion of *concurrent specification* developed by Burckhardt et al. (2014) has been used to prove the validity of several replicated data structure implementations. In future work, we would like to discover sufficient conditions relating concurrent and sequential specifications such that any implementation that is correct under the concurrent specification (as defined by Burckhardt et al. (2014)) will also be correct under the sequential counterpart (as defined here).

Acknowledgements. This paper has been greatly improved by the comments of the anonymous reviewers.

This material is based upon work supported by the National Science Foundation under Grant No. 1617175. Any opinions, findings, and conclusions or recommendations expressed in this material are those of the author and do not necessarily reflect the views of the National Science Foundation.

References

Alglave, J.: A formal hierarchy of weak memory models. Formal Methods Syst. Des. **41**(2), 178–210 (2012)

Alglave, J., Maranget, L., Tautschnig, M.: Herding cats: modelling, simulation, testing, and data mining for weak memory. ACM Trans. Program. Lang. Syst. **36**(2), 7:1–7:74 (2014)

Attiya, H., Burckhardt, S., Gotsman, A., Morrison, A., Yang, H., Zawirski, M.: Specification and complexity of collaborative text editing. In: Proceedings of the 2016 ACM Symposium on Principles of Distributed Computing, PODC 2016, Chicago, IL, USA, pp. 259–268, 25–28 July 2016

Bieniusa, A., Zawirski, M., Preguiça, N., Shapiro, M., Baquero, C., Balegas, V., Duarte, S.: Brief announcement: semantics of eventually consistent replicated sets. In: Aguilera, M.K. (ed.) DISC 2012. LNCS, vol. 7611, pp. 441–442. Springer, Heidelberg (2012). https://doi.org/10.1007/978-3-642-33651-5_48

Bouajjani, A., Enea, C., Hamza, J.: Verifying eventual consistency of optimistic replication systems. In: POPL 2014, pp. 285–296 (2014)

Brookes, S.D.: Full abstraction for a shared-variable parallel language. Inf. Comput. **127**(2), 145–163 (1996)

Budhiraja, N., Marzullo, K., Schneider, F.B., Toueg, S.: The primary-backup approach. In: Mullender, S. (ed.) Distributed Systems, 2nd edn., pp. 199–216 (1993)

Burckhardt, S.: Principles of eventual consistency. Found. Trends Program. Lang. **1**(1–2), 1–150 (2014). ISSN 2325-1107

Burckhardt, S., Leijen, D., Fähndrich, M., Sagiv, M.: Eventually consistent transactions. In: Seidl, H. (ed.) ESOP 2012. LNCS, vol. 7211, pp. 67–86. Springer, Heidelberg (2012). https://doi.org/10.1007/978-3-642-28869-2_4

Burckhardt, S., Gotsman, A., Yang, H., Zawirski, M.: Replicated data types: specification, verification, optimality. In: POPL 2014, pp. 271–284 (2014)

Chandy, K.M., Lamport, L.: Distributed snapshots: determining global states of distributed systems. ACM Trans. Comput. Syst. **3**(1), 63–75 (1985)

DeCandia, G., Hastorun, D., Jampani, M., Kakulapati, G., Lakshman, A., Pilchin, A., Sivasubramanian, S., Vosshall, P., Vogels, W.: Dynamo: Amazon's highly available key-value store. SIGOPS Oper. Syst. Rev. **41**(6), 205–220 (2007)

Diekert, V., Rozenberg, G. (eds.): The Book of Traces. World Scientific Publishing Co., Inc., River Edge (1995). ISBN 9810220588

Ellis, C.A., Gibbs, S.J.: Concurrency control in groupware systems. ACM SIGMOD Rec. **18**(2), 399–407 (1989)

Garcia-Molina, H., Wiederhold, G.: Read-only transactions in a distributed database. ACM Trans. Database Syst. **7**(2), 209–234 (1982)

Gilbert, S., Lynch, N.: Brewer's conjecture and the feasibility of consistent, available, partition-tolerant web services. SIGACT News **33**(2), 51–59 (2002)

Gotsman, A., Yang, H., Ferreira, C., Najafzadeh, M., Shapiro, M.: 'Cause i'm strong enough: reasoning about consistency choices in distributed systems. In: Proceedings of the 43rd Annual ACM SIGPLAN-SIGACT POPL, pp. 371–384 (2016)

Haas, A., Henzinger, T.A., Holzer, A., Kirsch, C.M., Lippautz, M., Payer, H., Sezgin, A., Sokolova, A., Veith, H.: Local linearizability. CoRR, abs/1502.07118 (2015)

Hansdah, R.C., Patnaik, L.M.: Update serializability in locking. In: Ausiello, G., Atzeni, P. (eds.) ICDT 1986. LNCS, vol. 243, pp. 171–185. Springer, Heidelberg (1986). https://doi.org/10.1007/3-540-17187-8_36

Herlihy, M., Wing, J.M.: Linearizability: a correctness condition for concurrent objects. ACM TOPLAS **12**(3), 463–492 (1990)

Higham, L., Kawash, J.: Memory consistency and process coordination for SPARC multiprocessors. In: Valero, M., Prasanna, V.K., Vajapeyam, S. (eds.) HiPC 2000. LNCS, vol. 1970, pp. 355–366. Springer, Heidelberg (2000). https://doi.org/10.1007/3-540-44467-X_32

Hoare, C.A.R.: Proof of correctness of data representations. Acta Informatica **1**(4), 271–281 (1972)

Jagadeesan, R., Riely, J.: From sequential specifications to eventual consistency. In: Halldórsson, M.M., Iwama, K., Kobayashi, N., Speckmann, B. (eds.) ICALP 2015, Part II. LNCS, vol. 9135, pp. 247–259. Springer, Heidelberg (2015). https://doi.org/10.1007/978-3-662-47666-6_20

Lamport, L.: Time, clocks, and the ordering of events in a distributed system. Commun. ACM **21**(7), 558–565 (1978)

Lamport, L.: Specifying concurrent program modules. ACM Trans. Program. Lang. Syst. **5**(2), 190–222 (1983)

Lynch, N., Vaandrager, F.: Forward and backward simulations. Inf. Comput. **121**(2), 214–233 (1995)

Perrin, M., Mostéfaoui, A., Jard, C.: Update consistency for wait-free concurrent objects. In: 2015 IEEE International Parallel and Distributed Processing Symposium, IPDPS 2015, Hyderabad, India, pp. 219–228, 25–29 May 2015

Plotkin, G., Pratt, V.: Teams can see pomsets. In: Workshop on Partial Order Methods in Verification. DIMACS Series, vol. 29, pp. 117–128. AMS (1997)

Saito, Y., Shapiro, M.: Optimistic replication. ACM Comput. Surv. **37**(1), 42–81 (2005)

Shapiro, M., Preguiça, N., Baquero, C., Zawirski, M.: A comprehensive study of Convergent and Commutative Replicated Data Types. TR 7506, Inria (2011a)

Shapiro, M., Preguiça, N.M., Baquero, C., Zawirski, M.: Conflict-free replicated data types. In: Proceedings of the 13th International Symposium on Stabilization, Safety, and Security of Distributed Systems, pp. 386–400 (2011b)

Shavit, N.: Data structures in the multicore age. Commun. ACM **54**(3), 76–84 (2011)

Tanenbaum, A., Steen, M.V.: Distributed systems. Pearson Prentice Hall, Upper Saddle River, NJ (2007)

Viotti, P., Vukolic, M.: Consistency in non-transactional distributed storage systems. ACM Comput. Surv. **49**(1), 19 (2016)

Vogels, W.: Eventually consistent. Commun. ACM **52**(1), 40–44 (2009)

Compiler Verification

A Verified Compiler from Isabelle/HOL to CakeML

Lars Hupel(✉) and Tobias Nipkow

Technische Universität München, Munich, Germany
lars.hupel@tum.de, nipkow@in.tum.de

Abstract. Many theorem provers can generate functional programs from definitions or proofs. However, this code generation needs to be trusted. Except for the HOL4 system, which has a proof producing code generator for a subset of ML. We go one step further and provide a verified compiler from Isabelle/HOL to CakeML. More precisely we combine a simple proof producing translation of recursion equations in Isabelle/HOL into a deeply embedded term language with a fully verified compilation chain to the target language CakeML.

Keywords: Isabelle · CakeML · Compiler
Higher-order term rewriting

1 Introduction

Many theorem provers have the ability to generate executable code in some (typically functional) programming language from definitions, lemmas and proofs (e.g. [6,8,9,12,16,27,37]). This makes code generation part of the trusted kernel of the system. Myreen and Owens [30] closed this gap for the HOL4 system: they have implemented a tool that translates from HOL4 into *CakeML*, a subset of SML, and proves a theorem stating that a result produced by the CakeML code is correct w.r.t. the HOL functions. They also have a verified implementation of CakeML [24,40]. We go one step further and provide a once-and-for-all verified compiler from (deeply embedded) function definitions in Isabelle/HOL [32,33] into CakeML proving partial correctness of the generated CakeML code w.r.t. the original functions. This is like the step from dynamic to static type checking. It also means that preconditions on the input to the compiler are explicitly given in the correctness theorem rather than implicitly by a failing translation. To the best of our knowledge this is the first verified (as opposed to certifying) compiler from function definitions in a logic into a programming language.

Our compiler is composed of multiple phases and in principle applicable to other languages than Isabelle/HOL or even HOL:

© The Author(s) 2018
A. Ahmed (Ed.): ESOP 2018, LNCS 10801, pp. 999–1026, 2018.
https://doi.org/10.1007/978-3-319-89884-1_35

- We erase types right away. Hence the type system of the source language is irrelevant.
- We merely assume that the source language has a semantics based on equational logic.

The compiler operates in three stages:

1. The preprocessing phase eliminates features that are not supported by our compiler. Most importantly, *dictionary construction* eliminates occurrences of type classes in HOL terms. It introduces dictionary datatypes and new constants and proves the equivalence of old and new constants (Sect. 7).
2. The *deep embedding* lifts HOL terms into terms of type term, a HOL model of HOL terms. For each constant c (of arbitrary type) it defines a constant c' of type term and proves a theorem that expresses equivalence (Sect. 3).
3. There are multiple *compiler phases* that eliminate certain constructs from the term type, until we arrive at the CakeML expression type. Most phases target a different intermediate term type (Sect. 5).

The first two stages are preprocessing, are implemented in ML and produce certificate theorems. Only these stages are specific to Isabelle. The third (and main) stage is implemented completely in the logic HOL, without recourse to ML. Its correctness is verified once and for all.[1]

2   Related Work

There is existing work in the Coq [2,15] and HOL [30] communities for proof producing or verified extraction of functions defined in the logic. Anand *et al.* [2] present work in progress on a verified compiler from Gallina (Coq's specification language) via untyped intermediate languages to CompCert C light. They plan to connect their extraction routine to the CompCert compiler [26].

Translation of type classes into dictionaries is an important feature of Haskell compilers. In the setting of Isabelle/HOL, this has been described by Wenzel [44] and Krauss *et al.* [23]. Haftmann and Nipkow [17] use this construction to compile HOL definitions into target languages that do not support type classes, e.g. Standard ML and OCaml. In this work, we provide a certifying translation that eliminates type classes inside the logic.

Compilation of pattern matching is well understood in literature [3,36,38]. In this work, we contribute a transformation of sets of equations with pattern matching on the left-hand side into a single equation with nested pattern matching on the right-hand side. This is implemented and verified inside Isabelle.

Besides CakeML, there are many projects for verified compilers for functional programming languages of various degrees of sophistication and realism (e.g.

---

[1] All Isabelle definitions and proofs can be found on the paper website: https://lars.hupel.info/research/codegen/, or archived as https://doi.org/10.5281/zenodo.1167616.

[4,11,14]). Particularly modular is the work by Neis *et al.* [31] on a verified compiler for an ML-like imperative source language. The main distinguishing feature of our work is that we start from a set of higher-order recursion equations with pattern matching on the left-hand side rather than a lambda calculus with pattern matching on the right-hand side. On the other hand we stand on the shoulders of CakeML which allows us to bypass all complications of machine code generation. Note that much of our compiler is not specific to CakeML and that it would be possible to retarget it to, for example, Pilsner abstract syntax with moderate effort.

Finally, Fallenstein and Kumar [13] have presented a model of HOL inside HOL using large cardinals, including a reflection proof principle.

3   Deep Embedding

Starting with a HOL definition, we derive a new, *reified* definition in a deeply embedded term language depicted in Fig. 1a. This term language corresponds closely to the **term** datatype of Isabelle's implementation (using de Bruijn indices [10]), but without types and schematic variables.

To establish a formal connection between the original and the reified definitions, we use a *logical relation*, a concept that is well-understood in literature [20] and can be nicely implemented in Isabelle using type classes. Note that the use of type classes here is restricted to correctness proofs; it is not required for the execution of the compiler itself. That way, there is no contradiction to the elimination of type classes occurring in a previous stage.

Notation. We abbreviate App t u to t \$ u and Abs t to Λ t. Other term types introduced later in this paper use the same conventions. We reserve λ for abstractions in HOL itself. Typing judgments are written with a double colon: $t :: \tau$.

Embedding Operation. Embedding is implemented in ML. We denote this operation using angle brackets: $\langle t \rangle$, where t is an arbitrary HOL expression and the result $\langle t \rangle$ is a HOL value of type **term**. It is a purely syntactic transformation, without preliminary evaluation or reduction, and it discards type information. The following examples illustrate this operation and typographical conventions concerning variables and constants:

$$\langle x \rangle = \text{Free "x"} \qquad \langle f \rangle = \text{Const "f"} \qquad \langle \lambda x.\, f\, x \rangle = \Lambda\, (\langle f \rangle\, \$\, \text{Bound } 0)$$

Small-Step Semantics. Figure 1b specifies the small-step semantics for **term**. It is reminiscent of *higher-order term rewriting*, and modelled closely after equality in HOL. The basic idea is that if the proposition $t = u$ can be proved equationally in HOL (without symmetry), then $R \vdash \langle t \rangle \longrightarrow^* \langle u \rangle$ holds (where $R :: (\text{term} \times \text{term})$ set). We call R the *rule set*. It is the result of translating a set of defining equations $lhs = rhs$ into pairs $(\langle lhs \rangle, \langle rhs \rangle) \in R$.

datatype term =
Const string |
Free string |
Abs term |
Bound nat |
App term term

$$\text{STEP}\ \frac{(lhs, rhs) \in R \qquad \text{match } lhs\ t = \text{Some } \sigma}{R \vdash t \longrightarrow \text{subst } \sigma\ rhs}$$

$$\text{BETA}\ \frac{\text{closed } t'}{R \vdash (\Lambda t)\ \$\ t' \longrightarrow t[t']} \qquad \text{FUN}\ \frac{R \vdash t \longrightarrow t'}{R \vdash t\ \$\ u \longrightarrow t'\ \$\ u}$$

$$\text{ARG}\ \frac{R \vdash u \longrightarrow u'}{R \vdash t\ \$\ u \longrightarrow t\ \$\ u'}$$

(a) Abstract syntax of
de Bruijn terms

(b) Small-step semantics

Fig. 1. Basic syntax and semantics of the **term** type

Rule STEP performs a rewrite step by picking a rewrite rule from R and rewriting the term at the root. For that purpose, match and subst are (mostly) standard first-order matching and substitution (see Sect. 4 for details).

Rule BETA performs β-reduction. Type term represents bound variables by de Bruijn indices. The notation $t[t']$ represents the substitution of the outermost bound variable in t with t'.

Our semantics does not constitute a fully-general higher-order term rewriting system, because we do not allow substitution under binders. For de Bruijn terms, this would pose no problem, but as soon as we introduce named bound variables, substitution under binders requires dealing with capture. To avoid this altogether, all our semantics expect terms that are substituted into abstractions to be closed. However, this does not mean that we restrict ourselves to any particular evaluation order. Both call-by-value and call-by-name can be used in the small-step semantics. But later on, the target semantics will only use call-by-value.

Embedding Relation. We denote the concept that an embedded term t corresponds to a HOL term a of type τ w.r.t. rule set R with the syntax $R \vdash t \approx a$. If we want to be explicit about the type, we index the relation: $\approx_\tau$.

For ground types, this can be defined easily. For example, the following two rules define $\approx_{\text{nat}}$:

$$\frac{}{R \vdash \langle 0 \rangle \approx_{\text{nat}} 0} \qquad \frac{R \vdash \langle t \rangle \approx_{\text{nat}} n}{R \vdash \langle \text{Suc } t \rangle \approx_{\text{nat}} \text{Suc } n}$$

Definitions of $\approx$ for arbitrary datatypes without nested recursion can be derived mechanically in the same fashion as for nat, where they constitute one-to-one relations. Note that for ground types, $\approx$ ignores R. The reason why $\approx$ is parametrized on R will become clear in a moment.

For function types, we follow Myreen and Owen's approach [30]. The statement $R \vdash t \approx f$ can be interpreted as "$t\ \$\ \langle a \rangle$ can be rewritten to $\langle f\ a \rangle$ for all a". Because this might involve applying a function definition from R, the $\approx$ relation must be indexed by the rule set. As a notational convenience, we define another relation $R \vdash t \downarrow x$ to mean that there is a t' such that $R \vdash t \longrightarrow^* t'$ and $R \vdash t' \approx x$. Using this notation, we formally define $\approx$ for functions as follows:

$$R \vdash t \approx f \leftrightarrow (\forall u\, x.\ R \vdash u \downarrow x \rightarrow R \vdash t\, \$\, u \downarrow f\, x)$$

Example. As a running example, we will use the map function on lists:

$$\text{map } f\ [] = []$$
$$\text{map } f\ (x \# xs) = f\, x \# \text{map } f\ xs$$

The result of embedding this function is a set of rules map':

map' =
  {(Const "List.list.map" $ Free "f" $ (Const "List.list.Cons" $ Free "x21" $ Free "x22"),
    Const "List.list.Cons" $ (Free "f" $ Free "x21") $ ...),
  (Const "List.list.map" $ Free "f" $ Const "List.list.Nil",
    Const "List.list.Nil")}

together with the theorem map' $\vdash$ Const "List.list.map" $\downarrow$ map, which is proven by simple induction over map. Constant names like "List.list.map" come from the fully-qualified internal names in HOL.

The induction principle for the proof arises from the use of the **fun** command that is used to define recursive functions in HOL [22]. But the user is also allowed to specify custom equations for functions, in which case we will use heuristics to generate and prove the appropriate induction theorem. For simplicity, we will use the term *(defining) equation* uniformly to refer to any set of equations, either default ones or ones specified by the user. Embedding partially-specified functions – in particular, proving the certificate theorem about them – is currently not supported. In the future, we plan to leverage the domain predicate as produced by **fun** to generate conditional theorems.

4   Terms, Matching and Substitution

The compiler transforms the initial term type (Fig. 1a) through various intermediate stages. This section gives an overview and introduces necessary terminology.

Preliminaries. The function arrow in HOL is $\Rightarrow$. The cons operator on lists is the infix $\#$.

Throughout the paper, the concept of *mappings* is pervasive: We use the type notation $\alpha \rightharpoonup \beta$ to denote a function $\alpha \Rightarrow \beta$ option. In certain contexts, a mapping may also be called an *environment*. We write mapping literals using brackets: $[a \Rightarrow x, b \Rightarrow y, \ldots]$. If it is clear from the context that σ is defined on a, we often treat the lookup $\sigma\, a$ as returning an $x :: \beta$.

The functions dom $:: (\alpha \rightharpoonup \beta) \Rightarrow \alpha$ set and range $:: (\alpha \rightharpoonup \beta) \Rightarrow \beta$ set return the *domain* and *range* of a mapping, respectively.

Dropping entries from a mapping is denoted by $\sigma - k$, where σ is a mapping and k is either a single key or a set of keys. We use $\sigma' \subseteq \sigma$ to denote that σ' is a sub-mapping of σ, that is, dom $\sigma' \subseteq$ dom σ and $\forall a \in$ dom σ'. $\sigma'\, a = \sigma\, a$.

Merging two mappings σ and ρ is denoted with $\sigma \mathbin{+\!\!+} \rho$. It constructs a new mapping with the union domain of σ and ρ. Entries from ρ override entries from σ. That is, $\rho \subseteq \sigma \mathbin{+\!\!+} \rho$ holds, but not necessarily $\sigma \subseteq \sigma \mathbin{+\!\!+} \rho$.

All mappings and sets are assumed to be finite. In the formalization, this is enforced by using subtypes of $\rightharpoonup$ and set. Note that one cannot define datatypes by recursion through sets for cardinality reasons. However, for finite sets, it is possible. This is required to construct the various term types. We leverage facilities of Blanchette *et al.*'s **datatype** command to define these subtypes [7].

Standard Functions. All type constructors that we use ($\rightharpoonup$, set, list, option, ...) support the standard operations map and rel. For lists, map is the regular covariant map. For mappings, the function has the type $(\beta \Rightarrow \gamma) \Rightarrow (\alpha \rightharpoonup \beta) \Rightarrow (\alpha \rightharpoonup \gamma)$. It leaves the domain unchanged, but applies a function to the range of the mapping.

Function rel_τ lifts a binary predicate $P :: \alpha \Rightarrow \alpha \Rightarrow$ bool to the type constructor τ. We call this lifted relation the *relator* for a particular type.

For datatypes, its definition is structural, for example:

$$\frac{}{\mathsf{rel}_{\mathsf{list}}\ P\ [\,]\ [\,]} \qquad \frac{\mathsf{rel}_{\mathsf{list}}\ P\ xs\ ys \qquad P\ x\ y}{\mathsf{rel}_{\mathsf{list}}\ P\ (x \mathbin{\#} xs)\ (y \mathbin{\#} ys)}$$

For sets and mappings, the definition is a little bit more subtle.

Definition 1 (Set relator). *For each element $a \in A$, there must be a corresponding element $b \in B$ such that $P\, a\, b$, and vice versa. Formally:*

$$\mathsf{rel}_{\mathsf{set}}\ P\ A\ B \leftrightarrow (\forall x \in A.\ \exists y \in B.\ P\ x\ y) \wedge (\forall y \in B.\ \exists x \in A.\ P\ x\ y)$$

Definition 2 (Mapping relator). *For each a, $m\, a$ and $n\, a$ must be related according to $\mathsf{rel}_{\mathsf{option}}\ P$. Formally:*

$$\mathsf{rel}_{\mathsf{mapping}}\ P\ m\ n \leftrightarrow (\forall a.\ \mathsf{rel}_{\mathsf{option}}\ P\ (m\ a)\ (n\ a))$$

Term Types. There are four distinct term types: term, nterm, pterm, and sterm. All of them support the notions of free variables, matching and substitution. Free variables are always a finite set of strings. Matching a term against a *pattern* yields an optional mapping of type string $\rightharpoonup \alpha$ from free variable names to terms.

Note that the type of patterns is itself term instead of a dedicated pattern type. The reason is that we have to subject patterns to a linearity constraint anyway and may use this constraint to carve out the relevant subset of terms:

Definition 3. *A term is* linear *if there is at most one occurrence of any variable, it contains no abstractions, and in an application $f\ \$\ x$, f must not be a free variable. The HOL predicate is called linear :: term $\Rightarrow$ bool.*

Because of the similarity of operations across the term types, they are all instances of the term type class. Note that in Isabelle, classes and types live in different namespaces. The term type and the term type class are separate entities.

Definition 4. *A term type τ supports the operations* match :: term $\Rightarrow \tau \Rightarrow$ (string $\rightharpoonup \tau$), subst :: (string $\rightharpoonup \tau$) $\Rightarrow \tau \Rightarrow \tau$ *and* frees :: $\tau \Rightarrow$ string set. *We also define the following derived functions:*

- matchs *matches a list of patterns and terms sequentially, producing a single mapping*
- closed t *is an abbreviation for* frees $t = \emptyset$
- closed σ *is an overloading of* closed, *denoting that all values in a mapping are closed*

Additionally, some (obvious) axioms have to be satisfied. We do not strive to fully specify an abstract term algebra. Instead, the axioms are chosen according to the needs of this formalization.

A notable deviation from matching as discussed in term rewriting literature is that the result of matching is only well-defined if the pattern is linear.

Definition 5. *An* equation *is a pair of a* pattern *(left-hand side) and a* term *(right-hand side). The pattern is of the form* $f \$ p_1 \$ \ldots \$ p_n$, *where f is a constant (i.e. of the form* Const *name). We refer to both f or name interchangeably as the* function symbol *of the equation.*

Following term rewriting terminology, we sometimes refer to an equation as *rule*.

4.1 De Bruijn terms (term)

The definition of term is almost an exact copy of Isabelle's internal term type, with the notable omissions of type information and schematic variables (Fig. 1a). The implementation of β-reduction is straightforward via index shifting of bound variables.

4.2 Named Bound Variables (nterm)

datatype nterm = Nconst string | Nvar string | Nabs string nterm | Napp nterm nterm

The nterm type is similar to term, but removes the distinction between *bound* and *free* variables. Instead, there are only named variables. As mentioned in the previous section, we forbid substitution of terms that are not closed in order to avoid capture. This is also reflected in the syntactic side conditions of the correctness proofs (Sect. 5.1).

4.3   Explicit Pattern Matching (pterm)

datatype pterm =
  Pconst string | Pvar string | Pabs ((term × pterm) set) | Papp pterm pterm

Functions in HOL are usually defined using *implicit* pattern matching, that is, the terms p_i occurring on the left-hand side $\langle f\ p_1\ \dots\ p_n \rangle$ of an equation must be constructor patterns. This is also common among functional programming languages like Haskell or OCaml. CakeML only supports *explicit* pattern matching using case expressions. A function definition consisting of multiple defining equations must hence be translated to the form $f = \lambda x.$ **case** x **of** $\dots$. The elimination proceeds by iteratively removing the last parameter in the block of equations until none are left.

In our formalization, we opted to combine the notion of abstraction and case expression, yielding *case abstractions*, represented as the Pabs constructor. This is similar to the **fn** construct in Standard ML, which denotes an anonymous function that immediately matches on its argument [28]. The same construct also exists in Haskell with the LambdaCase language extension. We chose this representation mainly for two reasons: First, it allows for a simpler language grammar because there is only one (shared) constructor for abstraction and case expression. Second, the elimination procedure outlined above does not have to introduce fresh names in the process. Later, when translating to CakeML syntax, fresh names are introduced and proved correct in a separate step.

The set of pairs of pattern and right-hand side inside a case abstraction is referred to as *clauses*. As a short-hand notation, we use $\Lambda\{p_1 \Rightarrow t_1, p_2 \Rightarrow t_2, \dots\}$.

4.4   Sequential Clauses (sterm)

datatype sterm =
  Sconst string | Svar string | Sabs ((term × sterm) list) | Sapp sterm sterm

In the term rewriting fragment of HOL, the order of rules is not significant. If a rule matches, it can be applied, regardless when it was defined or proven. This is reflected by the use of sets in the rule and term types. For CakeML, the rules need to be applied in a deterministic order, i.e. sequentially. The sterm type only differs from pterm by using list instead of set. Hence, case abstractions use list brackets: $\Lambda[p_1 \Rightarrow t_1, p_2 \Rightarrow t_2, \dots]$.

4.5   Irreducible Terms (value)

CakeML distinguishes between *expressions* and *values*. Whereas expressions may contain free variables or β-redexes, values are closed and fully evaluated. Both have a notion of abstraction, but values differ from expressions in that they contain an environment binding free variables.

Consider the expression $(\lambda x.\lambda y.x)\,(\lambda z.z)$, which is rewritten (by β-reduction) to $\lambda y.\lambda z.z$. Note how the bound variable x disappears, since it is replaced. This is contrary to how programming languages are usually implemented: evaluation does not happen by substituting the argument term t for the bound variable x, but by recording the binding $x \mapsto t$ in an environment [24]. A pair of an abstraction and an environment is usually called a *closure* [25,41].

In CakeML, this means that evaluation of the above expression results in the closure

$$(\lambda y.x, ["\texttt{x}" \mapsto (\lambda z.z, [])])$$

Note the nested structure of the closure, whose environment itself contains a closure.

To reflect this in our formalization, we introduce a type value of values (explanation inline):

datatype value $=$
  (* *constructor value: a data constructor applied to multiple values* *)
  Vconstr string (value list) |
  (* *closure: clauses combined with an environment mapping variables to values* *)
  Vabs ((term × sterm) list) (string $\rightharpoonup$ value) |
  (* *recursive closures: a group of mutually recursive function bodies with an environment* *)
  Vrecabs (string $\rightharpoonup$ ((term × sterm) list)) string (string $\rightharpoonup$ value)

The above example evaluates to the closure:

$$\mathsf{Vabs} \; \big[\, \langle y \rangle \Rightarrow \langle x \rangle \,\big] \; \big["\texttt{x}" \mapsto \mathsf{Vabs} \; [\langle z \rangle \Rightarrow \langle z \rangle] \; [] \big]$$

The third case for recursive closures only becomes relevant when we conflate variables and constants. As long as the rule set rs is kept separate, recursive calls are straightforward: the appropriate definition for the constant can be looked up there. CakeML knows no such distinction between constants and variables, hence everything has to reside in a single environment σ.

Consider this example of odd and even:

$$\text{odd } 0 = \mathsf{False} \qquad\qquad \text{even } 0 = \mathsf{True}$$
$$\text{odd } (\mathsf{Suc}\ n) = \text{even } n \qquad\qquad \text{even } (\mathsf{Suc}\ n) = \text{odd } n$$

When evaluating the term odd k, the definitions of even and odd themselves must be available in the environment captured in the definition of odd. However, it would be cumbersome in HOL to construct such a Vabs that refers to itself. Instead, we capture the expressions used to define odd and even in a recursive closure. Other encodings might be possible, but since we are targeting CakeML, we are opting to model it in a similar way as its authors do.

For the above example, this would result in the following global environment:

$$["\texttt{odd}" \mapsto \mathsf{Vrecabs}\ css\ "\texttt{odd}"\ [], "\texttt{even}" \mapsto \mathsf{Vrecabs}\ css\ "\texttt{even}"\ []]$$

$$\text{where } css = ["\texttt{odd}" \mapsto [\langle 0 \rangle \Rightarrow \langle \mathsf{False} \rangle, \langle \mathsf{Suc}\ n \rangle \Rightarrow \langle \text{even } n \rangle],$$
$$"\texttt{even}" \mapsto [\langle 0 \rangle \Rightarrow \langle \mathsf{True} \rangle, \langle \mathsf{Suc}\ n \rangle \Rightarrow \langle \text{odd } n \rangle]]$$

Note that in the first line, the right-hand sides are values, but in *css*, they are expressions. The additional string argument of Vrecabs denotes the selected function. When evaluating an application of a recursive closure to an argument (β-reduction), the semantics adds all constituent functions of the closure to the environment used for recursive evaluation.

5   Intermediate Semantics and Compiler Phases

In this section, we will discuss the progression from de Bruijn based term language with its small-step semantics given in Fig. 1a to the final CakeML semantics. The compiler starts out with terms of type term and applies multiple phases to eliminate features that are not present in the CakeML source language.

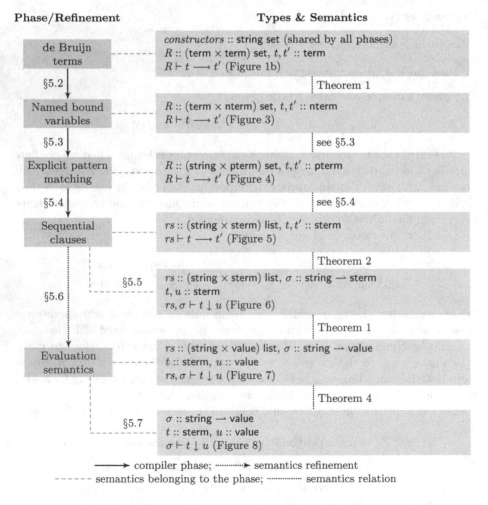

Fig. 2. Intermediate semantics and compiler phases

Types term, nterm and pterm each have a small-step semantics only. Type sterm has a small-step and several intermediate big-step semantics that bridge the gap to CakeML. An overview of the intermediate semantics and compiler phases is depicted in Fig. 2. The left-hand column gives an overview of the different phases. The right-hand column gives the types of the rule set and the semantics for each phase; you may want to skip it upon first reading.

$$\text{STEP} \ \frac{(lhs, rhs) \in R \qquad \text{match } lhs \ t = \text{Some } \sigma}{R \vdash t \longrightarrow \text{subst } \sigma \ rhs} \qquad \text{BETA} \ \frac{\text{closed } t'}{R \vdash (\Lambda x.\ t) \ \$ \ t' \longrightarrow \text{subst } [x \mapsto t'] \ t}$$

Fig. 3. Small-step semantics for nterm with named bound variables

5.1 Side Conditions

All of the following semantics require some side conditions on the rule set. These conditions are purely syntactic. As an example we list the conditions for the correctness of the first compiler phase:

- Patterns must be linear, and constructors in patterns must be fully applied.
- Definitions must have at least one parameter on the left-hand side (Sect. 5.6).
- The right-hand side of an equation refers only to free variables occurring in patterns on the left-hand side and contain no dangling de Bruijn indices.
- There are no two defining equations $lhs = rhs_1$ and $lhs = rhs_2$ such that $rhs_1 \neq rhs_2$.
- For each pair of equations that define the same constant, their arity must be equal and their patterns must be compatible (Sect. 5.3).
- There is at least one equation.
- Variable names occurring in patterns must not overlap with constant names (Sect. 5.7).
- Any occurring constants must either be defined by an equation or be a constructor.

The conditions for the subsequent phases are sufficiently similar that we do not list them again.

In the formalization, we use named contexts to fix the rules and assumptions on them (*locales* in Isabelle terminology). Each phase has its own locale, together with a proof that after compilation, the preconditions of the next phase are satisfied. Correctness proofs assume the above conditions on R and similar conditions on the term that is reduced. For brevity, this is usually omitted in our presentation.

5.2   Naming Bound Variables: From **term** to **nterm**

Isabelle uses de Bruijn indices in the term language for the following two reasons: For substitution, there is no need to rename bound variables. Additionally, α-equivalent terms are equal. In implementations of programming languages, these advantages are not required: Typically, substitutions do not happen inside abstractions, and there is no notion of equality of functions. Therefore CakeML uses named variables and in this compilation step, we get rid of de Bruijn indices.

The "named" semantics is based on the **nterm** type. The rules that are changed from the original semantics (Fig. 1b) are given in Fig. 3 (FUN and ARG remain unchanged). Notably, β-reduction reuses the substitution function.

For the correctness proof, we need to establish a correspondence between terms and nterms. Translation from **nterm** to **term** is trivial: Replace bound variables by the number of abstractions between occurrence and where they were bound in, and keep free variables as they are. This function is called nterm_to_term.

The other direction is not unique and requires introduction of *fresh* names for bound variables. In our formalization, we have chosen to use a *monad* to produce these names. This function is called term_to_nterm. We can also prove the obvious property nterm_to_term (term_to_nterm t) $= t$, where t is a term without dangling de Bruijn indices.

Generation of fresh names in general can be thought of as picking a string that is not an element of a (finite) set of already existing names. For Isabelle, the *Nominal* framework [42, 43] provides support for reasoning over fresh names, but unfortunately, its definitions are not executable.

Instead, we chose to model generation of fresh names as a monad α fresh with the following primitive operations in addition to the monad operations:

$$\text{run::}\ \alpha\ \text{fresh} \Rightarrow \text{string set} \Rightarrow \alpha$$
$$\text{fresh\_name::}\ \text{string fresh}$$

In our implementation, we have chosen to represent α fresh as roughly isomorphic to the state monad.

Compilation of a rule set proceeds by translation of the right-hand side of all rules:

$$\text{compile } R = \{(p, \text{term\_to\_nterm } t) \mid (p, t) \in R\}$$

The left-hand side is left unchanged for two reasons: function match expects an argument of type **term** (see Sect. 4), and patterns do not contain abstractions or bound variables.

Theorem 1 (Correctness of compilation). *Assuming a step can be taken with the compiled rule set, it can be reproduced with the original rule set.*

$$\frac{\text{compile } R \vdash t \longrightarrow u \qquad \text{closed } t}{R \vdash \text{nterm\_to\_term } t \longrightarrow \text{nterm\_to\_term } u}$$

We prove this by induction over the semantics (Fig. 3).

$$\text{BETA} \; \frac{(pat, rhs) \in C \qquad \text{match } pat \; t = \text{Some } \sigma \qquad \text{closed } t}{R \vdash (\Lambda \; C) \; \$ \; t \longrightarrow \text{subst } \sigma \; rhs}$$

$$\text{STEP'} \; \frac{(name, rhs) \in R}{R \vdash \text{Pconst } name \longrightarrow rhs}$$

Fig. 4. Small-step semantics for pterm with pattern matching

5.3 Explicit Pattern Matching: From nterm to pterm

Usually, functions in HOL are defined using *implicit* pattern matching, that is, the left-hand side of an equation is of the form $\langle f \; p_1 \; \ldots \; p_n \rangle$, where the p_i are patterns over datatype constructors. For any given function f, there may be multiple such equations. In this compilation step, we transform sets of equations for f defined using implicit pattern matching into a single equation for f of the form $\langle f \rangle = \Lambda \; C$, where C is a set of clauses.

The strategy we employ currently requires successive elimination of a single parameter from right to left, in a similar fashion as Slind's pattern matching compiler [38, Sect. 3.3.1]. Recall our running example (map). It has arity 2. We omit the brackets $\langle \rangle$ for brevity. First, the list parameter gets eliminated:

$$\begin{aligned} \text{map } f = \lambda \; [] &\Rightarrow [] \\ |\; x \mathbin{\#} xs &\Rightarrow f \; x \mathbin{\#} \text{map } f \; xs \end{aligned}$$

Finally, the function parameter gets eliminated:

$$\begin{aligned} \text{map} = \lambda \; f \Rightarrow (\lambda \; [] &\Rightarrow [] \\ |\; x \mathbin{\#} xs &\Rightarrow f \; x \mathbin{\#} \text{map } f \; xs) \end{aligned}$$

This has now arity 0 and is defined by a twice-nested abstraction.

Semantics. The target semantics is given in Fig. 4 (the FUN and ARG rules from previous semantics remain unchanged). We start out with a rule set R that allows only implicit pattern matching. After elimination, only explicit pattern matching remains. The modified STEP rule merely replaces a constant by its definition, without taking arguments into account.

Restrictions. For the transformation to work, we need a strong assumption about the structure of the patterns p_i to avoid the following situation:

$$\begin{aligned} \text{map } f \; [] &= [] \\ \text{map } g \; (x \mathbin{\#} xs) &= g \; x \mathbin{\#} \text{map } g \; xs \end{aligned}$$

Through elimination, this would turn into:

$$\begin{aligned} \text{map} = \lambda \; f \Rightarrow (\lambda \; [] &\Rightarrow []) \\ |\; g \Rightarrow (\lambda \; x \mathbin{\#} xs &\Rightarrow f \; x \mathbin{\#} \text{map } f \; xs) \end{aligned}$$

$$\text{STEP} \frac{(name, rhs) \in R}{R \vdash \textsf{Sconst } name \longrightarrow rhs} \qquad \text{BETA} \frac{\textsf{first\_match } cs\, t = \textsf{Some } (\sigma, rhs) \qquad \textsf{closed } t}{R \vdash (\Lambda\, cs) \, \$ \, t \longrightarrow \textsf{subst } \sigma\, rhs}$$

Fig. 5. Small-step semantics for sterm

Even though the original equations were non-overlapping, we suddenly obtained an abstraction with two overlapping patterns. Slind observed a similar problem [38, Sect. 3.3.2] in his algorithm. Therefore, he only permits *uniform* equations, as defined by Wadler [36, Sect. 5.5]. Here, we can give a formal characterization of our requirements as a computable function on pairs of patterns:

fun pat_compat :: term ⇒ term ⇒ bool **where**
pat_compat $(t_1 \, \$ \, t_2) \, (u_1 \, \$ \, u_2) \leftrightarrow$ pat_compat $t_1 \, u_1 \wedge (t_1 = u_1 \rightarrow$ pat_compat $t_2 \, u_2)$
pat_compat $t \, u \leftrightarrow$ (overlapping $t \, u \rightarrow t = u$)

This compatibility constraint ensures that any two overlapping patterns (of the same column) $p_{i,k}$ and $p_{j,k}$ are equal and are thus appropriately grouped together in the elimination procedure. We require all defining equations of a constant to be mutually compatible. Equations violating this constraint will be flagged during embedding (Sect. 3), whereas the pattern elimination algorithm always succeeds.

While this rules out some theoretically possible pattern combinations (e.g. the *diagonal* function [36, Sect. 5.5]), in practice, we have not found this to be a problem: All of the function definitions we have tried (Sect. 8) satisfied pattern compatibility (after automatic renaming of pattern variables). As a last resort, the user can manually instantiate function equations. Although this will always lead to a pattern compatible definition, it is not done automatically, due to the potential blow-up.

Discussion. Because this compilation phase is both non-trivial and has some minor restrictions on the set of function definitions that can be processed, we may provide an alternative implementation in the future. Instead of eliminating patterns from right to left, patterns may be grouped in tuples. The above example would be translated into:

$$\text{map} = \lambda \, (f, []) \Rightarrow []$$
$$\mid (f, x \,\#\, xs) \Rightarrow f \, x \,\#\, \text{map } f \, xs$$

We would then leave the compilation of patterns for the CakeML compiler, which has no pattern compatibility restriction.

The obvious disadvantage however is that this would require the knowledge of a tuple type in the term language which is otherwise unaware of concrete datatypes.

5.4   Sequentialization: From pterm to sterm

The semantics of pterm and sterm differ only in rule STEP and BETA. Figure 5 shows the modified rules. Instead of any matching clause, the first matching clause in a case abstraction is picked.

For the correctness proof, the order of clauses does not matter: we only need to prove that a step taken in the sequential semantics can be reproduced in the unordered semantics. As long as no rules are dropped, this is trivially true. For that reason, the compiler orders the clauses lexicographically. At the same time the rules are also converted from type (string × pterm) set to (string × sterm) list. Below, rs will always denote a list of the latter type.

$$\text{CONST} \; \frac{(name, rhs) \in rs}{rs, \sigma \vdash \text{Sconst } name \downarrow rhs} \qquad \text{VAR} \; \frac{\sigma \; name = \text{Some } v}{rs, \sigma \vdash \text{Svar } name \downarrow v}$$

$$\text{ABS} \; \frac{}{rs, \sigma \vdash \Lambda \; cs \downarrow \Lambda \, [(pat, \text{subst } (\sigma - \text{frees } pat) \; t \mid (pat, t) \leftarrow cs]}$$

$$\text{COMB} \; \frac{rs, \sigma \vdash u \downarrow u' \qquad \text{first\_match } cs \; u' = \text{Some } (\sigma', rhs) \qquad rs, \sigma + \!\!+ \, \sigma' \vdash rhs \downarrow v}{rs, \sigma \vdash t \, \$ \, u \downarrow v}$$

$$\text{CONSTR} \; \frac{name \in constructors \qquad rs, \sigma \vdash t_1 \downarrow u_1 \qquad \cdots \qquad rs, \sigma \vdash t_n \downarrow u_n}{rs, \sigma \vdash \text{Sconst } name \, \$ \, t_1 \, \$ \ldots \$ \, t_n \downarrow \text{Sconst } name \, \$ \, u_1 \, \$ \ldots \$ \, u_n}$$

Fig. 6. Big-step semantics for sterm

5.5 Big-Step Semantics for sterm

This big-step semantics for sterm is not a compiler phase but moves towards the desired evaluation semantics. In this first step, we reuse the sterm type for evaluation results, instead of evaluating to the separate type value. This allows us to ignore environment capture in closures for now.

All previous $\longrightarrow$ relations were parametrized by a rule set. Now the big-step predicate is of the form $rs, \sigma \vdash t \downarrow t'$ where $\sigma :: \text{string} \rightharpoonup \text{sterm}$ is a variable environment.

This semantics also introduces the distinction between *constructors* and *defined constants*. If C is a constructor, the term $\langle C \, t_1 \ldots t_n \rangle$ is evaluated to $\langle C \, t_1' \ldots t_n' \rangle$ where the t_i' are the results of evaluating the t_i.

The full set of rules is shown in Fig. 6. They deserve a short explanation:

CONST. Constants are retrieved from the rule set rs.

VAR. Variables are retrieved from the environment σ.

ABS. In order to achieve the intended invariant, abstractions are evaluated to their fully substituted form.

COMB. Function application $t \, \$ \, u$ first requires evaluation of t into an abstraction $\Lambda \, cs$ and evaluation of u into an arbitrary term u'. Afterwards, we look for a clause matching u' in cs, which produces a local variable environment σ', possibly overwriting existing variables in σ. Finally, we evaluate the right-hand side of the clause with the combined global and local variable environment.

CONSTR. For a constructor application $\langle C \, t_1 \ldots \rangle$, evaluate all t_i. The set *constructors* is an implicit parameter of the semantics.

$$\text{CONST} \; \frac{(name, rhs) \in rs}{rs, \sigma \vdash \mathsf{Sconst}\; name \downarrow rhs} \qquad \text{VAR} \; \frac{\sigma\; name = \mathsf{Some}\; v}{rs, \sigma \vdash \mathsf{Svar}\; name \downarrow v}$$

$$\text{ABS} \; \frac{}{rs, \sigma \vdash \Lambda\; cs \downarrow \mathsf{Vabs}\; cs\; \sigma}$$

$$\text{COMB} \; \frac{rs, \sigma \vdash u \downarrow v \qquad \text{first\_match}\; cs\; v = \mathsf{Some}\; (\sigma'', rhs) \qquad rs, \sigma' +\!\!+ \sigma'' \vdash rhs \downarrow v'}{rs, \sigma \vdash t \,\$\, u \downarrow v'}$$

with top premise $rs, \sigma \vdash t \downarrow \mathsf{Vabs}\; cs\; \sigma'$

$$\text{RECCOMB} \; \frac{\begin{array}{c} rs, \sigma \vdash t \downarrow \mathsf{Vrecabs}\; css\; name\; \sigma' \qquad css\; name = \mathsf{Some}\; cs \qquad rs, \sigma \vdash u \downarrow v \\ \text{first\_match}\; cs\; v = \mathsf{Some}\; (\sigma'', rhs) \qquad rs, \sigma' +\!\!+ \sigma'' \vdash rhs \downarrow v' \end{array}}{rs, \sigma \vdash t \,\$\, u \downarrow v'}$$

$$\text{CONSTR} \; \frac{name \in constructors \qquad rs, \sigma \vdash t_1 \downarrow v_1 \qquad \cdots \qquad rs, \sigma \vdash t_n \downarrow v_n}{rs, \sigma \vdash \mathsf{Sconst}\; name \,\$\, t_1 \,\$\, \ldots \,\$\, t_n \downarrow \mathsf{Vconstr}\; name\; [v_1, \ldots, v_n]}$$

Fig. 7. Evaluation semantics from sterm to value

Lemma 1 (Closedness invariant). *If σ contains only closed terms, frees $t \subseteq$ dom σ and $rs, \sigma \vdash t \downarrow t'$, then t' is closed.*

Correctness of the big-step w.r.t. the small-step semantics is proved easily by induction on the former:

Lemma 2. *For any closed environment σ satisfying frees $t \subseteq$ dom σ,*

$$rs, \sigma \vdash t \downarrow u \to rs \vdash \mathsf{subst}\; \sigma\; t \longrightarrow^* u$$

By setting $\sigma = []$, we obtain:

Theorem 2 (Correctness). $rs, [] \vdash t \downarrow u \wedge \mathsf{closed}\; t \to rs \vdash t \longrightarrow^* u$

5.6   Evaluation Semantics: Refining sterm to value

At this point, we introduce the concept of values into the semantics, while still keeping the rule set (for constants) and the environment (for variables) separate. The evaluation rules are specified in Fig. 7 and represent a departure from the original rewriting semantics: a term does not evaluate to another term but to an object of a different type, a value. We still use $\downarrow$ as notation, because big-step and evaluation semantics can be disambiguated by their types.

The evaluation model itself is fairly straightforward. As explained in Sect. 4.5, abstraction terms are evaluated to closures capturing the current variable environment. Note that at this point, recursive closures are not treated differently from non-recursive closures. In a later stage, when rs and σ are merged, this distinction becomes relevant.

We will now explain each rule that has changed from the previous semantics:

ABS. Abstraction terms are evaluated to a closure capturing the current environment.

COMB. As before, in an application $t\,\$\,u$, t must evaluate to a closure Vabs $cs\,\sigma'$. The evaluation result of u is then matched against the clauses cs, producing an environment σ''. The right-hand side of the clause is then evaluated using $\sigma' + \sigma''$; the original environment σ is effectively discarded.

RECCOMB. Similar as above. Finding the matching clause is a two-step process: First, the appropriate clause list is selected by name of the currently active function. Then, matching is performed.

CONSTR. As before, for an n-ary application $\langle C\,t_1\,\ldots\rangle$, where C is a data constructor, we evaluate all t_i. The result is a Vconstr value.

Conversion Between sterm and value. To establish a correspondence between evaluating a term to an sterm and to a value, we apply the same trick as in Sect. 5.2. Instead of specifying a complicated relation, we translate value back to sterm: simply apply the substitutions in the captured environments to the clauses.

The translation rules for Vabs and Vrecabs are kept similar to the ABS rule from the big-step semantics (Fig. 6). Roughly speaking, the big-step semantics always keeps terms fully substituted, whereas the evaluation semantics defers substitution.

Similarly to Sect. 5.2, we can also define a function sterm_to_value :: sterm $\Rightarrow$ value and prove that one function is the inverse of the other.

Matching. The value type, instead of using binary function application as all other term types, uses n-ary constructor application. This introduces a conceptual mismatch between (binary) patterns and values. To make the proofs easier, we introduce an intermediate type of n-ary patterns. This intermediate type can be optimized away by fusion.

Correctness. The correctness proof requires a number of interesting lemmas.

Lemma 3 (Substitution before evaluation). *Assuming that a term t can be evaluated to a value u given a closed environment σ, it can be evaluated to the same value after substitution with a sub-environment σ'. Formally: $rs, \sigma \vdash t \downarrow u \land \sigma' \subseteq \sigma \rightarrow rs, \sigma \vdash \text{subst } \sigma'\, t \downarrow u$*

This justifies the "pre-substitution" exhibited by the ABS rule in the big-step semantics in contrast to the environment-capturing ABS rule in the evaluation semantics.

Theorem 3 (Correctness). *Let σ be a closed environment and t a term which only contains free variables in dom σ. Then, an evaluation to a value $rs, \sigma \vdash t \downarrow v$ can be reproduced in the big-step semantics as rs', map value_to_sterm $\sigma \vdash t \downarrow$ value_to_sterm v, where $rs' = [(name, \text{value\_to\_sterm } rhs) \mid (name, rhs) \leftarrow rs]$.*

Instantiating the Correctness Theorem. The correctness theorem states that, for any given evaluation of a term t with a given environment rs, σ containing values, we can reproduce that evaluation in the big-step semantics using a derived list of rules rs' and an environment σ' containing sterms that are generated by the value_to_sterm function. But recall the diagram in Fig. 2. In our scenario, we start with a given rule set of sterms (that has been compiled from a rule set of terms). Hence, the correctness theorem only deals with the opposite direction.

It remains to construct a suitable rs such that applying value_to_sterm to it yields the given sterm rule set. We can exploit the side condition (Sect. 5.1) that all bindings define functions, not constants:

Definition 6 (Global clause set). *The mapping* global_css :: string $\rightharpoonup$ ((term $\times$ sterm) list) *is obtained by stripping the* Sabs *constructors from all definitions and converting the resulting list to a mapping.*

For each definition with name f we define a corresponding term $v_f = $ Vrecabs global_css f []. In other words, each function is now represented by a recursive closure bundling all functions. Applying value_to_sterm to v_f returns the original definition of f. Let rs denote the original sterm rule set and rs_v the environment mapping all f's to the v_f's.

The variable environments σ and σ' can safely be set to the empty mapping, because top-level terms are evaluated without any free variable bindings.

Corollary 1 (Correctness). $rs_v, [] \vdash t \downarrow v \rightarrow rs, [] \vdash t \downarrow$ value_to_sterm v

Note that this step was not part of the compiler (although rs_v is computable) but it is a refinement of the semantics to support a more modular correctness proof.

Example. Recall the odd and even example from Sect. 4.5. After compilation to sterm, the rule set looks like this:

$$rs = \{(\texttt{"odd"}, \text{Sabs } [\langle 0 \rangle \Rightarrow \langle \text{False} \rangle, \langle \text{Suc } n \rangle \Rightarrow \langle \text{even } n \rangle]),$$
$$(\texttt{"even"}, \text{Sabs } [\langle 0 \rangle \Rightarrow \langle \text{True} \rangle, \langle \text{Suc } n \rangle \Rightarrow \langle \text{odd } n \rangle])\}$$

This can be easily transformed into the following global clause set:

$$\text{global\_css} = [\texttt{"odd"} \mapsto [\langle 0 \rangle \Rightarrow \langle \text{False} \rangle, \langle \text{Suc } n \rangle \Rightarrow \langle \text{even } n \rangle],$$
$$\texttt{"even"} \mapsto [\langle 0 \rangle \Rightarrow \langle \text{True} \rangle, \langle \text{Suc } n \rangle \Rightarrow \langle \text{odd } n \rangle]]$$

Finally, rs_v is computed by creating a recursive closure for each function:

$$rs_v = [\texttt{"odd"} \mapsto \text{Vrecabs global\_css } \texttt{"odd"} [],$$
$$\texttt{"even"} \mapsto \text{Vrecabs global\_css } \texttt{"even"} []]$$

$$\text{CONST}\ \frac{name \notin constructors \qquad \sigma\ name = \mathsf{Some}\ v}{\sigma \vdash \mathsf{Sconst}\ name \downarrow v}$$

$$\text{VAR}\ \frac{\sigma\ name = \mathsf{Some}\ v}{\sigma \vdash \mathsf{Svar}\ name \downarrow v} \qquad \text{ABS}\ \frac{}{\sigma \vdash \Lambda\ cs \downarrow \mathsf{Vabs}\ cs\ \sigma}$$

$$\text{COMB}\ \frac{\sigma \vdash t \downarrow \mathsf{Vabs}\ cs\ \sigma' \quad \mathsf{first\_match}\ cs\ v = \mathsf{Some}\ (\sigma'', rhs) \quad \sigma' \mathbin{+\!\!+} \sigma'' \vdash rhs \downarrow v'}{\sigma \vdash t\ \$\ u \downarrow v'}$$

$$\text{RECCOMB}\ \frac{\begin{array}{c}\sigma \vdash t \downarrow \mathsf{Vrecabs}\ css\ name\ \sigma' \\ css\ name = \mathsf{Some}\ cs \quad \sigma \vdash u \downarrow v \quad \mathsf{first\_match}\ cs\ v = \mathsf{Some}\ (\sigma'', rhs) \\ \sigma' \mathbin{+\!\!+} \mathsf{mk\_rec\_env}\ css\ \sigma' \mathbin{+\!\!+} \sigma'' \vdash rhs \downarrow v'\end{array}}{\sigma \vdash t\ \$\ u \downarrow v'}$$

$$\text{CONSTR}\ \frac{name \in constructors \qquad \sigma \vdash t_1 \downarrow v_1 \quad \cdots \quad \sigma \vdash t_n \downarrow v_n}{\sigma \vdash \mathsf{Sconst}\ name\ \$\ t_1\ \$\ \ldots\ \$\ t_n \downarrow \mathsf{Vconstr}\ name\ [v_1, \ldots, v_n]}$$

Fig. 8. ML-style evaluation semantics

5.7 Evaluation with Recursive Closures

CakeML distinguishes between non-recursive and recursive closures [30]. This distinction is also present in the value type. In this step, we will conflate variables with constants which necessitates a special treatment of recursive closures. Therefore we introduce a new predicate $\sigma \vdash t \downarrow v$ in Fig. 8 (in contrast to the previous $rs, \sigma \vdash t \downarrow v$). We examine the rules one by one:

CONST/VAR. Constant definition and variable values are both retrieved from the same environment σ. We have opted to keep the distinction between constants and variables in the sterm type to avoid the introduction of another term type.

ABS. Identical to the previous evaluation semantics. Note that evaluation never creates recursive closures at run-time (only at compile-time, see Sect. 5.6). Anonymous functions, e.g. in the term $\langle \mathsf{map}\ (\lambda x.\ x) \rangle$, are evaluated to non-recursive closures.

COMB. Identical to the previous evaluation semantics.

RECCOMB. Almost identical to the evaluation semantics. Additionally, for each function $(name, cs) \in css$, a new recursive closure $\mathsf{Vrecabs}\ css\ name\ \sigma'$ is created and inserted into the environment. This ensures that after the first call to a recursive function, the function itself is present in the environment to be called recursively, without having to introduce coinductive environments.

CONSTR. Identical to the evaluation semantics.

Conflating Constants and Variables. By merging the rule set rs with the variable environment σ, it becomes necessary to discuss possible clashes. Previously, the syntactic distinction between Svar and Sconst meant that $\langle x \rangle$ and $\langle \mathsf{x} \rangle$ are not ambiguous: all semantics up to the evaluation semantics clearly specify where to look for the substitute. This is not the case in functional languages where functions and variables are not distinguished syntactically.

Instead, we rely on the fact that the initial rule set only defines constants. All variables are introduced by matching before β-reduction (that is, in the COMB and RECCOMB rules). The ABS rule does not change the environment. Hence it suffices to assume that variables in patterns must not overlap with constant names (see Sect. 5.1).

Correspondence Relation. Both constant definitions and values of variables are recorded in a single environment σ. This also applies to the environment contained in a closure. The correspondence relation thus needs to take a different sets of bindings in closures into account.

Hence, we define a relation $\approx_v$ that is implicitly parametrized on the rule set rs and compares environments. We call it *right-conflating*, because in a correspondence $v \approx_v u$, any bound environment in u is thought to contain both variables and constants, whereas in v, any bound environment contains only variables.

Definition 7 (Right-conflating correspondence). *We define $\approx_v$ coinductively as follows:*

$$\frac{v_1 \approx_v u_1 \quad \cdots \quad v_n \approx_v u_n}{\mathsf{Vconstr}\ name\ [v_1, \ldots, v_n] \approx_v \mathsf{Vconstr}\ name\ [u_1, \ldots, u_n]}$$

$$\frac{\forall x \in \mathsf{frees}\ cs.\ \sigma_1\ x \approx_v \sigma_2\ x \qquad \forall x \in \mathsf{consts}\ cs.\ rs\ x \approx_v \sigma_2\ x}{\mathsf{Vabs}\ cs\ \sigma_1 \approx_v \mathsf{Vabs}\ cs\ \sigma_2}$$

$$\frac{\forall cs \in \mathsf{range}\ css.\ \forall x \in \mathsf{frees}\ cs.\ \sigma_1\ x \approx_v \sigma_2\ x}{\forall cs \in \mathsf{range}\ css.\ \forall x \in \mathsf{consts}\ cs.\ \sigma_1\ x \approx_v (\sigma_2 +\!\!+ \mathsf{mk\_rec\_env}\ css\ \sigma_2)\ x}{\mathsf{Vrecabs}\ css\ name\ \sigma_1 \approx_v \mathsf{Vrecabs}\ css\ name\ \sigma_2}$$

Consequently, $\approx_v$ is not reflexive.

Correctness. The correctness lemma is straightforward to state:

Theorem 4 (Correctness). *Let σ be an environment, t be a closed term and v a value such that $\sigma \vdash t \downarrow v$. If for all constants x occurring in t, $rs\ x \approx_v \sigma\ x$ holds, then there is an u such that $rs, [] \vdash t \downarrow u$ and $u \approx_v v$.*

As usual, the rather technical proof proceeds via induction over the semantics (Fig. 8). It is important to note that the global clause set construction (Sect. 5.6) satisfies the preconditions of this theorem:

Lemma 4. *If name is the name of a constant in rs, then*

$$\mathsf{Vrecabs}\ \mathsf{global\_css}\ name\ [] \approx_v \mathsf{Vrecabs}\ \mathsf{global\_css}\ name\ []$$

Because $\approx_v$ is defined coinductively, the proof of this precondition proceeds by coinduction.

5.8 CakeML

CakeML is a verified implementation of a subset of Standard ML [24,40]. It comprises a parser, type checker, formal semantics and backend for machine code. The semantics has been formalized in Lem [29], which allows export to Isabelle theories.

Our compiler targets CakeML's abstract syntax tree. However, we do not make use of certain CakeML features; notably mutable cells, modules, and literals. We have derived a smaller, executable version of the original CakeML semantics, called *CupCakeML*, together with an equivalence proof. The correctness proof of the last compiler phase establishes a correspondence between Cup-CakeML and the final semantics of our compiler pipeline.

For the correctness proof of the CakeML compiler, its authors have extracted the Lem specification into HOL4 theories [1]. In our work, we directly target CakeML abstract syntax trees (thereby bypassing the parser) and use its big-step semantics, which we have extracted into Isabelle.[2]

Conversion from sterm to exp. After the series of translations described in the earlier sections, our terms are syntactically close to CakeML's terms (Cake.exp). The only remaining differences are outlined below:

- CakeML does not combine abstraction and pattern matching. For that reason, we have to translate $\Lambda [p_1 \Rightarrow t_1, \ldots]$ into $\Lambda x.$ **case** x **of** $p_1 \Rightarrow t_1 \mid \ldots$, where x is a fresh variable name. We reuse the fresh monad to obtain a bound variable name. Note that it is not necessary to thread through already created variable names, only existing names. The reason is simple: a generated variable is bound and then immediately used in the body. Shadowing it somewhere in the body is not problematic.
- CakeML has two distinct syntactic categories for identifiers (that can represent variables or functions) and data constructors. Our term types however have two distinct syntactic categories for constants (that can represent functions or data constructors) and variables. The necessary prerequisites to deal with this are already present in the ML-style evaluation semantics (Sect. 5.7) which conflates constants and variables, but has a dedicated CONSTR rule for data constructors.

Types. During embedding (Sect. 3), all type information is erased. Yet, CakeML performs some limited form of type checking at run-time: constructing and matching data must always be fully applied. That is, data constructors must always occur with all arguments supplied on right-hand and left-hand sides.

Fully applied constructors in terms can be easily guaranteed by simple pre-processing. For patterns however, this must be ensured throughout the compilation pipeline; it is (like other syntactic constraints) another side condition imposed on the rule set (Sect. 5.1).

---

[2] Based on a repository snapshot from March 27, 2017 (0c48672).

The shape of datatypes and constructors is managed in CakeML's environment. This particular piece of information is allowed to vary in closures, since ML supports local type definitions. Tracking this would greatly complicate our proofs. Hence, we fix a global set of constructors and enforce that all values use exactly that one.

Correspondence Relation. We define two different correspondence relations: One for values and one for expressions.

Definition 8 (Expression correspondence)

$$\text{VAR} \frac{}{\mathsf{rel\_e}\ (\mathsf{Svar}\ n)\ (\mathsf{Cake.Var}\ n)} \qquad \text{CONST} \frac{n \notin constructors}{\mathsf{rel\_e}\ (\mathsf{Sconst}\ n)\ (\mathsf{Cake.Var}\ n)}$$

$$\text{CONSTR} \frac{n \in constructors \qquad \mathsf{rel\_e}\ t_1\ u_1 \quad \cdots}{\mathsf{rel\_e}\ (\mathsf{Sconst}\ name\ \$\ t_1\ \$ \ldots \$\ t_n)\ (\mathsf{Cake.Con}\ (\mathsf{Some}\ (\mathsf{Cake.Short}\ name))\ [u_1, \ldots, u_n]))}$$

$$\text{APP} \frac{\mathsf{rel\_e}\ t_1\ u_1 \qquad \mathsf{rel\_e}\ t_2\ u_2}{\mathsf{rel\_e}\ t_1\ \$\ t_2\ \mathsf{Cake.App}\ \mathsf{Cake.Opapp}\ [u_1, u_2]}$$

$$\text{FUN} \frac{n \notin \mathsf{ids}\ (\Lambda\ [p_1 \Rightarrow t_1, \ldots]) \cup constructors \qquad q_1 = \mathsf{mk\_ml\_pat}\ p_1 \qquad \mathsf{rel\_e}\ t_1\ u_1 \quad \cdots}{\mathsf{rel\_e}\ (\Lambda\ [p_1 \Rightarrow t_1, \ldots])\ (\mathsf{Cake.Fun}\ n\ (\mathsf{Cake.Mat}\ (\mathsf{Cake.Var}\ n))\ [q_1 \Rightarrow u_1, \ldots])}$$

$$\text{MAT} \frac{\mathsf{rel\_e}\ t\ u \qquad q_1 = \mathsf{mk\_ml\_pat}\ p_1 \qquad \mathsf{rel\_e}\ t_1\ u_1 \quad \cdots}{\mathsf{rel\_e}\ (\Lambda\ [p_1 \Rightarrow t_1, \ldots]\ \$\ t)\ (\mathsf{Cake.Mat}\ u\ [q_1 \Rightarrow u_1, \ldots])}$$

We will explain each of the rules briefly here.

VAR. Variables are directly related by identical name.

CONST. As described earlier, constructors are treated specially in CakeML. In order to not confuse functions or variables with data constructors themselves, we require that the constant name is not a constructor.

CONSTR. Constructors are directly related by identical name, and recursively related arguments.

APP. CakeML does not just support general function application but also unary and binary operators. In fact, function application is the binary operator Opapp. We never generate other operators. Hence the correspondence is restricted to Opapp.

FUN/MAT. Observe the symmetry between these two cases: In our term language, matching and abstraction are combined, which is not the case in CakeML. This means we relate a case abstraction to a CakeML function containing a match, and a case abstraction applied to a value to just a CakeML match.

There is no separate relation for patterns, because their translation is simple.

The value correspondence ($\mathsf{rel\_v}$) is structurally simpler. In the case of constructor values (Vconstr and Cake.Conv), arguments are compared recursively. Closures and recursive closures are compared extensionally, i.e. only bindings that occur in the body are checked recursively for correspondence.

Correctness. We use the same trick as in Sect. 5.6 to obtain a suitable environment for CakeML evaluation based on the rule set *rs*.

Theorem 5 (Correctness). *If the compiled expression* sterm_to_cake *t terminates with a value u in the CakeML semantics, there is a value v such that* rel_v *v u and rs* ⊢ *t* ↓ *v.*

6   Composition

The complete compiler pipeline consists of multiple phases. Correctness is justified for each phase between intermediate semantics and correspondence relations, most of which are rather technical. Whereas the compiler may be complex and impenetrable, the trustworthiness of the constructions hinges on the obviousness of those correspondence relations.

Fortunately, under the assumption that terms to be evaluated and the resulting values do not contain abstractions – or closures, respectively – all of the correspondence relations collapse to simple structural equality: two terms are related if and only if one can be converted to the other by consistent renaming of term constructors.

The actual compiler can be characterized with two functions. Firstly, the translation of **term** to **Cake.exp** is a simple composition of each term translation function:

definition term_to_cake :: term ⇒ Cake.exp **where**
term_to_cake = sterm_to_cake ∘ pterm_to_sterm ∘ nterm_to_pterm ∘ term_to_nterm

Secondly, the function that translates function definitions by composing the phases as outlined in Fig. 2, including iterated application of pattern elimination:

definition compile :: (term × term) fset ⇒ Cake.dec **where**
compile = Cake.Dletrec ∘ compile_srules_to_cake ∘ compile_prules_to_srules ∘
  compile_irules_to_srules ∘ compile_irules_iter ∘ compile_crules_to_irules ∘
  consts_of ∘ compile_rules_to_nrules

Each function compile_* corresponds to one compiler phase; the remaining functions are trivial. This produces a CakeML top-level declaration. We prove that evaluating this declaration in the top-level semantics (evaluate_prog) results in an environment cake_sem_env. But cake_sem_env can also be computed via another instance of the global clause set trick (Sect. 5.6).

Equipped with these functions, we can state the final correctness theorem:

theorem compiled_correct:
  (* *If CakeML evaluation of a term succeeds ...* *)
  assumes evaluate False cake_sem_env *s* (term_to_cake *t*) (*s'*, Rval *mL_v*)
  (* *... producing a constructor term without closures ...* *)
  assumes cake_abstraction_free *mL_v*
  (* *... and some syntactic properties of the involved terms hold ...* *)
  assumes closed t **and** ¬ shadows_consts (heads *rs* ∪ *constructors*) t **and**
    welldefined (heads *rs* ∪ *constructors*) *t* **and** wellformed *t*
  (* *... then this evaluation can be reproduced in the term—rewriting semantics* *)
  shows rs ⊢ t →* cake_to_term *mL_v*

datatype 'a dict_add = Dict_add ('a ⇒ 'a ⇒ 'a)

class add =
  fixes plus :: 'a ⇒ 'a ⇒ 'a

fun cert_add :: ('a::add) dict_add ⇒ bool **where**
cert_add (Dict_add pls) = (pls = plus)

definition f :: ('a::add) ⇒ 'a **where**
f x = plus x x

fun f' :: 'a dict_add ⇒ 'a ⇒ 'a **where**
f' (Dict_add pls) x = pls x x

(a) Source program

lemma f'_eq: cert_add $dict$ → f' $dict$ = f
<$proof$>

(b) Result of translation

Fig. 9. Dictionary construction in Isabelle

This theorem directly relates the evaluation of a term t in the full CakeML (including mutability and exceptions) to the evaluation in the initial higher-order term rewriting semantics. The evaluation of t happens using the environment produced from the initial rule set. Hence, the theorem can be interpreted as the correctness of the pseudo-ML expression **let rec** rs **in** t.

Observe that in the assumption, the conversion goes from our terms to CakeML expressions, whereas in the conclusion, the conversion goes the opposite direction.

7   Dictionary Construction

Isabelle's type system supports *type classes* (or simply *classes*) [18,44] whereas CakeML does not. In order to not complicate the correctness proofs, type classes are not supported by our embedded term language either. Instead, we eliminate classes and instances by a dictionary construction [19] before embedding into the term language. Haftmann and Nipkow give a pen-and-paper correctness proof of this construction [17, Sect. 4.1]. We augmented the dictionary construction with the generation of a certificate theorem that shows the equivalence of the two versions of a function, with type classes and with dictionaries. This section briefly explains our dictionary construction.

Figure 9 shows a simple example of a dictionary construction. Type variables may carry *class constraints* (e.g. $\alpha ::$ add). The basic idea is that classes become *dictionaries* containing the functions of that class; class instances become dictionary definitions. Dictionaries are realized as datatypes. Class constraints become additional dictionary parameters for that class. In the example, class add becomes dict_add; function f is translated into f' which takes an additional parameter of type dict_add. In reality our tool does not produce the Isabelle source code shown in Fig. 9b but performs the constructions internally. The correctness lemma f'_eq is proved automatically. Its precondition expresses that the dictionary must contain exactly the function(s) of class add. For any monomorphic instance, the precondition can be proved outright based on the certificate theorems proved for each class instance as explained next.

Not shown in the example is the translation of class instances. The basic form of a class instance in Isabelle is $\tau::(c_1,\ldots,c_n)\ c$ where τ is an n-ary type constructor. It corresponds to Haskell's $(c_1\ \alpha_1,\ldots,c_n\ \alpha_n) \Rightarrow c\ (\tau\ \alpha_1\ldots\alpha_n)$ and is translated into a function $\mathsf{inst\_c\_\tau}::\alpha_1\ \mathsf{dict\_c_1} \Rightarrow \cdots \Rightarrow \alpha_n\ \mathsf{dict\_c_n} \Rightarrow (\alpha_1,\ldots,\alpha_n)\ \tau\ \mathsf{dict\_c}$ and the following certificate theorem is proved:

$$\mathsf{cert\_c_1}\ dict_1 \to \cdots \to \mathsf{cert\_c_n}\ dict_n \to \mathsf{cert\_c}\ (\mathsf{inst\_c\_\tau}\ dict_1\ \ldots\ dict_n)$$

For a more detailed explanation of how the dictionary construction works, we refer to the corresponding entry in the Archive of Formal Proofs [21].

8   Evaluation

We have tried out our compiler on examples from existing Isabelle formalizations. This includes an implementation of Huffman encoding, lists and sorting, string functions [39], and various data structures from Okasaki's book [34], including binary search trees, pairing heaps, and leftist heaps. These definitions can be processed with slight modifications: functions need to be totalized (see the end of Sect. 3). However, parts of the tactics required for deep embedding proofs (Sect. 3) are too slow on some functions and hence still need to be optimized.

9   Conclusion

For this paper we have concentrated on the compiler from Isabelle/HOL to CakeML abstract syntax trees. Partial correctness is proved w.r.t. the big-step semantics of CakeML. In the next step we will link our work with the compiler from CakeML to machine code. Tan et al. [40, Sect. 10] prove a correctness theorem that relates their semantics with the execution of the compiled machine code. In that paper, they use a newer iteration of the CakeML semantics (functional big-step [35]) than we do here. Both semantics are still present in the CakeML source repository, together with an equivalence proof. Another important step consists of targeting CakeML's native types, e.g. integer numbers and characters.

Evaluation of our compiled programs is already possible via Isabelle's predicate compiler [5], which allows us to turn CakeML's big-step semantics into an executable function. We have used this execution mechanism to establish for sample programs that they terminate successfully. We also plan to prove that our compiled programs terminate, i.e. total correctness.

The total size of this formalization, excluding theories extracted from Lem, is currently approximately 20000 lines of proof text (90 %) and ML code (10 %). The ML code itself produces relatively simple theorems, which means that there are less opportunities for it to go wrong. This constitutes an improvement over certifying approaches that prove complicated properties in ML.

References

1. The HOL System Description (2014). https://hol-theorem-prover.org/
2. Anand, A., Appel, A.W., Morrisett, G., Paraskevopoulou, Z., Pollack, R., Bélanger, O.S., Sozeau, M., Weaver, M.: CertiCoq: a verified compiler for Coq. In: CoqPL 2017: Third International Workshop on Coq for Programming Languages (2017)
3. Augustsson, L.: Compiling pattern matching. In: Jouannnaud, J.P. (ed.) Functional Programming Languages and Computer Architecture, pp. 368–381. Springer, Heidelberg (1985)
4. Benton, N., Hur, C.: Biorthogonality, step-indexing and compiler correctness. In: Hutton, G., Tolmach, A.P. (eds.) ICFP 2009, pp. 97–108. ACM (2009)
5. Berghofer, S., Bulwahn, L., Haftmann, F.: Turning inductive into equational specifications. In: Berghofer, S., Nipkow, T., Urban, C., Wenzel, M. (eds.) TPHOLs 2009. LNCS, vol. 5674, pp. 131–146. Springer, Heidelberg (2009). https://doi.org/10.1007/978-3-642-03359-9_11
6. Berghofer, S., Nipkow, T.: Executing higher order logic. In: Callaghan, P., Luo, Z., McKinna, J., Pollack, R., Pollack, R. (eds.) TYPES 2000. LNCS, vol. 2277, pp. 24–40. Springer, Heidelberg (2002). https://doi.org/10.1007/3-540-45842-5_2
7. Blanchette, J.C., Hölzl, J., Lochbihler, A., Panny, L., Popescu, A., Traytel, D.: Truly modular (co)datatypes for Isabelle/HOL. In: Klein, G., Gamboa, R. (eds.) ITP 2014. LNCS, vol. 8558, pp. 93–110. Springer, Cham (2014). https://doi.org/10.1007/978-3-319-08970-6_7
8. Boespflug, M., Dénès, M., Grégoire, B.: Full reduction at full throttle. In: Jouannaud, J.-P., Shao, Z. (eds.) CPP 2011. LNCS, vol. 7086, pp. 362–377. Springer, Heidelberg (2011). https://doi.org/10.1007/978-3-642-25379-9_26
9. Boyer, R.S., Strother Moore, J.: Single-threaded objects in ACL2. In: Krishnamurthi, S., Ramakrishnan, C.R. (eds.) PADL 2002. LNCS, vol. 2257, pp. 9–27. Springer, Heidelberg (2002). https://doi.org/10.1007/3-540-45587-6_3
10. de Bruijn, N.G.: Lambda calculus notation with nameless dummies, a tool for automatic formula manipulation, with application to the church-rosser theorem. Indag. Math. (Proceedings) **75**(5), 381–392 (1972)
11. Chlipala, A.: A verified compiler for an impure functional language. In: Hermenegildo, M.V., Palsberg, J. (eds.) POPL 2010, pp. 93–106. ACM (2010)
12. Crow, J., Owre, S., Rushby, J., Shankar, N., Stringer-Calvert, D.: Evaluating, testing, and animating PVS specifications. Technical report, Computer Science Laboratory, SRI International, Menlo Park, CA, March 2001
13. Fallenstein, B., Kumar, R.: Proof-producing reflection for HOL. In: Urban, C., Zhang, X. (eds.) ITP 2015. LNCS, vol. 9236, pp. 170–186. Springer, Cham (2015). https://doi.org/10.1007/978-3-319-22102-1_11
14. Flatau, A.D.: A verified implementation of an applicative language with dynamic storage allocation. Ph.D. thesis, University of Texas at Austin (1992)
15. Forster, Y., Kunze, F.: Verified extraction from coq to a lambda-calculus. In: The 8th Coq Workshop (2016)
16. Greve, D.A., Kaufmann, M., Manolios, P., Moore, J.S., Ray, S., Ruiz-Reina, J., Sumners, R., Vroon, D., Wilding, M.: Efficient execution in an automated reasoning environment. J. Funct. Program. **18**(1), 15–46 (2008)
17. Haftmann, F., Nipkow, T.: Code generation via higher-order rewrite systems. In: Blume, M., Kobayashi, N., Vidal, G. (eds.) FLOPS 2010. LNCS, vol. 6009, pp. 103–117. Springer, Heidelberg (2010). https://doi.org/10.1007/978-3-642-12251-4_9

18. Haftmann, F., Wenzel, M.: Constructive type classes in Isabelle. In: Altenkirch, T., McBride, C. (eds.) TYPES 2006. LNCS, vol. 4502, pp. 160–174. Springer, Heidelberg (2007). https://doi.org/10.1007/978-3-540-74464-1_11
19. Hall, C.V., Hammond, K., Jones, S.L.P., Wadler, P.L.: Type classes in Haskell. ACM Trans. Program. Lang. Syst. **18**(2), 109–138 (1996)
20. Hermida, C., Reddy, U.S., Robinson, E.P.: Logical relations and parametricity - a Reynolds programme for category theory and programming languages. Electron. Notes Theoret. Comput. Sci. **303**, 149–180 (2014)
21. Hupel, L.: Dictionary construction. Archive of Formal Proofs, May 2017. http://isa-afp.org/entries/Dict_Construction.html, Formal proof development
22. Krauss, A.: Partial and nested recursive function definitions in higher-order logic. J. Autom. Reason. **44**(4), 303–336 (2010)
23. Krauss, A., Schropp, A.: A mechanized translation from higher-order logic to set theory. In: Kaufmann, M., Paulson, L.C. (eds.) ITP 2010. LNCS, vol. 6172, pp. 323–338. Springer, Heidelberg (2010). https://doi.org/10.1007/978-3-642-14052-5_23
24. Kumar, R., Myreen, M.O., Norrish, M., Owens, S.: CakeML: a verified implementation of ML. In: POPL 2014, pp. 179–191. ACM (2014)
25. Landin, P.J.: The mechanical evaluation of expressions. Comput. J. **6**(4), 308–320 (1964)
26. Leroy, X.: Formal verification of a realistic compiler. Commun. ACM **52**(7), 107–115 (2009). http://doi.acm.org/10.1145/1538788.1538814
27. Letouzey, P.: A new extraction for Coq. In: Geuvers, H., Wiedijk, F. (eds.) TYPES 2002. LNCS, vol. 2646, pp. 200–219. Springer, Heidelberg (2003). https://doi.org/10.1007/3-540-39185-1_12
28. Milner, R., Tofte, M., Harper, R., MacQueen, D.: The Definition of Standard ML (Revised). MIT Press, Cambridge (1997)
29. Mulligan, D.P., Owens, S., Gray, K.E., Ridge, T., Sewell, P.: Lem: reusable engineering of real-world semantics. In: ICFP 2014, pp. 175–188. ACM (2014)
30. Myreen, M.O., Owens, S.: Proof-producing translation of higher-order logic into pure and stateful ML. JFP **24**(2–3), 284–315 (2014)
31. Neis, G., Hur, C.K., Kaiser, J.O., McLaughlin, C., Dreyer, D., Vafeiadis, V.: Pilsner: a compositionally verified compiler for a higher-order imperative language. In: ICFP 2015, pp. 166–178. ACM, New York (2015)
32. Nipkow, T., Klein, G.: Concrete Semantics. Springer, Cham (2014). https://doi.org/10.1007/978-3-319-10542-0
33. Nipkow, T., Wenzel, M., Paulson, L.C. (eds.): Isabelle/HOL—A Proof Assistant for Higher-Order Logic. LNCS, vol. 2283. Springer, Heidelberg (2002). https://doi.org/10.1007/3-540-45949-9. 218p.
34. Okasaki, C.: Purely Functional Data Structures. Cambridge University Press, Cambridge (1999)
35. Owens, S., Myreen, M.O., Kumar, R., Tan, Y.K.: Functional big-step semantics. In: Thiemann, P. (ed.) ESOP 2016. LNCS, vol. 9632, pp. 589–615. Springer, Heidelberg (2016). https://doi.org/10.1007/978-3-662-49498-1_23
36. Peyton Jones, S.L.: The Implementation of Functional Programming Languages. Prentice-Hall Inc., Upper Saddle River (1987)
37. Shankar, N.: Static analysis for safe destructive updates in a functional language. In: Pettorossi, A. (ed.) LOPSTR 2001. LNCS, vol. 2372, pp. 1–24. Springer, Heidelberg (2002). https://doi.org/10.1007/3-540-45607-4_1
38. Slind, K.: Reasoning about terminating functional programs. Ph.D. thesis, Technische Universität München (1999)

39. Sternagel, C., Thiemann, R.: Haskell's show class in Isabelle/HOL. Archive of Formal Proofs, July 2014. http://isa-afp.org/entries/Show.html, Formal proof development

40. Tan, Y.K., Myreen, M.O., Kumar, R., Fox, A., Owens, S., Norrish, M.: A new verified compiler backend for CakeML. In: Proceedings of 21st ACM SIGPLAN International Conference on Functional Programming - ICFP 2016. Association for Computing Machinery (ACM) (2016)

41. Turner, D.A.: Some history of functional programming languages. In: Loidl, H.-W., Peña, R. (eds.) TFP 2012. LNCS, vol. 7829, pp. 1–20. Springer, Heidelberg (2013). https://doi.org/10.1007/978-3-642-40447-4_1

42. Urban, C.: Nominal techniques in Isabelle/HOL. J. Autom. Reason. **40**(4), 327–356 (2008). https://doi.org/10.1007/s10817-008-9097-2

43. Urban, C., Berghofer, S., Kaliszyk, C.: Nominal 2. Archive of Formal Proofs, February 2013. Formal proof development: http://isa-afp.org/entries/Nominal2.shtml

44. Wenzel, M.: Type classes and overloading in higher-order logic. In: Gunter, E.L., Felty, A. (eds.) TPHOLs 1997. LNCS, vol. 1275, pp. 307–322. Springer, Heidelberg (1997). https://doi.org/10.1007/BFb0028402

Compositional Verification of Compiler Optimisations on Relaxed Memory

Mike Dodds[1] , Mark Batty[2], and Alexey Gotsman[3(✉)]

[1] Galois Inc., Portland, Oregon, USA
miked@galois.com
[2] University of Kent, Canterbury, UK
M.J.Batty@kent.ac.uk
[3] IMDEA Software Institute, Madrid, Spain
alexey.gotsman@imdea.org

Abstract. A valid compiler optimisation transforms a block in a program without introducing new observable behaviours to the program as a whole. Deciding which optimisations are valid can be difficult, and depends closely on the semantic model of the programming language. Axiomatic relaxed models, such as C++11, present particular challenges for determining validity, because such models allow subtle effects of a block transformation to be observed by the rest of the program. In this paper we present a denotational theory that captures optimisation validity on an axiomatic model corresponding to a fragment of C++11. Our theory allows verifying an optimisation compositionally, by considering only the block it transforms instead of the whole program. Using this property, we realise the theory in the first push-button tool that can verify real-world optimisations under an axiomatic memory model.

1 Introduction

Context and Objectives. Any program defines a collection of observable behaviours: a sorting algorithm maps unsorted to sorted sequences, and a paint program responds to mouse clicks by updating a rendering. It is often desirable to transform a program without introducing new observable behaviours – for example, in a compiler optimisation or programmer refactoring. Such transformations are called *observational refinements*, and they ensure that properties of the original program will carry over to the transformed version. It is also desirable for transformations to be *compositional*, meaning that they can be applied to a block of code irrespective of the surrounding program context. Compositional transformations are particularly useful for automated systems such as compilers, where they are known as *peephole optimisations*.

The semantics of the language is highly significant in determining which transformations are valid, because it determines the ways that a block of code being transformed can interact with its context and thereby affect the observable behaviour of the whole program. Our work applies to a relaxed memory concurrent setting. Thus, the context of a code-block includes both code sequentially

A. Ahmed (Ed.): ESOP 2018, LNCS 10801, pp. 1027–1055, 2018.
https://doi.org/10.1007/978-3-319-89884-1_36

before and after the block, and code that runs in parallel. Relaxed memory means that different threads can observe different, apparently contradictory orders of events – such behaviour is permitted by programming languages to reflect CPU-level relaxations and to allow compiler optimisations.

We focus on *axiomatic* memory models of the type used in C/C++ and Java. In axiomatic models, program executions are represented by structures of memory actions and relations on them, and program semantics is defined by a set of axioms constraining these structures. Reasoning about the correctness of program transformations on such memory models is very challenging, and indeed, compiler optimisations have been repeatedly shown unsound with respect to models they were intended to support [23,25]. The fundamental difficulty is that axiomatic models are defined in a global, non-compositional way, making it very challenging to reason compositionally about the single code-block being transformed.

Approach. Suppose we have a code-block B, embedded into an unknown program context. We define a *denotation* for the code-block which summarises its behaviour in a restricted representative context. The denotation consists of a set of *histories* which track interactions across the boundary between the code-block and its context, but abstract from internal structure of the code-block. We can then validate a transformation from code-block B to B' by comparing their denotations. This approach is compositional: it requires reasoning only about the code-blocks and representative contexts; the validity of the transformation in an arbitrary context will follow. It is also *fully abstract*, meaning that it can verify any valid transformation: considering only representative contexts and histories does not lose generality.

We also define a variant of our denotation that is *finite* at the cost of losing full abstraction. We achieve this by further restricting the form of contexts one needs to consider in exchange for tracking more information in histories. For example, it is unnecessary to consider executions where two context operations read from the same write.

Using this finite denotation, we implement a prototype verification tool, Stellite. Our tool converts an input transformation into a model in the Alloy language [12], and then checks that the transformation is valid using the Alloy* solver [18]. Our tool can prove or disprove a range of introduction, elimination, and exchange compiler optimisations. Many of these were verified by hand in previous work; our tool verifies them automatically.

Contributions. Our contribution is twofold. First, we define the first fully abstract denotational semantics for an axiomatic relaxed model. Previous proposals in this space targeted either non-relaxed sequential consistency [6] or much more restrictive operational relaxed models [7,13,21]. Second, we show it is feasible to automatically verify relaxed-memory program transformations. Previous techniques required laborious proofs by hand or in a proof assistant [23–27]. Our target model is derived from the C/C++ 2011 standard [22]. However, our aim is not to handle C/C++ per se (especially as the model is in flux in several respects; see Sect. 3.7). Rather we target the simplest axiomatic model rich enough to demonstrate our approach.

2   Observation and Transformation

Observational Refinement. The notion of *observation* is crucial when determining how different programs are related. For example, observations might be I/O behaviour or writes to special variables. Given program executions X_1 and X_2, we write $X_1 \preccurlyeq_{ex} X_2$ if the observations in X_1 are replicated in X_2 (defined formally in the following). Lifting this notion, a program P_1 *observationally refines* another P_2 if every observable behaviour of one could also occur with the other – we write this $P_1 \preccurlyeq_{pr} P_2$. More formally, let $[\![-]\!]$ be the map from programs to sets of executions. Then we define $\preccurlyeq_{pr}$ as:

$$P_1 \preccurlyeq_{pr} P_2 \quad \overset{\Delta}{\Longleftrightarrow} \quad \forall X_1 \in [\![P_1]\!].\, \exists X_2 \in [\![P_2]\!].\, X_1 \preccurlyeq_{ex} X_2 \qquad (1)$$

Compositional Transformation. Many common program transformations are *compositional*: they modify a sequential fragment of the program without examining the rest of the program. We call the former the *code-block* and the latter its *context*. Contexts can include sequential code before and after the block, and concurrent code that runs in parallel with it. Code-blocks are sequential, i.e. they do not feature internal concurrency. A context C and code-block B can be composed to give a whole program $C(B)$.

A transformation $B_2 \rightsquigarrow B_1$ replaces some instance of the code-block B_2 with B_1. To validate such a transformation, we must establish whether *every* whole program containing B_1 observationally refines the same program with B_2 substituted. If this holds, we say that B_1 observationally refines B_2, written $B_1 \preccurlyeq_{bl} B_2$, defined by lifting $\preccurlyeq_{pr}$ as follows:

$$B_1 \preccurlyeq_{bl} B_2 \quad \overset{\Delta}{\Longleftrightarrow} \quad \forall C.\, C(B_1) \preccurlyeq_{pr} C(B_2) \qquad (2)$$

If $B_1 \preccurlyeq_{bl} B_2$ holds, then the compiler can replace block B_2 with block B_1 irrespective of the whole program, i.e. $B_2 \rightsquigarrow B_1$ is a valid transformation. Thus, deciding $B_1 \preccurlyeq_{bl} B_2$ is the core problem in validating compositional transformations.

The language semantics is highly significant in determining observational refinement. For example, the code blocks B_1: store(x,5) and B_2: store(x,2); store(x,5) are observationally equivalent in a sequential setting. However, in a concurrent setting the intermediate state, x = 2, can be observed in B_2 but not B_1, meaning the code-blocks are no longer observationally equivalent. In a relaxed-memory setting there is no global state seen by all threads, which further complicates the notion of observation.

Compositional Verification. To establish $B_1 \preccurlyeq_{bl} B_2$, it is difficult to examine all possible syntactic contexts. Our approach is to construct a *denotation* for each code-block – a simplified, ideally finite, summary of possible interactions between the block and its context. We then define a *refinement relation* on denotations and use it to establish observational refinement. We write $B_1 \sqsubseteq B_2$ when the denotation of B_1 refines B_2.

Refinement on denotations should be *adequate*, i.e., it should validly approximate observational refinement: $B_1 \sqsubseteq B_2 \implies B_1 \preccurlyeq_{bl} B_2$. Hence, if $B_1 \sqsubseteq B_2$, then $B_2 \rightsquigarrow B_1$ is a valid transformation. It is also desirable for the denotation to be *fully abstract*: $B_1 \preccurlyeq_{bl} B_2 \implies B_1 \sqsubseteq B_2$. This means any valid transformation can be verified by comparing denotations. Below we define several versions of $\sqsubseteq$ with different properties.

3   Target Language and Core Memory Model

Our language's memory model is derived from the C/C++ 2011 standard (henceforth '*C11*'), as formalised by [5,22]. However, we simplify our model in several ways; see the end of section for details. In C11 terms, our model covers release-acquire and non-atomic operations, and sequentially consistent fences. To simplify the presentation, at first we omit non-atomics, and extend our approach to cover them in Sect. 7. Thus, all operations in this section correspond to C11's release-acquire.

3.1   Relaxed Memory Primer

In a sequentially consistent concurrent system, there is a total temporal order on loads and stores, and loads take the value of the most recent store; in particular, they cannot read overwritten values, or values written in the future. A *relaxed* (or *weak*) memory model weakens this total order, allowing behaviours forbidden under sequential consistency. Two standard examples of relaxed behaviour are *store buffering (SB)* and *message passing (MP)*, shown in Fig. 1.

```
       store(x,0); store(y,0);          store(f,0); store(x,0);
  store(x,1); ‖  store(y,1);       store(x,1); ‖  b := load(f);
  v1 := load(y); ‖  v2 := load(x);   store(f,1); ‖  if (b == 1)
                                                      r := load(x);
```

Fig. 1. *Left:* store-buffering (SB) example. *Right:* message-passing (MP) example.

In most relaxed models $v1 = v2 = 0$ is a possible post-state for SB. This cannot occur on a sequentially consistent system: if $v1 = 0$, then store(y,1) must be ordered after the load of y, which would order store(x,1) before the load of x, forcing it to assign $v2 = 1$. In some relaxed models, $b = 1 \wedge r = 0$ is a possible post-state for MP. This is undesirable if, for example, x is a complex data-structure and f is a flag indicating it has been safely created.

3.2   Language Syntax

Programs in the language we consider manipulate *thread-local variables* $l, l_1, l_2 \ldots \in \mathsf{LVar}$ and *global variables* $x, y, \ldots \in \mathsf{GVar}$, coming from disjoint sets

LVar and GVar. Each variable stores a value from a finite set Val and is initialised to $0 \in$ Val. Constants are encoded by special read-only thread-local variables. We assume that each thread uses the same set of thread-local variable names LVar. The syntax of the programming language is as follows:

$$C ::= l := E \mid \mathtt{store}(x, l) \mid l := \mathtt{load}(x) \mid l := \mathrm{LL}(x) \mid l' := \mathrm{SC}(x, l) \mid \mathtt{fence} \mid$$
$$C_1 \parallel C_2 \mid C_1; C_2 \mid \mathtt{if}\,(l)\,\{C_1\}\,\mathtt{else}\,\{C_2\} \mid \{-\}$$
$$E ::= l \mid l_1 = l_2 \mid l_1 \neq l_2 \mid \cdots$$

Many of the constructs are standard. $\mathrm{LL}(x)$ and $\mathrm{SC}(x, l)$ are *load-link* and *store-conditional*, which are basic concurrency operations available on many platforms (e.g., Power and ARM). A load-link $\mathrm{LL}(x)$ behaves as a standard load of global variable x. However, if it is followed by a store-conditional $\mathrm{SC}(x, l)$, the store fails and returns false if there are intervening writes to the same location. Otherwise the store-conditional writes l and returns true. The fence command is a *sequentially consistent fence*: interleaving such fences between all statements in a program guarantees sequentially consistent behaviour. We do not include *compare-and-swap* (CAS) command in our language because LL-SC is more general [2]. Hardware-level LL-SC is used to implement C11 CAS on Power and ARM. Our language does not include loops because our model in this paper does not include infinite computations (see Sect. 3.7 for discussion). As a result, loops can be represented by their finite unrollings. Our load commands write into a local variable. In examples, we sometimes use 'bare' loads without a variable write.

The construct $\{-\}$ represents a block-shaped hole in the program. To simplify our presentation, we assume that at most one hole appears in the program. Transformations that apply to multiple blocks at once can be simulated by using the fact our approach is compositional: transformations can be applied in sequence using different divisions of the program into code-block and context.

The set Prog of *whole programs* consists of programs without holes, while the set Contx of *contexts* consists of programs with a hole. The set Block of *code-blocks* are whole programs without parallel composition. We often write $P \in$ Prog for a whole program, $B \in$ Block for a code-block, and $C \in$ Contx for a context. Given a context C and a code-block B, the composition $C(B)$ is C with its hole syntactically replaced by B. For example:

$$C: \mathtt{load(x)};\ \{-\};\ \mathtt{store(y,11)}, \qquad B: \mathtt{store(x,2)}$$
$$\longrightarrow\quad C(B): \mathtt{load(x)};\ \mathtt{store(x,2)};\ \mathtt{store(y,11)}$$

We restrict Prog, Contx and Block to ensure LL-SC pairs are matched correctly. Each SC must be preceded in program order by a LL to the same location. Other types of operations may occur between the LL and SC, but intervening SC operations are forbidden. For example, the program $\mathtt{LL(x)};\ \mathtt{SC(x,v1)};\ \mathtt{SC(x,v2)};$ is forbidden. We also forbid LL-SC pairs from spanning parallel compositions, and from spanning the block/context boundary.

3.3   Memory Model Structure

The semantics of a whole program P is given by a set $[\![P]\!]$ of *executions*, which consist of *actions*, representing memory events on global variables, and several relations on these. Actions are tuples in the set $\mathsf{Action} \triangleq \mathsf{ActID} \times \mathsf{Kind} \times \mathsf{Option}(\mathsf{GVar}) \times \mathsf{Val}^*$. In an action $(a, k, z, b) \in \mathsf{Action}$: $a \in \mathsf{ActID}$ is the unique action identifier; $k \in \mathsf{Kind}$ is the kind of action – we use load, store, LL, SC, and the failed variant SC_f in the semantics, and will introduce further kinds as needed; $z \in \mathsf{Option}(\mathsf{GVar})$ is an option type consisting of either a single global variable $\mathsf{Just}(x)$ or None; and $b \in \mathsf{Val}^*$ is the vector of values (actions with multiple values are used in Sect. 4).

Given an action v, we use $\mathsf{gvar}(v)$ and $\mathsf{val}(v)$ as selectors for the different fields. We often write actions so as to elide action identifiers and the option type. For example, $\mathsf{load}(x, 3)$ stands for $\exists i.\,(i, \mathsf{load}, \mathsf{Just}(x), [3])$. We also sometimes elide values. We call load and LL actions *reads*, and store and successful SC actions *writes*. Given a set of actions $\mathcal{A}$, we write, e.g., $\mathsf{reads}(\mathcal{A})$ to identify read actions in $\mathcal{A}$. Below, we range over all actions by u, v; read actions by r; write actions by w; and LL, SC actions by ll and sc respectively.

$$\langle l := \mathtt{load}(x), \sigma \rangle \triangleq \{ (\{\mathsf{load}(x, a)\}, \emptyset, \sigma[l \mapsto a]) \mid a \in \mathsf{Val} \}$$

$$\langle \mathtt{store}(x, l), \sigma \rangle \triangleq \{ (\{\mathsf{store}(x, a)\}, \emptyset, \sigma) \mid \sigma(l) = a \}$$

$$\langle C_1; C_2, \sigma \rangle \triangleq \{ (\mathcal{A}_1 \uplus \mathcal{A}_2, \mathsf{sb}_1 \cup \mathsf{sb}_2 \cup (\mathcal{A}_1 \times \mathcal{A}_2), \sigma_2) \mid$$
$$(\mathcal{A}_1, \mathsf{sb}_1, \sigma_1) \in \langle C_1, \sigma \rangle \wedge (\mathcal{A}_2, \mathsf{sb}_2, \sigma_2) \in \langle C_2, \sigma_1 \rangle \}$$

$$\langle \mathtt{fence}, \sigma \rangle \triangleq \{ (\{ll, sc\}, \{(ll, sc)\}, \sigma) \mid ll = \mathsf{LL}(\mathit{fen}, 0) \wedge sc = \mathsf{SC}(\mathit{fen}, 0) \}$$

Fig. 2. Selected clauses of the thread-local semantics. The full semantics is given in [10, Sect. A]. We write $\mathcal{A}_1 \uplus \mathcal{A}_2$ for a union that is defined only when actions in $\mathcal{A}_1$ and $\mathcal{A}_2$ use disjoint sets of identifiers. We omit identifiers from actions to avoid clutter.

The semantics of a program $P \in \mathsf{Prog}$ is defined in two stages. First, a *thread-local semantics* of P produces a set $\langle P \rangle$ of *pre-executions* $(\mathcal{A}, \mathsf{sb}) \in \mathsf{PreExec}$. A pre-execution contains a finite set of memory actions $\mathcal{A} \subseteq \mathsf{Action}$ that could be produced by the program. It has a transitive and irreflexive *sequence-before* relation $\mathsf{sb} \subseteq \mathcal{A} \times \mathcal{A}$, which defines the sequential order imposed by the program syntax.

For example two sequential statements in the same thread produce actions ordered in sb. The thread-local semantics takes into account control flow in P's threads and operations on local variables. However, it does not constrain the behaviour of global variables: the values threads read from them are chosen arbitrarily. This is addressed by extending pre-executions with extra relations, and filtering the resulting *executions* using *validity axioms*.

3.4 Thread-Local Semantics

The thread-local semantics is defined formally in Fig. 2. The semantics of a program $P \in$ Prog is defined using function $\langle -, - \rangle$: Prog $\times$ VMap $\to \mathcal{P}($PreExec $\times$ VMap$)$. The values of local variables are tracked by a map $\sigma \in$ VMap $\stackrel{\Delta}{=}$ LVar $\to$ Val. Given a program and an input local variable map, the function produces a set of pre-executions paired with an output variable map, representing the values of local variables at the end of the execution. Let σ_0 map every local variable to 0. Then $\langle P \rangle$, the thread-local semantics of a program P, is defined as

$$\langle P \rangle \quad \stackrel{\Delta}{=} \quad \{ (\mathcal{A}, \mathsf{sb}) \mid \exists \sigma'. (\mathcal{A}, \mathsf{sb}, \sigma') \in \langle P, \sigma_0 \rangle \}$$

The significant property of the thread-local semantics is that it does not restrict the behaviour of global variables. For this reason, note that the clause for load in Fig. 2 leaves the value a unrestricted. We follow [16] in encoding the fence command by a successful LL-SC pair to a distinguished variable $fen \in$ GVar that is not otherwise read or written.

3.5 Execution Structure and Validity Axioms

The semantics of a program P is a set $[\![P]\!]$ of *executions* $X = (\mathcal{A}, \mathsf{sb}, \mathsf{at}, \mathsf{rf}, \mathsf{mo}, \mathsf{hb}) \in$ Exec, where $(\mathcal{A}, \mathsf{sb})$ is a pre-execution and $\mathsf{at}, \mathsf{rf}, \mathsf{mo}, \mathsf{hb} \subseteq \mathcal{A} \times \mathcal{A}$. Given an execution X we sometimes write $\mathcal{A}(X), \mathsf{sb}(X), \ldots$ as selectors for the appropriate set or relation. The relations have the following purposes.

- *Reads-from* (rf) is an injective map from reads to writes at the same location of the same value. A read and a write actions are related $w \xrightarrow{\mathsf{rf}} r$ if r takes its value from w.
- *Modification order* (mo) is an irreflexive, total order on write actions to each distinct variable. This is a per-variable order in which *all* threads observe writes to the variable; two threads cannot observe these writes in different orders.
- *Happens-before* (hb) is analogous to global temporal order – but unlike the sequentially consistent notion of time, it is partial. Happens-before is defined as $(\mathsf{sb} \cup \mathsf{rf})^+$: therefore statements ordered in the program syntax are ordered in time, as are reads with the writes they observe.
- *Atomicity* (at $\subseteq$ sb) is an extension to standard C11 which we use to support LL-SC (see below). It is an injective function from a successful load-link action to a successful store-conditional, giving a LL-SC pair.

The semantics $[\![P]\!]$ of a program P is the set of executions $X \in$ Exec compatible with the thread-local semantics and the *validity axioms*, denoted $\mathsf{valid}(X)$:

$$[\![P]\!] \quad \stackrel{\Delta}{=} \quad \{ X \mid (\mathcal{A}(X), \mathsf{sb}(X)) \in \langle P \rangle \wedge \mathsf{valid}(X) \} \tag{3}$$

The validity axioms on an execution $(\mathcal{A}, \mathsf{sb}, \mathsf{at}, \mathsf{rf}, \mathsf{mo}, \mathsf{hb})$ are:

- HBDEF: $\mathsf{hb} = (\mathsf{sb} \cup \mathsf{rf})^+$ *and* hb is acyclic.

  This axiom defines hb and enforces the intuitive property that there are no cycles in the temporal order. It also prevents an action reading from its hb-future: as rf is included in hb, this would result in a cycle.

- HBvsMO: $\neg \exists w_1, w_2.\ w_1 \overset{\mathsf{hb}}{\underset{\mathsf{mo}}{\rightleftarrows}} w_2$

  This axiom requires that the order in which writes to a location become visible to threads cannot contradict the temporal order. But take note that writes may be ordered in mo but not hb.

- COHERENCE: $\neg \exists w_1, w_2, r.\ w_1 \xrightarrow{\mathsf{mo}} w_2 \xrightarrow{\mathsf{hb}} r$ with $w_1 \xrightarrow{\mathsf{rf}} r$

  This axiom generalises the sequentially consistent prohibition on reading over-written values. If two writes are ordered in mo, then intuitively the second overwrites the first. A read that follows some write in hb or mo cannot read from writes earlier in mo – these earlier writes have been overwritten. However, unlike in sequential consistency, hb is partial, so there may be multiple writes that an action can legally read.

- RFVAL: $\forall r.\ (\neg \exists w'.\ w' \xrightarrow{\mathsf{rf}} r) \implies (\mathsf{val}(r) = 0 \wedge$
  $$(\neg \exists w.\ w \xrightarrow{\mathsf{hb}} r \wedge \mathsf{gvar}(w) = \mathsf{gvar}(r)))$$

  Most reads must take their value from a write, represented by an rf edge. However, the RFVAL axiom allows the rf edge to be omitted if the read takes the initial value 0 and there is no hb-earlier write to the same location. Intuitively, an hb-earlier write would supersede the initial value in a similar way to COHERENCE.

- ATOM: $\neg \exists w_1, w_2, ll, sc.\ w_1 \xrightarrow{\mathsf{mo}} w_2$ with $w_1 \xrightarrow{\mathsf{rf}} ll \xrightarrow{\mathsf{at}} sc \xleftarrow{\mathsf{mo}} w_2$

  This axiom is adapted from [16]. For an LL-SC pair ll and sc, it ensures that there is no mo-intervening write w_2 that would invalidate the store.

Our model forbids the problematic relaxed behaviour of the message-passing (MP) program in Fig. 1 that yields $\mathsf{b} = 1 \wedge \mathsf{r} = 0$. Figure 3 shows an (invalid) execution that would exhibit this behaviour. To avoid clutter, here and in the following we omit hb edges obtained by transitivity and local variable values. This execution is allowed by the thread-local semantics of the MP program, but it is ruled out by the COHERENCE validity axiom. As hb is transitively closed, there is a derived hb edge $\mathsf{store}(\mathsf{x}, 1) \xrightarrow{\mathsf{hb}} \mathsf{load}(\mathsf{x}, 0)$, which forms a COHERENCE violation. Thus, this is not an execution of the MP program. Indeed, any

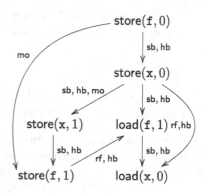

Fig. 3. An invalid execution of MP.

execution ending in $\mathsf{load}(\mathsf{x}, 0)$ is forbidden for the same reason, meaning that the MP relaxed behaviour cannot occur.

3.6 Relaxed Observations

Finally, we define a notion of observational refinement suitable for our relaxed model. We assume a subset of *observable* global variables, $\mathsf{OVar} \subseteq \mathsf{GVar}$, which can only be accessed by the context and not by the code-block. We consider the actions and the hb relation on these variables to be the observations. We write $X|_{\mathsf{OVar}}$ for the projection of X's action set and relations to OVar, and use this to define $\preccurlyeq_{\mathsf{ex}}$ for our model:

$$X \preccurlyeq_{\mathsf{ex}} Y \iff \mathcal{A}(X|_{\mathsf{OVar}}) = \mathcal{A}(Y|_{\mathsf{OVar}}) \wedge \mathsf{hb}(Y|_{\mathsf{OVar}}) \subseteq \mathsf{hb}(X|_{\mathsf{OVar}})$$

This is lifted to programs and blocks as in Sect. 2, def. (1) and (2). Note that in the more abstract execution, actions on observable variables must be the same, but hb can be weaker. This is because we interpret hb as a constraint on time order: two actions that are unordered in hb could have occurred in either order, or in parallel. Thus, weakening hb allows more observable behaviours (see Sect. 2).

3.7 Differences from C11

Our language's memory model is derived from the C11 formalisation in [5], with a number of simplifications. We chose C11 because it demonstrates most of the important features of axiomatic language models. However, we do not target the precise C11 model: rather we target an abstracted model that is rich enough to demonstrate our approach. Relaxed language semantics is still a very active topic of research, and several C11 features are known to be significantly flawed, with multiple competing fixes proposed. Some of our differences from [5] are intended to avoid such problematic features so that we can cleanly demonstrate our approach.

In C11 terms, our model covers release-acquire and non-atomic operations (the latter addressed in Sect. 7), and sequentially consistent fences. We deviate from C11 in the following ways:

- We omit *sequentially consistent* accesses because their semantics is known to be flawed in C11 [17]. We do handle sequentially consistent fences, but these are stronger than those of C11: we use the semantics proposed in [16]. It has been proved sound under existing compilation strategies to common multiprocessors.
- We omit *relaxed* (RLX) accesses to avoid well-known problems with thin-air values [4]. There are multiple recent competing proposals for fixing these problems, e.g. [14,15,20].
- Our model does not include infinite computations, because their semantics in C11-style axiomatic models remains undecided in the literature [4]. However, our proofs do not depend on the assumption that execution contexts are finite.

– Our language is based on shared variables, not dynamically allocated address-able memory, so for example we cannot write y:=*x; z:=*y. This simplifies our theory by allowing us to fix the variables accessed by a code-block up-front. We believe our results can be extended to support addressable memory, because C11-style models grant no special status to pointers; we elaborate on this in Sect. 4.
– We add LL-SC atomic instructions to our language in addition to C11's stan-dard CAS. To do this, we adapt the approach of [16]. This increases the observa-tional power of a context and is necessary for full abstraction in the presence of non-atomics; see Sect. 8. LL-SC is available as a hardware instruction on many platforms supporting C11, such as Power and ARM. However, we do not pro-pose adding LL-SC to C11: rather, it supports an interesting result in relaxed memory model theory. Our adequacy results do not depend on LL-SC.

4 Denotations of Code-Blocks

We construct the denotation for a code-block in two steps: (1) generate the *block-local* executions under a set of special cut-down contexts; (2) from each execution, extract a summary of interactions between the code-block and the context called a *history*.

4.1 Block-Local Executions

The block-local executions of a block $B \in$ Block omit context structure such as syntax and actions on variables not accessed in the block. Instead the context is represented by special actions call and ret, a set $\mathcal{A}_B$, and relations R_B and S_B, each covering an aspect of the interaction of the block and an arbitrary unre-stricted context. Together, each choice of call, ret, $\mathcal{A}_B$, R_B, and S_B abstractly represents a set of possible syntactic contexts. By quantifying over the possible values of these parameters, we cover the behaviour of *all* syntactic contexts. The parameters are defined as follows:

– *Local variables.* A context can include code that precedes and follows the block on the same thread, with interaction through local variables, but – due to syntactic restriction – not through LL/SC atomic regions. We capture this with special action call(σ) at the start of the block, and ret(σ') at the end, where σ, σ': LVar $\rightarrow$ Val record the values of local variables at these points. Assume that variables in LVar are ordered: $l_1, l_2, \ldots, l_n$. Then call(σ) is encoded by the action $(i, \text{call}, \text{None}, [\sigma(l_1), \ldots \sigma(l_n)])$, with fresh identifier i. We encode ret in the same way.
– *Global variable actions.* The context can also interact with the block through concurrent reads and writes to global variables. These interactions are rep-resented by set $\mathcal{A}_B$ of *context actions* added to the ones generated by the thread-local semantics of the block. This set only contains actions on the variables VS_B that B can access (VS_B can be constructed syntactically). Given an execution X constructed using $\mathcal{A}_B$ (see below) we write contx(X) to recover the set $\mathcal{A}_B$.

- *Context happens-before.* The context can generate hb edges between its actions, which affect the behaviour of the block. We track these effects with a relation R_B over actions in $\mathcal{A}_B$, call and ret:

$$R_B \subseteq (\mathcal{A}_B \times \mathcal{A}_B) \cup (\mathcal{A}_B \times \{\text{call}\}) \cup (\{\text{ret}\} \times \mathcal{A}_B) \qquad (4)$$

The context can generate hb edges between actions directly if they are on the same thread, or indirectly through inter-thread reads. Likewise call/ret may be related to context actions on the same or different threads.

- *Context atomicity.* The context can generate at edges between its actions that we capture in the relation $S_B \subseteq \mathcal{A}_B \times \mathcal{A}_B$. We require this relation to be an injective function from LL to SC actions. We consider only cases where LL/SC pairs do not cross block boundaries, so we need not consider boundary-crossing at edges.

Together, call, ret, $\mathcal{A}_B$, R_B, and S_B represent a limited context, stripped of syntax, relations sb, mo, and rf, and actions on global variables other than VS_B. When constructing block-local executions, we represent all possible interactions by quantifying over all possible choices of σ, σ', $\mathcal{A}_B$, R_B and S_B. The set $[\![B, \mathcal{A}_B, R_B, S_B]\!]$ contains all executions of B under this special limited context. Formally, an execution $X = (\mathcal{A}, \text{sb}, \text{at}, \text{rf}, \text{mo}, \text{hb})$ is in this set if:

1. $\mathcal{A}_B \subseteq \mathcal{A}$ and there exist variable maps σ, σ' such that $\{\text{call}(\sigma), \text{ret}(\sigma')\} \subseteq \mathcal{A}$. That is, the call, return, and extra context actions are included in the execution.

2. There exists a set $\mathcal{A}_l$ and relation sb_l such that (i) $(\mathcal{A}_l, \text{sb}_l, \sigma') \in \langle B, \sigma \rangle$; (ii) $\mathcal{A}_l = \mathcal{A} \setminus (\mathcal{A}_B \cup \{\text{call}, \text{ret}\})$; (iii) $\text{sb}_l = \text{sb} \setminus \{(\text{call}, u), (u, \text{ret}) \mid u \in \mathcal{A}_l\}$. That is, actions from the code-block satisfy the thread-local semantics, beginning with map σ and deriving map σ'. All actions arising from the block are between call and ret in sb.

3. X satisfies the validity axioms, but with modified axioms HBDEF$'$ and ATOM$'$. We define HBDEF$'$ as: $\text{hb} = (\text{sb} \cup \text{rf} \cup R_B)^+$ and hb is acyclic. That is, context relation R_B is added to hb. ATOM$'$ is defined analogously with S_B added to at.

We say that $\mathcal{A}_B$, R_B and S_B are *consistent with* B if they act over variables in the set VS_B. In the rest of the paper we only consider consistent choices of $\mathcal{A}_B$, R_B, S_B. The *block-local executions* of B are then all executions $X \in [\![B, \mathcal{A}_B, R_B, S_B]\!]$.[1]

---

[1] This definition relies on the fact that our language supports a fixed set of global variables, not dynamically allocated addressable memory (see Sect. 3.7). We believe that in the future our results can be extended to support dynamic memory. For this, the block-local construction would need to quantify over actions on all possible memory locations, not just the static variable set VS_B. The rest of our theory would remain the same, because C11-style models grant no special status to pointer values. Cutting down to a finite denotation, as in Sect. 5 below, would require some extra abstraction over memory – for example, a separation logic domain such as [9].

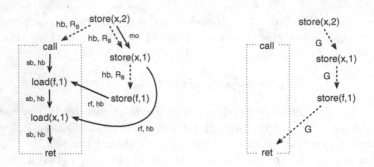

Fig. 4. *Left*: block-local execution. *Right*: corresponding history.

Example Block-Local Execution. The left of Fig. 4 shows a block-local execution for the code-block

$$l1 := \texttt{load}(f); l2 := \texttt{load}(x) \tag{5}$$

Here the set VS_B of accessed global variables is $\{f, x\}$, As before, we omit local variables to avoid clutter. The context action set $\mathcal{A}_B$ consists of the three stores, and R_B is denoted by dotted edges.

In this execution, both $\mathcal{A}_B$ and R_B affect the behaviour of the code-block. The following path is generated by R_B and the load of $f = 1$:

$$\mathsf{store}(\mathsf{x}, 2) \xrightarrow{\mathsf{mo}} \mathsf{store}(\mathsf{x}, 1) \xrightarrow{R_B} \mathsf{store}(\mathsf{f}, 1) \xrightarrow{\mathsf{rf}} \mathsf{load}(\mathsf{f}, 1) \xrightarrow{\mathsf{sb}} \mathsf{load}(\mathsf{x}, 1)$$

Because hb includes sb, rf, and R_B, there is a transitive edge $\mathsf{store}(\mathsf{x}, 1) \xrightarrow{\mathsf{hb}} \mathsf{load}(\mathsf{x}, 1)$. The edge $\mathsf{store}(\mathsf{x}, 2) \xrightarrow{\mathsf{mo}} \mathsf{store}(\mathsf{x}, 1)$ is forced because the HBvsMO axiom prohibits mo from contradicting hb. Consequently, the COHERENCE axiom forces the code-block to read $x = 1$.

4.2 Histories

From any block-local execution X, its *history* summarises the interactions between the code-block and the context. Informally, the history records hb over context actions, call, and ret. More formally the history, written $\mathsf{hist}(X)$, is a pair $(\mathcal{A}, G)$ consisting of an action set $\mathcal{A}$ and *guarantee relation* $G \subseteq \mathcal{A} \times \mathcal{A}$. Recall that we use $\mathsf{contx}(X)$ to denote the set of context actions in X. Using this, we define the history as follows:

- The action set $\mathcal{A}$ is the projection of X's action set to call, ret, and $\mathsf{contx}(X)$.
- The guarantee relation G is the projection of $\mathsf{hb}(X)$ to

$$(\mathsf{contx}(X) \times \mathsf{contx}(X)) \cup (\mathsf{contx}(X) \times \{\mathsf{ret}\}) \cup (\{\mathsf{call}\} \times \mathsf{contx}(X)) \tag{6}$$

The guarantee summarises the code-block's effect on its context: it suffices to only track hb and ignore other relations. Note the guarantee definition is similar to the context relation R_B, definition (4). The difference is that call and ret are

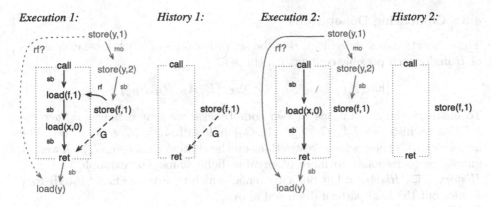

Fig. 5. Executions and histories illustrating the guarantee relation.

switched: this is because the guarantee represents hb edges generated by the code-block, while R_B represents the edges generated by the context. The right of Fig. 4 shows the history corresponding to the block-local execution on the left.

To see the interactions captured by the guarantee, compare the block given in def. (5) with the block 12:=load(x). These blocks have differing effects on the following syntactic context:

```
store(y,1); store(y,2); store(f,1)    ||    {-}; 13:=load(y)
```

For the two-load block embedded into this context, $11 = 1 \wedge 13 = 1$ is not a possible post-state. For the single-load block, this post-state is permitted.[2]

In Fig. 5, we give executions for both blocks embedded into this context. We draw the context actions that are not included into the history in grey. In these executions, the code block determines whether the load of y can read value 1 (represented by the edge labelled 'rf?'). In the first execution, the context load of y cannot read 1 because there is the path store(y, 1) $\xrightarrow{\text{mo}}$ store(y, 2) $\xrightarrow{\text{hb}}$ load(y) which would contradict the COHERENCE axiom. In the second execution there is no such path and the load may read 1.

It is desirable for our denotation to hide the precise operations inside the block – this lets it relate syntactically distinct blocks. Nonetheless, the history must record hb effects such as those above that are visible to the context. In Execution 1, the COHERENCE violation is still visible if we only consider context operations, call, ret, and the guarantee G – i.e. the history. In Execution 2, the fact that the read is permitted is likewise visible from examining the history. Thus the guarantee, combined with the local variable post-states, capture the effect of the block on the context without recording the actions inside the block.

---

[2] We choose these post-states for exposition purposes – in fact these blocks are also distinguishable through local variable 11 alone.

4.3   Comparing Denotations

The denotation of a code-block B is the set of histories of block-local executions of B under each possible context, i.e. the set

$$\{\mathsf{hist}(X) \mid \exists \mathcal{A}_B, R_B, S_B. X \in [\![B, \mathcal{A}_B, R_B, S_B]\!]\}$$

To compare the denotations of two code-blocks, we first define a *refinement relation* on histories: $(\mathcal{A}_1, G_1) \sqsubseteq_\mathsf{h} (\mathcal{A}_2, G_2)$ holds iff $\mathcal{A}_1 = \mathcal{A}_2 \wedge G_2 \subseteq G_1$. The history $(\mathcal{A}_2, G_2)$ places fewer restrictions on the context than $(\mathcal{A}_1, G_1)$ – a weaker guarantee corresponds to more observable behaviours. For example in Fig. 5, *History 1* $\sqsubseteq_\mathsf{h}$ *History 2* but not vice versa, which reflects the fact that History 1 rules out the read pattern discussed above.

We write $B_1 \sqsubseteq_\mathsf{q} B_2$ to state that the denotation of B_1 *refines* that of B_2. The subscript 'q' stands for the fact we *quantify* over both $\mathcal{A}$ and R_B. We define $\sqsubseteq_\mathsf{q}$ by lifting $\sqsubseteq_\mathsf{h}$:

$$B_1 \sqsubseteq_\mathsf{q} B_2 \quad \stackrel{\triangle}{\Longleftrightarrow} \quad \begin{aligned} &\forall \mathcal{A}, R, S. \forall X_1 \in [\![B_1, \mathcal{A}, R, S]\!]. \\ &\quad \exists X_2 \in [\![B_2, \mathcal{A}, R, S]\!]. \, \mathsf{hist}(X_1) \sqsubseteq_\mathsf{h} \mathsf{hist}(X_2) \end{aligned} \tag{7}$$

In other words, two code-blocks are related $B_1 \sqsubseteq_\mathsf{q} B_2$ if for every block-local execution of B_1, there is a corresponding execution of B_2 with a related history. Note that the corresponding history must be constructed under the same cut-down context $\mathcal{A}, R, S$.

Theorem 1 (ADEQUACY OF $\sqsubseteq_\mathsf{q}$). $B_1 \sqsubseteq_\mathsf{q} B_2 \implies B_1 \preccurlyeq_\mathsf{bl} B_2$.

Theorem 2 (FULL ABSTRACTION OF $\sqsubseteq_\mathsf{q}$). $B_1 \preccurlyeq_\mathsf{bl} B_2 \implies B_1 \sqsubseteq_\mathsf{q} B_2$.

As a corollary of the above theorems, a program transformation $B_2 \rightsquigarrow B_1$ is valid if and only if $B_1 \sqsubseteq_\mathsf{q} B_2$ holds. We prove Theorem 1 in [10, Sect. B]. We give a proof sketch of Theorem 2 in Sect. 8 and a full proof in [10, Sect. F].

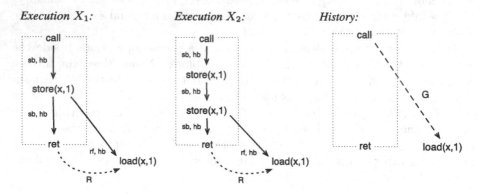

Fig. 6. History comparison for an example program transformation.

4.4   Example Transformation

We now consider how our approach applies to a simple program transformation:

$$B_2: \text{store(x,11); store(x,11)} \quad \leadsto \quad B_1: \text{store(x,11)}$$

To verify this transformation, we must show that $B_1 \sqsubseteq_q B_2$. To do this, we must consider the unboundedly many block-local executions. Here we just illustrate the reasoning for a single block-local execution; in Sect. 5 below we define a context reduction which lets us consider a finite set of such executions.

In Fig. 6, we illustrate the necessary reasoning for an execution $X_1 \in [\![B_1, \mathcal{A}, R, S]\!]$, with a context action set $\mathcal{A}$ consisting of a single load $\text{x} = 1$, a context relation R relating ret to the load, and an empty S relation. This choice of R forces the context load to read from the store in the block. We can exhibit an execution $X_2 \in [\![B_2, \mathcal{A}, R, S]\!]$ with a matching history by making the context load read from the final store in the block.

5   A Finite Denotation

The approach above simplifies contexts by removing syntax and non-hb structure, but there are still infinitely many $\mathcal{A}/R/S$ contexts for any code-block. To solve this, we introduce a type of context reduction which allows us to consider only finitely many block-local executions. This means that we can automatically check transformations by examining all such executions. However this 'cut down' approach is no longer fully abstract. We modify our denotation as follows:

– We remove the quantification over context relation R from definition (7) by fixing it as $\emptyset$. In exchange, we extend the history with an extra component called a *deny*.
– We eliminate redundant block-local executions from the denotation, and only consider a reduced set of executions X that satisfy a predicate $\text{cut}(X)$.

These two steps are both necessary to achieve finiteness. Removing the R relation reduces the amount of structure in the context. This makes it possible to then remove redundant patterns – for example, duplicate reads from the same write.

Before defining the two steps in detail, we give the structure of our modified refinement $\sqsubseteq_c$. In the definition, $\text{hist}_E(X)$ stands for the *extended history* of an execution X, and $\sqsubseteq_E$ for refinement on extended histories.

$$B_1 \sqsubseteq_c B_2 \quad \overset{\triangle}{\Longleftrightarrow} \quad \forall \mathcal{A}, S. \, \forall X_1 \in [\![B_1, \mathcal{A}, \emptyset, S]\!].$$
$$\text{cut}(X_1) \implies \exists X_2 \in [\![B_2, \mathcal{A}, \emptyset, S]\!]. \, \text{hist}_E(X_1) \sqsubseteq_E \text{hist}_E(X_2) \quad (8)$$

As with $\sqsubseteq_q$ above, the refinement $\sqsubseteq_c$ is adequate. However, it is not fully abstract (we provide a counterexample in [10, Sect. D]). We prove the following theorem in [10, Sect. E].

Theorem 3 (ADEQUACY OF $\sqsubseteq_c$). $B_1 \sqsubseteq_c B_2 \implies B_1 \preccurlyeq_{bl} B_2.$

5.1 Cutting Predicate

Removing the context relation R in definition (8) removes a large amount of structure from the context. However, there are still unboundedly many block-local executions with an empty R – for example, we can have an unbounded number of reads and writes that do not interact with the block. The cutting predicate identifies these redundant executions.

We first identify the actions in a block-local execution that are *visible*, meaning they directly interact with the block. We write $\mathsf{code}(X)$ for the set of actions in X generated by the code-block. Visible actions belong to $\mathsf{code}(X)$, read from $\mathsf{code}(X)$, or are read by $\mathsf{code}(X)$. In other words,

$$\mathsf{vis}(X) \triangleq \mathsf{code}(X) \cup \{u \mid \exists v \in \mathsf{code}(X). \, u \xrightarrow{\mathsf{rf}} v \vee v \xrightarrow{\mathsf{rf}} u\}$$

Informally, cutting eliminates three redundant patterns: *(i)* non-visible context reads, i.e. reads from context writes; *(ii)* duplicate context reads from the same write; and *(iii)* duplicate non-visible writes that are not separated in mo by a visible write. Formally we define $\mathsf{cut}'(X)$, the conjunction of cutR for read, and cutW for write.

$$\mathsf{cutR}(X) \overset{\triangle}{\iff} \mathsf{reads}(X) \subseteq \mathsf{vis}(X) \wedge$$
$$\forall r_1, r_2 \in \mathsf{contx}(X). \, (r_1 \neq r_2 \Rightarrow \neg \exists w. \, w \xrightarrow{\mathsf{rf}} r_1 \wedge w \xrightarrow{\mathsf{rf}} r_2)$$
$$\mathsf{cutW}(X) \overset{\triangle}{\iff} \forall w_1, w_2 \in (\mathsf{contx}(X) \setminus \mathsf{vis}(X)).$$
$$w_1 \xrightarrow{\mathsf{mo}} w_2 \Rightarrow \exists w_3 \in \mathsf{vis}(X). \, w_1 \xrightarrow{\mathsf{mo}} w_3 \xrightarrow{\mathsf{mo}} w_2$$
$$\mathsf{cut}'(X) \overset{\triangle}{\iff} \mathsf{cutR}(X) \wedge \mathsf{cutW}(X)$$

The final predicate $\mathsf{cut}(X)$ extends this in order to keep LL-SC pairs together: it requires that, if $\mathsf{cut}'()$ permits one half of an LL-SC, the other is also permitted implicitly (for brevity we omit the formal definition of $\mathsf{cut}()$ in terms of cut').

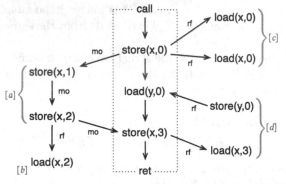

[a] *Forbidden by* $\mathsf{cutW}()$. Two non-visible stores without a visible store intervening in mo.

[b] *Forbidden by* $\mathsf{cutR}()$. Load is non-visible as it reads from a context store.

[c] *Forbidden by* $\mathsf{cutR}()$. Both reads are visible, but are duplicates, reading from the same write.

[d] *Allowed.* Visible load and store.

Fig. 7. *Left*: block-local execution which includes patterns forbidden by $\mathsf{cut}()$. *Right*: key explaining the patterns forbidden or allowed.

It should be intuitively clear why the first two of the above patterns are redundant. The main surprise is the third pattern, which preserves some non-visible writes. This is required by Theorem 3 for technical reasons connected to per-location coherence. We illustrate the application of cut() to a block-local execution in Fig. 7.

5.2 Extended History (hist$_E$)

In our approach, each block-local execution represents a pattern of interaction between block and context. In our previous definition of $\sqsubseteq_q$, constraints imposed by the block are captured by the guarantee, while constraints imposed by the context are captured by the R relation. The definition (8) of $\sqsubseteq_c$ removes the context relation R, but these constraints must still be represented. Instead, we replace R with a history component called a *deny*. This simplifies the block-local executions, but compensates by recording more in the denotation.

The deny records the hb edges that *cannot* be enforced due to the execution structure. For example, consider the block-local execution[3] of Fig. 8.

This pattern could not occur in a context that generates the dashed edge D as a hb – to do so would violate the HBvsMO axiom. In our previous definition of $\sqsubseteq_q$, we explicitly represented the presence or absence of this edge through the R relation. In our new formulation, we represent such 'forbidden' edges in the history by a deny edge.

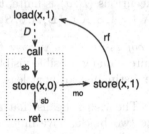

Fig. 8. A deny edge.

The *extended history* of an execution X, written hist$_E(X)$ is a triple $(\mathcal{A}, G, D)$, consisting of the familiar notions of action set $\mathcal{A}$ and guarantee $G \subseteq \mathcal{A} \times \mathcal{A}$, together with deny $D \subseteq \mathcal{A} \times \mathcal{A}$ as defined below:

$$D \triangleq \{(u,v) \mid \mathsf{HBvsMO\text{-}d}(u,v) \vee \mathsf{Cohere\text{-}d}(u,v) \vee \mathsf{RFval\text{-}d}(u,v)\} \cap$$
$$((\mathsf{contx}(X) \times \mathsf{contx}(X)) \cup (\mathsf{contx}(X) \times \{\mathsf{call}\}) \cup (\{\mathsf{ret}\} \times \mathsf{contx}(X)))$$

Each of the predicates HBvsMO-d, Cohere-d, and RFval-d generates the deny for one validity axiom. In the diagrammatic definitions below, dashed edges represent the deny edge, and hb* is the reflexive-transitive closure of hb:

HBvsMO-d(u,v): $\exists w_1, w_2.\ w_1 \xrightarrow{\ \mathsf{hb}^*\ } u \xdashrightarrow{\ D\ } v \xrightarrow{\ \mathsf{hb}^*\ } w_2$
$\overset{\longleftarrow}{\underset{\mathsf{mo}}{\qquad\qquad\qquad}}$

Coherence-d(u,v): $w_1 \xrightarrow{\ \mathsf{mo}\ } w_2 \xrightarrow{\ \mathsf{hb}^*\ } u \xdashrightarrow{\ D\ } v \xrightarrow{\ \mathsf{hb}^*\ } r$
$\underset{\mathsf{rf}}{\qquad\qquad\qquad\qquad}$

RFval-d(u,v): $\exists w, r.\ \mathsf{gvar}(w) = \mathsf{gvar}(r) \wedge$
$\neg\exists w'.\ w' \xrightarrow{\ \mathsf{rf}\ } r \wedge w \xrightarrow{\ \mathsf{hb}^*\ } u \xdashrightarrow{\ D\ } v \xrightarrow{\ \mathsf{hb}^*\ } r$

---

[3] We use this execution for illustration, but in fact the cut() predicate would forbid the load.

One can think of a deny edge as an 'almost' violation of an axiom. For example, if HBvsMO-d(u, v) holds, then the context cannot generate an extra hb-edge $u \xrightarrow{\text{hb}} v$ – to do so would violate HBvsMO.

Because deny edges represent constraints on the context, weakening the deny places fewer constraints, allowing more behaviours, so we compare them with relational inclusion:

$$(\mathcal{A}_2, G_2, D_2) \sqsubseteq_\mathsf{E} (\mathcal{A}_2, G_2, D_2) \xLeftrightarrow{\Delta} \mathcal{A}_1 = \mathcal{A}_2 \wedge G_2 \subseteq G_1 \wedge D_2 \subseteq D_1$$

This refinement on extended histories is used to define our refinement relation on blocks, $\sqsubseteq_\mathsf{c}$, def. (8).

5.3   Finiteness

Theorem 4 (FINITENESS). *If for a block B and state σ the set of thread-local executions $\langle B, \sigma \rangle$ is finite, then so is the set of resulting block-local executions, $\{X \mid \exists \mathcal{A}, S.\, X \in [\![B, \mathcal{A}, \emptyset, S]\!] \wedge \mathsf{cut}(X) \}$.*

Proof (sketch). It is easy to see for a given thread-local execution there are finitely many possible visible reads and writes. Any two non-visible writes must be distinguished by at least one visible write, limiting their number.   □

Theorem 4 means that any transformation can be checked automatically if the two blocks have finite sets of thread-local executions. We assume a finite data domain, meaning action can only take finitely many distinct values in Val. Recall also that our language does not include loops. Given these facts, any transformations written in our language will satisfy finiteness, and can therefore by automatically checked.

6   Prototype Verification Tool

Stellite is our prototype tool that verifies transformations using the Alloy* model checker [12,18]. Our tool takes an input transformation $B_2 \rightsquigarrow B_1$ written in a C-like syntax. It automatically converts the transformation into an Alloy* model encoding $B_1 \sqsubseteq_\mathsf{c} B_2$. If the tool reports success, then the transformation is verified for unboundedly large syntactic contexts and executions.

An Alloy model consists of a collection of predicates on relations, and an instance of the model is a set of relations that satisfy the predicates. As previously noted in [28], there is therefore a natural fit between Alloy models and axiomatic memory models.

At a high level, our tool works as follows:

1. The two sides of an input transformation B_1 and B_2 are automatically converted into Alloy predicates expressing their syntactic structure. Intuitively, these block predicates are built by following the thread-local semantics from Sect. 3.

2. The block predicates are linked with a pre-defined Alloy model expressing the memory model and $\sqsubseteq_c$.
3. The Alloy* solver searches (using SAT) for a history of B_1 that has no matching history of B_2. We use the higher-order Alloy* solver of [18] because the standard Alloy solver cannot support the existential quantification on histories in $\sqsubseteq_c$.

The Alloy* solver is parameterised by the maximum size of the model it will examine. However, our finiteness theorem for $\sqsubseteq_c$ (Theorem 4) means there is a bound on the size of cut-down context that needs to be considered to verify any given transformation. If our tool reports that a transformation is correct, it is verified in all syntactic contexts of unbounded size.

Given a query $B_1 \sqsubseteq_c B_2$, the required context bound grows in proportion to the number of internal actions on distinct locations in B_1. This is because our cutting predicate permits context actions if they interact with internal actions, either directly, or by interleaving between internal actions. In our experiments we run the tool with a model bound of 10, sufficient to give soundness for all the transformations we consider. Note that most of our example transformations do not require such a large bound, and execution times improve if it is reduced.

If a counter-example is discovered, the problematic execution and history can be viewed using the Alloy model visualiser, which has a similar appearance to the execution diagrams in this paper. The output model generated by our tool encodes the history of B_1 for which no history of B_2 could be found. As $\sqsubseteq_c$ is not fully abstract, this counter-example could, of course, be spurious.

Stellite currently supports transformations on code-blocks with atomic reads, writes, and fences. It does not yet support code-blocks with non-atomic accesses (see Sect. 7), LL-SC, or branching control-flow. We believe supporting the above features would not present fundamental difficulties, since the structure of the Alloy encoding would be similar. Despite the above limitations, our prototype demonstrates that our cut-down denotation can be used for automatic verification of important program transformations.

Experimental Results. We have tested our tool on a range of different transformations. A table of experimental results is given in Fig. 9. Many of our examples are derived from [23] – we cover all their examples that fit into our tool's input language. Transformations of the sort that we check have led to real-world bugs in GCC [19] and LLVM [8]. Note that some transformations are invalid because of their effect on local variables, e.g. skip $\rightsquigarrow l := \texttt{load}(x)$. The closely related transformation skip $\rightsquigarrow \texttt{load}(x)$ throws away the result of the read, and is consequently valid.

Our tool takes significant time to verify some of the above examples, and two of the transformations cause the tool to time out. This is due to the complexity and non-determinism of the C11 model. In particular, our execution times are comparable to existing C++ model *simulators* such as Cppmem when they run on a few lines of code [3]. However, our tool is a sound transformation verifier, rather than a simulator, and thus solves a more difficult problem: transformations

Introduction, validity, time (s)		
$\mathtt{skip} \rightsquigarrow \mathtt{fc}$	✓	76
$\mathtt{skip} \rightsquigarrow \mathtt{ld}(x)$	✓	429
$\mathtt{skip} \rightsquigarrow l := \mathtt{ld}(x)$	✗	18
$l := \mathtt{ld}(x) \rightsquigarrow l := \mathtt{ld}(x); \mathtt{st}(x,l)$	✗	72
$l := \mathtt{ld}(x) \rightsquigarrow l := \mathtt{ld}(y); l := \mathtt{ld}(x)$	?	∞
$l := \mathtt{ld}(x) \rightsquigarrow l := \mathtt{ld}(x); l := \mathtt{ld}(x)$	✓	20k
$\mathtt{st}(x,l) \rightsquigarrow \mathtt{st}(x,l); \mathtt{st}(x,l)$	✗	136
$\mathtt{fc} \rightsquigarrow \mathtt{fc}; \mathtt{fc}$	✓	248

Elimination, validity, time (s)		
$\mathtt{fc} \rightsquigarrow \mathtt{skip}$	✗	15
$l := \mathtt{ld}(x) \rightsquigarrow \mathtt{skip}$	✗	17
$l := \mathtt{ld}(x); \mathtt{st}(x,l) \rightsquigarrow l := \mathtt{ld}(x)$	✗	64
$l := \mathtt{ld}(x); l := \mathtt{ld}(x) \rightsquigarrow l := \mathtt{ld}(x)$	✓	2k
$\mathtt{st}(x,l); l := \mathtt{ld}(x) \rightsquigarrow \mathtt{st}(x,l)$	✓	9k
$\mathtt{st}(x,m); \mathtt{st}(x,l) \rightsquigarrow \mathtt{st}(x,l)$	✓	24k
$\mathtt{fc}; \mathtt{fc} \rightsquigarrow \mathtt{fc}$	✓	382

Exchange, validity, time (s)		
$\mathtt{fc}; l := \mathtt{ld}(x) \rightsquigarrow l := \mathtt{ld}(x); \mathtt{fc}$	✗	26
$\mathtt{fc}; \mathtt{st}(x,l) \rightsquigarrow \mathtt{st}(x,l); \mathtt{fc}$	✗	50
$l := \mathtt{ld}(x); \mathtt{fc} \rightsquigarrow \mathtt{fc}; l := \mathtt{ld}(x)$	✗	79
$\mathtt{st}(x,l); \mathtt{fc} \rightsquigarrow \mathtt{fc}; \mathtt{st}(x,l)$	✗	145
$l := \mathtt{ld}(x); \mathtt{st}(y,m) \rightsquigarrow \mathtt{st}(y,m); l := \mathtt{ld}(x)$	✗	28
$m := \mathtt{ld}(y); l := \mathtt{ld}(x) \rightsquigarrow l := \mathtt{ld}(x); m := \mathtt{ld}(y)$	✗	118
$\mathtt{st}(y,m); l := \mathtt{ld}(x) \rightsquigarrow l := \mathtt{ld}(x); \mathtt{st}(y,m)$	?	∞
$\mathtt{st}(y,m); \mathtt{st}(x,l) \rightsquigarrow \mathtt{st}(x,l); \mathtt{st}(y,m)$	✗	641

Fig. 9. Results from executing Stellite on a 32 core 2.3 GHz AMD Opteron, with 128 GB RAM, over Linux 3.13.0-88 and Java 1.8.0_91. load/store/fence are abbreviated to ld/st/fc. ✓ and ✗ denote whether the transformation satisfies $\sqsubseteq_c$. ∞ denotes a timeout after 8 h.

are verified for unboundedly large syntactic contexts and executions, rather than for a single execution.

7 Transformations with Non-atomics

We now extend our approach to *non-atomic* (i.e. unsynchronised) accesses. C11 non-atomics are intended to enable sequential compiler optimisations that would otherwise be unsound in a concurrent context. To achieve this, any concurrent read-write or write-write pair of non-atomic actions on the same location is declared a *data race*, which causes the whole program to have undefined behaviour. Therefore, adding non-atomics impacts not just the model, but also our denotation.

7.1 Memory Model with Non-atomics

Non-atomic loads and stores are added to the model by introducing new commands $\mathtt{store}_{\mathsf{NA}}(x, l)$ and $l := \mathtt{load}_{\mathsf{NA}}(x)$ and the corresponding kinds of actions: $\mathtt{store}_{\mathsf{NA}}, \mathtt{load}_{\mathsf{NA}} \in \mathsf{Kind}$. We let NA be the set of all actions of these kinds. We partition global variables so that they are either only accessed by non-atomics, or by atomics. We do not permit non-atomic LL-SC operations. Two new validity axioms ensure that non-atomics read from writes that happen before them, but not from stale writes:

```
    store(y,0); storeNA(x,1);              store(y,0); storeNA(x,1);
storeNA(x,1);  ‖ l1 := loadNA(x);       storeNA(x,1);  ‖ l1 := loadNA(x);
store(y,1);    ‖ l2 := load(y);         store(y,1);    ‖ l3 := loadNA(x);
               ‖ l3 := loadNA(x);                      ‖ l2 := load(y);
```

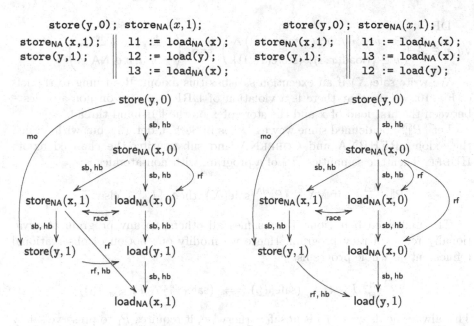

Fig. 10. *Top left*: augmented MP, with non-atomic accesses to x, and a new racy load. *Top right*: the same code optimised with $B_2 \rightsquigarrow B_1$. *Below each*: a valid execution.

- RFHBNA: $\forall w, r \in NA. \; w \xrightarrow{rf} r \implies w \xrightarrow{hb} r$
- COHERNA: $\neg \exists w_1, w_2, r \in NA. \; w_1 \xrightarrow{hb} w_2 \xrightarrow{hb} r$, $w_2 \xrightarrow{rf} r$

Modification order (mo) does not cover non-atomic accesses, and we change the definition of happens-before (hb), so that non-atomic loads do not add edges to it:

- HBDEF: $hb = (sb \cup (rf \cap \{(w,r) \mid w, r \notin NA\}))^+$

Consider the code on the left in Fig. 10: it is similar to MP from Fig. 1, but we have removed the if-statement, made all accesses to x non-atomic, and we have added an additional load of x at the start of the right-hand thread. The valid execution of this code on the left-hand side demonstrates the additions to the model for non-atomics:

- modification order (mo) relates writes to atomic y, but not non-atomic x;
- the first load of x is forced to read from the initialisation by RFHBNA; and
- the second read of x is forced to read 1 because the hb created by the load of y obscures the now-stale initialisation write, in accordance with COHERNA.

The most significant change to the model is the introduction of a *safety axiom*, *data race freedom* (DRF), This forbids non-atomic read-write and write-write pairs that are unordered in hb:

DRF:

$$\forall u, v \in \mathcal{A}. \begin{pmatrix} \exists x. \, u \neq v \land u = (\mathsf{store}(x, \_)) \land \\ v \in \{(\mathsf{load}(x, \_)), (\mathsf{store}(x, \_))\} \end{pmatrix} \implies \begin{pmatrix} u \xrightarrow{\mathsf{hb}} v \lor v \xrightarrow{\mathsf{hb}} u \\ \lor \, u, v \notin \mathsf{NA} \end{pmatrix}$$

We write $\mathsf{safe}(X)$ if an execution satisfies this axiom. Returning to the left of Fig. 10, we see that there is a violation of DRF – a race on non-atomics – between the first load of x and the store of x on the left-hand thread.

Let $[\![P]\!]_v^{\mathsf{NA}}$ be defined same way as $[\![P]\!]$ is in Sect. 3, def. (3), but with adding the axioms RFHBNA and CoherNA and substituting the changed axiom HBDEF. Then the semantics $[\![P]\!]$ of a program with non-atomics is:

$$[\![P]\!] \;\triangleq\; \text{if } \forall X \in [\![P]\!]_v^{\mathsf{NA}}.\, \mathsf{safe}(X) \text{ then } [\![P]\!]_v^{\mathsf{NA}} \text{ else } \top$$

The undefined behaviour $\top$ subsumes all others, so any program observationally refines a racy program. Hence we modify our notion of observational refinement on whole programs:

$$P_1 \preccurlyeq_{\mathsf{pr}}^{\mathsf{NA}} P_2 \;\stackrel{\triangle}{\Longleftrightarrow}\; (\mathsf{safe}(P_2) \implies (\mathsf{safe}(P_1) \land P_1 \preccurlyeq_{\mathsf{pr}} P_2))$$

This always holds when P_2 is unsafe; otherwise, it requires P_1 to preserve safety and observations to match. We define observational refinement on blocks, $\preccurlyeq_{\mathsf{bl}}^{\mathsf{NA}}$, by lifting $\preccurlyeq_{\mathsf{pr}}^{\mathsf{NA}}$ as per Sect. 2, def. (2).

7.2 Denotation with Non-atomics

We now define our denotation for non-atomics, $\sqsubseteq_{\mathsf{q}}^{\mathsf{NA}}$, building on the 'quantified' denotation $\sqsubseteq_{\mathsf{q}}$ defined in Sect. 4. (We have also defined a finite variant of this denotation using the cutting strategy described in Sect. 5 – we leave this to [10, Sect. C].)

Non-atomic actions do not participate in happens-before (hb) or coherence order (mo). For this reason, we need not change the structure of the history. However, non-atomics introduce undefined behaviour $\top$, which is a special kind of observable behaviour. If a block races with its context in some execution, the whole program becomes unsafe, for all executions. Therefore, our denotation must identify how a block may race with its context. In particular, for the denotation to be adequate, for any context C and two blocks $B_1 \sqsubseteq_{\mathsf{q}}^{\mathsf{NA}} B_2$, we must have that if $C(B_1)$ is racy, then $C(B_2)$ is also racy.

To motivate the precise definition of $\sqsubseteq_{\mathsf{q}}^{\mathsf{NA}}$, we consider the following (sound) 'anti-roach-motel' transformation[4], noting that it might be applied to the right-hand thread of the code in the left of Fig. 10:

$$B_2 \colon \mathtt{l1} := \mathtt{load_{NA}(x)}; \; \mathtt{l2} := \mathtt{load(y)}; \; \mathtt{l3} := \mathtt{load_{NA}(x)}$$
$$\rightsquigarrow \quad B_1 \colon \mathtt{l1} := \mathtt{load_{NA}(x)}; \; \mathtt{l3} := \mathtt{load_{NA}(x)}; \; \mathtt{l2} := \mathtt{load(y)}$$

---

[4] This example was provided to us by Lahav, Giannarakis and Vafeiadis in personal communication.

In a standard roach-motel transformation [25], operations are moved into a synchronised block. This is sound because it only introduces new happens-before ordering between events, thereby restricting the execution of the program and preserving data-race freedom. In the above transformation, the second NA load of x is moved past the atomic load of y, effectively *out* of the synchronised block, reducing happens-before ordering, and possibly introducing new races. However, this is sound, because any data-race generated by B_1 must have already occurred with the first NA load of x, matching a racy execution of B_2. Verifying this transformation requires that we reason about races, so $\sqsubseteq_q^{NA}$ must account for both racy and non-racy behaviour.

The code on the left of Fig. 10 represents a context, composed with B_2, and the execution of Fig. 10 demonstrates that together they are racy. If we were to apply our transformation to the fragment B_2 of the right-hand thread, then we would produce the code on the right in Fig. 10. On the right in Fig. 10, we present a similar execution to the one given on the left. The reordering on the right-hand thread has led to the second load of x taking the value 0 rather than 1, in accordance with RFHBNA. Note that the execution still has a race on the first load of x, albeit with different following events. As this example illustrates, when considering racy executions in the definition of $\sqsubseteq_q^{NA}$, we may need to match executions of the two code-blocks that behave differently after a race. This is the key subtlety in our definition of $\sqsubseteq_q^{NA}$.

In more detail, for two related blocks $B_1 \sqsubseteq_q^{NA} B_2$, if B_2 generates a race in a block-local execution under a given (reduced) context, then we require B_1 and B_2 to have corresponding histories *only up to the point the race occurs*. Once the race has occurred, the following behaviours of B_1 and B_2 may differ. This still ensures adequacy: when the blocks B_1 and B_2 are embedded into a syntactic context C, this ensures that a race can be reproduced in $C(B_2)$, and hence, $C(B_1) \prec_{pr}^{NA} C(B_2)$.

By default, C11 executions represent a program's complete behaviour to termination. To allow us to compare executions up to the point a race occurs, we use *prefixes* of executions. We therefore introduce the *downclosure* $X^{\downarrow}$, the set of $(hb \cup rf)^+$-prefixes of an execution X:

$$X^{\downarrow} \triangleq \{X' \mid \exists \mathcal{A}. \, X' = X|_{\mathcal{A}} \wedge \forall (u, v) \in (hb(X) \cup rf(X))^+. \, (v \in \mathcal{A} \Rightarrow u \in \mathcal{A})\}$$

Here $X|_{\mathcal{A}}$ is the projection of the execution X to actions in $\mathcal{A}$. We lift the downclosure to sets of executions in the standard way.

Now we define our refinement relation $B_1 \sqsubseteq_q^{NA} B_2$ as follows:

$$B_1 \sqsubseteq_q^{NA} B_2 \xleftrightarrow{\triangle} \forall \mathcal{A}, R, S. \forall X_1 \in [\![B_1, \mathcal{A}, R, S]\!]_v^{NA}. \exists X_2 \in [\![B_2, \mathcal{A}, R, S]\!]_v^{NA}.$$
$$(\mathsf{safe}(X_2) \implies \mathsf{safe}(X_1) \wedge \mathsf{hist}(X_1) \sqsubseteq_h \mathsf{hist}(X_2)) \wedge$$
$$(\neg\mathsf{safe}(X_2) \implies \exists X_2' \in (X_2)^{\downarrow}. \exists X_1' \in (X_1)^{\downarrow}.$$
$$\neg\mathsf{safe}(X_2') \wedge \mathsf{hist}(X_1') \sqsubseteq_h \mathsf{hist}(X_2'))$$

In this definition, for each execution X_1 of block B_1, we witness an execution X_2 of block B_2 that is related. The relationship depends on whether X_2 is safe or unsafe.

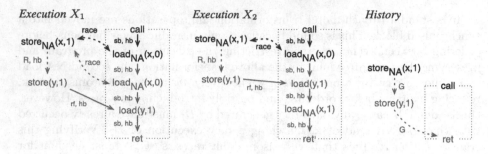

Fig. 11. History comparison for an NA-based program transformation

- If X_2 is safe, then the situation corresponds to $\sqsubseteq_q$ – see Sect. 4, def. (7). In fact, if B_2 is *certain* to be safe, for example because it has no non-atomic accesses, then the above definition is equivalent to $\sqsubseteq_q$.
- If X_2 is unsafe then it has a race, and we do not have to relate the whole executions X_1 and X_2. We need only show that the race in X_2 is feasible by finding a prefix in X_1 that refines the prefix leading to the race in X_2. In other words, X_2 will behave consistently with X_1 *until it becomes unsafe*. This ensures that the race in X_2 will in fact occur, and its undefined behaviour will subsume the behaviour of B_1. After X_2 becomes unsafe, the two blocks can behave entirely differently, so we need not show that the complete histories of X_1 and X_2 are related.

Recall the transformation $B_2 \rightsquigarrow B_1$ given above. To verify it, we must establish that $B_1 \sqsubseteq_q^{\mathsf{NA}} B_2$. As before, we illustrate the reasoning for a single block-local execution – verifying the transformation would require a proof for all block-local executions.

In Fig. 11 we give an execution $X_1 \in [\![B_1, \mathcal{A}, R, S]\!]$, with a context action set $\mathcal{A}$ consisting of a non-atomic store of $\mathsf{x} = 1$ and an atomic store of $\mathsf{y} = 1$, and a context relation R relating the store of x to the store of y. Note that this choice of context actions matches the left-hand thread in the code listings of Fig. 10, and there are data races between the loads and the store on x.

To prove the refinement for this execution, we exhibit a corresponding unsafe execution $X_2 \in [\![B_2, \mathcal{A}, R, S]\!]_v$. The histories of the *complete* executions X_1 and X_2 differ in their return action. In X_2 the load of y takes the value of the context store, so COHERNA forces the second load of x to read from the context store of x. This changes the values of local variables recorded in $\mathsf{ret'}$. However, because X_2 is unsafe, we can select a prefix X_2' which includes the race (we denote in grey the parts that we do not include). Similarly, we can select a prefix X_1' of X_1. We have that $\mathsf{hist}(X_1') = \mathsf{hist}(X_2')$ (shown in the figure), even though the histories $\mathsf{hist}(X_1)$ and $\mathsf{hist}(X_2)$ do not correspond.

Theorem 5 (ADEQUACY OF $\sqsubseteq_q^{\mathsf{NA}}$). $B_1 \sqsubseteq_q^{\mathsf{NA}} B_2 \implies B_1 \precsim_{\mathsf{bl}}^{\mathsf{NA}} B_2$.

Theorem 6 (FULL ABSTRACTION OF $\sqsubseteq_q^{\mathsf{NA}}$). $B_1 \precsim_{\mathsf{bl}}^{\mathsf{NA}} B_2 \Rightarrow B_1 \sqsubseteq_q^{\mathsf{NA}} B_2$.

We prove Theorem 5 in [10, Sect. B] and Theorem 6 in [10, Sect. F]. Note that the prefixing in our definition of $\sqsubseteq_q^{NA}$ is required for full abstraction—but it would be adequate to always require *complete* executions with related histories.

8   Full Abstraction

The key idea of our proofs of full abstraction (Theorems 2 and 6, given in full in [10, Sect. F]) is to construct a special syntactic context that is sensitive to one particular history. Namely, given an execution X produced from a block B with context happens-before R, this context C_X guarantees: (1) that X is the block portion of an execution of $C_X(B)$; and (2) for any block B', if $C_X(B')$ has a different block history from X, then this is visible in different observable behaviour. Therefore for any blocks that are distinguished by different histories, C_X can produce a program with different observable behaviour, establishing full abstraction.

Special Context Construction. The precise definition of the special context construction C_X is given in [10, Sect. F] – here we sketch its behaviour. C_X executes the context operations from X in parallel with the block. It wraps these operations in auxiliary wrapper code to enforce context happens-before, R, and to check the history. If wrapper code fails, it writes to an error variable, which thereby alters the observable behaviour.

The context must generate edges in R. This is enforced by wrappers that use watchdog variables to create hb-edges: each edge $(u, v) \in R$ is replicated by a write and read on variable $h_{(u,v)}$. If the read on $h_{(u,v)}$ does not read the write, then the error variable is written. The shape of a successful read is given on the left in Fig. 12.

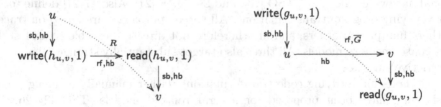

Fig. 12. The execution shapes generated by the special context for, on the *left*, generation of R, and on the *right*, errant history edges.

The context must also prohibit history edges beyond those in the original guarantee G, and again it uses watchdog variables. For each (u, v) *not* in G, the special context writes to watchdog variable $g_{(u,v)}$ before u and a reads $g_{(u,v)}$ after v. If the read of $g_{(u,v)}$ *does* read the value written before u, then there is an errant history edge, and the error location is written. An erroneous execution has the shape given on the right in Fig. 12 (omitting the write to the error location).

Full Abstraction and LL-SC. Our proof of full abstraction for the language with C11 non-atomics requires the language to also include LL-SC, not just C11's standard CAS: the former operation increases the observational power of the context. However, *without* non-atomics (Sect. 4) CAS would be sufficient to prove full abstraction.

9   Related Work

Our approach builds on our prior work [3], which generalises linearizability [11] to the C11 memory model. This work represented interactions between a library and its clients by sets of histories consisting of a guarantee and a deny; we do the same for code-block and context. However, our previous work assumed *information hiding*, i.e., that the variables used by the library cannot be directly accessed by clients; we lift this assumption here. We also establish both adequacy and full abstraction, propose a finite denotation, and build an automated verification tool.

Our approach is similar in structure to the seminal concurrency semantics of Brookes [6]: i.e. a code block is represented by a denotation capturing possible interactions with an abstracted context. In [6], denotations are sets of traces, consisting of sequences of global program states; context actions are represented by changes in these states. To handle the more complex axiomatic memory model, our denotation consists of sets of context actions and relations on them, with context actions explicitly represented as such. Also, in order to achieve full abstraction, Brookes assumes a powerful atomic `await()` instruction which blocks until the global state satisfies a predicate. Our result does not require this: all our instructions operate on single locations, and our strongest instruction is LL-SC, which is commonly available on hardware.

Brookes-like approaches have been applied to several relaxed models: operational hardware models [7], TSO [13], and SC-DRF [21]. Also, [7,21] define tools for verifying program transformations. All three approaches are based on traces rather than partial orders, and are therefore not directly portable to C11-style axiomatic memory models. All three also target substantially stronger (i.e. more restrictive) models.

Methods for verifying code transformations, either manually or using proof assistants, have been proposed for several relaxed models: TSO [24,26,27], Java [25] and C/C++ [23]. These methods are non-compositional in the sense that verifying a transformation requires considering the trace set of the entire program—there is no abstraction of the context. We abstract both the sequential and concurrent context and thereby support automated verification. The above methods also model transformations as rewrites on program executions, whereas we treat them directly as modifications of program syntax; the latter corresponds more closely to actual compilers. Finally, these methods all require considerable proof effort; we build an automated verification tool.

Our tool is a sound verification tool – that is, transformations are verified for all context and all executions of unbounded size. Several tools exist for testing (not verifying) program transformations on axiomatic memory models by searching for counter-examples to correctness, e.g., [16] for GCC and [8] for LLVM. Alloy was used by [28] in a testing tool for comparing memory models – this includes comparing language-level constructs with their compiled forms.

10   Conclusions

We have proposed the first fully abstract denotational semantics for an axiomatic relaxed memory model, and using this, we have built the first tool capable of automatically verifying program transformation on such a model. Our theory lays the groundwork for further research into the properties of axiomatic models. In particular, our definition of the denotation as a set of histories and our context reduction should be portable to other axiomatic models based on happens-before, such as those for hardware [1].

Acknowledgements. Thanks to Jeremy Jacob, Viktor Vafeiadis, and John Wickerson for comments and suggestions. Dodds was supported by a Royal Society Industrial Fellowship, and undertook this work while faculty at the University of York. Batty is supported by a Lloyds Register Foundation and Royal Academy of Engineering Research Fellowship.

References

1. Alglave, J., Maranget, L., Tautschnig, M.: Herding cats: modelling, simulation, testing, and data mining for weak memory. ACM Trans. Program. Lang. Syst. **36**(2), 7:1–7:74 (2014)
2. Anderson, J.H., Moir, M.: Universal constructions for multi-object operations. In: Symposium on Principles of Distributed Computing (PODC), pp. 184–193 (1995)
3. Batty, M., Dodds, M., Gotsman, A.: Library abstraction for C/C++ concurrency. In: Symposium on Principles of Programming Languages (POPL), pp. 235–248 (2013)
4. Batty, M., Memarian, K., Nienhuis, K., Pichon-Pharabod, J., Sewell, P.: The problem of programming language concurrency semantics. In: Vitek, J. (ed.) ESOP 2015. LNCS, vol. 9032, pp. 283–307. Springer, Heidelberg (2015). https://doi.org/10.1007/978-3-662-46669-8_12
5. Batty, M., Owens, S., Sarkar, S., Sewell, P., Weber, T.: Mathematizing C++ concurrency. In: Symposium on Principles of Programming Languages (POPL), pp. 55–66 (2011)
6. Brookes, S.: Full abstraction for a shared-variable parallel language. Inf. Comput. **127**(2), 145–163 (1996)
7. Burckhardt, S., Musuvathi, M., Singh, V.: Verifying local transformations on relaxed memory models. In: International Conference on Compiler Construction (CC), pp. 104–123 (2010)
8. Chakraborty, S., Vafeiadis, V.: Validating optimizations of concurrent C/C++ programs. In: International Symposium on Code Generation and Optimization (CGO), pp. 216–226 (2016)

9. Distefano, D., O'Hearn, P.W., Yang, H.: A local shape analysis based on separation logic. In: Hermanns, H., Palsberg, J. (eds.) TACAS 2006. LNCS, vol. 3920, pp. 287–302. Springer, Heidelberg (2006). https://doi.org/10.1007/11691372_19

10. Dodds, M., Batty, M., Gotsman, A.: Compositional verification of compiler optimisations on relaxed memory (extended version). CoRR, arXiv:1802.05918 (2018)

11. Herlihy, M.P., Wing, J.M.: Linearizability: a correctness condition for concurrent objects. ACM Trans. Program. Lang. Syst. **12**(3), 463–492 (1990)

12. Jackson, D.: Software Abstractions - Logic Language and Analysis, Revised edn. MIT Press, Cambridge (2012)

13. Jagadeesan, R., Petri, G., Riely, J.: Brookes is relaxed, almost! In: International Conference on Foundations of Software Science and Computational Structures (FOSSACS), pp. 180–194 (2012)

14. Jeffrey, A., Riely, J.: On thin air reads towards an event structures model of relaxed memory. In: Symposium on Logic in Computer Science (LICS), pp. 759–767 (2016)

15. Kang, J., Hur, C.-K., Lahav, O., Vafeiadis, V., Dreyer, D.: A promising semantics for relaxed-memory concurrency. In: Symposium on Principles of Programming Languages (POPL), pp. 175–189 (2017)

16. Lahav, O., Giannarakis, N., Vafeiadis, V.: Taming release-acquire consistency. In: Symposium on Principles of Programming Languages (POPL), pp. 649–662 (2016)

17. Lahav, O., Vafeiadis, V., Kang, J., Hur, C.-K., Dreyer, D.: Repairing sequential consistency in C/C++11. In: Conference on Programming Language Design and Implementation (PLDI), pp. 618–632 (2017)

18. Milicevic, A., Near, J.P., Kang, E., Jackson, D.: Alloy*: a general-purpose higher-order relational constraint solver. In: International Conference on Software Engineering (ICSE), pp. 609–619 (2015)

19. Morisset, R., Pawan, P., Zappa Nardelli, F.: Compiler testing via a theory of sound optimisations in the C11/C++11 memory model. In: Conference on Programming Language Design and Implementation (PLDI), pp. 187–196 (2013)

20. Pichon-Pharabod, J., Sewell, P.: A concurrency semantics for relaxed atomics that permits optimisation and avoids thin-air executions. In: Symposium on Principles of Programming Languages (POPL), pp. 622–633 (2016)

21. Poetzl, D., Kroening, D.: Formalizing and checking thread refinement for data-race-free execution models. In: International Conference on Tools and Algorithms for the Construction and Analysis of Systems (TACAS), pp. 515–530 (2016)

22. The C++ Standards Committee: Programming Languages – C++ (2011). ISO/IEC JTC1 SC22 WG21

23. Vafeiadis, V., Balabonski, T., Chakraborty, S., Morisset, R., Zappa Nardelli, F.: Common compiler optimisations are invalid in the C11 memory model and what we can do about it. In: Symposium on Principles of Programming Languages (POPL), pp. 209–220 (2015)

24. Vafeiadis, V., Zappa Nardelli, F.: Verifying fence elimination optimisations. In: International Conference on Static Analysis (SAS), pp. 146–162 (2011)

25. Ševčík, J., Aspinall, D.: On validity of program transformations in the Java memory model. In: Vitek, J. (ed.) ECOOP 2008. LNCS, vol. 5142, pp. 27–51. Springer, Heidelberg (2008). https://doi.org/10.1007/978-3-540-70592-5_3

26. Ševčík, J., Vafeiadis, V., Zappa Nardelli, F., Jagannathan, S.: Sewell, P.: Relaxed-memory concurrency and verified compilation. In: Symposium on Principles of Programming Languages (POPL), pp. 43–54 (2011)

27. Ševčík, J., Vafeiadis, V., Zappa Nardelli, F., Jagannathan, S., Sewell, P.: CompCertTSO: a verified compiler for relaxed-memory concurrency. J. ACM **60**(3), 22:1–22:50 (2013)

28. Wickerson, J., Batty, M., Sorensen, T., Constantinides, G.A.: Automatically comparing memory consistency models. In: Symposium on Principles of Programming Languages (POPL), pp. 190–204 (2017)

Author Index